THE
AMERICAN-BUILT CLIPPER SHIP

1850–1856

YOUNG AMERICA
NEW YORK

THE
AMERICAN-BUILT
CLIPPER SHIP
1850–1856

Characteristics, Construction, and Details

WILLIAM L. CROTHERS

INTERNATIONAL MARINE
CAMDEN, MAINE

International Marine

A Division of The McGraw-Hill Companies

10 9 8 7 6 5 4 3 2 1

Copyright © 1997, 2000 by International Marine

All rights reserved. The publisher takes no responsibility for the use of any of the materials or methods described in this book, nor for the products thereof. The name "International Marine" and the International Marine logo are trademarks of The McGraw-Hill Companies. Printed in the United States of America.

The Library of Congress has catalogued the cloth edition of this book as follows:

Library of Congress Cataloging-in-Publication Data
Crothers, William L., 1912–
    The American-built clipper ship, 1850–1856 : characteristics, construction, and details / William L. Crothers.
        p.   cm.
    Includes bibliographical references and index.
    ISBN 0-07-014501-6 (alk. paper)
    1. Clipper ships—United States—History.   I. Title.
VM23.C76   1996
623.8'224—dc20
                                                         96-7095
                                                            CIP

Paperback ISBN: 0-07-135823-4

Questions regarding the content of this book should be addressed to

International Marine
P.O. Box 220
Camden, ME 04843
http://www.internationalmarine.com

Questions regarding the ordering of this book should be addressed to

The McGraw-Hill Companies
Customer Service Department
P.O. Box 547
Blacklick, OH 43004
Retail customers: 1-800-262-4729; Bookstores: 1-800-722-4726

American-Built Clipper Ships is printed on 50-pound Pinehurst

This book was typeset in Adobe Garamond and Adobe Gill Sans.

Printed by Quebecor/Semline
Design by Patrice Rossi Caulkin
Production and page layout by Janet Robbins
Edited by Jonathan Eaton, Jane Crosen, Tom McCarthy
Illustrated by the author

CONTENTS

PART I
PRELUDE TO BUILDING THE SHIP

PART II
CONSTRUCTION OF THE HULL

PART III
COMPLETION OF THE SHIP

ILLUSTRATIONS

TABLES

All (152) vessels are named in each table except Tables 6.1, 9.2, 11.1, 12.1, and 29.2, which are abridged to include only specific vessels, and 30.1, which is arranged by items of rigging.

Lists of 152 American-Built Clipper Ships, 1850–1856

IN 1845, JOHN WILLIS GRIFFITHS built the fast ship *Rainbow,* and followed it the next year with the even faster *Sea Witch.* Both vessels would have tremendous impact on merchant hull design. *Sea Witch,* in fact, had more influence on the configuration of fast vessels than any ship built in the United States. Vessels built in general accordance with the *Sea Witch* model were known as clippers, a term already well entrenched in the language of fast vessels.

Historically these vessels appeared when trade to California was on the rise and speed was vital. Shipbuilding surged, and vessels with the potential for speed were built in ever-increasing numbers. The number of these ships increased annually, reaching a zenith in 1853, then declining until the last clipper was built in 1859.

Following are the names of 152 American-built clipper ships constructed through the period 1850–1856. These particular vessels are listed for the reason that detailed information, ranging from profuse descriptions in some cases, to merely a few isolated details in others, is available without the need for additional research. There is no doubt that considerable data may be found in many places when time and circumstance permit.

With only a few exceptions, none of the vessels were specifically chosen to be included in this volume; this probably results in a more representative cross-section of characteristics and details than would have been achieved by handpicking the entries. Procedures dictated by choice become governed by one's personal opinion and preference; thus, a certain objectivity is lost.

Many of these names will be very well known to anyone familiar with the subject. Others are of lesser magnitude; these are vessels that did not have the good fortune to perform outstandingly. Finally, there are some ships whose names have hardly been preserved for posterity. This book deals with the structural details and arrangements as reported from on-site descriptions rather than on the rudiments of design and development. It seems reasonable to believe that the ships included here cover all the structural details that were encountered in clipper ship construction. The names appear in two listings, the first alphabetically, the second chronologically.

In many cases no designer is named for a specific vessel. During this period many shipbuilders were designers in their own right. Among these were Ewall & Jackson, Samuel Hall, and Paul Curtis of Boston; Hayden & Cudworth and James O. Curtis of Medford, Massachusetts; George Raynes, Fernald & Pettigrew, and Toby & Littlefield of Portsmouth, New Hampshire; J. Westervelt, and Perrine, Paterson & Stack of New York—to mention a few. However, it is difficult to attribute the design of a specific vessel to a specific individual in such organizations. The space is therefore left blank, pending some future positive identification.

The fervor of the clipper ship era brought a dramatic change to the form and size of merchant vessels. This change was accompanied by a sudden rise in romanticism, and the consequent zealous search for names denoting beauty, speed, superior performance, grace and poetry. Thus, names suggestive of these attributes became the hallmark of the clipper ship. Almost every name stirred romantic notions in the minds of those who read them or saw the vessels in all their glory.

The alphabetical list, under "Signification of Name," includes, for many of the vessels, a brief statement concerning the name's origin, referring to a specific person, character, place, or animal life. Names that are purely romantic or indicative of natural phenomena have been left blank.

In the chronological list, the dimensions given, if known, are length between perpendiculars (pp), length on deck (od), or length overall (oa), as noted; beam; depth of hold; and old measurement tonnage.

During this period (1850–1856), old tonnage measurement, a practice of establishing a vessel's cubical capacity, was based on the English rule of measurement which was then in effect. The formula used by this rule was

$$\frac{(L - \frac{3}{5}B) \times B \times \frac{1}{2}B}{95}$$

the values being:

L = Length of vessel on the weather deck.

B = Maximum breadth of vessel to outside of planking.

95 = Cubic feet of space occupied by one ton of cargo.
(In this formula, the factor ½B replaced the original use of the "depth of hold from deck to ceiling of the hold.")

The above formula was in use in the United States until 1865, at which time it was superseded by the present-day Moorsom system.

It should be noted that in many instances, various sources and authorities quote differing figures for ships' dimensions. However, this diversity of values is rarely great enough to affect the general size classification of any vessel.

Vessel	Year	Class of Clipper	Signification of Name	Vessel	Year	Class of Clipper	Signification of Name
Note: All vessels are ship rig unless otherwise noted.				Electric Spark	1855	medium	
				Ellen Foster	1852	medium	Name of the wife of her builder Joshua T. Foster, Medford, Mass.
Alarm	1856	medium					
Amphitrite	1853	extreme	Greek mythological queen of the seas.	Empress of the Sea	1853	extreme	Contemporary spelling of the name using "Sea" in lieu of "Seas".
Andrew Jackson	1855	medium	Seventh president of the United States. Launched as Belle Hoxie, ref. 32.	Endeavor	1856	medium	
				Eringo Bark	1853	medium	Possibly named for the herb Eryngium or eryngo. The candied roots were believed to possess aphrodisiac properties. The name was also freely spelled eringo.
Antelope	1851	medium	This is Antelope built at Medford, Mass.				
Asa Eldridge	1856	medium	Named in memory of the captain of the lost Collins steamer Pacific.	Eureka	1851	extreme	
				Fair Wind	1855	medium	
Bald Eagle	1852	extreme	National bird in the United States coat of arms.	Fearless	1853	extreme	
Belle of the West	1853	extreme		Fleet Wing	1854	medium	
Beverly	1852	medium		Flyaway	1853	extreme	
Black Hawk	1856	medium	Launched 29 December 1856, vessel is generally listed as 1857.	Flying Arrow	1852	medium	(Built as Flying Yankee)
Blue Jacket	1854	medium	A term descriptive of a seaman.	Flying Childers	1852	medium	Famous undefeated English racehorse of the early 1700's.
Bonita	1853	medium					
Bounding Billow Bark	1854	medium		Flying Cloud	1851	extreme	
Celestial	1850	extreme		Flying Dragon	1853	medium	
Challenge	1851	extreme		Flying Dutchman	1852	extreme	A Dutch sailor condemned to sail the seas until Judgement Day.
Challenger	1853	extreme		Flying Eagle	1852	extreme	
Champion of the Seas	1854	extreme		Flying Fish	1851	extreme	
Charger	1856	medium		Flying Mist	1856	medium	
Charmer	1854	medium		Galatea	1854	medium	Greek mythological statue of a maiden, given life by Aphrodite after its sculptor, Pygmalion, fell in love with it.
Cleopatra	1853	medium	Queen of Egypt (51–49; 49–30 B.C.)				
Climax	1853	medium					
Coeur de Lion	1854	medium	Named after Richard I, King of England, 1189–1199.	Game Cock	1850	extreme	
				Gazelle	1851	extreme	
Comet	1851	extreme		Gem of the Ocean	1852	medium	
Cyclone	1853	medium		Golden Eagle	1852	extreme	
Daring	1855	medium		Golden Fleece (2nd)	1855	medium	Fleece of gold guarded by a dragon and taken away by Jason and the Argonauts.
Dauntless	1851	extreme					
Donald McKay	1855	clipper packet	Ship designer and builder in Boston, 1845–1869.	Golden Light	1853	medium	
				Golden West	1852	extreme	
Don Quixote	1853	medium	Chivalrous hero of novel of the same name by Miguel de Cervantes, 1547–1616.	Grace Darling	1854	medium	Named for Grace Horsley Darling, British heroine, daughter of a lighthouse keeper on the Farne Islands. She helped to rescue five persons from the wrecked Forfarshire in 1838.
Eagle	1851	extreme					
Eagle Wing	1853	medium					
Edwin Forrest	1853	medium	Famous American actor, 1804–1872.	Great Republic	1853	extreme	A reference to the United States of Ame
				Great Republic	1855	extreme	As re-built, razeed and with reduced rig.
				Henry Hill Bark	1856	medium	Named for the Treasurer of the American Board of Commissioners for Foreign Missions.
				Herald of the Morning	1853	medium	A reference to Eos (Greek) or Aurora (Roman) Goddess of Dawn.

Alphabetical List of Vessels, continued

Vessel	Year	Class of Clipper	Signification of Name
Hoogly	1851	medium	Name of the navigable Hooghly River, an arm of the Ganges in India.
Hurricane	1851	extreme	
Indiaman	1854	marginal	Intended to represent a native of Japan. (See Figureheads.)
Intrepid	1856	medium	
Invincible	1851	extreme	
James Baines	1854	extreme	Senior member of the owners, James Baines & Co., Liverpool.
John Bertram	1850	extreme	Well known sea captain and merchant of Salem, Mass.
John Gilpin	1852	medium	A London draper whose horseback riding is celebrated in the poem "The Diverting History of John Gilpin" by William Cowper, English poet, 1731-1800.
John Land	1853	medium	Named for Capt. John Land, once master of Rainbow and Challenge. (Built as an exact duplicate of Winged Arrow.)
John Stuart	1851	medium	
John Wade	1851	medium	Name of a well known sea captain.
Joseph Peabody	1856	medium	Named for prominent ship owner of Salem, Mass. in early 1800's.
King Fisher	1853	extreme	Contemporary spelling. (Two words.)
Lady Franklin	1852	medium	Name of the wife of Sir John Franklin, British explorer, 1786-1847. She outfitted a search expedition to the Arctic to trace his fate.
Lamplighter Bark	1854	marginal	
Lightfoot	1853	extreme	
Lightning	1854	extreme	
Mameluke	1855	medium	Member of a military caste which ruled Egypt from 1250 to 1517.
Mary Robinson	1854	medium	Name of the wife of E. M. Robinson, New Bedford, Mass., the owner of the ship.
Mastiff	1856	medium	
Mermaid Bark	1851	extreme	
Morning Light	1853	extreme	This is Morning Light built at Portsmouth, New Hampshire.
Mystery	1853	medium	
Nightingale	1851	extreme	Named for Swedish soprano Jenny Lind, 1820-1887.
Noonday	1855	medium	
Northern Light	1851	medium	
Ocean Express	1854	medium	
Ocean Pearl	1853	medium	
Ocean Telegraph	1854	extreme	
Onward	1852	medium	
Osborne Howes	1854	medium	Senior member of the owners, Howes & Crowell, Boston, Mass.
Panther	1854	medium	
Phantom	1852	medium	
Queen of Clippers	1853	medium	
Queen of the Pacific	1852	medium	
Queen of the Seas	1852	medium	
Quickstep (2nd) Bark	1855	medium	
Racehorse Bark	1850	medium	Classed as a clipper by Capt. Arthur H. Clark. Classification later refuted by scholars.
Racer	1851	medium	
Radiant	1853	medium	
Raven	1851	extreme	
Red Jacket	1853	extreme	Popular name of Sagoyewatha, Seneca Indian chief living at time of the American Revolution.
Robin Hood	1854	extreme	Legendary 12th century English outlaw who robbed the rich to help the poor.
Rocket Bark	1851	medium	
Roebuck	1851	medium	
Romance of the Sea	1853	extreme	A reference to Sir Walter Scott and James Fenimore Cooper
Santa Claus	1854	marginal	
Saracen	1854	medium	A member of the early nomadic tribes of the Middle East.
Sea Bird Bark	1851	medium	
Seaman's Bride	1851	extreme	Named to complement the clipper Seaman launched in 1850 by the same builders
Sea Serpent	1850	extreme	
Shooting Star	1851	extreme	
Sierra Nevada	1854	medium	Name changed from King of the Forest before launch.
Silver Star	1856	medium	
Southern Cross	1851	medium	
Sovereign of the Seas	1852	extreme	Named for the original ship of the same name built at Woolwich, England in 1637. (While on the stocks was named Enoch Train. See ref. 1, edition of 25 May 1852. Name changed prior to launch.)
Spitfire	1853	extreme	
Staffordshire	1851	clipper packet	English pottery district, source of much of Enoch Train's "Train Line" cargoes.
Stag Hound	1850	extreme	Contemporary spelling. (Two words)
Star of the Union	1852	extreme	A reference to Daniel Webster, U.S. statesman and orator.
Starr King	1854	medium	The Rev. Thomas Starr King, lecturer, writer and preacher of Boston, later San Francisco.

Vessel		Year	Class of Clipper	Signification of Name	Vessel		Year	Class of Clipper	Signification of Name
Storm King		1853	medium	Neptune, Roman god of the sea.	Whirlwind		1852	extreme	
Sultana	Bark	1850	marginal	Title of the wife, mother, sister or daughter of a Sultan.	Whistler		1853	medium	
Sunny South		1854	extreme		Wildfire	Bark	1853	medium	
Surprise		1850	extreme		Wild Pigeon		1851	extreme	
Swallow		1854	medium	Possibly named for Philomela, daughter of Pandion, King of Athens. She was turned into a swallow by the gods. (See Figureheads)	Wild Ranger		1853	medium	
					Wild Rover		1853	medium	
					Winged Arrow		1852	medium	
					Winged Racer		1852	extreme	Her figurehead carving suggests that the name refers to the winged horse Pegasus of Greek mythology. (See Figureheads)
Sweepstakes		1853	extreme						
Sword Fish		1851	extreme						
Syren		1851	medium		Witchcraft		1850	extreme	
Telegraph		1851	extreme		Witch of the Wave		1851	extreme	This is the first Witch of the Wave, built at Portsmouth, N.H. Second vessel, 1856, was not a clipper.
Thatcher Magoun		1856	medium	Senior member of the owners, T. Magoun & Son, Boston, Mass.					
Tornado		1850	medium	This is Tornado built at East Boston. Originally intended to be named Game Cock. (See Figureheads)	Wizard		1853	extreme	
					Young America		1853	extreme	A reference to the United States of America.
Uncowah		1856	medium	Possibly named after a small tribe of Indians located in the vicinity of Fairfield, Conn.	Young Turk	Bark	1856	medium	
War Hawk		1855	medium						
Water Witch		1853	extreme						
Western Continent		1853	medium						
Westward Ho		1852	extreme						
West Wind		1853	medium						

Vessel & Ref.#	Date of Launch	Designer	Builder	Original Owner
Notes: All dimensions are in feet and inches.				
* - Location of this dimension is not specifically stated.				
1850				
Celestial #18,42 158-9od x 35-6 x 20-6 860 tons 2 decks	10 June	Wm.H.Webb New York	Wm.H.Webb New York	Bucklin & Crane New York
Racehorse (Bark) #1 128oa x 30-6 x 16 514 tons 1 deck & hold beams partially decked	June	Samuel Hall+ East Boston +Sometimes attributed to S.H.Pook	Samuel Hall East Boston	J.M.Forbes Boston
Sultana (Bark) #1 121od x 28-4 x 15 434 tons 1 deck & hold beams	June	Donald McKay East Boston	Donald McKay East Boston	Edw. Lamb & Bro. Boston
Surprise #1 190oa x 39 x 22 1262 tons 2 decks	5 October	Sam'l.H.Pook Boston	Samuel Hall East Boston	A. A. Low & Bro. New York
Sea Serpent #4 212oa x 39-3 x 21 1337 tons 2 decks	20 November	Geo. Raynes Portsmouth, NH	Geo. Raynes Portsmouth, NH	Grinnell, Minturn & Co. New York
Stag Hound #1 226oa x 39-8 x 21 1534 tons 2decks	7 December	Donald McKay East Boston	Donald McKay East Boston	Geo.B.Upton, Sampson & Tappan Boston
John Bertram #1 190oa x 37 x 20 1050 tons 2 decks	9 December		Ewell & Jackson East Boston	Glidden & Williams, et al. Boston
Gamecock #1 200oa x 40 x 22 1391 tons 2 decks	21 December	Sam'l.H.Pook or Sam'l.Hall (disputed) Boston	Samuel Hall East Boston	Daniel C. Bacon Boston
Tornado #3 198od x 40 x 22 1320 tons 2 decks	21 December		Samuel Hall East Boston	Daniel C. Bacon, et al. Boston
Witchcraft #1 193oa x 39-4 x 22 1311 tons 2 decks	21 December	Sam'l.H.Pook Boston	Paul Curtis Chelsea, Mass.	Rogers & Pickman Salem,Mass.
1851				
Gazelle #4 181od x 40 x 21 1244 tons 2 decks	21 January	Wm.H.Webb New York	Wm.H.Webb New York	Taylor & Merrill New York
Shooting Star #1 171oa x 35 x 18-6 903 tons 2 decks	8 February	Capt. John Wade Boston	Jas.O.Curtis Medford, Mass.	Reed, Wade & Co. Boston
Eureka #4 173od x 36-6 x 21-6 1041 tons 2 decks	1 March		J.A.Wester- velt New York	Chambers & Heiser New York

Vessel & Ref.#	Date of Launch	Designer	Builder	Original Owner
1851				
Southern Cross #1 175oa x 36 x 21 938 tons 2 decks	19 March	E. & H.O. Briggs So. Boston	E. & H.O. Briggs So. Boston	Baker & Morrill Boston
Mermaid (Bark) #1 145oa x 29-3 x 15 533 tons 1 deck & hold beams partially decked	20 March	Samuel Hall East Boston	Samuel Hall East Boston	Hall, Gas- sell & May Boston
Witch of the Wave #1 220oa x 40 x 21 1498 tons 2 decks	5 April	Geo. Raynes Portsmouth, NH	Geo. Raynes Portsmouth, NH	Glidden & Williams, et al. Boston
Flying Cloud #1 235oa x 41 x 21-6 1783 tons 2 decks	15 April	Donald McKay East Boston	Donald McKay East Boston	Grinnell, Minturn & Co. New York
Syren #3 189oa x 36 x 22 1064 tons 2 decks	1 May		John Taylor Medford, Mass.	Silsbee & Pickman Salem,Mass.
Eagle #5 220oa x 38-6 x 22 1300 tons 2 decks	3 May		Perrine, Paterson & Stack Williams- burgh, NY	Harbeck & Co. New York
Challenge #1 252-6oa x 43 x 25-6 2006 tons 3 decks	24 May	Wm.H.Webb New York	Wm.H.Webb New York	N.L. & G. Griswold New York
Telegraph #1 178od x 36 x 21-6 1066 tons 2 decks	May	Sam'l.H.Pook Boston	Jas.O.Curtis Medford, Mass.	P. Sprague & Co. Boston
Nightingale #3 185od x 36-6 x 20 1070 tons 2 decks	16 June	Sam'l. Hans- com, Jr. & Capt.F.A. Miller Portsmouth, NH	Sam'l. Hans- com, Jr. Portsmouth, NH	Davis & Co., et al. Portsmouth, NH
Staffordshire #1 240oa x 41 x 29 1817 tons 3 decks	17 June	Donald McKay East Boston	Donald McKay East Boston	Enoch Train & Co. Boston
Racer #3 207oa x 42-6 x 28 1650 tons 3 decks	18 June		Currier & Townsend Newburyport, Mass.	David Ogden, et al. New York
Seaman's Bride #4,32 152od x 31-6 x 17-6 668 tons 2 decks	25 June		R. & E.Bell Baltimore	Thomas J. Handy & Co. New York
Raven #3 158* x 32-6 x 17 712 tons 2 decks	1 July		Capt.Jas.M. Hood Somerset, Mass.	Crocker & Warren, et al. NY & Boston
Comet #18,24 241oa x 41-4 x 22-2 1836 tons 2 decks	10 July	Wm.H.Webb New York	Wm.H.Webb New York	Bucklin & Crane New York
Wild Pigeon #1 184oa x 36-4 x 20 996 tons 2 decks	31 July	Geo. Raynes Portsmouth, NH	Geo. Raynes Portsmouth, NH	Olyphant & Co. New York
Invincible #4 235oa x 42-10 x 25-6 1769 tons 3 decks	6 August	Wm.H.Webb New York	Wm.H.Webb New York	James W. Phillips New York

Vessel & Ref.#	Date of Launch	Designer	Builder	Original Owner	Vessel & Ref.#	Date of Launch	Designer	Builder	Original Owner
	1851					**1852**			
John Wade #1 152oa x 32 x 16-6 660 tons 2 decks	August	Capt. John Wade Boston	Hayden & Cudworth Medford, Mass.	Reed, Wade & Co. Boston	Onward #1 175oa x 34 x 20-6 943 tons 2 decks	3 July		Jas.O.Curtis Medford, Mass.	Reed, Wade & Co. Boston
Sword Fish #24 170od x 36-6 x 20 1036 tons 2 decks	20 September	Wm.H.Webb New York	Wm.H.Webb New York	Barclay & Livingston New York	Winged Arrow #1 183oa x 36 x 22 1052 tons 2 decks	July	E. & H.O. Briggs So. Boston	E. & H.O. Briggs So. Boston	Baker & Morrill Boston
Northern Light #28 180oa x 36 x 21-9 1021 tons 2 decks	25 September	Sam'l.H.Pook Boston	E. & H.O. Briggs So. Boston	James Huckins Boston	Gem of the Ocean #1 153od x 33 x 20-6 730 tons 2 decks	August		Hayden & Cudworth Medford, Mass.	Wm.Lincoln & Co. Boston
Flying Fish #1 220oa x 39-6 x 22 1505 tons 2 decks	September	Donald McKay East Boston	Donald McKay East Boston	Sampson & Tappan Boston	Flying Dutchman #32 200oa x 38-6 x 21-6 1257 tons 2 decks	9 September	Wm.H.Webb New York	Wm.H.Webb New York	Geo. Daniels, et al. New York
John Stuart #4 228-6oa x 43 x 28 1670 tons 3 decks	October	Perrine, Paterson & Stack Williamsburgh, NY	Perrine, Paterson & Stack Williamsburgh, NY	B.A.Mumford, J.Smith, et al. New York	Whirlwind #1 175oa x 35 x 21-6 925 tons 2 decks	13 September		Jas.O.Curtis Medford, Mass.	W. & F.H. Whittemore Boston
Hurricane #4 230oa x 40 x 22 1608 tons 2 decks	25 October		Isaac C. Smith Hoboken, NJ	C.W. & H. Thomas New York	Westward Ho #1 220oa x 40-6 x 23-6 1600 tons 2 decks	14 September	Donald McKay East Boston	Donald McKay East Boston	Sampson & Tappan Boston
Antelope #1 140oa x 29 x 19 587 tons 2 decks	November		Jas.O.Curtis Medford, Mass.	Wm.Lincoln & Co. Boston	Queen of the Seas #1 214oa x 39 x 22 1356 tons 2 decks	18 September		Paul Curtis Medford, Mass.	Glidden & Williams Boston
Sea Bird (Bark) #1 115oa x 26 x 14 325 tons 1 deck & hold beams partially decked	November	Samuel Hall East Boston	Samuel Hall East Boston	Lombard & Co., et al. Boston	John Gilpin #1 205oa x 37 x 22 1084 tons 2 decks	September	Samuel Hall East Boston	Samuel Hall East Boston	Pierce & Hunnewell Boston
Dauntless #1 185oa x 33 x 21-6 800 tons 2 decks	December	W.N.Goddard Boston	Benjamin F. Delano Medford, Mass.	W.N.Goddard Boston	Golden Eagle #1,32 192oa x 36 x 22 1121 tons 2 decks	9 November		Hayden & Cudworth Medford, Mass.	Wm.Lincoln & Co. Boston
Hoogly #1 200oa x 39 x 25 1304 tons 2 decks & hold beams partially decked	December	Samuel Hall East Boston	Samuel Hall East Boston	D.C.Bacon & Sons Boston	Flying Childers #1,32 195oa x 36-4 x 22-6 1125 tons 2 decks	11 November	Samuel Hall East Boston	Samuel Hall East Boston	J.M.Forbes & Cunningham Bros. Boston
Rocket (Bark) #1 136od x 26 x 16-6 400 tons 1 deck	December	W.N.Goddard Boston	W.N.Goddard Boston		Golden West #1,32 210oa x 39 x 23-4 1441 tons 2 decks	16 November		Paul Curtis East Boston	Glidden & Williams Boston
Roebuck #1 170oa x 33 x 22 816 tons 2 decks	December		Bourne & Kingsbury Kennebunk, Maine	Nichols & Curtis Boston	Bald Eagle #1,32 225oa x 41-6 x 22-6 1705 tons 2 decks	25 November	Donald McKay East Boston	Donald McKay East Boston	Geo.B.Upton Boston
	1852				Queen of the Pacific #31 197* x 39-6 x 26-8 1356 tons 3 decks (probable)	November		Isaac Elwell Pembroke, Maine	Reed, Wade & Co. Boston
Beverly #3 152-6od x 32-6 x 21-6 676 tons 2 decks	19 April		Paul Curtis Medford, Mass.	Wm.Perkins & Israel Whitney Boston	Winged Racer #1 226oa x 42-6 x 23 1767 tons 2 decks	November	Sam'l.H.Pook Boston	Robert E. Jackson East Boston	Seccomb & Taylor Boston
Ellen Foster #1 180oa x 37 x 24 996 tons 2 decks	April		Joshua T. Foster Medford, Mass.	J. & A. Tirrell Boston	Phantom #1 200oa x 37-11 x 21-6 1300 tons 2 decks	8 December	Sam'l.Lapham Medford, Mass.(& John F.Lodge Boston)	Sam'l.Lapham Medford, Mass.	Crocker & Sturgis, et al. Boston
Sovereign of the Seas #1 265oa x 44 x 23-6 2421 tons 2 decks & hold beams	June	Donald McKay East Boston	Donald McKay East Boston	Donald McKay Boston	Star of the Union #1 200oa x 35 x 21-6 1200 tons 2 decks	9 December		Jas.O.Curtis Medford, Mass.	Reed, Wade & Co. Boston

Vessel & Ref.#	Date of Launch	Designer	Builder	Original Owner
1852				
Flying Arrow #1 170-8od x 37-10 x 23-4 1092 tons 2 decks	December		Geo. Dunham Frankfort, Maine	Manning, Stanwood & Co. Boston
Flying Eagle #1 195oa x 37 x 23 1097 tons 2 decks	December		Wm.Hitchcock Damariscotta, Maine	F.Nickerson, J. Beal, et al. Boston
Lady Franklin #31 133* x 27-6 x 18 475 tons 2 decks			Jarvis Pratt East Boston	Wm. Ropes Boston
1853				
Golden Light #1 193oa x 36 x 22-6 1150 tons 2 decks	8 January	E. & H.O. Briggs So.Boston	E. & H.O. Briggs So. Boston	Jas.Huckins & Sons Boston
Mystery #1 196oa x 37 x 23 1125 tons 2 decks	11 January	Samuel Hall East Boston	Samuel Hall East Boston	Crocker & Sturgis Boston
Empress of the Sea #1,31 240oa x 43 x 27 2197 tons 2 decks & hold beams partially decked	14 January	Donald McKay East Boston	Donald McKay East Boston	Wm. Wilson & Son Baltimore
Radiant #1 210oa x 40 x 24-4 1300 tons 2 decks	24 January		Paul Curtis East Boston	Baker & Morrill Boston
Storm King #1 216oa x 39 x 23 1400 tons 2 decks	February		John Taylor Chelsea, Mass.	Snow & Rich Boston
Belle of the West #1 182oa x 35 x 20-6 936 tons 2 decks	25 March	Sam'l.H.Pook Boston	Shiverick Bros. East Dennis, Mass.	Glidden & Williams Boston
John Land #32 183oa x 36 x 22 1052 tons 2 decks	26 March	E. & H.O. Briggs So. Boston	E. & H.O. Briggs So. Boston	Baker & Morrill Boston
Queen of Clippers #1 258oa x 44-6 x 24 2300 tons 2 decks	26 March		Robert E. Jackson East Boston	Zarega & Co. New York
(Bought from Seccomb & Taylor before launch.)				
Cleopatra #1,31 220oa x 41-6 x 23-4 1562 tons 2 decks	28 March		Paul Curtis East Boston	Benjamin Bangs Boston
Climax #1 180od x 36 x 22-9 1051 tons 2 decks	March		Hayden & Cudworth Medford, Mass.	Howes & Crowell Boston
West Wind #1,31 180od x 36-6 x 24 1071 tons 2 decks	March		Joshua Foster Medford, Mass.	J. & A. Tirrell Boston
Wild Ranger #1 175od x 35 x 23 1034 tons 2 decks	7 April		Jas.O.Curtis Medford, Mass.	Thatcher & Sears Boston
1853				
Young America #32 243od x 43-2 x 26-9 1961 tons 3 decks	30 April	Wm.H.Webb New York	Wm.H.Webb New York	Geo. Daniels New York
Wildfire (Bark) #1 138oa x 28 x 10-6 350 tons 1 deck & high quarter deck	April	Simeon McKay Boston	Simeon McKay Boston	A.L.Payson Boston
Wizard #1 225oa x 40-6 x 25-9 1650 tons 2 decks & hold beams partially decked	April	Samuel Hall East Boston	Samuel Hall East Boston	Slade & Co. New York
Water Witch #1 192oa x 38-3 x 21 1204 tons 2 decks	7 May		Fernald & Pettigrew Portsmouth, NH	Stephen Tilton, et al. Boston
Bonita #1 193oa x 36 x 22-6 1150 tons 2 decks	12 May	Capt. Jas. Huckins Boston	E. & H.O. Briggs So. Boston	Capt. Jas. Huckins Boston
Whistler #1,31 185oa x 36 x 22 820 tons 2 decks	15 June		George W. Jackman, Jr. Newburyport, Mass.	Bush & Wildes Boston
Sweepstakes #31 216-4od x 41-6 x 22 1735 tons 2 decks	21 June	Daniel Westervelt New York	D. & A. Westervelt New York	Grinnell, Minturn & Co. New York
Flyaway #24,31 190od x 38-3 x 21-6 1274 tons 2 decks	23 June	Wm.H.Webb New York	Wm.H.Webb New York	Schiff Bros. & Co. New York
Amphitrite #1 221od x 41 x 26-3 1687 tons 2 decks & hold beams partially decked	June	Samuel Hall East Boston	Samuel Hall East Boston	Samuel Hall Boston
Flying Dragon #1 187pp x 38 x 22 1137 tons 2 decks	June		Trufant & Drummond, Bath, Maine	Reed, Wade & Co. Boston
Fearless #31 191* x 36-5 x 22 1184 tons 2 decks	28 July	Sam'l.H.Pook Boston	A. & G.T. Sampson East Boston	William F. Weld & Co. Boston
Ocean Pearl #1 171od x 34-6 x 23 770 tons 2 decks	15 August	Elisha Stetson Boston	Jos. Magoun Charlestown, Mass.	Hardy, Sears, et al. Boston
Cyclone #1 183od x 36 x 22-6 1100 tons 2 decks	18 August	E. & H.O. Briggs So. Boston	E. & H.O. Briggs So. Boston	Curtis & Peabody Boston
King Fisher #1,31 217oa x 37-2 x 24 1300 tons 2 decks	18 August		Hayden & Cudworth Medford, Mass.	William Lincoln Boston
Morning Light #1 235oa x 43 x 27 1713 tons 3 decks	20 August		Tobey & Littlefield Portsmouth, NH	Glidden & Williams Boston
Lightfoot #1 237od x 42-6 x 23 1950 tons 2 decks	August		Robert E. Jackson East Boston	Seccomb & Taylor Boston

Vessel & Ref.#	Date of Launch	Designer	Builder	Original Owner	Vessel & Ref.#	Date of Launch	Designer	Builder	Original Owner
	1853					**1854**			
Spitfire #1 224oa x 40 x 23 1550 tons 2 decks	3 September		James Arey & Co. Frankfort, Maine	Gray, Manning & Stanwood Boston	Panther #31 193-7* x 37-5 x 24 1278 tons 2 decks	January or February		Paul Curtis East Boston	R.C.Mackay & Sons Boston
Don Quixote #1 225oa x 38-3 x 23-6 1450 tons 2 decks	September	Sam'l.Lapham Medford, Mass.	Sam'l.Lapham Medford, Mass.	J.E.Lodge Boston	Galatea #1 182od x 36-6 x 23 1100 tons 2 decks	16 March		Jos. Magoun Charlestown, Mass.	William F. Weld & Co. Boston
Eagle Wing #1,31 205oa x 39 x 23 1174 tons 2 decks	4 October		James O. Curtis Medford, Mass.	Chase & Tappan Boston	Ocean Telegraph #5,32 227oa x 41 x 26-6 1626 tons 2 decks	29 March	Sam'l.H.Pook Boston	Jas.O.Curtis Medford, Mass.	Reed, Wade & Co. Boston
Great Republic #31 335oa x 53 x 38 4555 tons 4 decks	4 October	Donald McKay East Boston	Donald McKay East Boston	Donald McKay Boston	Starr King #31 200oa x 39 x 22-6 1171 tons 2 decks	March		George W. Jackman, Jr. Newburyport, Mass.	Baker & Morrill, et al. Boston
Edwin Forrest #1 184od x 37 x 23-4 1074 tons 2 decks	5 October		Daniel D. Kelly East Boston	Crosby, Crocker & Co. New York	Swallow #1 210* x 39 x 23-4 1400 tons 2 decks	4 April		Robert E. Jackson East Boston	Dugan & Leland New York
Romance of the Sea #32 240-9oa x 39-6 x 20 1782 tons 2 decks	23 October	Geo.B.Upton Boston	Donald McKay East Boston	Geo.B.Upton Boston	Champion of the Seas #1 252od x 45-6 x 29 2447 tons 3 decks	19 April	Donald McKay East Boston	Donald McKay East Boston	Jas. Baines & Co. Liverpool
Red Jacket #14 241-6oa x 43 x 23 2305 tons 2 decks (originally); 3rd deck added 1860, Ref. 58	2 November	Sam'l.H.Pook Boston	Geo. Thomas Rockland, Maine	Seccomb & Taylor Boston	Robin Hood #31 186* x 37 x 23-6 1182 tons 2 decks	April		Hayden & Cudworth Medford, Mass.	Howes & Crowell Boston
Challenger #1 206oa x 38-4 x 23 1400 tons 2 decks	19 December	Sam'l.H.Pook Boston	Robert E. Jackson East Boston	W. & F.H. Wittemore Boston	Sierra Nevada #32 230oa x 44-4 x 26-4 1942 tons 3 decks	29 May		Tobey & Littlefield Portsmouth, NH	Glidden & Williams Boston
Eringo (Bark) #1 113od x 26-3 x 12-1 327 tons 1 deck & half poop	December		Brown & Lovell East Boston	Capt. Lewin, et al. Boston	Grace Darling #1 188od x 37-6 x 23 1230 tons 2 decks	May	E. & H.O. Briggs So. Boston	E. & H.O. Briggs So. Boston	Charles B. Fessenden Boston
Herald of the Morning #1 202od x 37 x 24 1300 tons 2 decks	December	Sam'l.H.Pook Boston	Hayden & Cudworth Medford, Mass.	Thatcher Magoun & Son Boston	Mary Robinson #31 215* x 38-6 x 22-6 1371 tons 2 decks	May		Trufant & Drummond Bath, Maine	E. M. Robinson New Bedford, Mass.
Western Continent #9 188' length of keel 1272 tons decks			H.E.Carter or S.C.Foster Pembroke, Maine	John M. Mayo & Co. Boston	Lamplighter (Bark) #1 121* x 27-7 x 12 365 tons 1 deck	June		Hayden & Cudworth Medford, Mass.	Lombard & Co., et al. Boston
Wild Rover #32 187* x 36 x 22 1100 tons 2 decks			Austin & Hall Damariscotta, Maine	Alpheus Hardy & Co. Boston	Ocean Express #1 240oa x 42-6 x 24-6 1697 tons 2 decks & hold beams from fore to mizzen	10 July		Jas.O.Curtis Medford, Mass.	Reed, Wade & Co. Boston
	1854				James Baines #31 266oa x 44-9 x 29 2515 tons 3 decks	25 July	Donald McKay East Boston	Donald McKay East Boston	Jas. Baines & Co. Liverpool
Coeur de Lion #1 198oa x 36 x 22 1100 tons 2 decks	3 January	Geo. Raynes Portsmouth, NH	Geo. Raynes Portsmouth, NH	William F. Parrott Boston	Osborne Howes #31 186* x 35-9 x 23-9 1100 tons 2 decks	27 July		Hayden & Cudworth Medford, Mass.	Howes & Crowell Boston
Lightning #1,31 243oa x 44 x 23 2084 tons 2 decks	3 January	Donald McKay East Boston	Donald McKay East Boston	Jas. Baines & Co. Liverpool	Blue Jacket #5 235oa x 41-2 x 24 1790 tons 2 decks	27 August		Robert E. Jackson East Boston	Seccomb & Taylor Boston
Fleet Wing #1 170od x 35-6 x 22 912 tons 2 decks	January		Hayden & Cudworth Medford, Mass.	Crowell, Brooks & Co. Boston	Santa Claus #1 194oa x 38-6 x 22-11 1255 tons 2 decks	5 September	Donald McKay East Boston	Donald McKay East Boston	William A. Harris Boston

Vessel & Ref.#	Date of Launch	Designer	Builder	Original Owner
1854				
#1 Bounding Billow (Bark) 125od x 27-6 x 12 360 tons 1 deck	September		Jotham Stetson Chelsea, Mass.	Lombard, Conant, et al. Boston
Sunny South #32 164-7oa x 31-4 x 16-6 776 tons 1 deck & possibly hold beams	7 October	Geo. Steers Williamsburg, New York	Geo. Steers Williamsburg, New York	Napier, Johnson & Co. New York
Saracen #1 200oa x 38-6 x 24 1300 tons 2 decks	October	E. & H.O. Briggs So. Boston	E. & H.O. Briggs So. Boston	Curtis & Peabody Boston
Charmer #1 203oa x 37 x 23 1083 tons 2 decks	November		George W. Jackman, Jr. Newburyport, Mass.	Bush & Wildes Boston
Indiaman #1 186pp x 37 x 22-4 1165 tons 2 decks	November		Hugh McKay East Boston	Sampson & Tappan Boston
1855				
War Hawk #1 193oa x 37 x 23 1074½ tons 2 decks	3 January		George W. Jackman, Jr. Newburyport, Mass.	Bush & Comstock, et al. Boston
Donald McKay #1 266od x 46 x 29 2588 tons 3 decks	January	Donald McKay East Boston	Donald McKay East Boston	Jas. Baines & Co. Liverpool
Great Republic #28,32 (rebuilt) 335oa x 53 x 29-6 3356 tons 3 decks (Spar deck omitted)	January	Rebuilding supervisor, N.B.Palmer New York	Sneeden & Whitlock Greenpoint, L.I.	A. A. Low & Bro. New York
Andrew Jackson #31,59 222* x 41-2 x 22-3 1679 tons 2 decks	March	Mason Cary Hill Mystic, Conn.	Irons & Grinnell Mystic, Conn.	John H. Brower & Co. New York
Noonday #1,31 197oa x 38-5 x 23-6 1177 tons 2 decks	25 August	Frederick W. Fernald (apparently) Portsmouth, NH	Fernald & Pettigrew Portsmouth, NH	Henry Hastings, et al. Boston
Mameluke #1 212oa x 38-10 x 24 1156 tons 2 decks	September	E. & H.O. Briggs So. Boston	E. & H.O. Briggs So. Boston	Curtis & Peabody Boston
Daring #1 193oa x 37-6 x 23 1100 tons 2 decks	8 October		George W. Jackman, Jr. Newburyport, Mass.	Bush & Comstock Boston
Fair Wind #1 204oa x 38-10 x 24 1303 tons 2 decks	12 October	E. & H.O. Briggs So. Boston	E. & H.O. Briggs So. Boston	Henry S. Hallett & Co. Boston
Electric Spark #1 185od x 40 x 24 1200 tons 2 decks	17 November		Hayden & Cudworth Medford, Mass.	Thatcher Magoun & Son Boston
#1 Golden Fleece (2nd) 222oa x 41 x 26 1500 tons 2 decks & hold beams	20 November		Paul Curtis East Boston	William F. Weld & Co. Boston
1855				
Quickstep (Bark) #1 143od x 29-6 x 18-9 530 tons 2 decks	November	Samuel Hall, Jr. Boston	Samuel Hall, Jr. Boston	Samuel Hall Boston
1856				
Mastiff #1 169pp x 37-6 x 22 1030 tons 2 decks	January	Geo.B.Upton Boston	Donald McKay East Boston	Geo.B.Upton Boston
Alarm #1 190oa x 38-6 x 24 1175 tons 2 decks & hold beams	18 March	E. & H.O. Briggs So. Boston	E. & H.O. Briggs So. Boston	Baker & Morrill Boston
Endeavor #1 1920a x 37 x 22 1136 tons 2 decks	April		Robert E. Jackson East Boston	Cunningham Bros. Boston
Silver Star #1 195oa x 38 x 24 1195 tons 2 decks	April		Jas.O.Curtis Medford, Mass.	Reed, Wade & Co. Boston
Thatcher Magoun #1,32 200oa x 40 x 24 1248 tons 2 decks	April		Hayden & Cudworth Medford, Mass.	Thatcher Magoun & Son Boston
Joseph Peabody #1 190oa x 38-6 x 24 1180 tons 2 decks & hold beams	7 June	E. & H.O. Briggs So. Boston	E. & H.O. Briggs So. Boston	Curtis & Peabody Boston
Henry Hill (Bark) #1 143oa x 31 x 14-8 550 tons 1 deck & hold beams partially decked	June	Donald McKay East Boston	Donald McKay East Boston	Charles S. Brown Boston
Intrepid #18,31 179-9* x 38 x 23 1173 tons 2 decks	June	Wm.H.Webb New York	Wm.H.Webb New York	Bucklin & Crane New York
Flying Mist #1 200oa x 39 x 24 1184 tons 2 decks	13 September		Jas.O.Curtis Medford, Mass.	Theodore & Geo. B. Chase Boston
Uncowah #18,31 169* x 36-6 x 22 988 tons 2 decks	15 October	Wm.H.Webb New York	Wm.H.Webb New York	Wakeman, Dimon & Co. New York
Charger #1 201oa x 39 x 23-6 1306 tons 2 decks	25 October		Elbridge G. Pierce Portsmouth, NH	Henry Hastings, et al. Boston
Asa Eldridge #1 204oa x 38-10 x 25 1198 tons 2 decks & hold beams	October	E. & H.O. Briggs So. Boston	E. & H.O. Briggs So. Boston	Henry S. Hallett, Esq. Boston
Young Turk (Bark) #1 116od x 28 x 13 350 tons 1 deck	November		Jas.O.Curtis Medford, Mass.	Alpheus Hardy & Co. Boston
Black Hawk #18,24 180od x 38 x 23 1175 tons 2 decks	29 December	Wm.H.Webb New York	Wm.H.Webb New York	Bucklin & Crane New York

ACKNOWLEDGMENTS

A BOOK SUCH AS THIS IS not the product of the author alone. Along the way, many individuals and institutions render invaluable services and facilities without which the end product could not have come into being. A statement of thanks and recognition is due those who contributed in measure great and small. To the following individuals and organizations, I am deeply indebted:

E. Ann Wilcox, Librarian, Independence Seaport Museum, Philadelphia, Pennsylvania (formerly the Philadelphia Maritime Museum), who furthered the progress of the work in many ways and who cannot be too highly commended. Edwin B. Leaf, The Philadelphia Ship Model Society, who provided essential information relative to steering the book in the proper direction. My wife, Marjorie, typist and research assistant on the many field trips undertaken in pursuit of well-hidden information.

Paige Lilly, Archivist/Librarian, Penobscot Marine Museum, Searsport, Maine; Paul J. O'Pecko, Reference Librarian, Mystic Seaport Museum, Mystic, Connecticut; and Ann Walsh, Library Assistant, Webb Institute of Naval Architecture, Glen Cove, New York; all contributed much information upon request, which was quite frequent.

Shipwrights Roger Hambidge, Mystic Museum Shipyard, Mystic Seaport Museum, Mystic, Connecticut; Melbourne Smith, International Historical Watercraft Society, Annapolis, Maryland; John Millar, Williamsburg, Virginia; Richard L. Miles, Aberdeen, Washington; Dana Story, Essex, Massachusetts; and Peter Stanford, National Maritime Historical Society; all provided practical answers to academic questions.

Robert and Grisel Leavitt, Miami, Florida; Michael Costagliola, Sea Cliff, New York; Erik A. R. Ronnberg, Jr., Rockport, Massachusetts; Merritt A. Edson, Bethesda, Maryland (deceased); Stephen D. Hopkins, New Rochelle, New York; Professor Richard Jagels, University of Maine, Orono, Maine; James Raines, Editor, *Seaways—Ships in Scale* magazine, San Jose, California; and William D. Thomas, Naval Architect, New York, New York; all provided information based on their own knowledge and expertise.

Finally, the facilities of the following organizations were indispensable: The Library of Congress, and the National Archives, Washington, D.C.; San Francisco Maritime National Historical Park, San Francisco, California; Mystic Seaport Museum, Mystic, Connecticut; William A. Farnsworth Library and Museum, Rockland, Maine; the National Maritime Museum, London, England; the City of Liverpool Museums, Liverpool, England; The Free Library of Philadelphia, Philadelphia, Pennsylvania; Webb Institute of Naval Architecture, Glen Cove, New York; the library of the Naval Academy Museum, Annapolis, Maryland; and the library of the Shelburne Museum, Shelburne, Vermont.

To all the above I express my appreciation.

WILLIAM L. CROTHERS

THE AMERICAN-BUILT CLIPPER SHIP and its structural details are the subject of this work, the word "ship" applying to all vessels in the category, whether rigged as ships or as barks.

The construction details and practices recorded here were applicable to shipbuilding in general. Wherever possible, those details that were applied to specific clipper ships have been listed and form the principal contents of this book.

The obvious features introduced to shipbuilding by clippers as a type were the pronounced flare of the clipper bow, generally fine lines, sleek appearance, and in action, an ability to reach and maintain speeds that were previously unmatched.

Shipmasters made their own contribution to clipper reputation by driving their ships as no ships had been driven before. They exacted the last ounce of strength and endurance that a vessel was capable of sustaining. Through this intense driving under every conceivable combination of wind and weather, the ships proved conclusively that the input of designers and artisans were not mere matters of chance and hope. Such hard driving underscored the fact that wooden ships, which for centuries had proved themselves in navigating the seas of the world, were capable of withstanding vast amounts of punishment not usually demanded of a ship.

Through a long period of history, ships had experienced improvement in seaworthiness, had undergone great increases in size, and had developed efficient sailing qualities. Along with these elements was a vast accumulated knowledge of the characteristics of timber and its most efficient usage.

Upon its arrival, the clipper ship was the beneficiary of centuries of seafaring experience. Unlike its predecessors, it did not develop over time; rather, it virtually burst upon the scene. It created an almost feverish sensation and frenzy and, like a meteor, just as quickly fell from grace.

Before the fall, however, the performance of the clipper ships was avidly followed in all the seafaring communities along the Eastern Seaboard of the United States. They became the subject of intense public interest, and their exploits were discussed and compared on a daily basis. The discussions were not private or quietly indulged in over a cup of tea or a glass of wine. The subject fed on itself until public interest gave way to civic pride. Communities began to champion the performances of their own vessels and were critical of any comments by other communities which appeared to belittle the accomplishments of the vessels.

A never-ending stream of boasting and defending became commonplace. Here follows a typical exchange between *The Boston Daily Atlas* and the *New York Herald* involving the performances of the clippers *Northern Light* and *Contest*, both articles being excerpted from the *Atlas* (see page *xxiv*).

The clipper period is generally considered to have flourished between 1845 and 1859. The bulk of construction, however, took place from 1850 to 1856, when 435 extreme and medium clippers were launched. The peak year of the period was 1853, when 120 clippers were launched.

While New York and Boston were the scenes of greatest activity, it appears that no suitable site between Maine and Virginia was without its shipyard.

The clipper fever was pervasive and generated a new type of thinking. Ships suddenly were christened with romantic names; interior decor of passenger-carrying vessels reached a new level of embellishment; masts were pushed skyward to carry ever-increasing clouds of sail.

The need which the clipper ship filled so well was the speedy transport of people and goods from the eastern United States to California and the Far East, especially China, for gold, tea, and exotic Oriental creations.

Some notable authorities have been very critical of the clipper ship and its design, citing the tremendous sacrifice of carrying capacity in order to achieve speed. This does not appear to be a proper evaluation when viewed in light of the conditions that prevailed during the clipper period. However, descriptions of the internal construction of the ships indicate an inordinate loss of space due to the great scantlings and profusion of such members. Nevertheless, it appears that no creation of man ever fulfilled its task of the moment more admirably than did the American-built clipper ship.

The price of speed was high. The ships required large crews and were reportedly costly to operate. Thus, when depression overtook the country in 1857 and world markets deteriorated, the clipper ship found it difficult to compete as a viable tool of commerce. The rocket that had ascended so swiftly and burned so brightly was slowly extinguished, a victim of the times.

The ships did not disappear from the surface of the sea. But, as the years went by, their assignments were downgraded and their tasks became menial. Some were dismasted and used as barges until, aged and broken, they met their end in flames or broken-backed on the rocks, or washed ashore to waste away at the discretion of the elements. Some, more mercifully, foundered and met their end at sea in the element for which they were conceived. Ships, by their nature, are born to die. There is no way they can go on forever.

JUNE 16, 1853.

CLIPPERS.

New York, June 13, 1853

To the Editors of the Atlas:—Gentlemen—Several statements having appeared in your city papers, to the effect that the clipper ship Northern Light had beaten the clipper ship Contest, on the last voyage to San Francisco and back, and as this is not the fact, I appeal to you to give the following communication, which was published in the Herald of the 4th inst., a place in your paper. The Boston papers were requested to copy it, but thus far, they have taken no notice of it whatever. Now as your paper is considered here the official organ of Clipperdom, I appeal to your sense of fair play to do the Contest justice.

THE CONTEST OF THE CLIPPERS.

New York, June 3, 1853.

To the Editor of the Herald:—As our Boston friends seem highly elated with the crack passages made by their ship Northern Light, from San Francisco, and are disposed to disparage her competitor, the Contest, perhaps it would be well to give a history of the voyages of the two ships, that the public may judge which came out the winner.

The Northern Light sailed from Boston, Oct. 29, 1852, and arrived at San Francisco, Feb. 23, 1853, making the passage in 117 days.

The Contest sailed from New York, Nov. 16, 1852, and arrived at San Francisco, Feb. 24, 1853, making the passage in 100 days. Difference in favor of the Contest, 17 days on the outer passage.

On the return voyage, the Contest sailed from San Francisco, March 12, and arrived at New York, May 31—making the passage home in 80 days. The Northern Light sailed from San Francisco, March 12, and arrived at Boston, May 29, making the passage in 77 days—a difference of 3 days in favor of the Northern Light. We now proceed to sum up:—Northern Light completed the voyage in precisely 7 months—average passage out and home, 97 days. Contest completed the voyage in six months and fourteen days—average passage, out and home, ninety days.

A number of squibs having appeared in the Boston papers in regard to the meeting of these two ships off Cape Horn—in one of which it is said the captain of the Northern Light "could not hold up his horse"—we will give some extracts from the log book of the Contest, that the public may judge which had occasion to hold up the strongest:

"April 29, discovered a ship off the lee bow. At meridian, ship abeam—made her out the Northern Light. April 21, Northern Light four points abaft the beam. April 22, Northern Light four miles astern. April 23, Northern Light fifteen miles astern, and out of sight in the course of the day."

As we have to make up the account with the Northern Light alone, we would only add, that the crack clippers Game Cock, Telegraph, Meteor, Whirlwind and Queen of the Seas, (belonging to Boston,) sailed on or before the Contest, all of which she beat from eight to seventeen days on the passage to San Francisco.

NAUTICON.

P. S. The Boston papers in their eagerness to glorify the Northern Light, seem to have forgotten that she is the only Boston vessel, except the John Bertram, which returned from San Francisco in ballast, and this ship on her outward passage beat the Northern Light 13 days. The Flying Fish, built about the same time, made her first passage to San Francisco in 100 days, and her second in 92, or both passages in 192 days; whereas the Northern Light made her first passage in 109 days, and her second in 117, or both passages in 226 days, having been beaten by the Flying Fish 34 days. The John Gilpin, too, a much fuller modelled ship than the Northern Light, beat her 19 days on the last passage to San Francisco. With these facts staring them in the face, it appears wonderfully strange that the Boston papers should be so silly as to call the Northern Light "their fastest ship." If the owners of the Northern Light feel inclined to bet a reasonable sum upon her next passage to San Francisco against the next passage of the Contest, I think a note to that effect addressed to her owners, would receive attention.

N.

We beg leave to inform our New York friend, that if, at any time, in the course of our glorification about the speed of our clippers, we should make mistakes, we will most cheerfully correct them when they are pointed out.

JUNE 24, 1853.

CLIPPER VOYAGES.

To the Editors of the Boston Atlas:

Gentlemen—We perused with pleasure an article in your daily of the 16th inst., copied at the *earnest* request of a New York correspondent, from the New York Herald of the 4th inst.

The writer appeals to your sense of fair play to do the New York clipper ship "Contest" justice, because, as he writes, several statements have appeared in the Boston papers, to the effect that the clipper ship "Northern Light" had beaten the clipper ship "Contest" on the last voyage to San Francisco and back, which he says is not the fact.

We have looked in vain to find a statement in any Boston paper that the "Northern Light" beat the "Contest" on the last voyage to San Francisco and back; but we do now state, and we believe it to be an indisputable fact, that the "Northern Light" beat the "Contest" on the passage back from San Francisco to Boston by four days of actual time, saying not a word about the difference in favor of a voyage from San Francisco to New York over one to Boston, which we claim to be as good as two days more.

Our New York friend, to prove, we suppose, that the "Contest" is the fastest sailer of the two ships, gives us extracts from the Log Book of the "Contest," which go to show that the two ships were in company several days, and in the course of the last day the "Contest" left the "Northern Light" at nightfall lost in the astern distance. We have not been favored with the Log of the "Northern Light," that we might compare accounts, but we have had the gratification of receiving information from a gentleman who came home a passenger in the "Contest," which is substantially this, that on the evening of the 19th of April, a large ship was discovered right astern, which he expressed his opinion as being the "Northern Light" from the fact of her carrying but one, that a main skysail; at meridian of the day following she was abeam—remained in company two or three days, and when last seen was a few miles ahead as night set in, and was not seen again. We make this statement, not to strengthen the fact that the Northern Light is a very fast sailer, but to show how exceedingly at variance are the facts as stated in the Log of the "Contest" and by one who was a present and disinterested observer of the affair.

We do not, with our New York friend, see anything "very silly" in the terming of the "Northern Light" a fast, a *very fast ship*, or even, if you please, "the fastest ship," if we may judge of her capabilities by her last passage, and we cannot see any unfairness in founding a decision upon this single passage, to prove the fact we now state, which is, that the Boston built clipper ship "Northern Light" has made the shortest passage between the port of San Francisco and the Atlantic States upon record, and that her performance justly entitles her to wear that Commodore's broad pennant, which flies at her main; which, by the by, if it should have the effect of causing clipper owners and builders to strive and produce a model which shall surpass, in its sailing and other qualities, that of the "Northern Light," will not have waved in vain, and we have no doubt but that the owners of the Northern Light would surrender it with a good grace to their conqueror whenever she comes along.

The gentleman to whom the Northern Light owes her beautiful and valuable model, was once heard to say that he believed 75 days would soon be a sufficient time for a clipper to accomplish her voyage in, from San Francisco to Boston; and we now congratulate him upon being so fortunate as to have already seen his prediction so nearly accomplished by a vessel constructed, in every respect, upon his own model. May she be to her owners as fortunate a vessel as she has proved herself FAST.

R.

To bring into one place a compilation of details of clipper ship construction, from conception to completion, these pages are written. Most information of this type has found its way into museums, libraries, universities, and historical organizations dedicated to the preservation of precious bits and pieces of our heritage.

The best overall descriptive source of the clipper ship as a finished product appears to be the articles written by marine reporter Duncan MacLean for *The Boston Daily Atlas* between the years 1850 and 1856. These were the result of on-board inspections of the various vessels, generally as they floated at dockside. They also contain details hidden from sight which could only have been provided by the builder or designer of the vessel.

There are, of course, other sources of information, many of which are included in this book, but no other single source covers so many vessels. Many ships have left behind little more than their names. The ships included here have been selected because information was reasonably available, appeared to be genuinely authentic, and serves the general purpose of describing how the clipper ship was constructed. The details discussed or illustrated here are typical and will enhance the overall detailed knowledge of the American-built clipper ship.

The ships were built without the benefit (or restraints) of an American code for building ships. However, almost without fail, an examination of the scantlings of materials used in the clippers tabulated in this book indicates that in general the vessels as built were consistent with the American rules that would be established a year or two later.

Immediately after our period (1850–1856), the rules for building ships in the United States were formalized. In 1857 a set of rules was promulgated in New York and was titled the *New York Marine Register: A Standard Classification of American Vessels, And of Such Other Vessels as Visit American Ports.* It was also known as *American-Lloyd's Universal* and became available in 1858. Thus, for the first time, the American shipbuilding industry had its own collection of rules by which it would be governed.

Then, in 1867, the American Shipmasters' Association, at the behest of the New York Board of Underwriters, compiled a book of *Rules of Classification* which covered, among other items, the details of construction and the evaluation of woods used in the construction of American vessels. This work was known as the *Record of American and Foreign Shipping.*

Finally, on August 25, 1870, two other shipping registers, *The American Lloyd's Universal Register of Shipping*, "purporting to be published by Thomas D. Taylor," and *The American Lloyd's Register of American and Foreign Shipping*, "purporting to be published by Hartshorne & King," were formally disavowed by the Board of Underwriters of New York. Thus the *Record of American and Foreign Shipping* became the sole recognized governing document pertaining to American shipbuilding. A detailed comparison of this document with the construction details of the clipper ships reveals that, in general, each followed the same path.

For the benefit of all who are seasoned and knowledgeable on the subject of nautical lore, and for the newcomer who is only now learning how addictive the subject can become, this book attempts to bring together the essence of far-flung details and information about the clippers that have been scattered like seeds before the wind into countless hidden repositories. The total story is interesting and beguiling and ready to be enjoyed.

A Note on References

References used for *The American-Built Clipper Ship* are identified throughout the text by superscript numerals, and are noted also in all tables. These references provide direct access to the author's basic sources, which are annotated and listed beginning on page 506.

THE
AMERICAN-BUILT CLIPPER SHIP

1850–1856

PART I
Prelude to Building the Ship

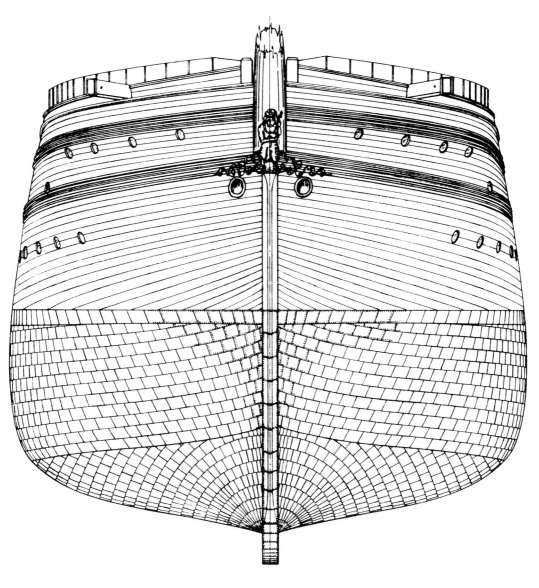

Bow view of
Lightning
1854

Chapter One

PREPARATION FOR CONSTRUCTION

THE LIFE OF A SHIP begins when an individual or organization decides upon the need or desire for such a vehicle to further the pursuit of pleasure or profit—in the case of the American-built clipper ship, the quest for profit in merchant shipping, and the quest for progress and product development on the part of the designer and shipbuilder.

The initial step, once the idea had germinated, was to determine the explicit purpose of the vessel. Other factors included the waters in which the ship was expected to sail, the depth of the water at ports where the ship would call, climatic conditions over her sailing routes, and many other considerations known to the ship's owner and designer.

After the client had formed his own picture of the ship he desired, he sought the services of an individual to design and build his ship; in many cases both skills lay with just one person. Suitable dimensions of length and breadth were determined, as was an estimated tonnage. A profile was developed, along with a *midship section*—the transverse shape of the hull at its widest and fullest dimensions, also known as the *dead flat* section. In clipper ships, the midship section varied widely in shape and location, as we will see in Chapter 6.

Around the midship section the hull form was developed until the stem and sternpost were reached. Many clients were retired shipmasters who had definite ideas about which characteristics they desired to see embodied in their new vessel. Thus the design and proportions of the ships and such characteristics as deadrise and tumblehome, the fullness or fineness of lines, and other pertinent details were determined between the designer and client, after which the designer took command and proceeded to develop the vessel. Designers were never altogether pleased with this arrangement.

The Half Model

The preferred method of developing the hull was by producing a *half model*: a three-dimensional model of the hull in profile, cut in half along its longitudinal, vertical centerline. The symmetry of ships about their centerline obviated the need for a complete hull. The half model, when completed, represented the skeletal form of the finished vessel—that is, the shape of the outer surface of the vessel's frames over which the hull planking would be laid. Thus, it was referred to as the *moulded* form, and in the building of ships reference was constantly made to moulded dimensions.

A flat board of suitable size might be selected as a mounting plaque, on which the silhouette form of the vessel was constructed and shaped. Generally, the height of a half model terminated at the main rail, with any minor structure above to be faired in later.

Half models were produced in a variety of forms. It was possible, though not very practical, to carve one from a single block of wood. A better, and the more preferred method, was to build a *waterline lift model*, "bread-and-butter" fashion, in lifts of a thickness corresponding to useful waterline planes. In this way it was easy to observe and understand the form of the hull at any given height above the moulded baseline. It was also a simpler matter to identify specific areas of the hull that might require modification.

As an improvement on the basic lift model, woods of contrasting color, commonly cedar and pine, were used for alternate lifts. With this construction, the form of the hull was apparent to even a passing glance. It was from this half model that the next preliminary step was taken.

Builders' half models abound in American museums,

historical collections, maritime schools, libraries, and other organizations whose interest is the preservation of such historical artifacts. The following list gives the locations of half models of some of the vessels included in this book.

Existing Half Models

Vessel	Location and Comments
Andrew Jackson[31]	Mr. Brower Hewitt, grandson of owner. (This information as of 1930.)
Belle of the West[31]	Mariners House, Boston.
Challenge[31]	Webb Institute of Naval Architecture, Glen Cove, New York.
Coeur de Lion[136]	Portsmouth Athenæum, Portsmouth, New Hampshire.
Comet[42]	Smithsonian Institution, Washington, D.C.
Fearless[136]	Weld family collection.
Golden West[31, 42]	Mariners House, Boston.
Great Republic[42]	Boston Museum of Fine Arts, Coolidge Collection.
Lightning[31]	Half model shown. Location not stated.
Morning Light[31]	Mariners House, Boston.
Nightingale[31]	Half model carved to line from The Monthly Nautical Magazine. Location not stated.
Red Jacket[31]	Builder's half model shown. Location not stated.
Sierra Nevada[78]	Portsmouth Athenæum, Portsmouth, New Hampshire.
Sovereign of the Seas[31, 42]	Mariners House, Boston.
Stag Hound[42]	Old State House Museum of the Marine Society, Boston.
Sunny South[136]	Mariners Museum, Newport News, Virginia.
Witch of the Wave[31, 42, 78]	Mariners House, Boston[31] and Portsmouth Athenaeum, Portsmouth, New Hampshire[78].
Wild Pigeon[42]	Noted but location not stated.
Young America[42]	Smithsonian Institution, Washington, D.C.

Once the half model was completed and approved, the task of replicating its form as a full-size hull was now at hand. To this end, appropriate markings were scribed on the half model, as indicated in Figure 1.1.

Frame spacing for the actual ship was selected and marked along the keel of the half model at the appropriate scale. The dimension between frames was known as "room and space," meaning the room occupied by the structural frame and the space remaining between it and the next frame—at the time, most frequently a uniform distance of 30 inches. There were deviations from this uniform spacing, most notably in some of the clippers of William H. Webb, who employed a variable spacing ranging from 30 inches amidships to 40 inches at the ends.

The midship frame was scribed on the half model; then, working forward and aft, frames were scribed at intervals of, perhaps, four to eight frames in the middle body and two frames at the ends. The frames thus marked were known as *frame stations* or *stations*. The waterline half-breadths at these stations would be used to fair the hull lines and provide preliminary offset readings.

The midship section was identified by the symbol ⦶ or a variation thereof. Then, progressing aft, the frames were given numeral designations—for example, 1, 2, 3, 4, etc. Frames forward of the midship section were identified alphabetically—A, B, C, D, etc. In large vessels, if the upper case alphabet was exhausted, the letters were continued in lower case letters until the stem was reached. It is important to note that it was customary in this period to omit frame designations "I" and "j" in order to avoid confusion with the numeral designation "1" in the after body and lower case "i" in the forward body. This system was followed until about 1870, by which time the size of ships had outdistanced the limits of the alphabet. A numerical system, usually starting at the bow, was then adopted to replace the alphanumerical system of frame designation.

At the intersection of each waterline with each frame station, a half-breadth measurement was made and recorded in a table. The same thing was done with the half-breadth and height of the main rail. The contour of the stem and sternpost, the shape of the counter or transom, and the location of the cross seam were also recorded. Step by step, the entire three-dimensional shape of the half model was transformed into a series of measurements and recorded in a preliminary table of offsets, which would be sent to the mould loft.

Once the required information was taken off the half model, its usefulness was ended. Generally it survived as a display in an office or a gallery, a mute reminder of the important part it had once played in the construction of a ship. Of course, many a half model did not come to such a fortunate end—possibly an omen for the ship it represented.

Lofting and Fairing of Lines

The mould loft, in which these preliminary measurements would be laid down at full size, was a room that ideally should be large enough to allow the body plan and at least half the vessel's longitudinal length to be laid down on the floor.

A baseline was laid down at one side of the loft, and a centerline perpendicular to the baseline was laid down to bisect it. After this, waterlines set apart to match those of the offsets were chalked in. This made up the grid upon which the body plan would be laid down and refined.

Every spot on the moulded surface of the hull is a point located in space, and must be fixed in three directions: vertically above the moulded baseline; horizontally at a distance from the centerline of ship; longitudinally at a distance

(text continued on page 6)

Figure 1.1. *Typical half model.*

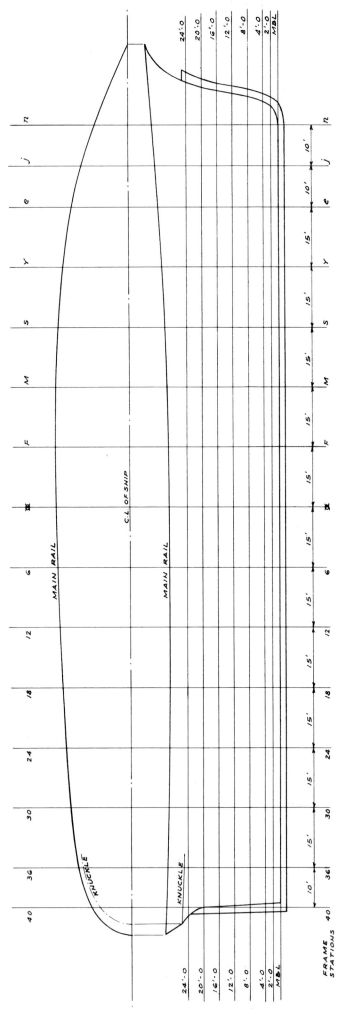

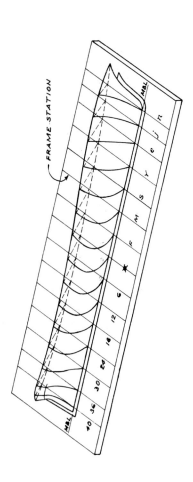

NOTES

1. FRAME SPACING UNIFORM AT 30 INCHES. FRAME SPACING AT TIMES MAY BE VARIABLE.

2. WATER LINES SPACED 4 FEET APART.

3. HALF BREADTH READINGS AT WATER LINES, KNUCKLE AND MAIN RAIL ARE LIFTED AT EACH FRAME STATION.

4. HEIGHTS FROM MOULDED BASE LINE TO KNUCKLE AND MAIN RAIL ARE LIFTED AT EACH FRAME STATION.

5. CONTOUR OF MAIN RAIL AND KNUCKLE ARE LIFTED FROM THE PLAN VIEW OF HALF MODEL.

6. PROFILE OF STEM, STERNPOST AND TRANSOM ARE TAKEN AT CENTER LINE OF SHIP.

FRAME DESIGNATIONS "I" AND "l" ARE CUSTOMARILY OMITTED TO AVOID CONFUSION WITH FRAME DESIGNATIONS "1" AND "1". IN SOME CASES "l" IS OMITTED AND "J" IS USED.

Figure 1.2. *Forms of keel rabbet.*

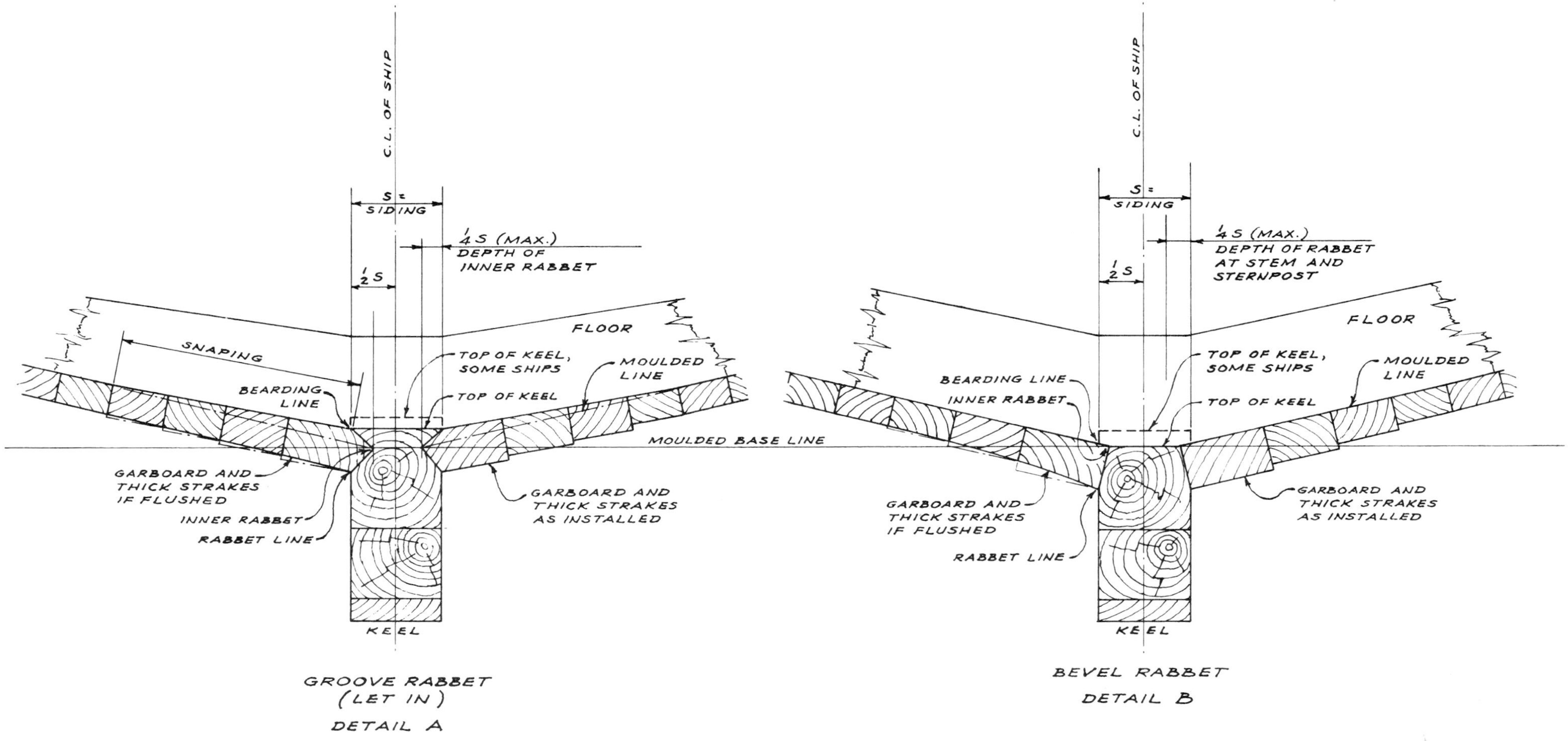

GROOVE RABBET
(LET IN)
DETAIL A

BEVEL RABBET
DETAIL B

C.L. OF SHIP

S = SIDING

1/2 S

4 S (MAX.)
DEPTH OF INNER RABBET

FLOOR

TOP OF KEEL, SOME SHIPS

MOULDED LINE

TOP OF KEEL

GARBOARD AND THICK STRAKES AS INSTALLED

KEEL

SNAPING

BEARING LINE

GARBOARD AND THICK STRAKES IF FLUSHED

INNER RABBET

RABBET LINE

MOULDED BASE LINE

C.L. OF SHIP

S = SIDING

1/2 S

4 S (MAX.)
DEPTH OF RABBET AT STEM AND STERNPOST

FLOOR

TOP OF KEEL, SOME SHIPS

MOULDED LINE

TOP OF KEEL

GARBOARD AND THICK STRAKES AS INSTALLED

KEEL

BEARDING LINE

INNER RABBET

GARBOARD AND THICK STRAKES IF FLUSHED

RABBET LINE

(text continued from page 3)

forward or aft of the midship section. These points are fixed by a given waterline height; a given waterline half-breadth; and a given frame spacing along the longitudinal moulded baseline.

Since the waterline heights and longitudinal locations have already been arbitrarily assigned, it remains only for the waterline half-breadths to be determined. This is accomplished by transferring the readings in the offset table to the grid on the mould loft floor and then fairing, or *penning*, them in by means of long, flexible battens. This requires considerable minor relocation of numerous points. Here the loftsman's skill is brought into play as he fairs the hull.

In many cases *buttocks*—vertical, longitudinal planes located parallel with the vertical centerline of the ship and extending the length of the vessel—are added to the grid. These planes are of great assistance in reproducing the shape of the hull between the keel and the turn of the bilges. Generally they are placed about 4 feet apart and are three or four in number.

In addition, *diagonals* are sometimes added. These are longitudinal planes, generally from one to three in number, which extend the entire length of the vessel and are inclined downward from the centerline of ship toward the floor heads and the butts in the *futtocks*, the name given to the individual segments of a vessel's frame. The diagonals are of sufficient extent to intersect the outline of the hull. These diagonals are useful in fairing the lines in way of the turn of the bilge and above. The readings of buttocks and diagonals seldom found their way into the final offset tables in the clipper ship era.

Before a body plan could be completely faired, it was necessary to know the sided dimension of the keel and the depth of the keel rabbet if a grooved rabbet was to be let into the keel. Some surviving tables of offsets include this depth of rabbet, which was generally one-half of the half-siding of keel. Also required was the proposed thickness of the *garboard* strake.

(text continued on page 9)

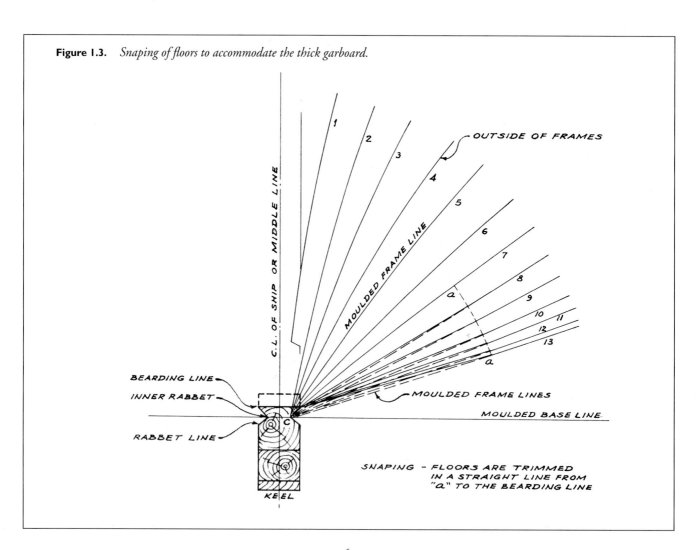

Figure 1.3. *Snaping of floors to accommodate the thick garboard.*

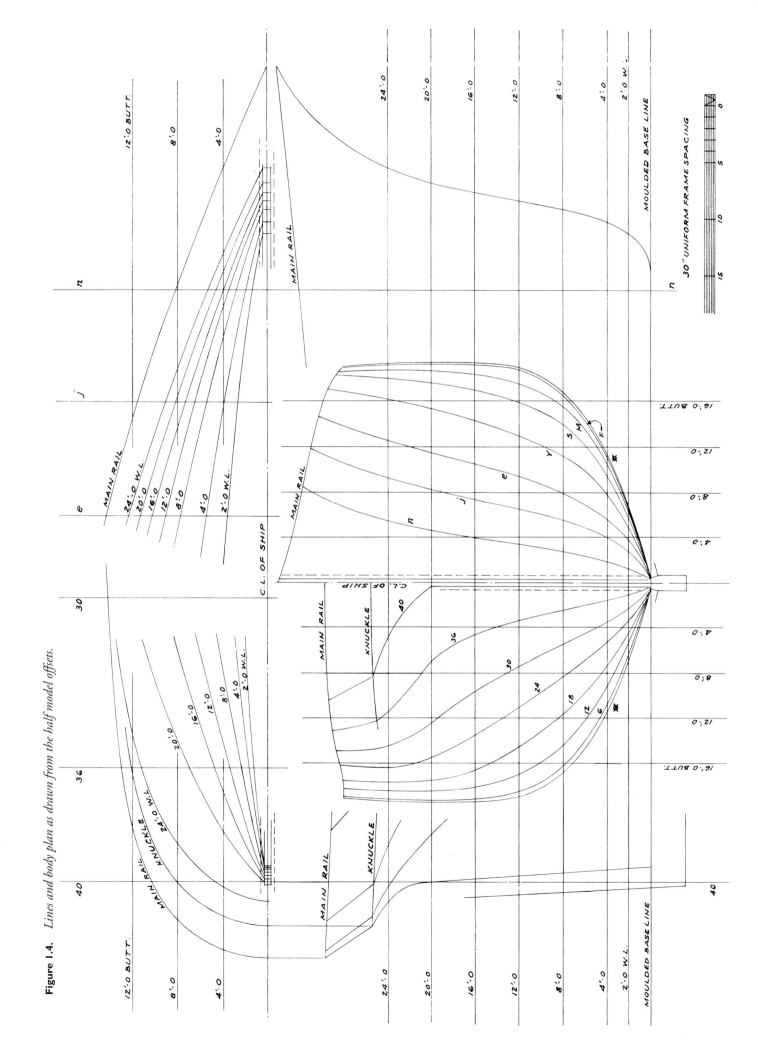

Figure 1.4. *Lines and body plan as drawn from the half model offsets.*

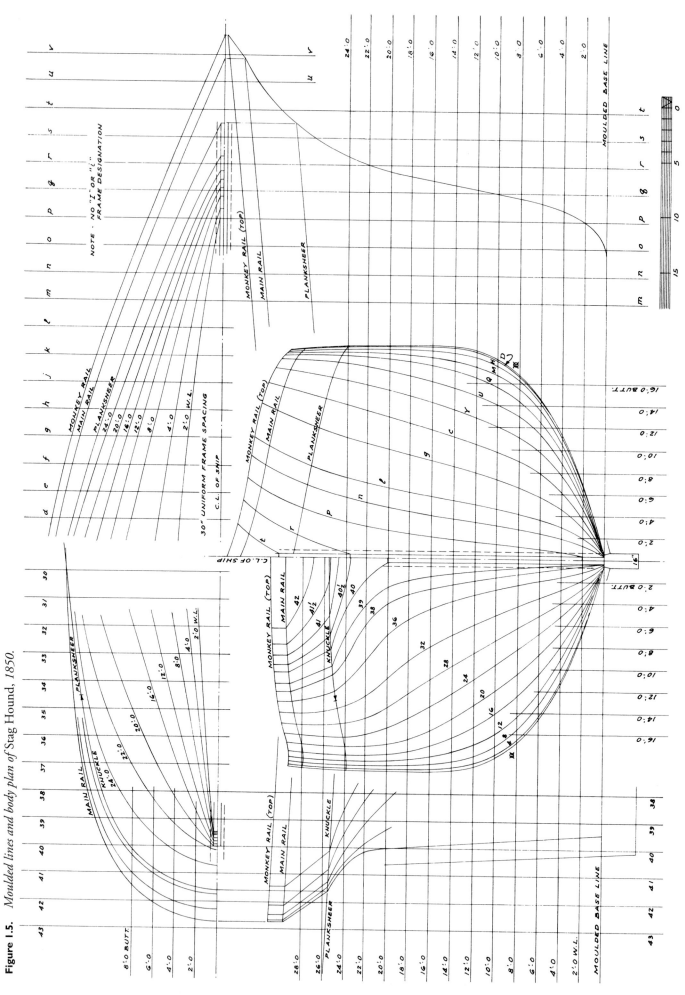

Figure 1.5. *Moulded lines and body plan of* Stag Hound, *1850.*

(text continued from page 6)

If the ship was to be built with a bevel keel rabbet, in lieu of the groove, this information must also be known since the shape of the ship's bottom was slightly different in each case. This is illustrated in Figure 1.2.

Clipper ships were generally built with garboard strakes about half again as thick as the bottom planking. This "thick" garboard was invented in a British naval dockyard by a master shipwright named Lang, around 1830, and was originally known as "Lang's safety keel." Little is recorded about the details of its installation.

However, a treatise[8] on laying off—laying down and building wooden and iron ships, written by an Englishman, S. J. P. Thearle, appeared in 1874, in which there appears a description of the laying out of keel and floors to accommodate the thick garboard. From the viewpoint of a draftsman at his drawing board, or a loftsman kneeling on the mould loft floor, this is clearly the most complete illustration of the development of the thick garboard and treatment of the keel to accommodate it. It cannot be definitely stated that the clippers were so treated, but the principal sketch (Figure 1.3) and the essence of the text are included here because they seem important, are explicit, and neatly clarify the procedure.

At the midship section the loftsman laid down the siding of the keel and the desired depth of rabbet, and the thickness of the bottom planking. The inner rabbet was established as shown in the figure, and the body lines were faired. The thickness of the bottom planking was then measured below the moulded frame line, establishing the location of the rabbet line. Upward from the rabbet line, the thickness of the garboard strake was laid on the side of the keel. This determined the location of the *bearding line*, which might also be the top of the keel, or the keel might extend upward yet another inch or two; which layout would be used was a matter of builder preference. A line drawn inward and upward from the rabbet line to the inner rabbet, then upward and outward from the inner rabbet to the bearding line, determined the profile of the groove, which was constant throughout most of the length of the thick garboard.

Using the inner rabbet as a center ("c") and a radius of sufficient length to include all diminishing strakes, an arc ("a-a" in the figure) was swung through the frames. (The center of this arc was sometimes located above the inner rabbet in order that the garboards would be wider at the ends than amidships.) From this arc, on each frame, the floor was *snaped* or trimmed in a straight line in to the bearding line. The resulting surface, the *angle of floor*, provided a straight, solid seat for the heavy garboard and diminishing strakes. Snaping also provided the space required by the extra thickness of these strakes.

The illustration shows that, toward the ends of the vessel, the snaping disappeared, generally at the frame where the upper angle of the groove coincided with the moulded line

of the frame. Technically, this location was the termination of the thick garboard. From this point, forward and aft, the inner rabbet remained straight while the rabbet line moved upward and the bearding line trended in to the depth of rabbet at stem and sternpost.

With details of the keel in place, the body plan could be fully developed. Customarily, the body forward of the midship section was laid out to the right of the centerline, while the after body was laid out to the left. The midship section itself was laid out on both sides so as to show, at this widest frame, a complete cross section of the hull.

The midship section was the first frame or station to be laid down. Offset dimensions were marked off using scratch awls and chalk. Battens were *penned* or bent around these marks, and the shape of the frame was transferred to the floor. Subsequently each frame station, forward and aft, was laid down in this same manner, as were the profiles of stem and sternpost on the sheer plan. A half-breadth plan was also laid down, particularly for the ends of the vessel.

With all the information transferred from the half model offsets to the mould loft floor, the final fairing of the lines was now in order. By checking each point as it appeared in each layout, the loftsman made appropriate adjustments by means of battens and ultimately finished with a layout similar to that shown in Figure 1.4, which uses Donald McKay's clipper *Stag Hound* as an example.

The loftsman now further refined his layout by penning in additional frame contours until the shape of every fourth frame from the midship section was shown on the floor. At the ends of the ship, where there was more shaping, this spacing was reduced to every two frames. Figure 1.5, also of *Stag Hound*, shows how this completed layout might have appeared.

These final lines and body plan remained on the mould loft floor until the ship's hull was complete. They were the constant reference from which was taken the size and shape of every piece of structural timber to be erected in the ship.

Figure 1.6 indicates the surfaces and lines from which offset dimensions were taken.

The Table of Offsets

From the complete hull form laid down on the mould loft floor, a final record was made of all the values of the lines and configurations that had been developed. Formally known as the *returned table of moulded offsets*, this tabulation, called the *table of offsets* for convenience, provided a numerical record of the ship's form which could be conveniently transported from place to place or copied as need required. Upon completion of the project, the table of offsets was retained for record purposes and future reference.

(text continued on page 14)

Figure 1.6. *Measurements required to determine the moulded hull form.*

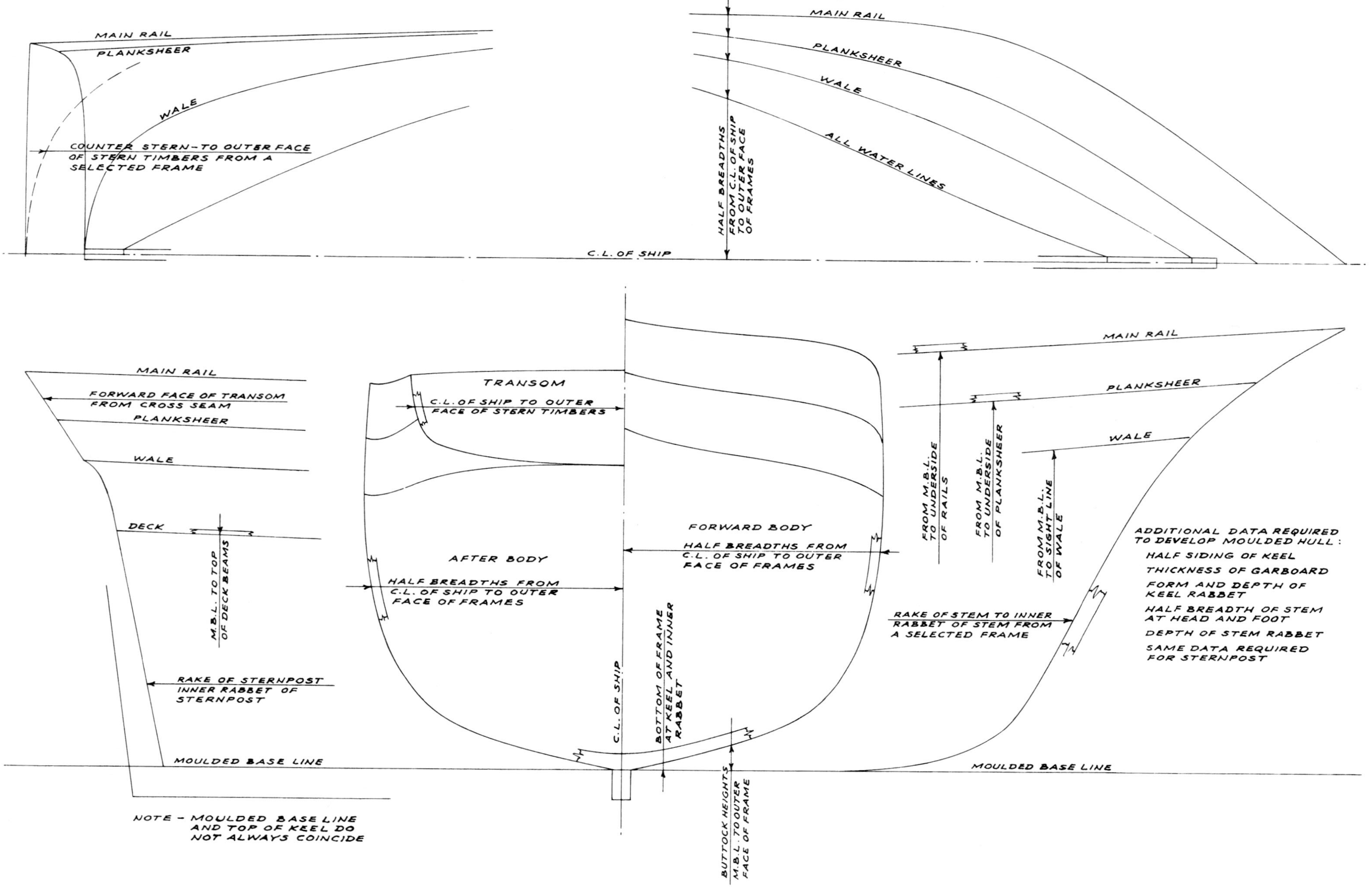

MAIN RAIL
PLANKSHEER
WALE
ALL WATER LINES

HALF BREADTHS FROM C.L. OF SHIP TO OUTER FACE OF FRAMES

C.L. OF SHIP

MAIN RAIL
PLANKSHEER
WALE

FROM M.B.L. TO SIGHT LINE OF WALE

FROM M.B.L. TO UNDERSIDE OF PLANKSHEER

FROM M.B.L. TO UNDERSIDE OF RAILS

RAKE OF STEM TO INNER RABBET OF STEM FROM A SELECTED FRAME

MOULDED BASE LINE

ADDITIONAL DATA REQUIRED TO DEVELOP MOULDED HULL:

HALF SIDING OF KEEL

THICKNESS OF GARBOARD

FORM AND DEPTH OF KEEL RABBET

HALF BREADTH OF STEM AT HEAD AND FOOT

DEPTH OF STEM RABBET

SAME DATA REQUIRED FOR STERNPOST

FORWARD BODY

HALF BREADTHS FROM C.L. OF SHIP TO OUTER FACE OF FRAMES

M.B.L. TO OUTER FACE OF FRAME

BUTTOCK HEIGHTS

BOTTOM OF FRAME AT KEEL AND INNER RABBET

C.L. OF SHIP

TRANSOM

C.L. OF SHIP TO OUTER FACE OF STERN TIMBERS

AFTER BODY

HALF BREADTHS FROM C.L. OF SHIP TO OUTER FACE OF FRAMES

MAIN RAIL
PLANKSHEER
WALE

COUNTER STERN-TO OUTER FACE OF STERN TIMBERS FROM A SELECTED FRAME

MAIN RAIL

FORWARD FACE OF TRANSOM FROM CROSS SEAM

PLANKSHEER
WALE
DECK

M.B.L. TO TOP OF DECK BEAMS

RAKE OF STERNPOST INNER RABBET OF STERNPOST

MOULDED BASE LINE

NOTE - MOULDED BASE LINE AND TOP OF KEEL DO NOT ALWAYS COINCIDE

Figure 1.7. *Moulded lines of Comet.*

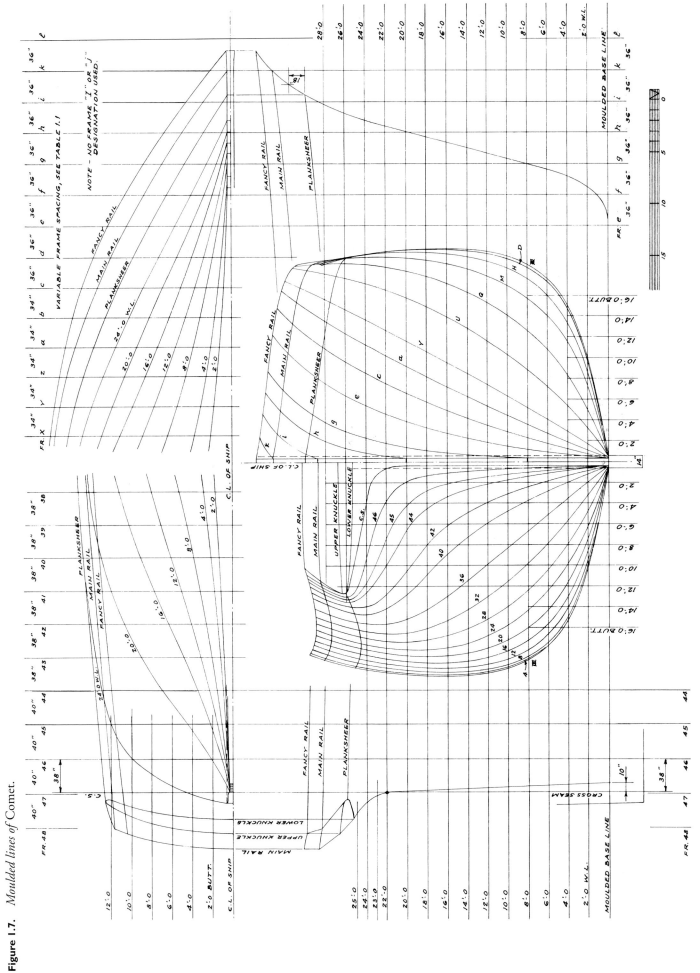

Table I.I. *Moulded offsets of* Comet.

COMET - 1851

WATER LINE

WATER LINE	CROSS SEAM	46	45	44	42	40	36	32	28	24	20	16	12	8	4
1st		0.3.7	0.5.0	0.6.4	0.9.7	1.1.6	2.0.5	3.4.4	4.11.2	6.4.6	7.9.0	8.10.2	9.7.5	10.1.4	10.4
2nd		0.4.0	0.6.4	0.9.5	1.3.7	1.11.4	3.7.7	5.9.1	8.0.6	9.11.7	11.7.0	13.1.5	14.2.4	14.11.4	15.4
3rd		0.5.6	0.9.0	1.1.0	1.10.1	2.9.5	5.2.6	7.9.7	10.4.4	12.6.0	14.3.6	15.7.5	16.7.7	17.4.0	17.8
4th		0.6.6	0.11.2	1.4.4	2.5.0	3.8.4	6.9.4	9.8.5	12.6.4	14.4.6	16.0.3	17.2.3	18.1.4	18.8.7	19.0
5th		0.7.6	1.1.5	1.8.5	3.0.7	4.8.6	8.4.3	11.5.0	13.11.4	15.9.4	17.2.4	18.2.5	19.0.0	19.6.2	19.9
6th		0.8.6	1.4.2	2.0.5	3.10.3	5.11.0	9.11.1	12.11.4	15.2.4	16.9.4	17.11.7	18.9.7	19.5.6	19.11.1	20.2
7th		0.10.1	1.8.0	2.7.6	4.11.0	7.4.2	11.5.7	14.3.2	16.1.7	17.5.5	18.5.1	19.1.6	19.8.4	20.1.2	20.4
8th		1.0.3	2.1.2	3.4.4	6.3.2	9.0.4	12.11.7	15.3.5	16.9.7	17.10.3	18.8.2	19.3.3	19.9.4	20.2.0	20.4
9th		1.4.0	2.9.7	4.7.3	8.2.4	10.11.6	14.3.5	16.0.3	17.2.2	18.0.4	18.9.0	19.3.0	19.9.2	20.1.3	20.4
10th		1.11.3	4.3.3	6.10.2	10.7.1	12.10.3	15.2.2	16.5.2	17.4.3	18.0.6	18.8.3	19.2.4	19.7.5	20.0.0	20.2
11th	0.6.6	3.10.4	7.7.7	10.1.6	12.10.0	14.1.6	15.7.2	16.6.2	17.3.4	17.11.1	18.6.1	18.11.6	19.4.6	19.9.0	20.0
12th	4.1.6	9.5.0	11.10.0	12.11.6	13.11.7	14.7.3	15.6.6	16.3.6	17.0.0	17.7.0	18.1.7	18.7.3	19.0.4	19.5.1	19.8
PLANK SHEER	12.7.2	12.10.0	13.2.3	13.5.7	14.0.1	14.6.2	15.5.0	16.2.0	16.10.5	17.5.7	18.0.6	18.6.1	18.11.1	19.3.3	19.6
MAIN RAIL	11.9.0	12.0.4	12.4.4	12.7.6	13.2.1	13.8.0	14.7.0	15.4.1	16.0.6	16.8.1	17.3.0	17.8.6	18.1.6	18.6.0	18.9
FANCY RAIL	FAIRED ⟶														

HEIGHTS A

	CROSS SEAM	46	45	44	42	40	36	32	28	24	20	16	12	8	4
13th															
14th															
PLANK SHEER 18" ABV. P.S	25.11.2	25.10.1	25.8.6	25.7.4	26.5.1	25.3.0	24.9.3	24.8.6	24.7.0	24.5.6	24.5.4	24.5.6	24.6.5	24.8.4	24.10
MAIN RAIL	28.5.5	28.4.5	28.3.3	28.2.2	28.0.0	27.10.3	27.7.4	27.5.7	27.4.7	27.4.4	27.4.6	27.5.3	27.6.4	27.8.2	27.10
FANCY RAIL	18 INCHES ABOVE MAIN RAIL ⟶														

BUTTOCK	ROUND OF STERN AFT FROM CROSS SEAM			HEIGHTS OF COUNTER TIMBERS ON KNUCKLES		HEIGHTS OF CROSS SEAM	RISE OF ⊠ FRAME ABV. B.L.
	MAIN RAIL	UPPER KNUCKLE	LOWER KNUCKLE	UPPER KNUCKLE	LOWER KNUCKLE		
CENTER LINE							0.0.0
SIDE LINE	5.5.1	3.11.0	2.7.0	26.8.5	25.2.6		
2 FT.	5.4.6	3.10.2	2.6.4	26.8.4	25.2.7	23.5.2	0.3.0
4	5.3.2	3.8.2	2.5.1	26.7.7	25.3.1	23.11.5	0.7.1
6	5.0.0	3.4.6	2.2.5	26.7.0	25.3.5	24.4.1	0.11.7
8	4.7.1	2.11.0	1.10.3	26.6.2	25.4.6	24.8.1	1.5.0
10	4.0.1	2.2.3	1.4.4	26.5.2	25.6.0	25.1.5	1.10.5
12	3.3.0	1.2.6	0.8.3	26.3.6	25.8.7	25.7.4	2.5.6
14							3.3.2
16 FT							4.7.0

CENTER TIMBERS		
WATER LINE	HEIGHT	RAKE AFT FROM CROSS SEAM
MAIN RAIL	28.8.1	5.5.1
UPPER KNUCKLE	26.8.5	3.11.0
LOWER KNUCKLE	25.2.7	2.7.0
25 FT.		2.2.4
24 FT.		1.0.2
23 FT.		0.3.6

...LF BREADTHS

⊠	D	H	M	Q	U	Y	a	c	e	g	h	i	k	HEIGHT ON STEM	RAKE OF STEM FROM FR.⊄
).4.4	9.11.4	8.10.3	7.2.7	5.1.4	3.2.3	1.8.0	1.1.4	0.8.3	0.5.4						3.8.4
).4.3	14.10.0	13.5.0	11.8.1	8.6.2	5.6.0	2.11.0	1.11.1	1.1.7	0.7.1						4.8.7
.9.1	17.3.3	16.0.3	13.10.3	10.9.7	7.5.1	4.1.4	2.9.1	1.8.0	0.9.7						5.4.7
.1.2	18.8.5	17.7.7	15.8.3	12.7.6	9.0.7	5.3.4	3.7.4	2.2.7	1.1.2	0.3.6					5.11.7
.10.4	19.7.0	18.8.4	16.11.7	14.1.3	10.6.2	6.4.7	4.6.2	2.10.2	1.5.0	0.4.5					6.6.2
).3.2	20.0.6	19.4.2	17.11.2	15.4.2	11.9.5	7.6.0	5.5.1	3.6.2	1.9.5	0.6.1					7.0.2
).5.3	20.3.4	19.9.0	18.6.7	16.4.2	12.11.6	8.7.0	6.4.0	4.2.5	2.2.6	0.8.0					7.6.2
).5.7	20.4.7	20.0.0	19.0.5	17.2.0	14.0.3	9.7.4	7.3.3	4.11.6	2.8.6	0.10.2					8.0.2
).5.6	20.5.2	20.1.6	19.4.7	17.9.7	14.11.6	10.8.0	8.2.6	5.9.1	3.3.3	1.1.4					8.6.2
).4.2	20.4.4	20.2.1	19.7.3	18.3.6	15.10.1	11.8.3	9.2.4	6.7.2	3.10.7	1.5.3					9.0.3
).2.3	20.3.1	20.1.6	19.8.6	18.8.2	16.7.2	12.8.6	10.3.0	7.6.3	4.7.2	1.10.3					9.7.0
.11.3	20.0.5	20.0.1	19.8.4	18.11.0	17.2.5	13.8.7	11.3.5	8.6.3	5.5.0	2.4.6					10.2.0
.9.0	19.10.2	19.9.6	19.7.0	19.1.3	17.10.3	15.5.4	13.5.7	11.0.2	7.11.3	4.6.3	2.8.6	0.10.0			
.11.6	19.1.7	19.2.7	19.2.5	19.0.0	18.4.5	16.9.5	15.4.2	13.2.5	10.5.0	6.9.7	4.9.7	2.8.4	0.5.4		
→→→				18.11.3	18.8.6	17.5.2	16.4.5	14.9.2	12.2.0	8.9.7	6.7.5	4.5.5	2.4.0		

...E BASE LINE

⊠	D	H	M	Q	U	Y	a	c	e	g	h	i	k	HEIGHT ON STEM	RAKE OF STEM FROM FR.⊄
															10.10.1
															11.7.5
.1.2	25.4.3	25.8.0	26.0.0	26.4.7	26.10.2	27.5.4	27.9.5	28.2.1	28.7.5	29.2.2	29.6.0	29.10.1		29.10.6	12.7.3
															13.6.7
.1.0	28.4.0	28.7.3	28.11.3	29.4.3	29.9.7	30.4.5	30.8.5	31.1.0	31.6.1	32.0.2	32.7.6	32.8.0	33.0.0	32.11.5	14.10.4
								→→→						34.8.4	16.10.6

FRAME SPACING

FRAMES	SPACE	CUMULATIVE LENGTH FROM FR. ⊄ TO FR.48
⊄ TO ⋉	36"	24'-0"
⋉ TO N	34	66 - 6
N TO M	32	69 - 2
M TO ⊠	30	99 - 2
⊠ TO 12	30	129 - 2
12 TO 20	32	150 - 6
20 TO 28	34	173 - 2
28 TO 36	36	197 - 2
36 TO 44	38	222 - 6
44 TO 48	40"	235'-10"

CUMULATIVE LENGTHS DO NOT APPEAR
IN ORIGINAL TABLE OF MOULDED OFFSETS

SPACING OF WATER LINES IS 2 FEET.

CROSS SEAM IS 38 INCHES AFT OF FR. 46.

STERNPOST RAKE FROM BASE LINE TO
11TH WATER LINE IS 10 INCHES.

KEEL SIDES 14 INCHES.

RABBET IS 4 INCHES AMIDSHIPS;
$3\frac{1}{2}$ INCHES FORWARD AND AFT.

COPIED FROM ORIGINAL OFFSETS, REF. 18

(text continued from page 9)

Traditionally, all measurements were made in feet, inches, and eighths. (At a later date, in steel ships, any dimension that did not fall on an exact eighth was appended with a "+" symbol, indicating that the line did not fall exactly on the mark. However, this refinement did not appear in the offset tables of wooden vessels.) A typical measurement is entered in the offset table as 21.4.7, which reads as 21 feet, 4⅞ inches.

In actual construction, any intervening frames that were not recorded were skillfully *dubbed off* by accomplished shipwrights, allowances having been provided by the mould loft.

Included are lines drawings of *Comet* and *Young America* (Figures 1.7 and 1.8, respectively), accompanied by their respective tables of offsets (Tables 1.1 and 1.2), which are copied from the originals.[18] Both vessels were products of William H. Webb and have been selected to show a vessel with a square or transom stern and one with a round or counter stern. Also illustrated is the use of variable frame spacing, as opposed to the uniform spacing in *Stag Hound* (Figure 1.5). The general format of the offset tables is similar except for the entries made at the stern. These portions, each made for a differently shaped stern, include entries peculiar to the stern in question, either transom or counter, in order to fashion the two different forms of structure.

Moulds and Templates

The time had now arrived where paper and planning could be converted into timber and construction. With appropriate information provided by the designer or builder, and the form of the hull laid out on the mould loft floor, the loftsman could begin to fabricate *moulds* or *templates* that would be patterns for the numerous items of structure that would be fitted together to form the ship.

These templates were made of wood about ¾ inch thick, shaped, marked, and cut to duplicate a piece of structure. Some moulds, where relatively small, were cut from solid material, while large ones were a fabrication of strips fastened together to form a latticework. The latter were known as "skeletal" moulds.

The moulds as developed, complete with their many markings and reference points, were the shipwright's road map. When completed, a mould contained all necessary scantlings, bevels, joints, and locations applicable to its use. The template could now be accurately "read."

Figure 1.9 shows the construction of a typical stem and forward deadwood assembly of a clipper ship; Figure 1.10 illustrates the construction and marking of moulds that could be made for such an assembly. The same general scheme was applicable to any other parts of a vessel. The academic process of lofting a vessel's hull is discussed and explained in finest detail in Thearle's treatise,[8] mentioned above, and in the books by Samuel M. Pook[22] and L. H. Boole,[55] as well as in many other articles extant on the subject.

Figure 1.8. *Moulded lines of Young America.*

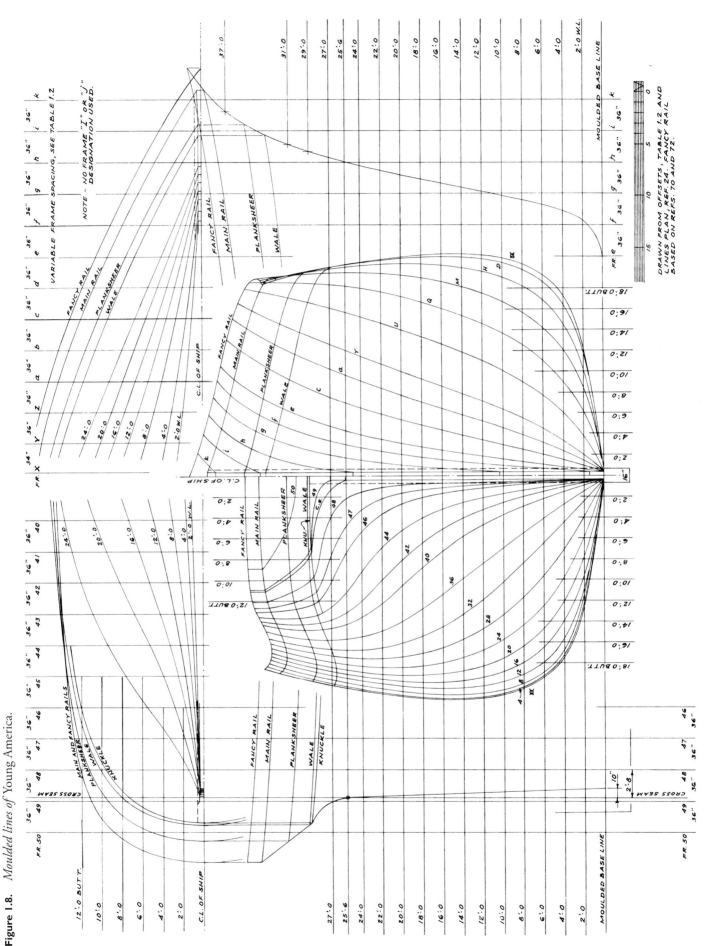

Table 1.2. *Moulded offsets of* Young America.

YOUNG AMERICA = 1853 — TABLE OF M...

WATER LIN...

WATER LINE	50	49	CROSS SEAM	48	47	46	44	42	40	36	32	28	24	20	16	12
1ST				0.3.7	0.4.5	0.5.3	0.7.2	0.9.2	0.11.7	1.7.3	2.8.2	4.2.5	6.1.6	8.1.5	9.11.2	11.4.2
2ND				0.4.4	0.5.5	0.6.6	0.10.0	1.1.6	1.7.0	2.9.6	4.9.3	7.2.5	9.11.0	12.3.1	14.3.3	15.10.3
3RD				0.4.6	0.6.2	0.8.1	1.0.6	1.6.7	2.2.6	4.1.0	6.9.2	9.8.4	12.6.3	14.9.1	16.6.6	17.11.3
4TH				0.5.1	0.7.1	0.9.6	1.4.1	2.0.5	2.11.3	5.5.3	8.7.5	11.9.0	14.4.7	16.4.5	17.11.4	19.1.3
5TH				0.5.4	0.8.1	0.11.4	1.8.0	2.7.2	3.9.3	6.10.7	10.4.6	13.4.7	15.9.2	17.5.7	18.9.6	19.9.5
6TH				0.6.1	0.9.4	1.1.4	2.0.4	3.3.2	4.9.2	8.4.7	11.11.6	14.8.7	16.9.4	18.3.0	19.4.3	20.2.2
7TH				0.6.7	0.11.0	1.4.2	2.6.4	4.1.0	5.11.2	9.11.1	13.4.5	15.9.1	17.6.0	18.8.6	19.7.7	20.4.4
8TH				0.7.7	1.0.7	1.7.6	3.2.0	5.1.4	7.3.5	11.5.0	14.6.2	16.6.3	17.11.6	19.0.0	19.9.5	20.5.0
9TH				0.8.7	1.3.4	2.0.6	4.0.2	6.5.0	8.10.2	12.9.7	15.5.1	17.0.6	18.2.7	19.1.3	19.9.5	20.4.2
10TH				0.10.5	1.7.6	2.8.3	5.3.2	8.0.6	10.6.7	14.0.1	16.1.0	17.4.7	18.4.4	19.1.5	19.8.7	20.2.5
11TH				1.1.0	2.2.6	3.8.2	6.11.7	10.0.3	12.2.7	14.10.6	16.5.6	17.6.4	18.4.3	19.0.2	19.6.6	20.0.8
12TH				1.6.0	3.3.4	5.4.5	9.3.4	11.11.7	13.7.1	15.5.4	16.8.0	17.6.5	18.3.2	18.10.0	19.3.6	19.9.0
13TH				2.2.6	4.10.0	7.6.0	11.3.2	13.2.1	14.3.2	15.8.0	16.8.0	17.5.4	18.1.1	18.7.0	19.0.7	19.5.7
14TH				4.1.0	7.10.3	10.4.6	12.9.0	13.10.6	14.7.6	15.8.6	16.7.2	17.3.4	17.10.3	18.4.2	18.9.4	19.2.3
WALE		7.6.4	7.11.4	10.1.1	11.5.2	12.2.2	13.4.3	14.1.5	14.9.0	15.8.7	16.7.3	17.3.7	17.7.3	18.6.0	18.11.2	19.3.2
PLANK SHEER	4.9.3	9.2.7	9.6.1	11.0.7	12.1.5	12.9.5	13.7.6	14.3.0	14.9.2	15.7.7	16.4.7	17.0.5	17.7.4	18.1.4	18.6.5	18.11.4
MAIN RAIL	8.9.6	11.0.4	11.2.2	12.1.1	12.8.2	13.1.1	13.8.4	14.2.2	14.7.2	15.4.1	15.11.7	16.6.1	16.11.7	17.5.1	17.10.0	18.2.2
FANCY RAIL	*· FAIRED ——————————————————→															
LOWER KNUCKLE		6.9.4	7.2.4	9.6.2	10.11.4	11.10.6	13.1.6									

HEIGHTS...

	50	49	CROSS SEAM	48	47	46	44	42	40	36	32	28	24	20	16	12
LOWER KNUCKLE		28.11.1	28.10.5	28.3.5	28.3.5	28.0.6	27.8.2									
WALE	29.4.7	29.2.2	29.2.0	29.0.0	28.9.6	28.7.6	28.3.7	28.0.4	27.9.2	27.4.0	27.0.0	26.9.2	26.7.2	26.6.1	26.5.6	26.5.6
PLANK SHEER	31.1.5	30.11.2	30.11.0	30.9.0	30.6.7	30.4.6	30.1.1	29.9.7	29.6.7	29.2.2	28.10.4	28.8.1	28.6.4	28.5.3	28.5.1	28.5.3
MAIN RAIL	33.6.3	33.4.1	33.3.7	33.2.0	33.0.1	32.10.3	32.7.0	32.4.0	32.1.5	31.9.2	31.6.4	31.4.6	31.3.7	31.3.4	31.4.0	31.4.7
FANCY RAIL	*- 15" ABOVE MAIN RAIL, FAIRED TO 18" ——————→									18	18	18	18	18	18	18

BUTTOCK	ROUND OF STERN AFT OF FR. 48				RISE OF [X] FRAME ABV. B.L.
	LOWER KNUCKLE	WALE	PLANK SHEER	MAIN RAIL	
CENTER LINE	5.0.5	5.2.1	6.9.2	8.10.0	
2 FT.	4.11.0	5.1.2	6.7.6	8.8.5	0.2.2
4	4.5.2	4.8.5	6.3.0	8.7.3	0.5.7
6	3.6.1	3.11.5	5.6.1	7.8.6	0.9.5
8	1.1.3	2.7.4	4.3.0	6.7.7	1.1.3
10		0.1.7	2.0.1	4.8.5	1.5.5
12				0.5.1	1.10.3
14					2.4.4
16					3.1.6
18 FT.					4.5.4

WATER LINE SPACING	
B.L. TO 12TH W.L.	2'-0"
12TH TO 13TH W.L.	1'-6"
13TH TO 14TH W.L.	1'-6"

*-FANCY RAIL IS NOT IN ORIGINAL TABLE O...
MOULDED OFFSETS. SCALED FROM PHOTO...

DED OFFSETS

LF BREADTHS

4	Ⅺ	D	H	M	Q	U	Y	a	c	e	f	g	h	i	k	HEIGHT ON STEM	RAKE OF STEM FROM FR.f
.7.7	12.7.1	12.1.5	10.9.6	8.9.2	6.4.5	4.0.5	2.2.6	1.6.4	1.0.2	0.7.3	0.5.0						0.6.4
5.2	17.5.0	16.8.1	14.10.5	12.3.2	9.3.3	6.2.3	3.7.1	2.5.6	1.6.7	0.10.1	0.6.3						1.5.2
4.7	19.4.5	18.8.4	16.11.3	14.3.7	11.2.5	7.9.5	4.8.4	3.3.5	2.1.1	1.1.0	0.7.6						1.11.7
5.1	20.5.4	19.10.0	18.2.4	15.8.3	12.7.5	9.1.0	5.7.7	4.0.3	2.7.1	1.3.7	0.9.3						2.5.4
.11.4	21.0.2	20.5.6	19.0.7	16.8.7	13.9.0	10.1.7	6.5.7	4.8.3	3.0.5	1.7.1	0.11.3	0.4.6					2.10.5
.2.3	21.3.1	20.9.7	19.7.5	17.6.5	14.8.0	11.0.7	7.3.1	5.3.6	3.6.0	1.10.2	1.1.1	0.5.4					3.3.4
3.1	21.4.1	21.0.2	20.0.2	18.2.2	15.5.6	11.11.1	8.0.0	5.11.0	3.11.4	2.1.7	1.3.7	0.6.7					3.8.3
.2.5	21.3.6	21.0.6	20.3.0	18.8.1	16.2.0	12.8.3	8.8.4	6.6.4	4.5.0	2.5.3	1.6.3	0.8.5					4.1.1
.1.2	21.2.5	21.0.5	20.4.5	19.0.3	16.9.4	13.5.2	9.4.2	7.1.3	4.10.6	2.9.2	1.9.3	0.10.2					4.6.0
.11.2	21.0.7	20.11.2	20.5.1	19.3.5	17.3.6	14.1.6	10.1.1	7.9.2	5.5.0	3.1.5	2.0.5	1.0.3					4.11.1
.8.3	20.10.1	20.9.3	20.4.6	19.5.6	17.9.0	14.9.3	10.9.7	8.5.1	5.11.5	3.6.4	2.4.3	1.3.0					5.4.3
.4.7	20.7.0	20.7.0	20.3.5	19.6.7	18.1.1	15.4.6	11.6.6	9.1.6	6.6.7	3.11.6	2.8.6	1.6.2	0.4.6				5.9.6
.1.4	20.4.0	20.4.1	20.1.7	19.7.1	18.3.6	15.10.1	12.1.5	9.8.4	7.1.0	4.4.3	3.0.4	1.9.0	0.6.3				6.2.1
.9.7	20.0.4	20.1.2	19.11.7	19.6.5	18.5.5	16.3.0	12.8.4	10.3.5	7.7.5	4.9.5	3.4.6	2.0.3	0.8.3				6.6.5 / 29'ABV.B.L. 7.1.3 / 31'ABV.B.L. 7.9.2
.11.2	20.1.4	20.1.5	19.11.6	19.6.3	18.6.6	16.8.3	13.9.4	11.8.6	9.3.5	6.6.1	5.0.2	3.5.7	1.11.1				
.6.1	19.8.3	19.9.2	19.8.3	19.4.4	18.8.1	17.2.2	14.7.3	12.7.6	10.3.3	7.5.2	5.10.5	4.3.2	2.7.7	1.0.0			
.9.0	18.11.5	19.1.3	19.1.7	19.0.4	18.8.0	17.9.4	15.11.1	14.2.5	12.0.6	9.3.3	7.9.2	6.2.2	4.6.4	2.10.0	1.1.6		

← ＊ FAIRED

VE BASE LINE

4	Ⅺ	D	H	M	Q	U	Y	a	c	e	f	g	h	i	k	HEIGHT ON STEM	RAKE OF STEM FROM FR.f
6.7.5	26.9.1	27.0.7	27.4.7	27.10.2	28.4.4	29.0.5	29.10.6	30.4.7	31.0.0	31.7.1	32.0.3	32.5.1	32.9.7			33.2.3	8.7.7
8.8.0	28.10.3	29.1.5	29.5.3	29.10.3	30.4.4	31.0.3	31.9.4	32.3.3	32.9.7	33.5.3	33.9.7	34.2.4	34.7.6	35.1.4		35.2.6	9.8.4 / 37'ABV.B.L. 10.11.7
.8.2	32.0.6	32.1.4	32.5.2	32.9.6	33.3.4	33.10.7	34.7.6	35.1.4	35.8.0	36.3.4	36.7.6	37.1.0	37.6.5	38.1.2	38.9.0	39.0.2	13.2.1
18	18	18	18" FAIRED TO 14"												14"		

FRAME SPACING

FRAMES	SPACE	CUMULATIVE LENGTH FROM FR.k TO FR.50
k TO Y	36"	33'-0"
Y TO Q	34	55-8
Q TO 24	32	162-4
24 TO 32	34	185-0
32 TO 50	36"	239'-0"

CUMULATIVE LENGTHS DO NOT APPEAR IN ORIGINAL TABLE OF MOULDED OFFSETS

CROSS SEAM IS 32 INCHES AFT OF FR.48.

STERNPOST RAKE FROM BASE LINE TO 13TH WATER LINE IS 10 INCHES. (SCALED FROM LINES PLAN, REF.24.)

STERNPOST INTERSECTS CROSS SEAM AT 13TH WATER LINE. (TAKEN FROM LINES PLAN, REF.24.)

COPIED FROM ORIGINAL OFFSETS, REF.18.

Figure 1.9. *Typical stem and forward deadwood assembly.*

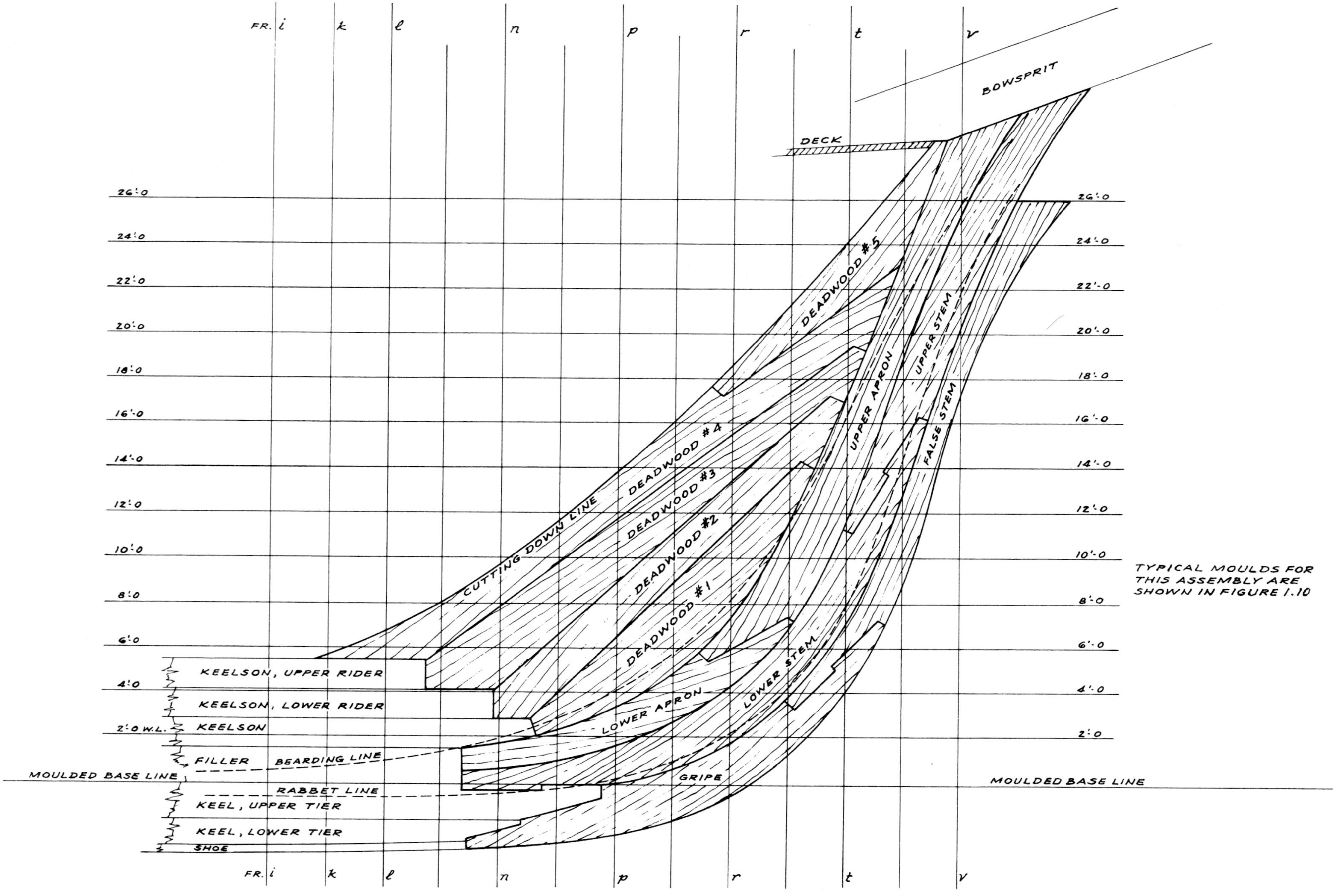

TYPICAL MOULDS FOR
THIS ASSEMBLY ARE
SHOWN IN FIGURE 1.10

BOWSPRIT

DECK

26'-0
24'-0
22'-0
20'-0
18'-0
16'-0
14'-0
12'-0
10'-0
8'-0
6'-0
4'-0
2'-0

MOULDED BASE LINE

FALSE STEM

UPPER STEM

UPPER APRON

LOWER STEM

DEADWOOD #5

DEADWOOD #4

DEADWOOD #3

DEADWOOD #2

DEADWOOD #1

LOWER APRON

GRIPE

DOWN LINE

CUTTING LINE

FR. i
k
l
n
p
r
t
v

KEELSON, UPPER RIDER
KEELSON, LOWER RIDER
KEELSON
FILLER
BEARDING LINE
RABBET LINE
KEEL, UPPER TIER
KEEL, LOWER TIER
SHOE

MOULDED BASE LINE

2'-0 W.L.

26'-0
24'-0
22'-0
20'-0
18'-0
16'-0
14'-0
12'-0
10'-0
8'-0
6'-0
4'-0
2'-0

Figure 1.10. *Representative moulds for typical stem and forward deadwoods.*

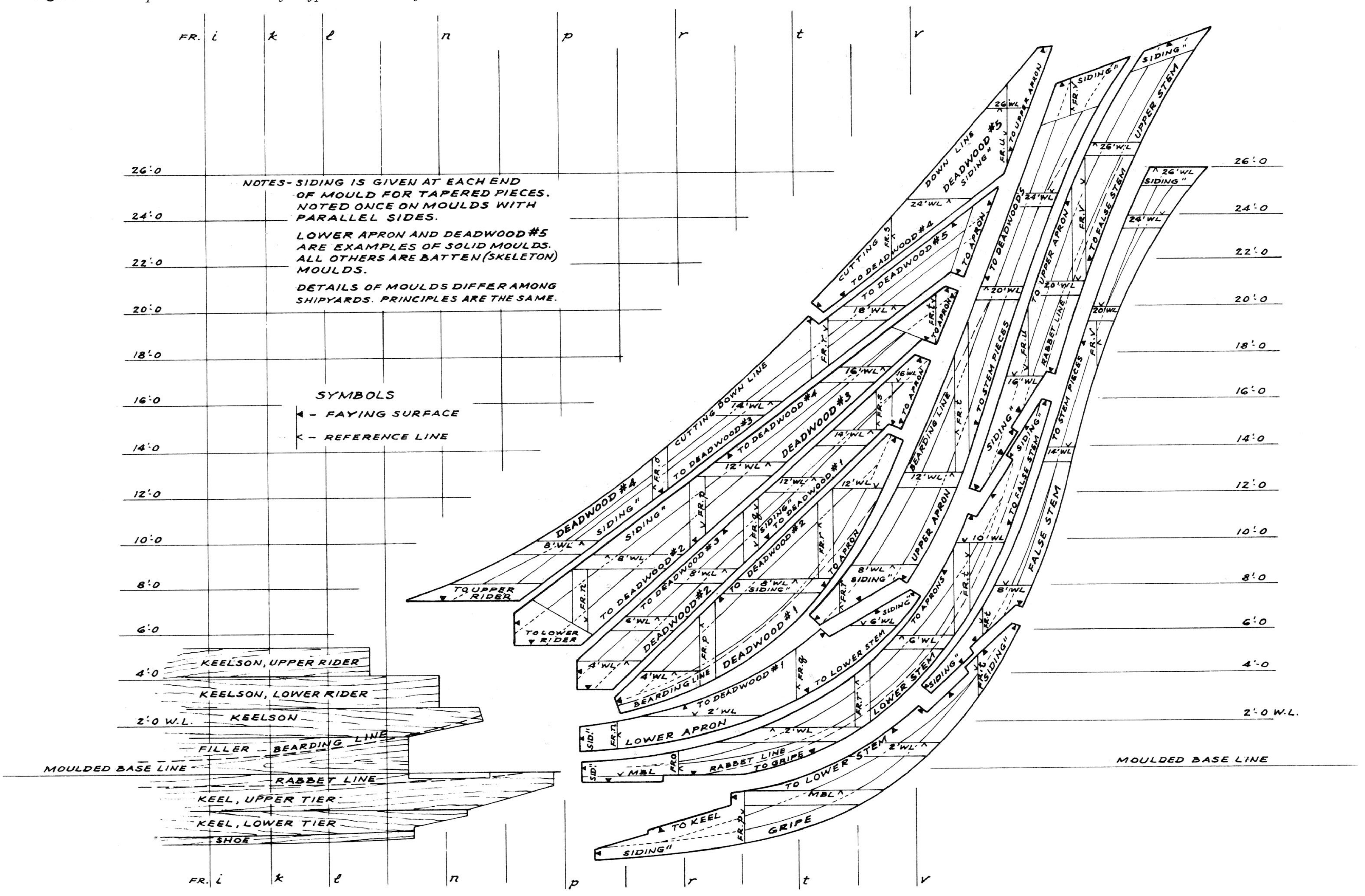

Chapter Two

WOODS USED IN CONSTRUCTION OF THE CLIPPERS

THE BUILDING OF A SHIP ultimately depended upon the availability of timber of suitable variety and size from which to fabricate its various parts. Timber, both structural and decorative, was purchased from dealers who dealt directly with the logging industry and with agents whose ships arrived laden with logs, either cargo or ballast. Procurement of acceptable timber was an important but little-regarded fact of shipbuilding.

American-built clippers were built from about a dozen types of structural timber. For the many parts of an individual vessel, all shapes and sizes, the quantities of wood involved were prodigious. It was therefore mandatory that the shipyard's inventory of wood be constantly kept abreast of its building schedule. This in turn required orderly record keeping and restocking. A large shipyard required an extensive, well-organized "holding" or storage area for its stockpiled timber. It seems safe to assume that timber was stored by configuration (knees, forks, logs, planks) and, within those categories, by species (oak, maple, pine, etc.).

There existed, between the function of the mould loft and the labor of the shipwrights, a group of men who are never accorded recognition in any treatise or composition which covers the subject of building wooden ships. These were the men who maintained a record of and monitored the various species and sizes of wood stockpiled by a shipyard. Their knowledge spelled the difference between the economical use of timber and costly random selection. Their awareness of the timbers on hand allowed for the fabrication of templates to suit specific logs, knees, and other odd shapes of wood that had been harvested and seasoned for use at some expeditious opportunity.

Many ships were built using unique combinations of structural shapes. This could only have come about through a detailed knowledge of the assorted odd and unusual pieces of timber that were on hand at the time. Substitutions of types and growths of woods were not uncommon, and many are noted throughout this book.

Many tree species grew abundantly in the eastern United States at this time. Each variety had its own characteristics of shape, grain, density, strength, durability, and beauty—all of which had been discovered through centuries of use and were catalogued in shipwrights' journals and records. The shipbuilding industry was acutely aware of and very particular in its choice of specific woods and shapes for various structural purposes.

The most desirable product was a tree whose natural growth corresponded with the required configuration of the proposed finished piece. Laying out the piece so that its shape followed the natural sweep of the grain gave the component its greatest possible strength, which in turn guaranteed the greatest degree of safety that could be built into a vessel. Such consideration was paramount, because at sea, small failures could become overwhelming disasters.

Of all wood used in wooden ship construction, the *knee* was the most important and had the most long-term influence. It is difficult to imagine how our ships would have developed and what form they would have taken had it not been for the natural-grown knee. It is a form of great strength, derived from the flow of the grain from one direction to another—generally of an angle approaching 90 degrees. In the process of growing on a tree, the fork from which a knee is cut is subject to a lifetime of proving itself superior to internal stresses of tension and compression, and surviving the external forces of wind and weight.

Shipbuilders from the earliest times had quickly discovered that straight timbers could be bound together, as in "made" masts, or bolted together, as in the huge keelson assemblies, and perform their tasks faultlessly. But in the long run it was the knee that allowed all these items to be assembled and connected to become a ship.

The strength advantage of using naturally curved timber applied to many other parts needed to build a ship. For the shipbuilder there were certain standard categories of shape for the parts of a hull, each of which had considerable variation—

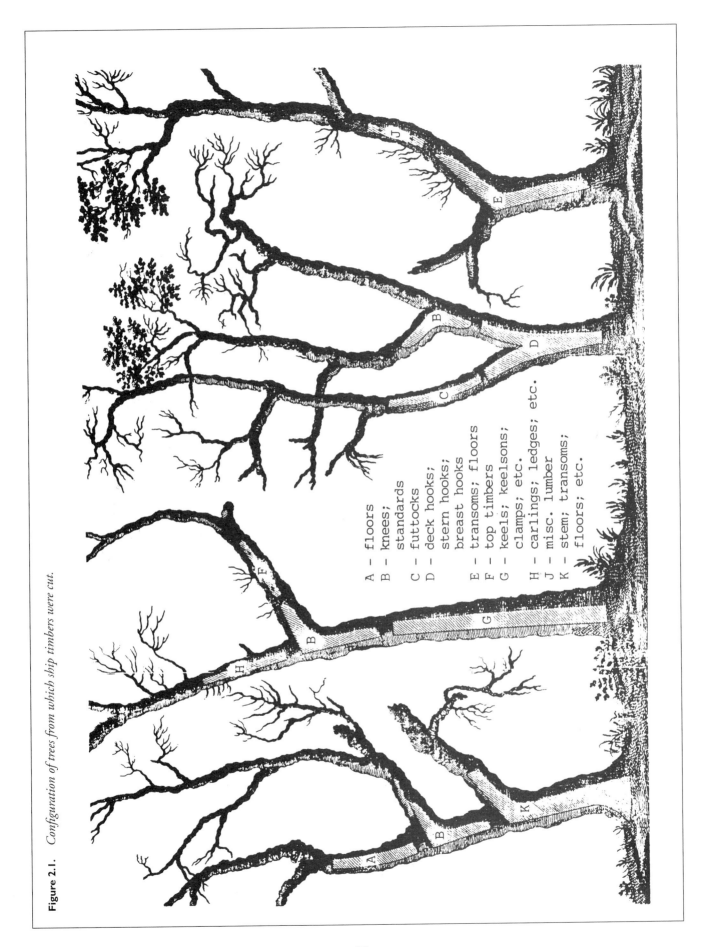

Figure 2.1. *Configuration of trees from which ship timbers were cut.*

A – floors
B – knees;
    standards
C – futtocks
D – deck hooks;
    stern hooks;
    breast hooks
E – transoms; floors
F – top timbers
G – keels; keelsons;
    clamps; etc.
H – carlings; ledges; etc.
J – misc. lumber
K – stem; transoms;
    floors; etc.

a factor very much in the shipbuilder's favor. Figure 2.1 depicts a variety of commonly needed shapes, without regard to the type of tree from which they might be cut. The letter designations (A, B, C, etc.) in the figure identify the uses to which each shape could be put.

Compass timbers are generally understood to be lengths or pieces of wood that have a natural curve, but are not straight. However, by strict definition a compass timber had a natural curve of at least 5 inches in a length of 12 feet. This was soon regarded as a technicality, and any timber that contained a noticeable natural curve was classed as a compass timber. In Figure 2.1 pieces A and C are compass timbers; B is a branch or *fork*; D is a *crotch*; E is a *crook*, a trunk that has grown in a crooked form for reasons known only to nature; F is a slender, straight branch; G is straight trunk timber from which the greatest dimensions are attainable; H is similar to F except that the *scantlings* (sizes) are greater; J provides a source of miscellaneous planks, boards, or *deal* (thin boards); K, as shown, is a trunk and branch which also contains a portion of the *bole* (base trunk) of a tree. This latter configuration of natural growth was greatly in demand in the period before the clipper ship, for fashioning the forefoot of a ship's stem, where it joins the forward end of the keel. The wood was extremely strong, tough, and durable, but the scarcity and expense of procuring such pieces rendered them rather impractical to specify.

The shipbuilders' demands rendered the oldest and largest trees most vulnerable. The huge timbers specified for keel logs, stem pieces, aprons, sternposts, and the like, could only be gotten from trees that had stood untouched for hundreds of years. There were thousands of these growing along the East Coast of the United States. With such proximity and numbers, it is little wonder that no one envisioned the supply as being exhaustible.

During the early nineteenth century, American shipbuilding flourished at a modest, consistent pace. Logging, from Maine to Georgia, was a well-established industry, and timber dealers were in business all along the coast, especially near seaports. Much of the timber harvested was brought by water, and most of the larger, naturally curved logs were used in the shipbuilding centers. Straight board timber, used in general construction, was sawn to size at the source and shipped rough, to be finished at the destination.

Figure 2.2 shows a typical ship timber dealer's advertisement of 1856. The ad emphasizes the variety of functional shapes, while listing the availability of planking and board lumber in routine fashion.

When, in 1850, the pace of shipbuilding quickened and a short time later became rampant, the onslaught on the forests was deadly. Timber was required in prodigious quantities. Trees were harvested in greater numbers for the reason that a certain percentage proved unfit for shipbuilding due to rot, internal injury, and a certain amount of destruction in logging.

Timbers for ship construction were categorized according to the scantlings of the material. The largest pieces of straight wood—those used in keels, stanchions, sternposts, etc.—were logs, which varied in size but were generally at least about 12 by 15 inches in cross section. Timber destined for planking and ceiling was designated according to thickness. Boards exceeding 4 inches in thickness (and generally not exceeding 8 inches) were classed as "thick stuff." Boards between 1½ and 4 inches were classed as "plank" or planking. Lumber properly classed as "boards" was less than 1½ inches thick. Finally, there was "deal," thin boards of various thicknesses.

Timbers cut from irregular shapes of natural growth were sided and left rough in order to allow the shipbuilder the maximum range of flexibility when suiting a given mould to the material at hand.

The largest pieces of timber to be specified for the ships listed in this book were the stem of *Challenge*, a single piece sided 18 inches, moulded 3 feet 6 inches, and approximately 35 feet long; a breasthook in *Westward Ho*, sided about 12 inches and 50 feet long; a section of keelson in *Spitfire*, 19 inches square and 41 feet long; the apron in *Great Republic*, sided 16 inches at the keel, 44 inches at the bowsprit, moulded 4 feet 3 inches, and 42 feet in length. All these timbers were of white oak and representative of the largest pieces that a shipbuilder could reasonably expect to obtain.

All the structural timbers needed to build a clipper were available along the Eastern Seaboard of the United States; however, the various woods used in fitting out such a ship were exotic and native only to foreign lands. They arrived in this country by ship, either as cargo or as ballast in vessels that might be sailing light. This also applied to woods that were useful or necessary to the operation of the ship after it had put to sea.

The following list examines in greater detail the varieties of wood specified for clipper ship construction of this period. The common and scientific names of each species are given, along with general characteristics, uses, and natural history of each variety. Weight per cubic foot is taken from contemporary (about 1850) sources, which vary widely, but the given weight is considered a representative dry weight. Diameters are measured at official "breast height" (DBH). Life span is the maximum age, unless otherwise noted. Strength is subject to many variables; however, the values given reflect a general comparison with white oak, even though individual sources cover a broad range of values.

Resistance to rot is a relative characteristic entered here as good, excellent, superior, and, in the case of teak, immune.

Figure 2.2. *Typical ship timbers sold by timber dealers.*

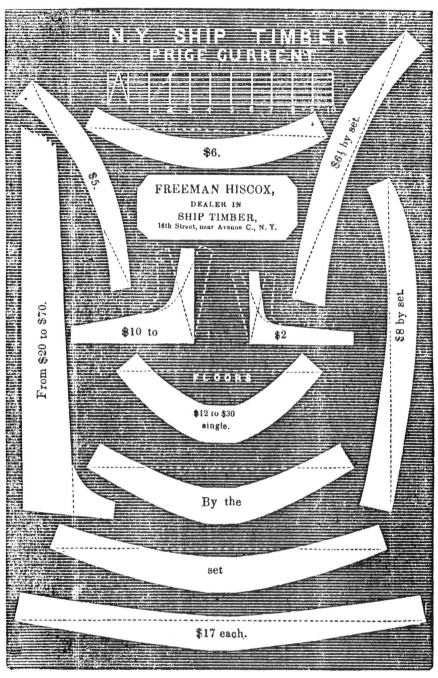

A set of floors and futtocks, $9 each Oak Flitch, 30 cents per cubic foot ; oak plank, $36¾ to $40 per M deck plank, $35 per M. ; hackmatack timber, 25 cents per cubic foot ; chestnut, ditto ; cedar, 30 to 50 cents yellow pine timber, rough, 35 to 45 cents per cubit foot ; ditto, sawed, $28 to $30 ; yellow pine plank, $27 to $30 per M.

Oak Knees— 5 inch $2 50 ; 6 inches, $5 ; 7 inches, $7¾; 8 inches, $10 ; 9 inches, $12 ; 10 inches, $15 above, $1 50 per inch.

Hackmatack Knees— 5 inches, $1.50 ; 6 inches, $2 50 ; 7 inches, $4 25 ; 8 inches, $6 00 ; 9 inches, $8 10 inches, $9 00 ; above, $1 per inch.

Yellow metal, 25 cents, at 6 months ; copper sheet, 28¼ cents, ditto ; copper bolts, 31 cents, ditto ; composition nails, 19 cents, ditto.

Structural Woods

Chestnut, *Castanea dentata*

Diameter	4 feet avg., 10 feet max.
Height	90 feet avg., 120 feet max.
Life span	Maximum life span has not been satisfactorily determined by dendrologists.
Weight	38 pounds per cubic foot
Strength	68, with white oak rated at 100

The American chestnut flourished in the eastern United States from the Great Lakes southward into Alabama. The wood is semi-hard, dense, tough, and strong; it can be worked well with tools and takes a beautiful finish. While suitable for shipbuilding, chestnut saw minimal use, possibly due to the abundance of the superior white oak. It was, however, quite acceptable for the construction of ship frames.

In 1904 a blight, starting in New York City, invaded these trees and began what was to be their ultimate destruction. At the time there was no great interest in a detailed study of the American chestnut; when, shortly thereafter, such an interest was generated, no first-growth timber was left standing to provide such information as a tree's age. Within forty years of the first appearance of the chestnut blight, all mature trees of the species had been wiped out. One known fact is that the American chestnut was a fast-growing species. At this time of writing (1990) it is slowly being hybridized in an effort to produce a blight-resistant strain, as previous efforts to conquer the blight have been unsuccessful.

Chestnut has good resistance to rot.

Fir, Balsam, *Abies balsamea*

Diameter	18 inches avg., 3 feet max.
Height	60 feet avg., 85 feet max.
Life span	150 years. These trees, when about 90 years of age, are prone to attacks by fungi.
Weight	35 pounds per cubic foot
Strength	56, with white oak rated at 100

Balsam fir is abundant throughout the northeastern United States and is the tree most used in this country as a Christmas tree. The wood is resinous, soft, straight-grained, lightweight, and easily worked with tools. Fir is not very strong, and its use in shipbuilding was limited almost exclusively to the making of stopwaters in the ends of scarphs that were constantly exposed to water, as in the keel. (Details of this are illustrated in Chapter 5.) When specified, this wood was simply referred to as "fir."

Fir has good resistance to rot.

Hackmatack, *Larix laricina*

Diameter	2 feet avg., 3 feet max.
Height	80 feet avg., 100 feet max.
Life span	200 years. These trees grow slowly after reaching 50 years of age.
Weight	37 pounds per cubic foot
Strength	75, with white oak rated at 100

Hackmatack (the name popular at the time for tamarack, the European larch) is abundant throughout the northeastern United States. The wood is tough and durable and is excellent for rough construction. In shipbuilding it was a major source of knees, which were cut from the base of the tree using the bole and the root. For this use, many of the trees were dug out of the ground rather than felled with axe and saw.

Hackmatack has good resistance to rot.

Locust, Black, *Robinia pseudo-acacia*

Diameter	2 feet avg., 5 feet max.
Height	60 feet avg., 100 feet max.
Life span	25 years
Weight	45 pounds per cubic foot
Strength	135, with white oak rated at 100

The principal habitat of this tree stretches along the Appalachian range from Pennsylvania to Alabama. Considered a small tree, black locust is fast-growing and short-lived, partly because it is subject to invasion by locust borers. The wood is very hard, strong, stiff, and very durable. It is difficult to work with hand tools, but machines well and takes a good finish. A tooled piece appears very polished and slippery.

In shipbuilding, black locust was used to make the finest *treenails* (pegs used as wooden nails) and, in rather rare cases, turned stanchions. Occasionally it was specified for some minor structural members. When specified it was simply referred to as "locust."

Locust has superior resistance to rot.

Maple, Rock, *Acer saccharum*

Diameter	2 feet avg., 5 feet max.
Height	80 feet avg., 135 feet max.
Life span	200 to 300 years
Weight	47 pounds per cubic foot
Strength	109, with white oak rated at 100

Rock maple (the generally specified name for sugar maple) is abundant from the Atlantic coast to the Mississippi River and from the Ohio River north to the Great Lakes, but is not limited to that area. It is in the half of the family referred to as hard maple, the other half being classed as soft maple. The wood is hard, dense, tough, strong, and works well with tools. Its use in shipbuilding was generally limited to large logs for fabricating portions of the ships' keels. When used structurally it was always referred to as "rock maple."

Rock maple has superior resistance to rot.

Oak, Live, *Quercus virginiana*

Diameter	4 feet avg., 11 feet max.
Height	50 feet avg., 60 feet max.
Life span	200 to 300 years
Weight	70 pounds per cubic foot
Strength	149, with white oak rated at 100

This species grows in the coastal areas of the United States stretching from Virginia south to Texas. It is not a forest tree but grows individually and sometimes in pure stands. Live oak trees are generally found within fifteen miles of the seacoast.

Individual specimens of great size survive today. One of the largest, standing in New Orleans, is 62 feet high, has a spread of 103 feet, and a trunk diameter of 9 feet 6 inches at official breast height (DBH).

Live oak is the most durable and valuable of the oaks, as well as the strongest. It is exceeded only by teak as being the most desirable wood for shipbuilding. It is fine-grained and compact, but due to its growth pattern does not lend itself to the production of long, straight-grained "board foot" lumber. However, its forks, branches, and varied shape growth made it admirably suited to shipbuilding. This was discovered very early in the American colonies, and in the first years of the United States the young government reserved live oak timber to be used in the construction of our early frigates and ships of the line. By the time of the clipper ships, there was not sufficient growth to be of general use, although live oak was occasionally specified.

Live oak has superior resistance to rot.

Oak, White, *Quercus alba*

Diameter	4 feet avg., 8 feet max.
Height	100 feet avg., 150 feet max.
Life span	500 to 600 years
Weight	45 pounds per cubic foot
Strength	Rated at 100 as a gauge against which other woods are measured

White oak is the wood by which other woods used in American shipbuilding were measured in determining their relative strength. For this purpose an arbitrary value of 100 was assigned to white oak as the basis for comparison.

White oak grows in abundance across the entire eastern United States, including the states bordering both sides of the Mississippi River, and is often found in pure stands.

Of all woods, white oak was the premier wood specified by American shipbuilders. It is durable, strong, and of coarse grain. Its growth pattern is such that it can provide planking timber and shapes such as knees, all from the same tree; compass timbers were also plentiful. For the clipper ships, every structural item could be obtained from white oak; thus it was specified for keels, frames, beams, and, in some cases, planking. Its abundance and proximity to shipyards rendered expensive searching and shipping from distant points unnecessary, and this contributed to its basic economical use.

All Eastern white oak has the same characteristics. However, in many instances the designer called for a variety grown in a specific locale such as New Hampshire, Virginia, or "Northern." And, in at least one vessel, the clipper *Southern Cross*, white oak specifically from Worcester County, Massachusetts, is recorded as being used.

The pores of white oak, filled with a substance known as *tyloses*, do not allow liquids to penetrate the wood. This characteristic contributed immeasurably to the permanency of the wood.

The best white oak has superior resistance to rot.

Pine, Hard, *Pinus palustris*

Diameter	2½ feet avg., 4 feet max.
Height	120 feet avg., 150 feet max.
Life span	150 years avg., 300 years max.
Weight	43 pounds per cubic foot
Strength	90, with white oak rated at 100

Known today as "longleaf pine," this species flourishes in the southeastern United States in coastal areas from Virginia to Texas. Ranking second only to white oak in use as a shipbuilding wood, when specified it was always referred to as "hard pine."

The wood is very resinous, durable, straight-grained, and hard. It is widely used in rough construction work. In shipbuilding it was specified for planking, knees, beams, and large timbers, but never for keels, stems, or sternposts.

The best hard (long leaf) pine has superior resistance to rot.

Pine, Norway, *Pinus resinosa*

Diameter	3 feet avg., 5 feet max.
Height	80 feet avg., 120 feet max.
Life span	350 years
Weight	41 pounds per cubic foot
Strength	60, with white oak rated at 100

Norway pine (a common, misleading name for red pine) ranges north from Pennsylvania into Canada, from the east coast of Maine westward through the Great Lakes region.

The wood is light, close-grained, and rather soft. The lumber is good for general building purposes and contains a high penetration of creosote, which makes it an enduring wood. In shipbuilding it was used for deck planking (except weather decks), masts, and spars. It was always specified as "Norway pine."

The best Norway pine has excellent resistance to rot.

Pine, Pitch, *Pinus echinata*

Diameter	3 feet avg., 4 feet max.
Height	100 feet avg., 146 feet max.
Life span	170 years avg., 400 years max.
Weight	43 pounds per cubic foot
Strength	75, with white oak rated at 100

This species, now known as "shortleaf pine" or "yellow pine," is abundant throughout all the Southern states from Virginia to eastern Texas. It is the tree which in the early 1700s was scored with the King's broad arrow and claimed by the English crown for use in making masts for the Royal Navy. Today is used extensively in millwork and construction, in the manufacture of plywood, and as pulpwood.

In the era of the clipper ship, the wood was widely used for keelsons, planking, beams, and other large inboard timbers, in addition to masts. It was always specified as "pitch pine." This tree should not be confused with the smaller Northern pitch pine, Pinus rigida, such as forms the famous Pine Barrens of New Jersey.

Pitch pine has superior resistance to rot.

Pine, Southern

This was, and still is, a common general name which could be applied to any of several varieties of pine tree indigenous to the southeastern United States. When specified it could presumably be any one of the following species: loblolly pine *(Pinus taeda)*; longleaf pine *(Pinus palustris)*; or shortleaf pine *(Pinus echinata)*.

Southern pine has superior resistance to rot.

Pine, White, *Pinus strobus*

Diameter	3½ feet avg., 6 feet max.
Height	100 feet avg., 220 feet max.
Life span	200 years avg., 450 to 500 years max.
Weight	30 pounds per cubic foot
Strength	55, with white oak rated at 100

White pine (the everyday name for Eastern white pine) was prolific throughout its original range, which covered the

northeastern United States from Maine westward beyond the Great Lakes. It was, in its prime period, the most valuable timber tree in the Northeast.

White pine is a soft, workable wood with straight, inconspicuous grain and excellent qualities for both hand and machine tooling. It also finishes well. In shipbuilding it was used in mast making and providing weather deck planking.

White pine has moderate to good resistance to rot.

Pine, Yellow

Like "Southern pine," "yellow pine" is a common general name that could be applied to any of several species of pine tree indigenous to the southeastern United States. When specified it could presumably be any one of the following: loblolly pine *(Pinus taeda)*; longleaf pine *(Pinus palustris)*; or shortleaf pine *(Pinus echinata)*.

Yellow pine has superior resistance to rot.

Sweetgum, *Liquidambar styraciflua*

Diameter	4 feet avg., 6 feet max.
Height	120 feet avg., 200 feet max.
Life span	200 to 300 years
Weight	37 pounds per cubic foot
Strength	72, with white oak rated at 100

Also known as "redgum," "sapgum," and "alligator wood," sweetgum is an important timber tree. Its growing range extends across the entire southeastern United States from Connecticut to Texas. In strength and elasticity it cannot compete with such woods as ash, maple, or oak; however, it is stable and easy to work with tools.

The wood, when green, is so heavy that it hardly floats; so, as with teak, the trees are often girdled and left to stand for about a year to season before they are harvested.

Sweetgum was not looked upon favorably in shipbuilding, and its use is noted here in only one instance, in the construction of the keel of the clipper ship *Santa Claus*, where it was used in combination with rock maple. When specified it was simply referred to as "gum wood."

Sweetgum has good resistance to rot.

Teak, *Tectona grandis*

Diameter	To 4 feet
Height	To 100 feet or more
Life span	Dendrologists have not satisfactorily ascertained the life span of teak due to the fact that tropical trees generally do not produce annual growth rings.
Weight	47 pounds per cubic foot
Strength	85, with white oak rated at 100

Without doubt, teak is the most desirable of shipbuilding woods. It is dense, strong, straight-grained, and has an oily surface. For use in ship structural work it is virtually indestructible and practically immune to rot.

Very little teak was specified for use in American-built clipper ships, and the reasons are worthy of note. The most compelling reason was the fact that teak is native to India, Java, Burma, and Thailand. These distances were in themselves reason to use white oak, which was close at hand and of an assured supply. Green teak is too heavy to float if cut with the expectation of transporting immediately. It is also so large that the logs, which in the forest are handled and moved by elephants, are prohibitively heavy, making the lumbering process exceedingly difficult.

Due to these physical problems, a unique harvesting process evolved. A tree chosen to be felled is first girdled by cutting a ring around the trunk completely through the bark into the heartwood. Thus cut, the tree is allowed to stand for about three years; as it dies, the moisture content deteriorates, and the wood becomes light enough to float.

Because of the magnitude of the logging process, it could take as long as eight years from the time of girdling to the time of arrival at a timber dealer or a shipyard in the United States. (Theoretically, the delivery of a log might not be accomplished within the time frame, 1850 to 1856, of this book.) Thus, it was almost imperative that a ship designer and/or builder have his supply of teak stockpiled if he intended to specify teak. A certain amount of teak was infrequently called for, generally limited to rails, such as fife rails and their stanchions, hatch coamings, belaying pins, and mast partners. On very rare occasions it was also specified for major structural items such as stems, sternposts, and deck planking.

An interesting sidelight concerning teak is that the tree's tough leaves are so rough and coarse that the natives use them in the same manner that we use sandpaper.

Fitting-Out and Decorative Woods

Ash

(See description under "Functional and Operational Woods.")

When it is flat-sliced or cut as veneer, ash shows a light brown, open figure characterized by thin, straight, closely spaced grain lines. Ash can be finished to a highly polished, refined surface and was one of the few varieties of native wood to be specified for interior decorative ornamentation in the great cabins and first-class dining saloons of the clippers and clipper packets.

Cherry, Black, *Prunus serotina*

Diameter	3 feet avg., 5 feet max.
Height	60 feet avg., 100 feet max.
Life span	150 to 200 years
Weight	44 pounds per cubic foot
Strength	84, with white oak rated at 100

Black cherry grows in the eastern United States, especially in the mountains of Pennsylvania. The wood is free from checking and warping; is stable after seasoning; and is moderately hard, stiff, and strong. It works well with tools and takes a fine finish. Its use in shipbuilding of this period was confined to rail stanchions to support a taffrail or similar rails surmounting the principal structural rails of the ship. When specified it was simply referred to as "cherry."

Mahogany, African, *Khaya ivorensis*

Diameter	To 6 feet
Height	To 150 feet; clear trunk to 90 feet
Life span	Well over 200 years
Weight	55 pounds per cubic foot
Strength	About 96, with white oak rated at 100

Mahogany, New World, *Swietenia macrophylla*

Diameter	To 12 feet, at base
Height	To 150 feet; clear trunk to 50 feet
Life span	Well over 200 years
Strength	About 96, with white oak rated at 100

The sizes noted above are at maturity, but trees may be harvested when only sixty years old, at which time their average diameter will exceed 30 inches.

As far back as the time of Cortez (early 1500s), mahogany was being used as a structural wood for shipbuilding. However, in the English colonies of North America, where there was a plentiful supply of suitable local timber for shipbuilding, mahogany was rarely used, generally only for such items as minor topside turned stanchions, ladder stringers, gangway boards, and rails.

Its principal use for interiors was in the great cabins and first-class dining saloons where it was employed as paneling, wainscoting, and elegant trim.

Maple, Bird's Eye, *Acer saccharum*

This wood, reported as being used for decoration and trim in some clipper ships, is the species known as "sugar maple." (See the earlier description of rock maple under "Structural Wood.") The bird's eye grain pattern was much desired for its beauty and the distinctive figure from which it derives its name. Another factor in bird's eye maple's desirability was its relative scarcity. Although the wood was plentiful and, being a native variety, could be obtained economically, generally only a small proportion of the trees harvested in a given locale contained the prized pattern.

At the time, there did not seem to be any logical explanation for this phenomenon, so it was accepted as a happening of nature with no explainable cause. Today (1990), the accepted belief is that the bird's eye figure is the result of stunted growth. Careful studies and markings observed over a period of years have shown that trees growing at a slow rate in dense areas, where there is a notable deficiency of light and air, are those that will produce wood containing the bird's eye pattern.

The wood, being hard and close-grained, as well as beautiful, can be brought up to a fine, smooth, brilliant finish. When available in sufficient quantity it was used in paneling and trim in combination with other decorative woods.

Rosewood

Rosewood, the most frequently mentioned wood used as decorative trim in the clipper ships, includes four species which could be considered under the name: Brazilian rosewood (*Dalbergia* spp); Honduras rosewood (*Dalbergia stevensonii*); Indian rosewood (*Dalbergia latifolia*); and Madagascar rosewood (*Dalbergia greveana*). Which of these was the principal variety, or whether there was any great demand for one over the other, is almost impossible to ascertain. The least likely variety would be Honduras rosewood, due to the fact that it does not take a high natural polish. Judging by their general qualities, the Brazilian and Indian varieties appear to be most qualified. However, it is a matter of record that a shipment of Honduras rosewood entered the United States in 1841, so this variety could well have been in use.

Regardless of variety, rosewood is one of the most beautiful, ornate woods to be found anywhere in the world and was the favorite decorative wood specified for appointing cabins and saloons; almost without exception it was specified for the more elite areas of the ships. Its color is basically a reddish brown; in any given piece, however, splendid streaks ranging from pink to black run side by side through its length, and there is never any appreciably large area that is any one color. The wood is very stable, works very well, and takes a brilliant finish.

Satinwood

Second only to rosewood in the frequency of being specified for first-class cabin and saloon trim, satinwood is obtainable in three varieties: Brazilian satinwood (*Euxylophora paraensis*); East Indian satinwood (*Chloroxylon swietenia*); and West Indies satinwood (*Zanthoxylum flavum*). Of these the finest variety is West Indies satinwood, both in quality and color. Logs were attainable as large as 22 inches in diameter, and the wood, at the time, was plentiful. It is golden yellow in color and, as its name suggests, has a sheen similar to that of satin.

East Indian satinwood featured more variable coloring, ranging from light yellow to dark brown, and was noted for the fanciful patterns that appeared on its surface after being processed into boards, panels, or veneers. This wood was plentiful and logs measuring as large as 30 inches in diameter and 20 feet in length were sometimes, although infrequently, obtainable. Generally the sizes were considerably smaller.

Brazilian satinwood was the same warm, yellow color, but of coarser grain than the other varieties. However, it was attainable in very desirable widths and lengths.

All satinwoods were amenable to a very fine finish, and all were most attractive. However, there is little way of determining whether one or all were in demand, because, when reported, it was merely specified as "satinwood."

Walnut, Black, *Juglans nigra*

Diameter	3 feet avg., 7 feet max.
Height	90 feet avg., 170 feet max.
Life span	150 years avg., 250 years max.
Weight	42 pounds per cubic foot
Strength	70, with white oak rated at 100; however, it is not regarded as structural timber

Also known as Eastern black walnut and American walnut, this species ranges over the entire eastern United States, even west of the Mississippi River. In spite of this range, it is considered a rather rare wood and has always been in great demand for making furniture, gun stocks, and veneers. Although a hard wood, it was never used in a structural sense, this being considered a waste of its aesthetic appeal. When cut as planking, black walnut displays very attractive and varied grain patterns. When cut as veneer, it contains an infinite variety of eye-catching figures, depending on the angle of the cut and the part of the tree being used. The color of the wood is spread through a range of warm, mellow browns and is very picturesque.

In spite of its universal appeal, this beautiful wood never found its way into widespread use as a decorative wood aboard ship. One reason was that rosewood, with its prominent red streaks and bright coloring, was the decorative wood that dominated the field of interior paneling and decoration and, even though an imported wood, was in plentiful, affordable supply.

Zebrawood, *Cynometra*

Zebrawood was the common name for zebrano, also known as zingana, a wood native to Africa. There are other

African and South American woods with zebra-like striping; thus a certain degree of confusion and uncertainty accompanies the identity of this wood.

The variety addressed here is from the west coast of Africa and features a striking pattern of light and black longitudinal stripes. It ranks behind rosewood and satinwood as the most frequently used decorative trim in the clippers.

The tree grows to large size, but its inaccessibility and hazardous harvesting rendered it very costly. Since the bark reaches 12 inches in thickness, it is always stripped at the site where the tree is felled.

There is no doubt that woods, both native and exotic, used in the interiors of clipper ships, were not restricted to those that have been described. In articles describing such ornamentation, the statement is generally made that "the cabin is tastefully decorated with rosewood, satinwood, and others." Any other species that may have been used are a subject of mystery and guesswork. The woods described in this section are representative.

Functional and Operational Woods

Ash, White, *Fraxinus americana*

Diameter	3 feet avg., 6 feet max.
Height	80 feet avg., 125 feet max.
Life span	200 to 250 years
Weight	45 pounds per cubic foot
Strength	95, with white oak rated at 100

White ash is the principal variety of a large group of the species which flourishes throughout the entire eastern United States, with the exception of Florida. The wood is strong, stiff, and extremely shock resistant. It also has excellent bending qualities. White ash has a long, straight grain and is light in color.

This wood is not used in general ship construction, but is used in the fabrication of the shells of blocks and is the primary material specified for oars for ships' boats, capstan bars, handspikes, belaying pins, and similar items. In extremely rare instances it was used for minor and incidental interior trim. When specified it was simply referred to as "ash."

Cedar, Atlantic White, *Chamaecyparis thyoides*

Diameter	14 inches avg., 5 feet max.
Height	85 feet avg., 120 feet max.
Life span	75 to 100 years
Weight	About 35 pounds per cubic foot
Strength	50, with white oak rated at 100

The range of this species is limited to a narrow coastal belt along the Atlantic Seaboard from Maine to northern Florida. The wood is soft, uniform in texture, close-grained, and extremely durable. The use of the wood was almost exclusively restricted to the fabrication of ships' boats. When specified it was simply referred to as "cedar."

White cedar has good resistance to rot, but not to the degree offered by Western Red Cedar.

Lignum Vitae, *Guaiacum officinale*

Diameter	To 3 feet
Height	To 35 feet
Life span	Dendrologists have not satisfactorily ascertained the life span of lignum vitae due to the fact that tropical trees generally do not produce annual growth rings.
Weight	83 pounds per cubic foot
Strength	90, with white oak rated at 100; however, it is not regarded as structural timber

This tree is native to the West Indies, the northern coast of South America, and the western coast of Central America. The wood is the heaviest and hardest known to man and will not float. It also has the closest grain and maintains tremendous resistance to crushing loads. Lignum vitae contains about 30 percent by weight of a natural resinous gum, and can be brought to a smooth, mirror-like finish.

When harvested, the average log is about 12 inches in diameter and rarely more than 6 feet long. Upon being cut into short lengths, it is best preserved by total immersion in water until the time of use.

In shipbuilding it was used for making deadeyes, fairleaders, bull's-eyes, and the sheaves of blocks. When used for sheaves, the tree must be cut so that a band of sap is preserved all around, as this prevents the sheaves from splitting from the outside inward toward the center.

One cannot conclude from this list that the woods described were the only varieties used in clipper ship construction. Hundreds of such ships were built in addition to those named in this book. It is entirely possible, indeed probable, that some builder who had obtained a stock of some different but acceptable timber would have used it in construction. However, documentation of such use is difficult to find and, in most cases, no longer survives.

Based on records, rules that were then in effect, and known practice, it is safe to assume that the woods described are representative of the entire shipbuilding industry in the United States during this period.

By the time 1857 arrived and the clamor for clipper ships had subsided, iron had found its way into ship construction: as iron straps, for reinforcing hulls diagonally; as iron fittings;

and aloft, in way of doublings. All in all, iron was soon to overtake wood in all phases of construction.

Timbermen who had once needed only to comb the seacoast for their material were now roaming far inland to find suitable trees. It was expensive and arduous work. Some of the desired timbers had been so decimated as to be unobtainable in the required quantities.

By this time the major damage to first-growth timber in the forests had been done. The great old majestic trees were, in essence, gone. For many lifetimes, if ever, they would not be seen again. When one considers that many hundreds of trees in excess of one hundred years old could be transformed into a clipper ship in only one hundred days, it is only a matter of simple arithmetic to arrive at the ultimate, sad conclusion. The supply of suitable timber was rapidly being exhausted. Necessity was propelling shipbuilding in a new direction.

Two outstanding instances of this prolific and speedy transformation of living trees into finished vessels are here noted. The extreme clipper *John Bertram*, a vessel of 190 feet length overall and 1,050 tons register, was launched sixty-one days after the keel was laid. The clipper ship *Golden Eagle*, built at Medford, Massachusetts, was 192 feet overall and 1,100 tons register. Only eighty-four days after the start of keel-laying she was alongside Lewis Wharf, Boston, ready to receive her cargo.

When one ponders the immense sizes and almost immeasurable life spans of the tree species noted in the preceding pages, it is very difficult to picture how magnificent the timber stands of the East Coast of the United States actually were. Also, the realization is forcefully brought home that when one of these trees was harvested it was gone forever, never to be replaced. The trees were unable to keep pace with man, and thus the battle was concluded. No quarter was given and, in effect, these giants are gone forever.

A current example of this overwhelming deforestation is evident in the fact that, as of 1990, the Commonwealth of Pennsylvania, a greatly forested area of forty-five thousand square miles, contains fewer than seven hundred trees that have been certified as being two hundred years of age or more. This figure is based upon a state registry of such trees.

Chapter Three

GENERAL CHARACTERISTICS OF CLIPPER SHIP HULLS

THE OUTSTANDING CHARACTERISTIC OF THE clipper ship was its long, lean hull form. Confined to that feature, it could be said that all clippers were alike. Obviously such a conclusion is faulty, because no mobile structure conceived and made by man can be summed up with such naive simplicity.

Many features were characteristic of all ships if considered in only the broadest sense, but ship designers were individuals, and each individual was steeped in his own peculiar ideas and preferences when it came to the inclusion and development of broad principles in his own designs.

As in most endeavors, in the building of ships there is no "one" inexorable way to accomplish a given objective. There are some absolute parameters, all of which are basic and quite obvious: The completed ship must float. It must also be maneuverable and seaworthy. It must be built with certain carrying capacity. It must be capable of propulsion by nature or machinery.

With these preconditions in place, the designer or client must enumerate his desires and start to work within and around them to achieve desired results. This is done, and has been for centuries, either by having a mental picture of what is wanted or by setting down the details in a list of specifications or a contract or both.

The very first man-made raft was very simple and easy to picture and produce from start to completion by the employment of mental images and applied native intelligence. From that first structure the path was long, slow, and arduous, fraught with much experimentation and failure. However, failure is a good teacher. It is one of the ways we learn how to avoid making the same mistake a second time.

Over a long period of time, as men developed their ships, they found that generally, broad, short vessels with fully rounded ends produced the best desired results. They would float, could be maneuvered, had carrying capacity, and could call on the wind at almost any time.

A great and well-known name in naval architecture in the 1700s was Fredrik Henrik af Chapman, of Sweden, who chronicled in great detail the types of vessels extant at the time and published his *Architectura Navalis Mercatoria*[25] in 1768. During this same period a young Englishman named Mark Beaufoy, who was only about fourteen years of age, devoted his precocious, inquisitive mind to the task of challenging some of the sacred nautical beliefs of the day, including the "solid of least resistance" theory of no less a figure than Sir Isaac Newton.

Young Beaufoy embarked on a series of unsophisticated but practical experiments having to do with the problems of bodies traveling through water and, over a period of years, produced some results and conclusions which disproved to a great extent some of the older theories. During the 1790s he was still testing the resistance of various solid forms, and ultimately expounded a most important discovery: that the length of an object moving through water has little effect on its resistance.

Beaufoy kept complete and accurate records of his findings, but it was not until 1834, some years after his death, that his son Henry gathered together his father's papers and published them on his own private press. One of the new breed of marine draftsmen who encountered this book was John Willis Griffiths, of New York, a young man twenty-five years of age. He was a free thinker, and eleven years later, in 1846, he would produce the renowned ship *Sea Witch*.

This was the long, slow, and devious path that ended in the hull form of the clipper ship. The length/breadth ratio of clippers was great by accepted standards. While the average figure was about 5:1, the ratios for specific vessels differed significantly, ranging from *Great Republic* with a slenderness ratio of about 6.14:1 down to the ratio of 4.30:1 for the virtually unknown *Eringo*. Table 3.1, which follows, lists the values for vessels appearing in this book. These values are representative of the type, but the possibility exists that some unlisted vessels may have exceeded the limits of the values noted in the table.

The most prominent and universal characteristics of the clipper hull were those visible to the eye when the hull was completed but was not yet in the water. All featured the protruding external keel found in the construction of all wooden ships; a stem that *raked* (inclined) forward in varying degrees and contours; sternposts that were almost universally upright or vertical; gently sweeping sheerlines that were low at the stern and noticeably higher at the bow; deadrise at the midsection ranging from moderate to extreme; tumblehome ranging from barely discernible to considerable; flare in the bow in varying extremes; small counters; and generally well-rounded bilges.

Each of these particular characteristics is worthy of some brief or definitive description, as addressed in the following pages.

The following paragraphs provide a key to the column headings or abbreviations in Table 3.1:

L/B. Ratio of length on deck (where known) to breadth. In some cases the length is overall or between perpendiculars. This distorts some of the ratios. However, the general comparison appears reasonable. A more accurate value is obtained by using a vessel's waterline length, which is rarely given. The value of breadth = 1.

Form of Keel. In this table the form referred to is the moulded shape in reference to the moulded baseline, as illustrated in Figure 3.1.

Rake of Stem. The moulded rake of the stem is given in degrees forward of vertical for ease of comparison. In actual practice the rake or contour of the stem was entered in the table of moulded offsets as feet, inches, and eighths forward of a given frame, each reading taken on a waterline. The rakes listed in this table are taken from offset tables, descriptions, or scaled from lines plans and are subject to reasonable differences due to varying interpretations.

Rake of Sternpost. The moulded rake of the sternpost is entered here in the same manner as recorded in a table of moulded offsets. The sternpost rake from the baseline to a given waterline is x inches. A line struck between these two points delineates the moulded rake of the sternpost, which is always raked aft.

Generally, the moulded scantlings of the sternpost are greater at the foot than at the head. As a result, the after edge of the post stands approximately vertical in most cases. The rakes in this table are taken from offset tables, descriptions, or lines plans.

The designation "upright" is from a description of the vessel and refers to the after edge of the sternpost.

Type of Profile. An examination of the hull form of many clipper ships results in arbitrarily allowing them to be assigned to one of ten distinctive types, which are illustrated in Figure 3.1. Profile type 2 overwhelmingly dominates the field of clipper ship design. The remaining types are found sparsely scattered through the list, some appearing only once or twice.

Sheer of Deck. A vessel's *sheer*, the term denoting the gentle, arced rise of the deck from its lowest point to its highest point forward at the knightheads, is referred to as a certain height measured in feet and inches, the measurement being the vertical difference between these two points.

In clippers, the lowest point was always located aft of the midship section, but the location varied greatly from vessel to vessel. A tabulation of these distances for a small number of well-known ships is listed later in this chapter under Sheer of the Deck. Aft of the lowest point, the sheer line rose gently until the stern was reached. The amount of this rise was a small but esthetically vital component of the sheerline and was helpful against pooping—waves breaking over the stern.

This figure is not always stated, and in some cases a contemporary source will note the sheer as being that of the planksheer. The sheer of deck, however, is not necessarily the same as the contour of the planksheer and the main rail, which latter two are generally, but not always, parallel.

Detail Sources. These columns apply to the details included in all sections of this book. Information of the type noted in the various columns can be found in many libraries and museums. Throughout Table 3.1 the greater the number of indications beside a vessel's name, the more information is generally available in the sources indicated.

The Keel

The *keel* of any vessel forms the base upon which the entire ship is built. The details of the keel were dictated by the ship's construction requirements. The ship's keel provided a meeting place for structural members such as frames. To give planking (which would sheathe the frames) a place to be fitted into in order to achieve a watertight structure, a *rabbet* (a groove shaped to receive the garboard strake) was cut into the keel; this called for sufficient depth of material in the keel timber. Clippers and other ship classifications were built with varying types of keel rabbet, a subject that will be discussed later.

The structural keel performed more functions than merely being a strongback for the ship. Deepened beyond the amount required for holding frames and plank ends, the keel was of immense importance in keeping a ship on a straight course when underway. In addition it protected the ship's bottom planking if shoal water or unseen obstacles lay hidden on the sea bed. The keel was helpful in diminishing excessive roll in a seaway and was indispensable for a ship attempting to hold her way when on a lee shore.

While always a major structural component, the keel lost some of its relative structural importance in the clipper ships *(text continued on page 38)*

Table 3.1. *Longitudinal characteristics of the clipper ship hull.*

Detail sources

Vessel & Ref.#	L/B	Form of keel	Rake of stem	Rake of sternpost	Type of profile, Figure 3.1	Sheer of deck	Offsets	Lines	Description	Half model	Photograph	Etching, etc.	Miscellaneous
Alarm #1	4.85		19°	upright	2	4'-0			D			E	
Amphitrite #1	5.39			upright	2, mod. fwd				D				
Andrew Jackson #31,59	5.34		11°	4"/24'	2	3'-0		L	D	H		E	
Antelope #1	4.52		15°	upright	2	2'-0			D				
Asa Eldridge #1	4.94		9°	upright	2	5'-6			D				
Bald Eagle #1	5.18	straight, arched forefoot	30°	nearly upright	3	3'-0			D				
Belle of the West #1,31	5.09		13°	6"/24'	2, mod. fwd	2'-3		L	D	H		E	
Beverly #3	4.69		11°	nearly upright	2				D				
Black Hawk #18,24,32	4.62		14°	10"/24'	2	2'-6	O	L	D		P	E	
Blue Jacket #5,32	5.70		25°	nearly upright	2	bold sheer			D			E	
Bonita #1,32	5.08		13°	upright	2, mod. fwd	3'-6			D			E	
Bounding Billow Bark #1	4.55			upright	2	1'-6			D				
Celestial #18,42	4.65	straight, rockered along shoe	19°	6"/20'	6	2'-0	O	L	D			E	
Challenge #1,18,24, 31,42,84	5.59		12°	9"/24'	2	3'-0	O	L	D	H			
Challenger #1	5.38			nearly upright	2	4'-6			D				
Champion of the Seas #1,86	5.54	straight, arched forefoot	16°	10"/24'	3	4'-6		L	D		P	E	
Charger #1	4.95		boldly raked	nearly upright	2	5'-0			D				
Charmer #1	5.16		slight rake	nearly upright	2	4'-5			D			E	
Cleopatra #1	4.94		slight rake	upright	2	4'-0			D			E	
Climax #1	5.00		pilot boat style	raked	5	2'-2			D				
Coeur de Lion #1,136	4.89		23°	nearly upright	2, mod. fwd	3'-0		L	D	H		E	
Comet #18,24	5.54		15°	10"/22'	2	4'-3	O	L	D			E	
Cyclone #1	5.14			nearly upright	2	3'-0			D				
Daring #1	4.83		12½°	nearly upright	2	3'-0			D				
Dauntless #1	5.30		6½°	upright	2	3'-0			D				

(Note in Form of keel column: "Keels are straight along top surface except as shown in Figure 3.1")

Vessel & Ref.#	L/B	Form of keel	Rake of stem	Rake of sternpost	Type of profile, Figure 3.1	Sheer of deck	Offsets	Lines	Descrip.	Half model	Photo.	Etching	Misc.
Donald McKay #30,32	5.75		9½°	3"/25'	2				D	H	P		M
Don Quixote #1,32, 84	5.19	straight, mld. 24" fwd mld. 18" aft	10°	12"/25'	8	4'-0		L	D		P	E	
Eagle #5	5.71		20°	nearly upright	2				D				
Eagle Wing #1	5.08		23°	nearly upright	2, mod. fwd	4'-0			D				M
Edwin Forrest #1	4.98		18½°		2	3'-6			D				
Electric Spark #1	4.63		nearly upright	nearly upright	2	1'-6			D				M
Ellen Foster #1	4.65		12°	nearly upright	2	2'-0			D				
Empress of the Sea #1,32	5.35		13°	nearly upright	3	3'-0			D			E	
Endeavor #1	5.05				2	4'-0			D				
Eringo Bark #1	4.30					1'-5			D				
Eureka #4	4.74				2				D				
Fair Wind #1	4.94		16°	nearly upright	2, mod. fwd	4'-0			D				
Fearless #29,136	5.23		12½°	10"/22'	2, mod. fwd	5'-0, plkshr.		L	D	H		E	
Fleet Wing #1	4.79		well raked	nearly upright	2	very slight			D				
Flyaway #18,24	5.14		14°	8"/22'	2	5'-0, plkshr.	O	L	D				
Flying Arrow #1	4.51		16°		2	2'-2			D				
Flying Childers #1 87	5.06				2	2'-6			D				
Flying Cloud #1,23, 87	5.53	straight, arched forefoot	21°	18"/24'	3	3'-0		L	D			E	
Flying Dragon #1	4.92			nearly upright	2				D			E	
Flying Dutchman #18, 24	4.94		14½°	6"/22'	2	4'-3, plkshr.			D				
Flying Eagle #1	4.93		12°	nearly upright	2	2'-6			D				
Flying Fish #1,30	5.31	straight, arched forefoot	11°	24"/24'	3	4'-6		L	D	H		E	M
Flying Mist #1	4.87		boldly raked	nearly upright	2	5'-0			D				
Galatea #1	4.99		well raked	nearly upright	2	very slight			D			E	
Game Cock #1	4.78		17°	upright	2	3'-0			D			E	

Table 3.1. *Continued.*

Vessel & Ref.#	L/B	Form of Keel	Rake of stem	Rake of sternpost	Type of profile, Figure 3.1	Sheer of deck	O	L	D	H	P	E	M
Gazelle #18,24	4.79		17°	9"/20'	2	3'-10, plkshr.	O	L	D			E	
Gem of the Ocean #1	4.90		10°	upright	2	1'-6			D			E	
Golden Eagle #1,5	5.14		17°	upright	2	2'-6			D			E	
Golden Fleece (2nd) #1	5.12		slight rake	nearly upright	2	4'-0			D			E	
Golden Light #1	5.06		17°	9"/24'	2, mod. fwd	3'-6			D			E	
Golden West #1,31	5.03		16°	upright	2, mod. fwd	3'-0			D	H		E	
Grace Darling #1	5.01		well raked	nearly upright	2	3'-6			D				
Great Republic (1853) #4,10,23,87	6.14	rockered forward, arched forefoot	25°	12"/25'	4	9'-0		L	D			E	
Great Republic (1855) #23,42,84,103	6.14	Same as original vessel						L	D		P	E	
Henry Hill Bark #1,42	4.45		20°	nearly upright	2, mod. fwd	4'-6		L	D			E	
Herald of the Morning #12	5.34	straight, arched forefoot	18°	14"/23'	3	4'-3, plkshr.		L	D			E	
Hoogly #1	4.87		10°	upright	2	3'-6			D				
Hurricane #4	5.38		15°	upright	2, mod. fwd				D			E	
Indiaman #1	5.03			nearly upright	2	4'-0			D				
Intrepid #18	4.77		19½°	10"/24'	2	4'-6, plkshr.	O		D				
Invincible #4,18,24	5.56		14°	6"/26'	2	4'-10, plkshr.	O	L	D				
James Baines #1,23	5.94	straight, arched forefoot	29°	12"/24'	3	7'-6, plkshr.		L	D			E	
John Bertram #1	4.86		17°	upright	2	2'-2			D			E	
John Gilpin #1	5.27		12°	upright	2, mod. fwd	2'-0			D			E	
John Land #1,32 (Built as a duplicate of Winged Arrow.)	4.89		12°	upright	2	2'-2			D			E	
John Stuart #4,31	5.31		12°	nearly upright	2	2'-0			D				
John Wade #1	4.53		16°	nearly upright	3	4'-6			D			E	
Joseph Peabody #1	4.75		20°	nearly upright	2	3'-6			D				
King Fisher #1	5.44		20°	nearly upright	3	3'-6			D				
Lady Franklin #31	4.84				2								M
Lamplighter Bark #1	4.38		very	nearly	2	very			D				
Lightfoot #1	5.58		pilot boat style	slightly inclined	5	3'-6			D			E	
Lightning #1,2,31,42	5.52	rocker fwd., arched forefoot	20°	10"/22'	4	4'-6		L	D			E	
Mameluke #1	4.88		14°	nearly upright	2				D				M
Mary Robinson #31	5.58				2				D				
Mastiff #1	4.63	straight, arched forefoot		upright	3	4'-0			D			E	M
Mermaid Bark #1	4.75	straight, 2' drag		upright	9	2'-1			D				
Morning Light #1,31	5.12	straight, arched forefoot	24°	upright	3	3'-6			D	H		E	M
Mystery #1	5.00			9"/24'	2	3'-0			D			E	
Nightingale #31,32,42	5.07		20°	10"/16-6	2	3'-2		L	D				
Noonday #1	4.73		12°	nearly upright	2, mod. fwd	6'-0			D			E	
Northern Light #32	4.76		10°	upright	2, mod. fwd				D			E	M
Ocean Express #1,32	5.41		well raked	nearly upright	2	3'-6			D				
Ocean Pearl #1	5.23		13°	nearly upright	2	2'-0			D				
Ocean Telegraph #5	5.54		boldly raked	nearly upright	2	moderate			D				
Onward #1	4.91		9°	nearly upright	2	2'-3			D				
Osborne Howes #31	5.20			nearly upright	2				D				
Panther #32	5.18				5 & 8				D				M
Phantom #1,32	5.15	straight, mld. 24" fwd 17" aft	pilot boat style	upright	2	2'-0			D			E	
Queen of Clippers #1,32	5.51		19½°	upright	2	4'-0			D			E	
Queen of the Pacific #31,32	4.99		13°	upright	2				D		P	E	
Queen of the Seas #1	5.06		17°	upright	2, mod. fwd	2'-6			D			E	
Quickstep Bark #1	4.85			nearly upright	2	2'-6			D			E	
Racehorse Bark #1,44	4.10	straight, 2' drag	20°	nearly upright	9	1'-8			D			E	
Racer #3,32	4.87		nearly straight	7'-0	2, mod. aft	slight			D			E	
Radiant #1,32	5.28		10°	upright	2	2'-6			D			E	
Raven #3	4.86				2				D				

Table 3.1. *Continued.*

Vessel & Ref.#	L/B	Form of keel	Rake of stem	Rake of sternpost	Type of profile, Figure 3.1	Sheer of deck	Offsets	Lines	Descrip.	Half model	Photo	Etching	Misc.
Syren #3,42,84	5.25		21°	nearly upright	2	slight			D		P	E	M
Telegraph #1	4.94		11°	nearly upright	2	2'-0			D			E	
Thatcher Magoun #1	4.75	straight, mld. 26" fwd mld. 18" aft		upright	2,mod. fwd	1'-8							
Tornado #3,83	4.95		30°	nearly upright	2				D			E	
Uncowah #18	4.73		19°	9"/22'	2	5'-7, plkshr.	O						
War Hawk #1,32	4.93		8°	upright	2,mod. fwd	3'-8			D			E	
Water Witch #1,84	4.80		10½°	upright	2	3'-0			D			E	
Western Continent #9,31		188' long											M
Westward Ho #1,87	5.19		8°	nearly upright	2,mod. fwd	2'-2			D			E	
West Wind #1	4.93			upright	2	2'-0			D				
Whirlwind #1	4.37		17°	upright	2,mod. fwd	3'-0, all fwd			D				
Whistler #1	4.75			upright	2,mod. fwd	2'-3			D				M
Wildfire Bark #1	4.61	rocker fwd., mld. 19" fwd mld. 42" aft	19°	nearly upright	10	4'-6			D				
Wild Pigeon #1,42	4.90	straight, angular forefoot	14°	36"/22'		3'-0		L	D	H		E	
Wild Ranger #1,32	5.00		12°	nearly upright	2				D			E	
Wild Rover #31	5.19												M
Winged Arrow #1	4.89		12°	upright	2	2'-2			D			E	M
Winged Racer #1,32	4.94		12°	upright	2,mod. fwd	3'-0			D			E	M
Witchcraft #1,32	4.89		12°	upright	2	2'-0			D			E	
Witch of the Wave #1,31,32,42,84	5.50	straight, angular forefoot, mld. 24" fwd mld. 22" aft	20°	16"/22'	1	2'-6		L	D	H		E	M
Wizard #1													
Young America #18, 24,32,87	5.63		12°	10"/25'-6	2	4'-0	O	L	D		P	E	
Young Turk Bark #1	4.14			nearly upright	2	3-0			D			E	

Vessel & Ref.#	L/B	Form of keel	Rake of stem	Rake of sternpost	Type of profile, Figure 3.1	Sheer of deck	Offsets	Lines	Descrip.	Half model	Photo	Etching	Misc.
Red Jacket #14,23, 31,32,83	5.70		11°	8"/22'	2,mod. fwd	3'-6	O	L	D	H	P	E	M
Robin Hood #32	5.03												M
Rocket Bark #1	5.23		12°	upright	2	2'-0			D				
Roebuck #1	4.85		9°	upright	2	1'-8			D				
Romance of the Sea #1,42	5.95		17°	8"/18'	2	4'-6		L	D	H			
Santa Claus #1	4.78			nearly upright	2	3'-6			D				
Saracen #1	4.94		dashy rake	nearly upright	2	3'-0			D				
Sea Bird Bark #1	4.23		9°	nearly upright	2	2'-0			D				
Seaman's Bride #4	4.76				2	2'-0			D				
Sea Serpent #4	5.40		30°	upright	2	2'-0			D				
Shooting Star #1,84	4.69		13°	upright	2	2'-0			D			E	
Sierra Nevada #1,78	5.01		nearly upright	upright	2	4'-6			D	H		E	M
Silver Star #1	4.91		14½°	upright	2	3'-6			D				
Southern Cross #1,32	4.72		14°	upright	2	1'-9			D			E	
Sovereign of the Seas #1,23,31,84,87	5.87		17°	15"/24'	2	4'-0		L	D	H		E	M
Spitfire #1	5.29			upright	2				D				
Staffordshire #1, 32,83	5.61		16°	nearly upright	2,mod. fwd	3'-0			D			E	
Stag Hound #1,23, 47,87	5.42		11°	16"/20'	2	4'-3		L	D	H			
Star of the Union #1.5	5.20		15°	nearly upright	2	2'-6			D				
Starr King #32	5.13			upright	2,mod. fwd	3'-0							M
Storm King #1	4.76		5°	36"/15'	2,mod. aft	nearly straight			D				
Sultana Bark #1	4.27			6'/13'	2	4'-0			D				
Sunny South #42,136	5.25	rocker full lgth., arched forefoot	18°	8"/20'	7	2'-6		L	D				
Surprise #1,32,42,83	4.74		9°	nearly upright	2	2'-6		L	D			E	
Swallow #1	5.38			8"/20'	2,mod. fwd	3'-0		L	D				
Sweepstakes #42,84	5.21	rocker fwd., arched forefoot	7°	10"/24'	4 mod.	2'-6		L		H		E	M
Sword Fish #18,24,32	4.64		14°	6"/18'	2	3'-6	O	L				E	

Figure 3.1. *Clipper ship moulded profiles.*

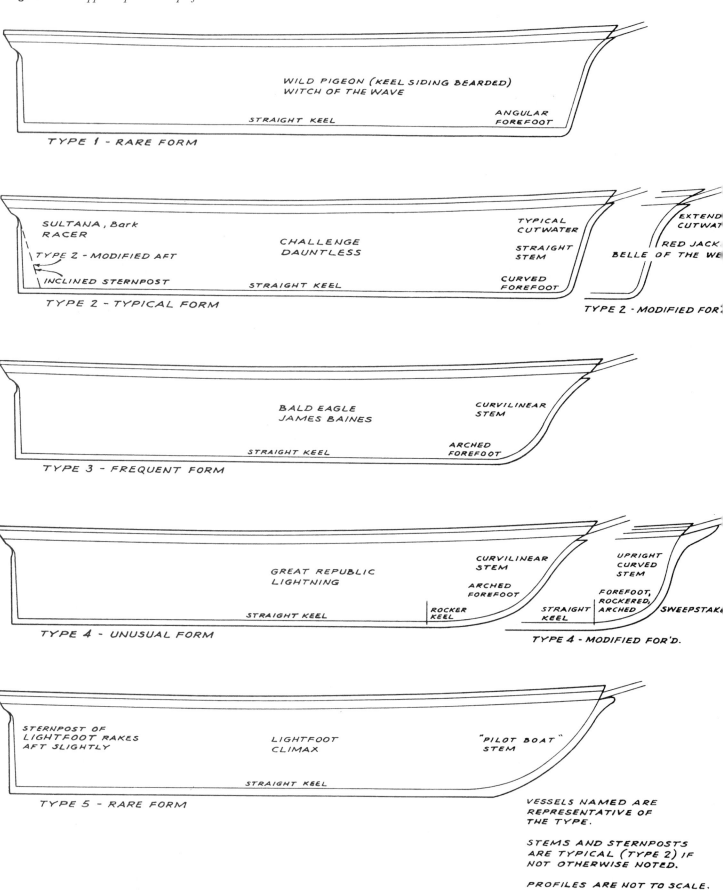

WILD PIGEON (KEEL SIDING BEARDED)
WITCH OF THE WAVE

STRAIGHT KEEL   ANGULAR FOREFOOT

TYPE 1 - RARE FORM

SULTANA, Bark
RACER

TYPE 2 - MODIFIED AFT

INCLINED STERNPOST

CHALLENGE
DAUNTLESS

STRAIGHT KEEL

TYPICAL CUTWATER

STRAIGHT STEM

CURVED FOREFOOT

TYPE 2 - TYPICAL FORM

EXTEND CUTWAT

RED JACK
BELLE OF THE WE

TYPE 2 - MODIFIED FOR

BALD EAGLE
JAMES BAINES

STRAIGHT KEEL

CURVILINEAR STEM

ARCHED FOREFOOT

TYPE 3 - FREQUENT FORM

GREAT REPUBLIC
LIGHTNING

STRAIGHT KEEL

CURVILINEAR STEM

ARCHED FOREFOOT

ROCKER KEEL

STRAIGHT KEEL

UPRIGHT CURVED STEM

FOREFOOT, ROCKERED, ARCHED

SWEEPSTAK

TYPE 4 - UNUSUAL FORM

TYPE 4 - MODIFIED FOR'D.

STERNPOST OF
LIGHTFOOT RAKES
AFT SLIGHTLY

LIGHTFOOT
CLIMAX

STRAIGHT KEEL

"PILOT BOAT" STEM

TYPE 5 - RARE FORM

VESSELS NAMED ARE
REPRESENTATIVE OF
THE TYPE.

STEMS AND STERNPOSTS
ARE TYPICAL (TYPE 2) IF
NOT OTHERWISE NOTED.

PROFILES ARE NOT TO SCALE.

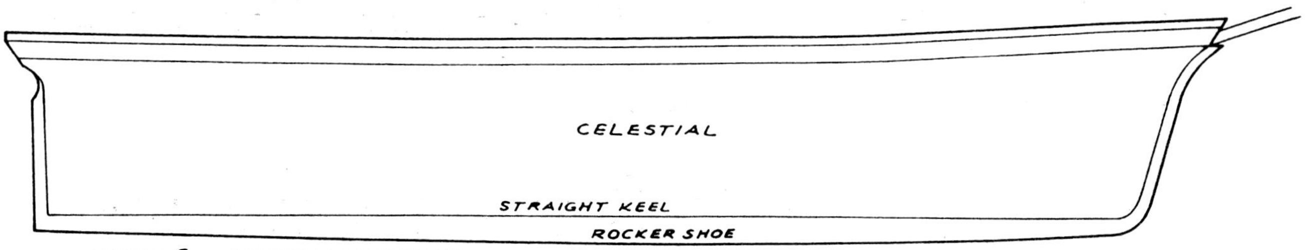

CELESTIAL

STRAIGHT KEEL

ROCKER SHOE

TYPE 6 - POSSIBLY UNIQUE

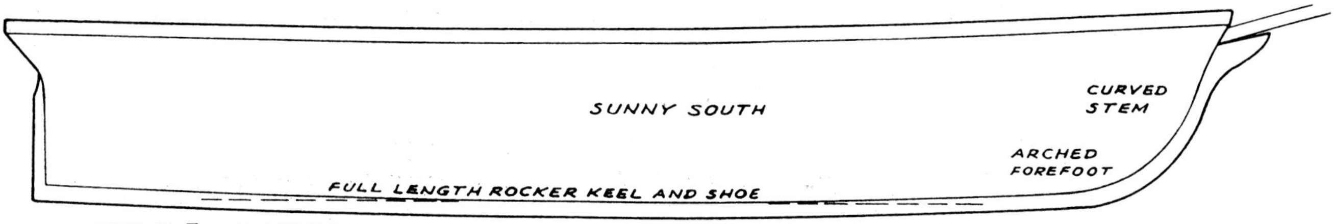

SUNNY SOUTH

CURVED STEM

ARCHED FOREFOOT

FULL LENGTH ROCKER KEEL AND SHOE

TYPE 7 - UNIQUE

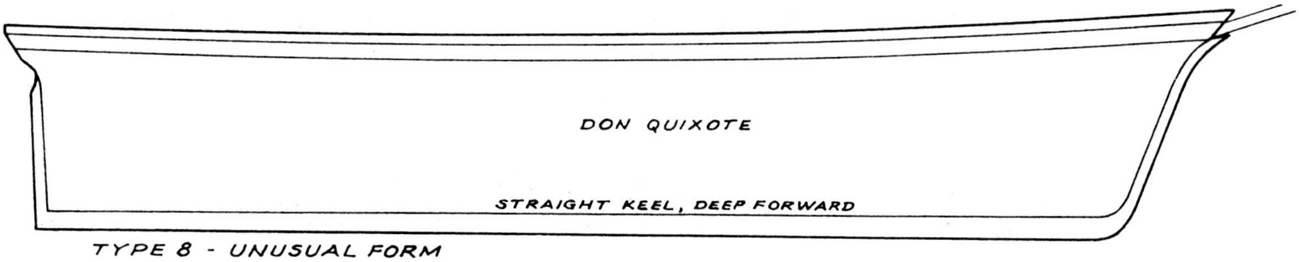

DON QUIXOTE

STRAIGHT KEEL, DEEP FORWARD

TYPE 8 - UNUSUAL FORM

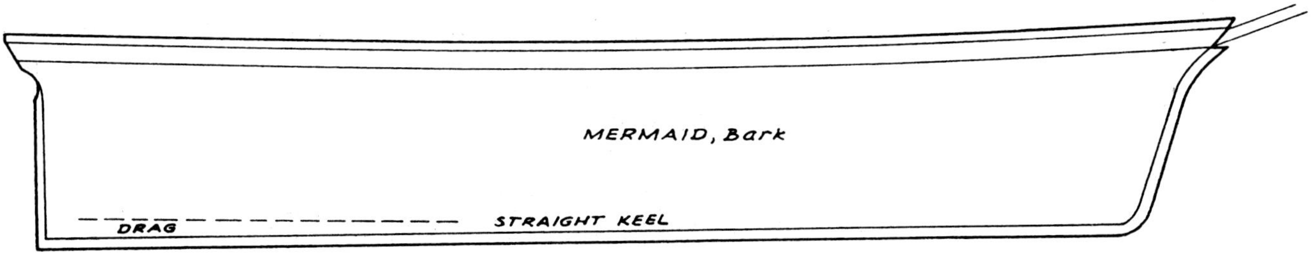

MERMAID, Bark

DRAG   STRAIGHT KEEL

TYPE 9 - UNUSUAL FORM

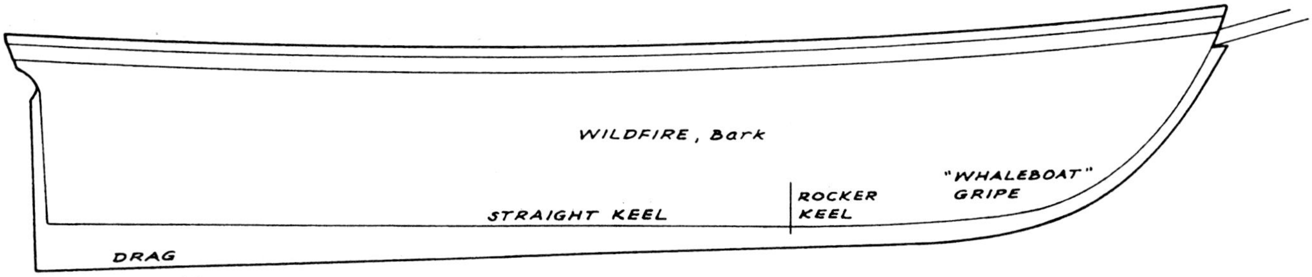

WILDFIRE, Bark

"WHALEBOAT" GRIPE

STRAIGHT KEEL   ROCKER KEEL

DRAG

TYPE 10 - RARE FORM

(text continued from page 32)

due to their fine lines and overall design. The necessary strength required to support these long vessels longitudinally was provided internally by massive keelson, rider keelson, and sister keelson assemblies, which will be discussed in detail in their proper sequence.

The clipper ship's keel was generally a structure of uniform depth below the moulded baseline, extending from the sternpost forward to the *gripe*, or meeting place with the foot of the stem, or *forefoot*. In this case, the transformation from keel to stem was a rather sharp, abrupt curve. This was the predominant configuration, but there were occasions where it was not followed.

The most prominent variation that occasionally found its way into design was a straight keel with an arched forefoot sometimes combined with a *rockered* (convexly curved) forward end. Rockering was achieved when the moulded line of the keel started to rise from the moulded baseline in a gentle curve which became a pronounced arc as it met its juncture with the stem. This easy blend of the two units resulted in a forefoot that was stronger than the normal, angular forefoot. It was also considered an advantage should the ship take the ground.

This form of construction always produced a stem with long, easy curves which resulted in a profile having an unusual forward rake and no straight lines.

Another positive result of this structural form was the saving of dead weight in the vessel's forefoot. In profile the angular forefoot extended farther forward than did the arced gripe of the rockered keel, and when one is compared to the other it can be calculated that about 3,000 pounds of structural material is eliminated with a rockered keel. This weight, while not great, was located where it was least desirable—that is, in the portion of the vessel that provided the least buoyancy. These apparent advantages notwithstanding, the rockered keel with its great curve was not built into the general run of clipper ships.

It is quite possible that the loss of lateral resistance vital to windward performance was a prominent factor in excluding this feature.

A third and most unusual form of keel to find its way into clipper construction was one that was rockered throughout its entire length from sternpost to stem. It cannot be truly stated that this form of keel ever found bona fide acceptance among shipbuilders. The only definite documented keel built this way was in the extreme clipper *Sunny South*. However, even though one example may not prove a case, the one example remains for posterity to ponder.

Her rocker curve rose from the moulded baseline amidships to a height of about 15 inches at the sternpost and to about 18 inches at a point immediately forward of the fore-

mast, terminating in the well-rounded forefoot and stem features associated with all the rockered keels.

This vessel, designed by George Steers, designer of the schooner-yacht *America*, was fast but unprofitable, being only 145 feet long. Steers also made a model along these same lines for a larger clipper ship. This vessel, however, never materialized, so justification for his keel treatment was never realized. Additional principal variations are illustrated in Figure 3.1.

The Stem

The *stem* of most clipper ships was designed with a moulded forward rake rising in essentially a straight line from the juncture with the keel to some point above the waterline, at which point it curved concavely forward until terminating at the main rail. While not uniform, the angle of forward rake of the straight portion of the stem, as measured in many typical vessels, ranged between 9 and 18 degrees forward of vertical. This form of stem was favored by William H. Webb and most other shipbuilders.

There were many variations of this configuration, some quite subtle and others very pronounced. Instances of the latter may be noted in the vessels designed by Samuel H. Pook where the curvature above the waterline was brought extremely far forward compared to the average vessel.

Exceptions to these stem profiles are notable among the designs of Donald McKay, most apparent in the vessels *Great Republic*, *Lightning*, and *James Baines*. Here the rounded or arched forefoot dominated the profile of the moulded stem and caused the apparent angle of rake to appear more pronounced, averaging about 26 degrees forward of vertical. This apparent angle of rake is an empirical rather than a factual value and is obtained by striking an arbitrary straight line through the forefoot upward to the main rail in a manner which divides the lower convex portions and the upper concave portions into roughly equal parts on the forward and after sides of the line. The resulting angle may quite obviously be read differently by each viewer, but to all it demonstrates the more pronounced forward rake.

This *apparent rake* is strictly a nontechnical term used to convey an idea of this relatively extreme rake which is made up of a combination of curves that in themselves defy measurement. It is not a term used in actual design or in naval architecture.

A point which appears significant in this stem design is that, of the fourteen occasions where clipper ships verifiably logged more than 400 miles in a sea day, the three aforementioned McKay ships accomplished this seven times between them.

The design appears to have been a definite contribution to a vessel's swiftness, but it never was adopted as a necessary characteristic, even by McKay, as well as the other major ship designers. Thus, what may have been a key ingredient to this class of ship never realized its potential destiny.

It is worthy of note that this feature is another one of the many characteristics of Griffiths's *Sea Witch* ultimately to find its way into clipper ship design.

These descriptions of the stem form have been based on the moulded dimensions, and note should be taken that rarely did the forward edge of the stem parallel this moulded line. Almost without exception, the moulded dimension of the structural stem was sided smaller above the waterline than it was at the turn of the forefoot.

While these stem configurations contributed to the æsthetic appeal of a ship, they also performed several very practical functions. As a vessel proceeded underway, especially under a full press of sail and at a high rate of speed, the raked stem diminished the impact of the sea as the stem cleaved the water. Another essential achievement was to allow the hawse holes to be moved forward in the eyes of the ship far enough, in combination with the flare of the bow, for the anchor to clear the forefoot when the anchor cable was "up-and-down"—that is, hanging from the hawse hole and clear of the ground. A third contribution was to add valuable space on the forecastle deck, this space being necessary to allow the crew to work ship. Also, the extended bow allowed the forecastle to be raised, thus facilitating the introduction of the long, gentle sweep of sheer, low aft and high forward, that was so necessary to the performance of the clippers.

The Sternpost

The *sternpost* was the third of the centerline structural elements that determined the skeletal profile of a ship. And, as the keel tied in the frames at the floor of the ship, and the stem tied together the forward structure, so did the sternpost tie together and secure the after end and stern. A broadside view of the sternpost gave the impression of its after edge, in way of the rudder, standing vertical. This was generally characteristic of clipper ship construction. There was, however, a subtle difference between vertical and "upright": A vertical sternpost was installed at a right angle with the moulded baseline. An "upright" sternpost was installed with a slight rake aft, perhaps as little as 3 or 4 inches in 24 feet.

Additionally, there were some ships, notably those designed by Donald McKay, built with pronounced rake to the sternpost, *Flying Cloud*, *Flying Fish*, and *Sovereign of the Seas* being examples.

Whether or not there was a structural or sailing advantage to one or the other of these configurations seems to defy a definite conclusion. It appears more likely that each builder had his own reason for his own installation.

However, the forward, or moulded, edge of the sternpost was always raked to some degree. This detail is supported by the fact that, wherever appropriate scantlings can be found, the moulded dimension of the sternpost at its foot was always recorded as 2 inches to 4 inches greater than at its head. In the same vein, the siding was generally greater at its head than at its foot by as much as 4 inches—the notable exception being an 8-inch difference in both versions of *Great Republic*, although this figure is subject to conspicuous contradictions.

In addition to this, the rake of the moulded forward edge of the sternpost was entered in the table of moulded offsets. This very slight, almost imperceptible rake, while always an entry in the offsets, was never discussed or explained. However, it had a very technical but definite verification for being included in the design of a vessel whose principal characteristic was speed. Its positive contribution to the forward progress of a ship is explained by Lauchlan McKay in his book *The Practical Shipbuilder, 1839*.[6]

In essence McKay states that if the stern is perpendicular it sinks directly into the water, and when the ship is underway it is deprived of the propelling action of the fluid angle that is obtained by a rake, however slight. When the level of the deck at the stern corresponds to that of the water to any considerable degree, the ship tends to slide both downward and forward, gaining a certain power to give headway as the ship's bow is about to ascend the next wave. Even though this action of the water may seem to be infinitely small and insignificant, it is an important element in making headway in heavy seas when a portion of the sails have been taken in.

This attribute would no doubt be of little assistance in vessels making short voyages or when not being urged on at their greatest capacity. However, for ships that were making passages as lengthy as those of the clipper runs, there can be no doubt that this feature contributed significantly to the sailing records made during this era.

In most cases the siding of the foot of the sternpost equaled the siding of the keel. However, where there was an exception to this rule, the lesser siding of the sternpost was given in the table of moulded offsets, and the siding of the keel was gradually tapered until the sidings are equal at the sternpost. This taper generally started at 1 foot forward of the post for every ¼-inch difference between the two basic sidings.[8]

In addition to being the support for the stern of the ship, the sternpost also was the structural member upon which the rudder was hung. Obviously, the well-being of a vessel was to a great extent dependent upon the reliability and stoutness of its sternpost.

Sheer of the Deck

Sheer of the deck was the original reference to the term *sheer*, and it was the difference between the low point of the deck in the ship's waist and its height at the stem. Accompanying this mathematical measurement was a second requisite: that this difference be arrived at in the form of a gentle, sweeping curve—never in the form of a straight-line slope, which would have been more economical to fabricate and install, but would have been very unattractive to behold.

In early times, when the outline of decks was enclosed by open rails rather than bulwarks, the sheer of a deck was of relatively little importance. Camber was all that was necessary to discharge boarding seas or torrential rains over the side. As time went on, ship form progressed from a series of short weather decks such as the waist, half deck, quarter deck, and poop deck, each one surmounting the other, to the institution of long, single flush decks that were enclosed by longitudinal bulwarks along the deck edge.

Water being thrown on a deck now presented a different problem. Boarding seas were trapped in a long trough, enclosed at both ends by planked bulwarks or ship structure. To discharge this trapped water, the bulwarks were pierced with a series of scuppers at the deck edge. In some vessels hinged freeing ports were cut in the bulwark planking.

The sheer of the weather deck, as quoted in various descriptions, did not necessarily run parallel with the sheerline of the *planksheer* (also called the *covering board*), and the main rail, the latter two generally, but not always, being parallel with each other. The deck sheer followed the trace of the planksheer from the stern through the length of the vessel to a point approximately abreast of the foremast. At this point, in ships where the two sheerlines diverged, the deck rose at a much flatter and slower rate than did the sheer of the covering board and main rail.

This divergence accomplished two objectives. First, a deck with the same steep incline as the covering board would, in many vessels, require a seaman to constantly walk up and down hill when working the forward end of the ship if she was sailing in normal trim. The situation would be exacerbated if she were trimmed by the stern. This of itself would not be very practical, and practicality was part and parcel of shipbuilding. The second result was that of achieving headroom under the topgallant forecastle deck. This allowed for housing one watch of the crew, handling of ground tackle, installation of the anchor windlass, and location of the hawseholes totally above the weather deck, a very practical accomplishment. Sufficient headroom beneath the topgallant forecastle deck was required, as it was an important working area.

A comparison of deck sheer measurements, when laid down on an outboard profile or sheer plan of many vessels, will generally but not always show this to be the case.

Briefly, as examples, *Flying Cloud* had a stated deck sheer of 3 feet, while the sheer of the rail was 7 feet 3 inches at the moulded stem; *Golden West*, deck sheer 3 feet, sheer of rail about 7 feet 6 inches; *Mastiff*, deck sheer 4 feet, sheer of rail about 7 feet.

Sheer of the Rail and Planksheer

Sheer of the rail and planksheer, as entered in the table of offsets, is the long, gentle sweep of the ship's main rail when viewed in profile. In the case of the clipper ships, the sheer seen in profile was developed from measurements entered in this table. Also, in the clipper ships, the sheer of deck and sheer of rail did not necessarily parallel each other throughout the length of the vessel. Any noticeable deviation occurred in way of the forecastle. This feature was considered in detail when discussing the sheer of the deck.

Sheer as we know it was introduced into shipbuilding in England in the early sixteenth century, and its reason for being was a very practical one. Shipwrights of the period were aware that raising the ends of a vessel was instrumental in reducing the forces acting against the motion of the vessel, thus furnishing easier passage through the water. In addition it promoted the seaworthiness of a ship in rough weather.

In this period the shapes of the various parts of ships were derived from a combination of arcs of circles drawn with diverse radii. And, in keeping with this fashion of design, the sheer of the deck was drawn in the form of a long sweep of an arc which had a radius of exceedingly large dimension. The center of this radius was placed forward of the dead flat section, resulting in an after end that sat higher than the forward end. The high stern provided considerable protection against the vessel being pooped or swamped by a following sea.

As ship design progressed and became more sophisticated, the center of the radius of the sheer arc was slowly moved aft, and as this was done the height of the stern diminished while the height of the bow increased. When the clipper ship appeared, the stern had reached its lowest practical freeboard. On many occasions it is reported that fast-sailing clippers buried their counters down to the rail.

In contrast, the bows of clipper ships stood high out of the water, in some cases being more than 6 feet higher at the knightheads than at the taffrail. This visible sheer was along the ship's main rail and did not represent the quoted sheer of a vessel, which technically was measured along the weather deck and was generally a noticeably different measurement.

It cannot be said that the sheer curve was still produced as the true arc of a circle, but it did remain as a smooth, fair, gentle curve which, in most cases, was pleasing to the eye. This æsthetic consideration was one that was never lost sight of by designer or client. Neither was ever able to forgo the opportunity to produce a vessel that was a pleasure to behold.

All clipper ships, due to each one being designed to accomplish similar missions, namely to deliver a cargo to a distant destination in a minimum amount of time, adhered in general to the same categorical configuration. However, in the less apparent details each designer still operated in his own individual style.

One phase of design that was known back in the sixteenth century and was carried on until the end of sail was the locating of the dead flat or midship section nearer to the bow than to the stern, thus making the forward section of the ship fuller and more buoyant. It would appear that this consideration was one generated through practical experience from the very earliest days of sail.

The forward progress of a hull is resisted by the water its prow is induced to part due to the force of the wind on its sails. This wind force is all concentrated high above the deck at a point termed the *center of effort*. The wind, quite naturally, is blowing faster than the forward progress of the ship, and this results in an *overturning moment*, a force which tends to bury the bow of the ship. To counter and compensate for this physical phenomenon, the most buoyant portion of the ship is moved forward to a specified location. As in all cases of design, each individual developed the proportions with which he was most comfortable; and, as might be expected, there was great diversity of thought among the various naval architects.

The following table gives, for a sampling of vessels, the locations of midship sections in reference to mid-length on the waterline.

Ship	Year built	Designer	Waterline length	℘ section feet forward of mid-length on waterline
Sea Witch	1846	John W. Griffiths	165'–1	14'–9½
Stag Hound	1850	Donald McKay	105'–0	-2'–6 (aft)
Flying Cloud	1851	Donald McKay	209'–6	2'–0
Challenge	1851	William H. Webb	225'–0	19'–6
Comet	1851	William H. Webb	223'–0	22'–0
Young America	1853	William H. Webb	231'–6	25'–0
Red Jacket	1853	Samuel H. Pook	225'–0	10'–0
Lightning	1854	Donald McKay	228'–0	1'–3
Black Hawk	1856	William H. Webb	173'–0	24'–0

Using the measurements of the few design examples listed in the table, it is apparent that Donald McKay preferred his midship sections close to the mid-length of the waterline of the ship. Conversely, William H. Webb shows a preference for locating the midship section well forward of the waterline

mid-length, while both Samuel H. Pook and John Willis Griffiths compromised between the two extremes.

It is entirely possible that a larger sampling of vessels might run contrary to this conclusion; but, since this is more of a random sampling than a hand-picked one, it is reasonable to conclude that each designer, including those not in this tabulation, adhered to his adopted philosophy.

As the line of rail sheer became lower aft and higher forward, the low point of the rail slowly moved farther aft, and in all cases it was located aft of the midship section. This fact is sustained in the following tabulation which indicates great variation in the choice of location except in the case of William H. Webb, who consistently favored a location well abaft the midship section.

Ship	Year built	Low point of main rail aft of 'midship section	Deadrise amidship in degrees
Sea Witch	1846	12'–0	14
Stag Hound	1850	30'–0	18½
Flying Cloud	1851	10'–0	11
Challenge	1851	40'–0	18
Comet	1851	62'–8	10½
Young America	1853	53'–4	9
Red Jacket	1854	40'–0	8
Lightning	1854	80'–0	8½
Black Hawk	1856	40'–0	5

There does not appear to be a consistent relationship between low point of rail and angle of deadrise.

Spring

Spring is a nontechnical term that was used to describe the curve of a ship's bow as the result of a combination of the vessel's sheerline at the bow, the rake of her stem, and the contour of her cutwater. All clipper ships had spring built into their structure due to the designed sweep of sheerline which resulted in the bow sitting high in the water. This, along with forward-leaning stems and extended cutwaters, gave an appearance of lightness and buoyancy to the bow. This effect of a bold, dashing, forward and upward movement, as when a vessel is under sail, was defined as *spring*.

However, this combination of details did not evoke the same impression in every vessel.

It might be expected that all vessels with considerable sheer along their rails would automatically be described as having spring. Such, however, was not necessarily the case. The required combination of ingredients was an elusive one.

Contemporary descriptions of the bows of those ships named in this book deal with this quality but in most instances skirt use of the word *spring*. Generally the appearance of the bow is described in a routine, rather glowing manner, in keeping with the description of the rest of the vessel being described.

Other instances where this lightness of appearance was apparently quite noticeable invited more descriptive terms. In the case of *John Bertram* the bow was "buoyant and dashing"; *Radiant* had "an air of lightness to the bow"; *Dauntless* was "bold and lively"; *Storm King* had a cutwater which "rakes boldly outwards and forms a graceful dashy curve as it rises."[1]

And finally, in instances so outstanding that they deserved the ultimate praise, the terminology was quite direct and the description phrased using the magic word. Of *Game Cock* it was written: "The spring of her cutwater, as it forms the heads is easy and graceful, and imparts a lively and buoyant air to its parent bow"; of *Don Quixote*, "The bow is very sharp, rakes boldly forward, and rises as it rakes into an easy and graceful spring"; of *Empress of the Seas*, "As the stem is boldly inclined outwards, and as the sheer of the bow springs buoyantly upwards"; of *Eagle Wing*, "Her cutwater springs boldly out, and curves up under the bowsprits."

Of the clipper ships that have been classed as "best" of their breed, some had spring and others did not. An examination of lines or paintings reveals that, of the vessels appearing in this book, *Sovereign of the Seas*, *Young America*, *Challenge*, and *Golden West* could easily be considered to possess this characteristic. And, of all clippers, including any not named in this book, the name *Red Jacket* is arguably the epitome of this elusive, beautiful element of the clipper form.

Performance of the clippers in their heyday indicates that spring was as much an element of beauty as it was an aid to sailing efficiency. The principal reason for including the characteristic of spring here is that its existence exactly paralleled the life span of clipper ship design. Once the fervor and clamor for such ships died out, the term was no longer applied in any great degree to the design of sailing ships.

Counter

The *counter* is the underside of the overhang of the stern in way of the sternpost. It is the result of the ship's run converging at the sternpost, along with the necessity of providing breadth on deck to work ship and to house and operate the vessel's wheel and the box that houses the steering mechanism, whatever its nature.

Long before the day of the clipper ship, the counter was the cause of distress among seamen. Due to the overhanging stern, the relatively flat area that developed in way of the rudderhead was exposed to enormous pounding when the ship's surging bow hammered her stern down upon the water's surface.

Water, free to run and find its own level when unrestricted, becomes as hard as a solid when pressed into a confined area. Such was the case under a ship's counter where the sea was trapped between the rudder, its stock, and the counter planking. The resulting crash in the most extreme conditions could shiver a ship from stern to stem.

The practical solution was to design counters that provided the minimum surface area against which the sea could impact. An examination of plans, where available, indicates two design modifications toward minimizing pounding: First, counters, transoms, and rounded sterns were designed with slopes ranging from about 45 degrees to 50 degrees with the baseline. The second trend was to reduce the amount of stern overhanging the rudderpost. This dimension was unbelievably small, being only about 4 feet in Webb's *Comet* and Pook's *Red Jacket*. The combination of these two factors all but eliminated the existence of a counter. This was a considerable asset to a ship making 15 knots or thereabouts, with the water's edge roaring by almost at planksheer level.

In addition, the breadth of the poop deck was diminished as much as was consistent with providing sufficient area on which to work ship. This breadth of deck, measured at the position of the steering wheel, was only 25 feet on the transom-sterned *Comet* and counter-sterned *Young America*.

Stern Knuckle

The *stern knuckle* in both square, transom-sterned and round, counter-sterned vessels (see the following section) represented the line of demarcation between the planking of the ship's body and the planking of her stern. However, the planking treatment differed in the two cases.

As we have just seen, all clipper ships were built to incorporate the smallest and most convex counters it was possible to attain in order to minimize the force of the sea impacting under a vessel's stern. In the case of the square stern, the lines of *Comet* (see Figure 1.7) graphically illustrate what was required to complete the form of the ship. A moulded line designated as the "lower knuckle" was drawn across the stern. This knuckle and the contour and rake of the transom proper were mutually adjusted to accommodate each other so that the lines of the after end of the ship resulted in a smooth and fair configuration. This fairing settled the final shape of the transom, with its upper boundary generally a line conforming to the camber of the weather deck and stretching across the ship at the height of the main rail. This treatment resulted in a single transom in which any buttock line drawn between the knuckle and the main rail was a straight line.

As a variation of the square, transom stern, a second knuckle, designated as the "upper knuckle" (this can also be seen in Figure 1.7) was introduced into the design. This second knuckle was located at the approximate height of the planksheer where compatible with structural considerations. Across the stern it followed the camber of the weather deck.

This knuckle, when viewed in the sheer plan, was placed so that it broke the plane of the single transom in a very subtle manner, resulting in the creation of two transoms, one extending from the lower knuckle to the upper knuckle, the other extending from the upper knuckle to the main rail. Sterns so treated had a very light and graceful appearance when compared to the single transoms, which were comparatively heavy and bulky.

This two-tiered working of the square transom was invariably a design element of William H. Webb's clippers. However, there were other designers who followed this practice.

The stern knuckle as incorporated into the round or elliptical counter stern is illustrated in Figure 1.8, the lines of *Young America*. The contour of the stern in plan view and its rake in the sheer plan were established, and the planksheer then plotted around the stern of the ship. A structurally acceptable distance below this, usually in way of timbers supporting the deck, the knuckle was laid down paralleling the line of the planksheer. In some cases the location of this knuckle coincided with the moulded line of the planksheer, as with *Stag Hound* (Figure 1.5), and in other cases it was located a noticeable distance below the planksheer, as in the case of *Young America* (Figure 1.8).

This knuckle delineated the aft termination of all the ship's body planking below it, serving the same purpose that the tuck played in the old, square-sterned ships. All the planks ending in way of the knuckle had their ends fastened in the most efficient and secure manner possible.

All the planking above the knuckle ran continuously around the stern of the ship in the manner of the planksheer and the main rail.

The forward extent of this knuckle was a development of the shape of the ship on her quarters. It eliminated itself at some point where a buttock line passing through the structure no longer formed a knuckle where the buttock crossed a frame or space between frames. The uppermost plank to be installed in this area required a great deal of fitting and coaxing to be shaped and adequately fastened into its final position.

Contour of the Stern

Contour of the stern, as seen in the plan view of a vessel, can be placed in one of three general categories of configuration: square, elliptical, and round. Of these three shapes, the square or "transom" stern predates the other two by centuries, it being the form of stern originally designed into large sailing vessels as we know them. Rounded sterns were referred to as "counter" sterns.

The square stern represented the weakest form of construction, and, in the case of naval vessels, the most vulnerable. In its earliest form the square or transom stern featured a square tuck, the *tuck* being the area where the ship's sides meet the stern. The square tuck was superseded by the round tuck, which, in general, followed the camber of the decks. In the early 1800s, the round tuck gave way to the development of the "round" stern in naval vessels; however, merchant vessels did not adopt this round or counter stern until the 1840s. One of the first clipper ships to be built with this round, counter stern was Samuel H. Pook's *Surprise* of 1850.

The contour of the stern was apparently determined solely by arbitrary choice on the part of the designer, the client, or both. According to sailing records none of the configurations had a significant effect on the sailing ability or performance of the vessels.

Contemporary descriptions of these stern contours at the deck are noted in Table 3.2 in finely divided form. In all, eighteen terms are mentioned—some very understandable, others leaving room for conjecture and interpretation as to exactly how the individual composing the description arrived at his conclusions. With the exception of those descriptions based on offsets, lines, half models, and other factual sources, all are of Duncan MacLean, marine reporter for the *Boston Daily Atlas*.[1] They are presented here in three principal categories progressing from "square" through "round."

Square Transom Stern	Elliptical Counter Stern	Round Counter Stern
square	curvilinear	nearly semicircular
arched	nearly oval	semicircular
convex	oval	rounded
	slightly elliptical	boldly rounded
	nearly semielliptical	round
	semielliptical	
	segment of an ellipsis	
	elliptic	
	boldly elliptic	
	elliptical	

Just exactly which details accounted for some of these fine distinctions is difficult to fathom; and just exactly what the viewer saw that determined his definition can never be known. However, since all the descriptions were written by the same person, it appears safe to conclude that there were small but discernible differences in the vessels he described and that the terms represent some definite pattern of consistency. Therefore an attempt will be made to adhere strictly to the descriptions as they were reported.

(text continued on page 46)

Table 3.2. *Transverse characteristics of the clipper ship hull.*

Vessel & Ref.#	Contour of stern at deck	Swell or round of stern at center line on deck		Deadrise	Swell of sides
		Aft of fashion piece	Aft of cross seam		
Alarm #1	oval			12"/6°	12"
Amphitrite #1	nearly semi-circular				
Andrew Jackson #31,59	semi-circular		4'-6	9"/4½°	4"
Antelope #1	square	very slight		8"/5°	6"
Asa Eldridge #1	oval			12"/6°	15"
Bald Eagle #1,4	slightly elliptical				slight
Belle of the West #1	nearly oval		3'-0	18"/9½°	4"
Beverly #3	square	slight		15"/9½°	
Black Hawk #18,24	square	2'-1		10"/5°	10"
Blue Jacket #5	square	rounded			5" abt.
Bonita #1	oval			27"/14°	
Bounding Billow Bark #1	nearly oval			12"/8°	6"
Celestial #18,42	square	1'-4		29"/18½°	13"
Challenge #18,24	elliptical		5'-6	36"/16°	18"
Challenger #1	nearly oval			20"/9½°	6"
Champion of the Seas #1,86	semi-elliptical		3'-0	18"/9°	10"
Charger #1	oval			12"/6½°	12"
Charmer #1	oval			15"/7°	6"
Cleopatra #1	oval			17"/9°	4"
Climax #1	nearly oval			15"/8°	7"
Coeur de Lion #1	nearly semi-circular	2'-2		23"/10½°	9"
Comet #18,24	square			26"/14°	6"
Cyclone #1	"same model as Northern Light"				
Daring #1	oval			12"/6°	12"
Dauntless #1	curvilinear			15"/9°	12"
Donald McKay #32	rounded			18"/7½°	
Don Quixote #1	square	very slight		very flat	9"
Eagle #5	rounded			30"/15°	slight
Eagle Wing #1	nearly semi-circular			14"/7½°	10"
Edwin Forrest #1	nearly oval			13"/7°	9"
Electric Spark #1	square	convex		18"/8½°	9"
Ellen Foster #1	square	very slight		15"/7½°	22"
Empress of the Sea #1,32	semi-elliptical			27"/11½°	12"
Endeavor #1	oval			12"/6°	6"
Eringo Bark #1	square	very slight		15"/11°	6"
Eureka #4	square				
Fair Wind #1	oval			18"/11°	9"
Fearless #29	round		2'-6		none
Fleet Wing #1	nearly oval				7"
Flyaway #18,24	square	1'-6		22"/13°	6"
Flying Arrow #1	square	boldly rounded		17"/9½°	6"
Flying Childers #1	rounded			18"/9½°	6"
Flying Cloud #1	elliptical		4'-0	30"/13½°	16"
Flying Dragon #1	oval			15"/7½°	slight
Flying Dutchman #18,24	square	2'-2		36"/17½°	6"
Flying Eagle #1	oval			15"/7°	6"
Flying Fish #1,32	semi-elliptical		4'-0	#1 20"/9° #32 25"/11°	12"
Flying Mist #1	rounded			15"/7°	12"
Galatea #1	oval				
Game Cock #1	elliptical			40"/20°	6"
Gazelle #18,24	square	2'-2		50"/24°	12"
Gem of the Ocean #1,32	square			14"/7½°	6"
Golden Eagle #1,5	arched			20"/11°	6"
Golden Fleece (2nd) #1	rounded			14"/6½°	12"
Golden Light #1	elliptical			27"/14°	6"
Golden West #1	"segment of an ellipsis"			20"/10°	6"
Grace Darling #1	oval			15"/9°	8"
Great Republic #4,10,23 (1853)	semi-elliptical		5'-0	#4 22"/8° #10 20"/7°	23"
Great Republic (rebuilt) #103	Similar to original vessel.				

Table 3.2. *Continued.*

Vessel & Ref.#	Contour of stern at deck	Swell or round of stern at center line on deck — Aft of fashion piece	Aft of cross seam	Deadrise	Swell of sides
Henry Hill Bark #1,42	round		beautifully rounded	12"/8°	12"
Herald of the Morning #12	arched	4'-0		14"/8°	12"
Hoogly #1	curvilinear			15"/12°	slight
Hurricane #4	elliptical			40"/19°	12"
Indiaman #1	rounded			10"/5°	12"
Intrepid #18	square		1'-6	10"/5°	12"
Invincible #4,18,24	round		3'-0	17"/8°	19"
James Baines #1,23	semi-elliptical		3'-0	18"/7°	12"
John Bertram #1	square	2'-0		40"/21°	6"
John Gilpin #1	nearly oval			20"/10½°	6"
John Land #32 (Built as a duplicate of Winged Arrow.)	square	very slight		20"/11°	6"
John Stuart #4	round			17"/10°	6"
John Wade #1	elliptical (taken from painting)			12"/6°	6"
Joseph Peabody #1	rounded			20"/10°	6"
King Fisher #1	nearly oval			15"/10°	
Lady Franklin #9					
Lamplighter Bark #1	square	slightly rounded			
Lightfoot #1	oval			20"/9°	6"
Lightning #1,42	semi-elliptical		4'-6	20"/8½°	10"
Mameluke #1	oval			20"/20½°	9" abt.
Mary Robinson #31	elliptical			14"/7°	
Mastiff #1	rounded			12"/6°	9"
Mermaid Bark #1	rounded	6'-0		24"/9½°	6"
Morning Light #1	nearly oval			20"/9°	6"
Mystery #1	semi-elliptical			19"/10°	6"
Nightingale #32,42	square	2'-0		36"/18½°	6"
Noonday #1	oval			12"/6°	6"
Northern Light #28,32	elliptical			40"/20½°	
Ocean Express #1	rounded			14"/7½°	8"
Ocean Pearl #1	nearly oval			13"/7°	
Ocean Telegraph #5	rounded				bold

Vessel & Ref.#	Contour of stern at deck	Swell or round of stern at center line on deck — Aft of fashion piece	Aft of cross seam	Deadrise	Swell of sides
Onward #1	curvilinear			20"/11½°	6"
Osborne Howes #9				17"/8½°	
Panther	boldly rounded			20"/10°	6"
Phantom #1	oval			18"/8°	4"
Queen of Clippers #1	square	very slight		18"/8°	
Queen of the Pacific #9	semi-elliptical			20"/9½°	6"
Queen of the Seas #1	oval			10"/6°	9"
Quickstep Bark #1	elliptical		beautifully rounded	28"/17°	4"
Racehorse Bark #1					
Racer #3,4	round			10"/4½°	
Radiant #1	square	very slight			
Raven #3,32	round			24"/14°	
Red Jacket #14,23	elliptical		3'-6	19"/8°	3"
Robin Hood #9				18"/9½°	
Rocket Bark #1	Built same style as Dauntless.			15"/11°	6"
Roebuck #1	square	very slight		15"/9°	13"
Romance of the Sea #1,42	nearly semi-elliptical		3'-6	15"/7°	6"
Santa Claus #1	rounded				slight
Saracen #1	nearly oval			14"/7°	7"
Sea Bird Bark #1	square	swells gracefully		18"/13°	6"
Seaman's Bride #4	elliptic			20"/11½°	
Sea Serpent #4	square (probable)			40"/21°	4"
Shooting Star #1	square	3'-0		24"/13°	12"
Sierra Nevada #1	oval			20"/9°	12"
Silver Star #1	rounded			15"/7½°	8"
Southern Cross #1	square	very slight		20"/10½°	6"
Sovereign of the Seas #1	curvilinear		5'-0	20"/9°	12"
Spitfire #1	oval			15"/7°	
Staffordshire #1	boldly elliptical			20"/9°	12"
Stag Hound #1,4	elliptical		4'-3	40"/18½°	4"
Star of the Union #1,5	elliptical		swells boldly	18"/9½°	6"

Table 3.2. *Continued.*

Vessel & Ref.#	Contour of stern at deck	Swell or round of stern at center line on deck		Deadrise	Swell of sides
		Aft of fashion piece	Aft of cross seam		
Starr King #9				16"/7°	
Storm King #1	semi-circular			20"/9½°	4"
Sultana Bark #1	square	swells boldly		32"/20°	2"
Sunny South #42	square	2'-6		38"/22°	17"
Surprise #1	elliptical		3'-6	30"/16°	9"
Swallow #1	nearly oval			14"/7°	6"
Sweepstakes #42	elliptical		2'-6	42"/18½°	9"
Sword Fish #18,24	square	2'-0		23"/12½°	4"
Syren #3	elliptical			20"/11°	
Telegraph #1	elliptical		like stern of Game Cock	27"/13°	4"
Thatcher Magoun #1	oval			18"/8½°	9"
Tornado #3	nearly square			slight (flat floor)	
Uncowah #18	square	1'-5		15"/8°	10"
War Hawk #1	oval			12"/6½°	12"
Water Witch #1,32	oval			24"/9½°	#1 6" #32 9"
Western Continent #9				17"/	
Westward Ho #1	semi-elliptical			20"/10°	6"
West Wind #1	square	very slight		15"/7½°	12"
Whirlwind #1	rounded			18"/10°	9"
Whistler #1	semi-circular			17"/9°	12"
Wildfire Bark #1	semi-circular			12"/8°	
Wild Pigeon #1,42	nearly oval	3'-6		26"/13°	6"
Wild Ranger #1	nearly semi-circular				
Wild Rover #9				19"/10°	
Winged Arrow #1	square	very slight		20"/11°	6"
Winged Racer #1,4	semi-elliptical			24"/9½°	6"
Witchcraft #1	curvilinear		8'-0	35"/17°	6"
Witch of the Wave #1	oval		See note below.	40"/19°	6"
Wizard #1,4	rounded				
Young America #18,24	round		4'-3	20"/9°	20"
Young Turk Bark #1	oval			12"/8°	6"

Note: Witch of the Wave builder's half model shows a square stern. Detailed description of completed vessel describes stern as being "perfectly oval." There are two half models; see refs. 31 and 78.

(text continued from page 43)

The "square," or "transom" stern is a definition governed specifically by the fact that the transom is relatively flat and is terminated by a distinct, hard "fashion piece" at the transom's juncture with the side of the vessel. The surface was never a plane, and its roundness aft of a straight line between the opposite fashion pieces, as illustrated in Figure 3.2, varied from some minimal curvature to a well-rounded 4 feet in the case of *Herald of the Morning*.

"Arched" and "convex" are interpreted as being modifica-tions of the basic square stern due to the fact that each de-scription is used only when hard fashion pieces are involved.

The "elliptical" group of definitions involves sterns with various degrees of curvature across the centerline of the vessel blending smoothly with the side of the ship by turning the transom through a tight curve in to the side planking. Its variations ranged freely between the true transom stern and the counter stern. From the previous listing it is obvious that this form of stern could attain many rather minute

(continued on page 48)

46

Figure 3.2. *Principal contours of the clipper ship stern.*

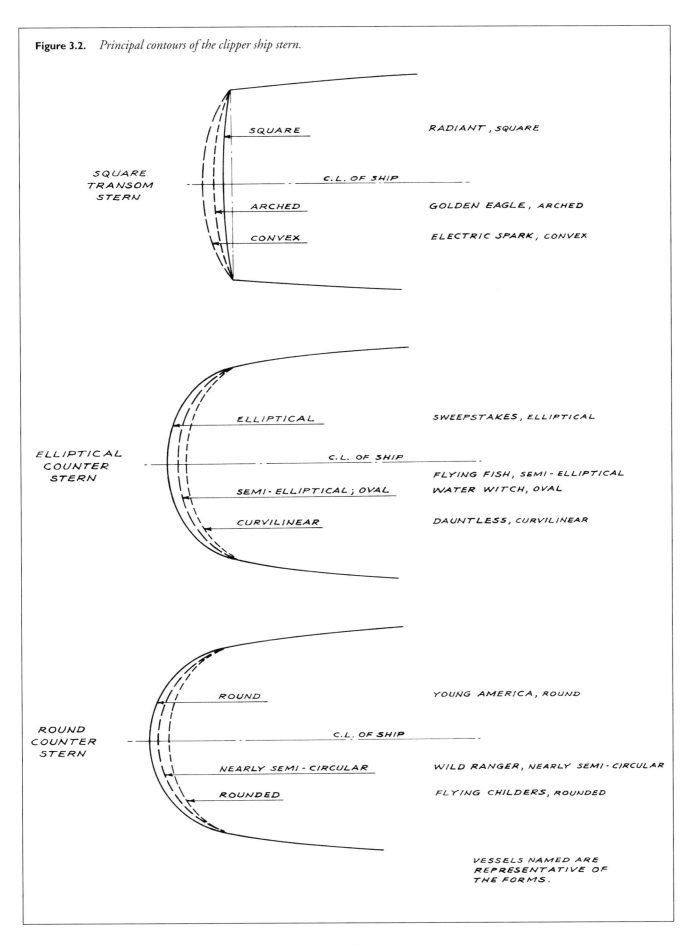

(text continued from page 46)
variations; its typical representation is shown in Figure 3.2. In its general form it was one of the most prominent configurations of the clipper ship stern.

"Round" was the furthest deviation from the square stern and more nearly represents the appearance of a semicircular form achieved by scribing a true arc with a uniform radius from one side of the ship to the other. Some of the sterns were slightly flatter than a semicircle but not to the extent of being elliptical. The form is illustrated in Figure 3.2.

Throughout the period covered in this book, the elliptical stern predominated.

Flare of the Bow

Flare of the bow in the clipper ships evolved as a direct result of the development of the fine, acute *entrance* (see the following section) of the ship's forefoot. There was not a great distance between the water's edge and the rail, which meant that a radical change of shape was imperative in this short space. It was achieved by gradually converting all waterline planes from a concave to a convex outline as they progressed upward, the result being the familiar pointed area that comprised the topgallant forecastle deck. Perhaps the easiest way to describe this shape in plan view would be to liken it to the form of a Gothic arch or the front end of an electric iron. The sharpness or fullness of this forecastle deck varied from ship to ship, but categorically it applied to all clippers.

The resulting flare of the bow fulfilled three major basic requirements of the ship's form. All three were essential, so no attempt is made here to note them in order of importance.

The most apparent result was formation of a deck area large enough to allow for working ship. This included the handling of headsails, the installation of the anchor windlass and the manning of its levers, the handling and stowing of anchors, and the installation of the forward warping capstan and the space required to operate the capstan bars.

Also achieved was the space required for weighing the ship's anchor when necessary. The marked increase in flare between the level of the weather deck and the main rail provided sufficient space outboard of the centerline of ship to install or cut the hawseholes well forward in the eyes of the ship so as to be in direct fore-and-aft alignment with the anchor windlass barrel. This outboard distance, combined with the considerable forward rake of stem and cutwater, prevented the flukes of the anchor from hanging up on the forefoot when the anchor was "up and down" as the ship was getting underway.

A third function had to do with the sailing qualities of the clipper ship. All ships underway are subject to roll and pitch, both of which are induced by the nature of wind and wave action along with the degree of stability built into each individual vessel. At the accelerated speeds of which the clippers were capable, pitching became a force of constantly increasing violence which subjected the ship's structure to incredible shock and stress. Such a ship, if built with uniformly increasing breadth from keel to rail when measured at a frame located closely abaft the stem, would slowly increase its forward buoyancy as the bow submerged but would still be subject to excessive plunging. The introduction of radically increasing flare tended to greatly ease this problem, although it could not totally eliminate it.

The concave configuration of flare, as it appears in any transverse section in the extremities of the bow, clearly indicates an accelerated rate of buoyancy as the ship buries her bow in and moves through the waves. The deeper the bow plows, the greater the rate of buoyancy that is brought into play. The total effect of this progressive action is to smooth the pitching action and tend to "level out the ride."

Great flare, however, was also considered to have a negative aspect. This was the buildup of atmospheric pressure under the extreme forward end where the overhanging forecastle deck tended to trap air in the area between rail and waterline. The resulting atmospheric pressure tended to lift the bow of a fast-moving clipper, which, in turn, caused her stern to settle and become buried. This unwanted deficiency was alleviated by giving the body of the ship more fullness aft and less flare (buoyancy) forward. An example of this is in the case of *Bald Eagle*,[1] in which the flare was modified to a more angular form.

Entrance and Run

Entrance and *run* are the terms applied, respectively, to the forward portion of a vessel which cleaves the water, specifically at the water's edge and below, and the after part of the vessel where her lines begin to converge toward the sternpost, again specifically at the water's edge and below. Both are illustrated in Figure 3.3.

In the sixteenth century the world moved at a very slow pace on land and sea. At that time the accomplishment of a task successfully far outweighed the consideration of accomplishing it swiftly. So, in most endeavors, conservatism was the ruling philosophy.

Shipwrights of the period were interested in building ships which featured carrying capacity. Naval architecture as we define it today was unknown except in its most basic form. Technology of the day was to a great extent modeled after the objects that man observed in nature. An outstanding example of this thinking is in the construction of an early

(continued on page 50)

Figure 3.3. *Extremities of the hull at the waterline.*

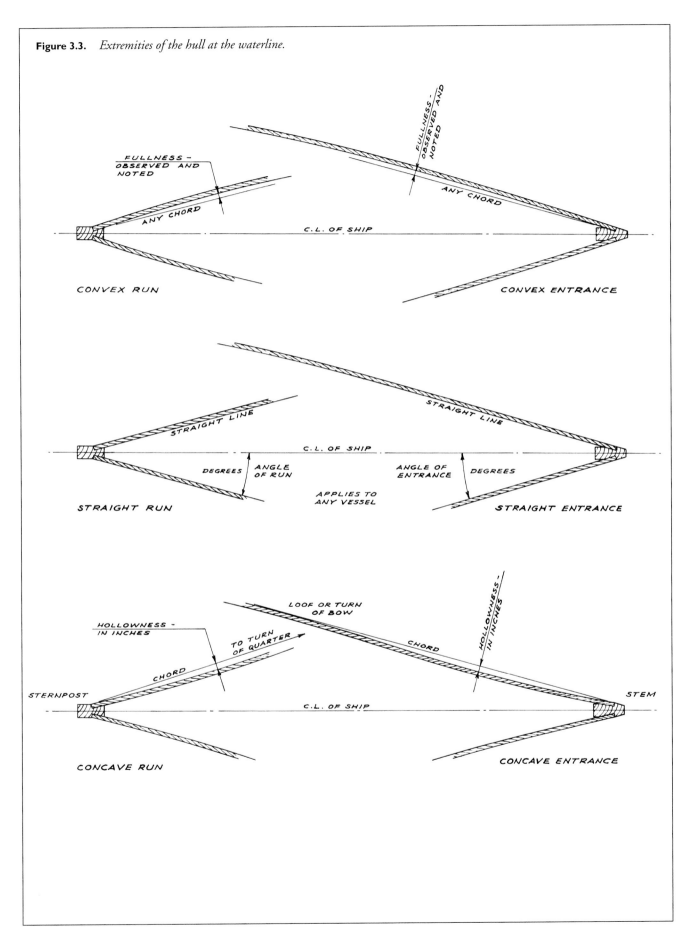

49

(text continued from page 48)
lighthouse on Eddystone Rocks in the English Channel, south of Plymouth. Its designers, noting the great strength and survival powers of the oak tree under all adverse conditions, recognized that a great portion of this strength was derived from the shape of the tree's trunk which flared out at the ground level, thus providing a greatly increased base on which to stand compared to trees whose trunks grew in a relatively straight line from the ground up. With this knowledge as a key, they made the outline of their new lighthouse conform exactly to the contour of a mature oak tree—so much so, that an etching illustrating the elevation of the completed structure included an accompanying outline of the model tree trunk to reinforce the comparison.

Similar thinking took place in ship design. Looking again to nature, man observed that fishes swam very well and that they had, in general, rather large rounded heads and long, slim tails. If a fish of this shape was able to swim well, could not a ship of somewhat similar shape also swim well? (In that early day it was common to refer to a ship as "swimming" rather than "sailing.") Applying the thought to the deed resulted in the underwater shape of a ship conforming to a "cod's head and mackerel tail."

The general results of this configuration were very satisfactory for the ships of the day. The fullness of the underbodies of both merchant vessels and ships-of-war allowed the former to carry large cargoes and the latter to support the great weight of broadside batteries ranged along their decks. The resultant limitation imposed on speed, perhaps optimistically in the range of 8 knots, occasioned little if any dissatisfaction.

The pursuit of progress, however, was not to be denied. Slowly, perhaps without a specified definite goal, ships became longer, finer, and increasingly larger. At the same time the location of the foremast was moved farther aft, thus offering compensation for the decreased buoyancy of the fine bows. Basically, large ships of a given design will sail faster than smaller ships of the same design. One of the findings along this path of progress was that, where the "cod's head and mackerel tail" form of underbody served well in ships that could attain a speed of about 6 knots, it became an impediment to ships that were becoming capable of greater speeds. Consequently, the fullness of the forebody gradually was reduced and the lines of the afterbody were modified. By the time the early clipper form put in its appearance, bows had become exceedingly fine, a necessary ingredient in ships that were now expected to attain 16 or 18 knots as part of their routine performance.

Ultimately, entrances and runs, although rarely the same, came to resemble each other, the entrance becoming very sharp, the run becoming fine but generally fuller than the entrance.

In the clipper ships the entrance, also known as the "entry," was almost evenly divided between concave and convex contours below the waterline, gradually developing into convex lines above the waterline up to the ship's rail. The same characteristic applied to the ship's run. However, while all the ships developed convex lines above the water's edge, the same cannot be said for the shapes of hull from water's edge to keel. A considerable percentage of the clippers were designed with completely convex lines throughout their underwater length. In addition, there were a rare few cases in which entrance and run did not fall within the same general description. Table 3.3 lists these characteristics, where known, for the ships which appear in this book.

In cases where offsets, lines, half models, or other factual sources are available, the waterline angles of the various ships' entrance and run have been listed measured in degrees. (The only exception occurs in the case of *Staffordshire*, for which the angular values of entrance and run are given in MacLean's description.)[1] Where only a description is available, it has been included in the table to indicate the general form of the ends of the vessel. As with all descriptions, individual interpretations will vary; however, it is not too difficult to use the entries for comparison with each other and with the general philosophy of the clipper ship hull form.

Some terms used in the table will benefit by additional brief explanation and reference to Figure 3.3. The sharpness of an entrance is determined by the angle of the bow as it breasts the sea when a vessel is underway. The water being parted is forced outward equally on either side of the cutwater, based on the shape of the hull at the stem; therefore the angle on both port and starboard sides is measured from the centerline of ship to the planking and is thus recorded in degrees. Sharpness of entrance is always recorded in this manner, as reflected in Table 3.3. The obvious reason for making this angular measurment at the waterline is the matter of convenience.

The angle of the run, also measured at the water's edge, represents the path of the passing sea as it once again converges toward the sternpost or rudder and is no longer parted by the structure of the vessel. The governing features of the run are similar to those of the entrance.

Concavity and convexity of the wetted hull do not, in themselves, necessarily determine the sharpness of a ship. While in the great majority of cases concave waterlines were sharper, there were ships that were sharp and, at the same time, maintained convex wetted surfaces, *Stag Hound* and *Wild Pigeon* being examples.

Convexity, or *fullness*, of lines was never recorded as a given measurement in inches; it was merely stated as an observed fact. This situation was brought about by the fact that

(text continued on page 53)

Table 3.3. *Waterline configurations at ships' extremities.*

Figures in inches denote hollowness at water line in a chord drawn from stem or sternpost to the turn of the hull. See Figure 3.3.

Vessel & Ref.#	Run	Entrance	Stern (Characteristics or angle at water line)	Bow (Characteristics or angle at water line)
Alarm #1	concave	concave		
Amphitrite #1	concave	concave		
Andrew Jackson #59	straight at W.L. concave below	straight at W.L. concave below	28°	25°
Antelope #1	concave	concave		
Asa Eldridge #1	convex at W.L. concave below	concave	long, clean	angular
Bald Eagle #1		straight		
Belle of the West #1,31	convex	concave, 2"	30°	22°
Beverly #3			moderate sharp	moderate sharp
Black Hawk #24	concave at W.L. concave below	convex at W.L. concave below	31°	30°
Blue Jacket #32			sharp	sharp
Bonita #1	convex	convex		
Bounding Billow Bark #1	concave	concave		
Celestial #18,42	concave, 4"	concave, 4"	39°	31°
Challenge #24	concave, 4"	concave, 7"	22°	15°
Challenger #1	convex	convex	convex	very sharp
Champion of the Seas #1,86	straight at W.L. concave below	concave, 2½"	32°	21°
Charger #1	convex	convex	clean	easy
Charmer #1	convex	convex		
Cleopatra #1	convex	convex		
Climax #1	concave	concave		
Coeur de Lion #1	convex	convex	20°	18°
Comet #24	concave, 6"	concave, 5"		
Cyclone #1	convex	convex		
Daring #1	convex	convex	fine, easy	fine, easy
Dauntless #1	concave	concave		
Donald McKay #1,30	concave	concave		
Don Quixote #1,32	concave	concave		
Eagle #5,32		concave		long, sharp
Eagle Wing #1	concave	concave		
Edwin Forrest #1	convex	convex		
Electric Spark #1	mildly concave	boldly concave		
Ellen Foster #1	convex	convex		
Empress of the Sea #1,32	concave	concave		
Endeavor #1	convex	convex		
Eringo Bark #1	concave		long, sharp	long, sharp
Eureka #4				very sharp
Fair Wind #1	concave	convex	long, clean	
Fearless #29	convex	convex at W.L. concave below	24°	26°
Fleet Wing #1	straight at W.L. concave below	convex		sharp
Flyaway #24	concave, 3"	slightly concave	30°	23°
Flying Arrow #1	convex	convex		
Flying Childers #1	convex	convex		
Flying Cloud #23	concave, 7"	concave, 5"	20°	16°
Flying Dragon #1	convex	concave		
Flying Dutchman #24	concave, 4"	concave, 2"	30°	22°
Flying Eagle #1	convex at W.L. concave below	convex at W.L. concave below		
Flying Fish #30	convex at W.L. concave below	concave, 2"	26°	19°
Flying Mist #1	convex	concave	clean	
Galatea #1	convex	convex	long, clean	long, clean
Game Cock #1	convex	convex		
Gazelle #24	convex	convex	36°	26°
Gem of the Ocean #1	convex	concave		
Golden Eagle #1,5	convex	convex		
Golden Fleece (2nd) #1	convex at W.L. concave below	convex at W.L. concave below	long, clean	
Golden Light #1	concave	concave		
Golden West #1,31	straight	straight		
Grace Darling #1	convex	convex	long, clean	

Table 3.3. *Continued.*

Vessel & Ref.#	Run	Entrance	Characteristics or angle at water line	
			Stern	Bow
Great Republic (1853) #23	concave, 6"	concave, 10"	13°	11°
Great Republic (rebuilt) #103	Similar to original vessel.			
Henry Hill Bark #42	concave, 5"	concave, 3"	28°	21°
Herald of the Morning #12	concave, 3"	concave, 2"	36°	22°
Hoogly #1	convex	convex		
Hurricane #4	concave	concave		
Indiaman #1	convex	convex	long, clean	short, sharp
Intrepid #18	concave, 5"	convex	35°	33°
Invincible #24	concave, 5"	concave, 2"	20°	24°
James Baines #23	convex at W.L. concave below	concave, 5"	38°	18°
John Bertram #1	convex	convex		
John Gilpin #1	convex	convex		
John Land #1,32 (Built as a duplicate of Winged Arrow.)	convex	convex		
John Stuart #4			sharp, clean	sharp
John Wade #1	convex	convex		
Joseph Peabody #1	convex	convex	fine	fine
King Fisher #1	slightly concave	slightly concave		
Lady Franklin				
Lamplighter Bark #1			moderate sharp	sharp
Lightfoot #1	concave	concave		
Lightning #1,42	concave, 2"	concave, 16"	26°	10°
Mameluke #1	convex	convex		
Mary Robinson				
Mastiff #1	convex	convex		
Mermaid Bark #1	convex	convex		
Morning Light #1,31	convex	convex		
Mystery #1	convex	convex		
Nightingale #42	convex	convex	42°	28°
Noonday #1	convex	convex	short, sharp	short, sharp
Northern Light #32	sharp	sharp		
Ocean Express #1	convex	convex	easy	easy

Vessel & Ref.#	Run	Entrance	Characteristics or angle at water line	
			Stern	Bow
Ocean Pearl #1	long, sharp	long, sharp	long, clean	
Ocean Telegraph #5				very sharp
Onward #1	convex	convex		
Osborne Howes				
Panther				
Phantom #1	straight	concave		
Queen of Clippers #1	concave	concave	quite sharp	quite sharp
Queen of the Pacific #32				
Queen of the Seas #1	convex	convex	long, clean	fine, sharp
Quickstep Bark #1	convex	convex	sharp	sharp
Racehorse Bark #1	convex	convex	sharp	sharp
Racer #3				
Radiant #1			easy, clean	
Raven #3			sharp	sharp
Red Jacket #14	concave, 2"	concave, 2"	23°	22°
Robin Hood				
Rocket Bark #1			very sharp	very sharp
Roebuck #1			easy, graceful	
Romance of the Sea #1,42	convex at W.L. concave below	straight at W.L. concave below	28°	16°
Santa Claus #1	convex	convex	long, clean	full, easy
Saracen #1	convex	convex	long, clean	long, clean
Sea Bird Bark #1	convex	convex	very sharp	very sharp
Seaman's Bride #4			very sharp	very sharp
Sea Serpent #4	convex	convex	very sharp	sharp
Shooting Star #1	convex	convex		
Sierra Nevada #1	concave	concave		
Silver Star #1	concave	concave		
Southern Cross #1	convex	convex		
Sovereign of the Seas #1,42	straight at W.L. concave below	concave, 2"	ref.#1 15½° / ref.#42 20°	14½°
Spitfire #1	convex	convex		
Staffordshire #1	concave	concave	20°	18°
Stag Hound #1,23	convex	convex	25°	24°

Table 3.3. *Continued.*

			Characteristics or angle at water line	
Vessel & Ref.#	Run	Entrance	Stern	Bow
Star of the Union #1,5	concave	concave	very sharp	very sharp
Starr King #32			clean run	
Storm King #1	concave	concave	sharp	very sharp
Sultana Bark #1	convex	convex		
Sunny South #42	concave, 4"	concave, 4"	45°	15°
Surprise #42	straight	convex at W.L. concave below	45°	30°
Swallow #1	convex	convex	long, sharp	long, sharp
Sweepstakes #42	concave, 10"	concave, 2"	23°	17°
Swordfish #24	concave, 6"	concave, 3"	19°	24°
Syren #3			long, clean	fairly sharp
Telegraph #1	convex	convex	sharper than Surprise	sharper than Surprise
Thatcher Magoun #1	concave	concave		
Tornado #3			moderate sharp	moderate sharp
Uncowah #18	concave, 8"	convex	29°	30°
War Hawk #1	convex	convex		
Water Witch #1	convex	convex		
Western Continent				
Westward Ho #1,32	concave	concave	24°	16½°
West Wind #1	convex	convex		
Whirlwind #1	concave	concave		
Whistler #1		convex		
Wildfire Bark #1	concave	concave	exceedingly sharp	exceedingly sharp
Wild Pigeon #1,42	convex	convex	37°	27°
Wild Ranger #1	concave	concave		
Wild Rover #32			sharp	sharp
Winged Arrow #1	convex	convex		
Winged Racer #1	convex	convex		
Witchcraft #1	convex	convex		
Witch of the Wave #1,32	convex at W.L. concave below	slightly concave	26°	26½°
Wizard #1	concave	concave		
Young America #24	concave, 10"	concave, 2"	15°	18°
Young Turk #1	concave	concave		sharp

(text continued from page 50)

there was no uniform method of striking a chord from the sternpost to some point on the vessel's side. Therefore, as shown in Figure 3.3, any arbitrary chord was struck and the fullness, if existent, then observed and noted. No measuring took place.

Concavity, or *hollowness*, was more easily recorded as an actual physical distance. Hollowness is the measurement taken between the most concave portion of the hull plank and a chord struck at the water's edge stretching from the stem or the sternpost to the turn of the hull. Forward, the portion of the ship where the body turns in toward the stem is termed the *loof*; aft it is loosely termed the *quarter*. This hollowness ranged between being an almost straight line that

followed this chord, to as much as 7 inches, as in Webb's *Challenge*. The general degree of the hollowness of entrance, however, ranged from 2 inches to about 4 inches.

The most noteworthy instances of extreme hollowness were built into two McKay vessels—*Great Republic*, with a 10-inch concavity, and *Lightning*, with a 16-inch concavity, which made her the hollowest of all American-built clipper ships. This feature was so pronounced in *Lightning* that, when delivered to her British owners, James Baines and Co., they took keen exception to it and also expressed grave concern about her sailing abilities. So troubled were they with this hollow waterline that, before she put to sea in their services they had the hollow filled in with a blanket of external planking. On her first outward-bound voyage to Australia, one side of this false bow was carried away. Upon arrival in Melbourne all of the remainder of the work was removed. Thus *Lightning*, as originally built, became one of the best-performing and fastest of American-built clippers, until she burned fifteen years later.

Typically a vessel would be either concave, convex, or straight in both her entrance and her run, but there were many exceptions to this rule. One end might be concave and the other end straight, or one end might be convex and the other end straight. However, when this detail of design did occur the difference between the configuration of the ends was minimal and, in some cases, hardly noticeable.

Deadrise and Swell of Sides (Tumblehome)

In addition to characteristics of a vessel's hull that are apparent only when viewed in profiles as illustrated in Figure 3.1 and Table 3.1, there are technical aspects that are apparent only when observed from above, in plan view, or when viewed transversely from forward or aft. The characteristics of outlines of stern, Figure 3.2, and deadrise and swell of sides, Figure 3.4, are enumerated in Table 3.2 with values where verified.

Deadrise is the transverse angle that the ship's floor makes with a horizontal plane. It is expressed as the number of inches between this plane and the hull at half floor. *Half floor* is one-half of the ship's half-breadth, or one-quarter of its beam. Deadrise is specified at the midship section, as shown in Figure 3.4, detail 1.

In the design of the clipper ship hull, no single source of disagreement rivaled the magnitude of that caused by the consideration of deadrise. There were two schools of thought: one, the belief espoused by John Willis Griffith, that moderate deadrise contributed significantly to the speed of a ship; the other, championed by Nathaniel B. Palmer, that minimal deadrise resulted in an equally swift vessel.

Rather than offer a lengthy technical discussion of deadrise, I will note some prevalent practical conditions discovered by contemporary observers. Actual sailing practice and records of various voyages gradually revealed that fuller-bodied ships with greater carrying capacity were performing as well as the very sharp vessels with their diminished carrying capacities. The result was that, at the end of the clipper ship era, the incorporation of steep deadrise into the design of the ships had virtually disappeared. Table 3.2 lists only thirty vessels with deadrise in excess of 12 degrees.

While, as previously noted, deadrise is always measured vertically in inches, the equivalent rise has also been entered in this column as the angle in degrees above the horizontal base. This allows an easier comparison between various vessels since the half-breadth dimension need not be considered. It should also be noted that there are the usual unfortunate discrepancies in values between one source and another.

A practical and necessary function of minimal deadrise was to allow a ship to sail and roll, or *heel*, with the wind abeam and still not increase her draft at the end of the roll.

The *swell of sides*, referred to at an earlier date as "housing-in," and also known as "rounding of the sides," is the term that was used to describe the characteristic we now refer to as "tumblehome." In the mid-1700s this characteristic was termed "tumbling home," which later became "tumblehome." However, throughout the descriptions of more than 150 clippers, packets, and freighters,[1] the term "tumblehome" is not to be found. Between the other two definitions, the "swell of sides" and "rounding of the sides," the former predominated. So, for that reason and for its relative conciseness, the term *swell of sides* will be used here as being a part of the language of the times.

The *swell of sides* is the measurement of the difference between a vessel's maximum breadth at midship section and the breadth of the uppermost or weather deck at that same section. It is expressed as the number of inches' difference per half-breadth of the section, as shown in Figure 3.4, detail 2.

The swell of sides is a throwback to the days when sailing men-of-war were armed with broadside batteries that lined the entire length of a ship's gun decks. The tremendous weight of these batteries which, by their nature and function, were installed at the deck edge, was carried in the most disadvantageous location for the stability of a vessel. In a heavy sea, or when sailing with the wind abeam or thereabouts, the weight of the batteries resisted the normal efforts of a ship to right itself. This was so serious a problem as to require special design considerations. The basic solution came in two forms, namely, to reduce the size of upper deck guns, and to reduce the breadth of the upper deck structure, thus alleviating to a considerable degree the ever-present overturning moment.

In earlier sailing days, tumblehome was also incorporated into the design of merchant craft, with apparent good reason, since the early ships were built with extremely high freeboard. As time went on and ship design progressed, freeboard was gradually reduced until, upon the arrival of the clipper ship, it had reached its lowest practical level.

However, the swell of sides was still a noticeable ingredient of hull form, and an important one, from the standpoint of the shipping merchant. It was of excellent use in circumventing the rules of the times for calculating a vessel's registry tonnage if the merchant was so inclined.

Whether or not swell of sides improved the sailing qualities of a vessel is questionable, since many successful vessels

(text continued on page 56)

Figure 3.4. *Midship sections illustrating deadrise and swell of sides.*

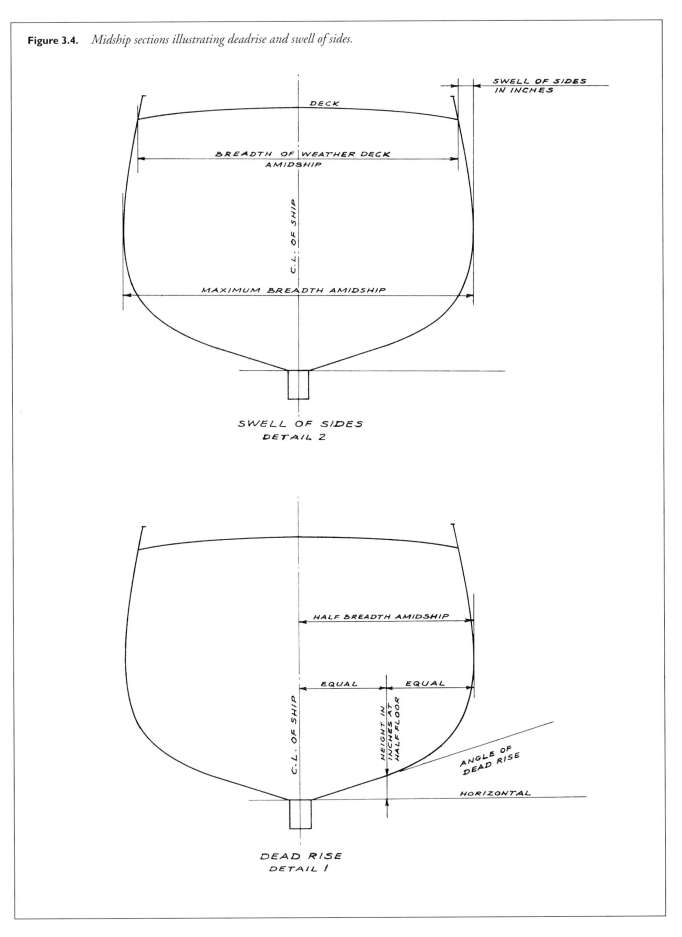

(text continued from page 54)

were built with no perceptible tumblehome, while others had the extreme tumblehome incorporated into their design.

And, finally, another reasonable assumption can be made, that æsthetics rather than any sense of necessity impelled a designer to mould the feature into the design of a new hull.

There are innumerable examples of the inclusion or omission of the swell of sides in ship design, and one can make a convenient comparison by inspecting the body plans of *Flying Cloud* (Figure 6.8), with her almost wall-sided dead flat section, and *Challenge* (Figure 6.16), with her marked roundness of side. To most viewers, the shape of *Challenge* is more attractive and refined than that of *Flying Cloud*. However, due to excessive shaping, *Challenge* would be the more expensive vessel to build.

The swell of sides made no contribution to the sailing qualities of a vessel, and yet, of all the vessels covered in this work, only *Fearless*, designed by Samuel H. Pook, appears to have been devoid of any degree of roundness.

One negative feature of this swell was the fact that when incorporated into the design of any ship, it was instrumental in reducing the spread of the shrouds where they were set up to the channels. This reduced span across a ship's breadth, while not large by measurement, introduced greater tensile load in a gang of shrouds whenever a ship was subject to excessive roll or to storm conditions. In ships that were sailed in an ordinary manner—that is to say, they were not called on to challenge or bully their way through murderous seas under extreme and critical conditions—this incidence of increased load on the gangs of shrouds was not of tremendous import. With the clippers, however, which were expected to be driven under all extreme circumstances and to the utmost of their structural endurance, this feature loomed larger than the diminished span would indicate. Indeed, under the fiercest conditions it could be the critical difference between survival and failure.

Nevertheless, the institution of swell of sides, unlike some other clipper features, persisted through the entire era. Table 3.2 lists values of swell of sides, where known, for vessels listed in this book.

Deck Camber

Deck camber, at one time referred to as "spring of the beam," and commonly described as "round up of the beam," is the transverse curvature of the deck surface. Its principal function is to facilitate the clearing of water that washes over a ship's weather deck. Its true form is the arc of a circle of extremely great radius, so great as to preclude its being conveniently drawn using the required radius. For this reason the designated arc is drawn by any one of several acceptable methods that can be confined to a relatively limited space.

In addition to providing a watershed for the deck, the arched span across the breadth of a vessel is physically stronger than a straight beam would be. Another effect of deck camber, serving a useful purpose in earlier ships-of-war, was that it helped lessen the recoil of broadside guns when they were fired.

Three methods of finding the proper curve for deck camber—one mathematical, one geometric, and one natural—are illustrated in Figure 3.5. In all cases the maximum moulded beam of the deck is the database. The second requirement is a determination of the height of desired camber at the centerline of ship. This was a figure that might typically be about 6 inches. With this information the proper curve can be developed on the mould loft floor.

Method No. 1 results in a curve that is mathematically correct, and was the method usually practiced in the mould loft.

Method No. 2, which is very simple to lay down, lacks the mathematical precision of the first method, but is very satisfactory for use in arriving at an acceptable camber curve.

Method No. 3 is not mathematical but rather the result of natural forces. A beam or spline of uniform rectangular cross section and density, when compressed by force applied at each end, will deflect in a uniform arc. If the pressure applied is sufficient to cause the spline to pass through the three points P, H, and S shown in method No. 3, the resulting arc will be a curve similar to the two previous curves. This particular method produces a uniform curve due to all portions of the spline being equally stressed under the compressive load. The established camber curve, or "round up," is constant throughout the length of the vessel.

Starting at the midship or dead flat frame, the surface of the beam is curved to the full extent of the camber curve PHS. As the beam mould is employed forward or aft toward the ends of the vessel, the breadth of the deck narrows. As this occurs, the dimension of the "round down" decreases, causing the sheer of the deck at the ship's side, points P and S, to rise in relation to the sheer of the centerline. The camber curve, however, remains constant throughout this process. As a result, the deck, as it approaches the ends of the vessel, appears to become flatter as it becomes narrower until, at the stem and taffrail, point P or S occupies the same position as does point H.

Initially the beam is shaped with a reduced height of camber at its center. At installation, after the ends have been secured, the center of the beam is "pumped"—jacked—up to the desired height of camber. It is then shored by a stanchion below to maintain the curve.[8, 133] The origin of this procedure is unknown.

In shipbuilding practice, the deck camber is progressively

(text continued on page 58)

Figure 3.5. *A beam mould for the camber curve.*

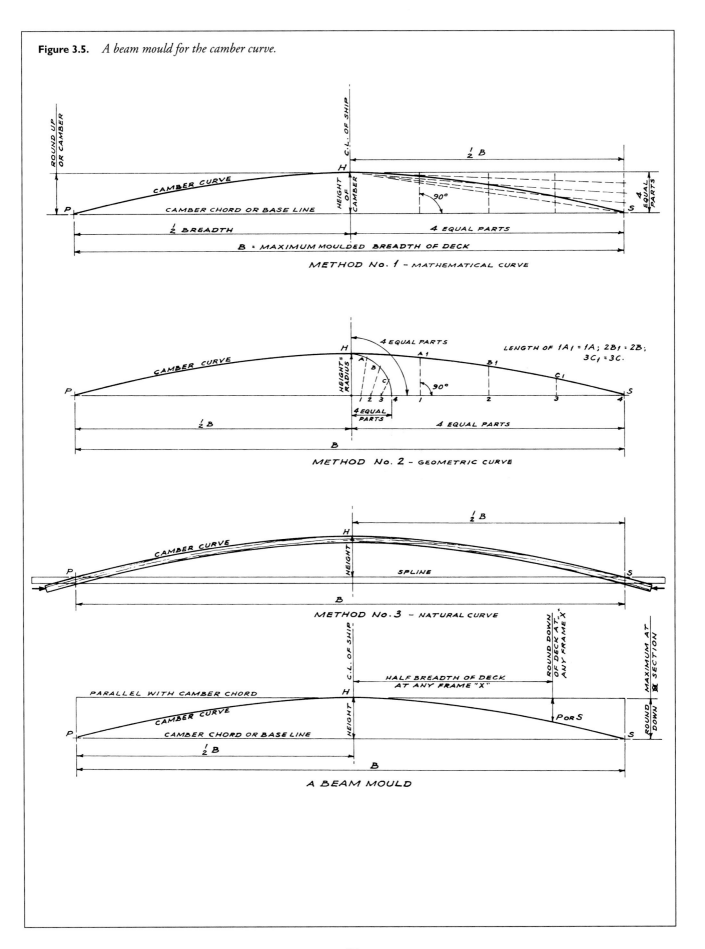

METHOD No. 1 – MATHEMATICAL CURVE

METHOD No. 2 – GEOMETRIC CURVE

METHOD No. 3 – NATURAL CURVE

A BEAM MOULD

(text continued from page 56)

less as decks are located lower in the ship. In very rare instances, where platforms were to be installed, camber might not be a consideration. A *platform* is a short section of deck that is laid in some particular area of a vessel.

Finally, camber is always referred to as the rise of the deck in inches in reference to its total maximum breadth in feet.

Only one-half of the camber curve need be laid down on the mould loft floor. If several decks are cambered, each needs a separate mould unless the round up and breadth of deck are identical to the previously described curve.

Hogging and Sagging

Hogging and sagging are inherent tendencies that are built into ships of all types and are directly attributable to the variance in buoyancy of a ship at any point throughout its length due to the continuing change of shape and submerged area at any frame.

Full-bodied ships with well-rounded ends were less subject to hogging and sagging than were the clippers, with their long, sleek lines and less-than-buoyant ends. *Hogging*, which was the drooping of the ship's ends, due principally to excessive dead load, was the great villain in the construction of the clippers. This very undesirable tendency was attacked in several ways, one of which was to incorporate mammoth keel and keelson assemblies through the length of the vessel in order to achieve structural rigidity. In addition to this use of sheer bulk, chocks were fitted in the spaces between adjacent floors or futtocks throughout the length of the vessels. McKay ships, for instance, had chocks fitted immediately above and below every floor and futtock butt in order to combat hogging.

The construction of a wooden sailing ship, by its nature, lacked any means of introducing triangulation, and thus rigidity, into its basic structure. Almost all pieces were connected to each other with square connections. The frames crossed the keel at a 90-degree angle; planking crossed the frames in the same manner; the same with deck beams intersecting carlings, carlings intersecting ledges, deck planking crossing deck beams.

This type of construction is never rigid, and, in the case of ships, which were subject to constant, repetitive motions of uneven magnitude, the weakness was exaggerated many times over. To ease the situation, diagonal wooden cross-braces were sometimes installed between frames at the ship's side between the weather deck and the next deck below. In addition, diagonal hooks and tremendous "pointers," some

of which were 50 feet in length, were installed diagonally in a ship's ends, resulting literally in a solid wooden mass of unusable space at her hood ends.

The next step in this stiffening process was introduced in the form of flat iron strapping diagonally fitted into the outer or inner surfaces of the frames in the form of a latticework. The outer type of installation was accomplished by fully letting the straps into the frames in order to bring them flush with the face of the frame. In the inner type of installation, half of the space required to accommodate the latticed ironwork was removed from both the inner surface of the frame and the outer surface of the ceiling.

Webb's clipper *Challenge* was reputedly the first American vessel to have this detail incorporated into her construction. However, in spite of the constant effort to overcome hogging, it was the rare and fortunate vessel that did not ultimately succumb to it in some considerable measure. The truth of this is very simply stated here:[7] "It is found in practice from the form given to the bow and quarters under the water being fine or sharp to ensure velocity in sailing, that these extreme portions of the ship are not water borne; and that thence the midship volume displaced must, to make up the whole displacement or weight, be on the contrary greater than equivalent to the weights placed over it. . . ."

Figure 3.6 illustrates the reason why a ship built of wood, was subject, because of its configuration, to eventual hogging even if it were to spend its entire lifetime tied up to a pier in quiet, undisturbed water.

Sagging, the second form of a ship losing her original shape, was generally the result of improper loading of cargo, or the natural wave motion of the sea. Both of these conditions could be termed *live load functions*.

In the first instance, indiscriminate distribution of a vessel's cargo in her hold, such as the undue concentration of very heavy items amidships, could so load a ship as to overreach her buoyancy amidships, in which case she would tend to settle excessively at that point while her ends would tend to resist settlement. In this manner the ends would provide support and the load would hang in the middle, thus introducing the elements necessary to induce sagging.

Sagging also occurred as a consequence of flexing underway. As a ship passed through a sea, the wave motion, alternately cresting and troughing, would intermittently support the ship—first at her ends, causing the hull to sag; then, in the next instant, at the center, causing the hull to hog.

The two alternating forces were instrumental in destroying the integrity of the connections and fastenings of the clipper ship.

Figure 3.6. *Hogging induced by structure and hull form.*

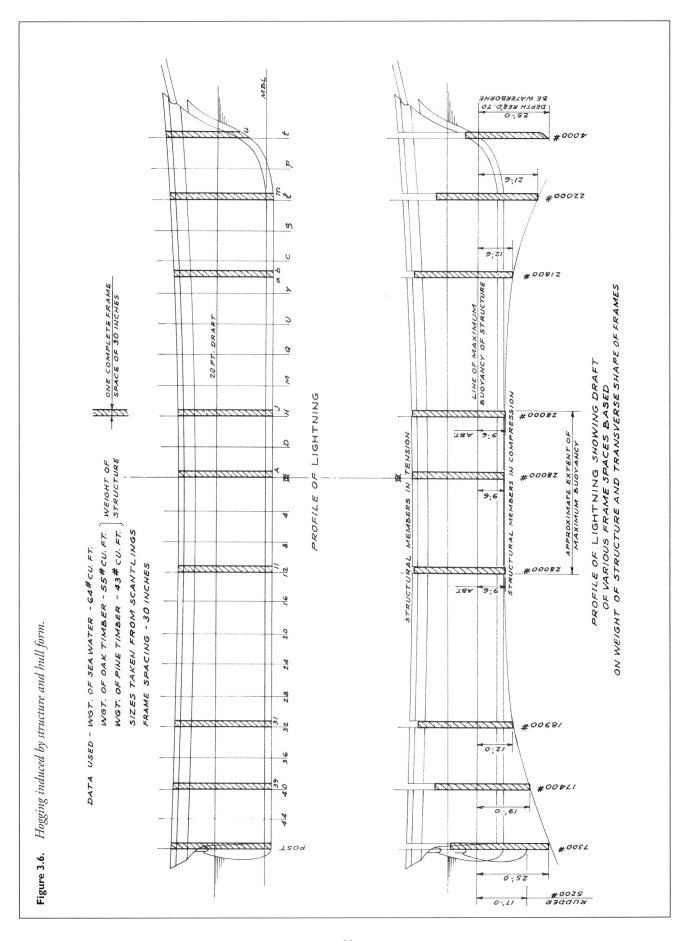

FASTENINGS, HOLE BORERS, AND FASTENERS

Fastenings

The fastenings driven into a ship were the means of making one huge creation out of many relatively small parts, holding them securely together to function as a unit. As a chain is no stronger than its weakest link, so the integrity of a ship is no greater than the soundness of its fastenings. All the care and skill that goes into a vessel's design would go for naught if the same care and skill were not carried over to the choice and selection of proper timber. And it follows that the choice of proper timber would be fruitless if the means of fastening the various components, one to another, was shrugged off as a dull and repetitive job to be meanly and crudely done. This was a fact well known throughout the history of shipbuilding, and over centuries the installation of fastenings was developed and improved and became a trade in its own right. The wooden clipper ships were among the beneficiaries of all that had been learned before.

If it had been possible to X-ray a clipper ship, the maze of metal fastenings revealed would have been astonishing. So numerous and close together were the fastenings, they would have appeared to foul each other and to occupy more space than the structural timbers could accommodate.

In addition to the almost countless quantity of metal fastenings such an X-ray would have revealed, were the literal thousands of wooden fastenings that would have remained unseen.

The types of fastenings used in the construction of clipper ships were wooden treenails (pronounced "trunnels"), bolts, spikes, and nails. The latter three categories were either iron, composition metal (brass), or copper, each to be used under specified conditions. Each of these items will be considered separately.

The clipper ship as a type offered nothing innovative in the matter of ship's fastenings, simply following the methods that had gone before. However, due to the fine configurations in the extreme ends of the vessels, the task of fastening

was probably aggravated by the constriction of space in which to work.

As with all other work performed in the construction of American-built clippers during these years, installation of fastenings was not controlled or governed by any American building code or system. They were installed in general accord with the rules laid down by Lloyd's, which in turn had been compiled and codified over the years as practice proved the merits of materials, construction methods, and scantlings. An American classification would not be forthcoming until 1858, in the form of the "New York Marine Register: A Standard of Classification of American Vessels, and of Such Other Vessels as Visit American Ports." Suffice it to say, however, that prevailing practice, Lloyd's Rules, and the American Standard of Classification all ended up within hailing distance of each other.

Even among those who are familiar with the history of wooden ships, there are many who have no real appreciation of the magnitude of the task of fastening a vessel or the sheer numbers involved. This lack of appreciation is due principally to a lack of need to know and also to the fact that such fastenings are, by their function, generally completely hidden from view and therefore go unnoticed.

To illustrate the immensity of the general element of fastenings in a ship, it is stated by Lauchlan McKay that "The average weight of fastenings for a ship's hull, rigging included, is 68 lbs. of iron per ton of measurement; 8 lbs. of copper per ton."[6] These figures were in reference to ships built between 1830 and 1839 when full, bluff hull forms were the rule.

It is recorded[10] that *Great Republic* contained 56 tons of copper, exclusive of sheathing; and 336½ tons of iron. (This figure for iron may have included her diagonal iron cross-strapping.)

Of the different types of fastenings, the bolt was the principal connector that held together securely the vast accumulation of parts that formed a ship. *Westward Ho* contained

1,325 bolts of 1-inch and 1¼-inch iron to secure her tween-decks waterways, beams, and timbers; *Winged Racer* required 1,452 bolts to perform this same function.

The clipper *Whistler* had 1¼-inch copper and 1-inch iron bolts driven through the keel and keelson assemblies at a distance of 7 inches apart along the full length of the vessel. *Dauntless* was fastened with 1¼-inch bolts spaced 6 inches apart along the full length of her keel. These were typical examples of clipper ship fastening.

Details of the treenails, bolts, spikes, and nails used throughout the construction of clipper hulls follow and are illustrated in Figure 4.1.

Table 4.1 lists the types, materials, and sizes of fastenings used in ships listed in this book, where such information is known. I have attempted to record each item verbatim from the source in order to accurately reflect the information as it is given. Blank spaces indicate that no data has surfaced; they do not signify that the missing item (treenails, for example) was not used in the construction of the particular vessel.

By the frequency or infrequency of entries, one can make a fairly accurate generalization as to the features of clipper ship fastenings. For instance, one can immediately see that dump bolts were rarely used in clipper ship construction. Also apparent is the overwhelming choice of locust as the material for treenails.

The method of fastening was not peculiar to clipper ships. It applied to all wooden vessels of comparable size, regardless of their intended use. However, in all cases, it is stated that the ships were "square fastened," "cross bolted," and "butt and bilge bolted."

Treenails

Treenails (Figure 4.1) are in essence long wooden dowels cut from hardwood, preferably locust, but also satisfactorily produced from white oak. Several other hardwoods—Osage orange, stringybark, and greenheart—were also suitable but apparently did not find their way into clipper ship construction.

The properties of locust made it ideal for treenails. The wood is straight-grained, dense, stronger than the woods it will hold together, and when its surface is tool-finished it becomes very smooth and slick, thus lending itself well to the stresses and blows of being driven deeply into wooden members. Another advantage of using locust for treenails is the fact that, when wet, this wood expands at a greater rate than does oak, allowing the treenail to achieve a tight fit in a bored hole.

The best treenails were made of wood cut from the top part of the tree, since this wood is the most free of knots and sap. Upon being made, the treenails were stored for an extended period in the driest place available, if possible near a boiler room or other heat-producing location, to dry out and

lose as much of their natural moisture as the ambient humidity would permit.

It was this storage period that allowed the treenail to achieve maximum expansion after being driven home in the structure of the ship. Here, where it was subject to normal atmospheric humidity, to the inherent dampness of a ship's interior, and to wetting from weather and the sea, the dried wood expanded as it absorbed its lost moisture and would thus tighten its hold against the wood fibers of the structure. In this way watertightness was assured, and the holding power of the treenail was almost indestructible.

The principal uses of treenails in a ship were to secure the outer planking and the ceiling to the frames; to hold together the pieces of floors, futtocks, and top timbers that were joined together to make up a ship's frames; and to aid in assembling the stem and sternpost.

The principal advantages in using treenails rather than spikes for securing ship's planking were fourfold. First, the treenail, being wood, eliminated any need for further labor and material in providing protection against corrosion and unsightly stain and discoloration. Second, being of wood, the same material as was the planking, the treenail, once expanded, worked with the twisting and straining of the ship's structure when underway, thus tending to remain watertight and secure. This might not have been achieved by the use of metal fastenings, which, being considerably harder than the wood which they were holding together, do not expand and contract; thus the surrounding wood runs the risk of loosening its grip around such a fastening by compacting the wood fibers and enlarging the hole around the metal fastening. Third is the matter of cost. Suitable metal fastenings were more expensive to procure and so were not economical to use unless absolutely necessary.

Fourth was the consideration of weight. When one looks at the overall magnitude of a completed ship, one's predominant impression centers around the grandeur of the structure; no conscious thought strays to the details, labor, and mental skills that make it all possible. And, when one finally realizes that this great structure is really the accumulation and consolidation of thousands of individual items, one knows that it must, naturally, be strong enough to perform its mission. Also the ship must be manageable, contain the necessary creature comforts, and be cost-effective.

However, a most vital and little-appreciated element built into any ship is control of its weight. Monitoring it was an ongoing process. So, even with the use of such massive amounts of timber as found their way into a clipper ship—or any other ship, for that matter—the weight of one spike received due consideration. Basically the elimination of one pound of structure translated into the addition of one pound of cargo.

(text continued on page 65)

Figure 4.1. *Types of fastenings.*

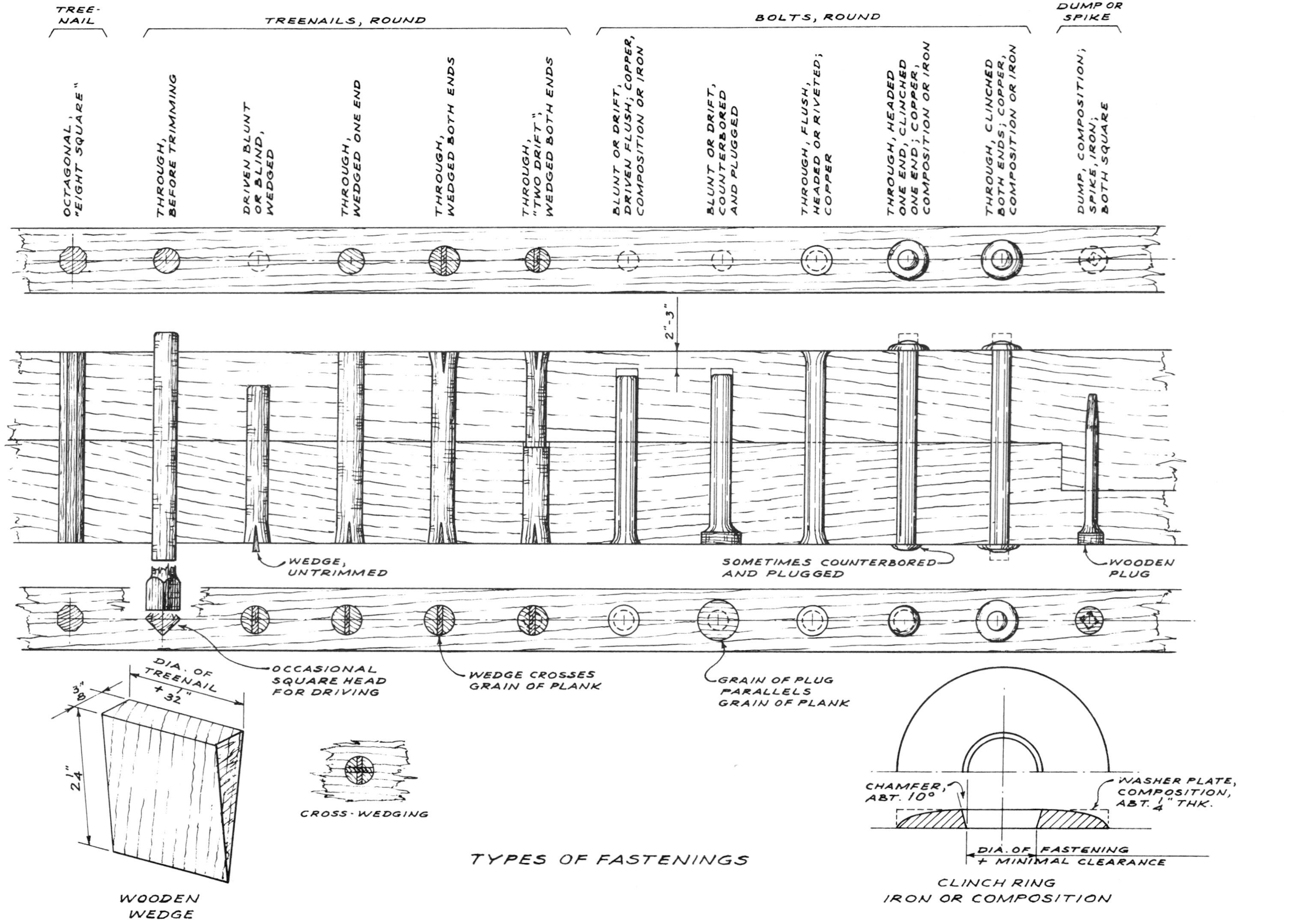

TREE-NAIL

TREENAILS, ROUND

BOLTS, ROUND

DUMP OR SPIKE

OCTAGONAL, "EIGHT SQUARE"

THROUGH, BEFORE TRIMMING

DRIVEN BLUNT OR BLIND, WEDGED

THROUGH, WEDGED ONE END

THROUGH, WEDGED BOTH ENDS

THROUGH, "TWO DRIFT", WEDGED BOTH ENDS

BLUNT OR DRIFT, DRIVEN FLUSH; COPPER, COMPOSITION OR IRON

BLUNT OR DRIFT, COUNTERBORED AND PLUGGED

THROUGH, FLUSH, HEADED OR RIVETED; COPPER

THROUGH, HEADED ONE END, CLINCHED ONE END; COPPER, COMPOSITION OR IRON

THROUGH, CLINCHED BOTH ENDS; COPPER, COMPOSITION OR IRON

DUMP, COMPOSITION; SPIKE, IRON; BOTH SQUARE

2"–3"

SOMETIMES COUNTERBORED AND PLUGGED

WOODEN PLUG

GRAIN OF PLUG PARALLELS GRAIN OF PLANK

WEDGE CROSSES GRAIN OF PLANK

WEDGE, UNTRIMMED

OCCASIONAL SQUARE HEAD FOR DRIVING

CROSS-WEDGING

WASHER PLATE, COMPOSITION, ABT. ¼" THK.

DIA. OF FASTENING + MINIMAL CLEARANCE

CHAMFER, ABT. 10°

CLINCH RING
IRON OR COMPOSITION

TYPES OF FASTENINGS

DIA. OF TREENAIL + 3/32"

3"
8

24"

WOODEN WEDGE

Table 4.1. *Fastenings used, material and size.*

Abbreviations
Cu - copper   Fe - Iron
Cn - composition   Ir - refined iron
Is - Swedish iron

Vessel & Ref.#	Treenails, Matl. & Dia.	Blunt bolts, Matl. & Dia.	Through bolts, Matl. & Dia.	Dump bolts, Matl.	Spikes, Matl.
Alarm #1	treenailed	Fe, $\frac{7}{8}$"to$1\frac{7}{8}$"	Cu,Cn,Fe,$\frac{7}{8}$"to$1\frac{1}{4}$"		Fe
Amphitrite #1	locust	Cu Fe	Cu Fe, $1\frac{1}{4}$"		
Andrew Jackson #20,47	treenailed	Fe	Cu Fe		
Antelope #1	treenailed	Fe, $1\frac{1}{8}$"	Cu Fe, $1\frac{1}{8}$"		
Asa Eldridge #1	locust, wedged both ends	Cu Ir, $1\frac{5}{8}$"	Cu,Cn,Fe, $1\frac{1}{4}$"	Cn	
Bald Eagle #1	treenailed	Fe, $1\frac{1}{4}$"	Cu Fe, 1",$1\frac{1}{4}$"		
Belle of the West #1		Cu Fe	Cu Fe		
Beverly #3		Cu Fe	Cu Fe		
Black Hawk	Iron and copper or composition fastenings.				
Blue Jacket #5	"Fastened in a most thorough manner."				
Bonita #1	locust and oak	Cu Fe, $1\frac{1}{4}$"	Cu Fe, $1\frac{1}{4}$"		Fe
Bounding Billow Bark #1	treenailed	Cn,Fe	Cn,Fe		Fe
Celestial					
Challenge #1	locust, wedged both ends	Cu Fe, $\frac{7}{8}$"to$1\frac{7}{8}$"	Cu Fe, 1",$1\frac{7}{8}$"	Cu	
Challenger #1	treenailed	Fe, $1\frac{3}{8}$"	Cu Fe, $1\frac{3}{8}$"		
Champion of the Seas #1	locust	Cu,Cn,Fe, 1"to$1\frac{3}{8}$"	Cu Fe, 1"to$1\frac{3}{8}$"		Fe
Charger #1	locust, wedged both ends	Cu Ir, $1\frac{5}{8}$"to$1\frac{3}{4}$"	Cu Ir, $1\frac{1}{4}$"	Cn	Cn,Fe
Charmer #1	locust	Fe	Cu Fe	Cu, in planking	
Cleopatra #1	treenailed	Cu Fe	Cu Fe		
Climax #1	treenailed	Cu Fe	Cu Fe		
Coeur de Lion #1	locust	Fe	Cu Fe	Cu, deck plkg.	
Comet					
Cyclone #1	"well built of good materials"	Cu Fe	Cu Fe		
Daring #1		Fe	Cn,Ir, $1\frac{1}{4}$"		
Dauntless #1	locust, wedged and plugged	Cu Ir, $1\frac{1}{8}$",$1\frac{1}{4}$"	Cu,Cn,Fe, $1\frac{1}{8}$",$1\frac{1}{4}$"		
	(Ceiling bolts plugged on inside.)				
Donald McKay #2	locust, $1\frac{1}{4}$"	Cu,Cn,Fe, 1"to$1\frac{3}{8}$"	Cu,Cn,Fe, 1"to$1\frac{3}{8}$"		Fe

Vessel & Ref.#	Treenails, Matl. & Dia.	Blunt bolts, Matl. & Dia.	Through bolts, Matl. & Dia.	Dump bolts, Matl.	Spikes, Matl.
Don Quixote #1	locust	Fe, $1\frac{3}{8}$"	Cu Fe, 1"to$1\frac{3}{8}$"		
Eagle #5	locust	Fe, $1\frac{1}{4}$",$1\frac{3}{4}$"	Cu Fe, 1"to$1\frac{3}{8}$"		Fe
Eagle Wing #1	many are locust, wedged both ends	Cu Fe	Cu Fe		
Edwin Forrest #1	treenailed		Cu Fe		
Electric Spark #1	treenails, wedged both ends	Fe	Cu Fe	Cn	
Ellen Foster #1		Cu Fe, $1\frac{1}{4}$"	Cu Fe, $1\frac{1}{4}$"		
Empress of the Sea #1,2	locust, $1\frac{1}{4}$"	Cu,Cn,Fe, 1"to$1\frac{3}{8}$"	Cu Fe, 1"to$1\frac{3}{8}$"		Fe
Endeavor #1	treenailed	Ir, $1\frac{1}{4}$"	Is		
Eringo Bark #1		Fe	Cu Fe		
Eureka #4	locust	Cu Fe, 1"to$1\frac{1}{4}$"	Cu,Cn,Fe, $\frac{7}{8}$"to $1\frac{1}{4}$"		
Fair Wind #1	locust	Ir	Cu,Cn,Ir, $1\frac{1}{4}$",$1\frac{5}{8}$"	Cn	
Fearless #47	iron and copper fastenings.				
Fleet Wing #1		Fe	Cu Fe		
Flyaway					
Flying Arrow #1	treenailed	Fe	Cu Fe		
Flying Childers #1	treenailed	Fe	Cu Fe, $1\frac{1}{4}$"		Fe
Flying Cloud #1,2	locust, wedged,$1\frac{1}{4}$"	Cu,Cn,Fe, 1"to$1\frac{3}{8}$"	Cu Fe, 1"to$1\frac{3}{8}$"		
Flying Dragon #1	locust	Fe	Cu Fe		
Flying Dutchman					
Flying Eagle #1	treenailed	Fe, $\frac{7}{8}$"to$1\frac{1}{4}$"	Cu Fe, $\frac{7}{8}$"to$1\frac{1}{4}$"		
Flying Fish #1,2	locust, $1\frac{1}{4}$"	Cu,Cn,Fe, 1"to$1\frac{3}{8}$"	Cu Fe, 1"to$1\frac{3}{8}$"		Fe
Flying Mist #1		Ir, $1\frac{1}{4}$",$1\frac{1}{2}$"to$1\frac{1}{2}$"	Cu,Cn,Ir, $1\frac{1}{4}$"		Cn,Fe
Galatea #1	"square fastened throughout"				
Game Cock #1		Fe, $1\frac{1}{4}$"	Cu Fe, $1\frac{1}{4}$"		
Gazelle #4		Fe	Cu Fe		
Gem of the Ocean #1	locust	Fe	Cu Fe		
Golden Eagle #1	treenails, many driven through	Cu Fe, $1\frac{1}{4}$"	Cu Fe, $1\frac{1}{4}$"	Cn, upper dk aft	
Golden Fleece (2nd) #1	treenails, wedged both ends	Fe	Cn,Fe		
Golden Light #1	locust and oak	Cu Fe, $1\frac{1}{4}$"	Cu Fe, $1\frac{1}{4}$"		
Golden West #1		Cu Fe	Cu Fe		
Grace Darling #1	locust	Fe	Cu Fe		Fe

Table 4.1. *Continued.*

Vessel & Ref.#	Treenails, Matl. & Dia.	Blunt bolts, Matl. & Dia.	Through bolts, Matl. & Dia.	Dump bolts, Matl.	Spikes, Matl.
Great Republic (1853) #2,4,10	locust, $1\frac{1}{4}$"	Cu Ir, $1\frac{1}{4}$"	Cu Ir, 1"to$1\frac{3}{8}$"	Cn	
Great Republic (rebuilt) #103	locust, $1\frac{1}{4}$"	Fe, 1"to$1\frac{3}{8}$"	Cu Fe, 1"to$1\frac{3}{8}$"		Fe
Henry Hill Bark #1		Cu,Cn,Fe	Cu,Cn,Fe		
Herald of the Morning #12		Fe, $1\frac{1}{4}$"	Cu,Cn,Fe, 1"to$1\frac{1}{4}$"		
Hoogly #1	locust, wedged and plugged		Cu Fe, 1"to$1\frac{1}{4}$"		
Hurricane #4		Fe	Cu $1\frac{1}{4}$"		
Indiaman #1		Fe	Cu,Cn,Fe		
Intrepid					
Invincible #4		Fe	Cu Fe		
James Baines #1	locust, $1\frac{1}{4}$"	Cu,Cn,Fe, 1"to$1\frac{3}{8}$"	Cu Fe, 1"to$1\frac{3}{8}$"		Fe
John Bertram #1	treenails, wedged both ends	Ir, $\frac{7}{8}$"to$1\frac{1}{4}$"	Cu,Cn,Fe, $\frac{7}{8}$"to$1\frac{1}{4}$"	Cn, upper dk. aft	Fe
John Gilpin #1		Fe	Cu Fe, $1\frac{1}{4}$"		
John Land #1,32 (Built as a duplicate of Winged Arrow.)		Fe, $1\frac{1}{4}$"	Cu Fe, $1\frac{1}{4}$"		Fe
John Stuart #4	locust	Fe	Cu Fe		
John Wade #1		Fe	Cu Fe		
Joseph Peabody #1	treenailed	Cn,Ir	Cn,Fe, $1\frac{1}{4}$"		
King Fisher #1		Fe	Cu Fe		
Lady Franklin					
Lamplighter Bark #1	treenailed	Fe	Cu Fe		
Lightfoot #1	treenailed	Fe	Cu Fe		
Lightning #1,2	locust, $1\frac{1}{4}$"	Cu,Cn,Fe, 1"to $1\frac{3}{8}$"	Cu Fe, 1"to $1\frac{3}{8}$"		Fe
Mameluke #1	treenails, wedged both ends	Fe	Cu Ir, $1\frac{1}{2}$"		Fe
Mary Robinson					
Mastiff #1		Fe	Cn,Fe		Fe
Mermaid Bark #1	locust	Fe	Cu,Cn,Fe		
Morning Light #1		Fe	Cu Fe		
Mystery #1	treenailed	Fe	Cu Fe, 1"to $1\frac{1}{4}$"		
Nightingale #3	"thoroughly copper fastened throughout."				
Noonday #1	locust, wedged both ends	Fe, $1\frac{1}{4}$"	Cu $\frac{7}{8}$" to $1\frac{1}{4}$"		Fe
Northern Light					
Ocean Express #1	treenailed	Fe	Cu Fe		
Ocean Pearl #1		Fe	Cu Fe		
Ocean Telegraph #5			Cu		
Onward #1	treenailed	Fe, $1\frac{1}{4}$"	Cu Fe, $1\frac{1}{4}$"		
Osborne Howes					
Panther					
Phantom #1	treenailed	Fe, $1\frac{3}{8}$"	Cu Fe, 1"to $1\frac{1}{4}$"		
Queen of Clippers #1	locust	Fe, $1\frac{1}{2}$"	Cu Fe, $1\frac{1}{2}$"		
Queen of the Pacific					
Queen of the Seas #1	treenailed	Fe, $1\frac{1}{4}$"	Cu Fe, $1\frac{1}{4}$"		
Quickstep Bark #1	treenails, wedged both ends	Fe	Cu Fe		
Racehorse Bark #1	treenails, wedged both ends	Fe	Cu Fe, $1\frac{1}{8}$"	Cn, deck	
Racer #3	"square bolted"	Fe, $1\frac{1}{4}$"	Cu $1\frac{1}{4}$"		
Radiant #1		Fe, $1\frac{1}{4}$"	Cu Fe, $1\frac{1}{4}$"		
Raven #3	"fastened in a superior manner."		Fe, $\frac{7}{8}$",1"		
Red Jacket #19	"square fastened throughout." Iron and copper fastenings.				
Robin Hood					
Rocket Bark #1	"built in the same style as Dauntless."				
Roebuck #1	treenailed	Fe	Cu Fe		
Romance of the Sea #1		Fe	Cu Fe		
Santa Claus #1	locust	Fe	Cu,Cn,Fe		
Saracen #1	locust, wedged both ends	Fe, $1\frac{1}{8}$"	Cu Fe, (Cu,$1\frac{1}{4}$"; Fe,1"to $1\frac{1}{2}$")		
Sea Bird Bark #1		Fe	Cu Fe		
Seaman's Bride #4	"square fastened throughout."		Fe		
Sea Serpent #4	"thoroughly bolted and fastened throughout with the best materials."				
Shooting Star #1	many are locust, wedged both ends	Ir, $1\frac{1}{4}$"	Cu Fe, $1\frac{1}{4}$"		Fe
Sierra Nevada #1	locust	Cu Fe, $1\frac{3}{4}$"	Cu		Fe
Silver Star #1	treenailed	Ir	Cu Fe	Cn	Fe
Southern Cross #1	treenailed	Fe, $1\frac{1}{4}$"	Cu Fe, $1\frac{1}{4}$"		Fe
Sovereign of the Seas #1,2	locust, $1\frac{1}{4}$"	Cu,Cn,Fe, 1"to $1\frac{1}{2}$"	Cu Fe, 1"to $1\frac{1}{2}$"		Fe
Spitfire #1	treenailed	Fe	Cu Fe		

Table 4.1. *Continued.*

Vessel & Ref.#	Treenails, Matl. & Dia.	Blunt bolts, Matl. & Dia.	Through bolts, Matl. & Dia.	Dump bolts, Matl.	Spikes, Matl.
Staffordshire #1,2	locust, 1", $1\frac{1}{4}$"	Cu,Cn,Fe, 1"to$1\frac{3}{8}$"	Cu Fe, 1"to$1\frac{1}{4}$"		Fe
Stag Hound #1,2	locust, 1", $1\frac{1}{4}$"	Fe, 1"to$1\frac{3}{8}$"	Cu Fe, 1"to$1\frac{1}{4}$"		Fe
Star of the Union #1	treenailed	Fe	Cu Fe		
Starr King					
Storm King #1	locust	Fe, $\frac{7}{8}$"to$1\frac{1}{4}$"	Cu Fe, $\frac{7}{8}$"to$1\frac{1}{4}$"		Fe
Sultana Bark #1		Fe, $1\frac{1}{8}$"	Cu Fe, $1\frac{1}{8}$"	Cn, deck	
Sunny South					
Surprise #1	treenailed	Fe	Cu Ir, $1\frac{1}{4}$"		Fe
Swallow #1		Fe	Cu Fe		
Sweepstakes					
Sword Fish					
Syren #3	"well fastened."		Cu		
Telegraph #1		Fe	Cu Fe		
Thatcher Magoun #1	many are locust	Fe	Cu,Cn,Fe, $1\frac{1}{4}$"		
Tornado					
Uncowah					
War Hawk #1		Cu Fe	Cu Fe, $1\frac{1}{4}$"		
Water Witch #1		Fe	Cu Fe		
Western Continent					
Westward Ho #1,2	locust, $1\frac{1}{4}$"	Cu,Cn,Fe, 1"to$1\frac{3}{8}$"	Cu Ir, 1"to$1\frac{7}{8}$"		Fe
West Wind #1	"strongly fastened, both inside and out."				
Whirlwind #1	treenailed	Fe, $1\frac{1}{4}$"	Cu Fe, $1\frac{1}{4}$"		
Whistler #1		Fe, $1\frac{1}{4}$"	Cu Fe, $1\frac{1}{8}$"		
Wildfire Bark #1	"well fastened."				
Wild Pigeon #1	treenailed	Fe	Cu Fe, $1\frac{1}{4}$" (Ceiling bolts plugged on inside.)		Fe
Wild Ranger #1	treenailed	Fe	Cu Fe		
Wild Rover					
Winged Arrow #1		Fe, $1\frac{1}{4}$"	Cu Fe, $1\frac{1}{4}$"		Fe
Winged Racer #1	treenailed	Ir, $1\frac{1}{4}$"	Cu Fe, $1\frac{1}{4}$"		Fe
Witchcraft #1	many are locust	Fe, $\frac{7}{8}$"to$1\frac{1}{4}$"	Cu Fe, $\frac{7}{8}$"to$1\frac{1}{4}$"		Fe
Witch of the Wave #1	treenailed, some wedged both ends	Fe, $1\frac{1}{4}$"	Cu Fe, $1\frac{1}{4}$"		Fe
Wizard #1	treenailed	Fe	Cu Fe		
Young America					
Young Turk Bark #1	treenailed	Cu	Cu	Cu	

(text continued from page 61)

The general progress of shipbuilding over several centuries had contrived to make the use of treenails universal in the fastening of planking to frames. But, even for all this universality, there had been significant diversity of opinion regarding the relative merits of the treenail versus the metal bolt or spike. That the treenail was lighter in weight was obvious and therefore a plus; that it was cheaper to produce and obtain also were positive contributions. Its tightness and immunity from deterioration due to wood acids and seawater were beyond dispute.

The strength of the treenailed connection compared to a bolted connection was the matter debated. The negative aspects of the treenail were its inferior resistance to shearing when a ship was working in a seaway, and the weakening of the frames as a result of drilling the large holes required to receive the treenails. There was also the tendency of the treenail to "draw," or back out of its position, when the adjacent planking seam was being caulked.

Another negative argument involving the use of treenails was their apparent tendency to decay. This was a factor about which little has ever been written or discussed, and never appeared to be a problem of enough magnitude to warrant investigation.

However, in their late-nineteenth-century works on naval

architecture, both James Peake[7] and Samuel J. P. Thearle[8] noted the fact that treenail fastening was nearly nonexistent in the British navy between 1834 and 1848, due to the decay that was said to be attendant to the use of the treenail. Also contributing to this disuse was the problem of treenails being subject to breaking or crippling, which was the shattering of a treenail while being driven. In such cases the treenail had to be bored out and a new one installed.

As a result, treenails were superseded by the use of copper bolts and short brass (mixed-metal or composition-metal) spikes, or *dumps*, as they were called at the time (see "Dump Bolts"). One of the great evils accompanying this system of fastening was the weight added to the hull by the use of the copper and composition metals, their weight being eight times that of wood. Added to this was a widely shared view that the composition dump, or "bolt-nail," as it was sometimes named, had no great grab or hold in the timbers and that, if not driven with great care and the exercise of good judgment, had a great tendency to split the plank and thus cause leaks.

So, after a period of fourteen years, many of the practical shipbuilders reverted to the use of wooden treenails, finally yielding to their combined advantages of good fastening grip and economy of weight.

On an individual basis, the weight saved appears to be a rather technical consideration, but when one considers that, for example, the clipper *Hoogly* had 5,000 treenails securing the planking to her frames, one's perspective changes and the case favoring treenailing becomes truly significant.

Ultimately, over a long period of time, the treenail, in spite of its academic weaknesses and drawbacks, performed so well that it became the accepted fastening for most ship planking. In this application, treenails did, however, receive an assist from metal fastenings; this subject is covered later in the discussion of exterior planking details.

The advantage of using treenails in interior construction such as the fabrication of frames, lay in the elimination of inadvertent interference with vital metal bolts. With the thousands of such fastenings needed for construction of a clipper ship, this was a consideration of sizable proportion.

Treenails were produced in many lengths and diameters and also in two cross-sectional shapes. The lengths of the treenails generally ranged from about 20 inches to 36 inches, thus allowing an economical choice, depending upon the combined thicknesses of the parts being secured together.

In earlier times, the diameter of the treenail had been dictated as 1 inch for every 100 feet of the vessel's length. Thus, a ship 100 feet long would use treenails 1 inch in diameter; a 150-foot ship would use 1½-inch-diameter treenails; a 200-foot ship would have 2-inch treenails; and so on. As time went on and ships became longer, the impracticality of this rigid system became apparent. Large ships, regardless

of their relative length, were being fabricated from material of similar scantlings and the fastening need only be of a size to securely hold the parts together. Treenails 1½ inches in diameter became the largest to be used in the clippers, and even this size was at the discretion of the individual builder. It is noteworthy that the largest treenails specified for the huge *Great Republic* were only 1¼ inch in diameter.

Treenails are generally perceived to be round, in the fashion of a broomstick. However, in days preceding the advent of the wood-turning lathe, this was not a fact. In those times it was much easier to make a treenail that was octagonal in section, or "eight-square." This was done by hand-splitting the logs, mostly oak or locust, in order to ensure straightness of grain and then sawing them to the desired square dimension. At this point the squares, of required length, were "eight-sided" by craftsmen who were accomplished in this skill, by chamfering the four corners by hand with axe, hatchet, or drawknife. This became one of the many skilled crafts that made up the art of shipbuilding.

By the time clipper ships were being built, the treenails, if round, were being turned in lathes or run through special machines that produced the proper diameter. If eight-sided, they were produced by machines that planed them to the desired cross section.

The eight-square treenail was regarded by some as having holding power or grip superior to that of round treenails, the reasoning being that the eight corners of the treenail would bite more tightly into the sides of the undersize hole that had been bored to receive it. Whether or not this was ever "proven" does not appear to have been recorded. Wherever noted in clipper ship specifications, the cross-sectional dimension of the treenail is given in inches, without reference to shape, but the probable assumption is that they were round.

Generally, treenails were cut in uniform section throughout their entire length, so either end could be used as the penetrating end. However, due to the vast quantities of treenails required, it is highly probable that this entering end was slightly chamfered in manufacturing, eliminating extra work for the "fastener."

Sometimes in manufacturing treenails, one end, the driving end, was left in the shape of the rough stock—that is, it would be left four-square for several inches of its length. This presented more surface to receive the blow of the maul and possibly resist damage to the treenail as a whole.

Another variation, found in round treenails of extended length, was the "two-drift" treenail[36] in which half the length of the treenail was turned to a diameter that would freely pass through the nominal-sized hole to be bored; this was the entering half-length. The driven half-length was of the specified diameter. Where the two parts met, a *stop* or shoulder was formed. Treenails of this configuration could be inserted into the bored hole for half their length before forceful driving was required.

In the actual building records of clipper ships, the only specifications found for treenails appear to be the required diameter and the type of wood to be used. Any other requirements were left to the discretion of the builder and the rules of practice.

As with all items that made up the clipper ship, the diameters of treenails were proportioned to adequately function with the part (usually planking) to be restrained. The following table lists the thickness of planking and a suitable size treenail to be used with it.

Planking thickness	Treenail diameter
1"	7/8"
2½"	1"
over 2½" to 3½"	1⅛"
over 3½" to 4½"	1¼"
over 4½" to 5½"	1⅜"
over 5½"	

Treenails larger than the quoted sizes could, naturally, achieve greater holding power. The deficiency therein lies in the fact that the boring of larger holes would weaken the ship's structure and was thus avoided.

While it is generally conceded that the premier wood for treenail production is locust, it was not the only wood considered acceptable. Of the ships listed in this book, descriptions by Duncan MacLean[1] of *Bonita* and *Golden Light* indicate that treenails were of both locust and oak, while those of *Edwin Forrest*, *Thatcher Magoun*, and *Shooting Star* record that "many of her treenails are locust." The assumption appears valid that the alternate wood was white oak. Many ships are specifically recorded as being locust treenailed throughout, and in many cases the particular wood is not identified in any manner.

The extensive use of treenails in wooden vessels is vividly brought into focus by the clipper *Charger*, into which 22,000 locust treenails, some of which were 28 inches long, were driven and wedged both ends. MacLean[1] also stated that many of her treenails were driven blunt and wedged.

Wedges

Wedges (Figure 4.1) were a necessary item in the treenailing process. Their function was to expand the ends of the driven treenail so that the wood of the treenail would flare against the side of the hole in which it had been driven.

When wedges were driven into the ends of the treenail it became immobilized, and it was virtually impossible for the fastening to back out of position in either direction.

Wedges were made of wood which, by specification, was required to be at least as hard as the treenail into which they were to be driven. In addition, the direction of the grain was to be parallel with the length of the wedge, not only to facilitate driving the wedge but also to prevent its breaking under a badly aimed hammer blow.

The last function of the wedge was to improve or ensure the watertightness of the treenailed connection by inducing expansion of the treenail.

The wedges, in general, were about ⅜ inch thick at the butt end and 2¼ inches in length; the fine or thin end was of hairline thickness. Between these two extremities the wedge was fashioned in a straight taper. The width of the wedge was 1/32 inch greater than the width of the treenail into which it would be inserted. This extra width ensured that the sides of the wedge would constantly press against the sides of the bored hole. The wedge shown in Figure 4.1 was measured at Mystic Seaport, Mystic, Connecticut.

Bolts

Bolts (Figure 4.1) were the glue that held the parts of the clipper ships together. Without quality bolts and their proper installation, a ship would soon return to its original state—a loose conglomeration of various types and shapes of timber.

Bolts, as referred to in wooden ship building, did not resemble bolts as we know them today. They were sometimes headed, never threaded, but were actually round rods of various diameters, lengths, and materials. However, in wooden ships, the term "bolt" was used, and that term is followed here. Bolts were provided in three basic materials, namely iron, brass (which was also called composition metal, mixed metal, or yellow metal), and copper. Since *composition* was the term most frequently used in specifying brass bolts, we will use that term. Of the three materials, the non-ferrous bolts were the quality members of the group, while iron bolts were the workhorses. Each is used in specified locations in a ship.

In practice, any bolt driven below a vessel's load waterline was required to be of copper or composition metal if its end would be in contact with seawater. A typical example of this is the bolts driven down through the lowest tier of the keel. Even though this tier would in turn be completely covered by the shoe protecting the bottom of the keel, the rule applied because the shoe was considered expendable, since it would scrape or contact underwater objects that might tear it away and thus expose the bottom of the keel and its fastenings.

Copper bolts sacrificed strength for resistance to corrosion. Copper bolts were the softest metal, perhaps three-quarters the strength of iron, and were the most expensive. Composition bolts were corrosion-resistant, stronger than either copper or iron, and were more expensive than iron but cheaper than copper.

The gripping power of composition and copper bolts—

that is, their facility for "grabbing" the sides of the hole in which they are driven—is quite inferior to that of iron bolts. All base metals are subject to surface corrosion. In the non-ferrous bolts this corrosion occurs in the form of a film of verdigris over its surface which allows certain slippage when a ship is working. This deficiency, if that term may be used, is more than compensated by the fact that, once the film is formed, the process of deterioration ceases and the bolt will last indefinitely.

The situation with iron bolts, however, is different. The corrosive action in iron, or "rusting" as we know it, is a continuing process if the iron is exposed to moisture. No matter how great the mass of metal, the corrosion relentlessly penetrates and destroys its integrity. Such was the case with iron bolts.

One of the greatest disasters that could befall a wooden vessel, clipper ship or any other, was for that ship to become "iron sick." This term denoted a situation in which the iron fastenings of a vessel have become corroded to a degree which causes a ship to leak due to progressive failure of her fastenings. Thus it is quite obvious that great care be taken in locating and driving iron bolts in order to ensure that they have no continuous contact with seawater and that they be driven true and tightly to prevent leakage.

The iron of those days was "pure," which means that the metal was obtained through the simple, unsophisticated process of smelting iron ore without further refinement. This "pure" product was about 95 percent iron, the remainder being mostly carbon. Considered size for size, iron bolts were stronger than copper but inferior to composition by about 25 percent.

After an iron bolt was driven and had been in place for an extended period, normal oxidation or rusting attacked its surface. This action fostered an interaction with the wood, and the iron bolt would then "grow fast" to the timber and thus increase its gripping power. Once this initial corrosion had taken place, the process slowed to a pace which, when used in locations not directly impinged upon by water, allowed the bolt to function with integrity throughout the life of a vessel. This grip was so great that driving an iron bolt out was impossible, whereas a copper or composition bolt could be backed out with little difficulty if such a need arose.

The sizes of bolts used in the ships included in this book, regardless of material, ranged in diameter from ⅞ inch to 1½ inches, generally increasing in ⅛-inch increments. The larger diameters were necessary not only to provide holding power, but to provide the stiffness required while the bolt was being driven and to restrict "backing out" of the bolt while being clinched. There were several principal forms of bolt.

Through-bolts completely penetrated all timbers into which they were driven. There were three forms of through-bolts. One form was made exactly as the blunt bolt except that its entering end would protrude beyond the timber when driven home. If the bolt was iron, it generally had a clinch ring under the head, and its end was always flattened over a second clinch ring; the purpose of the ring was to provide bearing surface against the timber to eliminate the possibility of compressing the wood during the clinching process. (Clinch rings essentially acted as washers; their use is described in detail in the following section.) One-half the diameter of the bolt extended beyond the clinch ring to allow for *upsetting* (deforming) the end of the bolt.

If the through-bolt was copper, the end could be riveted without a clinch ring due to the relative softness of the metal. However, composition bolts were difficult to peen over, and a clinch ring was a necessity. In some cases clinching over rings is specifically mentioned.

While it does not appear in the records, there is the possibility that, where copper and composition bolts were clinched over rings, these rings resembled thick, flat washers rather than true clinch rings, which had a specific form and shape as shown in Figure 4.1.

The following table lists the comparative weights of the basic materials from which fastenings were fabricated. The values are in pounds per foot.

Size (diameter)	iron	Bolts copper	composition	Treenails locust
½"	.672	.770	.752	.063
⅝	.960	1.100	1.074	.090
¾	1.440	1.650	1.611	.135
⅞	1.920	2.200	2.148	.180
1	2.592	2.970	2.900	.243
1⅛	2.880	3.300	3.222	.270
1¼	4.080	4.670	4.565	.383
1½	5.904	6.765	6.605	.554

While most vessels used copper in the wetted areas, there were some that used composition metal. In addition, while most vessels riveted or headed their copper fastenings, some employed clinch rings that were composition.

Finally, there was the iron through-bolt, which was simply a straight iron rod with its ends chamfered to facilitate driving. The bolt was used in locations where great stress could be expected. Clinch rings were placed over each end of the bolt to distribute the crushing load at the ends. Protection against the crushing of the wood fibers under the bolt ends was essential to the efficiency of a fastening in this situation.

The *blunt bolt*,[36] currently termed a *drift*, which regardless of material, might or might not be headed on the driven end, had a slight chamfer on the entering end, or point; this was to ease the driving force and eliminate the possibility of shearing the sides of the hole in the timbers into which the bolt was driven. This type of bolt was intended to stop short of full penetration of the timbers and was therefore driven into a "blind" hole, one that stopped 2 to 3 inches short of the holding member. The blunt bolt could be made from any of the metals.

Blunt bolts derived their holding power from the force of their grip upon the sides of the undersize holes into which they were driven. They were not exposed to the high tensile stresses to which through-bolts were subjected; therefore, the forming of heads of large area and the use of clinch rings was not a necessity. If not headed, the blunt bolt, when driven, would deform and acquire a head; this could be flattened flush with the surface of the timber when the bolt was driven home to its full length. This was important if a second tier of timber was to be fayed—fitted tightly—against the first, as in tiers of keel or keelson. Blunt bolts were also used where access to the entering end, or point, was not possible after being driven home; or, in the case of iron blunts, where complete penetration was not desired due to exposure to seawater.

The descriptions of most clippers[1] refer to iron bolts as simply being "iron." In the absence of any detailed information, it might be reasonable to assume that this form of iron was a basic pig iron from which impurities had been removed by means of melting the iron to burn off some of these undesirable elements. This resulted in a product similar in quality to wrought iron. However, there were certain clippers whose descriptions explicitly mention the use of "refined" iron fastenings. Again, lacking explicit details, one might make the assumption that this refined iron was the result of a more sophisticated heat-treatment process which results in a malleable iron of better quality.

At least one clipper, *Endeavor*, was fastened with "the best Swedish iron." This could be presumed to be the ultimate in iron fastenings.

It is noteworthy that the fibers of oak are so closely knit that an iron bolt subjected to a very great shear stress will not cut into the wood and damage the connection. However, were that same bolt driven through yellow pine and subsequently subjected to severe shear stress, the wood fibers would compress, the hole would elongate, and the bolt might eventually loosen.

Clinch Rings

Clinch rings (Figure 4.1) were essential to the successful fastening of a wooden vessel. They were basically washers that were used under the head or the point, or both, of a bolt; their function was to protect the wood during the clinching process and to distribute the compressive load around the head of the bolt.

While round in shape, their cross-sectional appearance was made up of one flat bearing surface and one low convex surface which was perhaps ¼ inch thick in the middle and rounded off in wafer shape toward the outer diameter where they were relatively thin.

The center of the ring was pierced by a hole that was of suitable diameter to accommodate a given bolt at the flat bearing surface. This hole, however, did not have parallel sides but rather was chamfered at about 10 degrees all around in the form of a countersink.

Clinch rings were cast in composition and iron in a range of sizes that would cover all the standard-diameter bolts used at the time, The composition rings were used with both composition and copper bolts, while the iron rings were used only with iron bolts. Both types of ring were manufactured and marketed by ship supply houses specifically for the ship-building industry and may be found advertised routinely in newspapers of the period.

Clinch rings were made in this particular form for reasons mentioned later under "Fasteners." This specific type of ring does not completely preclude the use of suitable round washer plates as a substitute, but with the rings being a standard stock item, this would not appear to be economical.

While blunt bolts could be used without the addition of a clinch ring, the same cannot be said for through-bolts. In texts and descriptions contemporary with the clipper period the language is sometimes ambiguous or nonexistent, but in general it appears that a through-bolt was generally clinched over a suitable ring. Discussions with present-day shipwrights who are engaged in building or preserving large wooden vessels indicate virtual complete agreement on this point.

Clinch rings were used principally to bear the forces of "draw" or compression that can be accumulated under the heads of through-bolts. Following is a simple example of these forces when an iron bolt is driven.

Using approximate values for the strength of materials involved, since there was considerable variation in composition of both the wood and the iron, the following values would apply. The greatest strength of the iron used was about 48,000 pounds per square inch, under which stress an iron bolt would part. The compressive strength of white oak, while very variable, was about 9,000 pounds per square inch; at this load the wood started to deform. The ratio of these two forces acting against each other was, therefore, 5.3 to 1 in favor of the iron.

Using a 1-inch-diameter iron bolt having a cross-sectional area of 0.785 square inch, it can be seen that this bolt will part under a load of 37,680 pounds. To resist this load it would require 4.19 square inches of oak. To obtain this area in a bolt by heading it would require a bolt head about 2½ inches in diameter, which is impracticably large; hence the introduction of the clinch ring, which in size would have a hole just large enough to slip neatly over the bolt and could be 2½ inches or greater in outside diameter. Theoretically the oak fiber would crush at the same time the iron bolt would part.

The above example grossly oversimplifies the technicalities of the actual conditions, but it illustrates the principle of the forces and stresses that had to be dealt with.

Dump Bolts

Dump bolts (Figure 4.1) or "dumps," as they were unceremoniously termed, were not bolts in the sense of the term used so far in this description of fastenings. Rather, they were spikes made from copper or composition metal. Like iron spikes (see below), they were formed with flat, round heads, were square across the shank, and were chisel-pointed. They were used mainly for fastening ship's planking, and their installation is covered under the headings "Spikes" and "Fasteners."

The pattern of "dump and bolt" installation is shown in Figure 20.1, detail I.

Spikes

Spikes (Figure 4.1) are the third and last of the major fastenings used in the building of wooden ships. Their principal use was in securing deck planking, ceiling planking, and the ends of wooden knees and scarphs. They were made from iron, composition, and copper. Their location in the ship determined which metal would be used.

For a long period prior to the clipper era, spikes had been used extensively but not exclusively in fastening planking and ceiling. However, as time progressed the twin considerations of cost and weight prevailed, and the treenail came into its own.

Spikes were manufactured in a variety of sizes, in all of which the cross-sectional area bore a relationship to the length. Spikes were square in section and were made with chisel points.

There were two outstanding advantages in the use of square spikes over round. The reasons, not necessarily in order of importance, were, first, that a chisel-pointed spike, when driven, acts as a punch when piercing the timber and thus is not likely to split the wood. A round spike with a conventional point acts as a wedge and is often the cause of splitting.

The second advantage of the square spike over the round one is in its "hold" or gripping power. Using a ½-inch spike as an example, the peripheral dimension of such a spike, if square, is 2 inches when measured around the four sides. In contrast, a round spike of the same dimension has a circumference of 1.57 inches. This results in a 25-percent superiority for the square spike.

The spike selected to hold a given plank is determined by the thickness of the plank, the intent being that the spike,

once driven, will not loosen and back out, and it cannot easily be drawn once it is seated. The general formula that satisfies this condition is that the spike should be in length two-and-one-half times the thickness of the plank being secured; for example, a plank 3 inches thick requires a spike 7½ inches in length. As stated before, the length will determine the sectional dimension of the spike.

Figure 4.2[29] lists some of the salient features and data relevant to spikes used in general ship work. This data was published in 1856 and was based upon the practices of many years.

Nails

Nails used in wooden ship building were a minority fastening little employed in the heavy structural work. They came into their own in joinery and small work such as carpentry in the construction of interior bulkheads, partitions, built-in furnishings, etc. These were "penny" nails from 1 to 4 inches in length, and their use was at the discretion of shipwrights and carpenters as the need arose. The terms *spike* and *nail* were sometimes rather loosely interchanged, but only in the way of small, light work. Nails had a specific use in the building of boats, which is outside the scope of this work. The relatively small size of boats precluded any great necessity for using bolts in the context of the previous discussion of fastenings.

Sheathing nails, as were used in fastening metal sheets to a ship's bottom, are covered in the chapter devoted to metal sheathing.

Hole Borers

Installation of treenails, bolts, and spikes was entrusted solely to skilled craftsmen who were trained and expert in this important trade. Each type of fastening was installed in its own particular manner.

The skills involved were assigned to two classes of craftsmen: one known as "hole borers," and the other as "fasteners." One should note that in shipbuilding, the term *fastening* always refers to a category of objects, while the term *fastener* always refers to a skilled craftsman.

The principal methods of fastening timbers together consisted of *square fastening*, in which case the borer pierced the timber to be fastened *normal* (at 90 degrees) to its surface and thence into the timber that would be the holding member—for example, a ceiling plank being held secure by a frame. Secondly, there was *edge-bolting*, in which the fastening entered the side of a member and was driven through its substance into the side of another or similar member. In addition, there was great use of *cross-bolting* or *diagonal-bolting* in such assemblies as the keelson and frames.

The process of installing a treenail or bolt, while not intricate, was one requiring great care, accuracy, and judgment. The procedure followed a set pattern, time-honored and well proven.

The hole borer had the responsibility of taking first action. First, the borer was given the size and particular type of hole to be bored for a given task in a given location. The size of the hole was dependent upon the type of wood to be bored through and the size of the fastening. The depth of the hole was important only in the use of a blunt fastening or the occasional "two-drift" treenail, described above.

The diameter of the hole would be ⅟₁₆ to ¼ inch smaller than the designated fastening depending upon the species of wood to be pierced, the material, and the diameter of the fastening. In rare cases, where all the wood involved was hardwood, oak for instance, the hole might be bored the same diameter as the fastening. This might also apply to the boring of holes to accept extraordinarily long bolts.

In situations requiring the use of long copper bolts, the diameter of the bored hole was not so markedly undersize due to the softness of the bolt material. If the difference in diameters between bolt and hole was too great, there was the considerable risk of "spoiling" the bolt as resistance of the wood built up before much of the bolt had entered the hole.

Much was left to the experience, judgment, and skill of both the borer and the fastener. As in all other trades there were rules and guidelines, but these were general, while judgment was specific.

In many instances the holes for through-fastening clamps, knees, and other inboard structures were bored from inside to outside. After the fastenings had been driven, it was possible to locate planking treenails in locations where they would not be driven into an impeding iron bolt, which would eliminate the holding power of the treenail. In this respect, installation of fastenings required considerable foresight and careful planning.

The augers and bits most often used by the borers were probably the spiral-ribbon bit, the nose auger, and the spoon bit.[102] The *spiral-ribbon bit* was on the general order of any spiral auger. It consisted of a long, helical ribbon of iron which had its cutting edge square across the bottom end. The *nose auger* was a long half-cylinder which also had its cutting edge square across the bottom end. The *spoon bit* was a long half-cylinder with a spoon-shaped cutting edge at the lower end.

These auger bodies were affixed to the end of a long iron rod which in turn had a T-handle secured across its uppermost end. Each bit scraped or cut the wood at the bottom of the hole. In the spiral-ribbon bit, the shavings were pulled up the hole as the spiral turned. In the half-cylinder-type bits, the shavings merely piled up until they were expelled when the bit was extracted.

Figure 4.2. *Common spikes used in shipbuilding.*

SHIP AND RAILROAD SPIKES, AND HORSE SHOES.

SHIP AND RAILROAD SPIKES.

NUMBER OF IRON SPIKES PER 100 POUNDS.

Manufactured by PHILIP C. PAGE, *Mass., and Sold by* PAGE, BRIGGS & BABBITT, *Boston.*

Ship Spikes or Hatch Nails 1-4 in. sq're.		Ship Spikes or Hatch Nails 5-16 in. sq.		Ship Spikes or Deck Nails 3-8 in. sq're.		Ship Spikes 7-16 inch square.		Ship Spikes 1-2 inch square.		Ship Spikes 9-16 inch square.		Ship Spikes 5-8 inch square.	
size in inc.	No. 100 lbs.	size in inc.	No. 100 lbs.	size in inc.	No. 100 lbs.	size in inc.	No. 100 lbs.	size in inc.	No. 100 lbs.	size in inc.	No. 100 lbs.	size in inc.	No. 100 lbs.
3	1900	3	1000	4	540	5	340	6	220	8	140	10	80
3½	1580	3½	960	4½	500	5½	310	6½	200	9	120	15	60
4	1320	4	800	5	460	6	300	7	190	10	110	—	—
4½	1220	4½	600	5½	420	6½	280	7½	180	11	100	—	—
5	1020	5	580	6	400	7	260	8	170	—	—	—	—
—	—	6	520	6½	320	7½	240	8½	160	—	—	—	—
—	—	—	—	—	—	8	220	9	150	—	—	—	—
—	—	—	—	—	—	—	—	10	140	—	—	—	—

Rail Road Spikes 9-16ths square 5½ inches 160 per 100 pounds.
Rail Road Spikes 1-2 inch " 5½ " 200 per 100 pounds.

BURDEN'S PATENT SPIKES AND HORSE SHOES.

Manufactured at the Troy Iron and Nail Factory, Troy, New York.

Boat Spikes.		Ship Spikes.		Hook Head.		Horse Shoes.	
Size in inches.	No. in 100 lbs.	Size in inches.	No. in 100 lbs.	Size in inches.	No. in 100 lbs.	Size in inches.	No. in 100 lbs.
3	1750	4	800	4 × ⅜	555	1	84
3½	1468	4½	650	4½ × 7-16	414	2	75
4	1257	5	437	5 × ½	252	3	65
4½	920	5½	430	5½ × ½	241	4	56
5	720	6	420	5½ × 9-16	187	5	39
5½	630	6½	377	6 × 9-16	172	—	—
6	497	7	275	6 × ⅝	138	—	—
6½	478	7½	250	7 × 9-16	140	—	—
7	362	8	174	8 × ⅝	110	—	—
7½	337	8½	163	—	—	—	—
8	295	9	155	—	—	—	—
8½	290	10	115	—	—	—	—
9	210	—	—	—	—	—	—
10	198	—	—	—	—	—	—

Number of Composition Spikes to the 100 lbs.		
5	inch. round head, ·	500
5	" " square, · ·	434
5½	" " " · ·	400
6	" " " · ·	377
6½	" " " · ·	295
7	" " " · ·	275
7½	" " " · ·	210
8	" " " · ·	200
8½	" " " · ·	148

The great advantage of the half-cylinder bits was their ability to bore in a straight line, due to the long, stiff character of the cylindrical body of the bit. The disadvantage of helical augers, when used to drill deep holes as in keelson assemblies or in the throats of knees, is the tendency of the relatively limber bit to drift or wander, especially when the cutting edge encounters material of varying densities.

The cylindrical bit also consistently produced holes that did not go out of round during the boring process.

Where many holes were to be bored, a can of grease was kept close at hand into which the end of the auger could be dipped. Frequent lubrication kept the auger cutting freely, with less frequent sharpening.

Often the location of the hole was spotted and started with a small center bit which guaranteed accuracy of the required location.

In general there were three types of hole bored to accept fastenings. The type most commonly used was the "through" hole which entered one side of the timbers to be joined, and exited on the other side, completely penetrating both or all members involved.

Next was the "blind" hole, which was bored completely through the member being attached but only penetrating the holding member to within 2 or 3 inches of its total thickness. This applied to keel and keelson assemblies.

Third was the "two-drift" hole, which was used only for the installation of very long treenails. As described under "Treenails," this system consisted of boring two holes, the first of which was smaller than required for the designated treenail and completely penetrated the timbers involved. Then, by a procedure known as *counter-boring*, another auger of the designated size was bored into the first hole to about half the total depth of the timbers. A treenail with two appropriate diameters was turned for this specific use. The result of this two-drift method was that the long treenail did not require hard driving for its entire length.

Many fastenings were installed in locations where the top of the bolt head must be flush with the surface of the timber in order to accommodate the faying surface of another timber, as in the case of one tier of a keelson building upon another. Here the borer would sink a shallow counterbore of appropriate diameter to accommodate the bolt head.

In other situations, such as exterior planking, ceiling, and deck planking, a deeper counterbore was required in order to allow insertion of a wooden plug after the fastening had been driven.

The hole bored for a spike was equal in diameter to the square dimension of the spike—for example, ½-inch diameter for a ½-inch-square spike. This hole would be bored through the plank, after which a pilot hole approximately one-half the size would be bored into the holding timber to an appropriate depth. This pilot hole not only eased the driving of the spike, but it also dictated the direction the spike would take. Ship's spikes had an uncanny inclination to deflect and follow the grain of the wood into which they were being driven; this tended to damage the counterbored hole and also to dislodge the plank being fastened.

Wherever possible, holes for fastenings were not bored until the actual driving of the fastening was at hand, due to the wood's tendency to swell and holes to shrink in diameter if left unfilled for any great length of time in the damp environment that is indigenous to shipbuilding.

The boring of thousands of holes into the framing of a ship was, indeed, one of the true marvels of the building of wooden ships. Anyone can start to bore a hole in a desired location, but if the hole is to be 5 or 6 feet deep, not everyone will be able to bring the bottom of the hole out where it is intended—especially when boring through three or four tiers of wood, as in a vessel's keelson. Yet such holes were bored in countless numbers in building wooden ships—by skilled craftsmen who were, after all, only boring holes. Much that is not obvious remains buried forever. Much that is not true remains known forever. With most of the old wooden ships, only the name of the builder survives.

Fasteners

The fastener was now called upon to apply the skills of his trade. In driving a treenail or bolt home there was more involved than the simple action of using brute strength to swing a maul, mallet, or sledge against the end of the fastening.

Particular care is required when driving long treenails. Their extreme length makes them very limber, and, as they enter the bored hole and the grabbing resistance builds up, there is a growing danger of their being shattered or "crippled," in which case they cannot be further driven.

If this occurs, the damaged treenail must be extracted (a near impossibility), driven through, or bored out, in which case the substituted treenail is generally less efficient than the original one would have been.

Another concern in driving a treenail is the possibility of splintering its length at some phase of its being driven deep in the hole. This occurs when the fastener strikes the end of the treenail with a blow that is not truly square. A splintered treenail is beyond repair and guaranteed function, thus it must be replaced in the same manner as a crippled treenail.

To protect the vulnerable (driven) ends of long treenails, an iron cap was used. This was, in effect, a socket of suitable diameter and metal thickness to be easily slipped over the end of the treenail, to remain through the entire driving process.

To facilitate driving, the entering end of the treenail was slightly chamfered. This assisted the passage of the treenail through the bored hole and eliminated the possibility of tearing the wood fiber around the hole. The end of the treenail was frequently coated with a light application of grease or creosote to further ease the driving process.

After the treenail had been driven home solid, where driving through was not possible or when the treenail had been driven completely through all members, the protruding ends were sawn off flush with the surface of the timbers thus joined. Then both the inboard and outboard ends of the treenail were split with a chisel cut, to receive the wedge as described earlier under "Wedges." This cut was always made across the grain of the joined timbers, to eliminate the possibility of splitting the member being secured when the wedge was driven into the chisel cut.

After the wedge had been driven home solid, it, too, was cut off flush with the surface of the plank or timber. If the completed fastening appeared to be of doubtful integrity, a second step, "cross-wedging," was resorted to. This consisted of making another chisel cut in the end of the treenail at 90 degrees to the first and then driving home a second wedge which was also cut off flush. Further insurance against leakage through a treenail could be achieved by caulking all around it.

In addition to these general fastening procedures, plugs were sometimes used in the construction of clippers and other ships. It is recorded that the clipper ship *Dauntless* had all her treenails driven through, wedged, and plugged. When plugs were installed they were always positioned with the grain of the wood running in the same direction as the timber in which they were inserted.

By far the most extensive and most difficult task of the fastener was that of driving the countless bolts that pierced the ship's timbers and bound them securely together. In addition to the sheer power required to force bolts through undersize holes of extreme depth were the obstacles of very limited space in which to work, in many cases, and also the disadvantageous position from which a heavy sledge or maul must be swung. A further challenge was the fact that every blow must be struck squarely in order to avoid damaging the fastening being driven. It is not difficult to realize that the trade of journeyman fastener was one with its own particular skills.

Bolts, as referred to in wooden shipbuilding of the period, were round rods of iron or nonferrous metal of any desired diameter and length. They were not threaded as we think of bolts in present-day terms.

There were a variety of ways in which bolts were installed in a ship, probably the simplest and easiest being the driving home of the "blunt" bolt. Such a bolt was sized in length so as to stop short of totally penetrating the piece of wood which was to do the holding. The borer had already bored the required hole and the appropriate blunt was on hand before the fastener began his work.

Composition or copper bolts, when driven through the tiers of multiple-tiered keels, might be headed beforehand or might start as merely a round rod, heading themselves as they were driven.

Heading of non-ferrous bolts in advance of their being driven was, in general, considered unnecessary in terms of labor and efficiency. The rule of thumb that had been handed down through the years was that, if the relationship between the diameter of the bolt and the diameter of the hole was in accordance with practice, the bolt would head itself perfectly while being driven. The progress of this heading depended upon the length of the fastening, and this was easily judged by the experienced fastener.

Since the holding power of the blunt bolt was contained in its grip upon the sides of the hole, it remained for the fastener to assure that the head was flush with the surface of the timber in order that no protrusion would interfere with the snug fit of any prospective faying surface.

Iron blunts were sometimes heated and headed prior to use (sometimes headed cold) due to the hardness of the iron and its relatively great resistance to deformity and self-heading while being driven. Heading a bolt generally consisted of placing a rod, cold or heated as might be considered necessary by the blacksmith, over a suitable form on an anvil and beating down the end until it was spread to the desired shape.

In the construction of a ship, composition and copper blunts were generally used in way of the lower false stem and gripe, and were driven into the stem from outside to inside. Iron blunts were driven through the upper false stem above the waterline into the stem, from outside to inside; through the stern knee into the keel; down through the keelson assembly into the keel; and in other locations as required.

Iron through-bolts were installed in two ways, depending on whether the bolt was the type that would be headed prior to driving, or simply a round rod of sufficient length to fully penetrate all members that were to be secured to each other. ("Sufficient" length included excess material at each end for cutting off and clinching.) The headed iron bolt was used in situations where the greatest stresses would not be expected. After being driven, a clinch ring or plate would be installed over the entering end or point. The non-headed bolt was used where the most extreme loads could be anticipated, and these bolts were clinched over a clinch ring at each end.

The gripping power of the wood around the bolts is very difficult to comprehend. An example that brings this into perspective is the fact that a 1-inch iron bolt driven 3 feet into a fir timber, in a properly bored hole, will hold so fast that the bolt will fail in tension before it will pull out of the hole.

Another accepted rule of practice followed by the fastener was that each fastening should not drive more than ¼ inch under each of the final six blows of the sledge.

After the iron bolt had been driven through, it was ready to be clinched at one or both ends, as the situation required. As has been described earlier (see "Clinch Rings"), the bolt was allowed to protrude the thickness of the clinch ring plus one-half the diameter of the bolt to allow for clinching.

Figure 4.3. *Clinching a through-bolt.*

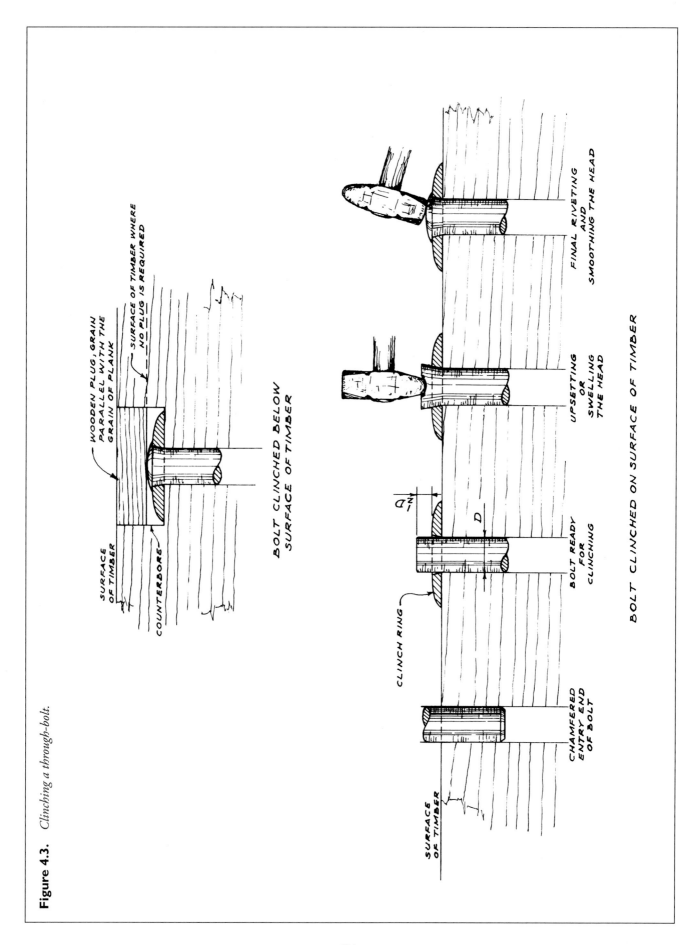

SURFACE OF TIMBER

WOODEN PLUG, GRAIN PARALLEL WITH THE GRAIN OF PLANK

SURFACE OF TIMBER WHERE NO PLUG IS REQUIRED

COUNTERBORE

BOLT CLINCHED BELOW SURFACE OF TIMBER

SURFACE OF TIMBER

CHAMFERED ENTRY END OF BOLT

CLINCH RING

BOLT READY FOR CLINCHING

D

a_1^2

UPSETTING OR SWELLING THE HEAD

FINAL RIVETING AND SMOOTHING THE HEAD

BOLT CLINCHED ON SURFACE OF TIMBER

A snug-fitting clinch ring was slipped over the end of the rod and solidly seated on the timber, or in the counterbore if the situation required one. An important part of the fastener's skill now came into play. We now see the reason for having a countersunk rather than a straight hole through the clinch ring, as illustrated in Figure 4.3.

The secret to the success of the clinching operation was to swell out or *upset* the bolt immediately at the bottom of the hole in the clinch ring in order to prevent the bolt's initial tendency to back out in the process of clinching. This was accomplished by striking the end of the bolt squarely in the center with several sharp blows of a peening hammer, dimpling the end of the bolt so that the deformed metal swelled out and jammed against the bottom of the hole in the clinch ring. (A different tactic was used with short bolts to prevent backing-out of the rod. Instead of upsetting the end of the bolt, the opposite end was "bucked up" by another worker.)

Once the end of the rod had been upset and thus fixed in position, clinching was accomplished by *peening* or rounding the remaining metal into the countersunk hole of the clinch ring, making a smooth button or flat head. This operation required care and skill in order to avoid splitting the iron bolt and thus jeopardizing the integrity of the head that had been formed.

The task of driving extremely long iron bolts is effectively brought into focus by the realization that some of the bolts in the navel timbers of *Great Republic* required the use of a pile-driving machine.

The driving of spikes and dumps was probably the easiest of the fastener's responsibilities. Spikes were required in laying deck planking, securing ceiling and exterior planking, in some instances building the keel assembly, and in the toes of knees.

In general spikes and dumps were driven until the head reached the bottom of the counterbore in the member. Where used to fasten deck and other planking they were then punched home with a *set*. This action had the effect of snugging down the planking as the fasteners progressed, and assured that the head was well beneath the surface of the plank in order to accommodate a tight-fitting wooden plug, which would cover the fastening for the sake of appearance or as protection against water and weather.

Spikes and dumps, made with chisel points (Figure 4.1), were driven with the broad part of the point at 90 degrees to the grain of the wood. In this position the point acted like a punch to force its way through the wood with little danger of splitting it. If the fastening were positioned so that the broad part of the point was parallel with the wood grain, it would act exactly as a wedge would be expected to act, and with the same results—the prospect of a split where least desirable.

Building wooden ships called for creating a huge structure from a vast accumulation of relatively small parts. It follows that these individual parts, once fashioned into their final form, must be assembled and securely held together to function as a unit—principally by the bolt.

In the course of assembly the number of bolts seemed countless. However, as representative examples, it is recorded that the clipper *Westward Ho* had 1,325 bolts driven through her waterways, beams, and timbers in the tween decks alone. The clipper *Bald Eagle* had 1,452 bolts driven through the same members.

Chapter Five

SCARPHS

A *SCARPH* IS THE JOINING of two lengths of timber by cutting matching tapers in the mating ends of the pieces of wood, and then securing them in a manner that achieves continuity of the completed assembly. Where necessary this process may be repeated with many pieces until the desired length is reached.

To satisfy the great length requirements of material for a ship, the scarph allows for the fabrication of long, strong structural timbers where only relatively short material is available. For this reason, the scarph has become almost uniquely associated with the construction of wooden vessels.

It is known to have been used by Egyptian and Phoenician shipbuilders. At a much later date tangible evidence was uncovered when an Anglo-Saxon burial mound that dated about 600 A.D. was excavated in 1939 near the town of Woodbridge, in Suffolk, England. Among the contents brought to light were the remains of a clinker-built (lap-strake) ship that proved to be 89 feet long, in which overlap scarphs were used to hold strakes of planking together endways by means of rivets. Both the stem and sternpost had been scarphed into the ends of the keel plank and were held in place by iron bolts. These examples constitute conclusive visual evidence that scarphing as we picture it is of quite ancient origin.

This discovery establishes a definite date of scarphing's existence. However, for actual origin we must reach much farther back in time. Exactly when or where the conventional tapered scarf first appeared will probably never be known. Still, it is known, as a general fact, that the Romans and, before them, the Phoenicians were well acquainted with the tapered scarph.

Let us advance to the year 1418, when King Henry V of England ordered that three ships be built. One of these, *Grace De Dieu*, was built at Southampton by Huggekyns, Master Carpenter of the King's Ships. In 1439 it burned and sank onto a mud flat at Bursledon. In 1933, when the Bursledon wreck was studied closely, one of the findings was

that the individual pieces of the built-up frames had been joined together by flat, tapered scarphs.

In 1605, Phineas Pett (1570–1647), one of a famous family of shipbuilders for the Royal Navy, was given his patent as a master shipwright by King James I, of England, and only two years later succeeded Matthew Baker as Master of the Shipwrights Company of England. In the same year, 1607, Phineas made a ship model for Prince Henry which so pleased the king that he ordered Pett to build a "great" ship in strict accordance with the model. A great ship was a capital ship, larger than a galleon. The keel, 115 feet long, was laid in October 1608, to the great consternation of all other master shipwrights, who were of the opinion—apparently well founded—-that Phineas Pett had never really learned his craft.

As work on the "great" ship proceeded, the master shipwrights became more and more resentful and finally submitted a written report to the king in May 1609, at which time he was holding his own royal inquiry. As might be expected, they fired a broadside which contained no diplomatic opinions, stating flatly that "her mould is altogether imperfect." From that sweeping statement, the six master shipwrights proceeded to dissect every aspect of the ship's form. They made certain that nothing about the ship was sound, safe, or well designed.

One complaint had to do with the working of the framing timbers. The master shipwrights reported, "The futtocks have not scarph enough with the floor timbers." The meaning of the statement, as we would put it, is that the floor timbers and the futtocks did not have sufficient *overlap* to develop proper strength; thus the definition of the word *scarph* is easily understood and verified in usage.

In 1711 scarphs were spoken of in detail as part of the structural procedure of shipbuilding, apparently for the first time. In that year William Sutherland, who called himself a shipwright and mariner, produced the first textbook for shipwrights, which he called *The Shipbuilders Assistant*. The book was divided into parts or essays, including one entitled "Solidity" in which Sutherland states that the keel is laid, trimmed, scarphed, and rabbeted on the keel blocks. He also states that the stem is scarphed to the keel, and that the keelson is scarphed and bolted through the floors to the keel.

From this time on until the demise of the great wooden ships as viable modes of transportation, the scarph was treated with great respect and consideration because it was, when all aspects were taken into account, the weakest part of even the strongest members. Like all other phases of shipbuilding, the scarph was subject to endless experimentation in an effort to improve its efficiency; so, while its configurations and details may not be innumerable, there were nevertheless many detailed forms of scarph.

Development of the Scarph

Shown in Figure 5.1 are some of the principal scarph forms that came into existence, ranging from the simplest to the more complex. They all had an identical function—namely, the transfer of the strength of one short piece of timber, through the scarphed joint to the next piece of timber until the final structural unit was formed.

Of the types of scarph shown, only a few are known with certainty to have been employed in American clipper ship construction. Each scarph type had merits and faults for various applications.

Except for the illustrations of plain and beam scarphs, which show the general method of securing the faying surfaces of the scarph in order to hold the two parts in position, the fastenings have been omitted in order to emphasize the form of the scarph. However, in every case, sufficient fastening was required, and this was generally dictated by the individual shipbuilder or designer according to his own version of what was necessary to form an efficient and successful joint.

Scarphs were generally fastened with a combination of bolts and spikes. The most universal method was to drive two spikes into each end of the scarph. To avoid damaging the timber, the spikes were always driven through the thin toe into the mating thick portion, thus achieving maximum grip. Whenever possible, bolts were also driven through the thin part of the scarph into the thick portion, at which end they were clinched or riveted. The bolting pattern varied, depending upon the location and use of the individual scarph.

Plain Scarph
The *plain scarph*, the simplest form, consisted merely of two matching slopes which, when fayed, combined to increase into one single length the combined lengths of several

timbers generally of the same cross-sectional size. Its principal asset was that it was very easy to fabricate, being composed of two matching plane surfaces that were obtained by merely making two straight cuts.

When joined together, the cross-sectional area of such a scarph is the same as that of the parent timbers. However, the efficiency of the joint, which is a mechanical connection, is not equal to the strength of the timbers thus connected. The loss of strength has two causes, one of which is the loss of material removed to allow installation of the fastenings. Also, all material that extends beyond the end fastening on each thin end of the slope is ineffective and, if it were practical to do so, could be removed without causing harm to the scarphed joint. Thus, these small areas of material must be deducted from the original sectional area of the timbers, which renders a transfer of 100-percent efficiency an impossibility.

This plain scarph was an effective connection when used in stationary construction—for instance, in the beams of a barn or other large structure—and could be used in either a horizontal or vertical plane when the beam was positioned. However, it was not acceptable in shipbuilding, for two principal reasons. One was the fact that the thin, feather edges of the joint were subject to splitting, splintering, and rot. The second was that a wooden ship, being a live and moving structure, induced alternating stresses in any mechanical connections. This meant that, in the plain scarph, the bolts were in a constantly changing shear pattern that had too great potential for failure. Therefore, this type of scarph was excluded from shipbuilding practice.

Beam Scarph
The *beam scarph*, a modified and improved form of the plain scarph, effectively eliminated the vulnerable feather edges of the plain scarph by offsetting the timbers to be scarphed. This resulted in only one level surface and required that the beam be installed with the scarph in the vertical plane; however, this limitation was acceptable without question since all beams when scarphed were generally installed with the scarph in that position.

Another asset of this particular scarph was that sufficient offset could be provided to allow the resultant cross section to equal or even exceed that of the parent timbers, thus transferring 100 percent of strength through the scarph.

In the plain scarph, the fastenings work in shear to resist the natural tendency of the timbers to slide along the slope; the beam scarph overcame this drawback by means of snug-fitting dowels let into each half of the joint. This allowed the fastenings to function solely in tension as they compressed the two halves of the joint against each other.

The beam scarph also featured a tie-bolt inserted through the thin end of each portion of the scarph. This secured the

Figure 5.1. *Some types of scarphs.*

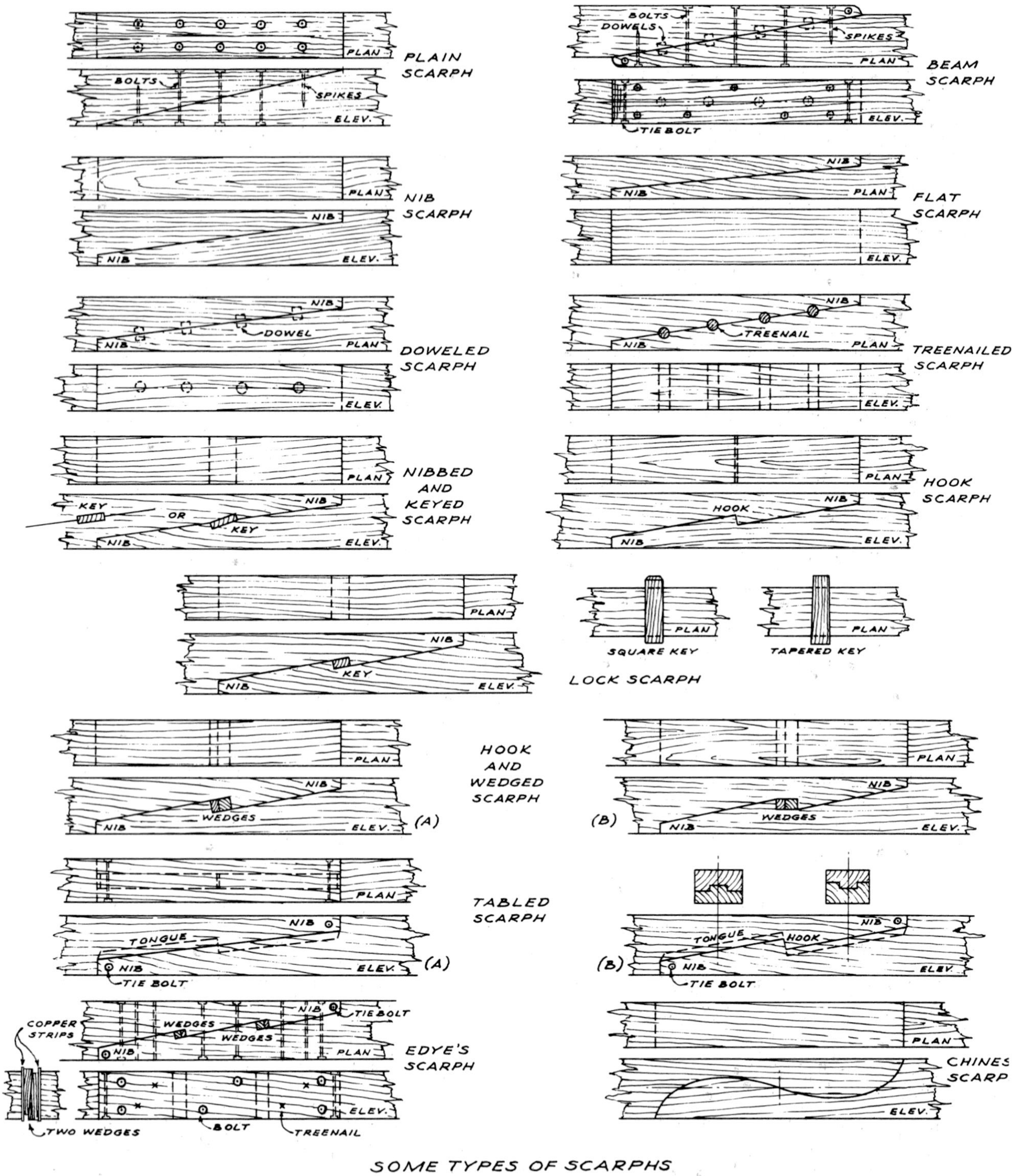

ends of the timbers against splitting due to stress, variation of the load, or aging of the wood.

A negative feature of this scarph was that it caused each component timber to have its own longitudinal centerline that was offset several inches from that of its neighbor. This could be a source of confusion in shipbuilding, which in most respects features absolute symmetry along each side of a ship.

A second objection was that any dowels inserted between the halves of the joint had to be installed with the utmost care and exactness of fit if they were to contribute to the well-being of the scarph. In addition, once the scarph was completed there was no assurance that the dowels would properly function throughout the life of the beam.

There is no specific instance noted where this scarph was used in the building of the clipper ships.

Nib Scarph

The *nib scarph*, as a development of the plain scarph, not only eliminated the objectionable feather ends of each cut, but was also the simplest form of scarph to find its way into certain phases of shipbuilding.

As with any other scarph, precision and accuracy were essential to the successful functioning of this joint. There were certain recognized rules governing its proportions. In length it was never less than five times the thickness of the timber being scarphed. This proportion could be exceeded where required to accommodate necessary fastenings. The depth of the nib is quoted in some cases as being one-eighth the thickness of the timber; other sources call for a nib to be as much as one-fifth of the thickness. In many instances the depth of the nib was dictated by the designer's personal preference; this also applied to the length of the scarph in excess of the minimum length.

An asset of the nib scarph is that, when skillfully made, with all faying surfaces achieving substantial, solid contact, it eliminates any shear load across the bolts if the scarph is subjected to any compressive load along its axis, as could take place when a ship was working heavily in a seaway. Instead, the compressive force would be resisted by the nibs butting against their fitted cutouts in the parent timbers, thus contributing greatly to the joint's strength and stability.

However, in the opposite situation, where the scarph is subject to tension loading, the nibs were of no benefit, and the fastenings were subject to shear except to the extent that friction in the joint absorbed some of the load. If taken to extremes, this might cause the scarph to work and thus diminish its integrity. (Much of this loading is theoretical and never comes to pass, but it does point out the relative strength and weakness of a given joint.)

Adversely, the nib scarph reduced the cross-sectional area of the beam by the depth of the cut. This reduced the bending strength of the entire assembly and became the area around which such strength would be calculated if such an occasion arose.

Finally, the introduction of the nib scarph allowed members that were decorative as well as functional—taffrails, as an example—to be joined in a pleasing and practical manner by avoiding short-graining the substance of the rail where sudden tight curves were required to accommodate any required contour.

Flat Scarph

The *flat scarph* was no more than a nib scarph formed and used in a vertical plane. This was referred to by the English as the "French system."

Shipbuilders felt that this particular scarph was effective in the construction of such members as bilge keelsons, shelves, and clamps. But, as in many other details, much was left to the discretion of the individual shipbuilder.

The flat scarph was also used in ceiling and other interior planking where the planks were relatively wide in relation to their thickness. Cutting the slope of the joint in the plane of the greatest width provided ample surface into which the fastenings could be inserted.

Doweled Scarph

The *doweled scarph* was the initial improvement to the original nib scarph. The nibs and slope were cut in the same manner as before so as to provide a tight, accurate fit. Then a series of dowels, perhaps four, were equally spaced along the centerline of the slope, and driven in *normal* (at a 90-degree angle) to the surface of the slope. Matching holes were bored in the faying piece to accept the dowel pins; then the scarphed pieces were assembled and appropriate bolts driven through the members, and headed or clinched as in the beam scarph. The dowels were helpful in maintaining alignment of the members while the holes were being bored to receive the fastenings.

In contrast to the nib scarph, which could resist only compressive end forces through the wood itself, the doweled scarph achieved a joint that could resist tensile forces because of the presence of the dowel pins, which could act in shear against such forces and thus relieve the bolts of any such loading. In this way the through-bolts, now working only in tension as they forced the members together, were relieved of any other function, and the scarphed joint effectively resisted any undue working caused by a ship laboring in heavy seas.

The principal deficiency in the doweled joint lay in the fact that, with the dowels completely hidden from view, there was no way of being certain that they were performing as was expected. The initial fit may not have been entirely perfect, and the dowels were subject to shrinkage. In either case, the scarph's efficiency was impaired.

Treenailed Scarph

The *treenailed scarph* was a further improvement to both the nib and the doweled scarphs. It was made in the same form as these scarphs; however, in lieu of dowels, treenails were fitted after the joint had been completely assembled and bolted.

Holes were bored for the treenails—generally four, as in the case of dowels—completely across the faying slope so that one-half of each hole pierced each timber. The holes were bored perpendicular to the surface of the timbers. Then treenails, usually locust, of appropriate diameter, were driven through the holes and their ends trimmed flush with the surface of the joined timbers. The treenails performed the same function as the dowels, resisting any tensile loading of the joint.

The obvious advantages of this scarph were that the bored holes were in guaranteed alignment and the treenails remained visible. Also the treenails now acted as stopwaters, effectively prohibiting the passage of water along the faying surfaces if the scarph was used in a wetted area.

Nibbed and Keyed Scarph

The *nibbed and keyed scarph* was a further improvement of the original nib scarph. After the timbers had been suitably cut and fitted, a *keyway*, perpendicular to the surface of the timbers but canted in reference to the sloping faces of the joint, was cut through the scarph.

Matching halves of the keyway were cut in each of the faying surfaces. Once assembled, a tight-fitting spline called a *key* was driven through and trimmed flush. This scarph then functioned in the same manner as the doweled and treenailed versions.

Hook Scarph

The hook scarph, in its various forms, was the most advanced and successful of all scarph developments. In any of its several forms it accomplished continuity of the joint under conditions of both compression and tension. As in all other nibbed scarphs, the nibs being jammed against each other resisted compressive forces. The new element, the hook, eliminated tensile forces. Thus, the nibs and hook combined to allow the fastenings to function solely in tension as they held the two parts of the joint together.

Greater accuracy and skill were required in order to assure perfect matching of the mating parts. This in itself made the hook scarph more expensive to form, but its structural advantages were so superior that the cost was tolerated with little or no question.

As in all scarphs containing internal corners, such as those at the bottom of the nibs and the hook, it was of paramount importance that the shipwright did not let his crosscut saw travel any deeper than required to form a sharp, square cor-

ner. To overcut the wood in any amount was to set up an area where great stresses could concentrate, much to the detriment of the structure.

The hook scarph, no matter what its detailed form, was used to join all principal structural members in every type of wooden vessel. It was in no way the sole province of the clipper ship.

Lock Scarph

The *lock scarph* was a hook scarph in which the hook in each piece of the joint was deliberately cut short of faying with its corresponding part. This separation or *keyway* was made large enough to allow a structurally stout batten, or *key*, to be driven completely through the resultant opening.

The function of the keyway was to allow expanding the two parts of the scarph so that the nibs seated with great force against their corresponding recesses. To accomplish this the keyway could be cut in one of two ways: either with parallel sides, or with a taper, the width of the entry side being slightly larger than the width of the exiting side.

If the sides of the keyway were parallel, the builder would cut a slightly oversize rectangular batten of sufficient length to span the width of the timbers, plus some working excess was cut. The entering end was chamfered, the batten possibly greased, and then it was driven home and trimmed flush on each side. This resulted in the buildup of tremendous pressures and a perfectly fitting scarph.

If the sides of the keyway were cut with a taper, the batten to be used as a key was cut with a corresponding taper and driven home in the same manner. This second method had two advantages, one being greater working tolerance, the other the possibility of achieving great compressive pressures that could be controlled by the judgment of the shipwright.

Hook and Wedged Scarph

The hook and wedged scarph was identical to the lock scarph, except for the manner of tightening the joint after the mating pieces were assembled but not yet fastened.

Here the keyway, instead of being filled by a single key, was filled by a pair of identical wedges whose faying surfaces were tapered to match each other and whose total cross-sectional area was a constant rectangle throughout its length. Each wedge was driven at its large end from opposite sides of the timbers until the compressive tightness satisfied the judgment of the shipwright. When the wedges had been driven home, the ends were trimmed flush with the surfaces of the scarphed timbers.

Little has been written about the details of scarphs actually used in clipper ship construction, other than the fact that certain members were scarphed. The most notable exception occurs in the tabulation of scantlings of the McKay clippers,[2] in which the keel scarphs are recorded as being "hooked and wedged." In addition, the lengths of the scarphs, the thickness of the nib ends, and the fastening details—namely types, size, and material—are also given. This same information is provided for scarphing the stem and the keelsons, with certain detailed exceptions.

There was at least one variation to the hook and wedged scarph, in which the hook was cut perpendicular to the outside surface of the timber, and the flat of the keyway was cut parallel to that surface. Both cuts were normal (perpendicular) to the sides of the affected timbers. As with all other hooked or keyed scarphs, this variation held great restraint against both tension and compression loads in the members, thus relieving the fastenings of shear stresses.

Tabled Scarph

The *tabled scarph* is probably the oldest of the scarphs used in the construction of very large structural members such as the keel. In the era of building wooden ships of the line, the keel was the backbone and principal longitudinal strength member of the ship. Ponderous keelsons and riders, such as were typical of the construction of clipper ships, had not yet appeared in hull construction. Therefore, the shipbuilders were very much aware of the need for utmost efficiency in the scarphing of keels. Their solution to the problem was the development of the tabled scarph. The details of its design resulted in a joint with longitudinal strength equal to that of any scarph subsequently developed, and lateral or transverse strength which exceeded that of scarphs yet to come. However, because of the precise fit of its mating parts, it was an expensive scarph to make due to the labor involved.

In later years, various designs of scarph were developed with the intention of maintaining structural strength and, at the same time, reducing the cost and precision required to achieve an effective joint. Thus, by the time the clipper ship arrived, the tabled scarph had apparently disappeared.

There is no reference to the tabled scarph in any descriptive texts or listings of structural requirements for the ships listed in this book. One reason for this is that, over a period of years, it was found that the transverse strength qualities of the scarph had been proven to be unnecessary. However, even though the scarph was not used, its general details should be noted here, if only for comparative purposes.

The tabled scarph was made in two basic forms. The simpler form was related to the nib scarph, whereas the more sophisticated form was designed around the hook scarph. Within the two forms there were variations in the proportions of the *tabling*, the raised portion or *tongue* of the joint (similar to the coak used in building up a made-mast). Basically, the tabling was one-half the length of the joint, and one-third the breadth of the siding of the parent timbers; the height of the tongue was about 1½ inches. Each of these di-

mensions was subject to the preferences of the individual shipbuilder.

The reason the tabling contributed to the transverse strength of the scarph was that when the joint was being tooled, this material was not removed. Thus the tongue remained as an integral part of the parent wood and was able to function even without fastenings.

To accommodate the tongue, a recess of corresponding size was dug out of the scarph of the timber to be joined. As with all other scarphs, the mating pieces of the scarph were cut to identical and symmetrical patterns. It is important to note that the tongue was always raised on the thin or nib end of the scarph.

The hooked variation of the tabled scarph was fabricated in the same manner as the previous type, the defining exception being that all tabling was done around the configuration of the basic hooked scarph.

Both variations of this scarph had a tie-bolt inserted through the end of each nib to ensure against splitting. The through-fastenings that connected the two parts of the scarph were placed sufficiently close to the centerline of the keel to ensure lack of interference with the cutting of the keel rabbet.

Edye Scarph

The *Edye scarph* was introduced into shipbuilding by a Mr. Edye who was Foreman of Shipwrights and Foreman of the Yard at the Plymouth (England) Dockyard from July 31, 1826, to December 31, 1829. The scarph was not Mr. Edye's invention, it having been used by house carpenters for many years prior to its adoption by the Royal dockyards, but Edye saw its potential for superior performance as a beam scarph on board ships where all joints were subject to constant working. After its initial adoption (the exact date is unknown), it was used in the dockyards, until wooden beams were superseded by iron.

The scarph was so efficient, it would reputedly allow a beam to deflect as one piece, even without fastenings, if it was accurately formed and assembled. It was an unusual scarph, being well removed from the more popular variations shown in Figure 5.1; for this reason it seems worthy of a brief description.

As with most scarphs, its length varied with the scantlings of the beam, but the average length was about 8 feet. This length was trisected after the nib depths had been laid off and connected by a straight line. Then, starting at one nib, three parallel faces were laid off, ending at the opposite nib. Hooks were cut short of and parallel with each other in order to provide two keyways of suitable size.

After assembly of the two members but before fastenings were installed, a strip of copper was placed along each side of each keyway; then a pair of wedges was inserted into opposite sides of each keyway and driven home. As in the beam scarph, a tie-bolt was inserted through the end of each nib, thus securing the nibs against the possibility of splitting. Final fastening was accomplished by installation of six bolts and four treenails, located as shown in the illustration.

Even though Edye's scarph was used for the duration of wooden ship building, it had its early detractors, one of them being James Peake, Assistant Master Shipwright at the Woolwich (England) Dockyard. Peake wrote a book on naval architecture in 1851[7] in which he expressed the opinion that this scarph was inferior to the doweled scarphs.

Whether or not the Edye scarph ever reached the shores of the United States cannot be verified. In the descriptions of clipper ship construction, little was written about their deckbeams, other than the scantlings and fastenings used. A reasonable assumption may be made that each individual builder used his own judgment in the matter.

Chinese Scarph

The *Chinese scarph* is shown only as a matter of interest. Its configuration could be classed as a cultural development, for so far as is known, it never found its way into American or European shipbuilding, the basic reason being that it was time-consuming to fabricate. The occidental penchant for haste was just as strong as the oriental fascination for skillful fitting and eye-catching lines, even at the cost of valuable time.

The worth and working of this scarph, however, should at least be observed. Even though the Chinese scarph contained no straight lines, except the flatness that occurred at any point across the faying surfaces, it had all the merits of plain, nib, and hook scarphs.

As in the plain scarph, the effective cross-sectional area was constant and proportionate in size to the timbers to be joined. There was no loss of area, such as occurs when a nib is cut in a member. However, unlike the plain scarph, the Chinese variation eliminated the vulnerable feather edges at the ends of the joint; likewise, it avoided the loss of area of the nib.

Compression stresses were taken up at each end of the scarph as the curves at the ends of the timbers jammed against their matching cutouts. Tension stresses were absorbed by the lobe of each member being curved across the centerline and back again, as shown in the illustration; this way the portions of the scarph at mid-point could not ride over one another under tensile loading unless the fastenings were to fail.

Another favorable feature of this scarph was the absence of sharp inside corners such as occur in the way of nibs and hooks. Such corners are always points of high structural stresses and are well avoided under most circumstances.

Chapter Six

REPRESENTATIVE MIDSHIP SECTIONS

SHIPBUILDING THROUGH THE AGES has been the product of three basic tenets: experience, proportion, and development, each phase encountered in the order stated.

Early man discovered that if he straddled a floating log, he did not have to do anything further to remain afloat—an ability he was quick to put to good use. However, a log is generally as broad as it is deep, and, therefore, basically unstable. The man astride the log soon found that he spent as much time under water as he did above it, due to this basic instability. This was experience.

With the aid of reasoning and, no doubt, considerable frustration, he discovered that if two logs were secured together side by side with vines or hide or other means, he could sit astride this structure, which now had a breadth twice as great as its depth, without concern about becoming wet. He had now introduced stability into his structure. At the same time he probably discovered that the length of the logs was of little consequence except as a matter of convenience or inconvenience, depending upon their size and weight. This was proportion.

Somewhat later, with the aid of experience and further reasoning, he learned that, by securing a greater number of logs side by side, his craft could accommodate a greater number of his fellows and support goods and materials as well.

Time passed and, as it did, this elementary floating craft became the beneficiary of countless experimentations and simple changes until it developed into a bona fide structure composed of many individual parts. Bringing greater size and refinement to the structure also suggested a new element as part of the fabrication: strength. After all, what would be the point of making a structure that could not survive in its appointed element? From this time onward it would now be necessary to factor in four basic considerations: experience, proportion, development, and strength.

By 1600, proportion was based upon the breadth of the ship at its widest point. This dimension was the unit around which practically all other measurements were determined.

Thus, a greater breadth allowed for a greater depth, and these two allowed for greater length. So, quite obviously, these larger structures required component members of greater strength in order to be self-supporting and to withstand the ferocity of hostile seas.

As shipbuilding advanced through the centuries and individual vessels increased in size, the structural members also grew in size and number, not by mathematical determination but according to the results of the most recent construction. In this manner the sizes of timbers—the *scantlings*—were increased by the amount deemed sufficient or necessary. Many successful vessels were constructed along this "try as you go" philosophy; but many vessels, though built using the same system, likely met an unhappy fate.

Two considerations were paramount: the structural strength of each individual wood, and its potential effective life span as a reliable structural member when exposed to all the elements associated with the sea. These considerations became an iron-bound premise of the trade; almost without exception the findings were religiously followed by the shipbuilding community.

Marine Insurance and Classification

While all this information was being gathered and informally catalogued, another activity was being carefully pursued and enlarged: the business of insurance. Since all phases of shipbuilding were commercial ventures involving large amounts of money by all parties concerned, it became a matter of business acumen for these interested parties to produce a vessel that would be readily acceptable to the insurers as a matter of reasonable risk. If this was done, then the entire venture involving a ship allowed each party to be protected against financial disaster.

As might be expected, the insurers were the ones to view the overall procedures with the most critical eye. To protect themselves, they ultimately collected all the known data concerning wood, fastenings, scantlings, distribution and general location of structural members, and all the other loosely followed parameters of shipbuilding, and assembled them into a formal table of ship classifications. This concerted action became a fact with the formation in London, in 1760, of Lloyd's Register of Shipping, an association that would control the construction of merchant vessels and determine their classification. All phases and requirements of shipbuilding that the association deemed acceptable were spelled out in a set of ship classifications with rules and specifications, ranging from the most highly qualified to the least qualified.

This British concept of shipbuilding reached America's shores as European-trained shipbuilders migrated to the United States and, in the glory years of American clipper ship construction, 1850–1856, were the rules by which American builders abided. It was not until 1858 that American-built ships became governed by their own rules in the form of the *New York Marine Register, A Standard of Classification of American Vessels.*

In reality, the various sets of rules and practices adhered to by the reputable shipbuilders were not very different, simply because the awesome powers of the world's oceans did not differentiate between the ships of various nations.

By the time these events transpired, the building of a large ship had become a great and complicated task. Woods of all types were being tested to their limits of strength. The means of fastening the many components together was becoming a considerable problem, and the great size of wooden ships was placing undue burdens on the very fabric of the ships themselves.

The vessels that were built, however, were in many cases the marvels of their time, regardless of size. The clipper ships, being large and formidable looking, were understandably the ones to attract the eye and to perform in historic fashion. However, the clipper ship was a type, based principally on hull form, and not all of them were of great size. Large or small, they were all built in the same general manner; the internal structures were quite similar except for magnitude.

The Midship Section and Variations of Hull Form

Being a creation of such variable configuration, absence of plane surfaces, and lack of straight lines, a vessel's hull immediately imparts to a viewer the fact that no single vantage point, picture, or hull section will suffice to reveal all the details within, to evaluate the qualities of a given ship. It is for this reason that so many views and details must be

drawn about the principal reference points used in the design and development of even the simplest of ship hulls.

However, there are occasions when one does not have access to all necessary plans, or perhaps one might only be hurriedly interested in a ship's characteristics. Taking this situation even further to its absolute basic minimum—the inspection of only one drawing or sketch that would indicate the vessel's most revealing characteristics—the selected view would no doubt be a section drawn through its midship frame, the *midship* or *dead flat section.*

No single view of a ship reveals so much of the individuality of the vessel. The first, most obvious detail is the amount of deadrise, indicating whether or not the hull is full bodied. Wide, hard bilges, if evident, would indicate carrying capacity. Swell of the sides or wall-sidedness can be seen and evaluated, along with such obvious details as the number of decks, structure of keel and keelsons, frames and interior structure. If this midship section is complete in all details, the scantlings of these members will be noted, thus revealing the strength of the ship's basic structure.

Of course, many qualities and details will not appear in the midship section due to the limitations of a one-plane view, but in shipbuilding very few unexpected surprises occur throughout the length and breadth of a ship of a given type such as a clipper, packet, or cargo carrier. So, based upon the common practices of an era, much that is not actually shown may be surmised with a great deal of general, if not detailed, accuracy.

This chapter includes illustrations of the midship sections of a selection of vessels. The information shown is taken from tables of moulded offsets, body plans, lists of scantlings, and descriptions of various ships as they floated at dockside.

Also included is Table 6.1, listing the various classifications of vessel starting with the smallest and concluding with the largest. The vessels referred to in this table are representative of the required hull structure based upon the depth of hold.

The various sources from which the information has been extracted are contemporary with the period of the vessels involved and are all of a reliable nature. This being the case, there will no doubt be questions raised and some puzzlement generated when, in several cases, the midship section of a ship appears twice with different internal details depicted in each. This situation is by no means rare, but it can be perplexing: if having no information to record leaves many blank areas in a volume such as this, having two or perhaps more descriptions of the same item that are not in agreement is vexing and unsettling. Where this occurs, some explanation will be attempted in order to rationalize, if not irrefutably clarify, the particular situation.

Not all of the ships have complete source material, and, unfortunately for posterity, there are many ships listed in this

Table 6.1. *Categories of hull classification based on depth of hold.*

Beams and decks	Depth of hold	Vessel	Remarks	Figure
One laid deck	12'-1	Eringo, bark	Half poop deck	6.3
One laid deck and hold beams	15'-0	Sultana, bark	Half poop deck	6.4
One laid deck and hold beams partially decked	16'-0	Racehorse, bark	Half poop deck. Hold beams decked at ends only.	6.5
Two laid decks	21'-0	Stag Hound		6.6 & 6.7
	21'-6	Flying Cloud		6.8 & 6.9
	23'-0	Lightning		6.10 & 6.11
	24'-0	Red Jacket		6.12
Two laid decks and hold beams	26'-0	Golden Fleece		6.13
Two laid decks and hold beams partially decked	25'-0	Hoogly	Hold beams decked at ends only.	6.14
	25'-9	Wizard	Hold beams decked at ends only; narrow gangway, P/S.	6.15
Three laid decks	25'-6	Challenge		6.16
	25'-9	Young America		6.17
	26'-4 (Also given as 28'-0)	Sierra Nevada	Open vent streak along center line, lower deck.	6.18
Four laid decks	39'-0	Great Republic	39'-0 is the whole depth.	6.19 & 6.20

Note: The depth of hold was the criterion by which the number of decks and beams was established.

book of which very little is known in the realm of details. However, the details shown are indicative and probably typical of the American-built clipper ship. Since ships are symmetrical about their longitudinal centerline, only one side of the ship is shown in each case. This is common practice, saving much time, space, and needless repetition.

Figure 6.1 represents the midship section of a typical clipper ship. The outline of the hull is not that of a particular vessel, and the figures that follow will show many similarities and just as many differences which appeared in clipper hulls.

The structural details shown and identified by the symbols in Figure 6.2, which complements Figure 6.1, are those that were most likely to be found in any randomly selected ship. There was great variation in the size, extent, and detailed location of many of these items, a notable example being the bilge keelsons, item E in the list of symbols. Similar variation was apparent in the formation of keelson assemblies, items C and D. In most cases, there were lesser differences throughout the complete structure.

(text continued on page 88)

Figure 6.1. *Midship section illustrating structural components.*

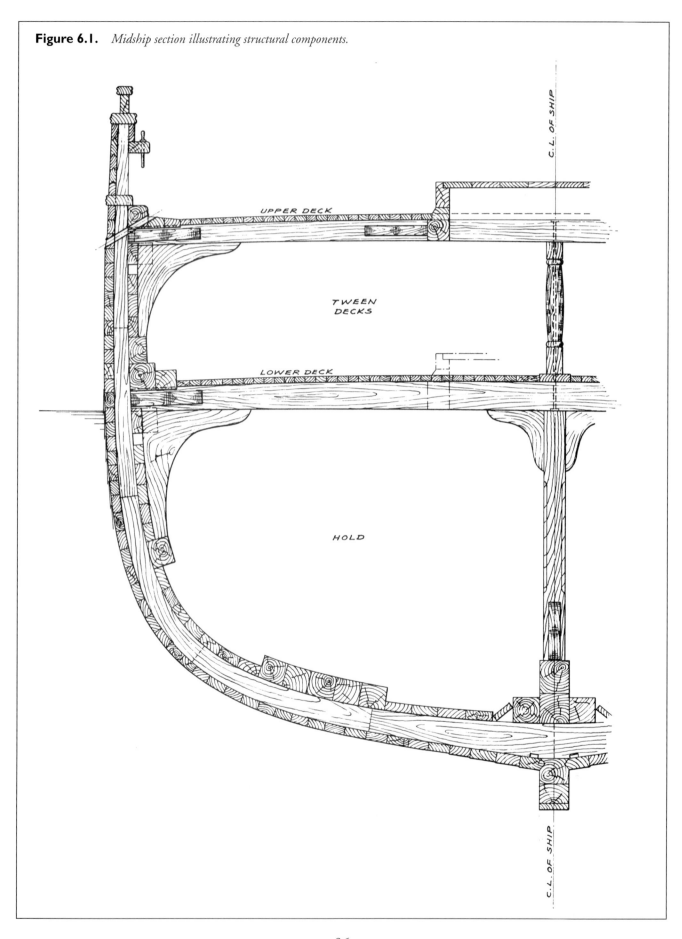

UPPER DECK

C.L. OF SHIP

TWEEN
DECKS

LOWER DECK

HOLD

C.L. OF SHIP

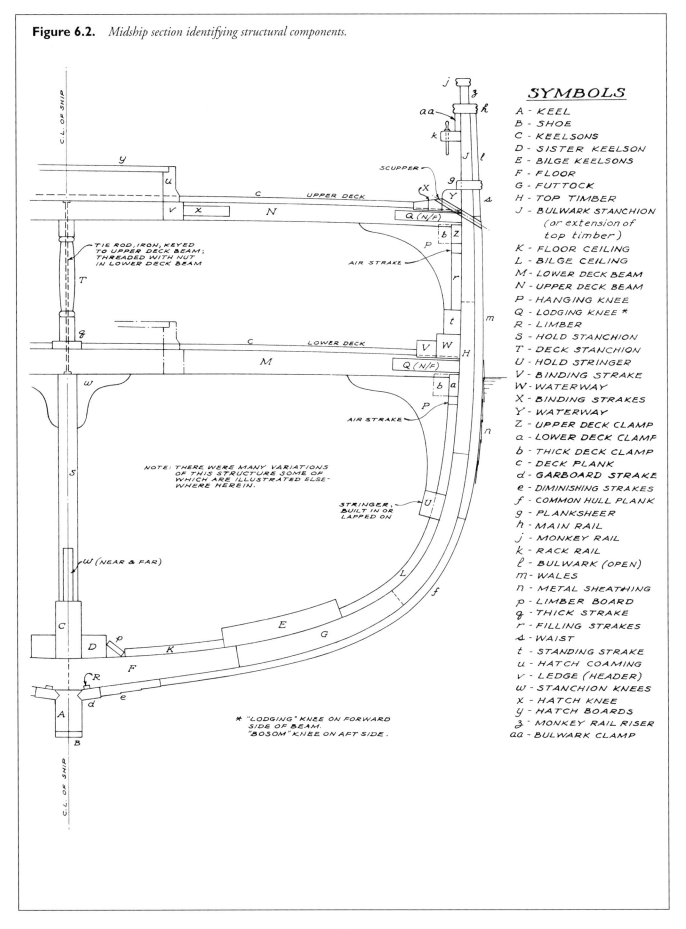

Figure 6.2. *Midship section identifying structural components.*

SYMBOLS

A - KEEL
B - SHOE
C - KEELSONS
D - SISTER KEELSON
E - BILGE KEELSONS
F - FLOOR
G - FUTTOCK
H - TOP TIMBER
J - BULWARK STANCHION
    (or extension of
    top timber)
K - FLOOR CEILING
L - BILGE CEILING
M - LOWER DECK BEAM
N - UPPER DECK BEAM
P - HANGING KNEE
Q - LODGING KNEE *
R - LIMBER
S - HOLD STANCHION
T - DECK STANCHION
U - HOLD STRINGER
V - BINDING STRAKE
W - WATERWAY
X - BINDING STRAKES
Y - WATERWAY
Z - UPPER DECK CLAMP
a - LOWER DECK CLAMP
b - THICK DECK CLAMP
c - DECK PLANK
d - GARBOARD STRAKE
e - DIMINISHING STRAKES
f - COMMON HULL PLANK
g - PLANKSHEER
h - MAIN RAIL
j - MONKEY RAIL
k - RACK RAIL
l - BULWARK (OPEN)
m - WALES
n - METAL SHEATHING
p - LIMBER BOARD
q - THICK STRAKE
r - FILLING STRAKES
s - WAIST
t - STANDING STRAKE
u - HATCH COAMING
v - LEDGE (HEADER)
w - STANCHION KNEES
x - HATCH KNEE
y - HATCH BOARDS
z - MONKEY RAIL RISER
aa - BULWARK CLAMP

C.L. OF SHIP

UPPER DECK

SCUPPER

TIE ROD, IRON, KEYED
TO UPPER DECK BEAM;
THREADED WITH NUT
IN LOWER DECK BEAM

AIR STRAKE

Q (N/F)

LOWER DECK

AIR STRAKE

Q (N/F)

NOTE: THERE WERE MANY VARIATIONS
OF THIS STRUCTURE SOME OF
WHICH ARE ILLUSTRATED ELSE-
WHERE HEREIN.

STRINGER,
BUILT IN OR
LAPPED ON

w (NEAR & FAR)

* "LODGING" KNEE ON FORWARD
SIDE OF BEAM.
"BOSOM" KNEE ON AFT SIDE.

C.L. OF SHIP

(text continued from page 85)

There were ships in which some members identified in Figure 6.2 were not installed, and other ships that had members installed that are not indicated in the figure. However, these differences notwithstanding, the overwhelming similarity of hull construction is apparent everywhere. It mattered little where a ship was built, by whom, or who designed her. The hull form of a clipper quietly and indelibly dictated the structure in general terms. It was a swift evolutionary development, and the form of the hull was the common denominator.

In three classifications of vessel—namely, two laid decks, the most common type; two laid decks and hold beams partially decked; and three laid decks—several examples of each have been included in order to provide a direct comparison of the range of hull forms that found favor among the various builders in their constant search to develop better ships.

The illustrations of the midship sections shown in Figures 6.3 through 6.20 are all drawn to the same scale and thus invite direct comparison of overall size and component details that were inherent in all sizable wooden vessels.

When viewing the figures, bear in mind that they appear in order of size classification, which disarranges any chronological sequence. Therefore, the figures do not represent the orderly advancement in progress that would be apparent in any chronological listing.

In all types of endeavor there are three groupings of individuals: those that are eminently successful and qualified; those that are obviously failures and thus unqualified; and those lying in the rather indeterminate gray area between the first two. Inclusion in the third group is always debatable, and opinions in such cases are at odds, each supported by one's own rationale. So it was with the clipper ship. Some vessels definitely were clippers; some were definitely not clippers; and then there were the inevitable few that did or did not quite fit, depending upon who was championing his own position or point of view. And since there was no rigid mathematical formula for determining precisely what design and construction characterized a clipper, quite a few ships spent their lives in a nautical limbo.

Two vessels included in these illustrations of midship sections are in this questionable category, the barks *Sultana* and *Racehorse*. The original description of *Sultana*[1] does not refer to her as a clipper, but in reciting her vital statistics it verges upon suggesting that her hull form contains the requisite characteristics. Nevertheless, she has never been given this descriptive classification.

The principal difference between bark rig and ship rig is that in a bark the mizzenmast carries fore-and-aft sails only, while a ship is square-rigged on all masts. Barks required smaller crews than comparably sized ships because fewer hands were needed to handle sail on the mizzen; thus they were more economical to operate. In general, barks were smaller and slower than the ships of the period, but they did have the advantage of entering shallow-water ports inaccessible to vessels with deeper drafts.

In this book, all vessels are ship-rigged unless specifically noted. Mast and spar arrangements are discussed in Chapter 29; rigging in Chapter 30.

While *Sultana* was being built by Donald McKay in East Boston, another small bark, *Racehorse*, was being built by Samuel Hall, also in East Boston. She, too, was described in the same general terms as *Sultana*, and in no instance was the word *clipper* included in her description.

The two vessels put to sea within a month of each other. *Sultana* sailed into her Mediterranean trade and performed well. *Racehorse* entered the romantic and much publicized California and Far Eastern trade and posted remarkable sailing records—so remarkable that Captain Arthur H. Clark, a man who had actually sailed in clipper ships, classed her as a clipper in his authoritative book *The Clipper Ship Era*.[28] Later scholars in their wisdom chose to refute this designation, each no doubt being able to overwhelmingly substantiate his conclusion.

However, if a vessel looks like a clipper, is built like a clipper, and sails like a clipper, she might possibly be a clipper. And, since it requires more than a prismatic coefficient to determine such a justification, it does not appear to be an act of heresy to include these two vessels and several others described as "marginal" in the pages of this book.

With the exception of *Wizard*, whose measurements were not reported, Table 3.2 gives the actual measurements of deadrise and swell of the sides for the vessels whose midship sections are shown in the illustrations that follow.

There is often confusion in the nomenclature of decks in a vessel, as various sources did not necessarily apply the same designation to a given deck in a particular ship (with the exception of the forecastle and poop decks). In general, the names applied are descriptive of their location in the hull, but this did not deter certain inconsistencies. To ensure order and consistency herein, the following designations apply to the various decks:

Vessels with	
One laid deck	The weather deck is the *main deck*.
One laid deck and hold beams	The weather deck is the *main deck*.
One laid deck and hold beams partially decked	The weather deck is the *upper deck*. The partial deck is the *lower deck*.
Two laid decks	The weather deck is the *upper deck*. The deck below is the *lower deck*.
Two laid decks and hold beams	The weather deck is the *upper deck*. The deck below is the *lower deck*.

Two laid decks and hold beams partially decked	The weather deck is the *upper deck*. The deck below is the *middle deck*. The partial deck is the *lower deck*.
Three laid decks	The weather deck is the *upper deck*. The deck below is the *middle deck*. The bottom deck is the *lower deck*.
Four laid decks (applies only to *Great Republic*, 1853)	The topmost deck is the *spar deck*. The next below, a true structural deck, is the *upper deck*. Below that is the *middle deck*. The bottom deck is the *lower deck*.

In regard to the areas between the various decks, the following designations apply:

Vessels with

One laid deck	The entire area is the *hold*.
One laid deck and hold beams	The entire area is the *hold*.
One laid deck and hold beams partially decked	The space between the upper deck and the partial deck is the *tween decks*. The space below the partial deck is the *hold*.
Two laid decks	The space between the upper deck and the lower deck is the *tween decks*. The space below the lower deck is the *hold*.
Two laid decks and hold beams	The space between the upper deck and the lower deck is the *tween decks*. The space below the lower deck is the *hold*.
Two laid decks and hold beams partially decked	The space between the upper deck and the middle deck is the *upper tween decks*. The space between the middle deck and the partial lower deck is the *lower tween decks*. The space below the partial lower deck is the *hold*.
Three laid decks	The space between the upper deck and the middle deck is the *upper tween decks*. The space between the middle deck and the lower deck is the *lower tween decks*. The space below the lower deck is the *hold*.
Four laid decks (applies only to *Great Republic*, 1853)	The space between the spar deck and the upper deck is the *upper tween decks*. The space between the upper deck and the middle deck is the *middle tween decks*. The space between the middle deck and the lower deck is the *lower tween decks*. The space below the lower deck is the *hold*.

Eringo, 1853, bark

Eringo, built by Brown and Lovell in their East Boston yard, is representative of the smallest class of clipper ship, her basic inboard structure consisting of one laid deck supported by stanchions footed and kneed on the keelson and headed with knees under each deck beam. Her depth of hold was 12 feet 1 inch.

She was a small vessel, measuring only 113 feet on deck, with a beam of 26 feet 3 inches. Her single deck was ended aft by a half poop deck, which is the nautical equivalent of a split-level house. In addition she was fitted with a small top-gallant forecastle and two small deckhouses. Her depth of hold approached the maximum allowable for a vessel with a single deck.

Along with moderate deadrise and extreme swell of the sides, which are apparent in Figure 6.3, she was described as having long, sharp ends and a long floor. All of these features were characteristic of the clipper as a type. The expectations were that she would be a fast sailer.

A detailed inspection of *Eringo*'s midship section indicates that the general construction was light and consistent with her diminutive overall dimensions. A comparison with larger vessels shown in succeeding plates will reveal that the size of knees that connect her beams to her frames seems to be rather large. This simply emphasizes the great importance that was placed on the integrity of connections pertaining to all the structural components of a ship, whether clipper or freighter.

Her structure was as simple as can be found in the construction of vessels of this type, and her scantlings were well within the established limits for her size. Her known details and sizes appear in appropriate tables where structural components are discussed later in this book. It is unusual to find actual sizes and descriptions of such small vessels which, by their size, would never be able to perform in a manner that would create noteworthy comment. For this, posterity is the fortunate beneficiary.

The basis for her overall small size was her commitment to the Mediterranean trade where her shallow draft would easily allow access to shallow ports of the area.

The contour of her midship section as drawn in Figure 6.3 is a reconstruction based upon the following given data: scantlings of the keel; deadrise at half floor; swell of the sides; depth of hold; and maximum beam. These dimensions, while not eliminating flexibility in the reconstruction of her midship configuration, especially in the immediate area of the turn of the bilge, are restrictive enough to guide a rational development of fair and reasonable curves. The net result is a section which appears to be compatible with other known details of her description.

Her structural members are drawn to scale from scantlings quoted in her description, some of which are actually

Figure 6.3. *Bark* Eringo, 1853.

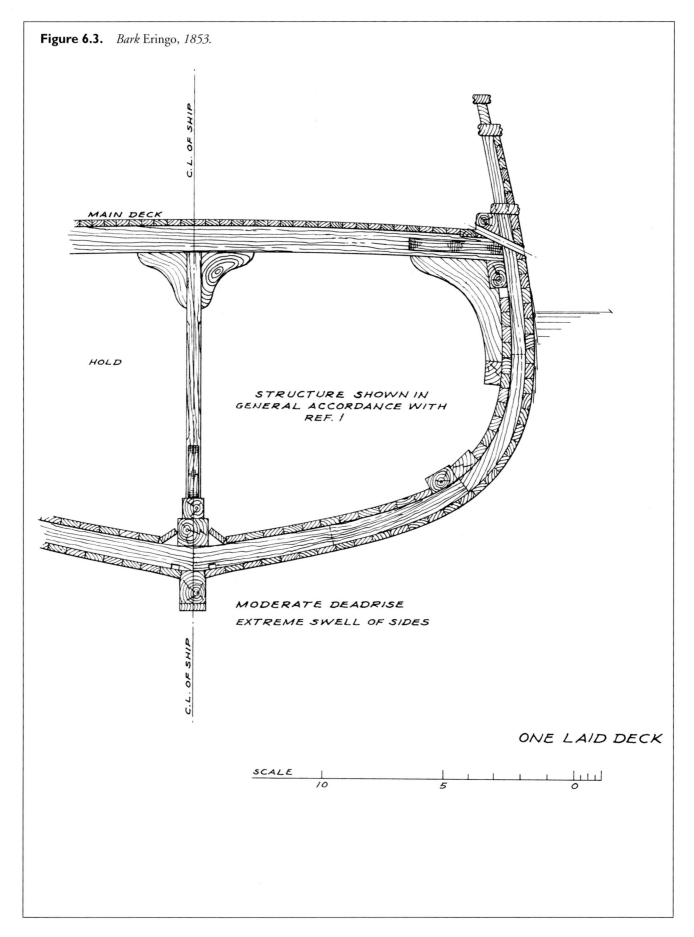

C.L. OF SHIP

MAIN DECK

HOLD

STRUCTURE SHOWN IN
GENERAL ACCORDANCE WITH
REF. 1

MODERATE DEADRISE
EXTREME SWELL OF SIDES

C.L. OF SHIP

ONE LAID DECK

SCALE   10   5   0

sized while others are general and accepted as an integral part of shipbuilding practice. Somewhat out of the ordinary are the scantlings of her rider keelson, which is sized noticeably smaller than the keelson itself.

Sultana, 1850, bark

Sultana is representative of the next-to-smallest ship classification based on depth of hold. At 15 feet this depth required the inclusion of hold beams in addition to the structure of the laid main deck. The purpose of these beams was to add stiffness to the hull immediately above the bilges, by dividing the unsupported span between the keel and the deck as measured along the frame; this added transverse strength to withstand the battering of heavy seas against a vessel's hull.

Donald McKay, *Sultana*'s designer and builder, had been constructing large vessels in his shipyard at East Boston since his arrival there in 1845. They were all packets or freighters of traditional design, specifically formed with little deadrise and maximum carrying capacity. All were considered to be successful vessels, and as a result Mr. McKay had become a highly regarded designer and builder.

Late in 1849 or early in 1850, he was approached by Mr. Edward Lamb and his brother, shipping merchants of Boston, who were in quest of a modestly dimensioned vessel that would be suited for the Mediterranean trade, particularly in the Smyrna area of west Turkey. The potential owners wanted a vessel with fast sailing qualities of foremost importance; carrying capacity was second in priority. Their new vessel should be able to work her way without problem through the Strait of Gibraltar in the face of headwinds and a steady inflow current of about 1.5 knots through the narrow 12-mile entrance of the Strait. This slot of sea was unceremoniously referred to as the "arse" of that body of water.

With these requirements laid before him, Mr. McKay was given carte blanche to design this vessel according to his own dictates. There is no way of ascertaining what train of thought went through his mind. Perhaps it was the ongoing philosophical contest between the proponents of the traditional flat-floored vessel, as staunchly favored by Nathaniel B. Palmer, and those who were swayed toward the sharp-bottomed vessels championed by John Willis Griffiths in the form of *Sea Witch* and *Rainbow*, both vessels of remarkable performance and far-flung reputation.

Donald McKay, who, to many personalities of the nautical scene, did not always appear to use the best business judgment, was definitely conservative in the matter of his ships' strength. Any study of the scantlings of his ships reveals that he was never reluctant to pour timber into his vessels. To expound that his vessels were well built would be an understatement; indeed, there is strong evidence that most of his vessels might have been overbuilt. Whatever the case in that regard, he was now on the verge of departing from his usual conservative practice in favor of embracing a new theory. This "new theory" was actually a venture into the hull form expounded by Griffiths since 1843. It appears reasonable to assume that McKay might have, for some time, felt the urge to point his talents in the direction of this new challenge. Up until then, his clients were chiefly interested in great capacity and respectable speed, in that order; but now, with carte blanche, he possibly thought of it as the opportunity to see what he could do.

Assumptions aside, this fact is most apparent: McKay changed his long-standing practice and developed a sharp, racy vessel with a relatively deep keel. This was the bark *Sultana*, brought into being six months prior to the launching of his famous clipper ship *Stag Hound*. It is noteworthy that, her sharpness notwithstanding, *Sultana* was not referred to as a clipper either while being built or after completion. But that she was built clipper fashion and contained the required attributes is amply indicated by the contour of her midship section and by the description of the lines of her hull, which contained the necessary sharp ends and long floor.

She was 121 feet long on deck, with a beam of 28 feet 4 inches, and her single deck was ended aft by a half poop deck. An examination of her midship section reveals that, while Donald McKay discarded his traditional conservatism as to design, the same cannot be said about her scantlings.

An opinion as to the sizing of her scantlings is given in this direct quote: "Of her materials and fastening, and the beautiful style in which she is finished, we cannot speak too highly, but still we think she is rather too heavily timbered, and has too much stout scantling in her hold. If designed to carry shot in bulk, it would not have been necessary to make her any stronger than she is. But we suppose her great strength may be in part attributed to the fact, that Mr. McKay has been in the habit of building large vessels, and found it difficult to pare his ideas down to a vessel of her size. If a merchant wishes to have a strong small vessel built, secure the services of a builder who has been in the habit of building large ships, and he will be sure to obtain his money's worth in timber and fastening."[1]

The contour of *Sultana*'s midship section as drawn in Figure 6.4 is a reconstruction based upon the following: scantlings of the keel; deadrise at half floor; swell of the sides; depth of hold; maximum beam; and height of bulwarks and monkey rail. As in the case of *Eringo* (Figure 6.3), this information does not indicate absolute reconstruction of her midbody, but the parameters do allow for reasonable conclusions as to the way her form might have appeared.

All her structural members are drawn to scale from scantlings quoted in her description. For reasons unknown, but probably obvious to the reporter, there is no mention made of stanchions having been installed along her centerline to

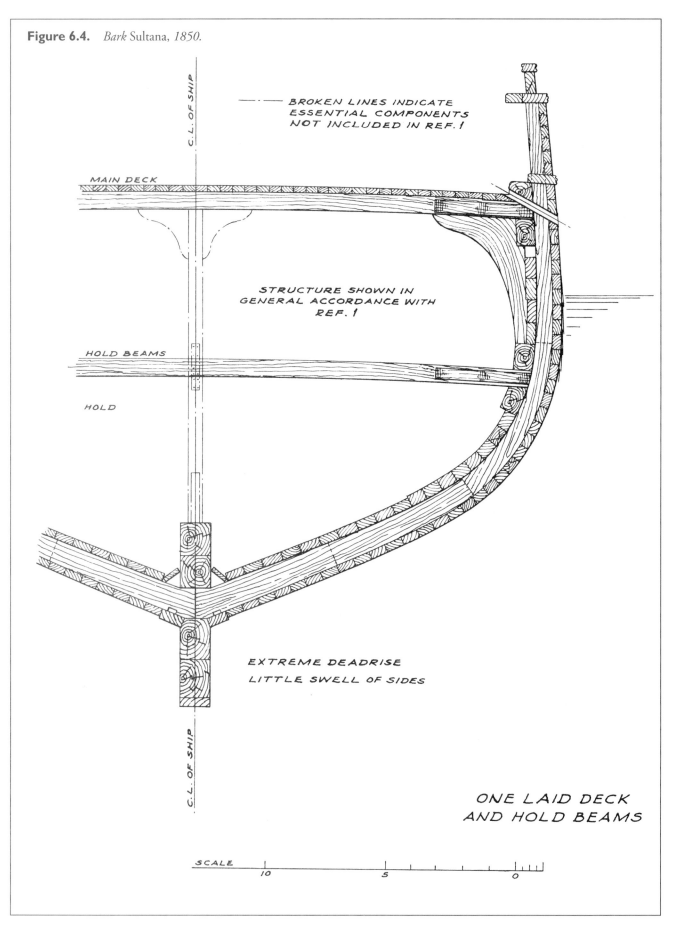

Figure 6.4. *Bark* Sultana, *1850.*

BROKEN LINES INDICATE
ESSENTIAL COMPONENTS
NOT INCLUDED IN REF. 1

C.L. OF SHIP

MAIN DECK

STRUCTURE SHOWN IN
GENERAL ACCORDANCE WITH
REF. 1

HOLD BEAMS

HOLD

EXTREME DEADRISE
LITTLE SWELL OF SIDES

C.L. OF SHIP

ONE LAID DECK
AND HOLD BEAMS

SCALE

10   5   0

support her hold beams and main deck. While the beams in question were not so large as to be difficult to obtain, nor was their span too great to function in an unsupported length, the stanchions in question were an absolute necessity for uniting the keel with the deck and thus forming a continuous girder along her centerline. In addition, such stanchions are required in order to restrain the deck beams from deforming upward when a broadside sea would tend to compress her sides in toward the center. These unmentioned stanchions are shown in broken lines in Figure 6.4.

The name of this bark, *Sultana*, appears to have been chosen as a subtle, or not so subtle, indication of friendliness toward the Sultan of Turkey and the Turkish people who, only a generation prior to this period, had seen their empire humiliated at the hands of the United States in the Tripolitan War which ended forever our payment of tribute to the Ottomans. Whether or not it promoted profitability is not recorded.

Racehorse, 1850, bark

Racehorse, built by Samuel Hall in his yard at East Boston, measured 16 feet depth of hold, which was well within the requirement of being fitted with hold beams and was considerably over the limit allowed for laying only a single deck.

She was a small vessel, measuring 125 feet on deck, with a beam of 30 feet 6 inches. Her single laid deck was ended aft by the usual half poop deck that invariably was built into vessels of this type. Extreme deadrise and moderate swell of her sides are clearly evident in her midsection. Her model was described as being sharp but well rounded throughout her length.

The contour of her midship section as drawn in Figure 6.5 is reconstructed using the following given data: deadrise at half floor; swell of the sides; depth of hold; maximum beam; and height of main and monkey rails. In the case of her keel only its depth is given, so the siding is assumed to be about 13 inches, which appears to be commensurate with other ships near her size. As with other vessels reconstructed using this same available, though limited, information, there is room for differences of opinion about the turn of the bilge. However, such differences are, by their nature and location, almost assuredly of a moderate nature.

The structural members are drawn to scale based on their given scantlings and indicate a vessel that is well found without being overburdened with excess timber. The available data states that her hold beams were decked over at each end of the ship. This decking, along with the specification that the stanchions between the upper deck and the hold beams were turned, allows for speculation that this deck might, at some future date, have been considered for planking throughout its entire length. No height between hold beams and upper deck is given, but the assumption must be made that adequate headroom would be required; for this reason a dimension of 7 feet moulded height between the beams has been arbitrarily selected and shown in Figure 6.5. Her bilge ceiling is of light construction, and although the hold beams are secured to the sides with lodging knees, no hanging knees have been installed. This omission is consistent with the fact that the hold beams are not subject to vertical loading.

An interesting and unusual feature of this vessel is apparent in the trace of her main and monkey rails, which are described as being contoured to run outboard of her lower deadeyes, thus, in effect, bringing all of her lower rigging inboard of the bulwarks. This same detail is built into the clipper *Dauntless*.

Stag Hound, 1850

(Structure in accordance with contemporary description by marine reporter Duncan MacLean in *The Boston Daily Atlas*)[1]

Stag Hound was Donald McKay's first large, rather belated entry into the fast-approaching clipper ship frenzy. At the time of her launching, December 7, 1850, she was the largest clipper ship afloat and was the precursor of what appeared to be McKay's basic philosophy, namely: Think big.

With 21 feet depth of hold, she was in the category of ships which, at that period, specified the installation of two laid decks. She measured 215 feet on deck, with an extreme beam of approximately 40 feet. Her midsection featured extreme deadrise and minimal swell of sides, as is evident in Figure 6.6. She was described as being uncommonly sharp with rounded lines. Figure 1.5 shows her moulded lines and body plan, which are the basis of her midship contour as drawn in Figure 6.6.

Her structure, as shown in this figure, is reputedly an onboard inspection of her as she floated at her pier while onloading her initial cargo prior to departing for New York. All structural members are shown as described.

It is quite obvious that certain portions of the ship could not have been described by sight due to their being hidden either by cargo already on board or by the fact that, even had the hull been empty, many members are not visible due to their location in the total structure. For these reasons it must be concluded that the reporter was given information by other knowledgeable persons.

Some statements have been made that such reporters were given false information of this type in order to mislead the competition and to retain certain secrets the builder might have had. However, a knowledge of shipbuilding practice, whether in the age of steel or in the age of wood, will not support that theory except in the area of some peculiar design characteristics. In the matter of materials and fastenings, it would be most difficult to incorporate something so radical as to warrant keeping it hidden from curious questioners.

The reasons for this brief digression will become apparent
(text continued on page 96)

Figure 6.5. *Bark* Racehorse, *1850.*

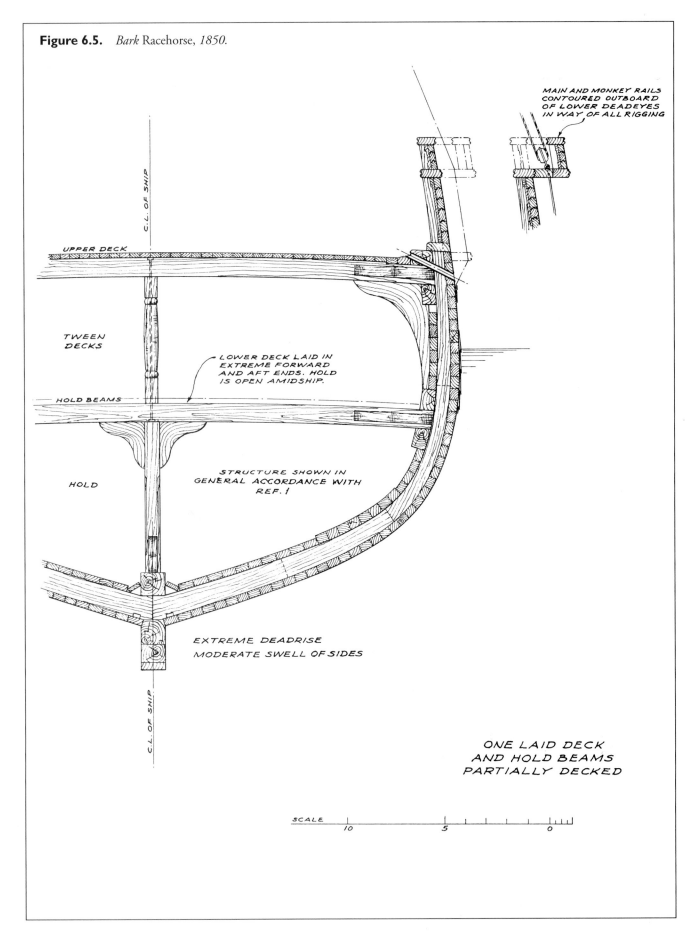

MAIN AND MONKEY RAILS
CONTOURED OUTBOARD
OF LOWER DEADEYES
IN WAY OF ALL RIGGING

C.L. OF SHIP

UPPER DECK

TWEEN
DECKS

LOWER DECK LAID IN
EXTREME FORWARD
AND AFT ENDS. HOLD
IS OPEN AMIDSHIP.

HOLD BEAMS

STRUCTURE SHOWN IN
GENERAL ACCORDANCE WITH
REF. 1

HOLD

EXTREME DEADRISE
MODERATE SWELL OF SIDES

C.L. OF SHIP

ONE LAID DECK
AND HOLD BEAMS
PARTIALLY DECKED

SCALE
10   5   0

94

Figure 6.6. Stag Hound, *1850—structure in accordance with description by Duncan MacLean.*

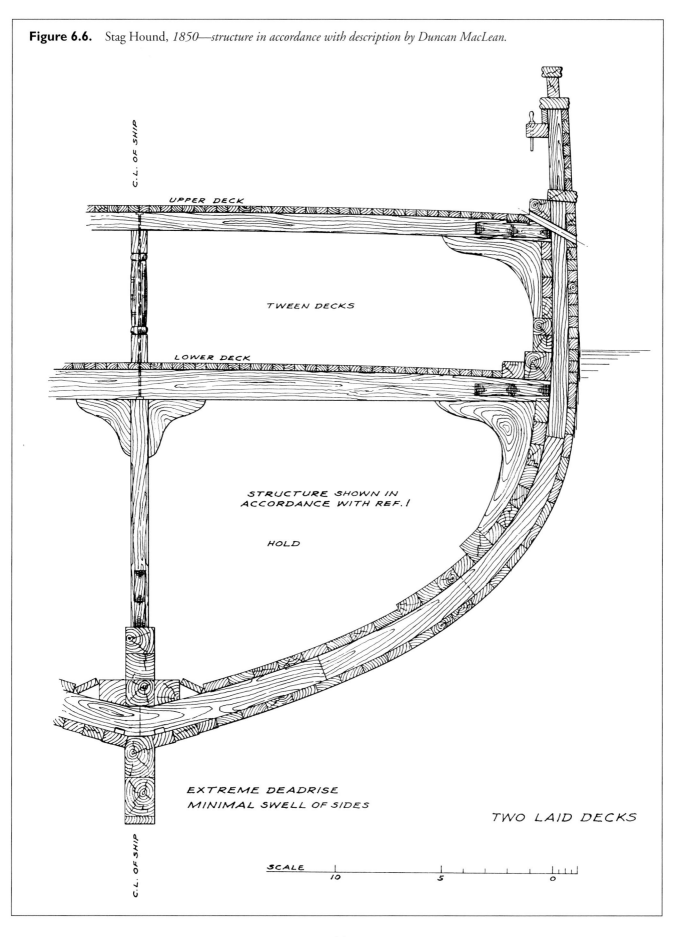

C.L. OF SHIP

UPPER DECK

TWEEN DECKS

LOWER DECK

STRUCTURE SHOWN IN
ACCORDANCE WITH REF. 1

HOLD

EXTREME DEADRISE
MINIMAL SWELL OF SIDES

TWO LAID DECKS

C.L. OF SHIP

SCALE

10   5   0

(text continued from page 93)

upon examination of Figure 6.7. The scantlings and construction of *Stag Hound* as shown in Figure 6.6 are very light as compared to later McKay vessels, particularly in way of the keelsons and the area of the bilges. The dimensions of such scantlings will be found later in tables dealing with the individual items of structure.

Added validity of MacLean's report is warranted by the detailed description of her bulwarks and rails (these do not appear in the list of scantlings of McKay vessels, the reference used for the following figure), and the arrangement of houses, fittings, and supplemental deck gear.

Overall, it appears that the choice of construction deemed acceptable lies with the reader after comparing one figure with the other.

The name *Stag Hound*, two separate words, is as it appears in the description, and apparently reflects the contemporary spelling.

Stag Hound, 1850

(Structure in accordance with scantlings given in *Models and Measurements* by Henry Hall, based on the papers of Donald McKay.)[2]

Stag Hound, as detailed in Figure 6.7, is drawn to the same contour that is shown in Figure 6.6. The tween-decks height is the same, and the structural members installed are essentially the same. Their scantlings, however, differ greatly. Thus the question is generated: How can two sources, both credible, present such conflicting evidence?

Perhaps it is a question that can never be satisfactorily answered, but one theory can be put forth which is characteristic of all boat and ship building. For a variety of reasons, it is an acknowledged tenet of shipbuilding that the ship "as built" will very likely be different than the ship "as designed." Such differences sometimes appear in the overall size of the vessel, but in the majority of cases the differences are in details. The following explanation will attempt, at the very least, to indicate that sources used for this comparison can, in their proper place, be correct or valid. Some background information is necessary in order to present the case.

Between 1845, when Donald McKay opened his shipyard in East Boston, and 1855, when the clipper *Donald McKay* was launched, he built approximately forty vessels, sixteen of which preceded the launching of *Stag Hound* in 1850—all designed as traditional packets. After *Stag Hound* came approximately fifteen clippers, culminating in *Donald McKay*, with a group of eight packets interspersed among the clippers.

Henry Hall's *Models and Measurements* is a tabulation of the scantlings specified for a total of twenty McKay vessels, eleven of which are universally regarded as true clippers while the remainder are packets. The tabulation is set down in

chronological sequence of building, regardless of classification, and, as might be expected, the vessels generally increased in size as the years advanced.

Two classes of specifications control the building of ships. The first is termed the *general specifications*. These spell out the necessary details that must be incorporated into any ship and identify structural members that must be included in the hull, along with minimum allowable scantlings. Also included are the acceptable types of wood; the material, size, and number of fastenings; types and sizes of deck equipment; and other details germane to the integrity of the finished product. Lloyd's Rules and the New York Marine Register of 1858 are, in effect, this type of general specification.

The second class is termed the *detail specifications*. These, in a formal or informal way, refine the requirements of the general specifications in a manner that is applicable to each specific ship. All items of structure, material, and procedure are covered by these specifications. It is not difficult to comprehend that, as a ship is being built, certain substitutions and deviations might become necessary. When this occurs, changes take place which are within the governing rules but are changes nevertheless. Thus, there are places where the ship will not agree with the plans. These detail specifications are, in essence, the contents of a final contract agreed to by the builder and the client.

Models and Measurements lists the names of five packets built between 1845 and 1850, identifying each major structural member—keel, frame, stem, etc.—and stating in detail the quantity, scantlings, material, and fastenings that were to be used in the building of each vessel. All five vessels ranged between 895 and 1,187 tons. In a word, they were comparable, and the aforementioned details (except in a few rare instances) were identical for all the vessels.

Then, starting with *Stag Hound* in 1850, the list continues through 1854, naming ten clippers and three packets which ranged between 1,505 and 2,515 tons. Only two of this group were less than 1,782 tons, so it is quite obvious that these later ships belonged in a different class of vessels when being judged by size. This increase in tonnage is accompanied by an increase in the scantlings of all the vessels in this group. The interesting fact is that, as in the previous group of packets, every ship was given the same scantlings, with only minor exceptions.

An example of the type of difference in scantlings between the two groups of vessels shows in the sizes of centerline stanchions. These, in the earlier, smaller packets, were sized at 10 inches square, while in the later, larger vessels they were uniformly increased in size to 7 inches by 22 inches.

Thus, it seems that a case may be made to support the assumption that the list of scantlings might be Donald McKay's own set of general specifications for ships categorized by size. If this were to be accepted, then the details

Figure 6.7. Stag Hound, *1850—structure in accordance with* Models and Measurements.

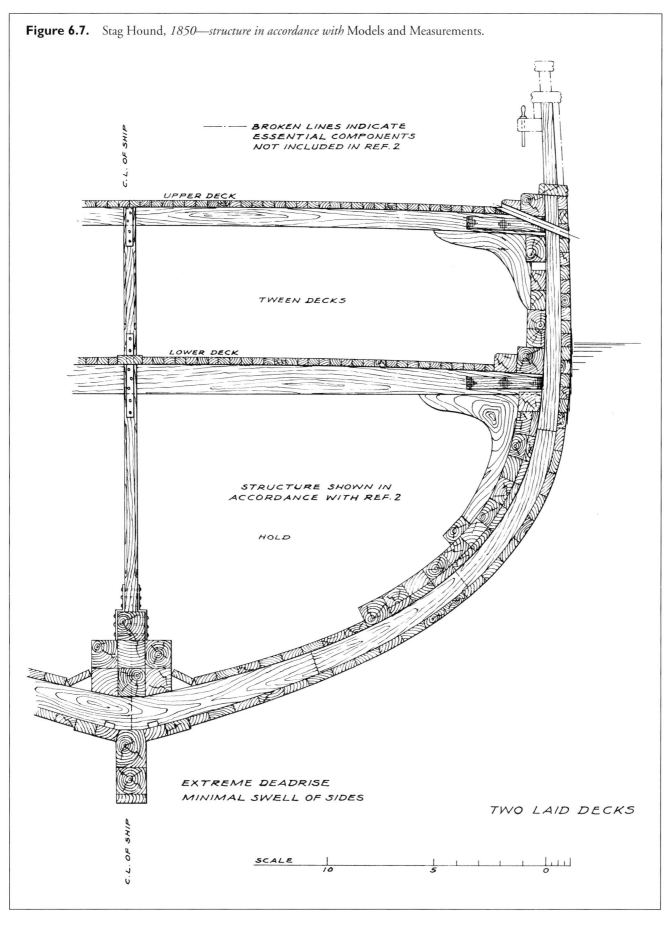

BROKEN LINES INDICATE
ESSENTIAL COMPONENTS
NOT INCLUDED IN REF. 2

C.L. OF SHIP

UPPER DECK

TWEEN DECKS

LOWER DECK

STRUCTURE SHOWN IN
ACCORDANCE WITH REF. 2

HOLD

C.L. OF SHIP

EXTREME DEADRISE
MINIMAL SWELL OF SIDES

TWO LAID DECKS

SCALE

10   5   0

spelled out in MacLean's description could be the result of a change in thinking on the part of the builder as to the bulk of wood that he wished to install in his ships; it could be that, in certain instances, the specified material was not available as needed; or it might be that space restrictions became apparent and must be dealt with on a case basis.

Note that although *Great Republic* is included in the list of ships recorded in *Models and Measurements*, she was a ship of unique proportions, and her scantlings were set up separately.

The major differences revealed between Figures 6.6 and 6.7 lie in the bulk of the keelson assembly; the bilge ceiling, noteworthy for its two-tier construction; the heavy tween-decks ceiling, all shown in Figure 6.7; and the size and connections of the centerline stanchions. The stanchion connections are plainly specified as being iron plates or straps, and there is a total absence of wooden knees. The remainder of the structure is similar, though not identical. McKay's list[2] also fails to make any mention of the structure above the plank sheer, which is indicated by broken lines in Figure 6.7.

Figure 6.7 should be compared with Figure 6.9, *Flying Cloud*, and with Figure 6.11, *Lightning*, in order to note the use of identical scantlings in all the clippers as recorded in *Models and Measurements*.

Flying Cloud, 1851

(Structure in accordance with description by Duncan MacLean)

Flying Cloud was another vessel requiring two laid decks and was without doubt the most famous of all American-built clippers. She was built by Donald McKay and is included here to illustrate the progression in thinking on the part of the builder—a progression that could generally be applied to any ship designer or builder. As was the case with *Stag Hound*, two figures are drawn, the first (Figure 6.8) featuring the details described in reports by Duncan MacLean,[1] and the second (Figure 6.9) drawn with details specified in *Models and Measurements*.[2]

The contour of the midsection of *Flying Cloud* is based on her lines and body plan as they are drawn in Henry Hall's *Report on the Ship building Industry of the United States*.[23] A comparison of the midship sections of *Flying Cloud* and *Stag Hound* reveals that in the six-month period between the launching of the two vessels, Donald McKay decided he could improve on *Stag Hound*. The new vessel, *Flying Cloud*, was built with greatly reduced deadrise and a slight increase in the swell of her sides. It is abundantly evident that, if McKay thought he was producing a vessel capable of greater speed, he was also producing one with relatively greater carrying capacity, as is evidenced by the fullness of her bilges.

As was the case with *Stag Hound*, Duncan MacLean inspected *Flying Cloud* at Boston as she was onloading her cargo prior to departure for New York. Except for the shape of her midsection, the most noticeable change from the general construction of *Stag Hound* is apparent in the great strengthening of her keelson assembly, which more nearly approaches the scantlings quoted in *Models and Measurements*. Also, iron plates and straps, in addition to wooden knees, were used for securing her centerline stanchions to the rider keelson and the lower deck beams. Her entire ceiling, from keelson to the upper deck clamp, is still of relatively light construction.

As with *Stag Hound*, included in this description are the scantlings of her bulwarks and rails.

Flying Cloud, 1851

(Structure in accordance with scantlings in *Models and Measurements*.)

Flying Cloud, as detailed in Figure 6.9, is drawn to the same contour that is shown in Figure 6.8. The tween-decks height is the same, and the structural members installed are essentially the same. The scantlings as listed in *Models and Measurements* are identical to those of all the other clippers in McKay's list, except for several minor differences that were controlled by the lines of her hull.

For all the ships listed in *Models and Measurements*, it seems apparent that the builder did not consider the structure above the planksheer to be of any great significance, so their scantlings are not mentioned.

A small detail that could easily go unnoticed is the fact that the planksheer of all McKay vessels, by his own instruction, was to be "laid inclined to the round of the beam." McKay was probably not the only builder to follow this practice, but he appears to be the only one to mention it explicitly.

Figure 6.9 should be compared with Figure 6.7, *Stag Hound*, and Figure 6.11, *Lightning*, in order to note the use of identical scantlings in all the clippers as recorded in *Models and Measurements*.

Lightning, 1854

(Structure in accordance with description by Duncan MacLean.)

Lightning, built by Donald McKay for James Baines and Co., Liverpool, was launched almost three years after *Flying Cloud* made her debut and, like her predecessor, was a vessel of two decks. Her midship section, as shown in Figure 6.10, is taken from a plan of her lines[11, 23] and demonstrates the extent of change that had, in general, taken hold of the thinking of the designers. The earlier high deadrise has given way to a relatively flat, wide floor with the bilges moved far outboard. As her sides rose and reached their maximum beam they were then brought noticeably inboard, resulting in great swell of the sides and, as an economic by-product, a means

(text continued on page 103)

Figure 6.8. Flying Cloud, *1851—structure in accordance with description by Duncan MacLean.*

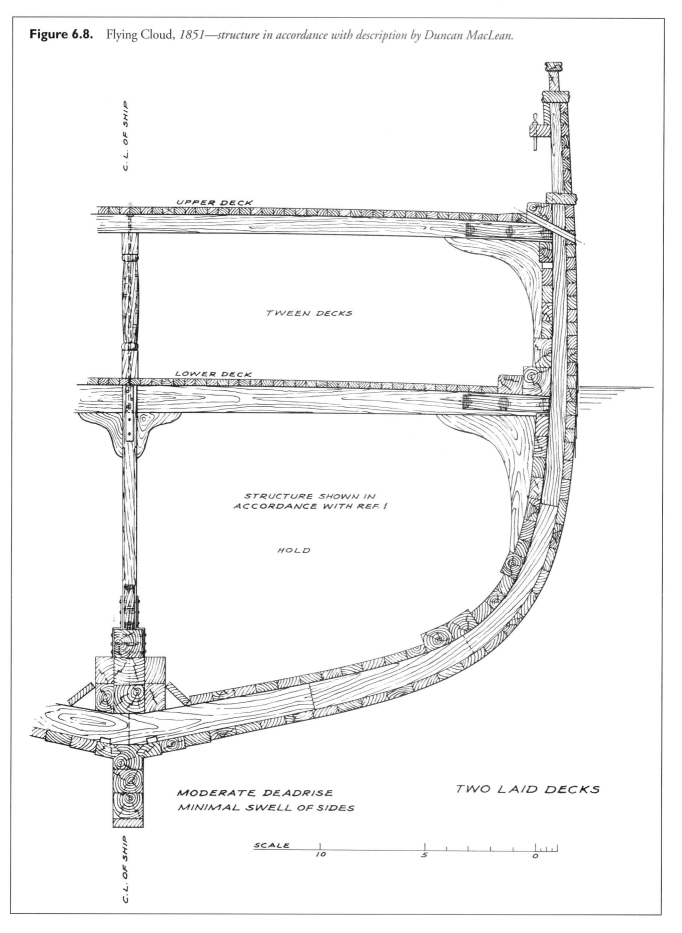

C.L. OF SHIP

UPPER DECK

TWEEN DECKS

LOWER DECK

STRUCTURE SHOWN IN
ACCORDANCE WITH REF. 1

HOLD

MODERATE DEADRISE
MINIMAL SWELL OF SIDES

TWO LAID DECKS

C.L. OF SHIP

SCALE
10   5   0

Figure 6.9. Flying Cloud, *1851—structure in accordance with* Models and Measurements.

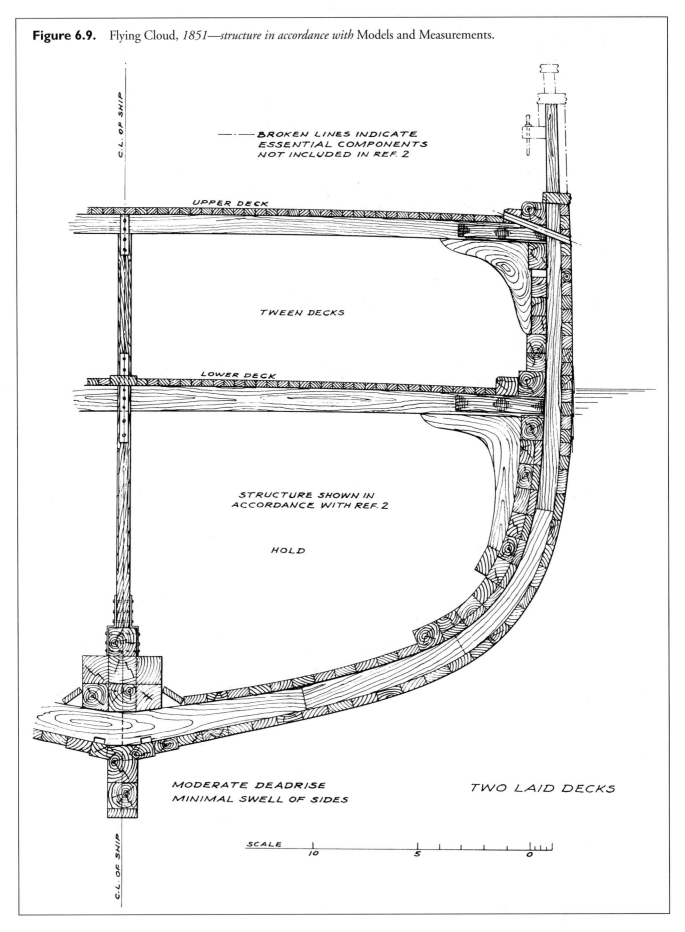

BROKEN LINES INDICATE
ESSENTIAL COMPONENTS
NOT INCLUDED IN REF. 2

C.L. OF SHIP

UPPER DECK

TWEEN DECKS

LOWER DECK

STRUCTURE SHOWN IN
ACCORDANCE WITH REF. 2

HOLD

MODERATE DEADRISE
MINIMAL SWELL OF SIDES

TWO LAID DECKS

C.L. OF SHIP

SCALE

10   5   0

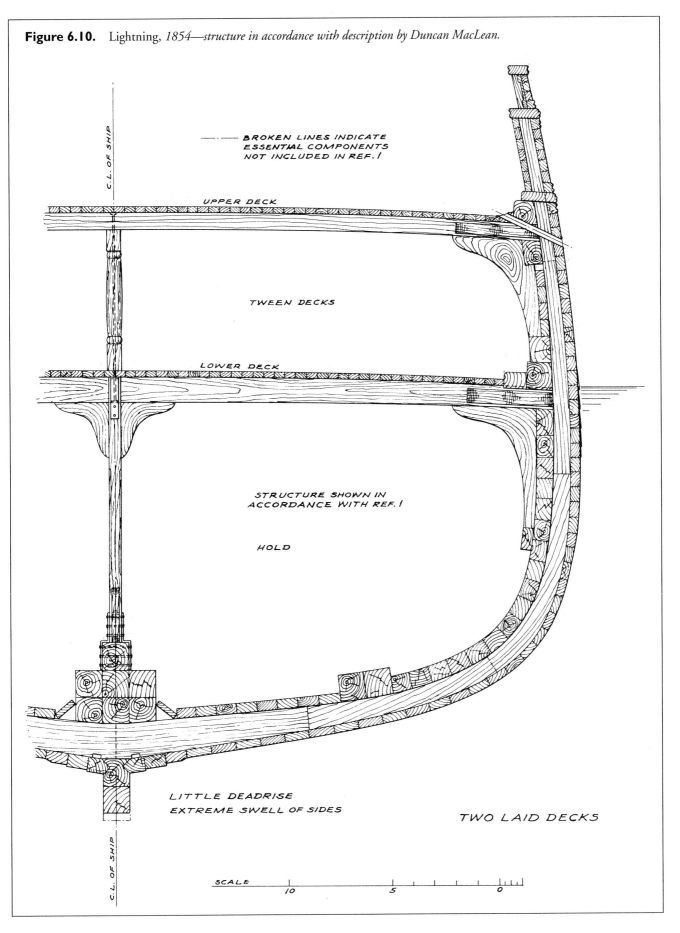

Figure 6.10. Lightning, *1854—structure in accordance with description by Duncan MacLean.*

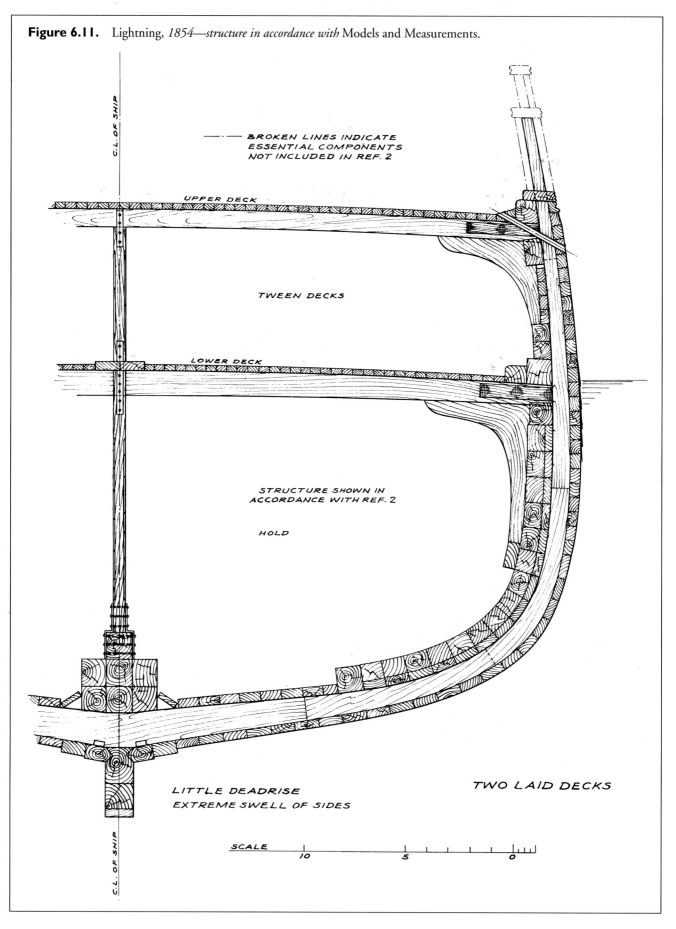

— · — BROKEN LINES INDICATE
ESSENTIAL COMPONENTS
NOT INCLUDED IN REF. 2

C.L. OF SHIP

UPPER DECK

TWEEN DECKS

LOWER DECK

STRUCTURE SHOWN IN
ACCORDANCE WITH REF. 2

HOLD

C.L. OF SHIP

LITTLE DEADRISE
EXTREME SWELL OF SIDES

TWO LAID DECKS

SCALE
10   5   0

(text continued from page 98)
of reducing her tonnage measurement. This is the hull form that had been adopted by the builders in 1853, and will prevail in the figures that follow.

The structure that was incorporated in *Lightning* is visibly ponderous, a hallmark of Donald McKay's ships. However, McKay was not alone in this practice, since the scantlings of most other vessels indicate a distinct propensity to apparently play it safe and err on the side of strength rather than weakness. On this score, history has very little data to actually determine or surmise how such excess material might have been used. The most well known builder to deviate from this philosophy was William H. Webb. An example of his structure, drawn from contemporary description,[1] is shown in Figure 6.16, the clipper *Challenge*.

Lightning, as described by MacLean, adheres quite closely to the scantlings in *Models and Measurements* except in way of the bilge ceiling and the heading of centerline stanchions under the lower deck beams. The bilge ceiling is very sturdy but laid in one thickness instead of being two-tiered. The heads of the centerline stanchions are still secured by knees in addition to iron straps.

Lightning, 1854

(Structure in accordance with scantlings in *Models and Measurements*.)

Lightning, as detailed in Figure 6.11, is drawn to the same contour that is shown in Figure 6.10. The tween-decks height is the same, and the structural members installed are essentially the same. The scantlings are identical to those of all the other clippers in McKay's list except for any minor differences that were dictated by the lines of her hull, as can be seen by comparing Figure 6.11 with Figure 6.7, *Stag Hound*, and Figure 6.9, *Flying Cloud*.

Red Jacket, 1853

Red Jacket, the handsome and remarkable masterpiece of designer Samuel Hartt Pook, was built by George Thomas at Rockland, Maine. Her depth of hold, 24 feet, required that she be built with two decks. Her midship section, which is contoured in accordance with her lines,[14] is somewhat similar to that of *Flying Cloud* in that she features little deadrise and minimal swell of the sides. The decrease in deadrise, resulting in flatter floors, also netted increased carrying capacity.

A close inspection of Figure 6.12 indicates that, while *Red Jacket* was substantially built, her scantlings were not as ponderous as those specified by Donald McKay, when one takes into consideration her significantly greater dimensions. Thus it is evident that each designer possessed his own idea of what should make up the general composition of his ships.

In 1860 *Red Jacket* underwent a very extensive overhaul in Liverpool. Her full proportions allowed the installation of an additional deck below her existing lower deck without changing the location of her upper deck. Her registry was then classed as a three-deck vessel.

Golden Fleece, 1855

Golden Fleece, built by Paul Curtis of Boston, was the second clipper to bear this name, the first having been built by the same man for the same owners, Weld and Baker of Boston, in 1852. She was a large ship, having a depth of hold of 26 feet which required, in addition to two laid decks, the installation of hold beams below her lower deck. Thirteen such beams were distributed through her length in order to buttress the bilges in the span measured along her frames between her keel and the lower deck clamp.

Her depth of hold was great in comparison to her beam, as may be seen in Figure 6.13. She was a full-bodied ship with little deadrise and moderate swell of sides. Her inboard construction, based on the description reported by Duncan MacLean, reveals a relatively light keelson assembly, but the construction of her bilge keelsons, bilge ceiling up to the lower deck, and her tween-decks ceiling can only be described as enormous. Her hold beams are secured to the frames by lodging knees. However, with no prospect of receiving vertical loading, hanging knees were omitted at the beam ends.

The contour of the midship section has been reconstructed from the following known data: scantlings of the keel; deadrise at half floor; swell of the sides; depth of hold; maximum beam; and the whole height of her bulwarks including the monkey rail. As with other vessels reconstructed from this same available, though limited, information, there is room for differences of opinion about the turn of the bilge; however, such differences would appear to be limited and of a moderate nature.

All structural members are drawn to scale. As in other clippers built in these later years, the centerline stanchions in way of beams were secured by iron straps, which occupied less space and were much lighter in weight than the ponderous wooden knees used previously.

Hoogly, 1851

The great clipper ship phenomenon was only a half-dozen years old when *Hoogly* was launched late in 1851 in the shipyard of Samuel Hall at East Boston. Already the infatuation with extreme deadrise was giving way to the adoption of flatter floors in even the most extreme clipper hulls. A few years of substantive experience had shown builders that flat bottoms combined with sharp ends provided vessels with a rewarding combination of speed and carrying capacity.

With these facts in mind, Samuel Hall forsook the acute hull and came forth with *Hoogly*, possibly named for an arm of the Ganges River, whose midship section is shown in Figure 6.14.

(text continued on page 107)

Figure 6.12. Red Jacket, *1853.*

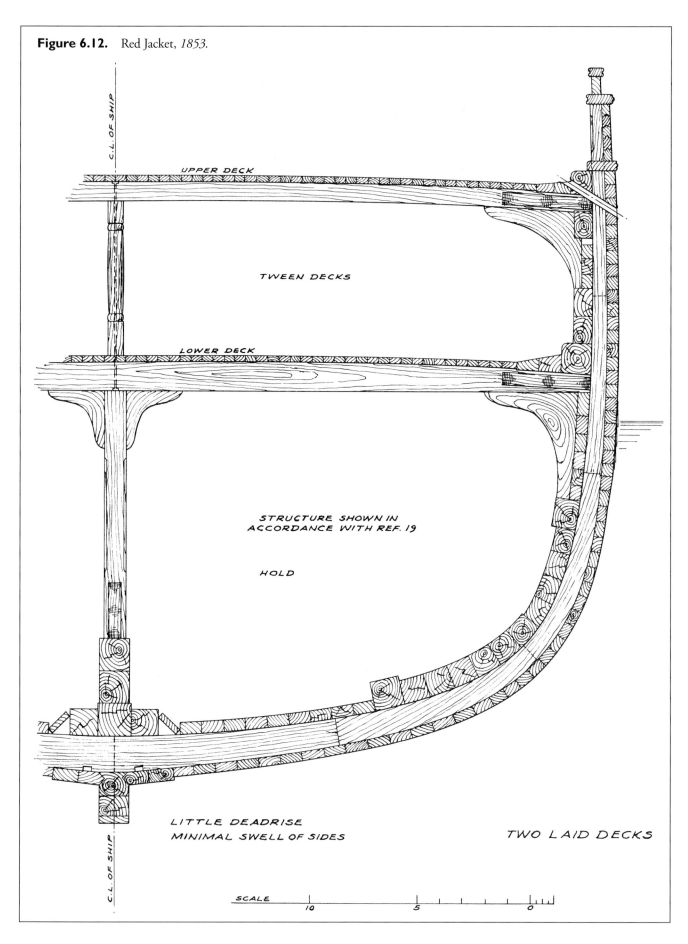

C.L. OF SHIP

UPPER DECK

TWEEN DECKS

LOWER DECK

STRUCTURE SHOWN IN
ACCORDANCE WITH REF. 19

HOLD

LITTLE DEADRISE
MINIMAL SWELL OF SIDES

TWO LAID DECKS

C.L. OF SHIP

SCALE
10   5   0

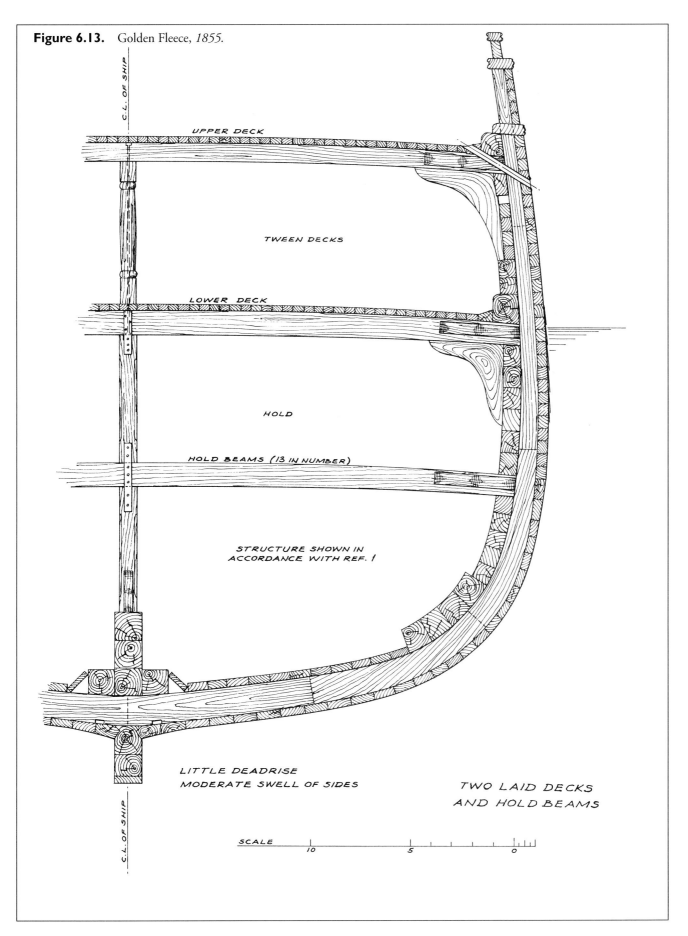

Figure 6.13. Golden Fleece, *1855.*

C.L. OF SHIP

UPPER DECK

TWEEN DECKS

LOWER DECK

HOLD

HOLD BEAMS (13 IN NUMBER)

STRUCTURE SHOWN IN
ACCORDANCE WITH REF. 1

LITTLE DEADRISE
MODERATE SWELL OF SIDES

TWO LAID DECKS
AND HOLD BEAMS

C.L. OF SHIP

SCALE   10   5   0

Figure 6.14. Hoogly, *1851.*

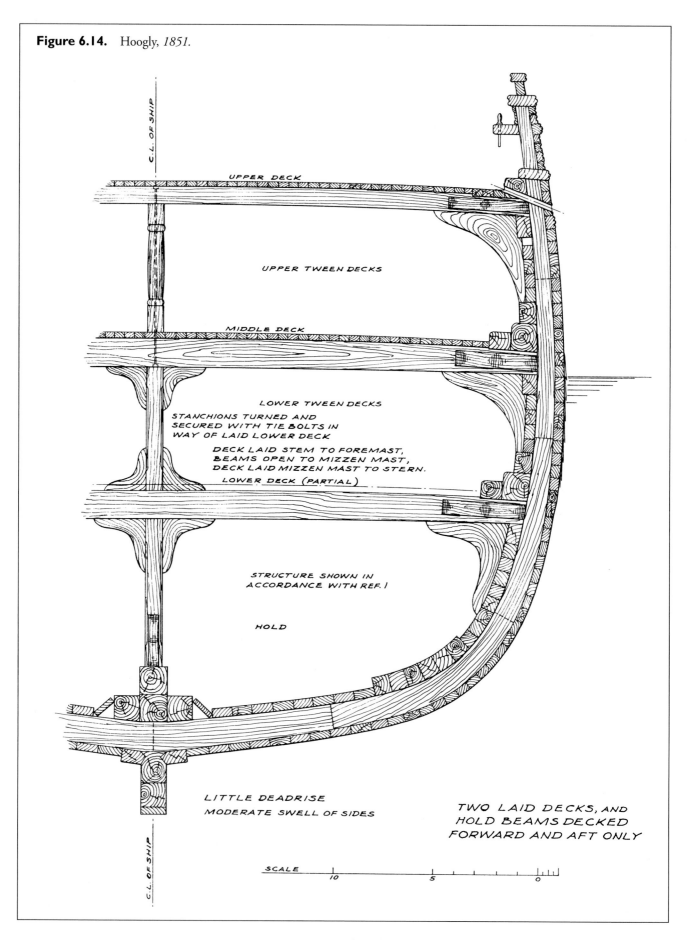

C.L. OF SHIP

UPPER DECK

UPPER TWEEN DECKS

MIDDLE DECK

LOWER TWEEN DECKS

STANCHIONS TURNED AND
SECURED WITH TIE BOLTS IN
WAY OF LAID LOWER DECK

DECK LAID STEM TO FOREMAST,
BEAMS OPEN TO MIZZEN MAST,
DECK LAID MIZZEN MAST TO STERN.

LOWER DECK (PARTIAL)

STRUCTURE SHOWN IN
ACCORDANCE WITH REF. I

HOLD

LITTLE DEADRISE
MODERATE SWELL OF SIDES

TWO LAID DECKS, AND
HOLD BEAMS DECKED
FORWARD AND AFT ONLY

SCALE

10   5   0

C.L. OF SHIP

(text continued from page 103)

It is refreshing to find detailed information about some clipper ships that were lesser remembered or, in some cases, not remembered at all. Much has been written and recorded about the famous vessels—mostly fact, but, unfortunately, much of it either unabashedly romantic or perhaps even fiction. With *Hoogly* we have an instance of extreme practicality supported by reliable detail. True, the information is not as complete as one could wish for; however, there is enough to support the case.

Figure 6.14 shows a well-rounded hull which, from the standpoint of appearance, combines all the positive elements of capacity and beauty. The contour of her midship section as shown in the plate is reconstructed using the following known data: scantlings of the keel; deadrise at half floor; depth of hold; maximum beam; and the whole height of her bulwarks, including the monkey rail. Unfortunately, the swell of her sides is not given as a measurement; all that is available here is the verbal description "and swells gracefully along her sides, both from the water to the rail, and fore and aft."[1] She was not unlike *Golden Fleece*, which would be built four years later by Paul Curtis of Boston.

Her depth of hold being 25 feet required the installation of hold beams in addition to her two laid decks, as would be the case with *Golden Fleece*. However, *Hoogly* was fitted with a complete complement of hold beams which were decked over from stem to foremast and from mizzenmast to stern. Amidships no deck was laid, yet the beams, knees, and waterways were installed to accommodate three complete decks if a decision might be made to do so.

Her construction in the hold, when examined closely and compared with the ships shown in other figures, indicates very clearly the thinking of the different builders as they approached the problems of achieving adequate strength combined with minimum weight. The keelson assembly in *Hoogly* is as minimal as can be found in a large clipper. On the other hand, the hold beams and those under the main or middle deck appear to be gargantuan in the area they occupy, namely the hold; the same may be said for the centerline stanchions installed between the middle deck and the hold beams. However, this was the necessary manner as perceived by Samuel Hall, who, as a designer and builder, was held in highest regard by his peers.

Any close inspection of this ship's structure and scantlings indicates without a doubt that here is a ship that will not fall apart under any conditions. What cannot be found is any apparent attempt to reduce weight by easing the size of her scantlings.

Wizard, 1853

Wizard, another product of Samuel Hall's shipyard at East Boston, had 25 feet 9 inches depth of hold, and thus—like *Hoogly* already built and *Golden Fleece* which would be built

in 1855 by Paul Curtis—fell in the class of vessels whose two laid decks also required the addition of hold beams.

Figure 6.15 shows her midship section as reconstructed according to contemporary descriptions by MacLean. Unfortunately for posterity, the only parameters noted are the scantlings of the keel; depth of hold; maximum beam; and the whole height of bulwarks including the monkey rail. With such incomplete information for guidance, the contour shown in the figure is of a mould which, in the year 1853, had become commonplace among the clippers of her size. This assumption is made with the full realization that the ship could have been built to different lines. The internal structure, however, has the virtue of being shown as described and dimensioned.

With the passage of time, advances were made in some details of construction; but each builder, feeling secure in his own strictly personal philosophy of structure, strayed very little from the basic path upon which he first set forth, and in many instances the peculiarities may be apparent in a study of the scantlings, the component parts, and, sometimes, in the methods of fastening that were favored.

The hold beams of *Wizard* were secured to the frames by lodging knees; but, since no deck was intended to be laid amidships, hanging knees were not installed. Only the beams forward of the foremast, reaching to the stem, and those between the mizzenmast and the stern were planked over. However, a narrow gangway four strakes wide ran along the waterway between the forward and aft planking, each side of the ship. This was an unusual treatment and must have been a welcome asset to any crewmen whose duty it was to inspect the hold or the cargo in that area.

Wizard, like most other clippers built between 1853 and the end of the phenomenon in 1857, had her centerline stanchions stoutly secured to the keelson by sturdy iron clasps and to the beams by equally sturdy flat iron straps. Simplicity of construction, an increase in available stowage space, a decrease in structural weight, and a growing scarcity of suitable knees all contributed to this inevitable bit of progress. Still, as in all types of ships built during these years, prodigious quantities of timber were poured into the never-ending stream of ships that were taking to the water.

Challenge, 1851

The saying "Man proposes but God disposes" could never be applied more appropriately than to the case of the great clipper *Challenge*, first of the 200-foot, three-deck marvels of her era.

In 1850, N. L. and G. Griswold, shipping merchants of New York, designed a huge ship with the express purpose of putting into the water the greatest merchant ship in existence. Once their goal had been set and their detailed desires

(text continued on page 110)

Figure 6.15. Wizard, *1853.*

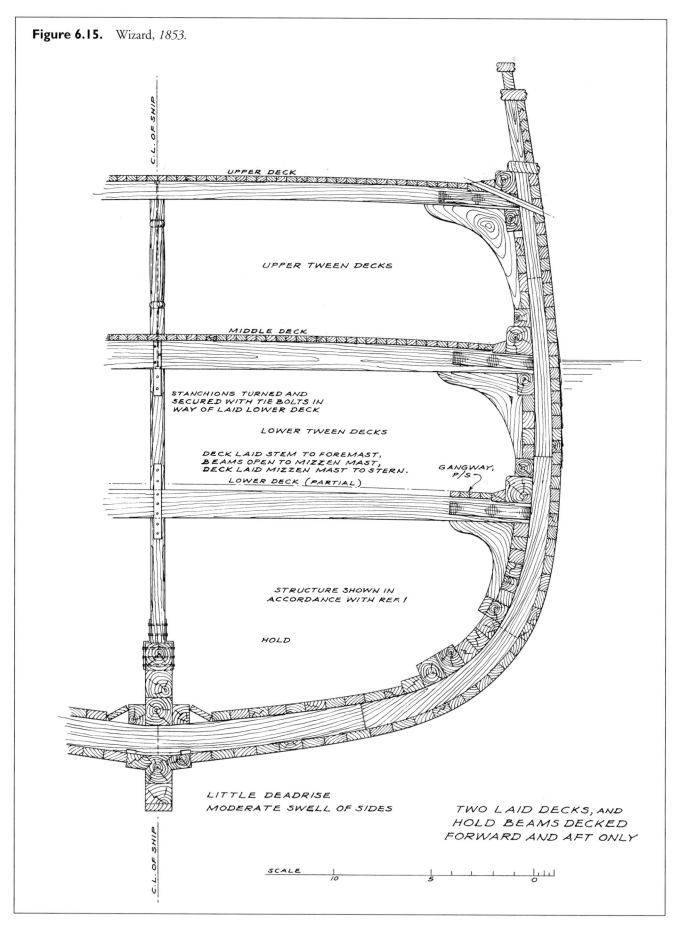

C.L. OF SHIP

UPPER DECK

UPPER TWEEN DECKS

MIDDLE DECK

STANCHIONS TURNED AND
SECURED WITH TIE BOLTS IN
WAY OF LAID LOWER DECK

LOWER TWEEN DECKS

DECK LAID STEM TO FOREMAST,
BEAMS OPEN TO MIZZEN MAST,
DECK LAID MIZZEN MAST TO STERN.

LOWER DECK (PARTIAL)

GANGWAY,
P/S

STRUCTURE SHOWN IN
ACCORDANCE WITH REF. 1

HOLD

LITTLE DEADRISE
MODERATE SWELL OF SIDES

TWO LAID DECKS, AND
HOLD BEAMS DECKED
FORWARD AND AFT ONLY

SCALE   10   5   0

C.L. OF SHIP

Figure 6.16. *Challenge, 1851.*

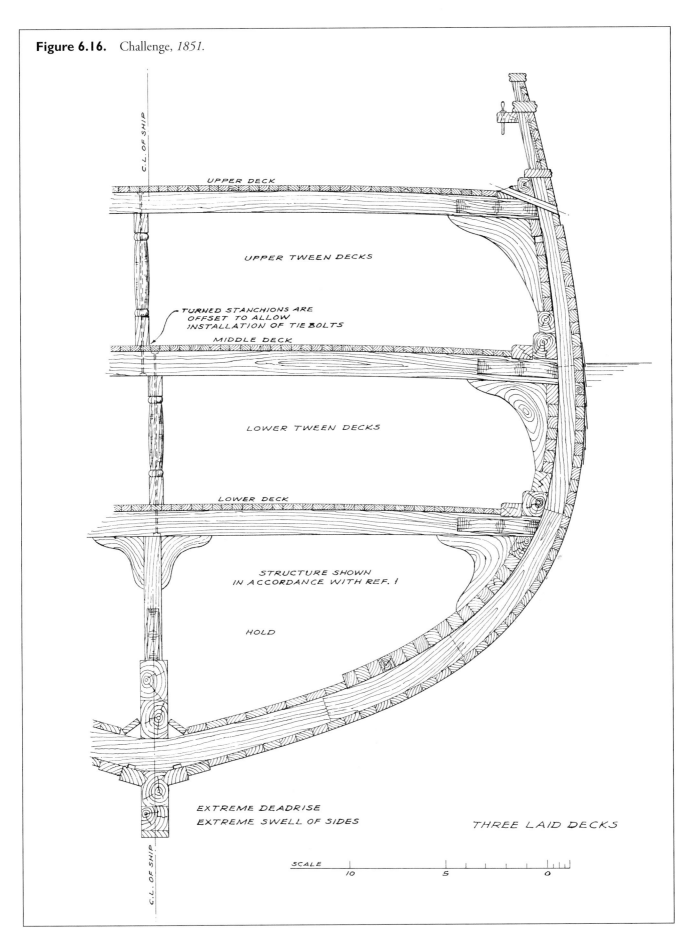

C.L. OF SHIP

UPPER DECK

UPPER TWEEN DECKS

TURNED STANCHIONS ARE
OFFSET TO ALLOW
INSTALLATION OF TIE BOLTS

MIDDLE DECK

LOWER TWEEN DECKS

LOWER DECK

STRUCTURE SHOWN
IN ACCORDANCE WITH REF. 1

HOLD

C.L. OF SHIP.

EXTREME DEADRISE
EXTREME SWELL OF SIDES

THREE LAID DECKS

SCALE   10   5   0

(text continued from page 107)

consolidated, they sought the services of William Henry Webb of New York, who, at this particular time, was regarded as America's premier designer and builder of ships. Their requirements were bare-boned: she must be the best sailing vessel in the world.

While the requirements were few, the responsibilities were enormous, and even a man of Webb's talent must have paused to reflect upon just how he could deliver the desired results of such a deliciously simple yet deceivingly complex proposal. No one knew more than he that many pitfalls lay between erecting the first timber and casting off the last line. He obviously had not gained his fine reputation by being a timid man, but neither had he foolishly jumped into impossible situations.

In any case, the Griswolds were determined and also prepared to go to any lengths to have their dream transformed into reality. They knew that William H. Webb was their man, and, what is of equal importance, they knew how to acquire his services. If their requirements were bare-boned, their restrictions were even less so, to the point of nonexistence. Her final model would be at the discretion of Webb. Cost would not enter into any phase of her construction or outfitting. Labor and materials were to be the best that money could buy. This was a dream proposal that probably could not have been refused by any shipbuilder and certainly not by Mr. Webb.

The ship as designed and built was a one-man show and created enthusiasm never before seen in nautical circles and among the public. *Challenge*—what Man had proposed—was launched May 24, 1851, in the presence of the largest audience to ever witness such an event in this country up to that time.

Upon putting to sea on her maiden voyage on July 13, 1851, "God's disposal" took over, and this splendid vessel embarked upon a sailing life that was plagued by disappointment and disaster. Throughout her entire career *Challenge* was dogged by unfavorable winds, dirty weather, untrained and mutinous crews, and a reputation as a "bad" ship. It was tacitly agreed by those who were knowledgeable of ships and the sea that she never actually realized her ultimate potential.

The most fortunate circumstance concerning *Challenge* is that she left to posterity one of the most complete records of statistics of building and appearance that can be found for any clipper ship.

Figure 6.16 shows her midship section as drawn using her table of moulded offsets[18] and her description in *The Boston Daily Atlas*. She was given all the characteristics considered desirable, namely, extreme deadrise at half floor, extreme roundness and ease of bilges, and extreme swell of sides. From the standpoint of refinement and grace, the midship

section of *Challenge* is a picture of sheer beauty and symmetry, one that might be difficult to improve upon.

A detail worthy of note is the way the turned stanchions in the tween decks were offset in reference to the centerline of ship and to each other. This offset was minimal and was spaced at the smallest distance that would allow the through-bolt of the upper stanchion to clear the head of the lower stanchion in order to provide access when installing the nut under the middle deck beam. The practice was followed only in cases where one turned stanchion surmounted another, and is illustrated in the construction plan of *Ocean Monarch*, 1856.[24]

With a depth of hold at 25 feet 6 inches, *Challenge* could easily accommodate the three laid decks with which she was fitted. Her inboard structure—that is, stanchions, deck beams and their knees, and deck planking—are all that one would expect in any large clipper. However, a comparison of the ship's ceiling, from keelson to planksheer, with those same components in any of the large clippers shown in other figures, reveals one of Webb's construction characteristics: a definite lightness of scantlings.

Of all the major shipbuilders, William H. Webb employed the most judicious use of timber in his vessels. His keelsons were of minimal but adequate scantlings, and he was not an advocate of bulky bilge keelsons. Apparently he relied on the structural value of hull planking and wales to function as longitudinal strength members in addition to forming the usual watertight envelope.[13] Webb also subscribed to the use of variable frame spacing, using close spacing amidships and increasing the distance as the frames progressed forward and aft. This stretching of the frame spacing eliminated the weight of four frames in each end of a 200-foot hull, amounting to about 25,000 pounds at the bow and stern of the ship. The lighter weight this achieved significantly inhibited a vessel's inherent tendency to hog.

Ironically, on July 10, 1851, a mere six weeks after the launching of *Challenge*, another Webb ship was launched without fanfare and with little publicity. This was his somewhat smaller clipper *Comet*, a ship whose midship section and lines were very similar to those of *Challenge*. No great expectations were retained for *Comet*, however; she was expected to perform as well as other ships being launched at the time.

The story of *Comet*'s successes are well known in the annals of the era, and the ship, in her life span of almost fifteen years, set more records, seven in all, over the recognized sailing courses of the clippers than any other clipper ever built. And, in addition to being fast, she was a general sailing favorite. Such is the whim of circumstance.

Young America, 1853

Young America, launched April 30, 1853, at the yard of William H. Webb in New York, was the last extreme clipper ship he would build and was considered by all to be his

Figure 6.17. Young America, *1853.*

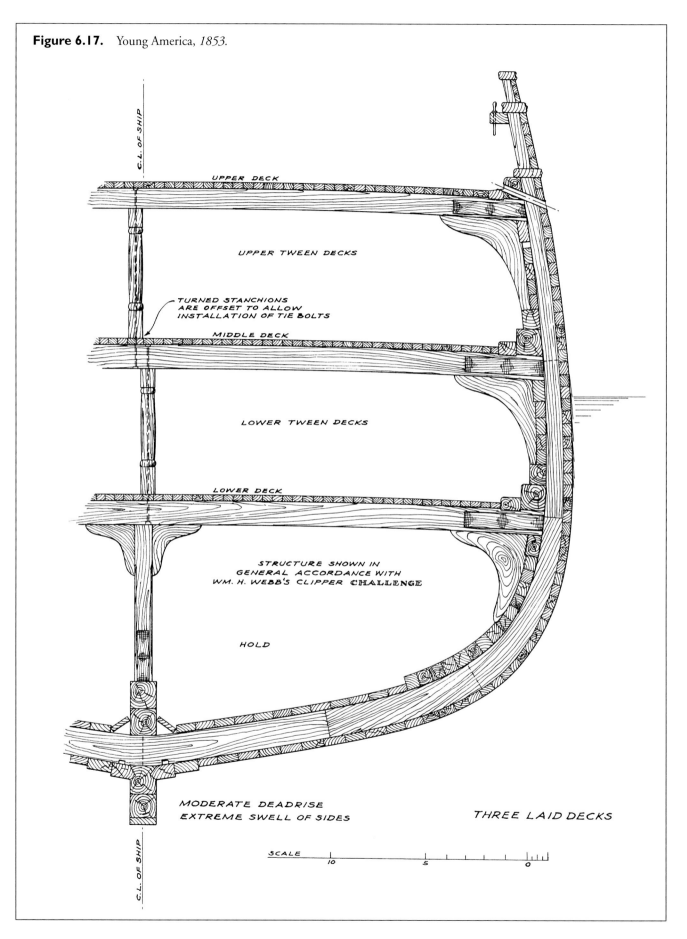

C.L. OF SHIP

UPPER DECK

UPPER TWEEN DECKS

TURNED STANCHIONS
ARE OFFSET TO ALLOW
INSTALLATION OF TIE BOLTS

MIDDLE DECK

LOWER TWEEN DECKS

LOWER DECK

STRUCTURE SHOWN IN
GENERAL ACCORDANCE WITH
WM. H. WEBB'S CLIPPER CHALLENGE

HOLD

MODERATE DEADRISE
EXTREME SWELL OF SIDES

THREE LAID DECKS

SCALE

10   5   0

C.L. OF SHIP

III

masterpiece. Her hull form, general appearance, sailing performances, and long life are ample testimonials to this accolade.

With 25 feet 9 inches depth of hold, she was fitted with three laid decks. Figure 6.17 illustrates the form of her midship section as drawn using her table of moulded offsets, recorded in Table 1.2 and photographs of her later in her career. A comparison with the midship section of *Challenge* (Figure 6.16) illustrates very plainly the change in thinking that took place in the short span of two years between 1851 and 1853. This change is brought home more forcefully by the fact that both vessels originated in the mind of the same builder, thus eliminating the consideration that two different philosophies might have been at work had these ships been designed and built by two distinct personalities.

The greatest divergence of form is apparent in the elimination of extreme deadrise at half floor, a design feature that had fallen from favor and usefulness by 1853; wider, sharper, though not hard, bilges were a direct result of this change. Swell of the sides was still extreme, allowing considerable advantage to the shipping merchant when the vessel was being measured for tonnage.

In my view, photographs are of use only to the extent of picking off the details of mouldings and rails. It is always unfortunate that such details rarely survive the actual vessel, but the reality of the situation was that such details were of no lasting value, and very little, if any, thought was given to the desires and wishes of posterity. With *Young America* being such a successful and long-lived vessel, this absence of information is particularly distressing. However, exhaustive research in all the logical institutions fails to bring to light much in the way of structural detail and nothing in the way of scantlings. The offset table verifies that her frame spacing was variable, being 32 inches throughout her mid-length and gradually increasing to 36 inches at stem and stern.

The midship section of *Young America* is drawn according to the known scantlings of *Challenge* and the contemporary description of *Comet*, while assuming that Mr. Webb's structural philosophy, which was eminently successful, would be followed in substance if not in identical detail. It provides a valid but not infallible means of studying the possible inboard structure as applied to a full-bodied hull. Others may have different opinions on this particular subject; one can only surmise. As was the case with *Challenge* and *Ocean Monarch*,[24] *Young America*, too, would require offset tween-decks stanchions.

That *Young America* was well built is a foregone conclusion. She sailed for thirty-three years—several lifetimes, by clipper ship standards—and in all that time was the victim of very little damage. She was a great favorite in all shipping circles and performed some astounding feats of sailing. Perhaps the most unbelievable of all her sailing accomplishments was that in her career she rounded Cape Horn approximately fifty times. No other clipper reached this astonishing figure.

There is a fitting postscript to the building of *Young America*. It is reported that one day in May or June, 1853, Mr. Webb wandered down to the dock, where she was onloading cargo for her maiden passage. He wanted a last look at his masterpiece. Catching sight of the mate, he is reported to have said, "Take good care of her, Mister, because after she's gone there will be no more like her."[26] Was this a salute to his pride and joy or was it possible his sense that the end of the extreme clipper was pending?

Sierra Nevada, 1854

While William H. Webb and Donald McKay were the acknowledged giants of the shipbuilding industry in the United States during the clipper ship era, it remains that the great majority of these ships, both large and small, well known and unknown, were the products of many smaller shipyards along the East Coast.

Sierra Nevada, a ship approaching 2,000 tons, was one of these vessels. She was built by the firm of Tobey and Littlefield, at Portsmouth, New Hampshire, one of their three clippers. Figure 6.18 shows her midship section, the contour of which is based upon the following known data reported by MacLean: scantlings of the keel; deadrise at half floor; maximum beam; swell of the sides; and height of bulwarks to the monkey rail. The depth of hold is taken from *Greyhounds of the Sea*,[31] by Carl C. Cutler, and *American Clipper Ships*,[32] by Howe and Matthews, and requires an explanation as to why this was done.

The bane of all research is to discover conflicting evidence about a subject. The depth of hold of *Sierra Nevada* is one of these instances. MacLean reports this figure to be 28 feet, while the two books just mentioned (which may have both used the same source material) give this dimension as 26 feet 4 inches. Using the 28-foot depth, along with the known tween-decks height of 6 feet 6 inches, gives an inordinately great depth of hold between floor ceiling and lower deck—much more than was consistent with prevailing practice. This does not conclusively demonstrate that the figure was wrong; it merely promotes suspicion. Using the 26-feet-4-inches dimension, as is done in Figure 6.18, results in a more acceptable height of this hold and is, therefore, the dimension selected. There is an old adage, aptly applicable to shipbuilding, that goes, "If it does not look right, check it, because it probably is not right." Since in this case a choice must be made, the adage provides some reasoning for the conclusion.

Sierra Nevada, as shown in Figure 6.18, includes several innovative features and, when compared to *Challenge* (Figure 6.16), provides a vivid contrast in the composition of scantlings and structure, thus emphasizing the differences between two designers setting out to accomplish the same goal.

Figure 6.18. Sierra Nevada, *1854.*

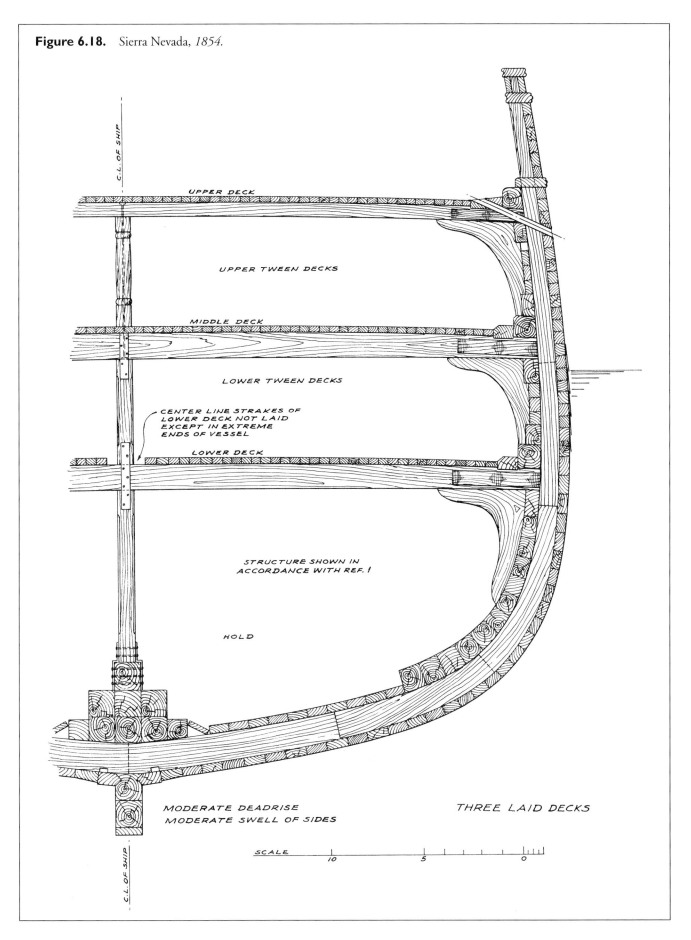

C.L. OF SHIP

UPPER DECK

UPPER TWEEN DECKS

MIDDLE DECK

LOWER TWEEN DECKS

CENTER LINE STRAKES OF
LOWER DECK NOT LAID
EXCEPT IN EXTREME
ENDS OF VESSEL

LOWER DECK

STRUCTURE SHOWN IN
ACCORDANCE WITH REF. 1

HOLD

C.L. OF SHIP

MODERATE DEADRISE
MODERATE SWELL OF SIDES

THREE LAID DECKS

SCALE   10   5   0

Most notable in *Sierra Nevada* is the large scale of her construction, both in scantlings and the sheer use of timber, which is easily noted in her keelson structure and her ceiling from bilge to middle deck. Three innovative details are shown in her structure. The first lies in the keelson assembly, which consists of the usual keelson and riders and sister keelsons. Then, faying against each sister keelson, is an additional member, designated as a "cousin" keelson,[1] about 40 feet in length, installed abreast of the pumps and mainmast. This "cousin" keelson cannot truly be called unique, because it may have been an integral part of the builder's general construction technique; however, the homespun designation seems undeniably applicable and is not a term that is easy to find in the building of wooden ships.

The second unusual construction feature is the treatment of the bilge ceiling. It is installed immediately outboard of the floor ceiling, below the first futtocks. The first strake is 14 inches square and is referred to as "ceiling," not as "bilge keelson." From this member up to the lower deck clamp, the ceiling is *bearded*—given a uniform taper, diminishing to 8 inches thickness at the clamp. Throughout the entire surface of the ceiling there are no projecting edges.

As a third unusual feature, the centerline strakes of planking were left out of her lower deck—a deliberate omission to facilitate the free flow of air through her lower hold.

With such sturdy construction, it might be assumed that *Sierra Nevada* would be fitted to carry an extraordinary amount of canvas, but such was not the case; she crossed nothing higher than royal yards. Throughout her career she is said to have sailed with easy motion, and was a popular passenger packet.

In nautical terms, "crossed" is applied to yards of square sails that are installed with their mid-portion located at the masts.

Royal yards are the fourth highest yards in square rig, being fitted above the lower, topsail, and topgallant yards. The unusual feature with *Sierra Nevada* is that, at this period, most large clippers were being fitted with square "skysail" yards, which were set above the royals to capture a bit more wind (see Chapters 29 and 30).

Great Republic, 1853

(Structure in accordance with *Description of the Largest Ship in the World*.)[10]

On December 26, 1853, Donald McKay's gigantic clipper *Great Republic* floated moored at her dock at the foot of Dover Street in New York where she had onloaded 6,000 tons of cargo preparatory to casting off on her maiden voyage, scheduled for the following day.

On December 28, 1853 only the skeletal remains of this, the largest monolithic, free-moving structure that man had produced up to this time, lay settled on the floor of the East River, the victim of an initially small fire that had ignited a block away.

Great Republic had floated unequaled in size, untried in performance, and underinsured, a monument to the ingenuity of man. Built at a cost of $300,000, she was insured for about $180,000. The value of her cargo, estimated also at $300,000, was insured for $275,000. The policies were fairly well distributed. Mutual Atlantic wrote $90,000; Mercantile Marine, Sun Mutual, and others were holding policies of $30,000 each. One policy for $20,000 was written in Philadelphia. The remainder was divided among offices in Boston and other localities. The small, wind-whipped fire became an uncontrollable conflagration that consumed nine neighboring stores, the clipper ship *White Squall*, and *Great Republic*. Her size was her undoing, because, laden as she was, she could only be moved at high tide. Three other vessels were towed into the stream, each sustaining little or no damage.

The remains would be raised, salvaged, resold, and rebuilt with cut-down hull and reduced sparring, and would live to sail a successful life until being abandoned at sea in 1872. However, the potential of the original *Great Republic* never had the chance to proclaim itself, and all that can now be done is to wonder and conjecture upon what phenomenal achievements this great vessel might have made. It was a sad fate for a ship that never put to sea. Figure 6.19 shows the midship section of the original *Great Republic* as drawn and described at the time of her launching.[10]

She is the only American-built clipper that had four laid decks, and was designed with little deadrise and extreme swell of the sides. The keelson assembly was monstrous, and all ceiling and structure was of large scantlings, even for a vessel of her size. Due to the extreme spread of her floor she was fitted with wing stanchions that were footed on the bilge keelsons and extended upward for two decks, being headed under the middle deck. All her stanchions below this deck were fitted with knees on the various keelsons, but were clasped to the lower and middle deck beams with iron plates and straps. Even so, her construction required 1,650 knees. Such care was devoted to her construction that all iron bolts in her frames, sternpost, keelson assembly, bilge keelsons, waterways, and thick strakes on all decks were *coaged*, or surrounded by a short dowel or plug of hardwood when installed. (The installation of coags will be covered later as a detail of construction; see Chapter 9.)

In a period when a large clipper ship required about 500,000 feet of pine in its construction, it is interesting to note that *Great Republic* required 1,500,000 feet of pine. In addition she used 2,056 tons of white oak, 336½ tons of iron, and 56 tons of copper. This last figure does not include the weight of her sheathing, which was yellow metal.

(text continued on page 117)

Figure 6.19. Great Republic, *1853.*

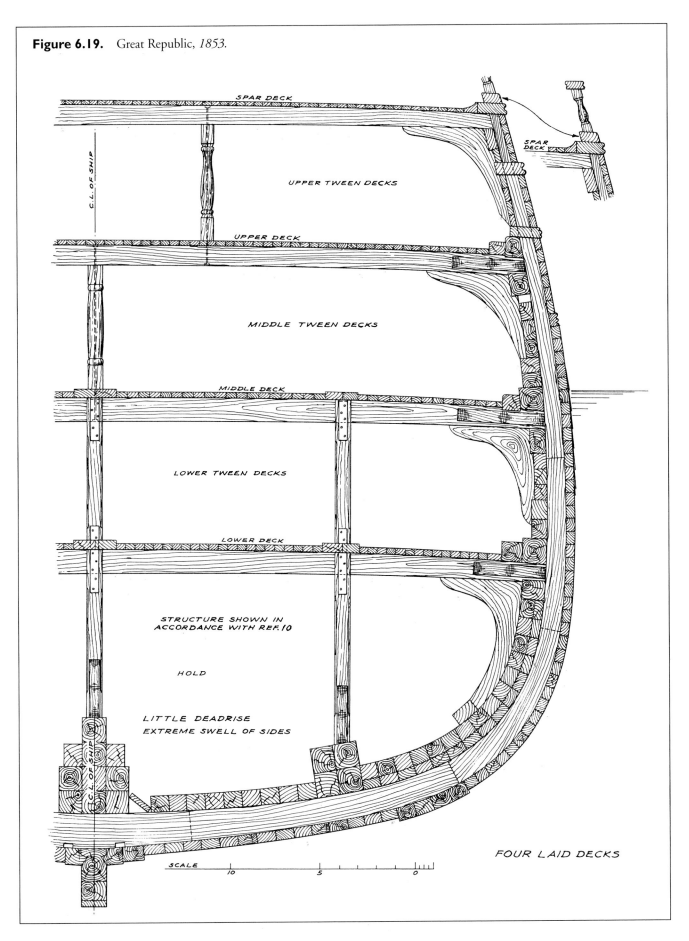

SPAR DECK

C.L. OF SHIP

UPPER TWEEN DECKS

SPAR DECK

UPPER DECK

MIDDLE TWEEN DECKS

MIDDLE DECK

LOWER TWEEN DECKS

LOWER DECK

STRUCTURE SHOWN IN
ACCORDANCE WITH REF. 10

HOLD

LITTLE DEADRISE
EXTREME SWELL OF SIDES

C.L. OF SHIP

FOUR LAID DECKS

SCALE
10   5   0

Figure 6.20. Great Republic, *1853—structure in accordance with scantlings in* Models and Measurements.

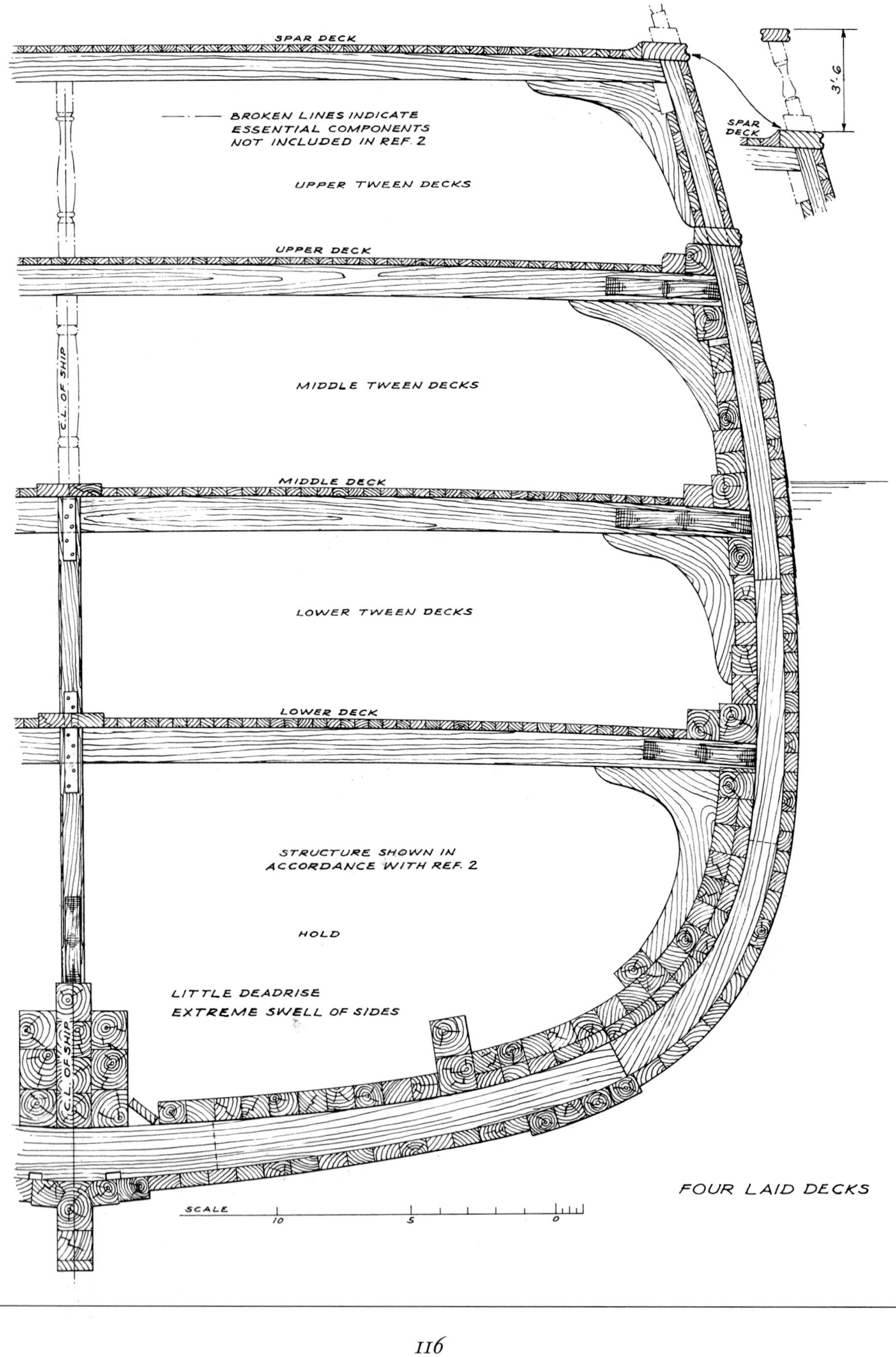

SPAR DECK

BROKEN LINES INDICATE
ESSENTIAL COMPONENTS
NOT INCLUDED IN REF. 2

UPPER TWEEN DECKS

3'.6

SPAR
DECK

UPPER DECK

C.L. OF SHIP

MIDDLE TWEEN DECKS

MIDDLE DECK

LOWER TWEEN DECKS

LOWER DECK

STRUCTURE SHOWN IN
ACCORDANCE WITH REF. 2

HOLD

LITTLE DEADRISE
EXTREME SWELL OF SIDES

C.L. OF SHIP

FOUR LAID DECKS

SCALE
10   5   0

(text continued from page 114)

A very unusual structural detail was built into the structure of *Great Republic*, a detail that is always avoided in construction if at all possible. This was the matter of locating a stanchion on a beam in a "soft" spot. A soft spot, in structural design, is a location under the foot of a column that is not supported by a vertical member. Normally, stiffness and rigidity of structure are maintained by the continuous support of columns one above the other, the lowest member being footed upon a solid base.

As illustrated in Figure 6.19, the turned stanchion in the upper tween decks stands greatly offset from the centerline stanchion below by about one-quarter the length of the unsupported span of the transverse upper deck beam. This is a condition that produces relative flexibility under any condition of loading.

The spar deck structure of this vessel was relatively light and was not intended to assume any severely loaded condition. Nevertheless, from a structural and engineering standpoint, locating a member in a "soft" spot is a practice which meets with general disapproval unless some means is provided to divert the load to a "hard" spot somewhere below.

Great Republic, 1853

(Structure in accordance with scantlings in *Models and Measurements*)

The construction details of *Great Republic* as specified in McKay's list of scantlings are not as complete as those reported in the previous reference[10] and, upon the surface at least, are not as palatable. As in several of the previously illustrated McKay vessels, certain items have not been included here, but their presence was absolutely essential to the well-being of a vessel. This statement refers to the lack of any information concerning stanchions between the middle deck and the spar deck. A minimum requirement would demand a stanchion on the centerline of ship on each deck in order to stiffen the 40-foot span of beams from one side of the vessel to the other.

A comparison between the vessel as shown in this figure and the details shown in Figure 6.19 reveals that the ship, even if strong enough with centerline stanchions, would have been excessively limber. Due to her tremendous size it can readily be assumed that her structural members would have been subjected to extreme "working" when underway. The interior space was too voluminous to remain stiff and rigid with so few large members located throughout this vast interior.

Hindsight apparently prevailed while she was on the ways. As can be seen in Figure 6.19, her bilge keelsons were doubled in scantlings and provided footing for newly considered wing stanchions which extended from the bilge to the middle deck. Also apparent in Figure 6.19 is a stanchion arrangement between the middle deck and the spar deck. While this arrangement is far from ideal, it definitely provided some much needed stiffness to the upper structure.

One might suppose that the structural arrangement depicted in Figure 6.20 was an original basic plan for the ship's construction. However, second thoughts could have decided that, for a vessel of such unprecedented bulk, extra consideration should be given to the potential limberness of her 300-foot length.

The principle, "If it does not look right, it probably is not right" seems to have been apropos the situation. A comparison of Figure 6.20 with, for instance, Figure 6.15 shows in full force how lacking in solid structure the ship appeared to be for her size.

However, regardless of arguments for and against certain items of structure, a comparison of *Great Republic*'s midship section with that of any other vessels depicted in the foregoing figures brings home with almost unbelievable emphasis the absolutely colossal proportions of this undertaking.

Part II

Construction of the Hull

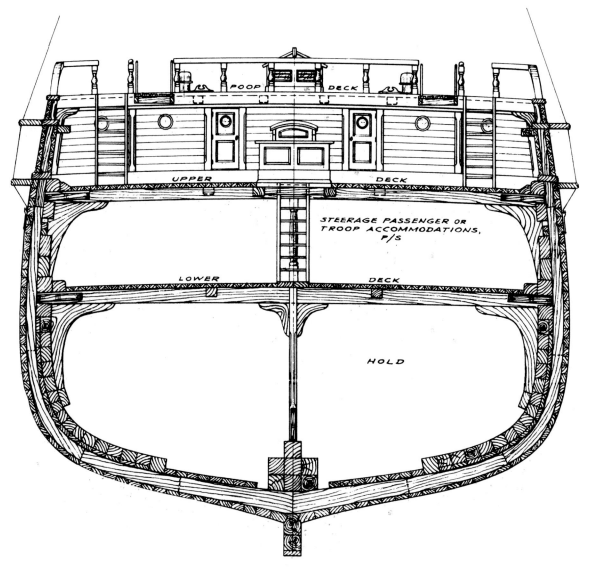

A section amidships,
Lightning
1854

Chapter Seven

KEEL ASSEMBLY

THE SMOOTH, NEWLY PAINTED HULL of a clipper ship moored at dockside as she onloaded her cargo concealed the intricacy of the hidden structure that supported the visible envelope—the enormous task of fabrication, assembly, and fastening that resulted in the final product.

This same deception applied to packets and freighters—and, to a lesser extent, to ships of war, although here the hull was generally pierced with gunports, which broke the sleek appearance of the hull lines.

Except for persons directly involved in the design and building of ships, very few people are aware of the sheer bulk of materials which constitute the framing of the wooden sailing ship. A better appreciation of this situation may be gained by reviewing of a few facts pertaining to the clipper ships *Challenge*, built by William H. Webb in 1851, and *Lightning*, built by Donald McKay in 1854—both typical of the imposing 200-foot clippers, though differing greatly in hull form.

The gross volume of *Challenge*'s hull, measured from the rabbet line of the keel to the underside of the upper deck, and from the rabbet line of the stem to that of the sternpost, was 161,570 cubic feet, figured to the outside of planking. Throughout her length, the thickness of structure—outside planking, moulded dimension of frames, and thickness of ceiling—averaged about 24 inches, based on construction as shown in Figure 6.16. Using these figures, the clear volume of space as bounded by her ceiling and the underside of the upper deck planking amounted to 129,000 cubic feet, or 80 percent of her gross volume; the remaining 20 percent is structure.

Applying the same parameters to *Lightning*, her gross volume was 157,840 cubic feet. Using the construction shown in Figure 6.10, which also indicates an average wall thickness of about 24 inches, her resulting net clear volume was 128,155 cubic feet, which is 81 percent of gross; her structure comprised the remaining 19 percent.

In both clippers, however, the inroads of structure on cargo space were still not complete. The net space was further diminished by the fabrication and installation of keelsons, stanchions, beams, knees, decks, and other structural components, leaving considerably less space for payload than the gross volume would indicate.

In comparing these two clippers, an obvious question is bound to arise. How could two vessels, each 240 feet long and of 44-foot beam, contain the same volume when one had such extreme deadrise and the other had such a relatively flat floor? The answer lies in a third dimension, namely the depth of hold, which in *Challenge* was 25 feet 6 inches, while in *Lightning* it was 23 feet.

The thrust of the comparison is to illustrate the extent and scale of the use of timber in wooden vessels and also to underscore one of the main factors that doomed vessels built with extreme deadrise—namely, the lack of carrying capacity.

In this section, Figures 6.1 and 6.2 will serve as the principal guides for naming various structural components of wooden vessels in general and clippers in particular, as we describe each item, its function, and the details of its construction.

European vs. American Construction

To become familiar with the construction of wooden ships in the 1800s, particularly clippers, is to see the evolution of certain basic procedures, techniques, and philosophies that motivated the various shipbuilders in America.

There were obvious differences at the time between European and American construction, although most of these were hidden from sight once the ship had been completed. European shipbuilding progressed at a slower, more casual pace than did shipbuilding in the United States—partly due to the cultural differences, and partly due to differing requirements in the way of speed.

For the European, the basic underlying philosophy was

founded on the tenet that what could not be finished today could be finished tomorrow. For that reason, certain time-consuming details and refinements were routinely included in European construction. Americans, on the other hand, were constantly obsessed with speed. They were not content with the fact that there was a tomorrow, and this penchant for constant hurry and speed began to appear in their methods of ship construction. The ties that bound the peoples together over the expanse of the ocean were slowly dissolving, and totally independent philosophies were being adopted by Americans.

Consequently, much of the refinement that was a part of European ship construction was discarded in the United States. The creed, "Don't force it—use a bigger hammer" became the accepted means of construction. And, in actuality, the results were highly successful.

In European vessels, mortise-and-tenon joints were used extensively in vital connections; tabling was widely used in scarphs; and an accepted practice was to use tabling, or fit a spline, between two pieces such as the main and inner sternposts. Not so with the Americans. Those refinements were eliminated by the simple expedient of increasing the number of fastenings that held two pieces together. Moreover, the United States had a plentiful supply of almost any species, size, and shape of timber needed to form a good ship in minimal time. As a result, many ships were constructed in a manner that accommodated the available timber. No one had even the remotest thought that it could not go on forever.

Keel Construction

The ship's keel (Figure 6.2, item A) was generally composed of two or more *tiers* or thicknesses. In some cases a keel might have sided and moulded dimensions small enough to allow its being constructed in only one tier. Figure 7.1 shows cross sections of the forms of keel construction that appear in this book.

For ships reaching 200 feet long on the keel, it is obvious that no timber was obtainable of sufficient length to form the keel without being pieced together. Thus, the use of scarphs was necessary and of paramount importance.

The maximum practical cross section of a keel which could be fashioned from a single tier was about 16 inches by 22 inches. And, since logs ranging between 40 feet to 50 feet in length were most desirable from the standpoint of handling and availability, this meant that, at a height of 50 feet above the ground, the tree must be a minimum of 28 inches in diameter. Allowing for taper, this required a tree about 3 feet in diameter at its base.

At the time of the clipper ships, this size tree was becoming a scarce commodity. Smaller trees were, however, still in

plentiful supply, so timbers 16 inches square were routinely specified in the construction of keels, and tiers were assembled one upon the other. Keel sidings ranged from a minimum of 12 inches to a maximum of 16 inches. Of course, there were exceptions to this generalization, such as, of the vessels covered in this volume, *Ellen Foster*, with a keel sided 17 inches.

When a clipper was begun, the first task was to piece together keel blocks of suitable dimension and workable height and place them in position on the shipways at predetermined intervals along the centerline of the proposed vessel. The topmost tier of the built-up keel block, the cap piece, was of a thickness which, when split out, or otherwise removed from beneath the keel which rested upon it, allowed insertion of the shoe or false keel.

Assuming that timbers of the proper length had been hewn and squared to their specified sided and moulded dimensions, the following information was provided to the field—that is, the activities or trades involved in actual construction as opposed to indoor work such as designing, drawing, or lofting, for example—by the mould loft: the scarph moulds, moulds for shaping the ends of the keel in way of the stem and the sternpost, moulds for sizing and shaping the keel rabbet, and the location of frame spacing. This information about the frame spacing was scribed or otherwise marked on a keel batten or battens of considerable length, perhaps 20 feet. In a ship having uniform frame spacing, such battens could be used throughout the length of the keel. In ships having variable frame spacing, as advocated by William H. Webb, specific battens were required for the various sections along the keel.

Since the top of the keel and the moulded baseline did not always coincide, this being a builder's prerogative, any moulds that pertained to the shaping of the keel rabbet would, of necessity, be obliged to indicate the dimensional difference between the two when it was a factor. It follows, therefore, that the top of the keel was not always a part of the moulded form of the hull. One of the difficulties with this situation is that no mention is made of it in specific descriptions of the various vessels. So, from a historical standpoint, one can only surmise.

It can be noted, however, that Lauchlan McKay wrote, when referring to some of his drawings in his book *The Practical Shipbuilder*, "Although I have represented the upper edge of the keel for the upper edge of the rabbett, I am far from approving the plan. . . ." He then goes on to aspire that future shipbuilders will avoid the practice and raise the substance of the keel to a nominal height above this line. This wish, however, did not wholly come to be a fact.

Any necessary markings and information that had been passed on to the field from the mould loft were appropriately transferred to the actual timbers to be used. When this

Figure 7.1. *Cross sections through keels.*

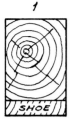

1
SHOE
SINGLE LOG
UNIFORM SIDING
UNIFORM MOULDING
2
SHOE
SINGLE LOG
UNIFORM SIDING
VARIABLE MOULDING, DEEP FORWARD
3
SHOE
TWO TIERS
UNIFORM SIDING
UNIFORM MOULDING
4
SHOE
TWO TIERS
BEARDED SIDING
UNIFORM MOULDING
BEARDING IS UNIFORM THROUGHOUT LENGTH OF KEEL
5
SHOE
TWO TIERS
UNIFORM SIDING
VARIABLE MOULDING, DEEP AFT
6
SHOE
TWO TIERS
UNIFORM SIDING
VARIABLE MOULDING, DEEP AMIDSHIP
KEEL ROCKERED
7
SHOE
THREE TIERS
UNIFORM SIDING
UNIFORM MOULDING
NOTE - IN A TIERED KEEL THE INDIVIDUAL TIERS WERE NOT NECESSARILY OF THE SAME MOULDED DIMENSION.

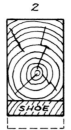

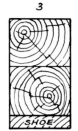

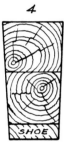

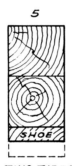

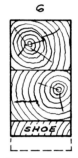

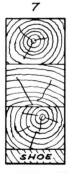

preparation was completed, actual work on the keel assembly could commence.

The shipbuilders of the time sometimes preferred to install a stem and sternpost sided slightly smaller than that of the keel. When this was done, the siding of the keel was diminished at the rate of ¼ inch per foot along the keel in a straight taper until the sidings of the members were equal. This procedure, when followed in way of the sternpost, accommodated the installation of a thinner rudder, which was considered an advantage in reducing resistance as the waters parted by the ship's entrance closed together behind the run as the ship moved forward. Although this practice was not generally followed in the construction of the clippers, it was not entirely unknown. For instance, the table of moulded offsets for William H. Webb's last medium clipper, *Black Hawk*, states that the keel was sided 15 inches, the stem and apron sided 14 inches, and the sternpost sided 14 inches at the heel, 16 inches at the head.

Table 7.1 is a compilation of keel construction details and material of the fastenings for vessels in this volume where such information has been found.

The shoe, which protects the bottom of the keel, is shown in Figure 6.2, item B, and is covered in Chapter 10.

Keel Scarph

The keel scarph, shown in Figure 7.2, was generally the first item to be cut and fitted in the prepared timbers. This operation included determining and recording the locations of every fastening that would be used in connecting the various logs. This knowledge became more and more important as construction progressed and the danger of a new fastening driving hard into one already installed increased. The quantity of metal bolts or rods that are driven into a total keel assembly is difficult to appreciate until the detailed steps have been followed. Metal interfering with metal produced disastrous results.

After the scarphs had been cut and fitted, the locations of holes to accommodate their fastenings were marked. In building multiple-tier keels, this was the only preparation required for any tiers that were not subject to the cutting of the rabbet to receive the garboard strake. See Figure 7.2, details B and C.

Most keels required from three to six scarphs, depending upon the length of the vessel being constructed. The scarphs ranged from 8 to 12 feet in length, which meant that as much as 24 feet of a given log could be subject to the cutting and shaping of the required scarphs. Thus it was most desirable that long timbers be used in order to have sound, solid scantlings throughout most of their length. There were other restrictions, one of which was the requirement that the scarphs in various tiers be shifted so as to lie substantially clear of each other. Also, practice and strength considera-

tions demanded that no scarph be located under a mast step.

The type and size of scarph was specified by the designer. With this information the mould loft determined the location of each scarph to avoid the mast steps and to accommodate the lengths of timber available. A mould was made to the configuration of the parts of the scarph. This mould would be used throughout the length of the ship for a tier of given sided and moulded dimension.

If the several tiers were of different scantlings, suitable moulds would be formed to account for the new dimensions. The moulds could be skeletal in form, as those shown in Figure 1.10, or of solid construction and would be used in the field when the scarph was fashioned. The mould loft laid out and noted all pertinent data and identification on each required mould. During this period, all scarphs in a single-log keel, and those in the lowest tier in keels of multiple-tier construction, were cut with the lower lip laid aft. One of the most complete descriptions of a specified keel scarph is provided by Donald McKay in his list of scantlings[2] and illustrated in Figure 7.2, detail A.

Keel Rabbet

A keel rabbet, grooved or beveled, was required in the keel of every ship to receive the garboard, or lowermost, strake. In the clippers this strake was universally quite a bit thicker than the bottom planking of the vessel and was known as a "thick garboard." Any exceptions were the smaller vessels in which the garboard and bottom planks were of the same thickness.

The thick garboard was "invented" to overcome the weakness of the keel in way of the keel rabbets. The effective thickness of material in way of the rabbets was only one-half of the keel siding. This is discussed in more detail later in this chapter. Garboards are discussed in Chapter 20.

In packets and freighters with very flat floors and long, full bodies, the thick garboard was merely butted against the side of the keel throughout the length of the vessel until an appropriate frame was reached near each end of the vessel, at which points the bevel rabbet was begun as a transition between the butted garboard and its ends which would be fashioned for fitting into the stem and sternpost rabbets. This rabbet treatment did not find its way into clipper construction due to the deadrise in such ships. However, at a later date the form was commonplace.

The forms of rabbet found in clippers are illustrated in Figure 1.2.

The type of rabbet that was to be cut was a discretionary matter for the designer or builder, and, unfortunately, detailed information as to which type was chosen is not as widely recorded as one would desire. However, it appears reasonable to conclude that in the smaller vessels which were built without thick garboards, the *bevel rabbet* was cut. In large vessels where the thick garboard was installed, the

Table 7.1. *Keel details.*

Notes: 1. * indicates that shoe is included in depth of keel.
2. Per ref.2 shoe is fastened with treenails and 1" composition bolts.
3. Abbreviations: S.= Sided; M.= Moulded.

Vessel & Ref.#	Form of keel, Fig.7.1	Size, S. x M.	Species of wood	Tier fastenings	Shoe	Remarks
Alarm #1	1	16"x24"	rock maple	none	*	
Amphitrite #1	3	15"x30"	rock maple	copper	*	Siding and moulding scaled from lines.
Andrew Jackson #20,47,59	3	15"x30"	oak	copper	*	
Antelope #1	1	13"x17"	rock maple	none	*	
Asa Eldridge #1	1	16"x24"	rock maple	none	*	12' scarphs
Bald Eagle #1	3	16"x30"	white oak	copper	*	
Beverly #3	1	15"x20"	rock maple	none	*	
Belle of the West #1,31	1	12"x22"	oak	none	*	Siding and moulding scaled from lines.
Black Hawk #18,24,47	3	15"x30"	oak	copper	*	Siding from offsets. Mldg. scaled from lines.
Blue Jacket #5			white oak			Construction reported similar to Golden Light.
Bonita #1			oak			
Bounding Billow Bark #1	1	14"x18"	white oak	none	*	Siding from offsets. Mldg. scaled from lines. See Figure 3.1, type 6.
Celestial #18,20,42	6	14"x42"max.	oak		*	#2- keel 16"x20", each 16"x16" tier 5 pieces, 12' scarphs, hooked and wedged, 10 1" bolts and 4 spikes. See note 2.
Challenge #1	3	16"x38"	white oak	copper	*	
Challenger #1	3	16"x32"	rock maple	copper	*	
Champion of the Seas #1,2	3	#1- 16"x16"/16"x16"	rock maple (& oak, ref.2)	copper	oak, 16"x4½"	Thickness of shoe not given.
Charger #1	3		rock maple	copper; treenails	*	Each tier 4 pieces with 10' scarphs.
Charmer #1	3		white oak	copper		Construction similar to New York packets of 1500 tons.
Cleopatra #1	3	15½"x36"	white oak	copper	*	
Climax #1	3	16"x26"	rock maple	copper	*	Thickness of shoe not given.
Coeur de Lion #1	3	16"x16"/16"x16"	New Hampshire white oak	copper	oak, 16"x	Siding from offsets. Mldg. scaled from lines.
Comet #18,24	3	14"x40"	oak		*	
Cyclone #1,3	1	15"x30"	Massachusetts white oak	copper	*	Made up of 4 pieces.
Daring #1	3	14½"x26"	white oak	yellow metal	oak, 14½"x4"	Tiers fastened every 4', 12' lock scarphs.
Dauntless #1	3	15"x36"	white oak	copper, 1⅛"	*	#2- keel 16"x20", each 16"x12" tier 5 pieces, fastened every 6' to 8' with 1" to 1⅛" bolts, 12' scarphs. See note 2.
Donald McKay #1,2	3	#1-16"x16"/16"x16"	rock maple (and white oak, ref.2)	copper	oak, 16"x4"	
Don Quixote #1	2	16"x24"fwd 18"aft	rock maple	none	*	See Figure 3.1, type 8.
Eagle #5	7	16"x44"	white oak	copper	*	
Eagle Wing #1	3	16"x27"	white oak	copper	*	12' scarphs
Edwin Forrest #1			white oak		*	Construction similar to a 1500 ton vessel.
Electric Spark #1	1	16"x24"	rock maple	none	*	
Ellen Foster #1	1	17"x22"	white oak	none	*	
Empress of the Sea #1,2	3	#1-16"x16"/16"x16"	white oak (and rock maple, ref.2)	copper, 1",1⅛"	oak, 16"x4½"	#2- keel 16"x20", each 16"x14" tier 5 pieces, 12' scarphs, hooked and 4 spikes. See note 2.
Endeavor #1	1	15"x26"	rock maple	none	*	
Eringo Bark #1	1	12"x15"	oak	none	*	10' keyed scarphs, ref.1.
Eureka #4	3	16"x17"/16"x17"	live oak	copper	*	Thickness of shoe not given.
Fair Wind #1	1	16"x23"	rock maple	none	*	
Fearless #29,47	1	12"x24"	oak	none	*	Siding and moulding scaled from lines.
Fleet Wing #1	1	15"x24"	rock maple	none	*	
Flyaway #18,24	3	14"x27"	rock maple	none	*	Siding from offsets. Mldg. scaled from lines.
Flying Arrow #1	1	16"x24"	rock maple	none	*	
Flying Childers #1	3	15"x36"	rock maple	copper	*	
Flying Cloud #1,2	3	16"x44"/16"x38½"	rock maple (and oak, ref.2)	copper, 1",1⅛"	oak, 16"x4½"	#2- keel 16"x20", each 16"x14" tier 4 pieces, 12' scarphs, hooked and wedged, 10 1" bolts and 4 spikes. See note 2.
Flying Dragon #1			white oak	copper		
Flying Dutchman #18,24	3	14"x30"			*	Siding from offsets. Mldg. scaled from lines.

Table 7.1. *Continued.*

Vessel & Ref. #	Form of keel, Fig. 7.1	Size, S. x M.	Species of wood	Tier fastenings	Shoe	Remarks
Flying Eagle #1	1	16"x24"	white oak	none	*	
Flying Fish #1,2	#1- 7 / #2- 3	16"x38"	oak and rock maple	copper, 1',⅛"	oak, 16"x4½"	#2- keel 16"x20", each 16"x14", tier 5 pieces, 12' scarphs, hooked and wedged, 10 1" bolts and 4 spikes. See note 2.
Flying Mist #1	1	16"x21"	rock maple	none	16"x3½"	Keel in 4 pieces, 12' scarphs.
Galatea #1			white oak			
Game Cock #1	3	16"x36"	rock maple	copper	*	
Gazelle #4,18,24	7	14"x42"	white oak	copper	* 14"x	Siding from offsets. Thickness of shoe not given.
Gem of the Ocean #1	1	16"x20"	oak	none	*	
Golden Eagle #1	3	15"x26"	rock maple	copper	*	
Golden Fleece (2nd) #1	3	16"x32"	rock maple	yellow metal	*	12' scarphs
Golden Light #1	3	15"x26"	rock maple	copper	*	
Golden West #1			white oak			
Grace Darling #1	3	16"x26"	white oak	copper	*	Keyed scarphs
Great Republic (1853) #2,4,10	3	#2-16"x20" / 16"x12"	#2,10-rock maple. #4-white oak	copper, 1",⅛"	oak, 16"x4½"	Each tier 7 pieces, 12' scarphs, hooked and wedged, 12 ⅛" copper bolts. See note 2. This data per refs. 2 and 10. Per ref.4, top tier is 8 pieces; scarphs also contain 8 composition spikes 12" long, driven one side, clinched other side.
Great Republic (rebuilt) #103	3	16"x20" / 16"x12"	rock maple	copper	16"x4½"	
Henry Hill Bark #1	3	12"x28"	rock maple	copper	*	
Herald of the Morning #12	1	15"x20"	rock maple	none	*	
Hoogly #1	3	15"x36"	rock maple	copper	*	
Hurricane #4			white oak			
Indiaman #1	1	15"x26"	rock maple	none	*	
Intrepid #18	3	15"x		copper	*	
Invincible #4,18	3	16"x34"	white oak	copper	* 16"x	Siding from offsets. Thickness of shoe not given.
James Baines #2	3	16"x20" / 16"x14"	oak and rock maple	copper, 1",⅛"	*	Each tier 5 pieces, 12' scarphs, hooked and wedged, 10 1" bolts and 4 spikes. See note 2.
John Bertram #1	3	15"x36"	rock maple	copper	*	8' scarphs
John Gilpin #1	3	15½"x32"	rock maple	copper	*	
John Land #1,32	3	16"x30"	white oak	copper	*	Built as a duplicate of *Winged Arrow*.
John Stuart #4			Virginia white oak			
John Wade #1			white oak			
Joseph Peabody #1	1	15"x22"	rock maple	none	*	12' scarphs
King Fisher #1			white oak			
Lady Franklin						
Lamplighter Bark #1			white oak			
Lightfoot #1	3	16"x16" / 16"x16"	white oak	copper	16"x	Thickness of shoe not given.
Lightning #1,2	3	#1-15"x15" / 15"x15"	white oak (and rock maple, ref.2)	copper	oak, 15"x4½" / 16"x14"	#2- keel 16"x20", each 16"x14", tier 5 pieces, 12' scarphs, hooked and wedged, 10 1" bolts and 4 spikes. See note 2.
Mameluke #1	3	16"x16" / 16"x16"	rock maple	copper	16"x	Thickness of shoe not given.
Mary Robinson						
Mastiff #1	1	14"x26"	rock maple	none	*	
Mermaid Bark #1	3	14"x28"	rock maple	copper	*	See Figure 3.1, type 9.
Morning Light #1	3	16"x16" / 16"x16"	New Hampshire white oak	copper	16"x	Thickness of shoe not given.
Mystery #1	3	15"x34"	rock maple	copper	*	
Nightingale #3			white oak			
Noonday #1	3	15"x15" / 15"x11"	rock maple	copper	15"x	Thickness of shoe not given.
Northern Light						
Ocean Express #1	3	16"x16" / 16"x16"	oak	copper	16"x	Thickness of shoe not given.
Ocean Pearl #1	1	15"x20"	rock maple	none	*	
Ocean Telegraph #5			white oak			
Onward #1	3	15"x32"	oak	copper	*	
Osborne Howes						
Panther			rock maple	none	*	
Phantom #1	2	16"x24"fwd / 17"aft	rock maple	none	*	See Figure 3.1, type 8.

Table 7.1. *Continued.*

Vessel & Ref.#	Form of keel, Fig. 7.1	Size, S. x M.	Species of wood	Tier fastenings	Shoe	Remarks
Queen of Clippers #1	3	16"x32"	white oak	copper	*	
Queen of the Pacific						
Queen of the Seas #1	3	16"x16" 16"x16"	white oak	copper	*	Shoe is not included in moulded depth.
Quickstep Bark #1	1	14"x24"	rock maple	none	*	Siding is not given.
Racehorse Bark #1	3	x27½"	white oak	copper	*	
Racer #3			white oak & rock maple	copper	*	
Radiant #1	3	15"x36"	white oak	copper	*	
Raven #3	3	15"x32"	white oak	copper	15"x	Thickness of shoe not given.
Red Jacket #14,19,46	3	14"x24"	Virginia white oak	copper	*	Siding and moulding scaled from lines.
Robin Hood /			oak			
Rocket Bark #47						
Roebuck #1	1	15"x20"	rock maple	none	*	
Romance of the Sea #1	3	15"x15" 15"x15"	white oak	copper	oak, 15"x	Thickness of shoe given.
Santa Claus #1	3	15"x14" 15"x14"	gumwood & rock maple	copper	oak, 15"x	12' scarphs, keyed. Thickness of shoe not given.
Saracen #1	1	16"x24"	rock maple	none	*	See Figure 3.1, type 9.
Sea Bird Bark #1			white oak			
Seaman's Bride #4			Chesapeake white oak			
Sea Serpent #47			oak			
Uncowah #18		14"x				
Shooting Star #1	3	15"x34"	rock maple	copper	*	
Sierra Nevada #1	3	16"x16" 16"x16"	New Hampshire white oak	copper	16"x	Thickness of shoe not given.
Silver Star #1	1	15"x20"	rock maple	none	*	12' scarphs
Southern Cross #1	3	16"x32½"	rock maple	copper	*	
Sovereign of the Seas #2	3	16"x20" 16"x14"	white oak	copper, 1",18	oak & maple, 16"x4½"	Each tier 6 pieces, 12' scarphs, hooked and wedged, 10 1" bolts and 4 spikes. See note 2.
Spitfire #1	3	16"x32"	white oak	copper	*	
Staffordshire #1,2	3	#1-16"x38" #2-16"x36½"	rock maple (and oak, ref.2)	copper	#1- * #2- 16"x4½"	#2- keel 16"x20", each 16"x12" tier 5 pieces, 12' scarphs, hooked and wedged, 10 1" bolts and 4 spikes. See note 2.

Vessel & Ref.#	Form of keel, Fig. 7.1	Size, S. x M.	Species of wood	Tier fastenings	Shoe	Remarks
Stag Hound #1,2	3	#1-16"x46"	oak and rock maple	copper	#1- * #2- 16"x4½"	#2- keel 16"x20", each 16"x14" tier 5 pieces, 12' scarphs, hooked and wedged, 10 1" bolts and 4 spikes. See note 2. 8' to 10' scarphs. ref.1.
Star of the Union #1			white oak			
Starr King						
Storm King #1	3	15"x36"	white oak	copper	*	
Sultana Bark #1	3	14"x40"	oak and rock maple	copper	14"x4"	
Sunny South #42	3	14"x40"	white oak	copper	*	Siding and moulding scaled from lines. See Figure 3.1, type 7.
Surprise #1	3	15"x38"	oak and rock maple	copper	*	10' scarphs bolted with 1" copper.
Swallow #1			white oak	copper	*	Siding and moulding scaled from lines.
Sweepstakes #42	3	16"x32"	white oak	copper	*	Siding from offsets. Mldg. scaled from lines.
Sword Fish #18,24	3	14"x28"	white oak	copper	*	Siding from offsets.
Syren #3	3		white oak	copper	*	
Telegraph #1			white oak			
Thatcher Magoun #1	2	16"x26"fwd 18"aft	rock maple	none	*	See Figure 3.1, type 8.
Tornado						
Uncowah #18		14"x				Siding from offsets. Moulding not given.
War Hawk #1	3	14½"x30"	rock maple	copper	*	
Water Witch #1	3	15"x32"	rock maple	copper	*	12' scarphs
Western Continent						
Westward Ho #1,2	3	#1-15"x30"	white oak (and rock maple,ref.2)	copper	#1- * #2- 16"x4½"	#2- keel 16"x20", each 16"x14" tier 5 pieces, hooked and wedged, 10 1" bolts and 4 spikes. See note 2.
West Wind #1			white oak			
Whirlwind #1	3	15"x30"	white oak	copper	*	
Whistler #1	3	14"x30"	rock maple	copper	*	
Wildfire Bark #1	5	x19"fwd 42"aft	oak	copper	*	Siding not given. See Figure 3.1, type 10.

Table 7.1. *Continued.*

Vessel & Ref.#	Form of keel, Fig. 7.1	Size, S. x M.	Species of wood	Tier fastenings	Shoe	Remarks
Wild Pigeon #1,42	4	15" top, 12" shoe, mld. 32"	rock maple	copper	*	Mldg. scaled from lines. See Figure 3.1, type 1.
Wild Ranger #1	3	15"x30"	rock maple	copper	*	
Wild Rover						
Winged Arrow #1	3	16"x30"	white oak	copper	*	
Winged Racer #1	3	16"x36"	rock maple	copper	*	
Witchcraft #1	3	15"x36"	rock maple	copper	*	
Witch of the Wave #1	7	15"x39"	rock maple	copper	*	
Wizard #1	3	16"x32"	rock maple	copper	*	
Young America #24,47	3	16"x31"	live oak	copper	*	Siding not given in offsets. Siding and moulding scaled from lines.
Young Turk Bark #1	1	13"x22"	white oak	none	*	

grooved rabbet, which was by its nature superior to but more expensive than the bevel, was used quite extensively, and many of these vessels are reported in the contemporary descriptions[1] and elsewhere as having their garboards "let into" the keel. The structural advantage of the grooved rabbet resided in the fact that the garboard was forced in against the back rabbet by the nature of the cut. This eliminated the necessity of relying totally upon the fastenings to hold the garboard assembly securely in position.

Another advantage of the grooved rabbet lay in its requiring a smaller seam to receive caulking due to the lesser depth of the surface between the keel and the garboard strake. This resulted in the use of less oakum to fill the joint and in less "horsing up," which was the process of pounding a beetle or mallet against a thin horsing iron in an effort to jam the oakum as firmly as possible into the seam. Excessive horsing resulted in too much stress being placed on adjacent fastenings in the garboard, sometimes to the detriment of the vessel.

On the unassembled sections of the keel, as they lay in the field, the grooved rabbet was cut or "run in" along both sides of the timber except in way of the scarphs. This portion of the rabbet was not cut until the keel had finally been assembled on the keel blocks.

James Peake's work on naval architecture,[7] mentioned earlier, describes in technical and academic detail the procedure for forming the grooved rabbet for thick garboards, and Samuel J. P. Thearle's treatise[8] expounds on its merits in matters of strength.

The mould loft required such basic information as the specified depth of rabbet, the desired thickness of the garboard strake, and the thickness of the bottom planking—information already forwarded to the mould loft by the designers. They, the designers, determined the shape of the rabbet, it being limited in depth by the rules to no more than one-fourth the siding of the keel. Its vertical dimension on the side of the keel was also determined by the designer and was generally about one-and-one-half times the thickness of the bottom planking. From this information the mould loft produced a wooden mould or pattern of the rabbet. Additional pertinent information, such as the extent of the rabbet, was taken from the body plan and forwarded to the field as required.

With this form of rabbet, only one template was needed throughout the midbody until the extremities of the keel were approached; see Chapter 1 for additional description.

Assembling the Keel

The assembling of the keel took place only after all scarphs had been accurately cut and each timber requiring a rabbet had received one. This work was all accomplished in the field while the components were in position, which best facilitated the extensive use of saw, axe, and adze.

The initial placement of the keel sections on the keel blocks was the same for single-log and multiple-tiered keels. They were placed in their proper position on the blocks with the scarphs engaged but not yet fastened. After this had been accomplished, the entire assembly was sighted or, to use the shipwright's term, "eyeballed" for alignment along its entire length. Once it was aligned, short treenails were driven into the keel blocks close against the sides of the keel, thus maintaining its position. After this was done, the wedges were driven home in way of the hooks, and the scarphs were now fixed in their final positions.

If the keel was built of multiple tiers, as shown in Figure 7.2, details B and C, there was no involvement of the

Figure 7.2. *Keel assembly and scarph details.*

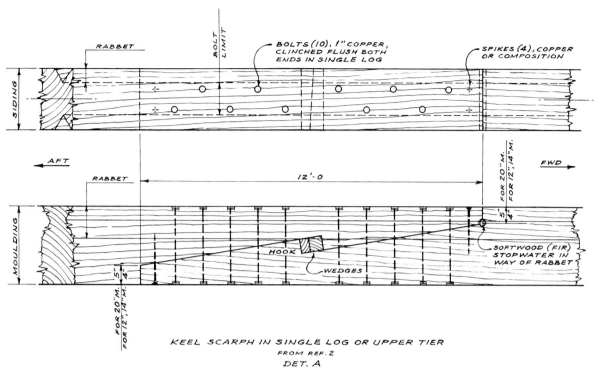

KEEL SCARPH IN SINGLE LOG OR UPPER TIER
FROM REF. 2
DET. A

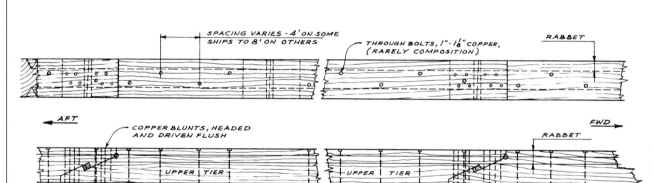

THREE TIER KEEL
DET. C

TWO TIER KEEL
DET. B

TYPICAL CONSTRUCTION OF MULTIPLE TIER KEELS

lower tiers with the keel rabbet, and thus the entire sided dimension of these tiers was available for boring and receiving fastenings. This condition provided the advantage of separating the bolts and spikes in the athwartship direction, and resulted in a superior joint. The fastening arrangement as shown in Figure 7.2, detail A, was followed except that the spread of bolts was not restricted.

If the keel was composed of a single log which, of necessity, contained the keel rabbet, then the details of fastening faced significant restrictions which were controlled by the depth of the rabbet. The limit to the spread of the scarph bolts meant that no bolt should break out in the rabbet. And, since for grooved rabbets this depth of cut was generally about one-quarter of the sided dimension of the keel on each side, there remained a spread equal to only one-half of the total siding. All bolts and spikes in this tier were therefore confined to a spread of about 8 inches, even in the largest of vessels. Figure 7.2, detail A clearly illustrates this restriction and the details of fastening.

Holes were bored through the assembled scarphs to accommodate the bolts, which were generally 1-inch-diameter copper. Smaller holes were bored through both nib ends to receive spikes; in some vessels, these fastenings were yellow metal in lieu of copper. The bolts were driven and riveted over yellow metal rings so that all parts were flush with the timber surfaces. The spikes, too, were driven flush. Iron fastenings were never used in these locations.

In assembling keels that were composed of three tiers, as shown in Figure 7.2, detail C, the method of bolting the scarphs as shown in detail A was obviously not feasible due to the inaccessibility of the lower surface of each tier. In this case the middle tier was set in place on the lower tier, due attention being paid to the proper shift of scarphs; then the scarphs were keyed together in the hooks, and the whole assembly was sighted for alignment, then temporarily dogged together pending final fastening.

As in the bottom tier, the scarphs were bored to accept the required bolts, while the spikes not needed for securing the nibs were omitted. Here, however, the bolts were blunts that were driven through the scarph well into the tier below, their holding power depending upon their grip in the surrounding wood. The blunts were headed and driven flush, either over clinch rings or without them, at the discretion of the builder. Such blunts, like the keel through-bolts, were invariably copper or yellow metal.

The top or rabbeted tier, in two- and three-tiered keels, was subject to the same breadth restrictions applicable to the single-log keel. The manner of installing the fastenings was the same as for the middle tier, with the exceptions of clearing the rabbet and driving spikes in the upper exposed nibs.

In vessels having a beveled keel rabbet, the breadth restrictions for driving bolts were not so severe, especially throughout the midbody, due to the form of the rabbet. However, as the ends of the vessel were approached, this available "seating" diminished until it became as restrictive as that for the grooved rabbet.

After the scarphs in the garboard tier were completely fastened and the various tiers were dogged in position one upon the other, a hole, perhaps 2 inches in diameter, was bored completely across the upper nib of the scarph in way of the rabbet, and a *stopwater*—a dowel of fir—was driven entirely through the breadth of the keel, as shown in Figure 7.2, detail A. Upon immersion of the hull after launching, the soft wood of the stopwater expanded and blocked the passage of water up through the scarph, thus preventing its penetrating behind the bottom planking.

The use of these stopwaters in the way of scarphs immersed in water (and, as will be seen later, with the installation of stem and sternpost) is an obscure detail that would generally go unnoticed, and should therefore be explained in order to clarify their necessity. All portions of the exterior hull planking are made watertight by the introduction of caulking to all seams between planks and to all portions of planking which engage the rabbets of keel, stem, and sternpost. Thus, all possible openings have been "plugged," with the exception of the faying surfaces across the two halves of scarphs that protrude outside the rabbet, as shown in Figure 7.2, detail A, and Figure 8.1; and, as will be seen later, the faying surfaces of the top of the keel and the junction of sternpost and inner post as shown in Figure 8.3. With the installation of the stopwater, this joint, too, became watertight.

With all tiers of the keel now completed and in place on the keel blocks, vertical holes were bored down through the entire assembly at intervals specified by the designer. These holes ranged from 4 feet to 8 feet apart along the keel and were staggered from one side of the centerline to the other within the restrictions imposed by the depth of rabbet. They were of a size to accommodate bolts 1 inch to 1⅛ inches in diameter, the purpose of which was to preserve alignment of the keel structure. The bolts were driven through and finished flush with the top and bottom surfaces of the keel, as shown in Figure 7.2, details B and C. These space restrictions that were caused by the keel rabbet resulted in an inherent weakness in way of the rabbet, which directly contributed to the invention and introduction of the thick garboard.

After the keel assembly had been fastened, the locations of frames and other required data were transferred from keel battens and moulds to the keel proper in anticipation of the work to follow.

The groove or bevel of the keel rabbet was now cut in way of the scarphs, where it had been initially omitted. This essentially completed the assembly of the keel in its entirety, with the exception of attaching the shoe.

STEM AND STERNPOST ASSEMBLIES

Stem Assembly

The stem assembly, usually the first structure to be erected on the keel of a clipper, consisted of four distinct and separate units: the stem, the apron, the false stem, and the gripe. Collectively they were to the forward end of the vessel what the keel assembly was to the bottom—namely, the meeting place and termination of all timbers which came in contact with their various surfaces. As with the keel, it was of paramount importance that the stem assembly be soundly formed and strongly fastened, especially at the forefoot where the two components were joined. Figure 8.1 illustrates a typical stem assembly as would be built for a large clipper ship. All of the parts and fastenings shown are based on details specified for *Lightning* by Donald McKay.[2] The stemson, because of its relative rarity, is not included in this figure, but is shown in Figure 8.2.

Table 8.1 gives known details of the stem assemblies of vessels included in this book.

The Stem

The *stem* is the principal member of this assembly, around which the remainder of the structure was built. Ideally the stem would be formed from a single tree if such a huge timber could be found and procured, but this happened so rarely that the typical specification called for two pieces to be scarphed together. This approach was practical not only from the standpoint of availability of suitably sized timber, but to take advantage of the natural sweep of the grain near the base of the trunk, for strength, as discussed in Chapter 2. For this reason, the form of tree considered best for shaping a stem was one that had been dug out of the ground rather than cut in the traditional manner. Such a log, when obtainable, could be worked so that the natural curves in the swelling of the bole would follow the turn of the foot of the stem near the keel, providing the strongest possible transition from upright to horizontal. (This was far preferable to "short-graining," in

which the direction of the grain and the direction of the structure tend to flow at right angles to each other, thus building in weakness.) A second advantage in using this type of log was that it allowed the shipwright to place the butt end of the log at the ship's forefoot. This was considered best practice since the bole of the tree was the least sound and could be better preserved by constant immersion in the sea.

In spite of the difficulty in obtaining and handling a timber large enough to form the stem in one piece, it was occasionally done. Duncan MacLean reported[1] that the stem of William H. Webb's *Challenge* was white oak, made in one piece sided 16 inches at the foot and 18 inches at the head, and moulded 3½ feet at the foot and 2½ feet at the head. This mammoth log was approximately 35 feet long.

The first step in constructing the stem was to obtain suitable moulds or templates from the mould loft. These would be fabricated and appropriately marked as illustrated in Figure 1.10. Upon completion they were delivered to the field where wood of the proper form and species was selected. Next the shipwrights sided and moulded the pieces to conform to their individual templates, and then fashioned the scarph and the extremities of each piece.

The lower end or *foot* of the lower piece was fashioned as a hook scarph, which would mate with a complementing hook cut in the top surface of the keel. The upper end or *head* of the upper piece was cut at the *angle of steeve* of the bowsprit and, along with the head of the apron, formed the bed upon which the bowsprit rested.

The two pieces that made up the length of the stem were always of a contour that would wholly contain the moulded line of the stem, which was the inner rabbet, and the rabbet line as indicated in Figure 8.1, without either line running outside the material selected.

The after edge of the stem timber was generally located at least 8 inches aft of the moulded line of the stem, to allow room for proper installation of fastenings in the planking

(text continued on page 134)

Figure 8.1. *Typical assembly of stem, apron, false stem, and gripe.*

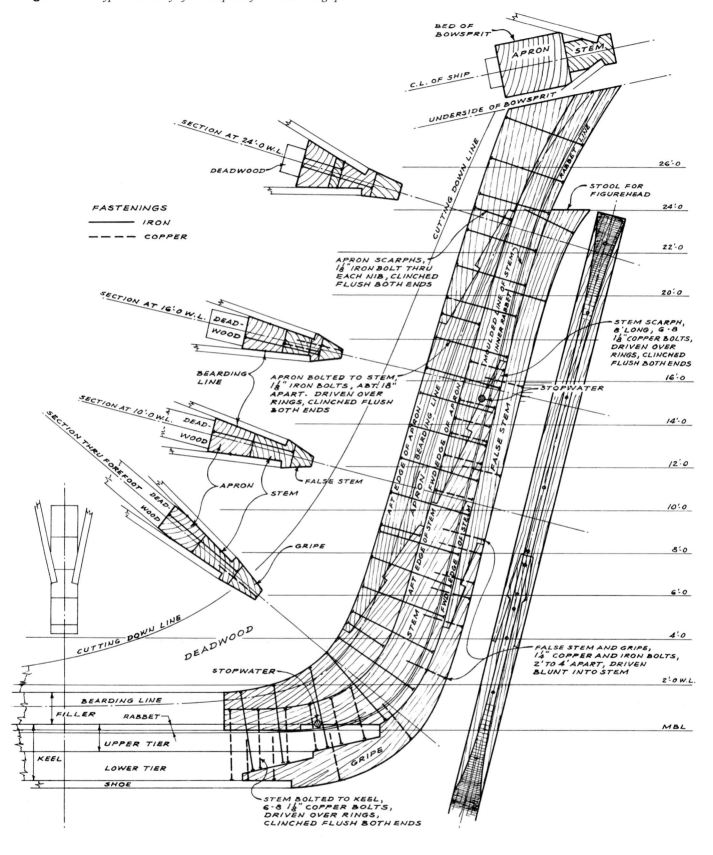

Table 8.1.   *Structural details of stem and sternpost assemblies.*

Abbreviations

Cu - copper	O - oak (variety not named)	NHWO - New Hampshire white oak
Cn - composition	LO - live oak	NWO - Northern white oak
Fe - iron	WO - white oak	VWO - Virginia white oak
Ir - refined iron	CWO - Chesapeake white oak	MDWO - Maryland white oak
Is - Swedish iron	MWO - Massachusetts white oak	
S - Sided		
M - Moulded		

Vessel & Ref.#	Stem assembly	Sternpost assembly
Alarm #1	stem, S. 16" thruout, M. 16" at head, M. 18" at foot. WO; Cu,Fe	sternpost, S. 16" thruout, M. 18" at head, M. 2'-4" at heel. stern knee, 6' body, 7' arm. WO; Cu (thru bolts)
Amphitrite #1	WO; Cu,Fe	WO; Cu,Fe
Andrew Jackson #20,47	O; Cu,Fe	O; Cu,Fe
Antelope #1	WO; Cu,Fe	WO; Cu,Fe
Asa Eldridge #1	stem, one piece. apron, built. WO; Cu,Fe	sternpost, one piece. inner post, built. WO; Cu,Fe
Bald Eagle #1	WO; Cu,Fe	WO; Cu,Fe
Belle of the West #1	O; Cu,Fe	O; Cu,Fe
Beverly #3	WO; Cu,Fe	WO; Cu,Fe
Black Hawk #18,47	stem, S. 14" thruout. WO; Cu,Fe	sternpost, S. 16" at head, S. 14" at heel. WO; Cu,Fe
Blue Jacket #5	WO	WO
Bonita #1	O; Cu,Fe	O; Cu,Fe
Bounding Billow Bark #1	WO; Cn,Fe	WO; Cn,Fe
Celestial #18,20	O; Siding not given in offsets.	O; Siding not given in offsets.
Challenge #1	stem, one piece, head, S.18",M.2'-6, foot, S.16",M.3'-6. apron, S. 34" at bowsprit. WO; Cu,Fe	sternpost, one piece, S. 18" at head, S. 16" at heel. WO; Cu,Fe
Challenger #1	WO; Cu,Fe	WO; Cu,Fe
Champion of the Seas #2	stem,S.16",two pcs., 8' hook scarph, M. 20" at head, M. 26" at foot. apron, S. 30" at bowsprit. false stem tapers to 4" on leading edge. WO; Cu,1"-1¼"; Fe,1⅛"-1¼"	sternpost, head, S.20",M.21", heel, S.16",M.24". inner post, head, S.20",M.20", heel, S.16",M.16". stern knee, S.16", 16' body, 7'-6 arm, 3'-10 thru throat. WO; Cu,1¼"; Fe,1¼"
Charger #1	stem, one piece. two aprons, foot of inner one is a knee. NHWO; Cu,Ir	sternpost is one piece. two stern knees, lower knee has 15' body. NHWO; Cu,Ir
Charmer #1	WO; Cu,Fe	WO; Cu,Fe
Cleopatra #1	WO; Cu,Fe	WO; Cu,Fe
Climax #1	WO; Cu,Ir	WO; Cu,Ir
Coeur de Lion #1	NHWO; Cu,Fe	NHWO; Cu,Fe
Comet #18	stem, S. 13" at foot.	sternpost, S.13" at heel.
Cyclone #1	WO; Cu,Fe	WO; Cu,Fe
Daring #1	built with a stemson. WO; Cn,Ir	WO; Cn,Ir

Vessel & Ref.#	Stem assembly	Sternpost assembly
Dauntless #1	built with a stemson. stem, one piece, S. 16" at foot. MWO; Cu,Fe (white oak is second growth.)	S. 16" at heel. MWO; Cu,Fe
Donald McKay #1,2	built with a stemson, (ref.1). stem,S.16",two pcs., 8' hook scarph, M. 25" at head, M. 30" at foot. apron, S. 32" at bowsprit. false stem tapers to 4" on leading edge. WO; Cn,1"-1¼"; Ir,1¼"	sternpost, head, S.20",M.22"; heel, S.16",M.25". inner post, head, S.20",M.16"; heel, S.16",M.20". stern knee, S.16", 16' body, 8' arm, 4'-2 thru throat. WO; Cn,1¼"; Ir,1¼"
Don Quixote #1	WO; Cu,Fe	two sternpost knees. WO; Cu,Fe
Eagle #5	LO,WO; Cu,Fe	LO,WO; Cu,Fe
Eagle Wing #1	WO; Cu,Fe	WO; Cu,Fe
Edwin Forrest #1	WO; Cu,Fe	WO; Cu,Fe
Electric Spark #1	WO; Cu,Fe	WO; Cu,Fe
Ellen Foster #1	stem, S.17" at foot. WO; Cu,Fe	sternpost,S.17" at heel. WO; Cu,Fe
Empress of the Sea #2	stem,S.16",two pcs., 8' hook scarph, M. 20" at head, M. 24" at foot. apron, S. 30" at bowsprit. false stem tapers to 4" on leading edge. WO; Cu,1"-1¼"; Fe,1⅛",1¼"	sternpost, head, S.20",M.20"; heel, S.16",M.21". inner post, head, S.20",M.20", heel, S.16",M.16". stern knee, S.16", 15' body, 7'-6 arm, 4' thru throat. WO; Cu,1¼"; Fe,1¼"
Endeavor #1	WO; Cu,Is	WO; Cu,Is
Eringo Bark #1	O; Cu,Fe	O; Cu,Fe
Eureka #4	LO; Cu,Fe	LO; Cu,Fe
Fair Wind #1	WO; Cu,Cn,Ir	WO; Cu,Cn,Ir
Fearless #47	O; Cu,Fe	O; Cu,Fe
Fleet Wing #1,47	WO; Cu,Fe	WO; Cu,Fe
Flyaway #18	stem, S. 14" thruout.	sternpost, S. 16" at head, S. 14" at heel.
Flying Arrow #1	WO; Cu,Fe	WO; Cu,Fe
Flying Childers #1	WO; Cu,Fe	WO; Cu,Fe
Flying Cloud #2	stem,S.16",two pcs., 7' hook scarph, M. 20" at head, M. 26" at foot. apron, S. 28" at bowsprit. false stem tapers to 4" on leading edge. WO; Cu,1"-1¼"; Fe,1⅛"-1¼"	sternpost, head, S.20",M.19"; heel, S.16",M.21". inner post, head, S.20",M.20", heel, S.16",M.16". stern knee, S.16", 14' body, 8' arm, 3'-6 thru throat. WO; Cu,1¼"; Fe,1¼"
Flying Dragon #1	WO; Cu,Fe	WO; Cu,Fe
Flying Dutchman #18	stem, S. 14" thruout.	sternpost, S. 16" at head, S. 14" at heel.
Flying Eagle #1	WO; Cu,⅞"-1¼"; Fe,⅞"-1¼"	WO; Cu,⅞"-1¼"; Fe,⅞"-1¼"
Flying Fish #2	stem,S.16",two pcs., 6' hook scarph, M. 20" at head, M. 24" at foot. apron, S. 28" at bowsprit. false stem tapers to 4" on leading edge. WO; Cu,1"-1¼"; Fe,1⅛"-1¼"	sternpost, head, S.20",M.19"; heel, S.16",M.21". inner post, head, S.20",M.20", heel, S.16",M.16". stern knee, S.16", 14' body, 8' arm, 3'-4 thru throat. WO; Cu,1¼"; Fe,1¼"
Flying Mist #1	built with a stemson. stem, one piece. NHWO; Cu,Ir	sternpost, one piece. NHWO; Cu,Ir

Table 8.1. *Continued.*

Vessel & Ref.#	Stem assembly	Sternpost assembly	Vessel & Ref.#	Stem assembly	Sternpost assembly
Galatea #1,47	WO; Cu,Fe	WO; Cu,Fe	Joseph Peabody #1	WO; Cn,Ir	WO; Cn,Ir
Game Cock #1	WO; Cu,Fe	WO; Cu,Fe	King Fisher #1	WO; Cu,Fe	WO; Cu,Fe
Gazelle #18,24,4	stem, MDWO, S. 14" thruout. apron, knightheads, LO	sternpost, MDWO, S.16" at head, 14" at heel. inner post, LO	Lady Franklin		
Gem of the Ocean #1	O; Cu,Fe	O; Cu,Fe	Lamplighter Bark #1	WO; Cu,Fe	WO; Cu,Fe
Golden Eagle #1	WO; Cu,Fe	WO; Cu,Fe	Lightfoot #1	WO; Cu,Fe	WO; Cu,Fe
Golden Fleece (2nd) #1	WO; Cn,Fe	WO; Cn,Fe	Lightning #2	stem,S.16",two pcs., 8' hook scarph, M. 20" at head, M. 24" at foot. apron, S. 30" at bowsprit. false stem tapers to 4" on leading edge. WO; Cu,1"-1¼"; Fe,1⅛",1¼"	sternpost, head, S.20",M.20", heel, S.16",M.21". inner post, head, S.20",M.20", heel, S.16",M.16". stern knee, S.16", 15' body, 8'-6 arm, 3'-6 thru throat. WO; Cu,1¼";Fe,1¼"
Golden Light #1	stem, S. 15" thruout, M. 14" at head, M. 26" at foot. WO; Cu,Fe	sternpost, S. 15" thruout, M. 18" at head, M. 2'-3 at heel. WO; Cu,Fe			
Golden West #1	WO	WO	Mameluke #1	built with a stemson. WO; Cu,Fe	WO; Cu,Fe
Grace Darling #1	O; Cu,Fe	O; Cu,Fe	Mary Robinson		
Great Republic (1853) #2,10	built with a stemson. stem,S.16",two pcs., 12' hook scarph, M. 30" at head, M. 26" at foot. apron, M. 4'-3 (max.), S. 44" at bowsprit. false stem tapers to 4" on leading edge. WO; Cu,1"-1¼"; Fe,1⅛",1¼"	sternpost, head, S.24",M.26", heel, S.16",M.30". inner post, head, S.24",M.20", heel, S.16",M.16". stern knee, S.16", 20' body, 8' arm, 5' thru throat. add'l. post above arm. WO; Cu,1¼"; Fe,1¼". (iron bolts are coaged).	Mastiff #1	WO; Cn,Fe	WO; Cn,Fe
			Mermaid Bark #1	WO; Cu,Fe	WO; Cu,Fe
			Morning Light #1	NHWO; Cu,Fe	NHWO; Cu,Fe
			Mystery #1	stem, S. 15" thruout, M. 15" at head, M. 27" at foot. WO; Cu,Fe	sternpost, S. 15" at keel, M. 18" at head, M. 29" at heel. WO; Cu,Fe
Great Republic (rebuilt) #103	stem, S. 16" thruout, M. 20" at head, M. 24" at foot. apron, M. 4'-3, made in several pieces. false stem tapers to suit lines of bow. WO; Cu,1¼";Fe,1¼"	sternpost, S. 16" thruout, M. 5' to 6', made in three pieces. stern knee, S.16", 20' body, 8' arm, 3' thru throat, scarphed to keelson. WO; Cu,1¼";FE,1¼" (iron bolts are coaged).	Nightingale #3	WO; Cu,Fe	WO; Cu,Fe
			Noonday #1	NHWO; Cu,Fe	NHWO; Cu,Fe
			Northern Light		
			Ocean Express #1	O; Cu,Fe	O; Cu,Fe
			Ocean Pearl #1	WO; Cu,Fe	WO; Cu,Fe
Henry Hill Bark #1	WO; Cu,Cn,Fe	WO; Cu,Cn,Fe	Ocean Telegraph #5	WO; Cu,Fe	WO; Cu,Fe
			Onward #1	O; Cu,Fe	O; Cu,Fe
Herald of the Morning #12,42	stem, S. 15" thruout. WO; Cn,Fe	sternpost, head, S.17",M.24", heel, S.15",M.15". WO; Cn,Fe	Osborne Howes		
			Panther		
Hoogly #1	WO; Cu,Fe	WO; Cu,Fe	Phantom #1	stem, S.16",M.21". apron, "stout". WO; Cu,Fe	sternpost, head, S.16",M.12", heel, S.16",M.16". stern knee, S.16", 14' body. also fitted with a second stern knee over the keelsons. WO; Cu,Fe
Hurricane #4	WO; Cu,Fe	WO; Cu,Fe			
Indiaman #1	WO; Cn,Fe	WO; Cn,Fe			
Intrepid #18	stem, S. 14" thruout. apron, S. 15" thruout.	sternpost, S. 16" at head, S. 14" at heel.			
			Queen of Clippers #1	WO; Cu,Fe	WO; Cu,Fe
Invincible #4,18	stem, WO, S. 14" thruout. apron, LO. LO,WO; Cu,Fe	sternpost, WO, S. 16" at head, S. 14" at heel. inner post, LO. LO,WO; Cu,Fe	Queen of the Pacific		
			Queen of the Seas #1	built with two stems, massive apron and a stemson. WO; Cu,Fe	WO; Cu,Fe
James Baines #2	stem,S.16",two pcs., 8' hook scarph, M. 20" at head, M. 26" at foot. apron, S. 30" at bowsprit. false stem tapers to 4" on leading edge. WO; Cu,1"-1¼"; Fe,1¼",1¼"	sternpost, head, S.20",M.21", heel, S.16",M.24". inner post, head, S.20",M.20", heel, S.16",M.16". stern knee, S.16", 16' body, 7'-6 arm, 3'-10 thru throat. WO; Cu,1¼";Fe,1¼"	Quickstep Bark #1	WO; Cu,Fe	WO; Cu,Fe
			Racehorse Bark #1	WO; Cu,Fe	WO; Cu,Fe
			Racer #3	NHWO; Cu,Fe	NHWO; Cu,Fe
			Radiant #1	WO; Cu,Fe	WO; Cu,Fe
			Raven #3	WO; Cu,Fe	WO; Cu,Fe
John Bertram #1	WO; Cu,Ir	WO; Cu,Ir	Red Jacket #19,46	VWO; Cu,Fe	VWO; Cu,Fe
John Gilpin #1	stem one piece. WO; Cu,Fe	sternpost, one piece. WO; Cu,Fe	Robin Hood		
John Land #1,32 (Built as a duplicate of Winged Arrow.)	WO; Cu,Fe	WO; Cu,Fe	Rocket Bark #47	O; Cu,Fe	O; Cu,Fe
			Roebuck #1	WO; Cu,Fe	WO; Cu,Fe
John Stuart #4	stem, WO. apron, LO. LO,WO; Cu,Fe	sternpost, WO. inner post, LO. LO,WO; Cu,Fe	Romance of the Sea #1	WO; Cu,Fe	WO; Cu,Fe
			Santa Claus #1	built with a stemson. WO; Cu,Fe	WO; Cu,Fe
John Wade #1	WO; Cu,Fe	WO; Cu,Fe			

Table 8.1. *Continued.*

Vessel & Ref.#	Stem assembly	Sternpost assembly	Vessel & Ref.#	Stem assembly	Sternpost assembly
Saracen #1	MWO; Cu,Fe	MWO; Cu,Fe	Western Continent		
Sea Bird Bark #1	WO	WO	Westward Ho #1,2	stem, one pc.(ref.1). stem,S.16",two pcs., 6' hook scarph, M. 20" at head, M. 24" at foot. apron, S. 28" at bowsprit. false stem tapers to 4" on leading edge. WO; Cu,1"-1¼"; Fe,1⅛",1¼"	sternpost is natural knee at bottom (ref.1). sternpost, head, S.20",M.19", heel, S.16",M.21". inner post is a second knee (ref.1). inner post, head, S.20",M.20", heel, S.16",M.16". stern knee, S.16", 14' body, 8' arm, 3'-4 thru throat. WO; Cu,1¼"; Fe,1¼"
Seaman's Bride #4	stem, CWO. apron, LO. LO,CWO; Cu,Fe	sternpost, CWO. inner post, LO. LO,CWO; Cu,Fe			
Sea Serpent #47	O; Cu,Fe	O; Cu,Fe			
Shooting Star #1	WO; Cu,1¼";Fe	WO; Cu,1¼";Fe			
Sierra Nevada #1	NHWO; Cu,Fe	NHWO; Cu,Fe			
Silver Star #1	WO; Cu,Ir	WO; Cu,Ir			
Southern Cross #1	MWO; Cu,Fe	MWO; Cu,Fe	West Wind #1	WO; Cu,Fe	WO; Cu,Fe
Sovereign of the Seas #2	stem,S.16",two pcs., 8' hook scarph, M. 24" at head, M. 28" at foot. apron, S. 30" at bowsprit. false stem tapers to 4" on leading edge. WO; Cu,1"-1¼"; Fe,1⅛",1¼"	sternpost, head, S.20",M.22", heel, S.16",M.26". inner post, head, S.20",M.22", heel, S.16",M.16". stern knee, S.16", 16' body, 7'-6 arm, 3'-10 thru throat. WO; Cu,1¼";Fe,1¼"	Whirlwind #1	O; Cu,Fe	O; Cu,Fe
			Whistler #1	NWO; Cu,Fe	NWO; Cu,Fe
			Wildfire Bark #1	O; Cu,Fe	O; Cu,Fe
			Wild Pigeon #1	NHWO; Cu,Fe	NHWO; Cu,Fe
			Wild Ranger #1	WO; Cu,Fe	WO; Cu,Fe
Spitfire #1	WO; Cu,Fe	WO; Cu,Fe	Wild Rover		
Staffordshire #2	stem,S.16",two pcs., 7' hook scarph, M. 20" at head, M. 26" at foot. apron, S. 30" at bowsprit. false stem tapers to 4" on leading edge. WO; Cu,1"-1¼"; Fe,1⅛",1¼"	sternpost, head, S.19",M.19", heel, S.16",M.24". inner post, head, S.19",M.19", heel, S.16",M.16". stern knee, S.16", 14' body, 8' arm, 3'-8 thru throat. WO; Cu,1¼";Fe,1¼"	Winged Arrow #1	WO; Cu,Fe	WO; Cu,Fe
			Winged Racer #1	stem, one piece, S. 16" thruout, is a natural knee at bottom. WO; Cu,Fe	sternpost, S. 16" at heel, is a natural knee at bottom. WO; Cu,Fe
			Witchcraft #1	WO; Cu,Fe	WO; Cu,Fe
Stag Hound #2	stem,S.16",two pcs., 6' hook scarph, M. 20" at head, M. 24" at foot. apron, S. 28" at bowsprit. false stem tapers to 4" on leading edge. WO; Cu,1"-1¼"; Fe,1⅛",1¼"	sternpost, head, S.18",M.19", heel, S.16",M.21". inner post, head, S.18",M.18", heel, S.16",M.16". stern knee, S.16", 14' body, 8'-6 arm, 3'-4 thru throat. WO; Cu,1¼";Fe,1¼"	Witch of the Wave #1	NHWO; Cu,Fe	NHWO; Cu,Fe
			Wizard #1	WO; Cu,Fe	WO; Cu,Fe
			Young America #24,47	stem, S. 16" thruout, (scaled from lines). WO; Cu,Fe	sternpost, S. 18" at head, S. 16" at heel. (scaled from lines). WO; Cu,Fe
Star of the Union #1	WO; Cu,Fe	WO; Cu,Fe	Young Turk Bark #1	WO; Cu,Fe	WO; Cu,Fe
Starr King					
Storm King #1	WO; Cu,Fe	WO; Cu,Fe			
Sultana Bark #1	WO; Cu,Fe	WO; Cu,Fe			
Sunny South					
Surprise #1	WO; Cu,1¼";Fe	WO; Cu,1¼";Fe			
Swallow #1	WO; Cu,Fe	WO; Cu,Fe			
Sweepstakes					
Sword Fish #18,20	stem, S. 14" thruout. O; Cu,Fe	sternpost, S. 16" at head, S. 14" at heel. O; Cu,Fe			
Syren #3	WO; Cu,Fe	WO; Cu,Fe			
Telegraph #1	WO; Cu,Fe	WO; Cu,Fe			
Thatcher Magoun #1	WO; Cu,Fe	WO; Cu,Fe			
Tornado					
Uncowah #18	stem, S. 13" thruout.	sternpost, S. 15" at head, S. 13" at heel.			
War Hawk #1	WO; Cu,Fe	WO; Cu,Fe			
Water Witch #1	NHWO; Cu,Fe	NHWO; Cu,Fe			

(text continued from page 129)

ends. The stem rabbet must be deep enough to allow smooth transition from the rabbet which had already been cut in the keel, as discussed in the previous chapter; this depth was approximately one-fourth of the stem siding on each side. (In some cases the specified depth has survived in the tables of offsets, as indicated in Table 1.1.)

The rabbet was cut in except in way of the scarph, hewing accurately to the rabbet line but only being roughly cut in depth to the back rabbet. The final trimming of this rabbet was generally deferred until installation of the planking which, in both ends of the vessel, was always thinned down from its nominal scantlings in order to fair into the stem or sternpost. This thinning of the planking began in the portion of the entrance or run where extreme bending would be encountered. It also allowed for deviations in dubbing the cant frames to accommodate the planks.

When the two parts were completed, they were joined at the scarph and fastened with copper bolts of a specified quantity and diameter. These bolts were always driven from the nib side of the scarph and were clinched over composition plates or rings at each end, this being a joint of the utmost importance. At this time, or after the stem was erected at the end of the keel, the rabbet was continued in way of the scarph. Figure 8.1 illustrates the completed form of the stem in place on the keel.

After the stem had been coaxed into its proper position and solidly braced, it was fastened to the keel scarph with copper bolts, driven through both parts and clinched flush over a ring at each end.

The general practice of the period was to have the stem sided to the same dimension as the specified siding of the keel. However, this practice was not followed in all cases. A known instance, among the ships listed in this book, is William H. Webb's clipper *Black Hawk*. For reasons not explained, Webb chose to side the stem 1 inch less than the keel. The actual dimensions have survived in her table of offsets. The keel is sided 15 inches while the stem is sided 14 inches. The siding of the keel was diminished at the forefoot as described in the previous chapter until the two parts were fair.

This same situation apparently existed with Webb's *Comet*. Her table of offsets specifies that the depth of rabbet of the stem was 3½ inches, compared to 4 inches of depth for the keel rabbet. The indication here is that the keel siding was one inch greater than that of the stem. It is probable that this practice was not rare in shipbuilding at the time. This difference is even more pronounced with his clipper *Invincible*. In this instance the table of offsets lists the siding of the keel as 16 inches, while the stem is sided 14 inches and the sternpost 14 inches at the keel and 16 inches at the head.

Two stopwaters were required, with installation similar to that described under the heading "Assembling of the Keel"

and shown in Figure 7.2, detail A, in the previous chapter. The first stopwater was in the upper scarph of the stem and could be installed immediately upon completion of the scarph. The second was installed at the junction of stem and keel after the stem had been erected and permanently secured in its final position; sometimes it was deferred until assembly with the apron had been accomplished.

The Apron

The *apron* was the second major component of the stem assembly, generally equal in bulk to the stem itself. In earlier times, when ships were built with *bluff* (having a rounded entry) or fuller bows, the sole function of the apron was to reinforce the scarph of the stem by giving generous shift to its own scarphs in reference to the stem scarph. In this way there was no place along the assembly which did not have at least one tier of solid wood in any cross section. If it had been possible to obtain a piece of timber large enough to form the complete backbone of the ship as represented by the stem assembly, the apron as an individual, identifiable piece would not have existed; the entire unit would then have been termed the stem.

When ships developed finer lines and ultimately reached the clipper form, the apron's original purpose was augmented by an additional function: it now provided a solid anchorage for the forward deadwood, which had become necessary in order to build up adequate substance for fastening the foremost frames, the cant frames in particular. (Framing will be addressed in the following chapter and in Chapter 11.) The apron eliminated the need to fasten the deadwood directly to the stem. In addition, it nearly doubled the dimensions of the ship's forward backbone.

The apron was always made of white oak or another similar strong hardwood. Its creation followed the same general procedure that applied to the stem: Moulds or patterns that were compatible with the after side of the stem were prepared by the mould loft. The moulded depth of the apron was, in its general length, approximately uniform, being almost parallel with the shape of the stem. However, at its head it tended to remain almost straight, while at its foot its dimension diminished until it faired with the filler piece that was an extension of the moulded depth of floors.

One condition which governed the moulded depth of the apron was that it be of sufficient dimension to allow the inboard face of the knightheads, which embraced the bowsprit, to extend downward in the ship until they finally heeled against the foremost cant frame while faying with the apron for their entire length.

The siding of the apron was arrived at using two different approaches, each at the discretion of the individual designer or builder and probably dependent to a great degree upon the suitability of the available timber.

The diameter of the bowsprit governed the sided dimension of the apron, since the bowsprit rested on the bed formed by the head of the apron. Some builders elected to cut the apron from a log of a size large enough to form this bed in one piece; Donald McKay specified such a log for all his clipper ships. When this procedure was followed, a mould was made delineating the forward edge of the apron, which was the after edge of the stem, and the shape at various significant waterlines. As the lower waterlines were approached, the substance of the apron diminished as it was shaped to conform with the moulded shape at each waterline until, at its lower extremity, it intersected the foremost cant frame at the siding of the stem. This configuration provided additional anchorage for securing the forward planking ends or *hoods*.

The predominant method of constructing the apron, however, was to side it to match the keel and mould it as previously described. In order that there would be effective shift between the scarphing of the apron and that of the stem, it was made up of three pieces. A mould was provided for each piece, complete with appropriate markings for locating and trimming to size, as illustrated in Figure 1.10. Two scarphs were required; these could be hooked, but in many cases plain nib scarphs, shown in Figure 5.1, were considered adequate.

After the three component parts had been fashioned in the field, they were aligned and fastened at the scarphs by driving a bolt through each end of both scarphs. These bolts were driven from the nib side and clinched at each end, and were always iron since they were not in contact with seawater. The complete apron was then raised into position behind the stem and eased into proper alignment. Temporary dogs were driven to hold the two units solidly together, after which iron bolts were driven through the assembly and clinched flush at both ends. These bolts were spaced about 18 inches apart throughout the entire length of the assembly.

The several uppermost bolts above the head of the false stem were well above the water's edge and were generally made of iron. They were not considered vulnerable, as would be bolts that were completely submerged. Thus the two principal components of the stem assembly were now in position and defined the forward profile of the vessel.

While it was customary to fashion the apron from several pieces of timber, the number depending on the shift of scarphs in reference to the scarph of the stem, it was possible on occasion to install an apron in one piece. Such an installation was very desirable since it eliminated the necessity of fashioning appropriate scarphs and was essentially a stronger member. However, the large size, coupled with the necessary configuration of the foot, rendered it impracticable to rigorously demand the use of a single log.

When this narrow apron was constructed, an additional member called a *stem piece* was installed on each side, of a thickness sufficient to allow the knightheads to clear the bowsprit. These stem pieces are described separately and are shown in Figure 11.4.

False Stem

The *false stem*, the third unit of the complete stem assembly, was not a member of structural importance and was considered an expendable installation. It was included principally as a protective piece that would tend to prohibit damage to the stem proper in the event of a relatively mild collision or unintentional contact with a wharf, pier, or other fixed object, the intent being that the false stem would be carried away without any significant damage to the stem.

The false stem was always made of white oak or similar hardwood and was a relatively small timber without complex form. As with the other parts of the stem assembly, the mould loft fashioned a suitable pattern from which the field could work. Sometimes this pattern would be provided in skeletal form, as illustrated in Figure 1.10, or it could be made in solid form if its size warranted. In either case, reference points, match marks, and other pertinent notations were laid on the pattern for the benefit of the shipwright.

The siding of the false stem was the same as that of the stem, and in many cases there was no further shaping after the scarph had been cut and the head trimmed to its proper alignment to allow proper seating of the ship's figurehead, if one were to be carried. However, many shipbuilders preferred to refine this piece by narrowing its forward or leading edge. In Donald McKay's clippers, the false stem was always reduced to a width of 4 to 5 inches across the leading edge, as shown in Figure 8.1. This *bearding* or tapering process could be accomplished before or after assembly on the ship at the discretion of the individual builders. In any event, upon completion the false stem was temporarily dogged in place on the stem to await the arrival of the gripe.

Figure 8.1 shows a hook scarph connecting with the upper end of the gripe, but this was a builder's prerogative, and, as with the apron, many considered a plain nib scarph to be adequate for the task.

The Gripe

The *gripe* was the final unit required to complete the stem assembly, and it was a piece which performed several functions. Structurally, being made of white oak or other wood similar to the remainder of the assembly, it protected the stem in the same way as did the false stem. In addition, if for some reason the ship should take the ground, the gripe, being easily carried away due to the manner of its being fastened to the main structure, could help the ship free itself. A third, nonstructural function of the gripe was its contribution to the sailing ability of the vessel, in keeping the ship from falling off the wind when the breeze was tending to blow the ship off course.

The mould for the gripe was no more carefully made than any other, but it was more complicated due to its multiplicity of curves and the flats to match the scarphs already formed in the false stem and the forward extremity of the keel. As with the false stem, the mould loft pattern could be skeletal or solid, and it would contain all markings, such as baseline and waterline, that were necessary to assure its proper positioning on the stem.

After proper location was verified, a copper bolt was driven through each end of the two scarphs. These bolts were driven blunt into the stem to perhaps half its moulded depth. The gripe thus secured in position, all the remaining blunts were driven into the stem to the same depth. Those below the water's edge were copper or composition, while those above were iron. These bolts were headed prior to being driven and were spaced from 2 feet to 4 feet apart. This extreme spacing ensured the probability of the parts breaking away if adverse circumstances were to develop.

Once all the parts of the stem assembly were fastened into a complete unit, there remained the installation of the stopwaters between the faying surfaces of keel and stem in way of the rabbet as shown in Figure 8.1, and the bearding of the stem assembly after the installation of the forward deadwood.

The Stemson

The foregoing description of components and fastenings was typical of clipper ship construction, but allowance must be made for variations of procedure and parts. There were two principal reasons for departure from the "standard" construction. The first was the inclination of individual shipbuilders to favor methods that they thought yielded better results. The second, based on the availability of required timber, is amply illustrated in the construction of Benjamin F. Delano's *Dauntless*, built at Medford, Massachusetts.

Her stem was of most unusual construction, apparently due solely to the fact that a large quantity of assorted knees was on hand at the shipyard. As a result it is reported[1] that her stem was of one piece with a natural knee at the lower end long enough to extend along the keel. The forward portion of the keelson was also a knee, and this extended along the apron. And, finally, over this combination of parts was installed a stemson, which was also a knee. This assembled structure was so large that it constituted all the forward deadwood required to secure the forward cant frames. It is possible that no other vessel contained this unique structural form.

The *stemson* was the least often installed member of a stem assembly. Originally, when ships were built with full, round bows, the function of the stemson was to reinforce the scarph of the apron and thus provide additional strength and rigidity to the stem assembly. In general, the stemson re-

quired scarphing that was located clear of any apron scarph. However, in smaller vessels it was possible at times to find a single timber of appropriate configuration.

Upon the advent of the clipper ship, with its narrow, sharp bow, crowded with almost solid timber due to structural requirements, the stemson acquired a second function: namely, to augment the buildup of the excessive forward deadwood required for securing the forward cant frames.

The clipper bow and stem configuration also changed the general shape of the stemson from a large, sweeping arc to a timber that was reasonably straight and could very often be obtained from a single tree. When installed it not only reinforced the apron but provided additional substance to which the deadwood could be secured. Its siding generally corresponded to the siding of the keel and deadwood. Its moulded dimension, however, appears to have been a discretionary matter, depending upon the lines of the bow and the whim of the builder.

If installed with through-bolts that completely penetrated the stem, the bolts below the waterline were copper or composition and those above were iron, all clinched flush at both ends. If installed separately as an independent unit with the bolts only partially penetrating the stem assembly, iron blunts, headed at one end, were driven flush into the stem assembly.

Of the vessels listed in this book, only eight have been specifically described as being fitted with stemsons. They are: *Daring*, 1855; *Dauntless*, 1851 (this stemson had a knee at the bottom); *Donald McKay*, 1855; *Flying Mist*, 1856; *Great Republic*, 1853; *Mameluke*, 1855; *Queen of the Seas*, 1852; and *Santa Claus*, 1854.

Figure 8.2 illustrates the stemson installation in *Great Republic*, built in 1853, based on McKay's scantlings[2] and contemporary description.[10] Discrepancies exist between the two references, but the principle is accurate.

The second source records the bolts as being spaced 6 inches apart. Due to space limitations along the stem assembly, this distance apparently also includes the bolting of stem and apron. This would allow a spacing of about 18 inches for the stemson bolts.

Sternpost Assembly

The sternpost assembly was generally erected immediately after or simultaneously with the stem assembly. By having both of them permanently in position on the keel, the reference points for alignment of members along the entire centerline of the vessel were assured. During the era of the clipper ship, this assembly typically consisted of the sternpost, the inner post, and the stern knee. Collectively they were to the after end of the ship what the stem assembly was to the forward end, namely the meeting place and termination
(text continued on page 139)

Figure 8.2. *Stemson as fitted in* Great Republic, *1853.*

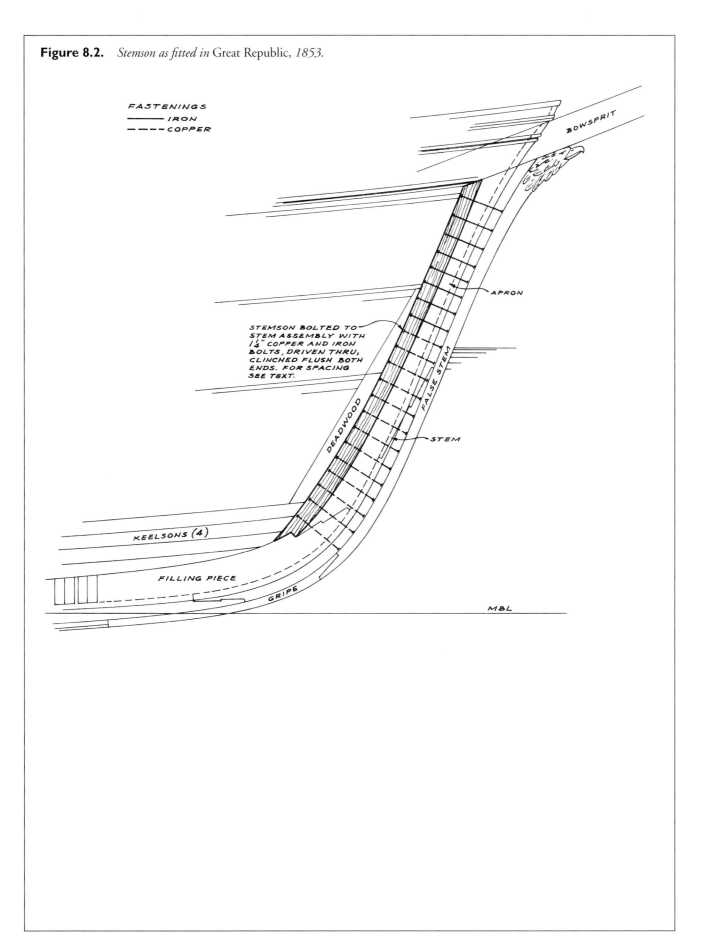

Figure 8.3. *Typical assembly of sternpost, inner post, and stern knee.*

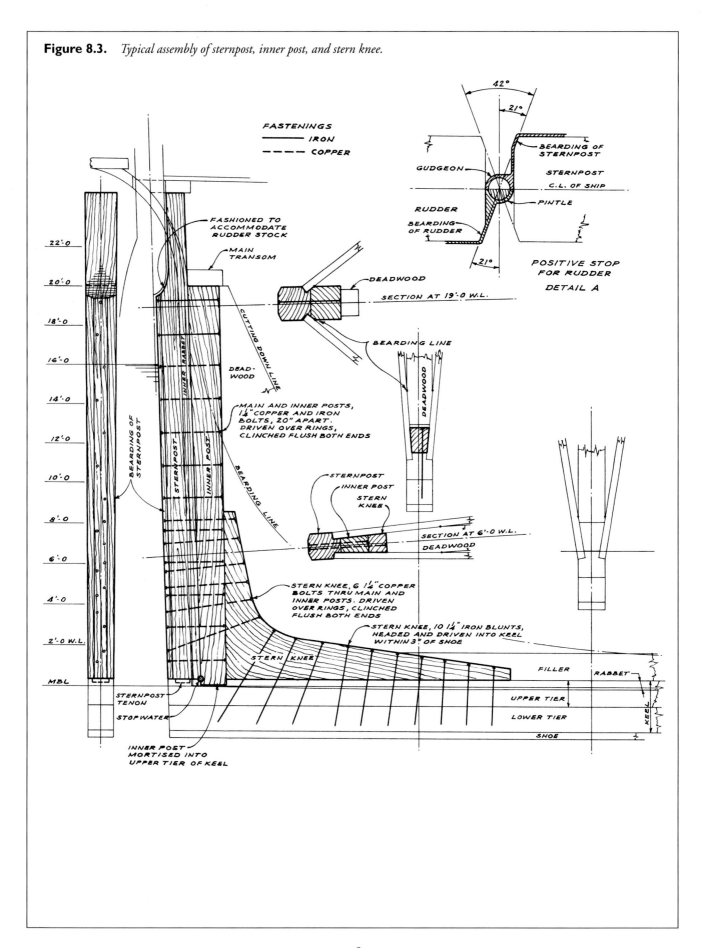

FASTENINGS
——— IRON
- - - - COPPER

42°
21°
BEARDING OF STERNPOST
GUDGEON
STERNPOST
C.L. OF SHIP
RUDDER
PINTLE
BEARDING OF RUDDER
21°

POSITIVE STOP FOR RUDDER

DETAIL A

FASHIONED TO ACCOMMODATE RUDDER STOCK

MAIN TRANSOM

DEADWOOD

SECTION AT 19'-0 W.L.

BEARDING LINE

DEADWOOD

CUTTING DOWN LINE

DEAD-WOOD

22'-0
20'-0
18'-0
16'-0
14'-0
12'-0
10'-0
8'-0
6'-0
4'-0
2'-0 W.L.
MBL

BEARDING OF STERNPOST

INNER RABBET

STERNPOST

INNER POST

BEARDING LINE

MAIN AND INNER POSTS, 1¼" COPPER AND IRON BOLTS, 20" APART. DRIVEN OVER RINGS, CLINCHED FLUSH BOTH ENDS

STERNPOST
INNER POST
STERN KNEE

SECTION AT 6'-0 W.L.
DEADWOOD

STERN KNEE, 6 1¼" COPPER BOLTS THRU MAIN AND INNER POSTS. DRIVEN OVER RINGS, CLINCHED FLUSH BOTH ENDS

STERN KNEE, 10 1¼" IRON BLUNTS, HEADED AND DRIVEN INTO KEEL WITHIN 3" OF SHOE

STERN KNEE

FILLER
RABBET

UPPER TIER
LOWER TIER
KEEL
SHOE

STERNPOST TENON
STOPWATER

INNER POST MORTISED INTO UPPER TIER OF KEEL

(text continued from page 136)

of all the ship's planking that ended below the main or wing transom. It was possibly the most important structural part of the ship, since it not only bound the stern to the body of the vessel but also provided the foundation upon which the rudder was hung. Figure 8.3, which is based on details for the McKay clipper *Lightning*,[2] illustrates a typical sternpost assembly that would be found in the large clippers.

Table 8.1 lists known details of the sternpost assemblies of vessels listed in this book.

The Sternpost

The *sternpost* is the principal unit of this assembly and, like the stem, is the structure around which the remainder of the assembly is constructed. Much care was exercised in selecting a proper timber for this item. The chosen log had to be of unquestionable soundness in order to withstand the variable stresses imposed upon it by the action of the rudder. Unlike the stem, it was essential that the sternpost be composed of only a single length of timber; no scarphing was acceptable.

Due to its size, the sternpost was almost exclusively fashioned from the lower trunk of a tree, and thus the butt or bole of the tree was placed at the heel of the post, for the same reason as explained for the stem. Due to the sternpost's straight form, there was a relatively limited choice of suitable timbers.

As was the case with all shaped timber in a ship, the first necessary information originated in the mould loft. Although the sternpost required a straight tree, fashioning this member was not as straightforward as its uncomplicated appearance would indicate. Invariably the moulded dimension at the heel was greater than it was at the head, and the siding at the top was greater than it was at the heel where its siding coincided with that of the keel. Therefore, the mould loft provided suitable moulds for shaping the sternpost. On these moulds were marked the necessary siding and moulding dimensions; the angle of rake, if any; the fashioning of the cutout in way of the rudder stock; the inner rabbet or moulded line, which was generally about 6 inches abaft the forward edge of the post; the form of the inner rabbet at the various waterlines; the size and location of the tenon that would be let into the keel; and a vertical line through the length of the mould. This latter line was used as a guide in placing the post in its final true position. The forward edge of the sternpost was always at least 6 inches forward of the inner rabbet line to ensure sound wood in which to drive the fastenings. The location of the fastenings to secure the inner post might also be included.

Another set of marks that might be included on the sternpost moulds were those that delineated the bearding lines on the after side of the post. The inclusion of these marks would depend upon how the ship's designer or builder intended to control the turning angle of the rudder.

In years prior to the advent of the clipper ship, theory and practice had concluded that for efficiency in turning a sailing ship around, the tiller, wheel, or steering mechanism should never be forced over beyond an angle of 42 degrees from a fore-and-aft line.[7] One method of preventing this was to beard both the sternpost and the rudder stock at an angle of 21 degrees on each side, as shown in Figure 8.3, detail A, thus providing a positive stop at the maximum angle. If this was the method chosen for a given vessel, the bearding lines would be included on the moulds so that the shipwrights could perform the bearding operation while the post was still on the ground. Any other method would be deferred until fabrication of the rudder, which is covered in Chapter 21.

After the sternpost had been shaped in accordance with the moulds, all necessary markings were transferred to it. Then the sternpost rabbet was cut in, following the same criteria as used in cutting the stem rabbet. The shipwright hewed accurately to the rabbet line but cut roughly the depth of the inner rabbet in order to leave suitable substance for fairing in the diminishing thickness of the planking from its nominal scantlings to the specified depth of the inner rabbet, which depth coincided with that of the keel rabbet. At this time the sternpost was ready for installation on the keel.

As stated before, the siding of the heel of the sternpost coincided with the siding of the keel, which was generally, but not always, uniform throughout its length. In some instances a vessel's sternpost was of lesser siding than the keel, and so the keel was tapered gradually aft to fair with the sternpost. Such was the case with Webb's *Black Hawk* and *Comet*. As with the stems of these vessels, as described earlier in this chapter under the heading "The Stem," their sternposts were sided 1 inch less at the heel than the siding of the keel.

Not all sternposts were shaped in accordance with the preceding descriptions. The clipper *Surprise* was reputed to have had many unusual details built into her structure, and one of these was incorporated into her sternpost. The *Boston Daily Atlas* edition of October 12, 1850, states that "Among these, the style in which her rudder is shipped is worthy of notice. The after part of the stern-post is concave, and into this cavity the rudder stock is fitted, so that when the rudder is amidships its sides form unbroken lines with the sternpost, leaving no space for the water to play between it and the rudder. This is equally strong and much neater than the plan now in general use."[1] This installation may not be unique, but it is the only mention of such treatment among the vessels included in this book. Further details are reconstructed in the section on rudders in Chapter 21.

Inner Post

The *inner post* was the second half of the sternpost assembly. Its several functions included strengthening the sternpost; providing substance for accepting the fastenings of the *hoods*, or after ends of the outside planking; providing a stout structure, along with the keel, to which the stern knee could be secured; and providing support at its upper end for the transoms and deadwood.

As was the case with the sternpost, the inner post was required to be of one piece, no scarphing being acceptable. Since the inner post was of a size approaching that of the sternpost, the choice of timber was very selective. In general its sided dimensions were the same as those of the sternpost, but in moulding the inner post was greater at the head than at the heel. While it required quite a length of straight tree trunk, no consideration was required as to the location of the butt of the tree. As the head of the inner post was larger than the heel, it readily lent itself to the butt being installed at the top, if desired, in direct contrast to the construction of the sternpost. This was possible since the entire substance of the inner post stood unexposed to the sea.

Suitable moulds for the inner post were provided to the field; these were relatively plain and simple, there being no additional working required once the piece was cut to shape. However, the heel of the inner post required neat squaring in order that the entire assembly preserve its position and alignment. To permanently fix the fore-and-aft location of the entire sternpost assembly, the keel was mortised about 2 inches deep to accept the extended heel of the inner post, as shown in Figure 8.3.

The two posts were fastened together with copper and iron bolts spaced about 20 inches apart along the entire length; as with the keel and stem bolts, these were staggered on either side of the centerline, care being taken that they did not break out in the rabbet. All the bolts were headed, driven clear through over rings, and clinched over rings at the point. Fastenings below the sheathing line were copper with composition rings; those above the sheathing line were iron over iron rings. It was sometimes the practice to drive alternate bolts from out to inside, or in to outside, and all were finished at or slightly below the surface.

The complete assembly was put in place with the extended end of the inner post snugly fitted into the keel mortises and then temporarily braced in proper alignment to await final installation with the stern knee.

Stern Knee

The *stern knee*, while not part of the actual sternpost assembly, was essential to its final installation. It was this knee which secured the sternpost to the keel, held it in true alignment, and provided additional substance to which the deadwood could be secured. Its siding was faired with that of the inner post and keel.

The stern knee was generally the largest knee used in the construction of an individual vessel. The principal components of a knee, which are considered in detail in Chapter 14, are the *body*, the longest part, which was fayed against the principal structure; the *arm*, which often was of lesser length and was placed against the structure that was to be held in place; and the *throat*, which was the thickness from the point of meeting of these two parts to the curve of the *bosom*, which flowed along the inner surface of the knee, as shown in Figure 14.1.

A mould was prepared by the mould loft in the usual manner, and the knee was hewn to dimension by the shipwrights, then placed in its proper position on the keel. Figure 8.3 illustrates this installation and is based on data specified for *Lightning*.[2] In this instance the body of the knee that is fayed along the keel is 15 feet long, the arm supporting the posts is 8½ feet long, and the mould of the throat is 3½ feet in depth.

Fastenings specified for this assembly are sixteen in number, copper and iron. No diameter is noted, but in keeping with the fastenings in the vicinity, 1¼-inch diameter appears to be appropriate. The proportions of the knee indicate a distribution of ten bolts along the body and six bolts along the arm. Following customary practice, the body bolts were iron blunts, headed and driven through the knee into the keel to within 3 inches of the shoe. By avoiding total penetration of the keel, which would have allowed contact between the iron bolt and seawater, considerable expense was avoided, and this was a practice followed throughout the ship wherever feasible. The heads were beaten flush with the surface of the knee to avoid interference with the installation of deadwood.

The arm of the knee, being shorter than the body, could accommodate the remaining six bolts. These, with their responsibility for holding the sternpost in position, were copper, driven over composition rings completely through the assembly, their points being clinched over similar rings. Counterbores of appropriate diameter and depth were cut in each end to permit sinking the bolts below the surface.

It may be appropriate to note at this time that in any grouping or row of driven bolts, the holding power of the assemblage is significantly increased when the bolts are driven at random angles with each other rather than being driven parallel.

With the physical installation of the sternpost assembly now permanently accomplished, there remained but two operations to be completed. First was the installation of a stopwater at the junction of the faying surfaces of the sternpost and the inner post with the top of the keel. This was done in a manner similar to that described under the heading "Assembling of the Keel" in Chapter 7 and shown in Figure 7.2, detail A. The stopwater prevented seawater from creeping along the exposed heel of the sternpost and thus entering behind the garboard plank.

Finally, the entire sternpost assembly would be bearded, or tapered, upon installation of the after deadwood.

The sternpost assembly described here can be considered typical among the clippers, a method that could be found in principle in almost any ship. The builders all marched along the same road, but they did not march in lockstep. In fact, some builders laid down their own specifications but did not slavishly follow them if some unusual circumstance should dictate otherwise. An excellent example of this is demonstrated by Donald McKay in the construction of *Westward Ho.*

According to the scantlings given for *Westward Ho* in *Models and Measurements,*[2] the sternpost assembly is similar to the one just described. However, as suggested earlier in Chapter 6, McKay's notes appear to be in the form of a general specification rather than a report of ships "as built"— and, in shipbuilding, "as specified" can be quite a bit different in detail than "as built." In any event, when *Westward Ho* was on the stocks and the time came to fashion her sternpost assembly, McKay reportedly found himself in possession of a timber of such size and shape that he was able to shape the sternpost and the stern knee from a single piece of wood.[1] In addition, this single unit was supported by a second knee that was worked in with the deadwood.

Another most unusual example of a builder accommodating his material to the design occurred with *Charger,* built by E. G. Pierce, at Portsmouth, New Hampshire. He had timber in stock large enough to fashion the vessel's sternpost from a single log. This post was secured to the keel with two stern knees, the lower one being fayed to the first keelson and the upper one being over the upper keelson. The total effect of this arrangement was to provide the ship with three aft uprights. Equally unusual, the siding of the lower knee was of such a dimension as to allow the body of the knee to form the aftermost portion of the garboard strake on each side of the ship. As a note of passing interest, the whaler *Charles W. Morgan,* preserved at Mystic Seaport Museum, in Mystic, Connecticut, shows a similar deviation from the usual construction. In this instance the garboard plank ends just short of the sternpost, leaving part of the stern deadwood exposed; the first broad strake runs by and over the top of the deadwood piece and butts against the sternpost.

There can be no doubt that this fortunate type of deviation was a routine occurrence when the availability of suitable timbers presented the opportunity. For this reason it is unwise to conclude that a certain detail applied to a specific ship without some pictorial or descriptive knowledge of its being. The only certain statement that can be made is that "it could have been" built in such a way.

Chapter Nine

SQUARE FRAMES AND FLOORS

Typical Framing Construction

The framing (Figure 6.2, details F, G, H, J) of a vessel followed the erection of stem and sternpost on the keel assembly, due to the location of the frames in the completed structure. It was the framing, cut to proper size and shape throughout the length of the vessel, which delineated the form of the hull. Each unit was so shaped as to accurately coincide with the designer's lines as laid down in the body plan on the mould loft floor.

During the period of the clipper ship when the vessels all

featured fine, sharp, almost knife-like ends, the frames were divided into three separate categories: square frames, half frames, and cant frames.

Square frames were those forward and aft of the midship or dead flat frame which completely spanned the vessel from one side to the other as a complete unit. The extent to which square frames were used in a ship was governed by the availability and economics involved in having timber of suitable shape on hand from which to fabricate them. They were set transversely at 90 degrees or perpendicular to the keel, although this rule was not absolute throughout general shipbuilding.

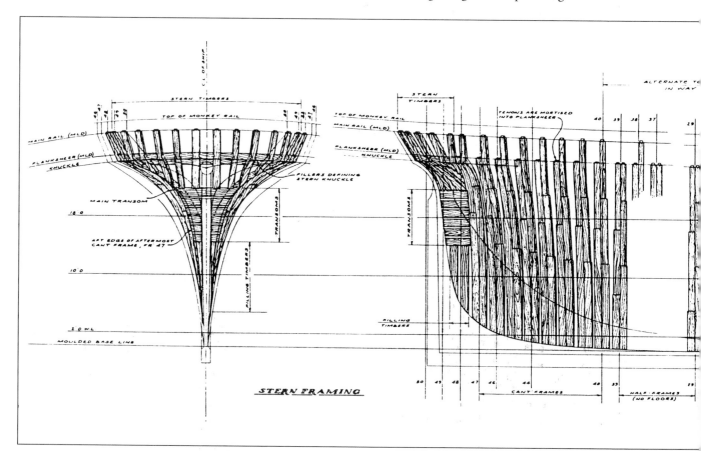

STERN FRAMING

The arrangement and construction of ship's frames are covered in detail in Chapter 11.

In the clipper ship period it was the custom to place all the floors on the same side of the frame line—that is, either on the forward side or after side, throughout the extent of the full square frames. There was no structural advantage to changing the arrangement in either the forward or after body. Such placement was at the discretion of the individual builder. However, it is possible that some ships were built in the older fashion of placing the floors on the midship side of the frame in both the forward and after body.

In the forward and after ends of a ship, where the angle of floor became steep as it rose from a horizontal attitude, the forms of timbers needed for floors became too acute to be readily available. In such cases deadwood was introduced into the construction. The deadwood, set up on the keelsons, with the same sided dimension as the keel, effectively divided the ship into two halves, port and starboard. At this point the full square frame was abandoned in favor of the *half frame*. This was a square frame made of two halves that were identical but to opposite hand. In way of each half frame the deadwood was built to a height sufficient to allow attachment of the half frame to the deadwood. This height of deadwood was termed the *cutting-down line*.

These square half frames continued forward and aft until, in the region of the stem and sternpost, the bevel of their substance became impracticably acute where it was to fay against the ship's planking. At this point they were superseded by the *cant frames*, which in reality were half frames set at varying angles with the keel rather than being set square. They were generally, but not exclusively, perpendicular to the moulded baseline. The faces of these frames tended to be more normal to the trace of the planking, thus reducing the incidence of thin, feather edges and increasing the capacity for sound fastening. Where cant frames were installed, care was taken to limit the distance between them at their uppermost extremities.

At the extreme ends of a vessel a point was reached where cant frames would no longer serve the required purpose of fulfilling the hull configuration. In the bow the cant frames were generally phased out at the point of junction between the forward end of the keel and the foot of the stem. Here the cants were feather-thin at the bearding line. At the upper end the foremost cant, in way of the planksheer and deck, had a half-breadth dimension from the centerline of ship that was perhaps as little as 8 or 10 feet. This was about the minimum space that could accommodate the placement of the ship's hawse holes and knightheads.

The frames were now displaced by a solid array of timbers called *hawse pieces*, which were installed parallel with the centerline of ship and were neatly fayed. Inboard of them were the knightheads, which in turn fayed against the inboard hawse

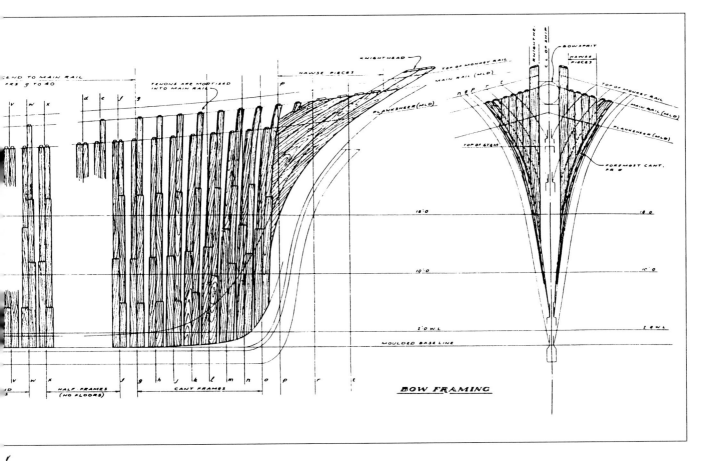

BOW FRAMING

piece. The inboard face of each knighthead was so located as to embrace the butt of the bowsprit and restrain it in a transverse direction. These pieces are illustrated in Figure 9.1.

The aftermost cant frame was located at a point along the keel so that, when projected upward to its extremity in way of the planksheer and rail, it intersected the tangent point where the side of the ship met the curve of the stern.

There were several methods of structuring the stern, the most usual consisting of a horizontal "wing transom" located at the top of the inner post. Below this a "flight" of as many as ten or more similar but smaller transoms were installed until at some point their installation was no longer practical. Below the lowest transom "filling timbers" were introduced where required. These were vertical timbers paralleling the trace of the aftermost cant on the deadwood.

Above the wing transom, vertical members called *stern timbers* were heeled onto the wing transom and positioned fan-like around the ship's transom and hewn to form the shape of the stern at the deck and the rail. These members were also fashioned to carry the stern knuckle around the planksheer, thus delineating the counter between the stern knuckle and the rudderhead.

Later pages describe in detail the form, fashioning, and fastening of these various members which when installed complete the skeletal form of the hull. Each member is described in its sequence of erection in the ship, except where interrupted after installation of the square frames by the construction and installation of deadwood and the keelson assemblies required for erecting the remainder of the framing.

Figure 9.1 illustrates these details of framing construction as applied to Samuel H. Pook's *Red Jacket* and may be considered as representative construction for vessels of the clipper type.

White oak was the overwhelming choice of wood used in the framing of American-built ships of all types. Table 9.1 lists the species of woods used in the general construction of clipper ship frames.

In addition to the vessels listed above, there are many whose timber content is not known and never will be uncovered except through much diligent research accompanied by some unexpected and fortunate discoveries.

The details of "long and short floor" framing (Figure 9.5 and Table 9.2), which was employed in the construction of *Great Republic* and *Donald McKay*, are described as separate items. This method was apparently little used in the building of clippers, generally finding favor in later construction which featured larger vessels with flatter floors.

Square Frames

The square frame (Figure 6.2, details F, G, H, J) was the predominant form of frame throughout the length of a vessel. In the average extreme clipper ship, full square frames and half frames could be expected to make up all the fram-

ing except the final six to ten cant frames approaching the stem or sternpost. These quantities were controlled, of course, by the form of the hull at its ends. The general extent of such frames is illustrated in Figure 9.1.

All square frames, due to the fullness of their form and the changes in direction from horizontal toward vertical, required the assembly of a number of separate pieces of timber in order to have the grain of wood run along the length of the piece in question. This applied to all large wooden ships, whether or not they were clippers.

Figure 9.2 shows the general construction of the midship or dead flat section of a typical clipper. It does not represent a specific vessel, but it is based on the listings in *Models and Measurements* of Donald McKay's clipper ships, their scantlings, and their fastenings.[2]

While the principle of frame construction is well known, there are not many instances in which the actual sided and moulded dimensions of frame members are specified. However, in records left by Donald McKay, this information has survived for twelve clippers and is listed in Table 9.2.

As Figure 9.2 indicates, the two halves of each frame were laid close together, with the frame line being the common faying surface. This type of construction was known as the "close-jointed" system. The total frame was made up of a floor which spanned the centerline of the ship, the first and second futtocks, the top timber, and the rail stanchion—all of which were installed on both sides of the ship to complete an entire frame.

The opposite of the "close-jointed" system, with its common faying surface, was the "open-jointed" system, in which the total width of the completed frame was constant from keel to rail, the decreasing siding of the ascending members creating an open space between the two halves. In this system only the floor and first futtocks fayed in way of the keel.

The members that made up any given frame were of prescribed scantlings and length, and were designed to include a generous shift of butts. However, the length of the members could be modified to accommodate available timber so long as the shift of butts did not decrease to a dimension the designer would not accept.

The moulded thicknesses of a given frame were set off inside the moulded frame line and diminished in size from keel to rail. As indicated in the figure, the depth of the moulded throat of the floor was given, along with the depth at the rail, this dimension being about one-third of the throat depth. Then dimensions were assigned at the turn of the bilge and at each deck, each decreasing as the rail was approached. Once these dimensions were laid out, a line was drawn through the given points in a regular, fair taper. It was important to adhere to these moulded dimensions throughout the length of the ship to ensure proper seating of the heavy

(text continued on page 148)

Table 9.1. *Continued.*

Vessel & Ref.#	Species of wood	Floors, S. x M.	Fastenings to keel, Figure 9.4
Lightfoot #1	WO	12" x 18"	Cu
Lightning #2	WO	12"to14" x 19"	Cu,1¼" No.2
Mameluke #1	WO	12" x 18"	Cu; probable No.1A
Mary Robinson			
Mastiff #1	WO	12" x 15"	Cn
Mermaid Bark #1,*	most WO	11" x 13"	Cu No.3A
Morning Light #1	NHWO		Cu No.1A
Mystery #1	WO	12"&13" x 16"	Cu,1¼" No.7
Nightingale #3	WO		Cu
Noonday #1	NHWO	14" x 16½"	Cu,1¼" No.3B
Northern Light			
Ocean Express #1	O	12" x 18"	Cu
Ocean Pearl #1	WO	11" x 16"	Cu
Ocean Telegraph #5	WO		Cu
Onward #1	O	11" x 15"	Cu,1¼" No.9
Osborne Howes			
Panther			
Phantom #1	WO	12"to13" x 17"	Cu,1",1¼" No.4
Queen of Clippers #1	WO	12" x 18"	Cu,1½" No.3B
Queen of the Pacific			
Queen of the Seas #1	WO	12" x 17"	Cu,1¼" No.4
Quickstep Bark #1	WO	12" x 14"	Cu No.1B
Racehorse Bark #1	WO	10"to11" x 13"	Cu,1⅛" No.2
Racer #3	NHWO		Cu
Radiant #1	WO	12" x 17"	Cu,1¼" No.3A
Raven #3	O	10" x 15"	Cu No.1A
Red Jacket #46,47	VWO		Cu
Robin Hood			
Rocket Bark #1	"similar to Dauntless"		Cu No.1A
Roebuck #1	WO	12" x 15"	Cu No.1A
Romance of the Sea #1	WO	12" x 17"	Cu
Santa Claus #1	WO	12½" x 16½"	Cu No.1A
Saracen #1	MWO	12"to13" x 17½"	Cu,1¼";Fe,1½" No.6
Sea Bird Bark #1	WO		Cu
Seaman's Bride #4	CWO		Cu
Sea Serpent #47,*	O, Hk		Cu
Shooting Star #1	WO	10"to12" x 15½"	Cu,1¼" No.3A
Sierra Nevada #1	NHWO	13" x 18"	Cu,1¾"
Silver Star #1	WO	12" x 16"	Cu
Southern Cross #1	MWO	10"to12" x 16"to17"	Cu,1¼" No.9
Sovereign of the Seas #2	WO	14" x 19"	Cu,1¼" No.2
Spitfire #1	WO	12" x 17"	Cu; probable No.1B
Staffordshire #1,2	WO	#1 12"to13" x 18" / #2 12"to14" x 19"	Cu,1¼" No.1A / Cu,1¼" No.2
Stag Hound #1,2,*	#1 WO, Hk / #2 WO	#1 10"to12" x 14"to16" / #2 12"to14" x 18"	#1,2 Cu,1¼" No.2
Star of the Union #1	WO		Cu
Starr King			
Storm King #1	WO	13" x 17"	Cu,1¼" No.7
Sultana Bark #1	WO	x 12"	Cu,1⅛" No.9
Sunny South			
Surprise #1	WO	12" x 15"to17"	Cu,1¼" No.1A
Swallow #1	WO		Cu
Sweepstakes			
Sword Fish #20	O		Cu
Syren #3	WO		Cu
Telegraph #1	WO		Cu
Thatcher Magoun #1	WO	12" x 18"	Cn,1¼" No.4
Tornado			
Uncowah #18		x 16"	
War Hawk #1	WO	12" x 16"	Cu,1⅛" No.1A
Water Witch #1	NHWO	12" x 18"	Cu,1¼"
Western Continent			
Westward Ho #1,2	WO	#1,2 12"to14" x 18"	#1 Cu No.4 / #2 Cu,1¼" No.2
West Wind #1	WO		
Whirlwind #1	O	11"to12" x 15½"	Cu,1¼" No.9
Whistler #1	NWO	12" x 15½"	Cu,1⅛" No.1A
Wildfire Bark #1	O		
Wild Pigeon #1	NHWO	12"to14" x 16"	Cu,1¼" No.3A
Wild Ranger #1	WO	12"to15½"	Cu No.3B
Wild Rover			
Winged Arrow #1	WO	12" x 16"	Cu,1¼" No.1A
Winged Racer #1	WO	12" x 18"	Cu,1¼" No.2
Witchcraft #1	WO	11"to12" x 17"	Cu,1¼" No.2
Witch of the Wave #1	NHWO	12" x 16"	Cu,1¼" No.3A
Wizard #1	WO		Cu
Young America #47,*	LO, WO		
Young Turk Bark #1	WO	12" x 14"	Cu

* The following are exceptions to complete white oak framing.

Vessel & Ref.#	
Andrew Jackson #20	Some portions of framing were chestnut.
Challenge #1	All frames forward of the foremast, all frames abaft the mizzen mast, all top timbers, all 4th futtocks amidships, and deadwoods in both ends were live oak.
Eagle #5	Some framing was live oak and locust.
Eureka #4	Apron, transoms, ends and deadwoods in both ends were live oak.
Flying Arrow #1	Top timbers were hackmatack.
Game Cock #1	Framing mostly white oak.
Gazelle #4	Top timbers (fore and aft only), some square frames, each end, and all cant frames were live oak.
Hurricane #4	Some top timbers were live oak and locust.
Invincible #4	Similar to Challenge.
John Bertram #1	Top timbers were hackmatack.
John Stuart #4	Apron and inner sternpost were live oak.
Mermaid Bark #1	Framing mostly white oak.
Sea Serpent #47	Some framing was hackmatack.
Stag Hound #1	Top timbers were hackmatack.
Young America #47	Some framing was live oak.

Table 9.1. *Continued.*

Vessel & Ref.#	Species of wood	Floors, S. x M.	Fastenings to keel, Figure 9.4
Lightfoot #1	WO	12" x 18"	Cu
Lightning #2	WO	12"to14" x 19"	Cu,1¼" No.2
Mameluke #1	WO	12" x 18"	Cu; probable No.1A
Mary Robinson			
Mastiff #1	WO	12" x 15"	Cn
Mermaid Bark #1,*	most WO	11" x 13"	Cu No.3A
Morning Light #1	NHWO		Cu No.1A
Mystery #1	WO	12"&13" x 16"	Cu,1¼" No.7
Nightingale #3	WO		Cu
Noonday #1	NHWO	14" x 16½"	Cu,1¼" No.3B
Northern Light			
Ocean Express #1	O	12" x 18"	Cu
Ocean Pearl #1	WO	11" x 16"	Cu
Ocean Telegraph #5	WO		Cu
Onward #1	O	11" x 15"	Cu,1¼" No.9
Osborne Howes			
Panther			
Phantom #1	WO	12"to13" x 17"	Cu,1",1¼" No.4
Queen of Clippers #1	WO	12" x 18"	Cu,1½" No.3B
Queen of the Pacific			
Queen of the Seas #1	WO	12" x 17"	Cu,1¼" No.4
Quickstep Bark #1	WO	12" x 14"	Cu No.1B
Racehorse Bark #1	WO	10"to11" x 13"	Cu,1⅛" No.2
Racer #3	NHWO		Cu
Radiant #1	WO	12" x 17"	Cu,1¼" No.3A
Raven #3	O	10" x 15"	Cu No.1A
Red Jacket #46,47	VWO		Cu
Robin Hood			
Rocket Bark #1	"similar to Dauntless"		Cu No.1A
Roebuck #1	WO	12" x 15"	Cu No.1A
Romance of the Sea #1	WO	12" x 17"	Cu
Santa Claus #1	WO	12½" x 16½"	Cu No.1A
Saracen #1	MWO	12"to13" x 17½"	Cu,1¼";Fe,1½" No.6
Sea Bird Bark #1	WO		Cu
Seaman's Bride #4	CWO		Cu
Sea Serpent #47,*	O, Hk		Cu
Shooting Star #1	WO	10"to12" x 15½"	Cu,1¼" No.3A
Sierra Nevada #1	NHWO	13" x 18"	Cu,1¾"
Silver Star #1	WO	12" x 16"	Cu
Southern Cross #1	MWO	10"to12" x 16"to17"	Cu,1¼" No.9
Sovereign of the Seas #2	WO	14" x 19"	Cu,1¼" No.2
Spitfire #1	WO	12" x 17"	Cu; probable No.1B
Staffordshire #1,2	WO	#1 12"to13" x 18" / #2 12"to14" x 19"	#1 Cu,1¼" No.1A / #2 Cu,1¼" No.2
Stag Hound #1,2,*	#1 WO, Hk / #2 WO	#1 10"to12" x 14"to16" / #2 12"to14" x 18"	#1,2 Cu,1¼" No.2
Star of the Union #1	WO		Cu
Starr King			
Storm King #1	WO	13" x 17"	Cu,1¼" No.7
Sultana Bark #1	WO	x 12"	Cu,1⅛" No.9
Sunny South			
Surprise #1	WO	12" x 15"to17"	Cu,1¼" No.1A
Swallow #1	WO		Cu
Sweepstakes			
Sword Fish #20	O		Cu
Syren #3	WO		Cu
Telegraph #1	WO		Cu
Thatcher Magoun #1	WO	12" x 18"	Cn,1¼" No.4
Tornado			
Uncowah #18		x 16"	
War Hawk #1	WO	12" x 16"	Cu,1⅛" No.1A
Water Witch #1	NHWO	12" x 18"	Cu,1¼"
Western Continent			
Westward Ho #1,2	WO	#1,2 12"to14" x 18"	#1 Cu No.4 / #2 Cu,1¼" No.2
West Wind #1	WO		
Whirlwind #1	O	11"to12" x 15½"	Cu,1¼" No.9
Whistler #1	NWO	12" x 15½"	Cu,1⅛" No.1A
Wildfire Bark #1	O		
Wild Pigeon #1	NHWO	12"to14" x 16"	Cu,1¼" No.3A
Wild Ranger #1	WO	12"to15½"	Cu No.3B
Wild Rover			
Winged Arrow #1	WO	12" x 16"	Cu,1¼" No.1A
Winged Racer #1	WO	12" x 18"	Cu,1¼" No.2
Witchcraft #1	WO	11"to12" x 17"	Cu,1¼" No.2
Witch of the Wave #1	NHWO	12" x 16"	Cu,1¼" No.3A
Wizard #1	WO		Cu
Young America #47,*	LO, WO		
Young Turk Bark #1	WO	12" x 14"	Cu

* The following are exceptions to complete white oak framing.

Vessel & Ref.#	
Andrew Jackson #20	Some portions of framing was chestnut.
Challenge #1	All frames forward of the foremast, all frames abaft the mizzen mast, all top timbers, all 4th futtocks amidships, and deadwoods in both ends were live oak.
Eagle #5	Some framing was live oak and locust.
Eureka #4	Apron, transoms, ends and deadwoods in both ends were live oak.
Flying Arrow #1	Top timbers were hackmatack.
Game Cock #1	Framing mostly white oak.
Gazelle #4	Top timbers (fore and aft only), some square frames, each end, and all cant frames were live oak.
Hurricane #4	Some top timbers were live oak and locust.
Invincible #4	Similar to Challenge.
John Bertram #1	Top timbers were hackmatack.
John Stuart #4	Apron and inner sternpost were live oak.
Mermaid Bark #1	Framing mostly white oak.
Sea Serpent #47	Some framing was hackmatack.
Stag Hound #1	Top timbers were hackmatack.
Young America #47	Some framing was live oak.

Figure 9.2. *Typical construction of a midship frame.*

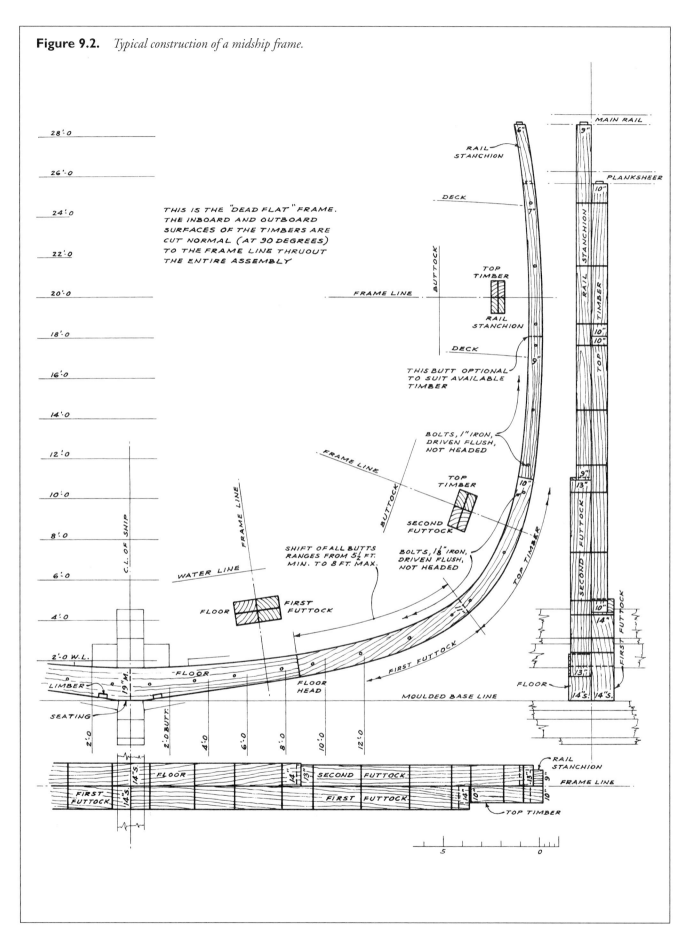

147

(text continued from page 144)

ceiling and bilge keelsons that would be installed on the frames. The moulding of the frames was constant until, at each end, it might become impractical to hold.

The sided dimension of each frame member decreased as the rail was approached but not in a manner that called for a taper. The governing dimension was the siding of the floor. With this assigned, each succeeding futtock or timber received a smaller siding until the rail was reached. Each piece was parallel-sided an inch or two less than its lower neighbor; this resulted in each butt being slightly offset. The procedure resulted in decreasing topside weight in the structure and also increased the opening between frames, thus facilitating salting and providing for greater air circulation within the structure. Salting is covered in Chapter 20.

It can be seen in the figure that the midship frame, throughout its entire structure, was not subject to any beveling, thus accounting for the designation of *dead flat*. In the midship area, the moulds or patterns that would be made by the mould loft and delivered to the field were very simple; one mould could be made and marked to serve many frames. But farther forward and aft of amidships, a point would be reached where all frames required beveling similar to that shown in Figure 11.1. These moulds would be more complex, as dictated by the fullness or sharpness of the vessel.

As the ends of the hull were approached and its shape began to change noticeably from frame to frame, the moulds became more and more individual. Their markings and reference points were carefully transferred in the field to appropriate timbers, which were then cut to proper shape.

After all the members of a given frame had been hewn to size and marked with all necessary information, they were laid in their proper position and fastened to become a single unit. In all frames the fastenings were iron bolts that ranged from 1 inch to 1¼ inches in diameter and were driven home unheaded. Once all the frames had been erected on the keel, it was expected that the fastenings of longitudinal timbers such as ceiling, bilge keelsons, clamps, and planking would firmly bind the frames together and in their designated positions.

Frame Futtocks

The number of futtocks used to make up a complete frame was dependent upon the size of the vessel, the philosophy of the designer, and, to some extent, the availability of suitable timber.

In actual construction, the availability of timber of proper size and shape exerted a certain amount of control over slavish adherence to the general details of construction, and as we have seen, convenient but harmless deviations were sometimes made to accommodate available pieces of timber. Frame construction was no exception. A representative example of this (now on exhibit at Mystic Seaport Museum, Mystic, Connecticut) is shown in Figure 9.3 where, rather than the typical junction of first futtocks on the keel near the extreme forward or aft full square frames, a convenient log of suitable shape was used.

Seating of Frames

In erecting a square frame on the keel, the keel was sometimes scored, or cut into, to a depth that lowered the seating of the floor to the bearding line of the grooved rabbet. On some occasions this was done by scoring the bottom of the

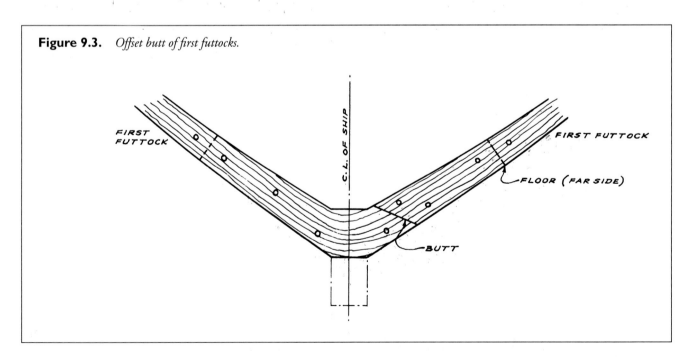

Figure 9.3. *Offset butt of first futtocks.*

Table 9.2. *Sided and moulded frame dimensions of McKay clippers.*

	Great Republic	Donald McKay	Sovereign of the Seas	Champion of the Seas / James Baines	Empress of the Seas	Lightning	Staffordshire	Flying Cloud	Westward Ho / Flying Fish	Stag Hound
Frames are all white oak.										
Frame spacing	28"	30"	30"	30"	30"	30"	30"	30"	30"	30"
Siding – floors	12"to15"	14"	14"	12"to14"	12"to14"	12"to14"	12"to14"	12"to14"	12"to14"	12"to14"
first futtocks	14"	14"	14"	12"to14"	12"to14"	12"to14"	12"to14"	12"to14"	12"to14"	12"to14"
second futtocks	13"	12"	12"to13"	12"to13"	11"to13"	11½"to13"	11"to13"	11"to13"	11"to13"	11"to13"
top timbers at planksheer	12"	10"	10"	10"	10"	10"	10"	10"	10"	10"
stanchions at rail	11"	9"	9"	9"	9"	9"	9"	9"	9"	9"
Each shift (of butts) diminishes from second futtocks.										
Moulding – over the keel	22"	20"	19"	20"	19"	19"	19"	18"	18"	18"
turn of bilge	14"	12"	11"	13"	11"	11"	11"	10½"	10"	10"
lower deck	12½"	10½"	9½"	11½"	10"	9"	10"	9"	9"	9"
middle deck	10½"	9½"	–	9"	9"	–	9"	–	–	–
upper deck	8"	7½"	7"	7"	7"	7"	7"	7"	7"	7"
at rail	7½"	6½"	6"	6"	6"	6"	6"	6"	6"	6"
Regular taper between these points.										
Length – long and short floors amidships	26',25'	24',22'								
floors amidships			18'to20'	24'	20'	18'	17'to18'	16'to17'	16'to17'	16'
Shift of – floors and futtocks	7'to10'	6'to8'	5½'to7'	5½'to7'	5½'to7'	5½'to7'	5½'to7'	5½'to7'	5½'to7'	5½'to7'
futtocks and top timbers	6'to10'	6'to 8'	6'to 8'	6'to 8'	6'to 8'	6'to 8'	6'to 8'	6'to 8'	6'to 8'	6'to 8'
Timbers of frame fayed close together.										
Frame bolts, each futtock	9 to 7	–	7 to 4	7 to 4	7 to 4	7 to 4	7 to 4	7 to 4	7 to 4	7 to 4
Dia. in bottom of ship	1¼"	1⅛"	1⅛"	1⅛"	1⅛"	1⅛"	1⅛"	1⅛"	1⅛"	1⅛"
Dia. in top of ship	1⅛"	1"	1"	1"	1"	1"	1"	1"	1"	1"

Horizontal keys (chocks) 5" thick between the frames at every butt, driven from inside to within 2" of the planking to prevent hogging. (See Figure 9.6)

Every second floor bolted to the keel with from 1" to 1⅛" bolts (1¼", Donald McKay), driven through the keel and riveted.

floor over the keel instead until it reached this line. A third option was to score both the keel and the floor, taking half the material out of each member, until the line was reached. Such scoring, or cutting, applied only to the floor of a given frame and did not apply to the first futtock. With the futtocks the material was always taken out of the futtocks in way of the keel in order to bring their moulded depth in throat to agree with the fayed floor. As might be expected, different yards adopted different procedures.

In keels which employed a beveled rabbet rather than a grooved rabbet, the frames could be seated directly upon the top of the keel when it coincided with the moulded baseline. It thus becomes obvious that there was considerable latitude in setting up these basic elements of a ship's hull.

From the dimensions tabulated in Table 9.2, it appears reasonable to conclude that, in the average large clipper, the moulded depth of the rail stanchion at its top was 6 inches. As is usual, however, there were exceptions, although the exceptions varied very little. Among such vessels listed herein are *Witch of the Wave*, *Black Hawk*, and *Herald of the Morning*, each at 6½ inches, and *Flying Childers*, at 7 inches.

Floors

The floors of square frames contained most of the fastenings that were used to secure the frames to the ship's keel. Bolting patterns varied according to the preferences of the builder. Some of the fastening systems were described by MacLean[1] and in McKay's scantlings,[2] and these are illustrated in Figure 9.4.

(text continued on page 152)

Figure 9.4. *Fastening of floors to keel and keelsons.*

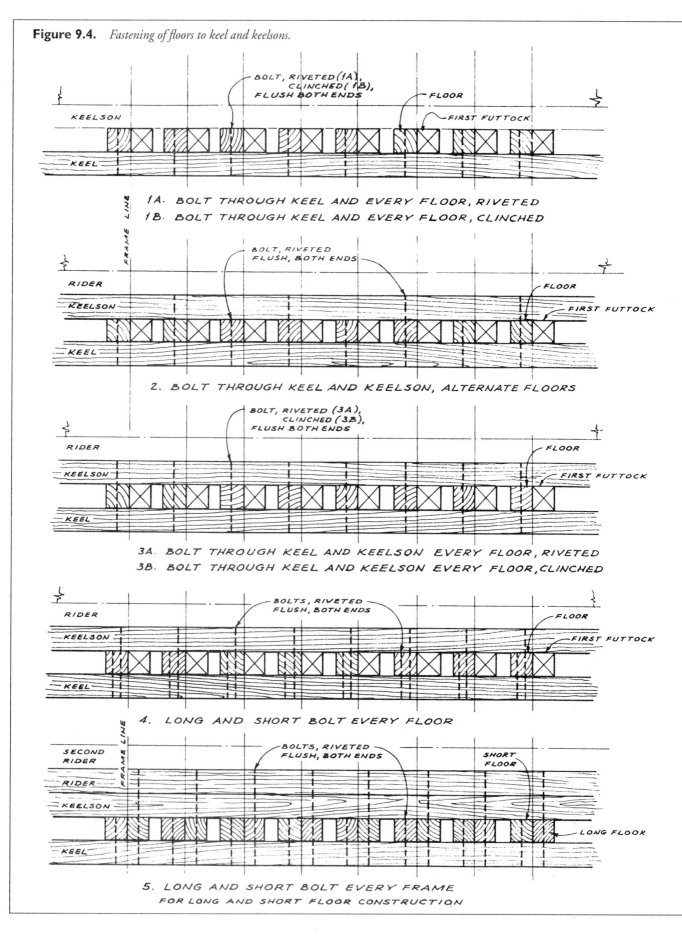

1A. BOLT THROUGH KEEL AND EVERY FLOOR, RIVETED
1B. BOLT THROUGH KEEL AND EVERY FLOOR, CLINCHED

2. BOLT THROUGH KEEL AND KEELSON, ALTERNATE FLOORS

3A. BOLT THROUGH KEEL AND KEELSON EVERY FLOOR, RIVETED
3B. BOLT THROUGH KEEL AND KEELSON EVERY FLOOR, CLINCHED

4. LONG AND SHORT BOLT EVERY FLOOR

5. LONG AND SHORT BOLT EVERY FRAME
FOR LONG AND SHORT FLOOR CONSTRUCTION

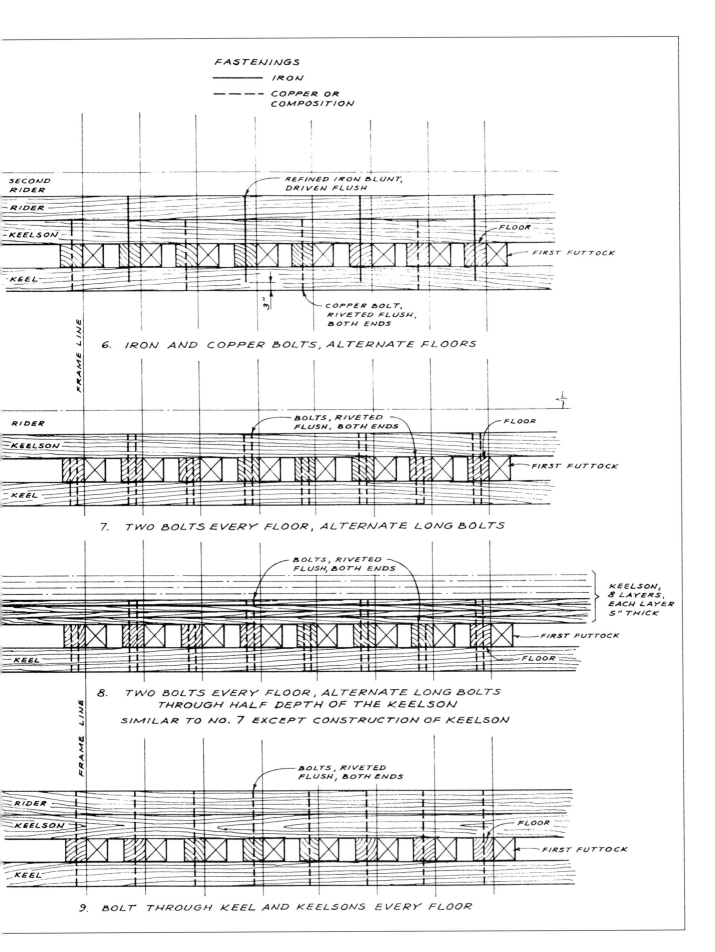

FASTENINGS
———— IRON
— — — COPPER OR COMPOSITION

SECOND RIDER
RIDER
KEELSON
FLOOR
FIRST FUTTOCK
KEEL
FRAME LINE
REFINED IRON BLUNT, DRIVEN FLUSH
3"
COPPER BOLT, RIVETED FLUSH, BOTH ENDS

6. IRON AND COPPER BOLTS, ALTERNATE FLOORS

RIDER
KEELSON
FLOOR
FIRST FUTTOCK
KEEL
BOLTS, RIVETED FLUSH, BOTH ENDS

7. TWO BOLTS EVERY FLOOR, ALTERNATE LONG BOLTS

BOLTS, RIVETED FLUSH, BOTH ENDS
KEELSON, 8 LAYERS, EACH LAYER 5" THICK
FIRST FUTTOCK
KEEL
FLOOR

8. TWO BOLTS EVERY FLOOR, ALTERNATE LONG BOLTS
THROUGH HALF DEPTH OF THE KEELSON
SIMILAR TO NO. 7 EXCEPT CONSTRUCTION OF KEELSON

FRAME LINE
BOLTS, RIVETED FLUSH, BOTH ENDS
RIDER
KEELSON
FLOOR
FIRST FUTTOCK
KEEL

9. BOLT THROUGH KEEL AND KEELSONS EVERY FLOOR

(text continued from page 149)

In many cases the descriptions are straightforward; unfortunately, however, quite a few of them seem to depend on what the reader decides is meant by the text, leaving room for diversity of interpretation. It is quite safe to state that the methods shown represent only a portion of the means employed.

The Limber

The *limber* (Figure 6.2, detail R) is a hole scored in the lower surface of every floor and first futtock, on either side of a vessel, throughout the length of the vessel. The word is believed to derive from the French *lumiere*, meaning "a hole." No mandatory size was specified for the limbers, but they were generally about 3 inches wide and 1½ inches deep. Their function was to provide a water course in which condensation, leakage of hull seams, spillage, and any water finding its way on board due to dirty weather would flow to the deepest portion of the body, there to be pumped overboard from the pump wells. The limber hole was located as closely adjacent to the siding of the keel as convenient access through the limber opening would permit, since there were occasions when the water course might require clearing of debris.

It was customary to reeve a close-link chain of small wire size through the limbers on each side so that if they became fouled or blocked on occasion, the chain could be racked back and forth to dislodge the blockage. The chain was, of course, not a part of the ship's structure, but an article in her list of outfit.

The "Long and Short Floor" System

The "long and short floor" system of frame construction was not widely incorporated into the building of clipper ships, the only known two in this book being *Great Republic* and *Donald McKay*. (This construction was not mentioned in reference to the rebuilt *Great Republic*, 1855.)[103]

The framing system was quite similar to one half of the "open-jointed" system of framing used in British naval construction of a period post-dating the American clipper era. That system was known as the "frame and filling frame" arrangement in which the type of construction of frames alternated through the length of the square body. Basically it consisted of constructing and erecting a "frame" which was made up of floor and futtock members similar to the typical construction found in American-built clippers. The adjacent frame space was occupied by a "filling frame" which was made up of long and short floors plus the usual assembly of futtocks. These two members alternated throughout the length of the square body, their purpose being to separate butts in adjacent frames when such butts were in alignment. However, at the time, this system did not flow over to the British merchant fleet and was not a part of American-built construction which adhered to the "close-jointed" type of frame in every frame space.

When specified, the "long and short floor" system applied to every frame in the square body and therefore was distinct from the "frame and filling frame" arrangement. Figure 9.5, detail A, shows an expanded arrangement of the system and the specifications recorded for *Great Republic* and *Donald McKay*.[2]

In 1867, when the American Shipmasters' Association was established, it included in its Rules for the Construction of Wooden Vessels the following: "Sec. 10, Floor timbers—The length of floor timbers amidships should not be less than three-fifths the breadth of beam. Long and short armed floor timbers are preferable, and in flat-bottomed vessels should always be used. These must lap each other one-third of their length in the body of the vessel, and one-fourth at the ends. If first futtocks or naval timbers are used; they must always butt close on the keel. . . ."

Coags

The use of coags was a practice not often indulged in, but they are an item of interest and were used extensively throughout the construction of the original *Great Republic*. For this reason it appears that, at the very least, they merit description and examples of their application.

Coags originated in ancient times, going back possibly as far as the Roman occupation of Britain. In his *History of Seafaring Based on Underwater Archeology*, George F. Bass describes how the wrecks of several Roman vessels apparently used something comparable to the coag of the clipper period, even though it is not designated by name.[80] In Roman times, as in the clipper period, the coag was used to protect iron fastenings that were in danger of direct contact with seawater.

The *coag* was a short dowel or plug of hardwood, generally white oak, which was used as a surround for iron bolts in the way of faying surfaces. Figure 9.5, detail B, shows a typical coag and representative use.

Coags were used for two reasons. First, the body of the coag bound the joints beyond the possibility of working; second, it protected the bolt from the corrosive action of salt water. It was a known fact that in the course of perhaps six to eight years, ships opened up for repairs to the outer hull and frames revealed corrosion of these iron frame bolts due to the slow seepage of salt water along the fayed joints. Condensation and moisture also contributed to this deterioration. The coag effectively prevented water from contacting iron by blocking this path taken by the water.

Great Republic, as originally built in 1853, had prolific use of coags. However, the shipbuilding industry in general apparently did not subscribe to the use of coags due to the cost,

Figure 9.5. *Long and short floor frames; details of coags.*

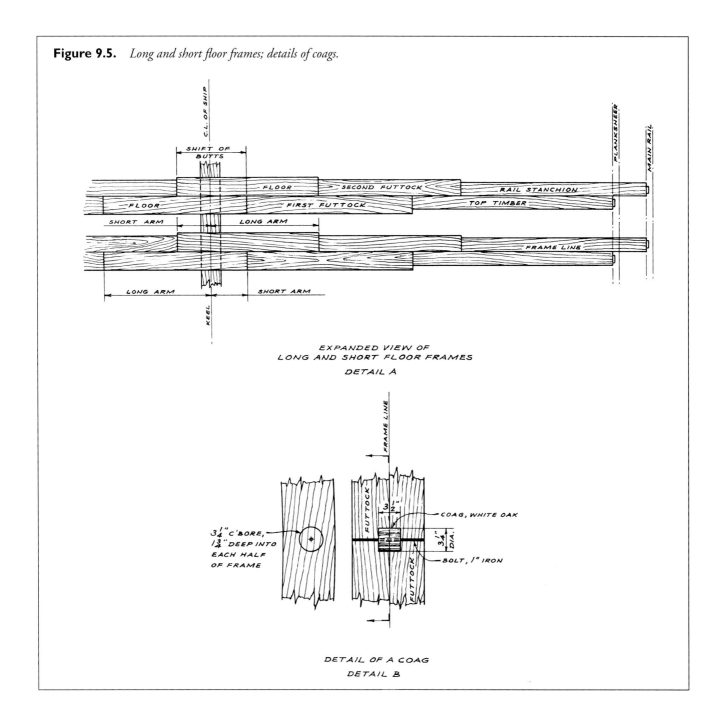

EXPANDED VIEW OF
LONG AND SHORT FLOOR FRAMES
DETAIL A

DETAIL OF A COAG
DETAIL B

time, and labor involved. Also known was the fact that a corroded iron bolt possessed greater holding power than a clean, newly driven one and that, once the iron surface had oxidized, the same oxidation, or rust, immediately retarded any further deterioration of the bolt.

Anti-hogging Chocks

The use of anti-hogging chocks or keys was resorted to in an almost vain attempt to eliminate or inhibit hogging of a clipper hull. As we have seen in Chapter 3, such hogging was an inherent characteristic of a vessel's hull form, in which the extreme forward and after ends lost much of their flotation capacity due to narrowing as the stem and sternpost were approached. In clipper ships, with their extremely slender midbodies and long, sharp entrances and runs, this fault was greatly accentuated.

In a 200-foot clipper ship, the foremost and aftermost 20 feet of structure at each end was of such configuration and weight that, when the ship was laden to her load waterline, these ends were not supporting themselves by flotation, but, rather, were hanging cantilevered from the main body of the ship. This undesirable condition is illustrated in Figure 3.6,

Figure 9.6. *Anti-hogging chocks.*

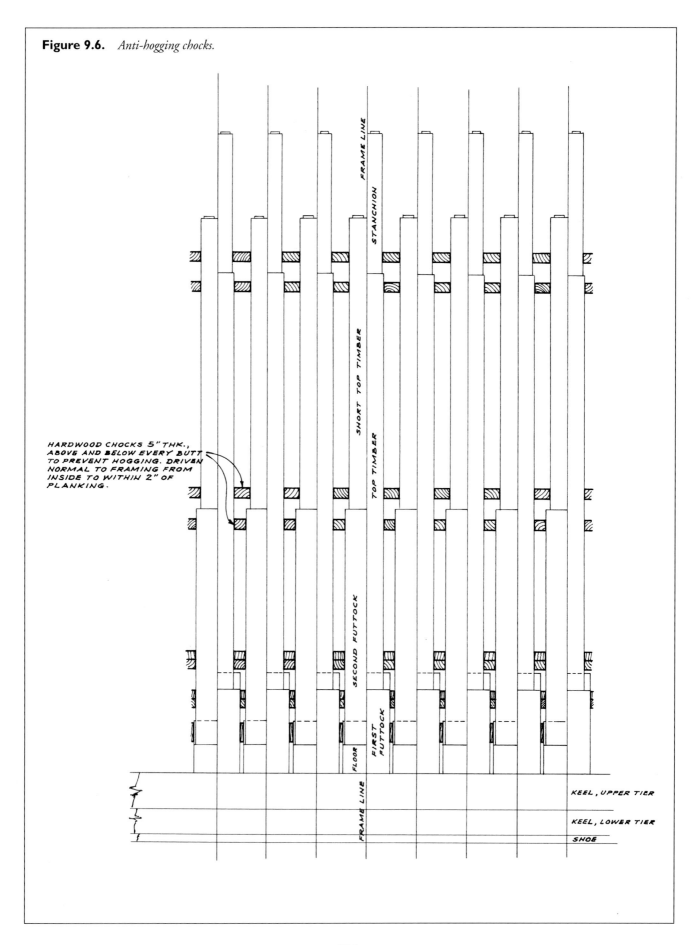

HARDWOOD CHOCKS 5" THK., ABOVE AND BELOW EVERY BUTT TO PREVENT HOGGING. DRIVEN NORMAL TO FRAMING FROM INSIDE TO WITHIN 2" OF PLANKING.

FRAME LINE

STANCHION

SHORT TOP TIMBER

TOP TIMBER

SECOND FUTTOCK

FIRST FUTTOCK

FLOOR

FRAME LINE

KEEL, UPPER TIER

KEEL, LOWER TIER

SHOE

in which it can be seen that, due to the wedge-like transverse sections of the end frames, their dead weight requires more displacement than their structure can provide. Since the ends cannot sink to their required depth to achieve flotation, they are left literally hanging in the water.

Wood is a strong but really quite elastic material. However, subject to the forces of alternating tensile and compressive stress at sea over an extended period of time, the ends of a hull start to droop or *hog*. It is not unusual for an old hull to have hogged as much as a foot in the length of her keel—not a minimal distortion.

Hogging did not necessarily damage a vessel, but it did have enormous influence on the sailing and handling qualities of the ship. With such knowledge gained through long experience, the designers and builders sought methods of eliminating hogging. One way was to increase the scantlings of the principal structural members such as keel, keelsons, clamps, etc. Another, later method, as discussed in Chapter 3, was to introduce rigidity by means of wooden cross-bracing or iron strapping.

An earlier approach was to install wooden keys or chocks in spaces between frames. These, as specified by Donald McKay,[2] are copied verbatim in Table 9.2 and illustrated in Figure 9.6. It can be seen in the figure that these chocks, in effect, completed the formation of two continuous longitudinal members in way of each butt in the frame structure throughout the length of the vessel.

It is probable that the chocks contributed to slowing of the hogging process; however, their actual effectiveness is difficult to evaluate and apparently not a subject of record.

Chapter Ten

KEELSON AND
DEADWOOD ASSEMBLIES

Keelson Assembly

The keelson assembly (Figure 6.2, details C and D), as installed in all but the very smallest clipper ships, was a far cry from the keelson that was installed in the full-bodied vessels of earlier periods, which were built with relatively great flotation capacity at their extremities. In such ships the principal function of the rather small keelson was to firmly secure the ship's frames in position on the keel, which constituted the major longitudinal structural member of the hull. With fastenings installed through keelson, frame floor, and keel, the foundation of the vessel was as sound as materials and craftsmanship could make it.

With the fine-ended clipper hull form, new structural elements were needed to compensate for the ever-decreasing flotation capacity of the ship's ends; this could only be done by increasing the longitudinal strength of the hull structure, the logical place being in way of the once diminutive keelson. Thus the keelson, which was originally an auxiliary member, now usurped the structural function of the keel as the principal strength member, relegating the keel to the essential function of aiding the sailing capability of a vessel. If there was any one structural feature proprietary to clipper ships, it was the keelson assembly.

As the ships became longer and larger, still maintaining their great length-to-breadth ratio, their tendency to hog increased proportionally; this was countered by building up a great bulk of keelson, which would act as a longitudinal beam extending from stem to sternpost. The basic element of keelson design was an increase in depth, which provided the greatest strength with the least gain in weight. However, there were limits to growth in this direction, so the builders installed additional members on either side of the central structure. Thus the keelson assembly grew to be made up of the keelson, keelson riders, sister keelsons, and sister riders. The strength of such assemblies was very great, but the additional weight and loss of cargo space was enormous.

The predominant but not exclusive choice of timber for keelson assemblies was any of the varieties of hard pine, sometimes in combination with another wood, generally oak.

As might be expected, each builder had his own ideas as to how the keelson assembly should be composed. In general, keelson assemblies were all very much alike; in detail there were innumerable differences. Figures 10.1 and 10.3 illustrate twenty-six actual cross-sectional examples of keelson assemblies that were described for vessels covered in this book. There are doubtless many more hidden away among various sources. The known examples, however, seem to cover all that might be expected in keelson design and magnitude.

The various forms are not drawn to an absolutely true scale, but proportionate one to another, arranged in a regular progression based on size, from one of the smallest vessels, *Racehorse* (number 1), to *Great Republic* (number 24 or 26). Most of the examples follow the same general type of assembly; however, four of them (numbers 4, 9, 11, and 12) deviate in ways that are unusual and unexpected.

In examples 4 and 11, the keelson proper and the keelson rider are made up of layers of planking throughout their entire length instead of each being made up of two separate logs. This method of construction was referred to as "naval style," probably indicating that naval construction favored this type of lamination; however, no explanation accompanies the statement. Example number 4 was built into *Golden Light*, while number 11 was used in *Romance of the Sea*. It is worthy of note that these vessels were built by different builders, so the merits of this method were not merely a matter of one builder's idiosyncrasies.

Example number 9, built into *Dauntless*, shows sister riders located 3 inches apart. This space was used to receive the foot of the hold stanchions, which were bolted horizontally through both riders. A second purpose served by this separation was to assist in seasoning the keelsons.

Example number 12 is found in *Witch of the Wave*, in

which the sister keelsons are flushed across until they meet the surface of the bottom ceiling.

Another unusual assembly is found in number 21, which was incorporated into *Sierra Nevada*. In this instance, "cousin" keelsons were installed for 40 feet in way of pumps and mainmast and were bolted both ways—that is, vertically and horizontally—into the floors and sister keelsons.

Whenever one of these rare or unusual installations appears, there is a tendency to refer to it as "unique." However, with so many ships having been built but leaving behind no trail of records, it is probably best to refrain from applying this term.

As with the keel, it was a matter of necessity that the total length of each member of the keelson assembly be made up of individual pieces, generally numbering about five timbers, connected by scarphs. Actual details of keelson scarphing are quite rare. However, the listing of McKay clippers and their scantlings[2] states that the main keelsons of all those ships will have "scarphs, generally eight feet [long], coaged and keyed." The only exception is *Great Republic*, whose scarphs were 10 feet long.

The same general rules that applied to keel scarphs were applicable to the keelsons. A generous shift was required between scarphs in adjacent tiers, and the topmost rider could not be scarphed in way of a mast step. Iron blunts were used in fastening the two parts of the scarphs.

In addition to the McKay ships, keelson scarphs are mentioned in the descriptions of only four other vessels in this book: *Endeavor*, *Joseph Peabody*, and the bark *Henry Hill*, all of which were "scarphed and keyed"; and *Water Witch*, of which it was noted that the keelson was scarphed. Coags appear to have been installed only in the ships of Donald McKay.

It goes without saying that the effectiveness of keelsons and keelson assemblies was dependent upon the integrity of their fastenings. The fastening patterns were governed by the composition of individual assemblies and also by the preferences of the various builders. Figure 10.2 illustrates bolting patterns for the assemblies shown in Figure 10.1. The bolts in the illustrations are arranged so as to be visible in each section. As in all descriptive matter, interpretation is needed for some of the wording accompanying these illustrations; however, this may be confined within a narrow range.

Keelson assemblies 25 and 26, listed separately in Figure 10.3, are as described in McKay's list of scantlings and general specifications. They are not in agreement with MacLean's descriptions in the *Boston Daily Atlas*,[1] and thus it is left to the reader to draw his own conclusions as to which is correct.

Another discrepancy between the two sources comes to light for *Sovereign of the Seas*. In a detailed description of the vessel in the *Boston Daily Atlas*, MacLean stated that her complete depth of backbone, including 1 foot 7 inches

moulded depth of floors, was 11 feet 8 inches. Allowing for the usual keel depth of 3 feet 2 inches in McKay clippers, this leaves a total depth of keelson and riders of 6 feet 11 inches, which, using the usual timber scantlings, would require five tiers to build up this height. Such a height does not appear to be compatible with construction found in any other large clipper; therefore, Table 10.1, which lists the keelson assemblies for all vessels in this book, where known, favors the scantlings given in McKay's list.[2] This is one of several instances where the recorded data conflict.

Figure 10.4 illustrates the keelson installation at the extremities of a clipper ship. Due to the changing form of the hull from one end of the ship to the other, certain changes took place in the keelson assemblies. As the vessel's extremities contracted toward the centerline of ship, the sister keelsons and sister riders gradually diminished in size as dictated by the fineness of the hull until, at some point, they disappeared entirely. However, the keelson and its riders remained intact until they were secured to the stem or sternpost assemblies.

After the forwardmost and aftermost full square frames had been erected, it was necessary to install a length of filler on the top of the keel to provide a seat for the keelson in those portions of the ship. This filler, of the same substance as the keelson, was sided to the same dimension as the keel and moulded to the same depth as the floors, and it extended forward to the apron and aft to the stern knee. Thus a continuous base for the keelson was provided from stem to stern. After being properly positioned, the fillers were secured to the keel with appropriately sized iron blunts, after which the entire keelson assembly could be installed.

The endings of the keelson were subject to some variations, examples of which are illustrated in Figure 10.4. At the stern the various tiers were generally terminated against the stern knee, and, due to the great similarity of sternpost construction, there was relatively little difference between one vessel and another.

The bow, with its many forms of forefoot and stem construction, offered more latitude to the builder in his choice of methods of connecting keelson, stem, and deadwood assemblies. The change from horizontal keel to more or less vertically inclined stem introduced a point of weakness, at least in the minds of designers and builders. For this reason the profiles of stems assumed quite a variety of subtly different forms ranging from truly angular changes, as in *Wild Pigeon*, to the long, graceful, sweeping arcs of *Sweepstakes* and *Lightning*, each of which is illustrated in Figure 3.1.

Along with this variation in stem profiles came variations in the endings of the keelson in this area. The simplest and most obvious termination was similar to detail A of Figure 10.4, in which each tier of keelson and riders simply abuts the after edge of the apron. A more elaborate treatment is

(text continued on page 169)

Figure 10.1. *Sections through keelson assemblies.*

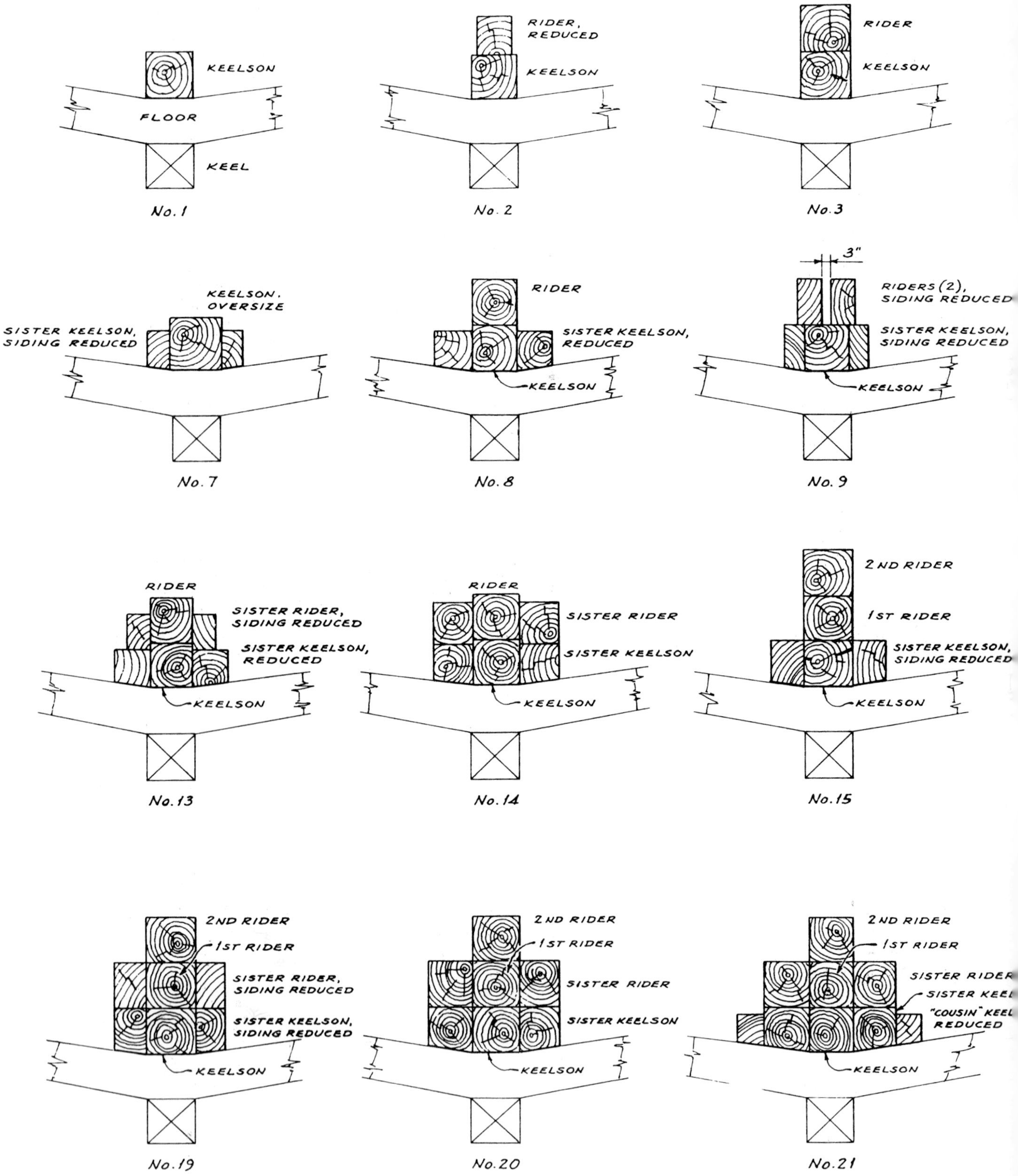

No. 1 — KEELSON / FLOOR / KEEL

No. 2 — RIDER, REDUCED / KEELSON

No. 3 — RIDER / KEELSON

No. 7 — KEELSON, OVERSIZE / SISTER KEELSON, SIDING REDUCED

No. 8 — RIDER / SISTER KEELSON, REDUCED / KEELSON

No. 9 — 3" / RIDERS (2), SIDING REDUCED / SISTER KEELSON, SIDING REDUCED / KEELSON

No. 13 — RIDER / SISTER RIDER, SIDING REDUCED / SISTER KEELSON, REDUCED / KEELSON

No. 14 — RIDER / SISTER RIDER / SISTER KEELSON / KEELSON

No. 15 — 2ND RIDER / 1ST RIDER / SISTER KEELSON, SIDING REDUCED / KEELSON

No. 19 — 2ND RIDER / 1ST RIDER / SISTER RIDER, SIDING REDUCED / SISTER KEELSON, SIDING REDUCED / KEELSON

No. 20 — 2ND RIDER / 1ST RIDER / SISTER RIDER / SISTER KEELSON / KEELSON

No. 21 — 2ND RIDER / 1ST RIDER / SISTER RIDER / SISTER KEEL / "COUSIN" KEEL, REDUCED / KEELSON

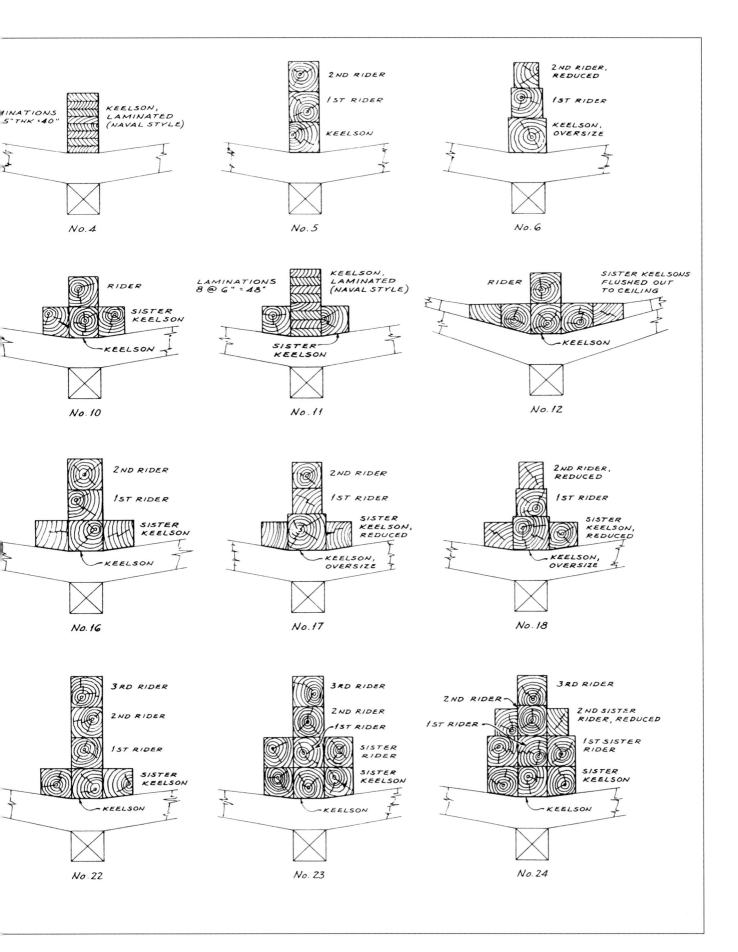

MINATIONS
5" THK =40"

KEELSON,
LAMINATED
(NAVAL STYLE)

No.4

2ND RIDER

1ST RIDER

KEELSON

No.5

2ND RIDER,
REDUCED

1ST RIDER

KEELSON,
OVERSIZE

No.6

RIDER

SISTER
KEELSON

KEELSON

No.10

LAMINATIONS
8 @ 6" = 48"

KEELSON,
LAMINATED
(NAVAL STYLE)

SISTER
KEELSON

No.11

RIDER

SISTER KEELSONS
FLUSHED OUT
TO CEILING

KEELSON

No.12

2ND RIDER

1ST RIDER

SISTER
KEELSON

KEELSON

No.16

2ND RIDER

1ST RIDER

SISTER
KEELSON,
REDUCED

KEELSON,
OVERSIZE

No.17

2ND RIDER,
REDUCED

1ST RIDER

SISTER
KEELSON,
REDUCED

KEELSON,
OVERSIZE

No.18

3RD RIDER

2ND RIDER

1ST RIDER

SISTER
KEELSON

KEELSON

No.22

3RD RIDER

2ND RIDER

1ST RIDER

SISTER
RIDER

SISTER
KEELSON

KEELSON

No.23

3RD RIDER

2ND RIDER

1ST RIDER

2ND SISTER
RIDER, REDUCED

1ST SISTER
RIDER

SISTER
KEELSON

KEELSON

No.24

159

Figure 10.2. *Fastenings through keelson assemblies.*

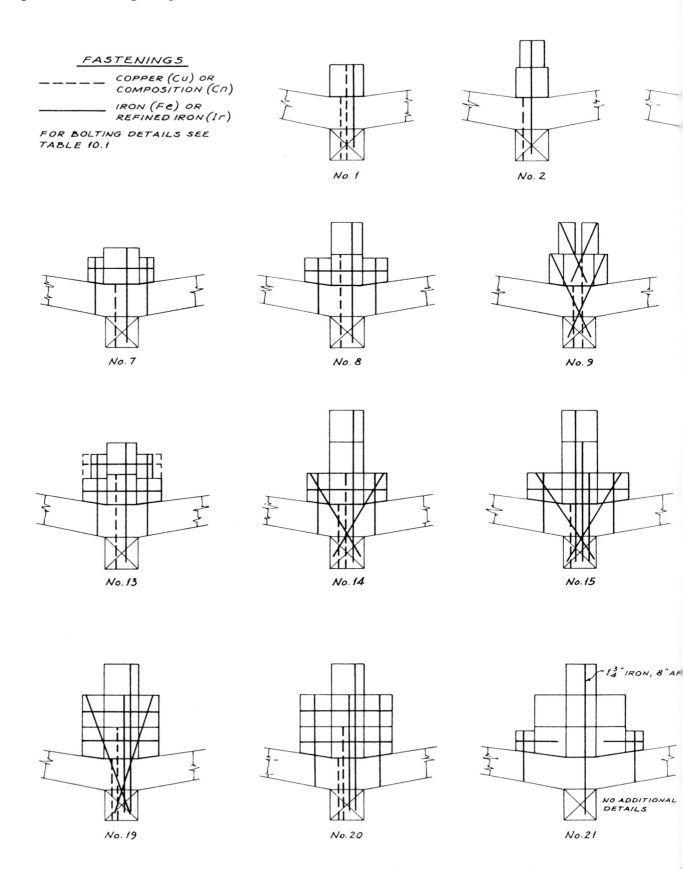

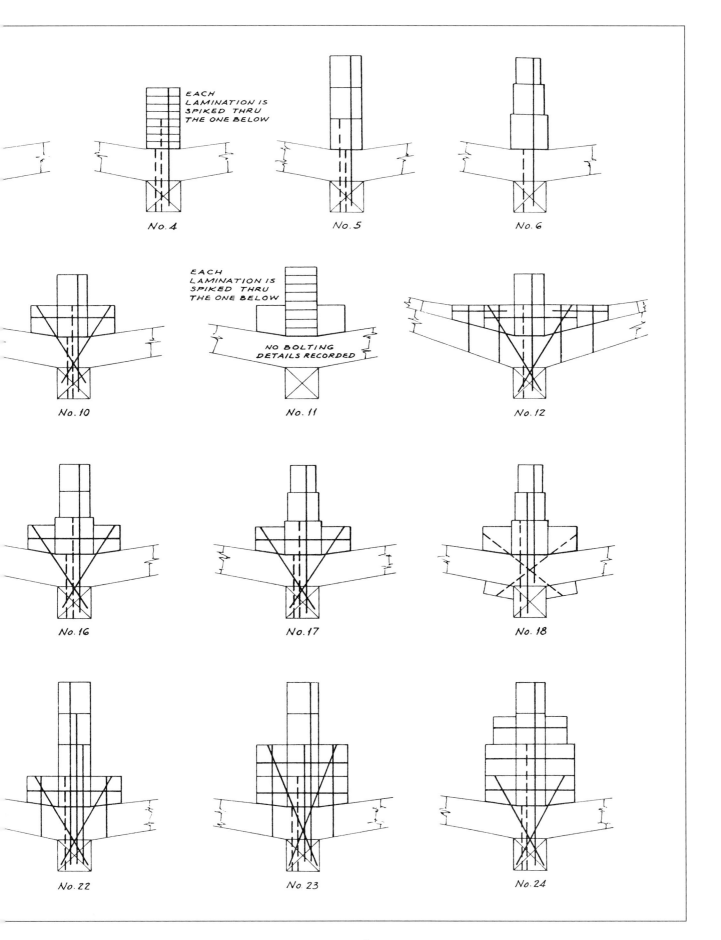

EACH LAMINATION IS SPIKED THRU THE ONE BELOW

No. 4

No. 5

No. 6

No. 10

EACH LAMINATION IS SPIKED THRU THE ONE BELOW

NO BOLTING DETAILS RECORDED

No. 11

No. 12

No. 16

No. 17

No. 18

No. 22

No. 23

No. 24

Figure 10.3. *Sections through keelson assemblies, McKay clippers.*

Vessel	Keelson Assembly	Fastenings data

Vessel list:
- *Champion of the Seas*
- *Donald McKay*
- *Empress of the Sea*
- *Flying Cloud*
- *Flying Fish*
- *James Baines*
- *Lightning*
- *Sovereign of the Seas*
- *Staffordshire*
- *Stag Hound*
- *Westward Ho*

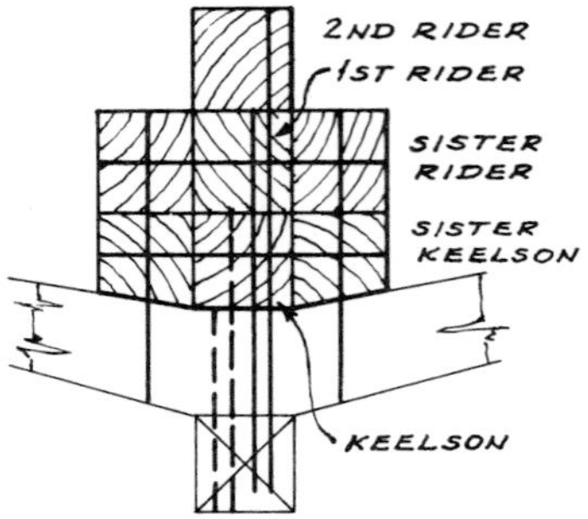

No. 25

Keelson, Fig. 6.2 :C,D

sister riders $\left.\begin{array}{c}\end{array}\right\}$ 14"S x 15"M ea.
sisters riders (2) $\left.\begin{array}{c}\end{array}\right\}$ 15" sq. each
keelson
all pitch pine

bolts into keel;
2nd rider, ea. navel, $1\frac{3}{8}"$.
1st rider, every 6', $1\frac{1}{8}"$.
keelson, see table 9.1
sister riders, V thru each navel, $1\frac{1}{4}"$.
sisters and sister riders, H thru each other, $1\frac{1}{4}"$, 4' to $4\frac{1}{2}'$ apart.

Great Republic

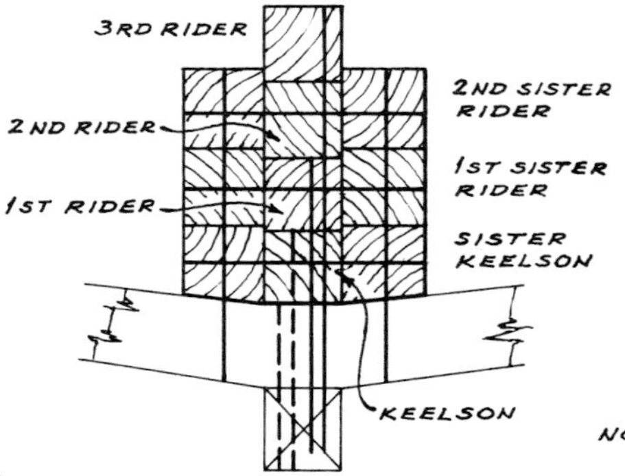

No. 26

2nd sister riders $\left.\begin{array}{c}\end{array}\right\}$ 16" sq.
1st sister riders $\left.\begin{array}{c}\end{array}\right\}$ each
sisters riders (3) $\left.\begin{array}{c}\end{array}\right\}$ 15" sq. each
keelson
all pitch pine

bolts into keel;
3rd rider, ea. navel, $1\frac{3}{8}"$.
2nd rider, same bolt
1st rider, every 6', $1\frac{1}{8}"$.
keelson, see table 9.1
sisters and sister riders, V thru each navel, $1\frac{1}{4}"$.
sisters and sister riders, H thru each other, $1\frac{1}{4}"$, 4' to $4\frac{1}{2}'$ apart.

NOTE: DUE TO APPARENT DISCREPANCIES IN ORIGINAL TEXT THIS ARRANGE-MENT HAS BEEN MODIFIED.

ASSEMBLIES NOS. 25 AND 26 ARE SHOWN AS TABULATED IN REF. 2 AND APPLY ONLY TO THE McKAY CLIPPERS NOTED.

FASTENINGS
- - - - COPPER (Cu)
———— IRON (Fe)

FOR ADDITIONAL BOLTING DETAILS SEE TABLE 10.1

Table 10.1. *Keelson assemblies.*

Abbreviations and Symbols

NHWO - New Hampshire white oak	Cu - copper	X - cross bolted
LO - live oak	Cn - composition	V - square bolted, vertical
PP - pitch pine	Fe - iron	H - square bolted, horizontal
navel - navel timber	Ir - refined iron	S - sided
		M - moulded

Vessel & Ref. #	Assbly. No., Fig. 10.1	Keelson, Fig. 6.2;C,D	Bolts	Bolt Arrgt. No., Fig. 10.2	Fastenings data
Alarm #1	22	sisters riders (3) keelson } 15" sq. ea. all pitch pine	Fe, $1\frac{1}{4}$"	22	bolts into keel; 3rd rider, spacing ? 2nd rider, ea. navel. 1st rider, ea. floor. keelson, see table 9.1. sisters X, ea. navel. sisters V, ea. floor; H thru each other.
Amphitrite #1	16	sisters riders (2) keelson } 16" sq. ea. all hard pine	Fe, $1\frac{1}{4}$"		
Andrew Jackson #20	16	sisters - riders (2) - keelson - all pine	Fe		
Antelope #1	3	rider keelson } 15" sq. ea. both pine	Fe, $1\frac{1}{8}$"	3	bolts into keel; rider, ea. navel. keelson, see table 9.1.
Asa Eldridge #1	22	sisters - 14"S x 15"M riders (3) keelson } 15" sq. ea. all pitch pine	Ir, $1\frac{5}{8}$"	sim. to 22 except no V thru sisters	bolts into keel; 3rd rider, every 3'. 2nd rider, every 1'. 1st rider, ea. floor. keelson, see table 9.1. sisters X, ea. navel, H thru each other.
Bald Eagle #1	15	sisters - 12"S x 14"M riders (2) keelson } 15" sq. ea. all hard pine	Fe, $1\frac{1}{4}$"	15	bolts into keel; 2nd rider 1st rider keelson } every 1'. sisters X, every 1'. sisters V, every 1'; H thru each other.
Belle of the West #1					"Details similar to a ship of 1200 tons."
Beverly					
Black Hawk					
Blue Jacket #5		hard pine			
Bonita #1					construction similar to Golden Light.
Bounding Billow Bark #1	3	rider - keelson -	Fe	sim. to 3	bolts into keel; rider, each navel. keelson, see table 9.1.
Celestial #20		oak			
Challenge #1	3	rider - 16"S x 24"M keelson - 16"S x 24"M 50' for'd. and 60' aft of each are live oak; other parts are hard pine.	Fe	3	bolts into keel; rider, each navel. keelson, each navel.
Challenger #1	20	sister riders sisters riders (2) keelson } 16" sq. each all hard pine	Cu, $1\frac{3}{8}$"; Fe, $1\frac{3}{8}$"		"fastened in the best style."
Champion of the Seas #1	23	sister riders sisters riders (3) keelson } 16" sq. each all hard pine Also see assembly no. 25, Figure 10.3	Fe, $1\frac{3}{4}$"		The whole assembly "fastened with $1\frac{3}{4}$" bolts, the bolts not more than 8" apart."
Charger #1	mod. 20	sister riders sisters } 15"S x 16"M each 2nd rider - 15"S x 9"M 1st rider keelson } 17" sq. each all hard pine	Fe, $1\frac{1}{8}$"; Ir, $1\frac{3}{4}$"	sim. to 20	bolts into keel; 2nd rider, ea. navel, $1\frac{1}{8}$"Fe. 1st rider keelson } alternate floors, $1\frac{3}{4}$"Ir. sister riders V, ea. navel. sisters & sister riders, H thru each other. keelson, see table 9.1.
Charmer #1					"Details similar to New York packets of 1500 tons."
Cleopatra #1	16	sisters riders (2) keelson } 16" sq. each all hard pine	Fe		"Fastened in the most approved style."
Climax #1	mod. 5	2nd rider - 14" sq. 1st rider keelson } 16" sq. each all hard pine	Fe	5	bolts into keel; 2nd rider 1st rider } spacing not known keelson, see table 9.1.
Coeur de Lion #1	8	sisters - 12" sq. rider keelson } 16 " sq. each all hard pine	Cn	8	bolts into keel; rider, each navel. keelson, see table 9.1. sisters V, each floor; H thru each other.
Comet					
Cyclone #3	5	riders (2) keelson } 16" sq. ea. all white oak	Cu, $1\frac{1}{4}$"; Fe, $1\frac{1}{4}$"	sim. to 5	bolts thru keel; keelson, ea. floor, $1\frac{1}{4}$"Cu. bolts into keel; keelson & riders, $1\frac{1}{4}$"Fe, each navel.
Daring #1	15	sisters - 10"S x 14"M riders (2) keelson } 15" sq. ea. type of wood not noted	Ir		"navel timbers and other keelsons bolted with refined iron."

Table 10.1. *Continued.*

Vessel & Ref.#	Assbly. No., Fig. 10.1	Keelson, Fig. 6.2;C,D	Bolts	Bolt Arrgt.No., Fig. 10.2	Fastenings data
Dauntless #1	9	sisters - 8"S x 16"M riders - 9"S x 16"M keelson - 16" sq. all white oak	Cu,1¼"; Ir,1¼"	9	bolts thru keel; keelson, ea.floor, 1¼"Cu. bolts into keel; sisters X with 1¼"Ir. bolts into keelson; riders X with 1¼"Ir.
Donald McKay #1	23	sister riders, sisters, riders (3), keelson } 16" sq. each all pitch pine Also see assembly no. 25, Figure 10.3	Ir,1¼" & 1⅝"		"bolted ----- in the most substantial style."
Don Quixote #1	5	riders (2), keelson } 16" sq. ea. all hard pine	Fe,1⅜"	5	bolts into keel; 2nd rider, 1st rider } each navel. keelson, see table 9.1.
Eagle #5	20	sister riders - sisters - riders (2) - keelson - all white oak	Cu,1¼"; Fe,1⅜"		"all bolted with 1¼" and 1⅜"Cu and Fe ----"
Eagle Wing #1	5	riders (2), keelson } 15" sq., each all hard pine	Fe	5	bolts into keel; 2nd rider, 1st rider } each navel. keelson, see table 9.1.
Edwin Forrest #1					"Details similar to a ship of 1500 tons."
Electric Spark #1	16	sisters, riders (2), keelson } 16" sq. ea. all pitch pine	Fe		"square fastened throughout."
Ellen Foster #1	2	rider - 16" sq. keelson - 17" sq. both hard pine	Fe,1¼"	2	bolts into keel; rider, each navel. keelson, see table 9.1.
Empress of the Sea #1	23	sister riders, sisters, riders (3), keelson } 15" sq. each all hard pine Also see assembly no. 25, Figure 10.3	Fe,1¼"	23	bolts into keel; 3rd rider, 2nd rider } each navel, same bolt. 1st rider, each navel. keelson, see table 9.1. sister riders & sisters X, each navel. sister riders & sisters V, thru each floor, H thru each other.
Endeavor #1	15	sisters - 12"S x 15"M riders (2), keelson } 15" sq. each all hard pine	Ir,1¾"	sim. to 15 except no V thru sisters	bolts into keel; 2nd rider, each navel. 1st rider, each floor. keelson, see table 9.1. sisters X, each navel. sisters H, thru ea. other.
Eringo Bark #1	2	rider - 11"S x 9"M keelson - 14"S x 13"M both oak	Fe	2	bolts into keel; rider, each navel. keelson, see table 9.1.
Eureka #4	14	sister riders, sisters } 12" sq. each rider, keelson } 16" sq. each all yellow pine	Cu,1¼"; Fe,1¼"	sim. to 13	bolts into keel; rider & keelson, 1¼"Cu, 14" apart. sisters & sister riders, V thru ea. navel, H thru each other, 1¼"Fe.
Fair Wind #1	22	sisters, 3rd rider, 2nd rider } 15" sq. ea. 1st rider, keelson } 16" sq. ea. all hard pine	Ir,1⅝"	sim. to 22 except no V thru sisters	bolts into keel; 3rd rider, every 3'. 2nd rider, each floor. 1st rider, each navel. keelson, see table 9.1. sisters X, each navel. sisters H, thru ea. other.
Fearless					
Fleet Wing #1	5	riders (2), keelson } 15" sq. each all hard pine	Fe	sim. to 5	"closely bolted."
Flyaway					
Flying Arrow #1	6	2nd rider - 13"S x 11"M 1st rider - 16"S x 12"M keelson - 22" sq. all hard pine	Fe	6	bolts into keel; 2nd rider, 1st rider } each navel. keelson, see table 9.1.
Flying Childers #1	8	sisters - 10"S x 14"M rider, keelson } 16" sq. each all hard pine	Fe	10	bolts into keel; rider, spacing ? keelson, see table 9.1. sisters X, each navel. sisters H, thru ea. other.
Flying Cloud #1	19	sister riders - 10"S x 14"M sisters - 10"S x 16"M 2nd rider - 15" sq. 1st rider, keelson } 17"S x 15"M each all southern pine Also see assembly no. 25, Figure 10.3	Fe.1¼"	19	bolts into keel; 2nd rider, each navel. 1st rider, each navel. keelson, see table 9.1. sister riders & sisters X, each navel. sister riders & sisters H, thru each other.
Flying Dragon #1	16	sisters - riders (2) - keelson - all hard pine	Fe		"built in the best style."
Flying Dutchman					
Flying Eagle #1	18	sisters - 12" sq. 2nd rider - 14" sq. 1st rider - 15"S x 16"M keelson - 17"S x 18"M all white oak	Fe,1¼"	17	bolts into keel; 2nd rider, 1st rider } each navel, same bolt. keelson, see table 9.1. sisters X, each navel. sisters H, thru ea. other.
Flying Fish #1	10	sisters - 14" sq. rider, keelson } 15" sq. each all hard pine Also see assembly no. 25, Figure 10.3	Fe,1¼"	10	bolts into keel; rider, each navel. keelson, see table 9.1. sisters X, each navel. sisters H, thru ea. other.

Table 10.1. Continued.

Vessel & Ref.#	Assbly. No., Fig.10.1	Keelson, Fig. 6.2.;C,D	Bolts	Bolt Arrgt.No., Fig.10.2	Fastenings data
Flying Mist #1	16	sisters - riders (2) - keelson - all hard pine	Ir,1½"	sim. to 15 except no V thru sisters	bolts into keel; 2nd rider, every 2'. 1st rider, each floor. keelson, see table 9.1. sisters X, each navel. sisters H, thru ea. other.
Galatea #1		white oak			
Game Cock #1	10	sisters - rider }16" sq. keelson }each all hard pine	Fe,1¼"	10	bolts into keel; rider, each navel. keelson, see table 9.1. sisters X, each navel. sisters H, thru ea. other.
Gazelle #4	3	rider }total depth, 30" keelson }both live oak, each end; middle parts PP (probable)	Fe	3 probable	
Gem of the Ocean #1	mod. 5	2nd rider - 1st rider }16" sq. keelson }each type of wood not noted.	Fe		"strongly built"
Golden Eagle #1	mod. 5	2nd rider - 15" sq. 1st rider }16" sq. keelson }each all hard pine	Fe,1¼"		"bolted in the most approved style."
Golden Fleece (2nd) #1	16	sisters - 15" sq. riders (2) }16" sq. keelson }each all hard pine	Fe		"bolted in the best style"
Golden Light #1	4	keelson - 16"S x 40"M laminated of 8 layers, each layer 5" thick. all hard pine	spikes & bolts, Fe	4	Each lamination spiked to the one below. Entire keelson bolted thru each navel, blunt into keel.
Golden West #1		white oak			
Grace Darling #1	mod. 15	sisters - 12" sq. 2nd rider - 15" sq. 1st rider }16" sq. keelson }each type of wood not noted.	Fe		"fastened in the most substantial style."
Great Republic #10	24	2nd sister riders - 12"S x 14"M 1st sister riders }15" sq. sisters } each riders (3) keelson } all hard pine	Cu,1¾"; Fe	24	bolts into keel; 3rd rider } each navel, 2nd rider } same bolt. 1st rider } keelson, see table 9.1. 2nd sister riders, 1st sister riders, and sisters H, thru ea. other.
Great Republic (rebuilt) #103	24	Assembly similar to original vessel. Also see assembly no. 26, Figure 10.3			

Vessel & Ref.#	Assbly. No., Fig.10.1	Keelson, Fig. 6.2.;C,D	Bolts	Bolt Arrgt.No., Fig.10.2	Fastenings data
Henry Hill Bark #1	3	rider }13"S x 14"M each keelson }both hard pine	Fe		"bolted in the best style"
Herald of the Morning #12	13	sister riders - 8"S x 12"M sisters - 12" sq. rider }15" sq. keelson }each all yellow pine	Fe,1¼"	13	bolts into keel; rider - keelson, see table 9.1. sister riders & sisters V, thru floors. sister riders & sisters H, thru ea. other. spacing of all bolts is unknown.
Hoogly #1	8	sisters - 15" sq. rider }16" sq. keelson }each all hard pine	Cu,1¼"; Fe		bolts into keel; rider } see table 9.1. keelson } sisters V, each navel, 1¼"Cu. sisters H,thru ea. other.
Hurricane #4	5	riders (2) }no sizes keelson }given all white oak	Cu,1¼"; Fe	5 probable	"thoroughly bolted"
Indiaman #1	16	riders - 13" sq. riders (2) }14"S x 40"M keelson }total all hard pine	Fe		"square fastened"
Intrepid					
Invincible #4	5	riders (2) }16"S x 17"M keelson }each ends of all are LO; middle parts are PP	Cu, Fe	5 probable	
James Baines #1	23	sister riders } sisters }16" sq. riders (3) }each keelson } all hard pine. Also see assembly no. 25, Figure 10.3	Fe,1¾"		"she is nearly the same in these particulars [construction] as Champion of the Seas."
John Bertram #1	8	sisters - 10"S x 12"M rider }15"S x 16"M keelson }each all hard pine	Ir,1¼"	10	bolts into keel; rider, each navel. keelson, see table 9.1. sisters X, each floor. sisters H, thru ea. other.
John Gilpin #1	8	sisters - 12"S x 14"M rider }16" sq. keelson }each all hard pine	Fe	sim. to 10	bolts into keel; rider, thru keelson, ea. navel. keelson, see table 9.1. sisters X, each floor. sisters H, thru ea. other.
John Land #1,32 (Built as a duplicate of Winged Arrow.)	mod. 5	2nd rider - 14" sq. 1st rider }16" sq. keelson }each all hard pine	Fe,1¼"	sim. to 2	bolts into keel; 2nd rider } each navel, 1st rider } same bolt. keelson, see table 9.1.
John Stuart #4		white oak			

Table 10.1. *Continued.*

Vessel & Ref.#	Assbly. No., Fig. 10.1	Keelson, Fig. 6.2;C,D	Bolts	Bolt Arrgt.No., Fig. 10.2	Fastenings data
John Wade					
Joseph Peabody #1	22	sisters - 14" sq. riders (3) } 15" sq. keelson } each all hard pine	Ir	sim. to 22	no details given. "her back bone throughout could not be more solid."
King Fisher #1	16	sisters - riders (2) } 16"S x 15"M keelson } each all hard pine	Fe	sim. to 15	sisters X, thru each navel into keel. sisters H, thru ea. other. no other details given.
Lady Franklin					
Lamplighter Bark #1		white oak			
Lightfoot #1	16	sisters } riders (2) } 16" sq. keelson } each all hard pine	Fe		"strongly bolted"
Lightning #1	20	sister riders } sisters } 15" sq. riders (2) } each keelson } all hard pine Also see assembly no. 25, Figure 10.3	Cu,1¼"; Fe,1¼"		"keelsons are bolted thru the timbers and keel with 1¼"Cu and 1¼"Fe, the bolts within a foot of one another."
Mameluke #1	22	sisters - 15" sq. riders (3) } 15" sq. x keelson } 16"M each all pitch pine except 3rd rider which is white oak.	Ir,1½"	sim. to 22 except no X bolting	bolts into keel; 3rd rider, 1' apart. 2nd rider } every 3', 1st rider } same bolt keelson, see table 9.1. sisters V, each navel. sisters H, thru ea. other.
Mary Robinson					
Mastiff #1	16	sisters - 14" sq. riders (2) } 14"S x keelson } 15"M each all hard pine	Fe		"the whole closely and strongly bolted"
Mermaid Bark #1	2	rider - 13" sq. keelson - 14" sq. all hard pine	Fe	2 probable	rider and keelson bolted into keel
Morning Light #1	20	sisters (2) - riders (2) - keelson - all yellow pine	Fe	sim. to 20	"best built"
Mystery #1	8	sisters - 10"S x 15"M rider } 16" sq. keelson } each all hard pine	Fe,1¼"	10, plus sisters V	bolts into keel; keelson, see table 9.1. sisters X, each navel. sisters V, each navel. sisters H, thru ea. other.
Nightingale #47		yellow pine	Cu		
Noonday #1	18	sisters - 12"S x 14"M 2nd rider - 15" sq. 1st rider - 16" sq. keelson - 17" sq. all yellow pine except 2nd rider which is NHWO.	Cu,1¼"; Fe,1¼"	18	bolts into keel; 1st rider, each navel, 1¼"Fe. keelson, see table 9.1. sisters X, alternate floors, thru keel and opposite garboards, 1¼"Cu, clinched outside. 2nd rider, V into each navel, 1¼"Fe.
Northern Light					
Ocean Express #1	16	sisters - riders (2) } 16" sq. keelson } each all hard pine	Fe		
Ocean Pearl #1	mod. 15or16	sisters - 2nd rider - 1st rider } 15" sq. keelson } each all hard pine	Fe		"strongly bolted"
Ocean Telegraph #5		hard pine	Cu		
Onward #1	3	rider } 14" sq. keelson } each apparently oak.	Fe,1¼"		
Osborne Howes					
Panther					
Phantom #1	5	riders (2) } 16" sq. keelson } each all hard pine	Fe,1⅜"	mod. 5	bolts into keel; 2nd rider, V thru keelson, each frame. 1st rider, each navel. keelson, see table 9.1.
Queen of Clippers #1	16	sisters - 15" sq. riders (2) } 16" sq. keelson } each all hard pine	Fe,1½"		
Queen of the Pacific					
Queen of the Seas #1	mod. 5	2nd rider - 18"S x 10"M 1st rider } 18" sq. keelson } each all white oak	Cu,1¼"; Fe,1¼"	mod. 5	bolts into keel; 2nd rider } same bolt thru 1st rider } keel, 1¼"Cu, riveted, spacing ? 2nd rider } same bolt each 1st rider } navel, 1¼"Fe. keelson, see table 9.1.
Quickstep Bark #1	2	rider - 12"S x 13"M keelson - 14" sq. both hard pine	Fe	2 probable	
Racehorse Bark #1	1	keelson - yellow pine	Fe	1	bolts into keel; keelson, each navel. also keelson, see table 9.1.

Table 10.1. *Continued.*

Vessel & Ref.#	Assbly. No., Fig.10.1	Keelson, Fig. 6.2 ;C,D	Bolts	Bolt Arrgt.No., Fig. 10.2	Fastenings data
<u>Racer</u>					
<u>Radiant</u> #1	5	riders (2) } 16" sq. keelson } each all yellow pine	Fe,1¼"	mod. 5	bolts into keel; 2nd rider } each navel. 1st rider } keelson, see table 9.1.
<u>Raven</u> #3	7	sisters - 10"S x 12"M keelson - 15"S x 14"M both white oak	Cu, Fe	7	keelson bolted into keel and H thru sisters. sisters bolted V thru floors.
<u>Red Jacket</u> #19	17	sisters - 15" sq. riders (2) - 17" sq. keelson - 18" sq. all white oak	Cu, Fe		"square fastened throughout"
<u>Robin Hood</u>					
<u>Rocket</u> Bark					
<u>Roebuck</u> #1	7	sisters - keelson - 18"S x 20"M all hard pine	Fe	7	bolts into keel; keelson, each navel. also keelson, see table 9.1. sisters V thru floors. sisters H thru ea. other.
<u>Romance of the Sea</u> #1	11	sisters - keelson - 15"S x 48"M, made up of planks bolted together. all hard pine	Fe		"thoroughly constructed".
<u>Santa Claus</u> #1	16	sisters } riders (2) } 15" sq. each keelson } type of wood not noted	Fe		bolts into keel; riders } "usual style". sisters } keelson, see table 9.1.
<u>Saracen</u> #1	mod. 15	sisters - 12"S x 14"M 2nd rider - 14"S x 15"M 1st rider } 16" sq. keelson } each all hard pine except 2nd rider which is white oak.	Fe,1½"	sim. to 15 except no V thru sisters	bolts into keel; 2nd rider, spacing ? 1st rider } see keelson } table 9.1. sisters X, each frame. sisters H, thru ea. other.
<u>Sea Bird</u> Bark #1		hard pine (probable)	Cu		
<u>Seaman's Bride</u> #4	mod. 7	sisters - keelson - type of wood not noted		7 probable	sisters H, thru ea. other. sisters V, thru frames. no add'l. details.
<u>Sea Serpent</u> #47		oak	Cu, Fe		
<u>Shooting Star</u> #1	2	rider - 15" sq. keelson - 16" sq. both southern pine	Ir,1¼"	2	bolts into keel; rider, each navel. keelson, see table 9.1.
<u>Sierra Nevada</u> #1	21	cousins - 12" sq. sister riders } sisters } 16" sq. riders (2) } each keelson } all hard pine	Fe,1¾"	21	cousin keelsons are 40' long; are in way of pumps and mainmast, and are bolted both ways; see arrgt. no. 21. bolts thru keelsons into keel, 8" apart; no add'l. details.
<u>Silver Star</u> #1	mod. 15	sisters - 12"S x 14"M riders (2) - 15" sq. ea. keelson - 16" sq. all hard pine	Cu,Ir		"the whole bolted with ...... and refined iron"
<u>Southern Cross</u> #1	3	rider } 16" sq. keelson } each both southern pine	Fe,1¼"	mod. 2	rider } 1¼"Fe, keelson } each navel. keelson, see table 9.1.
<u>Sovereign of the Seas</u> #2	20	sister riders } 14"S x sisters } 15"M ea. riders (2) } 15" sq. keelson } each all pitch pine Same as assembly no. 25, Figure 10.3	Fe,1⅛", 1¼", 1⅜"	20	bolts into keel; 2nd rider, ea. navel, 1⅜". 1st rider, every 6', 1⅛". keelson, see table 9.1. sister riders V, each navel, 1¼". sisters & sister riders H thru each other, 1¼", 4' to 4½' apart.
<u>Spitfire</u> #1	mod. 17	sisters - 14" sq. 2nd rider - 16" sq. 1st rider } 19" sq. keelson } each all hard pine	Cu,Fe		"all bolted with Cu and Fe thru the timbers and keel, the Cu clinched on the outside, and the Fe driven within 2" of the base of the keel."
<u>Staffordshire</u> #1	16	sisters - 15" sq. riders (2) } 15"S x keelson } 20"M each all hard pine Also see assembly no. 25, Fig. 10.3	Fe,1¼"	sim. to 15 except no V thru sisters	bolts into keel; 2nd rider, each navel. 1st rider, each navel. keelson, see table 9.1. sisters X, thru ea. navel. sisters H, thru ea. other.
<u>Stag Hound</u> #1	16	sisters - 15"S x 14"M riders (2) } 14" sq. keelson } each type of wood not noted. Also see assembly no. 25, Figure 10.3	Fe,1¼"	sim. to 15 except no V thru sisters	bolts into keel; 2nd rider, each navel. 1st rider, each navel. keelson, see table 9.1. sisters X, thru ea. navel. sisters H, thru ea. other.
<u>Star of the Union</u> #1		hard pine	Fe		
<u>Starr King</u>					
<u>Storm King</u> #1	mod. 15	sisters - 12" sq. 2nd rider - 16"S x 10"M 1st rider } 16" sq. keelson } each all hard pine except 2nd rider which is oak.	Fe,1¼"		sisters - riders - keelson, see table 9.1.
<u>Sultana</u> Bark #1	3	rider - keelson - 14"S x ? rider, hard pine keelson, white oak	Fe,1⅛"		bolts into keel; rider - spacing ? keelson, see table 9.1.

Table 10.1. *Continued.*

Vessel & Ref.#	Assbly. No., Fig.10.1	Keelson, Fig. 6.2;C,D	Bolts	Bolt Arrgt.No., Fig. 10.2	Fastenings data
Sunny South					
Surprise #1	10	sisters – rider } 16" sq. each keelson } all southern pine	Fe	sim. to 10	bolts into keel; rider } each navel keelson } same bolt. keelson, see table 9.1. sisters X, thru ea. navel. sisters H, thru ea. other.
Swallow #1	5	yellow pine	Cu		bolts into keel; 2nd rider – 1st rider – keelson, see table 9.1.
Sweepstakes					
Sword Fish					
Syren					
Telegraph					
Thatcher Magoun #1	5	riders (2) } 16" sq. keelson } each all hard pine	Fe,1¼"	sim. to 5	bolts into keel; 2nd rider, each navel. 1st rider, each navel. keelson, see table 9.1.
Tornado					
Uncowah					
War Hawk #1	15	sisters – 10"S x 15"M riders (2) } 15" sq. keelson } each type of wood not noted.	Fe		bolts into keel; sisters – riders – keelson, see table 9.1. "a bolt every 7" their whole length."
Water Witch #1	15	sisters – 12"S x 14"M riders (2) } 16" sq. keelson } each all hard pine	Cu,Fe		"every thru bolt is of Cu, clinched on outside."
Western Continent		Also see assembly no. 25, Figure 10.3			
Westward Ho #1	8	sisters – 12"S x 14"M rider } 15" sq. keelson } each all pitch pine	Ir	10	bolts into keel; rider, each navel. keelson, see table 9.1. sisters X, thru ea. navel. sisters H, thru ea. other.
West Wind #1		all hard pine	Fe		"strongly fastened both inside and out."
Whirlwind #1	3	rider } 15" sq. keelson } each type of wood not noted.	Fe,1¼"		rider – keelson –
Whistler #1	15	sisters – 10"S x 15"M riders (2) } 15" sq. keelson } each all hard pine	Fe,1¼"	sim. to 17	bolts into keel; 2nd rider } each navel, 1st rider } same bolt. keelson, see table 9.1. "a bolt every 7" along her back bone." sisters X, thru ea. navel. sisters H, thru ea. other.

Vessel & Ref.#	Assbly. No., Fig.10.1	Keelson, Fig. 6.2;C,D	Bolts	Bolt Arrgt.No., Fig. 10.2	Fastenings data
Wildfire Bark					
Wild Pigeon #1	10	rider – keelson – sisters – all hard pine	Fe	sim. to 10	bolts into keel; rider } each navel, keelson } same bolt. keelson, see table 9.1. sisters X, thru ea. navel. sisters H, thru ea. other.
Wild Ranger #1	5	riders (2) } 16" sq. each keelson – type of wood not noted.	Fe		bolts into keel; 2nd rider – 1st rider – keelson, see table 9.1.
Wild Rover					
Winged Arrow #1	mod. 5	2nd rider – 14" sq. 1st rider } 16" sq. keelson } each all hard pine	Fe,1¼"	sim. to 2	bolts into keel; 2nd rider } each navel, 1st rider } same bolt. keelson, see table 9.1.
Winged Racer #1	17	sisters – 15"sq. riders (2) – 16" sq. ea. keelson – 18" sq. all yellow pine except keelson which is white oak	Ir,1¼"	16	bolts into keel; rider } each navel keelson } same bolt. keelson, see table 9.1. sisters X, thru ea. navel. sisters H, thru ea. other.
Witchcraft #1	8	sisters – 12" sq. rider } 16" sq. keelson } each all hard pine	Ir,1¼"	10	bolts into keel; rider } each navel, keelson } same bolt. keelson, see table 9.1. sisters X, thru ea. navel. sisters H, thru ea. other.
Witch of the Wave #1	12	outer sisters – faired sisters – 15" sq. rider } 16"S x 18"M keelson } each all hard pine	Fe,1¼"	12	bolts into keel; rider } each navel, keelson } same bolt. keelson, see table 9.1. sisters X, thru ea. navel. sisters V, thru ea. navel and H thru each other. outer sisters V, thru each navel, and H into each sister.
Wizard #1	15	sisters – 10"S x 12"M riders (2) } 16" sq. keelson } each all hard pine	Fe		"the whole bolted in the most substantial style."
Young America					
Young Turk Bark #1	2	rider – 12" sq. keelson – 12"S x 14"M both hard pine	Fe		"the whole bolted in the best style."

(text continued from page 157)

illustrated in detail B, in which the endings are given slight shift so that each deadwood connects at a different point, to strengthen the joints at the forefoot.

Very little description and apparently no evaluations of any methods have survived through time.

Deadwood Assemblies

The deadwoods (Figure 10.6), which filled the angles between the apron and keelson, forward, and between the inner post and keelson, aft, could perhaps best be described as "necessary evils." They were composed of masses of timber which, while performing a required function, were not structural members in the same sense as the keel, keelsons, stem, sternpost, beams, and many other parts of a ship's structure. They owed their existence both to the fineness built into the extremities of the clipper ships, and to the fact that nature, which over the centuries had provided so many shapes of usable timber to the shipbuilding industry, balked at providing natural-grown timber of the configuration required in these areas. Due to the very acute angles between the sides at the extremities, the only trees that would have been found suitable were those that had grown with two relatively equal-sized trunks joined at or near the ground. Such growth was so uncommon that its use was discontinued a long time prior to the clipper ship era due to scarcity, expense, and inherent weakness.

As an alternative construction, the deadwood produced substance to which the half frames for each side of the vessel could be adequately secured and thus maintain the moulded form of the vessel in that area.

In detailed descriptions of the vessels' structure or in the information spelled out in specifications, there is very little detail prescribed for deadwood. The thickness or siding of the built-up assembly was the same as that of the keel, and each piece surmounted the one below in the same manner as riders were placed on keelsons. There was only one thickness, and it was uniform. Generally the individual timbers of a deadwood assembly formed the hypotenuse of the triangle formed by the stem or sternpost and the keelson. This had become a standard practice, based on a logical observation of that part of the structure; it is not spelled out in construction literature. The sizes of individual timbers were left to the discretion of the builder and depended to a great extent upon the form of material on hand in a shipyard at any given time.

In many cases the variety of wood to be used was not specified. However, it appears that the deadwood was generally considered to be an integral part of either the stem or the sternpost, and, when viewed in that context, it is safe to assume that deadwoods were constructed of oak. The general description usually is contained in the phrase "stoutly built." Of the vessels included here, the specific variety of wood is noted in only eight cases. MacLean stated that the deadwoods of *Antelope, Dauntless, Westward Ho*, and *Golden Light* were all of white oak, and that of *Challenge* was live oak. According to recorded specifications, *Donald McKay* had deadwood of white oak,[2] as did *Herald of the Morning*;[12] live oak was indicated for the deadwoods in *Gazelle*.[4]

Fastenings were more definitely specified, but, here too, generalities prevailed. The bolts were always iron, refined iron, copper, or composition, depending upon the type of metal used throughout the rest of the vessel. In most ships the fastenings that were driven completely through the assemblies were copper, riveted at each end. In later vessels, such as *Herald of the Morning*, composition was used in lieu of copper. In all cases where the fastening did not completely penetrate all members, iron blunts were driven to within about 3 inches or more of total penetration. The size of all such bolts was categorically 1¼ inches diameter; the spacing varied between 1 and 2 feet apart.

The height of the deadwood at any given frame, whether forward or aft, was determined by the fineness of a ship's entrance or run and by the moulded thickness of the futtock of the frame that would heel against the deadwood. This was the height of the inside of the timbers and was referred to as the "cutting-down line." Approaching the ends of a ship, this line ascended above the baseline in a fair curve until it terminated forward at the bowsprit and aft at the main transom. The substance of the deadwood was carried to a nominal measurement above this line, perhaps an inch or so, to accommodate the fastening of the half frames which opposed each other. Figure 10.5 represents a typical section through such a frame.

A second significant line that appeared on the deadwood, at both ends of the ship, was the trace of the bearding line that represented the lowest point on the deadwood, at any frame, at which the full siding of the deadwood could be retained. This line designated the lower end of the futtock at its moulded surface. From this point downward, the substance of the deadwood and the keelson was dubbed away in a smooth, fair fashion until it matched the depth of rabbet in the keel and stem or sternpost.

Figure 10.6 illustrates several accepted forms of deadwood construction. The simplest and most common construction was some variation of the forms shown in details A and C in the figure. If a builder wished to include a shift of butts in way of the keelson in the bow, a system similar to that shown in detail B might be introduced.

The greatest digression from these forms, however, occurred with the introduction of a knee to assist in the required buildup of deadwood. This type of installation is illustrated in detail D and is reconstructed directly from the

Figure 10.4. *Extent of keelson.*

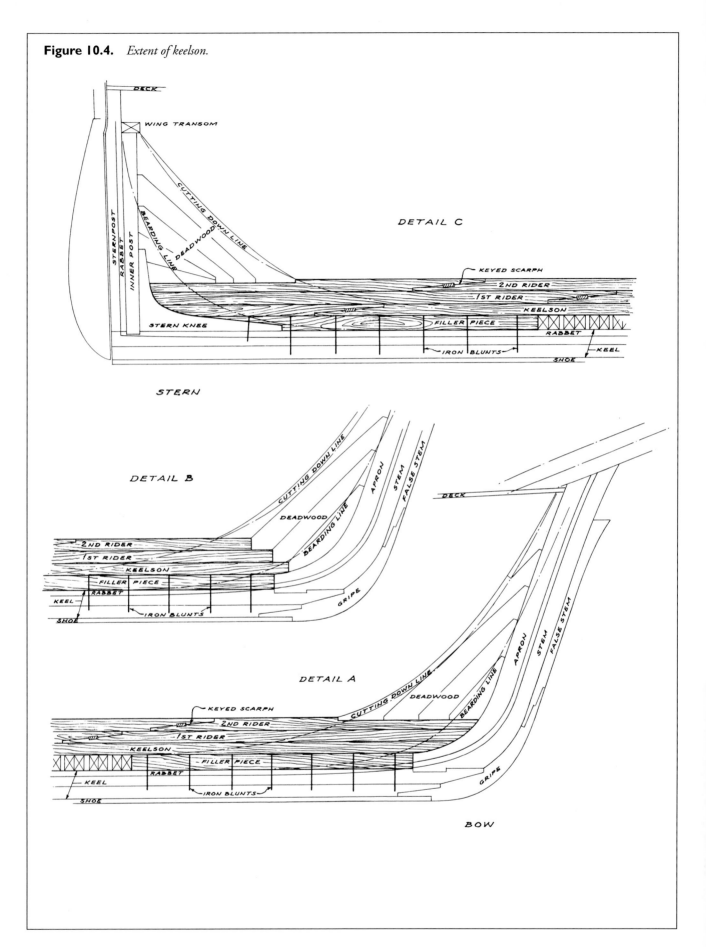

Figure 10.5. *Frame in way of deadwood.*

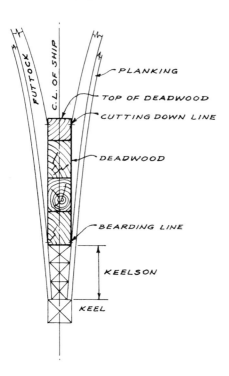

description of the clipper ship *Phantom*.[1] This second knee not only provided material with naturally contoured grain to fill the angle between sternpost and keelson, but also was considered to be a structural asset.

This structural feature was not confined to the stern of the ship. It appeared at the bow also, where the additional knee was fayed against the apron while it acted as a filler for the required deadwood. This practice was not commonplace, principally due to the scarcity of appropriate forms of timber, but apparently it was done quite often. MacLean described *Wild Pigeon*, *Whistler*, and *Donald McKay* as having "stern knees" (plural); *Phantom* and *Don Quixote* as being built with two stern knees, as illustrated in detail D; *Mystery* with "heavy knees" at the sternpost; and *Westward Ho* with a sternpost that was a natural knee at the lower end, supported by a second knee which was worked in with the deadwood. *Dauntless* had a stemson that was a knee installed over the apron; the two, when combined, formed the necessary substance of the forward deadwood. Also two knees were incorporated into the deadwood in way of the sternpost. *Charger* was built with two aprons, the inner one of which was a knee, and also two knees aft as in *Dauntless*. There were doubtless many more instances of the practice.

Regardless of which type of construction was selected, the mould loft fabricated a mould or pattern for each piece. Depending on the shape of the piece, the mould could be made up of battens—a skeletal mould—or solid. After its outline

had been fashioned, intermediate battens would be added, in the case of a batten mould, at significant locations on the mould, such as waterlines, frame lines, cutting-down line, and bearding line. Faying surfaces were designated and match marks added, all to ensure that each piece would neatly fit against its neighbor. When the individual timbers had been cut to shape, these marks were scratched into or chalked onto the timbers, after which the entire assembly was fastened piece by piece until the last member was finally in place.

The Shoe

The *shoe* (Figure 6.2, detail B), also referred to as the *worm shoe* or *false keel*, remained to be cut and fastened to the bottom of the structural keel, since no additional through-bolting was required which would penetrate the lowest tier of the keelson assembly.

The function of the shoe at this period was to protect the structural keel from damage should the ship take the ground or impact against some unseen submerged object. Since it was considered "sacrificial," the shoe was always installed in short lengths, perhaps 12 to 16 feet long, butted end-to-end and fastened to the keel with copper or composition spikes in such a way as to minimize the extent of damage if any portions were torn away from the keel.

The siding of the shoe corresponded to the siding of the keel, and its moulded dimension varied between approximately 3 and 5 inches. In McKay ships the depth was specified as 4 inches for all the vessels. For the vessels appearing in this book, all shoes were rectangular in section except that installed in *Wild Pigeon*, which was trapezoidal, made to fair with the siding of her keel. Table 7.1 contains all known shoe details for these ships.

The sequence of installation of the shoe depended upon whether or not the vessel was to be sheathed during her initial construction. If so, installation of the shoe was postponed until the keel had been completely sheathed, after which the shoe, itself sheathed, was positioned and permanently fastened.

If the ship was to sail prior to sheathing, not at all uncommon, the shoe could be installed immediately. Such was the case with *Lightning*, built in Boston and sailed to her owners in Liverpool, there to be sheathed after this maiden passage.

Since the function of the shoe was to protect the keel, there seems to be little doubt that a temporary shoe was installed and later removed to allow for sheathing the hull.

If the shoe was to be installed prior to sheathing the vessel, the best stage of construction for this was after the backbone assembly was rigidly complete and before additional framing was secured to the deadwoods at the extremities of the vessel;

Figure 10.6. *Deadwood assemblies.*

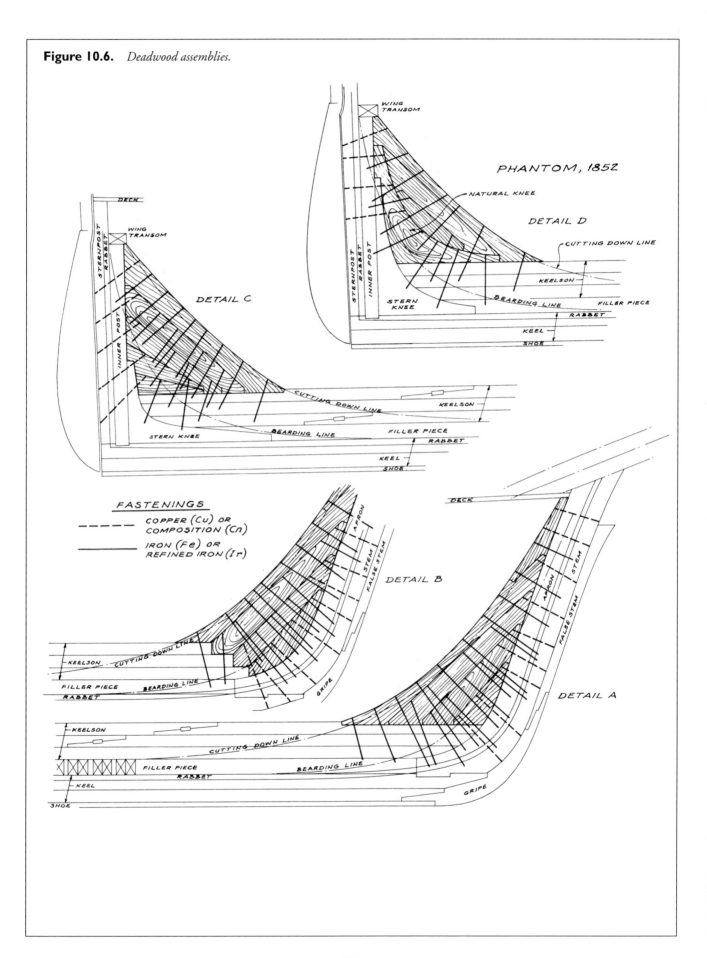

this would introduce the least disturbance of weight and structure. Appropriate lengths of hardwood were sized and readied for installation, after which the cap pieces of a certain number of keel blocks were split out; these cap pieces were always of a dimension greater than the thickness of the specified shoe. When a sufficient number of blocks had been thus treated—this might be only two or three, since they were spaced about 5 feet apart—the section of shoe was coaxed into position and fastened. After the fastenings were all driven home, the space between the bottom of the shoe and the top of the keel blocks was immediately filled with hardwood shims, which again brought the keel to rest on the blocks.

This procedure was followed throughout the length of the vessel. With the installation of the shoe, the longitudinal construction of the vessel's spine, from stemhead to the head of the sternpost, was complete.

In ships that were to be sheathed while still on the stocks, this same procedure was followed at the appropriate time.

Chapter Eleven

HALF FRAMES, CANT FRAMES; BOW AND STERN TIMBERING

Half Frames

As we have seen in Chapter 9, the square half frame became a necessity in the hull of a clipper ship when, proceeding either forward or aft from the midship section, the angle of deadrise of her bottom became so steep as to render the use of floors both impractical and uneconomical. The availability of natural-growth forks or crotches could not fill the industry's demand, and thus a structural change became necessary. The location of the first half frame closest to the midship section was not based upon a mathematical calculation, but rather was the product of physical conditions as they developed in individual vessels.

At an earlier date, as the full, round ends of ships began to be replaced by longer, finer lines, the *cant body*—that portion of the vessel shaped by cant frames—and the *square body*—the middle portion of the ship, shaped by square frames—began to move apart, and a space developed between them which required a new and special treatment. Initially the method chosen was to place "rising wood" under the floors in these areas and raise them so that they could cross the centerline of the ship and thus make up a complete square frame. This method was feasible when ships' keelsons were relatively minor structural members and when there were only a few such frames. However, as the distance increased and keelsons became larger and more important, this procedure was discarded. The solution to the problem was the introduction of the *half frame*, which was a square frame whose two opposite halves were interrupted by these greater keelsons and the addition of deadwood. These two halves were now made to heel against the centerline structure, to which they would be securely fastened, resulting in the equivalent of a full square frame. Their general extent in the framing of a ship is shown in Figure 9.1.

Being close to the ends of the ship allowed a certain diminution of the scantlings as the vessel's structure became more compact toward the extremities. In these areas the full, round bodies of the typical square frame gave way to a more triangular section as indicated in Figure 11.1, and long spans of deck beams were no longer encountered. With shorter spans to support and the advantage of a more rigid structural shape, it was now feasible to use smaller timbers while, at the same time, retaining adequate strength and, as a side benefit, saving weight.

Two procedures were followed to accomplish these results. First, the sided dimensions of the frames were uniformly decreased by perhaps 1 or 2 inches in each member from the keelson to the rail; the moulded dimensions, however, remained intact. These sizes were retained starting from the top of the rail stanchions and progressing downward through the top timbers and various futtocks. In so doing, the very stout members, such as floors with their great depth, were no longer a factor. At the junction of the frame with the keelson, certain accommodations might be made to the moulded depth of the half floor and first futtock in order to increase substance for the fastenings. If this was done, it was always accomplished in a smooth, fair manner in order to allow proper fitting of the floor ceiling to the inside of the frames.

As with all other structure, the mould loft provided properly shaped and marked moulds or templates for the half frames. At their locations in the ship significant beveling of the framing timbers was obligatory, and particular attention was devoted to transferring the degree of under bevel and standing bevel from the lines laid down on the mould loft floor to the patterns. Any particular frame pattern was formed to the shape of that frame as it appeared on the frame line, and the thickness or moulded dimension of the various timbers were scantlings specified by design.

As illustrated in Figure 11.1, an *under bevel* was the amount of material that was tapered off the frame member in relation to its nominal dimension, while a *standing bevel* was the amount of tapered substance that must be added to the nominal thickness. These bevels occurred on both inner and outer surfaces of the member in question, and at any given location they converted a rectangular section into

Figure 11.1. *Typical construction of a square half frame.*

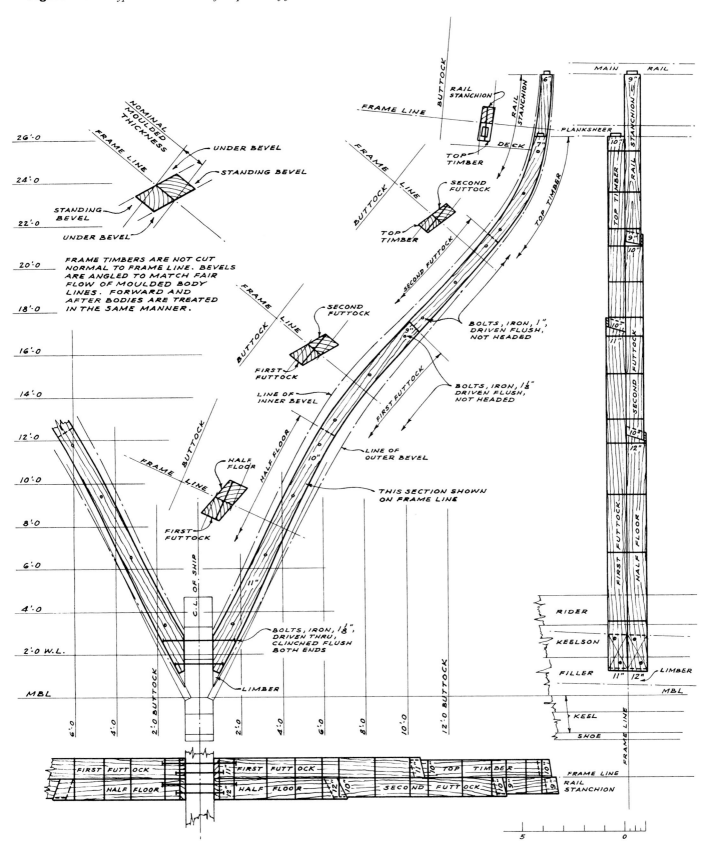

essentially a parallelogram. At appropriate locations on the moulds—waterlines, futtock heads, etc.—the loftsman indicated the amounts of material that must be provided in excess or cut away from the form of the frame line. It becomes quite obvious that the chosen timbers had to be excessively large to accommodate this shaping.

In each case, only one side of the ship was moulded, the other side being similar but to the opposite hand. Conversion from one hand to the other presented no problems to the journeyman shipwright in the field.

The pattern of bolting the various timbers of the half frame together was the same as that for the full square frames as shown in Figure 9.2. The separate halves of the frame were erected in their proper location on the keel and, after being temporarily secured, the two portions that heeled against the keelsons were bored completely through all members, after which iron bolts were driven and clinched, both ends. Generally, a minimum of four bolts was required. It was relatively easy to fabricate and install half frames due to their being square frames. For this reason they were installed as far forward and aft as was feasible. Progressing toward the ship's ends, the severity of the bevels increased and a limit was reached. The problem was governed not by the severity of the bevels but rather by the conditions that developed between the faying surfaces of each half frame.

The futtocks and other timbers that made up a half frame were fastened together with iron bolts driven completely through the sided thickness of the two members being held together. For efficiency in holding and to prevent one member from sliding along the other under the continuous impact of pounding seas, it was essential that such fastenings be driven normal (at 90 degrees) to the frame line. The cross-sectional views shown in Figure 11.1 indicate that the particular frame illustrated is as near to the extremities of the ship as is feasible for this angle of fastening; the ends of the fastenings are approaching a point where they will soon break out of the bevels. At this point the half frames gave way to the installation of cant frames, which, due to their positions in relation to normal frame lines, minimized the cutting of extreme bevels and allowed for the continued proper driving of fastenings through the faying members of the frames.

Cant Frames

Cant frames were erected immediately forward and aft of the last square half frames. In the bow of the ship, these frames, generally ranging between six to ten in number, extended forward to the stem, leaving only enough room for the hawse pieces and knightheads to be inserted between the foremost cant and the bowsprit. This point was generally at the heel of the bowsprit.

As with the square half frames, each cant was heeled against the keelsons or deadwood, generally (but not neces-

sarily) on a frame line. From this centerline location each cant fanned out forward and outboard, with the result that, at the rail, the space between each was greater there than at the heel. Figures 9.1 and 11.2 illustrate the typical progression of such frames. Due care was exercised that this space between cants did not become excessive.

Cant frames were needed principally to avoid the increasing amount of beveling required as progress was made toward the stem. As was the case with the beveled sections that developed through the foremost square half frames, it was essential that the bolts holding the various futtocks together could be driven completely through the sided dimensions normal (perpendicular) to the line of the individual cant frame. This allowed these bolts to act only in shear against the external force of pounding seas and eliminated any tendency for one futtock to slide across its neighbor. Figure 11.3 illustrates the construction of a typical cant frame forward as developed from details in McKay's specifications

In the early nineteenth century, when ships were full bodied with well-rounded bows, it had been customary to start the cant frames at about the location of the foremast step, heel them against the keelson, and then jam each cant frame hard against the one immediately aft of it. This resulted in a solid assembly of timbers along the keel throughout the entire cant frame installation. In clipper ship construction this procedure was abandoned, and the heels of the cant frames were placed near or on frame lines. It was also the practice to "box" or tenon every cant about 3 inches into the keelson or deadwood. Thus the forces that acted against the forward-sloping angle of the frame were absorbed by this abutment, eliminating any shear forces across the bolts whose sole function was to hold the cant frames securely against the centerline structure. As specified by McKay, each cant frame was secured to the ship by six bolts of 1⅛-inch iron which were driven blunt into the keelson assembly.

Bow Timbering

Stem Pieces

The *stem pieces*, when required, were not intended to provide additional structural strength to the bow of a ship. The contribution of these timbers was to provide filling on either side of the apron, when this member was installed with siding equal to that of the deadwood. In vessels that contained aprons of siding that could accommodate the seating of the bowsprit, the stem pieces were not necessary.

Stem pieces were cut from oak and were placed against the apron and deadwood, one on each side of the stem assembly, as shown in Figure 11.4. They were of thickness which, when combined with the siding of the apron, was

(text continued on page 179)

Figure 11.2. *Typical arrangement of forward cant frames.*

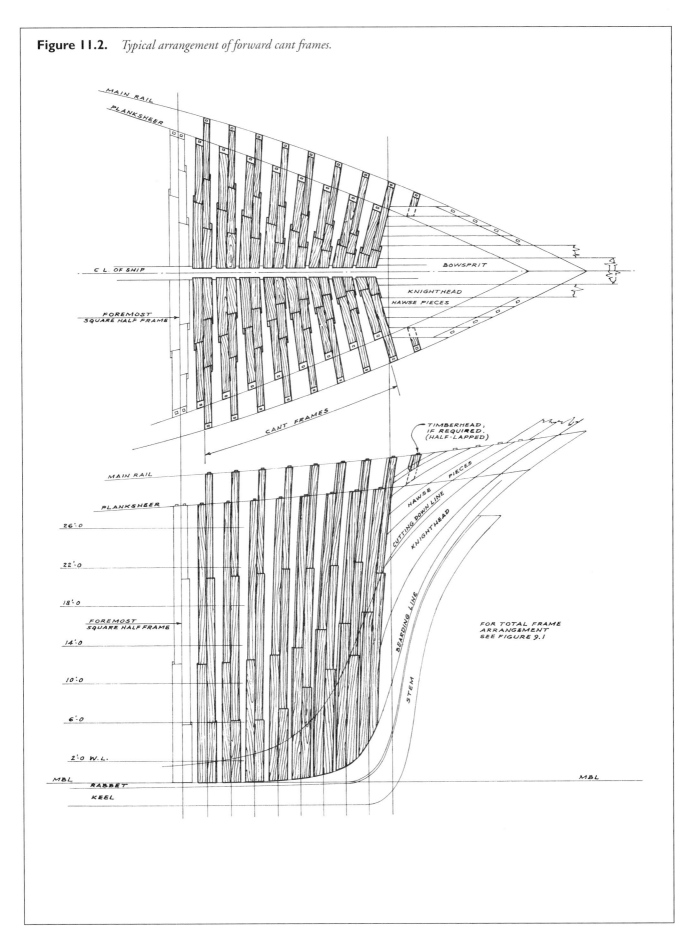

Figure 11.3. *Typical construction of a forward cant frame.*

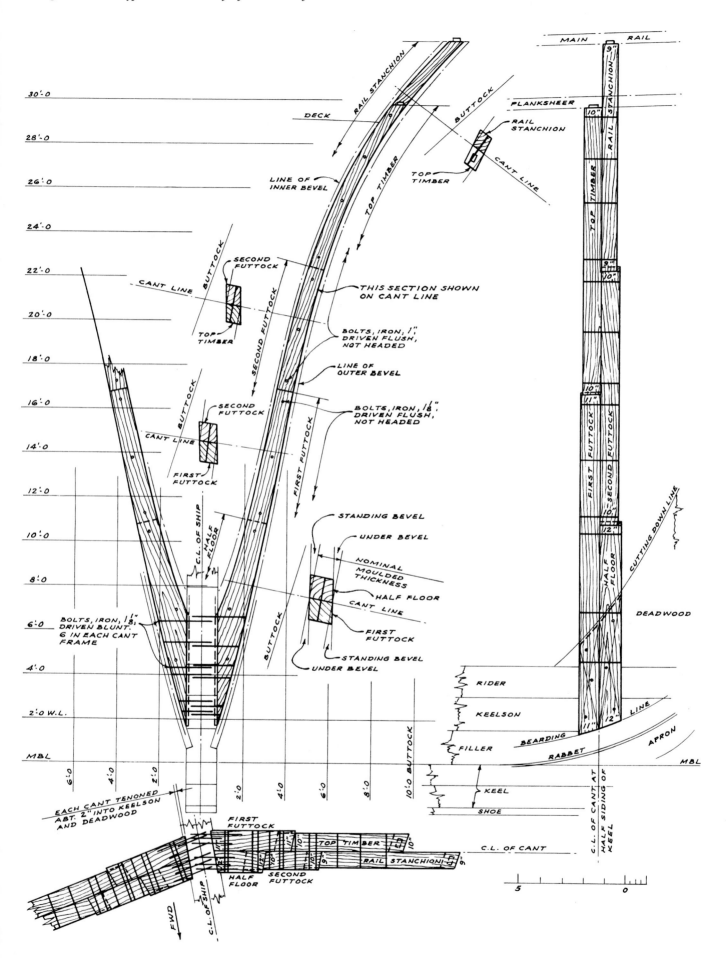

(text continued from page 176)

great enough to allow the inboard faces of the knightheads to fay with the outer surfaces of the stem piece at a distance off the ship's centerline sufficient to allow the bowsprit to be snugly fitted between the knightheads when seated upon the stemhead. This combination of timbering allowed the knightheads to be installed parallel with the longitudinal centerline of ship.

The mould loft provided moulds or patterns, generally of skeletal form, for the stem pieces. Since these pieces were similar but to opposite hand, only one mould was required. The configuration of the stem piece corresponded to the bearding line on its forward edge and to the cutting-down line on its after edge, from the seat of the bowsprit down to the point of intersection with the foremost cant frame. From this point the stem piece fayed with the cant frame down again to the bearding line, where it terminated. This mould provided the profile of the stem piece. Additional horizontal moulds were provided for a series of waterline planes as shown in Figure 11.4. These waterline moulds clearly indicated the required removal of material in order to maintain the moulded shape of the hull in this area. Also clearly indicated was the reduction of the substance of the knightheads as they reached deeper into the ship.

The profile shown in Figure 9.1 is that of Pook's *Red Jacket*, selected due to the fact that, of all major American-built clipper ships, her prow had the longest and most acute forward projection. This design feature compelled her knightheads to be installed with exaggerated forward rake, which in turn required very broad stem pieces for them to rest against as they extended downward in the ship. The stem piece as illustrated would probably be constructed of two planks due to its extraordinary width, but, if so, its efficacy would not have been affected. The final assembly was bolted together with 1-inch through-bolts, iron in areas that would be protected by the knightheads, copper where exposed to the sea, and all clinched or riveted flush at both ends.

Installation of the knightheads and hawse pieces, or hawse timbers, would complete the moulded outline of the bow. These framing timbers were installed in the space between the stem and the foremost cant frame, and resulted in this space being solidly filled with timber. This solidity provided ample substance through which the hawseholes could be cut and also to withstand the constant hammering of the chain cable when the anchor was let go.

Knightheads

The *knightheads* were the first pieces to be installed. In an earlier period, when ships were built with bluff, round bows, these members stood almost upright and fulfilled their intended function of restricting any movement of the bowsprit

in an athwartship direction. The upper extremity of the timber was often finished off in an ornamental fashion.

With the introduction of the slim clipper-type hull, the change in design brought with it a stem with very noticeable forward rake. As a natural side effect, the knightheads, while maintaining their same relative position in the ship, were inclined to the same degree in order to remain within the moulded confines of the bow.

This trend of lengthening the ship and at the same time increasing its length-to-breadth ratio also saw the location of the foremast slowly move aft. This increase in distance between the foremast and the stem was duly noted by the designers, who now saw an opportunity to alter their forward rigging. The knightheads became principal players in this change.

For countless years the forestay, due to the foremast being stepped so far forward in a ship, was set up outboard around the bowsprit in order to achieve an effective forward staying angle. This resulted in some very complex procedures of installation, and vulnerability due to the position and functions of the bowsprit.

Now, with the forward rake of the knightheads, it was seen that the foot of the forestay could be brought inboard and set up on the knightheads, thus allowing a distinct separation between the installation of the bowsprit and the rigging of the forestay. The result was that the knightheads could serve their original function and the additional task of anchoring the foremast. Their scantlings were appropriately increased and their installation precisely specified.

Figure 11.5 shows a typical pair of knightheads installed to suit the bow of Pook's *Red Jacket*, which we examined earlier in reference to her stem pieces. The details of installation and fastenings are as set down for the clippers of Donald McKay,[2] but may reasonably be presumed representative of such installations. Specifically it was required that the knighthead reach down to and heel against the foremost cant frame. Due to the installation of the stem pieces, it can be seen that in plan view the knightheads were disposed in a plane parallel with the centerline of ship, but contained considerable curvature when viewed in profile. Also their scantlings were considerably greater than those of the neighboring hawse pieces and they were, of necessity, gotten out of a single piece of compass timber.

The mould loft prepared a proper mould to this curvature and also noted the specified siding, which was uniform throughout the entire length. On the mould were marked the location of various pertinent waterlines, and separate moulds were made showing the hewn shape of the knighthead at each waterline plane. The two knightheads were similar but to opposite hand. After being positioned in their proper location on the stem pieces with temporary fastenings and dubbed off to very nearly their final shape, they were

Figure 11.4. *Location and extent of stem pieces.*

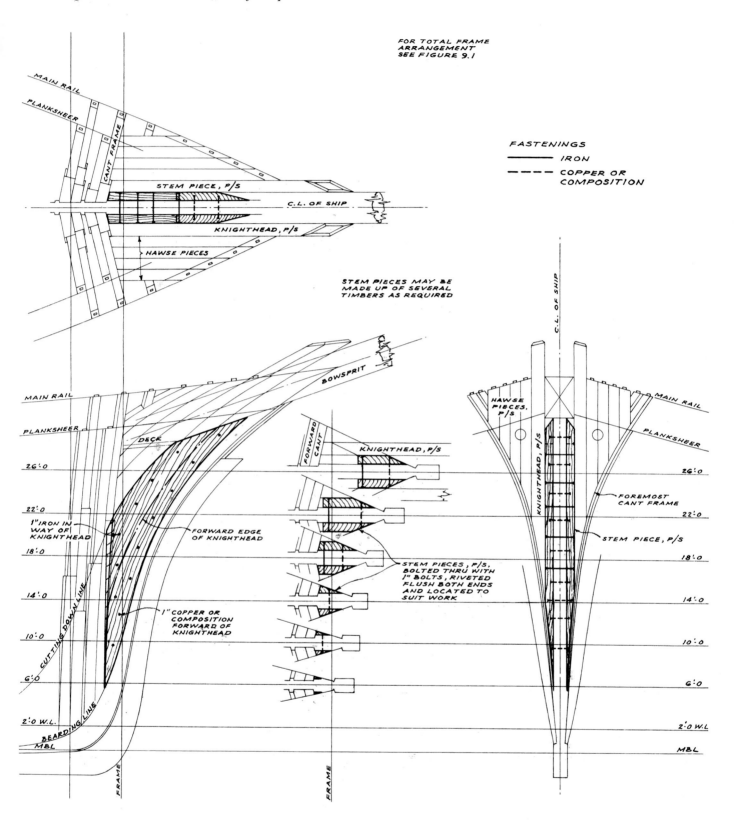

FOR TOTAL FRAME
ARRANGEMENT
SEE FIGURE 9.1

FASTENINGS
———— IRON
- - - - COPPER OR
COMPOSITION

MAIN RAIL

PLANKSHEER

CANT FRAME

STEM PIECE, P/S

C.L. OF SHIP

KNIGHTHEAD, P/S

HAWSE PIECES

STEM PIECES MAY BE
MADE UP OF SEVERAL
TIMBERS AS REQUIRED

BOWSPRIT

MAIN RAIL

PLANKSHEER

DECK

26'·0

22'·0

1" IRON IN
WAY OF
KNIGHTHEAD

FORWARD EDGE
OF KNIGHTHEAD

18'·0

14'·0

CUTTING DOWN LINE

1" COPPER OR
COMPOSITION
FORWARD OF
KNIGHTHEAD

10'·0

6'·0

2'·0 W.L.

BEARDING LINE

MBL

FRAME

FORWARD CANT

KNIGHTHEAD, P/S

STEM PIECES, P/S,
BOLTED THRU WITH
1" BOLTS, RIVETED
FLUSH BOTH ENDS
AND LOCATED TO
SUIT WORK

FRAME

C.L. OF SHIP

HAWSE
PIECES,
P/S

MAIN RAIL

PLANKSHEER

KNIGHTHEAD, P/S

26'·0

FOREMOST
CANT FRAME

22'·0

STEM PIECE, P/S

18'·0

14'·0

10'·0

6'·0

2'·0 W.L.

MBL

permanently fastened. Wherever possible the iron fastenings were driven completely through the entire assembly from one knighthead through the other. A general practice was to drive alternate through-bolts from opposite sides of the ship. The bolting arrangement is shown in Figure 11.5.

Hawse Pieces

The *hawse pieces* (Figure 11.5), or *hawse timbers* as they were sometimes called, were handled in much the same manner as were the knightheads. Their purpose was to solidly fill the space that now remained between the knightheads and the foremost cant frame—if not completely, at least to the extent that would allow the cutting of the hawseholes through their substance. There was a direct relationship between the location of the hawseholes and the athwartship length of the anchor windlass barrel on deck. This relationship could be satisfied if the total breadth across the hawse pieces was about 15 feet.

McKay specified four hawse pieces on each side of the ship, each sided 12 inches, the first one fayed with the knighthead and each succeeding one fayed with its neighbor. The number of pieces was at the discretion of the builder, and in some cases the space might not be entirely filled, as can be seen in the plan view of Figure 11.5. The forward angle of the foremost cant frame was the governing factor here, and if such was the case, a timberhead could be half-lapped into the outboard side of the last hawse piece.

By the nature of their position, the hawse pieces were each fastened separately, the inboard one being bolted to the knighthead and each succeeding one being bolted to the next. Moulds were provided for each item, and in fastening, great care was exercised that no fastening be driven in way of the hawseholes that would later be cut through. As can be seen in the plate, the fastenings were very numerous. After the last hawse piece had been installed, final dubbing of the entire assembly to the moulded line concluded the form of the bow.

The Hawseholes

The *hawseholes*, briefly mentioned in Chapter 3 under the heading "Flare of the Bow," could be cut during or after the installation of the hawse pieces, depending upon whether or not a length of hawsepipe might be required. If the holes were in a location which involved only the piercing of planking, framing, and ceiling, they could be cut through the completed structure. If they were in a location which required a pipe to guide the chain cable from the ship's side to its outlet on deck, it might necessitate installation of pipe and structure at the same time in order for one to accommodate the other.

In either situation, the hawsehole or hawsepipe was a true diameter in cross section. Its axis was straight and canted in a direction which would trend the chain toward the middle diameter of the windlass barrel.

While the mechanical process of cutting hawseholes through a ship's frame, or fitting cast iron pipes into their required locations, was basically a simple operation for a shipwright, the selection of location and size of the holes was determined by the mould loftsman and was based upon a series of considerations. The initial required ingredient was the size of the vessel in tons. From this tonnage figure the size of the ship's largest anchors, the bowers, was specified by Lloyd's or other marine authority. The size of the required anchor determined, in turn, the size of chain to be used with it. Chain size—stated as the diameter of the substance of a link, or the "wire size"—determines the overall dimensions of a given link of any chain, whether it be stud link (as is the case in anchor cable), long link, or common or close link chains. In each type of chain, the sizes of individual links are different.

The clear diameter of the hawsehole or hawsepipe was sized according to the chain's wire size. The width of a stud link was approximately three-and-a-half times the wire size; to this was added one wire diameter for clearance as the chain traveled through the opening. Thus, the total clear opening could be defined as the equivalent of four-and-a-half times the wire size of the anchor chain cable.

It was a rare clipper ship that required a chain as large as $2\frac{1}{8}$ inches. Such a chain required a hawsehole or hawsepipe a trifle less than 10 inches in diameter. The result was that hawseholes were smaller than is generally imagined. One reason for this is that the outboard opening was ringed with an iron rim or *lip* which was cast to fit the contour of the bow. This enlarged the apparent size of the hawsehole due to the fact that it was of a generally elliptical outline which exaggerated the true size of the hole. This cast iron rim was necessary to protect the ship's structure as the anchor chain rode out when the anchor was let go. Each link pounded the lip with a considerable "knock" as the chain traveled over the side. Without such protection, any wooden structure, no matter how high the quality, would have been chewed to bits in short order.

The above physical characteristics having been determined, a draftsman or mould loftsman could now locate the hawse opening in the side of the vessel. There were certain basic requirements and parameters. It was desirable to have the opening as far forward in the eyes of the ship as possible. Of all a ship's structure, this was the strongest location and the best to counter the load of the ship straining at her cable when the anchor was out. It was desirable and economical to have the hawsehole high enough on the side to avoid piercing the weather deck, if possible; this eliminated the task of ensuring watertightness. Another vital requirement was determined by the breadth of the flukes of the ship's largest anchor. When the anchor was "up-and-down" the location of the hawsehole must ensure two conditions. First, upon being raised, the

Figure 11.5. *Installation of knightheads and hawse pieces.*

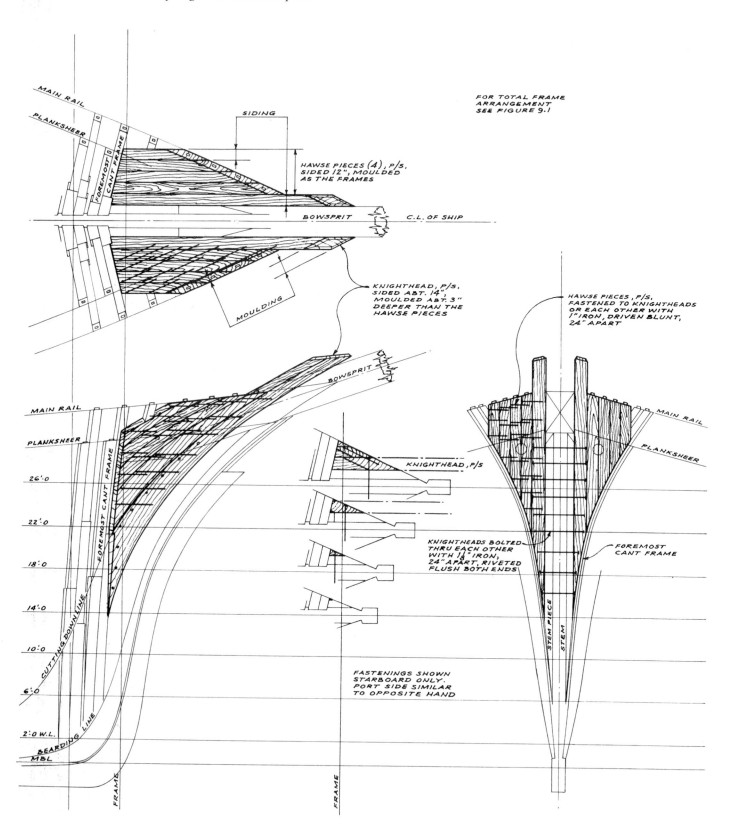

flukes of the anchor must not foul the forefoot of the stem and keel and thus hang up at that point. Second, upon breaking the surface and being in position to be catted, the anchor must not be so close to the ship's side as to place her sheathing or structure in danger. These were the details that must be considered in locating the hawsepipe or hawseholes.

All vessels were fitted with at least one hawsehole or hawsepipe in each side. This was universal practice in small ships but was also typical of many larger vessels. However, in large vessels there were sometimes two holes in one bow and one in the other, and, in some cases, four holes were fitted, two in each bow. In ships having two holes in a side, the aftermost hole was of a smaller diameter than the foremost since it would not be expected to service the large bower anchors.

The number of anchors a ship carried as a part of her outfit—generally bowers, stream, and kedge, by type and size—is known in many instances. This quantity, however, has no direct relationship to the number of hawseholes the vessel may have had in her sides, and cannot be used as a parameter.

Duncan MacLean reported[1] that *Challenge* and *Witch of the Wave* were each equipped with four hawseholes. There is a copy of a daguerrotype which shows four hawseholes in *Seaman's Bride*.[90] According to MacLean, the clippers *Asa Eldridge*, *Flying Childers*, and *Joseph Peabody* each contained three holes or pipes; the same applies to *Great Republic*,[10] and it seems reasonable to assume that the rebuilt *Great Republic* was fitted the same. Two holes are shown in the starboard profiles of the following Webb clippers: *Comet*, *Flyaway*, *Invincible*, *Sword Fish*, *Young America*, and *Black Hawk*.[24] Whether or not the port side can be presumed the same is inconclusive; however, each of these vessels would have had a minimum of three hawseholes.

Stern Framing

At the after end of the ship, the cant frames were installed in the same manner and with the same general considerations as for the bow. They started immediately aft of the aftermost square half frame and continued to the stern. Generally there were seven to ten of these frames at the after end of a vessel, much depending on the type of stern designed into the ship. Figure 11.6 illustrates the details of a typical aft cant frame, according to McKay's scantlings.

Transom and Counter Sterns
Many of the earlier clippers were built with the standard, time-tested square or *transom* stern, the rounded or *counter* stern having not yet come into its ultimate great favor. This square stern, which had been built into ships for several centuries, contained inherent structural weaknesses, as compared to the newly embraced counter stern. Nevertheless,

such builders as George Raynes of Portsmouth, New Hampshire, and William H. Webb of New York did not view the transom stern with disfavor. In fact, Webb's *Comet* was one of the most successful of all American-built clippers, and she had a transom stern. Figure 11.7 illustrates a typical arrangement of stern cant frames in such ships. As in all other phases of shipbuilding, the variations were many, but the principle was always the same.

In vessels with transom sterns, the aftermost cant frame sharply delineated the termination of the ship's side and its juncture with her transom. For this reason the canted angle of the frame and its contour dictated the configuration of her stern and was thus aptly designated as the *fashion piece*. The entire after end of the vessel's side above the waterline was carefully faired so as to conform to the outline of this particular frame. While the general details may be applied to any vessel, this rounded fairing, as shown in the partial view in Figure 11.6, is applicable to the square-sterned ship. This particular rounding of the aftermost cants occurred between the height of the rudderhead and the planksheer. The rounded or *counter* stern, developed as a result of general dissatisfaction with the construction of the transom stern, was not a product that could be attributed to the clipper ship. However, its adoption by clipper ship builders suited them very well since it allowed, in general, for smaller after ends which, in turn resulted in smaller counters and transoms, which were always subject to severe beatings in heavy seas.

The introduction of the round stern into shipbuilding can categorically be attributed to Sir Robert Seppings, during his tenure as master shipwright of the royal dockyard at Chatham, in Kent, England, between 1800 and 1832. The elliptical stern, which was the successor to the round stern, was initiated by another English master shipwright, Sir William Symonds, shortly thereafter.

By the time the clipper ship came into being, all three types of stern were being built into merchant vessels. The general trend, however, saw the transom stern disappear due to its structural weakness and be replaced by the stronger round stern. This stern was gradually superseded by the elliptical stern, which was considered the optimum form both for graceful appearance and comfort of the officers quartered aft in the ship.

The rounded stern caused some minor changes in the form of the aft cant frames, but there was very little difference in their arrangement in the ship when compared with the transom stern. Figure 11.8 illustrates a typical arrangement of the cants in the round-sterned vessel, and the only significant noticeable difference lies in the fact that, as the frames approached the stern, they pulled in more toward the centerline of ship; also, the aftermost frame no longer functioned as a fashion piece.

(text continued on page 186)

Figure 11.6. *Typical construction of an aft cant frame.*

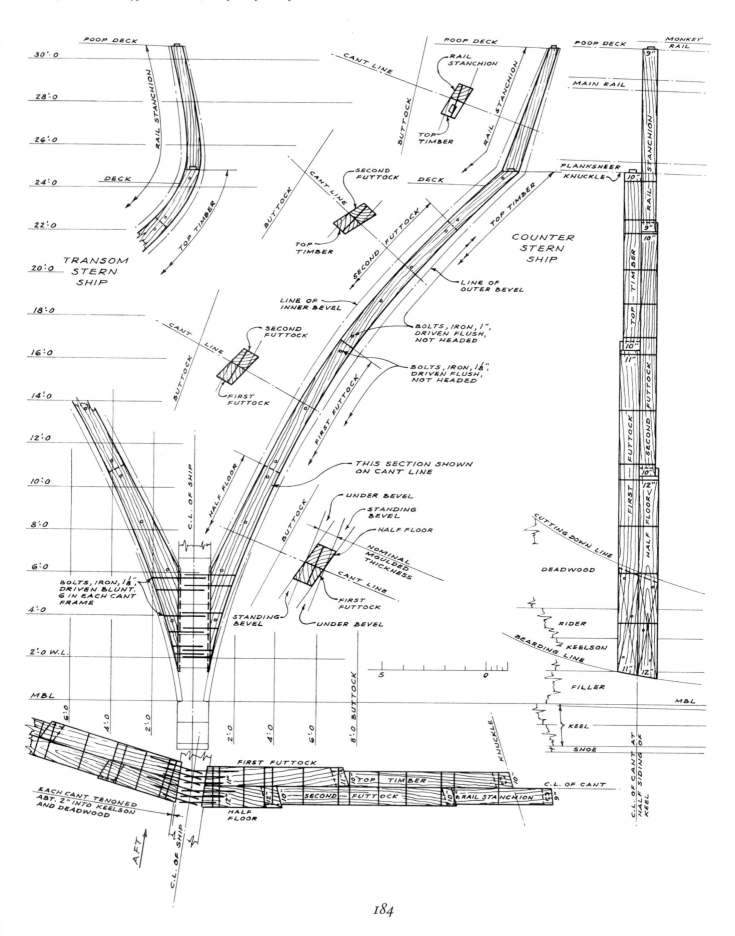

184

Figure 11.7. *Typical arrangement of cant frames for transom stern.*

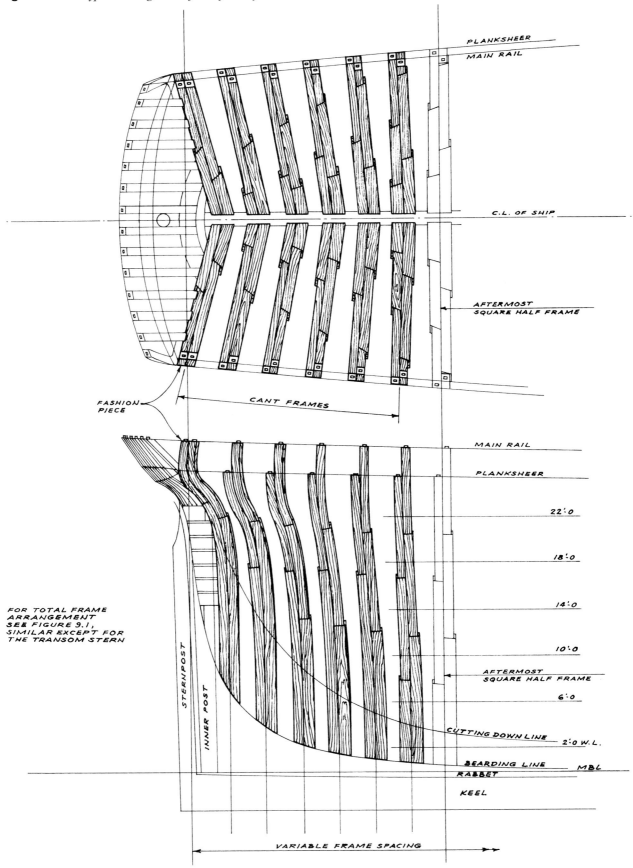

PLANKSHEER
MAIN RAIL

C.L. OF SHIP

AFTERMOST
SQUARE HALF FRAME

FASHION
PIECE

CANT FRAMES

MAIN RAIL

PLANKSHEER

FOR TOTAL FRAME
ARRANGEMENT
SEE FIGURE 9.1,
SIMILAR EXCEPT FOR
THE TRANSOM STERN

22'·0

18'·0

14'·0

10'·0

AFTERMOST
SQUARE HALF FRAME

6'·0

STERNPOST

INNER POST

CUTTING DOWN LINE

2'·0 W.L.

BEARDING LINE   MBL
RABBET

KEEL

VARIABLE FRAME SPACING

(text continued from page 183)

With the counter stern, the aftermost cant frame marked the termination of the ship's side by being located at the tangent of the side and the stern; there was no dramatic and sudden change of shape or direction. This allowed space for the installation of the structural stern timbers that would be fastened to this last cant frame and to the main transom if transoms were installed. Figure 11.8 illustrates the typical progression of such frames. After the external planking of the vessel was completed, there would be no visible evidence of this particular frame.

However, as was the case with ships having transom sterns, this aftermost cant frame was the member that anchored and supported the timbers that made up the structure of the stern itself. And in both instances care was taken to avoid excessive separation between frames at rail height. In general this created no great problem aft, where the lines of the planksheer and rail did not converge toward the centerline of ship nearly so much as they did in the bow.

Stern Knuckle

Figure 11.6 illustrates the details of a typical aft cant frame, according to McKay's specifications.[2] The notable difference in the total form of the frame, in comparison to its counterpart built into the transom-sterned ship, occurs approximately in way of the upper deck or planksheer where a *knuckle* develops in the frame, in lieu of the smooth fairing shown in the partial view in the same plate.

The stern knuckle that appears in vessels built with counter sterns provides for the same smooth, fair planking ending across the stern that is provided by the lower stern knuckle designed into the transom stern. However, due to the conformation of the after end of the ship and the need for a suitable and harmonious pattern of ending the ship's planking, a gradual transformation is necessary between the area of flush planking surface and the fully developed knuckle. For this reason, as the end of the ship becomes finer at the waterline and remains quite full at deck height, the extent of this stern knuckle along the side of the ship is a matter of development rather than of design. At some point on the side of the ship, the changing shape of each succeeding frame advancing toward the bow gradually diminishes the severity of the knuckle until it ultimately is eliminated by the shape of the ship's side. This point is not a mathematical consideration, and its location will differ from ship to ship, always in a smooth transition.

Transoms

The transoms structured into the stern of the ships were horizontal timbers fastened to the sternpost, inner post, and aftermost cant frame and were contoured to conform with the moulded lines of the vessel where they were fitted.

These transoms, when they were used, varied in number from ship to ship. Records show that, in both transom- and counter-sterned ships, they were not always installed (a subject which will be touched on later), being displaced by the installation of stern timbers which were, in effect, a continuation of cant frames completely across or around the stern. Collectively, a group of such transoms was termed a "flight."

The uppermost or principal member was the main transom, and it was the structural timber that supported much of the load generated by the stern structure, since many of these timbers were tenoned into and fastened to this transom and to the aftermost cant frame.

Figure 11.9 shows a transom installation reconstructed from Donald McKay's scantlings and represents this builder's typical installation of such timbers. Certain deviations have been included in this plate since many of the specifications applied to McKay's packets built between 1845 and 1850.

The main transom was of scantlings substantially greater than those of the other transoms, which were designated as "filling transoms" and performed the task of forming the moulded shape of the hull in their wake. The sizes and fastenings indicated in the plate may be considered typical for most clippers. The quantities, however, varied greatly throughout the roster of ships.

Figure 11.10 illustrates a flight of transoms as installed in a typical vessel with a counter stern. As can be seen, there is very little difference between the two except for the individual shapes due to the hull form of the ships.

The general installation of transoms varied but little. The massive main transom, sometimes sided and moulded 18 inches, was seated on the top of the inner sternpost, and then the main sternpost was let into its after side for a few inches. Holding it in position were four bolts of 1¼-inch iron, riveted on both ends. The wing ends of this transom spanned the stern of the vessel until the fashion piece or the last cant frame was reached. These frames were mortised to receive the ends of the transom, which was then fastened with iron bolts.

The filling transoms, of lesser siding, were cut and shaped to fit against the side of the inner post and the after side of the cant frames, to which they were then fastened with 1⅛-inch iron. Several inches of open space was allowed between transoms in a flight to provide for adequate ventilation. All the transoms were moulded in the same manner as the adjacent cant frames. Table 11.1 includes a list of the number of transoms installed in various ships in this book, where known.

Filling Pieces

The *filling pieces* were, as the name implies, used simply for filling in small spaces below the flight of transoms when such spaces did not fully warrant the installation of transoms in the area.

(text continued on page 190)

Figure 11.8. *Typical arrangement of cant frames for counter stern.*

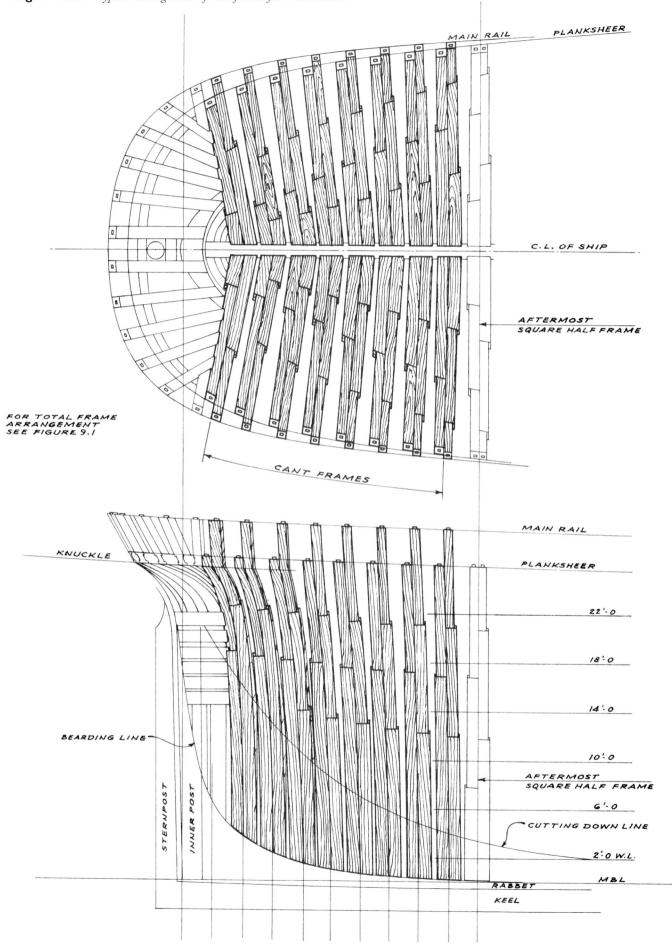

MAIN RAIL PLANKSHEER

C.L. OF SHIP

AFTERMOST
SQUARE HALF FRAME

FOR TOTAL FRAME
ARRANGEMENT
SEE FIGURE 9.1

CANT FRAMES

MAIN RAIL

KNUCKLE

PLANKSHEER

22'·0

18'·0

14'·0

10'·0

BEARDING LINE

AFTERMOST
SQUARE HALF FRAME

6'·0

CUTTING DOWN LINE

STERNPOST

INNER POST

2'·0 W.L.

RABBET   MBL

KEEL

Figure 11.9. *Typical arrangement of transom stern timbers and transoms.*

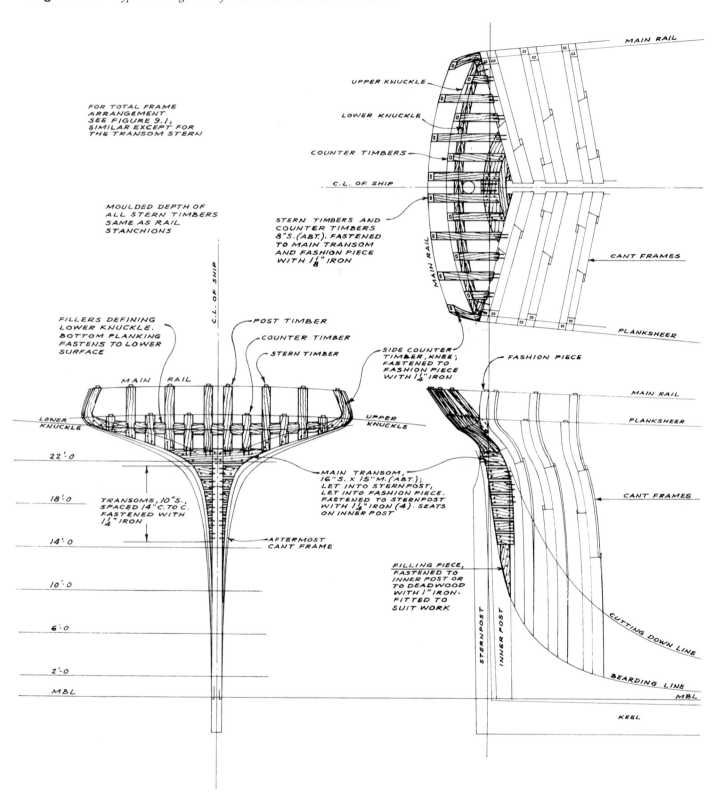

FOR TOTAL FRAME
ARRANGEMENT
SEE FIGURE 9.11,
SIMILAR EXCEPT FOR
THE TRANSOM STERN

MAIN RAIL

UPPER KNUCKLE

LOWER KNUCKLE

COUNTER TIMBERS

C.L. OF SHIP

MOULDED DEPTH OF
ALL STERN TIMBERS
SAME AS RAIL
STANCHIONS

STERN TIMBERS AND
COUNTER TIMBERS
8"S.(ABT.). FASTENED
TO MAIN TRANSOM
AND FASHION PIECE
WITH 1⅛" IRON

MAIN RAIL

CANT FRAMES

FILLERS DEFINING
LOWER KNUCKLE.
BOTTOM PLANKING
FASTENS TO LOWER
SURFACE

POST TIMBER

COUNTER TIMBER

STERN TIMBER

PLANKSHEER

C.L. OF SHIP

SIDE COUNTER
TIMBER, KNEE;
FASTENED TO
FASHION PIECE
WITH 1¼" IRON

FASHION PIECE

MAIN RAIL

MAIN RAIL

LOWER
KNUCKLE

UPPER
KNUCKLE

MAIN RAIL

PLANKSHEER

22'·0

MAIN TRANSOM,
16"S. x 15"M.(ABT.);
LET INTO STERNPOST,
LET INTO FASHION PIECE.
FASTENED TO STERNPOST
WITH 1¼" IRON (4). SEATS
ON INNER POST

18'·0

TRANSOMS, 10"S.,
SPACED 14" C. TO C.
FASTENED WITH
1¼" IRON

CANT FRAMES

14'·0

AFTERMOST
CANT FRAME

10'·0

FILLING PIECE,
FASTENED TO
INNER POST OR
TO DEADWOOD
WITH 1" IRON-
FITTED TO
SUIT WORK

6'·0

2'·0

CUTTING DOWN LINE

MBL

STERNPOST

INNER POST

BEARDING LINE

MBL

KEEL

188

Figure 11.10. *Typical arrangement of counter-stern timbers, transoms, and filling pieces.*

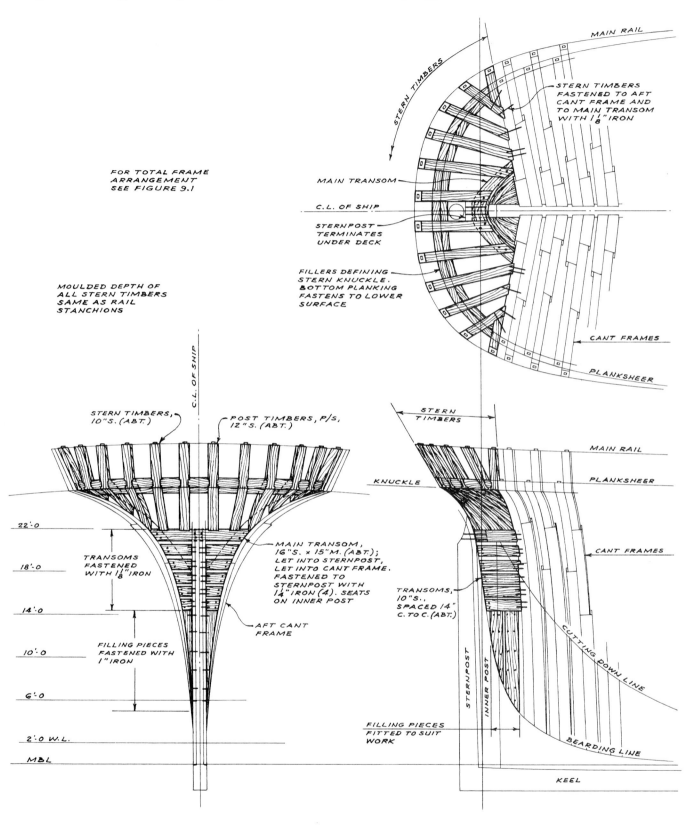

FOR TOTAL FRAME
ARRANGEMENT
SEE FIGURE 9.1

MOULDED DEPTH OF
ALL STERN TIMBERS
SAME AS RAIL
STANCHIONS

STERN TIMBERS

STERN TIMBERS
FASTENED TO AFT
CANT FRAME AND
TO MAIN TRANSOM
WITH 1⅛" IRON

MAIN TRANSOM

C.L. OF SHIP

STERNPOST
TERMINATES
UNDER DECK

FILLERS DEFINING
STERN KNUCKLE.
BOTTOM PLANKING
FASTENS TO LOWER
SURFACE

MAIN RAIL

CANT FRAMES

PLANKSHEER

C.L. OF SHIP

STERN TIMBERS,
10"S. (ABT.)

POST TIMBERS, P/S,
12"S. (ABT.)

STERN
TIMBERS

MAIN RAIL

KNUCKLE

PLANKSHEER

22'·0

18'·0

TRANSOMS
FASTENED
WITH 1⅛" IRON

14'·0

MAIN TRANSOM,
16"S. × 15"M. (ABT.);
LET INTO STERNPOST,
LET INTO CANT FRAME.
FASTENED TO
STERNPOST WITH
1¼"IRON (4). SEATS
ON INNER POST

AFT CANT
FRAME

CANT FRAMES

TRANSOMS,
10"S.,
SPACED 14"
C. TO C. (ABT.)

10'·0

FILLING PIECES
FASTENED WITH
1" IRON

6'·0

2'·0 W.L.

MBL

STERNPOST

INNER POST

FILLING PIECES
FITTED TO SUIT
WORK

CUTTING DOWN LINE

BEARDING LINE

KEEL

189

(text continued from page 186)

Figure 11.10 illustrates one method of installing these fillers, as vertical slabs that were suitably shaped and securely fastened to the deadwood between the lowest transom and the bearding line. These fillers provided solid seating for the exterior planking when it was installed.

Stern Timbers

The stern timbers were the final elements required to complete the moulded structural form of the hull. They were installed generally the same way in all ships, whether transom or counter sterned. In detail they differed with each builder and the contours of the individual ships.

There were two specific types of stern timbering, and both types were found in transom and counter sterns. The first system, no doubt carried over directly from the huge and intricate transoms of their predecessors, was applied to the greatly reduced and modified clipper ship transom stern, which was modeled after the earlier ships in that a flight of transoms was a major component of such construction. In this system the stern timbers were set up in a vertical plane and positioned parallel with each other and with the centerline of ship, as indicated in Figure 11.9; this represents only one variation of the system and is based largely on McKay's specifications.

The heel of each stern timber was let into the upper face of the main transom wherever these members came together. The timbers that lay outboard of the ends of the main transom were let into the after side of the fashion piece. The fine design of the clipper run and after end, combined with the great attention paid to making the counter and transom as small as was practicable, did not provide for the great span which was one of the characteristics of ships in earlier days. However, the details of this newer installation were far less complex, and each stern timber could easily be laid down on the mould loft floor.

The *outboard* or *side counter timber* was the only element in this structure that presented some relative degree of complexity. Its function was to delineate the trace of the juncture between the vessel's side and the transom proper. This was accomplished by installing a knee whose arm raked aft to a degree that matched the rake of the transom and at the same time rounded inward to match the contour of the upper end of the fashion piece. The body of the knee rested along the after side of the fashion piece, to which it was solidly fastened. In this manner the termination of the side and the stern of the ship became fixed.

In almost every vessel, this entire structure defining the configuration of her stern was a combination of shaped and secured timbers. However, in *Roebuck*—an 800-ton ship built by Bourne and Kingsbury, at Kennebunk, Maine—the builders departed from this practice and had her quarter

pieces cast in composition. These castings were so complete that the flowered decoration in their area was formed in the mould, thus being included as a part of the parent casting. This treatment of the stern may not have been unique, but it must have been very rare since it is the only such instance among the vessels included here.

Along the lower knuckle from one side of the ship to the other, a filling timber or filling pieces were required to receive the fastening of the ends of the ship's bottom planking. This is the construction illustrated in Figure 11.9 and represents a stern that was probably as diminutive as could be incorporated into a large clipper. This can be realized by comparing its size in relation to the distances between waterlines as shown. For ships with a deeper, more massive transom and fuller run, the main transom would be a much longer member and more stern timbers would be heeled into it, but the end result would be the same.

The stern timbers installed immediately adjacent to the sternpost were designated as *post timbers* and were sometimes of greater scantlings than the ordinary timbers, designated as *stern timbers* (the broad, general term for all such members) and *counter timbers*. Counter timbers were found only in vessels with square, transom sterns, and differed from stern timbers in that their upper length reached only to the planksheer rather than to the main rail; this was to eliminate unnecessary weight.

The counter timber supported the counter structure on the main transom and the aftermost cant frame, and also helped define the stern knuckle across the breadth of the transom. The transom itself was strong enough to eliminate the need for some of the vertical timbering. Customarily, alternate stern timbers were cut down to become counter timbers, as shown in Figures 11.9 and 11.11.

The stern timbers, when installed with round sterns and built with a flight of transoms, were assembled in a slightly different manner but with the same general concept. As with the square stern, each stern timber that met the main transom was let into it, while all remaining timbers were let into the aftermost cant frame. Each individual timber stood upright, but only the two timbers that framed the sternpost were installed parallel with the centerline of ship. Any other timbers, when seen in plan view, were fanned out around the stern, care being taken that the distance between each one at the rail was not excessive. This can be plainly seen in Figure 11.10.

The timbers were each laid down in the mould loft in a manner that developed the stern knuckle as a fair continuation of this knuckle where it ended at the aftermost cant frame. Along the stern knuckle a filling timber was installed to define the knuckle completely around the counter and to provide timber to which the ends of the bottom planking could be secured. In addition to superior structural strength,

(text continued on page 194)

Figure 11.11. *Typical arrangement of transom stern timbers without transoms.*

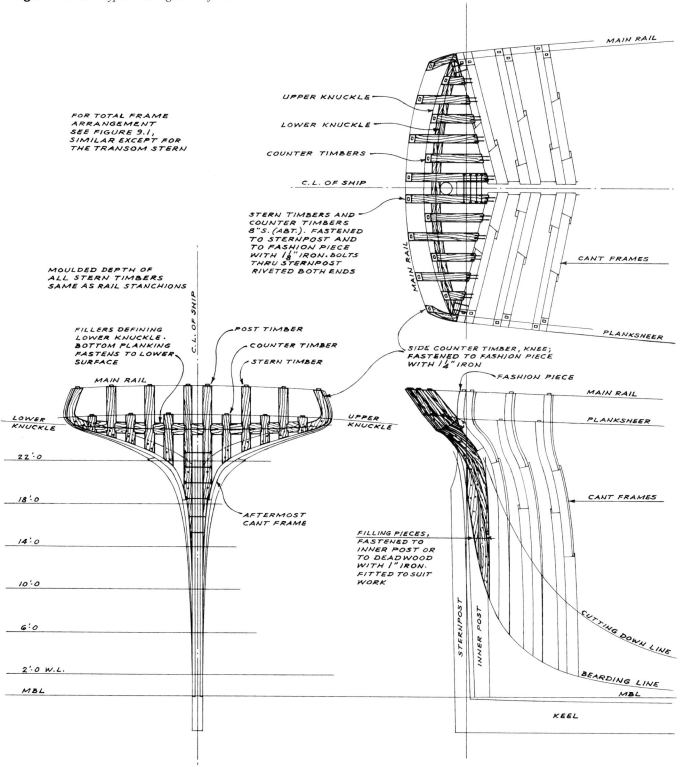

MAIN RAIL

UPPER KNUCKLE

LOWER KNUCKLE

COUNTER TIMBERS

C.L. OF SHIP

MAIN RAIL

CANT FRAMES

PLANKSHEER

FOR TOTAL FRAME
ARRANGEMENT
SEE FIGURE 9.1,
SIMILAR EXCEPT FOR
THE TRANSOM STERN

STERN TIMBERS AND
COUNTER TIMBERS
8"S. (ABT.). FASTENED
TO STERNPOST AND
TO FASHION PIECE
WITH 1⅛" IRON. BOLTS
THRU STERNPOST
RIVETED BOTH ENDS

MOULDED DEPTH OF
ALL STERN TIMBERS
SAME AS RAIL STANCHIONS

C.L. OF SHIP

FILLERS DEFINING
LOWER KNUCKLE.
BOTTOM PLANKING
FASTENS TO LOWER
SURFACE

POST TIMBER

COUNTER TIMBER

STERN TIMBER

SIDE COUNTER TIMBER, KNEE;
FASTENED TO FASHION PIECE
WITH 1¼" IRON

FASHION PIECE

MAIN RAIL

MAIN RAIL

PLANKSHEER

LOWER
KNUCKLE

UPPER
KNUCKLE

22'·0

18'·0

14'·0

10'·0

6'·0

2'·0 W.L.

MBL

AFTERMOST
CANT FRAME

CANT FRAMES

FILLING PIECES,
FASTENED TO
INNER POST OR
TO DEADWOOD
WITH 1" IRON.
FITTED TO SUIT
WORK

STERNPOST

INNER POST

CUTTING DOWN LINE

BEARING LINE

MBL

KEEL

Figure 11.12. *Typical arrangement of counter-stern timbers without transoms.*

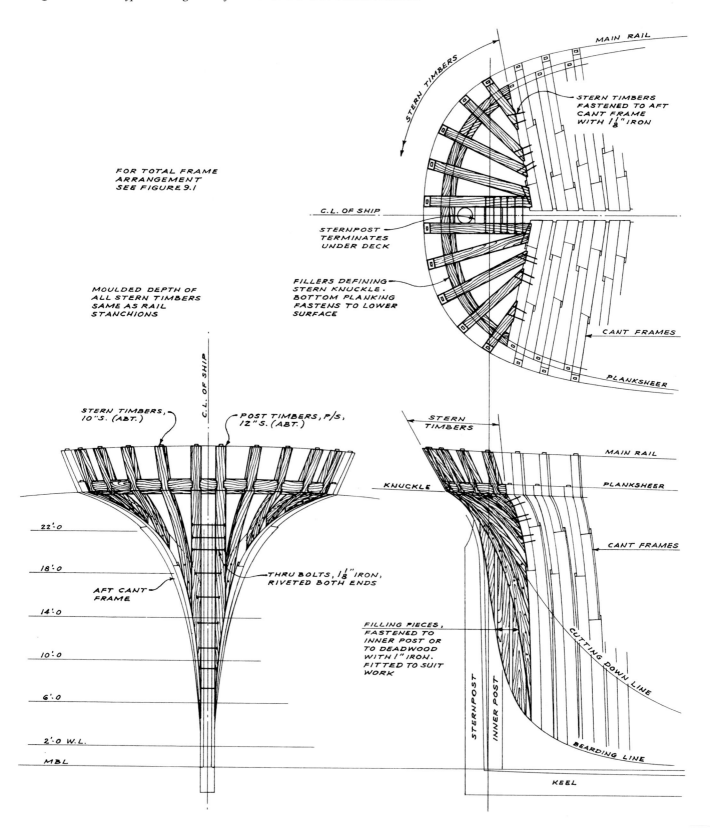

STERN TIMBERS

STERN TIMBERS FASTENED TO AFT CANT FRAME WITH 1⅛" IRON

FOR TOTAL FRAME ARRANGEMENT SEE FIGURE 9.1

C.L. OF SHIP

STERNPOST TERMINATES UNDER DECK

FILLERS DEFINING STERN KNUCKLE. BOTTOM PLANKING FASTENS TO LOWER SURFACE

MOULDED DEPTH OF ALL STERN TIMBERS SAME AS RAIL STANCHIONS

CANT FRAMES

PLANKSHEER

STERN TIMBERS

STERN TIMBERS, 10"S. (ABT.)

C.L. OF SHIP

POST TIMBERS, P/S, 12"S. (ABT.)

MAIN RAIL

KNUCKLE

PLANKSHEER

22'·0

18'·0

CANT FRAMES

AFT CANT FRAME

THRU BOLTS, 1⅛" IRON, RIVETED BOTH ENDS

14'·0

FILLING PIECES, FASTENED TO INNER POST OR TO DEADWOOD WITH 1" IRON. FITTED TO SUIT WORK

CUTTING DOWN LINE

10'·0

6'·0

2'·0 W.L.

MBL

STERNPOST

INNER POST

BEARDING LINE

KEEL

Table 11.1. *Transoms and stern timbers.*

Notes: "A flight" signifies an unspecified number of transoms.

Quantities indicated include the main transom.

Stern timbers are complete timbers without transoms.

Abbreviations

WO – white oak	NHWO – New Hampshire white oak
O – oak	MWO – Massachusetts white oak
LO – live oak	S – Sided
	M – Moulded

Vessel & Ref.#	Species of wood	Transoms or stern timbers	Remarks
Alarm #1	WO	A flight of 6; main, 18" sq.	Main transom kneed to the sides of ship
Antelope #1	WO	A flight; main, 14"x16"	Main transom extends along the sides of ship
Asa Eldridge #1	WO	A flight of 10; main, 18" sq.	Main transom kneed to the sides of ship
Black Hawk #2		A flight; main, 11½" S.	
Bald Eagle #1	WO	stern timbers (probable)	No additional details
Bonita #1	O		Similar to Golden Light
Champion of the Seas #2	WO	stern timbers	Post, 14"Sx10"M at knuckle; Others, 10"Sx10"M ditto
Charger #1	NHWO	A flight; main, 18" sq.	Double kneed to the sides of ship
Daring #1	WO	A flight of 11; main, 16"x17"	Main transom kneed to the sides of ship
Donald McKay #2	WO	stern timbers	Post, 14"Sx10"M at knuckle; Others, 10"Sx10"M ditto
Don Quixote #1	WO	A flight of 10; main, 18" sq.	Main transom kneed to the sides of ship
Ellen Foster #1	WO	A flight of 10; main, 18" sq.	Main transom kneed to the sides of ship, extending three beams
Empress of the Sea #2	WO	stern timbers	Post, 14"Sx10"M at knuckle; Others, 10"Sx10"M ditto
Endeavor #1	WO	A flight of 6; main, 18" sq.	Main transom kneed to the sides of ship
Eureka #4	LO		No additional details
Flying Childers #1	WO	A flight; main, 17" sq.	
Flying Cloud #2	WO	stern timbers	Post, 12"Sx10"M at knuckle; Others, 10"Sx10"M ditto
Flying Fish #2	WO	stern timbers	Post, 12"Sx10"M at knuckle; Others, 10"Sx10"M ditto
Gazelle #4	LO	A flight	No additional details
Gem of the Ocean #1	O	A flight of 8; main, 17" sq.	Main transom kneed to sides of ship with long knees
Golden Eagle #1	WO	A flight; main, 16" sq.	Main transom kneed to the sides of ship
Golden Light #1	WO	A flight; main, 18" sq.	
Great Republic #2	WO	stern timbers	Post, 14"Sx12"M at knuckle; Others, 12"Sx10"M ditto
Great Republic (rebuilt) #103			No specific data. Probably similar to original.
James Baines #2	WO	stern timbers	Post, 14"Sx10"M at knuckle; Others, 10"Sx10"M ditto
John Bertram #1	WO	A flight of 9; main, 17" sq.	Tween deck transoms supported by a standing knee on center line, bolted thru transoms and post
John Gilpin #1	WO	A flight of 10; main, 16" sq.	
John Land #1 (Built as a duplicate of Winged Arrow)	WO	A flight of 5; main, 18" sq.	Main transom kneed to sides of ship with stout knees
Lightning #2	WO	stern timbers	Post, 14"Sx10"M at knuckle; Others, 10"Sx10"M ditto
Mastiff #1	WO	stern timbers	No additional details
Mystery #1	WO	A flight; main, 19" sq.	Main transom braced to sides of ship with long wing transoms
Phantom #1	WO	A flight; main, 18" sq.	Main transom braced to sides of ship with long wing transoms
Romance of the Sea #1	WO	stern timbers	No additional details
Santa Claus #1	WO	stern timbers	No additional details
Shooting Star #1	WO	A flight; main, 18" sq.	Main transom is 25' long
Southern Cross #1	MWO	A flight; main, 18" sq.	Main transom kneed to sides of ship with long knees
Sovereign of the Seas #2	WO	stern timbers	Post, 14"Sx10"M at knuckle; Others, 10"Sx10"M ditto
Staffordshire #2	WO	stern timbers	Post, 12"Sx10"M at knuckle; Others, 10"Sx10"M ditto
Stag Hound #2	WO	stern timbers	Post, 12"Sx10"M at knuckle; Others, 10"Sx10"M ditto
Westward Ho #1,2	WO	stern timbers	Ref.1 – The stern is timbered round. Ref.2 – Post, 12"Sx10"M at knuckle; Others, 10"Sx10"M ditto
Whirlwind #1	O	A flight of 7; main, 16" sq.	
Winged Arrow #1	WO	A flight of 5; main, 18" sq.	Main transom kneed to sides of ship with stout knees

(text continued from page 190)

there was great beauty to this rounded stern, and the combination of these two assets foretold the solid future of the ultimate elliptical stern.

The second type of stern timbering is illustrated in Figures 11.11 and 11.12. It entirely eliminated the use of any horizontal transom structure. In lieu of the transoms, the stern timbers were treated in a manner which could conceivably allow them to be classed as stern cant frames. They found their way into the construction of both transom-sterned and counter-sterned ships, even though in the former style their use was rather limited. The famous ship *Sea Witch*, while built with a transom stern, was timbered with these stern timbers.

In this type of construction the two timbers that embraced the sternpost were slightly heavier than the others. They stood vertical, paralleled the centerline of the ship, and extended from the rail down to the bearding line, being bolted and riveted to the sternpost throughout their entire length. As they descended through the ship their outboard face was hewn to the moulded lines of the vessel, much as described for the knightheads in the bow. The remaining timbers, each of lesser scantlings than the post timbers, were installed parallel with the post timbers, as in Figure 11.11, or angled inboard toward the deadwood, as in Figure 11.12, at an angle that would provide good fastening surface for the hull planking. This arrangement was done in several ways, and Figures 11.11 and 11.12 illustrate the method that utilized the aftermost cant frame. This method was very effective in providing much needed ventilation among these members. The illustrations generally follow McKay's specifications.

Upon completion of the stern timbering, the moulded surfaces were dubbed fair using ribbands to expose high spots wherever they existed, as had been done throughout the length of the hull as work progressed. With this, the structural moulded form of the ship was achieved.

It is interesting to note that Donald McKay, who had built square sterns into his packets between 1845 and 1850, abruptly changed course with the building of his clipper *Stag Hound* in 1850. In this vessel and all of the twelve clippers built subsequently, he designed either round or elliptical sterns and completely ignored the construction of transom sterns. In addition, all of these clippers were built with stern timbering, to the total exclusion of the use of horizontal transoms, as illustrated in Figure 11.12.

William H. Webb, on the other hand, apparently remained very well satisfied with the transom stern. Of approximately the same number of clippers built by him during this same period, 1850–1856, only three were built with counter sterns. Also, from what is known it appears that he retained the installation of horizontal transoms and ignored the use of the cant frame type of stern timbering.

In Table 11.1 the column "Transoms or stern timbers" lists the number of transoms installed in various ships, where this information was verified by the author.[1,2] It goes without saying that the list does not pretend to cover all vessels. What appears to be significant in this list is that, after 1853, only six vessels—*Daring* (built in 1855), *Alarm, Endeavor, Black Hawk, Asa Eldridge,* and *Charger* (all built in 1856)—are noted as having been built with horizontal transoms.

MacLean's reports in the *Boston Daily Atlas* are very complete and detailed. In view of this, it appears reasonable to assume that any vessel described therein without mention of transoms was probably constructed with stern timbering. This, however, cannot be taken as a positive conclusion. A relevant point is that the fine run and particular lines of clipper sterns did not lend themselves very well to transom-type construction. The lack of adequate ventilation throughout a flight of transoms, and the fact that the main or wing transom, acting as a transverse beam supporting all the load of the stern, transferred this weight down through the stern timbers, were two powerful negatives.

On the other hand, stern timbering had the capability of transferring this same load down through the sternpost and aftermost cant into the heart of the ship's structure. In addition it lent itself to the most effective means of ventilation. The total result was the virtual elimination of transom-type construction.

Chapter Twelve

DIAGONAL IRON BRACING; HULL STIFFENING; HOLD CEILING

Diagonal Iron Bracing

The diagonal iron bracing (Figure 12.1), if specified as part of a ship's structure, would be installed now while the vessel was completely in frame but not yet cluttered with additional structure such as beams and knees.

As clippers grew in size, the ever-increasing length-to-breadth ratio resulted in a slenderness of hull which taxed the structure to its limits. The elasticity of the wood and the fiber stresses being developed were making it increasingly difficult to overcome the inherent tendency of vessels to hog—droop at the ends— because of diminished buoyancy in these areas.

Two Bracing Systems, Admiralty and Lloyd's

The problem of hogging (described in Chapter 3 under the heading "Hogging and Sagging") was one of long standing and had so plagued the Royal Navy that in about 1810 chocking the spaces between frames in ships' bottoms was introduced in order to make them stronger in compression. (These anti-hogging chocks have been covered in Chapter 9.) This was accompanied by the installation of diagonal timbers on the sides of the ship. While these were of some help, they greatly diminished the vessels' usable interior capacity. A Mr. Snodgrass, surveyor for the East India Company, was a great proponent of the idea that diagonal iron bracing, rather than wood, would be of vast help in strengthening a ship longitudinally. His arguments apparently had little impact on the solution of the problem, and the extended use of iron remained in limbo for a time.

About 1830 wooden structure had almost reached its limits, and iron once again reappeared in the form of "iron plate riders." These were diagonal straps installed at about 45 degrees, their upper ends in the forebody inclined aft and in the

afterbody inclined forward. Except for a few of these riders amidships, they did not form a latticework. In the Royal Navy, the British Admiralty made them an inboard installation, one half of the riders' substance being scored into the frames, the other half into the internal planking or ceiling.

At the same time, Lloyd's adopted a similar system, except here the iron plate riders were completely let into the outside of the frame and then boarded over by the ship's planking.

The Lloyd's system was decidedly the superior of the two in both strength and efficiency. If a ship tended to deform and elongate, the riders pressed against the frames, thus gaining a frictional advantage which relieved the considerable strain on the holding bolts. With the interior Admiralty system, the same external forces caused the iron riders to tend to separate from the ships' frames and thus transfer all the load into the heads of the holding bolts.

Ease and cost of installation, however, very heavily favored the Admiralty system. The interior of a vessel at this point in its construction was virtually uncluttered. In addition, all work was "down hand," so that in such tasks as cutting the frames to receive the riders—a procedure called "dapping"—the shipwrights were working with, rather than against, the force of gravity. Installation of riders using the Lloyd's system was hampered by scaffolding, stages, shores, and other gear. Much of the work was overhead and against gravity, thus more difficult.

Prior to 1850, however, diagonal iron latticework bracing had found its way into the Royal Navy. The iron used for this bracing was "pure," a term indicating that the molten metal had been stirred in furnaces until most of the carbon and other impurities were burned out. The resultant metal was relatively strong, with a tensile strength of about 48,000 pounds per square inch, and ductile enough so that a plate or bar ½ inch thick could be cold-bent to an angle of 35 degrees without fracture. Thus, with these properties, this type of iron presented no problems in being worked through the relatively long, smooth curves encountered throughout a ship's hull.

This subject is discussed at considerable length in Thearle's *Naval Architecture*, Part III, Chapter VII, under the heading "Iron Plate Riders."[8]

At about this time in the United States, ships were being built approaching the unheard-of length of 200 feet. The proportions were taxing American construction methods to the limit.

In 1850 the clipper ship fever began to ferment in America. The by-words of the phenomenon were "more speed" and "bigger ships." Toward the end of the year, the prominent New York shipping firm of N. L. & G. Griswold contracted with the equally prominent shipbuilder William H. Webb, also of New York, to build the biggest and best sailing ship in the world. Speed would be an admirable quality, but speed for speed's sake did not enter into the contract.

The result was that in May 1851, the longest, largest merchant ship built to that date was launched. More than 200 feet long, and of 2,006 tons, this ship, *Challenge*, ushered in the new breed of large ships. The proposed size of his new creation apparently provided Mr. Webb with food for thought about the details of her structure. The end result was the introduction of diagonal iron bracing along the entire length of her sides.

The historical misfortune, in this new development in ships' structure, lies in the fact that the two surviving descriptions are not in agreement as to the details of the bracing's installation. According to contemporary description in the *New York Commercial Advertiser*, *Challenge* had the early form of diagonal bracing in which the iron straps intersect only at amidships: "The frame is strengthened by diagonal iron braces placed four feet apart and intersecting each other amidship. Each bar is 35 feet in length and 7-8ths of an inch thick, and run from the floorhead to the upper deck."[5]

Duncan MacLean in the *Boston Daily Atlas* describes the later, or latticework installation: "The frames . . . sides, and are braced diagonally with iron 4 inches wide, and ¾ of an inch thick. These braces are 4 feet apart, and extend from the floorheads to the gunwales, are rivetted together at every intersection, bolted through every timber and form a complete network of iron, which binds the frame beyond the power of working. She is the first sailing vessel ever built in this country which has been braced with iron."[1]

Which account is true will possibly never be known, but the description of the diagonal strapping of *Invincible*, built later that same year, provides room for speculation: "The frame is braced diagonally from stem to stern, with iron plates four inches wide and three-fourths of an inch thick, extending from the gunwale to the floor timbers, and transversely with the same, except in the ends. These plates are riveted together at each intersection, and bolted through each timber. She is more thoroughly iron-braced than any sailing vessel before built."[4]

The last sentence of this quotation could indicate that *Challenge*, although first, might have been braced as in the first description. By extension this same condition might also have applied to *Comet*, since both vessels were built prior to *Invincible*. No conclusive evidence of any sort has surfaced as of this writing.

One important detail was not recorded, namely the method of installation—Lloyd's or Admiralty. This same omission applied to the other Webb clippers that were built with diagonal iron bracing.[32] What is known, however, is that Webb's ship *Ocean Monarch*, built in 1856, and later ships that were built with this bracing,[24] employed the Admiralty system of construction, which is shown in Figure 12.1.

Ten of the eighteen ships appearing in Table 12.1 are noted as having been braced with diagonal iron straps, but the method of installation was not recorded. The remaining eight ships are definitely described as being braced by the Admiralty system, four of them being built by Donald McKay. Such a small representation indicates that, of the hundreds of clipper ships built during the period 1850–1856, not many were thought to require this additional strength.

In 1858, after the building heyday of clipper ships in the United States, the American standard of classification described earlier, the *New York Marine Register*, was approved and published.[21] This register included diagonal iron plate bracing as one of the criteria of its highest classification; but, once again, there is no mention of the approved method of installation.

Finally, in March 1867, the *Record of American and Foreign Shipping*[47] was established and published by the American Shipmasters' Association, and was accepted as the standard source of vessel classification in the United States. The use of diagonal iron straps is covered in Section 33 of its rules for classifying wooden vessels; the straps were to be installed on the outside of frames. Thus the Lloyd's system became official, and the end had come for the Admiralty system.

Hull Stiffening

Lower Deck Clamp

The lower deck clamp (Figure 6.2, detail a or b) defined the upper limits of the ceiling in the hold. Its primary function was to provide a solid seat for the ends of the beams supporting the lower deck. The mould loft provided the field with the moulded heights of the deck sheer at the sides of the ship, and from these locations a line was struck on the inside of the frames at a distance below the moulded line equal to the moulded depth of beam at the side of the ship. In this manner the ends of successive beams throughout the length of vessel would fix the location of the deck at every frame.

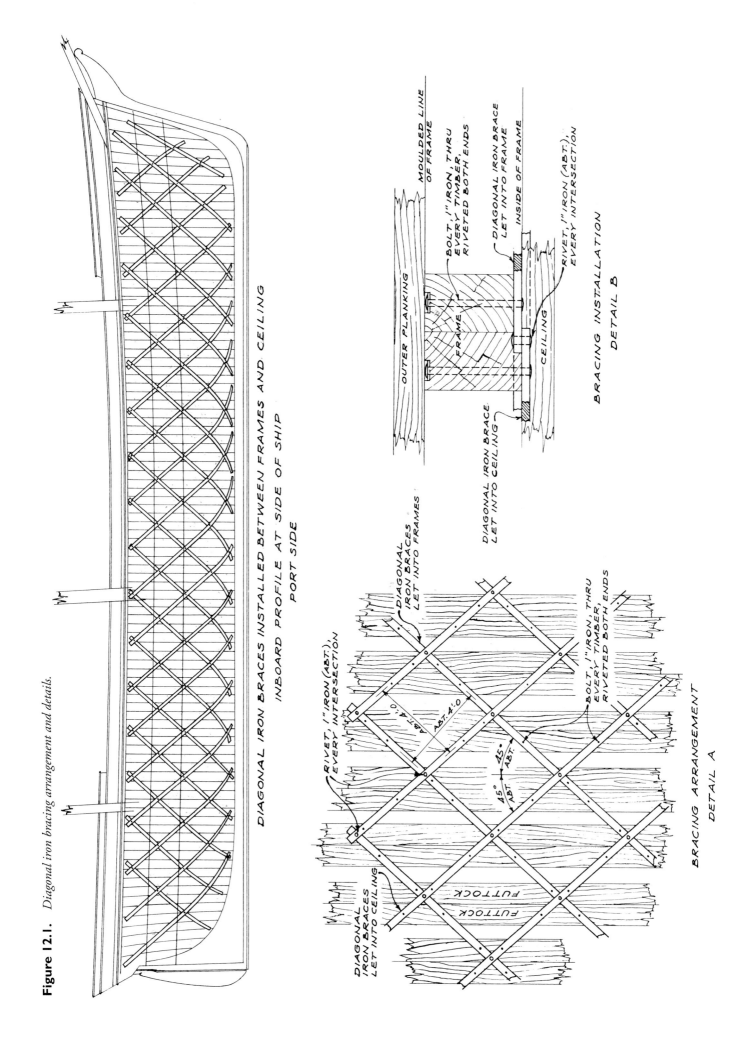

Figure 12.1. *Diagonal iron bracing arrangement and details.*

DIAGONAL IRON BRACES INSTALLED BETWEEN FRAMES AND CEILING

INBOARD PROFILE AT SIDE OF SHIP

PORT SIDE

MOULDED LINE OF FRAME

BOLT, 1" IRON, THRU EVERY TIMBER, RIVETED BOTH ENDS

DIAGONAL IRON BRACE LET INTO FRAME

INSIDE OF FRAME

OUTER PLANKING

FRAME

DIAGONAL IRON BRACE LET INTO CEILING

CEILING

RIVET, 1" IRON (ABT.), EVERY INTERSECTION

BRACING INSTALLATION

DETAIL B

DIAGONAL IRON BRACES LET INTO FRAMES

RIVET, 1" IRON (ABT.), EVERY INTERSECTION

ABT. 4'-0"

45° ABT.

45° ABT.

BOLT, 1" IRON, THRU EVERY TIMBER, RIVETED BOTH ENDS

FUTTOCK

FUTTOCK

DIAGONAL IRON BRACES LET INTO CEILING

BRACING ARRANGEMENT

DETAIL A

Table 12.1. *Vessels with diagonal iron bracing.*

Notes: Vessels are listed chronologically.

All straps are iron.

* – 4'-0" spacing insures each strap intersecting four cross straps. See Figure 12.1, detail A.

Vessel & Ref.#		Year built	Size of straps	Spacing	Bracing system	Extent of straps	Remarks
Challenge	#1	1851	¾"x4"	4'-0"	not noted	floorheads to gunwales	lattice throughout entire length of ship.
	#5	1851	⅞"x ?	4'-0"	not noted	floorheads to upper deck	lattice amidships only
Comet	#32	1851		*			no details given
Invincible	#4	1851	¾"x4"	*	not noted	floor timbers to gunwales	
Flying Dutchman	#32	1852		*			no details given
Phantom	#1	1852	11/16"x4"	*	not noted	floorheads to planksheer	
Young America	#32	1853	⅝"x3¾"	4'-0"	not noted		no additional details
Flyaway	#32	1853		*			no details given
Don Quixote	#1	1853	⅝"x4"	*	Admiralty	first futtocks to gunwales	
Eagle Wing	#1	1853		*	Admiralty	floorheads to upper deck clamp	
Great Republic	#10	1853	1"x4", 36' long	4'-0"	Admiralty	floorheads to top timbers	90 braces each side bolted with 1" iron
	#4	1853	⅞"x5", 36' long	5'-0"	not noted		description in edition of 18 June 1853
Panther	#32	1854		*			no details given
Champion of the Seas	#1	1854	⅞"x5" 38' long	*	Admiralty	first futtocks to top timbers	
James Baines	#1	1854	⅞"x5", 38' long	*	Admiralty	first futtocks to top timbers	
Blue Jacket	#5	1854					no details given
Sunny South	#42	1854		*			no details given
Donald McKay	#1	1855	⅞"x5"	*	Admiralty	first futtocks to top timbers	
Great Republic	#103	1855	1"x4", 38' long	*	Admiralty (probable)	floorheads to top timbers	90 braces each side bolted with 1" iron
Flying Mist	#1	1856	⅝"x4"	*	Admiralty	first futtocks to top timbers	

This was the simplest of such procedures, but it may not have been followed by all shipbuilders.

The most universally adopted method of setting the beams was to have them "let into" the clamps by about an inch or two. With this method, the location of the top surface of the clamp was raised to compensate for the amount the beam would be let in. Thus, in way of every deck beam the top of the clamp was cut away so the beam would fit snugly in the cutout and would be constrained from moving in a fore-and-aft direction. Donald McKay's ships are specifically noted[2] as being let in this way, although no dimension is given.

The clamp was installed in one of two forms, either as a single large squared log, or as an extension of the bilge ceiling. If the latter, it was about as thick as the ceiling. Figure 12.2 shows the general proportions (sizes are listed in Table 12.2, a or b) and extent of the clamps installed in the ships featured in this book.

Of these, only those clippers built by Donald McKay used the single-log clamp. In the McKay vessels, the clamps were square-fastened (see Figure 12.3) through every frame with 1⅛-inch iron, and then edge-bolted into the next strake below (the topmost bilge ceiling timber) with 1⅛-inch iron at every second frame. The clamps were also scarphed vertically, with scarphs approximately 5 feet long, located so that the exposed lip of each scarph was covered by the hanging knee under a beam. It was customary to gradually diminish the clamp's thickness near the bow and stern until it equaled that of the bilge ceiling, due to space restrictions in the ends of the vessels.

The second form of clamp was of the same thickness or very close to that of the bilge ceiling. This type of clamp, however, was of very variable proportions ranging from a single strake under the beam to a clamp made up of multiple strakes. *War Hawk*'s entire clamp consisted of six strakes, each 7 inches thick by 14 inches wide. Many other ships were built with this multiple type of clamp and, in some quarters, all the strakes that were encompassed by the body of the hanging knees were considered to be "the clamp."

As with the first type of clamp, all the strakes were square-fastened with 1-inch iron (about), but most were not edge-bolted. Figure 12.3 shows the typical method of fastening the several forms of lower deck clamp.

Bilge Keelson

The bilge keelson (Figure 6.2, detail E) was a single log, a group of logs, or an assembly of timbers with large scantlings, which extended throughout the length of the ship on each side. At amidships it was located outboard of the centerline, generally over the floorheads. At the extremities it terminated hard against the lower deck clamp. Through these three points it was laid in the straightest possible line fore-and-aft and was, in effect, an inverted arch that spanned the entire length of the vessel.

The bilge keelson was the only longitudinal member of the ship's structure which, due to its arch-like profile, was constantly working under compressive stress. This was a positive factor in resisting the clipper ship's propensity to hog due to the lack of buoyancy at the ends. The bilge keelson was also of great importance in the midship area in strengthening the hull against the pounding of surging seas under violent conditions.

The full extent of the bilge keelson very seldom appears in plans or inboard views of ships' holds, except in transverse views of the midship section. For this reason, relatively little information is included in texts dealing with the structure of wooden vessels. However, the trace of a single-log bilge keelson, developed for a McKay clipper, is shown in Figure 12.4.

In the inboard profile at the side of the ship, the bilge keelson traces a fairly uniform arc throughout the ship's entire length. This same trace, when transferred to the body plan of the same vessel, while still fair and without any abrupt changes, presents somewhat of a surprise, as indicated in Figure 12.5. The logical and most desirable path for this keelson would seem to be a straight line through the ship. Such installation, however, would require a shipwright to induce great twist, or "winding," in the member as it crossed the changing contour of each succeeding frame, so that one face of the log would fay against the inboard surface of each frame. This twist would inflict truly excessive forces upon both the timber and its fastenings, one of the least desirable conditions in all of shipbuilding.

A second reason for not attempting to adhere rigidly to an absolutely straight line is the fact that, in some locations, depending on the hull form of a particular vessel, there were impediments and difficulties in construction. Consequently, the mould loft would lay off the trace of the bilge keelson so that it crossed the frames at as normal an angle (90 degrees) as possible, thus necessitating a minimum of trimming and loss of substance. Figure 12.5 shows, in the body plan, the projected path of the bilge keelson as it progresses fore-and-aft through the vessel.

The bilge keelson, as discussed to this point, represents the member in its most basic and simple form—that of a single large log. As with all other extremely long ship timbers, it was made up of appropriate lengths connected by scarphs, most of which were hooked and/or keyed. The individual scarphs were about 5 feet long.

All such bilge keelsons were square-fastened to the frames with iron bolts that ranged from 1 inch to 1¼ inches. The preferred method of fastening was to drive the bolts alternately from inside to outside and outside to inside, with both ends being clinched or riveted.

As with the lower deck clamp described earlier, the bilge keelson was also installed as an assembly of logs, as well as a single unit, the maximum number being six laid side-by-side starting from the floorheads and working outboard toward the turn of the bilge. More generally, however, there were three or four, depending upon the builder's preference. Table 12.2 lists the bilge keelson data relating to vessels covered in this book.

When installed in "gangs" as mentioned above, the individual bilge keelsons, in addition to being square-fastened, were generally edge-bolted into their neighbors. The bolts were 1-inch to 1⅜-inch iron and were driven at distances varying between 3 and 5 feet apart. This cross-fastening virtually assured that the assembly would function as a unit.

In many vessels, the bilge keelsons were essentially heavy timbers that were installed, then faired into other heavy timbers at the turn of the bilge so that they became part of the bilge ceiling (see Table 12.2).

The general scope of bilge keelson installations is shown pictorially in Figure 12.2.

There was very little about a bilge keelson to attract attention. However, the bilge keelson installed in *Great Republic* was perhaps unique because of its size and structural details, listed in Table 12.2 and shown in Figure 12.2, number 17. *Great Republic* was apparently the only clipper whose bilge keelson was constructed in two tiers, each tier containing two logs side-by-side.

The reasons for this massive construction were two-fold, the first being the fact that the vessel itself was of such gigantic proportions. The second reason had to do with the

(text continued on page 207)

199

Figure 12.2. *Variations of ceiling in the hold.*

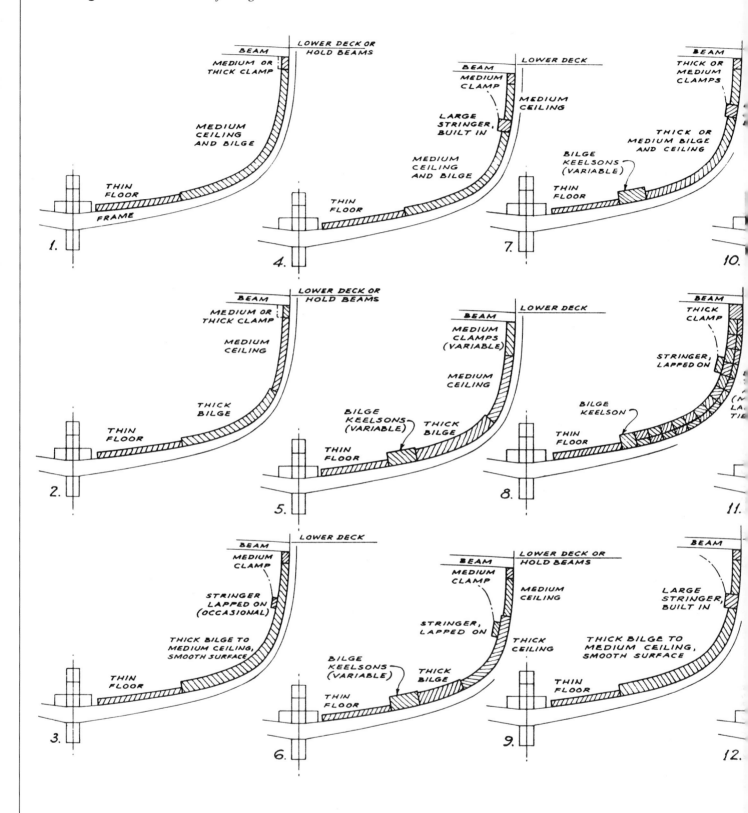

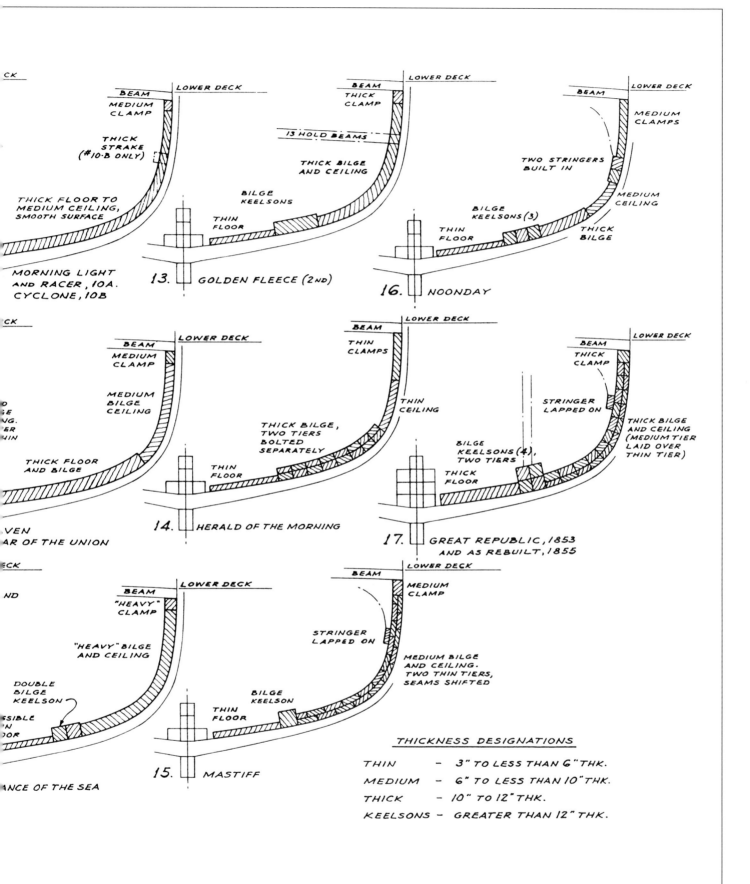

CK

BEAM
MEDIUM
CLAMP

LOWER DECK

THICK
STRAKE
(#10·B ONLY)

THICK FLOOR TO
MEDIUM CEILING,
SMOOTH SURFACE

MORNING LIGHT
AND RACER, IOA.
CYCLONE, IOB

BEAM
THICK
CLAMP

LOWER DECK

13 HOLD BEAMS

THICK BILGE
AND CEILING

BILGE
KEELSONS

THIN
FLOOR

13. GOLDEN FLEECE (2ND)

BEAM

LOWER DECK

MEDIUM
CLAMPS

TWO STRINGERS
BUILT IN

MEDIUM
CEILING

BILGE
KEELSONS (3)

THIN
FLOOR

THICK
BILGE

16. NOONDAY

CK

BEAM
MEDIUM
CLAMP

LOWER DECK

MEDIUM
BILGE CEILING

THICK FLOOR
AND BILGE

VEN
AR OF THE UNION

THICK BILGE,
TWO TIERS
BOLTED
SEPARATELY

THIN
FLOOR

14. HERALD OF THE MORNING

BEAM
THIN
CLAMPS

LOWER DECK

THIN
CEILING

BILGE
KEELSONS (4),
TWO TIERS

THICK
FLOOR

BEAM
THICK
CLAMP

LOWER DECK

STRINGER
LAPPED ON

THICK BILGE
AND CEILING
(MEDIUM TIER
LAID OVER
THIN TIER)

17. GREAT REPUBLIC, 1853
AND AS REBUILT, 1855

ECK

ND

BEAM
"HEAVY"
CLAMP

LOWER DECK

"HEAVY" BILGE
AND CEILING

DOUBLE
BILGE
KEELSON

SSIBLE
'N
OR

THIN
FLOOR

BILGE
KEELSON

ANCE OF THE SEA

15. MASTIFF

BEAM

LOWER DECK

MEDIUM
CLAMP

STRINGER
LAPPED ON

MEDIUM BILGE
AND CEILING.
TWO THIN TIERS,
SEAMS SHIFTED

THICKNESS DESIGNATIONS

THIN   — 3" TO LESS THAN 6" THK.
MEDIUM   — 6" TO LESS THAN 10" THK.
THICK   — 10" TO 12" THK.
KEELSONS — GREATER THAN 12" THK.

Table 12.2. *Details and scantlings of lower deck clamp, bilge keelson, stringer, and ceiling of the hold.*

Abbreviations

O – oak	HP – hard pine
WO – white oak	GHP – Georgia hard pine
CWO – Chesapeake white oak	PP – pitch pine
NHWO – New Hampshire white oak	SP – Southern pine
? – Species not specific	YP – yellow pine

( ) – See Figure 6.2

Vessel & Ref.#	Species of wood	(K) Floor ceiling (thk)	(E) Bilge keelsons	Bilge ceiling (L) Stringer (U)	(a),(b) Clamp (thk)	Fig.12.2 Form of ceiling
Alarm #1	PP	5"	4 strakes 12" x 14"	diminished smooth 10", 9" to 8" thk	8"	3
Amphitrite #1	HP	4½"	12" thick	not less than 8"	8"	2
Andrew Jackson #20	YP		12" thk in bilges	stringer built in		
Antelope #1	YP	3½"	2 strakes 7" thk then 2 strakes @ 6"	5" thk	5"	2
Asa Eldridge #1	PP	5"	strakes 12"x14" to 10"x12" over whole turn of bilge	9" thk diminished to 8" thk	8"	2
Bald Eagle #1	HP	4½"	3 strakes 12" x 14"	8"; a 6" stringer lapped on	8"	2
Belle of the West #1	O					
Beverly #3	HP					
Black Hawk #5	HP					
Blue Jacket #5	HP					
Bonita #1	O			"built similar to Golden Light"		3
Bounding Billow Bark #1	O	4"	2 strakes 8" x 14"	6" thk, then a stringer built in, then 5" thk	5"	3
Celestial	HP					
Challenge #1	HP	4"		8" thk graduated to 7" thk	8"	3
Challenger #1	HP	5"	1 @ 16" sq., then 5 @ 12" x 16"	8" x 14"	8"	5
Champion of the Seas #1,2	HP	#1-5"	2 @ 15" sq	strakes graduated from 12" to 10", a stringer lapped on	10"	6
	PP	#2-5"x12"	1 @ 14"x14" to 10"M at lower deck clamp	two tiers; lower pcs 4½"x14½"; upper pcs 10"x14½"; a stringer 15"x8"; lapped on	10"x13½",	8
Charger #1	WO,HP	4",WO	3 @ 12" x 14"	3 strakes 10" thk, 3 @ 9", 3 @ 8", then 2 stringer strakes @ 12"x13" built in. An air strake provided.	4 @ 7"	5
Charmer #1	O					
Cleopatra #1	HP	4½"	17" sq (no quantity given but more than one.)	10" thk graduated to 7" thk	7"	5
Climax #1	HP	4"	6 @ 12" thk	12" thk graduated to 8" thk	8"	2
Coeur de Lion #1	HP	5"	3 @ 10" x 12"	12" thk graduated to 7" thk	7"	2
Comet						
Cyclone #3				Entire ceiling 10" thk graduated to 8" thk at lower deck clamp. A 10"x12" stringer built in.	8"	10B
Daring #1	?	4", oak	2 @ 10"x14" then 2 @ 9"x14"	6" thk up to a 10"x14" stringer built in, then 6"	several @ 7"x13"	7
Dauntless #1	HP,WO	4",HP		9" thk graduated to 8" thk, WO	several @ 6½",HP	2
Donald McKay #1,2	PP	#1-5"	2 @ 16" sq then 12" thk	10" thk above turn of bilge. A stringer lapped on.	10"	6
	PP	#2-5"x12"	1 @ 14" sq	two tiers; lower pcs 4½"x14½"; upper pcs 10"x14½"; a stringer 15"x8"; lapped on	12"x13½",	8
Don Quixote #1	HP	4½"	3 @ 12"x15" then 3 @ 10"x14"	8", no stringer	8"	2
Eagle #5	WO	4"	4 @ 13" sq., hook scarphed			
Eagle Wing #1	HP	4½"	10" thk over entire bilge	10" thk graduated to 8" thk	8"	2
Edwin Forrest #1	HP	6"	2 @ 12" x 14"	6", then 2 stringers 10"x12" built in, then 6"	6"	7

Table 12.2. Continued.

Vessel & Ref.#	Species of wood	(K) Floor ceiling (thk)	(E) Bilge keelsons	Bilge ceiling (L) / Stringer (U)	(a),(b) Clamp (thk)	Fig.12.2 Form of ceiling
Electric Spark #1	PP	4"	12"x14" (no quantity given but more than one.)	9", no stringer	9"	2
Ellen Foster #1	HP	4½"	3 strakes 12" thk, then 3 @ 8" thk	7", then a stringer 10"x12" built in, then 7"	several @ 8"	7
Empress of the Sea #1,2	HP	#1-5"	4 @ 14" sq then 4 @ 12"x14"	10", no stringer	10"	2
	PP	#2-5" x12"	1 @ 14"x14" to 10"M at lower deck clamp.	two tiers; lower pcs 4½"x14", upper pcs 8"x14"; a stringer 15"x7" lapped on	12"x13½"	8
Endeavor #1	HP	4½"	4 @ 12" x 14"	3 strakes 10" thk, 4 @ 8". A stringer lapped on	7"	6
Eringo Bark #1	O	3"	1 @ 8" x 14" and 1 @ 7" x 12"	4", no stringer	4"	2
Eureka #4	YP	7"	uniform thickness up to lower deck clamp		7"	similar to 10A
Fair Wind #1	HP	5"	2 @ 14" sq	diminishes smoothly from 14" to 9" at lapped on stringer, then 8"	8"	3
Fearless						
Fleet Wing #1	HP		2 @ 15" sq	8" to a stringer built in, then 8" to clamp	several 8"	7
Flyaway						
Flying Arrow #1	HP	4"	3 strakes @ 10½"x13", 4 @ 7½" thk, 3 @ 6" thk, built in, then 6" to lower deck clamp	4 @ 8½" thk, a 10" stringer built in, then 8"	2 @ 7"	7
Flying Childers #1	HP	4"	4 strakes 10" thk, 5 @ 9" thk, 4 @ 8" thk, diminished smoothly to 6" at lower deck clamp	6"	3
Flying Cloud #1,2	SP	#1-4½"	2 @ 10" x 16"	7", then a stringer 10"x16" built in, then 7"	7"	7
		#2-5" x12"	1 @ 14"x14" to 10"M at lower deck clamp	two tiers; lower pcs 4"x14", upper pcs 8"x14"; a stringer 15"x7" lapped on	12" sq	8
Flying Dragon #1	HP		no bilge keelsons, no dimensions	not less than 8"	9"	1
Flying Dutchman						
Flying Eagle #1	oak in the ends	4"	12" sq (no quantity given but more than one.)	8" minimum	8"	2
Flying Fish #1,2	HP	#1-4½"	2 @ 14" x 15"	4 @ 10"x14" graduated to 8" thk, a stringer 14"x12" built in, then 8"	8"	7
	PP	#2-4½" x12"	1 @ 14"x12" to 10"M at lower deck clamp	two tiers; lower pcs 4"x14", upper pcs 8"x14"; a stringer 15"x7" lapped on	12" sq	8
Flying Mist #1	HP	5"	strakes 12"x14" diminishing to 10" thk over the whole turn of the bilge	8", no stringer	8"	5
Galatea #1	HP					
Game Cock #1	HP	4½"	4 @ 12" x 13" then 4 @ 10" x 13"	8", no stringer	8"	2
Gazelle #4	PP					
Gem of the Ocean #1	O	4"	1 strake 14" sq	14" thk graduated to 8" thk at lower deck clamp	8"	3
Golden Eagle #1	HP	4½"	3 @ 12" x 14"	diminished to 8", a stringer 12"x15" built in, then 8"	8"	7
Golden Fleece (2nd) #1	HP	4½"	15" sq (no quantity given but more than one.)	10" minimum	10"	13
Golden Light #1	YP	4"	6 @ 8"x12", then graduated to 7" thk	6" thk, then a stringer 12"x14" built in, then 6"	6"	sim. to 4
Golden West #1	HP	4½"	strakes 14" sq (no quantity given but more than one.)	14" thk diminished smoothly to 8" thk, a stringer built in, then 8"	8"	9
Grace Darling #1	O					

Table 12.2. *Continued.*

Vessel & Ref.#	Species of wood	(K) Floor ceiling (thk)	(E) Bilge keelsons	Bilge ceiling (L) / (U) Stringer	(a),(b) Clamp (thk)	Fig.12.2 Form of ceiling
Great Republic #2,4,10	PP	#2-12"x10" thk	2 @ 15" sq (2 tiers)	two tiers; lower pcs 6"x12", upper pcs 9"x12"; a stringer 15"x8" lapped on	12"x15" thk	sim. to 17
	SP,YP	#4-7 @ 12" sq	4 @ 15" sq (2 on 2) YP	two tiers; lower pcs 6" thk, upper pcs 10"x12"; no stringer	12"x16"	sim. to 17
	HP	#10-9 @ 10"x12"	4 @ 15" sq (2 on 2)	two tiers; lower pcs 6" thk, upper pcs 15" thk; a stringer 6"x15" lapped on. See note at the end of this table.	1 pc 6", 1 pc 10"	sim. to 17
Great Republic (rebuilt) #103	HP	9 @ 10"x12"	4 @ 15" sq (2 on 2)	two tiers; lower pcs 6" thk, upper pcs 15" thk; a stringer 6"x15" lapped on. See note at the end of this table.	1 pc 6", 1 pc 10"	sim. to 17
Henry Hill Bark #1	HP	3"	6" uniform thickness	to lower deck clamp	6"	1
Herald of the Morning #12	YP	4"	10", in 2 thicknesses bolted separately	5 @ 5½" x 12"	several 5½"	14
Hoogly #1	HP	4½"	6 @ 10" thk	8", no stringer	8"	2
Hurricane	HP	#1-5"	2 @ 14" sq	14" thk diminished smoothly to 7½" thk, a stringer lapped on, then 7½"	7½"	3
Indiaman #1	HP	#2-5"x12"	1 @ 14"x12" to 10"M at lower deck clamp	two tiers; lower pcs 4½"x14½", upper pcs 10"x14½"; a stringer 15"x8" lapped on	10"x13½"	8
Intrepid						
Invincible #4	GHP	4"	8" thk at floorheads to 7" deck clamp	8" thk at floorheads to 7" thk at lower deck clamp	8"	1
James Baines #1,2	HP	4½"	1 @ 14"x14½" to 10"M at lower deck clamp	strakes graduated from 12" to 10", a stringer lapped on	10"	6
John Bertram #1	HP	4"	4 @ 10' x 13" then 4 @ 8" x 13"	all 6" thk x13", no stringer	6"x13"	2
John Gilpin #1	HP	4½"	1 strake @ 11"x14", 7 @ 10" thk, 2 @ 9" thk, 2 @ 8" thk, diminished smoothly to 7" at lower deck clamp	diminished smoothly to 7" at lower deck clamp	7"	3
John Land #1,32 (Built as a duplicate of Winged Arrow.)	HP	4"	10" thk over floor-heads	strakes graduated from 10" to 7" thk 5' from lower deck; a stringer 10"x14" built in, then 7"	several 7"	7
John Stuart						
John Wade #1	HP					
Joseph Peabody #1	?	5"	strakes 12"x14" over whole turn of bilge	9" thk to 8" thk at lower deck clamp; a lap stringer under the hold beams	8"	3
King Fisher #1	HP	4"	strakes 12"x14" over whole turn of bilge	strakes 12"x14" over whole turn of bilge	several 8"	2
Lady Franklin						
Lamplighter Park #1	O,HP	3½"	6" thk, then 6" to lower deck clamp. All seams of thick work wedged with HP.	6" thk, a stringer 9"x14" built in.	6"	4
Lightfoot #1	HP	4½"	2 @ 16" sq	10" thk graduated to 9" thk at lower deck clamp	9"	5
Lightning #1,2	HP	#1-5"	2 @ 15" sq	strakes 9"x12" up to lower deck clamp; a stringer 6"x12" lapped on	9"	5
	PP	#2-5"x12"	1 @ 14"x12" to 10"M at lower deck clamp	two tiers; lower pcs 4½"x14", upper pcs 10"x14"; a stringer 15"x7"; lapped on	12"x13½"	8
Mameluke #1	PP	4½"	13" thk over the whole turn of bilge	8" thk, then a stringer 13"x14" built in, then 8"	several 8"	7
Mary Robinson						
Mastiff #1	HP	4½"	1 @ 14" sq	8" thk (2 tiers, each 4" thk.) Seams of lower tier are clear of seams of upper tier, up to the clamp. A stringer lapped on	8"	15
Mermaid Bark #1	HP	3"	1@5" thk; 2@6" thk	4½", no stringer	7½"	2
Morning Light #1	YP		12" thk diminished smoothly to 9" thk at lower deck clamp	diminished smoothly to 9" thk at lower deck clamp	9"	10A

Table 12.2. *Continued.*

Vessel & Ref.#	Species of wood	(K) Floor ceiling (thk)	(E) Bilge keelsons	Bilge ceiling (L) / Stringer (U)	(a),(b) Clamp (thk)	Fig.12.2 Form of ceiling
Mystery #1	HP	4½"	5 @ 10"x13", 5 @ 9"x13", then diminished smoothly to 6" thk at lower deck clamp		6"	3
Nightingale #3	O,YP					
Noonday #1	O,YP	4½"	3 @ 12" x 14"	10" thk graduated to 8" thk; then 2 strakes 11"x14" built in (1 oak, 1 YP)	several 7"	16
Northern Light						
Ocean Express #1	HP		14" thk (no quantity given but more than one.)	14" thk graduated to 10" thk, then a massive stringer built in, then 10"	10"	7
Ocean Pearl #1	HP	4"	2 strakes @ 13" thk	2 strakes @ 9" thk, 3 @ 8", then graduated to 7" thk at lower deck clamp. A stringer 10" thk lapped on	several 7½"	6
Ocean Telegraph #5	HP					
Onward #1	?	5"	9" thk over the whole turn of bilge	5", no stringer	5"	2
Osborne Howes						
Panther						
Phantom #1	HP	4½"	3 @ 12" x 14" then 3 @ 10" x 14"	8", no stringer	8"	2
Queen of Clippers #1	HP	5"	16" sq (no quantity given but more than one.)	6 @ 12"x14" graduated to 8" thk at lower deck clamp, a stringer lapped on	8"	6
Queen of the Pacific						
Queen of the Seas #1	?	4"	1 @ 16" sq	5 strakes @ 10" thk, 5 @ 8", then a stringer built in	5 @ 7"	5
Quickstep Bark #1	HP	3"	5" uniform thickness to lower deck clamp	5", no stringer	5"	1
Racehorse Bark #1	HP	3½"	8 strakes @ 5" thk graduated to 4½" thk	4 @ 4" thk, no stringer	8"	2
Racer #3	SP			12" thk graduated to 8½" thk at lower deck clamp	8½"	10A
Radiant #1	SP	4½"	15"x16" (no quantity given but more than one.)	8 @ 10"x14" then 3 @ 9"x14", no stringer	6@6" thk	5
Raven #3	YP	10"	8 strakes 10" thk graduated to 7" thk	5" thk to lower deck clamp	5"	11
Red Jacket #19,46	SP		1 @ 16" sq	6 @ 12" x 14", 4 @ 10" x 14", then a stringer 13"x15" built in	several 8"	7
Robin Hood #3						
Rocket Bark #1			"styled similar to Dauntless"			
Roebuck #1	HP	3½"	12"x14" (no quantity given but more than one.)	6" thk, then a stringer 12"x14" built in, then 6" to lower deck clamp	2 @ 7"	7
Romance of the Sea #1	HP		"double", no sizes given	"heavy", no sizes given		12
Santa Claus #1	?	4½"	14" thk (no quantity given.)	14" thk diminished smoothly to 8" thk, a heavy stringer built in, then 8" thk to lower deck clamp	8"	9
Saracen #1	WO,HP	4",WO	14" thk over the whole turn of bilge	14" thk diminished smoothly to 8" thk, a stringer 12"x14" built in, then 8" to lower deck clamp	8"	9
Sea Bird Bark #1	HP	3"	5" uniform thickness to lower deck clamp		5"	1
Seaman's Bride #4	CWO		strakes 5" thk			
Sea Serpent						2
Shooting Star #1	SP	4"	2 strakes @ 10" thk, 3 @ 8" thk, then 6" thk up to lower deck clamp		6"	2
Sierra Nevada #1	HP	4½"	14" thk over the whole turn of bilge	14" thk diminished smoothly to 8" thk at lower deck clamp	8"	3
Silver Star #1	HP	4½"	3 @ 12" x 14"	10" thk graduated to 9" thk, then a stringer 5"x14" lapped on, then 8"	8"	6
Southern Cross #1	SP	4"	2 @ 12" x 8"	6", no stringer	6"	2
Sovereign of the Seas #1,2	HP	#1-5"		14" thk diminished smoothly to 10" thk, then a stringer 14" thk built in, then 10"	10"	9
	PP	#2-5" x12"	1 @ 14"x14" to 10"M at lower deck clamp	two tiers; lower pcs 4½"x14½"; upper pcs 10"x42"; a stringer 15"x8" lapped on	12"x10"	8
Spitfire #1	HP		2 @ 14" sq	strakes diminish ½" per strake from 14" to 9" thk, then a stringer 13" sq built in, then 9"	9"	7

Table 12.2. *Continued.*

Vessel & Ref.#	Species of wood	(K) Floor ceiling (thk)	(E) Bilge keelsons	Bilge ceiling (L) Stringer (U)	(a),(b) Clamp (thk)	Fig.12.2 Form of ceiling
Staffordshire #1,2	?	#1-4½"	3 @ 14" x 12" then 3 @ 12" x 10"	6 @ 14"x8", then a clamp 15"x14" under the hold beams, then 7". A strake 12"x5" lapped on over the hold beams.	7"	2
	PP	#2-4½" x12"	1 @ 14"x12" to 10"M at lower deck clamp	two tiers; lower pcs 4½"x14", upper pcs 8"x14"; a stringer 15"x7" lapped on	12" sq	8
Stag Hound #1,2	HP	#1-4½"	7" thk over the whole turn of bilge	7" thk, then a stringer 12"x15" built in, then 7"	7"	3
	PP	#2-4½" x12"	1 @ 14"x12" to 10"M at lower deck clamp	two tiers; lower pcs 4"x14", upper pcs 8"x14"; a stringer 15"x7" lapped on	12"x10"	8
Star of the Union #1	HP	10" thk	10" thk over the whole turn of bilge	none less than 6"thk, no stringer	6"	11
Starr King						
Storm King #1	YP	4½"	15" sq over the whole turn of bilge	6 @ 10" thk, 4 @ 8"; a thick stringer built in, then 6"	several 6"	7
Sultana Bark #1	HP	3½"	8 strakes @ 5" thk x 8" to the clamp under the hold beams	these reach the hold beams	"massive"	1
Sunny South						
Surprise #1	SP	5"	4 @ 12" x 13"	5 strakes @ 10"x12", then 7" thk, no stringer	7"	2
Swallow #1	YP					
Sweepstakes #1						
Sword Fish #3						
Syren #3	HP	4½"	9 @ 10" thk	6" to lower deck clamp, no stringer	6"	2
Telegraph	YP					
Thatcher Magoun #1	HP	4½"	5 @ 12" x 14"	strakes 10" thk, then 9" thk. The change in thickness forms ledge for toes of hanging knees	several 9"	2
War Hawk #1	O,?	4", oak	2 @ 10"x14", 2 @ 9"x14"	2 @ 10"x14", then 6"thk to a stringer 10"x14" built in, then 6"	6 @ 7"x14"	7
Water Witch #1	HP	4"	2 @ 12" x 14"	7" thk to lower deck clamp; a stringer 5" thk lapped on	7"	variant of 6
Western Continent						
Westward Ho #1,2	HP	#1-4"	3 @ 12" x 14"	8" thk to lower deck clamp; a stringer 6" lapped on	8"	variant of 6
	PP	#2-4½" x12"	1 @ 14"x12" to 10"M at lower deck clamp	two tiers; lower pcs 4"x14", upper pcs 8"x14"; a stringer 15"x7" lapped on	12" sq	8
West Wind #1	HP					
Whirlwind #1	HP	4"	4 @ 9"x12", 4 @ 8" thk to lower deck clamp	6" thk, then 6" thk	6"	2
Whistler #1	O,HP	4",oak	2 @ 10"x14", 2 @ 8"x14" built in	2 @ 10"x14", then 6" thk to a stringer 10"x14" built in, then 6"	several 7"x14"	7
Wildfire Bark #1	O					
Wild Pigeon #1	O,HP	4",oak	10" thk diminished smoothly to 7" thk over turn of bilge	7", no stringer	7"	3
Wild Ranger #1	O	4"	10" thk over the whole turn of bilge	7" thk graduated to 6" thk at lower deck clamp	6"	2
Wild Rover						
Winged Arrow #1	HP	4"	10" thk over floor-heads	strakes graduated from 10" to 7" thk 5' from lower deck; a stringer 10"x14" built in, then 7"	several 7"	7
Winged Racer #1	HP	4½"	1 @ 16" sq	5 strakes @ 12"x14", then 8" thk, then a stringer 12"x14" built in, then 8"	8"	7
Witchcraft #1	O,HP	4½"	4 @ 12"x14" (the lowest strake is oak), 4 @ 10" thk x12"	6" thk x 12" to clamp	6"	2
Witch of the Wave #1	HP	4½"	12" thk diminished smoothly to 7" at clamp		7"	3
Wizard #1	HP	5"	1 @ 8"x12" then 2 @ 14" sq	12" thk graduated to 9" thk under hold beams; a stout stringer lapped on	9"	6

Table 12.2. *Continued.*

Vessel & Ref.#	Species of wood	(K) Floor ceiling (thk)	(E) Bilge keelsons	Bilge ceiling (L) Stringer (U)	(a),(b) Clamp (thk)	Fig.12.2 Form of ceiling
Young America						
Young Turk Bark #1	HP	3"	5" thk over the whole turn of bilge	4½", no stringer	several 4½"	1

Note for Great Republic:

The thickness (15") of the upper pieces
of ceiling is taken directly from refs. 10
and 103. This, combined with the 6" thickness of the lower pieces, provides a ceiling
whose total scantling is 21". This dimension
is much greater than that of the lower deck
clamp - a condition which finds little support in any contemporary rules of shipbuilding. In the opinion of the author the 15"
thickness may be an error and should possibly
be either 9" or 10" as is recorded in refs. 2
and 4, and is in agreement with the midship
section shown in ref. 10.

(text continued from page 199)
bilge keelson's function as a hard foundation for the bilge or wing stanchions that were built into the ship. These stanchions were kneed onto the bilge keelson on both the forward and after side of the stanchions (referred to as "double-kneeing") and reached upward to the middle deck.

These bilge keelsons were coaged (see Figure 9.5), key-scarphed, square-fastened with bolts of 1¼-inch refined iron, and bolted edgeways. The square-fastenings were driven completely through both tiers of keelson and the frame.

In the overall detail of a ship's structure, the bilge keelson in actuality became an integral portion of the vessel's ceiling. Due to its relatively massive proportions, regardless of the form it took, and to its great strength, it was laid down before any other portions of the ceiling in order to install it in the most effective alignment along the frames. Once it was in place and securely fastened, the remainder of the ceiling was installed according to the individual builder's practice.

The list of ships covered in this book illustrates the great variation in bilge keelson structure. In form, bilge keelsons ranged between the great two-log, two-tiered mass found in *Great Republic*, to thick timbers which were an indistinguishable continuation of the floor ceiling through its conjunction with the bilge ceiling. However, in spite of the variations, the general system of fastening applied to all vessels, large or small. Figure 12.3 shows the representative mode of securing the bilge keelsons to the vessel's framing.

The Stringer

The stringer (Figure 6.2, detail U) was installed to provide a shelf upon which the toe (or foot) of the lower deck hanging knees could rest, thereby eliminating shear forces in the fastenings that secured the body of this knee to the framing of the vessel. Thus these bolts were called on to act only in tension as they clasped the knee hard against the lower deck clamp and ceiling assembly.

This stringer was installed in most, but not all of the clippers, and it had two forms. One type, the "built in" stringer, was a square timber of thickness perhaps 50 percent greater than that of the ceiling in which it was placed. This figure was not fixed and varied from ship to ship. The important consideration was that it provided a shelf upon which the hanging knees could rest. In this type of installation the stringer became an integral part of the bilge ceiling.

Near the midship section, the height of the upper edge of the stringer was struck on a frame that would bear a beam, in such a location as to accommodate the selected length of the body of the hanging knee. From this point, advancing both forward and aft, a fair line was marked on succeeding frames until the ends of the vessel were reached. An inspection of Figure 12.4 shows that, while this line was fair and was intended to service the lower deck, it did not parallel the moulded line of the deck at side of ship but rather ascended toward it as the hood ends were approached. This trace of the stringer was based on the fact that knees were always made smaller in the ends of a ship, for two reasons. One consideration was the lack of interior space in which to work and to accommodate the sheer bulk of material to be installed. Secondly, from the standpoint of structural requirements, a knee installed under the short span of the beams in the ship's ends could never be required to carry the load that the long beams in the midbody could induce. Therefore, the sizes of the knees were gradually diminished at a rate deemed appropriate by the designer or builder. As for the ever-present consideration of saving weight, there was no more effective location to do this in a ship than in her extremities. At each end of the vessel, the stringer terminated in a "hook" which bound the two sides of the ship together (see Figure 15.1, detail D).

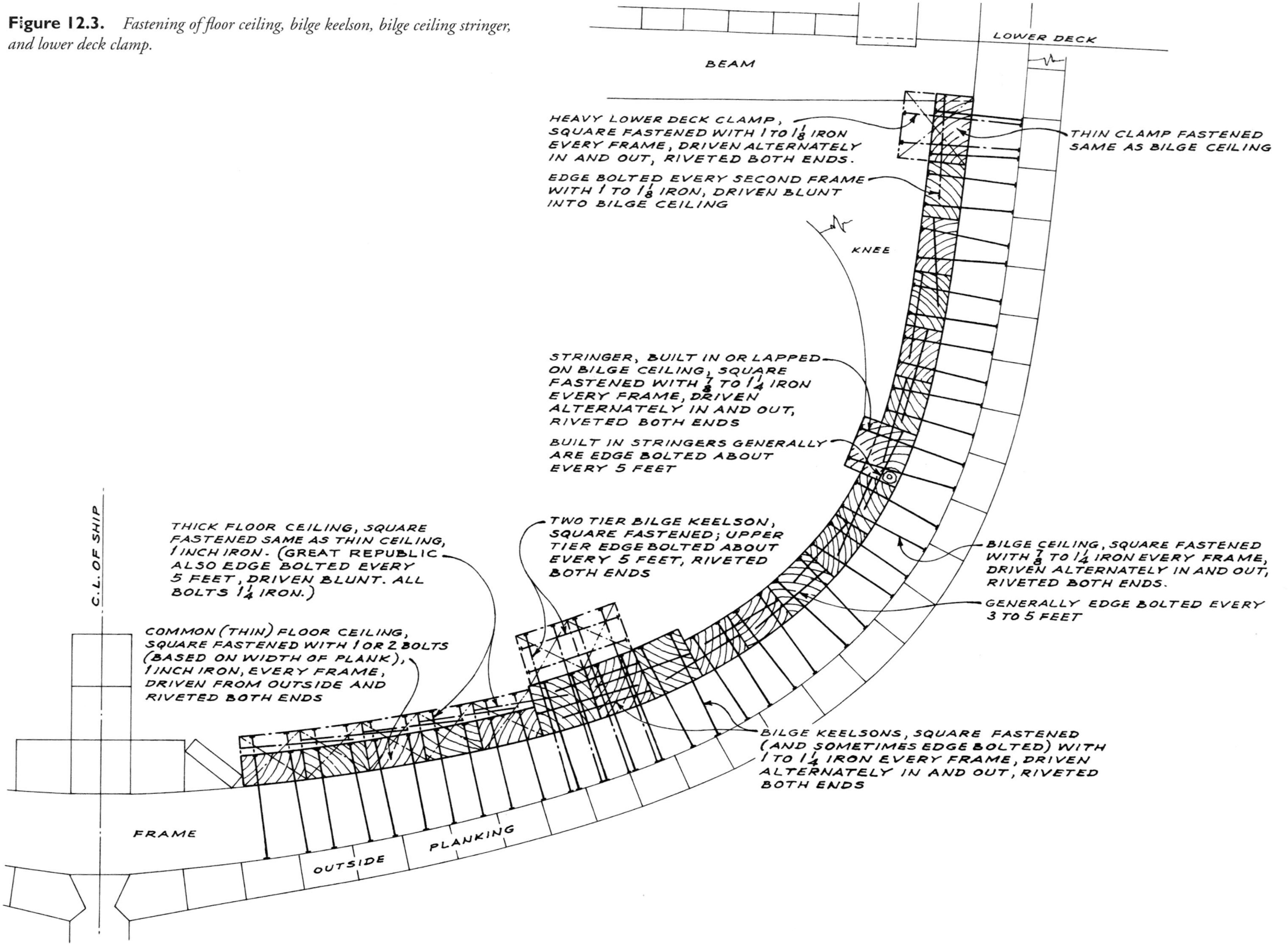

Figure 12.3. *Fastening of floor ceiling, bilge keelson, bilge ceiling stringer, and lower deck clamp.*

THIN CLAMP FASTENED SAME AS BILGE CEILING

LOWER DECK

BEAM

BILGE CEILING, SQUARE FASTENED WITH 7 TO 14 IRON EVERY FRAME, DRIVEN ALTERNATELY IN AND OUT, RIVETED BOTH ENDS.

GENERALLY EDGE BOLTED EVERY 3 TO 5 FEET

HEAVY LOWER DECK CLAMP, SQUARE FASTENED WITH 1 TO 1⅛ IRON EVERY FRAME, DRIVEN ALTERNATELY IN AND OUT, RIVETED BOTH ENDS.

EDGE BOLTED EVERY SECOND FRAME WITH 1 TO 1⅛ IRON, DRIVEN BLUNT INTO BILGE CEILING

KNEE

STRINGER, BUILT IN OR LAPPED ON BILGE CEILING, SQUARE FASTENED WITH ⅞ TO 1¼ IRON EVERY FRAME, DRIVEN ALTERNATELY IN AND OUT, RIVETED BOTH ENDS

BUILT IN STRINGERS GENERALLY ARE EDGE BOLTED ABOUT EVERY 5 FEET

TWO TIER BILGE KEELSON, SQUARE FASTENED; UPPER TIER EDGE BOLTED ABOUT EVERY 5 FEET, RIVETED BOTH ENDS

BILGE KEELSONS, SQUARE FASTENED (AND SOMETIMES EDGE BOLTED) WITH 1 TO 1¼ IRON EVERY FRAME, DRIVEN ALTERNATELY IN AND OUT, RIVETED BOTH ENDS

THICK FLOOR CEILING, SQUARE FASTENED SAME AS THIN CEILING, 1 INCH IRON. (GREAT REPUBLIC ALSO EDGE BOLTED EVERY 5 FEET, DRIVEN BLUNT. ALL BOLTS 1¼ IRON.)

COMMON (THIN) FLOOR CEILING, SQUARE FASTENED WITH 1 OR 2 BOLTS (BASED ON WIDTH OF PLANK), 1 INCH IRON, EVERY FRAME, DRIVEN FROM OUTSIDE AND RIVETED BOTH ENDS

FRAME

OUTSIDE   PLANKING

C.L. OF SHIP

The stringer was made up in the longest practical lengths, scarphed vertically and square-fastened with iron generally of the same diameter as the other thick work in the hold, ranging from ⅞ inch to 1¼ inches.

While most ships with built-in stringers had only one installed on each side, there were exceptions to this practice. The clippers *Edwin Forrest, Noonday,* and *Charger* were all fitted with two stringers fayed against each other side-by-side, thus forming two strakes of ceiling.

The second type of hold stringer was the "lapped on" version, installed after the ceiling was laid up and thus independent of it. The trace of the lapped member was the same as that of the built-in stringer, but it was a much thinner timber, its thickness roughly corresponding to the projection of the large built-in type and generally being about 6 to 8 inches thick.

An advantage of the lapped stringer was that it allowed the hold to be completely ceiled without having to fair the strakes to accommodate the stringer. It was made up of several lengths—each generally, but not exclusively, scarphed at the ends—and was square-fastened in the same manner as was the built-in stringer. At the ends of the ship it, too, was terminated within the confines of a hook. All McKay clippers utilized this form of lapped stringer.

The two types of stringer were about evenly divided in usage throughout the clipper fleet, according to the available data; however, such data remains unknown for the majority of vessels, so there is no conclusive means of ascertaining the total preference.

In one known instance, the clipper *Thatcher Magoun,* the use of any stringer was avoided. In her case the bilge ceiling, which was 10 inches thick, was installed up from the bilge keelsons to the required location, at which line the ceiling thickness was decreased to 9 inches, and it was upon this thin ledge that the toe of the hanging knees rested. It seems highly probable that this same procedure may have been followed in other vessels.

Table 12.2, U, lists the types and dimensions, when known, of the stringers installed in ships included in this book. Figure 12.3 covers the fastenings of both the built-in and lap stringer.

Hold Ceiling

The *ceiling* (Figure 6.2, details K and L) of a ship, whether or not the vessel was a clipper, was the timbering laid on the inboard surface of the ship's frames and, in general, was considered to extend from the keelson assembly to the underside of the lower deck. In effect it was the lining of the ship's hold. There was similar lining above this level, but the terminology was different and had its own connotations.

There was nothing complex about such ceiling, but it was installed in many forms and combinations of sizes. Figure 12.2 illustrates a variety of such installations encountered in the vessels covered herein. Examples 1 through 9 represent arrangements which categorically apply to many ships, while examples 10 through 17 apply to specific vessels. In the first group, ships constructed with the same general timbering arrangement appear under a given example, regardless of whether the ship was large or small; for this reason, timber thicknesses would vary, and are thus relative rather than absolute. In the group of individual vessels, the illustrations are shown in order to portray the great diversity among the shipbuilders' methods of accomplishing a given result.

The nautical term *ceiling* is at odds with the land-based concept of the word, where we are accustomed to ceiling being an overhead detail. In architecture, ceiling is used to cover the joists or rafters which support floors or roof surfaces overhead. In shipbuilding, the purpose is still the same: a covering of beams (frames) which, due to the nature of a ship's form, are underfoot or on the side. The word apparently is derived from the Old French *celer,* which means "to conceal."

Floor Ceiling

The floor ceiling (Figure 6.2, detail K) was generally the thinnest timber used to ceil a vessel. In most cases the thickness ranged between 4 inches to something less than 6 inches, except in very small ships, where 3-inch or 3½-inch material was most commonly used.

There were, however, exceptions to these general practices. Among the ships listed in this book, *Star of the Union, Morning Light,* and *Great Republic* were all built with floor ceiling 10 inches or greater in thickness. The first two vessels did not have individual bilge keelsons; instead, the builder opted to gain strength from the floor ceiling by straking thick timbers from the midship keelson to the turn of the bilge. *Great Republic* was apparently thought to warrant this great thickness as a contribution to the strength of her structure. These particulars are illustrated in Figure 12.2, numbers 10, 11, and 17.

The functions of the floor ceiling were not structural except in rare instances, one of which was *Great Republic*. With longitudinal strength in mind, her unusually thick floor ceiling was square-fastened, edge-bolted every 5 feet, and also scarphed. In her case it is also probable that due care was exercised in giving ample shift to the scarphs.

In the general run of clippers, the floor ceiling served three purposes, strength not being one of them. The first, or at least the most obvious function was that of providing a smooth, strong platform in the bottom of the hold. This

(text continued on page 213)

Figure 12.4. *Outboard, inboard, and centerline profiles of a clipper ship.*

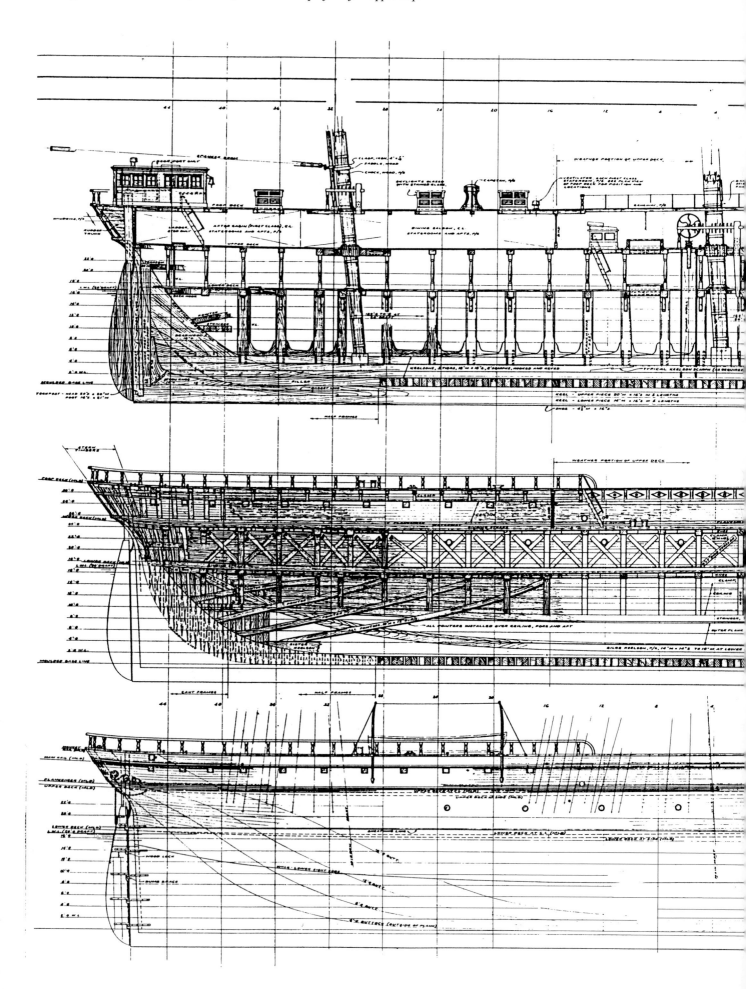

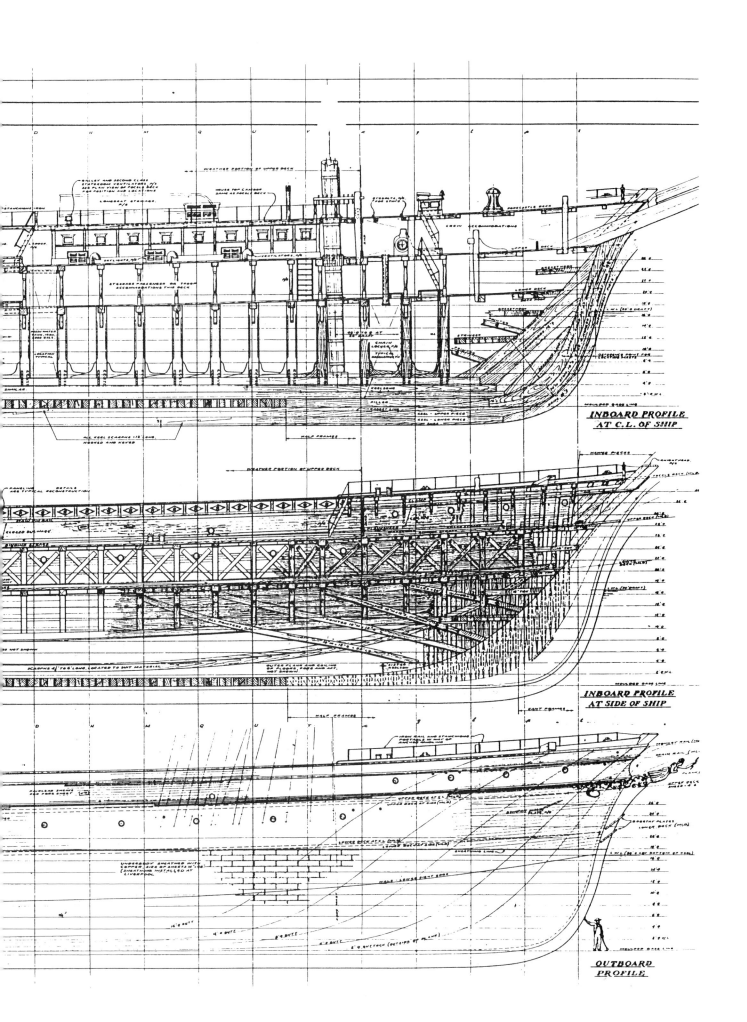

**INBOARD PROFILE
AT C.L. OF SHIP**

**INBOARD PROFILE
AT SIDE OF SHIP**

**OUTBOARD
PROFILE**

Figure 12.5. *Typical trace of a bilge keelson through a ship.*

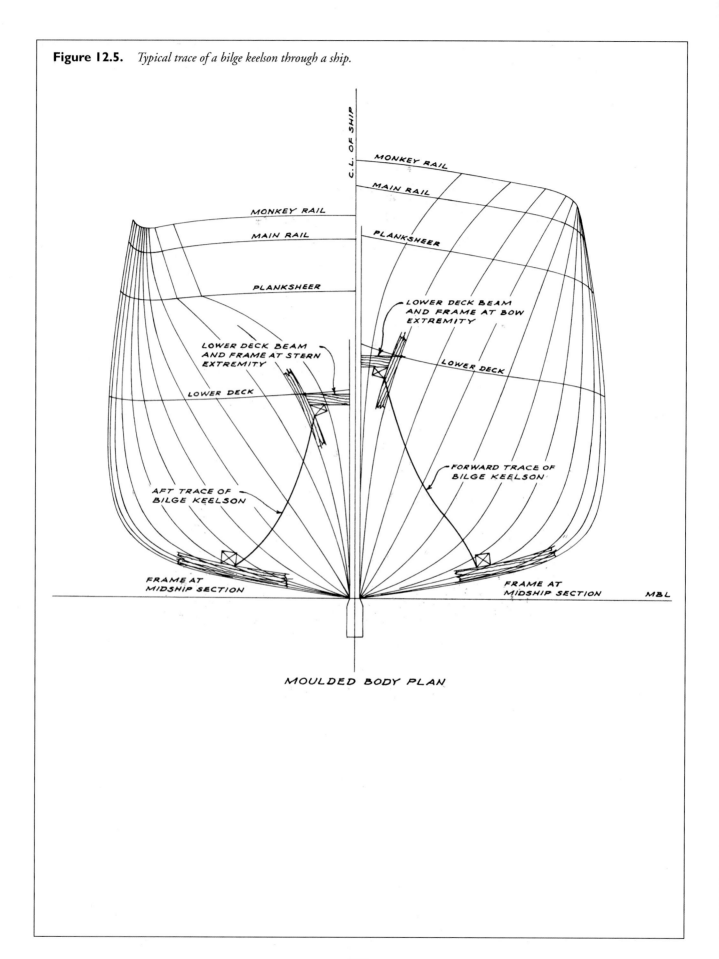

MOULDED BODY PLAN

(text continued from page 209)

facilitated working in the area and also promoted the safe and secure stowage of cargo.

A second function of floor ceiling was to provide protection against the possibility of the limbers and space between frames becoming clogged if sacks, bags, crates, or other containers filled with grain, tea, mineral crystals, or other cargo being shipped in particle form, should be damaged or accidentally opened. Without the protection of a solid ceiling, the task of cleaning up, if such an accident should occur, would be costly due to the difficulty of gaining complete access to spaces between frames, and also because of the steps necessary to render the hold free of contamination.

The third function was that the floor ceiling helped insulate the cargo from condensation which formed in the hold due to the difference in temperature between the ship's interior and that of the surrounding water, which went through a wide range of extremes as a vessel proceeded through successive degrees of latitude. Even in given latitudes, the water temperature was subject to different constants of warmth and cold.

As in almost every other phase of shipbuilding, the installation of floor ceiling varied from ship to ship. The areas to be covered were of relatively simple configuration, so it was a simple matter to cover the floors with relatively wide planks, the maximum width being about 12 inches. The first, or limber strake, which was closest to the sister keelsons, was laid at a distance of perhaps 10 inches from those members, leaving an access opening which would later be covered by a loose row of boards identified as *limber boards*.

The planks were square-fastened, usually with iron bolts driven from outside and riveted inside. In many ships, the bolts were driven through every frame, alternately from inside and outside. While most of the floor ceilings were butt-bolted—that is, the ends of the timbers simply butted tightly against each other—there were some ceilings, especially those in the thick range, in which the ends were joined by scarphs.

As usual, there were exceptions to these general rules. In the clipper *Noonday*, the floor ceiling was fastened with a spike and a treenail in every strake and every timber (floor or first futtock). No bolts were driven in her floor ceiling.

The clipper *Charger* had her floor ceiling fastened with one spike and two treenails in every strake and every timber, also eschewing the use of bolts.

In all the McKay vessels, the fastenings for the floor ceiling were simply stated as being fastened with treenails and spikes.[2] In the case of the small clipper *Sultana*, built for use in the Mediterranean fruit trade, her entire ceiling was square-fastened, after which every seam was caulked and payed. In effect, her ceiling was finished off in the same manner as would be any vessel's weather deck.

The sequence of installing ships' planking, whether hold ceiling or external hull planking, was not of technical importance, and, no doubt, some procedures were based on the individual builder's preference and some may have been governed by the overall state of construction. However, the most practical sequence was to install the ceiling before installing the exterior planking. In this way the process was self-cleaning, since all chips and accumulation of any dirt would by nature fall to the ground unobstructed.

Fastenings of both the thin (common) and thick form of floor ceiling are illustrated in Figure 12.3. As shown, they may be considered as typical but subject to individual preferences.

Limber Boards

The limber board (Figure 6.2, detail p) was functional but not structural in nature. Its dimensions were such that its thickness could withstand considerable load and abuse, while its width was determined by the open space it was intended to cover in the lowest depths of the hold.

The first or lowest strake of floor ceiling was known as the *limber strake* due to its location in the ship. In general it paralleled the outboard side of the sister keelsons for a considerable portion of the vessel's length at a distance of perhaps 10 inches. This opening facilitated access to the limbers if ever required.

In order to eliminate the possibility of dirt and foreign objects falling into the spaces between frames and in order to provide a complete platform on which to place cargo, this opening was covered with a collection of relatively short, loose boards. These were the *limber boards*.

Their length was governed by convenience in handling and by stability in maintaining their position when placed in the opening. Their width was made wider than the opening, the result being that they invariably rested at a considerable angle in relation to horizontal, thus lightly wedging themselves in place without producing a problem in lifting them out. There were various methods of installing the boards, but the simplest installation, a board that was cut four-square, performed as well as any other when the proper angle of repose was attained as shown in the figure.

The limber boards, if secured at all, were sparsely stuck with spikes which were easily removed when the situation required.

Bilge Ceiling

The bilge ceiling (Figure 6.2, detail L) was categorically made up of heavier material than was the floor ceiling, due to its dual function as ceiling and as a longitudinal strength installation. In this book, the only known exceptions to this rule are *Morning Light*, *Raven*, and *Star of the Union*, which were all built without specific bilge keelsons and are shown in Figure 12.2, numbers 10 and 11.

The thickness and general characteristics of the bilge ceiling are listed in Table 12.2, L, while arrangements are illustrated in Figure 12.3.

The installation of bilge ceiling received special consideration due to the bulk of the individual timbers, their function as structural members, and the restrictions of their placement between the bilge keelsons and the clamp of the lower deck, which was the upper limit of this ceiling.

Structurally, the bilge ceiling augmented the function of the bilge keelsons, namely, to stiffen the entire bilge area against the surge of pounding seas. Due to its position on the lower portion of the ship's side, the bilge ceiling was very often indirectly positioned between wind and water and thus received punishment transmitted through the frames by the impact of seas as a ship rolled and lunged during her forward progress.

As ceiling, it performed as did the bilge keelsons and the floor ceiling: it was an effective means of putting distance and insulation between the internal hold and the external sea.

This ceiling was generally fastened with as much care and precision as was applied to keelson assemblies. The minimum installation in the large clippers consisted of square-fastening with iron bolts ranging between ⅞ inch and 1¼ inches. These bolts, in most ships, were alternately driven from outside and inside, with the leading end being riveted in all cases.

In addition to the square-fastening, edge-bolting was very common, the bolts, generally about 1-inch iron, being driven into the adjacent member from 3 to 5 feet apart. All McKay ships specify this procedure, as do *Lightfoot, Saracen, Daring, Electric Spark, Fair Wind, Golden Fleece, Mameluke,* and *Alarm.* There can be no doubt that through the entire litany of clipper ships, many more were probably built in this same fashion.

In addition to the fastenings mentioned above, all bilge ceiling, so far as can be ascertained, was scarphed, sometimes with keyed scarphs and, in other cases, with lock scarphs, these scarphs being 4 to 5 feet long. Every attempt was made to ensure continuity of the individual strakes; this included ample shift between scarphs in adjoining strakes.

All individual timbers and combinations of timbers were fitted with utmost care—and the fitting required some expertise, when one considers the assemblies shown in Figure 12.2.

Regardless of the detailed make-up of the ceiling, the uppermost strake was fayed against the clamp or clamp assembly. Between that uppermost strake and the bilge keelson, the individual strakes were tapered as they approached the ends of the ship; and, where necessary, certain strakes were dropped out until in the hoods or extreme ends, sufficient strakes remained to properly fill the existing space.

Worked into the bilge ceiling of many vessels was the heavy stringer, or, in lieu of an inserted stringer, a lighter stringer was "lapped" onto the ceiling. Both of these have been covered earlier on this chapter under the heading of "The Stringer."

While all strakes of bilge ceiling were scarphed in their connecting ends, sometimes even more detail was expended on their installation. *Quickstep* had this ceiling caulked, and several ships were treated to an even more refined ceiling: Duncan MacLean reported that *Sovereign of the Seas* and *Westward Ho*, both built by Donald McKay, and *Queen of the Seas*, built by Paul Curtis of Boston, were not only caulked but also payed from bilge keelson to the lower deck. This procedure no doubt found its way into many other vessels; but, unfortunately, such finite detail has not survived in great amount and can only be gleaned a piece at a time, if at all.

Figure 12.3 illustrates the general method of fastening the bilge ceiling from the bilge keelson to the lower deck clamp.

Chapter Thirteen

STANCHIONS

THE STANCHION (Figure 6.2, details S and T) was a pillar or column whose principal function was to support a vessel's transverse beams and, by extension, its laid decks. As a structural unit it was not peculiar to the clipper ship or any other form of vessel. In fact, stanchions (or columns) are basic to all forms of engineered structures that require this type of support.

In a ship the beams that spanned her entire breadth could very well be strong enough, with their given scantlings, to support any load that might be expected, such as cargo, or boarding seas if the deck was a weather deck. However, such beams are very limber and elastic and are thus subject to excessive deflection. This deflection, in the mobile and flexible structure which constitutes a ship, would ultimately prove to be disastrous if not fatal to the vessel.

The introduction of a stanchion under a beam at midspan eliminates this objectionable situation. By supporting the beam at the ship's centerline, the stanchion not only divides the full span into two equal parts, but it converts the beam from a "simple" beam that is supported at each end to a "continuous" beam which spans the vessel's breadth as an uninterrupted unit. In engineering, this type of beam is a very efficient component. When applied to a ship, the beam becomes rigid rather than limber, and its end connections, generally knees, are no longer subject to extreme working. This protects the integrity of the fastenings and thus the safety of the vessel as a whole.

Onboard ship stanchions were generally grouped into two configurations. The first and most widely used was the squared stanchion, which was installed in the holds of vessels and, in many cases, in some of the tween-decks. In section these stanchions were either square or rectangular and, except for trimming to fit them into their final position, received no tooling except for the chamfering of the corners for most of their length. The chamfer served two purposes. First, it kept the corners of the timbers from splintering and being constantly damaged. Second, it removed sharp corners that could easily open up a sailor's head should he be thrown against one. In all probability, this was not dwelt upon as being too important a consideration; however, it should be stated that, in shipbuilding, sharp corners are always avoided where possible so as to prevent injuries. After all, an incapacitated seaman is of no value to the working of a ship—and he still must be fed.

The second form of stanchion was the "turned" stanchion, which was generally installed in the tween-decks where living quarters and other passenger facilities were located. These stanchions were turned with graceful forms and numerous variants of ogee, torus, and ovolo mouldings, along with slender neckings, all to suit the eye of the designer. At their upper and lower extremities their form was generally round but in some cases square in the form of a post.

Both forms of stanchions performed the same obvious duty, namely the supporting of one deck above another. However, in ships, especially of the clipper type with their extreme slenderness ratio, another duty was performed, and that was to restrain the deck beams from lifting off the stanchions when the ship's breadth was compacted by the crushing force of broadside seas. This was accomplished through the installation of suitable fastenings, which will be described in sequence for the installation of the stanchions from keel to deck, without reference to any beams or decking.

Because ships were built from the ground up, the stanchions to be installed first were those in the hold, and these, in most vessels, were installed atop the midship keelson. Although these were always square or rectangular, like all else in shipbuilding there was great diversity in the details of construction. Figures 13.1 and 13.2 illustrate the various structural assemblies of stanchions used in the vessels in this book where such information can be obtained or reasonably reconstructed. Figure 13.3 illustrates the principal details involved in the installations.

The terms "strapped" and "clasped" are used in many
(text continued on page 221)

Figure 13.1. *Stanchion assemblies, one- and two-deck vessels.*

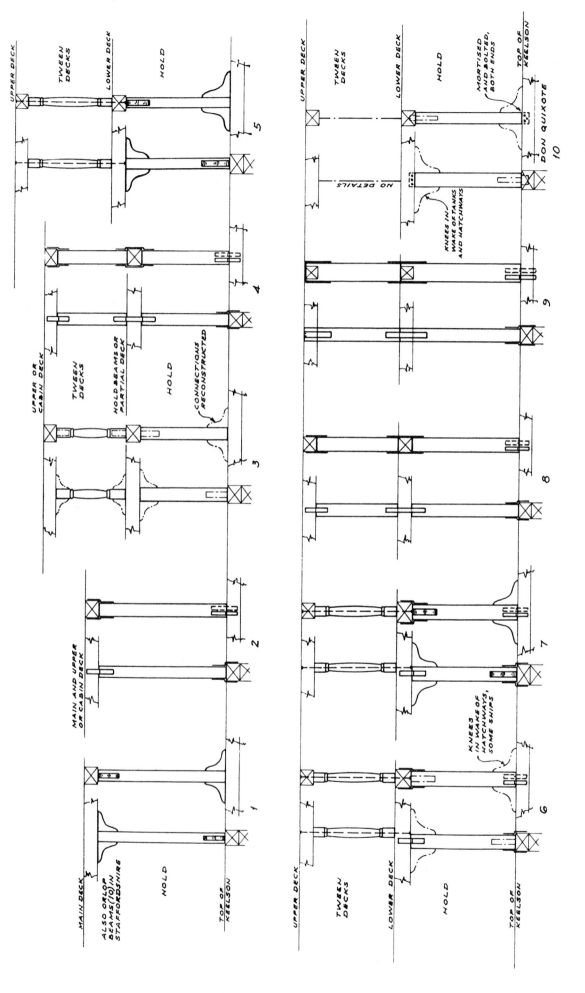

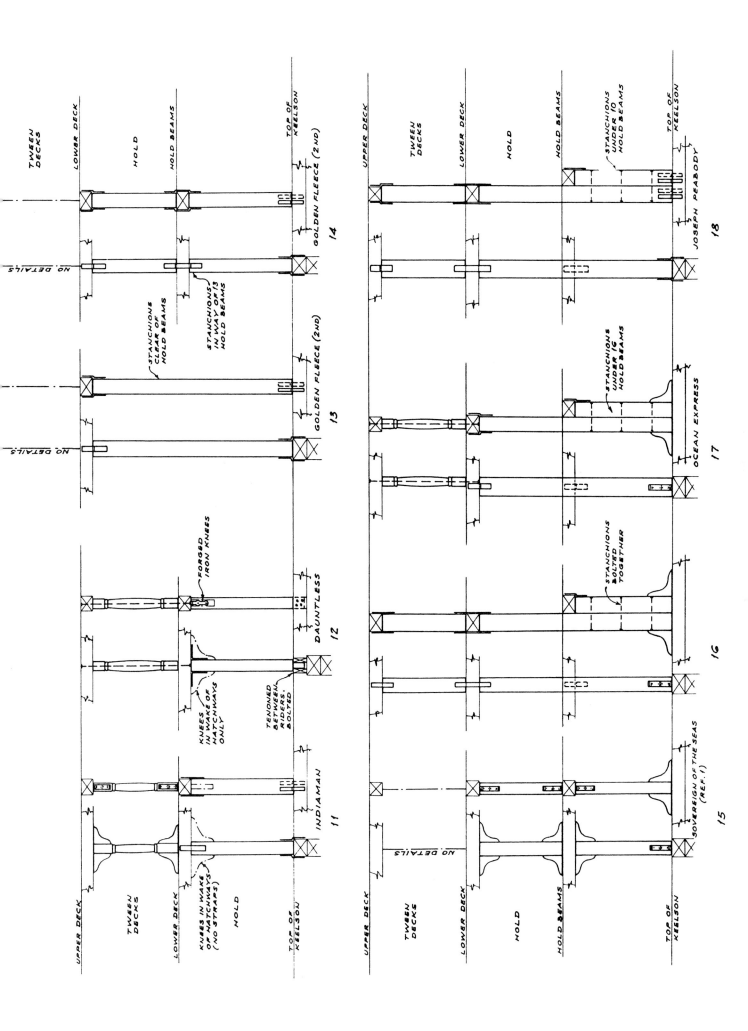

Figure 13.2. *Stanchion assemblies, three- and four-deck vessels.*

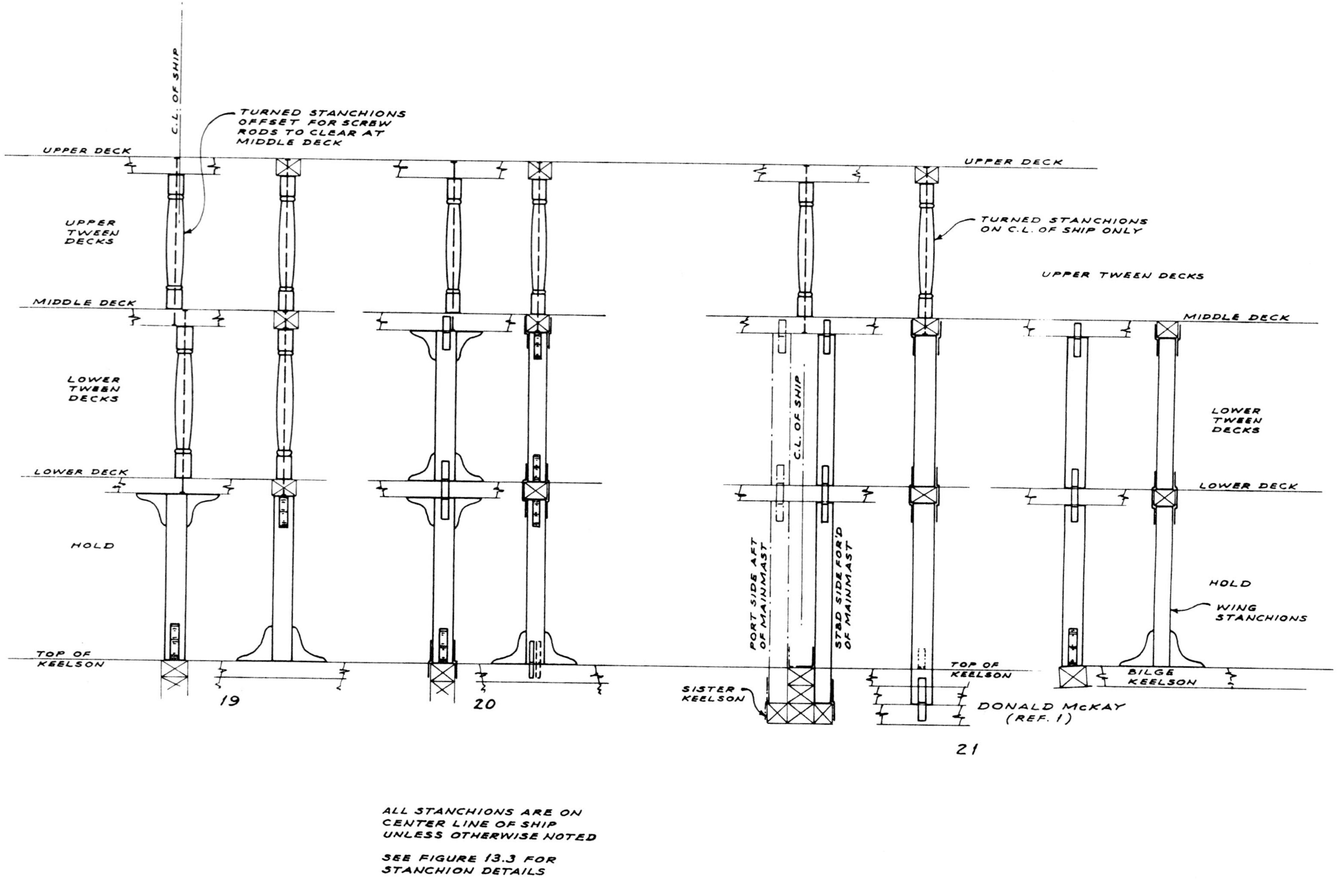

MIDDLE DECK

LOWER TWEEN DECKS

LOWER DECK

HOLD

WING STANCHIONS

BILGE KEELSON

UPPER TWEEN DECKS

UPPER DECK

TURNED STANCHIONS ON C.L. OF SHIP ONLY

TOP OF KEELSON

DONALD McKAY (REF. 1)

21

STBD SIDE FOR'D OF MAINMAST

C.L. OF SHIP

PORT SIDE AFT OF MAINMAST

SISTER KEELSON

20

TURNED STANCHIONS OFFSET FOR SCREW RODS TO CLEAR AT MIDDLE DECK

19

C.L. OF SHIP

UPPER DECK

UPPER TWEEN DECKS

MIDDLE DECK

LOWER TWEEN DECKS

LOWER DECK

HOLD

TOP OF KEELSON

ALL STANCHIONS ARE ON CENTER LINE OF SHIP UNLESS OTHERWISE NOTED

SEE FIGURE 13.3 FOR STANCHION DETAILS

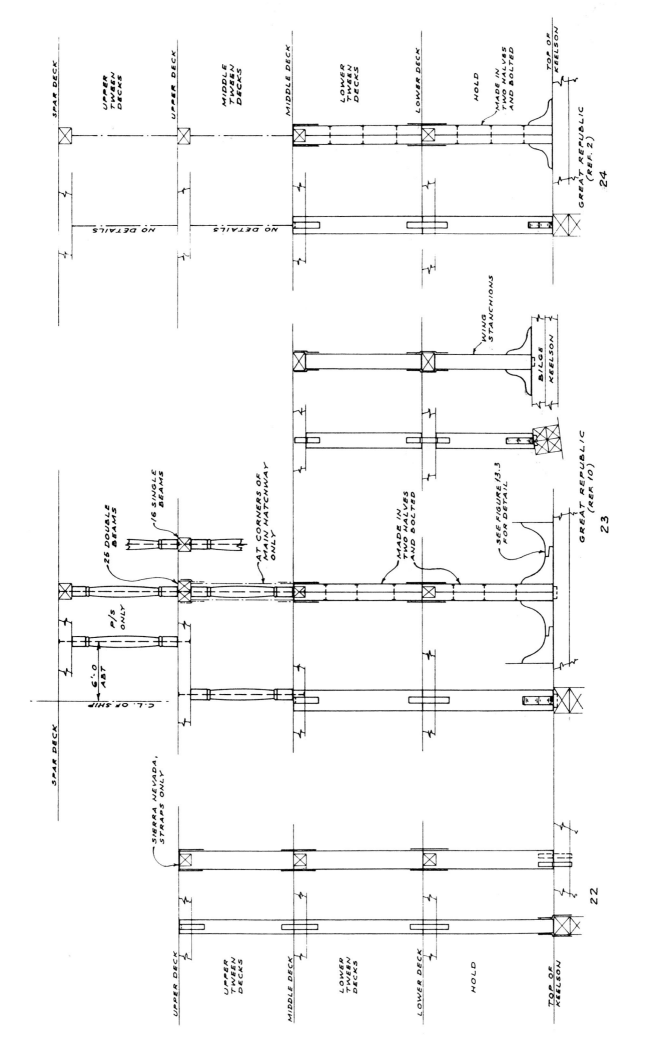

Figure 13.3. *Stanchion details.*

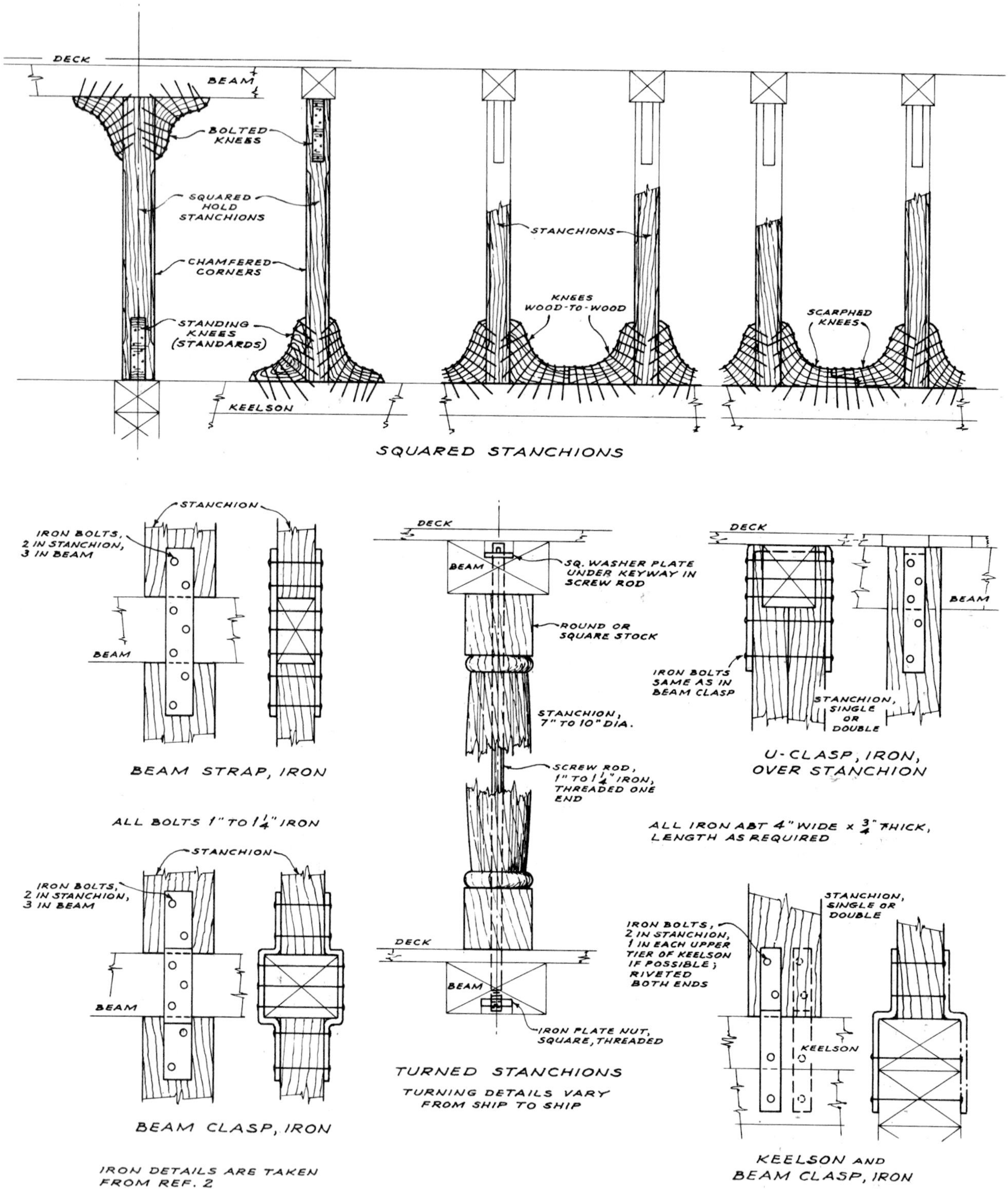

DECK
BEAM
BOLTED KNEES
SQUARED HOLD STANCHIONS
CHAMFERED CORNERS
STANDING KNEES (STANDARDS)
STANCHIONS
KNEES WOOD-TO-WOOD
SCARPHED KNEES
KEELSON

SQUARED STANCHIONS

STANCHION
IRON BOLTS, 2 IN STANCHION, 3 IN BEAM
BEAM

BEAM STRAP, IRON

ALL BOLTS 1" TO 1¼" IRON

STANCHION
IRON BOLTS, 2 IN STANCHION, 3 IN BEAM
BEAM

BEAM CLASP, IRON

IRON DETAILS ARE TAKEN FROM REF. 2

DECK
BEAM
SQ. WASHER PLATE UNDER KEYWAY IN SCREW ROD
ROUND OR SQUARE STOCK
STANCHION, 7" TO 10" DIA.
SCREW ROD, 1" TO 1¼" IRON, THREADED ONE END
DECK
BEAM
IRON PLATE NUT, SQUARE, THREADED

TURNED STANCHIONS

TURNING DETAILS VARY FROM SHIP TO SHIP

DECK
BEAM
IRON BOLTS SAME AS IN BEAM CLASP
STANCHION, SINGLE OR DOUBLE

U-CLASP, IRON, OVER STANCHION

ALL IRON ABT 4" WIDE x ¾" THICK, LENGTH AS REQUIRED

STANCHION, SINGLE OR DOUBLE
IRON BOLTS, 2 IN STANCHION, 1 IN EACH UPPER TIER OF KEELSON IF POSSIBLE; RIVETED BOTH ENDS
KEELSON

KEELSON AND BEAM CLASP, IRON

(text continued from page 215)

texts to describe methods of connecting stanchions to a vessel's structure, but the terminology is sometimes inconsistent. To avoid confusion, let us adhere to the following definitions: A *strap* is a piece of iron that is cut to proper length and width, punched or drilled, and remains flat without further working. A *clasp* is a piece of iron that, in addition to the above, is bent with a single or a double joggle, or is in the form of an inverted U. This terminology is applied throughout Table 13.1, which appears at the end of this chapter.

Two valuable illustrations of stanchion installation exist today. A contemporary article about William H. Webb's *Ocean Monarch*[15] features a description of the vessel along with a masterfully drafted midship section and longitudinal centerline section of the ship. It is difficult to conceive of any single drawing that could contain more detailed and general information than does this one. A drafted painting of the McKay packets *Star of Empire* and *Chariot of Fame*[54] shows the same views in a different manner. Both drawings verify and give credence to certain details that might otherwise have remained in limbo.

As the 1850s approached, the simplest and most common stanchion on the scene was number 1 in Figure 13.1. It consisted of a square stanchion kneed to keelson and beam with wooden knees. In each arm of the knee, spaced about 6 inches apart, were iron bolts, 1 inch to 1¼ inches, headed and driven blunt. This feature of fastening secured the stanchion firmly in position and also overcame any tendency of the beam to lift. A detail is shown in Figure 13.3.

With larger ships, those having two decks, this essential stanchion was augmented by a stanchion above it in the tween-decks. This stanchion, being in an area occupied by personnel, was generally more refined and finished, and was the turned stanchion found throughout all of merchant shipping except, perhaps, in ships designed wholly as freighters.

Still larger ships, those with three decks, required an extension of the above installations, and these took many forms throughout the American clipper fleet. Figures 13.1 and 13.2 illustrate the many variants found among the vessels appearing in this book. Of those illustrated, forms 5 and 6 were by far the most prevalent, mainly due to the predominance of two-deck vessels. Of interest is the fact that in 1850 form 5, fabricated with wooden knees as connectors, was the common choice. By 1856 it had been superseded by form 6, which featured iron clasps as connectors. This was one of the disturbing indicators that foreshadowed the oncoming shortage of suitable select timbers.

Throughout the entire period, 1850–1856, the use of the turned stanchion in the tween decks remained constant but not necessarily exclusive. It was in use many years prior to this period and would remain in use until the demise of the wooden ship. One of its principal features in clippers and packets of the period was the iron screw rod, which passed completely through the center of its length as illustrated in Figure 13.3. The stanchion itself functioned as a column and resisted the compressive load of the deck above. The iron screw rod which passed through its center acted in tension when external forces tended to lift the deck by compressing the beams at their ends. The rod passed completely through the beams above and below the stanchion. As illustrated in Figure 13.3, the beam below was recessed on its underside to receive a squared plate nut whose surface was of sufficient area to resist crushing the fiber of the beam. The rod was screwed into this nut, which was about ¾ inch thick. A somewhat similar recess was cut into the upper surface of the beam above. A plate with an unthreaded hole was placed in this recess, and the upper end of the screw rod, being pierced with a keyway, protruded sufficiently above the plate to accommodate an iron key which was driven home against the surface of the plate. This detail would ultimately be covered by the laid deck. This assembly of a turned stanchion is reported in the contemporary description of *Lightning*;[1] also see Table 13.1.

The two illustrations just described show very plainly the types of stanchion arrangements that were employed in a ship. The drafted painting[54] reveals that squared stanchions were normally installed directly over each other from keelson to upper deck, no reason for offsetting being apparent. However, the installation of a turned stanchion directly over a squared one was influenced by the necessity of having the fastenings of the strap or clasp below the foot of the turned stanchion fall clear of the hole bored to accommodate the iron screw rod.

In the lines of *Ocean Monarch*,[15] the midship section clarifies the solution to the problem of installing one turned stanchion immediately over another. If this were attempted, the iron screw rod of one would foul the screw rod of the other. To avoid this, the stanchions were offset about one diameter in reference to each other. Stanchion assembly 19, Figure 13.2, illustrates this solution.

Before closing the subject of stanchions, it seems appropriate to point out the details of some of the rare or unusual installations which occur in vessels covered in this book.

Don Quixote, built by Samuel Lapham of Medford, Massachusetts, had her stanchions mortised into the keelson and beams without benefit of knees or straps for additional restraint. This mortising technique was generally looked upon with disfavor, being regarded as a potential danger to the integrity of the keelson assembly. The tenon in each end was made large enough to allow several bolts to be driven through the beam and upper tier of the keelson and riveted at both ends; see Figure 13.1, number 10.

Indiaman, built by Hugh McKay of East Boston, was

(text continued on page 227)

Table 13.1. *Stanchion installation and details.*

Notes: "Assbly. #" refers to Figures 13.1 and 13.2.

See Figure 6.2,S and T, for typical stanchion locations.

( ) = Reconstruction based on year, size of vessel and general
     practice.

Abbreviations

WO - white oak	HP - hard pine
NHWO - New Hampshire white oak	PP - pitch pine
MWO - Massachusetts white oak	SP - Southern pine Loc - locust

Vessel, Ref.#, Assbly. #

Alarm   #1   #16

Hold - PP; 7"x15" (width of beams), kneed to keelson, iron strapped
     across lower deck beams to stanchions above.

Hold beams - PP; stanchions (10) fayed and bolted to lower deck stanchions
     and iron clasped to hold beams. Stanchions squared.

Tween decks - PP; 7"x15" (width of beams), iron strapped to lower deck
     stanchions and to upper deck beams.

Amphitrite   #1   #(6)

Hold - HP; "very stout and strongly bound to beams."

Tween decks -

Andrew Jackson

Antelope   #1   #6

Hold - Oak; kneed in wake of hatchways; elsewhere iron clasped both ends.

Tween decks - Oak; turned and secured with iron screw rods through
     centers, through lower and upper deck beams.

Asa Eldridge   #1   #16

Hold - PP; 7"x15" (width of beams), kneed to keelson and iron strapped
     across lower deck beams to stanchions above.

Hold beams - PP; stanchions (17) fayed and bolted to lower deck stanchions
     and iron clasped to hold beams. Stanchions squared.

Tween decks - PP; 7"x15" (width of beams), iron strapped to lower deck
     stanchions and to upper deck beams.

Bald Eagle   #1   #7

Hold - HP; 10"x12", kneed and iron clasped to keelson and to
     lower deck beams. "Through bolted."

Tween decks - WO; turned and secured with iron screw rods through
     centers, through lower and upper deck beams.

Belle of the West

Beverly

Black Hawk

Blue Jacket

Bonita   #1 - Described as being "similar to Golden Light."

Bounding Billow   Bark   #1   #2

Hold (one deck vessel) - (HP); "well stanchioned."

Celestial

Challenge   #1   #19

Hold - HP; kneed to keelson and to lower deck beams. Stanchions squared.

Lower tween decks - Loc; turned and secured with iron screw rods
     through centers, through lower and middle deck beams.

Upper tween decks - Loc; turned and secured with iron screw rods
     through centers, through middle and upper deck beams.

Challenger   #1

Hold - WO; "stout."

Tween decks - WO; "stout."

Vessel, Ref.#, Assbly.#

Champion of the Seas   #1,2   #20,22

Ref.1, Assbly. #20
Hold - HP; 10"x22", kneed and iron clasped to keelson and clasped
     across lower deck beams to stanchions above. Wing stanchions (12)
     on bilge keelson, secured in same manner.

Lower tween decks - HP; 10"x22", kneed and iron clasped to lower deck
     beams and to middle deck beams over midship and wing stanchions
     in hold.

Upper tween decks - No midship stanchions. WO wing stanchions, turned and
     secured with iron screw rods through centers, through middle and
     upper deck beams.

Ref.2, Assbly. #22
Hold - PP; 7"x22", iron clasped to keelson and strapped across lower deck
     beams to stanchions above.

Lower tween decks - PP; 7"x22", iron strapped across lower and middle
     deck beams to stanchions above.

Upper tween decks - PP; 7"x22", iron strapped across middle deck beams
     and iron clasped over upper deck beams with "U" clasp.

Charger   #1   #(6)

Hold - HP; 10"x12", bolted with iron.

Tween decks - NHWO; turned and secured with iron screw rods through
     centers, through lower and upper deck beams.

Charmer

Cleopatra   #1   #5

Hold - WO; squared, kneed to keelson and to lower deck beams.

Tween decks - WO; turned and secured with iron screw rods through centers,
     through lower and upper deck beams.

Climax   #1   #(3)

Hold - WO; squared, "secured with very stout knees and stanchions."

Tween decks - Same as hold except stanchions probably turned.

Coeur de Lion

Comet

Cyclone

Daring   #1   #(6)

Hold - (HP); 10" square, secured to keelson and to lower deck beams.

Tween decks - WO; turned and secured with iron screw rods through
     centers, through lower and upper deck beams.

Dauntless   #1   #12

Hold - MWO; 10"x12", stepped between keelson riders; secured to lower
     deck beams with forged iron knees except in wake of hatchways, in
     which locations the knees are hackmatack.

Tween decks - MWO; turned and secured with iron screw rods through
     centers, through lower and upper deck beams.

Donald McKay   #1,2   #21,22

Ref.1, Assbly. #21
Hold - PP; squared, stepped on starboard sister keelsons forward of
     mainmast, on port sister keelsons aft of mainmast. Iron clasped to
     keelsons and lower deck beams. Squared wing stanchions (11), kneed
     to bilge keelsons, iron clasped to lower deck beams.

Lower tween decks - PP; squared, stepped directly over hold beams. Clasped
     to lower and middle deck beams. Squared wing stanchions (11), iron
     clasped to lower and middle deck beams.

Upper tween decks - WO; turned and secured with iron screw rods through
     centers, through middle and upper deck beams. Located on center line
     of ship. No wing stanchions.

Ref.2, Assbly. #22
Hold - PP; 7"x22", iron clasped to keelson and strapped across lower deck
     beams to stanchions above.

Lower tween decks - PP; 7"x22", iron strapped across lower and middle
     deck beams to stanchions above.

Upper tween decks - PP; 7"x22", iron strapped across middle deck beams
     and iron clasped over upper deck beams with "U" clasp.

Don Quixote   #1   #10

Hold - WO; squared, kneed in wake of tanks and hatchways. All others
     mortised into keelson and lower deck beams, then bolted.

Tween decks -

Eagle

Eagle Wing   #1

Hold - WO; squared.

Tween decks -

Table 13.1. *Continued.*

Vessel, Ref.#, Assbly.#

Edwin Forrest   #1   #5
   Hold - HP; squared, kneed to keelson and to lower deck beams.
   Tween decks - WO; turned and secured with iron screw rods through centers, through lower and upper deck beams.

Electric Spark   #1   #(6)
   Hold - PP; "very stout and well fastened." Stanchions squared.
   Tween decks -

Ellen Foster   #1   #5
   Hold - WO; 10" square, kneed to keelson and to lower deck beams.
   Tween decks - WO; turned and secured with iron screw rods through centers, through lower and upper deck beams.

Empress of the Sea   #1,2   #20(mod.),22
   Ref.1, Assbly. #20(mod.)
   Hold - HP; ?x16"(width of beams), kneed to keelson and to hold beams. Iron strapped across hold beams to stanchions above.
   Hold beams, decked 8' wide along the waterways - HP; ? x16" (width 0f beams), kneed and iron strapped to hold stanchions and to middle deck beams above.
   Upper tween decks - WO; turned and secured with iron screw rods through centers, through middle and upper deck beams.
   Ref.2, Assbly. #22
   Hold - PP; 7"x22", iron clasped to keelson and strapped across lower deck beams to stanchions above.
   Lower tween decks - PP; 7"x22", iron strapped across lower and middle deck beams to stanchions above.
   Upper tween decks - PP; 7"x22", iron strapped across middle deck beams and iron clasped over upper deck beams with "U" clasp.

Endeavor   #1   #(6)
   Hold - HP; 10"x12", keelson to lower deck beams. (No additional details.)
   Tween decks - WO; turned and secured with iron screw rods through centers, through lower and upper deck beams.

Eringo   Bark   #1   #(2)
   Hold (one deck vessel) - Oak; "stout stanchions."

Eureka

Fair Wind   #1   #8
   Hold - HP; 10"x15" (width of beams), clasped with iron to keelson and strapped across lower deck beams to stanchions above.
   Tween decks - HP; 10"x15" (width of beams), iron strapped to lower and upper deck beams.

Fearless

Fleet Wing   #1
   Hold - WO
   Tween decks -

Flyaway

Flying Arrow   #1
   Hold - HP; "very stout and well secured."
   Tween decks -

Flying Childers   #1   #5
   Hold - WO; 10" square, kneed to keelson and to lower deck beams.
   Tween decks - WO; turned and secured with iron screw rods through centers, through lower and upper deck beams.

Flying Cloud   #1,2   #7,9
   Ref.1, Assbly. #7
   Hold - SP; squared, kneed and iron clasped to keelson and to lower deck beams.
   Tween decks - WO; turned and secured with iron screw rods through centers, through lower and upper deck beams.
   Ref.2, Assbly. #9
   Hold - PP; 7"x22", iron clasped to keelson and strapped across lower deck beams to stanchions above.
   Tween decks - PP; 7"x22", iron strapped to lower deck stanchions and iron clasped over upper deck beams with "U" clasp.

Flying Dragon   #1
   Hold - HP; "very stout."
   Tween decks -

Flying Dutchman

Vessel, Ref.#, Assbly.#

Flying Eagle   #1   #8
   Hold - WO; ? x15" (width of beams), iron clasped to keelson and strapped across lower deck beams to stanchions above.
   Tween decks - WO; ? x15" (width of beams), iron strapped to lower deck stanchions and to upper deck beams.

Flying Fish   #1,2   #6,9
   Ref.1, Assbly. #6
   Hold - SP; 10" square, kneed in wake of hatchways; elsewhere iron clasped to keelson and to lower deck beams.
   Tween decks - WO; turned and secured with iron screw rods through centers, through lower and upper deck beams.
   Ref.2, Assbly. #9
   Hold - PP; 7"x22", iron clasped to keelson and strapped across lower deck beams to stanchions above.
   Tween decks - PP; 7"x22", iron strapped to lower deck stanchions and iron clasped over upper deck beams with "U" clasp.

Flying Mist   #1   #8
   Hold - HP ; 8"x15" (width of beams), iron clasped to keelson and strapped across lower deck beams to stanchions above.
   Tween decks - HP ; 8"x15" (width of beams), iron strapped to lower deck stanchions and to upper deck beams.

Galatea

Game Cock   #1 - "stanchions_____best materials, well fastened."

Gazelle   #4 - "stanchions are of locust." (These stanchions are not identified.)

Gem of the Ocean

Golden Eagle   #1   #5 (Hold only)
   Hold - Oak; squared, kneed to keelson and to lower deck beams.
   Tween decks -

Golden Fleece (2nd)   #1   #13,14
   Hold, #13 - HP; squared, iron clasped to keelson and to lower deck beams.
   Hold beams, #14 - HP; iron clasped to keelson and across hold beams (13) to stanchions above, then iron clasped to lower deck beams.
   Tween decks -

Golden Light   #1   #6
   Hold - WO; 10" square, kneed in wake of hatchways; elsewhere iron clasped to keelson and to lower deck beams.
   Tween decks - WO; turned and secured with iron screw rods through centers, through lower and upper deck beams.

Golden West   #1   #(5)(Hold only.)
   Hold - WO; squared.
   Tween decks -

Grace Darling   #1   #(6)
   Hold - WO; squared.
   Tween decks - WO

Great Republic   #2,4,10   #23,24
   Refs.10,4, Assbly. #23 (These references differ in description.)
   Hold - HP; 10"x23" (in two halves), tenoned into keelson and scarph kneed fore and aft, iron strapped across lower deck beams to stanchions above. Wing stanchions tenoned into bilge keelsons, kneed fore and aft and iron clasped across lower deck beams to stanchions above.
   Lower tween decks - HP; 10"x23" (in two halves), iron strapped across lower deck beams; "U" clasped over middle deck beams. Wing stanchions iron clasped across lower deck beams and iron clasped to middle deck beams.
   Middle tween decks - WO; 10" dia., turned and secured with iron screw rods through centers, through middle and upper deck beams. Located on center line of ship only.
   Upper tween decks - WO; 10" dia., turned and secured with iron screw rods through centers, through upper and spar deck beams. Located about 6' to port and stbd only. No stanchions on center line of ship.
   Ref.2, Assbly. #24
   Hold - PP; 10"x24" (in two halves), kneed to keelson fore and aft, iron strapped across lower deck beams to stanchions above.
   Lower tween decks - PP; 10"x24" (in two halves), iron strapped to lower deck stanchions and clasped over middle deck beams with "U" clasp.
   Middle tween decks -
   Upper tween decks -

Table 13.1. *Continued.*

Vessel, Ref.#, Assbly.#

Great Republic (rebuilt) #103 #(23) No spar deck installed.

    Stanchions below middle deck same as in original ship. Stanchions between middle deck and upper deck, oak, 10" dia., turned and secured with iron screw rods through centers, through middle and upper deck beams. Locations not specified.

Henry Hill Bark #1 #2,4

    Assbly. #2
    Hold - HP; squared, iron clasped to keelson and to upper deck and cabin deck beams.

    Assbly. #4
    Hold beams (11), (Laid deck in forward end only, from 5' abaft foremast.) HP; squared, iron clasped to keelson and across beams to stanchions above.

    Tween decks - HP; iron clasped to stanchions below and to upper or cabin deck beams.

Herald of the Morning

Hoogly #1 #5

    Hold - HP; 10" square, kneed to keelson and to lower deck beams.

    Tween decks - WO; turned and secured with iron screw rods through centers, through lower and upper deck beams.

Hurricane

Indiaman #1 #11

    Hold - HP; 10"x15" (width of beams), kneed in wake of hatchways, elsewhere iron clasped to keelson and strapped to lower deck beams.

    Tween decks - WO; turned and secured to lower and upper deck beams with stout knees, strongly fastened.

Intrepid

Invincible #4 #19

    Hold - PP; squared, kneed to keelson and to lower deck beams.

    Lower tween decks - Loc; turned and secured with iron screw rods through centers, through lower and middle deck beams.

    Upper tween decks - Loc; turned and secured with iron screw rods through centers, through middle and upper deck beams.

James Baines #1,2 #20,22

    Ref.1, Assbly. #20
    "nearly the same _____ as Champion of the Seas."

    Ref.2, Assbly. #22
    Hold - PP; 7"x22", iron clasped to keelson and strapped across lower deck beams to stanchions above.

    Lower tween decks - PP; 7"x22", iron strapped across lower and middle deck beams to stanchions above.

    Upper tween decks - PP; 7"x22", iron strapped across middle deck beams and iron clasped over upper deck beams with "U" clasp.

John Bertram #1 $5,6

    Hold - WO; 10" square, kneed to keelson and to lower deck beams in body of vessel (Assbly. #5) and iron clasped to keelson and to lower deck beams in the ends of vessel (Assbly. #6).

    Tween decks - WO; 10" dia., turned and secured with iron screw rods through centers, through lower and upper deck beams.

John Gilpin #1 # 5

    Hold - WO; squared, kneed to keelson and to lower deck beams.

    Tween decks - WO; turned and secured with iron screw rods through centers, through lower and upper deck beams.

John Land #1,32 #6 (Built as a duplicate of Winged Arrow.)

    Hold - Oak; 11" square, kneed in wake of the hatchways, elsewhere iron clasped to keelson and to lower deck beams.

    Tween decks - Oak; turned and secured with iron screw rods through centers, through lower and upper deck beams.

John Stuart #4

    Hold - "Three rows of stanchions, doubly sealed."

    Lower tween decks -

    Upper tween decks -

John Wade

Vessel, Ref.#, Assbly.#

Joseph Peabody #1 #18

    Hold - HP; 7"x15" (width of beams), iron clasped to keelson and strapped across lower deck beams to stanchions above.

    Hold beams - HP; stanchions (10) fayed and bolted to lower deck stanchions, iron clasped to keelson and strapped to hold beams.

    Tween decks - HP; 7"x15", iron strapped to lower deck stanchions and clasped to upper deck beams.

King Fisher #1

    Hold - WO

    Tween decks - WO

Lady Franklin

Lamplighter Bark #1 #(2)

    Hold (one deck vessel) - WO; squared.

Lightfoot #1

    Hold - HP

    Tween decks -

Lightning #1,2,32 #7,22

    Ref.1, Assbly. #7
    Hold - HP; squared, "very stout", kneed and iron clasped to keelson and to lower deck beams.

    Tween decks - WO; turned and secured with iron screw rods through centers, through lower and upper deck beams. "The rods have nuts and screws under the lower deck beams, and keys on the upper deck beams."

    Ref.2, Assbly. #22
    Hold - PP; 7"x22", iron clasped to keelson and strapped across lower deck beams to stanchions above.

    Lower tween decks - PP; 7"x22", iron strapped across lower and middle deck beams to stanchions above.

    Upper tween decks - PP; 7"x22", iron strapped across middle deck beams and iron clasped over upper deck beams with "U" clasp.

Mameluke #1 #8

    Hold - PP; ? x15" (width of beams; some beams are sided 17"), iron clasped to keelson and iron clasped or strapped across lower deck beams to stanchions above.

    Tween decks - PP; ? x15" (width of beams), iron strapped or iron clasped to lower deck stanchions, and strapped to upper deck beams.

Mary Robinson

Mastiff #1 #6

    Hold - HP; 7"x12", iron clasped to keelson and to lower deck beams.

    Tween decks - Oak; turned and secured with iron screw rods through centers, through lower and upper deck beams.

Mermaid Bark #1

    "Stanchions are strongly secured."

Morning Light

Mystery #1 #7

    Hold - Oak; 10" square, kneed and iron clasped to keelson and to lower deck beams.

    Tween decks - Oak; turned and secured with iron screw rods through centers, through lower and upper deck beams.

Nightingale

Noonday #1 #(6)

    Hold - "very stout and strongly secured to keelson and lower deck beams."

    Tween decks - Oak; turned and secured with iron screw rods through centers, through lower and upper deck beams.

Northern Light

Ocean Express #1 #17

    Hold - HP; squared, kneed to keelson, iron clasped to lower deck beams.

    Hold beams - HP; stanchions (16) fayed and bolted to lower deck stanchions, kneed to keelson and clasped to hold beams.

    Tween decks - Oak; turned and secured with iron screw rods through centers, through lower and upper deck beams.

Table 13.1. *Continued.*

Ocean Pearl   #1   #(6)

    Hold - HP; squared, "kneed in wake of the hatchways."

    Tween decks -

Ocean Telegraph   #5

    Hold - HP; squared.

    Tween decks -

Onward   #1

    Hold - Oak; squared.

    Tween decks -

Osborne Howes

Panther

Phantom   #1   #6

    Hold - HP; 11" square, kneed in wake of the hatchways and mast partners, iron clasped to keelson and to lower deck beams.

    Tween decks - WO; turned and secured with iron screw rods through centers, through lower and upper deck beams.

Queen of Clippers   #1

    Hold - WO; squared.

    Tween decks -

Queen of the Pacific

Queen of the Seas   #1   #6

    Hold - Oak; 10"x12", kneed in wake of the hatchways, iron clasped to keelson and to lower deck beams.

    Tween decks - Oak; turned and secured with iron screw rods through centers, through lower and upper deck beams.

Quickstep   Bark   #1   #(6)

    Hold - HP; 8" square.

    Tween decks - Oak.

Racehorse   Bark   #1   #3

    Hold - Oak; squared from keelson to hold beams.

    Hold beams (partially decked forward and aft) - Oak; turned, in tween decks between partial deck and upper deck.

Racer   #3   #(20)

    Hold - WO; squared, kneed to keelson and to lower deck beams.

    Lower tween decks - WO; squared, kneed to lower deck beams and to middle deck beams.

    Upper tween decks -

Radiant   #1   #(6)

    Hold - Oak; "very stout_____kneed in wake of the hatchways and clasped with iron elsewhere."

    Tween decks -

Raven

Red Jacket

Robin Hood

Rocket

Roebuck   #1   #5

    Hold - Oak; squared, kneed to keelson and to lower deck beams.

    Tween decks - Oak; turned and secured with iron screw rods through centers, through lower and upper deck beams.

Romance of the Sea   #1

    HP; "stanchions are all of the most substantial kind."

Santa Claus   #1

    "very stout."

Saracen   #1   #(5)

    Hold - MWO; squared, kneed to keelson and to lower deck beams.

    Tween decks -

Sea Bird   Bark   #1   #(3)

    HP; "very stout stanchions."

Seaman's Bride   #1   #6

    Hold - HP; squared, iron clasped to keelson and to lower deck beams.

    Tween decks - (Oak); turned and secured with iron screw rods through, through lower and upper deck beams.

Sea Serpent

Shooting Star   #1   #(6)

    Hold - WO; kneed in wake of the hatchways (and iron clasped to the keelson and to lower deck beams elsewhere.) Stanchions squared.

    Tween decks - WO; turned and secured with iron screw rods through centers, through lower and upper deck beams.

Sierra Nevada   #1   #22 (mod.)

    Hold - NHWO; ? x16" (width of beams), iron clasped to keelson and iron strapped across lower deck beams to stanchions above.

    Lower tween decks - NHWO; ? x16" (width of beams), iron strapped across lower deck beams, and across middle deck beams to stanchions above.

    Upper tween decks - NHWO; ? x16" (width of beams), iron strapped across middle deck beams and iron strapped to upper deck beams. (No "U" clasp installed in way of upper deck beams.)

Silver Star   #1   #(6)

    Hold - WO; 10"x12", kneed in wake of the hatchways and iron clasped to keelson and to lower deck beams elsewhere.

    Tween decks -

Southern Cross   #1   #(6)

    Hold - MWO; squared, kneed in wake of the hatchways and iron clasped to keelson and to lower deck beams elsewhere.

    Tween decks -

Sovereign of the Seas   #1,2   #(1),(15),22

    Ref.1, Assbly. #(1)
    Hold - WO; squared, kneed to keelson and to lower deck beams.

    Assbly. #(15)
    Hold beams (5 beams) - WO; lower stanchions kneed to keelson and to hold beams. Upper stanchions kneed to hold beams and to lower deck beams.

    Tween decks -

    Ref.2, Assbly. #22
    Hold - PP; 7"x22", iron clasped to keelson and strapped across lower deck beams to stanchions above.

    Lower tween decks - PP; 7"x22", iron strapped across lower and middle deck beams to stanchions above.

    Upper tween decks - PP; 7"x22", iron strapped across middle deck beams and iron clasped over upper deck beams with "U" clasp.

Spitfire   #1   #(5)

    Hold - WO; squared, kneed to keelson and to lower deck beams.

    Tween decks -

Staffordshire   #1,2   #1,19,22

    Ref.1, Assbly.19
    Hold - (HP); 10"x12", kneed to keelson and to lower deck beams.

    Assbly. #1
    Orlop beams (10 beams) - (HP); kneed to keelson and to the orlop beams.

    Lower tween decks - WO; turned and secured with iron screw rods through centers, through lower and middle deck beams.

    Upper tween decks - WO; turned and secured with iron screw rods through centers, through middle and upper deck beams.

    Ref.2, Assbly.#22
    Hold - PP; 7"x22", iron clasped to keelson and iron strapped across lower deck beams to stanchions above.

    Lower tween decks - PP; 7"x22", iron strapped across lower and middle deck beams to stanchions above.

    Upper tween decks - PP; 7"x22", iron strapped across middle deck beams and iron clasped over upper deck beams with "U" clasp.

Table 13.1. *Continued.*

Vessel, Ref.#, Assbly.#

Stag Hound   #1   #5,9
> Ref.1, Assbly. #5
> Hold – (HP); 10" square, kneed to keelson and to lower deck beams.
>
> Tween decks – Oak; turned and secured with iron screw rods through centers, through lower and upper deck beams.
>
> Ref.2, Assbly. #9
> Hold – PP; 7"x22", iron clasped to keelson and iron strapped across lower deck beams to stanchions above.
>
> Tween decks – PP; 7"x22", iron strapped to lower deck stanchions and iron clasped over upper deck beams with "U" clasp.

Star of the Union   #1   #(5)
> Hold – WO; squared.
>
> Tween decks –

Starr King

Storm King   #1   #5
> Hold – Oak; squared, kneed to keelson and to lower deck beams.
>
> Tween decks – Oak; turned and secured with iron screw rods through centers, through lower and upper deck beams.

Sultana   Bark

Sunny South

Surprise   #1   #5
> Hold – WO; 10" square, kneed to keelson and to lower deck beams.
>
> Tween decks – Oak; turned and secured with iron screw rods through centers, through lower and upper deck beams.

Swallow

Sweepstakes

Sword Fish

Syren

Telegraph

Thatcher Magoun   #1   #(6)
> Hold – WO; squared, "strongly secured."
>
> Tween decks – WO; "strongly secured."

Tornado

Uncowah

War Hawk   #1   #(6)
> Stanchions under lower and upper deck beams "secured in the best style."

Water Witch   #1   #5
> Hold – Oak; squared, kneed to keelson and to lower deck beams.
>
> Tween decks – Oak; turned and secured with iron screw rods through centers, through lower and upper deck beams.

Western Continent

Westward Ho   #1,2   #6,9
> Ref.1, Assbly. #6
> Hold – HP; squared, kneed in wake of the hatchways; elsewhere iron clasped to keelson and to lower deck beams.
>
> Tween decks – Oak; turned and secured with iron screw rods through centers, through lower and upper deck beams.
>
> Ref.2, Assbly. #9
> Hold – PP; 7"x22", iron clasped to keelson and strapped across lower deck beams to stanchions above.
>
> Tween decks – PP; 7"x22", iron strapped to lower deck stanchions and iron clasped over upper deck beams with "U" clasp.

West Wind

Whirlwind   #1   #6
> Hold – Oak; 10"x12", kneed in wake of the hatchways; elsewhere iron clasped to keelson and to lower deck beams.
>
> Tween decks – Oak; turned and secured with iron screw rods through centers, through lower and upper deck beams.

Whistler   #1
> Hold – Oak; "very strongly stanchioned."
>
> Tween decks – Oak.

Vessel, Ref.#, Assbly.#

Wildfire   Bark

Wild Pigeon   #1   #5
> Hold – WO; 9" square, kneed in wake of the hatchways to keelson and to lower deck beams. No other details.
>
> Tween decks – WO; 7" dia., turned and secured with iron screw rods through centers, through lower and upper deck beams.

Wild Ranger   #1   #(6)
> Hold – Oak; squared.
>
> Tween decks –

Wild Rover

Winged Arrow   #1   #6
> Hold – Oak; 11" square, kneed in wake of the hatchways; elsewhere iron clasped to keelson and to lower deck beams.
>
> Tween decks – Oak; turned and secured with iron screw rods through centers, through lower and upper deck beams.

Winged Racer   #1   #6
> Hold – HP; 10"x12", kneed in wake of the hatchways; elsewhere iron clasped to keelson and to lower deck beams. "Bolted through-and-th
>
> Tween decks – Oak; turned and secured with iron screw rods through centers, through lower and upper deck beams.

Witchcraft   #1   #5
> Hold – Oak; 12" square to 10" square in ends of ship, kneed to keelson and to lower deck beams.
>
> Tween decks – Oak; 9" dia., turned and secured with iron screw rods through centers, through lower and upper deck beams.

Witch of the Wave   #1   #7 (mod.)
> Hold – WO; 10" square, kneed and iron clasped to keelson and to lower deck beams.
>
> Tween decks – Oak; turned and secured with 1¼" dia. iron screw rods through centers, through lower and upper deck beams. Both ends of turned stanchions are fitted with cast iron sockets.

Wizard   #1   #19 (mod.)
> Hold – Oak; squared, iron clasped to keelson and to lower partial deck beams. Lower deck is laid forward from 3' abaft foremast, and aft from 3' afore the mizzen mast.
>
> Lower tween decks – Oak; turned and secured with iron screw rods through centers, through all lower partial deck beams and middle deck beams.
>
> Upper tween decks – Oak; turned and secured with iron screw rods through centers, through middle deck and upper deck beams.

Young America

Young Turk   Bark   #1   #2
> Hold (one deck vessel) – HP; 8"x9", iron clasped to keelson and to main deck beams.

226

(text continued from page 221)

fitted with turned stanchions in the tween-decks. The unusual feature in this vessel was that, even at this relatively late date, these stanchions were kneed to the beams above and below, while the customary iron screw rod was omitted. This type of installation would also indicate that the base and the head of the stanchions were square in order to accommodate fitting of the knees. See Figure 13.1, number 11.

Dauntless, built by Benjamin F. Delano of Medford, contained two unusual features. The lower ends of her hold stanchions were tenoned between the two oak keelson riders, which were sided 9 inches, moulded 16 inches, and spaced 3 inches apart along the top of the keelson; see Figure 13.1, number 12, and Figure 10.1, number 9. The stanchion tenon was probably no more than 15 inches long in order to ensure seating on the shoulders, and bolts were driven through and riveted at both ends.

In addition, the upper ends of her hold stanchions were secured to the deck beams by forged iron knees, except for those stanchions in the wake of hatchways. These were secured by conventional wooden knees, which was the general practice.

According to MacLean's description, McKay's *Donald McKay* featured a very unusual arrangement of her midship stanchions. Her stanchions were apparently stepped on the sister keelsons rather than on the riders. Those afore the mainmast were stepped on the starboard side, while those abaft the mainmast were stepped on the port side; see Figure 13.2, number 21.

McKay's *Great Republic* was noted principally for the magnitude of her many parts. Her stanchions were stepped into both her main keelson and her bilge keelsons.[10] Also, as illustrated in Figure 13.2, number 23, the midship keelson knees were scarphed in every berth which, in effect, amounted to the installation of an additional keelson rider.

Finally, a rare installation of turned stanchions occurred in *Witch of the Wave*, in which each end of every such stanchion was fitted into a cast iron socket.

Such diversity of methods used to accomplish a given function accents the diffusion of preferences among the many shipbuilders. Obviously, there were many different ways to do the job. The only real consistency that seems apparent was the increasing use of iron as the connection medium and the gradual disappearance of wood in certain phases of construction.

Table 13.1 lists the stanchion assemblies applicable to each vessel and describes the general details of each individual installation.

Chapter Fourteen

BEAMS AND KNEES

THE BEAMS OF A SHIP are the third of three units which, when assembled, confine the hull to the form laid down by her designer, the other two units being the keel and the frames. The beams' primary function is to hold the two sides of the ship together, whether or not the vessel is laden. The second essential function—the one we are sometimes inclined to think of as their sole function—is that of supporting the deck planking and any loading that is placed upon it. This loading is designated the *live load*, due to the fact that it is intermittent, variable, and, on occasion, almost totally absent. The *dead load*—that is, the weight of permanent objects such as deck houses, helm, windlass, capstans, and other shipboard items—was, in the day of the sailing ship, of relatively little significance; such was the nature of these ships.

In general, beams installed in given locations, such as the lower deck or the upper deck in different vessels, all conformed to similar broad characteristics. Material, scantlings, quantity, spacing, and other basic elements followed the same generally accepted rules that had been handed down through years of experience. However, as in all other phases of shipbuilding, there were variations from the normal practice, reflecting preferences of the designer and builder. Some of these variations were bold and rather unusual, while others were very subtle and minute.

Table 14.1 is a tabulation of beam details for vessels included in this book. With some ships there is a wealth of detailed information, while with others there is hardly a word, the data having gone the way of the vessel. Tabulations such as this are, by their very nature, long, repetitive, tedious, and perhaps uninteresting. However, when a categorical study of a subject is attempted, it cannot be centered around the statistics that apply to only one or two related units. It must encompass as broad a field as can be obtained, or at least must cover enough examples of the subject as to be considered representative of that subject.

The table contains probably every form of beam installation used in the construction of wooden clippers. A broad, superficial scanning of the contents shows, in many cases, a constant repetition of what has already been recorded. A close examination, however, reveals many minute and unusual diversions from normal, and this, after all, is what a detailed study is about.

Details enumerated in the table indicate that the choice of woods followed a generally accepted rule. Beams were invariably cut from one of several varieties of pine tree, although oak was used on rare occasion in smaller vessels.

Knees connecting the beams to the frames were generally cut from white oak or hackmatack and were installed in definite locations based on strength considerations. In small vessels built with one deck, the knees were of white oak. In vessels of two decks, the knees of the lower deck beams were of white oak, this being considered the primary strength connection that held the two sides of the ship together. In such vessels the knees of the upper deck beams were of hackmatack, which was adequately strong for the purpose intended and helped conserve the dwindling sources of suitable white oak. In larger vessels of three decks, the knees of the lower and middle decks were of white oak, the middle deck being considered the primary strength connection, and the knees of the upper deck were of hackmatack. There were numerous cases where this pattern was not followed, and these show up throughout the table.

Fabrication of Beams

The distance between beams developed over the years and was determined by the desire to use a minimum of material to provide the required strength and stiffness. Ultimately the spacing evolved to a distance ranging between 5 and 7 feet, depending, to a great extent, upon the installation of carlings and ledges, with the added consideration that each end of a beam should butt against the substance of a frame.

All beams had their upper surfaces shaped to the designated camber (curve) for a specific vessel. Once this had been accomplished, the underside of the beam was shaped. Hold beams and lower deck beams appeared in two forms. In the most basic concept, the lower side of the beam was left as a straight, flat surface; this resulted in a beam that was of nominal scantling at the center, tapering toward the clamps by the amount of camber at the beam location. In the second form, material was removed from the underside of the beam so that the moulded dimension of the beam was constant throughout its length. All beams were formed with constant siding.

Beams under the middle, upper, spar, and main decks were always of constant siding, generally, uniform moulded dimension. This, while requiring considerable labor, saved weight, and gave extra headroom between decks. In many vessels the shorter beams required in the ends of vessels were of lesser scantlings than those installed toward amidships.

The underside of beam ends, in the way of the clamps upon which they were to rest, were *snaped*—that is, cut so that the surface was flat and parallel to a waterline. This is illustrated in Figure 14.2, detail A. Of course, in beams whose lower surface was straight, this procedure was not necessary.

The clamp on which the beam was to rest also required scoring in way of the beam in order to obtain a flat seating surface. Such scoring eliminated the effects of sheer and slope of the ship's side. In addition to this basic treatment, some builders went a step further by specifying that the lower deck beams be "let into" the clamp. This was actually the same treatment just described, except that the seat was cut about 1 inch deep into the clamp, thus effectively locking the beam in place. Donald McKay specifically called for this procedure,[2] and there seems little doubt that many other builders followed the practice, perhaps routinely.

In fitting a beam, the actual length was taken from the work, and this was augmented by a very comprehensive mould fashioned by the mould loft accounting for all bevels that would be encountered at the beam ends. Every effort was made to have the butt end of the beam fay against the inboard face of the frame. This, properly done, eliminated shear load from the bolts that secured the beam to the clamp. The number of such bolts varied among the builders, but Donald McKay called for four bolts through each beam end, driven blunt into the clamp.

The only operation remaining to complete the basic fabrication of a beam was its preparation for salting; this was applicable only to beams that supported the weather deck. In this area, the upper surface of the planking was subject to great variations in temperature. This promoted condensation on the underside of the deck. The introduction of salt into the top surface of the beam contributed to the preservation of the wood. Salting is covered in Chapter 20.

A center groove about 1 inch wide and 1 inch deep was chased along the entire length of the upper surface of such beams. The work could be performed at assembly, but the easier way would appear to be while the beam was being fashioned on the ground. These grooves were progressively filled with salt as the weather deck was being laid.

In the various texts dealing with clipper ships, nothing is mentioned about scarphs in the fabrication of beams. This leaves one with the reasonable assumption that, in spite of shipbuilding's voracious appetite for timber, there was an ample supply of timbers long enough and stout enough to allow cutting beams in a single length. This may or may not have been the case. However, it is a known fact that in England during this period, both the Royal Navy and the merchant fleet routinely scarphed beams. The scarph of choice was Edye's scarph,[8] Figure 5.1, described in Chapter 5. This scarph was introduced about 1830 and, due to its efficiency, could easily have found its way across the Atlantic to America's shores between that date and the clipper period.

Whatever the case and whatever type of scarph was used, certain general rules were followed. First, the scarph was always formed vertically. Second, it was always located clear of any stanchion or fixed obstacle; to place it over the head of a stanchion involved a potential clash of fastenings and rendered it inaccessible for possible tightening should its keys work loose for any reason.

When a beam was in position, its ends seated on and bolted to the clamps, the time for actually connecting the beam to the ship's structure was at hand. This was accomplished by the installation of knees, which were, in reality, the linchpins of ship construction.

Wooden Knees

The knee (Figure 14.1), a natural form of growth in various species of timber (as described in detail in Chapter 2), was without question the most essential structural unit used in the construction of large wooden vessels, be they clipper, packet, or cargo carrier. By its form, a knee transferred the flow of structural strength from one leg to another via the included angle between the two legs.

The principal function of the knee was to provide a mechanical connection between two parts which worked in different directions but were located in one plane, a notable example being the sternpost knee. Perhaps the most visible and familiar use of the knee on board ship was as a connector between the ship's frame and her deck beams. In this respect, the knee was the wooden counterpart of the steel angle of today.

The modern steel angle, regardless of size and proportions, is described in its own terminology, as are many other individual items. The principal parts of an angle are its *legs* which join at the *heel* on the outside of the angle, forming a

(text continued on page 239)

Table 14.1. *Deck beams and knees.*

Notes: Tops of weather deck beams are generally grooved and salted.

Abbreviations

WO – white oak	HP – hard pine	S – Sided
MWO – Massachusetts	PP – pitch pine	M – Moulded
white oak	SP – Southern pine	
NWO – Northern white oak	YP – yellow pine	
VWO – Virginia white oak	GP – Georgia pine	
NHWO – New Hampshire	Hk – hackmatack	
white oak		

Vessel & Ref.#

Alarm #1

Hold - Beams (10), PP, 15"S x 15"M.
    Hanging knees, WO, 10" to 12"S, 22" throat. 16 bolts and
        4 spikes, iron, in each knee.
    Lodging knees, WO. Scarphed in every berth.

Lower deck - Beams (26), PP, 15"S x 15"M.
    Hanging knees , WO, same as hold.
    Lodging knees , WO, same as hold.

Upper deck - Beams (27), PP, 15"S x 10"M.
    Hanging knees, Hk, 10" to 12"S, 22" throat. 18 bolts, iron, in each knee.
    Lodging knees, Hk. Scarphed in every berth. All lodging
        knees are bolted through the frames with 1" iron.

Amphitrite #1

Lower deck - Beams, HP.
    Hanging and lodging knees, WO.

Upper deck - Beams, HP.
    Hanging and lodging knees, Hk.

Andrew Jackson #20

Lower deck - Beams, ?
    Hanging knees, WO, standing on a stringer.
    Lodging knees, WO.

Upper deck - Beams, ?
    Hanging and lodging knees, WO.

Antelope #1

Lower deck - Beams, YP, 14"S x 13"M.
    Hanging and lodging knees, oak, securely bolted.

Upper deck - Beams, YP, 14"S x 8"M.
    Hanging and lodging knees, oak, securely bolted.

Asa Eldridge #1

Hold - Beams (17), PP, 15"S x 10"M. Beam ends rest on a lap stringer.
    Hanging knees, none.
    Lodging knees, WO, every berth.

Lower deck - Beams (26), PP, 15"S x 15"M.
    Hanging knees, WO. 18 bolts, iron, driven from outside, clinched inside.
    Lodging knees, WO. 12 bolts, iron, in every berth.

Upper deck - Beams (27), PP, 15"S x 7"M.
    Hanging knees, Hk, fastened in same style as lower deck.
    Lodging knees, Hk, every berth.

Bald Eagle #1

Lower deck - Beams, HP, 16"S x 16"M.
    Hanging knees, oak. 18 to 20 bolts, iron, in each knee.
    Lodging knees, WO.

Upper deck - Beams, HP, 15"S x 9"M.
    Hanging knees, Hk. 18 to 20 bolts, iron, in each knee.
    Lodging knees, Hk.

Belle of the West

Beverly #3

Lower deck - Beams, ?
    Hanging knees, oak.

Upper deck - Beams, ?
    Hanging knees, Hk.

Black Hawk

Blue Jacket #5

All beams, HP.

Bonita #1

Described as being similar to Golden Light."

Vessel & Ref.#

Bounding Billow Bark #1

Main deck - Beams, oak, 14"S x 10"M.
    Hanging knees, oak, 8" to 10"S. Foot rests on a built-in stringer.
        18 bolts and 4 spikes, iron, in each knee.
    Lodging knees, oak. Scarphed in every berth.

Celestial

Challenge #1,5

Lower deck - Beams, HP, 15" to 17"S x 14"M.
    Hanging knees, WO, 10" to 12"S x 22" to 28" throats. 16 to 18 bolts,
        driven from outside, clinched inside. Knees diminish in size
        toward the ends of the ship.
    Lodging knees, PP, 12" to 14"S.

Middle deck - Beams (28), HP, about 15" to 17"S x 14"M.
    Hanging knees, WO, similar to lower deck.
    Lodging knees, PP, 12" to 14"S.

Upper deck - Beams, HP, 13" to 15"S x 12"M.
    Hanging knees, WO, 8" to 10"S. 15 bolts, 1" iron, in each knee.
    Lodging knees, PP, 6"S.

Ref.5 - Ship contains over 150 hanging knees and 350 deck knees.

Challenger #1

Lower deck - Beams, HP, 16"S x 16"M.
    Hanging knees, oak. 28 bolts, 1⅛" iron, in each knee.
    Lodging knees, oak.

Upper deck - Beams, HP, 15"S x 10"M.
    Hanging knees, Hk. 28 bolts, 1⅛" iron, in each knee.
    Lodging knees, Hk.

Champion of the Seas #1,2

Ref.1
Lower deck - Beams (32), HP, 16"S x 15"M.
    Hanging and lodging knees, WO.

Middle deck - Beams (34), HP, 15"S x 12"M.
    Hanging and lodging knees, Hk.

Upper deck - Beams (35), HP, 15"S x 8"M.
    Hanging and lodging knees, Hk.

Ref.2
Lower deck - Beams, PP, 15"S x 14"M at center, 10½"M at clamps. Let into
    clamp and secured with 4 bolts, iron.
    Hanging knees, WO, 11" to 12"S, 6½' to 7' body, 4½' to 5' arm,
        24" throat. Foot rests on a lap stringer. 20 bolts in each
        knee, 1⅛" iron in body, 1" iron in arm.
    Lodging knees, WO, 7" to 8"S, 3½' to 4' arm and body, 26", 28" and
        30" throats. 8 bolts, iron, in beam.

Middle deck - Beams, PP, 15"S x 15"M at center, 10½"M at clamps. Secured
    to clamp with 4 bolts, iron.
    Hanging knees, WO, 10" to 11"S, 4' to 4½' arm and body, 22" and 24"
        throats. Foot rests on standing strakes. 18 bolts in each knee,
        1" and 1¼" iron.
    Lodging knees, WO, 10" to 11"S, 4½' to 5' arm and body, 28" throat.
        Bolt nearest the end of bodies goes through both and is riveted

Upper deck - Beams, PP, 16"S x 10"M. Secured to clamp with 4 bolts, 1⅛"
    and 1¼", iron.
    Hanging knees, Hk, 10" to 12"S, 4½' arm and body, 21" throat. Foot
        rests on standing strakes. 15 and 16 bolts, 1⅛" and 1¼" iron,
        through each knee.
    Lodging knees, Hk and WO, 7"S, 3½' to 4' arm and body.

Charger #1

Lower deck - Beams (26), HP, 16"S x 15"M.
    Hanging knees, WO· 16 bolts, iron, in each knee.
    Lodging knees, WO, 8"S. Bolts in body are clinched.

Upper deck - Beams (27), HP, 15"S x 10"M.
    Hanging knees, Hk, 10" to 12"S, 3½' arm, 4'-8" body, 22" throat.
        Secured with 22 bolts. Some in body are driven from outside,
        clinched on knee. 4 bolts in arm driven through beam, clinched
        on knee. All bolts are iron.
    Lodging knees, Hk, 7"S. Scarphed in every berth, driven in through
        frame, clinched on knee.

Charmer

Table 14.1. *Continued.*

Cleopatra   #1

    Lower deck - Beams, HP, 16"S x 16"M.
        Hanging and lodging knees, oak.

    Upper deck - Beams, HP, 16"S x 10"M.
        Hanging and lodging knees, Hk.

Climax   #1

    Lower deck - Beams, HP, 15"S x 15"M.
        Hanging and lodging knees, WO.

    Upper deck - Beams, HP, 15"S x 9"M.
        Hanging and lodging knees, Hk.

Coeur de Lion   #1

    Lower deck - Beams, HP, 14"S x 14"M.
        Hanging and lodging knees, NHWO.

    Upper deck - Beams, HP, 14"S x 10"M.
        Hanging and lodging knees, Hk.

Comet

Cyclone   #3

    Lower deck - Beams, ?
        Hanging knees, MWO, 9" to 13"S, well fastened. Body rests on a
           built-in stringer, 12" x 14".
        Lodging knees, MWO.

    Upper deck -

Daring   #1

    Lower deck - Beams, ?, 16"S x 15"M.
        Hanging knees, WO. Body rests on a built-in stringer. "Stout
           and strongly fastened."
        Lodging knees, WO. "Stout, strongly fastened."

    Upper deck - Beams, ?, 16"S x 8½"M.
        Hanging and lodging knees, WO. "Stout and strongly fastened."

Dauntless   #1

    Lower deck - Beams, HP, 16"S x 16"M.
        Hanging knees, MWO, 13" to 11"S, 4½' arm, 6' body, 20" to 24"
           throats. 24 bolts, iron, in each knee.
        Lodging knees, MWO, 10"S. Scarphed in every berth. Closely bolted.

    Upper deck - Beams, HP, 16"S x 10"M.
        Hanging knees, Hk, 24 bolts, iron, in each knee.
        Lodging knees, Hk, in proportion.

Donald McKay   #1,2

    Ref.1
    Lower deck - Beams, PP, 17" sq. to 15" sq.
        Hanging knees, WO, 18 iron bolts in each. Foot rests on a lap
           stringer.
        Lodging knees, WO.

    Middle deck - Beams, PP, 17" sq. to 15" sq.
        Hanging knees, WO. 18 iron bolts in each.
        Lodging knees, WO.

    Upper deck - Beams, PP, 15"S x 10"M.
        Hanging and lodging knees, Hk.

    Note: A total of 96 beams under the three decks.

    Ref.2
    Lower deck - Beams, PP, 15"S x 15"M to 11"M at clamps. Let into clamp
        and bolted.
        Hanging knees, WO, 12" to 11"S, 4½' to 5' arm, 6½' to 7' body,
           24" throat. 20 bolts 1⅛" iron in throat, all others 1" iron.
           Foot rests on a lap stringer.
        Lodging knees, WO, 8"S, 3½' and 4' arms, 30" throat. 8 bolts,
           1" iron, through beams.

    Middle deck - Beams, PP, 16"S x 15"M at center, 10½"M at clamps.
        Hanging knees, WO, 10" to 11"S, 3½' arm, 4' body, 24" throat.
           Foot rests on standing strakes. 18 bolts in each knee,
           1" and 1¼" iron.
        Lodging knees, WO, 10"S, 4½' to 5' arms, 28" throat.

    Upper deck - Beams, PP, 16"S x 10"M.
        Hanging knees, Hk, 12"S, 4½' arms, 20" to 22" throats. 16 bolts,
           1⅛" and 1¼" iron.
        Lodging knees, 7"S, 3½' and 4' arms.

Don Quixote   #1

    Lower deck - Beams, HP, 16"S x 16"M.
        Hanging and lodging knees, WO. "Stout and closely bolted."

    Upper deck - Beams, HP, 16"S x 10"M.
        Hanging and lodging knees, Hk. "Stout and closely bolted."

Eagle   #5

    All deck beams, GP. All knees, WO.

Eagle Wing   #1

    Lower deck - Beams, HP, 16"S x 16"M.
        Hanging and lodging knees, WO. "Stout and closely bolted."

    Upper deck - Beams, HP, 16"S x 9"M.
        Hanging and lodging knees, HP. "Stout and closely bolted."

Edwin Forrest   #1

    Lower deck - Beams, ?
        Hanging knees, WO. Foot rests on a built-in stringer.
        Lodging knees.

    Upper deck - Beams, ?
        Hanging and lodging knees.

Electric Spark   #1

    Lower deck - Beams, PP or YP.
        Hanging and lodging knees, WO. "Stout and well fastened."

    Upper deck - Beams, PP or YP.
        Hanging and lodging knees, "stout and well fastened."

Ellen Foster   #1

    Lower deck - Beams (22), HP, 17"S x 16"M.
        Hanging knees, WO, 12" to 9"S, 4' arm, 5½' body, 22" throat. Foot
           rests on a built-in stringer. 14 to 18 bolts, iron, in each knee.
        Lodging knees, WO. Scarphed in every berth.

    Upper deck - Beams (24), HP, 15"S x 9"M.
        Hanging and lodging knees, Hk.

Empress of the Sea   #1,2

    Ref.1
    Lower deck - Beams, HP, 16"S x 15"M at center, tapered toward clamps.
        Hanging knees, WO, 10" to 13"S, 20" to 22" throats.
        Lodging knees, WO. Scarphed in every berth.

    Middle deck - Beams, HP, 16"S x 15"M at center, tapered toward clamps.
        Hanging knees, WO, 10" to 13"S, 20" to 22" throats.
        Lodging knees, WO. Scarphed in every berth.

    Upper deck - Beams, HP, 16"S x 10"M.
        Hanging knees, Hk.
        Lodging knees, Hk. Scarphed in every berth.

    Ref.2
    Lower deck - Beams, PP, 15"S x 14"M at center, 10½"M at clamps. Let into
        clamp and secured with 4 bolts, iron.
        Hanging knees, WO, 11" to 12"S, 4½' to 5' arm, 6' to 6½' body,
           24" throat. Foot rests on a lap stringer. 20 bolts in each
           knee, 1⅛"iron in body, 1" iron in arm.
        Lodging knees, WO, 7" to 8"S, 3½' to 4' arm and body, 26", 28" and
           30" throats. 8 bolts, iron, in beam.

    Middle deck - Beams (28), PP, 15"S x 15"M at center, 10½"M at clamps.
        Secured to clamp with 4 bolts, iron.
        Hanging knees, WO, 10" to 11"S, 4½' to 4' arm and body, 22" and 24"
           throats. Foot rests on standing strakes. 18 bolts in each knee,
           1" and 1¼" iron.
        Lodging knees, WO, 10" to 11"S, 4½' to 5' arm and body, 28" throat.
           Bolt nearest the end of bodies goes through both and is riveted.

    Upper deck - Beams, PP, 16" and 15"S, 10" and 9"M. Secured to clamp with
        4 bolts, 1⅛" and 1¼", iron.
        Hanging knees, Hk, 10" to 12"S, 4½' arm and body, 21" throat. Foot
           rests on standing strakes. 15 or 16 bolts, 1⅛" and 1¼" iron,
           through each knee.
        Lodging knees, Hk and WO, 7"S, 3½' to 4' arm and body.

Table 14.1. *Continued.*

Vessel & Ref.#

Endeavor #1

Lower deck - Beams, HP, 15"S x 14"M at center, tapered toward the
     clamps and bolted.
   Hanging knees, WO, 10" to 12"S, 20" to 22" throats. Foot rests
      on a lap stringer. 20 bolts, iron, in each knee.
   Lodging knees.

Upper deck - Beams, HP, 16"S x 10"M.
   Hanging knees, Hk. 20 bolts, iron, in each knee.
   Lodging knees.

Eringo Bark #1

Main deck - Beams, oak, 14"S x 12"M.
   Hanging and lodging knees, oak.

Eureka #4

Lower deck - Beams, YP, 15"S x 13"M, spaced 3' apart.
   Hanging knees, oak, 11"S, 24" throat.
   Lodging knees, oak, 7"S.
   Bosom knees, oak, 7"S.

Upper deck - Beams, YP, 14"S x 10"M.
   Hanging knees, oak, 11"S, 24" throat.
   Lodging knees, oak, 7"S.
   Bosom knees, oak, 7"S.

Fair Wind #1

Lower deck - Beams (27), HP, 15"S x 15"M.
   Hanging knees, WO, 10" to 13"S, 20" to 24" throats. 15 to 18 bolts,
      iron, in each knee.
   Lodging knees, WO.

Upper deck - Beams (28), HP, 15"S x 10"M.
   Hanging knees, WO, 10" to 13"S, 20" to 24" throats. 15 to 18 bolts,
      iron, in each knee.
   Lodging knees, WO.

Fearless

Fleet Wing #1

Lower deck - Beams, HP.
   Hanging knees, WO. "Stout and closely bolted." Foot rests on a
      built-in stringer.
   Lodging knees, WO. "Stout and closely bolted."

Upper deck - Beams, HP.
   Hanging and lodging knees, WO. "Stout and closely bolted."

Flyaway

Flying Arrow #1

Lower deck - Beams, HP, 16"S x 14"M.
   Hanging knees, WO. "Stout and well secured." Foot rests on a
      built-in stringer.
   Lodging knees, WO. "Stout and well secured."

Upper deck - Beams, HP, 15"S x 9"M.
   Hanging and lodging knees, Hk. "Stout and well secured."

Flying Childers #1

Lower deck - Beams, HP, 16"S x 14"M at center, tapered toward clamps.
   Hanging knees, WO, 12"S, 3½' arm, 4½' body, 20" to 22" throats.
      16 bolts, iron, in each knee.
   Lodging knees, WO, 9"S. Scarphed in every berth.

Upper deck - Beams, HP, 15"S x 10"M at center, tapered toward clamps.
   Hanging and lodging knees, Hk. "About same size as those below."

Flying Cloud #1,2

Ref.1
Lower deck - Beams, SP, 15"S x 15"M.
   Hanging knees, WO. "Very stout and closely fastened." Foot rests
      on a built-in stringer.
   Lodging knees, WO. "Very stout and closely fastened."

Upper deck - Beams, SP, 16"S x 9½"M amidships.
   Hanging and lodging knees, ?. "Very stout and closely fastened."

Ref.2
Lower deck - Beams, PP, 15"S x 14"M at center, 10½"M at clamps. Let into
      clamp and secured with 4 bolts, iron.
   Hanging knees, WO, 11" to 12"S, 4½' to 5' arm, 6' to 6½' body,
      20" to 24" throats. Foot rests on a lap stringer. 20 bolts
      in each knee, 1⅛" iron in body, 1" iron in arm.
   Lodging knees, WO, 7" to 8"S, 3½' to 4' arm and body, 26", 28" and
      30" throats. 8 bolts, 1" iron, in beam

Upper deck - Beams, PP, 15" and 16"S x 10"M. Secured to clamp with
      4 bolts, 1⅛" and 1¼", iron.
   Hanging knees, Hk, 10" to 12"S, 4½' arm and body, 21" throat. Foot
      rests on standing strakes. 15 or 16 bolts, 1⅛" and 1¼" iron,
      through each knee.
   Lodging knees, Hk, 7"S, 3½' to 4' arm and body.

Vessel & Ref.#

Flying Dragon #1

Lower deck - Beams, HP.
   Hanging and lodging knees, WO. "Very stout."

Upper deck - Beams, HP.
   Hanging and lodging knees.

Flying Dutchman

Flying Eagle #1

Lower deck - Beams, ?, 15"S x 15"M.
   Hanging knees, Hk, some 15"S, 24" throat.
   Lodging knees.

Upper deck - Beams, ?, 15"S x 9½"M.
   Hanging knees, Hk.
   Lodging knees.

Flying Fish #1,2

Ref.1
Lower deck - Beams, SP, 16"S x 15"M.
   Hanging knees, WO. Foot rests on a built-in stringer. 18 bolts
      and 4 spikes, iron, in each knee.
   Lodging knees, WO. Scarphed in every berth.

Upper deck - Beams, SP, 16"S x 10"M.
   Hanging knees. 18 bolts and 4 spikes, iron, in each knee.
   Lodging knees.

Ref.2
Lower deck - Beams, PP, 15"S x 14"M at center, 10½"M at clamps. Let into
      clamp and secured with 4 bolts, iron.
   Hanging knees, WO, 11" to 12"S, 4½' to 5' arm, 6' to 6½' body,
      24" throat. Foot rests on a lap stringer. 20 bolts in each
      knee, 1⅛" iron in body, 1" iron in arm.
   Lodging knees, WO, 7" to 8"S, 3½' to 4' arm and body, 26", 28" and
      30" throats. 8 bolts, 1" iron, in beam.

Upper deck - Beams, PP, 15" and 16"S x 10"M. Secured to clamp with
      4 bolts, 1⅛" and 1¼", iron.
   Hanging knees, Hk, 10" to 12"S, 4½' arm and body, 20" throat. Foot
      rests on standing strakes. 15 or 16 bolts, 1⅛" and 1¼" iron,
      through each knee.
   Lodging knees, Hk, 7"S, 3½' to 4' arm and body.

Flying Mist #1

Lower deck - Beams, HP, 15½"S x 15½"M at center, tapered toward clamps.
   Hanging knees, NHWO, 12"S, 3½' arm, 4½' body, 22" throat. 16 bolts
      and 4 spikes, iron, in each knee.
   Lodging knees, NHWO. Scarphed in every berth and bolted from the
      outside.

Upper deck - Beams, HP, 15"S x 9½"M.
   Hanging and lodging knees, Hk. "Nearly the same as those below in
      size and fastening."

Galatea #1

Lower deck - Beams, HP.
   Hanging and lodging knees, WO.

Upper deck - Beams, HP.
   Hanging and lodging knees, WO.

Game Cock #1

Lower deck - Beams, HP.
   Hanging and lodging knees, WO. "Well fastened."

Upper deck - Beams, HP.
   Hanging and lodging knees "well fastened."

Gazelle #4

Lower deck - Beams, PP.
   Hanging knees, WO.
   Lodging (deck) knees, WO.

Upper deck - Beams, PP.
   Hanging knees, WO.
   Lodging (deck) knees, WO.

Gem of the Ocean #1

Lower deck - Beams.
   Hanging and lodging knees, oak.

Upper deck - Beams.
   Hanging and lodging knees, Hk.

Golden Eagle #1

Lower deck - Beams, HP, 15"S x 15"M.
   Hanging knees, WO. Foot rests on a built-in stringer.
   Lodging knees, WO.

Upper deck - Beams, HP, 15"S x 9"M.
   Hanging and lodging knees, Hk. "Finely fitted and well bolted."

Table 14.1. *Continued.*

Golden Fleece (2nd) #1
    Hold - Beams (13), HP.
        Hanging and lodging knees, WO.

    Lower deck - Beams, HP.
        Hanging and lodging knees, WO. "Very stout and well fastened."

    Upper deck - Beams, HP.
        Hanging and lodging knees, ?. "Very stout and well fastened."

Golden Light #1
    Lower deck - Beams, HP, 15"S x 14"M. Ends bolted through the clamps.
        Hanging knees, WO, 10" to 12"S, 3½' arm, 5' body, 20" to 23" throats.
            Foot rests on a built-in stringer. 16 to 18 bolts, iron, in each knee.
        Lodging knees, WO. Scarphed in every berth.

    Upper deck - Beams, HP, 15"S x 10"M. Ends bolted through the clamps.
        Hanging knees, Hk, 10" to 12"S, 3½' arm, 5' body, 20" to 23" throats.
            (Foot probably rests on standing strakes.) 16 to 18 bolts, iron,
            in each knee.
        Lodging knees, Hk. Scarphed in every berth.

Golden West #1
    Lower deck - Beams, HP.
        Hanging and lodging knees, WO.

    Upper deck - Beams, HP.
        Hanging and lodging knees.

Grace Darling #1
    Lower deck - Beams, ?, 15"S x 15"M.
        Hanging knees, WO, 10" to 13"S, 3' arm, 5' body, 20" to 24" throats.
            Foot rests on a built-in stringer. 20 bolts and 4 spikes, iron,
            in each knee.
        Lodging knees, WO.

    Upper deck - Beams, ?, 15"S x 9"M.
        Hanging and lodging knees, WO.

Great Republic #10,2
    Ref.10
    Lower deck - Beams (38), HP, 16"S x 15"M.
        Hanging knees, WO, 10" to 13"S, 4' to 4½' arm, 5' to 6' body, 22" to
            24" throats. Foot rests on a lap stringer. 20 bolts, 1¼" iron,
            and 4 spikes, iron, in each knee.
        Lodging knees, WO, 8"S, 18" throat, 1½" iron bolts. Long scarph in
            every berth.

    Middle deck - Beams (40), HP, 16"S x 15"M.
        Hanging knees, WO, 10" to 13"S, 4' to 4½' arm, 5' to 6' body, 22" to
            24" throats. 20 bolts, 1¼" iron, and 4 spikes, iron, in each knee.
        Lodging knees, WO, 8"S, 18" throat, 1¼" iron bolts. Long scarph in
            every berth.

    Upper deck - Beams (41 total), HP; 16 @ 15"S x 12"M, 25 doubled @ 22"S x
        12"M, bolted together.
        Hanging knees, Hk, 10" to 13"S, 4' to 4½' arm, 5' to 6' body, 22" to
            24" throats. 20 bolts, 1¼" iron, and 4 spikes, iron, in each knee.
        Lodging knees, Hk. Long scarph in every berth.

    Also lodging knees long scarphed in every berth to both sides of a center
        line longitudinal beam, 14"S x 8"M.

    Spar deck - Beams (89), HP, variable sizes, closely spaced.
        Dagger knees, Hk, all of very light scantlings.
        Lodging knees, Hk, 8"S. Scarphed in every berth and closely bolted.

    Ref.2
    Lower deck - Beams, PP, 15"S x 15"M at center, 12"M at clamps. Let into
        clamp and secured with 4 bolts, iron.
        Hanging knees, WO, 11" to 14"S, 4½' to 5' arm, 7' to 7½' body,
            26" throat. Foot rests on a lap stringer. 20 bolts, iron, in
            each knee, 1⅛" in body, 1" in arm.
        Lodging knees, WO, 7" to 8"S, 3½' to 4' arm and body, 26", 28" and
            30" throats. 8 bolts, iron, in beam.

    Middle deck - Beams (40), PP, 15"S x 15"M at center, 11"M at clamps.
        Secured to clamp with 4 bolts.
        Hanging knees, WO, 10" to 11"S, 4½' arm, 6' body, 22" to 24" throats.
            Foot rests on standing strakes. 18 bolts, 1" and 1¼"iron,through each knee.
        Lodging knees, WO, 10" to 11"S, 4½' to 5' arm and body, 28" throat.
            Bolt nearest the end of bodies goes through both and is riveted.

    Upper deck - Beams, PP, 20"S x 12"M. Secured to clamp with 4 bolts, 1⅛" or
        1¼" iron.
        Hanging knees, Hk, 13"S, 4½' arm and body, 22" to 24" throats. Foot
            rests on standing strakes. 15 or 16 bolts, 1⅛" and 1¼" iron,
            through each knee.
        Lodging knees, Hk and WO, 7"S, 3½' to 4' arm and body.

Great Republic (rebuilt) #103
    Apparently rebuilt similar to original vessel (See Ref.10) except for
        elimination of the spar deck.

Henry Hill Bark #1
    Hold - Deck laid forward only, from 5' abaft the foremast.
        Beams (11), HP, 14"S x 10"M.
        Hanging knees, none installed.
        Lodging knees, WO.

    Upper deck - Beams (16), ?, 11 under upper deck, 5 under cabin deck.
        Hanging knees.
        Lodging knees.

Herald of the Morning #12
    Lower deck - Beams, YP, 15"S x 13"M.
        Hanging knees, WO, 7", 8" and 10"S. Secured with 1⅛" bolts, iron,
            riveted.
        Lodging knees, WO. Same as above.

    Upper deck - Beams, YP, 13"S x 9"M.
        Hanging knees, WO. Same as lower deck.
        Lodging knees, WO. Same as lower deck.

Hoogly #1
    Lower deck - Deck laid forward of foremast and abaft the mizzen mast only.
        Beams, HP, 16"S x 14"M.
        Hanging knees, WO, 12"S, 24" throat.
        Lodging knees, WO.

    Middle deck - Beams, HP, 16"S x 14"M.
        Hanging knees, WO, 12"S, 24" throat.
        Lodging knees, WO.

    Upper deck - Beams, HP, 14"S x 10"M.
        Hanging knees.
        Lodging knees.

Hurricane

Indiaman #1
    Lower deck - Beams, HP, 16"S x 15"M.
        Hanging knees, WO. "Very stout." Foot rests on a lap stringer.
        Lodging knees, WO. "Very stout."

    Upper deck - Beams, HP, 15"S x 10"M.
        Hanging knees, "very stout."
        Lodging knees, "very stout."

Intrepid

Invincible #4
    Lower deck - Beams, HP, "very large."
        Hanging knees, WO, 22" to 25" throats. "Heavily bolted."
        Lodging knees - WO.

    Middle deck - Beams, HP, "very large."
        Hanging knees, WO, 22" to 25" throats. "Heavily bolted."
        Lodging knees, WO.

    Upper deck - Beams, HP, "very large."
        Hanging knees, WO, 22" to 25" throats. "Heavily bolted."
        Lodging knees, WO.

James Baines #1,2
    Ref.1
    "Nearly the same as Champion of the Seas."

    Ref.2
    Lower deck - Beams, PP, 15"S x 14"M at center, 10½"M at clamps. Let into
        clamp and secured with 4 bolts, iron.
        Hanging knees, WO, 11" to 12"S, 6½' to 7' body, 4½' to 5' arm,
            24" throat. Foot rests on a lap stringer. 20 bolts in each
            knee, 1⅛" iron in body, 1" iron in arm.
        Lodging knees, WO, 7" to 8"S, 3½' to 4' arm and body, 26", 28" and
            30" throats. 8 bolts, iron, in beam.

    Middle deck - Beams, PP, 15"S x 15"M at center, 10½"M at clamps. Secured
        to clamp with 4 bolts, iron.
        Hanging knees, WO, 10" to 11"S, 4' to 4½' arm and body, 22" and 24"
            throats. Foot rests on standing strakes. 18 bolts in each
            knee, 1" and 1¼" iron.
        Lodging knees, WO, 10" to 11"S, 4½' to 5' arm and body, 28" throat.
            Bolt nearest the end of bodies goes through both and is riveted.

    Upper deck - Beams, PP, 16"S x 10"M. Secured to clamp with 4 bolts,
        1⅛" and 1¼", iron.
        Hanging knees, Hk, 10" to 12"S, 4½' arm and body, 21" throat. Foot
            rests on standing strakes. 15 and 16 bolts, 1⅛" and 1¼", iron,
            through each knee.
        Lodging knees, Hk and WO, 7"S, 3½' to 4' arm and body.

Table 14.1. *Continued.*

Vessel & Ref.#

John Bertram   #1
    Lower deck - Beams, HP, 16"S x 14"M.
        Hanging knees, Hk, 8" to 12"S, 3'-8" arm, 4'-5" body, 20" throat.
            Secured with 16 to 18 bolts, iron, in each knee.
        Lodging knees, Hk. "Well fitted and strongly bolted."

    Upper deck - Beams, HP, 16"S x 9½"M.
        Hanging knees, Hk, 8" to 12"S, 3'-8" arm, 4'-11" body, 20" throat.
            Secured with 18 to 20 bolts, iron, in each knee.
        Lodging knees, Hk. "Well fitted and strongly bolted."

John Gilpin   #1
    Lower deck - Beams, HP, 15"S x 15"M.
        Hanging knees, WO, 12"S. 18 bolts, iron, in each knee.
        Dagger knees, WO. Opposite foremast and mainmast only.
        Lodging knees, WO. Scarphed in every berth.

    Upper deck - Beams, HP, 15"S x 10"M.
        Hanging knees, Hk, 12"S. 18 bolts, iron, in each knee.
        Lodging knees, Hk. Scarphed in every berth.

John Land   #1,32   (Built as a duplicate of Winged Arrow."
    Lower deck - Beams, HP, 16"S x 16"M.
        Hanging knees, WO, 9" to 12"S, 3'-3" arm, 5'-2" body, 22" throat.
            Foot rests on a built-in stringer. 15 bolts and 4 spikes,
            iron, in each knee.
        Lodging knees, WO. Scarphed in every berth.

    Upper deck - Beams, HP, 15"S x 10"M.
        Hanging knees, WO, 9" to 12"S, 3'-3" arm, 5'-2" body, 22" throat.
            18 bolts and 4 spikes, iron, in each knee.
        Lodging knees, WO. Scarphed in every berth.

John Stuart   #4
    Lower deck - Beams.
        All knees, WO.

    Middle deck - Beams.
        All knees, WO.

    Upper deck - Beams.
        All knees, Hk.

John Wade   #1
    Lower deck - Beams, HP.
        Hanging knees, WO.
        Lodging knees, WO.

    Upper deck - Beams, HP.
        Hanging knees, WO.
        Lodging knees, WO.

Joseph Peabody   #1
    Hold - Beams (10), HP.
        Hanging knees, none installed.
        Lodging knees, WO.

    Lower deck - Beams, HP, 15"S x 14"M.
        Hanging knees, WO, 10" to 12"S, 22" throat. 18 bolts, iron, in
            each knee, driven alternately from either side.
        Lodging knees, WO, 7½"S. Scarphed in every berth. "Closely bolted."

    Upper deck - Beams, HP, 14"S x 10"M.
        Hanging knees, Hk, 10" to 12"S, 22" throat. 18 bolts, iron, in
            each knee, driven alternately from either side.
        Lodging knees, Hk, 7½"S. Scarphed in every berth. "Closely bolted."

King Fisher   #1
    Lower deck - Beams, HP, 15"S x 15"M.
        Hanging knees, WO.
        Lodging knees, WO.

    Upper deck - Beams, HP, 14"S x 9"M at center, 7½"M at clamps.
        Hanging knees, Hk.
        Lodging knees, Hk.

Lady Franklin

Lamplighter   Bark   #1
    Main deck - Beams.
        Hanging knees, WO. Foot rests on a built-in stringer.
        Lodging knees.

Lightfoot   #1
    Lower deck - Beams, HP.
        Hanging knees, WO.
        Lodging knees, WO.

    Upper deck - Beams, HP.
        Hanging knees, Hk. "Very stout and strongly bolted."
        Lodging knees, Hk. "Very stout and strongly bolted."

Vessel & Ref.#

Lightning   #1,2,32
    Ref.1
    Lower deck - Beams (30), HP, 16"S x 14"M at center, 12"-13"M at clamps.
        Hanging knees, WO, 10" to 12"S, 4' arm, 5½' body, 22" throat. Foot
            rests on a lap stringer. 20 bolts and 4 spikes, iron, in each
            knee.
        Lodging knees, WO, 8"S. Scarphed in every berth. "Closely bolted."

    Upper deck - Beams (32), HP, 14"S x 9"M.
        Hanging knees, Hk, 10" to 12"S, 4' arm, 5½' body, 22" throat.
            20 bolts and 4 spikes, iron, in each knee.
        Lodging knees, Hk, 8"S. Scarphed in every berth. "Closely bolted."

    Ref. 32
        Lightning was built with 2 decks and gangways extending between the
            forecastle and long poop deck. This upper structure was later
            modified to become a third deck.

    Ref.2 (records scantlings for 3 decks.)
    Lower deck - Beams, PP, 15"S x 14"M at center, 10½"M at clamps. Let into
            and bolted to clamp with 4 bolts, iron.
        Hanging knees, WO, 11" to 12"S, 4½' to 5' arm, 6' to 6½' body,
            24" throat. Foot rests on a lap stringer. 20 bolts in each
            knee, 1⅛" iron in body, 1" iron in arm.
        Lodging knees, WO, 7" to 8"S, 3½' to 4' arm and body, 26", 28" and
            30" throats. 8 bolts, iron, in beam.

    Middle deck - Beams (30), PP, 15"S x 15"M at center, 10½"M at clamps.
            Secured to clamp with 4 bolts, iron.
        Hanging knees, WO, 10" to 11"S, 4' to 4½' arm and body, 22" to 24"
            throats. Foot rests on standing strakes. 18 bolts, 1" and 1¼"
            iron, in each knee.
        Lodging knees, WO, 10" to 11"S, 4½' to 5' arm and body, 28" throat.
            Bolt nearest the end of bodies goes through both and is riveted

    Upper deck - Beams, PP, 15" and 16"S, 9" and 10"M. Secured to clamp with
            4 bolts, 1⅛" or 1¼", iron.
        Hanging knees, Hk, 10" to 12"S, 4½' arm and body, 21" throat. Foot
            rests on standing strakes. 15 or 16 bolts, 1⅛" and 1¼" iron,
            in each knee.
        Lodging knees, Hk and WO, 7"S, 3½' to 4' arm and body.

Mameluke   #1
    Lower deck - Beams, PP, vary from 17" sq. to 15" sq.
        Hanging knees, WO. Foot rests on a built-in stringer. 18 bolts and
            4 spikes, iron, in each knee.
        Lodging knees, WO. Scarphed in every berth.

    Upper deck - Beams, PP, 15"S x 9"M.
        Hanging knees, WO. 18 bolts and 4 spikes, iron, in each knee.
        Lodging knees, WO. Scarphed in every berth.

Mary Robinson

Mastiff   #1
    Lower deck - Beams, HP, about 15"S x 15"M at center, tapered toward the
            clamps.
        Hanging knees, WO, 10" to 12"S, 3' arm, 5' body, 18" to 22" throats.
            Foot rests on a lap stringer. 16 bolts and 4 spikes, iron, in
            each knee.
        Lodging knees, WO.

    Upper deck - Beams, HP, 14"S x 10"M.
        Hanging knees, Hk, 10" to 12"S, 3' arm, 5' body, 18" to 22" throats.
        Lodging knees, Hk.

Mermaid   Bark   #1
    Lower deck - Deck laid forward of fore hatchway and aft of main hatchway.
        Beams, HP, 13"S x 12"M. (13"S x 7"M under the decking.)
        Hanging knees, none installed.
        Lodging knees, WO.

    Upper deck - Beams, HP, 13"S x 7"M.
        Hanging knees.
        Lodging knees.

Morning Light   #1
    Lower deck - Beams, YP.
        Hanging knees, NHWO.
        Lodging knees, NHWO.

    Upper deck - Beams, YP.
        Hanging knees.
        Lodging knees.

Table 14.1. *Continued.*

Vessel & Ref.#

Mystery #1

    Lower deck - Beams, HP or YP, 15"S x 14"M. Partner beams are 1" larger
        on the square.
        Hanging knees, WO, 10" to 12"S, 24" throat. Secured with 1" iron,
           driven both ways.
        Lodging knees, WO.

    Upper deck - Beams, HP or YP, 15"S x 10"M.
        Hanging knees, Hk, 10" to 12"S, 24" throat.
        Lodging knees, Hk.

Nightingale

Noonday #1

    Lower deck - Beams, YP, 16" to 16½" sq.
        Hanging knees, NHWO, 9" to 12"S, 45" arm and body, 21" throat.
           14 bolts, iron, clinched and 4 bolts, iron, driven blunt in
           each knee.

    Upper deck - Beams, YP, 15"S x 10"M.
        Hanging knees, Hk, 9" to 12"S, 20" throat. 17 bolts, iron, clinched
           and 1 bolt, iron, driven blunt in throat, in each knee.

Northern Light

Ocean Express #1

    Hold - Beams (16), HP, 16"S x 16"M, between foremast and mizzen mast.
        Hanging knees, none installed.
        Lodging knees, WO.

    Lower deck - Beams (29), HP, 16"S x 16"M.
        Hanging knees, WO, 10" to 12"S, 20" to 22" throats. Foot rests on
           a built-in stringer. 16 to 19 bolts, iron, in each knee.
        Lodging knees, WO.

    Upper deck - Beams (30), HP, 16"S x 10"M.
        Hanging knees, ?, 10" to 12"S, 20" to 22" throats. 16 to 19 bolts,
           iron, in each knee.
        Lodging knees.

Ocean Pearl #1

    Lower deck - Beams, HP, 15"S x 15"M.
        Hanging knees, WO. Foot rests on a lap stringer.
        Lodging knees, WO.

    Upper deck - Beams, HP, 15"S x 9"M.
        Hanging knees, Hk.
        Lodging knees, Hk.

Ocean Telegraph #5

    All beams, HP.

Onward #1

    Upper deck - Beams.
        Hanging knees, WO.
        Lodging knees, WO.

    Lower deck - Beams.
        Hanging knees, Hk.
        Lodging knees, Hk.

Osborne Howes

Panther

Phantom #1

    Lower deck - Beams, HP, 16"S x 16"M.
        Hanging knees, WO and Hk, 12" to 13"S, 20" to 24" throats.
        Lodging knees.

    Upper deck - Beams, HP, 16"S x 10"M at center, tapered toward the clamps.
        Hanging knees, WO and Hk. "Nearly the same size as lower deck knees."
        Lodging knees.

Queen of Clippers #1

    Lower deck - Beams, HP, 16"S x 16"M.
        Hanging knees, WO. "Very stout."
        Lodging knees, WO. "Very stout."

    Upper deck - Beams, HP, 16"S x 10"M.
        Hanging knees, Hk. "Very stout."
        Lodging knees, Hk. "Very stout."

Queen of the Pacific

Queen of the Seas #1

    Lower deck - Beams, HP, 16"S x 16"M.
        Hanging knees, WO, 12"S, 20" throat. Foot rests on a built-in stringer.
           16 to 18 bolts, iron, in each knee.
        Lodging knees, WO. Scarphed in every berth.

    Upper deck - Beams, HP, 16"S x 9"M.
        Hanging knees, Hk, 12"S, 20" throat. Foot rests on standing strakes.
           22 bolts, iron, in each knee, except those in ends which rest
           on hooks.
        Lodging knees, Hk. Scarphed in every berth.

Vessel & Ref.#

Quickstep Bark #1

    Lower deck - Beams, HP, 14"S x 14"M.
        Hanging knees, WO, 10"S, 18" throat. 14 bolts, iron, in each knee.
        Lodging knees, WO.

    Upper deck - Beams, HP, 13"S x 7"M.
        Hanging knees, Hk.
        Lodging knees, Hk.

    Note: A total of 43 beams under the decks.

Racehorse Bark #1

    Hold - Deck laid forward and aft only; midships open.
        Beams, HP, 10"S x 11"M.
        Hanging knees, none installed.
        Lodging knees, WO. Scarphed in every berth.

    Upper deck - Beams, HP, 10"S x 11"M.
        Hanging knees, WO. Foot rests on standing strake over hold beams.
        Lodging knees.

Racer #3

    Lower deck - Beams, SP.
        Hanging knees, oak, 10" to 12"S.
        Lodging knees, oak, 10" to 12"S.

    Middle deck - Beams, SP.
        Hanging knees, half oak, half SP. 20 bolts, iron, in each knee.
        Lodging knees, half oak, half SP. 20 bolts, iron, in each knee.

    Upper deck - Beams, SP.
        Hanging knees.
        Lodging knees.

Radiant #1

    Lower deck - Beams, YP, 16"S x 16"M.
        Hanging knees, WO, 10" to 12"S. 18 bolts, iron, in each knee.
        Lodging knees, WO.

    Upper deck - Beams, YP, 16"S x 10"M.
        Hanging knees, "very stout."
        Lodging knees, "very stout."

Raven #3

    Lower deck - Beams, YP, 14"S x 12"M.
        Hanging knees, WO, 7"S. 14 bolts, $\frac{7}{8}$" iron, in each knee.
        Lodging knees.

    Upper deck - Beams, YP. Ends rest on stringer (clamp).
        Hanging knees, none installed.
        Lodging knees.

Red Jacket #19,46

    Lower deck - Beams, SP, 15"S x 15"M.
        Hanging knees, VWO, 12"S.
        Lodging knees.

    Upper deck - Beams, SP.
        Hanging knees.
        Lodging knees.

Rocket Bark

Robin Hood

Roebuck #1

    Lower deck - Beams, HP, 15"S x 12"M.
        Hanging knees, WO. Foot rests on a built-in stringer.
        Lodging knees, WO.

    Upper deck - Beams, HP, 15"S x 8"M.
        Hanging knees.
        Lodging knees.

Romance of the Sea #1

    Lower deck - Beams, HP or YP.
        Knees. Some are WO.

    Upper deck - Beams, HP or YP.
        Knees. Some are WO.

Santa Claus #1

    Lower deck - Beams.
        Hanging knees, WO.
        Lodging knees, WO.

    Upper deck - Beams.
        Hanging knees, WO.
        Lodging knees, WO.

Table 14.1. *Continued.*

Vessel & Ref.#

Saracen #1

    Lower deck – Beams, HP, 15"S x 15"M.
        Hanging knees, MWO, 11" to 13"S, 22" throat. Foot rests on a built-in
            stringer. 20 bolts, 1" to 1⅛" iron, in each knee.
        Lodging knees, MWO, 8"S. Scarphed in every berth.

    Upper deck – Beams, HP, 15"S x 10"M.
        Hanging knees, MWO, 11" to 13"S, 22" throat.
        Lodging knees, MWO, 8"S. Scarphed in every berth.

Sea Bird Bark #1

    Hold – Half-deck laid aft of main hatchway; deck laid forward of fore
        hatchway. Remainder of hold is open.
        Beams, HP and Hk.
        Hanging knees, none installed.
        Lodging knees, WO. "Strong."

    Main deck – Beams, HP and Hk.
        Hanging knees.
        Lodging knees, WO. "Strong."

Seaman's Bride #4

    Lower deck – Beams.
        Hanging knees.
        Lodging knees.

    Upper deck – Beams dovetailed into clamps.
        Hanging knees. "A full set".
        Lodging knees. "A full set."

Sea Serpent #47

    Beams, Hk. Knees, WO.

Shooting Star #1

    Lower deck – Beams, HP, 16"S x 16"M amidships. (Apparently tapered
        toward the clamps.)
        Hanging knees, WO, 10" to 12"S, 20" to 22" throats. 14 to 16 bolts
            and 4 spikes, iron, in each knee.
        Lodging knees, WO. Scarphed in every berth.

    Upper deck – Beams, HP, 15½"S x 8½"M.
        Hanging knees, Hk, 10" to 12"S, 20" to 22" throats. 14 to 16 bolts
            and 4 spikes, iron, in each knee.
        Lodging knees, Hk. Scarphed in every berth.

Sierra Nevada #1

    Lower deck – Beams, HP, 16"S x 16"M at center, tapered toward the clamps.
        Hanging knees, NHWO, 12"S, 18" to 22" throats. 18 bolts and 4 spikes,
            iron, in each knee.
        Lodging knees.

    Middle deck – Beams, HP, 16"S x 16"M at center, tapered toward the clamps.
        Hanging knees, NHWO, 12"S, 18" to 22" throats. 18 bolts and 4 spikes,
            iron, in each knee.
        Lodging knees.

    Upper deck – Beams, HP, 16"S x 8"M.
        Hanging knees, NHWO.
        Lodging knees.

    Note: A total of 90 beams under the three decks.

Silver Star #1

    Lower deck – Beams, HP, 15"S x 15"M at center, tapered toward the clamps.
        Hanging knees, WO, 10" to 12"S, 20" to 22" throats. Foot rests on a
            lap stringer. 15 bolts and 4 spikes, iron, in each knee.
        Lodging knees.

    Upper deck – Beams, HP, 14"S x 10"M.
        Hanging knees, Hk. Foot rests on standing strakes.
        Lodging knees, Hk. Scarphed in every berth.

Southern Cross #1

    Lower deck – Beams, SP, 15"S x 14"M.
        Hanging knees, MWO, 10" to 12"S, 3½' arm, 5' body, 18" to 22" throats.
            16 to 19 bolts and 4 spikes, iron, in each knee.
        Lodging knees, MWO. Scarphed in every berth.

    Upper deck – Beams, SP, 15"S x 9"M.
        Hanging knees, Hk. Foot rests on standing strakes.
        Lodging knees, Hk.

Vessel & Ref.#

Sovereign of the Seas #1,2

    Ref.1
    Hold – Beams (5), HP. 3 forward and 2 aft.
        Hanging knees, WO.
        Lodging knees.

    Lower deck – Beams, HP, 15"S x 15"M.
        Hanging knees, WO. Foot rests on a built-in stringer.
        Lodging knees.

    Upper deck – Beams, HP, 16"S x 10"M.
        Hanging knees, Hk. 20 bolts and 4 spikes, iron, in each knee.
        Lodging knees.

    Ref.2
    Lower deck – Beams, PP, 15"S x 14"M at center, 10½" at clamps. Let into
        and bolted to clamp with 4 bolts, iron.
        Hanging knees, WO, 11" to 12"S, 4½' to 5' arm, 5½' to 7' body,
            24" throat. Foot rests on a lap stringer. 20 bolts, iron, in
            each knee, 1⅛" in body, 1" in arm.
        Lodging knees, WO, 7" to 8"S, 3½' to 4' arm and body, 26", 28" and
            30" throats. 8 bolts, iron, in beam.

    Middle deck – Beams (31), PP, 15"S x 15"M at center, 10½" at clamps.
        Secured to clamp with 4 bolts, iron.
        Hanging knees, WO, 10" to 11"S, 4' to 4½' arm and body, 22" to 24"
            throats. Foot rests on standing strakes. 18 bolts, 1" and 1¼"
            iron, in each knee.
        Lodging knees, WO, 10" to 11"S, 4½' to 5' arm and body, 28" throat.
            Bolt nearest the end of bodies goes through both and is riveted.

    Upper deck – Beams, PP, 15" and 16"S x 10"M. Secured to clamp with 4 bolts,
        1⅛" or 1¼" iron.
        Hanging knees, Hk, 12"S, 4½' arm and body, 20" to 22" throats. Foot
            rests on standing strakes. 15 or 16 bolts, 1⅛" and 1¼" iron,
            in each knee.
        Lodging knees, Hk and WO, 7"S, 3½' to 4' arm and body.

Spitfire #1

    Lower deck – Beams, HP, 16"S x 16"M.
        Hanging knees, WO. "Long arms and bodies." 20 bolts, iron, in each
            knee, except toward the ends of vessel.
        Lodging knees, WO.

    Upper deck – Beams, HP, 16"S x 10"M.
        Hanging knees, ?. "Long arms and bodies."
        Lodging knees.

Staffordshire #1,2

    Ref.1
    Hold – Beams (10), HP.
        Hanging knees, WO, 12"S, 24" throat. 16 to 18 bolts, iron, in each
            knee.
        Lodging knees, WO. Scarphed in every berth.

    Lower deck – Beams, HP, 16"S x 16"M.
        Hanging knees, Hk, 12"S, 24" throat. 16 to 18 bolts, iron, in each
            knee.
        Lodging knees, Hk. Scarphed in every berth

    Middle deck – Beams, HP, 16"S x 12"M.
        Hanging knees.
        Lodging knees.

    Upper deck – Beams, HP, 16"S x 10"M.
        Hanging knees.
        Lodging knees.

    Ref.2
    Lower deck – Beams, PP, 15"S x 14"M at center, 10½"M at clamps. Let into
        and secured to clamp with 4 bolts, iron.
        Hanging knees, WO, 10" to 11"S, 4½' to 5' arm, 6' to 6½' body, 22" to
            23" throats. Foot rests on a lap stringer. 20 bolts in each
            knee, 1⅛" iron in body, 1" iron in arm.
        Lodging knees, WO, 7" to 8"S, 3½' to 4' arm and body, 26", 28" and
            30" throats. 8 bolts, iron, in beam.

    Middle deck – Beams, PP, 15"S x 15"M at center, 10½"M at clamps. Secured
        to clamp with 4 bolts, iron.
        Hanging knees, WO, 10" to 11"S, 4' to 4½' arm and body, 22" to 24"
            throats. Foot rests on standing strakes. 18 bolts, 1" and 1¼"
            iron, in each knee.
        Lodging knees, WO, 10" to 11"S, 4½' to 5' arm and body, 28" throat.
            Bolt nearest the end of bodies goes through both and is riveted.

    Upper deck – Beams, PP, 15" and 16"S x 10"M. Secured to clamp with 4 bolts,
        1⅛" or 1¼", iron.
        Hanging knees, Hk, 10" to 12"S, 4½' arm and body, 20" throat. Foot
            rests on standing strakes. 15 or 16 bolts, 1⅛" and 1¼" iron,
            in each knee.
        Lodging knees, Hk and WO, 7"S, 3½' to 4' arm and body.

Table 14.1. *Continued.*

Vessel & Ref.#

Stag Hound   #1,2

    Ref.1
    Lower deck - Beams, HP, 17"S x 16"M.
        Hanging knees, Hk, 10" to 11"S, 24" to 26" throats. Foot rests on
            a built-in stringer. 16 bolts and 4 spikes, iron, in each
            knee.
        Lodging knees, Hk.

    Upper deck - Beams, HP, 16"S x 10"M.
        Hanging knees, Hk, 10"S, 20" to 22" throats. 18 bolts and 4 spikes,
            iron, in each knee.
        Lodging knees, Hk.

    Ref.2
    Lower deck - Beams, PP, 15"S x 14"M at center, 10½"M at clamps. Let into
            and secured to clamp with 4 bolts, iron.
        Hanging knees, WO, 11" to 12"S, 4½' to 5' arm, 6' to 6½' body, 24"
            throat. Foot rests on a lap stringer. 20 bolts in each knee,
            1⅛" iron in body, 1" iron in arm.
        Lodging knees, WO, 7" to 8"S, 3½' to 4' arm and body, 26", 28" and
            30" throats. 8 bolts, iron, in beam.

    Upper deck - Beams, PP, 15" and 16"S x 10"M. Secured to clamp with 4 bolts,
            1⅛" or 1¼", iron.
        Hanging knees, Hk, 10" to 12"S, 4½' arm and body, 19" throat. Foot
            rests on standing strakes. 15 or 16 bolts, 1⅛" and 1¼" iron,
            in each knee.
        Lodging knees, Hk and WO, 7"S, 3½' to 4' arm and body.

Star of the Union   #1

    Lower deck - Beams, HP.
        Hanging knees, WO.
        Lodging knees, WO.

    Upper deck - Beams, HP.
        Hanging knees, Hk.
        Lodging knees, Hk.

Starr King

Storm King   #1

    Lower deck - Beams, YP, 16"S x 16"M.
        Hanging knees, WO, 12"S, 17" to 22" throats. Foot fitted over a thick
            strake. 18 bolts and 4 spikes, iron, in each knee.
        Lodging knees, WO. Scarphed in every berth. "Closely bolted."

    Upper deck - Beams, YP, 16"S x 9"M.
        Hanging knees, Hk, 12"S, 17" to 22" throats. 18 bolts and 4 spikes,
            iron, in each knee.
         Lodging knees, Hk. Scarphed in every berth. "Closely bolted."

Sultana   Bark   #1

    Hold - Beams, HP, 13"S x 8"M.
        Hanging knees, none installed.
        Lodging knees, Hk. Scarphed in every berth.

    Main deck - Beams, HP, 13"S x 8"M. Included are the partner beams and
            three others of equal size - one is between mainmast and mizzen
            mast, two are between foremast and mainmast.
        Hanging knees, Hk. Foot rests on a thick strake. Bolted from outside
            and riveted.
        Dagger (diagonal) knees, Hk. Fitted only in way of oversize beams
            under the main deck.
        Lodging knees, Hk. Scarphed in every berth. Bolted from outside and
            riveted.

Sunny South

Surprise   #1

    Lower deck - Beams (24), SP, 16"S x 14"M.
        Hanging knees, WO, 12"S, 3½' arm, 5' body (docked), 22" to 24"
            throats. 18 bolts and 4 spikes, iron, in each knee.
        Lodging knees, WO. "Stout in proportion and equally well fastened."

    Upper deck - Beams (27), SP, 16"S x 10"M.
        Hanging knees, Hk, 9" to 11"S. Foot rests on standing strakes.
            18 bolts and 4 spikes, iron, in each knee.
         Lodging knees, Hk.

Swallow   #1

    Lower deck - Beams, YP.
        Hanging knees, mostly WO.
        Lodging knees, mostly WO.

    Upper deck - Beams, YP.
        Hanging knees.
        Lodging knees.

Vessel & Ref.#

Sweepstakes

Sword Fish

Syren   #3

    "Knees between decks half oak and half Hk. Fastened with copper bolts."

Telegraph

Thatcher Magoun   #1

    Lower deck - Beams, HP, 16"S x 15"M.
        Hanging knees, WO. Foot rests on a thick strake of bilge ceiling.
            "Strongly secured."
        Lodging knees, WO.

    Upper deck - Beams, HP, 15"S x 10"M.
        Hanging knees, Hk.
        Lodging knees, Hk.

Tornado

Uncowah

War Hawk   #1

    Lower deck - Beams, HP, 16"S x 15"M.
        Hanging knees, WO, 9" to 12"S, 18" to 20" throats. Foot rests on a
            built-in stringer. 16 bolts, iron, in each knee.
        Lodging knees, WO.

    Upper deck - Beams, HP, 16"S x 8½"M.
        Hanging knees, ?, 9" to 12"S, 18" to 20" throats. 16 bolts, iron,
            in each knee.
        Lodging knees.

Water Witch   #1

    Lower deck - Beams, HP, 16"S x 16"M.
        Hanging knees, NHWO. Foot rests on a lap stringer.
        Lodging knees.

    Upper deck - Beams, HP, 15"S x 9"M.
        Hanging knees, Hk.
        Lodging knees, Hk.

Western Continent

Westward Ho   #1,2

    Ref.1
    Lower deck - Beams, HP, 16"S x 16"M.
        Hanging knees, WO, 12"S, 22" throat. Foot rests on a lap stringer.
            20 bolts and 4 spikes, iron, in each knee.
        Lodging knees, WO. Scarphed in every berth.

    Upper deck - Beams, HP, 15"S x 8"M.
        Hanging knees, Hk, 12"S, 22" throat. 20 bolts and 4 spikes, iron,
            in each knee.
        Lodging knees, Hk. Scarphed in every berth.

    Ref.2
    Lower deck - Beams, PP, 15"S x 14"M at center, 10½"M at clamps. Let into
            clamp and secured with 4 bolts, iron.
        Hanging knees, WO, 11" to 12"S, 4½' to 5' arm, 6' to 6½' body,
            24" throat. Foot rests on a lap stringer. 20 bolts in each
            knee, 1⅛" iron in body, 1" iron in arm.
        Lodging knees, WO, 7" to 8"S, 3½' to 4' arm and body, 26", 28" and
            30 " throats. 8 bolts, 1" iron, in beam.

    Upper deck - Beams, PP, 15" and 16"S x 10"M. Secured to clamp with
            4 bolts, 1⅛" and 1¼", iron.
        Hanging knees, Hk, 10" to 12"S, 4½' arm and body, 20 " throat. Foot
            rests on standing strakes. 15 or 16 bolts, 1⅛" and 1¼" iron,
            through each knee.
        Lodging knees, Hk, 7"S, 3½' to 4' arm and body.

West Wind   #1

    Lower deck - Beams, HP.
        Hanging knees, WO.
        Lodging knees, WO.

    Upper deck - Beams, HP.
        Hanging knees.
        Lodging knees.

Whirlwind   #1

    Lower deck - Beams, HP, 15"S x 15"M.
        Hanging knees, oak.
        Lodging knees, oak.

    Upper deck - Beams, HP, 15"S x 8½"M.
        Hanging knees, Hk.
        Lodging knees, Hk.

Table 14.1. *Continued.*

Vessel & Ref.#

Whistler   #1

    Lower deck – Beams, HP, 16"S x 15"M.
        Hanging knees, Hk and NWO , 12"S. 16 bolts, iron, in each knee.
        Lodging knees, Hk and NWO.

    Upper deck – Beams, HP, 15"S x 8"M.
        Hanging knees, Hk.
        Lodging knees, Hk.

Wildfire   Bark

Wild Pigeon   #1

    Lower deck – Beams, HP, 15"S x 14"M.
        Hanging knees, NHWO.
        Lodging knees, NHWO.

    Upper deck – Beams, HP, 15"S x 9"M.
        Hanging knees, Hk, 9" to 11"S, 3½' arm, 5' body, 20" throat. Foot
            rests on upper edge of thick work. 20 bolts, iron, in each knee.
        Lodging knees, Hk. Scarphed in every berth.

Wild Ranger   #1

    Lower deck – Beams.
        Hanging knees, WO.
        Lodging knees, WO.

    Upper deck – Beams.
        Hanging knees, Hk.
        Lodging knees, Hk.

Wild Rover

Winged Arrow   #1

    Lower deck – Beams, HP, 16"S x 16"M.
        Hanging knees, WO, 9" to 12"S, 3'-3" arm, 5'-2" body, 22" throat.
            Foot rests on a built-in stringer. 15 bolts and 4 spikes,
            iron, in each knee.
        Lodging knees, WO. Scarphed in every berth.

    Upper deck – Beams, HP, 15"S x 10"M.
        Hanging knees, WO, 9" to 12"S, 3'-3" arm, 5'-2" body, 22" throat.
            18 bolts and 4 spikes, iron, in each knee.
        Lodging knees, WO. Scarphed in every berth.

Winged Racer   #1

    Lower deck – Beams, HP, 16"S x 16"M.
        Hanging knees, WO, 12"S, 23" throat. Foot rests on a built-in
            stringer. 20 to 24 bolts, iron, in each knee.

        Lodging knees, WO, 9"S. Scarphed in every berth. "Closely bolted."

    Upper deck – Beams, HP, 16"S x 10"M.
        Hanging knees, Hk, 12"S, 23" throat. 20 to 24 bolts, iron, in
            each knee.
        Lodging knees, Hk, 9"S. Scarphed in every berth. "Closely bolted."

Witchcraft   #1

    Lower deck – Beams, SP, 16"S x 16"M.
        Hanging knees, WO, 12"S, 4½' arm, 6' body, 23" throat. 18 bolts
            and 4 spikes, iron, in each knee.
        Lodging knees, WO.

    Upper deck – Beams, SP, 16"S x 10"M.
        Hanging knees, Hk, 12"S, 4½' arm, 6' body, 23" throat. 18 bolts
            and 4 spikes, iron, in each knee.

    Note: "Toward the ends of the ship the sizes of all knees are diminished."

Witch of the Wave   #1

    Lower deck – Beams (40), HP, 16"S x 14"M.
        Hanging knees, NHWO, 10" to 12"S, 3'-8" arm and body, 18" to 21"
            throats. 18 bolts and 4 spikes, iron, in each knee.
        Lodging knees, NHWO, 8"S. Scarphed in every berth. "Closely bolted."

    Upper deck – Beams (42), HP, 14"S x 8½"M.
        Hanging knees, NHWO, 10"S, 3'-7" arm, 4' body, 20" throat. Foot
            rests on standing strakes. 20 bolts and 4 spikes, iron, in
            each knee.
        Lodging knees.

Vessel & Ref.#

Wizard   #1

    Lower deck – Deck laid forward of the foremast and abaft the mizzen
            mast only.
        Beams, HP, 16"S x 16"M at center, tapered toward the clamps.
        Hanging knees, none installed.
        Lodging knees, WO. Scarphed in every berth.

    Middle deck – Beams, HP, 16"S x 16"M at center, tapered toward the clamps.
        Hanging knees, WO. "Very stout and closely bolted."
        Lodging knees, WO. "Very stout and closely bolted."

    Upper deck – Beams, HP, 16"S x 10"M.
        Hanging knees, WO. "Very stout and closely bolted."
        Lodging knees, WO. "Very stout and closely bolted."

    Note: A total of 85 beams under the three decks.

Young America

Young Turk   Bark   #1

    Main deck – Beams, HP, 14"S x 12"M (6 are partner beams, 2 to each mast.)
        Hanging knees, WO. "Strongly secured."
        Lodging knees, WO. "Strongly secured."

(text continued from page 229)

hard, sharp corner or *knuckle*. The end of each leg is termed the *toe*. On the inside of the angle, the curved portion at the intersection of the two legs is the *bosom*.

The development of knees as connectors encompassed three stages: the original wooden knee; its immediate successor, the iron knee; and, ultimately, the modern iron or steel angle that came into existence after the clipper area.

The iron knee existed but found very limited use in clipper ship construction. One example is in *Dauntless*, where such knees were used to secure the head of hold stanchions to the lower deck beams (Figure 13.1, number 12).

The wooden knee, like the modern angle, had specific names for its various parts. It was basically an angle whose legs were identified as the *body* and the *arm*. They could be of equal or unequal length. The projection known as the body was the portion that would be attached to the member of a ship—for example, a frame—which was stout enough to act as a support. If the projections were of unequal length, it was customary to refer to the longer one as the body. The body was invariably secured to the structure first. The unit to be attached and supported—for instance, a beam or a post—was positioned on or against the remaining projection or arm, there to be fastened. The substance of the wood between the heel and bosom of the steel angle was termed the *throat* in the wooden knee.

When calling for a wooden knee, it was necessary to specify the length of body, length of arm, *mould* (dimension) through the throat, the dimension of siding, and the species of wood. In addition, either a *mould* (pattern) or the number of degrees in the included angle must be stated. Any required bevels, as would be needed to fit dagger knees, were specified and accounted for by the mould loft.

Figure 2.1 illustrates the great diversity that existed between the extremes of acuteness and obtuseness of wooden knees. Symbol B in this plate illustrates the most common form of knee to be found on board ship. The included angle between its arms could be anywhere from 45 to 120 degrees, depending upon its location in the vessel. When the included angle was less than 45 degrees, as shown by symbol D, these knees became known as *hooks*. When the angle opened wider than 120 degrees, the older term in ships that preceded the clipper era was "breast hook" due to the fact that this member held the two sides of the ship together across the bluff, well-rounded bows of such ships. (The term survives today, being applicable to the construction of steel ships and small boats alike.) Hooks of this type were virtually unknown to the clipper ship. However, the acute hooks were used in every clipper that was ever built, both in the forward and after ends.

Knees were made in every conceivable size. They ranged from pieces that a man could hold in one hand (such as

knees tying the clamp and transom of a dinghy together) to the sternpost knee used in *Great Republic*, with 20-foot body, 8-foot arm, 5-foot mould through the throat, and 16-inch siding.

Considering that an average large wooden ship with a hull 200 feet long required as many as 1,500 knees of various sizes and configurations, it was inevitable that the supply of such a unique growth as the natural wooden knee would be exhausted in a relatively short length of time. This shortage was felt in Europe long before it became a factor in the United States. Compared to the vast forestation of America, the European sources were quite limited and had been in the process of depletion for many years, until, about the year 1800, the shortage of such "grown" timber reached crisis proportions and forged iron knees were produced to take their place, as described below under the heading "Iron Knees."

The initial use of iron for production of various parts of ships that had been made of wood since time immemorial was approached with great suspicion and caution. The prevailing sentiment was that iron was too rigid and unyielding to be used as a structural component of a wooden ship. This, of course, quickly proved to be a fallacious premise, and iron soon found everlasting favor due to its availability, superior strength, economy of space, and weight-saving features.

The "inexhaustible" supply of shipbuilding timbers in the United States, coupled with the already depleted sources in Europe, resulted in much more rapid ship development overseas where iron was used with increasing success. Thus, for many years, American builders lagged behind their European counterparts.

Beam Knees

The *beam knees* installed in American-built ships of this period were the traditional wooden knees formed by natural growth of trees. They were principally white oak, which made the strongest connections, followed by hackmatack, which was used in the tween-decks where such superior strength was not required.

All knees were of the same general shape, their two arms and the included angle formed by these arms being proportioned and shaped individually to suit a given location. Their designations were determined by the positions they would assume when installed on board a vessel.

There were four such major designations. The first and probably the most familiar was the *hanging knee*, so named because, placed vertically beneath a beam, it appeared to hang from that beam.

The second major designation was that of *lodging knee*. These were installed in a horizontal plane at each end of a beam. Such knees were also installed in wake of hatchways,

Figure 14.1. *Typical wooden knee.*

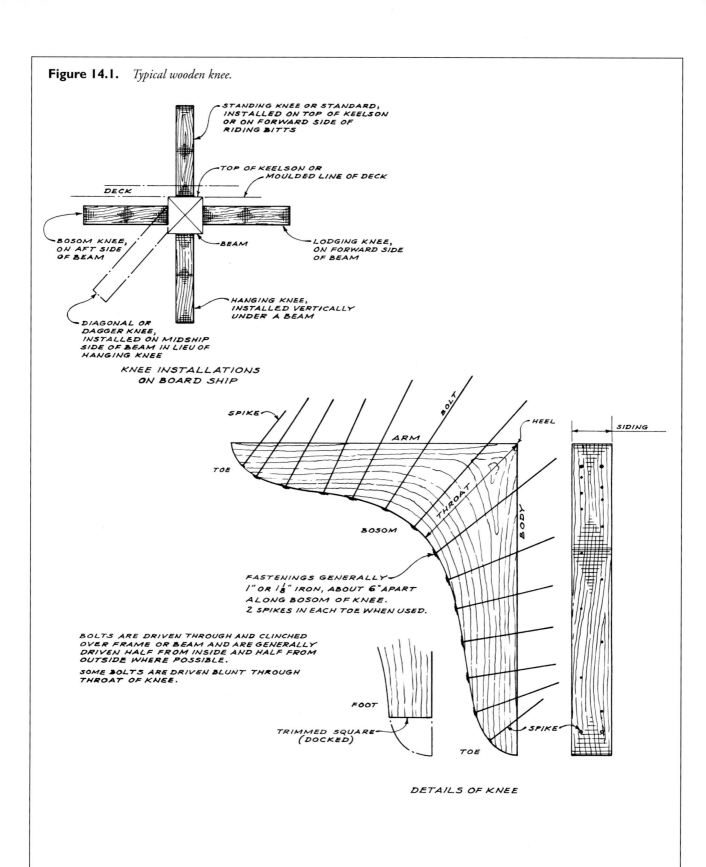

STANDING KNEE OR STANDARD, INSTALLED ON TOP OF KEELSON OR ON FORWARD SIDE OF RIDING BITTS

TOP OF KEELSON OR MOULDED LINE OF DECK

DECK

BOSOM KNEE, ON AFT SIDE OF BEAM

BEAM

LODGING KNEE, ON FORWARD SIDE OF BEAM

HANGING KNEE, INSTALLED VERTICALLY UNDER A BEAM

DIAGONAL OR DAGGER KNEE, INSTALLED ON MIDSHIP SIDE OF BEAM IN LIEU OF HANGING KNEE

KNEE INSTALLATIONS ON BOARD SHIP

SPIKE

BOLT

ARM

HEEL

SIDING

TOE

THROAT

BODY

BOSOM

FASTENINGS GENERALLY 1" OR 1⅛" IRON, ABOUT 6" APART ALONG BOSOM OF KNEE. 2 SPIKES IN EACH TOE WHEN USED.

BOLTS ARE DRIVEN THROUGH AND CLINCHED OVER FRAME OR BEAM AND ARE GENERALLY DRIVEN HALF FROM INSIDE AND HALF FROM OUTSIDE WHERE POSSIBLE.

SOME BOLTS ARE DRIVEN BLUNT THROUGH THROAT OF KNEE.

FOOT

TRIMMED SQUARE (DOCKED)

TOE

SPIKE

DETAILS OF KNEE

as transverse supports for mast partners, and other specific locations throughout a vessel. A lodging knee, by most definitions, was installed on the forward side of the beam. Its counterpart, the *bosom knee*, also by most definitions, was installed on the after side of the beam.

Finally, there was the *dagger knee*, which was secured to the beam at its ends and was angled downward in a position between the hanging knee and the lodging knee. Such knees found great use in ships-of-war since they provided much-needed diagonal bracing and, in addition, helped distribute the considerable load occasioned by the firing of ships' cannon and the resultant recoil impact of the gun carriage on the deck over a beam.

Hanging Knee

The hanging knee, if not the most important type of knee in a ship, was the most visible and obvious. It, along with its fastenings, supported the beam to which it was attached and any load on deck, at the same time tying the two sides of the vessel securely together. The fastenings were iron bolts, generally sixteen to twenty per knee, sometimes augmented by two iron spikes driven through each toe. The knee was located directly under the beam that it was to support, except in unusual cases where it might be necessary to move it toward one or the other of the beam's sides.

The mode of fastening was relatively uniform but not necessarily the same with various builders. Figure 14.2, detail B, illustrates the general bolting patterns. In all cases the through-bolts were headed, then driven and their ends clinched. Some builders drove all bolts from one side, while others favored driving alternately in and out. And, in the fullest thickness of the throat, there were sometimes bolts that were driven blunt.

As this plate shows, there were three usual types of hanging knee installation. The first and simplest consisted of a suitably fitted knee which, when installed, was held in position solely by the strength of its fastenings.

The second type of installation was a knee of the same form as that previously described but with some of its substance removed to allow its body to rest on a ledge formed by thick strakes of the vessel's ceiling. This knee was neatly fitted so that the various surfaces fayed tightly against each other. Seated in this fashion, the bolts do not support the knee but, rather, they expend their energy by holding the various units tightly together.

The final, and by far most frequently used, type of hanging knee installation was made with the foot of the body resting solidly on a built-in stringer or a lap stringer when installed in the hold, or resting solidly on a standing strake when installed in the tween-decks.

As the hold was being ceiled, a squared stringer of scantlings approximately twice the thickness of the ceiling was installed at a suitable distance below the clamp. The ceiling strakes were fitted to accommodate this stringer. The projection provided the solid seat for the knee.

The alternative to the above procedure was to completely ceil the hold, after which a stout stringer was securely *lapped*—laid tightly against—the surface of the ceiling in the same location that would be selected for a built-in stringer (see Figure 12.3).

In cases where hold beams were installed, upon which no deck was to be laid, the general practice was to forgo the installation of any hanging knees because of the lack of any potential vertical load.

Lodging Knee

The lodging knee, also referred to as a *deck knee*, was installed in various fashions, the principal ones being illustrated in Figure 14.2, detail C. These knees accomplished two results. The first and most obvious was to fix the ends of beams so that they were rendered immobile. The second was reinforcement of the ship's sides when the knees were cut and installed with long scaphs as shown in Figure 14.2, detail C (long scarph).

The simplest of these installations was to have one lodging knee and one bosom knee in every *berth* (space) between beams. The toe of each arm was faired to a smooth curve as shown in the figure. The upper surface of any knee was located about 1 inch below the top of beam to allow for circulation of air between the knee and the deck planking.

Fastening followed the same general procedure as with the hanging knees, but with certain differences of detail dictated by arrangement. At each beam end the bolts were generally driven completely through the beam and both knees, driving alternately from one side and then the other; the ends were then riveted. Through-bolts were driven into the bodies and the ship's frames, one bolt piercing each futtock; these, too, were riveted. Finally, in the thickness of the throat one bolt was usually driven blunt.

This particular style of installation was not generally used in the way of clamps due to space limitations and the luxury of having a choice of several superior and stronger methods. However, this installation was used extensively in securing mast partners, half-beams, or headers, and in the wake of hatchways.

A more common practice in securing beam ends was that of providing knees whose bodies were of sufficient length to allow *docking* or trimming the end square. In such cases the lengths of the bodies were cut so that the knees met in every berth, thus completely filling the space. Fastening of the knees was accomplished as before. This installation provided substance over the clamp but did not provide continuity of the assembly due to there being no actual connection of the butted ends.

Figure 14.2. *Beam and knee details.*

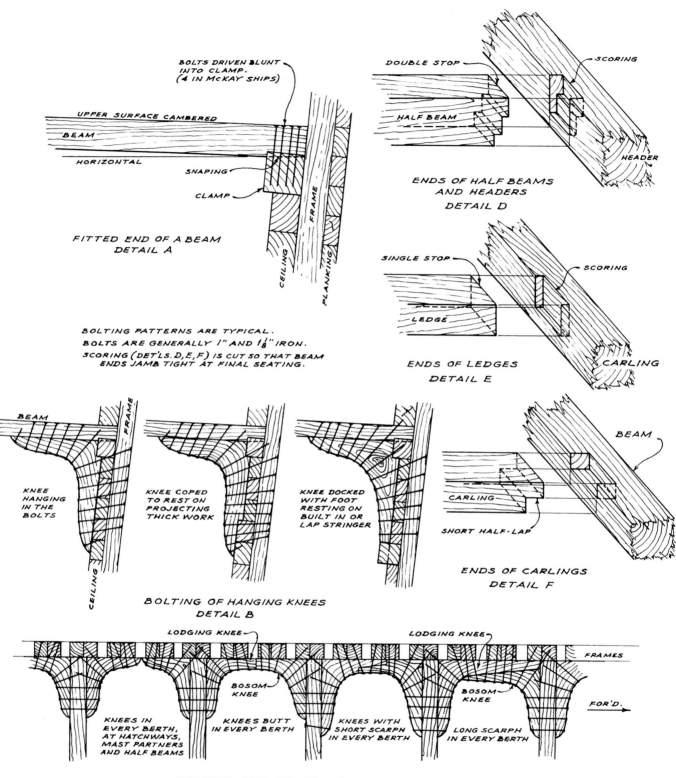

BOLTS DRIVEN BLUNT INTO CLAMP. (4 IN McKAY SHIPS)

UPPER SURFACE CAMBERED

BEAM

HORIZONTAL

SNAPING

CLAMP

CEILING

FRAME

PLANKING

FITTED END OF A BEAM
DETAIL A

BOLTING PATTERNS ARE TYPICAL.
BOLTS ARE GENERALLY 1" AND 1⅛" IRON.
SCORING (DET'LS. D,E,F) IS CUT SO THAT BEAM
ENDS JAMB TIGHT AT FINAL SEATING.

DOUBLE STOP

SCORING

HALF BEAM

HEADER

ENDS OF HALF BEAMS
AND HEADERS
DETAIL D

SINGLE STOP

SCORING

LEDGE

CARLING

ENDS OF LEDGES
DETAIL E

BEAM

FRAME

KNEE HANGING IN THE BOLTS

CEILING

KNEE COPED TO REST ON PROJECTING THICK WORK

KNEE DOCKED WITH FOOT RESTING ON BUILT IN OR LAP STRINGER

BOLTING OF HANGING KNEES
DETAIL B

BEAM

CARLING

SHORT HALF-LAP

ENDS OF CARLINGS
DETAIL F

LODGING KNEE

LODGING KNEE

FRAMES

BOSOM KNEE

BOSOM KNEE

FOR'D.

KNEES IN EVERY BERTH, AT HATCHWAYS, MAST PARTNERS AND HALF BEAMS

KNEES BUTT IN EVERY BERTH

KNEES WITH SHORT SCARPH IN EVERY BERTH

LONG SCARPH IN EVERY BERTH

BOLTING AND SCARPHING OF LODGING KNEES
DETAIL C

A third and more effective installation of lodging knees employed the use of a short scarph through which the ends of each knee were connected. This scarph, when secured in position, provided a continuous belt throughout the length of the vessel. The continuity was achieved by bolts driven through the scarph and futtocks.

The ultimate installation of lodging knees was achieved when the body of the knee was of sufficient length to completely fill the berth between two beams. After it was fitted and temporarily held in position, the bosom knee was cut to shape so that it fayed against the lodging knee and extended along the body until it fitted hard against the throat of the lodging knee, as shown in Figure 14.2, detail C (long scarph). The total assembly was then fastened as previously described. These assemblies, installed in every berth, extended forward and aft along the sides of the vessel and terminated in hooks at stem and stern. Such a structure provided the vessel with an additional belt of tremendous strength, and was universally used.

A detailed inspection of this form of beam end connection discloses a situation where form and terminology seem to be at odds. As stated before, the lodging knee was defined as being installed on the forward side of the beam; the bosom knee was installed on the after side. Figure 14.2, detail C, is drawn with this in mind and appears to accurately portray the above descriptions. However, a question can arise concerning the use of the terms compared to their location, made apparent by two very clear examples.

The packets *Star of Empire* and *Chariot of Fame*,[54] both built by Donald McKay, and the freighting ship *Ocean Monarch*,[24] built by William H. Webb, were built with lapped knees as previously described. However, in each of these vessels the knee arrangement was applied to the forward body only. Aft of amidships the juxtaposition of the two knees was transposed so that the outer knee was now attached to the after side of the beam and the lapped knee was secured to the forward side of the beam. There is no indication that this changed the designation of the two knees. This practice also appears in plans of other Webb vessels.[24] Whether or not other builders adhered to it is difficult to say, since such information is scarce and, in most cases, well hidden if existent at all.

Dagger Knee

The dagger knee, when installed, was pointed downward toward amidships. In the forebody of a vessel, this knee would point down and aft, while in the afterbody the knee would point down and forward.

The reason for this mode of installation was not based on strength but rather on practicality. Installing the dagger knees in this manner allowed the bosom or included angle of the arms to increase as the ends of the ship were approached.

This was essential for providing sufficient room for shipwrights to drive the many fastenings associated with the installation of knees. If the knee were positioned in the opposite direction, the bosom angle would close as the ends of the vessel were approached and accessibility for fastening would soon be nonexistent or, at the very least, extremely limited.

It is interesting to note that this feature or practice of opening the bosom between the legs of an angle was an important consideration in all iron and steel ship construction during the entire period in which mechanical connectors such as rivets or bolts were used to fasten two pieces together. And the reason was the same, namely to allow sufficient room to insert and drive the fastening. Not until the advent of welding, in the 1930s, did this consideration cease to be a factor.

While the dagger knee was widely used in ships-of-war, it found little favor in the building of clipper ships. Throughout the list of ships covered in this book, the specific use of dagger knees is mentioned in only three vessels, and in two instances their use was limited to specific installations. The bark *Sultana* had them installed in way of partner beams and three oversize beams, while in the ship *John Gilpin* it is stated that dagger knees were installed opposite the foremast and mainmast; no other details are noted. The third vessel noted as having dagger knees is *Great Republic*, which is described as being fitted with hackmatack dagger knees of very light scantlings under the beams of her spar deck. These were installed in lieu of hanging knees. When this ship was rebuilt in 1855, these knees disappeared due to the elimination of her old spar deck.

That is the extent of the use of the dagger knee, and, while it cannot be concluded that all other clippers were built without them, it does justify the conclusion that they were apparently thought to be unnecessary.

Iron Knees

Iron knees found little favor in American-built ships of the period, the principal reason being the abundance of naturally formed wooden knees. These were readily available and inexpensive when compared to those made of iron. In addition, they could not always suitably be fabricated for use in all locations where knees were required. For example, the fabrication of a hanging knee suitable for supporting the end of a beam at a frame could have become a complex and costly expedient, especially if such a member was required in great quantities. The use of iron in this form was therefore quite restricted.

Of the vessels included in this book, only one is reported to have had iron knees installed. Paradoxically this vessel was built in the earlier years of the clippers when there was no question or concern about the exhaustive use of timber. She was *Dauntless*, built by Benjamin F. Delano at Medford, Massachusetts, and launched in December 1851.

In this vessel the knees that were fabricated for connecting the hold stanchions to the hold beams were iron forgings. They were used on all stanchions except those in wake of the hatchways. Figure 13.1, assembly 12, illustrates this specific installation. It is obvious that the use of the iron knees consumed minimal space under the beams when compared to the bulk of wooden knees; this saving of space converted directly into space available for cargo. The installation of iron knees required less labor than for wooden knees since fewer bolts were required. Where the wooden knee had a bolt spacing of about 6 inches along the throat, the iron knee could be fastened with bolts spaced about 12 inches apart.

It appears safe to conclude that, categorically, the iron knee was not a factor in clipper ship construction.

Additional Deck Framing

There remained some additional timbers to complete the general complement of beam structure under a vessel's decks. These were half beams, headers, ledges, and carlings, none of which were complex, but each had its individual assignment and general proportions. Figure 14.3 illustrates a typical installation of these members under the deck of a clipper ship.

Half Beams

The *half beam* was the largest of these structural components. It contained no distinction in its own right, since it was merely a deck beam that was interrupted in its complete span of the deck. Its installation in clipper ships occurred only at one location on each deck, namely in the wake of the main hatchway.

In a vessel's construction it was a cardinal rule that no deck opening be of a size whose longitudinal dimension should require the elimination of more than one continuous beam; this was to maintain the vessel's structural integrity. For this reason, only the main hatchway was large enough to require this treatment. Any additional hatchways, companionways, and other openings were constrained to a size that could be accommodated between beams. Due to the general spacing of beams, this consideration limited the greatest fore-and-aft opening to approximately 10 feet. There was no definite limitation to the transverse dimension. However, any size which would exceed approximately one-third of the vessel's breadth was impractical due to the restricted space for handling cargo in the tween-decks and in the hold. In cases where vessels were expected to carry long materials, such as timber, side-loading facilities were provided.

The half beam, at the end that rested on the clamp, was installed, kneed, and fastened in the same manner as all other beams that ranged along the length of the ship. Its inboard, or butt end was cut at the required length to accommodate the proposed hatchway, at which point the end was picked up by a longitudinal header which transferred the load to the beams immediately forward and aft of the half beam. This member was not installed permanently at either end until the header, beams, and associated knees had been fashioned and trimmed to accommodate the entire assembly.

Prior to installation the butt end of the beam was trimmed with a "double stop"[8] which is shown in Figure 14.2, detail D. It cannot be construed that this double stop was the only manner in which the half beam was fashioned at the end. There were numerous variants, all capable of fulfilling the requirements of an adequate connection.

Half beam installations are shown for *Great Republic*,[10] Webb's *Ocean Monarch*,[24] and in the *New York Marine Register*.[21]

Headers

The *header* (Figure 6.2, detail v) which was to support the butt end of the half beam was of approximately the same scantlings as that beam and made of the same variety of wood. It was installed longitudinally, as were carlings, and its purpose was to support the half beam and to transfer one-half of its load to each adjacent deck beam. It was essential that it not only be strong enough to do this but stiff enough so as to not be limber.

The length of the header was equal to the distance between the supporting beams plus the amount of material required to fill the scoring of each beam for a double stop. This "scoring" was the amount of substance removed from the beams in order to provide a seat for the ends of the header, as shown in Figure 14.2, detail D. A double stop was generally reserved for units of considerable depth and snug fit, the relatively shallow depth of each step shortening the distance that the header had to be driven before seating itself solidly on the stops.

After the beams had been scored and the butts of the header shaped, similar scoring was applied to the header where it would receive the half beam. The various units were then placed in position in the ship and driven home permanently. The butt end of the half beam and the ends of the header were secured to the structure with knees (Figure 6.2, detail x) in the same manner as the ends of the beams at the clamps.

Generally the only other use of large headers was as part of the mast partner assemblies. One known exception was in *Great Republic*,[10] where a line of intercostal headers was installed along the centerline of the upper deck from stem to stern. Presumably, this structure was also used when the vessel was rebuilt in 1855.

Header installations are shown for *Great Republic*,[10] *Ocean Monarch*,[24] and in the *New York Marine Register*.[21]

Figure 14.3. *Deck framing arrangements.*

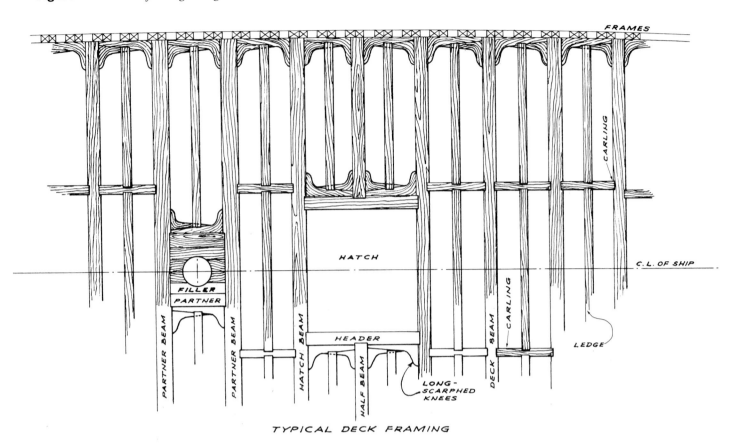

TYPICAL DECK FRAMING

MIDDLE DECK FRAMING, GREAT REPUBLIC, 1853

245

Carlings

The *carlings* were longitudinal timbers, which in the typical clipper ship were located so as to divide the breadth of the ship into three approximately equal parts. Generally they were installed in a line in the broad midbody, but as the ends of the ship were approached their location was shifted to suit the decreasing breadth until, in the vessel's extremities, they might be eliminated.

They were of the same material as the deck beams, and their purpose was to support the transverse ledges and, by reducing the unsupported length of the ledges, allow them to be made with slighter scantlings, thus reducing dead weight. Attention to saving weight was as integral to building a vessel as was the selection and proper sizing of her timbers.

Scantlings of carlings are not often recorded. However, McKay's notes contain the sizes as specified for the McKay clippers.[2] When plans of other ships are scaled, no dimensions being given, it appears that the McKay data is typical for these members. The scantlings are: lower deck carlings, sided 10 inches, moulded 7 inches; middle deck, sided 10 inches, moulded 8 inches; upper deck, sided 10 inches, moulded 6 inches. The material was always the same as that specified for the deck beams.

The moulded dimension of carlings was less than the thickness of the beams into which their ends would be scored. This virtually dictated that such connections would be simple half-laps let into each member to a depth which brought the top surface of the carling down to the top of the beam. This connection is shown in Figure 14.2. detail F.

While in most vessels the carlings were implied to be installed normal (at 90 degrees) to the beams, a different installation was employed in *Great Republic*. At the quarterbreadth of her upper deck amidships, the carlings were positioned in a line that extended the length of the vessel on both port and starboard sides; this distance from the centerline was maintained throughout. However, the line is a theoretical one, since the carlings were installed diagonally between beams in what might be called a herringbone pattern.

Starting at the half beam at the side of the main hatchway, the ends of the ledges were scored into this beam at an angle of approximately 30 degrees with the centerline of ship. The scores were opposite each other, both the forward and after score angling outward toward the side of the ship. The carling on the after side of the beam was extended outboard until it reached the next beam, and there it was installed. The next carling started at this same point but pointed inboard at 30 degrees until it reached the next beam aft. This procedure was followed all the way to the turn of the counter. Conversely , the same procedure was followed forward until the windlass bitts were reached. The same pattern of installation was applied to the second side of the ship but to the opposite hand, resembling the herringbone method of climbing a slope on skis.

This approach provided additional diagonal bracing, which was always welcome. However, it was laborious and expensive, and apparently other shipbuilders did not believe it to be worth the expense. Like many other unusual practices in shipbuilding, it would be unwise to conclude that this one was unique. Figure 14.3 illustrates this installation as copied from the description of *Great Republic*.[10]

In the various texts, no mention is made of the manner in which the carlings were fastened to the deck beams, except that the beams were scored to a size which required that the carlings be pounded home to achieve solid seating at their proper level.

Ledges

The ledges were timbers that ran athwartships midway between deck beams. Their ends were supported by carlings, as described above, installed in order to shorten the unsupported length of each individual ledge as the breadth of the vessel was spanned. This allowed the scantlings of the ledges to be reduced, with the result of more weight saving.

The purpose of a ledge was to shorten the span between deck beams across which the deck planking was laid. With the beams approximately 6 feet apart, deck planking when laid would be amply strong, but it would also be limber and subject to deflection under varying loads. On a weather deck, this limberness would make it almost impossible to maintain watertightness due to springing of caulking.

The scantlings of ledges were much smaller than those of the few headers that were installed in a vessel. They were substantially smaller than deck beams. Donald McKay specified that ledges for his clipper ships be of pitch pine, moulded 6 inches and sided 10 inches on the lower deck and 9 inches on the upper deck and the middle deck of ships having three decks.

As to the manner in which the ends of ledges were fashioned and secured, nothing is mentioned about any of the vessels included here. However, Thearle states that they were installed with the "single stop" method,[8] which is illustrated in Figure 14.2, detail E. Here the ends of the ledge are shown finished off square. The sides of the carlings are scored down to snugly receive these ends. The ledge is thus resting on a single stop, as opposed to the two scores that are cut into a double stop (described above under the heading "Half Beams").

Ledges, in their own right, did not merit the installation of kneed connections, although many were secured to knees that had been installed for other purposes.

Mast Partners

The *mast partners*, shown in Figure 14.3, were one of the two structural units essential to retaining the masts in their assigned positions. The second unit was the mast step, which surmounted the keelson and is covered in Chapter 16 under its own heading.

If a complete mast assembly is considered to be a beam standing in an upright position, then the mast step is the fixed anchorage, the wind at the center of effort on the sails is the variable load acting upon this beam, and the mast partners are the fulcrum about which the beam will tend to move out of position. These partners were generally, but not always, installed as an integral part of the highest structural deck in the vessel, and were included in the general installation of deck beams.

During the building of American clipper ships between 1850 and 1856, there were no actual mandatory rules for scantling sizes, although a general practice was followed throughout the shipbuilding industry. The desire to build a ship that was insurable was the best controller of construction with integrity.

As a practice, the partner beams immediately forward of and aft of a mast were sized a nominal percentage larger than the general run of beams that ranged along a deck. However, even in texts that are profuse with such information, it is very rare that these beams are ever mentioned when the scantlings are recorded. One fortunate deviation from this fact is found in the listed details of McKay vessels.[2] The number of vessels does not warrant a separate table, so they are covered here as follows:

	Partner beams and partners	
Vessel	Fore and Main	Mizzen
Stag Hound	15"S × 14"M	15"S × 15"M
Flying Cloud	15"S × 14"M	15"S × 15"M
Staffordshire	15"S × 14"M	15"S × 15"M
Flying Fish	15"S × 14"M	15"S × 15"M
Westward Ho	15"S × 14"M	15"S × 15"M
Sovereign of the Seas	15"S × 15"M	15"S × 15"M
Empress of the Sea	15"S × 15"M	15"S × 15"M
Lightning	15"S × 15"M	15"S × 15"M
Champion of the Seas	15"S × 15"M	15"S × 15"M
James Baines	15"S × 15"M	15"S × 15"M
Donald McKay	15"S × 15"M	15"S × 15"M
Great Republic	not given	not given

NOTE: All partner beams and partners are kneed with knees 6" × 8" and 10" throats, bolted into beams with 3 and 4 bolts.

Within the confines of these partners were fitted stout fillers of similar thickness which completely filled the enclosed space. Out of their substance, a hole was cut to house the appropriate mast; this was, in larger vessels, about 6 inches greater in diameter than was the mast. This area around the mast would be filled with tapered oak wedges which were driven tightly in place, thus restraining any movement of the mast; they were not, however, fixed in the same manner as was the mast step, which held but one permanent position. The wedges could be backed out to varying degrees, which allowed disenchanted shipmasters to trim the entire mast assembly, even while underway—a not uncommon practice.

Chapter Fifteen

HOOKS AND POINTERS

Hooks

The hooks (Figure 15.1) were installed in all vessels, whatever class or type—freighter, packet, or clipper—because they performed a function necessary to all ships, this being to securely bind the sides of the vessel together at her ends. Hooks were given names descriptive of their location. Thus, there were *deck hooks*; *breast hooks*, also known as *forward hooks* or *stem hooks*; and *stern hooks*, also known as *after hooks*. All hooks were made of oak and, in their simplest form, were cut from the natural growth of trees.

Natural and "Made" Hooks

Figure 2.1 illustrates the various shapes of timber that could be obtained as natural growth from trees used in shipbuilding. Piece D in this plate, a crotch, was available for use in the lower portions of a vessel's ends which were very sharp and confined. Piece B, a fork, was useful higher up in the ship where the ends were more divergent. Piece E, a crook, was required for the ends of the vessel in areas above the waterline in way of the upper decks. From pieces such as this the typical open breast hook was cut. Finally, various conformations of piece C, compass timbers, were used in the fuller, rounder aft end of a vessel in way of her transom.

All the above configurations of natural growth were in ample supply in days preceding the clipper ship, but, due to excessive demand, an increase in the size of vessels, and drastic changes in hull form, a great deal of timber was increasingly in short supply. The result was that, in many cases, the use of natural growth was supplanted by "made" hooks to alleviate the problem which was becoming more serious literally on a day-to-day basis.

"Made" hooks were fabrications of timbers, beams, and knees that were assembled to occupy the space and perform the function of a natural growth. They required a maximum of labor and fastenings but functioned as ably as did their natural counterparts. And, due to their form, there was never a question of supply.

Typical forms of hooks are illustrated in Figure 15.1. The simplest of these is shown in detail B, in which a basic hook, cut from a crotch or fork of a tree, is properly sided and then trimmed to suit the angle it is intended to fill. Its arms terminate in its own extremities, these being finished off in smooth fashion without protruding corners. Such hooks were used for deck, breast, and stern hooks, especially in the lower portions of the ship where space was extremely limited in way of her entrance and run.

Detail A is a hook more often to be found in the after end of a ship where space between the ship's sides was opened due to the run not being as fine as the entrance. In the case of deck hooks, a natural growth was fitted between the deadwood aft and the aftermost deck beam, with the ends of the arms docked to fay to the beam.

When necessary the space between the sternpost assembly and the beam was "eked out," or filled with timber as shown in the detail. Any finishing, such as rounding up to align with the surface of the beam, was done if required by the vessel's breadth at that level.

Details C and D show "made" hooks which might be found as deck hooks, stem and stern hooks, hooks securing the ends of horizontal stringers, and hooks securing the ends of pointers that did not fay to the keelsons. In both details the strength of the assembly lies in the scarphed knees which connect the sides of the ship. Detail C shows fillers fitted abaft the knee assembly, while detail D employs timbers to form any necessary landing when installed as deck hooks.

Detail E illustrates a deck hook aft, which in this case is a deck transom and is cut from a single large crook that completely spans the round of the stern. Its ends are docked to fay against the aftermost deck beam and are kneed to that beam. This is a typical example of a hook which requires rounding up in order to be in line with deck beams and planking. By its extreme form it is obvious that, in many

Figure 15.1. *Common forms of hook construction.*

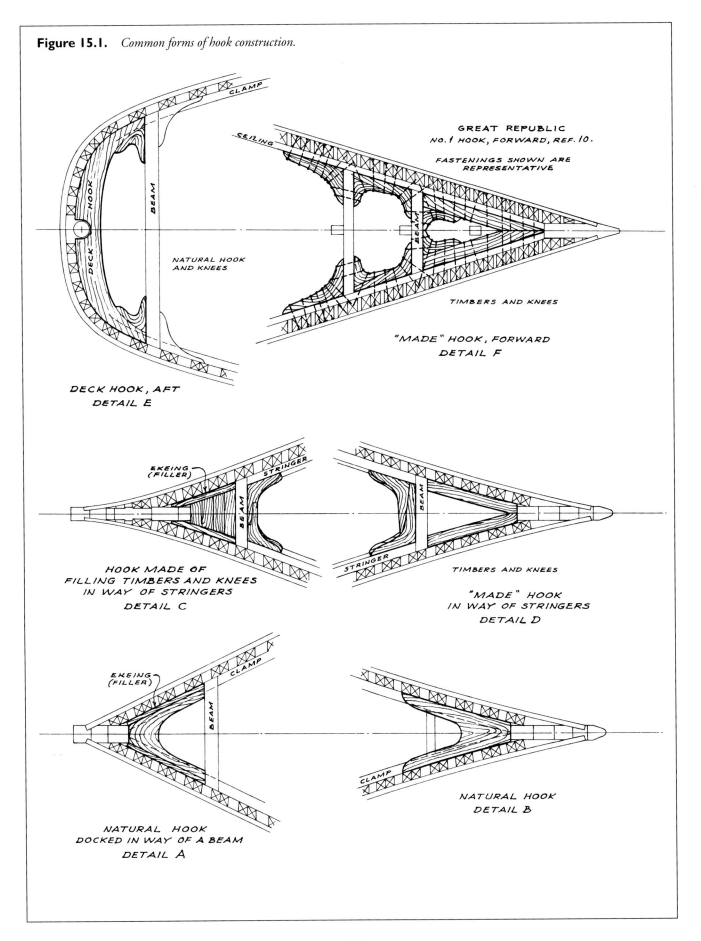

GREAT REPUBLIC
NO. 1 HOOK, FORWARD, REF. 10.

FASTENINGS SHOWN ARE
REPRESENTATIVE

CEILING

BEAM

BEAM

NATURAL HOOK
AND KNEES

TIMBERS AND KNEES

CLAMP

DECK HOOK

BEAM

"MADE" HOOK, FORWARD
DETAIL F

DECK HOOK, AFT
DETAIL E

EKEING
(FILLER)

STRINGER

BEAM

BEAM

STRINGER

TIMBERS AND KNEES

HOOK MADE OF
FILLING TIMBERS AND KNEES
IN WAY OF STRINGERS
DETAIL C

"MADE" HOOK
IN WAY OF STRINGERS
DETAIL D

EKEING
(FILLER)

CLAMP

BEAM

CLAMP

NATURAL HOOK
DETAIL B

NATURAL HOOK
DOCKED IN WAY OF A BEAM
DETAIL A

249

instances, such a hook might require two pieces scarphed together to span the same location. It is a visual example of the reason that so many differences appeared throughout the various ships in the matter of detail. Such timbers would be scarce and difficult for most shipbuilders to obtain. However, when speculating upon the reality of such timbers even existing, it is well to refer to Figure 2.2 and observe the scope of natural growths that were routinely offered for sale by timber dealers. In our era, at the writing of this book, our imagination must be coaxed to believe that any such timber could be had in quantity and as a normal commodity. Such was the nature of our forests at that period.

Detail F is an example of a "made" hook as fabricated for *Great Republic*. With this outsize vessel of giant proportions, all thought of filling her ends with hooks only of natural growth was apparently discarded from the outset. Thus, her hooks actually were structures composed of beams, timbers, and knees. She contained five hooks of this same general construction in each end, including her deck hooks.[10]

It goes without saying that all hooks, whatever their form and function, were only as reliable as the fastenings that secured their component parts to the ship's structure. The general scope of such fastenings appears throughout Table 15.1 and can reasonably be regarded as applicable to all vessels.

Table 15.1 is a tabulation of the hooks installed in vessels included in this book. The data is based on descriptions found in the references; however, additional information may exist in other sources.

Figure 12.4, an inboard profile at the side of *Lightning*, illustrates the locations of her hooks.[1, 2] These locations and general details are typical and would apply to a great extent to other similar vessels.

Deck Hooks

The deck hooks are the hooks that required the most exact installation and finishing. They were located in the extremities of the vessel, this being the nature of all hooks, and, like the beams of the deck they served, rested on the clamps that ran along either side of the ship. In positioning the hook, the upper surface was set in alignment with the top of the deck beams, since the hooks provided support and substance to which the ends of the deck planking would be fastened. In the uppermost portions of the ship, particularly aft in the vicinity of the transom, where relatively great breadth occurred, the upper surface of such hooks required trimming to the round-up or camber of the beams in order to accommodate the ends of planking. In such locations they were termed *deck transoms*.

Every deck in a ship required the installation of deck hooks, and generally they spanned the angle of the deck until the ends of their arms reached a deck beam to which they were fayed. At this point they may or may not have been kneed to the beam, this being at the discretion of the builder.

All the forms of knee shown in Figure 15.1 found their way into the construction of deck hooks.

Breast Hooks and Stern Hooks

The breast hooks and stern hooks are those hooks which, at either end of the vessel, are located approximately midway (vertically, see centerline profile, Figure 12.4) between the deck hooks. In the hold below the lower deck structure there was generally one hook at each end and, in some cases, two in the bow due to the greater height generated by her sheer. These were always located higher than hooks that terminated the pointers, which stretched diagonally along the sides of the hold and are described later.

The general practice was to install those hooks square, or nearly so, to the curvature of the forward or aft deadwood so as to allow the arms to lie diagonally across the cants. Generally, they were located 4 to 5 feet apart. Unlike deck hooks, their location and angle of inclination were not restricted in any manner, so particular skill and exactness were not required in order to achieve strong and effective installation.

Except in the very highest reaches of the hull, as in way of the bowsprit, breast hooks did not achieve an opening that allowed the use of compass timbers. In an earlier era, when ships were built with bluff, well-rounded bows, it was not unusual to find many of the upper breast hooks to be cut nearly in an arc of a great circle. Timbers of this sort were easily obtained and just as easily installed. In the clippers, however, the greatest included angle of the bow one might reasonably expect to find was about 60 degrees. This effectively eliminated the use of compass timbers and forced attention to hooks of natural growth or of "made" construction.

The general exception to placing hooks in a diagonal attitude was in the areas between decks where low headroom rendered such inclining to be rather impractical and of little use. In these instances the hooks paralleled the deck or were installed horizontally.

The lower hooks were made with the longest arms that would conveniently fit into the location in which they were installed, generally terminating with the ends of the arms fayed to a knee under the lower deck beams. This diagonal trace added some triangulation to the general structure of the frames, thus contributing to much-needed rigidity and strength.

All hooks were fastened with ⅞-inch to 1¼-inch iron. Some were fastened with the iron driven from outside or inside, and many were fastened with the iron driven alternately from inside and outside. Most fastenings were riveted, and a general practice was to drive at least one fastening through every frame. Fastenings were also driven blunt into the deadwoods where possible.

(text continued on page 256)

Table 15.1. *Hooks and pointers, details and locations.*

Abbreviations

WO – white oak
LO – live oak
NHWO – New Hampshire
     white oak

Hk – hackmatack
MWO – Massachusetts
     white oak
NWO – Northern white oak

S – Sided
M – Moulded

Vessel & Ref.#

Alarm   #1

Hooks – Oak; 2 forward and 2 aft. Stem hook is beamed and kneed afore and abaft the windlass bitt stepped in the lower deck.

Pointers – Oak; 3 pairs in each end of hold. All cross the cants diagonally and extend to lower deck. Ends of ship are filled with hooks, oak. Bolts are driven alternately in and out.

Amphitrite   #1

"Well secured with hooks, oak, and pointers."

Andrew Jackson   #20

Hooks –
Pointers – 3, forward in the hold.

Antelope   #1

Hooks – Oak; 6 forward and 5 aft. Completely span the angles of her ends.

Pointers –

Asa Eldridge   #1

Hooks – Tween decks breast hook, WO, 14"S, 5' throat. Supported by two beams kneed together over hook in the bays. After hook the same size. 84 bolts in each. 1 hook over and 1 under bowsprit, both WO.

Pointers – WO; 3 pairs in each end of hold. All cross the cants diagonally and extend to lower deck. Ends of ship are filled with hooks, WO.

Bald Eagle   #1

Hooks – WO; span both ends of ship. 1 hook over and 1 under bowsprit, both WO.

Pointers – WO; 3 pairs forward. All cross the cants diagonally and extend almost to lower deck. Those above the keelson are filled with hooks, WO.

Belle of the West

Beverly

Black Hawk

Blue Jacket

Bonita

Described as being "similar to Golden Light."

Bounding Billow   Bark

Celestial

Challenge   #1

Hooks – WO; 3 breast hooks in hold. All deck hooks are LO.
Pointers –

Challenger   #1

Hooks – WO. All are stout.

Pointers – WO. All are stout.

Champion of the Seas   #1,2

Ref.1
Hooks – WO. Tween decks hooks beamed and kneed. Fastened through all.

Pointers – Ends almost filled with massive hooks and pointers. Pointers all cross the cants diagonally and fay to the lower deck beams.

Ref.2
Hooks – All WO, 10" and 12"S.

Pointers – All WO, 10" and 12"S.

Vessel & Ref.#

Charger   #1

Hooks – NHWO; tween decks, 12"S x 16"M, bolted from inside and outside, 122 bolts. Breast hook has Hk knee bolted in throat. After hook, NHWO, bolted from outside of timbers and transom. 1 hook over and 1 under bowsprit, both NHWO.

Pointers – NHWO; 2 pairs in each end of hold. Filled in throats with Hk hooks. Cross-hook above each, clinch bolted.

Charmer   #1

Hooks – WO

Pointers – WO

Cleopatra   #1

Hooks – WO; 8 forward, 6 aft. They cross all the cants diagonally and horizontally. Completely span the angles of her ends.

Pointers – (Apparently fitted in combination with the hooks in the hold.)

Climax   #1

Hooks – WO; 8 forward, 5 aft. Completely span the angles of her ends.

Pointers –

Coeur de Lion   #1

"Massive hooks and pointers, NHWO, cross all the cants diagonally and horizontally in both ends."

Comet

Cyclone   #3

Hooks – MWO; 7 forward, 5 aft.

Pointers –

Daring   #1

Hooks – WO; 3 in each end of hold. A breast hook forward in the tween decks, bolted alternately from inside and outside. Also a hook in each angle of the transom to strengthen the stern frame.

Pointers – WO; 3 pairs in each end of hold.

Dauntless   #1

Hooks – MWO; 8 forward, 6 aft.

Pointers –

Donald McKay   #1,2

Ref.1
Hooks – WO; fill in stringer in hold at both ends of ship. 1 hook, WO, between each deck at both ends. WO hook under bowsprit.

Pointers – WO; 3 pairs in each end of hold. Angles filled in with hooks.

Ref.2
Hooks – All WO, 10" and 12"S.

Pointers – All WO, 10" and 12"S.

Don Quixote   #1

Hooks – WO; between decks, both ends of ship. Bolted alternately from inside and outside.

Pointers – WO; 4 pairs forward. 1st pair, 20' long each side. 2nd pair, 25' long. 3rd and 4th pairs, 35' long. All vary between 14" and 10" square (no tapers). All cross the cants diagonally and fay against lower deck beams or knees. Bolts spaced apart 8" maximum. Also WO, 3 pairs aft, installed in the same fashion.

Eagle   #5

Hooks – WO, breast and stern hooks. LO deck hooks.

Pointers –

Table 15.1. *Continued.*

Vessel & Ref.#

Eagle Wing   #1

   Hooks – WO; 9 massive hooks and pointers forward, 7 hooks and pointers
      aft. These include all the deck hooks.

   Pointers – Included in combination with the hooks in the hold.

Edwin Forrest   #1

   "Her ends are well secured with hooks and pointers, all WO."

Electric Spark   #1

   "Her ends are strongly secured with hooks and pointers, all WO.

Ellen Foster   #1

   Hooks – WO; 9 forward, 6 aft. The tween decks breast hook is secured
      with 89 bolts.

Empress of the Sea   #1,2

   Ref.1
   Hooks – WO; 10 forward, 8 aft.

   Pointers – WO; cross all the cants diagonally and extend well along the
      body.

   Ref.2
   Hooks – All WO, 10" and 12"S.

   Pointers – All WO, 10" and 12"S.

Endeavor   #1

   Hooks – WO; tween decks breast hook, 13"S, 4' throat, fastened with
      86 bolts. Also a breast hook, WO, under the bowsprit.

   Pointers – WO; 3 pairs forward, 2 pairs aft. All are filled with hooks,
      WO, bolted from both sides.

Eringo Bark   #1

   "She has heavy hooks, oak, forward and aft."

Vessel & Ref.#

Eureka

Fair Wind   #1

   Hooks – WO; tween decks breast hook completely spans angle of bow and
      is supported with beams kneed to it. Another hook, same size,
      unkneed, spans the stern. 70 to 80 bolts in each hook.

   Pointers – WO; 3 pairs in hold forward, 2 pairs aft, all filled in
      with massive hooks.

Fearless

Fleet Wing   #1

   "She has heavy hooks and pointers, WO, which span the angles of her
      ends completely."

Flyaway

Flying Arrow   #1

   Hooks – WO; 7 forward, 5 aft.

Flying Childers   #1

   Hooks – WO; 8 forward, 5 aft. All in the tween decks are horizontal
      and span the angles of the ends. All are closely bolted.

   Pointers – WO; 2 in each end of hold. Ends are filled with hooks. All
      cross the cants diagonally and fay against the knees under the
      lower deck beams.

Flying Cloud   #1,2

   Ref.1
   Hooks – WO; 1 long stout hook forward in the tween decks.

   Pointers – WO; almost fill her ends, some extending 40' along her skin.
      Ends of the pointers are filled with hooks.

   Ref.2
   Hooks – All WO, 10" and 12"S.

   Pointers – All WO, 10" and 12"S.

Flying Dragon   #1

   Hooks – WO. Very stout.

   Pointers –

Flying Dutchman

Flying Eagle   #1

   Hooks – 8 forward, 5 aft. Cross all the cants and span the angles of
      her ends. Hooks in the tween decks are 13"S, 3' to 4' throats.

   Pointers – WO; some are extensions of her hooks in the hold.

Flying Fish   #1,2

   Ref.1
   Hooks – WO; massive, in both ends of the tween decks.

   Pointers – WO; 4 pairs in each end of hold. Ends of all are filled in
      with hooks. Some extend 30' along her skin and all are at least
      12" square.

   Ref.2
   Hooks – All WO, 10" and 12"S.

   Pointers – All WO, 10" and 12"S.

Flying Mist   #1

   Hooks – NHWO; massive, in both ends of the tween decks. 1 over and
      1 under the bowsprit, both NHWO.

   Pointers – NHWO; 3 pairs in each end of hold. Cross all the cants
      diagonally and extend to the lower deck. Ends of all are filled
      in with hooks.

Galatea

Game Cock   #1

   Hooks – WO; all breast hooks and after hooks.

   Pointers –

Gazelle

Gem of the Ocean   #1

   Hooks – WO

   Pointers – WO

Golden Eagle   #1

   Hooks – WO; 6 forward, 3 aft. Tween decks strongly braced with hooks,
      fore and aft.

   Pointers – WO; 2 pairs forward and 2 pairs aft, in hold. All cross
      the cants diagonally and fay against the knees under the lower
      deck beams.

Golden Fleece (2nd)   #1

   Hooks – WO; heavy. Bolted from both sides.

   Pointers – WO; heavy. Bolted from both sides.

Golden Light   #1

   Hooks – WO; 7 forward, 5 aft.

   Pointers –

Golden West   #1

   Hooks – WO; all breast hooks.

   Pointers –

Grace Darling   #1

   Hooks – WO; 8 forward, 5 aft.

   Pointers – WO; some are extensions of her hooks in the hold.

252

Table 15.1. *Continued.*

Great Republic   #2,4,10

    Ref.10
    Hooks - WO; 1 horizontal forward, 1 horizontal aft, in hold. Both
        shored off with 2 beams and 4 knees each side. Lower tween decks,
        fore and aft, hooks reach to 4th beam and are similar to hooks in
        hold. Upper tween decks, forward, same as lower tween decks. Upper
        tween decks, aft, hook is built double around curve of the stern,
        otherwise same as lower tween decks. All decks are fitted with
        hooks. Heavy hooks fill the angles over and under the bowsprit.
        Hooks of hold and lower deck, both ends, and middle deck, forward,
        are "made". All other hooks contain some natural growth.

    Pointers - WO; 3 pairs forward in hold, 30' to 40' long, 9" x 11" squared.
        Lowest pair fays into the angles between keelson and skin. 2 upper
        pairs cross all the cants diagonally and fay to the lower deck beams.
        Their ends are filled in with hooks. 2 pairs aft in hold, 9" x 11"
        squared. Cross all cants diagonally and fay to keelson and lower
        deck beams. Ends are filled in with hooks.

    Ref.2
    Hooks - All WO, 10" and 12"S.

    Pointers - All WO, 10" and 12"S.

    Ref.4
    Hooks - A total of 10 beamed hooks, forward and aft.

    Pointers - WO; 4 pairs in each end, 20' to 50' long, 1¼" bolts, iron,
        clinched.

Great Republic (rebuilt)   #103

    Apparently rebuilt similar to original vessel (See ref.10) except for
        elimination of the spar deck.

Henry Hill   Bark   #1

    Hooks -

    Pointers - WO; "Her ends are well braced with heavy pointers which cross
        all the cants diagonally and are filled in with oak hooks."

Herald of the Morning   #9

    Hooks -

    Pointers - WO; 3 pairs forward, 3 pairs aft. Kneed and well fastened at
        ends, angled diagonally up and fayed to lower deck beams.

Hoogly   #1

    Hooks - WO; 9 forward, 6 aft. Also LO, the hook under the upper deck, aft,
        which is 13"S and forms a complete arch around her stern. (A total
        of 7 hooks aft.)

    Pointers - WO; some are extensions of her hooks in the hold.

Hurricane

Indiaman   #1

    Hooks - WO; a massive hook, 14"S, 4' throat, in each end of tween decks.
        80 to 90 bolts in each.

    Pointers - WO; 3 pairs in each end of hold. Cross all cants diagonally
        and fay to lower deck beams.

Intrepid

Invincible   #4

    Hooks - WO; 3 breast hooks in lower hold. LO, deck hook at each deck.

    Pointers - WO; lined up with each breast hook in lower hold.

James Baines   #1,2

    Ref.1
    "Nearly the same as Champion of the Seas."

    Ref.2
    Hooks - All WO; 10" and 12"S.

    Pointers - All WO; 10" and 12"S.

John Bertram   #1

    Hooks - WO; 1 breast hook in hold. 1 breast hook in the tween decks,
        13"S, 3' to 4' throat, extends well aft. Closely bolted.

    Pointers - WO; 2 pairs in each end of hold. Cross all cants diagonally
        and fay to lower deck beams.

John Gilpin   #1

    Hooks - The tween decks breast hook is stout and completely spans the
        angle of the bow.

    Pointers - WO; massive, 3 pairs forward, 2 pairs aft. Cross all cants
        diagonally and fay to lower deck beams.

John Land   #1,32   (Built as a duplicate of Winged Arrow.)

    Hooks - WO; 8 forward, 5 aft.

    Pointers - WO

John Stuart

John Wade   #1

    Hooks - WO; forward and aft.

    Pointers -

Joseph Peabody   #1

    Hooks - WO; the tween decks breast hook completely spans the angle of
        the bow, is double beamed and secured with lodging knees. The
        tween decks after hook is very stout and closely bolted.

    Pointers - WO; 3 pairs forward, 2 pairs aft. Cross all cants diagonally
        and fay to lower deck beams or knees.

King Fisher   #1

    Hooks - WO; ends completely spanned by massive hooks, strongly fastened
        through all.

    Pointers - WO; 3 pairs in each end of hold. Cross cants diagonally and
        connect with knees under lower deck beams. Bolted through all.

Lady Franklin

Lamplighter   Bark   #1

    Hooks - WO

    Pointers -

Lightfoot   #1

    Hooks - WO; fill her ends.

    Pointers -

Lightning   #1,2

    Ref.1
    Hooks - WO; the tween decks hooks, forward and aft, are beamed and kneed.

    Pointers - WO; 4 pairs in each end, 20' to 50' long, 12" square. All
        bolted through cants and timbers from inside and outside. 2 in
        each end fay to keelsons below and two are filled with hooks in the
        ends. All angle up to lower deck beams.

    Ref.2
    Hooks - All WO; 10" and 12"S.

    Pointers - All WO; 10" and 12"S.

Table 15.1. *Continued.*

Vessel & Ref.#

Mameluke   #1

    Hooks - WO; 3 forward, 2 aft, in hold. 1 hook in each end of the tween
    decks, each completely spanning the angles of the ends. The breast
    hook has two beams secured at the ends with knees. 1 hook over and
    1 hook under the bowsprit, alternately bolted from inside and outside.

    Pointers -

Mary Robinson

Mastiff   #1

    Hooks - WO; large hooks in each end of the tween decks. 1 hook over
    and 1 hook under the bowsprit.

    Pointers - WO; 3 pairs in each end of ship. Ends are filled with hooks
    and bolted from inside and outside.

Mermaid   Bark   #1

    Hooks - WO

    Pointers -

Morning Light   #1

    Hooks - NHWO; her ends are strongly spanned by massive hooks.

    Pointers - NHWO; massive.

Mystery   #1

    Hooks - WO; 9 forward, 5 aft. All completely span the angles of her ends.

    Pointers - WO; some are extensions of her hooks. Cross cants diagonally
    and fay to lower deck beams. Bolted alternately from inside and
    outside and riveted.

Nightingale

Noonday   #1

    Hooks - NHWO; 4 forward in hold, 3 aft in hold, all filling in the ends
    of stringers. 1 breast hook forward in the tween decks, 12½"S x 28"M,
    scarphed to a pair of stringers 4" thick, NHWO. Bolted through every
    timber and clinched on the inside.

    Pointers - NHWO; 4 pairs of diagonal stringers in forward hold, 3 pairs
    aft in hold, same size as those forward. 1 pair of pointers aft in
    hold. All of the above square fastened and clinch bolted. 1 pair
    of stringers aft in the tween decks, the end filled with a hook.
    Clinch bolted.

Northern Light

Ocean Express   #1

    Hooks - WO; 1 hook forward in the tween decks. Completely spans the angle
    of the bow. Secured with 136 bolts. 1 hook aft secured with 100 bolts.
    Both hooks 14"S, 24" throat.

    Pointers - WO; 4 pairs forward in hold, 3 pairs aft in hold, all filled
    in the angles with hooks. 2 pairs in each end are 30' long each
    side. All are 12" to 14" square.

Ocean Pearl   #1

    "Her ends are strongly secured with hooks and pointers, WO."

Ocean Telegraph   #5

    Hooks - Oak, massive.

    Pointers - Oak, massive.

Onward   #1

    "All her hooks and pointers are of oak."

Osborne Howes

Panther

Vessel & Ref.#

Phantom   #1

    Hooks - WO; 9 forward, 6 aft. Hooks above the lowest two in both
    ends of hold are horizontal. All very closely bolted.

    Pointers - WO; 2 lowest pairs in each end of hold cross cants diagonally
    and fay to knees under lower deck beams. All are very closely
    bolted.

Queen of Clippers   #1

    "Her ends are well secured with massive hooks and pointers, WO."

Queen of the Pacific

Queen of the Seas   #1

    Hooks - WO; 1 in each end of the tween decks. Both span the ends
    completely and contain about 80 bolts each. 1 hook over and
    1 hook under the bowsprit.

    Pointers - WO; 3 pairs in each end of hold, ends filled in with hooks.
    Cross cants diagonally and fay to lower deck beams. Bolted
    through all.

Quickstep   Bark   #1

    Hooks - WO; 1 in each end of the tween decks. Both span the ends.

    Pointers - WO; 2 pairs in each end of hold, ends filled in with hooks.

Racehorse   Bark   #1

    "Forward and aft she is well secured with hooks, WO, which cross all
    the cants and are bolted from outside."

Racer

Radiant   #1

    Hooks - WO; 8 forward, 5 aft.

    Pointers - (Apparently included with the hooks.)

Raven   #3

    Hooks - WO; 5 breast hooks.

    Pointers - WO; 2 pairs.

Red Jacket

Robin Hood

Rocket   Bark

Roebuck   #1

    "Her ends are well secured with massive hooks, WO."

Romance of the Sea   #1

    "Her hooks, WO, are all of the most substantial kind."

Santa Claus   #1

    Hooks - WO; strongly fastened.

    Pointers - WO; strongly fastened.

Saracen   #1

    Hooks - MWO; 3 forward, 2 aft, in hold. 1 breast hook in the tween
    decks, extends aft to the foremast and is supported by two beams
    which are kneed.

    Pointers - MWO; are filled in the ends by some of the hooks.

Sea Bird   Bark   #1

    "Her ends are well secured with massive hooks, WO."

Seaman's Bride

Sea Serpent

Table 15.1. *Continued.*

Vessel & Ref.#

Shooting Star #1

   Hooks - WO; 7 forward, 5 aft, including deck hooks. The tween decks
      hook in each end is secured with 67 bolts and 4 spikes.

   Pointers - WO; 2 pairs in each end of hold are filled in the ends with
      hooks. Cross the cants diagonally and fay to the knees under the
      lower deck beams.

Sierra Nevada #1

   "Her ends are strongly secured with heavy hooks and pointers, NHWO."

Silver Star #1

   Hooks - WO; 7 forward, 6 aft, including deck hooks. The tween decks
      hook in each end completely fills the angle and is secured with
      100 bolts driven from both sides. The hooks vary between 12" to
      14"S and 3' to 4' throats.

   Pointers - WO; some are filled in the ends with hooks.

Southern Cross #1

   Hooks - MWO; the tween decks breast hook spans the bow completely and
      is securely bolted from the outside.

   Pointers - MWO; 3 pairs forward, 2 pairs aft. Cross the cants diagonally
      and fay to the knees under the lower deck beams.

Sovereign of the Seas #1,2

   Ref.1
   "Her ends are literally filled with massive hooks and pointers, WO."

   Ref.2
   Hooks - All WO; 10" and 12"S.

   Pointers - All WO; 10" and 12"S.

Spitfire #1

   Hooks - WO; ends well secured with massive hooks, particularly in the
      tween decks. All bolted alternately from both sides.

   Pointers -

Staffordshire #1,2

   Ref.1
   Hooks - WO; bow and stern in upper and lower tween decks are spanned
      by massive hooks which extend well along the sides.

   Pointers - WO; 5 pairs forward, 4 pairs aft, in the hold. Some are
      40' long on each side and are no less than 12" square.

   Ref.2
   Hooks - All WO; 10" and 12"S.

   Pointers - All WO; 10" and 12"S.

Stag Hound #1,2

   Ref.1
   Hooks - WO; 3 breast hooks, 3 stern hooks, all closely bolted. The
      tween decks breast hook extends well aft. 1 hook over and 1 hook
      under the bowsprit, very stout and well secured.

   Pointers - WO; 1 pair forward, 1 pair aft, in the hold. Each 30' long.

   Ref.2
   Hooks - All WO; 10" and 12"S.

   Pointers - All WO; 10" and 12"S.

Star of the Union #1

   Hooks - WO

   Pointers -

Starr King

Storm King #1

   Hooks - WO; 9 forward, 8 aft, including deck hooks.

   Pointers -

Sultana Bark #1

   "Her ends are well secured with massive hooks and pointers, WO."

Sunny South

Vessel & Ref.#

Surprise #1

   Hooks - WO; the tween decks breast hook has a 3' throat. Closely bolted.

   Pointers - WO; 3 pairs forward, 2 pairs aft, in the hold. Cross cants
      diagonally and fay to the knees under the lower deck beams.

Swallow #1

   Hooks - WO

   Pointers -

Sweepstakes

Sword Fish

Syren

Telegraph

Tornado

Thatcher Magoun #1

   Hooks - WO; 7 forward, 5 aft, including deck hooks. All bolted from
      inside and outside.

   Pointers -

Uncowah

War Hawk #1

   Hooks - WO; the tween decks spanned by stout hooks in both ends.

   Pointers - WO; 3 pairs forward, 2 pairs aft, in the hold. All bolted
      from inside and outside. Cross all cants diagonally and fay to
      the knees under the lower deck beams.

Water Witch #1

   Hooks - NHWO; the tween decks breast hook is 14"S x 36' long on each
      side of the apron. Strongly bolted.

   Pointers - NHWO; 4 pairs forward, in the hold. Cross all cants
      diagonally and completely span the angle of the bow. Equally
      well secured aft.

Western Continent

Westward Ho #1,2

   Ref.1
   Hooks - WO; 8 forward, 5 aft, including deck hooks. The tween decks
      breast hook is 50' long.

   Pointers - WO; in both ends of the hold they are filled with some hooks.
      They are 12" square, 30' to 35' long, bolted through all. 1 long
      diagonal on each side, opposite the foremast, reaches from the
      floor heads nearly to the lower deck. Bolted through all.

   Ref.2
   Hooks - All WO; 10" and 12"S.

   Pointers - All WO; 10" and 12"S.

West Wind

Whirlwind #1

   Hooks - WO; 7 forward, 5 aft, including deck hooks. The tween decks
      hook is massive and completely spans the angle of the bow.

   Pointers - WO; 2 pairs in each end. Their ends are filled with some of
      the hooks. Cross all cants diagonally and fay to the knees under
      the lower deck beams.

Whistler #1

   "Her hooks and pointers are very stout and strongly fastened, NWO."

Wildfire Bark

Wild Pigeon #1

   "Her ends are literally filled with massive hooks and pointers, NHWO,
      very stout and strongly secured."

Wild Ranger #1

   "Her deck frames are well secured with massive hooks and pointers, WO."

Table 15.1. *Continued.*

```
Vessel & Ref.#

Wild Rover

Winged Arrow   #1

     Hooks - WO; 8 forward, 5 aft, including deck hooks.

     Pointers - WO

Winged Racer   #1

     Hooks - WO; 8 forward, 7 aft, including deck hooks.  The tween decks
          hooks, forward and aft, completely span the angles of the ends.
          Closely bolted through all.

     Pointers - WO; 3 pairs in each end.  Their ends are filled by some of
          the hooks.  Cross all cants diagonally and fay to the knees under
          the lower deck beams.  Closely bolted through all.

Witchcraft   #1

     Hooks - WO; 7 forward, 5 aft, including deck hooks.

     Pointers - WO; 2 pairs in each end.  Their ends are filled by some of
          the hooks.  Cross all cants diagonally and fay to the knees under
          the lower deck beams.

Witch of the Wave   #1

     Hooks - NHWO; the tween decks breast hook is 11"S, 4' throat.  Extends
          15' on each side of the apron.  Secured with 46 bolts, 1⅛" to 1¼", iron.

     Pointers - NHWO; 3 pairs in each end. Two of these in each end cross all
          cants diagonally and fay to the knees under the lower deck beams.
          All are bolted in substantial style.

Wizard   #1

     Hooks - WO; massive hooks, forward and aft.  Completely span the angles
          of her ends.

     Pointers - WO; run diagonally and fay to the knees under the lower
          deck beams.

Young America

Young Turk   Bark   #1

     Hooks - WO

     Pointers - 2 pairs forward, 1 pair aft, in the hold.  All are filled
          in with hooks in the angles of the ends.  Bolted alternately
          from both sides.
```

(text continued from page 250)

Pointers

The *pointers*, which were long, diagonally installed timbers in the forward and after holds, were an integral part of clipper ship construction. They appear as shown in Figure 12.4, although the quantity and scantlings varied from ship to ship at the discretion of the individual builders.

Pointers were very prominent in the construction of the clipper hulls, but were not confined to such ships. The packets and freighters of the period made use of them almost in the same profusion.

It apparently cannot be determined when and by whom they were introduced into ship structures of this period. However, it appears probable that they first appeared (or reappeared) in the early 1840s when the slenderness of ships' hulls started to become more pronounced and developed into a general characteristic. Pointers were the last of the many (then) modern innovations that were built into the structure of wooden ships in the persistent but futile attempt to overcome the characteristic of hogging.

"Reappearance" refers to the fact that, in general concept, pointers had been introduced into British naval construction in 1814 by Sir Robert Seppings, surveyor or chief constructor of the Royal Navy. At the time they were referred to as "diagonal braces" and were part of a complex latticework built into the holds of British ships-of-war. Brian Lavery's work

The Ship of the Line, Volume II shows an inboard profile at the side of a hypothetical British vessel in which these diagonal braces, which would become known as *pointers* in the clipper period, may be plainly observed in the ends of the ship.[56]

If shipbuilding was a craft to which axioms might readily be applied, the following would be near the head of the list: "If a wooden ship lasts long enough, she will hog." The lack of buoyancy in the extremities of large ships had been a plague from the time the first ship with pointed ends had been built. And from that day until the day the last wooden ship was built, the phenomenon was fought but never really overcome. In the intervening ages many schemes had been introduced, as we have seen in previous chapters. Some were failures; some were helpful; and some effectively, but not completely, retarded the process.

Before the age of the clipper ship arrived in 1845, it is known that pointers had been installed in many vessels. The intent of their installation was, in everyday terms, to let the extreme ends of the vessel hang from the midbody structure and thus avoid distortion by hogging. The pointers, as installed, were stressed in tension, the load at their extreme ends being transferred toward amidship by the fastenings, which secured them to the ship's structure. They were, in effect, stretched along the ceiling of the ship, angling up and toward amidships in each end of the hull. There were innumerable variations in their installation, since there was no mathematical formula. Thus, the number of pointers, the angle of inclination, the scantlings and length, their termination at each extremity, and the fastening pattern differed to a great degree.

However, there were also general similarities. In a typical hull the lower ends of the lowest pointers were secured to the sides of keelson or deadwood without resorting to the use of hooks. They were fayed to these members and fastened directly to them. The lower ends of the pointers that were installed in more open areas terminated in hooks which confined the entire assembly and bound it to the sides of the ship. The pointers roughly paralleled each other and were located 4 to 5 feet apart, depending upon individual conditions. The upper ends of the pointers fayed to the hanging knees at the lower deck beams, and they diagonally crossed as many cant and square frames as their lengths would allow. They were invariably cut from white oak.

While scarphing was acceptable, the preferred practice was to install the pointer in a single piece. Such an installation was a considerable achievement, since these members were sized about 12 inches square and ranged up to a length of 50 feet. In Figure 12.4 the pointers appear to be positioned in long, graceful curves; this is due to the view being a projection. In actual installation the practice was to lay them up in as straight a line as possible, both for ease in bending them to fay against the ceiling and also to avoid the troublesome problem of having twist in their fiber.

Hooks used in way of pointers were similar to that shown in Figure 15.1, detail B. The pointers were positioned with their lower ends in position, and the natural-grown hook was inserted between them, forcing them against the ceiling. This assembly did not consume as much space in the hold as the other forms required. It is readily seen that the lower portions of the hold in either end of the vessel were veritable forests of massive timbers which occupied a great amount of valuable space and added a huge amount of undesirable weight.

The fastening of pointers followed a fairly uniform practice. The bolts, all approximately 1-inch iron, were generally driven alternately from inside and outside through frame, ceiling, pointer, and, at the lower end, the hook. All were riveted or clinched and, in most instances, there was one bolt driven through every futtock crossed by the pointer.

Diagonal Braces

In one case, diagonal braces of white oak were installed in the ends of a clipper. This system, if not unique, was very rare in these ships. The specific vessel was *Bald Eagle*, designed and built by Donald McKay at Boston. The installation consisted of pointers augmented by parallel diagonal braces in the ship's ends, crossed in turn by additional diagonal braces angled across the others, an arrangement that formed a wooden lattice-work in the ends of the vessels. This construction was, in essence, a throw-back to the diagonal bracing system introduced into the British Navy by Sir Robert Seppings earlier in the century.[56]

Rather than attempt an abbreviated description of this installation, the following is quoted from a report by Duncan MacLean: "She has three massive pointers forward, which cross all the cants diagonally, and extend almost to the deck, and those above the keelson are filled in with hooks. Diagonal braces of oak, varying from 10 to 12 inches square, extending from the floorheads to the deck, and nearly parallel to the after pointer, are continued to abaft the foremast, and these, as well as the pointers, are crossed by diagonals of the same size, all bolted through the ceiling and timbers. Abaft these again, are other diagonals, extending from the lower strake of the thick work over the first futtocks to the stringer upon which the lower ends of the hanging knees rest, forming a series of acute-angled triangles, with the projecting line of the thick work for a common base. In this bracing there are over 600 one-inch bolts. Her after end is also diagonally braced, and spanned with hooks bolted through all."[1]

The scantlings of Donald McKay's vessels were always very generous, no matter how small or large the ship, and in this instance, he appeared to outdo himself. No other description within the scope of this book approaches the magnitude of the above structure.

MAST STEPS, TRUSSES, AND BRACING

Mast Steps

The mast step, while an essential element of a vessel's integrity, is not the subject of frequent or elaborate descriptions. Generally it is pictured as a platform of oak, large enough to accommodate the heel of the mast it is to support, thick enough to receive the squared tenon cut into the foot of the mast, and solidly secured atop or astride the keelson. This concept was basically correct and more or less accurate for centuries. In some cases where restoration of old vessels has been accomplished, a few photographs support this over-simplified description. However, the fact remains that, in ship structure, no details are more elusive than those dealing with the construction of mast steps.

This type of mast step was highly successful over a long period, one reason being that keelsons of the times were not of great moulded dimension and thus the step rested at the very bottom of the ship's structure. (This statement is general since the mizzenmast of many vessels was stepped on the orlop deck due to the relatively minor proportions of the mast.) In such a location the mast step accepted the crushing weight of the total mast assembly, and the bolts which secured the step to the structure needed only to act in shear as the ship rolled and pitched as she made her way under a press of sail.

By the time clipper ships put in their appearance, some drastic structural changes had taken place in ships' structures. As the vessels became longer and more slender, they required deeper backbones in order to hold their form without distortion. Structure was modified to satisfy the need, and the most obvious and drastic departure from what had gone before probably lay in the construction of keelsons.

At least as early as 1845, and probably prior to that date, keelsons were being constructed two tiers high, a height of about 30 inches above the floors. In 1850, keelsons three tiers high, about 45 inches, were routinely being built, as described in Chapter 10. Ultimately, in some of the very large vessels,

four tiers were installed, raising the height of the keelson and rider assembly to 60 inches above the floors. Even this structural assembly was exceeded, but not in the clipper ships.

This increase in height impacted on the stepping of masts. As the depth of keelsons became greater, the location of the mast step was raised higher off the floors and new stresses were introduced into the ship's structure. The foot of a mast, now solidly stepped on the topmost rider, was anywhere from 3 feet to 5 feet above its basic foundation, which was the ship's floors. Now, when the ship rolled and pitched, the foot of the mast, secured in position by its tenon, worked in an athwartship direction and the load was resisted by the multiple-tiered keelson construction. The resulting stresses were transmitted through the bolts, the final result being that the planking in way of the masts also worked in an infinitesimal way. Consequently, the seams in this area were vulnerable and prone to straining, thus loosening the caulk, which ultimately led to leakage.

A logical assumption would be that the mast step was supported on either side of the keelson by some form of structure. One must search diligently to find factual evidence of the form such structure took. Illustrations are, to all intent, nonexistent. Plans and drawings such as those of *Great Republic*,[10] *Ocean Monarch*,[24] *Star of the Empire*,[54] and *Chariot of Fame*[54] give no details. Among the nomenclature, scantlings, material, and fastening listed for all structural members of Donald McKay's clipper ships,[2] nowhere is there the mention of a mast step. Marine reporter Duncan MacLean was equally silent on this, except in one instance. His description of the clipper *Endeavor*, a vessel of moderate size built by Robert E. Jackson at East Boston, is concise and quite complete, with enough detail to allow a reasonable reconstruction to be developed (see Figure 16.1): "The steps of her masts are built solid, of oak, alongside and over the keelsons, and each step is braced by four standing knees, bolted through it, and through the floor ceiling and timbers, so that the weight of the masts will not press wholly upon the keelsons."[1]

To this description several assumptions must be added: the actual fastening pattern; a reasonable sizing of the knees; and the spacing of the knees to ensure that the fastenings would pass through the floor timbers. It is also probable that the side chocks which fayed to the keelsons were fitted with the grain running vertically so that the weight of the mast assembly would bear on the end-grain of the wood. The compressive value of white oak in this position is approximately 1,000 pounds per square inch, as compared with 500 when the load is across the grain. In the case of yellow pine, the compressive values are 1,000 pounds per square inch on end-grain and 300 across the grain.[50] (These values vary among sources.)

Due to the concentrated weight of masts, which were stepped on the cross-grain of pine keelsons, the masts, in due course of time, were prone to settle as the fibers of the wood in the keelson, which was not always well seasoned, compacted under the load. Thus the mast steps were designed to distribute this load. Innovative steps to do so were initiated prior to the building of *Endeavor*, and they are detailed later in this chapter under separate headings.

Some weights involved are of interest in realizing the magnitude of the problem. The mainmast of *Endeavor* was approximately the size of the mizzenmast of *Donald McKay*, and a reasonably comparable dead weight was 32 long (2,240 pounds) tons, after one of the two topsail yards of the McKay vessel was deducted; this was the constant or "dead" load. The heel of *Endeavor*'s 31-inch-diameter mast was about 26½ inches in diameter. Included in this weight were the masting, yards, iron hoops for all, and lower yard truss. Not included were intermittent or "live" loads such as the weights of sails (wet), studdingsail booms and yards, blocks and gear, chain rigging, and the vertical component of the forces induced in the shrouds by the downward pull of the lanyards at the channels.

Thus, a "dead" load of 71,680 pounds was funneled into the heel area of 551 square inches, or 130 pounds per square inch. This, if transferred to the top surface of the keelson rider, which was sided 15 inches, becomes 181 pounds per square inch. This value, added to the rather indeterminate "live" load, along with loads induced by the ship's motions under sail, can be seen as fast approaching the safe strength of the pine keelson. The concentration of weight was considerable, and this step design was one attempt at distributing it.

Whether or not this particular type of step was in general use cannot be substantiated due to the absence of any available information. Suffice it to say that, considering all the ships that were ever built, the problem was dealt with, even though not overcome.

The detailed weights of the masting of *Donald McKay* are given in Chapter 29.

Briggs Mast Truss

The Briggs mast truss was a unique innovation introduced into shipbuilding apparently about November 1854 by the brothers E. and H. O. Briggs, who had opened their own shipyard at South Boston in 1848. These men were descendants of a shipbuilding family that was well established in Colonial times. The family remained continuously in shipbuilding, over the years carefully handing down to each succeeding generation their building proficiency and design expertise. As a result, the two brothers established their own business and brought into it not only this accumulated knowledge, but also a keen scientific and analytical approach to all the problems that confronted the shipbuilders of the day. They apparently possessed considerable engineering acumen.

One of these outstanding problems was the inherent weakness of a ship in the area of the mast steps where the great concentrated load of a fully rigged and fitted mast brought inordinately high stresses to bear in all the timbers, fastenings, and seams in the immediate area.

The brothers apparently devoted much thought to some means of overcoming the problem, and their interest finally brought results sometime between October 1854 and September 1855. The clipper *Saracen*, which they designed and built, was launched in October 1854 and, according to her description,[1] was constructed in the usual manner of the period. In September 1855 they launched another product of their own design, the clipper *Mameluke*. This vessel contained a revolutionary treatment of the keelson structure, namely the addition of a truss-like arrangement of timbers which were securely fastened to the sides of the keelson along the entire length of the vessel and which rose to form the apex of a triangle under the step of each mast. It was greeted with highest regard by all knowledgeable people before it had ever gone to sea. It was quickly adopted and in its earliest existence was known as the Briggs mast truss—sometimes referred to as the Briggs mast bridge or, incorrectly, the Briggs mast brace. The material was hard pine, and the fastenings were iron, driven through all members and clinched.

Although *Mameluke* is the first vessel included in this book to be identified by name as having these mast trusses installed, there is evidence that she may not have actually been the first vessel for which they were designed. This statement may be considered in light of the wording of the original description: "She also has trusses fitted to the side of the keelson, and these extend from the stem to the sternpost—meet under the heel of each mast, and are bolted through and through and are clinched. The Messrs. Briggs, who built this vessel, are the originators of this plan, which has been applied to four other vessels, now in the course of construc-

Figure 16.1. *Detail of mast steps built in* Endeavor, *1856.*

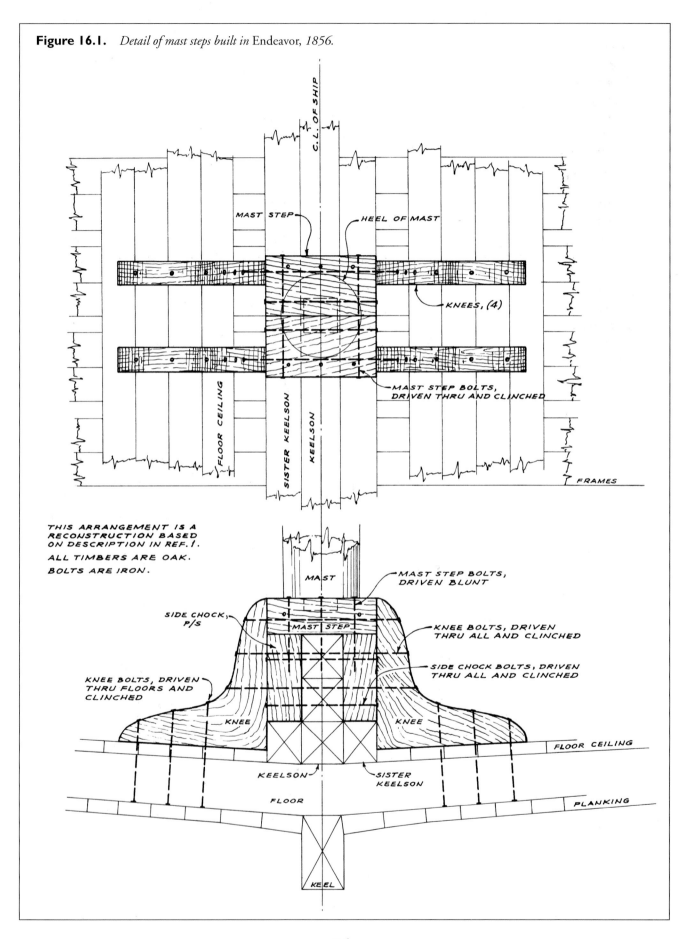

tion in this vicinity. These braces or trusses are designed to prevent the masts settling, and taken in connection with the partner beams, make her unusually strong in the bottom. The marine inspectors and all others, who have seen this plan, speak of it in the highest terms, as a very valuable improvement."[1]

The "partner beams" mentioned in the above description are covered later as a separate item under their own heading.

In October 1855, one month after the launching of *Mameluke*, the brothers Briggs launched another clipper, *Fair Wind*. The report on this vessel states that there were now six other vessels under construction in the vicinity, all having mast trusses applied in the same style.

Finally, in October 1856, they launched the clipper *Asa Eldridge*, and included in the description of the ship is the statement that ". . . [the trusses] are now applied to almost every new ship."[1]

The following nine vessels included in this book are described as being fitted with the Briggs mast truss: *Mameluke, Fair Wind, Daring, Electric Spark*, and *Alarm*, all built in 1855; *Thatcher Magoun, Joseph Peabody, Asa Eldridge*, and *Flying Mist*, all built in 1856. In *Fair Wind* and *Thatcher Magoun* the scantlings of the truss were 8 inches thick by 14 inches wide; in *Alarm, Joseph Peabody*, and *Asa Eldridge* the scantlings were 7 inches thick by 14 inches wide; in the remaining four vessels no sizes are reported. A comparison between the sided dimensions of the various keelsons and the thickness of the truss timbers suggests that the truss thickness was approximately equal to the half-siding of the keelson.

An indication that this new feature was well received is illustrated in William H. Webb's *Ocean Monarch*, launched in September 1856. This ship was a freighter rather than a clipper, but the function and advantages of fitting the mast truss applied to any class of vessel. Fortunately for posterity, the form of the truss as fitted in this ship may be plainly seen in the inboard profile of *Ocean Monarch*[24]; the arrangement and details are shown in Figure 16.2. The only apparent difference between this and the usual installation is the absence of sister keelsons in *Ocean Monarch*. This, however, would have had no effect on the distribution of forces that the mast truss generated.

It functioned as follows: The weight of the completely installed mast came to rest on the mast step, as it always did. With the truss in place and its general proportions already known, the load was now divided into three parts. One-half rested on the keelson rider, and one-quarter rested on the apex of each truss, port and starboard. The portion of the load bearing on the keelson was vertical, as was always the case, but reduced by half. The portion of the load bearing on each truss element was divided into two parts, one-part being diverted forward and one part di-

verted aft; thus each portion of the truss supported one-eighth of the mast load. Due to the angle of the members forming the apex, vertical and horizontal components were set up, the magnitude of each being governed by the vertical component which was one-eighth of the mast load. Relatively great stresses were developed in the diagonal truss member which carried the resultant force of this loading. Acting in compression as a column, its foot abutted the horizontal member that was secured alongside the keelson and, since it was tightly fayed to the sides of the keelson, it was in no danger of buckling.

The result of this additional structure was that, while half of the mast load bore directly down on the keelson, the remaining portion was diverted to points considerably distant from the mast location. Thus, not only was the great stress under the mast relieved, but also the total load was distributed to various points along the keelson. An additional benefit was the easing of forces that tended to strain the seams and caulking in way of the masts.

Briggs Partner Beams

The installation of Briggs partner beams, another innovation of the Briggs brothers, first occurred in *Mameluke* in 1855. It appears to be the first deliberate attempt to contribute to the lateral stability of masting, the problems of which were discussed under the heading "Mast Steps."

Their engineering minds had already devised the highly regarded mast truss which for a while would bear their name, but apparently they were never content with merely building a good ship. It seems that their philosophy was to constantly pursue and resolve problems inherent in ship construction.

Having relieved the high concentration of stresses on the keelson due to mast weight, they turned their attention to alleviating the tendency of the masts to strain the fiber and fastenings of the keelson at the mast steps when a ship was rolling in heavy seas. Their early solution, the installation of mast partner beams, seems so obvious that one wonders why it had not appeared much sooner.

Mast partner beams were actually two stout timbers laid athwartships atop the keelson in way of each mast. The ends of these timbers butted against the heavy bilge ceiling on both sides of the ship. They were then kneed to the sides and securely fastened with iron bolts. Amidships, stout iron bolts were driven down through each partner beam into the keelson.

This system appeared a second time when they launched the clipper *Fair Wind*, on October 12, 1855. These are the only two clipper ships included in this book that were fitted out with mast partner beams. Figure 16.3, detail A, illustrates this installation as described by MacLean.[1]

The text of the description of this unique construction detail is much the same for both vessels. However, that for

(text continued on page 264)

Figure 16.2. *Briggs mast truss as installed in Ocean Monarch, 1856.*

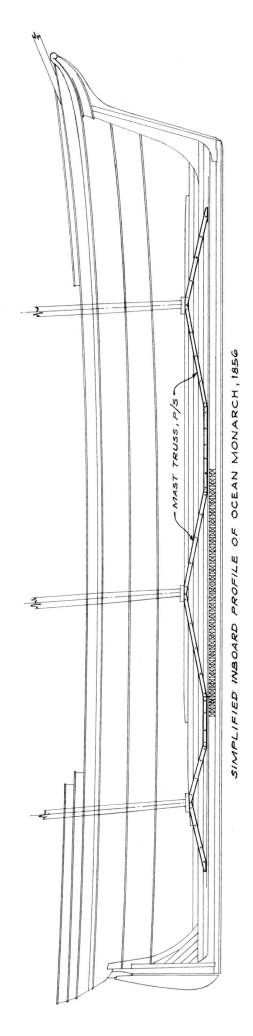

SIMPLIFIED INBOARD PROFILE OF OCEAN MONARCH, 1856

MAST TRUSS, P/s

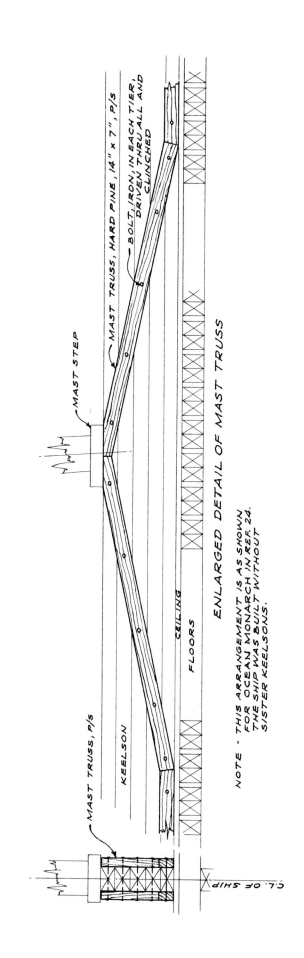

MAST STEP

MAST TRUSS, HARD PINE, 14" × 7", P/s

BOLT, IRON, IN EACH TIER, DRIVEN THRU ALL AND CLINCHED

MAST TRUSS, P/s

KEELSON

CEILING

FLOORS

C.L. OF SHIP

ENLARGED DETAIL OF MAST TRUSS

NOTE - THIS ARRANGEMENT IS AS SHOWN FOR OCEAN MONARCH IN REF. 24. THE SHIP WAS BUILT WITHOUT SISTER KEELSONS.

Figure 16.3. *Briggs partner beams and mast braces.*

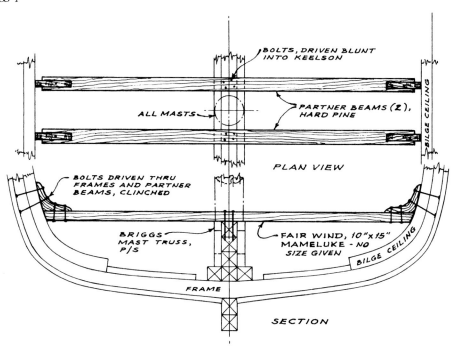

BOLTS, DRIVEN BLUNT
INTO KEELSON

ALL MASTS

PARTNER BEAMS (2),
HARD PINE

BILGE CEILING

PLAN VIEW

BOLTS DRIVEN THRU
FRAMES AND PARTNER
BEAMS, CLINCHED

BRIGGS
MAST TRUSS,
P/S

FAIR WIND, 10"x15"
MAMELUKE - NO
SIZE GIVEN

BILGE CEILING

FRAME

SECTION

PARTNER BEAMS

MAMELUKE, 1855 AND FAIR WIND, 1855

DETAIL A

ALL BOLTS ARE IRON

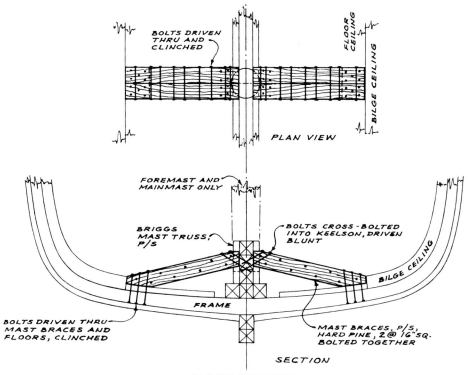

BOLTS DRIVEN
THRU AND
CLINCHED

FLOOR
CEILING

BILGE CEILING

PLAN VIEW

FOREMAST AND
MAINMAST ONLY

BRIGGS
MAST TRUSS,
P/S

BOLTS CROSS-BOLTED
INTO KEELSON, DRIVEN
BLUNT

BILGE CEILING

FRAME

BOLTS DRIVEN THRU
MAST BRACES AND
FLOORS, CLINCHED

MAST BRACES, P/S,
HARD PINE, 2@ 16"SQ.
BOLTED TOGETHER

SECTION

MAST BRACES

JOSEPH PEABODY, 1856 AND ASA ELDRIDGE, 1856

DETAIL B

(text continued from page 261)

Fair Wind is the more complete and, since interpretations of written descriptions are subject to great variation, I quote MacLean directly so that each reader may derive his own conclusion: "To each mast there are also two partner beams of 10 × 15 inches, which are bolted to the keelson and kneed to the sides. The application of these beams and trusses, for strengthening the bottom and supporting the masts, is the invention of the Messrs. Briggs, who designed and built this ship. Six other vessels, now in the course of construction in this vicinity, are also having them applied in the same style."[1]

Since six other vessels being built elsewhere were installing similar mast partner beams, there can be little doubt as to their effectiveness in solving the problem that was addressed, but they were quite obviously cumbersome, space-consuming, and in locations that must have generated many a mouthful of picturesque longshoreman's invective.

Apparently the Briggs partner beams met with only limited approbation in this form. Within a year the ingenious brothers Briggs had discarded this design and brought forth a revised version which is covered below.

Briggs Mast Braces

A new bit of construction, Briggs mast braces appeared in mid-1856. The Briggs brothers were apparently intent upon improving their solution to a problem previously resolved, namely the mast partner beam introduced the preceding year.

A detailed examination of Figure 16.3, detail A, easily shows that the old mast partner beams, while extremely effective, also possessed nuisance value of the highest order. A keelson four tiers high was, in effect, a longitudinal partial bulkhead along the centerline of the ship and as such presented an inconvenience and, in the eyes of the Briggs brothers, was a source of potential damage to the ship due to the high location required for the mast step. The brothers were apparently unhappy on this score, but at the same time they were still intent on retaining the function of these timbers. Their improved structure appeared in the clipper *Joseph Peabody,* which they launched June 7, 1856.

The new structure could no longer be termed a partner beam due to its location, so it was referred to as a mast brace. It consisted of a diagonal brace on each side of the ship with its outboard end butted against the bilge keelson or the first strake of thick bilge ceiling and its inboard end fayed to the sides of the two topmost keelson riders. The braces opposed each other immediately below the mast step and were installed only in way of the foremast and the mainmast.

Even though these new components were of massive proportions, their improvements were three-fold. The new location eliminated the objections to their considerable interference in lading the hold; they were placed in the lowest possible location in the ship, thus reducing their overall size; and they contributed a new element, namely additional support for the deadweight of the masts, this being accomplished by the angle at which they were installed, which introduced a vertical component force under the mast steps.

Apparently pleased with the success of these new mast braces, the Briggs brothers built a second ship containing them. This was the clipper *Asa Eldridge,* launched in October 1856. The two vessels are the only clippers included in this book to have this style of mast brace. Figure 16.3, detail B, illustrates this installation as described by MacLean.[1]

Duncan MacLean[1] notes in his description of *Joseph Peabody* that almost all new ships were being built with Briggs mast braces. However, he does not mention the ships or their builders by name.

His detailed description of the mast braces in that vessel is: "The steps of this ship's fore and mainmasts are supported by double angle-pieces, combined, measuring 16 × 32 inches. These pieces are of hard pine, butt up against the thickwork on the bilge, rest upon the floor ceiling, and are fayed to the keelsons, bolted through them, and also through the ceiling and the timbers. These cross braces share the weight of the masts with the keelsons, and have also a tendency to confine the garboards to the keel, at points where they are most liable to open."[1]

This particular report is one of very few which, in its last sentence, specifically addresses the fact that straining the seams of the garboard strake in way of the masts was actually a matter of ongoing concern.

A similar report in reference to mast braces was also written for *Asa Eldridge* and tends to clarify certain details of their positioning. The description is brief: "The steps of the fore and mainmasts, in addition to the bridge are supported by angular crosspieces of 16 × 32 inches, which butt against the inner strake of the bilge keelson, and against the two upper midship keelsons, and are very strongly bolted together and at the ends."[1]

This second description indicates that, at the keelson, the details of both the mast truss and the mast brace were slightly modified to accommodate each other at the point where they met.

Figure 16.3, detail B, is one interpretation of the construction of the mast braces. The two descriptions may provide a basis for other interpretations, if such seem to be warranted.

Chapter Seventeen

WATERWAYS, BINDING STRAKES, AND TWEEN-DECKS CEILING

Tween-Decks Structure

The inboard structure of the tween-decks typically appears as shown in Figure 6.2, details V, W, Z, b, r, and t. The sizes, quantities, and materials for each of these items, along with upper deck structural members X and Y, are listed in Table 17.1 where known. While the fine details vary in accordance with the philosophy of each individual builder, the construction in the various ships is similar, and, in one form or another, each of the included members was basic to the strength and integrity of the ship. An inspection of Table 17.1 reveals that, throughout the entire list of ships, the scantlings for any given component vary but little between vessels of comparable size.

Second only to the keel/keelson assembly, in providing longitudinal strength to a vessel, was the group of timbers clustered around the ends of the lower deck beams in vessels with more than two decks. These areas together formed the girder that maintained the form of the ship throughout its length. The upper deck and its relevant structure provided tightness against water and weather, and strength to support the ship's top hamper.

The construction sequence of members listed in the table was not absolutely rigid. However, an inspection of Figure 17.1, detail A, which is devoted to fastenings, reveals that some components needed to precede others in assembly. The two controlling members were the lower deck waterway and the upper deck clamp. Once these members had been installed, there was certain flexibility in assembling the remaining structure.

Upper Deck Clamp

The upper deck clamp (Figure 6.2, detail Z or b) was the one item of tween-decks structure that had to be positioned in an exact and precise location. It had to be accurately cut and trimmed, and its upper edge scored to suit the snaping of every beam end. After this had been accomplished, the clamp was located so that the top surface of each upper deck beam was coincident with the moulded line of that deck at the side of the ship. Once in position, it was securely fastened and ready to perform its function of supporting the beam ends.

This clamp was made up in three basic forms. The most common form was a timber of thickness equal to that of the filling strakes; this occurred in about half of the vessels listed in this book when such detail is known. The second form was a clamp of thickness from 1 to about 3 inches greater than the filling strakes; this form was used in about one-third of the ships herein. The third form was a true log whose thickness approached twice that of the filling strakes. This massive clamp was specified consistently for the clippers of Donald McKay,[2] who laid wood on with a very heavy hand. Only a few additional isolated cases of this massive clamp are found.

As with all ship timbers, the longest possible lengths, 40 to 50 feet, were desired in order to minimize the number of butts that would occur throughout the vessel. None of the ships listed, including those with heavy upper deck clamps, are noted as having the clamps scarphed together. All were fastened through the frames and, in the case of heavy clamps, were also bolted vertically in way of the beams, one bolt being driven completely through the clamp and the beam end, as shown in Figure 17.1, detail A.

The clipper *Charger*, in addition to the above fastenings, also had one treenail driven horizontally through the clamp and every timber.

A very rare clamp installation is found in *Raven*, whose upper deck clamp was installed as a stringer, 14 by 17 inches, which substituted for the hanging knees that usually supported deck beams. This stringer was fastened with a 1-inch square bolt through every timber, apparently to achieve greater support and grip, the square bolt having 25 percent more area than a round bolt of similar dimension. This use of square bolts, while rare, was not unique.

(text continued on page 271)

Figure 17.1. *Waterways and tween-decks ceiling.*

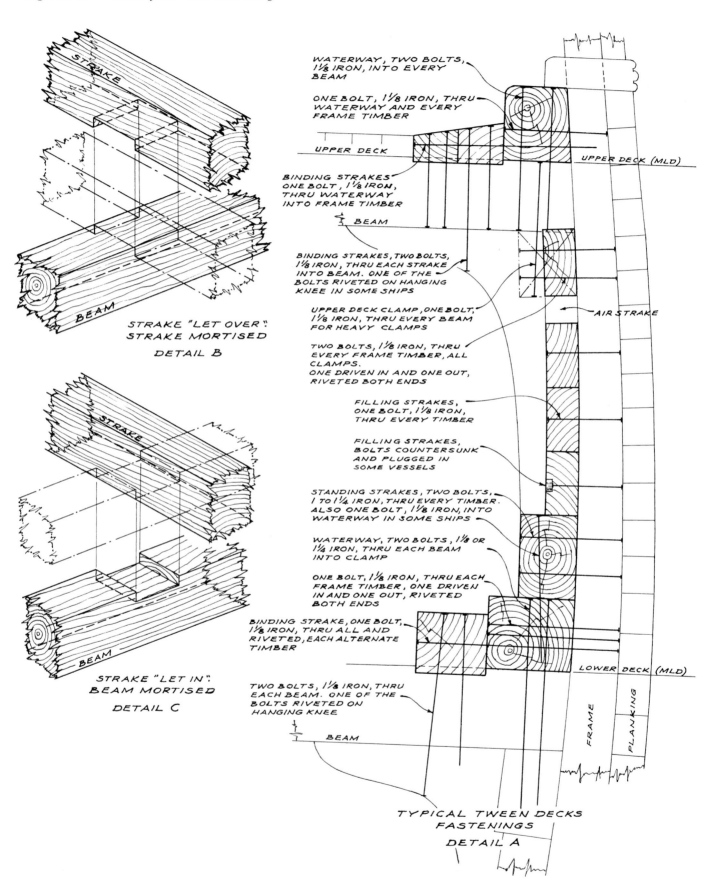

STRAKE "LET OVER":
STRAKE MORTISED
DETAIL B

STRAKE "LET IN":
BEAM MORTISED
DETAIL C

WATERWAY, TWO BOLTS,
1⅛ IRON, INTO EVERY
BEAM

ONE BOLT, 1⅛ IRON, THRU
WATERWAY AND EVERY
FRAME TIMBER

UPPER DECK

UPPER DECK (MLD)

BINDING STRAKES
ONE BOLT, 1⅛ IRON,
THRU WATERWAY
INTO FRAME TIMBER

BEAM

BINDING STRAKES, TWO BOLTS,
1⅛ IRON, THRU EACH STRAKE
INTO BEAM. ONE OF THE
BOLTS RIVETED ON HANGING
KNEE IN SOME SHIPS

AIR STRAKE

UPPER DECK CLAMP, ONE BOLT,
1⅛ IRON, THRU EVERY BEAM
FOR HEAVY CLAMPS

TWO BOLTS, 1⅛ IRON, THRU
EVERY FRAME TIMBER, ALL
CLAMPS.
ONE DRIVEN IN AND ONE OUT,
RIVETED BOTH ENDS

FILLING STRAKES,
ONE BOLT, 1⅛ IRON,
THRU EVERY TIMBER

FILLING STRAKES,
BOLTS COUNTERSUNK
AND PLUGGED IN
SOME VESSELS

STANDING STRAKES, TWO BOLTS,
1 TO 1¼ IRON, THRU EVERY TIMBER.
ALSO ONE BOLT, 1⅛ IRON, INTO
WATERWAY IN SOME SHIPS

WATERWAY, TWO BOLTS, 1⅛ OR
1¼ IRON, THRU EACH BEAM
INTO CLAMP

ONE BOLT, 1⅛ IRON, THRU EACH
FRAME TIMBER, ONE DRIVEN
IN AND ONE OUT, RIVETED
BOTH ENDS

BINDING STRAKE, ONE BOLT,
1⅛ IRON, THRU ALL AND
RIVETED, EACH ALTERNATE
TIMBER

LOWER DECK (MLD)

FRAME

PLANKING

TWO BOLTS, 1⅛ IRON, THRU
EACH BEAM. ONE OF THE
BOLTS RIVETED ON
HANGING KNEE

BEAM

TYPICAL TWEEN DECKS
FASTENINGS
DETAIL A

Table 17.1. *Waterways, binding strakes, and tween-decks ceiling.*

Notes: All vessels have two decks unless otherwise noted.
"Let in", the beam is mortised; "let over", the strake is mortised. (See Figure 17.1)
Scantling dimensions are copied as noted in the references.

Abbreviations

PP – pitch pine   SP – Southern pine
HP – hard pine   GHP – Georgia hard pine
YP – yellow pine

( ) – See Figure 6.2

Vessel & Ref.#	Species of wood	Waterways, Upper deck (Y) / Lower deck (W)	Binding strakes, Upper deck (X) / Lower deck (V)	Standing strakes, thick (t)	Filling strakes, thick (r)	Upper deck clamp, thick, (Z) or (b)
Challenge #1 (Three decks.)	HP	Upper 11"x12" Middle 15"x15" Lower 15"x15"	1 @ 8" thk 1 @ 8" thk	1 @ 10"x12" 1 @ 10"x12"	5" 6"	6" 7"
Challenger #1	HP	Upper 14"x14" Lower 16"x16"	1 @ 10"x14"	1 @ 10"x16"	6"	6"
Champion of the Seas #1,2 (Three decks.) — Ref.1	HP	Upper 14"x15" Middle 15"x15" Lower 15"x15"	thk, rounded 1 @ 10"x12"	1 @ 10"x12" 1 @ 10"x12"	5" 5"	heavy 7"
Ref.2	PP	Upper 12"x14" Middle 15"x14" Lower 14"x15"	1 @ 10"x 8" 1 @ 12"x10"	2 @ 18"x10" 2 @ 20"x10"	14"x 8", as req'd.	15"x10" 14"x10"
Charger #1	YP, HP, oak	Upper 14"x14" Lower 17"x17"; oak at ends of ship.	1 @ 10"x14"	1 @ 10"x14"	5", an air strake left open.	2 @ 6" thk; oak at bow
Charmer						
Cleopatra #1	HP	Upper 12"x14" Lower 16"x16"	2, thk, let in. massive	massive	5"	5"
Climax #1	HP	Upper 12"x14" Lower 15"x15"	2, thick	1 @ 10"x12"	5"	5"
Coeur de Lion #1	HP	Upper 12"x14" Lower 14"x14"	1 @ 8"x10"	1 @ 8"x14"	5"	5"
Comet	"Work compares with any ship of 1300 tons."					
Cyclone #3	PP	Upper 10"x12" Lower 15"x15"	1 @ 10"x14"	2 @ 10"x14"	5"	5"
Daring #1	HP, oak	Upper 12"x12" Lower 16"x16", curved inside to blend in with the binding strake	2 @ 4½" thk, let over 1 @ 9"x 8", oak, let in	1 @ 10½"x12" over 1 @ 11"x12"	5½"	6"
Dauntless #1						
Donald McKay #1,2 (Three decks.) — Ref.1	PP	Upper 14"x14" Middle 16"x16" Lower 16"x16"	1 @ 10"x12", rounded 1 @ 10"x12" 1 @ 10"x12"	1 @ 10"x16" 1 @ 10"x16"	6" 6"	6"
Ref.2	PP	Upper 12"x14" Middle 15"x16" Lower 15"x16"	1 @ 10"x 8" 1 @ 10"x12"	2 @ 18"x10" 2 @ 20"x10"	14"x 7", as req'd.	15"x10" 14"x10"
Don Quixote #1	HP	Upper 12"x14" Lower 16"x16"	2, thk, let over 1 @ 12"x14", let over	2 @ 10"x14"	6"	6"
Eagle #5	GHP					

Vessel & Ref.#	Species of wood	Waterways, Upper deck (Y) / Lower deck (W)	Binding strakes, Upper deck (X) / Lower deck (V)	Standing strakes, thick (t)	Filling strakes, thick (r)	Upper deck clamp, thick, (Z) or (b)
Alarm #1 (Two decks and hold beams.)	PP	Upper 10"x14" Lower 15"x15"	1 @ 10"x12"	2 @ 10"x12"	5"	6"
Amphitrite #1 (Two decks and hold beams partially decked.)	HP	Upper 12"x14" Middle 15"x15" Partial 15"x15"	thick thick	thick thick	5" 5"	5" 5"
Andrew Jackson						
Antelope #1	YP	Upper 12"x 8" Lower 14"x14"	1, thk, let in 1 @ 8"x12", let in	2 @ 8"x12"	5"	5"
Asa Eldridge #1 (Two decks and hold beams.)	PP	Upper 10"x14" Lower 15"x16", let over	1 @ 10"x13"	2 @ 9"x13"	6"	6"
Bald Eagle #1	HP	Upper 12"x12" Lower 16"x16"	2, thk, let over 1 @ 12"x14"	1 @ 10"x14"	5"	7"
Belle of the West						
Beverly #3	HP					
Black Hawk						
Blue Jacket #5	HP	"Nearly the same as Golden Light."				
Bonita #1		Main 14"x14"				
Bounding Billow Bark #1 (One deck.)						
Celestial						

Table 17.1. *Continued.*

Vessel & Ref.#	Species of wood	Waterways, Upper deck (Y) / Lower deck (W)	Binding strakes, Upper deck (X) / Lower deck (V)	Standing strakes, thick (t)	Filling strakes, thick (r)	Upper deck clamp, thick, (Z) or (b)
Eagle Wing #1	HP	Upper 12"x14"; Lower 16"x16"	1, thick	2, thick	6"	6"
Edwin Forrest #1	HP	Upper 15"x15"	1 @ 8"x14"	1 @ 9"x14"	5"	5"
Electric Spark #1	YP, PP	Upper; Lower	1, thick	2, thick	6"	7"
Ellen Foster #1	HP	Upper 10"x12"; Lower 15"x15"	2, thick; 1 @ 9" thk, let in	2 @ 9" thk	5"	6"
Empress of the Sea #1,2 (Two decks and hold beams partially decked.)	HP	Ref.1 Upper 12"x12"; Middle 15"x15"; Partial 15"x15"	2, thk, let over; 1 @ 10"x12", let in	2, thick; 1 @ 10"x16"	5"; 14"x 8", as req'd.	2, thick; 6"
	HP	Ref.2 Upper 12"x14"; Middle 15"x14"; Partial 14"x15"	1 @ 10"x12", let in	1 @ 10"x12"	6"	15"x10"; 14"x10"
Endeavor #1	HP	Upper 12"x12"; Lower 16"x16", let over	1 @ 10"x 8"; 1 @ 12"x10"	2 @ 18"x10"	6"	6"
Eringo Bark (One deck and half poop.)				2 @ 20"x10"		
Eureka #4	YP	Upper 13"x14"; Lower 15"x16"	1 @ 10"x13"	2 @ 11"x11"	6"	6"
Fair Wind #1	HP	Upper 10"x14"; Lower 15"x16"	2, thick; 1 @ 9"x13"	2 @ 9"x13"	5"	6"
Fearless	HP	Upper 12"x14"; Lower 15"x15"	1, thick	2, thick	6"	6"
Fleet Wing #1	HP	Upper 13"x13"; Lower 15"x15"	2, thick; 1 @ 7"x12", let in	2 @ 9"x12"	6"	6"
Flyaway #2,4,10	HP	Upper 10"x14"; Lower 15"x15"	2 @ 4½"x 6", let in; 1 @ 10"x14", let in	2 @ 10"x14"	6"	6"
Flying Arrow #1	PP	Ref.2 Upper 12"x14"; Lower 15"x15"	2, thick; 1 @ 10"x14"	2 @ 10"x14"	6"	6"
Flying Childers #1	SP	Upper 12"x14"; Lower 15"x15"	2, thick; 1 @ 10"x14"	1 @ 10"x16"	5½"	7"
Flying Cloud #1,2	PP	Ref.2 Upper 12"x14"; Lower 14"x15"	1 @ 10"x 8"; 1 @ 12"x10"	2 @ 20"x10"		14"x10"
Flying Dragon #1	HP	Upper; Lower	2, thk, let in	2, thick	8"	9"
Flying Dutchman						

Vessel & Ref.#	Species of wood	Waterways, Upper deck (Y) / Lower deck (W)	Binding strakes, Upper deck (X) / Lower deck (V)	Standing strakes, thick (t)	Filling strakes, thick (r)	Upper deck clamp, thick, (Z) or (b)
Flying Eagle #1		Upper 12"x12"; Lower 16"x16"	1 @ 10"x14"	1 @ 10"x20", finished with moulded top corner	6"	7"
Flying Fish #1,2	HP	Ref.1 Upper 12"x12"; Lower 15"x15"	2 @ 4½" thk, let in; 1 @ 9"x12"	1 @ 10"x16"	5"	5"
Flying Mist #1	PP; HP	Ref.2 Upper 12"x14", Lower 14"x15"; Upper 12"x14", Lower 16"x16"	1 @ 10"x 8", 1 @ 12"x10"; 2, thk, let in 1 @ 9"x13"	2 @ 20"x10"; 2 @ 10"x13"	6"	14"x10"; 6"
Galatea #1	HP				6"	
Game Cock #1	HP	Upper 15"x15"			6"	6"
Gazelle #4	PP	Upper 15"x15"; Lower			6"	
Gem of the Ocean #1	HP	Upper 16"x16"; Lower		2, thick	6"	6"
Golden Eagle #1	HP	Upper 15"x15"; Lower	1 @ 10"x15", let over	2 @ 10"x15"	5"	7"
Golden Fleece (2nd) #1 (Two decks and hold beams.)	HP	Upper 12"x14"; Lower 16"x16"	2 @ 4"x6", let in; 1 @ 8"x12"	2, thick	6"	7"
Golden Light #1	YP	Upper 10"x12"; Lower 14"x16"	1 @ 9"x12"	2 @ 8"x12"	4"	6"
Golden West #1	HP	Upper 10"x13"; Lower 15"x16"	1 @ 9"x12"	2 @ 9"x12"	5"	6"
Grace Darling #1	HP	Ref.10 Spar; Upper 12"x13"; Middle 16"x16"; Lower 16"x16"	1 @ 8"x13"; 1 @ 10"x12"; 1 @ 10"x12"	3½"; 1 @ 12"x18"; 1 @ 12"x18"	3½"; 8"; 8"	6"x14"; 12"x15"; 8"
Great Republic #2,4,10 (Four decks.)	HP	Ref.2 Spar; Upper 12"x15"; Middle 16"x16"; Lower 16"x16"	1 @ 10"x 8"; 1 @ 12"x10"	2 @ 18"x12"	14"x 8", as req'd.	15"x12"; 16"x10"
Great Republic (rebuilt) #103 (Three decks.)	PP, SP	Ref.4 Spar; Upper 16"x16"; Middle 16"x16", 6' scarphs; Lower 16"x16", 6' scarphs	1 @ 14"x12"; 1 @ 12"x14" / 1 @ 12"x14"	2 @ 24"x10"; 1 @ 12"x14" / 1 @ 12"x15"	10"; 8", scarphed	

Apparently rebuilt similar to original vessel (See ref.10) except for elimination of the spar deck.

Table 17.1. *Continued.*

Vessel & Ref.#	Species of wood	Waterways, Upper deck (Y) / Lower deck (w)	Binding strakes, Upper deck (X) / Lower deck (v)	Standing strakes, thick (t)	Filling strakes, thick (r)	Upper deck clamp, thick, (z) or (b)
Henry Hill Bark #1 (One deck and hold beams partially decked.)	HP	Upper 10"x12"; Partial		1, thick	4½"	thick
Herald of the Morning #12	YP	Upper 12"x12"; Lower 15"x15"	1 @ 7"x12", let over, 1" deep	2 @ 10"x10"		2 @ 5½"
Hoogly #1 (Two decks and hold beams partially decked.)	HP	Upper 12"x14"; Middle 16"x16"; Partial 16"x16"	3 @ 4½" thk; 1 @ 10" thk; 1 @ 10" thk	1 @ 10" thk; 1 @ 10" thk	6"; 6"	6"; 6"
Hurricane						
Indiaman #1	HP	Upper 10"x12"; Lower 15"x15"	1 @ 10"x15"	1 @ 10"x15"	6"	8"x14"
Intrepid		"Very heavy and thoroughly bolted."				
Invincible #4 (Three decks.)	GHP					
James Baines #1,2 (Three decks.)	PP	Ref.1 "Nearly the same as Champion of the Seas." Ref.2 Upper 12"x14"; Middle 15"x14"; Lower 14"x15"	1 @ 10"x 8"; 1 @ 12"x10"; 1 @ 12"x10"	2 @ 18"x10"; 2 @ 20"x10"	14"x 8", as req'd.	15"x10"; 14"x10"
John Bertram #1	HP	Upper 12"x12"; Lower 15"x15"	1 @ 9"x12", let over, 1½" deep	1 @ 9"x14"	5"	5"
John Gilpin #1	HP	Upper 10"x12"; Lower 15"x15"	2 @ 6½" thk, let in; 1 @ 12"x 9"	2 @ 10" thk	6"	6"
John Land #1,32 (Built as a duplicate of Winged Arrow.)	HP	Upper 10"x12"; Lower 15"x16"	1 @ 12"x 8", let in	2 @ 8"x13"	5"	6"
John Stuart (Three decks.)	HP					
John Wade #1	HP	Upper 10"x12"; Lower 15"x15"	1 @ 9"x14"	2 @ 9"x14"	6"	7"
Joseph Peabody #1 (Two decks and hold beams decked.)	HP	Upper 12"x14"; Lower 16"x16"	2, thk,let in.	2, thick	6"	6"
King Fisher #1			2, thk,let in.	2, thick	6"	6"
Lady Franklin	HP		1, thick			
Lamplighter Bark (One deck.)				massive	6"	6"
Lightfoot #1	HP	Upper 12"x14"; Lower 16"x16"	2, thk,let in	massive		
Lightning #1,2 (Built with two decks, third deck added later.)	HP	Ref.1 Upper 12"x14"; Lower 16"x16" Ref.2 Upper 12"x14"; Lower 14"x15"	1, thick, chamfered; 1 @ 9"x12", let over; 1 @ 10"x 8"; 1 @ 12"x10"	1 @ 12"x14"; 2 @ 20"x10"	6"	9"x14"; 15"x10"; 14"x10"
Mameluke #1	PP	Upper 14"x14"; Lower 15"x15"	2, thick; 1,thk,let over	2, thick	6"	6"
Mary Robinson						
Mastiff #1	HP	Upper 10"x12"; Lower 14"x14"	1 @ 10"x12"	1 @ 10"x22"	5"	6"x14"
Mermaid Bark #1 (One deck and hold beams partially decked.)	HP	Upper 9"x13"; Partial 10½" in two thicknesses	2 @ 4" thk	4½"	4½	4½"
Morning Light #1,3 (Three decks.)	YP	"All work very stout. Strongly bolted with copper and iron."				
Mystery #1	YP	Upper 10"x14"; Lower 15"x15"	2 @ 6" thk, let over; 1 @ 10"x13", let over	2 @ 10"x13"	5"	6"
Nightingale #1	YP					
Noonday #1	HP	Upper 14"x14"; Lower 17"x17"	2, thick; 1 @ 14"x14" outside of 1 @ 6" thk	1 @ 10"x12" over 1 @ 11"x14"	6"	6"
Northern Light						
Ocean Express #1 (Two decks and hold beams from foremast to mizzen mast.)	HP	Upper 16"x16"	1, thick	2, thick	6"	6"
Ocean Pearl #1	HP	Upper 12"x12"; Lower 15"x15"	thick	thick	5"	5"
Ocean Telegraph #5	HP	Upper; Lower				5"
Onward #1	HP	Upper; Lower			5"	5"
Osborne Howes						
Panther						
Phantom #1	HP	Upper 12"x15"; Lower 16"x17"	2, thk,let in; 1 @ 10"x14"	2 @ 12"x14"	6"	6"
Queen of Clippers #1	HP	Upper 13"x13"; Lower 17"x17"	2 @ 4½" thk; 1 @ 10"x14"	1 @ 10"x16"	6"	6"
Queen of the Pacific (Three decks probable.)						
Queen of the Seas #1	HP	Upper 12"x14"; Lower 16"x16"	2, thk,let in; 1 @ 11"x10", let in	1 @ 10"x14"	6"	6"
Quickstep Bark #1	HP	Upper 12"x12"; Lower 14"x15"	1 @ 7"x14"	1 @ 7"x14"	3½"	4½"x12"

Table 17.1. *Continued.*

First group (Racehorse – Silver Star)

"Vessel & Ref.#	Species of wood	Waterways, Upper deck (Y) / Lower deck (W)	Binding strakes, Upper deck (X) / Lower deck (V)	Standing strakes, thick (t)	Filling strakes, thick (r)	Upper deck clamp, thick, (Z) or (b)
Racehorse Bark #1 (One deck and hold beams - partially decked.)	YP	Upper 9"x14"; Partial	1 @ 5½" thk outside of 1 @ 4" thk	1 @ 8" thk	4"	4"
Racer #3 (Three decks.)	SP	Upper; Middle; Lower 16"x16"	1 @ 7"x13" / 1 @ 7"x13"	1 @ 7"x13"	7"x13", as req'd.; 7"x13", as req'd.	7"x13"; 7"x13"
Radiant #1	YP	Upper 10"x12"; Lower 16"x16"	1 @ 10"x14"	2 @ 10"x14"	6"	6"
Raven #3	YP	Upper; Lower 14"x14"	1 @ 10"x14"	4½"	4½"	14"x17", 1" square bolts, iron
Red Jacket #19,46 (Built with two decks. An add'l. deck was installed in late 1860.)	SP	Upper 16"x16"; Lower 16"x16"	2 @ 9"x12"	2 @ 10"x15"	6"	6"
Robin Hood	PP					
Rocket Bark #1 (One deck.)	HP					
Roebuck #1	HP	Upper 11"x14"; Lower 14"x14"	2, thick / 1 @ 6½" thk	2 @ 8" thk	3½"; an air strake left open	1 @ 7" thk over 1 @ 6" thk
Romance of the Sea #1	HP,YP	Upper; Lower				
Santa Claus #1	HP	Upper 15"x15"; Lower 15"x15"	1 @ 9"x14"	2 @ 9"x14"	6"	6"
Saracen #1	HP	Upper 10"x14"; Lower 16"x16"	1 @ 9"x12"	2 @ 9"x12"	6"	6"
Sea Bird Bark #1 (One deck and hold beams partially decked.)	HP	Upper 9"x12"; Partial 9"x12"			5"	5"
Seaman's Bride #4	HP	Upper; Lower				13"
Sea Serpent	SP	Upper; Lower				
Shooting Star #1	HP	Upper 12"x12"; Lower 15"x15"	2, thk, let in / 1 @ 9" thk	1 @ 8½" thk	5"	5"
Sierra Nevada #1 (Three decks.)	HP	Upper 12"x14"; Middle 15"x15"; Lower 15"x15"	2, thk, let over; thick; thick	thick; thick	5"; 5"	7"; 7"
Silver Star #1	HP	Upper 12"x12"; Lower 15"x15", let over	1 @ 9"x14"	2 @ 10"x14"	6"	6"

Second group (Southern Cross – Thatcher Magoun)

Vessel & Ref.#	Species of wood	Waterways, Upper deck (Y) / Lower deck (W)	Binding strakes, Upper deck (X) / Lower deck (V)	Standing strakes, thick (t)	Filling strakes, thick (r)	Upper deck clamp, thick, (Z) or (b)
Southern Cross #1	SP	Upper 12"x12"; Lower 15"x15"	1 @ 5" thk, let in / 1 @ 8"x12"	1 @ 9"x12"	5"	6"
Sovereign of the Seas #1,2 (Two decks and hold beams.)	HP	Ref.1 Upper 14"x14"; Lower 16"x16" — Ref.2 Upper 12"x14"; Lower 15"x16"	Ref.1 2, thick / 1 @ 10"x12" — Ref.2 1 @ 10"x 8" / 1 @ 12"x10"	1 @ 11"x16"	6"	7"
Spitfire #1	PP	Upper 12"x12"; Lower 16"x16"	1 @ 12"x14"	2 @ 20"x10"	7"	15"x10"
Staffordshire #1,2 (Three decks.)	HP; PP	Ref.1 Upper 8" thk; Middle 12"x14"; Lower 15"x15" — Ref.2 Upper 12"x14"; Middle 15"x14"; Lower 14"x15"	Ref.1 1 @ 12"x14" — Ref.2 1 @ 10"x 8" / 1 @ 12"x10"	Ref.1 2 @ 12"x14"; 1 @ 10"x16" — Ref.2 2 @ 18"x10"	4"; 6"; Ref.2 14"x 8", as req'd.	Ref.1 7" — Ref.2 1 @ 6" thk over 1 @ 5" thk; 14"x10"; 14"x10"
Stag Hound #1,2	HP; PP	Ref.1 Upper 12"x12"; Lower 15"x15" — Ref.2 Upper 12"x14"; Lower 14"x15"	Ref.1 2 @ 4½"x 6", let over / 1 @ 9"x12" — Ref.2 1 @ 10"x 8" / 1 @ 12"x10"	Ref.1 2 @ 10"x 9" — Ref.2 2 @ 20"x10"	5"	Ref.1 5" — Ref.2 14"x10"
Star of the Union #1	HP	Upper; Lower				thick
Starr King #1	HP					
Storm King #1	HP	Upper 12"x14"; Lower 16"x16"	2, thk, let in / 1 @ 10"x16"	1 @ 10"x16"	6"	6"
Sultana Bark #1 (One deck and hold beams.)	HP	Main 10"x12"; Hold beams	2, thk, let in	1, thick	2 @ 4" thk	2 @ 5" thk
Sunny South (One deck and possibly hold beams.)						
Surprise #1	SP	Upper 12"x14"; Lower 15"x15"	2 @ 4½"x 6", let in / 2 @ 9"x 7", let in	1 @ 10"x12"	6"	6"
Swallow #1	HP					
Sweepstakes						
Sword Fish	YP					
Syren						
Telegraph						
Thatcher Magoun #1	HP	Upper 12"x14"; Lower 16"x16", let over	1 @ 9"x14"	2 @ 9"x14"	5"	7"

Table 17.1. *Continued.*

Vessel & Ref.#	Species of wood	Waterways, Upper deck (Y) Lower deck (W)		Binding strakes, Upper deck (X) Lower deck (V)	Standing strakes, thick (t)	Filling strakes, thick (r)	Upper deck clamp, thick, (Z) or (b)
Tornado							
Uncowah							
War Hawk #1	HP	Upper	12"x14"				5"
		Lower	15"x15"	1 @ 10"x14"	2 @ 10"x14"	5"	
Water Witch #1	HP	Upper	10"x12"	2, thick			5"
		Lower	15"x15"	1 abt 9"x14", let in	2 @ 9"x14"	5"	
Western Continent							
Westward Ho #1,2	HP	Ref.1		2, thk,let in			7"
		Upper	12"x12"	1 @ 10"x12",	1 @ 10"x14"	5"	
		Lower	16"x16"	let over			
	PP	Ref.2					14"x10"
		Upper	12"x14"	1 @ 10"x 8"			
		Lower	14"x15"	1 @ 12"x10"	2 @ 20"x10"		
West Wind #1	HP						
Whirlwind #1	HP	Upper	9"x12"				5"
		Lower	15"x15"	1 @ 9"x12"	2 @ 8"x12"	5"	
Whistler #1	HP	Upper	11"x14"				5½"
		Lower	15"x15"	1 @ 10"x13"	2 @ 10"x13"	5½"	
Wildfire Bark (One deck and high quarter deck.)							
Wild Pigeon #1	HP	Upper	14"x14"	2, thk,let in			5"
		Lower	16"x16"	1 @ 9"x16"	1 @ 9"x16"	5"	
Wild Ranger #1	HP	Upper	10"x12"				6"
		Lower	15"x15"	1 @ 9" thk	2 @ 8½" thk	6"	
Wild Rover							
Winged Arrow #1	HP	Upper	10"x12"				6"
		Lower	15"x16"	1 @ 12"x 8", let in	2 @ 8"x13"	5"	
Winged Racer #1	HP	Upper	14"x14"	2, thk,let in			6"
		Lower	16"x16"	1 @ 10"x16"	1 @ 10"x16"	6"	
Witchcraft #1	HP	Upper	12"x12"	2,thk,let over			6"x11"
		Lower	15"x15"	1 @ 9"x12", let over	1 @ 10"x16"	6"x11", as req'd.	
Witch of the Wave #1	HP	Upper	14"x14"				5"
		Lower	15"x15"	1 @ 12"x 9"	1 @ 9"x14"	5"	
Wizard #1 (Two decks and hold beams partially decked.)	HP	Upper	14"x14"	2, thick			7" 7"
		Middle	16"x16",abt	1, thick	1, thick	5"	
		Partial	16"x16",abt	1, thick	1, thick	5"	
Young America (Three decks.)							
Young Turk Bark #1 (One deck.)	HP	Main	12"x14"				4½", several

(text continued from page 265)

Waterways

The *waterways* (Figure 6.2, details W and Y) occupied similar locations on the decks upon which they were installed, but their functions were not totally identical. Those on the upper, or weather deck, functioned as the name implied. In their location along the sides of the ship these members, which were at the low point of the round-up of the deck, provided a channel to carry off water toward the scuppers which pierced the sides of the ship. The lower deck waterway, so called because of its location in reference to other structure, quite obviously was not installed to provide a watercourse. If this had been the only function of these components, their scantlings could have been greatly reduced.

The primary function of the waterway was to connect the sides of the ship to her decks. Consequently, the waterways' scantlings were of considerable magnitude, especially those of the lower decks. In general these waterways were carefully fashioned so that their lower and outer surfaces fayed against the top of the beam and the inboard face of the frame timbers. They were cut from the longest possible timbers, and their ends were scarphed or butted snugly together. The butts of these pieces were given ample shift with the butts or scarphs of the lower deck clamps. When located in position, these waterways were square-fastened through each frame timber and bolted through every beam, sometimes into the clamp below as shown in Figure 17.1, detail A.

There were exceptions to the above installation. The upper deck waterways of *Great Republic* were vertically scarphed,[10] and the lower deck waterways of *Witch of the Wave* and *Charger* were fitted with vertical scarphs at their ends rather than with square butts.[1] Also, in the clippers *Asa Eldridge, Endeavor, Silver Star,* and *Thatcher Magoun,* these waterways were all let over the lower deck beams instead of being fayed on them.

In addition to the above-mentioned fastenings, the lower deck waterways of *Charger* had treenails driven through every timber.

Binding Strakes

The *binding strakes* (Figure 6.2, details V and X) are shown in their most common form of installation, namely one large strake on the lower deck (or decks) and two smaller strakes on the upper or weather deck. While this scheme was overwhelmingly adhered to, there were several variations which can be found in the listing in Table 17.1.

The binding strakes reinforced the position of the waterways, but among the various shipbuilders there was the usual difference of opinion as to how these strakes should be installed. Figure 17.1, details B and C, illustrate two of the three methods of installing these strakes. Both involve scoring in way of the ship's beams. When the strake was to be "let over" the beam, a mortise, generally about 1 inch deep and of width to accommodate the beam, was scored in the strake, as shown in detail B. When the strake was to be "let into" the beam, the mortise was scored in the beams, as shown in detail C. The third method did not involve scoring of either member, the two units being fayed across their surface and then fastened. The specific types of installation, as indicated in the various references, are noted in Table 17.1.

A fourth procedure, which is not referred to at all in the references, involved the scoring of both beam and strake to one-half the total depth of the mortise. This method would seem to be the best of both worlds in that the binding strake would be captive in both longitudinal and transverse directions, any tendency to move being obstructed by the shoulders of the scoring, even without consideration of the fastenings. This, however, was an expensive process since each member would require the same amount of tooling. Apparently the builders were of the opinion that the end did not

justify the means. It cannot be concluded that no ship was ever built in this manner, but specific evidence is not included in any descriptions that are available.

The most specific description of fastening is found in McKay's notes.[2] The bolting of the lower deck binding strake is specified, and the details are reflected in Figure 17.1, detail A. The size of the bolts shown, 1⅛-inch iron, is typical throughout MacLean's ship descriptions, with, as always, variations. The fastenings of the upper deck binding strakes were, where possible, driven in the same manner.

When installing the binding strakes, the ends of each individual length of timber, whether butted or scarphed, were given ample shift with the joints of the waterways.

Standing Strakes

The *standing strakes* (Figure 6.2, detail t) were the major items of thick work in the tween-decks, effectively adding the mass of their scantlings to the strength of the ship's sides. The figure shows the installation of a single strake over the lower deck waterway; however, the listing of vessels in Table 17.1 shows that approximately half (where such details are known) were fitted with two such strakes, one secured over the other.

In either case, the practice was to fasten the standing strake at every frame, square-fastening it with two bolts through its substance and the frame timber, then riveting the ends. In all except the smallest ships, the strake was also edge-bolted through itself into the lower deck waterway. Where two strakes were installed the upper edge bolt was driven blunt into the lower strake. This pattern of fastening is illustrated in Figure 17.1, detail A.

These standing strakes were important longitudinal strength members and, as such, the ends were cut with vertical scarphs about 4 feet long, as specified by McKay.[2] The scarphs were given shift with the waterways and each other throughout the length of the ship.

In his descriptions, Duncan MacLean specifically stated that *Witch of the Wave* and *Silver Star* had scarphed standing strakes; also that *Witch of the Wave, Mystery,* and *Grace Darling* had all their heavy work scarphed.

Charger also had a treenail driven through the standing strake and every timber.

Tween-Decks Ceiling

Filling Strakes

The *filling strakes* (Figure 6.2, detail r) were the final members of the ceiling of the typical vessel. Their thickness was on the order of that of her exterior planking in way of the wales, ranging between 5 and 6 inches in most ships. Naturally, there were exceptions to this practice, two notable exceptions in two-deck clippers being *Spitfire*, a 1,550-ton vessel whose filling strakes were 7 inches thick, and *Flying Dragon*, a ship of only 1,137 tons, fitted with filling strakes 8 inches thick. At the other extreme was *Golden Light*, a vessel of 1,150 tons and filling strakes that were only 4 inches thick. Table 17.1 lists the thickness of filling strakes for vessels in this book.

These strakes were installed solely as covering for the frame timbers and protection of cargo; they were not considered as contributing to the longitudinal strength of the vessel. Their width was limited to about 8 inches, which allowed them to be suitably fastened with just one bolt through each timber, the end then being riveted. The usual attention was given to neat fit of the seams and adequate shift of butts.

A further refinement appeared in a few ships. In *Wild Pigeon* and *Dauntless* the bolts were countersunk on the inside and then plugged in order to guard her cargoes against iron rust.

In most vessels the filling strakes were installed until all the space between the standing strakes and the upper deck clamp had been completely filled. However, there were certain exceptions to this rule wherein the topmost filling strake was not brought up as high as the clamp. The resulting narrow space, about 4 inches, was left open and was termed an *air strake*. MacLean reported that the small ship *Roebuck* had an air strake in her tween-decks, and the 1,306-ton *Charger* had an air strake in her tween-decks and also one under the lower deck clamp in the hold. Air strakes are covered briefly below under their own heading.

The number of bolts driven in this portion of the average 200-foot clipper is not apparent when the bolts are considered one by one as they are being driven, but in the aggregate picture the quantities become rather unbelievably great. Following are two entries of MacLean, both referring to clippers built by Donald McKay. In *Westward Ho*: "The between decks. . . . Through the waterways and the beams and timbers there are no less than 1,325 bolts of inch and inch and a quarter size, and in a section of 7½ by 10 feet in the between decks there are 165 bolts." In *Bald Eagle*: "Through the between decks waterways, the timbers and beams, there are 1,452 bolts, and in a section of 8 feet by 10, also in the between decks there are 165 bolts."[1]

Unfortunately, figures from ships constructed by other builders are not to be found, but it appears reasonable to assume that the above examples are representative of typical construction.

In one vessel, *Lightning*, which was one of four ships McKay built specifically for James Baines and Co. in 1854–55, he attempted to reinforce the ship against hogging by installing wooden diagonal cross braces directly on the ceiling of the tween-decks. MacLean stated: "In every berth between the hanging knees she is diagonally cross-braced with hard pine 9 by 7 inches over the ceiling and these braces are bolted through the ceiling and the timbers."

This system of diagonal bracing is directly traceable back to the early 1800s when Sir Robert Seppings introduced such bracing into the construction of ships for the British navy. It is possible that it was viewed with second thoughts and possible misgivings as to its ultimate effectiveness, because it was not included in the structure of the three succeeding ships, all of which were fitted with external diagonal iron strapping.

Air Strakes

The use of *air strakes* (Figures 6.2 and 17.1) in the ceiling is a subject that receives but little attention in available texts, and among the clippers included in this book, they appear in the reports of Duncan MacLean as having been used in only two instances. The first vessel mentioned is *Roebuck*, in which the tween-decks ceiling is described thus: ". . . The strake above the thick work is 3½ inches thick, above it there is an air strake, and then above, her clamps which are of 6 and 7 inches thickness." This vessel was launched at the end of 1851. Air strakes were not reported again by MacLean until December 29, 1856, when he wrote of *Charger* that: "She is also ventilated through the bitts, and has an air-strake open in the between-decks and in the hold."

It cannot be presumed that these two vessels were the only ships that allowed for an air strake in the ceiling of either the tween decks or the hold. However, since both the detailed descriptions of MacLean and the structural specifications of McKay make no other mention of provision for air strakes, the conclusion may be drawn that, at this period, allowing for these openings was a matter of builder preference.

During this period of the early 1850s, ships' structures were routinely salted as an aid to structural preservation (this is covered in detail in Chapter 20). It is conceivable that builders, knowing the value of proper salting, allowed the value of structural ventilation to disappear from their thinking.

In describing the clipper *Electric Spark*, MacLean offered the best discussion found in the available references of the general problem of ventilating ships' interiors. Among other things, he recognized that the air in the hold was warmer and not as heavy as that on deck, allowing outside air to rush in and downward, thus creating a certain amount of slow circulation. Thus, if air strakes were provided, this circulation would penetrate the opening occasioned by the air strake, and air could very slowly circulate between frames and ultimately escape through the same open strake or through the opening in way of loosely installed limber boards. However insignificant this form of circulation might be, it would eliminate the negative effects of trapped, stagnant air.

Chapter Eighteen

Planksheer, Rails, and Bulwarks

Assuming That Construction Had progressed from the keel upward in a strictly uninterrupted sequence (this was not always so), the vessel was now in frame, and, once the weather deck waterways and binding strakes had been permanently fastened, the major strength structure was almost complete. Above this point most of the remaining structure was devoted to the purpose of preventing the elements—wind, water, and climate—from penetrating the vessel. The outer planking was, of course, vital to this purpose and is covered under its own heading. (Deck planking is discussed in Chapter 19.)

Topside Structure

With topside construction, as well as most other elements of the hull structure, the individual builders inserted their personalities into the details of construction, within certain time-tested parameters. Added to their own preferred methods were the demands of the owners for whom the ships were being built, and perhaps an even greater controlling factor: the amount of money that was to be spent on the project. The owners were practical businessmen intent on turning a profit, but it is rather surprising to find that they were rarely loath to pour capital into the venture. In fact, they, too, seem to have been caught up in the clipper phenomenon, and this became apparent when the topsides of a vessel became a structural reality. It was here that functional simplicity was often abandoned in favor of artistic treatment and structural overindulgence, many examples of which are evidenced throughout this representative gathering of ships. However, nothing was ever done that might contribute to the lessening of the vessel's ultimate integrity.

The typical structure above the weather deck is illustrated in Figure 6.2, details c, g, h, j, k, l, and z. Data pertinent to these items—sizes, quantities, materials, and details peculiar to some of the vessels—are listed in Table 18.1, where

known. Some indulgence must be rendered in connection with the word "typical," since there is so much variation in the details of the parts involved. In the long list of ships included, it is entirely possible that no single vessel will adhere to the "typical" illustration. Some clippers contained more structure than is indicated, some contained less, and the term implies some mystical balance between the extremes of reality. Since one drawing or sketch will not totally fill the picture, the term "typical" presents the best single means of portraying the intent.

Figure 18.1 illustrates a series of structural details encountered in the topside construction of all ships of the clipper configuration. The various details are all interchangeable; almost any combination of structure was possible, and this variety is reflected in the listing in Table 18.1 in which the details are noted in their proper combination in each vessel where known.

Planksheer

The *planksheer* (Figure 6.2, detail g), sometimes referred to as the *covering board*, was the structural member that closed all the openings between frames along the sides of the hull between the outer surface of the ceiling and the inner face of the exterior planking. It rested on top of, and fayed close against, the upper deck waterway, the ends of any framing that did not extend up to the main rail, and the sheerstrake of the exterior planking. It was laid in one of two ways. As shown in Figure 6.2, the surface of the planksheer was set parallel with the waterlines; in Figure 18.1 it is inclined with the round-up of the beams. No advantage appears to be evident in either case, and in none of MacLean's ship descriptions is mention made of either method. A fair assumption may be made that the manner of installation was the option of the builder. The only definite statement of procedure occurs in McKay's list of specifications, in which all twelve clippers were noted as having the planksheer inclined with the round-up of the beams.[2]

There were two methods of installing the planksheer, both illustrated in Figure 18.1. The first, shown in detail A, has the planksheer mortised in way of each top timber or stanchion and shipped over these members in one piece of the longest practical dimension, taking care that there was ample shift of the butts with those of the waterways. The width of the timber allowed sufficient substance inboard of the stanchion for an iron bolt to be driven through the planksheer and the waterway and riveted at both ends. Obviously these bolts were driven clear of the weather deck beams.

The projection outboard of the stanchion was generally great enough to allow the edge of the planksheer to extend beyond the surface of the sheerstrake and also to take a moulded edge. The timber was then fastened by bolts driven blunt down into the outer planking and, finally, received a bolt driven horizontally through the plank in way of each stanchion, riveted both ends and plugged.

The second method involved fabricating the planksheer in two pieces, as shown in detail B. A planksheer of the same total width as for the first method was made up of an inboard portion and an outboard portion, with cutouts in each of the pieces to accommodate the top timbers or stanchions. The two pieces were then assembled from inside and outside rather than being shipped over the timberheads. The fastening was similar to that of the one-piece construction, but required one extra bolt to be driven horizontally through the planksheer between stanchions, riveted at both ends and plugged.

An exception to the projection of the planksheer beyond the outer plank occurred in Samuel Hall's small clipper bark *Racehorse*. She was described as being perfectly smooth from keel to the rail, the planksheer being flush with the side and without moulding.

In the large clippers the prevalent thickness of the planksheer was 6 inches, proportionately less in the smaller vessels. Where considerable shape was encountered at the ends of a vessel, the planksheers were never bent to shape but, rather, were cut from suitable lengths of compass timber so that the wood grain would follow the contour of the individual piece.

As was discussed in Chapter 3, under the heading "Sheer of the Deck" and in Table 3.1, the sheer of the deck and the trace of the planksheer were not always the same; the trace of the planksheer followed that of the main rail, both rising at a faster rate than the deck. In such cases the waterway and the planksheer parted company in the vicinity of the foremast. The waterway proceeded forward in its normal fashion, secured to the deck beams. The planksheer, however, rose at the same rate as the main rail and, in so doing, left a space between itself and the waterway. This gap was filled in by a filler piece or *stealer strake* which was secured in the manner of any

bulwark planking and then caulked to ensure tightness.

The general material used in bolting the planksheer to the structure appears to be iron. However, in the clipper bark *Mermaid*, the planksheer fastenings were composition and, in *Saracen*, the planksheer was bolted to the structure with copper bolts.[1]

Rails

Main Rail

The *main rail* (Figure 6.2, detail h) was the last major structural member to be installed above the weather deck, and it defined the upper trace of the bulwarks. In general its width and thickness matched those of the planksheer; however, there were many clippers that deviated from the usual in minor details, especially in width and in the moulding and beading of the edges.

Transversely, the main rail was usually set parallel with the waterline, as shown in Figure 18.1. In profile its sheer, paralleling that of the planksheer, ascended forward to a height which invariably approached the level of the forecastle deck, imparting to the clipper its characteristic "spring."

Like the planksheer, the main rail was fabricated from the longest available pieces of timber, and wherever possible, in the portions of the vessel where extreme curvature was encountered, it was always cut from grown timber rather than being forced to shape by artificial means such as steaming. Unlike the planksheer, whose ends were bolted very closely together, the pieces of the main rail were scarphed together with long, vertical hook scarphs that were bolted together horizontally, the bolts being sunk into counterbores, riveted and plugged, inside and outside. In effect, the main rail became one continuous member which encircled the ship, its continuity contributing to the vessel's longitudinal strength.

In many vessels both the inboard edge and the outboard edge were moulded with pleasing rounded beadings, except for the outboard edges in way of the channels. In these areas the edge of the rail was left square in order to receive the faying surface of the channel.

There were several treatments applied to the installation of the main rail, the simplest being that shown in Figure 18.1, detail C. In this case all frame top timbers which had been extended above the planksheer were trimmed to the proper rail sheer height, with due allowance being made for a tenon about 1 inch long fashioned into the end to engage a suitable mortise which had been cut in the underside of the main rail. The stops thus formed were located at the moulded height of the rail and provided solid seating for the rail when it was settled into place. The rail was secured by iron blunts, or drifts, which were driven into the timber

(text continued on page 285)

Figure 18.1. *Planksheer, rails, and bulwarks; details and fastenings.*

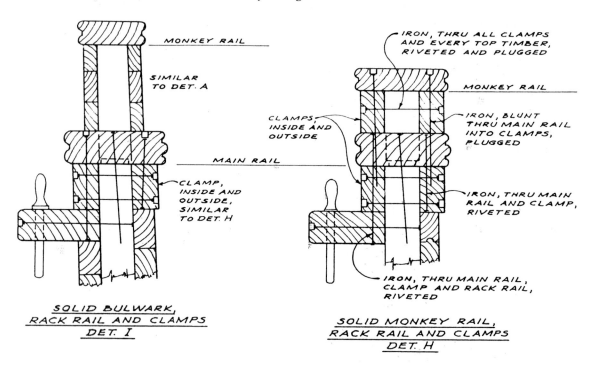

MONKEY RAIL

SIMILAR TO DET. A

MAIN RAIL

CLAMP, INSIDE AND OUTSIDE, SIMILAR TO DET. H

SOLID BULWARK, RACK RAIL AND CLAMPS DET. I

IRON, THRU ALL CLAMPS AND EVERY TOP TIMBER, RIVETED AND PLUGGED

CLAMPS, INSIDE AND OUTSIDE

MONKEY RAIL

IRON, BLUNT THRU MAIN RAIL INTO CLAMPS, PLUGGED

IRON, THRU MAIN RAIL AND CLAMP, RIVETED

IRON, THRU MAIN RAIL, CLAMP AND RACK RAIL, RIVETED

SOLID MONKEY RAIL, RACK RAIL AND CLAMPS DET. H

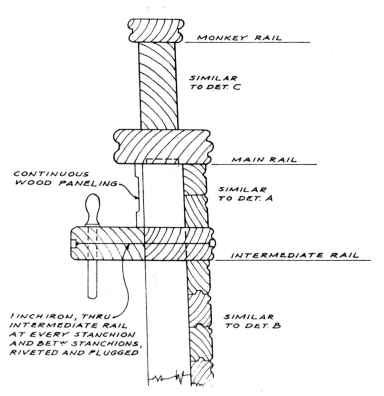

MONKEY RAIL

SIMILAR TO DET. C

MAIN RAIL

CONTINUOUS WOOD PANELING

SIMILAR TO DET. A

INTERMEDIATE RAIL

1 INCH IRON, THRU INTERMEDIATE RAIL AT EVERY STANCHION AND BET'N STANCHIONS, RIVETED AND PLUGGED

SIMILAR TO DET. B

RACK RAIL ON INTERMEDIATE RAIL DET. J

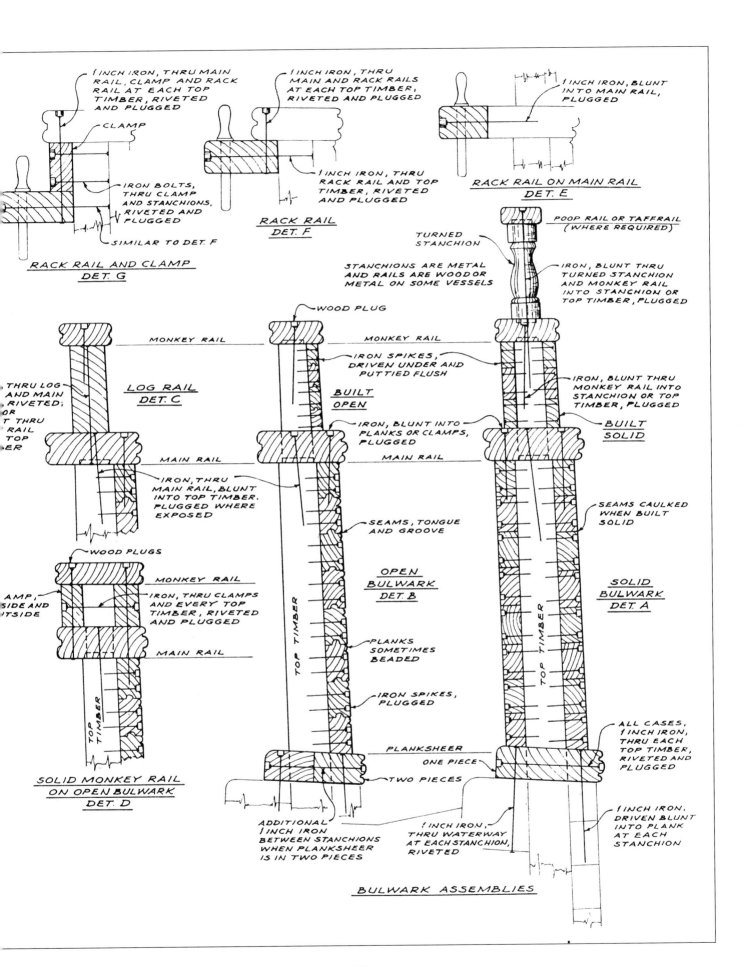

1 INCH IRON, THRU MAIN RAIL, CLAMP AND RACK RAIL AT EACH TOP TIMBER, RIVETED AND PLUGGED

CLAMP

IRON BOLTS, THRU CLAMP AND STANCHIONS, RIVETED AND PLUGGED

SIMILAR TO DET. F

RACK RAIL AND CLAMP
DET. G

1 INCH IRON, THRU MAIN AND RACK RAILS AT EACH TOP TIMBER, RIVETED AND PLUGGED

1 INCH IRON, THRU RACK RAIL AND TOP TIMBER, RIVETED AND PLUGGED

RACK RAIL
DET. F

1 INCH IRON, BLUNT INTO MAIN RAIL, PLUGGED

RACK RAIL ON MAIN RAIL
DET. E

TURNED STANCHION

STANCHIONS ARE METAL AND RAILS ARE WOOD OR METAL ON SOME VESSELS

POOP RAIL OR TAFFRAIL (WHERE REQUIRED)

IRON, BLUNT THRU TURNED STANCHION AND MONKEY RAIL INTO STANCHION OR TOP TIMBER, PLUGGED

WOOD PLUG

MONKEY RAIL

LOG RAIL
DET. C

THRU LOG AND MAIN RIVETED; OR T THRU RAIL TOP ER

MAIN RAIL

IRON, THRU MAIN RAIL, BLUNT INTO TOP TIMBER. PLUGGED WHERE EXPOSED

MONKEY RAIL

IRON SPIKES, DRIVEN UNDER AND PUTTIED FLUSH

BUILT
OPEN

IRON, BLUNT INTO PLANKS OR CLAMPS, PLUGGED

MAIN RAIL

SEAMS, TONGUE AND GROOVE

OPEN
BULWARK
DET. B

PLANKS SOMETIMES BEADED

IRON SPIKES, PLUGGED

MONKEY RAIL

IRON, BLUNT THRU MONKEY RAIL INTO STANCHION OR TOP TIMBER, PLUGGED

BUILT
SOLID

SEAMS CAULKED WHEN BUILT SOLID

SOLID
BULWARK
DET. A

ALL CASES, 1 INCH IRON, THRU EACH TOP TIMBER, RIVETED AND PLUGGED

WOOD PLUGS

MONKEY RAIL

IRON, THRU CLAMPS AND EVERY TOP TIMBER, RIVETED AND PLUGGED

AMP, SIDE AND TSIDE

MAIN RAIL

TOP TIMBER

SOLID MONKEY RAIL
ON OPEN BULWARK
DET. D

TOP TIMBER

TOP TIMBER

PLANKSHEER

ONE PIECE

TWO PIECES

ADDITIONAL 1 INCH IRON BETWEEN STANCHIONS WHEN PLANKSHEER IS IN TWO PIECES

1 INCH IRON, THRU WATERWAY AT EACH STANCHION, RIVETED

1 INCH IRON, DRIVEN BLUNT INTO PLANK AT EACH STANCHION

BULWARK ASSEMBLIES

277

Table 18.1. Plankshear, rails and bulwarks, deck planking.

Notes: All vessels have two decks unless otherwise noted.

Height of bulwarks is from deck to main rail plus monkey rail, or to whole height of both, and is measured in the waist of the vessel.

Abbreviations

HP - hard pine	SP - southern pine	GP - Georgia pine
NP - Norway pine	WP - white pine	GHP - Georgia hard pine
PP - pitch pine	YP - yellow pine	WO - white oak
		Cu - copper

( ) - See Figure 6.2

Vessel & Ref.#	Decks (c,q) and Tween dk hgts, Thk & Matl	Plankshear (g) Thk & Matl	Main rail (h) Thk & Matl	Bulwarks (1) Type,Thk,Matl See Figure 6.2	Monkey rail; Rack rail (j,k,z) See Figure 18.1	Remarks
Alarm #1 (2 decks & hold beams.)	Upper, 3½"pine 7'-9"; Lower, 3½"pine	6" PP	6" PP	open, whole height 5'-6"	Detl C, all HP	
Amphitrite #1 (2 decks & hold beams partially decked.)	Upper, pine 7'-3"; Middle, pine 7'-3"; Partial, pine	6" HP	6" HP	open, oak stanch'ns; whole height 5'-4"	Detl B, all HP	Mahogany monkey rail stanchions
Andrew Jackson						
Antelope #1	Upper, 3" WP 7'-0"; Lower, 3" HP	5" YP	5" YP	open, 2" YP, oak stanch'rns 8"x6"; hgt 3'-10" + 1'-0"	Detl B, all YP	Bulwarks beaded.
Asa Eldridge #1 (2 decks & hold beams.)	Upper, 3½" WP; Lower, 3½" HP	6" HP	6" HP	open, HP, oak stanch'ns, spaced 2'; whole height 5'-0"	Detl A, Detl C, all HP	Upper deck fastened with composition. Has a taffrail.
Bald Eagle #1	Upper, 3½" WP 8'-0"; Lower, 3½" HP	6" HP	6" HP	solid, HP, hgt 4'+ low rail.	Detl A, all HP	Bulwarks beaded outside and pierced with ports. See text.
Belle of the West #1	Upper, pine 7'-7"; Lower, pine	6" HP	6" HP	open, whole height 4'-6"	Detl B,	
Beverly #3	Upper, pine 7'-6"; Lower, pine	HP	HP			Iron rail and stanchions around poop deck.
Black Hawk #62,63	Upper, pine 8'-0"; Lower, pine			HP		A wooden rail on metal stanchions around poop deck.
Blue Jacket #5	Upper, pine 8'-0"; Lower, pine	HP	HP			
Bonita #1	Upper, pine 7'-6"; Lower, pine	HP	HP	open, paneled inside.	Detl B	Mahogany monkey rail stanchions
Bounding Billow #1 (One deck.) Bark	Main, 3" pine	5"	5"	open, paneled inside.	Detl B	Teak monkey rail stanchions
Celestial						
Challenge #1 (Three decks.)	Upper, 3½" WP 7'-8"; Middle, 3½" WP 7'-8"; Lower, 3½" WP	5" HP	6" HP	open, HP, locust stchns; whole height 4'-6"	Detl A, B and F, all HP except oak rack rail	Bulwarks and monkey rail paneled inside.
Challenger #1	Upper, pine; Lower, pine	6½" HP	6½" HP	open, HP, "low bulwarks and monkey rail"	Detl B, all HP	Mahogany monkey rail stanchions
Champion of the Seas #1,2 (Three decks.)	Ref.1 Upper,3½" WP 7'-6"; Middle,3½" HP 7'-6"; Lower,3½" HP — Ref.2 Upper,3½"x6"YP; Middle,3½"x7" PP & YP; Lower,3½"x6"YP	7" HP; 6"x15" PP	7" HP; PP	solid, HP, height 4'-6"+ monkey rail.; 3" PP	Detl A, all HP; all PP	
	Middle deck has thick strakes, 2 @ 5"x 14" along center line of ship. Lower deck has thick strakes, 2 @ 6" x 14" along center line of ship.					
Charger #1	Upper, 3½" WP 8'-0"; Lower, HP	6" HP	6" HP	open, HP	Detl A, B and D, all HP	Oak bulwark stanchions, every other timber. A taffrail but solid.
	Note: Half poop planks are all the length of the deck and are graduated in width to conform to the shape of the vessel.					
Charmer #1	Upper, pine 8'-0"; Lower, pine	6" HP	PP	open	Detl B	
Cleopatra #1	Upper,3½"pine 7'-8"; Lower,3½"pine	6" HP	6" HP	open, HP, whole height; abt. 5'-6"	Detl A, Detl B, all HP	Bulwarks beaded; oak stanchions, close together. A poop rail on turned stanchions.
Climax #1	Upper, 7'-10" WP; Lower, HP	6" HP	6" HP	open, HP	Detl B, all HP	
Coeur de Lion #1	Upper, 3½" WP; Lower, 3½" WP Decks fastened with copper	6" HP	HP	open, HP, height 4'-6" + solid monkey rail	Detl A, modified, all HP	Monkey rail is planked to full width of main rail.
Comet						

Table 18.1. *Continued.*

Vessel & Ref.#	Decks (c,q) and Tween dk hgts, Thk & Matl	Planksheer (g) Thk & Matl	Main rail (h) Thk & Matl	Bulwarks (1) Type,Thk,Matl See Figure 18.1	Monkey rail; Rack rail (j,k,z) See Figure 18.1	Remarks
Cyclone #1	Upper, pine 7'-6"; Lower, pine			open	Detl B	
Daring #1	Upper, 3½"pine 8'-6"; Lower, 3½"pine	6"		open, whole height 4'-10"	Detl C	Bulwark stanch'ns bright and varnished on outer square
Dauntless #1	Upper, 3½" WP 7'-9"; Lower, 3½" HP	6" HP	6" HP	open, HP, whole height 5'-6"	Detl B, Detl G, all HP	Monkey rail similar to Racehorse. See Figure 6.5
Dauntless :	Decks fastened with composition at every butt. Bulwark stanchions 6½"x10", every third timber and fastened with composition. Monkey rail lined with yellow metal; runs outside of deadeyes.					
Donald McKay #1,2 (Three decks.)	Ref.1 Upper, 3½"pine 7'-0"; Middle, 3½"pine 7'-6"; Lower, 3½"pine; Ref.2 Upper, 3½"x6"YP 7'-0"; Middle, 3½"x7"PP; Lower, 3½"x6"PP	PP; 6"x15"PP	PP; PP	solid, PP, whole height 7'-0"; 3" PP	Detl A, all PP; all PP	An oak poop rail on turned stanchions.
	Middle deck has thick strake, 5" x 14" along center line of ship. Lower deck has thick strakes, 2 @ 6" x 14" along center line of ship.					
Don Quixote #1	Upper, 3½" WP 8'-0"; Lower, 3½" WP	6" HP	6" HP	open, HP, hgt 3'-8" + 1'-2"	Detl B, all HP	Main rail moulding covered with yellow metal
Eagle #5	Upper, pine 8'-0"; Lower, pine	6" GP	6" GP	open, 2½" GP	Detl B, all GP	
Eagle Wing #1	Upper, 3½"pine 8'-0"; Lower, 3½"pine	6" HP	6" HP	open, HP, hgt 4'-0" + 1'-4"	Detl B, all HP	
Edwin Forrest #1	Upper, 3½" WP 7'-6"; Lower, 3½" HP	6" HP	6" HP	open, HP, whole height 5'-4"	Detl B, all HP	Monkey rail is 4" thk
Electric Spark #1	Upper, 3½" WP 8'-0"; Lower, 3½" HP	6" HP	HP	open, YP or PP, whole height 5'-0"	Detl C, Detl F, all HP	Rack rail is oak, covered with yellow metal
Ellen Foster #1	Upper, 3½" WP 8'-0"; Lower, 3½" HP	6"x14" HP	6"x14" HP	open, HP, hgt 3'-10" + 1'-3"	Detl B, all HP	
	Lower deck has 6" thick strake along center line of ship.					
Empress of the Sea #1,2 (2 decks and hold beams partially decked.)	Ref.1 Upper, 3½" WP 7'-10"; Middle, 3½" HP 7'-7"; Partial, 3½" HP	6" HP	6" HP	solid, 2" HP, hgt 4'-8" + 1'-8"	Detl A, all HP	Monkey rail is paneled inside. A railing around the poop deck. Part'l. dk plank'g is 8" wide along each side from bow to stern.
(Three decks.)	Ref.2 Upper, 3½"x6"PP 6"x15"PP; Middle, 3½"x7"PP; Lower, 3½"x6"PP	6"x15"PP	PP	3" PP	all PP	Deck is completely planked.
	Lower deck has thick strakes, 2 @ 6" x 14" along center line of ship.					
Endeavor #1	Upper, 3½" WP 8'-0"; Lower, 3½" HP	6" HP	6" HP	open, HP, hgt 3'-2" + 1'-3"	Detl B, all HP	Poop deck is protected by railings
Eringo Bark #1 (1 deck and half poop.)	Main, 3" pine		PP	open	Detl B	
Eureka #4	Upper, pine; Lower, pine	YP	YP	YP	YP	
Fair Wind #1	Upper, 3½"pine 7'-9"; Lower, 3½" HP	6" HP	6" HP	open, 2½" HP, stanchions 8" x 10"; hgt 4'-0" + 1'-1"	Detl C, all HP	Bulwark plank fastened with composition
Fearless						
Fleet Wing #1	Upper, pine 8'-0"; Lower, pine	6" HP	6" HP	open, HP, whole hgt abt 5'-0"	Detl B, all HP	Monkey rail stanchions are mahogany
Flyaway						

Table 18.1. *Continued.*

Vessel & Ref.#	Decks (c,q) and Tween dk hgts, Thk & Matl	Planksheer (g) Thk & Matl	Main rail (h) Thk & Matl	Bulwarks (1) Type, Thk, Matl See Figure 18.1	Monkey rail; Rack rail (j,k,z) See Figure 18.1	Remarks
Gazelle #4	Upper, pine; Lower, pine	PP	PP	PP	PP	
Gem of the Ocean #1	Upper,3½"pine "nearly 8'-0.". Lower, 3½"pine	6"	6"	open	Detl B	
Golden Eagle #1	Upper, 3½" WP 7'-10"; Lower, 3¼"	6" HP	6" HP	open, HP, oak stanch'ns; whole hgt abt 5'-0"	Detl B, all HP	Upper deck plank fastened with composition aft
Golden Fleece (2nd) #1 (Two decks and hold beams.)	Upper,3½"pine "lofty". Lower, 3½" HP	6" HP	6" HP	open, whole hgt 5'-0"	Detl B, all HP	
Golden Light #1	Upper, 3½" WP 7'-6"; Lower, 3½" HP	6" YP	6" YP	open, YP, paneled inside; hgt 4'-0" + 1'-3"	Detl B, all YP	Monkey rail stanchions are cherry
Golden West #1	Upper, pine 7'-6"; Lower, pine	HP	HP	open, HP, whole hgt 5'-0"	Detl A, Detl B, all HP	A poop rail on stanchions
Grace Darling #1	Upper,3½"pine 7'-9"; Lower,3½"pine	6"	6"	open	Detl B	
Great Republic #2,4,10 (Four decks.)	Ref.10 Spar, 3" WP 7'-0"; Upper, 3" HP 8'-0"; Middle, 3½" HP 8'-0"; Lower, 3½" HP. Ref.4 YP. Ref.2 Spar,3"x6"WP	Spar deck, 7"x20"HP; Upper,7"HP. Spar dk, 7"x20"PP	7" HP. YP	solid, abt 4"HP; 3½" ceiling inside from Upper deck to Spar dk. solid, 4" PP; 3½" ceiling inside	Chock 6" x 12" sits on Spar deck plansheer; supports turned stanchions 3½' high and a rail 5"x12" completely around Spar deck for the length of the vessel to the fore hatch. sim. to Detl A, all PP except oak stanch'ns	Monkey rail is 12"x5". Its top is 3½' above the Spar deck.
Great Republic #103 (Three decks, rebuilt.)	Lower,3½"x6"YP. Middle deck has thick strakes, 2 @ 5" x 14" along center line of ship. Lower deck has thick strakes, 2 @ 6" x 14" along center line of ship.					Probably similar to original vessel except for elimination of spar deck and rail on turned stanchions. If so, bulwarks are built solid with 3½" HP inside and 4" HP outside. See Detl A. Height possibly cut down between forecastle deck and spar deck.

Vessel & Ref.#	Decks (c,q) and Tween dk hgts, Thk & Matl	Planksheer (g) Thk & Matl	Main rail (h) Thk & Matl	Bulwarks (1) Type,Thk,Matl See Figure 18.1	Monkey rail; Rack rail (j,k,z) See Figure 18.1	Remarks
Flying Arrow #1	Upper,3½"pine 8'-0"; Lower,3½"pine	6" HP	6" HP	open, HP, planks beaded; hgt 4'-3" + 1'-6"	Detl B, all HP	Inside of main rail covered with yellow metal
Flying Childers #1	Upper, 3½" WP 7'-9"; Lower, 3½" WP	6" HP	6" HP	open, 2½" HP, oak stanch'ns; whole hgt 5'-3"	Detl B, all HP	Bulwarks beaded
Flying Cloud #1,2	Ref.1 Upper, 3½" WP 7'-8"; Lower, 3½" HP. Ref.2 Upper,3½"x6"YP; Lower,3½"x6"YP	6"x16"SP; 6"x15"PP	6"x16"SP; PP	open, SP, oak stanch'ns; hgt 5'-0" + 1'-4"; 3" PP	Detl A, B and G, all SP; all PP	A poop rail on turned stanchions. Lower deck has thick strake, 5" x 14" along center line of ship.
Flying Dragon #1	Upper, pine; Lower, pine	HP	HP	open, HP	Detl B, all HP	
Flying Dutchman						
Flying Eagle #1	Upper,3½"pine 8'-0"; Lower,3½"pine	6"	6"	open, oak stanch'ns; hgt 3'-6" + 1'-3"	Detl B	Bulwark planks are beaded
Flying Fish #1,2	Ref.1 Upper, 3½" WP 7'-10"; Lower, 3½" HP. Ref.2 Upper,3½"x6"YP; Lower,3½"x6"YP	6" HP; 6"x15"PP	6" HP; PP	open, HP, hgt 4'-6" + 1'-4"; 3" PP	Detl A, B and F, all HP; all PP	Rack rail 5" thk. A poop rail on turned stanchions. Lower deck has thick strake 5" x 14" along center line of ship.
Flying Mist #1	Upper, 3½" WP 8'-0"; Lower, 3½" WP	HP	HP	open, HP, hgt 5'-6"	Detl A, Detl D, all HP	Upper deck plank fastened with composition. A poop rail on turned stanchions
Galatea #1	Upper, pine 8'-0"; Lower, pine	HP	HP	open, HP	Detl B, all HP	
Game Cock #1	Upper, pine 6'-7"; Lower, pine	6" HP	6" HP	open, whole hgt 4'-0"	Detl C, all HP	

Table 18.1. *Continued.*

Vessel & Ref.#	Decks (c,q) and Tween dk hgts, Thk & Matl	Planksheer (g) Thk & Matl	Main rail (h) Thk & Matl	Bulwarks (1) Type,Thk,Matl See Figure 18.1	Monkey rail; Rack rail (j,k,z) See Figure 18.1	Remarks
Henry Hill Bark #1 (1 deck and hold beams partially decked.)	Upper, 3" WP; Partial, 3" WP	5" HP	5" HP	open, HP	Detl A, B and F, all HP	Rack rail is covered with yellow metal. A rail around poop deck.
Herald of the Morning #1,12	Upper, 3" WP; Lower, 3" WP	7" WO	7" WO	open (probable)	Detl B, Detl F	Rack rail is covered with yellow metal
Hoogly #1 (2 decks and hold beams partially decked.)	Upper, 3½" WP 7'-3"; Middle, 3½" HP 7'-3"; Partial, 3½" HP	6" HP	6" HP	open, HP; intermediate rail 6" HP, 1' below mn rail; whole hgt 5'-7". Space between main rail and rack rail is "tastefully paneled". Bulwark planking is grooved and moulded.	Detl J, all HP	Poop has bulwarks around stern above sheer of monkey rail
Hurricane #4	Upper 8'-3"; Lower	6" HP	6" HP	open, HP, whole hgt 5'-0"	Detl B, all HP	A heavy brass rail around the poop deck.
Indiaman #1	Upper, 3½" WP 7'-10"; Lower, 3½" HP					
Intrepid						
Invincible #4,32 (Three decks.)	Upper, pine 7'-6"; Middle, pine 7'-6"; Lower, pine	GHP	GHP	open, GHP, whole hgt 4'-6"	Detl B, all GHP	
James Baines #1,2 (Three decks.)	Ref.1 Upper, 3½" WP 7'-6"; Middle, 3½" HP 7'-6"; Lower, 3½" HP; Ref.2 Upper,3½"x6"YP; Middle,3½"x7" PP & YP; Lower,3½"x6"YP	6"x15"PP	7" HP	solid, HP, whole hgt abt 6'-0"	Detl A, all HP	Monkey rail is paneled inside. A poop rail on turned stanchions
	Middle deck has thick strakes, 2 @ 5" x 14" along center line of ship. Lower deck has thick strakes, 2 @ 6" x 14" along center line of ship.					
John Bertram #1	Upper, 3½" WP 7'-3"; Lower, 3½" HP; Upper deck fastened with composition.	6"x14"HP	6"x14"HP	open, HP; stanchions, 7" x 10", Cu fastened; hgt 4'-3" + 1'-6"	Detl B, Detl E, all HP, except oak rack rail	Bulwarks fastened with composition and ornamented inside

Vessel & Ref.#	Decks (c,q) and Tween dk hgts, Thk & Matl	Planksheer (g) Thk & Matl	Main rail (h) Thk & Matl	Bulwarks (1) Type,Thk,Matl See Figure 18.1	Monkey rail; Rack rail (j,k,z) See Figure 18.1	Remarks
John Gilpin #1	Upper, 3½" WP 8'-0"; Lower, 3½" WP	6" HP	6" HP	open, whole hgt 5'-10"	Detl B, all HP	Monkey rail goes around the poop
John Land #1,32	Built as a duplicate of Winged Arrow.					
John Stuart #4 (Three decks.)					Detl B	Monkey rail is around the poop
John Wade #1	Upper, pine; Lower, pine	HP	HP	open, HP	Detl B, all HP	Bulwarks are paneled inside
Joseph Peabody #1 (Two decks and hold beams.)	Upper, 3½" WP 7'-9"; Lower, 3½" HP	6" HP	6" HP	open HP, oak stanch'ns	Detl A, Detl B, all HP	Bulwark stanchions varnished on outer square. A poop rail on mahogany turned stanchions
King Fisher #1	Upper, 3½" WP 8'-0"; Lower, 3½" HP	6" HP	6" HP	open, HP, whole hgt 5'-6"	Detl B, all HP	Monkey rail stanchions are East India teak
Lady Franklin						
Lamplighter Bark #1 (One deck.)	Main, pine			open	Detl B	
Lightfoot #1	Upper, pine 8'-0"; Lower, pine	6" HP	6" HP	open, HP	Detl B, all HP	
Lightning #1,2 (Built with two decks, third deck added later.)	Ref.1 Upper, 3½" WP 7'-6"; Lower, 3½" HP; Ref.2 Upper,3½"x6"YP; Lower,3½"x6"YP	HP	HP	solid, HP, hgt 5'-0" + 2'-0"	Detl A, all HP	Monkey rail paneled inside. Poop rail and turned stanch'ns are mahogany.
	Lower deck has thick strakes, 2 @ 5" x 14" along center line of ship.					
Mameluke #1	Upper,3½"pine; Lower,3½"pine	6" PP	6" PP	open, PP	Detl B, all PP	
Mary Robinson						
	Lower deck has thick strakes, 2 @ 5" x 14" along center line of ship.					
Mastiff #1	Upper, 3½" WP 7'-8"; Lower, 3½" HP	6" HP	6" HP	open, HP, oak stanch'rns whole hgt 5'-6"	Detl B, all HP	Main rail is brass covered

Table 18.1. *Continued.*

(First group)

Vessel & Ref.#	Decks (c,q) and Tween dk hgts, Thk & Matl	Planksheer (g) Thk & Matl	Main rail (h) Thk & Matl	Bulwarks (1) Type, Thk, Matl See Figure 6.5	Monkey rail; Rack rail (j,k,z) See Figure 18.1	Remarks
Mermaid Bark #1 (1 deck and hold beams partially decked.)	Upper, 3" WP; Partial, 3" WP	5" HP, fastened with composition	5" HP, fastened with composition	open, HP, hgt 2'-6" + 1'-5"	Detl B, all HP	Bulwarks and monkey rail paneled inside
Morning Light #1 (Three decks.)	Upper, 7'-4", pine; Middle, 7'-4", pine; Lower, pine	YP	YP	solid, YP	Detl I, without rack rail; Detl A, all YP	A poop rail on turned stanchions
Mystery #1	Upper, 7'-9", 3½" WP; Lower, 7'-9", 3½" HP	6" HP	6" HP	open, HP, oak stanch'ns; hgt 4'-3" + 1'-3"	Detl A, Detl B, all HP	Bulwarks are beaded. Has a taffrail.
Nightingale #3	Upper, pine; Lower, pine	YP	YP	YP	all YP	Inside of monkey rail ornamented with carved branch work.
Noonday #1	Upper, 8'-2" WP; Lower, YP	6" YP	YP	open, YP	Detl D, all YP	
Northern Light						
Ocean Express #1 (2 decks and hold beams from foremast to mizzen mast.)	Upper, 3½" WP; Lower, 3½" HP	HP	HP	solid, HP	Detl A, all HP	Monkey rail paneled inside
Ocean Pearl #1	Upper, 8'-0", 3½"pine; Lower, 3½"pine	6" HP	6" HP	open, HP	Detl B, all HP	
Ocean Telegraph #5	Upper, 9'-0"	HP	HP	HP	all HP	
Onward #1	Upper, 7'-10", pine; Lower, pine	6"	6"	open, whole hgt abt 4'-6"	Detl B	
Osborne Howes						
Panther						
Phantom #1	Upper, 7'-10", 3½" WP; Lower, 3½" WP	6" HP	6" HP	open, HP, oak stanch'ns; whole hgt 5'-4" amidships	Detl A, Detl B, all HP	Main rail is covered with yellow metal. A poop rail on turned stanchions

(Second group)

Vessel & Ref.#	Decks (c,q) and Tween dk hgts, Thk & Matl	Planksheer (g) Thk & Matl	Main rail (h) Thk & Matl	Bulwarks (1) Type, Thk, Matl See Figure 6.5	Monkey rail; Rack rail (j,k,z) See Figure 18.1	Remarks
Queen of Clippers #1	Upper, 8'-0", 3½" HP; Lower, 3½" HP	6½" HP	HP	open, HP, whole hgt 5'-4"	Detl B, all HP; mahogany stanch'ns	Bulwark stanchions, oak, at every other top timber.
Queen of the Pacific (3 decks, probable)						
Queen of the Seas #1	Upper, 7'-10", 3½" WP; Lower, 4" HP	6"	6"	solid, 3", whole hgt 7'-3"	Detl A, Detl G	Monkey rail paneled inside. A poop rail on turned stanchions
Quickstep Bark #1	Upper, 6'-10", 3" pine; Lower, 3" pine	5" HP	5" HP	open, HP, whole hgt 4'-6"	Detl B, all HP	
Racehorse Bark #1 (1 deck and hold beams partially decked.)	Upper, 3" pine; Partial, pine, fastened with composition	4½" YP	4½" YP	open, YP, hgt 4'-0" + 1'-2"	Detl B, all YP	Bulwarks and monkey rail are paneled between stanchions.
Racer #3 (Three decks.)	Upper, 7'-0", WP; Middle, SP; Lower, 7'-0", SP	SP	SP	SP	all SP	
Radiant #1	Upper, 3½"pine, 7'-8"; Lower, 3½"pine	6" YP	6" YP	open, YP	Detl B, all YP	
Raven #3	Upper, 3½" WP; Lower, 3½" YP	YP	YP	YP	4½"x10"YP, mortised into stanchions	
Red Jacket #19,46 (2 decks. Add'l. deck added in late 1860.)	Upper, 8'-0"; Lower, pine, pine	Ref.# 19, HP 46, SP	HP SP	HP, SP	Detl B, all HP & YP	
Robin Hood						
Rocket Bark #1 (One deck.)	Main, pine	open	open	open	Detl B	Built similar to *Dauntless*
Roebuck #1	Upper, 7'-6", 3½" WP; Lower, 3½" YP	5½" HP	5½" HP	open, HP	Detl B, all HP	

Notes: Bulwarks are pierced with several gunports. See text.
Outside of planksheer is flush with planking, without any moulding. See Figure 6.5.
Monkey rail runs outside of deadeyes. See Figure 6.5.

Table 18.1. *Continued.*

Vessel & Ref.#	Decks (c,q) and Tween dk hgts, Thk & Matl	Planksheer (g) Thk & Matl	Main rail (h) Thk & Matl	Bulwarks (1) Type,Thk,Matl See Figure 18.1	Monkey rail; Rack rail (j,k,z) See Figure 18.1	Remarks
Romance of the Sea #1	Upper, 8'-0", pine; Lower, pine	YP or HP	YP or HP	solid,YPorHP, hgt 4'-6" + 1'-4"	Detl A, all YP or HP	A poop rail on turned stanchions
Santa Claus #1	Upper, pine; Lower, pine	6"	6"	open, oak stanch'ns	Detl B	Bulwark stanchions fastened with composition. See text.
Saracen #1	Upper, 3½"pine 7'-6"; Lower, 3½" HP, planking butts fastened with composition.	6" HP, copper bolted	6" HP	open, HP, oak stanch'ns 2'-0" apart.	Detl A, B and F, all HP except taffrail & oak rack rail	Main rail is covered with yellow metal. Has a taffrail.
Sea Bird Bark #1 (1 deck and hold beams partially decked.)	Main, pine Partial, pine	4½" HP	4½" HP	open, HP	Detl B, all HP	
Seaman's Bride #4	Upper; Lower			open, hgt 5'-10" + 1'-1"		Bulwark stanchions are all locust
Sea Serpent						
Shooting Star #1	Upper, 3½" WP 7'-0"; Lower, 3½" HP	6"x14"SP	6"x17½"SP	open, stanch'ns, 8" x 12"; hgt 3'-8" + 1'-3"	Detl A, Detl B, all SP	Bulwarks and monkey rail paneled inside. A brass railing around poop deck
Sierra Nevada #1 (Three decks.)	Upper, 3½" WP 6'-6"; Middle, 3½" HP 6'-6"; Lower, 3½" HP	6" HP	HP	open, HP, oak stanch'ns; whole hgt 5'-0"	Detl A, Detl D, all HP	Inside of main rail covered with yellow metal. A poop rail on turned stanchions
	Note: Center of lower deck is open for nearly the length of the ship.					
Silver Star #1	Upper, 3½" WP 8'-6"; Lower,3" PP	6" HP	6" HP	open, HP, hgt 3'-6", + 1'-2"	Detl A, B and F, all HP	Rack rail is oak, covered with Cu. A poop rail on turned stanchions
Southern Cross #1	Upper, 3½" WP 7'-0"; Lower, 3½" SP	6"x15"SP	6"x15"SP	open, SP, oak stanch'ns; hgt 4'-0" + a monkey rail	Detl B, all SP	

Vessel & Ref.#	Decks (c,q) and Tween dk hgts, Thk & Matl	Planksheer (g) Thk & Matl	Main rail (h) Thk & Matl	Bulwarks (1) Type,Thk,Matl See Figure 18.1	Monkey rail; Rack rail (j,k,z) See Figure 18.1	Remarks
Sovereign of the Seas #1,2 (Two decks and hold beams.)	Ref.1 Upper,3½"pine 8'-0"; Lower, 3½"pine	7" HP	7" HP	open, 2½" HP, hgt 5'-2" + 1'-4"	Detl B, Detl G, all HP	
	Ref.2 Upper,3½"x6"YP; Lower,3½"x6"PP	6"x15"PP	PP	solid, 3" PP	all PP	
	Lower deck has thick strakes, 2 @ 6" x14" along center line of ship.					
Spitfire #1	Upper, 3½" WP 9'-0"; Lower, 3½" HP	HP	HP	open, HP	Detl B, all HP	
Staffordshire #1,2 (Three decks.)	Ref.1 Upper, 3" WP; Middle, 3½" HP; Lower, 3½" HP	5"	5"	open, upper bulw'ks, whole height is 4'-6". See text.	Detl B	Main rail is covered with yellow metal inside
	Ref.2 Upper,3½"x6"YP; Middle,3½"x7" PP & YP; Lower,3½"x6"YP	6"x15"PP	PP		all PP	
	Lower and middle decks have a 5" x 14" thick strake along center line of ship.					
Stag Hound #1,2	Ref.1 Upper, 3½" WP 7'-0"; Lower, 3½" WP	6"x16"HP	6"x16"HP	open, HP, fastened with composition; whole hgt 6'-6"	Detl A, B and G, all HP	Bulwark stanchions WO, 8"x10". A poop rail on turned stanchions
	Ref.2 Upper,3½"x6"YP; Lower,3½"x6"YP	6"x15"PP	PP	3" PP	all PP	
Star of the Union #1	Upper, 7'-9"; Lower,	HP	HP	open, whole hgt 5'-0"	Detl B, Detl B, all HP	
	Lower deck has a 5" x 14" thick strake along center line of ship.					
Starr King						
Storm King #1	Upper, 3½" WP 7'-7"; Lower, 3½" HP	6" YP	6" YP	open, YP, oak stanch'ns; whole hgt 5'-4"	Detl B, all YP	Main rail is covered with yel-low metal inside. A poop rail on turned stanchions
Sultana Bark #1 (One deck and hold beams.)	Main, 3" WP, fastened with composition	4" HP	4" HP	open, HP, hgt 3'-10" + 10"	Detl C, Detl E, all HP	Bulwarks are beaded

Table 18.1. *Continued.*

Vessel & Ref.#	Decks (c,q) and Tween dk hgts, Thk & Matl	Planksheer (g) Thk & Matl	Main rail (h) Thk & Matl	Bulwarks (1) Type,Thk,Matl See Figure 18.1	Monkey rail; Rack rail (j,k,z) See Figure 18.1	Remarks
Sunny South #42 (One deck and possibly hold beams.)				open	Detl B	
Surprise #1	Upper, pine 7'-2"; Lower, pine	6"x16"SP	6"x16"SP	open, SP, hgt 3'-0" + 1'-11"	Detl B, all SP	Bulwarks and monkey rail wainscoted inside.
Swallow #1	Upper, pine 8'-0"; Lower, pine	YP	YP	open, YP	Detl B, all YP	Monkey rail stanchions are polished mahogany
Sweepstakes						
Sword Fish (One deck and high quarter deck.)						
Syren #3	Upper, pine 7'-6"; Lower, pine					
Telegraph #1	Upper, pine 8'-0"; Lower, pine	6" HP	6" HP	open	Detl B	
Thatcher Magoun #1	Upper, 3½" WP 8'-0"; Lower, 3½" HP	6" HP	6" HP	open, HP, whole hgt 5'-6"	Detl A, Detl B, all HP	A poop rail on turned stanchions
Tornado						
Uncowah						
War Hawk #1	Upper, 3" WP 8'-6"; Lower, 3" HP	6" HP	HP	open, HP, locust stanchions; hgt 4'-8" + 1'-2"	Detl D, all HP	Monkey rail is a solid outline 14" square.
Water Witch #1	Upper, 3½" WP 7'-9"; Lower, 3½" HP	HP	HP	solid, HP, whole hgt 5'-4"	Detl I, all HP	
Western Continent		6"x15"PP	PP	3" PP	all PP	
Westward Ho #1,2	Ref.1 Upper, 3½" WP 7'-8"; Lower, 3½" HP; Ref.2 Upper,3½"x6"YP; Lower,3½"x6"YP Lower deck has a 5"x14" thick strake along center line of ship.	6" HP	6" HP	open, 2½" HP, oak stanch'ns 7" x 10", 20" apart. Whole hgt 5'-6"	Detl A, B and G, all HP	A poop rail on turned stanchions
West Wind #1	Upper, pine 8'-0"; Lower, pine	HP	HP	open, HP	Detl A, Detl B, all HP	Has a taffrail
Whirlwind #1	Upper, 3½" WP 7'-9"; Lower, 3½" HP	6" HP	6" HP	open, HP, whole hgt 5'-3" amidships, 6' high for d.	Detl A, Detl B, all HP	Main rail covered with yellow metal. A brass railing around poop deck.
Whistler #1	Upper,3½"pine 7'-6"; Lower, 3½" HP	6" HP	6" HP	open, HP, hgt 4'-9" + a monkey rail	Detl D, all HP	
Wildfire Bark #1 (One deck and high quarter deck.)	Main, pine			open, whole hgt 4'-2"	Detl B	
Wild Pigeon #1	Upper, 3½" WP 7'-3½"; Lower, 3½" HP	5½" HP	5½" HP	open, HP, oak stanch'ns 6"x8", 22" apart. Whole hgt 5'-4"	Detl B, Detl G, all HP	Rack rail is 1'-0" below main rail
Wild Ranger #1	Upper,3½"pine 8'-0"; Lower, 3½"pine	6"	6"	open	Detl B	
Wild Rover						
Winged Arrow #1	Upper,3½"pine 8'-0"; Lower,3½"pine	6" HP	6" HP	open, HP, whole hgt 5'-0"	Detl B, all HP	Mahogany monkey rail stanchions, bright & varnished
Winged Racer #1	Upper, 3½" WP 7'-10"; Lower, 3½" NP	6½" HP	6½" HP (abt)	open, HP, planks beaded; hgt 4'-0" + 1'-3"	Detl B, all HP	Mahogany monkey rail stanchions
Witchcraft #1	Upper,3½"pine 7'-8"; Lower,3½"pine	6" HP	6" HP	open, HP, oak stanch'ns, close together; hgt 4'-6" + 1'-8"	Detl B, all HP	
Witch of the Wave #1	Upper,3½"x6"WP 7'-0"; Lower, 3½" HP	5½" SP	5½"x20"SP	open, HP, whole hgt 6'-0", small mldgs outside	Detl H, all HP	Inside of rack rail is covered with yellow metal
Wizard #1 (2 decks and hold beams partially decked.)	Upper, 3½" WP 7'-8"; Middle,3½" HP 7'-2"; Partial, pine	6" HP	6" HP	open, HP, whole hgt 6'-0"	Detl A, Detl B, all HP	A poop rail on mahogany turned stanchions
Young America #71,72 (Three decks.)						
Young Turk Bark #1 (One deck.)	Main, 3" pine	4" HP	4" HP	open, HP	Detl B or C	A wooden rail on metal stanchions around poop deck

(text continued from page 275)

heads, always at an angle in reference to the grain of the wood, this increasing the holding power of the bolt and decreasing the possibility of splitting the top timber. If such a fastening was in an exposed location, it was sunk and covered with a wooden plug. Additional fastening was provided by blunts, or drifts, being driven into the bulwark planking or clamps, if such were installed, one fastening on either side of the top timber in close proximity to it, after which they were plugged. With the main rail in place, the sheer of the vessel was permanently delineated.

This particular form of installation of the main rail applied to vessels that were to be fitted with single-log monkey rails; vessels fitting this category are included in Table 18.1. (The monkey rail, a cap for the main rail, is covered below under its own heading.)

As was the case with fastenings of the planksheer, iron was used almost universally. One known exception is the clipper bark *Mermaid*, where composition was the metal specified.

When seen in plan view, the main rail conformed exactly with the outline of any vessel, no projections being visible unless the channels that would later be installed to spread the lower rigging were considered. But, here again, as in all other details of shipbuilding, can be found exceptions to the general rule. Such exceptions are found in *Racehorse* and *Dauntless*, each designed and built by different men, in which the outboard edge of the main rail was carried outboard to the edge of the channels so that the monkey rail lay outside of the deadeyes of the lower rigging and backstays; thus, all such rigging lay within the vessel's structure. Figure 6.5, showing the midship section of *Racehorse*, includes an illustration of this detail.

(The unusual detail noted above is an excellent illustration of the dangers inherent in attempting, no matter how earnestly, to indulge in reconstruction when actual detail is not to be found. Having provided reconstructed details many times in my own development of ships' plans, the nagging thought that the educated guess, made because general practice supported the idea, may be blatantly incorrect, lurks constantly in the background. It appears entirely reasonable to believe that no one attempting a reconstruction of either *Racehorse* or *Dauntless* would include this rare detail without having some prior knowledge of its existence. It is for this reason that many blank spaces appear in this volume. Without exact knowledge at the moment, the hope always persists that at some future time such blank spaces may be filled with factual data. Until that time, sincere but always questionable reconstruction must suffice. The best solution is to admit the shortcoming.)

In vessels that were to be fitted with monkey rails that were either "built open" or "built solid," as covered below under the heading "Monkey Rail," the treatment of the main

rail was similar to that described before, except for the mortising to receive stanchions or top timbers that would pass through and extend above the main rail as risers for the monkey rail structure.

In many ships the inboard surface on the face of the main rail was covered with yellow metal. This detail is appropriately noted where applicable in Table 18.1.

Rack Rail

The rack rail (Figure 6.2, detail k), sometimes referred to as the *pin rail*, was a vital component of any ship's sailing function, it being the location of most of the belaying points of the vessel's running rigging. While not considered to be part of the vessel's structural strength, it had, nevertheless, the mass and proportions of a structural member due to the constant and varying loads introduced into it by the forces that acted on the running rigging with unpatterned intensity and frequency. By its nature the rack rail demanded absolute solidity, and absolute reliance was entrusted to its fastenings.

The rack rail was generally of the same thickness as the main rail of the ship. The thickness, in addition to providing the required sturdiness, also allowed the holes for the belaying pins to be bored minimally greater than the pin diameter; this kept the pins in a vertical position whether or not they were under load.

The width of the rack rail was subject to details of other structure existing in way of the rail. Figure 18.1, details E through J, illustrates the various installations of a rack rail. The main factor to be considered was clearance between the head of the belaying pin and the nearest encroaching structure; such structure dictated the width necessary to facilitate simple, efficient working of a line around the pin. For the casting of a figure-of-eight knot around a pin in order to belay a line, and space to allow excess line to be looped over the pin, at least 6 inches clearance would be prudent. Add to this the space required by the pin itself, which could be 2 to 2½ inches, plus additional substance between the pin and the edge of the rail and to reach back to solid structure, and a rack rail might easily attain a width of 14 inches. Examination of the details identified in the figure shows clear indications of the factors that must be considered.

If no interferences were present, the rack rail extended from the break of the forecastle to the break of the poop. As in most other ship's structure, it was made of the longest convenient lengths with the ends scarphed in locations that were not subject to being drilled through to accept belaying pins.

Rack rails were generally installed with their topmost surface about 4 feet 6 inches above the deck. This was a convenient height to allow men to haul on a line and also allowed a reasonable distance for the loops of line to drape between the rail and the deck without becoming unduly cumbersome. There was, however, considerable latitude in this dimension.

Various methods were employed to make the height of the main rail and that of the rack rail compatible, and these are clearly illustrated in details E through J, along with the various methods of fastening each.

For most of the ships listed in Table 18.1, the lack of mention of a rack rail is very apparent. However, the rail was an absolute necessity, so it cannot be ignored. With known heights of main rail and monkey rail, or known whole height of the bulwarks, one may proceed to reconstruct a typical rack rail if certain basic considerations are borne in mind. First, the rack rail was never higher than the main rail. If this main rail were less than about 4 feet 6 inches above the deck, it would be reasonable to construct the rail as shown in Figure 18.1, detail E. The second condition supposes the main rail to be nominally higher than this, in which case the rack rail would be secured to the underside of the main rail as shown in detail F. Finally, in vessels having an unusually high main rail, the rack rail was located at the desired height and the intervening space between the two rails was filled with a stout clamp as shown in details G, H, and I.

In many vessels the rack rail was covered with yellow metal. This detail is appropriately noted, where applicable, in Table 18.1. In one very rare instance, that of *Silver Star*, the rack rail was covered with copper. This was most unusual since, by 1856, the year in which the vessel was built, yellow metal had superseded the use of copper in every situation that had, only a few years earlier, specified copper.

Monkey Rail

The monkey rail (Figure 6.2, details j and z) surmounted the main rail and was the topmost item of hull structure in way of the framing. It was the structure which, when viewed in profile, defined the long, smooth, graceful trace of the hull, setting it off from all other gear, deck structures, and masting. The monkey rail represented the flowing form we associate with the clipper ship as a type.

The term *monkey rail* is generally assumed to have applied to the cap portion as an individual unit. MacLean's contemporary descriptions, however, consistently indicate that reference to the monkey rail was intended to include all units of the structure mounted upon the main rail, such as any stanchions or risers, top timbers, and planking, in addition to the rail cap proper.

Details A, B, C, and D of Figure 18.1 illustrate the forms in which the monkey rail was constructed and the terminology applied to each of these forms.

Detail B in the figure illustrates the form of monkey rail construction that was, by far, the most prominent in ships of all categories, clipper or otherwise. This type was known as an "open" rail. The first impression is, generally, that such a rail must have been supported by stanchions and could be looked through. Such was not the case. The term refers to the fact that it was planked on the outboard side only, thus assuring that every surface of the structure was open to view and inspection.

Monkey rails that were built "open" consisted of an extended top timber or a stanchion which protruded through the main rail up to the monkey rail proper, and an outer sheathing of small-scantling tongue-and-groove planks which were adequate for protection since tightness was not a factor. As in the installation of all tongue-and-groove planking, the tongue was in the upper edge of the plank in order to ensure drainage. Monkey rails built in this fashion were generally a good bit higher than solid-log rails, and this made boarding them up a more practical method of construction than installing a rather large single timber.

The top end of the stanchion was cut as a tenon, the shoulder of which provided a stop on which the rail proper rested. The rail was fastened with an iron bolt driven blunt into each stanchion at an angle crossing the stanchion grain, after which the counterbore was tightly plugged.

The width of the rail was equal to the moulded dimension of the stanchion, plus the thickness of the outside boarding that was to be installed and, at a minimum, sufficient substance for the rail to have overhanging beading or moulding both inside and outside.

The boarding of the monkey rail was fastened as illustrated in detail B of the figure.

Due to its exposed location, the monkey rail was installed with care and appropriate finish. The joint between any two sections was a carefully cut and fitted scarph of any form free of minor or vulnerable protrusions.

Most open monkey rails were finished with a coat of paint the same color as the bulwarks and, in some cases, were highlighted by paint of a contrasting color. However, there were vessels in which the space between the stanchions was fully paneled and then decorated with colorful mouldings, geometric patterns, or even artistic floral designs and motifs. Such vessels are noted in Table 18.1, as is the fact that the monkey rail cap proper of *Dauntless* was lined with yellow metal and the boarding fastened with composition (yellow metal). Other vessels having boarding fastened with composition were *Fair Wind*, *John Bertram*, and *Stag Hound*.

Detail A in the figure illustrates the "solid" monkey rail, a version that could not be considered as rare, although it was not too frequently encountered. Once again the term used is misleading since it does not mean that these rails were made of wood "through-and-through" but rather that they were planked both inside and outside. Actually, they were described as "built solid," which term was shortened to "solid" and is dealt with in detail under the heading of "Bulwarks."

The construction of a solid monkey rail was on the order of the construction of the open rail but required considerably more labor and material. As with the open rail, detail B, the stanchion or the extended top timber reached through the main rail to the moulded height of the monkey rail, at which point it was tenoned to engage the rail and provide a stop upon which the rail would rest. The monkey rail proper could be of the same proportions as before, namely about 4 inches thick and wide enough to span the stanchion, two thicknesses of boarding, and some nominal excess to allow for moulding or beading on each edge.

After the rail had been assembled on the stanchions, an iron bolt was driven down through a counterbore into each stanchion at an angle, as was described previously for the "open" rail, after which it was plugged as shown in detail A.

The boarding-up of a solid monkey rail was a more precise task than boarding the open rail with tongue-and-groove strakes. Because the interior of the assembly would be closed in, it was requisite that it be rendered watertight. This required fitting and caulking, as was applied to other tight planking in the vessel—a laborious and expensive procedure. In spite of these considerations it was, however, often done.

Detail A illustrates this installation. The planking differs from that of the open monkey rail in that its edges were treated for caulking and it was rarely beaded. Fastenings were similar to those used in an open rail, namely spikes, driven under and puttied flush.

Detail C in the figure presents a third form of monkey rail to be encountered in clipper ship construction. This was the "log" rail, a truly solid structure which consisted of a solid timber as a riser, topped by the monkey rail cap proper. This type of rail was found only where the monkey rail was of minimal height, perhaps 15 inches. Its use, noted in Table 18.1, appears to have been limited to small vessels such as *Sultana* and to ships in which the whole height of the bulwarks was in the vicinity of 5 feet.

It appears to be a relatively simple installation, most of the work centering around the principal log, shaping and contouring it to fair with the curvature of the ship's main rail and the slope of her sides.

As indicated in the detail, fastening the log could be achieved in one of two ways. The monkey rail cap was installed in the same manner as the preceding rails.

Details D and H illustrate the final and rarest form of monkey rail installation that has been found among the vessels included herein. It has no recognizable name or designation and is usually referred to as a "solid belt." This form of rail was made up of inside and outside clamps, rather than relatively thin planking. These clamps were located near the extreme inner and outer edges of the main rail, and the monkey rail cap completely spanned the space across the two clamps. This rail structure was deliberately intended to add to the strength of the vessel. Its configuration, when assembled atop the main rail, formed a box girder which in essence girdled the vessel and contained considerable inherent strength. Proper development of such strength was assured by providing ample shift of scarphs with those of the main rail, and by the manner in which the fastenings were installed. With iron fastenings driven as depicted in details D and H, the assembly became an important addition to the longitudinal strength of the vessel.

Of the vessels listed in this book, only four are known to have had this installation: *Sierra Nevada*, *Witch of the Wave*, *Noonday*, and *War Hawk*. In the case of *War Hawk*, the assembly was reported as being 14 inches square, the clamps blending into the edges of the monkey rail cap.

The term *monkey rail* appears to be the accepted contemporary nomenclature for the uppermost rail that surmounted the main rail of clippers, packets, and freighters of the period. However, the term *fancy rail* is occasionally encountered as the designation for this same rail, as can be found in some of the tables of moulded offsets of the clippers of William H. Webb.[18]

Bulwarks

The bulwarks (Figure 6.2, detail l) of a merchant vessel served two purposes. One function was to keep seas from washing over the deck each time a wave broke against her hull. The other function was to prevent members of the crew from falling overboard while performing their normal duties or from being swept over the side when the ship was sailing in heavy or stormy seas.

The given height of a ship's bulwarks was the height measured in the waist of the vessel, from which point it increased toward the bow to fair with the edge of the forecastle deck, and decreased toward the stern where it would meet with the poop deck or half poop, depending upon the design of the vessel. There were cases, however, where bulwarks had a whole height of as much as 7 feet, the bulwark structure being of uniform height throughout its entire length. The whole height was the height from the deck to the top of the monkey rail. The height of the bulwark itself was limited by the location of the main rail. The bulwark planking consisted of the strakes of planking fitted between the upper surface of the planksheer and the lower surface of the main rail. This latter surface was located at the moulded height of the main rail, a location always dictated by the table of moulded offsets.

There were two basic types of bulwarks built into the clipper ships, both of which are illustrated in Figure 18.1. The predominant one was known as an "open" bulwark. The second type was the "solid" bulwark, which found its way into about 10 percent of the vessels. As with the two forms of monkey rail just described, these terms referred not to the solidity of the planking but to the visibility of the structure. An "open" bulwark, detail B in the figure, was not open in the sense of a picket or pale fence which protects and restricts but can be seen through; rather, it was a wall composed of horizontal strakes of planking that were about 3 to 4 inches thick and of optional width. Narrow planks required a bit more work but fewer fastenings than did wide strakes.

Planking an open bulwark was a relatively quick and easy method of constructing the bulwarks since there was no need for their being watertight. The planks were generally beaded and were cut with tongue-and-groove edges that were always installed with the tongue uppermost in order to avoid having water drain into the groove and settle there. These planks were not intended to contribute to the longitudinal strength of the vessel, and so the usual stringent rules pertaining to fastenings and the shifting of butts (for exterior planking below the planksheer) did not apply. However, every effort was expended upon appearance and adherence to the accepted construction practices.

The fastenings used were generally iron spikes driven through the planks into the top timbers, the heads sunk in counterbores in the planks and then covered with wooden plugs. There were exceptions to this general practice; *Fair Wind*, *John Bertram*, *Dauntless*, and *Stag Hound* all were reported as having their bulwarks fastened with composition spikes, termed *dumps*. The use of such fastenings eliminated the need for wooden plugs over the heads.

In the case of *Santa Claus*, the bulwark stanchions were reportedly "fastened with composition in wake of the planksheer."[1] An examination of the structure in this area of a ship renders this statement rather enigmatic, there being no readily identifiable fastenings which fit this description.

Although this open bulwark construction was not as expensive as that of the solid bulwark, it presented an opportunity to adorn a vessel with considerable artistic treatment, as with the monkey rail. Many vessels had the inboard surface of the bulwark planking covered with paneling which was then embellished with artistic designs, geometric patterns, and floral tracery, all in an attempt to transform the vessel into a truly artistic, albeit costly, creation.

A peculiarity in open bulwark construction occurred in the building of Donald McKay's clipper *Staffordshire*. Originally designed to have two decks, a poop deck, and a topgallant forecastle, she was modified toward the completion of her construction. Due to the increase in the packet trade in 1851, Enoch Train & Co., her owners, apparently decided that they wanted her to have a third deck. When the decision was made, the ship was already bulwarked (with open bulwarks) up to her monkey rail, which coincided with the height of the poop and forecastle decks. The additional deck was built to connect these two decks, and thus she became a three-decker, the weather deck being flush as was the case with *Great Republic*, which would be built two years later.

The third deck brought the problem of maintaining an attractive appearance. This was satisfactorily done by adding an additional bulwark and monkey rail only 4 feet 6 inches in height which completely encircled the ship. The vessel, when completed, appeared to have the bulwarks and monkey rail of a two-deck ship and, above these, the new bulwarks and a monkey rail of minimal height.

The second type of bulwark was the "solid" or "ship-of-war" bulwark, detail A in the figure, in which the bulwark was boarded inside and outside. Such construction was more meticulous and expensive inasmuch as all seams and butts required caulking to render them watertight in order to exclude the elements and prevent rot. Beading of the planks was generally dispensed with in this construction. As with the open bulwark, the fastenings were generally iron spikes driven through the planks into the stanchions, the heads buried in counterbores and plugged with wood.

In ships-of-war this solid bulwark was installed as protection for the gun crews stationed at the ship's main battery along her sides. The two thicknesses of planking were effective protection against shot that impacted the ship's sides in battle. While the solid bulwark could not totally resist close-range assault, it was a valuable asset where distance was involved.

Surmounting the bulwarks above the main rail in ships-of-war was the *hammock trough*, a wood or iron and rope channel which ran along the main rail and into which the crew's hammocks, rolled and stopped, were stowed. This stowage offered considerable protection against musket balls, small-arms fire, and flying splinters that might result from a direct hit. In merchant vessels the monkey rail took the place of this hammock trough.

With the merchant vessel needing no consideration as to matters of warfare, it appears rather incongruous that solid bulwarks would be constructed. However, it is pointed out in the description of *Bald Eagle* that this method of constructing the bulwarks gave solidity where a vessel was most liable to warp from the effects of the sun in warm weather; it was also considered to be neater and cleaner.[1] Neither of the above statements seemed to impress the majority of shipbuilders. Of the vessels included herein, only about 10 percent had solid bulwarks, and most of these were in ships built by Donald McKay. Once again, it was apparently a case of the builder's own personal philosophy.

To a certain extent the sequence of boarding up the bulwarks was controlled by the type of rack rail and monkey rail construction proposed for a given vessel. In Figure 18.1, details F, G, H, I, and J illustrate conditions that must be satisfied prior to the final installation of bulwark planking both inside and outside. Each of these details is applicable to one or more vessels listed in Table 18.1 and may be used with either open or solid bulwarks, although the detail is drawn showing only one of the types.

In some vessels, long, heavy clamps were installed immediately below the main rail both inside and outside, as in details H and I, to increase the ship's longitudinal strength. In other vessels a clamp was added on the inboard side only, as in detail G, filling in the space between main rail and rack rail. Sometimes the rack rail was secured directly to the underside of the main rail, as in detail F. And finally, the clipper *Hoogly* was built with a rack rail installation unique among the vessels covered in this volume. As illustrated in detail J, the ship was described as being built with an intermediate rail installed 1 foot below the main rail;[1] the rack rail was then secured as shown in the detail. When any one of these installations had been completed, the final boarding-up of the bulwarks could be undertaken.

As in any other phase of shipbuilding—or, for that matter, any endeavor which lends itself to written description—terms will become customary but will seem to be incongruous. Such a term is found in MacLean's description of *Joseph Peabody* in which it is stated that the "outer square" of her bulwark stanchions was varnished.[1] One might think of "outer" and "outboard" as the same, but such is not the case. Here the term applies to the exposed face of the stanchion. The situation is not unique to this vessel or to this detail, since the term was also often used in reference to the "outer" or under side of beams.

Two vessels in this list had their bulwarks pierced with gunports and fitted with tackle bolts in bulwarks and deck, breeching bolts in the deck, and breeching rings in the bulwarks. The first, the bark *Racehorse*, was built for the India and China trade where, even in the 1850s, piracy was still an ever-present danger. The number of ports and size of armament are not recorded,[1] but a painting in the Smithsonian Institution depicts her with three ports each side, located between the mainmast and the mizzenmast. Since she was a small vessel her owner probably slept more soundly with the knowledge that his diminutive ship could defend herself.

The second, the large ship *Bald Eagle*, was pierced with four ports each side, completely fitted with the necessary bolts and ringbolts to accommodate her intended long six-pounders.

Poop Rail or Taffrail

A *poop rail* or *taffrail* (Figure 18.1, detail A) was required on any vessel whose weather deck aft did not have the protection of bulwarks (in the case of flush-decked vessels) or a high monkey rail (in vessels with a half poop or poop deck, described in the next chapter).

These rails, which surmounted the monkey rail, were most generally husky handrails secured to the top of sturdy, sometimes ornately turned stanchions fashioned from hardwoods such as mahogany, cherry, or teak. The more elaborate rails enhanced the appearance of even the most pleasing of sterns.

However, there were exceptions where wood was either totally absent or was restricted to the handrail only. There are six known instances among the ships in this volume, and they are noted in Table 18.1. *Young America* and *Black Hawk* were fitted with wooden handrails mounted on metal stanchions. *Shooting Star* and *Whirlwind* featured railings made completely of brass. *Hurricane* is reported as having a "heavy" brass rail, and *Beverly*, alone among the ships, had a rail composed completely of iron stanchions and handrail.

In most of the vessels listed in Table 18.1 no poop rail or taffrail is noted, but since the principal function of such rails was to protect the crew from being swept over the side, it may safely be assumed that the rails were installed on a case basis. The materials, of course, are subject to educated guess. An additional function of the rails was to accommodate belaying pins which were required for use with rigging that led far aft.

When installed, the turned wooden stanchions were generally raked inboard to fair with the slope of the vessel's side at the stern; this presented the most pleasing appearance. However, in the case of metal rails, which were much less obtrusive to the eye, the stanchions were invariably installed in a vertical stance.

The wooden handrail was 4 to 5 inches thick, about 8 inches wide, and its upper surface was located about 3 feet 6 inches above the deck. There was considerable latitude in these dimensions. The use of butt joints was shunned.

When noted at all, the existence of these protective rails receives only a cursory comment in the descriptions of the clipper ships, but their necessity is self-evident.

Ships with topgallant forecastles were very often fitted with protective rails and stanchions along the sides of such decks. These were invariably metal in both rail and stanchions. In many cases the stanchions were made portable for convenience in boarding the anchors. In these locations the metal rails were replaced by lengths of close-link chain which were easily unshipped and temporarily stowed until they would be reinstalled at an appropriate time.

BITTS; HATCH COAMINGS; DECK PLANKING; FORECASTLE AND POOP DECKS

Deck Structure

Bitts

Certain *bitts* are required on board ship for performing a variety of functions. These timbers, usually of rather generous scantlings, are not, strictly speaking, a part of the ship's structural form; even though permanently fixed in their locations, they are actually functional components. Their use throughout the entire register of ships was quite universal, only differing in size, quantity, and exact location. It was convenient to install them after the beams were in position since in most cases they were scored into or lapped onto beams in order to be securely anchored. Installation of bitts at this time also allowed decks to be planked around them later.

Beginning at the bow and proceeding aft through the length of a vessel, the first pair of bitts was installed in way of the heel of the bowsprit. They stood astride the heel and were scored into it, extending to a beam or a breasthook immediately below, onto which they were lapped and bolted. Above the heel they extended upward to the forecastle deck beams and generally through the deck itself to a height of several feet, where they functioned as mooring and general-purpose bitts. Their primary purpose was to restrain the heel of the bowsprit in its assigned position, which they did both transversely and vertically.

Next aft on the forecastle deck, installed one on each side of the ship near the rail, were another, smaller pair of bitts used for mooring the vessel. Generally, they were pierced through with *norman pins*, which were horizontal iron rods projecting a short distance beyond each side of the bitt head. These pins prevented the bight of a mooring line from accidentally slipping the bitt.

Larger vessels such as *Lightning* had massive riding bitts located on the deck where the anchor cable exited the hawsehole or hawsepipe. They were in line between the hawsehole and the middle of the windlass barrel and about halfway be-

tween the two fore-and-aft. In general they penetrated to the deck below where they were lapped onto a beam and bolted.

Next aft was the samson post, about which the windlass assembly was located. This was located on the centerline of the ship and securely anchored between its deck and the forecastle deck, above which it extended about 2 to 3 feet in order to accommodate the pivot of the pump brake handle. Outboard of the samson post, one on each side of the ship, were the side posts that supported the ends of the windlass axle. These extended up to the forecastle deck, sometimes projecting several feet above it.

These members of the total windlass assembly were not actually bitts. However, their being installed at this time contributed to the orderly laying of deck planking.

A relatively rare installation of bitts, especially in the earliest years of the clipper, were those used to support *lever winches*, which were gypsy heads mounted about 3 feet above the weather deck. The bitts extended about 4 feet above this deck and down to the beams of the deck next below where they were secured in the customary manner. These bitts were located to port and starboard of the fore and main rigging, 4 to 5 feet from the rail, and were used for raising and lowering yards, and for general working of ship. Their name derives from the fact that the gypsy heads were mounted to large gears which were operated in turn by hand levers perhaps 4 feet in length. The gearing developed great mechanical advantage and eased the work of the crew when put to use. An outstanding example of this installation is found in the clipper *Challenge*.

Along the waterways of some ships, in locations nearly abreast of each mast, pairs of mooring bitts were installed. The bitts of each pair were spaced a few feet apart, fitted with norman pins and anchored to the beams of the deck next below the weather deck. They were always located about 8 feet forward or aft of the mooring holes cut through the ship's bulwarks. This distance allowed ease of line handling and fleeted the line in the most advantageous direction for the bitts to counteract the load of the ship moving at its berth.

Many vessels were fitted with *cavils* rather than bitts. These were large wooden cleats which spanned the mooring hole in the bulwarks and reached to the top timbers on each side of the hole. They were securely bolted to these timbers and their ends were extended to accommodate the turns of belayed mooring lines.

All ships had a pair of topsail sheet bitts installed on the weather deck immediately forward of the foot of each mast. At the foremast and the mainmast these bitts anchored the fife rail assembly, while at the mizzen they usually stood alone. The force acting on these bitts was vertical since they reacted against the considerable load generated through the topsail sheets when those sails were pulling in a stiff breeze. For this reason these bitts also extended to the beams of the deck next below, where they were let in and bolted.

Finally, far aft on the weather deck, almost abreast of the rudderpost, were a pair of bitts on each side of the ship which served a dual purpose. Being located within a few feet of the rail, they functioned as mooring bitts, but in addition they provided the inboard restraint for the aft bumkins in the same manner that the bowsprit bitts restrained the heel of that stick. These were important components, since the outboard portion of each bumkin was fitted with eyebolts to which the main and main topsail braces were set up. These braces induced high and variable loads in the bumkins and were utterly indispensable to the successful operation of a ship.

Hatch Coamings

Hatch coamings (Figure 6.2, detail u) surrounded all hatchways that penetrated a ship's weather deck. MacLean consistently referred to these members as "combings." In most of the large vessels there were three hatchways installed, one forward, one aft, and one amidships; the latter was called the *main hatch* and was routinely larger than the others. Some of the very large vessels had more than three of these cargo hatches, and most ships had several other types such as companionway hatches. All required coamings to prevent water from washing across the deck and flooding the ship's interior.

The hatch coamings of major importance were those located on a vessel's weather deck, illustrated in Figure 19.1. They served not only to prohibit the ingress of water, but to protect against men falling into the hatchway when it was open and the crew were working in the vicinity. Such a fall could be a serious misfortune since the hatches in the different decks "plumbed" each other and a fall could end in the bottom of the hold.

The sides of the hatchways were coamings which ran longitudinally and were supported by *headers* (the members placed under the hatch coamings) and *head ledges* which ran transversely and were supported by the deck beams. Collectively these members were referred to as *hatch coamings*. In

the clear opening, the sides of beams and these assemblies were made flush so as to avoid interference by protrusions when cargo was being lowered into the hold. On the outside the upper surfaces of beams and headers were of sufficient scantling to provide a surface or surround upon which the butts of deck planks could rest and be fastened.

As discussed under the heading "Half Beams" in Chapter 14, there were limits placed upon the size of openings through the deck, based upon structural considerations. In the fore-and-aft direction it was permissible to interrupt only one beam, resulting in an opening of about 10 feet; the inboard end of the half beam was supported by a header. Athwartships, the size of opening could be as much as one-third of the ship's breadth; but this size hatch was rarely, if ever, chosen for a merchant ship due to encroachment upon the working area on deck, also due to the type of cargo generally carried in such ships. In most instances the clear opening was square or slightly rectangular, the greater dimension lying athwartships.

A known exception to this general rule occurred in *Great Republic*, whose main hatch measured 11 feet transversely and 14 feet fore-and-aft—an unusually large hatch in an unusually large vessel.[10]

The scantlings of hatch coamings were structural in nature since they were essential to the watertight integrity of a vessel. In addition, they were subject to certain abuse when cargo was being onloaded or offloaded. However, they did not provide strength to the ship's structure, this function being accounted for in the assembly of beams and headers upon which the coamings rested.

Typical coamings on the weather deck were from 6 to 8 inches thick and from 18 to 24 inches high. The thickness allowed the installation of substantial fastenings; the height was considered adequate to prevent water from penetrating the hatchway under all except the most extreme conditions.

Each side of the coaming was composed of timber in a single length, preferably of one tier in height. This provided the ultimate assurance of tightness in the structure. The joining of the corners presented the greatest problem in constructing a completely watertight coaming, and the inclusion of double dovetail joints on each corner provided the best assurance of a reliable joint. Figure 19.1 illustrates this construction. When the assembly was held down snugly on the framing below by adequate fastenings, this joint could not separate in either direction, athwartships or fore-and-aft, due to the dovetail cuts in each direction. The configuration of these cuts is clearly shown in the figure.

One unusual feature of this double dovetail is that it cannot be assembled in any horizontal direction due to the angles of the cuts. After each of the sides was fashioned, bored, and counterbored to receive the fastenings, the coaming pieces were required to be located in position on the headers.

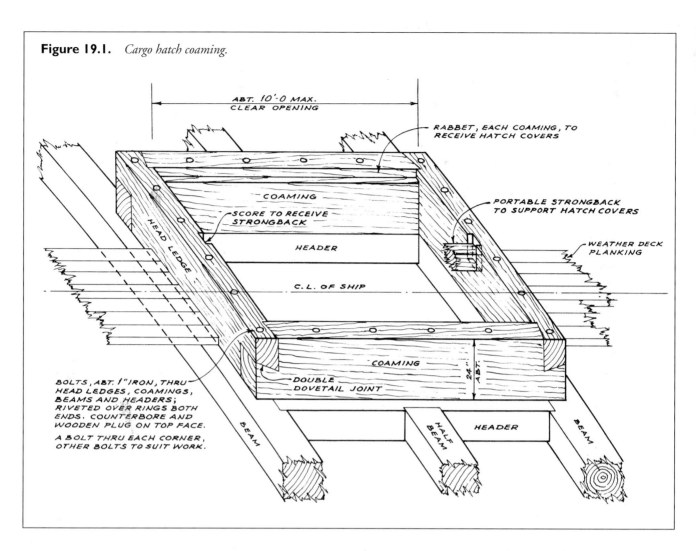

Figure 19.1. *Cargo hatch coaming.*

When this was done, the head ledges were slipped down over them and solidly seated. The entire assembly was then coaxed into its final position over the beams and the fastenings driven. Once completed, the joint could not separate unless there was failure of the fastenings or the wood fiber from external causes.

All hatches of this type were provided with covers (Figure 6.2, detail y) about 3 inches thick made up into panel sections or possibly as individual hatch boards. In either case, lifting facilities, usually recessed in the covers, were provided. In cases of large hatches such as the main hatch, a portable strongback was settled into recesses scored into the inner face of the head ledges as shown.

There no doubt were variations in the fabrication of the corner joints, and the cross-sectional shape of each part of the coaming was probably moulded and contoured into more graceful shape on the outside surfaces. Details such as these, however, are rarely depicted. The details of construction were always essentially as shown.

Coamings surrounding cargo hatchways in the tween-decks and the hold required no such detailed fabrication and were usually merely protective rims around the perimeter of the hatchways. They were about 6 inches high and 8 inches wide, laid on beams that were sided large enough to allow the butts of deck planks to be fastened. Covers could be laid within their boundaries if cargo was to be stowed on them. Tightness was not considered to be a problem.

There were miscellaneous coamings on the weather deck in addition to those already described. These were coamings in the way of manned accesses and structures such as companionway hatches, deck houses, and exterior bulkheads. For all of these coamings, the heights were about 12 inches. Their purpose was the same as that of the cargo hatch coamings, namely to prevent the entry of water into the ship's interior. There were, however, two differences. First, they had to be of a height that would allow a person to step over them. Second, these weather deck coamings were in locations that were constantly visible to crew or other personnel. If trouble developed, it was readily spotted and remedied. With cargo hatches, battened down for the duration of a voyage, this was not the case.

Despite the fact that hatch coamings, like beams and other stationary structures, were working parts of a ship's structure, they were sometimes the subject of unusual treatment of one sort or another. All the weather deck hatch coamings in *Challenge* and *Star of the Union*, as well as the aft hatch in *Bonita*, were constructed of mahogany. Those in *Hoogly* were mahogany lined with composition. The ship *Whirlwind* had her coamings covered with yellow metal. Finally, *King Fisher* had coamings of East India teak. This was one of the relatively rare appearances of teak in an American-built clipper, other than in small turned stanchions.

It was also reported of *Challenge* that the framing of the hatchways (and of the mast partners on deck) was constructed of East India teak, certainly a most uncommon practice.[1]

Deck Planking

The *deck planking* (Figure 6.2, details c and q) served two purposes, both of them quite obvious. First, all decks were laid to provide a surface upon which people could walk; and second, the weather deck was made tight, thus forming the topside portion of the watertight envelope of the vessel. Either could be installed anytime after the waterways and binding strakes were in place. This applied to any class or type of vessel. The details of planking the decks of a clipper ship did not differ from any other ships.

Certain general rules were applicable. These included the installation of a *nib strake* or thin waterway faying against the inboard binding strake which was cut to accept the nib ends of planks that might terminate in pointed shim ends. These nibs were cut a minimum of 2 inches wide across the ends to allow for caulking and sufficient substance to receive one spike in the end of the plank. This nibbing requirement was necessitated by the outline of the hull converging toward the centerline of the ship forward and by the rounding of the stern.

In the ends of a vessel, some planking terminated on deck hooks which were installed with their top surface coincident with the top surface of the beams, as described in Chapter 15. In such cases the seating was solid and the planks could be spiked directly to the hooks. However, there were locations in which planks ended in mid-space between beams. To provide for this shortcoming a strake of heavy timber was fitted between beam ends in all locations where it occurred. The top surface of this strake was fitted to coincide with the top surface of the beams and provided a landing to receive the spikes that fastened the ends of planks.

As we have seen, there were no codified American rules for building ships during the clipper period, but an examination of details shows that, in general practice, Lloyd's rules prevailed. This applied to the shifting of butts in laying the deck planking, taking care to avoid a succession of butts that suggested a "ladder step." Butts could not be closer than 5 feet to each other unless there was a strake between them, in which case 4 feet was allowed. No butts could terminate on the same beam unless there were three strakes between them.

This general information is not included in typical descriptions of individual vessels. However, there are many books which deal with the subject, rendering it superfluous and repetitive to cover it here. We will deal only with detailed information applicable to the vessels included herein.

American-built clipper ships were decked with pine planking, typically 3 to 3½ inches thick and 6 inches wide. The upper or weather deck was white pine, while the lower decks were generally hard pine. There were exceptions to both material and size of the planks. The planking details are listed in Table 18.1, and some of the unusual differences and details are now noted.

The vessels built by Donald McKay generally featured thick strakes on the lower decks along the ship's centerline in way of the deck stanchions.[2] The only other ship in this list to include this feature was *Ellen Foster*, built with a 6-inch-thick strake along the centerline of her lower deck.

Planking thickness was remarkably consistent, the only listed deviation occurring in *Queen of the Seas*, which featured a lower deck of hard pine 4 inches thick.

White pine was the overwhelming choice for weather deck planking, but there were some unusual exceptions, the most notable being Donald McKay's specifications, calling for yellow pine on most of the decks[2]; this does not agree with MacLean's reports, which state that white pine was installed on the upper deck.

All the clipper ship planking was laid parallel to the centerline of the ship. As usual, however, there was the inevitable exception, in *Charger*. The planks of her half poop deck were each laid in one piece the full length of the deck. In addition, this planking was graduated in width to conform to the shape of the vessel. This is a costly method of shaping planks, a fact that is pointedly brought out in her description as being the most costly vessel of her size ever belonging to Boston.

This curvilinear tapering of deck planks was of cosmetic rather than practical value. Its purpose was to neutralize the optical illusion of curved deck edges that is produced when parallel straight seams approach a side of considerable curvature. This was a practice not uncommon in naval vessels that were built with long, flush decks, such as the steam frigates *Mississippi* and *Missouri*, built in 1841. It is quite probable that the availability of public money made this practice even more attractive than it was to the profit-motivated merchant owner.

The specific purpose of this book is to compile a record of components, materials, and sizes that were actually built into the clippers listed. Such information serves as a broad indication of what might be reasonably expected in any such vessels that are not included.

There is no intention of trying to record the manner in which any of this work was accomplished. However, in such a plain and simple sounding procedure as planking a deck, it seems appropriate to explain some of the details involved in bringing the job to a successful and attractive conclusion. It quite obviously involved more than cutting a quantity of boards and hammering a lot of spikes.

The first step involved a sketch of the planks which would show the disposition of plank edges and butts. It was also paramount that the width of plank be cut at a constant dimension to ensure that seams be straight and true. Some practice involved positioning perhaps four strakes at the same time, aligning and fastening them collectively; this was a very effective method of achieving fair and even seams.

After the planks had been cut to the desired width, their edges were beveled to "allow the seam" for inserting caulking. Figure 20.1, detail A, shows one method of determining this opening or groove, which was directly proportionate to the thickness of the planking. The shipwright's practical method of obtaining the proper seam for the thickness of plank was to open a 2-foot folding rule to a space of ⅝ inch between the extreme inner edges of the 12-inch arms of the rule. The "allowance," for any planking thickness, could then be read directly by measuring the planking thickness along the arms of the rule, starting at the apex of the angle, and noting the amount of opening at that point.

Normally, each plank was secured with two spikes through the butt of the plank and two through the plank into each beam. In McKay vessels of three decks, a single spike was also driven through each plank of the middle deck into each ledge.[2]

For the planking used in vessels listed in Table 18.1, the spikes, square in section with chisel points, were about 7½ inches long and ⅝ inch square, the length being two-and-one-half times the thickness of the plank to be secured. In preparation to being fastened, a ⅝-inch-diameter hole was bored in way of each required spike, this hole receiving a counterbore to accommodate the spike head and a wooden plug. A pilot hole of smaller diameter, centered in this hole, was bored into the beam below. The spike was then positioned in the top of the hole with its chisel point directed across the grain of the beam below, after which it was driven home and snugged down with a "set" until the head was solid against the bottom of the counterbore. At a later time all counterbores would be tightly filled with wooden plugs. The grain of the plugs ran parallel with the grain of the plank.

Generally, the spikes used for fastening decks were iron. Exceptions to this rule are noted in Table 18.1, which indicates that some vessels employed composition fastenings called *dumps* (see Chapter 4) and that the decks of *Coeur de Lion* were fastened with copper.

After fastening was completed, all decks were subject to caulking and paying of the seams. The procedure was the same as that used in the installation of the exterior planking;

however, the number of threads of oakum differed, and they are tabulated below.

Plank thickness	No. of threads
2"	2, small
3"	2, small
4"	3, small
5"	4, small

Forecastle and Poop Decks

Topgallant Forecastle

The *topgallant forecastle* was a standard installation on virtually all clipper ships (see also Chapter 26). Figure 19.2 is a reconstruction based on general data including typical details. However, in some instances the structure was omitted, leaving the forward end of the weather deck flush.

The raised forecastle deck served two obvious purposes. First, it added a certain protection against seas breaking over a ship's bow; and second, it provided a greater area of working space for the crew to carry out their duties forward. The handling of ground tackle was made easier because of this larger work space.

Although forecastle decks were for all intents and purposes universally used, they were constructed in a variety of sizes, as tabulated in Table 19.1. These are based on photographs and descriptions which, for the most part, are extremely reliable, and on prints and paintings, some of which allow room for individual interpretation.

The most usual form of structure was open between its level and the weather deck below, and it was short or of medium length, extending only about halfway to the foremast. This allowed for the installation of a capstan, the usual pair of catheads, and the upper projection of the samson post to receive the handles for operating the pump-brake windlass which was located on the weather deck under the break of the forecastle.

Some open forecastle decks were built with most of these general features, compacted into a much smaller area. In such cases the windlass might not be under the forecastle deck, but rather would stand exposed on the weather deck. In general descriptions these diminutive structures were merely mentioned as being "small."

The final forecastle deck was the "long" deck, which could be so extensive as to extend aft to the foremast. This type, like the small forecastle, was not often encountered.

In height there were two general types. The most extensive was the forecastle deck built to the height of the main rail. Most forecastle decks at this height were open below, and the space was used for lockers and stowage. The crew was quartered below deck or in their own deck house abaft the foremast.

Figure 19.2. *A topgallant forecastle.*

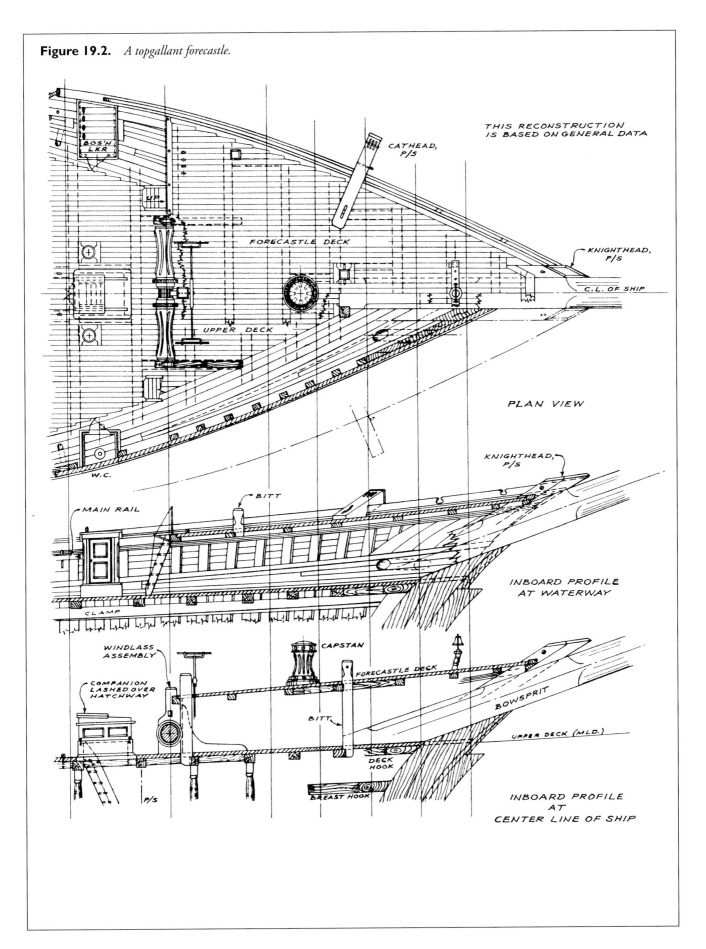

BOS'N LKR

CATHEAD, P/S

THIS RECONSTRUCTION IS BASED ON GENERAL DATA

FORECASTLE DECK

KNIGHTHEAD, P/S

C.L. OF SHIP

UPPER DECK

PLAN VIEW

W.C.

MAIN RAIL

BITT

KNIGHTHEAD, P/S

INBOARD PROFILE AT WATERWAY

CLAMP

WINDLASS ASSEMBLY

CAPSTAN

FORECASTLE DECK

COMPANION LASHED OVER HATCHWAY

BITT

BOWSPRIT

UPPER DECK (MLD.)

DECK HOOK

P/S

BREAST HOOK

INBOARD PROFILE AT CENTER LINE OF SHIP

High forecastle decks were built at the height of the monkey rail. This allowed for headroom under the beams, in which case the area was usually closed and fitted out with quarters for at least one watch of the crew. There were a few variations to the above types of installation, and these are noted in Table 19.1.

Descriptions of ships which include scantlings, fastenings, and other structural details of the vessels content themselves with statements that are cursory and contain only information as outlined above. Generally, one learns little more than what is stated in the accompanying table. While this is very frustrating and unsatisfactory from the standpoint of research and reconstruction, it is plainly understandable. By the time a ship's forecastle can be built, the structural elements of the ship have been completely assembled. The vessel's strength has already been built into its fabric, and its structural integrity is assured. The forecastle is only required to support itself and its fittings against the forces of the sea; it is not counted on as a structural portion of the ship's frame.

Apparently the rule for building such structures as a forecastle deck can be summed up in the axiom "If it looks right, it probably is right." Years of experience in the many shipyards resulted in rule-of-thumb procedures that had proven themselves over time. In the forecastle there were no lengthy spans of unsupported beams, no great deck loads to be accounted for, and no sense of reliance upon this structure to hold the bow of the ship together. Consequently, the scantlings of beams were relatively small, being about 6 or 7 inches moulded and 8 or 9 inches sided. Their spacing approximated that of the beams under the deck below. This alignment of beams was useful in securing vertical posts and members passing upward through the decks.

While Figure 19.2 approximates a typical forecastle deck structure, it must be added that there were numerous variations.

The height of the forecastle deck of *Coeur de Lion* was at the main rail and the space under the deck was enclosed, containing quarters for her crew. In order to achieve sufficient headroom in the space, the floor was dropped a few feet below the upper deck.

The clipper *Wild Pigeon* was built with a rack rail 1 foot below the main rail. The forecastle deck, along with the half poop deck, was planked at this level. In order to afford accommodations for her crew, the floor below the forecastle deck was dropped below the level of the upper deck in order to attain adequate headroom.

An unusual treatment of what was basically an open forecastle was built into *Witch of the Wave*. In her case the deck was built full height, and the space below was divided amidships on either side of the bowsprit, each enclosed side outfitted with accommodations for the crew. Included was a water closet in the after end of each wing.

In *Lightning* the top of the forecastle deck was built at the same level as the top of the deck house, and the two were built together as a continuous unit at this level; Figure 12.4 includes this detail. A year later the same feature was built into *Donald McKay*.

Catheads

The *catheads*—see Figures 12.4 and 19.2—one on each side of the forecastle deck, were an essential structural item, although they did not contribute to the integral strength of the ship. Their purpose was to keep the anchor away from the side of the ship after it had been fished from the anchor cable to the catfalls in the process of bringing it on board.

The sizes of catheads differed depending upon the size of the vessel that carried them. A large clipper of 1,500 to 2,000 tons might be expected to be fitted with oak catheads that were about 15 inches square and 10 feet in length; these could be expected to handle an anchor weighing as much as 5,000 pounds.

The cathead functioned as a cantilevered beam. Its downward load outboard was contained in the three sheaves that were fitted in mortises cut near the end of the cathead; these sheaves formed the upper block of the cat tackle. The ship's rail was the fulcrum about which this load worked. The practical considerations of the installation were dictated by two requirements: one, to keep the anchor outboard far enough to eliminate damage to the ship's side by the flukes as they swung above the water's edge; the other, to keep the outreach to a minimum in order to reduce the load on the inboard fastenings whose job it was to hold the cathead down on the deck.

Restraint of the cathead in any horizontal direction was of no great magnitude, since all the load to be encountered—the weight of the anchor—was vertical. To adequately ensure securing the inboard portion of the cathead, the beam structure was appropriately reinforced with stout headers, which in combination with the beams could receive iron bolts of sufficient size and quantity to permanently hold the cathead in position.

There was a working relationship between the location of the hawseholes, the catheads, and a capstan which was always installed on the deck. The initial controlling factor was the location of the hawseholes, since these were already cut in the ship's bows. Locating the catheads well forward facilitated the task of fishing the cat tackle hook to the anchor ring or shackle in preparation for unshipping the bending shackle; this would then leave the chain cable unencumbered. When a probable location had been selected, the cathead was positioned across the rail normal (at 90 degrees) to the rail. This position allowed for equal clearance of the ship's sides both forward and aft of the cathead sheaves.

With this settled, the capstan could be located on the
(text continued on page 300)

296

Table 19.1. *Forecastle and poop decks.*

Notes:
1. Height of the topgallant forecastle deck is the main rail unless noted as "full height".
2. "Short" or "small" forecastle indicates the usual extent of such a deck which is about half the distance between the knightheads and the foremast.
3. "Open" forecastle indicates that the area has no closing bulkhead and is fitted with stowages, etc. Crew is quartered below deck or in a deck house.
4. Height of half poop deck is generally the main rail.
5. "Short" or "small" poop deck extends about half the distance between the stern and the mizzen mast.
6. "Medium" poop deck extends forward approaching the mizzen mast.
7. "Long" poop deck encloses the mizzen mast.

Vessel & Ref.#	Poop deck	Forecastle deck	Remarks
Alarm #1	Half poop, in excess of 40' long	Tglt, open, short	
Amphitrite #1	Half poop, medium	Tglt, open, short	
Andrew Jackson #82	Half poop, medium	Full height, closed, long	Painting in ref.82
Antelope #1	Half poop, medium	Tglt, open, small	
Asa Eldridge #1	Half poop, about 38' long	Tglt, open, short	
Bald Eagle #1	Upper deck flush aft	Tglt, open, short	
Belle of the West #1	Half poop, medium	Tglt, open, short	
Beverly #3	Half poop, 24' long	Tglt, open, short	
Black Hawk #32,62,63	Half poop, very long	Full height, open, short	Half poop extends forward to include mainmast
Blue Jacket #5,32	Full height, 80' long	Full height, closed, short	
Bonita #1	Half poop, medium	Tglt, open, short	
Bounding Billow Bark #1	Half poop, long	Tglt, open, short	Half poop extends to aft part of main rigging
Celestial #42	Raised quarter deck, long	Tglt, open, short	
Challenge #1	Half poop, 20' long	Tglt, open, short	
Challenger #1	Half poop, medium	Tglt, open, short	
Champion of the Seas #1	Upper deck flush aft	Full height, closed, spacious	
Charger #1	Half poop, medium	Full height, closed, large	Poop deck planks laid in single lengths. See Table 18.1
Charmer #1	Half poop, medium	Tglt, open, short	
Cleopatra #1	Half poop, medium	Tglt, open, small	
Climax #1	Half poop, short	Tglt, open, small	
Coeur de Lion #1	Half poop, medium	Tglt, closed, spacious	Crew quartered in the tglt focsle; floor is a few feet lower than the upper deck
Comet #32,64,92	Half poop, about 108' long	Tglt, open, short	Half poop extends forward to include mainmast. The break of the poop deck is curved
Cyclone #3	Officer and crew accommodations all on deck.		Described as similar to Northern Light
Daring #1	Half poop, 36' long	Tglt, open, 22' long	
Dauntless #1	Half poop, medium	Tglt, open, short	Crew quartered below the upper deck, forward
Donald McKay #1	Full height, long	Full height, closed, long	Tglt focsle is same height as the deck house and is built with it
Don Quixote #1	Half poop, medium	Tglt, open, short	
Eagle #5	"Drop" poop, 40' long	Full height, closed, short	Cabin floor is below level of upper deck
Eagle Wing #1	Half poop, medium	No tglt focsle noted	All accommodations are in houses on upper deck
Edwin Forrest #1	Half poop, medium	Tglt, open, short	
Electric Spark #1	Half poop, medium	Tglt, open, short	
Ellen Foster #1	Half poop, 42' long	Tglt, open, small	
Empress of the Sea #1	Half poop, medium	Full height, closed, short	
Endeavor #1	Poop deck, short; Half poop, 38' long	Tglt, open, short	Description of aft end is confusing and subject to interpretation. See Ref.1
Eringo Bark #1	Half poop, short	Tglt, open, small	
Eureka			
Fair Wind #1	Half poop, long	Tglt, open, short	
Fearless #32	Full height, medium	Full height, closed, short	Painting in Ref.32
Fleet Wing #1	Half poop, medium	Tglt, open, short	
Flyaway			
Flying Arrow #1	Half poop, long	Tglt, open, short	

Table 19.1. Continued.

Vessel & Ref.#	Poop deck	Forecastle deck	Remarks
Flying Childers #1	Half poop, small	Upper deck flush for'd	Crew quartered below deck
Flying Cloud #1	Half poop, 68' long	Full height, closed, 30' long	
Flying Dragon #1	Half poop, medium	Tglt, open, short	
Flying Dutchman #24	Half poop, long	Tglt, open, small	
Flying Eagle #1	Half poop, small	Tglt, open, short	
Flying Fish #1	Half poop, long	Tglt, open, short	
Flying Mist #1	Half poop, long	Full height, open, short	
Galatea #1	Half poop, medium	Upper deck flush for'd	
Game Cock #1	Half poop, medium	Tglt, open, short	
Gazelle #4	Half poop, medium	Tglt, open, short	Poop deck reaches forward close to mizzen mast
Gem of the Ocean #1	Half poop, medium	Tglt, open, short	
Golden Eagle #1	Half poop, medium	Tglt, open, short	
Golden Fleece (2nd) #1	Half poop, long	Tglt, open, short	
Golden Light #1	Half poop, 30' long	Tglt, open, short	
Golden West #1	Half poop, long	Tglt, open, 40' long	
Grace Darling #1	Half poop, medium	Tglt, open, short	
Great Republic #10	Spar deck flush	Spar deck flush	
Great Republic (rebuilt) #32,75	Full height, medium	Full height, medium	
Henry Hill Bark #1	Full height, 38' long	Tglt, open, short	
Herald of the Morning #12	Half poop, medium	Tglt, open, small	
Hoogly #1	Full (6½') height, 60' long	Tglt, open, short	
Hurricane #4,65	Half poop, extends forward of mizzen mast	Tglt, open, short	
Indiaman #1	Half poop, short	Tglt, open, short	
Intrepid			
Invincible #4,24	Half poop, 22' long (Given in ref.4)	Full height, open. (No tglt focsle noted in ref.4)	Tglt focsle deck is 18" above monkey rail. Scaled from ref.24
James Baines #1,32	Full (over 7') height, long	Full height, closed, long	Focsle deck extends to foremast. Poop deck extends forward of mizzen mast.
John Bertram #1	Half poop, short	Tglt, open, small	
John Gilpin #1	Half poop, short	Tglt, open, short	
John Land #32 (Built as a duplicate of Winged Arrow.)	Half poop, short	No tglt focsle noted	Crew quartered in a deck house amidships
John Stuart #4	Poop with sunken floor, long	Tglt, open, short	
John Wade #1	Half poop, short	Tglt, open, small	
Joseph Peabody #1	Half poop, short	Tglt, open, short	
King Fisher #1	Half poop, short	Tglt, open, short	
Lady Franklin			
Lamplighter Bark #1	Full height, 60' long	Tglt, open, small	Poop deck extends forward to include mainmast
Lightfoot #1			"The usual deck arrangement of houses, etc."
Lightning #1	Full (7') height, 90' long	Full (7') height, closed, long	Focsle deck extends to foremast
Mameluke #1	Half poop, long	Tglt, open, short	
Mary Robinson			
Mastiff #1	Half poop, medium	Full height, open, short	
Mermaid Bark #1	Half poop, 35' long	Tglt, open, small	Main deck is depressed 4' in way of poop deck
Morning Light #1	Half poop, short	Tglt, open, large	This is Morning Light of Boston
Mystery #1	Half poop, short	Tglt, open, short	
Nightingale #3	Half poop, 60' long	Full height, open, short	
Noonday #1	Half poop, short	Full height, closed, short	
Northern Light #32	Full height, short	Tglt, open, small	Paintings in ref.32
Ocean Express #1,66	Half poop, short	Tglt, open, short	
Ocean Pearl #1	Half poop, short	Tglt, open, short	
Ocean Telegraph #5	Half poop, short	Upper deck flush for'd	No tglt focsle noted in description
Onward #1	Half poop, long	Tglt, open, small	
Osborne Howes			
Panther			
Phantom #1	Half poop, medium	Tglt, open, short	

Table 19.1. *Continued.*

Vessel & Ref.#	Poop deck	Forecastle deck	Remarks
Queen of Clippers #1	Half poop, small	Tglt, open, small	
Queen of the Pacific #32	Half poop, short	No visible details	Painting in ref.32
Queen of the Seas #1	Full height, 91' long	Full height, closed, 40' long	Poop deck extends forward to include mainmast. Break of poop curves forward amidships
Quickstep Bark #1	Half poop, short	Tglt, open, short	
Racehorse Bark #1	Half poop, 32' long	No tglt focsle noted	
Racer #3,97	Half poop, short	Tglt, open, small	
Radiant #1	Half poop, short	Tglt, open, short	
Raven #3	Half poop, medium	No tglt focsle noted	
Red Jacket #32,67,68	Full height, short	Full height, open, short	
Robin Hood			
Rocket Bark #1	Half poop, short	Tglt, open, small	
Roebuck #1	Half poop, medium	Tglt, open, long	
Romance of the Sea #1	Half poop, medium	Tglt, open, long	Tglt focsle extends aft nearly to the foremast
Santa Claus #1	Full height, long	Tglt, open, short	
Saracen #1	Half poop, short	Tglt, open, short	
Sea Bird Bark #1	Half poop, short	Tglt, open, small	
Seaman's Bride #4	Half poop, short	Tglt, open, short	
Sea Serpent #4	Half poop, 55' long	Full height, closed, short	
Shooting Star #1	Half poop, medium	Tglt, open, small	
Sierra Nevada #1	Half poop, short	Tglt, open, short	
Silver Star #1	Half poop, long	Tglt, open, short	
Southern Cross #1,32	Half poop, 26' long	Tglt, open, short	Crew quartered in a deck house amidships
Sovereign of the Seas #1	Half poop, short	Full height, closed, long	All accommodations are on the upper deck
Spitfire #1			
Staffordshire #1	Upper deck flush	Upper deck flush	
Stag Hound #1	Half poop, 44' long	Tglt, open, short	
Star of the Union #1	Half poop, medium	Tglt, open, short	
Starr King			
Storm King #1	Half poop, short	Tglt, open, short	Crew quartered below deck forward
Sultana Bark #1	Half poop, long	No tglt focsle indicated	
Sunny South #42	Raised quarter deck	Tglt, open, short	Quarter deck extends forward to include mizzen mast
Surprise #1	Half poop, 42' long	Tglt, open, small	
Swallow #1	Full height, medium	Tglt, open, short (Not certain)	All accommodations are on the upper deck
Sweepstakes #42,69	Half poop, long	Tglt, open, short	
Sword Fish #32	Half poop, medium	Full height, closed, long	Tglt focsle extends aft nearly to the foremast. Painting in ref.32
Syren #3	Half poop, short	Tglt, open, short	
Telegraph #1	Half poop, short	No tglt focsle	Crew quartered in a deck house amidships
Thatcher Magoun #1	Half poop, 75' long	Full height, open, short	Tglt focsle has staterooms for the boys in the crew
Tornado #3	Half poop, short	Upper deck flush forward	
Uncowah			
War Hawk #1	Half poop, short	Tglt, open, short	
Water Witch #1	Half poop, short	Tglt, open, short	
Western Continent			
Westward Ho #1	Half poop, long	Tglt, open, short	
West Wind #1	Half poop, short	Upper deck flush forward	
Whirlwind #1	Half poop, medium	Tglt, open, short	
Whistler #1	Half poop, short	Tglt, open, short	
Wildfire Bark #1	Raised quarter deck, 48' long	Tglt, open, small	
Wild Pigeon #1,42	Half poop, 45' long, includes mizzen mast	Tglt, closed, short	Focsle deck and poop deck are height of rack rail; floors of both drop below upper deck level
Wild Ranger #1,32	Half poop, long	Full height, closed, short	Painting in ref.32
Wild Rover			

Table 19.1. *Continued.*

Vessel & Ref.#	Poop deck	Forecastle deck	Remarks
Winged Arrow #1	Half poop, short	No tglt focsle noted	Crew quartered in a deck house amidships
Winged Racer #1	Half poop, medium	Tglt, open, short	
Witchcraft #1	Half poop, 45' long	Tglt, open, small	
Witch of the Wave #1	Half poop, height of rack rail, includes mizzen mast	Full height, 32' long	Closed only on each side outboard of bowsprit
Wizard #1	Half poop, long	Tglt, open, small	
Young America #32,70,71	Full height, 42' long	Full height, open, short	
Young Turk Bark #1	Half poop, medium	No tglt focsle noted	

(text continued from page 296)

centerline of the ship. Ideally this location was at the point where the extended centerlines of the catheads converged at the centerline of the ship. If the capstan could be located at this convergence, the hauling end of the catfalls, when taken around the capstan barrel, would come off the after cathead sheave in a line parallel with the sheave. This provided for ease of working and eliminated any chafing of the tackle as it passed over the sheave.

With these considerations having been met, it now remained to ascertain that there was sufficient room on deck for the crew to man the capstan bars when boarding the anchor. If this could not be done properly, certain shifting of these elements might be attempted. If such shifting was undesirable or the desired alignment was to be disrupted, then provisions might be made to secure a snatch block or a tail block to act as a fairleader when needed.

As has been described, it can be seen that the catheads were structural in nature and specific in function. However, from the earliest days of their appearance they offered a tempting target for decoration. In the clippers this inclination was fulfilled by various carvings on the outboard end. Some known designs are illustrated in Figure 24.6.

Half Poop

The *half poop*, shown in Figure 19.3, was constructed in as many variations as the topgallant forecastle deck and was found in almost all clipper ships. However, there were exceptions to this rule in which a poop deck was not built, thus leaving the weather deck flush aft.

The most prevalent form of this deck was the half poop, its height being that of the main rail. In length it ranged from "short," as shown in the figure, to a length of 91 feet in *Queen of the Seas* and 108 feet in *Comet*. In these cases, which were unusual, the entire poop deck, being in reality an extension of each ship's upper deck, was regarded as a structural deck and was built to the same scantlings as the upper deck

forward of the mainmast. In this type of configuration the partners of the mizzenmast were built into this deck.

The example shown in Figure 19.3 represents an average half poop deck in area and general features regarding lightness of structure. Beams were generally slightly heavier than those under the forecastle deck due to the greater breadth of the stern. Most of this increase was added to the sided dimension of the beam in order to avoid encroaching on much-needed headroom.

Once again, details are almost nonexistent, but beams moulded 6 to 7 inches and sided about 10 inches appear to fill all obligations. The spacing of the beams was somewhat optional and was determined to a great extent by the location of accesses and skylights.

Provision was made to properly support the bumkins, port and starboard, and to allow room for a steering stand immediately over the head of the rudderpost.

The half poop shown in the figure is encroached upon by a trunk cabin which, to varying degrees, occurred in almost half of the clippers built. Cabin details are discussed in Chapter 28.

There was an occasional ship whose steering wheel was not located in the usual exposed location at the taffrail. One of these was *Challenge*, in which the wheel was located naval fashion on the quarter deck afore the break of the poop. This location gave the helmsman great protection against seas thrashing over the taffrail. In naval vessels, which were always conned by officers on the quarter deck who passed their orders directly to the helmsman, this was the most convenient location. In addition, the men at the wheel were not openly exposed to enemy musket fire, a situation which, fortunately, was not a consideration in the merchant service.

Another vessel with this unusual arrangement of her poop deck was *Hoogly*. She was built more nearly to naval fashion than was *Challenge*. In the case of *Hoogly* her poop deck, built to full height, had a projecting front, under which there was a stateroom on each side of the ship, forming a recess amidships. In this recess, protected by the overhang, the

Figure 19.3. *A half poop.*

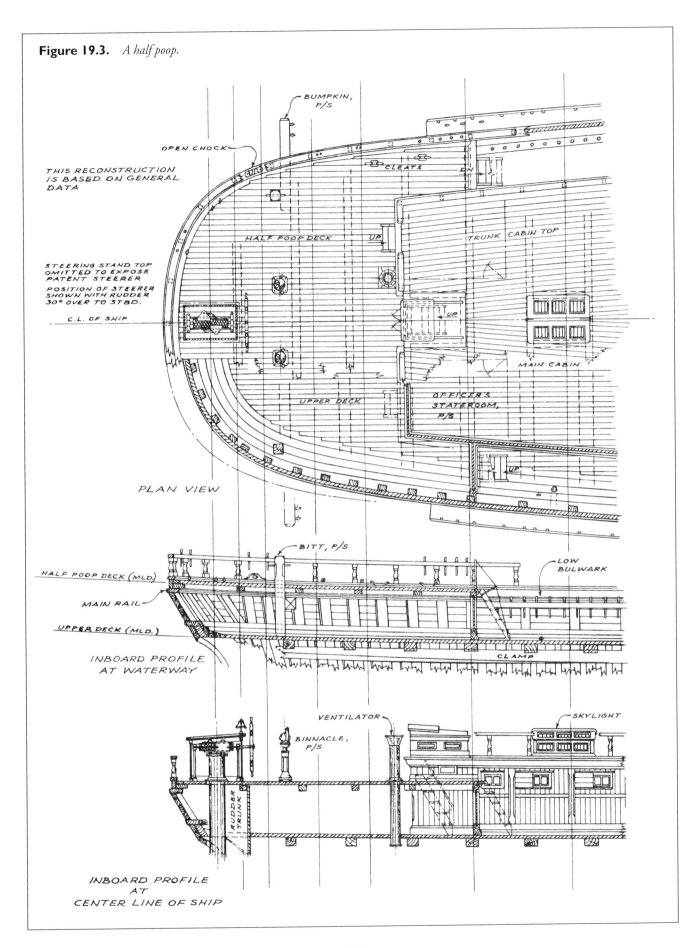

BUMPKIN, P/S

OPEN CHOCK

CLEATS

DN

THIS RECONSTRUCTION
IS BASED ON GENERAL
DATA

HALF POOP DECK

UP

TRUNK CABIN TOP

STEERING STAND TOP
OMITTED TO EXPOSE
PATENT STEERER
POSITION OF STEERER
SHOWN WITH RUDDER
30° OVER TO STBD.

C.L. OF SHIP

UP

MAIN CABIN

UPPER DECK

OFFICER'S
STATEROOM,
P/S

PLAN VIEW

UP

BITT, P/S

LOW
BULWARK

HALF POOP DECK (MLD.)

MAIN RAIL

UPPER DECK (MLD.)

INBOARD PROFILE
AT WATERWAY

CLAMP

VENTILATOR

SKYLIGHT

BINNACLE,
P/S

RUDDER
TRUNK

INBOARD PROFILE
AT
CENTER LINE OF SHIP

ship's wheel was installed, completely under cover. Her gun tackle steering purchase was then led along below the upper deck and connected with a yoke fitted on the rudderhead below the deck. This was the same arrangement that had been built into American 74-gun ships of the line in the earlier 1800s. Except for steering from a wheelhouse, as in *Lightning*, a helmsman could not be provided with greater protection against the elements.

The clipper *Wild Pigeon* was built with a rack rail 1 foot below the main rail. The half poop deck, along with the forecastle deck, was planked at this level. To afford accommodations for her officers, the floor below the poop deck was dropped below the level of the upper deck in order to attain adequate headroom.

Many of the half poop decks surrounded long trunk cabins, which reduced these decks to gangways along each side of the ship until the break forward. This configuration eliminated much of the work of the shipwright in favor of the joiner or jointer.

In rare instances vessels were built with raised quarter decks, which were essentially a compromise between a flush deck aft and a half poop. These raised decks were about 2 to 3 feet above the weather deck. Three vessels in this book—the ships *Celestial* and *Sunny South*, and the bark *Wildfire*—were built in this manner.

A relatively few vessels were constructed with full-height poop decks which were at the level of the monkey rail and were generally quite long. Their structural details did not differ from the half poop.

In Donald McKay's *Lightning* the poop deck was built at the same height as the connected forecastle deck and deck house. In order to eliminate the need for the crew to descend to the upper deck when passing from one end of the ship to the other, two gangways were installed, one port and one starboard, between the poop deck and the deck house top, thus providing full run of the ship at this one level.

Later, when *Donald McKay* was built, the same feature was built in except that only one gangway was provided.

Bumkins

The *bumkins*, at the stern of the vessel, one port and one starboard, were located at the same level as the beams that supported the weather deck. In vessels built with square sterns they were installed a few feet forward of the fashion piece; in vessels featuring round or elliptical sterns they were located about at the meeting of the ship's side and its stern. Since their function was to keep the several braces of the main yards from fouling the mizzen rigging when the yards were braced hard up, care was taken that they were not installed too far aft around this stern curvature.

Like the catheads on the forecastle, the bumkins were cantilevered beams. The rail or structure of the deck edge was the fulcrum, the strain in the main brace and main topsail brace was the load, and the inboard end was the anchorage. However, unlike the catheads, the bumkins did not resist major vertical forces. Instead, the load was mostly horizontal and, to a small extent, vertical since the load of the braces combined these two forces into one resultant force which was variable in direction, depending on the bracing of the yards, and in intensity, depending upon the prevailing force of the wind.

Typically, the bumkin stood off the ship's side about 4 feet and reached inboard under the deck another 4 or 5 feet. A cross section of 9 by 12 inches, the large dimension being horizontal, was ample to receive the eyebolts to which the brace pendants would be set up. The inboard end of the bumkin was sometimes fitted against a bitt, into which it was scored. In many cases these bitts protruded up through the deck for about 2 feet. Norman pins were inserted through the bitt heads, and they then functioned as mooring bitts. With the inboard end of the bumkin firmly restrained in a fore-and-aft direction and the scoring preventing any upward movement, the installation was able to withstand the loading produced by sails that were filled and pulling.

Chapter Twenty

SALTING; EXTERIOR HULL PLANKING; HEADBOARDS; MOULDINGS

THE PRACTICE OF *SALTING* OR "seasoning" ships with salt was firmly entrenched by the time of the clipper ship. The use of salt as a preservative, both in liquid and dry crystalline form, had been known for countless ages, and through observation and experiment had, at some unknown date, been applied to ship construction.

The salt was placed in confined areas lacking ventilation—essentially, spaces bounded on the outside by the ship's planking and on the inside by her ceiling. In these constricted interstices, filled mostly with the substance of the frames of the vessel, there remained innumerable relatively small air pockets between the frames which, when the planking had been closed up, were trapped forever. Subjected to extreme changes of temperature and humidity, these areas became stagnant and damp or wet—thus, the timbers were vulnerable to fungous decay and the ravages of condensation.

If a ship were fortunate enough to be constructed of sound, well-seasoned timber, it was off to a reasonably good start in the battle against dry rot and decay. However, with the burst of shipbuilding beginning in 1850, the normal quantity of seasoned timber to be found in shipyards was quickly exhausted, and by the height of the clipper-building frenzy in 1853, it was an unusual ship that enjoyed the luxury of being constructed with well-seasoned timber. Trees were felled and converted into sized logs at such a pace that they found themselves shaped and bolted into the structure of some ships while their cells were yet alive.

Wet, green wood such as this exacerbated a situation that even at its best was fraught with potential disaster. There was no way that green wood forced into such conditions could lose its moisture and function as sound, reliable material for any long period of time. If no precautions were taken, such timber would ultimately succumb to dry rot and, with the deterioration of its fibrous structure, lose all of its structural strength and value, no longer able to hold its fastenings.

Dry rot is a rather parodoxical term, since it is a disease which thrives in dampness, humidity, and warmth rather than in a dry environment or where there is free circulation of air. It is a fungous decay and occurs in almost all except some rather exotic woods, the most notable of which (for shipbuilding) is teak, a timber rarely used in American-built ships of the period. Salt was the element introduced to impede this fungal onslaught.

The application of salt was accomplished as the ship's structure was being closed in by the outer planking. *Salt stops*, relatively thin pieces of perforated wood, were secured in line between each frame and of a size to fill the space between the ceiling and the outer planking. The lowest of these stops was located close to the floorheads, below which no salt was introduced. The intent here was to eliminate any possibility of choking the limbers along the line of the keel.

Other necessary stops were required immediately above any air strake that was left open in the ceiling. These open strakes usually were located next below a deck clamp as shown and noted in Figure 6.2. The obvious purpose of these stops was to prohibit salt from being poured into the bottomless pit of the ship's hold or tween-decks. Additional stops might be added at the discretion of the individual builder.

Since salting the ship was a critical process, the manner of application was extremely vital. Fine salt, dampened to a consistency that would ultimately allow it to dissolve into the exposed timber surfaces, was introduced into the spaces after the planking had reached a point higher than a row of stops. Coarse salt, which was less expensive and hence more attractive, was nevertheless frowned upon since there was the strong possibility of it not dissolving, thus clogging the perforations and prohibiting any possible air circulation. The process was repeated until the interstices had all been filled and boarded over by the external planking.

The proper salting of a ship was universally recognized as a strong deterrent to decay and a contributor to the prospective life of the vessel. This reflected in her classification; the underwriters deemed salting sufficient to allow her to keep her classification for an additional year.

In addition to its purely preservative properties, salt has the faculty of absorbing relatively large amounts of moisture; this is why we become thirsty after eating salty foods. This property was also put to good use in shipbuilding.

As has been described earlier, each weather deck beam had a groove chased along its upper surface. As the deck was being laid, this groove was packed with granular salt which, once the deck had been completed, was totally contained in the groove. All weather decks were exposed to vast changes in climatic conditions. In summer the exposed surface of the deck could become extremely hot, while in the tween-decks the temperature was relatively cool. Conversely, in winter the deck could be freezing while the tween-decks was relatively warm. Either condition promoted the formation of condensation which became trapped between the faying surfaces of the top of the beam and the bottom of the deck planking. The absorption capability of the salt in the groove was enough to eliminate the probability of this juncture of materials rotting out due to this "sweating."

Even in such a routine procedure as salting a vessel, there were certain deviations from the usual practice. A good example is encountered in *Dauntless*, a vessel built with a unique keelson structure that is illustrated in Figure 10.1, detail 9. After her keelson had been assembled and the stanchions inserted and secured between the twin riders, holes were bored down into the keelson every 2 feet in the space between the riders. This space and the holes were then filled with salt, allowing seasoning of the main keelson. The top of each sister keelson was grooved close to the riders, and these grooves were also filled with salt. Such was the reliance upon adequate seasoning of a vessel.

However, it cannot be assumed that all vessels were salted. In building his great clipper *Challenge*, William H. Webb decided that the vessel should not be salted, as reported in her description: "In this vessel the builder has dispensed entirely with the use of salt, under the belief that salt cannot penetrate the pores of the wood except by capillary action, at the ends. Instead of packing the interstices of the frame with this article, as usual, all is left open to the action of the air, and large holes have been made in the planksheer, through which the air can circulate when the vessel is in port."[5]

This quote sounds as though it reflects a distinct philosophy on the part of the builder. Whether or not this is so cannot be accepted without question since detailed descriptions of Webb clippers are very rare. Six months later when his *Invincible* was launched, her description makes no mention of salt.[4] Whether or not it was used cannot be ascertained, so there is little possibility of determining whether *Challenge* represented a philosophy or a one-time experiment.

The description of *Water Witch* includes the statement, "She is seasoned with salt."[78] The process is referred to as an ancient process brought to America by the earliest English

shipwrights, saying further that the technique of seasoning against dry rot was as follows: "The process is to wash the timbers by means of a syringe with strong brine and then fill the spaces between them from the gunwale to the turn of the bilge with rock or common rough salt and if the first dose is administered effectually, it seldom requires repetition for the incipient fungus is usually destroyed once and forever."[105] Among other things, this quote serves to show that the relatively simple process of seasoning a ship with salt could be done in a variety of ways.

Exterior Hull Planking

The exterior hull planking (Figure 6.2, details d, e, f, m, and s) of any ship is the planking installed between the keel and the planksheer. Its function being to provide a watertight envelope around the ship, it is fitted with great care and, generally, in a given pattern.

The nomenclature of this planking is distinctive, and the locations of the planks may be visualized by their various names without actually looking at a picture or a plan. During the period of the clipper ships, planking had evolved into forms and installation which differed in detail from what had gone before. There were now five plank designations to be found in almost all clippers, progressing upward from the keel: the garboard, diminishing strakes, bottom or common planking, wales, and waist. Each will be considered under its own heading and particular details noted where applicable.

Whatever their location on the hull, all types of planks shared the obvious necessity of being watertight. This was accomplished in the same manner in wooden ships for many years before and after the clipper ship, and was not distinctive in any type of vessel, whether a commercial ship or a ship-of-war. There were occasional departures from the general rule, but exterior planking was generally installed the same way from ship to ship.

For all planking on a ship's bottom and sides, regardless of the width, thickness, or type of wood from which a plank was cut, once it had been sized the edges were subjected to the same treatment, the only exception being the fitting of the garboard to the keel, which was its own distinct operation. Figure 20.1, details A and B, show two formulae for edge-treating planks to "allow the seam," by leaving an opening at the outer edge of adjoining planks to allow insertion of oakum for achieving watertightness. The two rules provide essentially the same opening between planks and are based solely upon the thickness of the individual planks in question.

An important requirement in planking was that, when fastened to the ship's frames, the inner edges of adjacent planks must be tightly butted together, to eliminate any strain or cross-sectional movement of the fastenings which were, for the most part, locust treenails. When caulking was forced into the narrow seam and "horsed up," or pounded, deep into the wedge-shaped opening, tremendous forces were exerted between the planks. These forces could be of such magnitude as to cripple the fastenings due to movement in the planks, which had a tendency to spread apart. If such a situation occurred, the driving of new fastenings might be called for—a costly, time-consuming repair.

The oakum used in caulking seams between planks might be made up of "junk"—unserviceable rope or cable, picked apart and twisted into threads—or available from ship chandlers in ready-to-use form, which, at the peak of ship construction, was by far the most practical means of obtaining it.

The thickness of the planking dictated the number of threads of oakum to be worked into the seam. The numbers are as follows:

Plank thickness	No. of threads
2"	2
3"	4
4"	5
5"	6
6"	7
7"	9
8"	10
9"	11
10"	13

The caulking process generally consisted of opening any seams with large iron wedges, called *reaming irons*, if the seams were undersize. After this the required number of threads were forced into the seams, using caulking iron and mallet. The final step was to "horse up" the seam with a *meeking iron* and *beetle*; this was a two-man job, one man handling each tool. The seam was now ready to be payed with melted pitch.

Due to the tremendous forces that could build up across the planking seams, it was customary to caulk any undersize seams first to ensure that they would not close up. An additional advantage was that this tended to decrease the opening of oversize seams.

Table 20.1 lists the known material, sizes, fastenings, and specific details of the planking of vessels included in this book. The peculiarities applicable to each type of planking follow.

Garboard Plank

The *garboard* (Figure 6.2, detail d, and Figure 20.1, details D and E) was a principal structure of all large vessels, whether or not they were clippers. Traditionally, all bottom planking of ships had been of uniform thickness from the keel out to the turn of the bilge. Under normal sailing con-

ditions, including heavy weather, this area was the least prone to external damage, and the accepted theory was that the thickness of planking need only be great enough to satisfy the requirements dictated by adequate fastening and caulking. Practical considerations resulted in bottom planking being limited to a general minimum of 3 inches.

This form of planking was very efficient for the function it was called upon to fulfill. However, it was accompanied by an inherent weakness built into all ships, at the inner rabbet line at or near the top of the keel, where there was the least sectional area of keel. This area was vulnerable and often resulted in the keel being torn out if the ship accidentally took the ground, especially when making leeway. While such damage was not often heard of, it was a perplexing problem for ship builders and repairers alike.

The solution, or at least a step toward reducing the frequency of this problem, along with reducing the effect of sagging strains, came about sometime between 1826 and 1832 when a Mr. Lang, Master Shipwright at the Woolwich Royal Dockyard in England, invented "Lang's safety keels," which were later to become known as *thick garboards*.[7, 8, 73] Between 1812 and 1826, Lang had served as Foreman at the Deptford Dockyard, Assistant Master Shipwright at Plymouth Dockyard, and Master Shipwright at Sheerness prior to his appointment at Woolwich. He was obviously well acquainted with the problem and decided that it could be resolved by increasing the substance of material in way of the keel. He did this by making the garboard strake approximately one-and-one-half times the thickness of bottom planking, and sometimes *flushing*, or fairing, the thickness of the two adjacent strakes down to the thickness of the bottom planking. These strakes, which later came to vary in number from one to three or more, became known as *diminishing strakes*.

The typical cross sections of these new "safety keels" are shown in Figure 1.2, details A and B, and Figure 20.1, details D and E. Lang's solution was a sound one and was quickly adopted by the Royal Navy and, at the same time, highly recommended for use by merchant sail. After this initial period, all large vessels incorporated these thicker garboards into their structure. Whether or not all clipper ships having thick garboards were built with the modified form of grooved rabbet is a matter of conjecture. However, in Table 20.1, about forty vessels are noted as having their garboards "let into" the keel. Also, in the same table, eight smaller vessels are listed as being built with common planking of uniform thickness from wales to keel. These, based on early common practice, may be assumed to have beveled rabbets, as indicated in Figure 6.5.

The nominal size of the garboard at amidships is given in Table 20.1. And, although complete information is missing for a great number of vessels, it can be observed that a garboard

(text continued on page 308)

Figure 20.1. *Exterior planking details.*

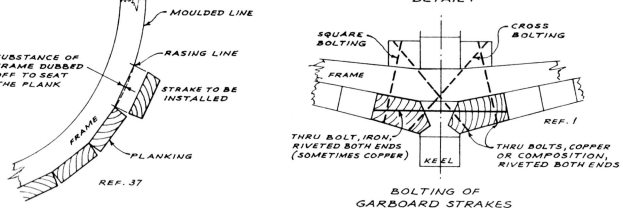

10"

THICKNESS OF
PLANK = X

WIDTH OF OPENING
FOR CAULK

DETERMINATION OF
"ALLOWING THE SEAM"

DETAIL A

FRAME

d   e   f

REF. 1

CONCAVITY
OF BOTTOM

GARBOARD AND
DIMINISHING STRAKES
DUBBED OFF FLUSH

KEEL

GARBOARD ASSEMBLY
FLUSHED FAIR

DETAIL D

PLANK STRAKES
BUTT TOGETHER

FRAME

1"
16 OPENING PER
INCH OF PLANK
THICKNESS, TO
RECEIVE CAULK

6" MAXIMUM
THICKNESS

REF. 8, 37

A FORMULA FOR
"ALLOWING THE SEAM"

DETAIL B

FRAME

REF. 21

CORNERS
CHAMFERED

KEEL

GARBOARD ASSEMBLY
STRAKES CHAMFERED

DETAIL E

FRAME

RABBET, ABT. 1"

REF. 8

KEEL

GARBOARD ASSEMBLY
ALTERNATE SEAMS

DETAIL F

MOULDED LINE

SUBSTANCE OF
FRAME DUBBED
OFF TO SEAT
THE PLANK

RASING LINE

STRAKE TO BE
INSTALLED

FRAME

PLANKING

REF. 37

DUBBING OF FRAMES

DETAIL C

SQUARE
BOLTING

CROSS
BOLTING

FRAME

REF. 1

THRU BOLT, IRON,
RIVETED BOTH ENDS
(SOMETIMES COPPER)

KEEL

THRU BOLTS, COPPER
OR COMPOSITION,
RIVETED BOTH ENDS

BOLTING OF
GARBOARD STRAKES

DETAIL G

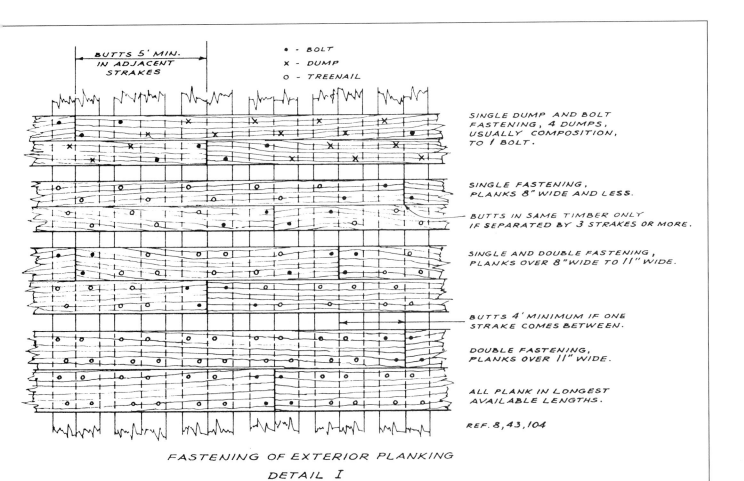

BUTTS 5' MIN.
IN ADJACENT
STRAKES

• – BOLT
x – DUMP
o – TREENAIL

SINGLE DUMP AND BOLT
FASTENING, 4 DUMPS,
USUALLY COMPOSITION,
TO 1 BOLT.

SINGLE FASTENING,
PLANKS 8" WIDE AND LESS.

BUTTS IN SAME TIMBER ONLY
IF SEPARATED BY 3 STRAKES OR MORE.

SINGLE AND DOUBLE FASTENING,
PLANKS OVER 8" WIDE TO 11" WIDE.

BUTTS 4' MINIMUM IF ONE
STRAKE COMES BETWEEN.

DOUBLE FASTENING,
PLANKS OVER 11" WIDE.

ALL PLANK IN LONGEST
AVAILABLE LENGTHS.

REF. 8, 43, 104

FASTENING OF EXTERIOR PLANKING

DETAIL I

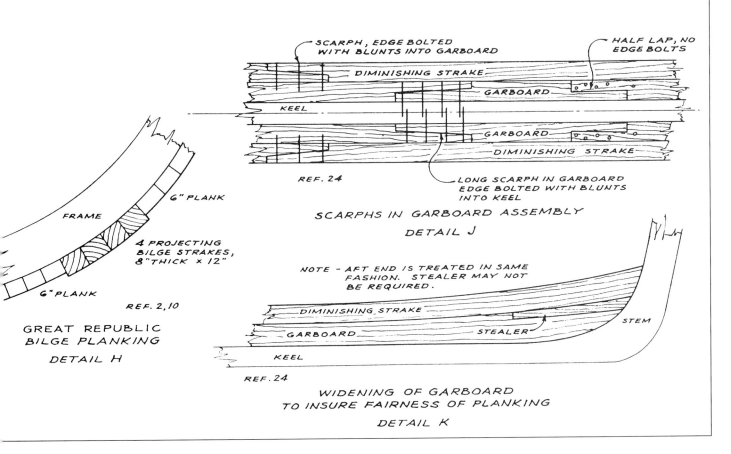

SCARPH, EDGE BOLTED
WITH BLUNTS INTO GARBOARD

HALF LAP, NO
EDGE BOLTS

DIMINISHING STRAKE

GARBOARD

KEEL

GARBOARD

DIMINISHING STRAKE

REF. 24

LONG SCARPH IN GARBOARD
EDGE BOLTED WITH BLUNTS
INTO KEEL

SCARPHS IN GARBOARD ASSEMBLY

DETAIL J

FRAME

6" PLANK

4 PROJECTING
BILGE STRAKES,
8" THICK x 12"

6" PLANK

REF. 2, 10

GREAT REPUBLIC
BILGE PLANKING

DETAIL H

NOTE – AFT END IS TREATED IN SAME
FASHION. STEALER MAY NOT
BE REQUIRED.

DIMINISHING STRAKE

GARBOARD

STEALER

STEM

KEEL

REF. 24

WIDENING OF GARBOARD
TO INSURE FAIRNESS OF PLANKING

DETAIL K

(text continued from page 305)

7 inches thick and 14 inches wide is representative of this strake. The inner edge was shaped to suit the rabbet that had been cut in the keel for the specific vessel, and the outer edge was squared and beveled to allow the seam.

The introduction of the thicker garboard also produced a new treatment for the outer edge of the strake, as illustrated in Figure 20.1, detail F.[8] A rabbet, perhaps 1 inch in depth, was scored along the outer edge of the plank, to provide a stop for the caulking since only the outer portion of the plank thickness was opened to allow the seam. This resulted in great saving of time, labor, and caulking material along the joint. The edges of diminishing strakes were finished in the same fashion, except for the edge that abutted the bottom planking.

The garboard was fitted into the keel rabbet as a squared timber, Figure 20.1, detail D, and fastened as shown in detail G and in Table 20.1. Every effort was made to unite the keel and the garboards into one solid assembly. Through-bolting of the garboards with the keel and each other, and square-bolting through the floors or timbers and sister keelsons, was considered standard practice.

The cross-bolting shown in Figure 20.1, detail G, was specified for *Charger*, *Eureka*, and *Noonday*, the only ships in this book to have this feature recorded.

A rare and unusual method of fastening the garboards occurred in *Don Quixote*, which used copper bolts and locust treenails, the use of treenails in this situation possibly being unique.

The nominal size given for any garboard was the size at amidships; from here forward and aft its thickness gradually diminished as the vessel's angle of floor began to rise from the horizontal, even though the form and dimensions of the rabbet, if grooved, remained constant. This thinning of the strake continued throughout the length of the vessel until at some point forward and aft, the garboard thickness was the same as that of the bottom planking; here the grooved keel rabbet also started to change its shape as it approached the end rabbets.

All the planking then proceeded toward the *hood ends*, which would be set in the stem and sternpost rabbets. The thickness of the garboard was gradually reduced further until its thickness and the depth of the end rabbets were the same. Thus the junctures of the stem, sternpost, and garboard were flush.

While the garboard thickness was diminished at the extreme ends of the strake, its width was gradually increased near the extremities of both bow and stern in order to keep the planking edges fair in those areas. This sometimes required the insertion of a *stealer*, or partial strake, especially at the forefoot, if the planks tended to become too wide. This detail is clearly indicated in the plan of *Ocean Monarch*[24] and illustrated in Figure 20.1, detail K.

Little is mentioned about the type of connection that was worked into the ends of individual lengths of garboard, and the assumption must be that simple butt joints were commonly used. If this was not the case, there was usually a description or comment concerning the particular type of detail. However, it is known that some ships, which were not clippers, employed scarphed connections to join the various lengths. This scarphing is also shown in the plan of *Ocean Monarch*[24] and illustrated in Figure 20.1, detail J.

Whether the connections were simple butts or scarphs, care was taken that there was ample shift with the scarphs of the keel. This was a practice religiously observed in the joining of ends of all structural timbers installed in ships.

The garboard, the most important and requiring the most fitting, was generally the first strake of planking to be installed. However, at times, the sheer strake might be installed first. In other cases, the uppermost wale might be installed first if the ship was fitted with waist planking (see Figure 6-2, detail S). It was the shipbuilder's option. With the latter procedure the location of the topmost wale was *rased*—marked or etched—on a plan or model to ensure its being fair and parallel with the planksheer. The location was transferred to the ship's frames and the wale installed, followed by several additional wales. These strakes, being located in way of beam ends and deck clamps, became substantially solid and helped the ship hold her form while the rest of the planking was being fitted.

The garboard was next fitted and installed, followed by the diminishing strakes. After these components had been fastened, the remainder of the planking was installed simultaneously, working up from the keel and down from the planksheer.

Diminishing Strakes

The *diminishing strakes* (Figure 6.2, detail e) were several strakes of thick planking installed alongside the garboard, and considered part of the *garboard assembly*. By definition there can be only one garboard, and if a timber of sufficient width could be obtained, the entire assembly would be constructed in a single width and correctly referred to as the *garboard*. Such was not the case, however, and these so-called diminishing strakes were needed to reduce the garboard dimension from its large thickness at the keel to a lesser thickness that conformed with that of the bottom planking.

Table 20.1 indicates a range of one to three of these strakes alongside each garboard, the most common number being two. In many cases no quantity is recorded. Whatever the number, the installation procedure was quite universal. Each diminishing strake was fitted to the ship as a squared timber of lesser thickness than its inboard neighbor. If the garboard had been rabbeted on its outer edge, the inner edge of the first diminishing strake was rabbeted to fit; this might also be done

(text continued on page 314)

Table 20.1. *Exterior planking.*

Notes:
1. Garboard assembly "flushed", Figure 20.1, detail D; "chamfered", Figure 20.1, detail E.
2. Strakes "tapered" are flushed down to the thickness of the common plank.
3. The waist, Figure 6.2, s, is the thin planking between the topmost wale and the planksheer and is not a feature of all vessels.
4. Only one diminishing strake unless otherwise indicated.
5. Treenails are locust; butt bolts are copper, square fastened. Both apply to all vessels unless otherwise noted.

Abbreviations

HP – hard pine	GHP – Georgia hard pine
YP – yellow pine	WO – white oak
PP – pitch pine	MWO – Massachusetts white oak
SP – Southern pine	NHWO – New Hampshire white oak

( ) – See Figure 6.2

Vessel & Ref.#	Species of wood	Garboard, thickness (d)	Diminishing strakes, No. & thk. (e)	Common plank, thk. (f)	Wales, thk. & width (m)	Remarks
Alarm #1	WO	7"	6", tapered	5"	5½" x 7"	Butt bolts yellow metal.
Amphitrite #1	HP	8" x 14"	5"	5"	6" x 7"	
Andrew Jackson #20	YP				oak	
Antelope #1	YP	3½"	3½"	3½"	5" x 7"	Narrow waist, 3½" thk.
Asa Eldridge #1	WO	7", let in, chamfered	6", 5", chamfered	4½"	5" x 7"	Treenails driven thru, wedged both ends.
Bald Eagle #1	HP	7", let in	4½"	4½"	5" x 7"	Garboard bolted with copper thru timbers and keel.
Belle of the West	HP					
Beverly #3	HP	let in;				
Black Hawk #18	HP					
Blue Jacket #5	HP					"Nearly the same as Golden Light."
Bonita #1						
Bounding Billow Bark #1		4"	4"	4"	5"	Butt bolts yellow metal.
Celestial						
Challenge #1	HP	8", let in	6"	4" to 4½"	5"	Narrow waist, 4" thk. Garboard bolted with copper thru timbers and keel. Diminishing strake bolted with copper thru timbers. All other planking fastened with copper spikes and locust treenails, wedged both ends.
Challenger #1	HP	8"	7", 6", flushed	5"	6" x 7"	
Champion of the Seas #1,2 (Ref.1)	HP	9" x 15"	8"x14",7"x14"	5"	6" x 7"	Waist, 4½" thk.
Champion of the Seas (Ref.2)	PP	9" x 15", let in	8", 7"	5½" to bilge	24 @ 6" x 7"	Garboard bolted thru keel into opposite garboard with 1⅛" iron, spaced 5 feet apart. Thru every 3rd frame into sister keelson with 1¼" copper and iron. Next strake bolted into garboard every 5 feet with 1⅛" iron and into timbers with 1⅛" copper and iron. All planking tapers toward the end rabbets. All planking over 8" wide is square treenailed; under 8" wide, double and single. Butt bolts are copper.
Charger #1	WO	7"	6", 5"	4"	5½" x 6"	Narrow waist, 4" thk. Garboard cross bolted thru timbers into opposite sister keelsons with copper bolts 5 feet apart. Also bolted every 5 feet thru the frames. Two and three treenails in every timber. Diminishing strakes are treenailed into the timbers. All other planking is thru treenailed and butt bolted with copper.
Charmer #1	WO,pine	WO	WO	WO	WO,pine	Copper spike driven between every two locust treenails.
Cleopatra #1	HP	7"	4½"	4½"	5½" x 7"	
Climax #1	HP	7"	6", 5"	4½"	5½" x 7"	
Coeur de Lion #1	HP, oak	7"	6", tapered	5"	oak, 6" x 8"	
Comet #18		let in				
Cyclone #1						"similar to Northern Light."
Daring #1	WO, pine	7" x 14"	5½" x 14", tapered	4½"	WO, 5½" x 7"	
Dauntless #1	MWO	7" x 14", "grubbed in"	5"	5"	5½"	Waist, 4" thk. Garboard is bolted thru keel into opposite garboard with 1¼" copper. Also bolted thru every floor with 1¼" copper. Locust treenails are driven thru, wedged and plugged. All planking is second growth, laid up sap side out.

Table 20.1. *Continued.*

Vessel & Ref.#	Species of wood	Garboard, thickness (d)	Diminishing strakes, No. & thk. (e)	Common plank, thk. (f)	Wales, thk. & width (m)	Remarks
Donald McKay #1,2	Ref.1 PP	8" x 14", let in	7", 6"	5"	6" x 7"	Butt bolts yellow metal. Garboard is bolted thru keel into opposite garboard and upward thru the timbers.
	Ref.2 PP	10" x 14", let in	8", (probable)	4½"	6"	Fastenings and details same as <u>Champion of the Seas</u>.
Don Quixote #1	HP	8" x 14", flushed	7"x12",5"x12", flushed	4½"	5½" x 6"	Garboards are fastened with copper bolts and locust treenails.
Eagle #5	WO	8"	7", 6"	4½"	22 @ 5½" thk.	
Eagle Wing #1	HP	7"	6", 5", outer strake chamfered	4½"	5" x 7"	
Edwin Forrest #1	WO	7"	6"	4"	5½" x 6½"	Waist, 4 strakes, each 3½" x 4" thk.
Electric Spark #1	PP or YP	8" x 14", let in	7", 6", 5"	4½"	5½" x 7"	Planks square fastened with locust treenails, many driven thru and wedged both ends. Treenails driven thru, wedged both ends.
Ellen Foster #1	HP,WO	9", let in	4¼"	4¼"	5½" x 7" (8 are WO)	Waist, 4" thk.
Empress of the Sea #1,2	Ref.1 HP	8" x 16", let in, flushed	6", 5", flushed	4½"x14"	6" x 7"	Garboard is bolted thru keel into opposite garboard and upward thru the timbers. Waist, 5 strakes, 4½" thick.
	Ref.2 PP	8" x 16", let in	6"	4½"	24 @ 6"x7"	Fastenings and details same as <u>Champion of the Seas</u>.
Endeavor #1	WO	6"	4½"	4½"	5" x 7"	
Eringo Bark #1	oak	4"	3"	3"	4"	
Eureka #4	YP	8"	4"	4"	5"	Garboard is bolted thru keel into opposite garboard with 1" iron and cross bolted with 1¼" composition driven from outside. Planks square fastened with locust treenails, wedged both ends.
Fair Wind #1	WO	7", let in	6", 5", outer strake tapered	4"	5½" x 7"	Garboard is bolted thru keel into opposite garboard and upward thru the timbers.
Fearless						
Fleet Wing #1	HP	8"	7", 6"	5"	6" x 8"	
Flyaway						
Flying Arrow #1	HP,WO	7"	6", 5"	4½"	17 @ 5½"x7", mostly WO.	Narrow waist, 4½" thk.
Flying Childers #1	HP	7", flushed	6", 5" flushed	4"	5½" x 7"	Waist, 3 strakes, 4½" thick.
Flying Cloud #1,2	Ref.1 SP	7"	6", 5"	4½"	18 @ 5½"x7"	Treenails driven thru, wedged both ends.
	Ref.2 PP	7" x 14"	6"	4½"x14"	18 @ 5½"x7"	Fastenings and details same as <u>Champion of the Seas</u>. Waist, 6 strakes.
Flying Dragon #1	mostly WO					
Flying Dutchman						
Flying Eagle #1	WO, pine	WO, 7", let in	pine, 6",5"	pine, 4"	5½" x7½", probably WO	Waist, 9 strakes, 4" thk, possibly pine.
Flying Fish #1,2	Ref.1 HP	7", let in	4½"	4½"	6" x 7"	Garboard is bolted thru keel into opposite garboard and upward thru the timbers.
	Ref.2 PP	7" x 14", let in	7"	4½"x14"	16 @ 5½"x7"	Fastenings and details same as <u>Champion of the Seas</u>.
Flying Mist #1	NHWO	7"	6", 5", outer strake chamfered	4½"	5½" x 7"	
Galatea #1	HP		graduated to 4½"	4½"		
Game Cock #1	HP	7"		4½"	5½" x 7"	Narrow waist, 4" thk.

Table 20.1. *Continued.*

Vessel & Ref.#	Species of wood	Garboard, thickness (d)	Diminishing strakes, No. & thk. (e)	Common plank, thk. (f)	Wales, thk. & width (m)	Remarks
Gazelle #4	PP					
Gem of the Ocean #1	oak	4"	4"	4"	5" x 7"	Waist, 4" thk.
Golden Eagle #1	HP	7" x 14"	4"	4"	5" x 7"	Some treenails driven thru, wedged both ends
Golden Fleece (2nd) #1	HP	7"	6", tapered	4½"	6" x 7"	Butt bolts yellow metal
		Treenails are driven thru and wedged both ends.				
Golden Light #1	YP	7" x 12", flushed	6" x 12", flushed	4"	5" x 7"	Waist, 3 strakes, 4" thick.
		Garboard is bolted thru keel into opposite garboard and upward thru the timbers.				
Golden West #1	HP					
Grace Darling #1	oak	7" x 14"	6", 5", outer strake tapered	4"	23 @ 5"x7"	
Great Republic #2,10	Ref.10 HP	10" x 14", let in	9", 8", outer strake tapered	6"	6" x 8"	Waist, 9 strakes, 4½" thick.
		Garboard is bolted thru keel into opposite garboard and upward thru the timbers. Bilge is planked with 8" thk protruding planks, Figure 20.1, detail H.				
	Ref.4 SP	8"	7½" to 7"	7"	7" x 8"	Bilge plank same as in Refs.2,10.
	Ref.2 PP	10" x 14", let in	9" x 14"	6"x14"	6" x 8"	
		Square treenailed with 1¼" locust and a copper bolt thru every 4th timber. Other fastenings similar to Champion of the Seas. Bilge is planked with 4 protruding strakes, 8" x 12", see Figure 20.1, detail H. Planking from wales down to the bilge planking is 12" wide.				
Great Republic (rebuilt) #103	HP	10" x 14", let in	9", 8", outer strake tapered	6"	6" x 8"	Waist, 9 strakes, 4½" thick.
		Bilge planking is 8" thick.				

Vessel & Ref.#	Species of wood	Garboard, thickness (d)	Diminishing strakes, No. & thk. (e)	Common plank, thk. (f)	Wales, thk. & width (m)	Remarks
Henry Hill Bark #1	HP	5"	3½"	3½"	4½" x 6"	Butt bolts copper and yellow metal.
Herald of the Morning #12		let in				Narrow waist,
Hoogly #1	HP	7", let in	4½"	4½"	5½" x 7"	3 strakes, 4½" thk.
		Garboard is bolted thru keel into opposite garboard and upward thru the timbers. Vessel has 5000 locust treenails driven thru all, wedged and plugged.				
Hurricane #1						
Indiaman #1	HP	8" x 14"	7", 6", outer strake tapered	4½"	5½" x 7"	Butt bolts yellow metal.
Intrepid						
Invincible #4	GHP	8", let in	6"	4" to 5"	5"	Planking free from sap or shakes.
James Baines #2	PP	9" x 15", let in	8", 7"	5½" to bilge	24 @ 6"x7"	Fastenings and details same as Champion of the Seas.
John Bertram #1	HP	7", let in	graduated to 4"	4"	5½"	Garboards "alternately bolted through each other and the keel and upward through the floor timbers into the hold." Many of her treenails are driven thru and wedged both ends.
John Gilpin #1	HP	6", flushed	4½"	4½"	5" x 7"	Waist 16" wide, 4" thk.
John Land #1,32 (Built as a duplicate of Winged Arrow.)	HP	7"	4"	4"	5" x 7"	Narrow waist, 3 strakes.
John Stuart						
John Wade #1	HP					
Joseph Peabody #1	WO	7", let in	6", 5", outer strake tapered	4"	5½" x 7"	Butt bolts yellow metal.
		Garboard is bolted thru keel into opposite garboard and upward thru the timbers.				
King Fisher #1	HP	7", flushed	"flushed out to 4" at the 3rd strake."	4"	5½" x 7"	"The planking fore and aft is bolted alternately through stem and sternpost ----.'

Table 20.1. *Continued.*

Vessel & Ref.#	Species of wood	Garboard, thickness (d)	Diminishing strakes, No. & thk. (e)	Common plank, thk. (f)	Wales, thk. & width (m)	Remarks
Lady Franklin						
Lamplighter Bark #1	oak	3½"	3½", flushed	3½"	4½"	
Lightfoot #1	HP	7"	6", flushed	4½"	5½" x 7"	
Lightning #1,2	Ref.1 HP	8" x 12"	7"x12",6"x12", outer strake chamfered	4½"	5½" x 8"	
	Ref.2 PP	8" x 16", probable	7", 6"	4½"x14"	24 @ 5½"x8"	Fastenings and details same as Champion of the Seas.
Mameluke #1	WO	7", chamfered	6", 5", chamfered	4½"	5½" x 7"	Many of her treenails driven thru and wedged both ends.
Mary Robinson						
Mastiff #1	HP	7" x 13"	4½"	4½"	5½" x 6"	Butt bolts yellow metal.
Mermaid Bark #1	HP	5"	3½"	3½"	4"	
Morning Light #1	YP					"Outside planking is stout and square fastened."
Mystery #1	HP	7" x 13", let in	6", 5"	4"	5½" x 7"	Garboard is bolted thru keel into opposite garboard and upward thru the timbers.
Nightingale #3	oak,YP					Copper fastened.
Noonday #1	NHWO	7", flushed	6", 5", flushed	4"	6"	Bilge plank, 6" thk. Waist, 4" thk.
						Garboard is bolted thru keel into opposite garboard and also cross bolted thru opposite sister keelsons in every other timber with 1¼" copper.
Northern Light						
Ocean Express #1	HP		4½"	4½"	5½"	
Ocean Pearl #1	HP	7"			5" x 7"	Waist, 6 narrow strakes, 4" thk.
Ocean Telegraph #5	HP					
Onward #1	oak	6"	4"	4"	5" x 7"	
Osborne Howes						
Panther						

Vessel & Ref.#	Species of wood	Garboard, thickness (d)	Diminishing strakes, No. & thk. (e)	Common plank, thk. (f)	Wales, thk. & width (m)	Remarks
Phantom #1	HP	8" x 14", flushed	5"x12",5"x4½", flushed	4½"	6" x 6"	
Queen of Clippers #1	HP	7", flushed	6", 5", flushed	4½"	5½" x 7"	
Queen of the Pacific						
Queen of the Seas #1	oak	7", let in	4"	4"	5" x 7"	All treenails driven thru, wedged both ends.
Quickstep Bark #1	HP,WO	6"	3"	3"	WO, 5"	Many treenails driven thru, wedged both ends.
Racehorse Bark #1	YP	3½"	3½"	3½"	4¾" x 6½"	
Racer #3	NHWO,SP				NHWO,SP	
Radiant #1	YP	7", flushed	2 strakes, flushed to 4½"	4½"	5½" x 7"	
Raven #3	WO	7"	3½"	3½"	10 @ 5"	
Red Jacket #19,46	SP or HP	7"	7"	5"	6"	
Robin Hood Bark						
Rocket Bark						
Roebuck #1	HP,WO	4"	4"	4"	WO, 5" x 7"	
Romance of the Sea #1	YP,HP					
Santa Claus #1		7", flushed	6", 5", flushed	4" or 4½",	5½" x 7"	
Saracen #1	HP	7"	6", 5", outer strake tapered	4½"	5½"	All treenails driven thru, wedged both ends.
Sea Bird Bark #1	HP	3"	3"	3"	5"	
Seaman's Bride						
Sea Serpent						
Shooting Star #1	HP	6"	5", tapered	4"	5" x 7"	Many treenails driven thru, wedged both ends.
Sierra Nevada #1	HP	7"	6", flushed	5"	6½" x 7"	
Silver Star #1	WO	7"	6", 5", outer strake chamfered	4½"	5" x 7"	Upper wales flushed to 4½" thickness of waist.
Southern Cross #1		7"	graduated to 4"	4"	19 @ 5"x7"	Narrow waist, 3 strakes, abt. 4" thick.

Table 20.1. *Continued.*

Vessel & Ref.#	Species of wood	Garboard, thickness (d)	Diminishing strakes, No. & thk. (e)	Common plank, thk. (f)	Wales, thk. & width (m)	Remarks
Sovereign of the Seas #1,2	Ref.1 HP	8"	6", flushed to 5"	5"	25 @ 6" x 7"	
	Ref.2 PP	10" x 14"				Fastenings and details same as Champion of the Seas.
Spitfire #1	HP	8"	4"	4"	5½" x 7"	
Staffordshire #1,2	Ref.1 HP	7", let in	6", 5",	4½"	6" x 7"	Garboards "alternately bolted thru the keel and each other and square fastened thru the timbers."
	Ref.2 PP	7" x 14", let in	6"	4½"x14"	20 @ 5½"x7"	Fastenings and details same as Champion of the Seas.
Stag Hound #1,2	Ref.1 HP, probable	7", let in	2 strakes, graduated to 4½"	4½"	16 @ 5½" x 6"	Garboard is bolted thru keel into opposite garboard and upward thru the timbers. Planking along upper part of the run is of uniform width and terminates at the planksheer. Below, the planking from opposite sides meets and forms a series of angled butts on center line down to the sternpost.
	Ref.2 PP	7" x 14", let in	7"	4½"x14"	16 @ 5½"x7"	Fastenings and details same as Champion of the Seas.
Star of the Union #1	HP	"heavy"	4½"	4½"	5½"	
Starr King						
Storm King #1	WO	7" x 13", flushed	6" x 13", flushed	4½"	20 @ 5½" x 7"	
Sultana Bark #1	HP,WO	5"	3¾"	3¾"	4"	
Sunny South						
Surprise #1	SP	7", let in	6", 5"	4½"	5½" x 7"	Narrow waist, 4 strakes, 3½" wide x 4" thk.
	YP					Garboards and the diminishing strakes are bolted thru keel and opposite members, and upward thru the timbers.
Swallow #1	YP					Fastenings and details same as Champion of the Seas.
Sweepstakes						
Sword Fish #18		let in				
Syren #3		9"				
Telegraph						
Thatcher Magoun #1	HP	7", let in	6", 5", tapered	4½"	5½" x 7"	Garboard is bolted thru keel into opposite garboard with copper bolts. Also bolted upward thru the timbers.
Tornado						
Uncowah						
War Hawk #1	WO up to 18 feet	8" x 14", let in	5"	5"	5½" x 7"	Garboard is bolted thru keel into opposite garboard and upward thru the timbers. Wood in planking above 18 feet is not identified.
Water Witch #1	HP,NHWO	7", let in	4"	4"	NHWO, 5½" x 7"	Garboard is bolted thru keel into opposite garboard and upward thru the timbers.
Western Continent						
Westward Ho #1,2	Ref.1 HP	7", let in	4½"	4½"	5" x 5"	Garboards "bolted thru the keel and alternately thru each other and upward thru the timbers."
	Ref.2 PP	7" x 14", let in	7"	4½"x14"	16 @ 5½"x7"	Fastenings and details same as Champion of the Seas.
West Wind #1	HP					Fastenings and details same as Champion of the Seas.
Whirlwind #1	oak	6"	4"	4"	5" x 7"	
Whistler #1	HP	7" x 14"	2 @ 5½"x14"	4"	22 @ 6" x 7"	
Wildfire	Bark					

Table 20.1. *Continued.*

Vessel & Ref.#	Species of wood	Garboard, thickness (d)	Diminishing strakes, No. & thk. (e)	Common plank, thk. (f)	Wales, thk. & width (m)	Remarks
Wild Pigeon #1	HP	7", let in	4"	4"	5" x 6½"	
			Garboard is bolted thru keel into opposite garboard and upward thru the timbers.			
Wild Ranger #1		7", let in	4"	4"	5½" x 7"	
Wild Rover						
Winged Arrow #1	HP	7"	4"	4"	5" x 7"	Waist, 3 strakes.
Winged Racer #1	HP	8"	7", 6", 5", outer strake tapered	4½"	6" x 7"	
Witchcraft #1	HP	7½"	6", 5", outer strake tapered	4½"	5½" x 6½"	Narrow waist, 18" wide, 3 strakes.
			Garboard is bolted thru keel into opposite garboard and upward thru floor timbers and ceiling.			
Witch of the Wave #1	HP	7"	graduated to 4"	4"	5½" x 7"	
Wizard #1	HP	8"	5"	5"	5½" x 7"	
Young America						
Young Turk Bark #1	HP	3"	3"	3"	4½"	Planking fastened with treenails and spikes.

(text continued from page 308)

to the outer edge if excessive thickness warranted it. The result was a series of steps, as shown in Figure 20.1, detail D. The strakes were fastened with oak or locust treenails and copper or composition bolts which were riveted both ends. No rigid uniformity was followed in driving the treenails, but in many cases they were driven completely through planking, frame, and ceiling and wedged at both ends.

There were exceptions to this form of fastening the diminishing strakes, notable examples being found in McKay's clippers, William H. Webb's *Challenge*, and in Samuel Hall's *Surprise*. McKay specified that each thick (diminishing) strake be bolted edgeways into the garboard with 1⅛-inch iron at intervals of 5 feet and into the timbers with 1⅛-inch copper and iron.[2] Webb required that, in *Challenge*, the single diminishing strake should be bolted with copper through the timbers.[1] (This could also have applied to his other clippers, but no such details are recorded.) In the case of *Surprise*, Hall called for both diminishing strakes to be bolted through the keel and the opposite members in addition to being bolted upward through the timbers.[1]

The garboard assembly was finished in three different fashions. The simplest of these was to leave each of the heavy timbers in its installed square configuration as indicated in Figure 1.2.

The two remaining treatments were as shown in Figure 20.1, details D and E. Detail D, reconstructed principally from contemporary descriptions,[1] shows how the protrud-

ing surface of each strake, starting at the rabbet line on the keel, was dubbed off until the strakes were flushed fair with the thickness of the common, or bottom, planking. The detail shows a resulting concavity of the vessel's bottom. This is a little-noted detail of hull form, and not of any great significance. Approaching the ends of the vessel, as the heavy planks diminished in thickness, the feature disappeared entirely.

Detail E, based on an illustration in the *New York Marine Register*,[21] shows how the protruding corners of the garboard and diminishing strakes were chamfered so as to align with the next strake. The practical advantages are self-evident. First, by cutting off the square projecting shoulder, vulnerability to hanging up on some underwater object was eliminated or, at the very least, minimized. Second, the sheathing gang was not left with the formidable task of neatly fitting and fastening the strakes of sheathing in areas where they crossed the strakes of planking.

Descriptions by MacLean[1] indicate that many vessels were built with a combination of all three treatments, so this was evidently very much a matter of builder's preference.

As with the garboards, there is very little if any detailed information available in regard to the end connections of the individual diminishing strakes. However, the plan of *Ocean Monarch*[24] illustrates that there was some use of scarphs in connecting the various lengths of, at least, the inner strake. Such scarphs were edge-bolted into the garboard and located with ample shift in reference to the garboard scarphs.

Bottom Planking

The *bottom planking* or *common planking* (Figure 6.2, detail f) covered a ship's bottom from the diminishing strakes out to the wales, which nearly always involved making the turn of the bilge. These planks, due to their protected location, were the thinnest of the exterior hull planking, excluding waist planking if called for. Table 20.1 lists the thickness of bottom planking for vessels listed in this volume. Also entered is the width of the planks for McKay's ships, specified in McKay's notes as 14 inches[2]—a relatively large dimension for planking in general. This is the only source which specifically gives this dimension, all other sources confining themselves to the thickness only.

Bottom or common planking was easily cut to required width and easily installed due to the relative consistency of hull form, especially in the middle length of the vessel. Each plank was cut to match the *rasing line* and fitted to the frames in accordance with Figure 20.1, details B and C. In many areas the surfaces across adjacent frames were flat enough to allow direct application of the planks to the frames. Reaching the turn of the bilge, where the surface of the frames formed an arc, the rasing line was marked on the frame, which was then dubbed off flat as shown in detail C. This provided a solid seat for the plank, thus avoiding the possibility of *spring* in the plank, which made it impossible to successfully drive and secure treenails.

The general method of fastening planking is shown in Figure 20.1, detail I, the particulars being determined by plank width. Most fastenings were locust treenails with copper bolts riveted at both ends in way of the butt ends of the planks. This information is listed in Table 20.1, and exceptions are noted when known.

As the width and thickness of planks decreased approaching the ends of the ship to match the depth of the stem and sternpost rabbets, it sometimes became necessary to steam the planks until they were pliable enough to bend to the more acute curves of the ship's form. The general formula for steaming was one hour of immersion for every inch of plank thickness.

When the planks in any portion of a vessel were considered ready for final installation, they were located in position and "stuck" in place with preliminary fastenings, which were usually standard ship spikes about ½ inch square and 8 or 10 inches long.

When planking was being installed, whether common planking or wales, it was customary to fasten the end lengths into the rabbets forward and aft before fitting the rest of any given strake. Therefore, the final "shutter in" plank (later shortened to "shutter") was chosen for a location that required a minimum of shaping and fitting.

All planking was procured in the longest attainable lengths, and butts and fastenings installed in accordance with details shown in Figure 20.1, detail I.

Some variations to the general rules of fastening are found among the vessels listed in this book. The planking of *Challenge* was reportedly fastened with locust treenails and copper spikes. The use of copper bolts to secure the butts is not mentioned, but, of necessity, it can be assumed that this was done. This explicit use of spikes is the closest example to the old dump-and-bolt system which had been widely used at one time and is illustrated in Figure 20.1, detail I.

Dauntless and *Hoogly* had their planking fastened with treenails that not only were wedged at both ends, but the exterior ends were plugged as well. In addition, the planking of *Dauntless* was Massachusetts white oak, all installed "sap side out."

As we have seen in other contexts, *Great Republic*, a ship unique due to her overwhelming size, was possessed of many peculiarities and digressions from normal in the details of her construction. One of these was in the form of her exterior planking, having bottom planking of the same thickness as her wales. Between these two planking categories, she was fitted with four projecting strakes of bilge planking that was not faired into the adjacent planking except at her extremities, as shown in Figure 20.1, detail H. However, it seems reasonable to assume that the upper and lower protruding shoulders might have been chamfered.

Wales

The *wales* (Figure 6.2, detail m) were thick, relatively narrow strakes that covered a vessel's sides from the planksheer to a location at or near the upper turn of the bilge. When a ship was built with waist planking, the uppermost wale might be as much as 18 inches below the lower edge of the planksheer. By their bulk and extra thickness, the wales provided stiffness and strength to the sides of the vessel.

Table 20.1 lists the sizes of these strakes, in most cases both the width and thickness being given. Also, in eighteen vessels the number of individual strakes is recorded. From these statistics it can be seen that the thickness of these members ranged between 5 and 6 inches, while the widths were between 6 and 8 inches. These proportions applied to all the large clippers. The reduction in width made these strakes more amenable to bending and compensated for their extra thickness.

The number of strakes, where such information is given, varied from sixteen to twenty-four. The total width of this assembled band of strakes ranged from 16 feet in *Lightning* to about 9 feet 6 inches in *Stag Hound* and several other vessels. This brought the heavy protective planking down to some level below the waterline.

The wales of most clippers were of the same type of wood as the remainder of the planking. However, some vessels made use of superior wood for the wales. *Andrew Jackson*,

Coeur de Lion, *Daring*, *Flying Arrow*, *Roebuck*, and *Water Witch* all had wales of white oak and common planking of yellow or hard pine. *Ellen Foster* and *Racer* each contained some white oak wales.

Again, *Great Republic* differed from conventional practice. While all her exterior planking was pine, she was built without clearly defined wales. Her sides above the external bilge planks to her waist, and her bottom below these same planks to her keel, were covered uniformly with 6-inch planking.

All the installation details applicable to other planking applied to the wales, including extreme narrowing of their thickness as they approached the rabbets.

The Waist

The *waist* (Figure 6.2, detail s), when installed in a vessel's planking, consisted of several strakes of thickness less than that of common planking but greater than that of the bulwarks. These planks were narrow and filled the space between the topmost wale and the planksheer. Using figures based upon the number of vessels listed and known to have had waist planking, it appears that approximately 20 percent incorporated the feature, while the remaining 80 percent were planked flush up to the planksheer.

Table 20.1 lists this information, and from the table it is evident that the width of this band of planking varied greatly if one uses the number of strakes as the criterion. This number varied from three to nine strakes; however, the total width in most cases is indeterminate. Definite widths are available for a few vessels, they being *Edwin Forrest*, four strakes, each 4 inches wide; *Surprise*, four strakes, each 3½ inches wide; *Witchcraft*, three strakes, each 6 inches wide; *John Land* and *Winged Arrow*, width 16 inches. *Great Republic*, as usual operating in her own waters, had a waist of nine strakes whose combined width, scaled from her midship section, totaled 48 inches.

No outstanding reason presents itself to explain the use of waist planking. Any weight saving would be minimal and of little consequence; if a ship was built with this as a factor, she was surely headed for far greater trouble at some time in her life. An individual builder's opinion that waist planking was an asset to the vessel can be understood, even if not agreed with.

An apparently valid rationale can be advanced that, in their location in the ship, where fastenings of the waterway, planksheer, upper deck clamp, and lodging knees occurred in great profusion, waist planks did not require the same solid fastening that was needed for fastening wales. This would seem to be an acceptable argument in favor of installing such slender timbers. However, if this was a fact, the advantage was not pursued by the majority of shipbuilders.

Due to their narrow width, these waist strakes were single-fastened as shown in Figure 20.1, detail I. However, it is not inconceivable that some liberties could have been taken without affecting the ship's structural integrity.

Headboards

The *headboards*, illustrated in Figure 24.2, were the only exterior planking remaining to be fitted in the ship. They did not constitute a part of the structural hull, even though, due to their exposed position on the bows, they required sufficient substance to enable them to withstand the heavy battering of rough seas. Their structure, stoutly supported by transverse timbers called *cheeks*, which were anchored into the stemhead, was heavy and cumbersome, even though their appearance to an observer was graceful and pleasing. They served no purpose other than to ornament the bow and render the forward endings of the planksheer and the main rail more pleasing to the eye. In general, the upper rail projected forward in a line which continued fair with the sheer of the main rail while the lower rail continued as an extension of the planksheer, sweeping forward and upward in a graceful curve until the two rails converged immediately abaft the figurehead. Between these rails, the transverse cheek timbers supported suitable framing to which the headboarding was fastened.

Detailed information on the subject of headrails and headboards in merchant vessels is very scarce and difficult to find. This, as is the case with much intimate detail concerning commercial ships, is due to the fact that, in early days, such ships were constructed as individual enterprises. There were no precise rules in place, so each shipbuilder followed his own initiative and inclination. With no central policy or control, it was inevitable that there would be great variation of detail among merchantmen. However, the general rules of construction were followed by all shipbuilders and thus, at any given period, all ships being built were constructed in a like manner and they all took on the same general appearance, adhering to the same general details.

Therefore, the evolution of the headboard, from a series of headrails to its ultimate demise, is best followed in naval vessels, which were built according to "establishment" and very faithfully recorded, step by step. With almost endless money available, the state was not motivated to be austere. On the other hand, the merchantmen, while following the same general construction, were required to consider economics, the result being a plain edition of an ornate treatment of the ship's head. The progression and changes as applied to naval vessels provide a clear overview of the ship's head, allowing for a reasonable translation of the subject as applied to merchantmen and the clipper ships.

Headboards were the direct descendants of the headrails

which surged into prominence in the early 1600s, when the ruling monarchs of western European naval powers convinced themselves that the dignity and prestige of their states could boldly be proclaimed through intricate and costly decoration of their ships in locations that were most visible, namely the bow and stern.

In this early period the bows of ships below the waterline were full and well rounded. The forward hull above the waterline, however, ended abruptly in a vertical, flat transverse bulkhead—the *beakhead bulkhead*. This type of construction was inherently weak, a condition that would later be rectified by the introduction of the round bow.

Forward of this bulkhead was the *beakhead deck*, completely outside of the hull and unprotected from the elements and the sea. This deck was made up as a grating and was nestled between the headrails on either side of the ship. The entire structure was fabricated as open-work which eliminated any possibility of the structure spooning up water when the ship pitched in heavy seas, or retaining water during violent storms.

The beakhead and headrails were, as stated before, ornamental showcases. They did, however, serve two practical purposes. One of these purposes was to support the fore tack *bumkins*, or *boomkins*. These bumkins, one on each side of the bowsprit, pointed outboard at about 45 degrees from the centerline of the ship, in a horizontal attitude. Their function was to hold the fore tack block when sailing conditions demanded that the clew of the foresail be extended forward in order to catch the breeze. This situation was caused by the fact that, at this time, a ship's foremast was crowded very far forward, almost to the point of encroaching upon the beakhead bulkhead. In later periods the problem was eliminated as foremasts were slowly moved farther aft.

The second purpose was equally practical but utterly different. The headrails not only satisfied the vanity of kings, they also provided for the needs of men, for within the confines of these rails were installed the toilet facilities for the crew—euphemistically referred to as "seats of ease." They were located on the level of the beakhead deck grating and consisted basically of a wide plank raised on enclosed sides, and perforated with round openings of a size to accommodate a man when seated. Quite obviously, the bottom of these assemblies was left open. Their number and location varied from ship to ship. However, some known examples are: HMS *Victory*, 1765, three seats each side, two located beside the bowsprit, one located at the rail near the hood ends; the American Continental frigate *Confederacy*, 1778, two seats each side midway between bowsprit and upper headrail; the United States ship of the line *Columbus*, 1819, six seats each side located along the rail; and the United States sloop-of-war *Germantown*, 1843, four seats each side, located along the rail at the hood ends.

Being located on the beakhead deck, it likely was not very long before a ship's toilet facilities were inevitably referred to as "the head," whatever the location, and this convenient term has ever since been understood and handed down throughout the nautical world.

The design and location of the head facilities in their unprotected situations were uncomfortable and rather forbidding, and were not conducive to long absences by even the most malingering of sailors. The situation improved with the passage of time.

From the early 1600s to the late 1700s, the beakhead bulkhead was a fixture. It took on many detailed variations but always remained basically the same. About 1800 it gave way to the completely round bow whose planking terminated in the hood ends. Concurrently, the expense of the ornate headrail treatment overcame the vanity of kings, and plainer headrails were installed. Obviously, the head facilities in merchant vessels, which carried significantly smaller complements, were not as extensive as those in their naval counterparts. However, in other respects, they were alike.

About the year 1815 a new feature appeared at the ship's head, namely headboards. A new straight rail, uniformly tapered from its after end to the forward end, was installed between the catheads and the figurehead. The space between this new rail and the old upper rail was boarded in. This detail is very apparent in the United States ship of the line *Columbus*. The ship's head had finally received a very small improvement.

By 1840 the old individual, graceful headrails were superseded by more predominant boarding. The topmost rail was an extension of the main rail and the lower rail was an extension of the planksheer. By this time, foremasts were located abaft the forecastle and the ship's head was moved under cover.

In 1850, headboards were regularly built into the bows of large merchant vessels. However, it was a time when shipbuilders and owners, pressed by demand and economics, looked for ways to speed construction and reduce costs without sacrificing a ship's seaworthiness. By decreasing the structural work required to install headboards, they saved both weight and labor, which, along with the elimination of excessive and useless structure, fitted nobly into the design of the clipper ship.

And so began the demise of headboards, particularly in clippers. Of the vessels included in this book, only twenty-two are definitely known to have been built with headboards. Between 1851 and 1853 the number of ships built with headboards declined uniformly until they disappeared entirely. After 1853 the only clipper ship built with headboards and included in this list was *Noonday*, launched August 25, 1855.

Naturally, the fact that new ships might no longer be built with headboards did not mean that these structures would

(text continued on page 320)

Figure 20.2. *Mouldings and beaded edges.*

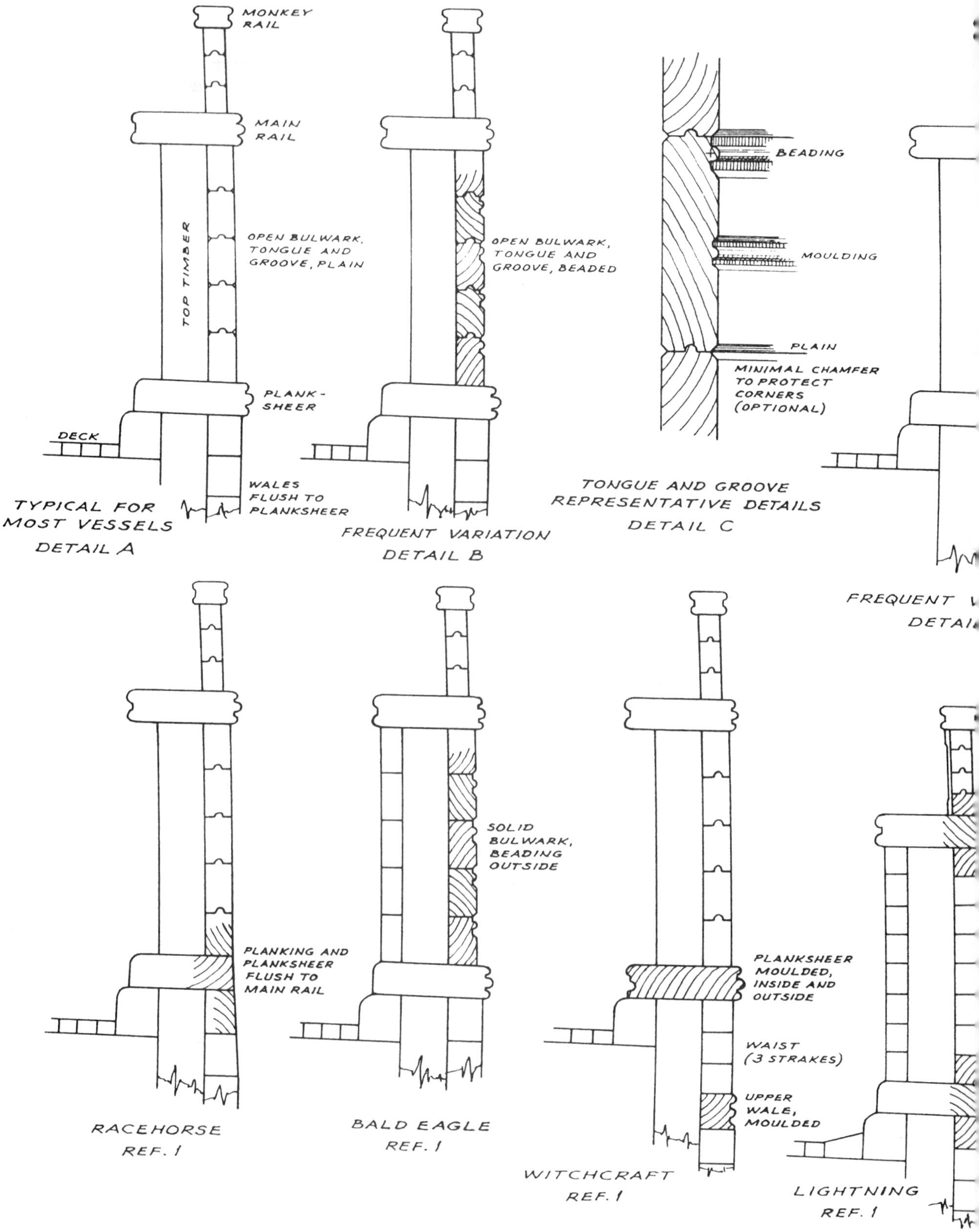

MONKEY RAIL

MAIN RAIL

TOP TIMBER

OPEN BULWARK, TONGUE AND GROOVE, PLAIN

PLANK-SHEER

DECK

WALES FLUSH TO PLANKSHEER

TYPICAL FOR MOST VESSELS
DETAIL A

OPEN BULWARK, TONGUE AND GROOVE, BEADED

FREQUENT VARIATION
DETAIL B

BEADING

MOULDING

PLAIN

MINIMAL CHAMFER TO PROTECT CORNERS (OPTIONAL)

TONGUE AND GROOVE REPRESENTATIVE DETAILS
DETAIL C

FREQUENT V
DETAI

PLANKING AND PLANKSHEER FLUSH TO MAIN RAIL

RACEHORSE
REF. 1

SOLID BULWARK, BEADING OUTSIDE

BALD EAGLE
REF. 1

PLANKSHEER MOULDED, INSIDE AND OUTSIDE

WAIST (3 STRAKES)

UPPER WALE, MOULDED

WITCHCRAFT
REF. 1

LIGHTNING
REF. 1

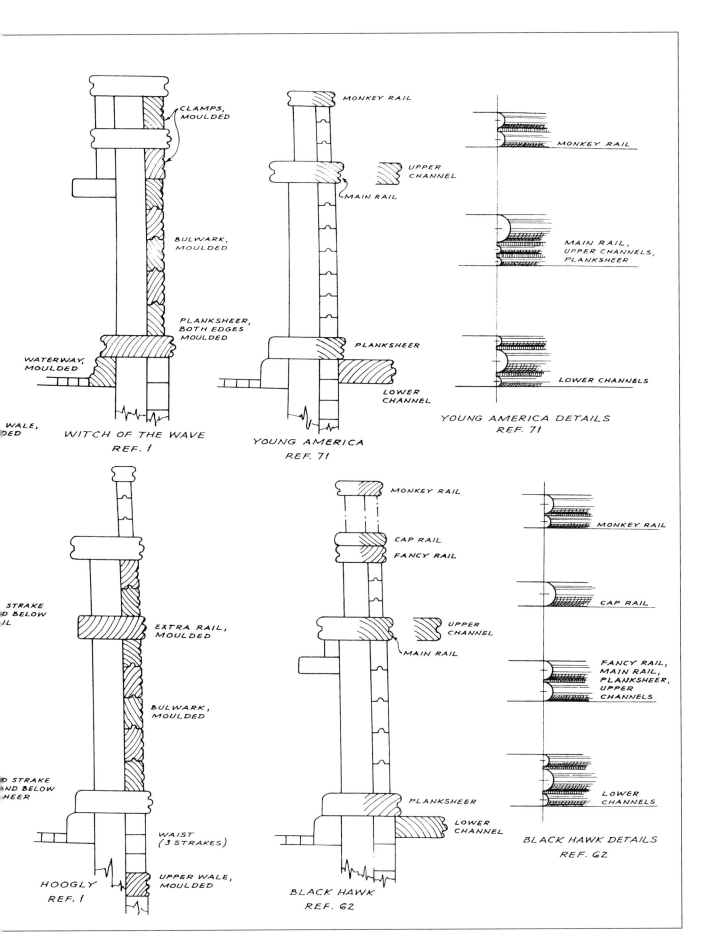

CLAMPS,
MOULDED

BULWARK,
MOULDED

PLANKSHEER,
BOTH EDGES
MOULDED

WATERWAY,
MOULDED

WALE,
ED

WITCH OF THE WAVE
REF. 1

MONKEY RAIL

UPPER
CHANNEL

MAIN RAIL

PLANKSHEER

LOWER
CHANNEL

YOUNG AMERICA
REF. 71

MONKEY RAIL

MAIN RAIL,
UPPER CHANNELS,
PLANKSHEER

LOWER CHANNELS

YOUNG AMERICA DETAILS
REF. 71

STRAKE
D BELOW
L

EXTRA RAIL,
MOULDED

BULWARK,
MOULDED

D STRAKE
ND BELOW
HEER

WAIST
(3 STRAKES)

UPPER WALE,
MOULDED

HOOGLY
REF. 1

MONKEY RAIL

CAP RAIL

FANCY RAIL

UPPER
CHANNEL

MAIN RAIL

PLANKSHEER

LOWER
CHANNEL

BLACK HAWK
REF. 62

MONKEY RAIL

CAP RAIL

FANCY RAIL,
MAIN RAIL,
PLANKSHEER,
UPPER
CHANNELS

LOWER
CHANNELS

BLACK HAWK DETAILS
REF. 62

319

(text continued from page 317)

no longer be seen. While most of the clippers had unfortunately brief life spans (see Chapter 32), there were a few which experienced amazing longevity to the extent of being afloat for as long as fifty years. Among those were *John Bertram*, launched in December 1850 and reported sinking at sea on March 17, 1883, a life duration of thirty-two years; *Nightingale*, launched in June 1851, abandoned at sea April 17, 1893, after a life of forty-two years; and the longest-lived clipper of all, *Syren*, launched May 1, 1851 and still listed in *Lloyd's Register* in 1920, at sixty-nine years of age.

Whether or not these aged ships retained their headboards throughout their entire lives cannot be stated with absolute certainty. Such structure could have been lost or damaged at sea over the years. What does appear certain is that no ship owner was likely to spend money removing something unless dictated by necessity.

Mouldings and Beaded Edges

All of the hull construction has now been accounted for. When the last "shutter" strake was cut, fastened, and caulked, the structural hull was a completed unit.

Mouldings and beaded edges (Figure 20.2), while not contributing to the strength of a vessel, were very much a part of her structural composition. In spite of the obvious expense of cutting artistic trim and contoured edges, very few vessels were built without such adornment. If the hull was the picture, the mouldings and trim were the frame.

The items that were generally moulded were the inner and outer edges of the monkey rail and the main rail; the outer edge of the planksheer and the channels. Occasionally, the outer face of the top and bottom strakes of the monkey rail planking and bulwark planking, and one or more strakes of the waist or upper wale planks, were also moulded. The tongue-and-groove planking of open bulwarks was sometimes, but not always, fashioned with beading at the tongue edge, which was always the top edge when installed.

In most cases these minor details have been lost to posterity. However, through descriptions and photographs, some of these moulded features have survived. Figure 20.2 illustrates a few of the known treatments and some that have been reconstructed. A reasonable assumption might be made that these are typical examples.

Neither the application nor pattern of the mouldings was consistent, but, by the nature of their locations, they were restricted to certain general forms and contours.

The typical extent of the moulded edges depended generally upon the form of the vessel's stern. In vessels built with transom sterns, the main rail and any rails above continued with their moulded form across the stern of the vessel. The planksheer terminated at the fashion piece. There were, of course, exceptions to this practice. In vessels having counter sterns, all the rails were continuous around the stern, thus forming moulded bands completely around the ship.

At the bow, the moulded traces of the rails generally terminated in way of the bowsprit. In vessels with a stem and bow arrangement compatible to the feature, these rails were gracefully faired closer together and worked into the extremity of the stem.

In Figure 20.2, details A, B, and D illustrate the most frequently used moulded details. The beading and moulding shapes, as shown, are representative of such details, and are not taken from actual vessels. The same applies to detail C.

The details of mouldings indicate the actual locations of moulded edges as described by MacLean.[1] The finite details are only imaginative. Obviously, in these cases each individual is free to reconstruct his own version of the appearance of the mouldings.

In the cases of *Young America* and *Black Hawk*, both the locations and details of the mouldings are taken from photographs of the vessels.[71,62] From these it is not difficult to envision the general forms that might be encountered in most of the clippers.

The bark *Racehorse*, unusual in her simplicity, represents the only instance among the ships in this book in which the definition of the outboard edge of the planksheer was lost due to its being flushed off to the surface of its neighboring planking.

Chapter Twenty One

CARGO PORTS; SCUPPERS; CHANNELS; RUDDER

Cargo Ports

Cargo ports, or *side ports,* as they were sometimes called, generally but not exclusively, were found in the larger clippers. Their mention is confined to relatively few vessels, however, and details were not considered worthy of note. In concept they resembled gunports. They required sills, lintels, and side frames, all of which protruded into the opening in order to provide solid seating of the port cover and to help maintain watertightness.

There were certain restrictions to their size and location. For a ship to retain its maximum classification for insurance purposes, any such port was required to be in the tween-decks in two-deck vessels, and in the upper tween-decks in three-deck vessels. Structurally, the height of the opening was restricted by the upper deck clamp at the top and one standing strake over the lower or middle deck waterway at the bottom, which prescribed an opening about 4 feet high. The width was usually cut to accommodate the ship's frames. The result was a rectangular opening that was slightly long on either its vertical or horizontal axis, depending on the ship's framing and the cargo port's location.

The cover was made of planking that matched the lines of the ship's exterior planking, backed by vertical strakes on the inside, the combined thickness equaling that of the ship's side. Any moulded edges on the ship were carried across the breadth of the cover.

While all cargo ports were installed for the basic purpose of onloading or offloading a vessel's contents, the covers were secured in one of two ways. Simplest and most usual was the cover that, when the onloading of cargo was completed, was put into place permanently. It was secured by hooks, strongbacks, wedges, caulking, or other means compatible with the immediate surrounding structure. The perimeter thus sealed against the elements, the cover would remain thus until the ship arrived at her destination, at which time the port would be broken out.

The second installation was in the manner of a gunport cover, complete with hinges, hooks, and some temporary or permanent means of breaking the cover open in fair weather as an additional means of interior ventilation. Permanent but removable iron bars or gratings were placed over the inside of the opening for the safety of personnel. Such port covers were gasketed when closed in order to render them sufficiently tight against water and weather. When installed in a ship, the cargo ports were most often located abreast of a hatch.

Of the ships included herein, there were very few in which cargo ports are mentioned, and for these only the quantity and location are recorded. Details are negligible, probably due to the fact that the mechanics of such installations were routine.

The following two-deck ships were fitted with the first type of cargo port, each located in the tween-decks, one on each side of ship opposite the main hatch: *Ellen Foster, John Gilpin, Fair Wind, Mastiff, Joseph Peabody,* and *Asa Eldridge.*[1] The three-deck *Champion of the Seas* was fitted in similar fashion in the upper tween-decks, this being visible in a photograph.[61]

Challenge, a three-deck ship, was fitted with three ports with protective iron bars on each side of the ship approximately abreast of her principal hatches and located in her upper tween-decks.[1] *Staffordshire,* also a three-deck vessel, was fitted in a like manner. Her forward ports, however, were provided with appropriate bolts and ring bolts to accommodate the two nine-pounders with which she was armed.[1]

Last, but certainly not least, was *Great Republic,* the only four-deck clipper. Her spar deck was very lofty in relation to her waterline, so her mooring bitts were located on the next deck below, which was the upper deck—a truly structural deck. In way of these bitts, located forward, amidships and aft, her sides were fitted with ports for line handling while making the ship fast when moored alongside a wharf. These ports were approximately 2 feet 6 inches high and 5 feet long. It is quite probable that these openings would be sealed at sea since the space between upper and spar decks was otherwise solidly planked.

Immediately below these line handling ports were her cargo ports, cut into her sides. For such a large ship the cargo ports seem to be uncommonly small, measuring about 2 feet 6 inches high by 3 feet 9 inches long. The covers for these were apparently of the first type.[10]

Scuppers

The *scuppers* (shown in Figure 6.2) were a necessary installation on the weather decks of all vessels built with bulwarks rather than with open rails. They did not fit the category of structure, and they did not qualify as deck furniture. They were, rather, passive permanent fittings which could be grouped with other items such as catheads, bumkins, and bitts.

The function of the scupper was to eliminate the possibility of water collecting in the low points of the weather deck. These locations differed depending upon the trim of the ship and possible listing or heeling. For this reason, the usual locations on the weather deck, along each side of the ship, were at the break of the topgallant forecastle, at the break of the poop deck, at the low point in the waist, and approximately halfway between that point and the topgallant forecastle, thus totaling four scuppers on each side. The number of scuppers installed was dictated by the individual shipbuilder, but their general locations were universal. By their presence it became impossible for water to accumulate for any period longer than it took the scuppers to handle any runoff from rain or boarding seas.

A typical scupper was a lead pipe about 4 inches in diameter. It ran between frames, its upper end cutting through the waterways, the bottom edge being at deck level. The downward angle was such that the scupper exited the hull through the center of a plank, so that it did nothing to jeopardize a caulked seam. Each end of the lead pipe was rolled and flattened until it formed a flange which fayed against the ship's structure and could be rendered watertight.

Channels

The *channels* (Figure 6.1 and Figure 30.1) were the outermost structural components on a ship's hull. Their function was to add spread to the rigging and allow it to stand clear of the uppermost rail. While not considered a structural necessity for the ship's hull, they were of sufficient scantlings to withstand the crushing transverse load induced by the angle of a gang of shrouds set up taut and as rigid as iron rods. Channels were generally constructed of oak.

The channels in the clippers were arranged in the same manner as those installed in packet or cargo vessels, since their purposes were identical. Typically the upper channel was lined up on the main rail and the lower channel was fayed against the lower edge of the planksheer. On occasion this lower channel was placed about one strake below the edge of the planksheer; such was the case with the clipper *Nightingale*.[74]

In size the channels, both upper and lower, were as thick as the main rail and the planksheer, respectively, and of length which could comfortably accommodate the spacing of deadeyes for the rigging and the backstays of each individual mast. The forward end of the channel was located about abreast of the mast so as to allow the foremost deadeye to be set up slightly abaft the mast.

The breadth of the channel was controlled by the angle of the shrouds set up around the masthead, and was sufficient to provide minimum but ample clearance between the lanyards and uppermost rail. Both upper and lower channel at a given mast were of the same breadth, or very nearly so. If made up of more than one width of timber, the pieces were doweled together and the assembly was through-bolted to the ship's side with iron bolts spaced about 3 feet apart.

Unlike men-of-war, which were fitted with one very wide channel abreast of each mast on each side of the ship, merchant sail had two relatively narrow channels per mast on each side of the ship. One practical reason for this was the fact that merchant vessels were subject to crowded dockside conditions when in port, which would make any excessive protrusion a liability.

Reasons for some structures are very seldom given, and channels were no exception. However, some conjecture appears reasonable. The tension in a gang of shrouds descending from masthead to the side of ship was transmitted through the lanyards to the lower deadeyes, thence through the chainplates to the fastenings on the hull. The angle at which the shrouds descended induced a horizontal component which tended to squeeze the ship's rail in toward the centerline of the ship. By placing the channel on the rail, the strongest possible structural unit was formed, resulting in added local stiffness to the rail. It also was a means of providing the narrowest suitable channel.

Placing the lower channel below the planksheer allowed it to be secured through or into the waterway, which was much sturdier than the planksheer itself. Below this the fastenings for the ends of the chainplates were driven into the hull, thus counteracting the induced vertical component.

These forces could be of great magnitude merely through the procedure of being set up. However, it was their reliability when at sea under rough conditions that made installation of the channels a task of the utmost importance.

One vessel which departed from the channel locations

previously discussed was *Great Republic* as rebuilt in 1855. In her case the upper channels for the fore, main, and mizzen masts were fastened midway between the main rail and the planksheer. The upper channel for the aft, or spanker mast, was fayed against the lower edge of the main rail. The lower channels for all masts were located about 4 feet below the planksheer. These locations are plainly visible in a photograph of the vessel taken in 1860 at San Francisco.[75]

Perhaps the most unusual treatment of channels occurred in the bark *Racehorse* and the ship *Dauntless*. In both vessels all upper channels were installed at their customary width, which was similar to the width of the lower channels. However, added to this was the width of the main rail which, along with the monkey rail, was contoured outboard of the lower deadeyes, thus enclosing the lower shrouds and all the backstays.[1] This arrangement is illustrated in Figure 6.5.

Rudder

The rudder (Figure 21.1), which was not a part of the structural hull, was an indispensable structural appendage without which no vessel could cast off from dockside. It was the unit which made the ship a viable operational creation.

The shape of rudders differed during various periods, the form being based upon the configuration of a ship's underwater lines aft and the number of knots at which a vessel could be expected to sail. Ships preceding the clipper era, notably naval vessels, were fitted with rudders that had a straight taper on their after edge and were very broad at the sole, or bottom. This placement of the broad surface at the lowest point was an effort to reach for "solid" water that was not affected by any turbulence or slack water dragged behind the ship.

For the clipper ships, which developed speeds previously unheard of, the established rudder design no longer embodied the most effective shape. The smooth, virtually undisturbed flow of water along the fine lines of the clipper underbody allowed the broadest part of the blade surface to be raised until it was found to be most efficient at a height about midway between the keel and the waterline. A related result of this rudder reshaping was the elimination of the broad sole which was always prone to damage should the vessel take the ground.

Along with this progressive change of shape, the immersed area of the rudder was reduced, this in direct relation to the vessel's ability to sail at great speeds. A study of ships' sheer plans reveals that this area was smaller in the fastest ships. This variation in size can be observed when the immersed area of the rudder is expressed as a percentage of the area of the ship's immersed centerline plane. The following values are general but representative of the relative sizes. In

extreme clippers the value was 1.68 percent; in medium clippers, 2.06 percent; in marginal clippers, such as *Black Hawk*, 2.50 percent.

In terms of the proportions between the rudder's greatest width and the beam of the vessel, this being one of the accepted forms of measurement, in extreme clippers it ranged between one-tenth to one-ninth; in medium clippers, one-ninth to one-eighth; and in marginal vessels, one-eighth of the beam.

The configuration of gunstock rudders followed one general pattern on the order of that shown in Figure 21.1, which is actually a composite of a half dozen forms taken from the lines drawings of specific clippers. Since the shape of the rudder was not based upon a mathematical formula but rather was one born of experience, the only source of such information is generally the lines plan of the vessel itself. In the absence of such detail it is very safe and reasonable to accept the rudder shown in the plate, since very few strayed far from the efficient shape.

As we have seen earlier, proportion and nature had been the governing considerations in shipbuilding for several centuries. Over this extended period of time, any relationship between the size and strength of two related items which proved successful and reliable was carefully noted and handed down for further use. In reference to rudder scantlings, Lauchlan McKay noted that "the diameter of the rudder head should be about three-eighths of the rudder's width."[6] It was a sound finding, based on experience, and, as such, was accepted and handed down. Similarly, a diameter of 3 inches had proven to be reliable for pintles secured to a rudder, and became the accepted proportion. Such was the case with countless components of the average vessel.

Meanwhile, nature had constantly been observed and, through logical thought and reasoning, had been applied to hull form, extending to rudder design. Lauchlan McKay stated, "If we acknowledge the perfection of the fish, let us copy his form and adapt it to the rudder; for the fact of the fish's tail being tapered to a thin edge goes directly and positively to prove that it is the easiest possible form to afford speed. The greatest opposition to this improvement is that the vessel requires more helm."[6] A taper of 2 degrees was bearded on each side of the centerline of the rudder, making it thinner along its after edge. In addition, the siding of the rudder was reduced from top to heel, paralleling similar siding of the sternpost.

Lauchlan McKay's observations were published in 1839, and this date marked the beginning of the end of the philosophy based on experience, proportion, and nature. In the 1840s science intruded and in a very few years governed almost every phase of shipbuilding.

The principal components of the rudder were the stock (A), the coning (B), and the main piece (C). Either the rudder

Figure 21.1. *Typical form of gunstock rudder.*

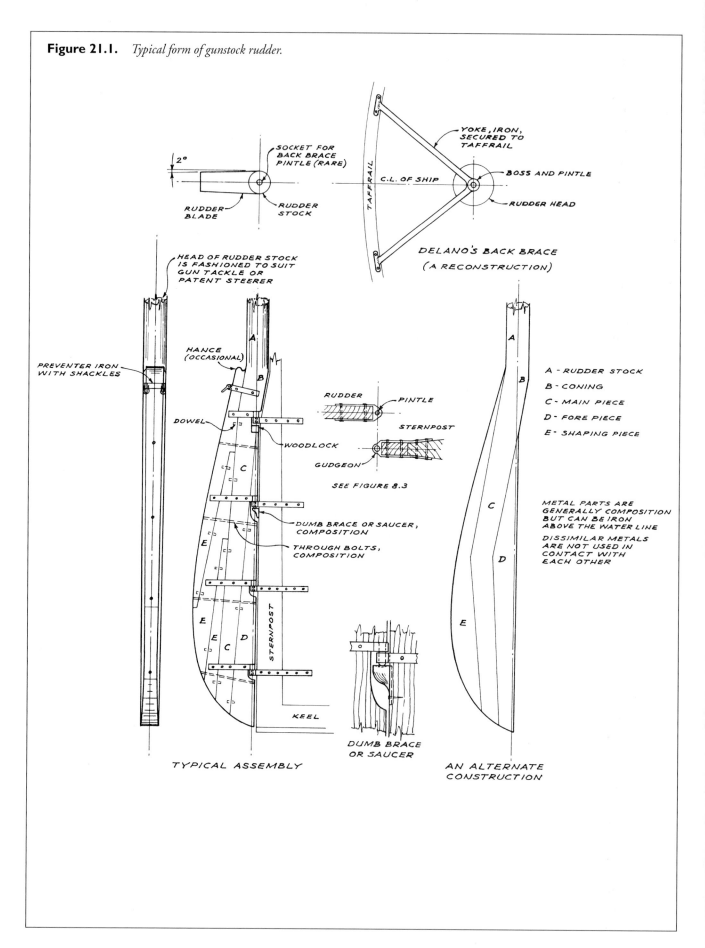

2°

SOCKET FOR
BACK BRACE
PINTLE (RARE)

RUDDER
BLADE

RUDDER
STOCK

YOKE, IRON,
SECURED TO
TAFFRAIL

TAFFRAIL

C.L. OF SHIP

BOSS AND PINTLE

RUDDER HEAD

DELANO'S BACK BRACE
(A RECONSTRUCTION)

HEAD OF RUDDER STOCK
IS FASHIONED TO SUIT
GUN TACKLE OR
PATENT STEERER

PREVENTER IRON
WITH SHACKLES

HANCE
(OCCASIONAL)

A

B

DOWEL

WOODLOCK

RUDDER

PINTLE

STERNPOST

GUDGEON

SEE FIGURE 8.3

C

DUMB BRACE OR SAUCER,
COMPOSITION

THROUGH BOLTS,
COMPOSITION

E

E

E

C

D

STERNPOST

KEEL

A

B

A - RUDDER STOCK
B - CONING
C - MAIN PIECE
D - FORE PIECE
E - SHAPING PIECE

METAL PARTS ARE
GENERALLY COMPOSITION
BUT CAN BE IRON
ABOVE THE WATER LINE
DISSIMILAR METALS
ARE NOT USED IN
CONTACT WITH
EACH OTHER

C

D

E

TYPICAL ASSEMBLY

DUMB BRACE
OR SAUCER

AN ALTERNATE
CONSTRUCTION

could be formed in one piece, or the stock and *coning* (a transition from the stock to the blade) could be worked into the main piece. This combination of stock and coning, no matter how shaped and fabricated, was consistently made of oak because of its strength. Its form and shape evolved so as to bring the stock-coning into the middle part of the blade to protect it from external injury and weakening by the cutting of the *gullets* necessary to make room for the pintles. The length of each gullet was about 1 inch greater than the depth of the braces, to allow clearance to unship the rudder. The fore piece (D), also of hardwood, was placed in position to accept this work. The total profile of the rudder was achieved by assembling the pieces E, which were hard pine or similar wood. These pieces were all doweled one to the other and then bound together by through-bolts which were composition below the waterline, but could be iron above the waterline.

A few rudders were fashioned with a *hance*, or break, in the upper end of the smooth trailing edge as it approached the rudder stock. This bit of decor had no effect upon the action of the rudder and was one of the few nonessential details to find its way into a finished vessel.

Pintles and gudgeons, on which the rudder hung, and their straps were composition below the waterline and were secured with similar fastenings to avoid electrolytic interaction, which occurs between dissimilar metals that are in contact with salt water. Above the waterline they could be iron.

The *preventer fitting* and its shackles were iron, secured with iron rivets. The purpose of this fitting was to accept chains, one in each shackle, which hung slack and were secured on the port and starboard sides of the stern in the vicinity of the knuckle to prevent loss of the rudder if it should become unshipped through some unforeseen circumstance.

The *gudgeon straps* were secured to the sternpost and hull in positions which brought the foot of the rudder to a height clear of the shoe which was attached to the keel, this being a position which offered protection in case of grounding of the vessel.

Immediately below one of the gudgeons, usually the second from the top, a *dumb brace* or *saucer* was fastened to the sternpost, a detail of which is shown in the plate. This was a composition casting upon which the end of one pintle transferred the weight of the rudder onto the dumb brace, thus eliminating undue wear and friction between the surfaces of the pintle and gudgeon straps.

After the rudder was shipped and hanging in place, the gulleting in way of the topmost pintle was hollowed out square and then filled in with a piece of wood called the *wood lock*. This was firmly nailed in the opening, its purpose being to prevent the rudder from floating up and out of the gudgeons when the ship was laden and sitting deep in the water,

or when heavy seas were wildly tossing the ship. When necessary it could be easily removed since it was fastened with nails only.

Experience had shown that the extreme hard-over angle of the rudder in sailing ships was about 40 to 42 degrees. To put the helm over further circumvented the function of steering, and the rudder acted more as a brake and deterrent to the vessel's forward progress. This extreme angle was rarely resorted to in steering a ship, but there were always *positive stops* installed to restrict the travel of the tiller if set up to a gun tackle purchase, or to the threaded rods of patent steering devices. Positive stops could also be built into the rudder and sternpost by bearding their edges as shown in Figure 8.3, detail A.

The function of the rudder, very briefly put, was to steer the ship by increasing the water pressure at the after end of the side of the ship toward which it was turned. Pushing the stern in this manner, for instance to starboard, swung her bow to port, the side to which the rudder had been turned.

The elasticity of wood became apparent in a large wooden sailing vessel when, underway, the bow and the stern of a ship did not necessarily maintain the built-in alignment that prevailed at dockside. This was especially so among the clippers, whose extraordinary slenderness ratio, combined with their high rates of speed under a full press of sail, were more than ever subject to this constant working of the fibers of her wooden structure.

This elasticity was actually helpful in preserving the structural integrity of a vessel inasmuch as it provided a shock-absorbing quality to the total structure. However, at the sternpost in way of the pintles on which the rudder hung, there were problems. This was the only area on the hull where two separate wooden parts, namely the rudder and the sternpost, were required to function together. For this to take place, constant alignment was essential but, at the same time, was difficult to achieve and maintain. Consequently, the pintle and gudgeon assemblies were fabricated with a "sloppy" fit between each part. It was essential that the rudder, once it had been hung on the pintles, be free to swing at all times without the possibility of the pintles binding in the gudgeons and producing destructive forces on the fastenings.

This loose fit resulted in excessive knocking and wear over a period of time. To what extent this feature caused concern among builders and sailors is not known. However, it is a fact that, at the very least, the problem did not go unnoticed, and in a few rare instances an effort was made to diminish, if not eliminate, this undesirable condition.

Benjamin F. Delano, a shipbuilder in Medford, Massachusetts, invented a restraining device designed to compel the rudder to swing fair upon its hinges. Known as "Delano's back brace," it consisted of an iron yoke in the form of two legs of a triangle, the apex of which was fitted with a large *boss* or hub into which a pintle (pointing downward) was fitted. This pintle was inserted into a socket bored in the center of the rudderhead. The end of each leg of the yoke was flattened and formed to a configuration compatible with the shape of the taffrail to which the assembly was secured. Four vessels included herein were fitted with Delano's back braces: *Climax* and *Thatcher Magoun*, both built by Hayden & Cudworth, at Medford, Massachusetts; *Don Quixote*, built by Samuel Lapham, also at Medford; and *War Hawk*, built by George W. Jackman, at Newburyport, Massachusetts. The minimal use of this invention suggests that it did not improve the condition to an extent that fostered wide acceptance throughout the shipbuilding community. A reconstruction of this device is shown in Figure 21.1.

With the hanging of the rudder on its pintles and gudgeons, the structural hull was now a complete unit. The rudder was considered part of the structural hull, even though it was a separate appendage without which no vessel could be considered as a complete, self-contained structure.

There was still much to be accomplished on the hull in the category of nonstructural work. The following chapters detail this phase of construction. Deckhouses (see Chapter 26), for example, while structural in nature, were items that need only be substantial enough to sustain themselves under all adverse conditions that could be encountered at sea. They contributed nothing to the structural integrity of a ship. In fact, many ships contained deckhouses that were portable, and some were secured over hatchways, being removed only at a time when the hatch was to be broken out at journey's end.

Figure 12.4 illustrates the completed hull of Donald McKay's clipper *Lightning*. The three profiles shown account for virtually every major structural member that found its way into her construction. In addition, her deck structures and some of her items of outfit and decoration are included. Essentially, the structures and fittings shown in this figure apply to all vessels of the type. Naturally, the details and their locations would vary; however, these views contain all that might be encountered within the confines of the wooden hull of a merchant sailing vessel.

PART III

Completion of
the Ship

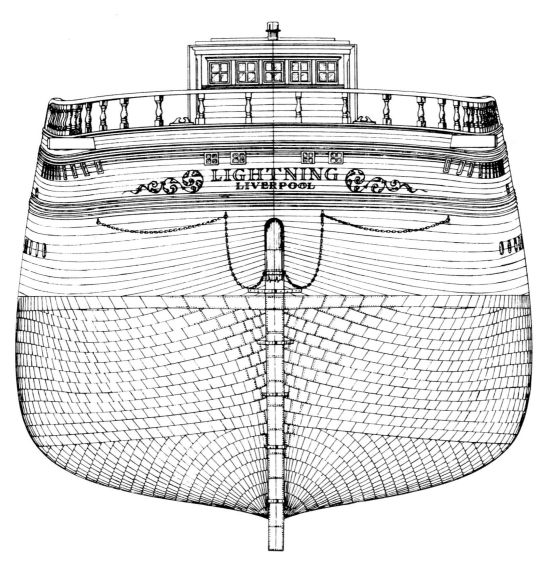

Stern of
Lightning
1854

Chapter Twenty-Two

METAL SHEATHING

THE METAL SHEATHING (Figure 6.2, detail n), which was installed on all large vessels of this period, was the ultimate method of protecting the bottoms of wooden ships from the ravages of teredoes (shipworms) and fouling by the growth of marine matter such as barnacles and sea vegetation.

The sea vegetation most usually encountered growing on ships' submerged surfaces consists of a type that grows in thin threadlike filaments, easily visible on stationary pilings and other wooden items built into a seashore environment. When these minute growths accumulate in great numbers on a ship's hull, their effect on the ship's speed is very significant. Painted, untreated wood, used in ship construction since earliest times, is the perfect host for such growth, which, while universally unwelcome, is not destructive to the ship's structure.

Accompanying the marine vegetation was the crustacean we know by the common name of barnacle. The class of barnacle found on ships' hulls was the gooseneck variety (Lepas), which has a leathery stalk and a flattened shell and looks very much like a small clam attached by its siphon. The shell is hard, rocklike limestone, and the barnacle holds tenaciously to the wooden hull. Its uncontrolled growth and accumulation are disastrous to the achievement of a ship's potential speed. However, like marine vegetation, barnacles are not destructive to the wooden hull.

The third parasite is the shipworm, *Teredo navalis*. The teredo's main food consists of wood particles. It is not a worm but rather a greatly elongated clam and is classified as a mollusk. Its two shells enclose the front end of its body and function as a tool, rather than as protection to the animal. These shells, rough and ridged, are used for boring through hull planking. Its burrow, begun when the animal is in its larval stage, becomes lined with a calcerous coating produced by the clam's mantle and is constantly enlarged as the animal grows. Although its shells remain ½ inch long, the worm itself can reach a length of 2 feet. Once started, the great number of burrows can be disastrous to the integrity of any ves-

sel. Shipworms can be deterred by chemicals, but control is achieved only by constant effort.

These three problems were the direct cause of the many attempts to protect ships' bottoms over the centuries.

Another incentive to discovering an effective method of protecting the hulls was indirect, but of the utmost long-range importance: the growing shortage of available ship timbers. Even as early as the latter part of the sixteenth century, this situation was recognized in England as a serious menace to the continuing enlargement and replacement of ships in the Royal Navy.

As early as 1670, lead was experimented with as a sheathing, but the results were less than satisfactory. Following that, various coatings were applied to the underwater planking: vegetable tar; tar or pitch liberally covered with loose animal hair (applied after charring the hull); tallow laced with soot, pulverized charcoal, or brimstone (sulfur). All of these applications were apparently poisonous to the shipworm, but proved at best to be only mildly successful. Studding the bottoms with black iron nails driven closely together was also tried, the reasoning being that the rusting nails would defeat the attack of worms. The last, partially successful, attempt to thwart *Teredo navalis* consisted of applying a layer of wood sheathing about 2 inches thick over a coating of tar or tallow mixed with hair, sulfur, ground glass, or other substance not acceptable to the voracious worm, the premise being that the shipworm would dine on the layer of sheathing and not penetrate beneath the undercoat thus protecting the ship's planking.

While all these protective measures were being used with and without appreciable success, sheet metal, occasionally zinc but mostly copper, was tentatively experimented with, and finally, in 1761, the British thirty-two-gun frigate *Alarm* was sheathed with copper, the result being one of success. The principal deterrent to absolute acceptance of this method was the failure of iron fastenings and fittings, along with the copper sheets, when the dissimilar metals were in contact in salt water, due to characteristic electrolytic action under such conditions.

However, additional effort and study ensued, and by 1783 this problem had been solved in a very simple manner. Bronze fittings replaced iron in way of the copper sheathing. Where this was not possible a layer of wood was placed between the two metals, effectively insulating one from the other. Thus it was at this date that copper sheathing became standard practice in the building of large wooden ships.

About 1800 a General Bentham, once a shipwright's apprentice at the Woolwich Dockyard, who later achieved his rank while doing service in the army in Russia, became a Commissioner of the Navy and was given charge of works. Among other projects, he set up metal mills at Portsmouth, and the manufacture of metal sheathing began in earnest.

The first metal to be extensively rolled in the English mills was copper. The finished sheets were 14 inches wide and 48 inches long. These two dimensions could possibly have been derived from the capacity of the rolling machines or the practical features such as ease of handling, freedom from undue damage to the sheets, and reasonable coverage per sheet. The accepted thicknesses were as shown in Figure 22.1, ranging from 14 ounces to 32 ounces per square foot, the latter weight being .046 inch in thickness.[9] The copper used was termed "pure," which, in the context of the times, meant that it was not alloyed with another metal. The quality-control techniques and approach of today were, of course, unknown, so the pure copper possessed certain impurities which resulted in a product of very variable quality.

Technically, copper is classed as a malleable metal, the next designation above soft. Easily worked, it can be bent and shaped to accommodate the gentle curves encountered on the hull of a ship, and corners and edges can be tucked down and will hold their form.

The characteristic of copper which made it so efficient as a sheathing for ships' hulls was the process of *exfoliation* in which the surface of the metal takes on a *scale* due to oxidation. This scale does not work into the metal in the manner that iron rusts deeper and deeper over a period of time. The formation of the scale, which was so effective in the sheathing, is the very property which prevents copper or brass fastenings from obtaining a good "grab" when used in ship construction. Where an iron fastening has the capacity to secure a good hold in the parts being held together, a copper or composition fastening always has the surface scale present between the wood and the fastening. However, the great asset of the copper is that it will not deteriorate due to contact with salt water, whereas the iron, in due course, will disintegrate.

This exfoliation was the process which kept the sheathed bottoms clean. Any growth, whether animal (such as the barnacle and teredo) or vegetation (such as seaweed), could only grip onto the scale, which would soon lose its hold and

Figure 22.1. *Metal sheathing data.*

SHEATHING VESSELS WITH COPPER, YELLOW AND ZINC METAL.

It was not until the latter end of the last century that Copper was introduced for covering the immersed portions of ships. This coating of Copper is extended over the whole intended immersed portion of the bottom. It is formed of sheets of copper of 4 feet in length, and 14 inches in breadth, the lower edges of the upper sheets lapping over the upper edges of those below them, and the after end of each sheet lapping over the fore end of the one immediately following it.

Yellow sheathing metal, has been of late generally used, it being less expensive when compared with copper.

Zinc Sheathing, manufactured by La Veille Montagne Zinc Mining Company, of Leige, in France, has lately been introduced for sheathing vessels. It is said to be considerably cheaper than copper, or yellow metal, lasts longer; and many shipmasters certify that it continues as clean as yellow metal.

––––––

MODE OF SHEATHING VESSELS.

The Copper, or Metal, used in sheathing vessels is divided into three thicknesses, consisting of twenty, twenty-four, and twenty-eight ounce; but oftener it is equally divided into four thicknesses of twenty-two, twenty-four, twenty-six, and twenty-eight ounce,—and is applied in the following manner :—The twenty-eight ounce should cover the bows diagonally from the fore-mast, at load line, to the heel of the forefoot; the twenty-six ounce should run parallel from the heel of the fore-mast to the main-mast; the twenty-four ounce should run from the heel of the main-mast to the load line at the mizen-mast; and the twenty-two ounce should cover all abaft the mizen-mast, except the rudder, which should be sheathed with twenty-six ounce, the beardings with twenty-eight ounce, and the keel with twenty-six ounce.

To ascertain the quantity of Copper required to sheath a vessel, measure the length of the keel, and find how many sheets it will take to extend the whole length, allowing 3 feet 11 inches for the length of a sheet of copper; then ascertain the number of courses from the bottom of the keel to the copper-line, allowing 1 foot 1 inch for one course of copper; then multiply the number of courses by the number of sheets on the keel, and the product gives the number of sheets required for each side.

A full built Ship requires about 1-20th more Copper than a Clipper.

Sheets of Copper are usually punched for three and five rows of nails.

The sheets punched with three rows require 39 nails.

The sheets punched with five rows require 49 nails.

WEIGHT OF SHEATHING COPPER, AND YELLOW SHEATHING METAL, PER SHEET.

Size.	Lb.	oz.	Size.	Lb.	oz.	Size.	Lb.	oz.
14 oz.	4	1	20 oz.	5	13	26 oz.	7	9
16 "	4	10	22 "	6	7	28 "	8	3
18 "	5	4	24 "	7		30 "	8	12
						32 "	9	5

NUMBER OF COMPOSITION SHEATHING NAILS IN A POUND.
(By actual count.)

Size.	Number.	Size.	Number.	Size.	Number.
$\frac{7}{8}$ to a lb.	230	$1\frac{1}{4}$ to a lb.	186	$1\frac{3}{4}$ to a lb.	112
1 "	190	$1\frac{1}{2}$ "	169	2 "	105

separate from the parent metal. This was a slow form of erosion, and no sheathing was everlasting, but in the life of ships it served its purpose well.

There was no "one" way to apply the sheets of sheathing to the hull of a ship, but the pattern shown in the details in Figure 22.2 and the text printed in Figure 22.1 appear to describe the method most typical of American vessels. As with all other phases of shipbuilding, the rules and standards, as prescribed, were used as guides rather than as gospel.

In general, the heaviest-gauge sheathing was installed between the stem and the foremast as shown in Figure 22.2; this was the area which breasted the sea in the headlong rush of the ship being pulled under a press of sail. From here the gauge of sheathing metal was decreased toward the stern. These various gradations were not always as shown and in some instances were ignored entirely. The clipper *Raven* is described as being sheathed with 26-ounce copper throughout her length.[3]

The height of sheathing on the hull fitted into one of two principal categories. In one the sheathing line was parallel with the load waterline but extended approximately the width of one course above this line, thus ensuring that the hull was protected under all conditions. In the second the sheathing line was higher aft than it was forward, generally about 1 foot. This was apparently done to protect against the tendency of a clipper's bow to rise or plane at high speeds, thus forcing her stern low in the water. Table 22.1 indicates that these conditions were about evenly divided throughout the American-built clipper fleet.

In most vessels the sheets that represented the actual height of sheathing were trimmed to shape to match this predetermined level. This resulted in most of such sheets being cut into more or less triangular shapes, some of which tended to become long, vulnerable slivers. In this case a ship might have a "dressing course" applied which would consist of a belt of full-size, untrimmed sheets girdling the vessel and defining the sheathing line. This installation was strictly optional and at the discretion of the builder.

The generally accepted practice was to install the metal over a thick layer of tarred felt laid over a coating of tar applied to the ship's bottom. This could be done on the ways before launching or in a drydock after launching. Some vessels built at one site, Boston for instance, were moved to New York to be sheathed; others were sailed to a further destination. Of the four clippers built by Donald McKay to order for James Baines and Co. of Liverpool, it is definitely reported that *Lightning* and *James Baines* sailed unsheathed to Liverpool and were metaled there; the other two, *Champion of the Seas* and *Donald McKay*, were probably treated in the same fashion. Another vessel, *Red Jacket*, also was reputedly sheathed after her arrival at Liverpool. The practice was not rare, since some owners were of the opinion that a ship should "work" at sea prior to receiving her metal.

The application of a tarred underlayment was sometimes dispensed with, but this was considered poor practice. The installation of one layer of felt was the accepted method of applying underlayment to a ship's bottom and was regarded as a definite asset, if not an absolute requirement. In the case of *Grace Darling*, after being caulked on the stocks, she was hove out, every seam again horsed and payed, and two tiers of felt placed under the sheathing. The report of this unusual treatment concluded that "consequently she will be tight as a bottle."[1]

The shoe, or false keel, was sheathed separately from the structural keel, and there was a practice of placing a layer of 16- or 18-ounce copper between these members in order to protect the structural keel from the worm should the shoe be torn away.[7] The practice appears to be sound, but whether it was followed in American-built clippers cannot be ascertained.

Three elements were considered negative in the use of copper as sheathing, two of which were inherent in the metal itself. These were, first, the elemental softness of pure copper. This characteristic accounted for an accelerated rate of erosion by the seawater as it scoured the metal's surface when the ship was underway. Second, was the inconsistency of the content of the metal sheets. This factor promoted uneven deterioration of the individual sheets, some of which disintegrated in a matter of months while others remained almost intact. The result was that the underbody was a surface of ragged and torn fragments of metal, all deteriorated in a piecemeal fashion. It is reported that Webb's clipper *Challenge* required drydocking for sheathing repairs only fifteen months after her launching.

The third negative did not involve the metal's properties, but its cost. Even though the bottom problem was resolved, the cost of procuring and applying sheathing was tremendous, as much as one-tenth the cost of the hull. This was an initial expense and did not count maintenance, which would periodically be required as the ship grew older.

All of these factors were well known, and during the years much effort was expended in improving the product. One objective was to discover or manufacture a metal whose rate of exfoliation was slower than that of pure copper. This product came into being in 1830 when, in Birmingham, England, George Frederick Muntz invented and patented an alloy consisting of fifty parts copper and fifty parts zinc. This new product, "yellow metal," became an overwhelming success and began immediately to supersede copper as the sheathing of choice. It was tougher and longer wearing than copper since its rate of exfoliation was slower, and it was also less expensive than copper, a feature dear to the hearts of ship owners.

(text continued on page 335)

Figure 22.2. *Metal sheathing, arrangement and details.*

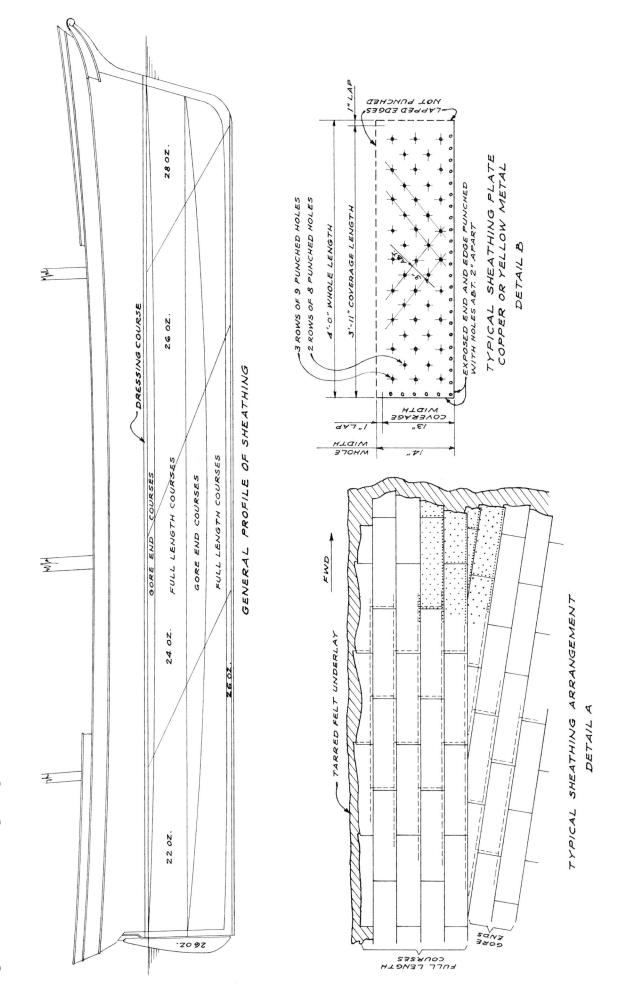

DRESSING COURSE

28 OZ.

26 OZ.

GORE END COURSES

FULL LENGTH COURSES

GORE END COURSES

FULL LENGTH COURSES

24 OZ.

26 OZ.

22 OZ.

26 OZ.

GENERAL PROFILE OF SHEATHING

3 ROWS OF 9 PUNCHED HOLES

2 ROWS OF 8 PUNCHED HOLES

4'-0" WHOLE LENGTH

3'-11" COVERAGE LENGTH

1" LAP

LAPPED EDGES NOT PUNCHED

EXPOSED END AND EDGE PUNCHED WITH HOLES ABT. 2" APART

TYPICAL SHEATHING PLATE COPPER OR YELLOW METAL

DETAIL B

3"

13" COVERAGE WIDTH

14" WHOLE WIDTH

1" LAP

FWD

TARRED FELT UNDERLAY

GORE ENDS

FULL LENGTH COURSES

TYPICAL SHEATHING ARRANGEMENT

DETAIL A

Table 22.1. *Metal sheathing.*

Notes:
1. Height of sheathing is generally one course of sheathing above the load water line (L.W.L.).
2. Quantities shown in "Remarks" column are from ref.9.
3. Metal sheathing is indicated in Figure 6.2.n.

Vessel & Ref.#	Sheathing metal	Height of sheathing Aft	Height of sheathing Forward	Remarks
Alarm #1	yellow metal	19'-0	19'-0	
Amphitrite				
Andrew Jackson #20	yellow metal			
Antelope				
Asa Eldridge #1	copper	20'-0	20'-0	
Bald Eagle #1	yellow metal	21'-0	20'-0	
Belle of the West #1,31	yellow metal	21'-0 about	21'-0 about	Hgt. based on lines drawing
Beverly #3	yellow metal			
Black Hawk #24,47	yellow metal	22'-6	22'-6	Hgt. based on lines drawing
Blue Jacket				
Bonita #1	yellow metal			
Bounding Billow Bark #1	copper			
Celestial #20,31,42	copper	21'-0 about	21'-0 about	Hgt. scaled from ref.42
Challenge #1	yellow metal	21'-0	20'-0	
Challenger #1	yellow metal	20'-0	20'-0	
Champion of the Seas #86		23'-6 about	23'-6 about	May have been sheathed after delivery to Jas. Baines & Co., Liverpool
Charger #1	yellow metal	19'-0	19'-0	
Charmer #1	yellow metal	19'-0	18'-0	
Cleopatra #1	yellow metal			
Climax #1				
Coeur de Lion #1	yellow metal			
Comet #24		22'-6 about	22'-6 about	Hgt. based on lines drawing
Cyclone #3	copper			
Daring #1	yellow metal	19'-0	19'-0	
Dauntless #1	copper	17'-0	16'-0	
Donald McKay #47				May have been sheathed after delivery to Jas. Baines & Co., Liverpool. New yellow metal sheathing installed in September 1879.
Don Quixote #1	yellow metal	21'-0	21'-0	
Eagle				
Eagle Wing #1	yellow metal	20'-0	19'-0	
Edwin Forrest #1,9	Ref.1 yellow metal	19'-0	19'-0	
	Ref.9 copper	17'-0	16'-0	2156 sheets
Electric Spark #1	yellow metal	20'-0	20'-0	
Ellen Foster #1,9	Ref.1 yellow metal	19'-6	18'-6	
	Ref.9 copper	18'-0	17'-0	2350 sheets
Empress of the Sea #1	yellow metal	21'-6	20'-6	
Endeavor #1	copper	19'-6	18'-6	Cold rolled copper
Eringo Bark #1	yellow metal	11'-0	11'-0	
Eureka				
Fair Wind				
Fearless #47				
Fleet Wing #1	yellow metal	18'-0	18'-0	New yellow metal sheathing installed in December 1879
Flyaway #24		21'-3 about	21'-3 about	Hgt. based on lines drawing
Flying Arrow #1	yellow metal	19'-0	18'-0	
Flying Childers #1	copper	19'-0	18'-0	
Flying Cloud #23	copper	21'-0 about	21'-0 about	Hgt. based on lines drawing
Flying Dragon #1	yellow metal	20'-0	19'-0	
Flying Dutchman #24		21'-6 about	21'-6 about	Hgt. based on lines drawing
Flying Eagle #1	yellow metal	18'-0	18'-0	
Flying Fish #1,9	Ref.1 yellow metal	19'-0	18'-6	
	Ref.9 copper	19'-0	18'-0	2556 sheets
Flying Mist #1	yellow metal	20'-6	20'-6	
Galatea #1	yellow metal	18'-0	18'-0	

Table 22.1. *Continued.*

Vessel & Ref.#	Sheathing metal	Height of sheathing Aft	Height of sheathing Forward	Remarks
Game Cock #1	copper	18'-6	17'-6	
Gazelle #24,32	copper	21'-0 about	21'-0 about	Hgt. based on lines drawing
Gem of the Ocean #1,9	Ref.1 yellow metal	18'-0	17'-0	
	Ref.9 copper	18'-0	17'-6	1558 sheets
Golden Eagle #1,5	yellow metal	19'-6	18'-6	
Golden Fleece (2nd) #1	yellow metal	20'-0	20'-0	
Golden Light #1	yellow metal	16'-6	16'-6	
Golden West #1	copper	20'-0	19'-0	
Grace Darling #1	yellow metal	19'-0	19'-0	Two layers of felt underlay
Great Republic #4,10	yellow metal	25'-0	25'-0	
Great Republic (rebuilt)	yellow metal			Assumed same as original sheathing
Henry Hill Bark #1,42	copper	16'-3 about	12'-3 about	Built with 4'-6 drag of keel. Hgt. based on lines drawing.
Herald of the Morning #1	yellow metal			
Hoogly #1	copper	19'-6	18'-6	
Hurricane				
Indiaman #1	yellow metal	18'-0	18'-0	
Intrepid				
Invincible #4,24	Ref.4	21'-0	21'-0	Estimated draft 20'-0.
	Ref.24	23'-6 about	23'-6 about	Hgt. based on lines drawing
James Baines #23	copper	23'-3 about	23'-3 about	Coppered after delivery to Jas. Baines & Co., Liverpool. Hgt. based on lines drawing.
John Bertram #1	copper	18'-0	17'-0	
John Gilpin #1	yellow metal	18'-0	17'-0	
John Land #32 (Built as a duplicate of Winged Arrow.)	yellow metal or copper			See Winged Arrow
John Stuart #32	copper	25'-6	25'-6	Height based on draft in 1854
John Wade #1	yellow metal			
Joseph Peabody #1	copper	19'-6	19'-6	
King Fisher #1	yellow metal	19'-0	19'-0	

Vessel & Ref.#	Sheathing metal	Height of sheathing Aft	Height of sheathing Forward	Remarks
Lady Franklin #9	copper	15'-0	18'-0	1258 sheets. (Forward sheathing height appears to be in error.)
Lamplighter Bark				
Lightfoot #1	yellow metal			Coppered after delivery to Jas. Baines & Co., Liverpool. Hgt. based on lines drawing.
Lightning #1,11	copper	18'-0 about	18'-0 about	
Mameluke #1	yellow metal	20'-0	20'-0	2509 sheets
Mary Robinson #9	copper	18'-0	17'-6	
Mastiff #1	yellow metal			
Mermaid Bark #1	copper	15'-0	13'-0	Built with 2'-0 drag of keel
Morning Light #9	copper	20'-6	20'-0	2795 sheets
Mystery #1	copper	19'-0	18'-0	
Nightingale #42,47		20'-3 about	19'-3 about	New yellow metal sheathing installed in May 1878. Water line not parallel to base line. Hgt. based on lines drawing.
Noonday #1	yellow metal	18'-6	18'-6	
Northern Light #9	copper	16'-6	16'-0	1852 sheets
Ocean Express #1	yellow metal			
Ocean Pearl #1	yellow metal			
Ocean Telegraph #5	copper	18'-6	18'-0	1665 sheets
Onward #1	yellow metal	16'-0	15'-0	
Osborne Howes #9	copper			
Panther #1				
Phantom #1	copper	20'-0	19'-0	
Queen of Clippers #1	yellow metal	20'-0	20'-0	2570 sheets
Queen of the Pacific #9	copper	20'-0	19'-0	
Queen of the Seas #1	yellow metal	20'-6	19'-6	
Quickstep Bark #1	yellow metal	15'-6	15'-6	
Racehorse Bark #1	copper	15'-0	13'-0	Built with 2'-0 drag of keel
Racer #1	yellow metal			
Radiant #1	copper			
Raven #3	yellow metal	16'-6	16'-0	26 ounce copper throughout

Table 22.1. *Continued.*

Vessel & Ref.#	Sheathing metal	Height of sheathing Aft	Height of sheathing Forward	Remarks
Red Jacket #14,47		19'-0 about	19'-0 about	Reputedly received her sheathing in Liverpool. New yellow metal sheathing installed in January 1879. Hgt. based on lines drawing.
Robin Hood #9	copper	17'-0	16'-0	1985 sheets
Rocket Bark #47	yellow metal	17'-0	16'-0	New yellow metal sheathing installed in September 1874
Roebuck #1	yellow metal	19'-6 about	19'-6 about	Hgt. based on lines drawing
Romance of the Sea #1,42				
Santa Claus	yellow metal	18'-6	18'-6	
Saracen #1	copper	12'-6	11'-0	Built with 1'-6 drag of keel
Sea Bird Bark #1				"Coppered high with cold rolled copper."
Seaman's Bride #4	copper			
Sea Serpent #47				New yellow metal sheathing installed in November 1876
Shooting Star #1	copper	17'-0	16'-0	
Sierra Nevada #1,9	Ref.1 yellow metal; Ref.9 copper	19'-0	18'-6	2730 sheets
Silver Star				
Southern Cross #1,3	Ref.1 yellow metal; Ref.3 yellow metal	17'-6	16'-6	
Sovereign of the Seas #1	yellow metal	17'-0	16'-0	
Spitfire #1,9	Ref.1 yellow metal; Ref.9 copper	21'-6	20'-6	2440 sheets
Staffordshire #32	copper	20'-6	19'-0	Based on draft of 19'-6 aft and 18'-6 forward.
Stag Hound #4,23	copper	22'-0 about	22'-0 about	Hgt. based on lines drawing
Star of the Union #1	copper	19'-6	18'-6	
Starr King #9	copper	20'-0	20'-0	2146 sheets
Storm King #1	yellow metal			

Vessel & Ref.#	Sheathing metal	Height of sheathing Aft	Height of sheathing Forward	Remarks
Sultana Bark #1	copper	13'-6	13'-6	Ref.1 states she will draw 16' aft and 13' forward when fully loaded.
Sunny South #42	varnished	18'-9	18'-9	Hgt. scaled from lines plan at midship due to rockered keel
Surprise #1	copper	17'-6	16'-6	
Swallow #47				New yellow metal sheathing installed in September 1881
Sweepstakes #42		23'-0 about	23'-0 about	Hgt. based on lines drawing
Sword Fish #20,24	yellow metal	20'-3 about	20'-3 about	Hgt. based on lines drawing
Syren #3	copper	17'-0	16'-6	"Coppered with heavy metal."
Telegraph #1	copper			
Thatcher Magoun #1	yellow metal	20'-6	19'-6	
Tornado #3	copper			
Uncowah				
War Hawk #1	yellow metal	19'-0	19'-0	
Water Witch #1	copper	20'-0	19'-0	
Western Continent #9	copper	16'-0	15'-0	1812 sheets
Westward Ho #1	yellow metal	20'-0	20'-0	
West Wind #1	yellow metal			
Whirlwind #1	yellow metal	18'-6	17'-6	
Whistler #1,9	Ref.1 yellow metal; Ref.9 copper			
Wildfire Bark	copper	21'-0	20'-0	2500 sheets
Wild Pigeon #1,42	copper	20'-6 about	20'-6 about	Hgt. based on lines drawing
Wild Ranger #1	yellow metal	18'-6	17'-6	2196 sheets
Wild Rover #9	copper	18'-0	17'-0	
Winged Arrow #1,3,9	Ref.1 yellow metal; Ref.3,9 copper	18'-0	17'-0	2450 sheets
Winged Racer #1,9	Ref.1 yellow metal; Ref.9 copper	21'-0	20'-0	
	copper	20'-0	19'-0	2693 sheets

Table 22.1. *Continued.*

Vessel & Ref.#	Sheathing metal	Height of sheathing Aft	Height of sheathing Forward	Remarks
Witchcraft #1	copper	18'-6	17'-6	
Witch of the Wave #1,9	Ref.1 copper	19'-3	18'-9	
	Ref.9 copper	19'-6	18'-6	2310 sheets
Wizard #1	yellow metal			
Young America #24,47		21'-6 about	21'-6 about	New yellow metal sheathing installed in November 1879. Hgt. based on lines drawing.
Young Turk Bark #1	yellow metal			

(text continued from page 330)

After its introduction, Mr. Muntz spent much time and effort in trying to improve on his new alloy, and by 1846 the composition had been changed to sixty parts copper and forty parts zinc. This became the final sheathing material, which was known as yellow metal, patent metal, composition metal, and, last but far from least, especially in the eyes of its inventor, Muntz metal. This is a perfect example of being able to profit through name recognition, because the general product was referred to generically as yellow metal, and all yellow metal was "Muntz metal." Even today the brass composition of sixty parts copper and forty parts zinc is called Muntz metal.

Under the patent, various manufacturers throughout Britain produced the metal for consumption at home and extensive export to the United States. This fact can be attested by the advertisements that appeared in various newspapers in the 1850s, several of which are reproduced in Figure 22.3. These advertisements suggest that, even at the advanced period of the clippers, American shipbuilders were still greatly dependent upon these imports, even though some native manufacturers were producing sheathing metal.

Even as yellow metal was being used and improved, copper still retained a place on the scene, and many clippers were sheathed with it. In fact, some descriptions make a particular point of noting that a certain vessel was "sheathed with copper not yellow metal" as though to imply that no cheap material was being used in her construction.

Two ships in this list, *Endeavor* and *Seaman's Bride*, are both described as having been sheathed with cold-rolled copper. This may have been a longer-lasting class of material than hot-rolled metal, due to the fact that cold-rolling does not affect the crystalline structure of the metal and results in a hardening of its surface.

Zinc sheathing, manufactured in France and noted in Figure 22.1, was stated to be as effective as both copper and yellow metal, was longer lasting, and was considerably less expensive to purchase and maintain. It was introduced into the United States in the first quarter of the nineteenth century, and before the appearance of the clippers was being manufactured here. An advertisement appeared in *The Boston Daily Atlas* of Tuesday, January 1, 1850 that Wm. Thomas & Co., No. 79 State Street, had for sale, among other sheathing items, "Sheet zinc, of American manufacture."

However, at that time and throughout the entire clipper period, copper and yellow metal were being imported from England in great quantities, as indicated in Figure 22.3. Very little exposure is given to the use of zinc, in spite of the "factual" advantages noted above.

One of the negative aspects of the use of zinc sheathing was that it required the use of zinc nails as fastenings due to electrolytic action of dissimilar metals in salt water. Copper and yellow metal sheathing and fastenings were interchangeable, but such fastenings could not be used with zinc, for the following reasons, explained briefly and simply.

Metals are listed in an *electromotive series* which places them in relative compatibility with each other. Arranged in sequence of compatibility is a partial list of these metals: zinc, chromium, iron, nickel, lead, copper (or its alloy, yellow metal), silver. Only zinc and copper are of interest in sheathing; the others are included to help in presenting the erosion problem when these metals are immersed in salt water and electrolysis takes place. Any two metals that are listed next to each other are least subject to electrolytic action regardless of their position in the list; any two metals listed far apart are most subject to this phenomenon.

As can be seen, zinc and iron are relatively close in the chain, but the swift corrosion of iron in seawater eliminates its suitability as a fastening. Zinc and copper, both suitable separately, are widely separated in the list, and this renders them unsatisfactory when underwater in close proximity to each other. Thus, if zinc sheathing were fastened with copper or yellow metal fastenings, it would not take long for the zinc sheet to disintegrate in way of the fastening and become a casualty. It remains that the only suitable fastenings for zinc sheathing were zinc nails, and these were evidently in limited or inconvenient supply.

Figure 22.3. *Metal sheathing, newspaper advertisements.*

mechanical propulsion, and then its use was confined to certain specific functions.

From the earliest days of the use of metal sheathing, in the late eighteenth century, the procedure was accomplished with copper sheets, and the terms "coppering the ship" or "her coppering" were literal and specific. By the time yellow metal came into use, the terms were deeply imbedded in the shipbuilding profession and in the minds of any who were remotely interested in marine matters. The result was that ships sheathed in yellow metal were still being "coppered," the term now having become generic. Historically, and from the researcher's point of view, this can be at best confusing and at worst incorrect. Fortunately, the descriptions of clippers derived from references used in this volume are very specific in the mention of the metal used in the sheathing of the various vessels. In a certain number of vessels no mention is made of the sheathing material; one can only surmise or make an educated guess, which is not very satisfactory and definitely not conclusive.

An example of this possible shortcoming in terminology is found in the description of *Stag Hound*, built in Boston by Donald McKay: ". . . She will be docked in New York, to be coppered, and then your mechanics will have a fair chance to examine her thoroughly. . . ."[4] The wording of the statement can be taken literally or generically. Hopefully, for the sake of historical accuracy, the report is literal. It is reassuring that almost every description which mentions sheathing identifies the metal used.

Another quandary arises when two sources are not in agreement. Table 22.1 lists nine vessels described in both *The Boston Daily Atlas* and *The Merchant's and Mechanic's Assistant* by I. R. Butts.[9] In the former, reporter Duncan MacLean definitely identifies the sheathing as being yellow metal in all nine instances. The latter source contains two listings of vessels—one by Capt. S. B. Hobart, Superintendent of the late Marine Railway, Boston, Massachusetts, and the second by Capt. Barstow, Superintendent of East Boston Dry Dock—headed "Sheathing Vessels with Copper," in which appear the same nine vessels. This leaves one wondering which metal is correct, since the general time frame is the same. Table 22.1 clearly identifies the vessels in question, but the answer will apparently always be subject to doubt.

It is not my intent to cover the many small but interesting or important details associated with the use of metal sheathing. To do so would prove repetitive, incomplete, and outside the intended scope of coverage. Much detail of the subject may be learned from the following: Butts's *The Merchant's and Mechanic's Assistant*[9]; Campbell's *China Tea Clippers*,[51] Ronnberg's *The Coppering of 19th-Century American Merchant Sailing Ships*,[77] and (very briefly) Peake's *Rudiments of Naval Architecture*.[7]

Throughout the entire list of clippers, packets, and freighters included in contemporary newspaper descriptions,[1,3,4,5] only one vessel is described as being sheathed with zinc. This was the 366-ton packet bark *Edisto*, launched in the spring of 1851 by Hayden & Cudworth at Medford for the Lombard Line of Boston and Charleston packets.[1]

Actually, the use of zinc in underwater locations did not come into its own until the advent of iron construction and

Chapter Twenty-Three

COLORS OF THE SHIPS

THE HULL COLORS OF CLIPPER ships, as covered in this chapter, include the exterior colors of the hull, the inboard works above the weather deck, some structures on the weather deck, and certain tween-decks color schemes. (Fittings and deck furniture, general cabin decoration, and exterior ornamentation are covered separately in later chapters, as are the painting of masts and spars.)

Table 23.1 lists the colors of the clippers included in this book, based principally upon observation of the actual vessels by *Boston Daily Atlas* reporter Duncan MacLean,[1] augmented by descriptions found in some other newspapers of the period.[3, 4, 5] Several color schemes are taken from paintings and etchings that were contemporary with the particular vessels, and a few are based on actual photographs of vessels. These photographs are, of course, black-and-white, and as such are not irrefutably conclusive.

In museums, libraries, public institutions, and private collections there are countless paintings depicting the clipper ship in all its glory, none of which is noted in the table as a prime source of information. Most of these were painted in a period which succeeded that of the clipper ship, and in such cases the artist was obliged to discover his own source of detail; artistic license being a recognized privilege of the artist, interpretation could then enter into the subject. This is not meant to be derogatory of a work or to cast doubt on the integrity of the artist. It only means that the information is not prime in itself.

For the vessels in the table for which there is no apparent source information, no entry has been made, since opinion and logic are not absolute substitutes for actual information. No doubt, some details exist which have either not been discovered or have not been included. Hopefully, such faults may be rectified as time passes.

The coloration described in this chapter is based on rather concise and brief factual data, as reported. No attempt is made here to describe methods of painting, composition of the paints themselves, interpretations of the colors, wearing qualities of the paints, or the many technical aspects of painting as a trade. Much of such detail is nebulous, at best. Descriptive records are relatively scarce, and personal evaluations of given colors are subject to variables so numerous that what one person sees is not the same as what is seen by another person describing the same article. An instance of this is brought into evidence when the color "buff" is noted. Such an observation appears innocent and straightforward until one suddenly finds buff described, in certain cases, as "light buff." This is further confounded by the appearance of "dark buff." Thus, buff now has three distinct variations. The guessing game could proceed ad infinitum.

However, the color descriptions in the table do supply an understandable and clear vision of general coloration of the vessels. The contrasts between the treatments of the various vessels allow for relatively clear visions of their sameness and differences. And, generally speaking, what emerges is a satisfactory picture of the vessels' appearances.

In the interest of providing any student of nautical lore with the best available information on the subject, *Paint and Colors for American Merchant Vessels, 1800–1920*, by Eric A. R. Ronnberg, Jr.,[88] is most highly recommended. It is a compilation of data extracted from prime sources and has the added feature of containing more than eighty color chips which allow one to study, compare, and arrive at his own conclusions about the aspect of color in ships.

With no attempt at being technical, it can be pointed out that the variety of colors, or hues, which found their way into clipper ship structure was very limited, unexciting, and, considering the clipper fleet as a whole, rather monotonous. Even a superficial perusal of Table 23.1 will quickly bear this out. This, of course, does not apply to paints used in a vessel's scheme of ornamentation, a subject covered separately in the next chapter.

Considering the use to which the various paints were put and the basic colors that were chosen allows one to wonder

(text continued on page 343)

Table 23.1. *Colors of the ships.*

Vessel & Ref.#	Hull, outside	Inboard structure
Alarm #1	black	Bulwarks: cream relieved with white. Waterways: upper deck, blue. Tween decks: thick work, blue; ceiling and overhead, white. Deck houses: cream relieved with white; skylight and window frames, mahogany.
Amphitrite #1	black	Bulwarks: buff relieved with white. Waterways: upper deck, buff.
Andrew Jackson		
Antelope #1	black	Bulwarks: dark buff. Waterways: upper deck, blue.
Asa Eldridge #1	black	Bulwarks: cream color. Waterways: upper deck, cream color. Skylight frames, mahogany.
Bald Eagle #1	black	Bulwarks: pearl color, and pierced with gun ports. Waterways: upper deck, pearl color.
Belle of the West #1	black	Bulwarks: buff relieved with white. Waterways: upper deck, buff.
Beverly #3	black, with a small belt of red on her load line.	Bulwarks: dark buff. Waterways: upper deck, blue; lower deck, blue. Tween decks: ceiling,dark buff; overhead, white(probable). Deck house: painted imitation oak.
Black Hawk #62,63	black	Deck houses: white.
Blue Jacket		
Bonita #1	black	Bulwarks: buff. Waterways: upper deck, blue. Aft hatchway coamings, mahogany.
Bounding Billow Bark #1	black	Bulwarks: pearl color. Waterways: upper deck, blue.
Celestial		

Vessel & Ref.#	Hull, outside	Inboard structure
Challenge #1,28	black, with the moulded upper wale gilded from the extended ta_ of her eagle figurehead com_ pletely around the stern an_ along the opposite side in _ same fashion.	Bulwarks: white, with stan_ ions bright on the outer(i_ board) square. Rack rail a_ bright. Waterways: upper deck, gre_ middle deck, blue; lower de_ lead color. Tween decks: upper and low_ ceilings, overheads, white_ hanging knees, stanchions, lower squares of beams, ca_ and ledges, bright and var_ ed. Deck structures: Hatchway frames and fife rails Eas_ ia teak; hatch coamings, m_ hogany.
Challenger #1	black	Bulwarks: buff relieved wi_ white. Waterways: upper deck, buf_
Champion of the Seas #1	black	Bulwarks: white. Waterways: upper deck, blu_ Deck structures: skylight frames are polished mahoga_
Charger #1	black	Bulwarks: buff relieved wit_ white. Waterways: upper deck,lower deck, red. Tween decks: thick work gre_ stone color;ceiling and ove_ head, white; stanchions and undersquares of beams are b_ and varnished.
Charmer #1	black	Bulwarks: buff relieved wit_ white. Waterways: upper deck, buff
Cleopatra #1	black	Bulwarks: pearl color relie_ with white. Waterways: upper deck, pear_ color.
Climax #1	black	Bulwarks: buff relieved wit_ white. Waterways: upper deck, buff
Coeur de Lion #1	black, with planksheer gilded aroun_ the ship.	Bulwarks: white. Waterways: upper deck, whit_
Comet #64	black	Bulwarks: cream or light bu_ Waterways: upper deck, crea_ buff. Deck structures: cream reli_ with white.
Cyclone		

Vessel & Ref.#	Hull, outside	Inboard structure	Vessel & Ref.#	Hull, outside	Inboard structure
			Flyaway		
Daring #1	black	Bulwarks: buff; stanchions bright and varnished on their inside square. Waterways: upper deck, blue.	Flying Arrow #1	black	Bulwarks: "nearly" white. Waterways: upper deck, "nearly" white. Deck structures: deck houses "nearly" white.
Dauntless #1	dark bronze, with a white ribbon along the waist. (Her waist is narrow, three strakes, and this ribbon apparently covers one strake.) Bulwarks: buff. Waterways: upper deck, blue.		Flying Childers #1	black	Bulwarks: pearl color. Waterways: upper deck, pearl color.
			Flying Cloud #1	black	Bulwarks: pearl color. Waterways: upper deck, pearl color.
Donald McKay #1	black	Bulwarks: buff. Waterways: all three decks, blue. Tween decks: thickwork in upper and lower tween decks, blue. Ceiling and overhead in both tween decks, white. Deck structures: the rise and railings of the poop deck are white. Skylight frames are mahogany.	Flying Dragon #1	black	
			Flying Dutchman		
			Flying Eagle #1	black	Bulwarks: pearl color. Waterways: upper deck, pearl color. Deck structures: houses, pearl color.
Don Quixote #1	black	Bulwarks: white, except the moulding of the main rail which is covered with yellow metal. Waterways: upper deck, white.	Flying Fish #1	black	Bulwarks: pearl color. Waterways: upper deck, blue. Deck structures: houses, pearl color, apparently. Description vague.
Eagle					
Eagle Wing #1	black	Bulwarks: buff relieved with white. Waterways: upper deck, buff.	Flying Mist #1	black	Bulwarks: white. Waterways: upper deck, blue. Deck structures: houses, white; skylight frames, mahogany.
Edwin Forrest #1	black	Bulwarks: dark buff. Waterways: upper deck, blue.	Galatea #1	bronze	Bulwarks: buff relieved with white. Waterways: upper deck, buff.
Electric Spark #1	black	Bulwarks: light lead color. Waterways: upper deck, light lead color.	Game Cock #1	black	Bulwarks: buff relieved with white. Waterways: upper deck, lead color. Deck structures: houses, buff relieved with white.
Ellen Foster #1	black, with a red stripe at the sheathing line. Bulwarks: buff relieved with white. Waterways: upper deck, blue; lower deck, blue. Tween decks: thick work, blue; ceiling and overhead, white.		Gazelle		
			Gem of the Ocean #1	black	Bulwarks: buff relieved with white. Waterways: upper deck, blue.
Empress of the Sea #1	black				
Endeavor #1	black		Golden Eagle #1	black	Bulwarks: pearl color relieved with white. Waterways: upper deck, pearl color.
Eringo Bark #1	black				
Eureka			Golden Fleece (2nd) #1	black	Bulwarks: pearl color relieved with white. Waterways: upper deck, pearl color.
Fair Wind #1	black	Bulwarks: buff. Waterways: upper deck, blue.			
Fearless #32	dark green, referred to as "tea color" by painters of these ships.				
Fleet Wing #1	black	Bulwarks: buff relieved with white. Waterways: upper deck, blue.			

Table 23.1. *Continued.*

Vessel & Ref.#	Hull, outside	Inboard structure	Vessel & Ref.#	Hull, outside	Inboard structure
Golden Light #1	black	Bulwarks: buff. Waterways: upper deck, buff; lower deck, blue. Tween decks: thickwork, blue; ceiling and overhead, white; stanchions, natural oak. Hold: noted as being unpainted. This was the usual treatment.	John Bertram #1	black	Bulwarks: buff relieved with white. Waterways: upper deck, buff.
			John Gilpin #1	black	Bulwarks: buff. Waterways: upper deck, buff; lower deck, blue. Tween decks: thick work, blue; ceiling and overhead, white; lower squares of beams, bright and varnished.
Golden West #1	black	Bulwarks: buff relieved with white. Waterways: upper deck, blue. Deck structures: houses, buff relieved with white.			
			John Land #1 (Built as a duplicate of Winged Arrow.)	black	Bulwarks: buff relieved with white. Waterways: upper deck, buff.
Grace Darling #1	black	Bulwarks: buff relieved with white. Waterways: upper deck, buff.	John Stuart #4	black	Bulwarks: light brown. Waterways: upper deck, light brown.
Great Republic #4	black	No bulwarks above the spar-deck. Outline of deck is formed by a wide plate which supports turned stanchions and the spar deck rail all of which are "nearly" white.	John Wade #1	black	Bulwarks: white. Waterways: upper deck, white.
			Joseph Peabody #1	black	Bulwarks: white, with stanchions bright and varnished on the outer (inboard) square. Waterways: upper deck, blue; lower deck, blue. Tween decks: thick work, blue; ceiling and overhead, white; lower squares of beams, bright and varnished. Deck structures: houses, white.
Great Republic (rebuilt) #84	black,	apparently (in black and white photo, 1860).			
Henry Hill Bark #1	black	Bulwarks: white. Waterways: upper deck, blue. Deck structures: houses, white.			
Herald of the Morning #1	black	Bulwarks: white. Waterways: upper deck, blue.	King Fisher #1	black	Bulwarks: pearl color. Waterways: upper deck, blue. Deck structures: hatchway coamings, East India teak.
			Lady Franklin		
Hoogly #1	black,	with a red stripe at the sheathing line. Poop bulwarks above the monkey rail: white, inside and outside. Bulwarks: buff. Waterways: upper deck, blue; lower deck, blue. Tween decks: ceiling and overhead, white; lower squares of the beams are bright and varnished. Deck structures: house, buff; hatchway coamings, mahogany, lined with composition.	Lamplighter Bark		
			Lightfoot #1	black	
			Lightning #1	black	Bulwarks: pearl color relieved with white. Waterways: upper deck, lead color. Deck structures: skylight frames, mahogany.
Hurricane					Note: Vessel was built with her bottom painted copper color. The sheathing was applied after her arrival in Liverpool.
Indiaman #1	black	Bulwarks: buff relieved with white. Waterways: upper deck, buff.			
Intrepid			Mameluke #1	black	Bulwarks: buff. Waterways: upper deck, blue; lower deck, blue. Tween decks: thick work, blue; ceiling and overhead, white.
Invincible #4,28	black,	with a crimson stripe, (location not stated). Deck structures: hatch coamings and mast partners, mahogany.	Mary Robinson		
James Baines #1	black	Rise of poop deck above monkey rail, white. Bulwarks: white. Waterways: upper, middle and lower decks, blue. Tween decks: upper and lower, thickwork, ceilings and overheads, white. Deck structures: houses, white.			

340

Table 23.1. *Continued.*

Vessel & Ref.#	Hull, outside	Inboard structure	Vessel & Ref.#	Hull, outside	Inboard structure
Mastiff #1	black	Bulwarks: light pearl color. Waterways: upper deck, blue; lower deck, blue. Tween decks: thickwork, blue; ceiling and overhead, white; stanchions and lower squares of beams bright and varnished. Deck structures: houses, light pearl color.	Panther		
			Phantom #1	black	Bulwarks: buff relieved with white. Waterways: upper deck, blue; lower deck, blue. Tween decks: thickwork, blue; ceiling and overhead white. Deck structures: houses, buff relieved with white.
Mermaid Bark #1	black,	with moulded edges of plank-sheer bronzed Bulwarks: white. Waterways: main deck, white. Deck structures: hatchway coamings, polished mahogany, lined with composition.	Queen of Clippers #1	black	Bulwarks: pearl color relieved with white. Waterways: upper deck, pearl color.
			Queen of the Pacific		
Morning Light #1	black	Bulwarks: white. Waterways: upper deck, white.	Queen of the Seas #1	black	Bulwarks: Waterways: upper deck, lower deck, blue. Tween decks: thickwork, blue; ceiling and overhead, white.
Mystery #1	black	Bulwarks: pearl color relieved with white. Waterways: upper deck, white; lower deck, blue. Tween decks: thickwork, blue; ceiling and overhead, white; lower squares of beams bright and varnished.	Quickstep Bark #1	black	
			Racehorse Bark		Bulwarks: pierced with gun ports. No color scheme given.
			Racer #3	black	
Nightingale #4	black	Bulwarks: Waterways: upper deck, lower deck, white. Tween decks: thickwork, ceiling and overhead, white.	Radiant #1	black	Bulwarks: buff relieved with white. Waterways: upper deck, blue.
			Raven #3	black	
Noonday #1	black	Bulwarks: dark buff relieved with white. Waterways: upper deck, dark buff. Deck structures: "The front of the aft cabin, facing the deck, is wainscotted and painted in imitation of mahogany and other fancy woods, which has quite a showy effect upon her aft."	Red Jacket #67	black	
			Robin Hood		
			Rocket Bark		
			Roebuck #1	black,	with a tier of painted black ports on a white belt around her waist. Bulwarks: buff. Waterways: upper deck, blue.
Northern Light					
Ocean Express #1	black	Bulwarks: light pearl color. Waterways: upper deck, blue.	Romance of the Sea #1	black	Bulwarks: pearl color relieved with white. Waterways: upper deck, pearl color.
Ocean Pearl #1	black	Bulwarks: buff relieved with white. Waterways: upper deck, blue. Deck structures: houses, buff relieved with white.	Santa Claus #1	black	Bulwarks: "light" in color. Waterways: upper deck, "light" in color.
Ocean Telegraph #5	black	Bulwarks: white. Waterways: upper deck, blue.	Saracen #1	black	Bulwarks: buff. Waterways: upper deck, buff.
Onward #1	black	Bulwarks: white. Waterways: upper deck, blue.	Sea Bird Bark #1	black	Bulwarks: pearl color. Waterways: main deck, blue.
Osborne Howes			Seaman's Bride #4		"In painting the vessel, wherever white was required, white zinc paint is used throughout the ship, it being considered of a more durable character and less liable to be affected by the gases generated below".

Table 23.1. *Continued.*

Vessel & Ref.#	Hull, outside	Inboard structure	Vessel & Ref.#	Hull, outside	Inboard structure
Sea Serpent #4	black, with a narrow yellow stripe at the sheathing line.		Sunny South #42	black	topsides, with varnished bottom.
Shooting Star #1	black	Bulwarks: buff. Waterways: upper deck, blue.	Surprise #1	black	
Sierra Nevada #1	black	Bulwarks: dark buff relieved with white. Waterways: upper deck, lead color; middle deck, stone color; lower deck, white. Tween decks: upper thickwork, lead color; ceiling and overhead, white; stanchions, hanging knees and lower squares of beams imitation mahogany. Tween decks: lower; all white and ornamented.	Swallow #1	black	Bulwarks: cream color relieved with white. Waterways: upper deck, cream color. Deck structures: houses, cream color relieved with white; skylight frames mahogany.
			Sweepstakes #28,84	black, with a gold stripe. (Location not stated).	
			Sword Fish		
Silver Star #1	not noted	Bulwarks: buff. Waterways: upper deck, buff. Deck structures: forward houses, buff; skylight frames, polished mahogany.	Syren #3	black	
			Telegraph #1	black	Bulwarks: buff. Waterways: upper deck, buff.
Southern Cross #1	black	Bulwarks: buff. Waterways: upper deck, blue.	Thatcher Magoun #1	Black	Bulwarks: Waterways: Deck structures: skylight coamings and frames, polished mahogany.
Sovereign of the Seas #1	black	Bulwarks: buff. Waterways: upper deck, buff.			
			Tornado #83	black	
Spitfire #1	black	Bulwarks: Waterways: upper deck, lower deck, blue. Tween decks: thickwork, blue; ceiling and overhead, white.	Uncowah		
			War Hawk #1	black	Bulwarks: white, with outer (inboard) squares of stanchions bright and varnished. Waterways: upper deck, white.
Staffordshire #1	black	Bulwarks: white. Waterways: upper deck, white. Deck structures: houses, white; skylight frames, mahogany.	Water Witch #1	black	Bulwarks: buff. Waterways: upper deck, buff.
Stag Hound #1	black	Bulwarks: pearl color relieved with white. Waterways: upper deck, pearl color.	Western Continent		
			Westward Ho #1	black	Bulwarks: buff relieved with white. Waterways: upper deck, blue.
Star of the Union #1	black	Bulwarks: white. Waterways: upper deck, blue; lower deck, blue. Tween decks: thickwork, blue; ceiling and overhead, white. Deck structures: houses, white; hatchway coamings, mahogany.	West Wind #1	black	Bulwarks: buff. Waterways: upper deck, buff.
Starr King			Whirlwind #1	black	Bulwarks: buff relieved with white. Waterways: upper deck, blue; lower deck, blue. Tween decks: thickwork, blue; ceiling and overhead, white.
Storm King #1	black	Bulwarks: buff relieved with white. Waterways: upper deck, buff.	Whistler #1	black	Bulwarks: buff relieved with white. Waterways: upper deck, blue. Deck structures: houses, buff relieved with white.
Sultana Bark #1	black, with planksheer painted red forward to her head.		Wildfire Bark		
			Wild Pigeon #1	black	

Table 23.1. *Continued.*

Vessel & Ref.#	Hull, outside	Inboard structure
<u>Wild Ranger</u> #1	black	Bulwarks: buff. Waterways: upper deck, buff.
<u>Wild Rover</u>		
<u>Winged Arrow</u> #1	black	Bulwarks: buff relieved with white. Waterways: upper deck, buff.
<u>Winged Racer</u> #1	black	Bulwarks: buff relieved with white. Waterways: upper deck, blue. Deck structures: houses, buff relieved with white.
<u>Witchcraft</u> #1	black	Bulwarks: buff relieved with white. Waterways: upper deck, buff.
<u>Witch of the Wave</u> #1	black,	with a red stripe at the sheathing line. Bulwarks: white. Waterways: upper deck, white; lower deck, blue. Tween decks: thickwork, granite color; ceiling and overhead, white; hanging knees, grained; lower squares of beams, bright and varnished. Deck structures: forward house, white; aft house, in front of cabin, white with carved cornices interwoven with gilding. It also has a stained glass window in front.
<u>Wizard</u> #1	black	Bulwarks: buff. Waterways: upper deck, blue; lower deck, blue. Tween decks: thickwork, white; ceiling and overhead, white; lower squares of beams, bright and varnished. Deck structures: houses, buff.
<u>Young America</u> #84	black	
<u>Young Turk</u>	Bark	

(text continued from page 337)

how much attention was given to *value* (lightness) and *saturation* (chroma, or intensity). The descriptions of the coloring are restricted to naming the basic hue; gradations are left to the imagination.

Hull Exterior (Topsides) and Trim (Mouldings)

A possible "best" way to discuss the colors of the vessels is to imagine that the viewer is approaching a vessel that is tied up at dockside. Categorically, the outside hull will be black from the sheathing line to the rail. Duncan MacLean, describing *Flying Fish*, remarked that "her hull is black outside . . . a color peculiar to clippers and the clergy."[1] While no definite explanations are given in the description for the choice of color, there do appear to be some obvious reasons.

First, to state it in oversimplified fashion, black is black. This is very true until one black is compared side-by-side with another; in some cases the difference almost amounts to two different colors. In paints of the period, lampblack was the standard pigment used in the mixing of black paint. Lampblack is a very consistent, deep, one-value hue—and it goes a long way, a fact to which anyone who has ever encountered it in some unwanted fashion can attest.

Once mixed, the black paint provided good, intense coverage when applied to a surface. It also possessed maximum spreading capability. Another advantage was that no mixing of pigments was required to achieve a desired value.

343

Finally, of all colors, it was the easiest one to provide or mix.

Not too much data is available concerning the make-up of such paint. However, the composition for a paint used to blacken *bends*, or wales, is given as the following "recipe" (a rather quaint title): "Combine, one pound lamp-black mixed for paint, one pound red lead, one gallon paint oil, half pound litharge, and half an ounce of indigo, boiled for half an hour, and stirred at intervals. Care should be taken that the composition boils that length of time. After it has cooled a little, add one pint of spirits of turpentine; apply when warm, and it will dry in a short time with a beautiful gloss, and be perfectly limber. This last mixture has been found very suitable for yards, and also the bends."[89] The *bends* (wales) of a clipper ship constitute the entire side of the ship, generally numbering from sixteen to twenty-four strakes, which is greater than the entire area of freeboard.

The "limber" characteristic of the above paint was an obvious asset when used on a ship's hull in light of the constant intra-structural workings of a ship under full sail. The area that the above mixture would be expected to cover is not stated.

As shown at right, advertisements in contemporary newspapers verify that ready-made constituents of paints—white lead, black lead, whiting, coach varnish, linseed oil, and pigments such as French yellow, ivory black, and Venetian red—were readily available for the production of paints made by other methods. In any case, the process was quite a bit different and more difficult than the convenience of opening a 55-gallon drum.

Black, of itself, is not a color to excite one's interest. However, its application to the hull of a clipper ship resulted in a grand silhouette when viewed against a backdrop of sea or sky. Capt. Arthur H. Clark, a man who knew and sailed in clippers, made a point of commenting on the stately beauty of the American clipper fleet as it lay at anchor in the harbor of Hong Kong during the autumn of 1858.[28]

However, not all clipper hulls were painted black. Some—a very few—were of a different color, and it is generally conceded that these were less impressive than the black hulls.

In this book's gathering of ships, those known to have a hull that was not black are *Dauntless*, described as being dark bronze; *Galatea*, bronze; and *Fearless*, dark green, a color known to the painters as "tea color," a reference to the color of Imperial and Hyson teas. *Fearless* was built for William F. Weld & Co., Boston, whose large fleet was all painted this green color.[32]

While the overwhelming number of clipper hulls were of one solid, unrelieved color, a small number were adorned with a painted stripe at some level above the sheathing—in most cases, a thin line immediately above the sheathing line. The stripe was not referred to as boottopping and was not wide enough to be *boottopping* in the accepted sense of the term, which basically was the width of a belt rather than a stripe. *Beverly* is the only vessel herein whose description fits the boottop concept. She is described as having "a small belt of red on her load line."[3]

Sea Serpent was relieved with a yellow stripe along her sheathing line. *Ellen Foster*, *Witch of the Wave*, and *Hoogly* were all trimmed with a thin red stripe in the same location. In addition, *Hoogly* had poop deck bulwarks above her monkey rail, which were painted white inside and outside. The same construction and finish applied to *James Baines*.

Sultana had her planksheer moulding painted red; in *Mermaid* the planksheer moulding was bronzed; and in *Coeur de Lion* it was gilded around the ship. The upper wale of *Challenge* was gilded from the extended talons of her eagle figurehead completely around the stern and along the opposite side in the same fashion. *Dauntless*, in addition to her non-black hull, featured a white ribbon along her waist, apparently one strake in width. *Invincible* carried a thin crimson stripe and *Sweepstakes* a thin gold stripe, but in both cases the location of the striping is not defined.

Roebuck departed entirely from the above scheme and was trimmed with a tier of painted black ports on a white belt around her waist. Built for the New York–to–San Francisco run, it is not known whether this was done as a defensive scheme or was purely a matter of the owner's desires.

Finally, there was the bark *Racehorse*, whose bulwarks were actually pierced with gunports, but no information on a paint scheme is given.

The subject of exterior hull color ends here, since all other hulls were pure, unrelieved black.

Inboard Works Above the Weather Deck

Inboard, the colors of structure included those of the weather deck waterway, the planksheer surfaces, the bulwarks and stanchions, the main rail, the monkey rail, and, in a relatively few instances, the rise of the poop or half poop deck.

Descriptions of bulwark colors generally include the planksheer, the inner surface of the bulwark planking, and, in open bulwarks (those with no ceiling installed on the stanchions), the exposed squares of the stanchions. If the bulwark was solid (ceiled in with planking), the surface of such planking is included. Waterways, when not identified as being of a specific color, were painted as the bulwarks. This is a general concept and obviously could be subject to many detailed variations.

An apparent prevailing perception is that most bulwarks were painted white or an attractive, delicate color designated "pearl." This, however, was not the case. The descriptions of the ships in this volume indicate that about 50 percent of the inboard works were painted buff; 20 percent each were pearl or white; and the remaining 10 percent were generally a light color.

Buff, by definition, is a brownish-yellow color, generally regarded as a "soft" color. It is not a color that stands alone but is, like the majority of colors, a mix of pigments. If two pigments are combined, the "color" that is achieved will depend upon proportions of the mixture. With this in mind, combined with the fact that there was no reason to achieve a standard hue, it is difficult to conclude that various ships described as having buff bulwarks would be painted the same color. The latitude for deviation was almost endless. Nevertheless, MacLean designated some bulwarks as being "light buff" and some being "dark buff." This differentiation seems to indicate that the vast majority of vessels with buff bulwarks were somewhere in mid-range. This cannot, however, be regarded as fact. Color is, to say the least, what the viewer perceives it to be.

More than half of the bulwarks that were painted buff color were also described as being "relieved with white." This treatment was not ornate and intricate, as were some of the more decorative schemes. The type of relief was accomplished in more geometric and straight-line applications such as tipping the chamfered corners of the outside (inboard) squares of stanchions with white; painting white borders around the perimeters of bulwark planking between the stanchions; perhaps trimming those same areas with mouldings which were painted white; and other basic applications that would not necessarily be considered as truly artistic.

This same relief treatment was often applied to bulwarks that were "pearl," a pleasant light color on the grayish side which stood out well when trimmed with white. The same was applicable to cream-colored bulwarks.

White bulwarks, which comprised 20 percent of the total, were left plain and unrelieved, their solid color being considered suitable by itself. There were a few vessels, however, which relieved the monotonous expanse of white by finishing the inboard squares of the bulwark stanchions without paint, leaving them natural, or *bright*, and varnished. *Chal-*

lenge, Joseph Peabody, and *War Hawk* effected this treatment, as did *Daring*, a vessel whose bulwarks were buff.

The descriptions give the impression of the colors of most vessels' bulwarks being tasteful and pleasant in appearance. There were, however, some which to most viewers might not sound appealing. *Antelope* and *Beverly* were dark buff, while *John Stuart* was light brown, none of them relieved in any fashion.

Of the 10 percent of ships with bulwarks painted a "light" color, half were cream, a very pleasant color, and the remainder were almost one-of-a-kind treatments. *Electric Spark* was light lead color; *Santa Claus*, "light in color"; *Flying Arrow*, "nearly" white. This last description also applied to the wooden plate, turned stanchions, and spar deck rail of the original *Great Republic*, whose bulwarks were under cover.

The coloring of waterways on the weather deck represented the most prominent paint contrast in the external structure. They were blue in almost half the vessels, and half of those with buff bulwarks had them complemented with blue waterways. The variants of what we designate as "blue" can normally range from sky blue to navy blue, and, since no gradation is given in the descriptions, it once again becomes a matter of drawing personal conclusions. All other bulwarks that were buff featured buff waterways, with the exception of two vessels, *Game Cock* and *Sierra Nevada*, both of which carried lead-color waterways below their buff-color bulwarks. This does not sound like a combination with great appeal.

It is noteworthy that in the descriptions of the vessels there are many instances in which no color is noted for the waterways, so the conclusion is that these were painted the same as the bulwarks.

Of the bulwarks that were pearl, cream, white, or another light color, many featured blue waterways or waterways the color of the bulwarks. There were three known exceptions, they being *Challenge*, white bulwarks, green waterways; *Lightning*, pearl bulwarks, lead waterways; *Mystery*, pearl bulwarks, white waterways.

The bulwarks of some vessels were embellished with

highly decorated panels and flowing, carved floral and leafy motifs. Unfortunately for posterity, there is little intimate detail of such ornamentation left to show exactly what was included in individual vessels. Any descriptions are very general and only alert us to the fact that the decoration was included in a certain ship.

Of the ships included in this book, the general wording of MacLean's descriptions reveals that fifteen vessels were definitely embellished with this type of decoration:

Golden Light—Bulwarks paneled inside.

John Wade—Bulwarks beautifully paneled inside.

John Bertram—Bulwarks tastefully ornamented inside.

Empress of the Sea
James Baines
Lightning ⎯ Monkey rail paneled inside.
Ocean Express
Queen of the Seas

Challenge—Bulwarks and monkey rail paneled inside.

Shooting Star—Bulwarks and monkey rail paneled inside.

Racehorse—Bulwarks and monkey rail paneled between stanchions.

Mermaid—Bulwarks and monkey rail are set off inside with panels and mouldings.

Surprise—"Her bulwarks and monkey rails inside are wainscoted, and may be ornamented by a skillful painter in such a style as to make her rival a royal yacht in beauty, on deck."

Hoogly—Space between rack rail and main rail is "tastefully paneled."[1]

A description of *Nightingale* provides the best inkling of this sort of decoration. While not in fine detail, it still allows one to grasp the type of motif and method of application: "The inside of her monkey rail is ornamented with carved branch work, running fore and aft, which adds much to her beauty on deck."[3] In this case, one is at least able to grasp a general idea of what was done.

I have not attempted to illustrate any of the above decorative treatments since, at best, it would represent the thinking of a single individual. However, George F. Campbell's *China Tea Clippers* devotes a chapter to these artistic touches which is well worth reading for an overall view. The chapter also contains sketches appropriate to the subject. The book deals mainly with the later British tea clippers and tends to depict the American clippers as being more colorful than

their specific descriptions indicate; however, in principal it is most informative.

Additional structural items that received what could be described, at least in part, as artistic treatment were the main rail, the rack rail, and, in several cases, hatchway coamings. The treatment of these members mainly consisted of finishing them natural, or bright, and varnished. After this they would be trimmed or capped with yellow metal shaped to fit their specific contours and then kept polished and bright as the sun itself. This trim, in addition to being decorative, was also protective in situations where normal abuse might occur.

Table 18.1 gives particulars on decoration of rails and coamings where applicable. Of note is the fact that one vessel, *Silver Star*, had her rack rail covered with copper rather than the usual yellow metal.

As noted earlier under the heading of "Hatch Coamings," the coamings of *Hoogly* and *Whirlwind* were protected with yellow metal linings.

The final paint work above the weather deck, which could be designated as structural coverage, was the rise of the half poop or poop deck where the difference in height between the weather deck and these deck levels was planked with heavy planking strong enough to resist the battering of heavy seas. This does not include any cabin or deckhouse structures, which were built as independent units not associated with the structural integrity of the hull (see Chapter 26).

White, as the inboard color of structure above the weather deck, was introduced in the early 1800s in the packets, which, competing with each other for passenger trade, were made as attractive and pleasing as possible in appearance. White, and in some cases cream, were the chosen colors. As time passed, white, being the easier paint to acquire, became the standard, to the point that in the clipper period, little mention was made of the color when used for structures such as deckhouses. Its use was regarded as a given unless specifically superseded by another color.

The same applied to the rise of the poop. A rare instance of the mention of white in this capacity appears in the description of *Donald McKay*. Even more unusual is the treatment of *Noonday*'s after cabin: "The front of the cabin, facing the deck, is wainscotted and painted in imitation of mahogany and other fancy woods, which has quite a showy effect upon her aft."[1] The foremost cabin bulkhead was also the structural rise of her half poop.

Decks and Deck Structures

Decks in American-built clippers were planked with pine, the most selected variety being unblemished white pine for weather decks, and hard pine or yellow pine for the lower decks. No paint was applied to deck surfaces. The raw wood was kept clean by constant scrubbing and mopping with brooms, swabs, and water. If some untoward accident occurred, the decks would be scoured with blocks of sandstone. Preservation was achieved by an occasional application of oil to repel water.

Since the vessels listed in Table 23.1 represent a randomly selected group, chosen principally because of the information available, it appears reasonable to select the external color scheme of a "typical" American-built clipper ship. This would consist of a black hull, from sheathing to rail; buff bulwarks relieved with white; blue weather deck waterways; white deckhouses; and polished mahogany trim on such items as the frames of skylights. These would be basic colors, or hues, but one is left to wonder how many of these "typically" colored ships would look alike when the colors were compared with each other.

Most descriptions of ships' deck arrangements do not mention a specific color for deckhouses. When color is mentioned, it is a color other than white. Following the same logic, it seems reasonable to assume that the unnamed color was white.

Duncan MacLean, in his marine reports, made many general observations about the ships of the day. Regarding color, he comments in his report of *Star of the Union* that he personally thought white to be the best color for the inside of a ship, but sailors had decided that white was "no color at all." Little did they know or care that their complaint was actually a statement of scientific truth.

Even though white predominated in the coloring of deckhouse structure, there were a considerable number of deviations. Table 23.1 shows that the deckhouses of *Flying Eagle*, *Flying Fish*, and *Mastiff* were pearl or light pearl; those of *Alarm*, *Comet*, and *Swallow* were cream relieved with white; those of *Game Cock*, *Golden West*, *Ocean Pearl*, *Phantom*, *Whistler*, and *Winged Racer* were buff relieved with white; those of *Hoogly*, *Silver Star*, and *Wizard* were buff. *Beverly* departed the general color schemes in singular fashion by having her entire house painted in imitation of oak. *Flying Arrow* is described in a nebulous manner as being "nearly" white. *Seaman's Bride* was covered with zinc white wherever white was required throughout the ship, "it being considered of a more durable character and less liable to be affected by the gases generated below."[4]

The color of trim and small work receives but scant attention and is thus left to the imagination of the individual.

Tween-Decks

Much less information is available dealing with the coloring of structure in the tween-decks of clipper ships, possibly because relatively few people ever saw these portions of a vessel.

However, enough detail has been recorded to give a general idea of the scope and selection of such coloring.

Where such information is tabulated in Table 23.1, the predominant color scheme in the tween-decks (exclusive of cabins and other living accommodations) emerges as a combination of blue waterways, blue thick work, white ceiling, and white overhead. The most frequent departures from this are in the substitution of white in lieu of blue for the thick work, and the practice of leaving the lower square of deck beams natural, or bright, and varnishing them. Some of this brightwork was also extended to include stanchions and hanging knees. In *Challenge* the lower squares of carlings and ledges were also finished in this manner. A further refinement is found in *Sierra Nevada*, whose stanchions and beam lower squares of the upper tween-decks were stained mahogany color and then varnished, while the hanging knees in the same space were finished with graining. This same graining was employed in *Witch of the Wave*.

The table reveals some additional variations in coloring, none of which are in any way unusual, with the exception of *Charger*, in which the tween-decks ceiling and overhead were white; the stanchions and lower squares of beams bright and varnished; the thick work gray stone color; and the waterways red. The last detail might well be one of the great surprises in clipper ship painting.

The holds of the ships were left unpainted. Painting in such areas, which were subject to great fluctuations of moisture, condensation, and dampness, would have had an adverse effect on the continued long-term soundness of the timbers and would have been subject to considerable abuse. The description of *Golden Light* makes note of this fact in the following manner: "This ship's hold, though not painted, is just as well turned out of hand as the between decks."[1]

Bottom Painting or Sheathing

A final phase of hull exterior finishing was the painting of hulls below the waterline in such ships as were sent to sea without sheathing. Detailed information is not plentiful; however, some does exist, mostly for packets and freighters rather than for the clippers. The principles, however, would apply in any case.

An accepted practice in shipbuilding was to send a ship to sea for a voyage, or sometimes more, to let the ship work itself into shape, squeeze the caulking into final working condition, and "work out the kinks," after which the hull would be inspected, the paint touched up if necessary, and then sheathed. This practice was routine when ships were built at a normal pace and the completion of the project was not dictated by extreme time limitations.

The philosophy that governed the clipper ship—"speed

above all else"—did not begin when the vessel cast off on her maiden voyage. The penchant for speed started at the drawing board, worked itself into the shipbuilding yards where ships were constructed in three months or even less (rather than the ten months that could be put into a packet), and continued until the vessel was driven under or arrived panting at her destination. This philosophy precluded the refinement of a breaking-in period.

According to most records, the average clipper ship was sheathed before she went to sea. A known departure from this occurred with Donald McKay's *Lightning*, which received her copper after delivery to her owners James Baines & Co., in Liverpool. She sailed her maiden passage with her bottom painted copper color. The three other McKay vessels built in the same time frame for the same owner—*James Baines, Champion of the Seas,* and *Donald McKay*—all were probably coppered after delivery. However, no record of bottom paint for any of the three appears to exist. The same applies to *Red Jacket*, which was reportedly sheathed in Liverpool, but no paint record has survived.

Ship model makers ask what color the bottoms of ships in this period were when they went to sea unsheathed. Little can be found in clipper ship reports. Of the vessels covered in this book, only *Lightning*, as previously stated, was painted copper color,[1] and *Sunny South,* varnished bright,[42] are specifically noted.

The best record of the actual colors of bottom paint is found in MacLean's descriptions of packets and freighters, which accompanied his reports of clipper ships.[1] Of approximately fifty such vessels, sixteen are recorded as to the colors of their unsheathed bottoms. The predominant color was green, given for twelve vessels: *Winfield Scott, Samuel Lawrence, Caroline,* and *Winchester,* 1851; *J. Montgomery* and *Orient,* 1852; *Chatsworth* and *Commodore Perry,* 1854; *Cathedral* and *Harry Bluff,* 1855; *Orion,* 1856; and *Dione,* 1857. The second known color was copper color, applied to *Lightning,* 1853; *Star of Empire,* 1853; *Defender,* 1855; and *Plutarch,* 1856.

An anomaly appears in the description of the cargo vessel *Elvira,* built in 1855 by Messrs. Pratt & Osgood, at East Boston. She was, incidentally, their first ship and, according to the description, was painted black over her entire hull. This was most unusual, if not unique, but the article states: "She is butt and bilge bolted with copper, finely finished, and painted black. After she has performed a European voyage she will be coppered."[1]

Of all the ships named above, including *Lightning*, a direct statement about future coppering is made in six instances. In the remaining descriptions the fact is assumed.

It is also correct to conclude that the height of the bottom paint did not necessarily denote the final height of sheathing when installed. This fact is borne out by the bottom painting of the packet ship *Cathedral*, built by Samuel Badger of Portsmouth, New Hampshire, in 1855. Her bottom paint line was cut in only to the height of her light load waterline.[1]

This discussion of bottom painting of packets and freighters is admittedly a departure from the principal subject of this book, the construction of clippers. However, since many vessels of all categories were built by the same builders, this conclusion appears to be valid.

Chapter Twenty-Four

HULL ORNAMENTATION

DESPITE THE FACT THAT THE building and operation of a clipper ship was a strictly commercial and competitive enterprise, it was a rare vessel that put to sea totally devoid of ornamental trim embellishing its plain, rather severe, sleek hull. Even the most hard-nosed, money-conscious owner was unable to resist the urge to impart to his ship a certain bit of distinctive personality.

This was accomplished in a rather standard manner throughout the clipper fleet. Such ornamentation was present in a variety of applications that followed generally accepted categories and could be found in any class of merchant vessel.

Ships' Names

The ship's name was the most universal form of artistic work to be found on all vessels, either in the form of a nameboard or, more often, simply carved into the surface of the planking. The obvious purpose was to identify a vessel, since, even to the experienced and seasoned eye, only a very few ships were built with details and features so unusual as to make them recognizable on sight; *Great Republic* might be considered an example due to her unusual size.

Ships' names, if carved, were located on both bows, both quarters, and the stern. The carving was generally located between the monkey rail and the main rail, or between the main rail and the planksheer. The name on the bows was located forward of the catheads and, on the quarters, forward of the bumkins. When the names were carved on boards, those forward were referred to as *headboards*. (This term should not be confused with the structural headboards, described in the Chapter 20, which were a common installation on ships of an earlier period.) Those aft were referred to as *quarter boards*.

Inevitably, there were exceptions to these general rules, and some of these are illustrated in Figure 24.1. There can be no doubt that many variations found their way into the

ships. Unfortunately, much information of this type has gone the way of the ships themselves and probably will never be known.

The style of lettering was not prescribed; however, incised, modified Roman letters were artistic and the most impressive. Block letters, not so artistic but possibly more practical, were also to be found. Both were easily carved and, especially if gilded, reflected light very well and showed off to great advantage against the black or dark background of the hull.

"Gilding" is the only term used in reference to gold color in the clippers. However, if brilliance and permanence are the criteria, it appears safe to assume that the term was a convenient word meaning the application of gold leaf. This is a craft that is centuries old and was probably a stock-in-trade of sign painters, ship carvers, and others engaged in decorative woodwork.

Where nameboards were installed, the lettering was, perhaps, embellished with a border worked around the edge of the board. Some provision was made for shipping and unshipping such boards in order to preclude their being lost at sea and to facilitate bringing them inboard for retouching if such treatment became necessary.

Names located on the bows were generally sloped or raked to harmonize with the rake of the vessel's stem, and this necessitated a minor but most noticeable and important difference in the cutting of the letters. Names appearing on the starboard side of the ship were sloped forward to match this rake, while those on the port side of the vessel were sloped backhand to achieve the same alignment. Examples of this feature are shown in Figure 24.1.

The names on the quarters or on quarter boards did not necessarily require this difference in the letters since the sternposts of most vessels stood upright. This allowed the name to be carved in vertical letters; thus both quarter boards could be made the same.

(text continued on page 352)

Figure 24.1. *Placement and forms of ship names.*

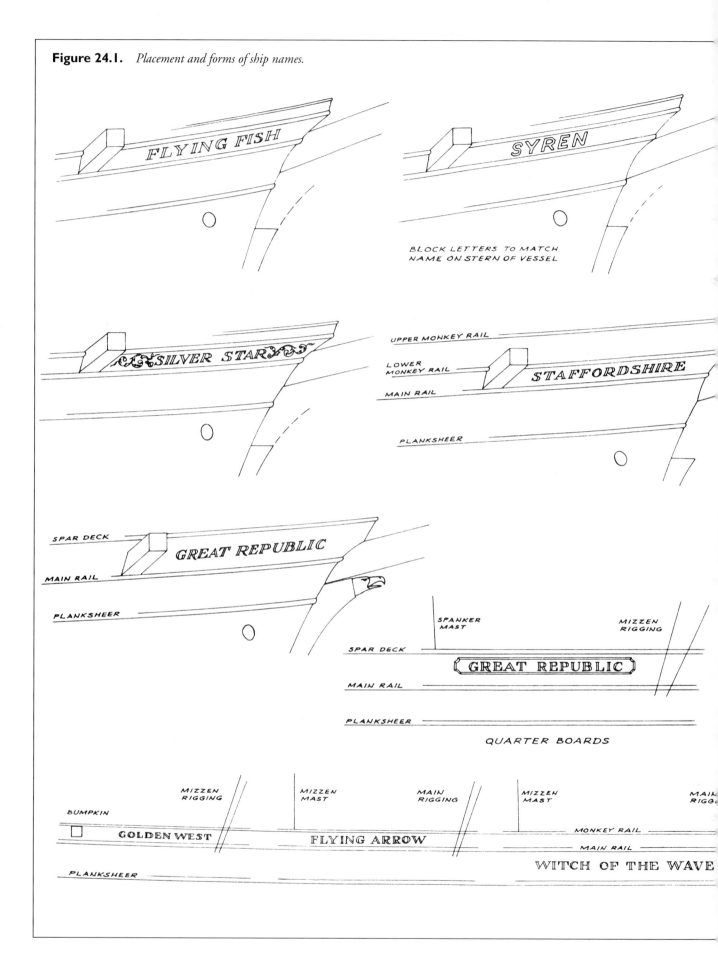

350

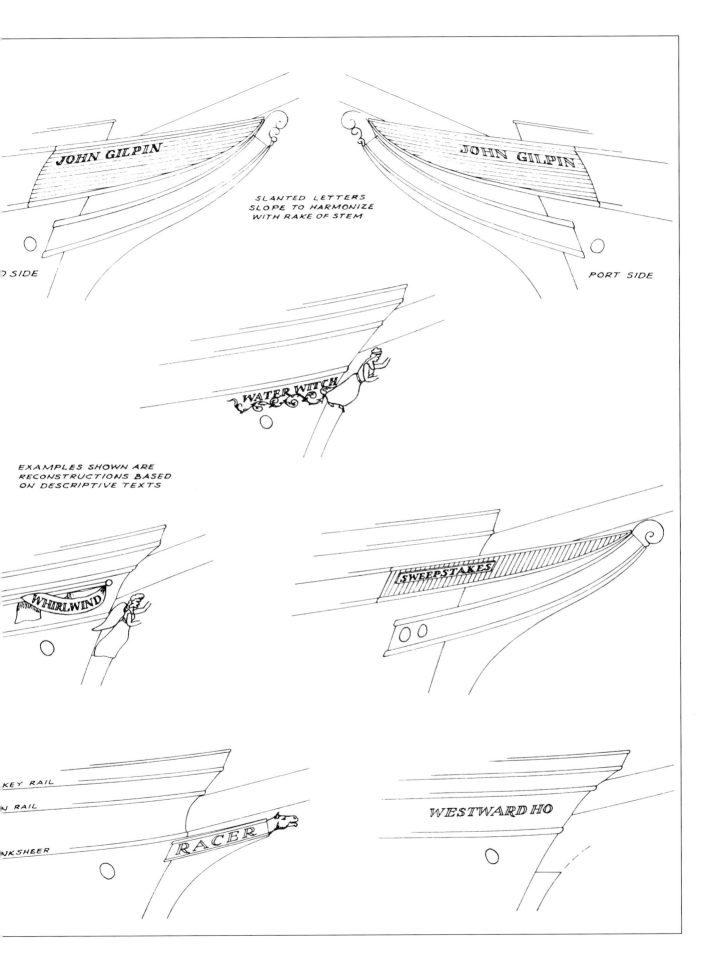

JOHN GILPIN

JOHN GILPIN

SLANTED LETTERS
SLOPE TO HARMONIZE
WITH RAKE OF STEM

SIDE

PORT SIDE

WATER WITCH

EXAMPLES SHOWN ARE
RECONSTRUCTIONS BASED
ON DESCRIPTIVE TEXTS

WHIRLWIND

SWEEPSTAKES

KEY RAIL

N RAIL

NKSHEER

RACER

WESTWARD HO

(text continued from page 349)

Every vessel had her name spread across the stern in letters large or small, accompanied by her port of hail. The latter was a mandatory feature in merchant vessels of the period. Lettering was almost exclusively white or gilded.

Trailboards

The *trailboard* was the foremost ornamental unit to embellish a ship except for the figurehead itself. In clippers the forward end of the trailboard began at the foot of the vessel's figurehead, or at the bottom of her billethead if there was no figurehead, and swept aft in a graceful curve until it finally embraced the hawseholes, aft of which it was terminated. In some instances its sweep did not include the hawseholes.

The upper and lower edges of the trailboard consisted of slender rails secured to the stem and to the navel planking. At the point where the stem met the hull these rails followed the expanding contour of the bow in the form of *cheek pieces* which were built up to smooth the knocking of the anchor chain cable as it traveled in or out of the vessel. Between the upper and lower rails there was inserted a flat plank, cut to fit neatly into the space. On this plank were carved picturesque vines or leafy tracery, or sometimes an ornate, stylized version of the classic acanthus or a fern-like motif. All were very graceful and a delight to the eye. This, the most ornate and complicated form of trailboard, went into decline with the appearance of the clipper ship, for practical and economic reasons.

These trailboards, with their long rails and extra substance, while minor compared to the bulk of a clipper hull, represented additional weight. Unfortunately, this weight was installed in the least affordable location in the clipper ship. These vessels, with their long, fine entrances and extremely thin cutwaters, by their own design already lacked buoyancy in the bow. The trailboards' placement in the least advantageous of locations spelled their ultimate demise.

While the classic, traditional style of trailboard did not disappear entirely, it did not accommodate well to the sharp bow of this new class of ship. Consequently, the complexity of this ornamentation was replaced by simpler decorative schemes ranging from carvings that trailed the figurehead in a line almost parallel with the planksheer, to carvings that descended from the figurehead downward along the stem toward the cutwater.

In some instances the stem was left utterly bare, leaving the entire bow with the figurehead—or the billethead—as the lone adornment forward.

The clipper *Whistler* was a very rare vessel, wearing neither trailboards nor figurehead. Her bow was totally naked, as shown in Figure 24.2. This figure also illustrates some actual and reconstructed examples of trailboard treatment.

Common styles of trailboard ornamentation are shown in Figure 24.3. All except *Seaman's Bride*, which is from a photograph, are based on descriptive texts.

Generally speaking, all ornamentation was presented on both sides of a ship, the details being similar but to the opposite hand. A known exception to this practice was the bow treatment of *Young America*. In this vessel the motifs adorning the bow were alike in concept but different in detail and are illustrated in Figure 24.4. This instance, if not unique, was extremely rare, occurring only once in this list of vessels so far as can be verified.

Oculi

The *oculus* was another form of hull ornamentation found in clipper ships. This was the carved or painted representation of a peering eye, gazing either ahead in the direction of travel of the vessel, or sometimes gazing abeam as if to scan the horizon on either side of the ship.

These oculi, one on each bow, were generally placed immediately above or below the planksheer and forward of the hawseholes. These were the objects which, in antiquity, were the genesis of the term *the eyes of the ship*. Their original, superstitious functions were to allow the ship to see ahead of the path in which she was "swimming," and to let an enemy know that he was being watched by the vessel. Their use can be traced back as far as the Egyptian Pharaoh Sahure, circa 2400 B.C., and possibly earlier.

Their placement on the bows of large vessels, such as the clippers, was a rarity. However, in many parts of the world they were, and still are, frequently included in the decoration of small craft.

The practice of adorning ships with oculi that were to perform their original function degenerated over the ages and fell into disuse except for decorative purposes. Long before the clipper era, the *eyes of the ship* had become a term meaning a vessel's most forward structure, which term is well understood today.

The occasional appearance of oculi in clipper ships was based in part on business considerations. A few owners, whose ships traded in the Far East, were of the opinion that the adornment was a detail with which Oriental merchants might empathize. Whether or not this expectation was fulfilled cannot be known; however, it was certainly an inexpensive public-relations gesture. Figure 24.5 shows general illustrations of oculi on the hulls.

(text continued on page 360)

Figure 24.2. *Principal forms of bow ornamentation.*

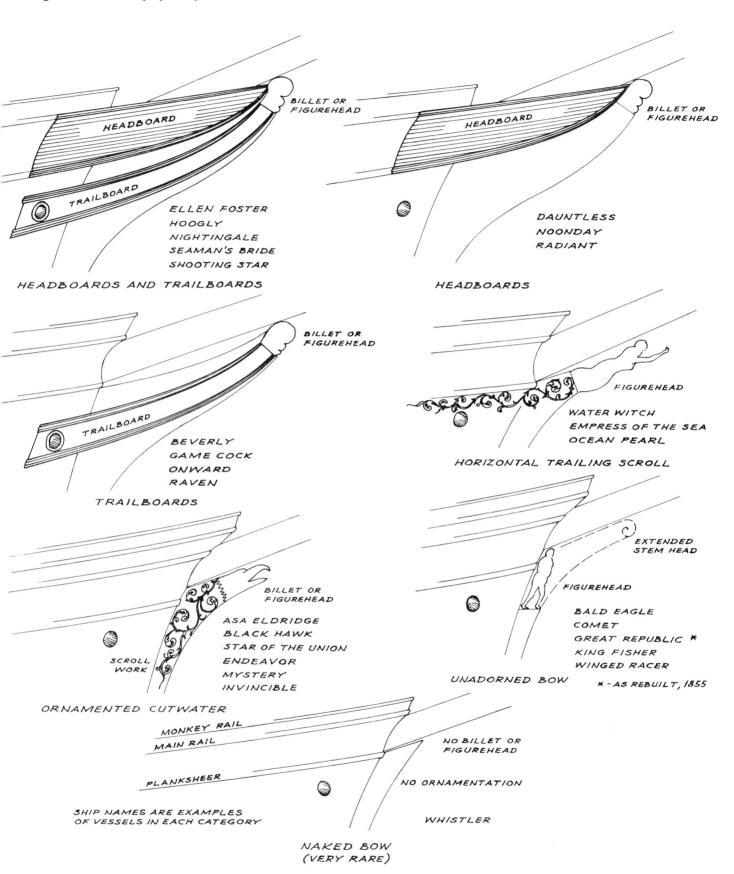

HEADBOARD
BILLET OR FIGUREHEAD
TRAILBOARD

ELLEN FOSTER
HOOGLY
NIGHTINGALE
SEAMAN'S BRIDE
SHOOTING STAR

HEADBOARDS AND TRAILBOARDS

HEADBOARD
BILLET OR FIGUREHEAD

DAUNTLESS
NOONDAY
RADIANT

HEADBOARDS

BILLET OR FIGUREHEAD
TRAILBOARD

BEVERLY
GAME COCK
ONWARD
RAVEN

TRAILBOARDS

FIGUREHEAD

WATER WITCH
EMPRESS OF THE SEA
OCEAN PEARL

HORIZONTAL TRAILING SCROLL

BILLET OR FIGUREHEAD

ASA ELDRIDGE
BLACK HAWK
STAR OF THE UNION
ENDEAVOR
MYSTERY
INVINCIBLE

SCROLL WORK

ORNAMENTED CUTWATER

EXTENDED STEM HEAD
FIGUREHEAD

BALD EAGLE
COMET
GREAT REPUBLIC *
KING FISHER
WINGED RACER

UNADORNED BOW   * - AS REBUILT, 1855

MONKEY RAIL
MAIN RAIL

PLANKSHEER

SHIP NAMES ARE EXAMPLES
OF VESSELS IN EACH CATEGORY

NO BILLET OR FIGUREHEAD

NO ORNAMENTATION

WHISTLER

NAKED BOW
(VERY RARE)

Figure 24.3. *Styles of trailboard ornamentation.*

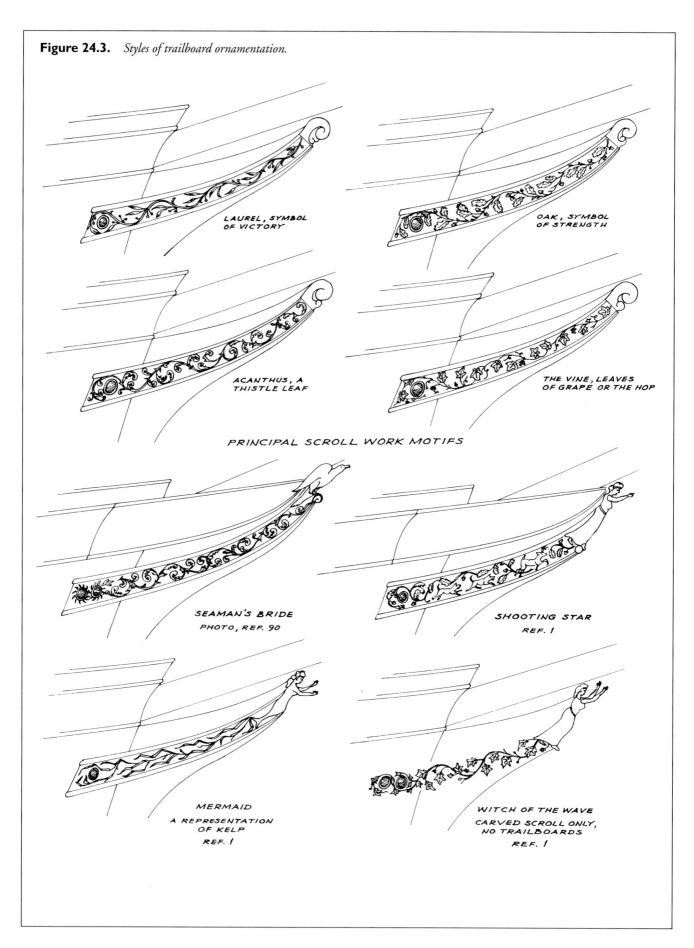

LAUREL, SYMBOL
OF VICTORY

OAK, SYMBOL
OF STRENGTH

ACANTHUS, A
THISTLE LEAF

THE VINE, LEAVES
OF GRAPE OR THE HOP

PRINCIPAL SCROLL WORK MOTIFS

SEAMAN'S BRIDE
PHOTO, REF. 90

SHOOTING STAR
REF. 1

MERMAID
A REPRESENTATION
OF KELP
REF. 1

WITCH OF THE WAVE
CARVED SCROLL ONLY,
NO TRAILBOARDS
REF. 1

354

Figure 24.4. *Cutwater and unusual bow ornamentation.*

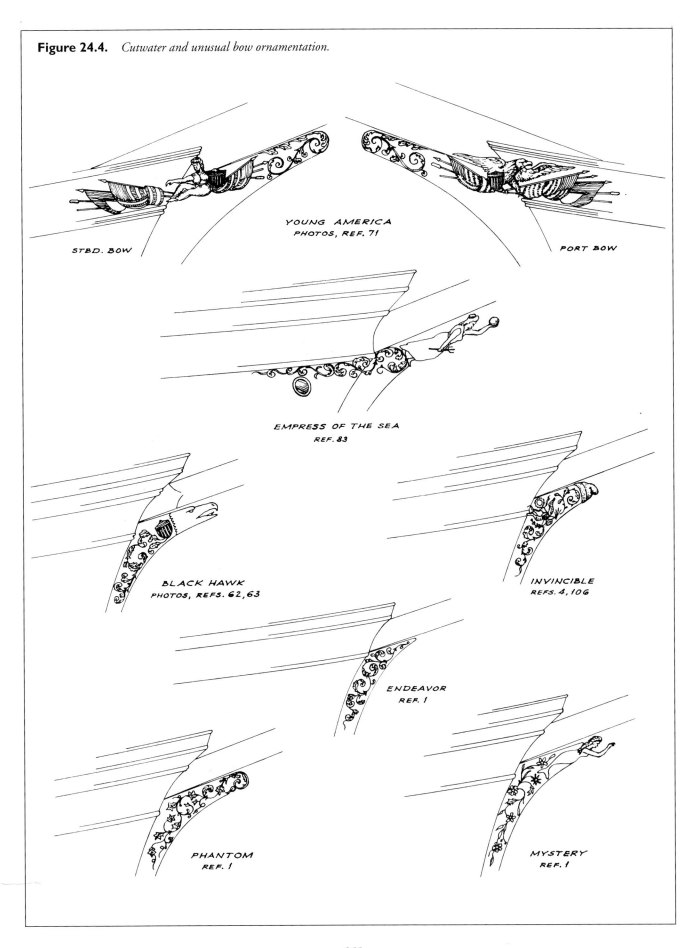

STBD. BOW

YOUNG AMERICA
PHOTOS, REF. 71

PORT BOW

EMPRESS OF THE SEA
REF. 83

BLACK HAWK
PHOTOS, REFS. 62,63

INVINCIBLE
REFS. 4,106

ENDEAVOR
REF. 1

PHANTOM
REF. 1

MYSTERY
REF. 1

Figure 24.5. *Applications of the oculus.*

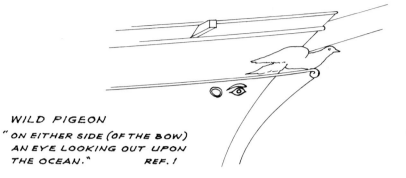

WILD PIGEON
"ON EITHER SIDE (OF THE BOW)
AN EYE LOOKING OUT UPON
THE OCEAN."   REF. 1

WITCH OF THE WAVE

WITCH OF THE WAVE
"ONE (EYE) GLOWERING FROM
EACH BOW AS IF SCANNING
THE FOAMING DEEP BEFORE."
                    REF. 1

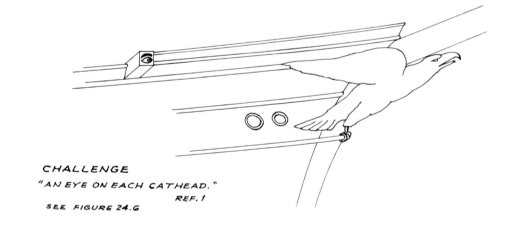

CHALLENGE
"AN EYE ON EACH CATHEAD."
                    REF. 1
    SEE FIGURE 24.6

Figure 24.6. *Cathead devices.*

BLACK HAWK
FLYING MIST

CHALLENGE

ELLEN FOSTER

WITCH OF THE WAVE

INVINCIBLE

ONWARD

BALD EAGLE
DAUNTLESS
FLYING CHILDERS
FLYING FISH
JOHN BERTRAM
SOUTHERN CROSS
STAFFORDSHIRE
STAG HOUND
STAR OF THE UNION
STORM KING
WHIRLWIND

QUEEN OF THE SEAS
RADIANT

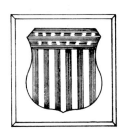

YOUNG AMERICA

Figure 24.7. *Stern ornamentation.*

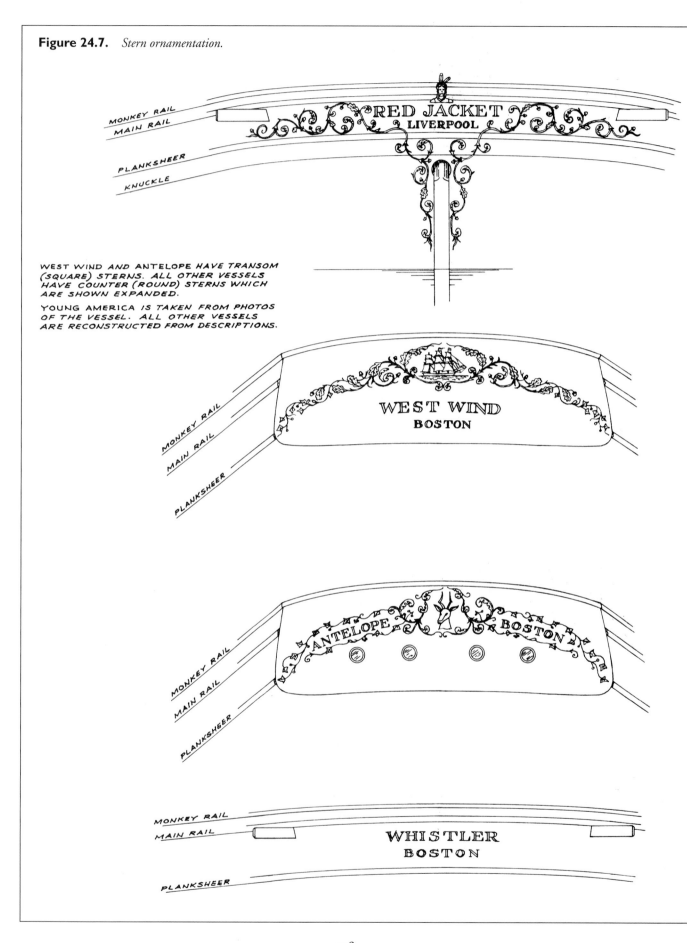

MONKEY RAIL
MAIN RAIL

RED JACKET
LIVERPOOL

PLANKSHEER

KNUCKLE

WEST WIND *AND* ANTELOPE *HAVE TRANSOM
(SQUARE) STERNS. ALL OTHER VESSELS
HAVE COUNTER (ROUND) STERNS WHICH
ARE SHOWN EXPANDED.*

YOUNG AMERICA *IS TAKEN FROM PHOTOS
OF THE VESSEL. ALL OTHER VESSELS
ARE RECONSTRUCTED FROM DESCRIPTIONS.*

MONKEY RAIL

MAIN RAIL

WEST WIND
BOSTON

PLANKSHEER

MONKEY RAIL

MAIN RAIL

ANTELOPE   BOSTON

PLANKSHEER

MONKEY RAIL

MAIN RAIL

WHISTLER
BOSTON

PLANKSHEER

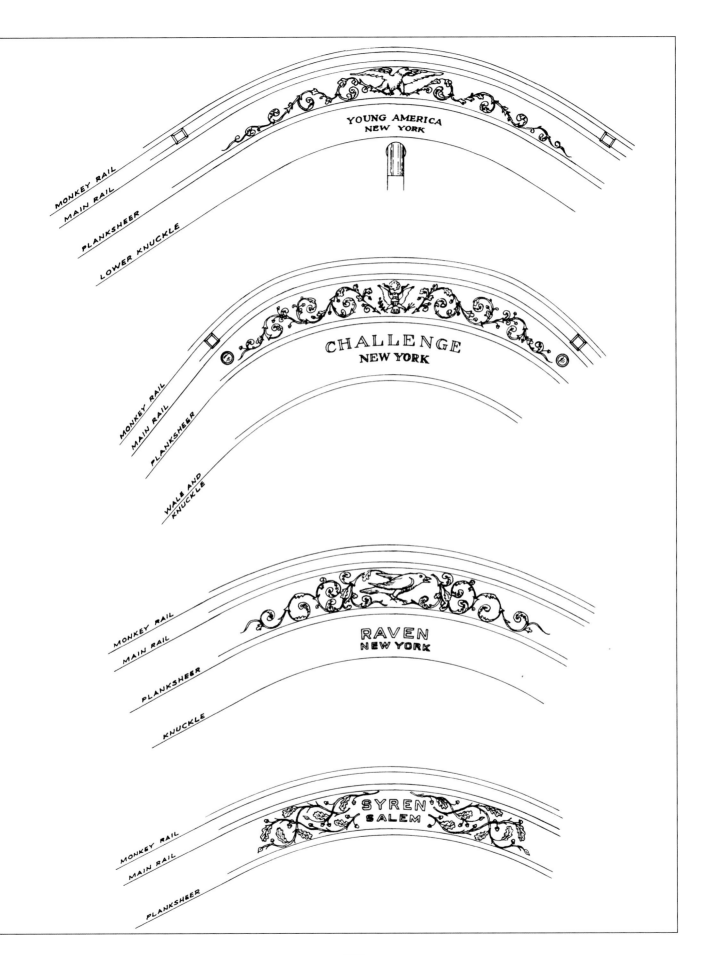

(text continued from page 352)

Catheads

The *catheads* on many vessels were subject to decorative artistry, usually confined to their ends. These small squares presented an irresistible opportunity for embellishment. Not every vessel received such treatment; however, the practice was followed with a frequency which made it commonplace or, at the very least, not unusual.

The variety of cathead embellishment did not cover a great range. A basic motif was that of a five-pointed star. Another elementary design was the sunburst. A third type of the simpler treatments was a carved wreath. Due to their relative simplicity, all of the above designs could conceivably be carved into the end of the cathead prior to its being installed in the ship. If done at this time, the carving could be protected simply by temporarily covering it with a board nailed in place until all work of installation was completed.

The second means of applying the decoration was to carve it separately in a suitable block of wood. The carvings were executed in cameo (relief) or intaglio (incised) form at the woodcarver's whim or instructions, and fastened to the end of the cathead after it had been installed on the ship.

The most ornate form of decoration was that of a feline face, either cat or lion, in either natural or stylized form. Such faces offered the woodcarver unlimited opportunity to impart detail and expression to his heart's content. His imagination was the only limit to stand in his path. These faces were invariably executed in the woodcarver's shop, sculpted from solid blocks of wood. Being three-dimensional, they were developed in depths ranging from bas-relief to almost full round, although the latter form at this date was rather infrequent. Upon completion they were taken to the ship and suitably spiked in position on the end of the cathead.

In addition to decorating the end of the cathead, artistry was sometimes applied to the projecting length of the cathead timber, in the form of vines or leafy tracery. If the cathead was supported by a knee at the ship's side, this knee might also be artfully carved. This particular detail, however, was extremely rare in the clipper ship.

Some cathead carvings, based on photographs of vessels and descriptions in the various references, are shown in Figure 24.6. Additional coverage of the general subject can be found in Marion V. Brewington's *Shipcarvers of North America*.[90]

Gangway Boards

The *gangway boards*, located in the ship's waist above the main rail, were generally decorated with as much carving as their broad surfaces would permit. These boards could be found in all classes of ships and existed from the introduction of solid bulwarks in ships' sides. In function they bounded the ends of the monkey rail assembly, which had been cut away to allow convenient access for boarding or disembarking from a vessel in its mid-length area.

Such gangway boards did not fit specifically into any single category of ship structure. They were stout pieces of wood, ranging between 3 and 5 inches in thickness, but did not contribute to the structural integrity of the ship. They performed no shipkeeping function in the fashion of such items as bitts and fife rails, but could not be considered fittings. And finally, they could not, strictly speaking, be considered hull ornamentation. However, they were usually made of exotic or furniture-quality woods, were intricately and artistically carved, and were well finished and highly polished. Using these last features as criteria, they are superficially mentioned in this chapter dealing with hull ornamentation.

In American-built clippers the wood most used for gangway boards was mahogany or, on rare occasion, teak. Favorite motifs included some form of the eagle and shield, as found in the American coat of arms; draped flags; ribbands gracefully spread, containing the name of the vessel; floral tracery; and the inevitable star or sunburst themes.

Actual gangway board descriptions, as installed in clippers, are very rare, and the descriptions usually are restricted to brief phrases such as "ornately carved," "tastefully decorated," etc.

Stern Carvings

The *stern carvings* of a vessel, especially one with a transom stern, were the answer to a woodcarver's prayer—an invitation for the carver to run amok. That broad, clean, clear expanse of bare planks sang a siren song to which all good woodcarvers responded.

Prior to the era of the clipper ship, such sterns were usually covered with a highly decorated *archboard* which was made up of three or more panels—always an odd number, so that the central figure could be carved as a single segment—which would span the transom from the port counter timber to the starboard counter timber. The panels, when assembled, would appear as a single unit covered with every form

(text continued on page 369)

Table 24.1. *Hull ornamentation.*

Vessel & Ref.#	Hull ornamentation
Alarm #1	Stern - Ornamented with gilded branches.
Amphitrite #1	Stern - Female bust amidship, flanked by gilded carved work on either side.
Andrew Jackson	
Antelope #1	Headboards - Lower edge formed by the extended planksheer. Trailboards - Decorated with ornamental carved work. Stern - An arch of carved work with the bust of an antelope amidship. Her name is carved into the archboard along with her port of hail (Boston), painted white. All worked over four circular plate glass airports. See Figure 24.7.
Asa Eldridge #1	No headboards or trailboards. Stem - Gilded carved work below the figurehead. Stern - Tastefully ornamented with gilded carved work. Included are representations of American and British flags, united by a wreath of myrtle. [The flags are probably colored proper.]
Bald Eagle #1,32	No headboards or trailboards. Catheads - Ends ornamented with gilded carved work. Stern - Tastefully ornamented.
Belle of the West #1	No headboards or trailboards. Stern - Tastefully ornamented with a neat female bust in bas-relief amidship, flanked on either side with gilded carved work.
Beverly #3	Trailboards - Ornamented with finely carved gilded work. Stern - An arch of massive carved and gilded work beautifully executed. Name carved in gilded letters.
Black Hawk #62	No headboards or trailboards. Name - No name carved on bows or quarters. Stem - A United States shield of stars and stripes, colored proper, with gilded carved work below. All aft of the figurehead. See Figure 24.4 Catheads - Five-pointed star incised in end, white or gilded. See Figure 24.6.
Blue Jacket #5,86	Trailboards - On either side of the figurehead a scroll saying "Keep a Sharp Lookout." Stern - Ornamented with an arch of gilded carved work in the center of which are representations of fruits and flowers.

Vessel & Ref.#	Hull ornamentation
Bonita #1	No headboards or trailboards. Stem - Cutwater is flowered with carved gilt work on both sides. Stern - Finely ornamented with gilded carved work, consisting of the horn of plenty, Spanish grape vines, the rose, thistle and shamrock, and a variety of other devices. Name - Located, with port of hail (Boston) below the stern decoration. Executed in raised gilded letters.
Bounding Billow Bark #1	Stem - Gilded carved work below the figurehead. Stern - Ornamented with an arch of gilded carved work.
Celestial #42	Trailboards - Gilded carved scroll work from the figurehead downward and aft to embrace the hawse holes. (Ref.42 is not an original source.)
Challenge #1,42	No headboards or trailboards. No chocks [bolsters] around the hawse holes. Catheads - An oculus (eye) on the end of each cathead. See Figure 24.6. Stern - Ornamented with gilded branches above the planksheer, with the arms of the United States, in bas-relief, probably colored proper, amidship. Name - Located with port of hail (New York) below the stern decoration. Executed in gilded letters. See Figure 24.7.
Challenger #1	Stern - Finely ornamented with an arch of gilded carved work.
Champion of the Seas #1,61	Trailboards - Ornamented with carved scroll work. Stern - Ornamented with the Australian coat of arms. (Port of hail is Liverpool.)
Charger #1	No headboards or trailboards. Stern - A mounted charger, in full career (galloping), and other carved work, tastefully set off with gilding. (The wording appears to imply that the central motif is colored proper.)
Charmer #1	Stern - Amidship, a female figure represented as reclining in a circular frame, relieved with gilding.
Cleopatra #1	No headboards or trailboards. Stern - Lower part beautifully ornamented with gilded carved work.
Climax #1	Stern - Spanned by an arch of gilded carved work.
Coeur de Lion #1	Stern - Amidship, the escutcheon of King Richard I blazoned proper, in the apex of an arch of gilded carved work.
Comet #24,42,92	No headboards or trailboards. Stern - Carved tracery across the transom. Name - Surrounded by the transom tracery.
Cyclone #3	Stern - Decorated with splendid scroll work.
Daring #1	Stern - Ornamented with gilded carved work.

Table 24.1. *Continued.*

Vessel & Ref.#	Hull ornamentation
Dauntless #1,32	Headboards; no trailboards.
	Catheads - Decorated with gilded carved work.
	Stern - Spanned by an arch of gilded carved work, with a bust in its center, and this arch is divided by smaller arches, which form so many apparent supporters to the main arch above them.
Donald McKay #1	Stern - Tastefully ornamented with gilded carved work. (Port of hail is Liverpool.)
Don Quixote #1	No headboards or trailboards.
	Stem - A sprig of gilded carved work on each side of the cutwater, below the bowsprit, is her only ornament forward.
	Stern - Chastely ornamented with gilded branches.
Eagle #5	No headboards.
	Trailboards - Formed by the spread wings of her eagle figurehead. The feet rest on the planksheer moulding.
	Stern - Embellished with a spread eagle of most beautiful proportions.
Eagle Wing #1	No headboards or trailboards.
	Stem - Cutwater ornamented with gilded branches.
	Stern - Ornamented with a gilded eagle on the wing, and other fancy work.
Edwin Forrest #1	Stern - Tastefully ornamented with gilded carved work.
Electric Spark #1	Stern - Finely ornamented with gilded carved work.
Ellen Foster #1	Headboards - Outline formed by the sweep of the main rail and the planksheer which terminate in a point at the head.
	Name - Carved in gilded letters in the headboards.
	Trailboards - Descend downward and aft to embrace the hawse holes. Embellished by gilded branches of carved work, including the perimeter of the hawse holes.
	Catheads - A lion grins in gold from the end of each cathead. See Figure 24.6.
	Stern - Spanned by an arch of carved work. In the apex amidship is a finely executed bust of her namesake (wife of the builder), in bas-relief, painted white and edged with gold. Ornamented with gilded drops (clusters of flowers, leaves, ribbons, etc.) between the cabin windows. Her name and port of hail (Boston) are painted white on the archboard.
Empress of the Sea #1,83	No headboards.
	Trailboards - Only carved work from the figurehead to the navel hoods, paralleling the planksheer. No built-in trailboards. See Figure 24.4.
	Name - Carved in the bows between the main rail and the monkey rail cap forward of the catheads.
	Stern - Tastefully ornamented with gilded carved work.
Endeavor #1	No headboards or trailboards.
	Stem - A few scrolls of carved work upon the cutwater below the bowsprit.
Eringo Bark #1	Stern - Ornamented with gilded carved work.

Vessel & Ref.#	Hull ornamentation
Eureka #4	Stern - Ornamented with some neat gilt work.
Fair Wind #1	Stern - Tastefully ornamented with gilded carved work.
Fearless	
Fleet Wing #1	Stern - Spanned by an arch of gilded carved work. In the apex amidship is a gilded eagle. Her name and port of hail (Boston) are carved the archboard.
Flyaway #24,32	Stem - Ref.24: Lines plan indicates fanciful carved scroll work on the elongated stemhead under the bowsprit from billet to planking. Ref.32: States that there was no decoration.
Flying Arrow #1	Headboards - Ornamented, with the ship's name carved in.
	Name - Carved in gilded letters in the headboards.
	Trailboards - Ornamental gilding along the trailboard
	Quarters - Ship's name carved in gilded letters. See Figure 24.1.
	Stern - Ornamented with an arch of gilded work.
Flying Childers #1	No headboards or trailboards.
	Catheads - Gilded ornaments on the ends.
	Stern - Tastefully ornamented with gilded carved work, etc.
Flying Cloud #1	No headboards or trailboards.
	Name - Carved in gilded letters into the curve of her bows, between the mouldings of the rails.
	Quarters - Ship's name carved in gilded letters.
	Stern - Ship's name and port of hail (New York) ca and gilded upon it, surrounded by finely designed ornamental work.
Flying Dragon #1	No headboards or trailboards.
	Stern - Ornamented with three gilded flying dragons.
Flying Dutchman	
Flying Eagle #1	No headboards or trailboards.
	Stern - Ornamented with an arch of gilded carved work, in the apex of which is a gilded eagle, with a female figure on each side of it, represented emerging from sea-shells.
Flying Fish #1,3	Ref.1 No headboards or trailboards.
	Name - Carved into the monkey bulwarks along the curve of her bows, and is gilded. See Figure 24.1.
	Hawse holes - No chocks surround the hawse holes.
	Catheads - Gilded carved work on the ends.
	Stern - A beautiful arch of carved work, and her name, etc. ornament the stern.
	Ref.3 - Describes the stern only, stating it to be "ornamented with a fine circle of carved work, as well as her name."

Table 24.1. *Continued.*

Vessel & Ref.#	Hull ornamentation	Vessel & Ref.#	Hull ornamentation
Flying Mist #1	No headboards or trailboards. Name - In gilded letters on each curve of the monkey rail. Catheads - A gilded star on the end of each cathead. See Figure 24.6. Stern - Spanned by an arch of gilded carved work.	Great Republic #10, 93,94	No headboards or trailboards. Stem - No ornamentation. Name - Carved in gilded letters in the curve of the bows between the main rail and the spar deck. See Figure 24.1. Quarters - Ship's name on quarter boards located above main rail between mizzen mast and spanker mast. See Figure 24.1. Stern - Spanned by a large, gilded eagle, with the American shield in his talons, and extends thirty-six feet between the tips of its wings. [The American shield is probably colored proper.] Her name and port of hail (Boston) are also on the stern.
Galatea #1	No headboards or trailboards. Stern - Ornamented with gilded carved work in the center of which is a female figure, painted white.		
Game Cock #1	No headboards. Trailboards - Descend down and aft from the feet of the figurehead to embrace the hawse holes and are ornamented with branches of gilded carved work. Stern - Spanned by an archboard tastefully ornamented with carved and gilded branches. Her name and port of hail (Boston) are carved into the archboard and painted white.	Great Republic #97 (re-built) Henry Hill Bark #1,42	Ornamentation of the re-built vessel was possibly the same as the original ship of 1853. Port of hail was New York. See Figureheads. No headboards or trailboards. Name - Carved and gilded upon each side of the bow. Stern - Tastefully ornamented with gilded carved work.
Gazelle #4,24	No headboards or trailboards. Stem - Ref.4: Ornamented with but little carved work on the cutwater. Ref.24: Shows ornamental carved leafy branches along the short cutwater under the bowsprit, extending from the billet to the planking. Stern - Ref.4: Ornamented with a carved representation of a gazelle.	Herald of the Morning #1,32 Hoogly #1	No headboards or trailboards. Stern - Finely ornamented with gilded carved work. Headboards - Outline formed by the planksheer and the first rail above (this rail is one foot below the main rail. See Table 18.1) which are carried forward to the extreme and terminate in a point at the head. Trailboards - Descend down and aft from the pedestal of the figurehead and are ornamented with richly flowered carved work, relieved with gilding. Stern - Her name and port of hail (Boston) are in gilt letters between the stern knuckle and the planksheer. Above, between the planksheer and first rail, are beautifully designed branches, covered with gilding. Next above, between the first rail and the main rail, are four circular plate glass ports.
Gem of the Ocean #1	No headboards or trailboards. Stern - Ornamental gilded carved work.		
Golden Eagle #1	Stem - No ornamentation. Stern - Arched in outline and ornamented with gilded carved work.		
Golden Fleece (2nd) #1	Stem - No ornamentation. Stern - Ornamented with gilded carved work.	Hurricane #4	Stem - No ornamentation.
Golden Light #1	No headboards or trailboards. Stem - No ornamentation. Stern - Beautifully ornamented with gilded carved work, and other devices.	Indiaman Intrepid Invincible #4	
Golden West #1,97	No headboards or trailboards. Stem - No ornamentation. Quarters - Ship's name carved above main rail, aft of mizzen rigging. See Figure 24.1. Stern - Beautified with elaborate ornamental work.		No headboards or trailboards. Stem - The American coat-of-arms fills the space between the figurehead and the planking. [This ornament is probably colored proper.] See Figure 24.4. Catheads - A star, surrounded by a wreath of laurel and oak, adorn the end of each cathead. See Figure 24.6 Stern - Ornamented with an eagle and scroll work.
Grace Darling #1	Stem - No ornamentation. Stern - Neatly ornamented with gilded carved work.		

Table 24.1. *Continued.*

Vessel & Ref.#	Hull ornamentation	Vessel & Ref.#	Hull ornamentation
James Baines #1	No headboards or trailboards. Stem – Gilded carved work continues where the figurehead blends with the cutwater. Stern – Ornamented with carved representations of "the great globe itself", between the arms of Britain and the United States, surrounded with fancy scroll work. Carved and gilded drops are draped between the cabin windows. Her name is carved above all. (Her port of hail is Liverpool.) The whole is tastefully gilded and painted. [The arms of the two nations and the globe are probably colored proper.]	Mameluke #1	No headboards or trailboards. Stern – Tastefully ornamented with gilded carved work.
		Mary Robinson	
		Mastiff #1	No headboards or trailboards. Stern – The head of a mastiff appears from the gilded scroll work.
John Bertram #1	Vessel has headboards. Name – Carved in gilded letters in the headboards. Trailboards – Descend down and aft from the feet of the figurehead to embrace the hawse holes, and are ornamented with gilded branches. Catheads – Gilded devices on the ends. Her cathead knees are carved and gilded. Stern – Spanned by an arch of gilded carved work. In the apex is a medallion bust of John Bertram. The ornamental work ends in two busts of eagles, represented gazing at each other.	Mermaid Bark #1	No headboards. Trailboards – Descend down and aft from the pedestal of the figurehead and are ornamented with bronzed representations of kelp. See Figure 24.3. Stern – Decorated with bronzed ornamental work.
		Morning Light #1,3	No headboards or trailboards. Stern – Spanned by an arch of gilded carved work. In the arch is the goddess of the day (Aurora), represented seated in a chariot of light, drawn by fleet coursers. Her name and port of hail (Boston) are also on the stern.
John Gilpin #1,32	Vessel has headboards. Name – Ornaments the headboards in gilded letters. See Figure 24.1. Trailboards – Descend down and aft from the billet, taking in the navel hoods, and are decorated with ornamental work. Quarters – Ship's name is gilded on quarter boards. Stern – Ornamented with a representation of John Gilpin on horseback, galloping at full speed. Also other fancy work, all tastefully carved and gilded.	Mystery #1	No headboards or trailboards. Stem – The figurehead is relieved with flowered gilding and other ornamental work on the cutwater; otherwise the bow is plain to nakedness. See Figure 24.4. Stern – Finely ornamented with gilded carved work.
		Nightingale #3,42	Vessel has headboards. Trailboards – Descend down and aft from the figurehead to embrace the hawse holes, and are ornamented with carved gilded scroll work. Name – Carved and gilded in the bows between the main rail and the monkey rail cap, forward of the catheads. Quarters – Ship's name carved and gilded above the main rail aft of the mizzen rigging. Stern – Ornamented with a carved figure of Jenny Lind reposing on a couch, in flowing dress and waving hair [all possibly colored proper]; on each side of which is a gilded representation of a cornucopia. The whole is surrounded by branch work, interlined with clusters of grapes. Her name is also on the stern in blue and gold. (Port of hail is Boston.)
John Land #32	Vessel was built as an exact duplicate of Winged Arrow, and was fitted with headboards but no trailboards. No description of ornamentation is given and it might differ from Winged Arrow. Stern – Vessel's own name appeared on stern.		
John Stuart #4	Her head is ornamented with neatly carved and gilt scroll work.		
John Wade #1,95	No headboards or trailboards. Stem – Ornamented with scroll work down the cutwater. Stern – Ornamented with neat and beautiful carved work.	Noonday #1	Vessel has headboards; no trailboards. Name – Blazoned on the headboards in letters of gold. Stern – Ornamented with gilded carved work, conspicuous among which are representations of the American flag and eagle [both probably colored proper], her name and port of hail (Boston).
Joseph Peabody #1	No headboards or trailboards. Name – Carved and gilded upon each side of the bow.		
King Fisher #1	No headboards or trailboards.	Northern Light	
Lady Franklin		Ocean Express #1	No headboards or trailboards. Stern – Ornamented with gilded carving.
Lamplighter Bark #1	No headboards or trailboards. Stern – Ornamented with an arch of gilded carved work, in the center of which is a medallion bust of a sage.		
Lightfoot #1	Stern – Ornamented between the archboard and rail with gilded carved work.		
Lightning #1,42	No headboards or trailboards.		

Table 24.1. *Continued.*

Vessel & Ref.#	Hull ornamentation	Vessel & Ref.#	Hull ornamentation
Ocean Pearl #1	No headboards. Trailboards - Blended into the navel hoods and are ornamented with carved work. Stern - Ornamented with gilded carved work, in the center of which are representations of pearl shells, and her name and port of hail (Boston) are also in gilded letters, upon a scroll from each side of the arch.	Racehorse Bark #1,44	Vessel has headboards and trailboards. Trailboards - Descend down and aft to embrace the hawse holes and are ornamented with carved scroll work. Stern - Ornamented with gilded work.
Ocean Telegraph #5	Apparently no headboards or trailboards. Stern - Gracefully ornamented with gilded carved work, in the center of which is old Neptune, with the emblems of his empire.	Racer #3,4,96	No headboards. Trailboards - Extend from the figurehead to the navel hoods, their upper moulding paralleling the planksheer. Their only ornamentation is her name which engages their complete expanse. See Figure 24.1. Name - Carved in large gilded letters on the trailboards. See Figure 24.1. Stern - Ornamented with a carved and gilded spread eagle under which is carved her name and port of hail (New York), also gilded.
Onward #1,32	No headboards. Trailboards - Ornamented with gilding. Name - Carved in gilded letters in each bow. Catheads - A gilded hand, pointed forward, on the end of each cathead. See Figure 24.6. Quarters - Ship's name is carved in gilded letters on each quarter. Stern - Ornamented with an American Indian, surrounded with gilt work. Her name is carved and painted white, "according to law." [Presumably her port of hail (Boston) is also included.] Note: Ref.32 interprets "according to law" as a phrase "According to Law", in carved white letters under the name.	Radiant #1,32	Headboards - Outlined by the extended mouldings of her main rail and planksheer which terminate in a point aft of her figurehead. No trailboards. Catheads - A gilded representation of the sun ornaments the end of each cathead. See Figure 24.6. Stern - Ornamented with an arch of gilded carved work.
Osborne Howes		Raven #3	No headboards. Trailboards - Descend down and aft to embrace the hawse holes and are ornamented with carved and gilded scroll work. Stern - Ornamented with gilded scroll work, in the center of which, on a white ground work, is also a beautifully carved representation of the Raven. Beneath is her name and port of hail (New York), in gilt block letters. See Figure 24.7.
Panther			
Phantom #1	No headboards or trailboards. Stem - A simple carved vine, terminating in a billet, forms the head. See Figure 24.4. Stern - Tastefully ornamented with gilded carved work.		
Queen of Clippers #1	No headboards or trailboards. Stern - Tastefully ornamented with gilded carved work.	Red Jacket #19,31, 46,47	No headboards or trailboards. Stern - Amidship, on the moulding, the bust of an [American] Indian, which surmounted her name. Carved and gilded scroll work, chastely executed, extended a total of forty-eight feet around her stern, also running vertically on each side of the sternpost. See Figure 24.7.
Queen of the Pacific #32	Vessel has headboards and trailboards. Name - Appears high on headboards. Trailboards - Descend down and aft to the location of the hawse holes and are ornamented with graceful carved work. The above information is taken from a painting reproduced in Ref.32.	Robin Hood	
		Rocket Bark	
Queen of the Seas #1,32	No headboards or trailboards. Stem - The pedestal upon which the figurehead stands is ornamented with gilded carved work. Catheads - On the end of each cathead is the representation of the sun (probably gilded). See Figure 24.6. Stern - Ornamented with gilded fancy work.	Roebuck #1	Apparently no headboards or trailboards. Quarter pieces - Of cast composition metal, flowered and edged with gilding. Stern - Splendidly ornamented with carved gilt work, conspicuous among which is the head of a roebuck, in bas-relief.
		Romance of the Sea #1,42	No headboards or trailboards. Stern - Tastefully ornamented with gilded carved work.
		Santa Claus #1	No headboards or trailboards. Stern - Tastefully ornamented.
Quickstep Bark		Saracen #1	No headboards or trailboards. Stern - Ornamented with shields and other implements of Eastern warfare, all gilded.

Table 24.1. *Continued.*

Vessel & Ref.#	Hull ornamentation	Vessel & Ref.#	Hull ornamentation
<u>Sea Bird</u> Bark #1	Headboards - Outlined by the extended mouldings of her main rail and planksheer which terminate in a point aft of her figurehead. Trailboards - Descend down and aft terminating around her navel hoods. They are ornamented with gilded carved work. Stern - Ornamented with an arch of gilded carved work. An eagle is in its apex and below, her name and port of hail (Boston) are painted white.	<u>Southern Cross</u> #1,3	Headboards - Outlined by the extended mouldings of her main rail and planksheer which terminate in a point aft of her figurehead. Name - Carved in gilded letters on her headboards. Trailboards - Descend down and aft to embrace the hawse holes and are ornamented with gilded carved work which also encircles the hawse holes. Catheads - Gilded carved work on the ends. Quarters - Ship's name is carved in gilded letters on quarter boards, each side. Stern - Beautifully ornamented with carved and gilded scroll work.
<u>Seaman's Bride</u> #4,57	Headboards - Outlined by the extended mouldings of her main rail and planksheer which terminate in a point aft of her figurehead. Trailboards - Descend down and aft to embrace the hawse holes and are ornamented with carved and (apparently) gilded scroll work. Carved sunbursts surround the hawse holes. See Figure 24.3. Stern - Ornamented with a carved representation, in heraldic colors, of the arms of the State of Maryland.	<u>Sovereign of the Seas</u> #1,97	No headboards or trailboards. Stem - No ornamentation on the cutwater.
<u>Sea Serpent</u> #4,32,78	Apparently no headboards or trailboards. Stern - Tastefully decorated with two green and gold, carved full length, representations of the shiny, slivery, glistening great American sea serpent, intertwined across her stern. ["Slivery" may have been intended to mean "slithery".]	<u>Spitfire</u> #1	Apparently no headboards or trailboards. Stern - Tastefully ornamented.
		<u>Staffordshire</u> #1,3	No headboards or trailboards. Name - Carved into the lower monkey rail with gilded letters. See Figure 24.1. Stem - Ref.1: No ornamentation on the cutwater. Ref.3: Gilded scroll work down and around the hawse holes. Hawse holes - Ref.1: Surrounded with gilded fleurs-de-lis. Catheads - Ref.1: Ornamented with gilded devices on the end of each cathead. Stern - A beautiful arch of gilded carved work spans its lower division, and contains a manufacturing scene of Staffordshire, and opposite, a representation of Train & Co's. store, on the end of Lewis' wharf, with a lion's head on each side, and other devices below. Her name and port of hail (Boston) follow the sweep of the arch, and are inside of it.
<u>Shooting Star</u> #1,90	Headboards - Outlined by the extended mouldings of her main rail and planksheer which terminate in a point aft of her figurehead. Name - Carved in gilded letters on the headboards. Trailboards - Descend to the area of the hawse holes and are ornamented with gilded carved work, interwoven with which are representations of the chase. See Figure 24.3. Stern - Ornamented amidship with a female figure represented feeding an eagle, relieved with stars on each side, and other tasteful ornaments; and her name and port of hail (Boston) are carved and painted white on the archboard.		
<u>Sierra Nevada</u> #1,78	No headboards or trailboards. Stern - Tastefully ornamented with the representation of an eagle on the wing, bearing in his beak a scroll, upon which are engraved the ship's name and port of hail (Boston).	<u>Stag Hound</u> #1,4,42	No headboards or trailboards. Stem - No ornamentation on the cutwater. Hawse holes - Surrounded by chaste carved work. Catheads - Ends ornamented with gilded carved work. Stern - Ornamented with a stag, her name and other devices, neatly executed.
<u>Silver Star</u> #1	No headboards or trailboards. Name - Carved into the monkey rail of each bow and tastefully gilded. See Figure 24.1. Stern - Is spanned with an arch of gilded carved work, in the center of which is the representation of a star. The upper strake of her waist forms the base of her stern, and into this strake is carved her name and port of hail (Boston), both painted white.	<u>Star of the Union</u> #1,5	No headboards or trailboards. Stem - Cutwater relieved on each side by the American shield [probably colored proper] and other gilded carved work immediately aft of figure Catheads - Ornamented with gilded carved work. Stern - Finely ornamented with gilded carved work and a medallion bust of our great statesman (Daniel Webster).

Table 24.1. *Continued.*

Vessel & Ref.#	Hull ornamentation	Vessel & Ref.#	Hull ornamentation
Starr King		Tornado	
Storm King #1,32	No headboards or trailboards. Stem - Cutwater, at the base of the figurehead, is ornamented with carved work. Catheads - Ornamented with gilded carved work on the end. Stern - Spanned by an arch of beautiful carved work. Her name and port of hail (Boston) are painted white below.	Uncowah War Hawk #1	No headboards or trailboards. Stern - Ornamented with a circular picture representing a war-hawk picking up an unfortunate fish.
Sultana Bark #1	No headboards. Trailboards - Ornamented with gilded carved work. Stern - Spanned by an arch of carved work. A full figure of a lady in reclining posture, amidship; the horn of plenty, bales, etc. surrounding the figure.	Water Witch #1,32,97	No headboards or trailboards. Stem - On either side of the cutwater the angles are filled with gilded carved work, embracing her name. See Figure 24.1. Name - Carved into the gilded work aft of the cutwater. See Figure 24.1. Stern - Elaborately ornamented with carved work, embracing a sea scene with three water witches in the center.
Sunny South #32,42	Trailboards - Her elongated figurehead may have developed into trailboards.	Western Continent	
Surprise #1,28,32, 42,83	Refs.1,28: No headboards or trailboards mentioned. Ref.32: Two paintings which are not in agreement. Ref.42: Plan includes headboards and trailboards. Ref.83: Reproduction of painting shows headboards, trailboards, and name on bow and quarters. Note: Ref.1 is an on-site description of the ship.	Westward Ho #1,4	No headboards or trailboards. Stem - The pedestal upon which the figurehead stands is decorated with ornamental flowering. Name - Carved on the curve of each bow. See Figure 24.1. Stern - Ornamented with some handsome gilt scroll work, twining around the letters composing her name.
Swallow #1	No headboards or trailboards. Stern - Tastefully ornamented with gilded carved work.	West Wind #1,32	No headboards or trailboards. Stern - Spanned by an arch of gilded carved work, in the apex of which is the representation of a ship, under all drawing sail, by the wind. See Figure 24.7.
Sweepstakes #42,97	Headboards - Outlined by the extended mouldings of her waist rail (located midway between the planksheer and main rail) and her planksheer. Name - Carved on a name board located on the aft end of the headboards. See Figure 24.1 Trailboards - Descend down and aft to embrace the hawse holes and are ornamented with carved work which includes the hawse holes.	Whirlwind #1	No headboards or trailboards. Stem - The pedestal from which the figurehead seems to fly is beautifully ornamented with flowered carved work, tastefully gilded.
Sword Fish #24,32	No headboards or trailboards.		Name - On each bend of the bow is a representation of a blue flag, hung in curved folds from a gilded staff, and her name in gilded letters is on the flag. See Figure 24.1. Catheads - Tastefully ornamented on the end. Stern - Ornamented with a beautiful spread eagle covered with gilding.
Syren #3,32,97	Apparently had headboards. Trailboards - Ornamented with carved gilded scroll work. Name - Carved into the monkey rail of each bow forward of the catheads. Stern - Finely carved representation of oak branches interwoven and gilded,in the center of which are her name and port of hail (Salem) in gilded block letters. See Figure 24.7.	Whistler #1	No headboards or trailboards. Bow - No ornamentation forward, including the omission of a figurehead. See Figure 24.2. Stern - No ornamentation. Her name and port of hail (Boston) carved in gilt letters. See Figure 24.7. Note: Whistler may have been the most naked of all clippers.
Telegraph #1	Headboards - Outlined by the extended mouldings of her main rail and planksheer which were carried forward in excellent style to the figurehead. Trailboards - May have been installed. The only vague reference is that "Her ornamental work fore and aft, corresponds well with the beauty of her hull."	Wildfire Bark #1	Stern - Ornamented with carved work.
Thatcher Magoun #1	No headboards or trailboards. Stern - Tastefully ornamented with gilded carved work.		

Table 24.1. *Continued.*

Vessel & Ref.#	Hull ornamentation	Vessel & Ref.#	Hull ornamentation
Wild Pigeon #1,32,42	No headboards or trailboards. Oculi – An oculus (eye) in the eyes of the ship below the planksheer moulding on each bow, looking out upon the ocean. (Probably carved and painted in natural colors.) See Figure 24.5. Stern – Beautifully ornamented with gilded carved work and two gilded pigeons.	Young America #71,72, 97	No headboards. Trailboards – No conventional trailboards. Instead carved patriotic themes, colored proper, were located between the main rail and the planksheer, on each bow, immediately abaft the figurehead. Port and starboard representations were not alike. See Figure 24.4. The designs are drawn from photographs of the vessel. Name – Carved into the monkey rail of each bow forward of the catheads. Catheads – End of each cathead is ornamented with a United States shield of stars and stripes colored proper. From photo. See Figure 24.6 Stern – A gilded spread eagle, facing to starboard, in bold relief amidship, between the main rail and planksheer, flanked by ornate gilded scroll work extending to the bumkins. Her name and port of hail (New York) below between the planksheer and the stern knuckle. From photograph. See Figure 24.7.
Wild Ranger #1	No headboards or trailboards. Stern – Tastefully ornamented with gilded carved work, in the center of which is a woodland scene, with a hunter, rifle in hand, just about rising to follow the chase.		
Wild Rover			
Winged Arrow #1	Headboards – Outlined by the extended mouldings of her main rail and planksheer, making a neat finish in the rear of the head. No trailboards. Stern – Ornamented with gilded carved work, emblematical of her name.	Young Turk Bark #1	No headboards or trailboards. Stern – Is set off with gilded carved work.
Winged Racer #1,4	No headboards or trailboards. Stern – Tastefully ornamented with gilded carved work.		
Witchcraft #1	Headboards – The mouldings of her main rail and planksheer are carried forward in unbroken sweep, until they terminate in the head. Trailboards – Descend down and aft to embrace the hawse holes and are ornamented with carved branches along their length and around the hawse holes, all tastefully bronzed. Stern – Ornamented with a huge serpent, which is represented in the act of uncoiling himself for a march. (Quite a mix of metaphors.)		
Witch of the Wave #1,42	No headboards. Trailboards – In place of trailboards branches of gold descend from the figurehead pedestal and encircle the hawse holes. See Figure 24.3. Name – Carved into the monkey rail in gilded letters, close abaft the bowsprit, on each bow. Oculi – An oculus (eye) glowering from each bow, as if scanning the foaming deep before. (Probably carved and painted in natural colors.) See Figure 24.5. Catheads – A gilded head on the end of each cathead. Quarters – Her name is carved in her bulwarks in gilded letters between the main and mizzen rigging. See Figure 24.1. Stern – Ornamented with a representation of her name (a witch), floating in a shell, with an imp, on the larboard side, riding a dolphin, and on the opposite side other members of the finny family sporting in the sea. Above these is her name, in gilded letters, and below it her port of hail (Salem), with a star on each side and a wreath of roses below, the whole enclosed in a gilded frame. The principal figures are painted white, relieved with gilding on either side.		
Wizard #1,4,32	Apparently no headboards or trailboards. Stern – Tastefully ornamented with gilded carved work.		

368

(text continued from page 360)

of actual and mythological representation of life, all painted "proper," the heraldic term denoting natural color, and generally depicting a theme.

This extravagance was superseded in the clipper ships by more modest embellishments. The ornate archboard, with its colorful story, was superseded to a great extent by carved garlands, vines, scrolls, and tracery that surrounded the vessel's name and port of hail, which were generally centered on the transom. White or gilding were the new colors of choice.

Some vessels featured central figures or, perhaps, medallions having a specific significance. Many of these central motifs were carved and painted "proper." However, this was an occasional rather than a usual occurrence.

This newer form of ornamentation lent itself well to vessels with round or elliptical counter sterns, and most ships had some sort of decoration in this area.

In many cases the personality of the shipbuilder was apparent in the subject matter of ornamentation. William H. Webb was most partial to patriotic themes, and his patriotism was conveyed through the use of flags, shields, official seals, and eagles, and, in the case of *Young America*, in the name of the vessel itself. Figure 24.7 illustrates a selection of stern motifs, some reconstructed from verbal descriptions and one taken from photographs.

The reports of Duncan MacLean provide the most profuse and far-reaching record of the ornamentation of many of the vessels included in this book. Table 24.1 compiles these descriptions and those from other sources and represents a well-rounded picture of clipper ship ornamentation. Figureheads are covered separately in Chapter 25.

Except for ornamentation drawn from photographs, all illustrations in Figures 24.1 through 24.7 have been reconstructed by the author from descriptions appearing in the noted references. There is no pretense that these designs are factual. However, the references generally spell out the principal parts of the design motifs, and from these descriptions it is not difficult to develop the designs into a picture form which, if nothing else, will portray the intention of the scheme, conveying a credible concept of the artistry that embellished each vessel. In such reconstruction, each reader or artist will have his own opinion of the final result.

Chapter Twenty-Five

FIGUREHEADS AND CARVED STEMHEADS

THE FIGUREHEAD, IN ONE FORM or another, can be traced back to antiquity. In the earliest times it might hardly be recognizable as such. As ship's form developed over the centuries, the evolving treatment of the prow led to changes in such decorations, mostly to accommodate the changes in the hull. However, the figurehead as we now know it was a definite ornamental appendage greatly in evidence by the time the ships of the Spanish Armada engaged in battle with the English fleet of Queen Elizabeth I in 1588. Ships of both fleets were adorned with figures which fit our present-day depiction of a figurehead.

Merchant ships, not having at their disposal the considerable riches of the royal exchequer, generally did not indulge in the luxury of the ornamental figurehead until about the year 1800. It was, however, an appealing bit of decoration which served to identify a particular vessel, to display the skill of its carver, and to show off the pride and prestige of the vessel's owner.

Ship owners, however pragmatic and tight-fisted they might be, generally took great pride in their ships and saw them as extensions of themselves or their companies. With this attitude they were very critical, being well satisfied with what pleased their eye and very unhappy with anything that disturbed them; an example of this is related later in this chapter, concerning the figurehead of *Gazelle*.

Figurehead design passed through various stages, beginning in the seventeenth century. Except for some relatively few ships which carried very ornate and fanciful figureheads, the first standard form was that of the lion. This was later superseded by carvings that were representative of the name of the ship, generally a famous man. Toward 1800 classical names were introduced, and this opened the Pandora's box of the shipcarvers' imagination. The art of figurehead carving flourished during the era of the clipper ship. As in every other facet of this class of ship, excess was the norm.

It was probably in the clippers that the female figure as a subject for figurehead carving reached its zenith. It has been noted that "Women were, if anything, rather more popular than men; and very often reflected a superstition of seamen by having one or both breasts bared. Women in general were thought to be unlucky on board ship, but a naked woman was supposed to be able to calm a storm at sea."[40] Maybe. Naked women are not noted for calming anything. However, other observations notwithstanding, it is interesting to note that, of the ships in this book, the following quantities are pertinent. Excluding figureheads of human form that were carved to represent the vessel's namesake, there are twenty-nine females, either bust or full length, and only eleven males. This number of females exceeds any other form, since the always-popular American eagle appears in twenty instances, and the *billet* (see Figure 25.1) in all of its plain or fancy forms, is noted in twenty-one vessels. The remainder of the ships were fitted with a random assortment of creatures and fanciful themes. With certain ships, no record remains.

Between 1850 and 1856, the bows of the clippers generally became plainer as each year went by. The cumbersome headboards, which were subject to destruction at sea, and the graceful trailboards, with their expensive carvings, were diminished for pragmatic reasons, as described in Chapter 24. However, the practice of decorating a ship's bow did not disappear completely. Figureheads and stemheads often received lavish treatment at the hands of the carvers. These treatments, where known, are listed in Table 25.1.

In general, the choice of coloring—white, gilded, or proper—was a matter settled between the ship owner and the woodcarver. The choice of wood to be used was probably the carver's option. Little appears to be recorded on this score. However, such material can be identified in any one of many figureheads that survive in museums. It is known generally that white pine, oak, and cherry lend themselves well to this purpose.

Figureheads are a subject in their own right and much detailed information can be found in *Shipcarvers of North America*[90] and *Figureheads and Ship Carvings at Mystic Seaport*.[91]

(text continued on page 377)

Table 25.1. *Figureheads and carved stemheads.*

Note: The descriptions in this table are taken verbatim from the various
appropriate references unless otherwise qualified.

Vessel & Ref.#	Description
Alarm #1,98	Ref.1 A full female figure, represented blowing a trumpet. Ref.98 Also states "in flowing drapery."
Amphitrite #1	A full female figure, rather fashionably decked, intended to represent the Rib of Neptune, trident and all.
Andrew Jackson #32	An image of the soldier-statesman for whom she was named.
Antelope #1	A carved and gilded billet which grows out of the ornamental work upon the trailboards.
Asa Eldridge #1	A bust of Capt. Eldridge, relieved by gilded carved work.
Bald Eagle #1	A large gilded eagle on the wing, for a head, and it forms the best and most beautiful head that we have yet seen upon any clipper.
Belle of the West #1	A graceful full female figure, robed in vestments of white, fringed with gold.
Beverly #3	A finely carved and gilded billet head.
Black Hawk #62,63	A carved stem head representing a hawk's head. Sketched from photographs which are black and white but indicate that the figure was colored proper. See Figure 25.2.
Blue Jacket #5,86	Ref.5 A carved figure of a sailor, with a blue jacket. In the left hand he holds the American flag, in the right a cutlass. Ref.86 "On Decmeber 8, 1871 the Blue Jacket's figure head was found washed up on the shore of Rottnest Island, off Tremantle, Western Australia. Part of it was charred by fire, but there was no mistaking its identity, which was described as a man from the waist up in old sailor's costume, a blue jacket with yellow buttons, the jacket open at the front, no waistcoat, loose shirt and large knotted handkerchief around the neck, a broad belt and large square buckle and cutlass hilt at the side."
Bonita #1	A neatly carved and gilded billet, formed of the cutwater itself. Additional comment by the reporter - "How beautifully the dashing clipper Westward Ho would have looked, end on, with such a head, instead of the poor Indian slung by the middle, which now mars her bow. We hope, for the honor of Boston, that Neptune will appropriate the said Indian to himself , before the ship returns to the United States."

Vessel & Ref.#	Description
Bounding Billow Bark #1	A bust of Neptune.
Celestial #2	A flying bird head.
Challenge #1,32,99	Ref.1 A gilded eagle represented on the wing. Ref.99 An Admiralty take-off of her lines at London, in November, 1852 shows this bird to be seventeen feet long, from tip of beak to tip of extended wings. This take-off is noted in Ref.32. See Figure 25.2.
Challenger #1	A full female figure, in vestments of white fringed with gold.
Champion of the Seas #1,28	Ref.1 A full figure of a sailor, with his hat in his right hand, and his left hand extended. Ref.28 A tall, square-built sailor, with dark curly hair and bronzed clean-shaven face. A black belt with a massive brass buckle supported his white trousers, which were as tight about the hips as the skin of an eel, and had wide, bell-shaped bottoms that almost hid his black polished pumps. He wore a loose-fitting blue-and-white checked shirt, with wide, rolling collar, and black neck handkerchief of ample size, tied in the most rakish of square knots with long flowing ends. But perhaps the most impressive of this mariner's togs were his dark-blue jacket, and the shiny tarpaulin hat which he waved aloft in the grip of his brawny, tattoed right hand.
Charger #1	A carved and gilded billet head.
Charmer #1	A gilded serpent. Additional comment by the reporter - "whose tongue sticks out as if he had just swallowed a tumbler of lake Cochituate."
Cleopatra #1	A full figure of Cleopatra, in robes of purest white, edged with gold and other ornaments.
Climax #1	A gilded eagle on the wing.
Coeur de Lion #1	A full figure of the lion-hearted monarch [Richard I, of England], in armor.
Comet #24,92	A carved stem head representing a shooting star. See Figure 25.2.
Cyclone #3	An elegantly carved female figure.
Daring #1,32	Ref.1 A full figure of an ancient free-trader, with the implements of his craft. Ref.32 The representation of a pirate. (The origin of this description is unknown.)

Table 25.1. *Continued.*

Vessel & Ref.#	Description	Vessel & Ref.#	Description
Dauntless #1	The full figure of an aerial nymph, with outstretched wings, and robed in flowing vestments of white, confined around the waist with a girdle of gold; and on her head a chaplet of flowers, also blazoned with gold. She is placed to correspond with the flare of the bow.	Endeavor #1	No figurehead. Her cutwater is ornamented.
		Eringo Bark #1	A gilded sea-crow, or some other new bird, unknown to natural history.
		Eureka	
Donald McKay #1,87, 91	Ref.1 A full figure of a Highlander, "all plaided and plumed in the tartan array" of the ancient McKay. Ref.91 A Scottish Highlander in Balmoral bonnet and kilt, a red jacket and plaid stockings. His left hand is on chest, right hand clenching the hilt of a claymore. See Figure 25.3. This figurehead is prominently displayed in the Stillman Building at Mystic Seaport, and wears the following color scheme: Red jacket with brown buttons; green plaid kilt (the McKay tartan); knee stockings matching the kilt; blue Balmoral bonnet with green head band; black belt with silver buckle, worn bandolier fashion; black Balmorals (laced walking shoes); silver claymore with brown basket hilt; tawny complexion; "reddish" hair and beard. Color photos appear in refs. 87 and 91.	Fair Wind #1	A full figure of Aurora, represented lifting the veil of night to usher in the morning, _____. The figure is well executed, is painted white, relieved with gilding, and is placed to correspond with the rake of the bow.
		Fearless	
		Fleet Wing #1	A gilded eagle on the wing.
		Flyaway #2	A giant pair of bird wings straddling the stem, one wing on each side, indicating flight over the waves.
		Flying Arrow #1	A carved and gilded billet-head.
		Flying Childers #1	Emblematical of her name, she has the representation of a race-horse for a head.
		Flying Cloud #1,98	Ref.1 The full figure of an angel on the wing, with a trumpet raised to her mouth. (There is no indication as to which hand holds the trumpet.) Ref.98 The white robed figure of an angel blowing a long, slender trumpet.
Don Quixote #32	A billet head.		
Eagle #5	A beautifully carved spread eagle, the wings forming the trailboards, the feet resting on the planksheer moulding.		
Eagle Wing #1	No figurehead. Her cutwater is ornamented.	Flying Dragon #1,32	Ref.1 A gilded bird with a dart in its mouth. Ref.32 A typical Chinese dragon, with open mouth, from which a dart-like tongue protruded.
Edwin Forrest #1	A full figure of the great tragedian [Edwin Forrest], represented in the character of Spartacus, painted white and relieved with gilding. The face is slightly turned to port, the right foot is advanced and in his hand is the appropriate sword. _____ The expression of the countenance, the form of the head, neck and chest are admirable, and although the lower parts of the figure and its attitude are rather stiff, yet these were controlled by the limited space of the pedestal, and the fore rake of the vessel.	Flying Dutchman #24	Apparently a billet head.
		Flying Eagle #1	A gilded eagle on the wing.
		Flying Fish #1,28,98	Ref.1 The representation of a flying fish for a head, neatly carved and burnished with gold and green. Ref.28 A fish on the wing, of life-like color and giving a vivid sense of speed. Ref.98 A beautifully carved green and gold fish arched just the shape of the stem as if shooting up out of the sea.
Electric Spark #1	A full female figure, painted white, relieved with gilding, represented directing the lightning. It is inclined forward, and completes the outward spring of the cutwater.		
Ellen Foster #1,32	Ref.1 A full figure of the lady whose name she bears. Ref.32 A representation of the wife of the builder.		
Empress of the Sea #1,4	Ref.1 A full female figure, arrayed in flowing vestments of white, fringed with gold, placed in an easy and airy attitude, and forming a beautiful ornament to the bow. Her left hand extended grasps the globe - her right hand, reposing by her side, holds the sceptre of the sea. Ref.4 Describes the globe as "a golden sphere".	Flying Mist #1	A full female figure, in vestments of flowing white fringed with gold.
		Galatea #1	A full female figure, standing on tip-toe, and robed in vestments of flowing white, fringed with gold. See Figure 25.3. (Ref.87 contains a color plate of this figurehead.) This figurehead is displayed in The Mariners Museum, Newport News, Virginia.

Table 25.1. *Continued.*

Vessel & Ref.#	Description	Vessel & Ref.#	Description
Game Cock #1,28,32	Ref.1 A large, carved and gilded Game Cock, represented in the act of crowing, perched on the forward extreme. Ref.28 A fighting bird with outstretched neck and head, apparently eager for combat. Ref.32 A game cock, with outstretched neck and head as though ready for any contest.	Great Republic #4,10, 87,91	Ref.4 The representation of an eagle, as if emerging from below the bowsprit. Ref.10 Refers to "the national eagle". (See comments in text.) Ref.87 A color plate of the original figurehead. Brown head feathers, tawny beak. See Figure 25.2. Ref.91 The eagle's head ____ with beak curving over the open mouth, remarkable detail in the feathers, and is over five feet long by two feet six inches high. The original figurehead is now displayed in the Mallory Building, Mystic Seaport.
Gazelle #2,32	Ref.2 A gazelle head. Ref.32 A billethead. Robert L. Taylor, of Taylor & Merrill, her owners, was very emphatic in his condemnation of the inartistic figurehead originally attached, so it was removed and a billet substituted.	Great Republic #28 (rebuilt)	A carved billet head. (See comments in text.)
		Henry Hill Bark #1	A gilded eagle, with her name upon a scroll in its beak.
Gem of the Ocean #1,32	Ref.1 A carved and gilded head. Ref.32 A billet substituted for a figurehead.	Herald of the Morning #1	A full figure of Aurora for a head, placed to correspond with the inclination of the cutwater.
Golden Eagle #1	A gilded eagle on the wing.	Hoogly #1	A full female figure head, placed to correspond with the rake of the stem, painted white in flowing vestments, with her right arm extended, and a gilded globe in her hand.
Golden Fleece (2nd) #1,32	Ref.1 A full figure of a warrior knight, placed to correspond with the rake of the stem, and painted white. Ref.32 States "a knight in armor".	Hurricane #4,32	Ref.4 A very handsome eagle's head with a ribbon flowing from its mouth, upon which is her name in gilt letters. Ref.32 States "a gilded eagle's head".
Golden Light #1	A torch-staff, grasped by a golden hand, and from the end blazes a golden light. The design is certainly original for a ship's head, and its workmanship is really excellent. It looks strangely, but it is so well made that no one can find fault with it.	Indiaman #1	A full figure, intended to represent a native of Japan.
		Intrepid #2	An eagle head.
Golden West #1	A gilded eagle on the wing.	Invincible #4,32	Ref.4 The liberty cap with the American coat of arms, forming the space from head to stem. See Figure 24.4. Ref.32 A liberty cap as a billet head, backed by the American coat of arms.
Grace Darling #1	A full female figure in vestments of flowing white, fringed with gold.		
		James Baines #1	A bust of her namesake, which was carved in Liverpool, and which is said by those who know the original, to be an excellent likeness. It is blended with the cutwater, is relieved with gilded carved work, and forms a neat and appropriate ornament to the bow.
		John Bertram #1	She has a long and rakish head, with an eagle perched on its extreme. The noble bird is represented with outstretched wings, ready to soar aloft.

Table 25.1. *Continued.*

Vessel & Ref.#	Description	Vessel & Ref.#	Description
John Gilpin #1	A carved and gilded billet head.	Nightingale #3,28,32	Ref.3 A finely carved figure of Jenny Lind, painted white, set off with gilded ornaments; in the right hand, which is extended, is a gilded bird, representing the nightingale with half spread wings.
John Land			
John Stuart #4	No figurehead or billethead. Her head is ornamented with neatly carved and gilt scroll work.		Refs.28,32 Both describe her figurehead as being a bust of Jenny Lind, for whom the ship was named.
John Wade #1	A bust of her namesake for her head; but we think the artist has failed to produce a correct likeness.		Note: The description quoted in ref.3 suggests that it may be suspect and inadvertently includes some details of her stern ornamentation.
Joseph Peabody #1	The king of birds for a head.		
King Fisher #1	The continuation of the cutwater carved and gilded into a neat billet head.	Noonday #1	A neatly carved billet-head.
Lady Franklin		Northern Light #28	The full-length figure of an angelic creature in flowing white drapery, one graceful arm extended above her head, and bearing in her slender hand a torch with golden flame.
Lamplighter Bark #1	A gilded eagle, represented as about spreading his wings for a soar aloft.		
Lightfoot #1	A full female figure, in flowing vestments of white, fringed with gold.	Ocean Express #1	A large gilded spread eagle.
Lightning #1,28	Ref.1 A full female figurehead, placed to correspond with her fore rake.	Ocean Pearl #1	A neatly carved and gilded billet, and its lower outline is the continuation of the moulding of the planksheer.
	Ref.28 A beautiful full-length figure of a young woman holding a golden thunder-bolt in her outstretched hand, the flowing white drapery of her graceful form and her streaming hair completing the fair and noble outline of the bow.	Ocean Telegraph #5	A beautiful full length female figure represented emerging from a cloud, while the lightning plays around.
		Onward #1	The Goddess of Liberty, robed in the American ensign, is placed to correspond with the fore-rake of the vessel, the right hand pointing forward while the left grasps the emblems of harvest, and one foot on the globe.
Mameluke #1	The full figure of a Mameluke warrior, placed to correspond with her fore rake.		
Mary Robinson		Osborne Howes	
Mastiff #1	A full figure of a well-fed mastiff, on the lookout.	Panther	
Mermaid Bark #1	A mermaid, with comb and glass [mirror] in hand, as if in the act of saying - "Sheer off, sheer off, bold mariner, you are too nigh the land". It is placed to correspond with the rake of the stem.	Phantom #1	A billet forms her head, entwined in a simple vine.
		Queen of Clippers #1	A queenly figure for a head, decked in right regal style.
Morning Light #1	The full figure of an archer, "With bended bow, and quiver full of arrows", placed to correspond with her fore rake. See Figure 25.3.	Queen of the Pacific	
Mystery #1	The representation of a mermaid emerging from the sea, with a hand raised over her head, as if beckoning her lover to approach.	Queen of the Seas #1	A full female figure, crowned, and robed in flowing vestments of white, the folds of which are gathered in front, and held in the right hand, while in the left she holds her wand, which, instead of a trident, bears on its end a glittering star, as much as to say - "Westward the star of empire takes its way".
		Quickstep Bark #1	A female figure, placed to correspond with the rake of the stem.
		Racehorse Bark #1	A carved and gilded billet head.

Table 25.1. *Continued.*

Vessel & Ref.#	Description	Vessel & Ref.#	Description
Racer #3,4,32,98	Ref.3 A finely carved and gilded representation of a horse's head. Ref.4 A carved and gilded figure of a racehorse. Refs.32,98 (Neither is a contemporary source.) A gilded head only, of a race horse.	Sea Serpent #4,28, 32	Ref.4 A large gilded eagle, with outstretched wings. Ref.32 An eagle. Ref.28 A long slender serpent, whose life-like, slimy-looking body, picked out in shades of green and gold, suggested his recent escape from the waters of one of the summer resorts along the Atlantic coast. Note: The description in ref.28 appears to be more applicable to her stern ornamentation as described in refs.4 and 32.
Radiant #1	A carved and gilded billet head.		
Raven #3,32	Ref.3 A finely carved figure of the Raven, painted black. Ref.32 A billet head.		
		Shooting Star #1	A full female figure ____ represented in white vestments, spangled with gilded stars upon the waist; her hair is confined by a gilded zone, in front of which the hair descends loosely over the shoulders - her right foot is advanced, and rests upon a gilded globe, and her right arm is extended, with the hand pointing onward. She is placed to correspond with the rake of the stem.
Red Jacket #19,46	Ref.19 A massive, full figurehead of the Indian Chief whose name she bears. Ref.46 Sagoyewatha, a Seneca Indian chieftain who always wore a red jacket.		
Robin Hood #32	A life-size image of Robin Hood showing his bended bow.	Sierra Nevada #1	A full figure of an Indian warrior, appropriately colored, is placed to correspond with her fore rake.
Rocket Bark		Silver Star #1	A full female figure in flowing vestments of white fringed with gold.
Roebuck #1	A carved and gilded billet.	Southern Cross #1	A gilded eagle on the wing forms the termination of the head.
Romance of the Sea #1,28	Ref.1 A small female figure, intended to represent Romance, with the name of Scott (Sir Walter) on one side, and Cooper (James Fenimore) on the other - the greatest romancers of the century. Ref.28 The full length figure of an ancient navigator, whose original might have stood on the high poop of Magellan's flag-ship, with head bent forward and right hand raised to shade his eager eyes, as he gazed upon an unknown land in an uncharted sea.	Sovereign of the Seas #1,32	Ref.1 The figure of a sea god, half man, half fish, with a conch shell raised to his mouth, as if in the act of blowing it. The figure accords with the sheer of the bow. Ref.32 States that the figurehead was painted bronze.
		Spitfire #1	A gilded eagle.
Santa Claus #1	A full figure of the imaginary gentleman whose name she bears, laden with presents in every pocket, and represented smoking a gilded pipe.	Staffordshire #1,3	Ref.1 An angelic witch upon the wing, robed in white vestments. Ref.3 An angelic witch, painted white. Note: The term "angelic witch" appears to be the perfect oxymoron.
Saracen #1	The full figure of a Saracen warrior, placed to correspond with the rake of the stem.		
Sea Bird Bark #1	A gilded eagle on the wing.	Stag Hound #1	A carved and gilded stag hound, represented panting in the chase.
Seaman's Bride #4,57, 90	Ref.4 A gilt eagle, with wings thrown back, as though stooping for flight, raked in line with the stem. Ref.57 A daguerreotype of the vessel's bow. This is reproduced in ref.90. See Figure 25.2. This daguerreotype is in the Maryland Historical Society.	Star of the Union #1	A bust of Daniel Webster, which is a good likeness.
		Starr King	

Table 25.1. *Continued.*

Vessel & Ref.#	Description	Vessel & Ref.#	Description

Storm King #1,32

Ref.1
A full figure of the King of Storms, pointing
with his right hand to the deep, while his left
hand, by his side, holds the trident of the sea.
The figure corresponds in attitude with the rake
of the bow.

Ref.32
The reproduction of a "shipping card" advertising
the sailing of Storm King from New York for San
Francisco. The card, in color, features a representation of the figurehead and is in the collection
of the Peabody Museum, Salem, Mass.

Note: The position of the arms in ref.32 is depicted
opposite to the description in ref.1.

Sultana Bark #1   A carved and gilded billet-head.

Sunny South #32,42

Ref.32
A scaly monster.

Ref.42
A gilded sea-serpent figurehead.

Surprise #1,28

Ref.1
An eagle, represented in the act of spreading his
wings for a soar aloft.

Ref.28
A finely carved and gilded flying eagle.

Swallow #1,32

Ref.1
A full female figure.

Ref.32
A woman draped in white.

Sweepstakes

Sword Fish #2   A billet head.

Syren #3,32

Ref.3
A finely carved and gilded representation of a
Mermaid.

Ref.32
Originally the image of a mermaid for a figurehead,
but this was carried away at an early date and an
eagle's head was substituted.

Telegraph #1   A female figure, placed in a graceful and airy
attitude.

Thatcher Magoun #1   A full bronzed figure of Thatcher Magoun, placed to
correspond with the rake of the stem - an excellent
likeness.

Tornado #3   A neatly carved figure of a game-cock.

Note: This was originally intended to be her name.

Uncowah #2   An eagle head.

War Hawk #1   A war-hawk on the wing.

Note: "War-hawk" is an Americanism which has the
same meaning as "hawk".

Water Witch #1   A female figure, in flowing vestments, tastefully
bronzed.

Western Continent

Westward Ho #1   The full figure of an Indian warrior, represented
as advancing rapidly in the chase.

Note: See Bonita for the reporter's unflattering
personal opinion of the figurehead of
Westward Ho.

West Wind #32   This vessel carried no figurehead or billethead.

Whirlwind #1   The goddess of the wind, with extended wings of gold
and robed in flowing vestments of white, fringed with
gold, and bearing a torch in her left hand.

Whistler #1   This vessel carried no figurehead or billethead.

Wildfire Bark #1   Apparently built without figurehead or billethead.

Wild Pigeon #1   A wild pigeon on the wing, represented as ready
for a soar aloft.

Wild Ranger #1   A gilded hound.

Wild Rover

Winged Arrow #1   A large gilded flying dragon displays his length
along the trailboards, and grins, with outspread
wings, a flying arrow issuing from his mouth, and
forms the termination of the head. The moulding of
the planksheer forms the lower outline of the head
boards, and makes a neat finish in the rear of the
head.

Winged Racer #1   The representation of a flying horse with extended
wings, tastefully gilded.

Witchcraft #1,28

Ref.1
A tiger, represented crouched, ready for the spring.

Ref.28
A grim Salem witch riding upon her aerial broomstick.

Witch of the Wave
#1,3,78

Ref.1
A female figure, beautiful as an houri, and placed to
correspond with the spring of the bow, ornaments her
forward. The figure is represented in flowing vestments of white, fringed with gold; and she bears
aloft a scarf, half unfurled by the breeze.

Ref.3
A finely carved female, in drapery, shielded by a
broad shell.

Ref.78
The figurehead represents a beautiful female, in
gossamer drapery, shielded by a broad shell like a
canopy, gracefully and lightly stepping on the crest
of a wave.

Table 25.1. *Continued.*

Vessel & Ref.#	Description
Wizard #1,4,32	Ref.1 The full figure of an oriental magician, with a book under his right arm, and his face is turned to the right or starboard. The figure is finely executed, stands in an easy and graceful attitude, and forms a beautiful ornament to the bow. Ref.4 Refers to the book as "his book of fate". Ref.32 Refers to the book as "his book of spells".
Young America #71	A carved stem head, substituting for a figurehead. See Figure 25.2.
Young Turk Bark #1	A full figure of a young Turk, placed to correspond with the rake of the cutwater.

(text continued from page 370)

Stemhead Decoration

During the 1850–1856 clipper period, woodcarvers remained as much a part of the nautical scene as did shipwrights and riggers, and seldom did a vessel put to sea without some form of decoration on her stemhead. There were, however, three clippers which, by contemporary description, were built with utterly naked stemheads. These were *West Wind*, *Whistler*, and the bark *Wildfire*. This, of course, does not account for vessels for which there is no description or other authentic evidence.

Closely following these three in the absence of ornament were *Comet* and *John Stuart*. *Comet* had a stemhead decorated as shown in Figure 25.2.[24, 92] This plain and self-explanatory ornamentation was probably quite accurate since, in November 1863, the ship was sold British and renamed *Fiery Star*, a name very appropriate to the rather stark head carving. *John Stuart* was described as having minimal scrollwork in the area of the stemhead.

Then followed two more vessels, *Eagle Wing* and *Endeavor*, both with some decoration on the cutwater, but naked at the head. The amount of decoration on the remaining ships could only be measured relative to each other.

In nautical terminology "nakedness," in reference to a ship's hull, particularly in the prow, refers to the absence of incidental structure and decoration. It has nothing to do with "nudity" as applied to the human body.

Billetheads and Fiddleheads

As to intricacy, the next rung on the ladder of stemhead decoration was the billethead. An apparent, but by no means conclusive, derivation of the word *billet* is from the Old French word *billette*, meaning "tree trunk." Possibly the spiral *volute* of the billethead was reminiscent of the annular rings across a section of such a piece of the tree trunk.

A form of design somewhat similar to that of the billethead was the fiddlehead, which was also known to have adorned ships' heads. The basic construction form of both of these is shown in Figure 25.1.

Based on this form, the development of the volute around the eye is the same for both types of head, with the exception that the spiral evolves in opposite directions as can be seen in the figure. The scroll, as indicated for the billethead, is of ancient origin, having been the principal feature of the capital of Greek (Ionic) columns.

Second in frequency to only the female figure as the adornment of a ship's stemhead, the billethead was a happy compromise between unimpressive nakedness and the eye-catching detail of the more glamorous figureheads. Billethead scrolls ranged from a few graceful, curling acanthus leaves following the trace of the volute, without fillets, as was the case of *Young America*, shown in Figure 25.2, to the ornate and fully exploited billethead shown in Figure 25.1. Heads like that of *Young America* were most often carved directly in the wood of the structural stemhead. The more ornate billets, like that shown in the figure, were generally larger and were fashioned by the woodcarver in his shop, after which they were fitted and bolted in the assigned position on the stem. With no prescribed rules governing the design of billetheads, there is the distinct possibility that, of

Figure 25.1. *The billethead and the fiddlehead.*

NOTE –
THIS SIMPLIFIED VOLUTE IS BASED ON THE CLASSICAL VOLUTE (REF. 107) IN WHICH THE HEIGHT IS DIVIDED INTO EIGHT PARTS, 0 THRU VIII. THE DIA- METER OF THE EYE IS FROM IV TO V. THE DIAGONALS 1–3 AND 2–4 ARE THEN DIVIDED INTO SIX PARTS EACH. THE VOLUTE IS THEN DEVELOPED IN THE MANNER SHOWN HERE. THIS RESULTS IN ONE ADDITIONAL SPIRAL.

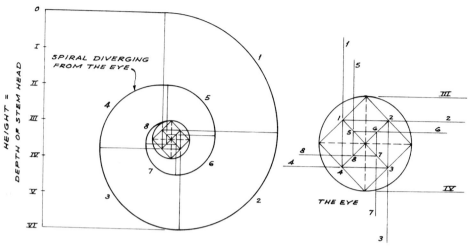

HEIGHT = DEPTH OF STEM HEAD

SPIRAL DIVERGING FROM THE EYE

THE EYE

DEVELOPMENT OF A SIMPLIFIED VOLUTE

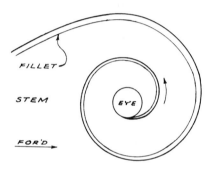

FILLET

STEM

FOR'D

EYE

FILLET SPIRALS OUT FROM EYE AND UPWARD

A BILLETHEAD VOLUTE

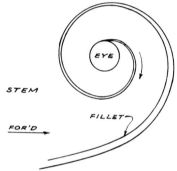

EYE

STEM

FOR'D

FILLET

FILLET SPIRALS OUT FROM EYE AND DOWNWARD

A FIDDLEHEAD VOLUTE

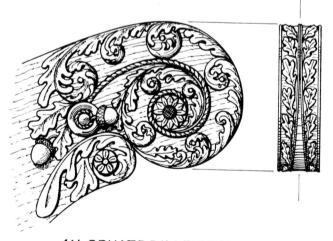

AN ORNATE BILLETHEAD

A FIDDLEHEAD DESIGN
REF. 12

all clipper ships taking to the water, no two carried identical adornment.

The fiddlehead is more easily but less satisfactorily disposed of. In all the descriptions of clipper ships and packets alike, there is no statement of any ship being adorned with a fiddlehead. In the case of the clippers, the only rather vague appearance of the fiddlehead occurs in the lines of *Herald of the Morning*.[12] As shown in her lines plan, the draftsman intended to embellish her stemhead with the design shown in Figure 25.1, which is enlarged and copied directly from the plan. This drawing illustrates the general form of the fiddlehead design. Unfortunately, this design never was perpetuated on the ship, a female figure, that of Aurora, being installed instead.

It is possible that the term *billethead* may have evolved into a generic term. If so, some ships that were described as having billetheads might actually have had fiddleheads. This, however, is supposition only and as such cannot be read into any descriptions.

Figureheads

Animals and Birds

The penultimate form of stemhead decoration was that of animal life, as exemplified in the ships that carried replicas of dragons, serpents, fishes, horses, dogs, and birds. One of these is the representation of a hawk's head from the clipper *Black Hawk*. A drawing of this head, copied from photographs of the vessel, is included in Figure 25.2.[62, 63] Even though these photographs are black-and-white, it is evident that the figurehead was colored *proper* (true to life).

There remains the American eagle, one of the three predominant forms of figurehead. The manner in which eagles were carved and the attitudes in which they were depicted were almost as numerous as the vessels that carried them. From the list of ships covered herein, three examples are portrayed in Figure 25.2. First, and perhaps foremost, is the eagle head of *Great Republic*, preserved for posterity in the Mystic Seaport Museum. It has been referred to as the "national eagle,"[10] but technically such is not the case, no matter how sincerely intended. The national or American eagle is the white-headed or bald eagle, while the color scheme of the figurehead is entirely of brown feathers, which are found in the golden eagle.

An unusual story surrounds this figurehead, a story that shows the fallibility of research sources that would ordinarily be considered reliable. As has been told earlier, *Great Republic* was set on fire at her berth on December 26, 1853, about midnight, by blazing cinders carried from another waterfront fire. Several days later she was settled on the bottom of the East River, a burned-out hulk. She was purchased, refloated,

and rebuilt. In his book *The Clipper Ship Era*, Capt. Arthur H. Clark states that the rebuilt vessel was fitted with a carved billethead and scroll, the original eagle figurehead having been destroyed.[28] The first portion of this statement is true—the rebuilt ship wore a billethead. However, fortunately for Mystic Seaport Museum and posterity, the stated loss of her original figurehead in the disastrous fire is in error. One of the facts of the fire is that it wreaked no destruction to the vessel in the area forward of the fore chains. Actually, the figurehead was removed and placed in storage when the rebuilding began, and was never reinstalled. This in itself is a fortunate incident, since, in 1872, sailing under the British flag and renamed *Denmark*, she began to leak and was abandoned at sea not far from Bermuda. The main point of this story is that, sometimes, sources that are regarded as reliable might not be correct. It is one of the pitfalls of research, and all research is made up of bits and pieces, not all of which are correct.

The second actually verifiable eagle figurehead is that of the ship *Seaman's Bride*. This was a complete bird, perched on the stemhead with wings extended. The sketch shown in Figure 25.2 is taken from a daguerreotype.[90]

Finally, there is the figure of an eagle on the wing which graced the bow of *Challenge* and is illustrated in Figure 25.2. This representation is copied from the lines plan taken off for the Admiralty when the ship was drydocked in London in 1852.[99] In this instance the assumption is that the draftsman drew what he saw.

Human Figures

The epitome of the woodcarver's art was achieved in the human figure, particularly the female figure, as noted earlier in this chapter. Here the craftsman devoted all his knowledge and skill to the vivid and accurate portrayal of his subject. Figures of specific personages, such as ship owners, shipmasters, and the wives of both, were carefully carved as accurate, recognizable likenesses of the subject. In some cases the results were not all that could be desired, but in most instances, if descriptions are to be accepted on their merit, the results were a positive endorsement of the artistry of the craftsman.

The most outstanding achievements were those figures representing mythical females, where the craftsman was free to indulge in his own ideas of beauty and grace. Out of this freedom were produced many exquisite pieces of work. Reputedly one of the finest examples of such work was the robed, female figurehead of the clipper *Shooting Star*. The ship was built by James O. Curtis at Medford, Masssachusetts, and the ornamental work was executed by Messrs. S. W. Gleason & Sons of Boston. The marine reporter describing the work made specific note that "to Mr. W.B. Gleason belongs the sole credit of having made her figurehead. He is

(text continued on page 382)

Figure 25.2. *Figureheads and carved stemheads.*

STEM HEAD
COMET
REF. 92

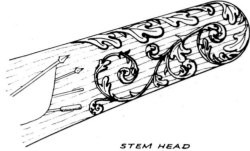

STEM HEAD
YOUNG AMERICA
REF. 71

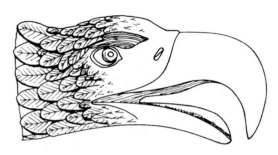

GREAT REPUBLIC
REF. 87

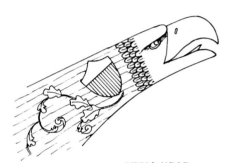

STEM HEAD
BLACK HAWK
REF. 62, 63

CHALLENGE
REF. 32, 99

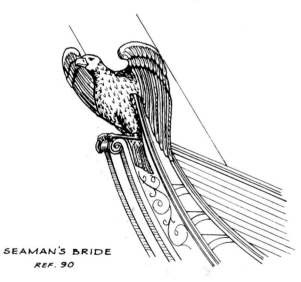

SEAMAN'S BRIDE
REF. 90

Figure 25.3. *Full-length figureheads.*

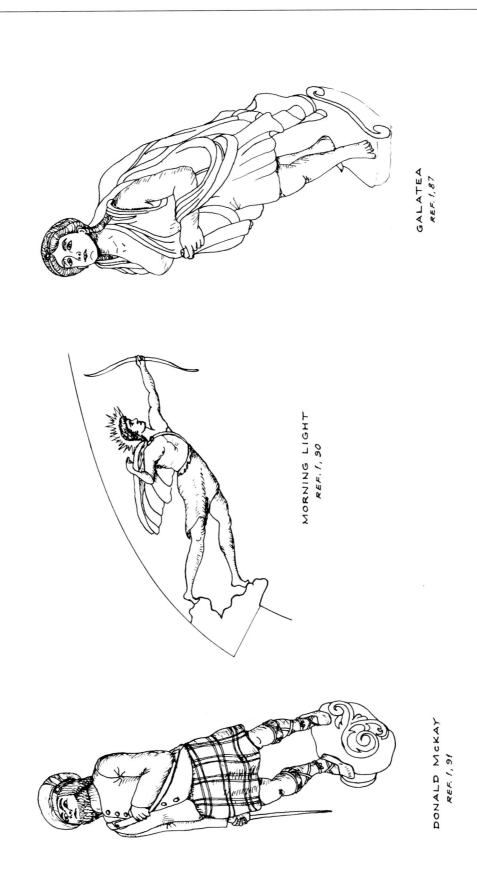

GALATEA
REF. I, 87

MORNING LIGHT
REF. I, 90

DONALD McKAY
REF. I, 91

381

(text continued from page 379)

a young artist devotedly attached to his profession, and exhibits a more refined taste in the execution of his work than is common to carvers."[1]

Figure 25.3 illustrates two typical forms of full-length figurehead which have survived to provide glimpses into the predominant treatment of figureheads as a group. The *Galatea* carving portrays the graceful beauty of a figure which is stylized in the sense that the carver was intent only upon producing the general appearance of female beauty and expression without being limited to producing a likeness of a known individual. In most figureheads of this type, the finished product was usually painted white or given a gilded finish; this tended to accent the romantic aspect of the carver's craft. The ship *Donald McKay* shows an excellent example of the realistic approach to the subject. In this type of carving the figures were made as lifelike as possible, sheer beauty for beauty's sake being shunned. As can be seen in this figure, robust, stern features replaced the smooth, serene countenance. In addition, such figures were colored proper, bringing amazing realism to the finished work.

The final illustration in Figure 25.3 is that of a proposed design of the figurehead for *Morning Light*. By its form it can be seen to present a challenge to the carver. Also evident is the potential for destruction at sea. However, when compared to the figurehead actually installed on the ship,[1] it is apparent that this design was perpetuated in wood by the carver, Mr. J.W. Mason of Boston.

Even a casual review of the figureheads described in this chapter reveals the extent to which the carvers went to produce their masterful works.

The figureheads that were carved as representations of animal life and miscellaneous subjects exhibited all of the skill and even more imagination than did the figures of humans, a form with which all viewers could readily relate. As reported in the descriptions in this chapter, the color schemes ranged from white, through gilt, to proper.

While figureheads were in no way considered to be expendable, it was not a rare occurrence for one to be carried away by the force of the elements. When this happened, its replacement appears to have been one of simpler design. It is not unreasonable to believe that such replacement may have been based on the availability of a figurehead that was already carved but had not yet been consigned. Two specific examples of this are found herein, one being *Gazelle*, the second being *Syren*. In the case of the Webb clipper *Gazelle*, the original figurehead, the head of a gazelle, was judged to be extremely inartistic by one of the ship's owners, Robert L. Taylor, of Taylor & Merrill; he had the offending figure removed from the vessel and a billet substituted. With *Syren*, the longest-lived clipper of the vessels herein, the original mermaid figure was carried away early in her career, subsequently being replaced by an eagle's head.

Most of these figurehead descriptions are taken verbatim from the reports of Duncan MacLean.[1] Written in the romantic glowing prose of the period, the articles sometime border on sentimentality and exaggerated statement. Probably in the context of the language of the times, and considering the overall excellence of the work, these reports are consistent and not overdone. However, there were occasions when even Mr. MacLean was so unimpressed that he could not forgo the opportunity to voice an adverse or unflattering opinion of the work. Three of these are noted in the list of vessels in this chapter. One was in the case of *Bonita*, whose billethead impressed him favorably and, at the same time, caused him to write quite disparagingly of the figurehead which adorned *Westward Ho*. Then there was *Charmer*, whose serpent figurehead apparently impressed him as being the image of a rather sick serpent. Finally there was the little-known clipper bark *Eringo*, whose figurehead he describes as "A gilded sea crow, or some other new bird, unknown to natural history."

The subject of figureheads, like many other reported details of the clipper ship, suffers from the discrepancies that exist between two or more descriptions of the same detail. When such a situation develops, the reader is faced with making a choice—and, in the case of figureheads, the choice cannot necessarily be resolved by the application of logic. Many figureheads bear no resemblance to the name of the vessel on which they were installed. The reader is left in a quandary tempered only by the fact that his educated guess might be the correct one. Ten ships in this table fall into this category—a rather large percentage, when one considers that the subjects were apparently described on site. For *Daring*, *Flying Dragon*, *Gazelle*, *Nightingale*, *Racer*, *Raven*, *Romance of the Sea*, *Sea Serpent*, *Witchcraft*, and *Witch of the Wave*, the enigma as to their true figurehead probably cannot be resolved beyond question. Additional information that might surface could possibly remove some ships from the list.

Chapter Twenty-Six

WEATHER DECK ARRANGEMENTS

THE WEATHER DECK ARRANGEMENTS OF the clippers were almost as varied as the number of ships in the clipper fleet. However, the variations were controlled by certain parameters, governed by the configuration of ships in general. Vessels by their nature are long and slender, to a greater or lesser degree, and must be balanced about their longitudinal centerline in order to retain stability. From earliest times, this requirement resulted in structures being symmetrically aligned about the centerline of the vessel from bow to stern.

Vessels built for specific services were arranged in a manner designed to best accommodate the service, but there developed a general scheme that could be found in almost any ship chosen at random. That there was a typical deck arrangement is not quite a fact. However, the arrangement most usually encountered among the clippers is easily ascertained from the surviving descriptions of those ships. This arrangement, starting at the bow and proceeding aft to the stern, was as follows: topgallant forecastle with capstan on and windlass under; fore hatch; foremast; large deckhouse; main hatch; mainmast; pumps; capstan; after hatch; mizzenmast; half poop deck, with or without a trunk cabin built into it; and steering apparatus at the taffrail.

The major items that influenced the weather deck arrangement were fixed structures that were relatively large, such as superimposed decks and houses, and masts which were located to suit the vessel's sailing capabilities. However, proper consideration was due the placement of the windlass, the capstans, and the steering apparatus, even though they were properly in the category of ship's outfit rather than being structures. Their function and size dictated that ample space in the proper locations be considered as vital to the operation of the vessel. With other, minor items, there was a certain amount of latitude in location along the deck.

Where known, specific identity and some details (such as size) of fittings and items of outfit are included in Chapter 27.

From this most general arrangement, of which *Cleopatra* is a typical example, there blossomed a vast array of varia-tions which appealed to the individual designers. In some vessels the topgallant forecastle was eliminated in favor of a flush deck forward. In other, rare cases the raised poop was omitted in favor of a flush deck aft. And, finally, there were vessels built with a flush weather deck, all accommodations being located in the tween-decks. There were countless minor variations in the deck arrangements, but all were accomplished in a manner guaranteed to not endanger the integrity of the ship as a whole.

The weather deck arrangements of all the ships included in this book are shown in the figures where such information is available; the sources of information are listed with each vessel. Minor embellishment, such as the indication of a companionway where one is obviously necessary, is resorted to only in instances where omission would appear to be a blatant error.

The arrangements illustrated invite comparisons between the various vessels. It becomes apparent as the list is perused that, in general, the deck arrangements were very much alike. Conversely, the ships that deviated substantially from the usual arrangement stand out very plainly. Among these are *Black Hawk* and *Comet*, with their extraordinarily long half poop decks; *Challenge*, notable for her lack of any large deck structures; *Donald McKay*, *Lightning*, and *Queen of the Seas*, all having elevated gangways connecting the forecastle deck, housetop, and poop deck, thus relieving the crew from climbing ladders when working ship; *Great Republic* (the original ship) and *Staffordshire*, both having flush weather decks; *Bald Eagle* and *Champion of the Seas*, flush deck aft; *Flying Childers*, *Tornado*, and *West Wind*, flush deck forward; and *Mameluke*, *West Wind*, *Winged Racer*, *Winged Arrow*, and *John Land*, all having movable houses secured over their three hatches.

The arrangement of the illustrations, all drawn to the same scale, provides an immediate picture of the sizes of the vessels in reference to each other. In the case of *Great Republic*, both the original and the rebuilt edition, the enormity of the size of the hull is brought into vivid visual focus when compared with any of the other large clippers.

Following the conclusion of the illustrations there is a brief discussion of the principal structures and furniture found on deck.

Topgallant Forecastle

The *topgallant forecastle*, the major structure forward above the weather deck, appeared in most vessels and was built in a variety of forms (see also Chapter 19). The most prevalent type was usually described as short or small, and built to the height of the main rail. It was usually left open at the after end, or *break*, leaving the space within subject to the elements. This space between its deck and the weather deck was generally fitted with lockers, miscellaneous stowages, and, in its after wings, water closets for the use of the crew. In rare instances the space, with its extremely low headroom, was partially enclosed and fitted with sleeping quarters for at least one watch of the crew. In practically all cases, the fitting out of this area was designed around the necessary space required for anchor handling.

The length of this short or small topgallant forecastle was about half the distance between the knightheads and the foremast. In turn, this location was determined to a great extent by the breadth of the windlass, which was of a size compatible with the outboard location of the hawseholes. In the fashioning of a ship there was very little that could be done with complete independence from some other consideration.

Two of the more notable exceptions to this low, short topgallant forecastle were *Golden West* and *Romance of the Sea*, each of which had extremely long structures that extended aft almost to the foremast. As in the other vessels, the resulting space was devoted to miscellaneous stowages.

Two ships, *Coeur de Lion* and *Wild Pigeon*, were both built with low topgallant forecastles that were closed and in which the crews were quartered. The apparent lack of headroom was, in both cases, overcome by the floors of each space being sunk about 2 feet below the level of the upper deck.

Many vessels were built with full-height topgallant forecastles, this height corresponding with the height of the monkey rail. (In contemporary descriptions this latter height is referred to as "the rail," whereas the height at the main rail is always specifically stated as such.) Vessels built with this feature covered a variety of forms and functions. Most of these decks were short and were closed, thus providing living quarters for the crew. However, many remained open, even with adequate headroom available, the crew being quartered in the deckhouse or below in the forecastle and tween-decks. Other vessels, notably McKay clippers, and also *Queen of the Seas* and *Charger*, were built with long, full-height topgallant forecastles which provided spacious accommodations for their crews. An unusual arrangement occurred in *Witch of the Wave*, in which a separate enclosure was built on either side of the bowsprit, each fitted out to accommodate part of the crew. The space between the two enclosures remained as an open passage from bowsprit to windlass.

Whatever the advantages of the raised forecastle, some vessels were designed with their weather decks flush forward, such as *Flying Childers*, *Tornado*, and *West Wind*. This feature is shown in the illustrations in this chapter.

Poop Deck

A *poop deck* was the predominant superstructure at the stern of a vessel and, like the topgallant forecastle, it assumed a variety of forms, the most prevalent being the half poop, generally built at the height of the main rail. The apparent principal advantages of a half poop were that it elevated the steering stand to a height which allowed both the helmsman and the officer of the watch a clear view of all the ship before them, and it did not tend to break a vessel's sheer when viewed from broadside. (This should not be confused with a ship breaking her sheer while riding at anchor.)

Half poops were built in a multitude of sizes, ranging from merely adequate steering space to a length which extended forward far enough to embrace the mainmast, as was the case with *Black Hawk*, *Comet*, and *Queen of the Seas*.

The simplest form of half poop had all accommodations for officers and passengers enclosed below. This resulted in a minimum of structure encumbering the deck itself, the largest item generally being a small house built into the break of the half poop and providing access to the tween-decks cabins and staterooms. This was a very popular arrangement.

More frequent, however, was the half poop that had a trunk cabin or cabinhouse built into it, the floor of the cabin being on the same level as the weather deck. These structures provided headroom above the deck, and had entry directly from the quarter deck and a companionway aft to access the half poop deck and steering stand. There was no uniformity in the sizes of these trunks, some being minimal in size and others being very large, depending upon the number of cabins and staterooms within their confines. Available descriptions very often contain dimensions of these structures, and where this is the case, the dimensions are given in the deck arrangements shown in this chapter.

The most unusual half poop arrangements appear to have been in *Comet*, *Nightingale*, and *Thatcher Magoun*, each being very long, plain, and without clutter.

The full-height poop, built at about the height of the monkey rail, was the second form of structure that occupied a vessel's stern above the weather deck. Due to their height,

(text continued on page 416)

Figure 26.1. *Weather deck arrangements.*

NOTES

All vessels are drawn to the same scale.

All dimensions are in feet and inches except certain house sizes.

Longitudinal dimension is first when more than one dimension is given.

Vessels are generally fitted with three hatchways.

Skylights are installed over interior cabins and passages.

Dimensions given below certain hulls indicate known locations or distances between masts.

*OA = over all; OD = on deck; PP = between perpendiculars; * = location of dimension is not specified.*

SYMBOLS

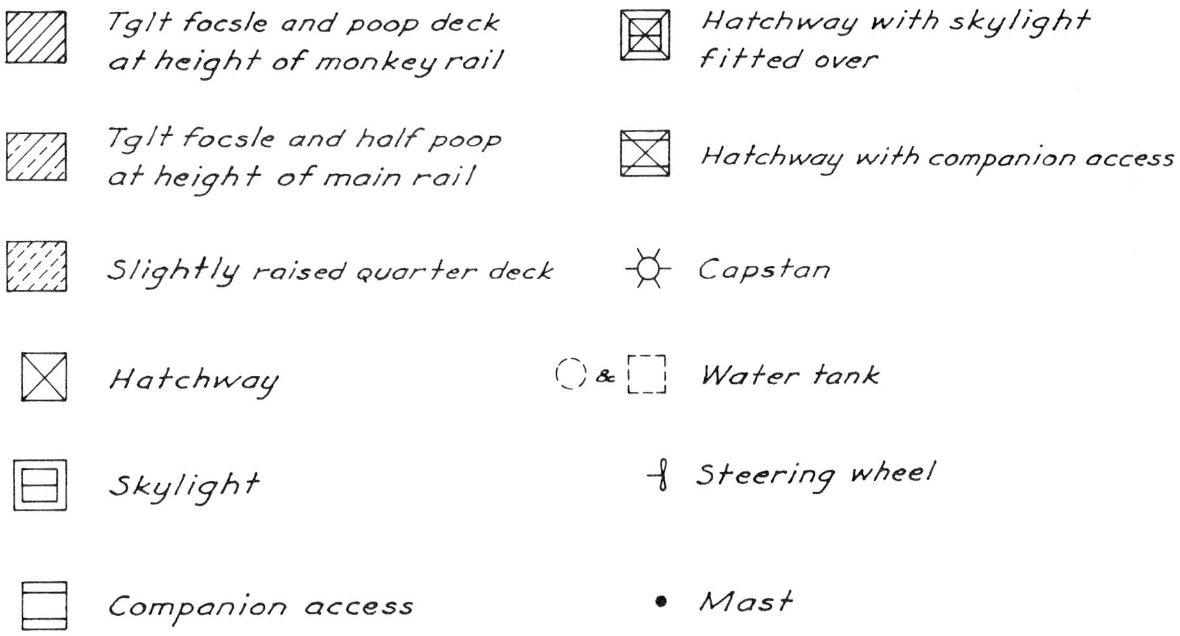

▨	*Tg/t focsle and poop deck at height of monkey rail*	⊠	*Hatchway with skylight fitted over*
▨	*Tg/t focsle and half poop at height of main rail*	⊠	*Hatchway with companion access*
▨	*Slightly raised quarter deck*	☼	*Capstan*
⊠	*Hatchway*	◯ & ▢	*Water tank*
⊟	*Skylight*	⚓	*Steering wheel*
⊟	*Companion access*	•	*Mast*

NOTES AND SYMBOLS FOR WEATHER DECK ARRANGEMENTS

Figure 26.2. *Weather deck arrangements.*

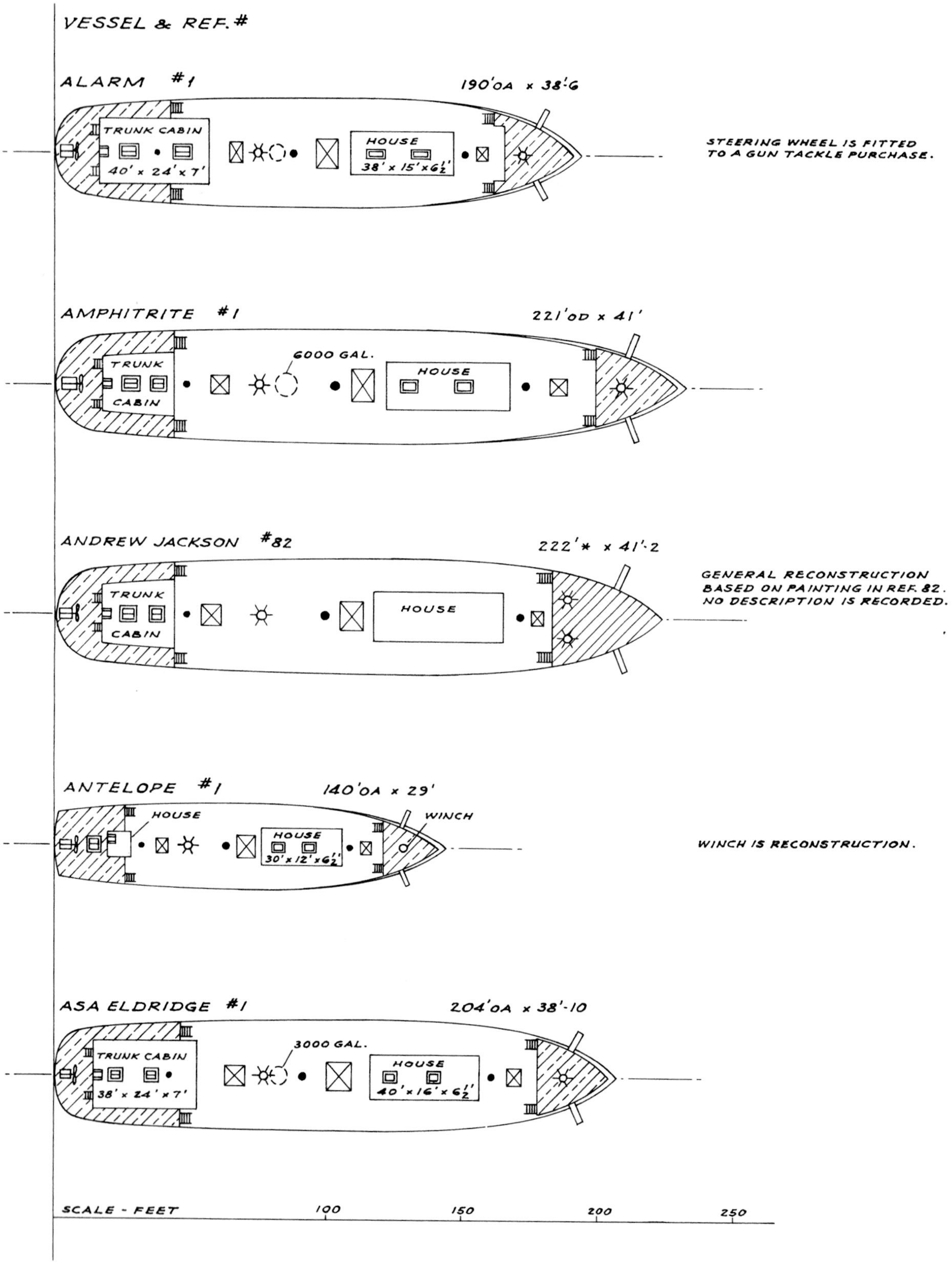

VESSEL & REF. #

ALARM #1 — 190' OA × 38'-6

TRUNK CABIN 40' × 24' × 7'
HOUSE 38' × 15' × 6½'

STEERING WHEEL IS FITTED TO A GUN TACKLE PURCHASE.

AMPHITRITE #1 — 221' OD × 41'

TRUNK CABIN
6000 GAL.
HOUSE

ANDREW JACKSON #82 — 222'* × 41'-2

TRUNK CABIN
HOUSE

GENERAL RECONSTRUCTION BASED ON PAINTING IN REF. 82. NO DESCRIPTION IS RECORDED.

ANTELOPE #1 — 140' OA × 29'

HOUSE
HOUSE 30' × 12' × 6½'
WINCH

WINCH IS RECONSTRUCTION.

ASA ELDRIDGE #1 — 204' OA × 38'-10

TRUNK CABIN 38' × 24' × 7'
3000 GAL.
HOUSE 40' × 16' × 6½'

SCALE - FEET   100   150   200   250

386

Figure 26.3. *Weather deck arrangements.*

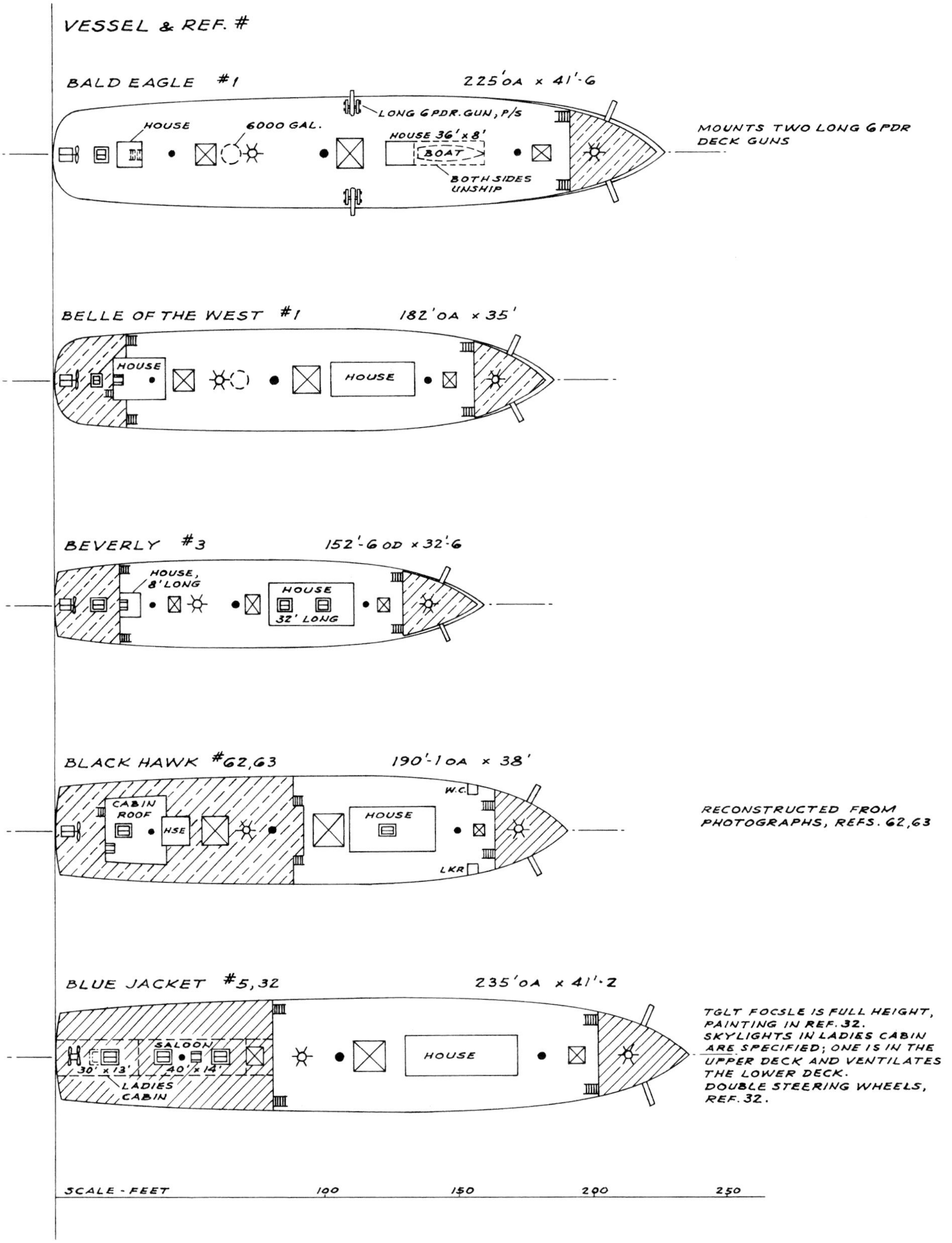

VESSEL & REF. #

BALD EAGLE #1   225'OA × 41'·6

HOUSE   6000 GAL.   LONG 6 PDR. GUN, P/S   HOUSE 36' × 8'   BOAT   BOTH SIDES UNSHIP

MOUNTS TWO LONG 6 PDR DECK GUNS

BELLE OF THE WEST #1   182'OA × 35'

HOUSE   HOUSE

BEVERLY #3   152'·6 OD × 32'·6

HOUSE, 8' LONG   HOUSE 32' LONG

BLACK HAWK #62,63   190'·10 OA × 38'

CABIN ROOF   HSE   W.C.   HOUSE   LKR

RECONSTRUCTED FROM PHOTOGRAPHS, REFS. 62,63

BLUE JACKET #5,32   235'OA × 41'·2

SALOON 40' × 14'   30' × 13'   LADIES CABIN   HOUSE

TGLT FOCSLE IS FULL HEIGHT, PAINTING IN REF. 32. SKYLIGHTS IN LADIES CABIN ARE SPECIFIED; ONE IS IN THE UPPER DECK AND VENTILATES THE LOWER DECK. DOUBLE STEERING WHEELS, REF. 32.

SCALE - FEET   100   150   200   250

387

Figure 26.4. *Weather deck arrangements.*

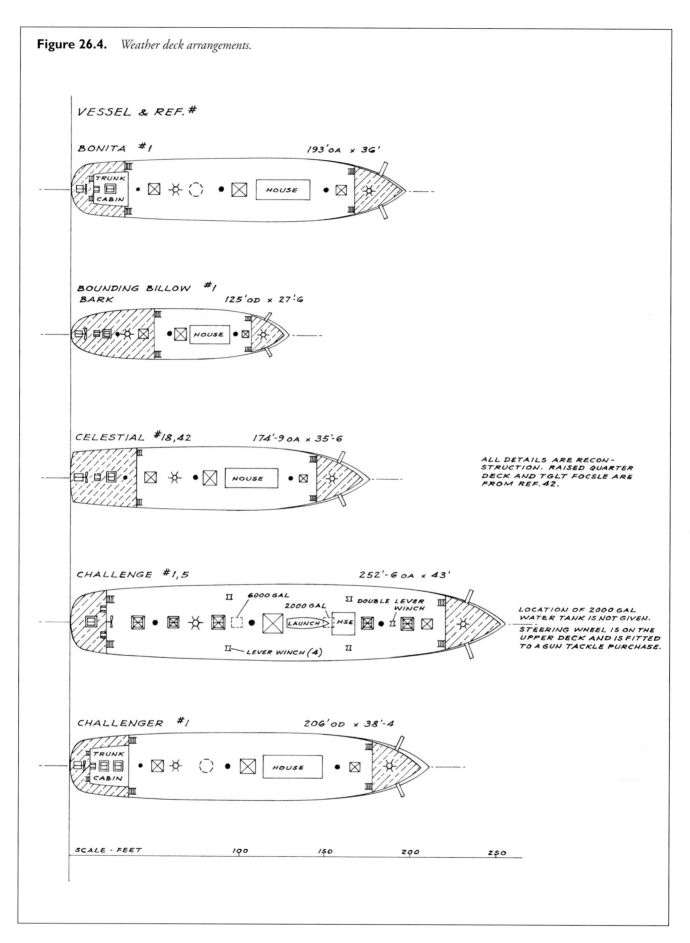

VESSEL & REF.#

BONITA #1   193'OA x 36'

BOUNDING BILLOW #1
BARK   125'OD x 27'6

CELESTIAL #18,42   174'-9 OA x 35'-6

ALL DETAILS ARE RECON-
STRUCTION. RAISED QUARTER
DECK AND TGLT FOCSLE ARE
FROM REF.42.

CHALLENGE #1,5   252'-6 OA x 43'

6000 GAL   DOUBLE LEVER
                                          WINCH
2000 GAL   LAUNCH   HSE

LEVER WINCH (4)

LOCATION OF 2000 GAL
WATER TANK IS NOT GIVEN.
STEERING WHEEL IS ON THE
UPPER DECK AND IS FITTED
TO A GUN TACKLE PURCHASE.

CHALLENGER #1   206'OD x 38'-4

TRUNK
CABIN   HOUSE

SCALE - FEET   100   150   200   250

Figure 26.5. *Weather deck arrangements.*

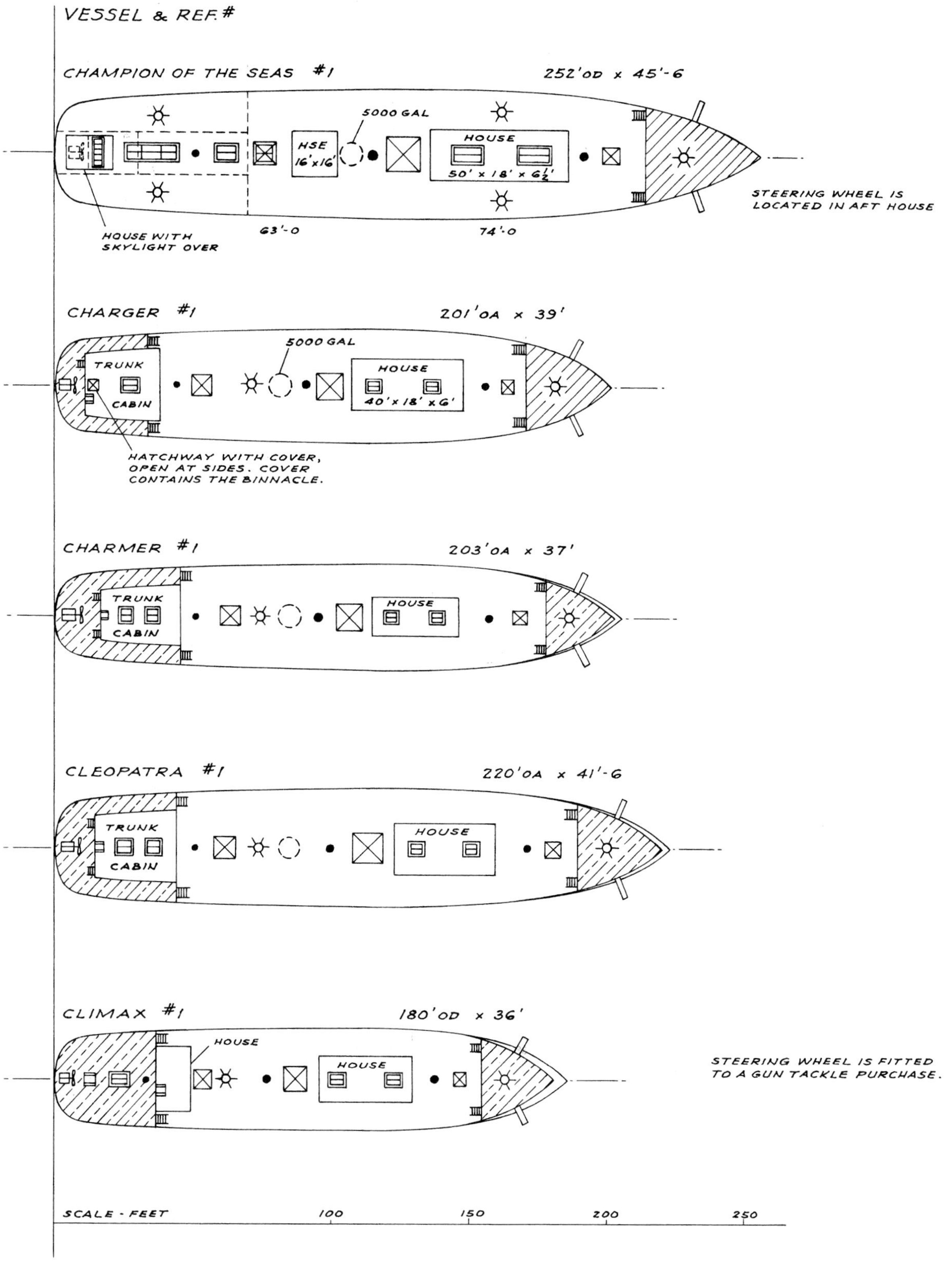

VESSEL & REF. #

CHAMPION OF THE SEAS #1   252' OD x 45'-6

HSE 16' x 16'
5000 GAL
HOUSE 50' x 18' x 6½'

STEERING WHEEL IS
LOCATED IN AFT HOUSE

HOUSE WITH
SKYLIGHT OVER

63'-0   74'-0

CHARGER #1   201' OA x 39'

TRUNK
CABIN
5000 GAL
HOUSE 40' x 18' x 6'

HATCHWAY WITH COVER,
OPEN AT SIDES. COVER
CONTAINS THE BINNACLE.

CHARMER #1   203' OA x 37'

TRUNK
CABIN
HOUSE

CLEOPATRA #1   220' OA x 41'-6

TRUNK
CABIN
HOUSE

CLIMAX #1   180' OD x 36'

HOUSE
HOUSE

STEERING WHEEL IS FITTED
TO A GUN TACKLE PURCHASE.

SCALE - FEET   100   150   200   250

389

Figure 26.6. *Weather deck arrangements.*

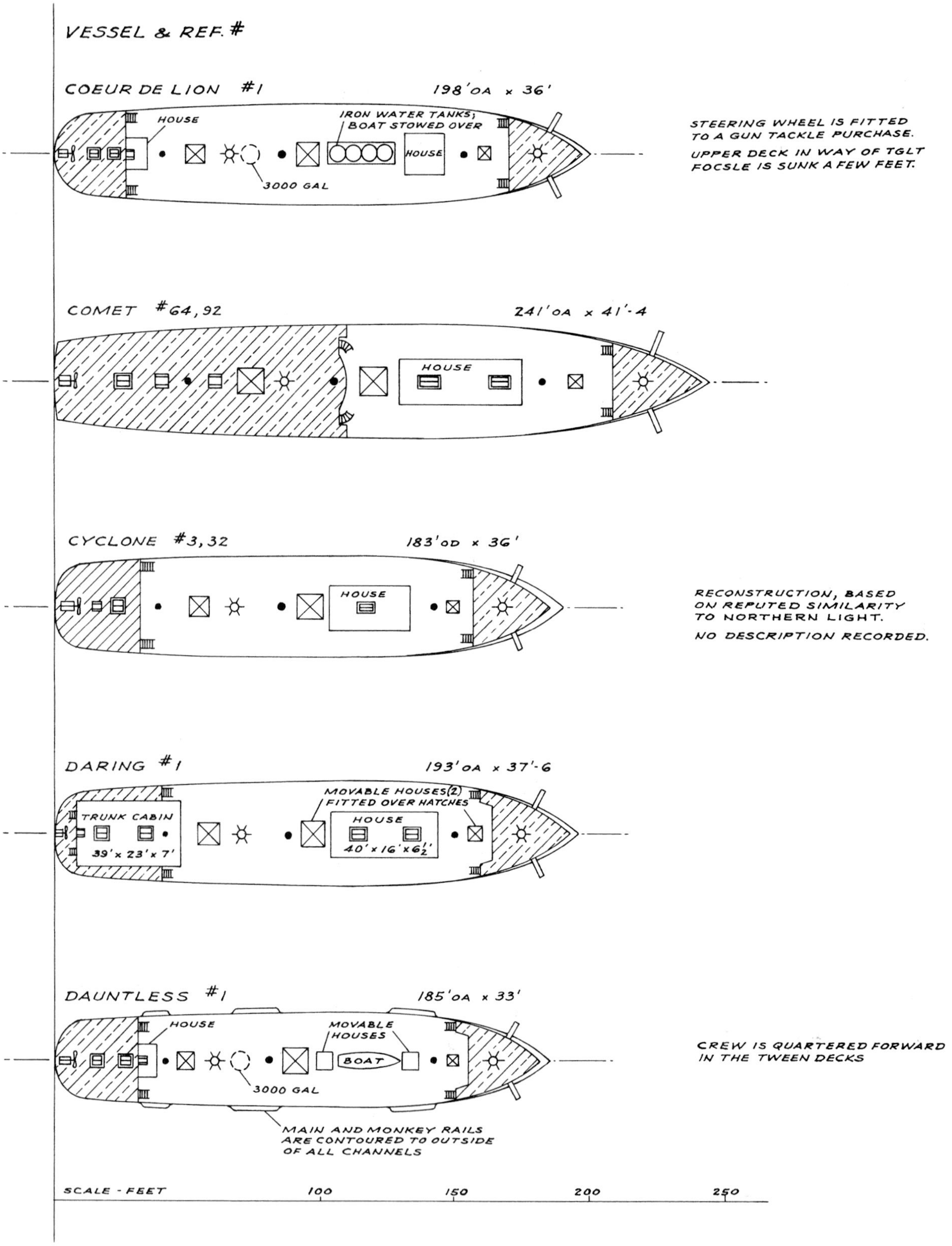

VESSEL & REF. #

COEUR DE LION #1   198' OA x 36'

HOUSE   IRON WATER TANKS, BOAT STOWED OVER   HOUSE

3000 GAL

STEERING WHEEL IS FITTED TO A GUN TACKLE PURCHASE.

UPPER DECK IN WAY OF TGLT FOCSLE IS SUNK A FEW FEET.

COMET #64, 92   241' OA x 41'-4

HOUSE

CYCLONE #3, 32   183' OD x 36'

HOUSE

RECONSTRUCTION, BASED ON REPUTED SIMILARITY TO NORTHERN LIGHT.

NO DESCRIPTION RECORDED.

DARING #1   193' OA x 37'-6

MOVABLE HOUSES(2) FITTED OVER HATCHES

TRUNK CABIN 39' x 23' x 7'

HOUSE 40' x 16' x 6½'

DAUNTLESS #1   185' OA x 33'

HOUSE   MOVABLE HOUSES

BOAT

3000 GAL

CREW IS QUARTERED FORWARD IN THE TWEEN DECKS

MAIN AND MONKEY RAILS ARE CONTOURED TO OUTSIDE OF ALL CHANNELS

SCALE - FEET   100   150   200   250

Figure 26.7. *Weather deck arrangements.*

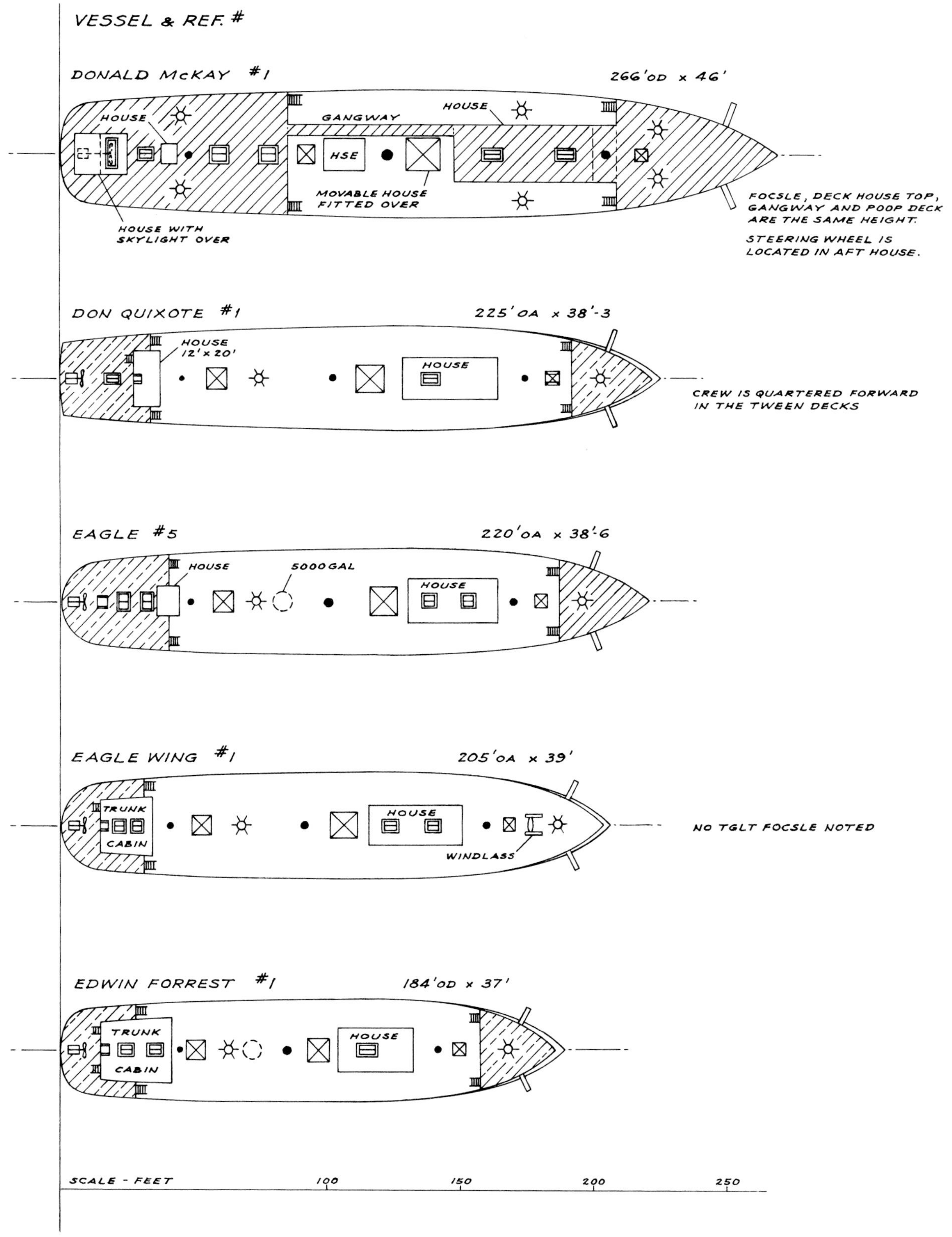

VESSEL & REF. #

DONALD McKAY #1   266'OD x 46'

HOUSE
GANGWAY
HOUSE
HSE
MOVABLE HOUSE
FITTED OVER
HOUSE WITH
SKYLIGHT OVER

FOCSLE, DECK HOUSE TOP,
GANGWAY AND POOP DECK
ARE THE SAME HEIGHT.

STEERING WHEEL IS
LOCATED IN AFT HOUSE.

DON QUIXOTE #1   225'OA x 38'-3

HOUSE
12' x 20'
HOUSE

CREW IS QUARTERED FORWARD
IN THE TWEEN DECKS

EAGLE #5   220'OA x 38'-6

HOUSE
5000 GAL
HOUSE

EAGLE WING #1   205'OA x 39'

TRUNK
CABIN
HOUSE
WINDLASS

NO TGLT FOCSLE NOTED

EDWIN FORREST #1   184'OD x 37'

TRUNK
CABIN
HOUSE

SCALE - FEET   100   150   200   250

391

Figure 26.8. *Weather deck arrangements.*

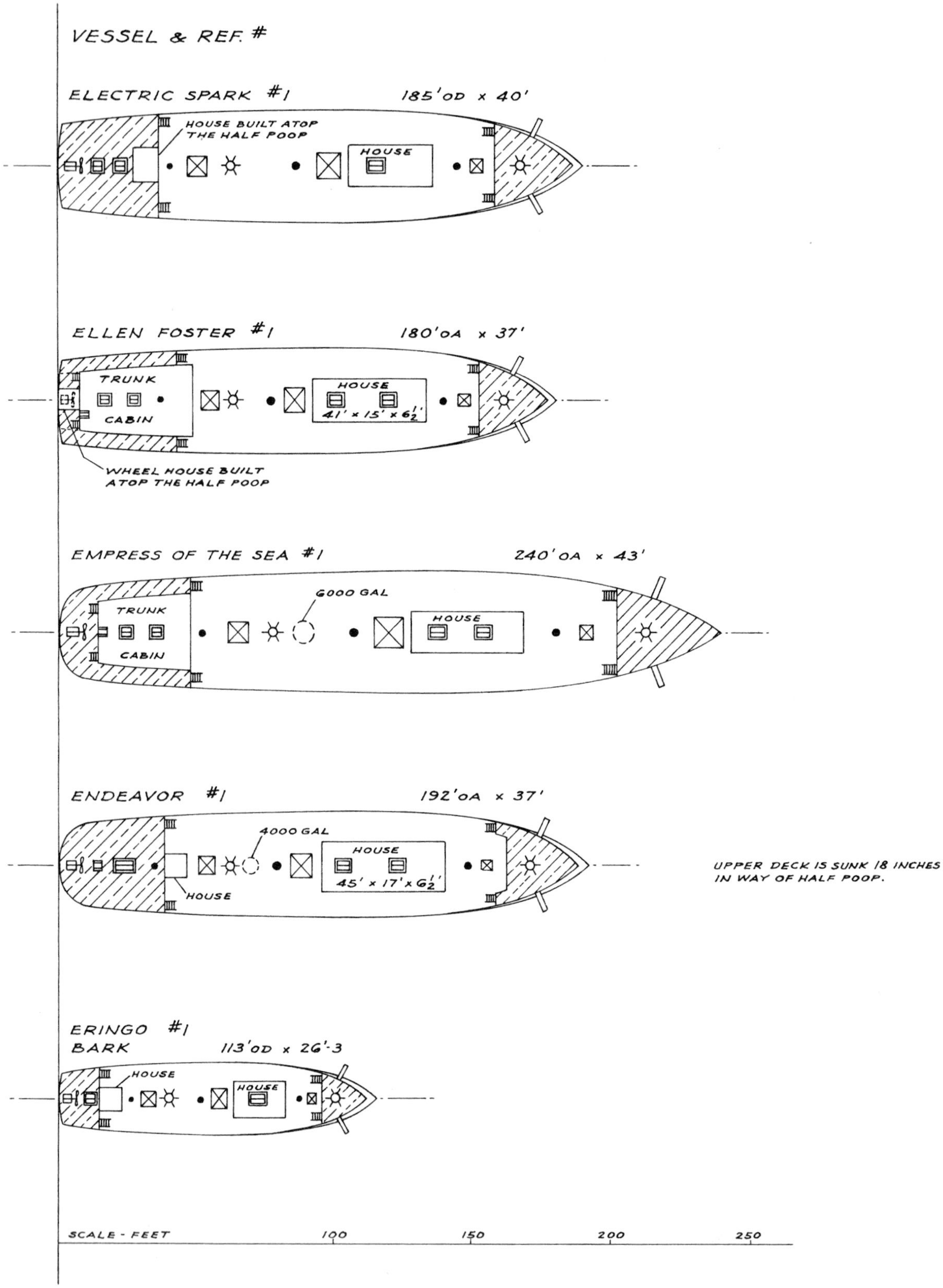

VESSEL & REF. #

ELECTRIC SPARK #1   185'OD × 40'

HOUSE BUILT ATOP
THE HALF POOP

HOUSE

ELLEN FOSTER #1   180'OA × 37'

TRUNK

CABIN

HOUSE

41' × 15' × 6½'

WHEEL HOUSE BUILT
ATOP THE HALF POOP

EMPRESS OF THE SEA #1   240'OA × 43'

6000 GAL

TRUNK

CABIN

HOUSE

ENDEAVOR #1   192'OA × 37'

4000 GAL

HOUSE

45' × 17' × 6½'

HOUSE

UPPER DECK IS SUNK 18 INCHES
IN WAY OF HALF POOP.

ERINGO #1
BARK   113'OD × 26'-3

HOUSE

HOUSE

SCALE - FEET   100   150   200   250

Figure 26.9. *Weather deck arrangements.*

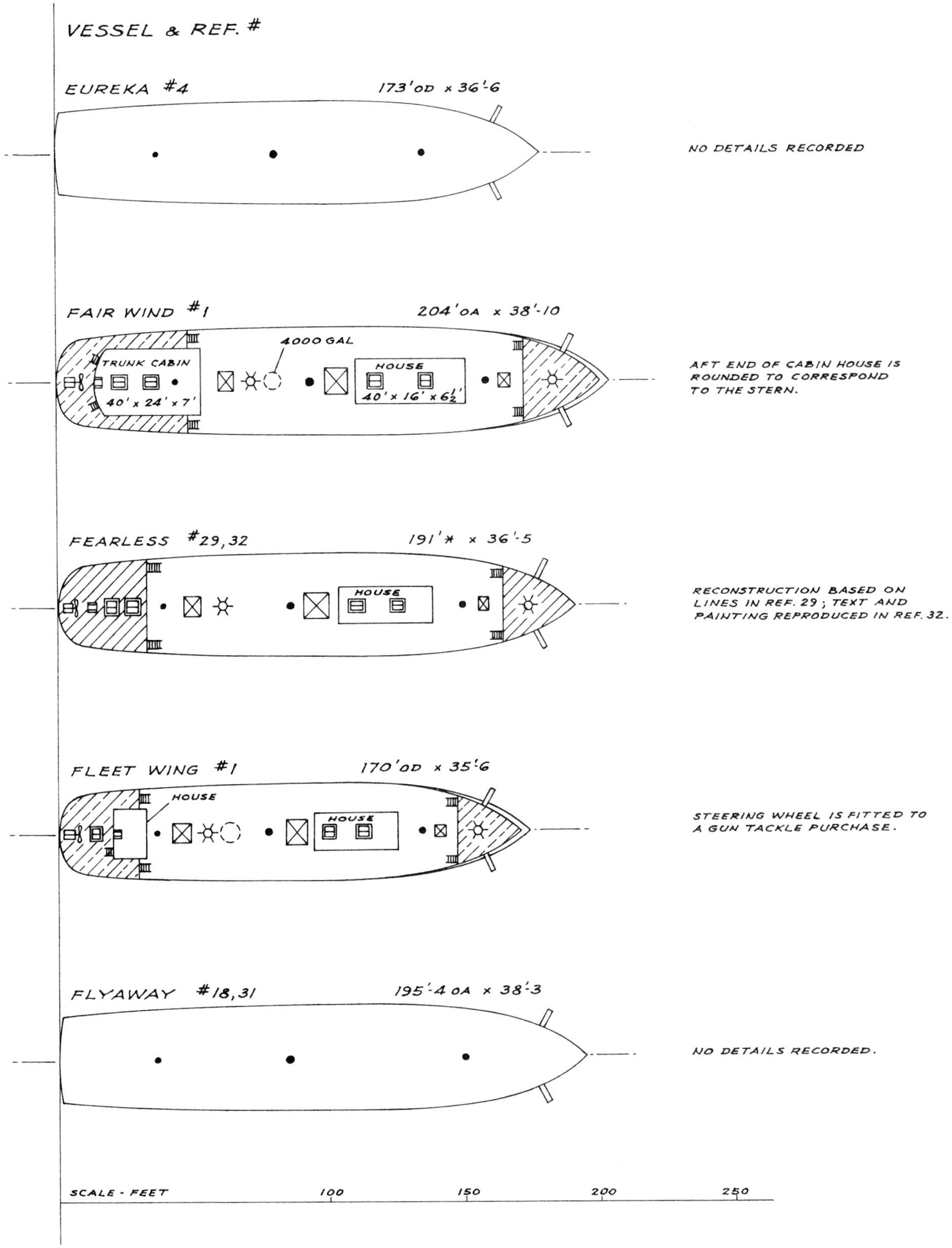

VESSEL & REF. #

EUREKA #4   173' OD x 36'-6

NO DETAILS RECORDED

FAIR WIND #1   204' OA x 38'-10

TRUNK CABIN

4000 GAL

HOUSE

40' x 24' x 7'

40' x 16' x 6½'

AFT END OF CABIN HOUSE IS
ROUNDED TO CORRESPOND
TO THE STERN.

FEARLESS #29,32   191'* x 36'-5

HOUSE

RECONSTRUCTION BASED ON
LINES IN REF. 29; TEXT AND
PAINTING REPRODUCED IN REF. 32.

FLEET WING #1   170' OD x 35'-6

HOUSE

HOUSE

STEERING WHEEL IS FITTED TO
A GUN TACKLE PURCHASE.

FLYAWAY #18,31   195'-4 OA x 38'-3

NO DETAILS RECORDED.

SCALE - FEET   100   150   200   250

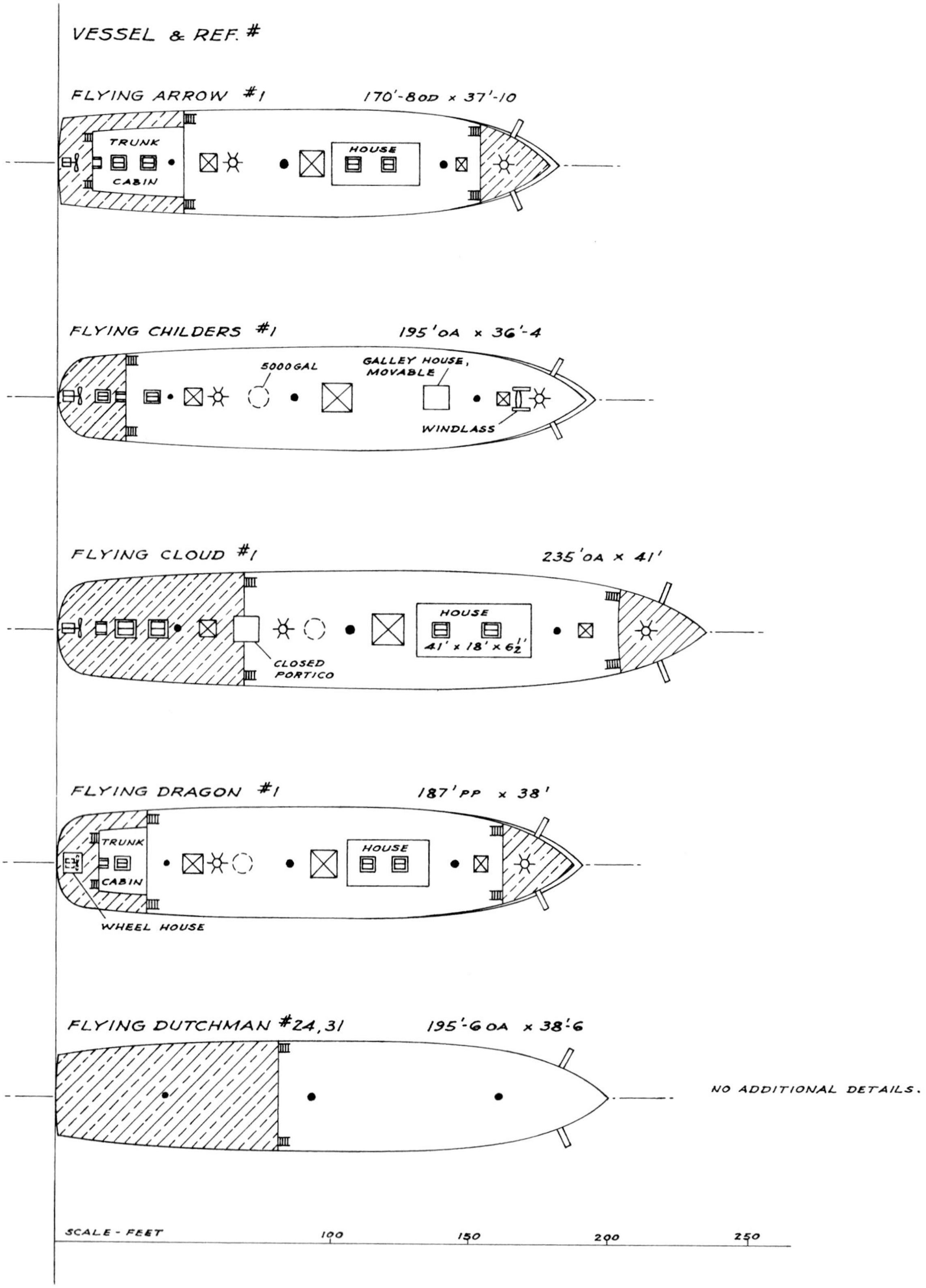

Figure 26.10. *Weather deck arrangements.*

VESSEL & REF. #

FLYING ARROW #1   170'-80D × 37'-10

TRUNK
CABIN
HOUSE

FLYING CHILDERS #1   195'OA × 36'-4

5000 GAL   GALLEY HOUSE, MOVABLE

WINDLASS

FLYING CLOUD #1   235'OA × 41'

HOUSE
41' × 18' × 6½'

CLOSED PORTICO

FLYING DRAGON #1   187'PP × 38'

TRUNK
CABIN
HOUSE

WHEEL HOUSE

FLYING DUTCHMAN #24,31   195'-6 OA × 38'-6

NO ADDITIONAL DETAILS.

SCALE - FEET   100   150   200   250

Figure 26.11. *Weather deck arrangements.*

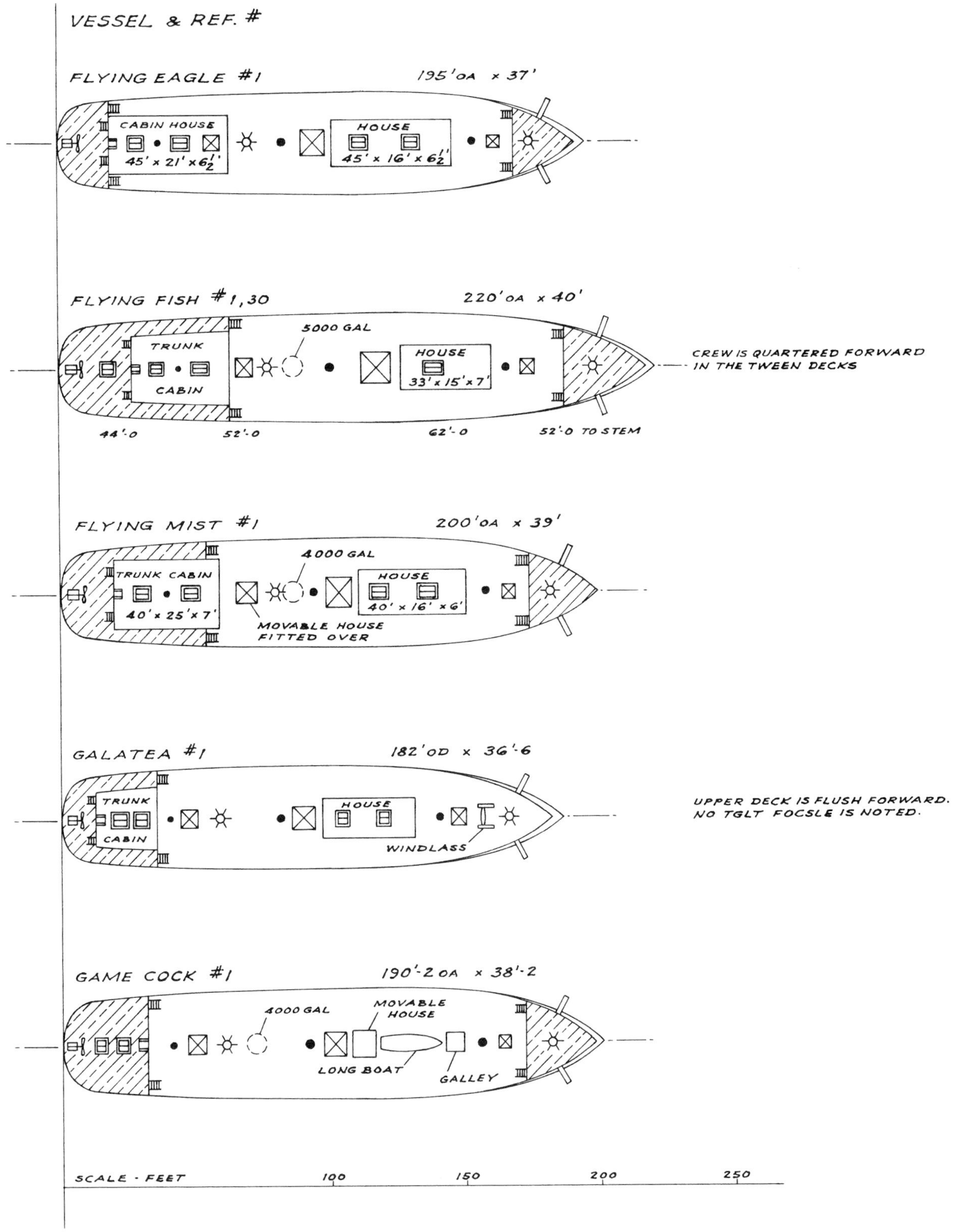

VESSEL & REF. #

FLYING EAGLE #1   195' OA x 37'

CABIN HOUSE
45' x 21' x 6½'

HOUSE
45' x 16' x 6½'

FLYING FISH #1,30   220' OA x 40'

5000 GAL

TRUNK
CABIN

HOUSE
33' x 15' x 7'

CREW IS QUARTERED FORWARD
IN THE TWEEN DECKS

44'·0   52'·0   62'·0   52'·0 TO STEM

FLYING MIST #1   200' OA x 39'

4000 GAL

TRUNK CABIN
40' x 25' x 7'

HOUSE
40' x 16' x 6'

MOVABLE HOUSE
FITTED OVER

GALATEA #1   182' OD x 36'·6

TRUNK
CABIN

HOUSE

WINDLASS

UPPER DECK IS FLUSH FORWARD.
NO TGLT FOCSLE IS NOTED.

GAME COCK #1   190'·2 OA x 38'·2

4000 GAL

MOVABLE
HOUSE

LONG BOAT   GALLEY

SCALE · FEET   100   150   200   250

395

Figure 26.12. *Weather deck arrangements.*

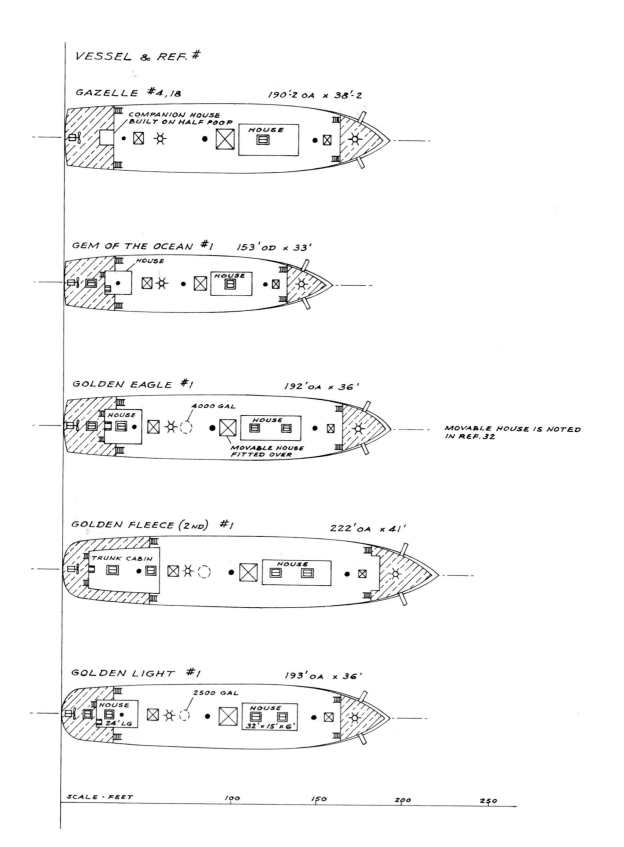

Figure 26.13. *Weather deck arrangements.*

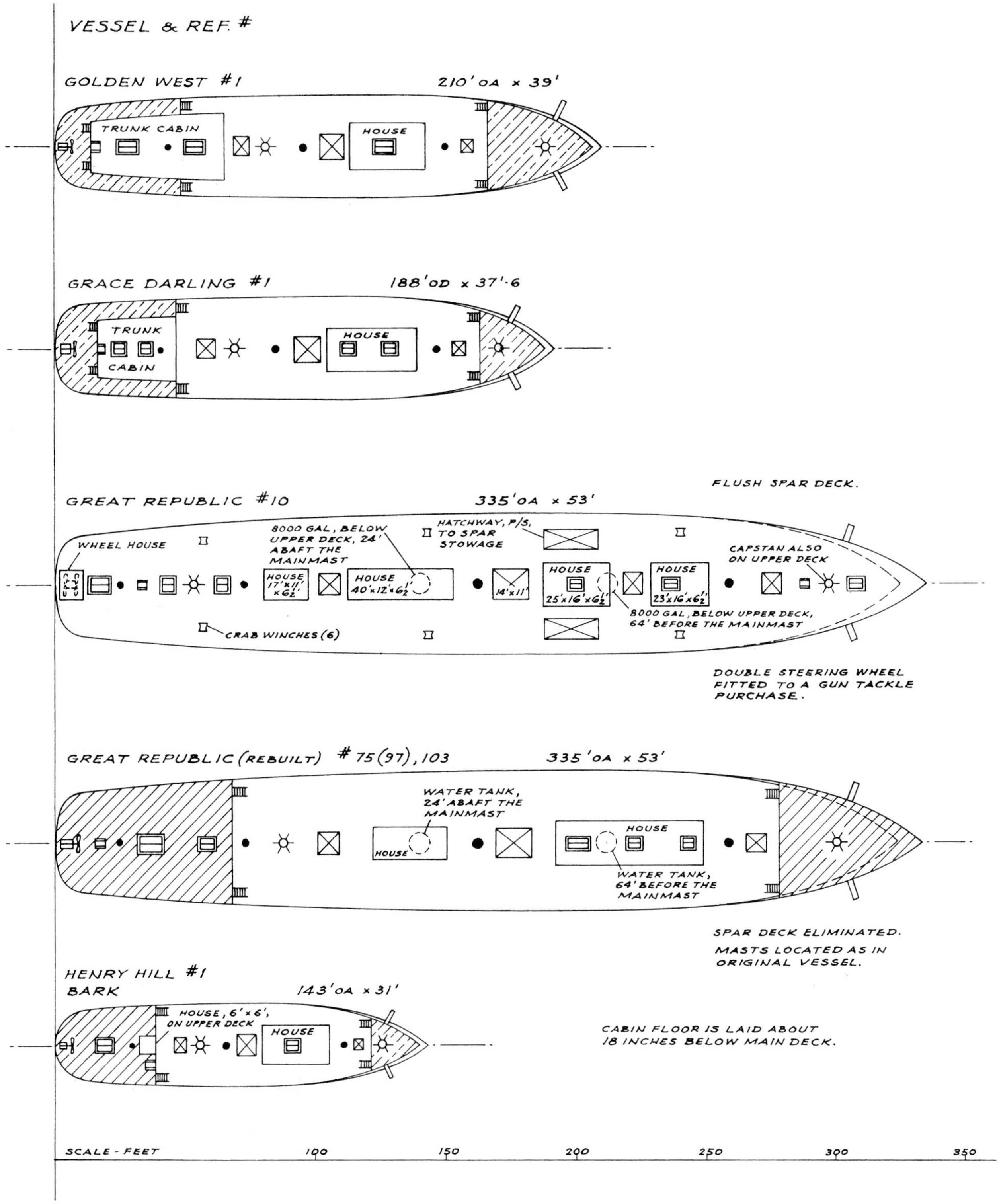

VESSEL & REF. #

GOLDEN WEST #1   210' OA × 39'

TRUNK CABIN   HOUSE

GRACE DARLING #1   188' OD × 37'·6

TRUNK CABIN   HOUSE

GREAT REPUBLIC #10   335' OA × 53'   FLUSH SPAR DECK.

WHEEL HOUSE

8000 GAL, BELOW UPPER DECK, 24' ABAFT THE MAINMAST

HATCHWAY, P/S, TO SPAR STOWAGE

CAPSTAN ALSO ON UPPER DECK

HOUSE 17'×11' ×6½'

HOUSE 40'×12'×6½'

14'×11'

HOUSE 25'×16'×6½'

HOUSE 23'×16'×6½'

CRAB WINCHES (6)

8000 GAL, BELOW UPPER DECK, 64' BEFORE THE MAINMAST

DOUBLE STEERING WHEEL FITTED TO A GUN TACKLE PURCHASE.

GREAT REPUBLIC (REBUILT) #75 (97), 103   335' OA × 53'

WATER TANK, 24' ABAFT THE MAINMAST

HOUSE

HOUSE

WATER TANK, 64' BEFORE THE MAINMAST

SPAR DECK ELIMINATED.
MASTS LOCATED AS IN ORIGINAL VESSEL.

HENRY HILL #1 BARK   143' OA × 31'

HOUSE, 6'×6', ON UPPER DECK

HOUSE

CABIN FLOOR IS LAID ABOUT 18 INCHES BELOW MAIN DECK.

SCALE - FEET   100   150   200   250   300   350

Figure 26.14. *Weather deck arrangements.*

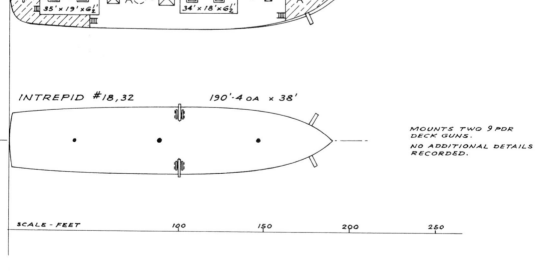

VESSEL & REF. #

HERALD OF THE MORNING #1,12   202' OD × 37'

5000 GAL
HOUSE
HOUSE
ABT. 40' LG.

FANCY BRASS
CANNON, P/S

HOOGLY #1   200' OA × 39'

5000 GAL
HOUSE
42' × 17' × 6'

STEERING WHEEL IS ON UPPER
DECK IN RECESS UNDER FRONT
END OF POOP DECK AND IS
FITTED TO A GUN TACKLE
PURCHASE.

HURRICANE #4,65   230' OA × 40'

ABT. 2500 GAL   ABT. 2500 GAL
HOUSE

45'·0   57'·6   72'·6   52'·6 TO KNIGHTHEADS

INDIAMAN #1   186' PP × 37'

4000 GAL
TRUNK CABIN   HOUSE
35' × 19' × 6½'   34' × 18' × 6½'

INTREPID #18,32   190'-4 OA × 38'

MOUNTS TWO 9 PDR
DECK GUNS.
NO ADDITIONAL DETAILS
RECORDED.

SCALE - FEET   100   150   200   250

Figure 26.15. *Weather deck arrangements.*

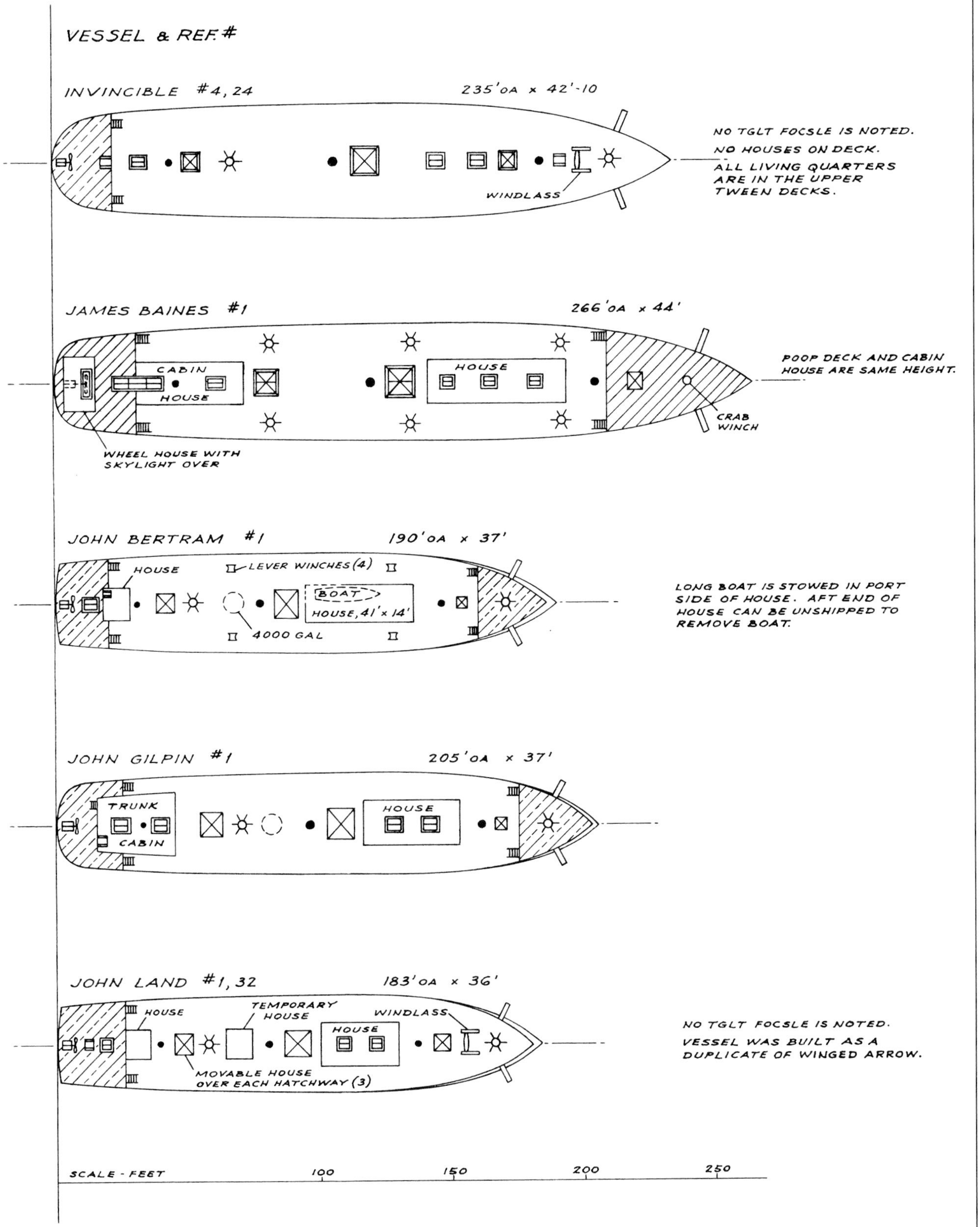

VESSEL & REF. #

INVINCIBLE   #4, 24   235' OA x 42'-10

NO TGLT FOCSLE IS NOTED.
NO HOUSES ON DECK.
ALL LIVING QUARTERS
ARE IN THE UPPER
TWEEN DECKS.

WINDLASS

JAMES BAINES   #1   266' OA x 44'

CABIN
HOUSE

HOUSE

POOP DECK AND CABIN
HOUSE ARE SAME HEIGHT.

CRAB
WINCH

WHEEL HOUSE WITH
SKYLIGHT OVER

JOHN BERTRAM   #1   190' OA x 37'

HOUSE   LEVER WINCHES (4)

BOAT
HOUSE, 41' x 14'

4000 GAL

LONG BOAT IS STOWED IN PORT
SIDE OF HOUSE. AFT END OF
HOUSE CAN BE UNSHIPPED TO
REMOVE BOAT.

JOHN GILPIN   #1   205' OA x 37'

TRUNK

HOUSE

CABIN

JOHN LAND   #1, 32   183' OA x 36'

HOUSE   TEMPORARY
               HOUSE   WINDLASS

HOUSE

MOVABLE HOUSE
OVER EACH HATCHWAY (3)

NO TGLT FOCSLE IS NOTED.
VESSEL WAS BUILT AS A
DUPLICATE OF WINGED ARROW.

SCALE - FEET   100   150   200   250

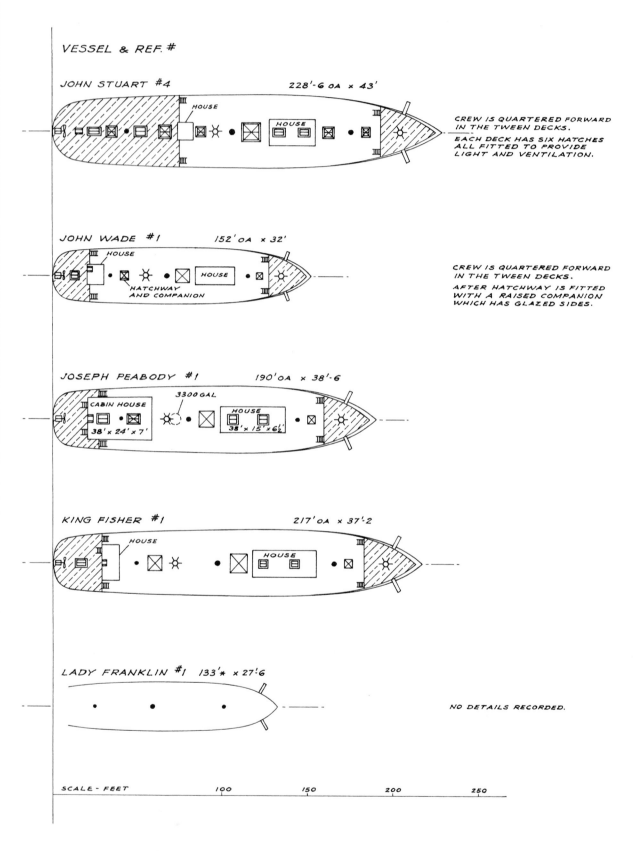

Figure 26.16. *Weather deck arrangements.*

VESSEL & REF. #

JOHN STUART #4   228'-6 OA × 43'

HOUSE   HOUSE

CREW IS QUARTERED FORWARD
IN THE TWEEN DECKS.

EACH DECK HAS SIX HATCHES
ALL FITTED TO PROVIDE
LIGHT AND VENTILATION.

JOHN WADE #1   152' OA × 32'

HOUSE   HOUSE

HATCHWAY
AND COMPANION

CREW IS QUARTERED FORWARD
IN THE TWEEN DECKS.

AFTER HATCHWAY IS FITTED
WITH A RAISED COMPANION
WHICH HAS GLAZED SIDES.

JOSEPH PEABODY #1   190' OA × 38'-6

CABIN HOUSE   3300 GAL   HOUSE

38' × 24' × 7'   38' × 15' × 6½'

KING FISHER #1   217' OA × 37'-2

HOUSE   HOUSE

LADY FRANKLIN #1   133'* × 27'-6

NO DETAILS RECORDED.

SCALE - FEET   100   150   200   250

Figure 26.17. *Weather deck arrangements.*

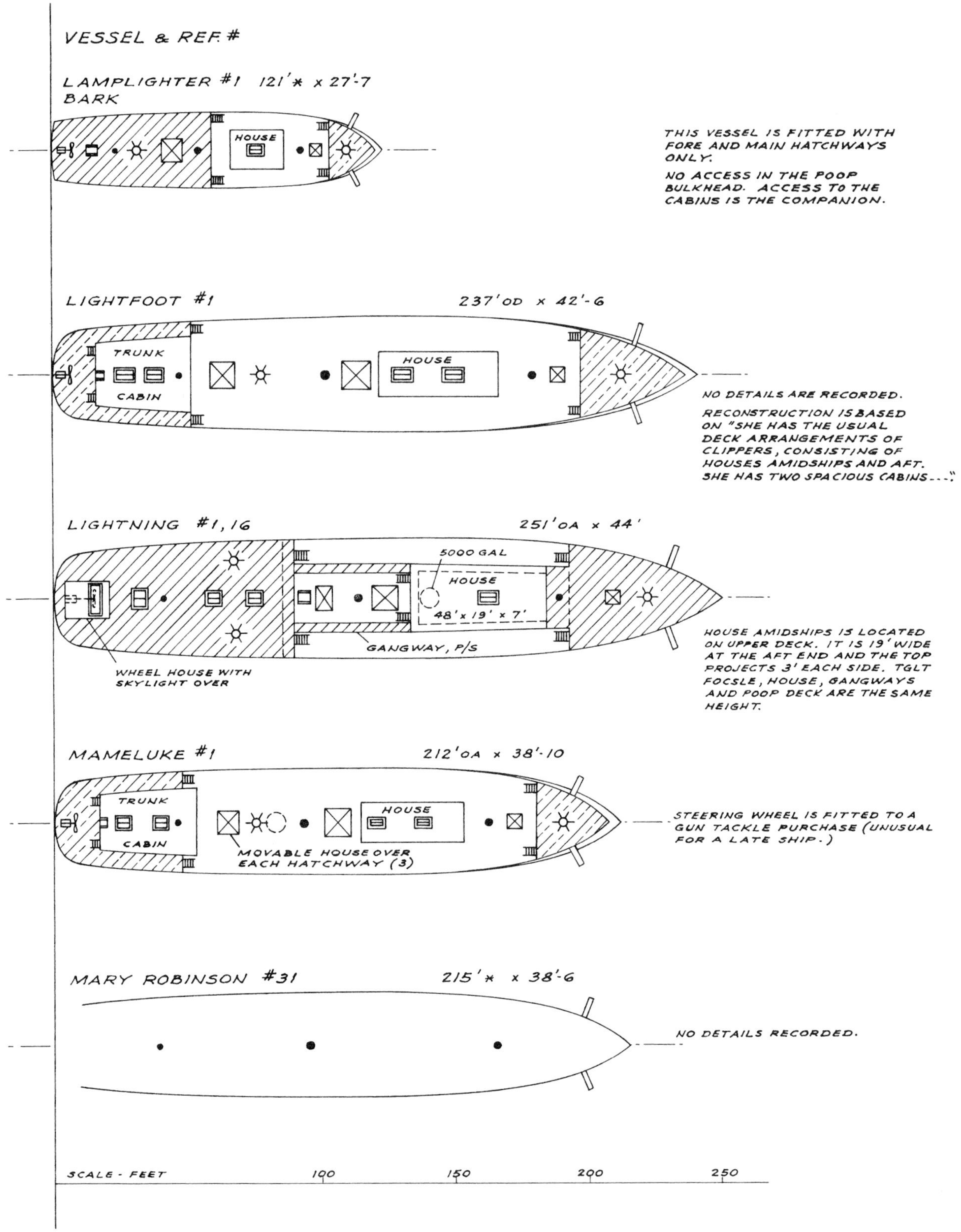

VESSEL & REF. #

LAMPLIGHTER #1   121'ᵡ x 27'-7
BARK

THIS VESSEL IS FITTED WITH
FORE AND MAIN HATCHWAYS
ONLY.

NO ACCESS IN THE POOP
BULKHEAD. ACCESS TO THE
CABINS IS THE COMPANION.

LIGHTFOOT #1   237'OD x 42'-6

NO DETAILS ARE RECORDED.

RECONSTRUCTION IS BASED
ON "SHE HAS THE USUAL
DECK ARRANGEMENTS OF
CLIPPERS, CONSISTING OF
HOUSES AMIDSHIPS AND AFT.
SHE HAS TWO SPACIOUS CABINS.…".

TRUNK
CABIN
HOUSE

LIGHTNING #1,16   251'OA x 44'

5000 GAL
HOUSE
48' x 19' x 7'

GANGWAY, P/S

WHEEL HOUSE WITH
SKYLIGHT OVER

HOUSE AMIDSHIPS IS LOCATED
ON UPPER DECK. IT IS 19' WIDE
AT THE AFT END AND THE TOP
PROJECTS 3' EACH SIDE. TGLT
FOCSLE, HOUSE, GANGWAYS
AND POOP DECK ARE THE SAME
HEIGHT.

MAMELUKE #1   212'OA x 38'-10

TRUNK
CABIN
HOUSE

MOVABLE HOUSE OVER
EACH HATCHWAY (3)

STEERING WHEEL IS FITTED TO A
GUN TACKLE PURCHASE (UNUSUAL
FOR A LATE SHIP.)

MARY ROBINSON #31   215'ᵡ x 38'-6

NO DETAILS RECORDED.

SCALE - FEET   100   150   200   250

Figure 26.18. *Weather deck arrangements.*

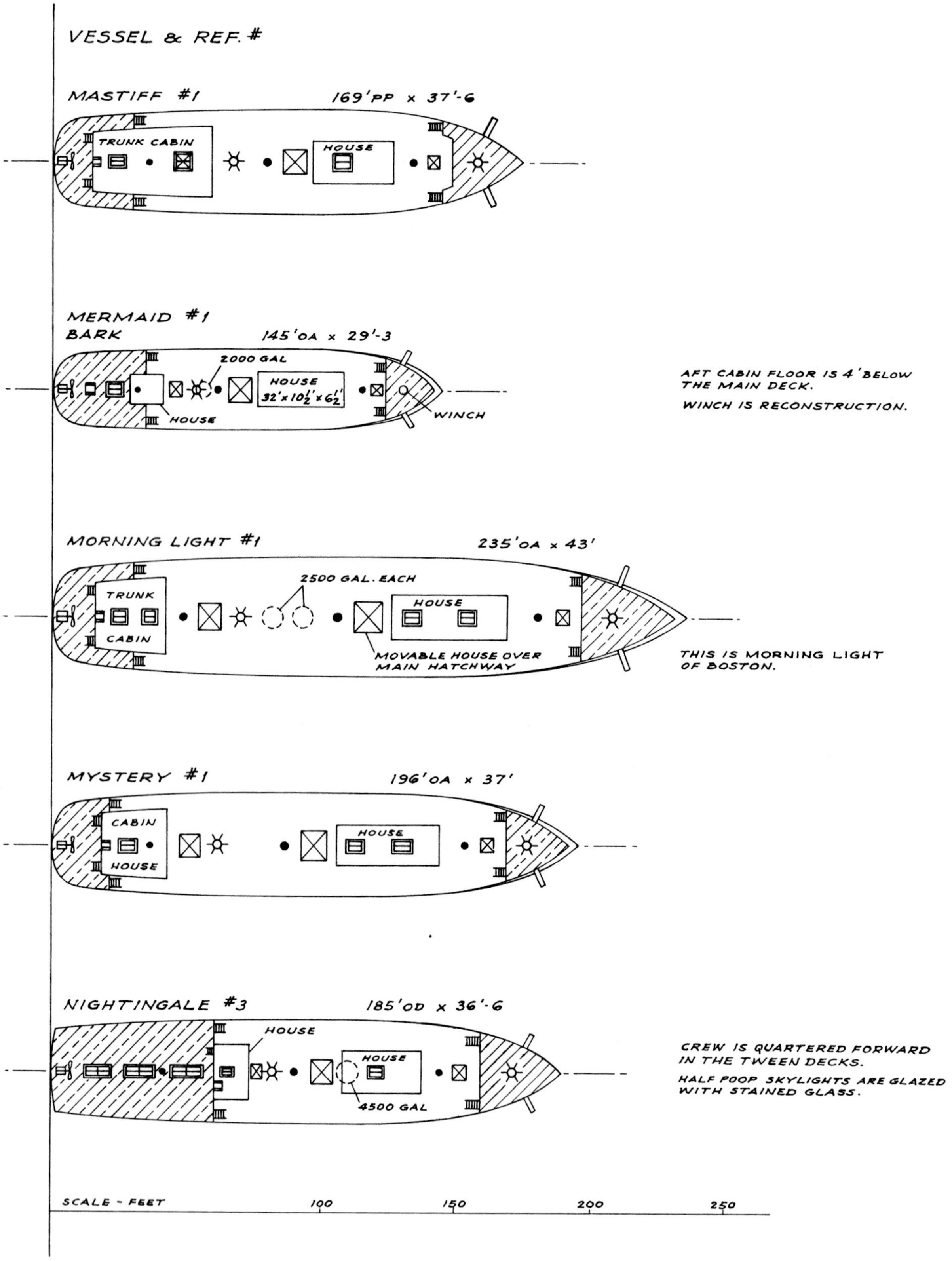

VESSEL & REF. #

MASTIFF #1   169'PP × 37'-6

TRUNK CABIN   HOUSE

MERMAID #1
BARK   145'OA × 29'-3

2000 GAL

HOUSE   HOUSE
                 32'×10½'×6½'

WINCH

AFT CABIN FLOOR IS 4' BELOW
THE MAIN DECK.

WINCH IS RECONSTRUCTION.

MORNING LIGHT #1   235'OA × 43'

2500 GAL. EACH

TRUNK   HOUSE

CABIN

MOVABLE HOUSE OVER
MAIN HATCHWAY

THIS IS MORNING LIGHT
OF BOSTON.

MYSTERY #1   196'OA × 37'

CABIN   HOUSE

HOUSE

NIGHTINGALE #3   185'OD × 36'-6

HOUSE

HOUSE

4500 GAL

CREW IS QUARTERED FORWARD
IN THE TWEEN DECKS.

HALF POOP SKYLIGHTS ARE GLAZED
WITH STAINED GLASS.

SCALE - FEET   100   150   200   250

Figure 26.19. *Weather deck arrangements.*

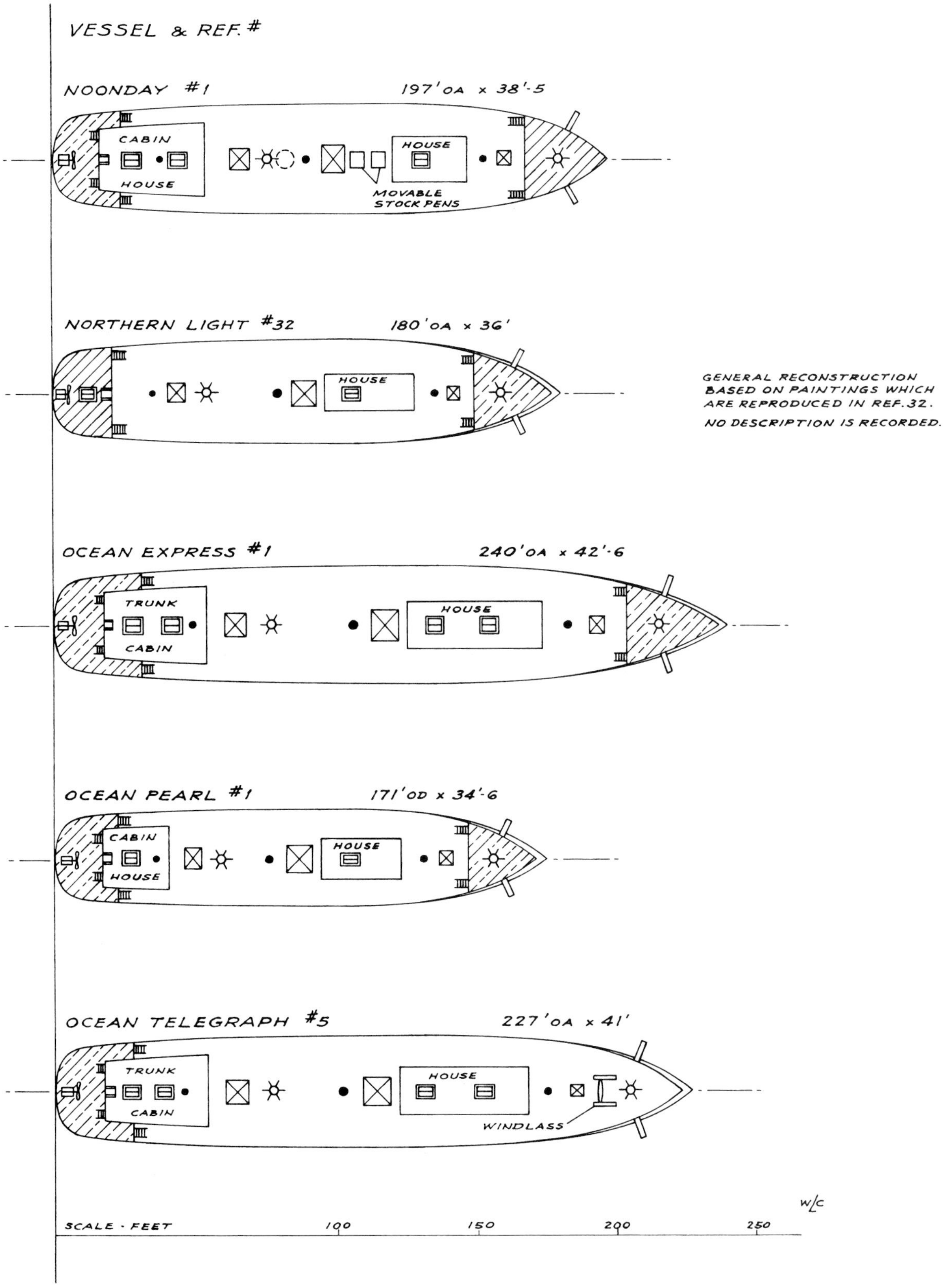

VESSEL & REF. #

NOONDAY #1   197'OA × 38'-5

CABIN
HOUSE
MOVABLE
STOCK PENS

NORTHERN LIGHT #32   180'OA × 36'

HOUSE

GENERAL RECONSTRUCTION
BASED ON PAINTINGS WHICH
ARE REPRODUCED IN REF.32.

NO DESCRIPTION IS RECORDED.

OCEAN EXPRESS #1   240'OA × 42'-6

TRUNK
CABIN
HOUSE

OCEAN PEARL #1   171'OD × 34'-6

CABIN
HOUSE
HOUSE

OCEAN TELEGRAPH #5   227'OA × 41'

TRUNK
CABIN
HOUSE
WINDLASS

w/c

SCALE · FEET   100   150   200   250

403

Figure 26.20.   *Weather deck arrangements.*

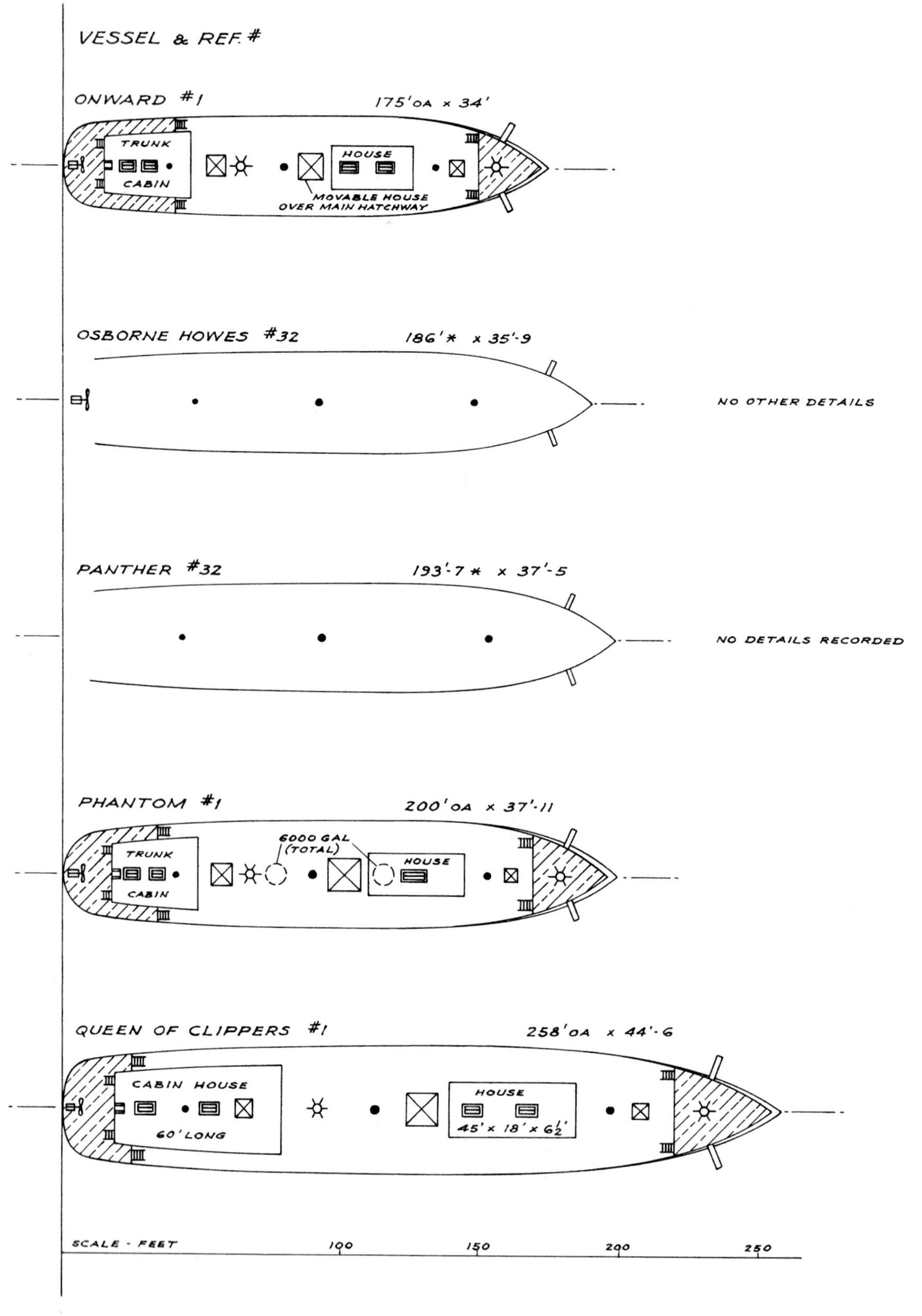

VESSEL & REF. #

ONWARD #1   175'OA × 34'

TRUNK
CABIN

HOUSE

MOVABLE HOUSE
OVER MAIN HATCHWAY

OSBORNE HOWES #32   186'* × 35'-9

NO OTHER DETAILS

PANTHER #32   193'-7 * × 37'-5

NO DETAILS RECORDED

PHANTOM #1   200'OA × 37'-11

TRUNK
CABIN

6000 GAL
(TOTAL)

HOUSE

QUEEN OF CLIPPERS #1   258'OA × 44'-6

CABIN HOUSE

60' LONG

HOUSE

45' × 18' × 6½'

SCALE - FEET   100   150   200   250

Figure 26.21. *Weather deck arrangements.*

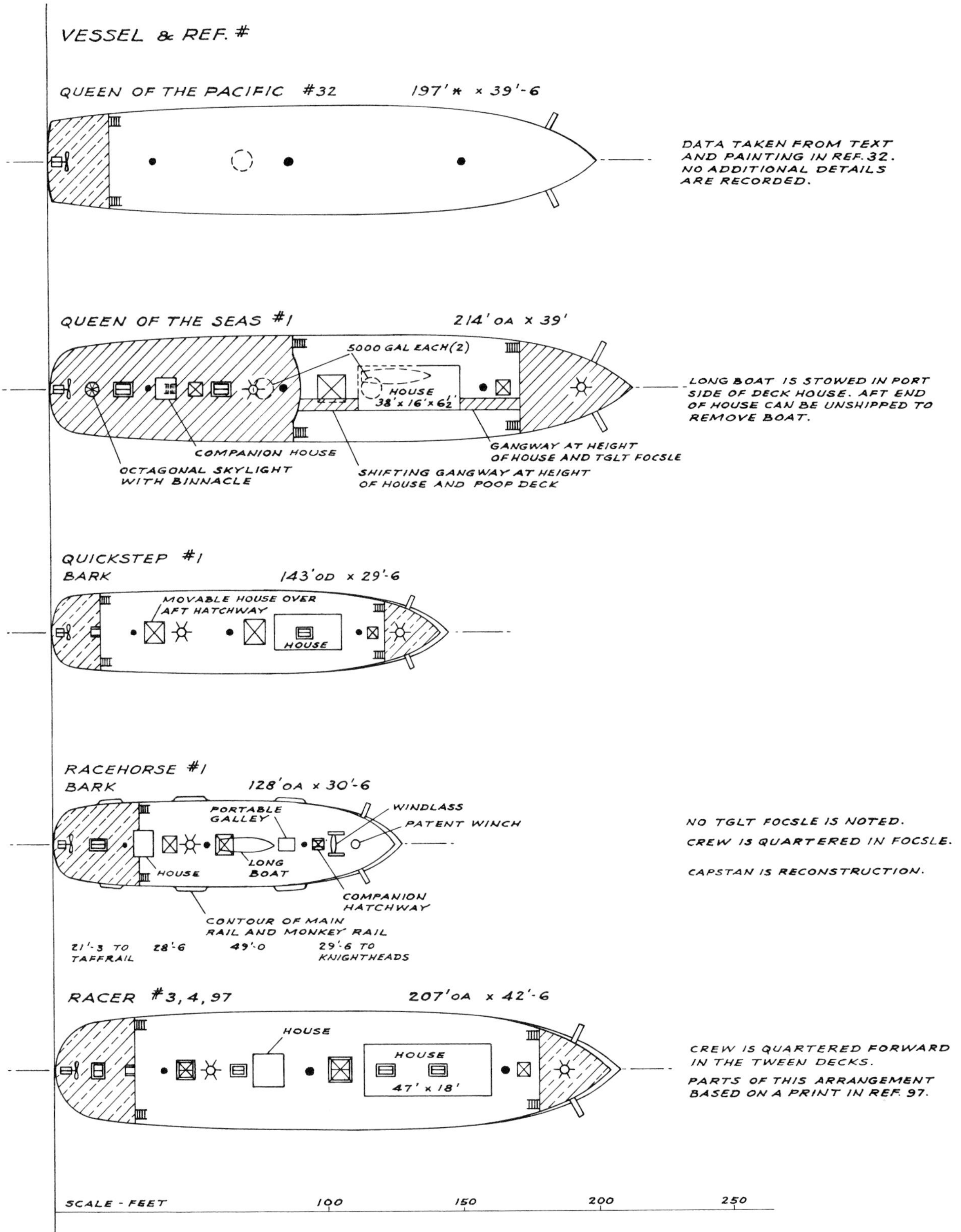

VESSEL & REF. #

QUEEN OF THE PACIFIC #32   197'ж × 39'-6

DATA TAKEN FROM TEXT
AND PAINTING IN REF. 32.
NO ADDITIONAL DETAILS
ARE RECORDED.

QUEEN OF THE SEAS #1   214'OA × 39'

5000 GAL EACH (2)

HOUSE
38' × 16' × 6½'

LONG BOAT IS STOWED IN PORT
SIDE OF DECK HOUSE. AFT END
OF HOUSE CAN BE UNSHIPPED TO
REMOVE BOAT.

COMPANION HOUSE

OCTAGONAL SKYLIGHT
WITH BINNACLE

GANGWAY AT HEIGHT
OF HOUSE AND TGLT FOCSLE

SHIFTING GANGWAY AT HEIGHT
OF HOUSE AND POOP DECK

QUICKSTEP #1
BARK   143'OD × 29'-6

MOVABLE HOUSE OVER
AFT HATCHWAY

HOUSE

RACEHORSE #1
BARK   128'OA × 30'-6

PORTABLE
GALLEY

WINDLASS
PATENT WINCH

NO TGLT FOCSLE IS NOTED.
CREW IS QUARTERED IN FOCSLE.

CAPSTAN IS RECONSTRUCTION.

HOUSE   LONG
BOAT

COMPANION
HATCHWAY

CONTOUR OF MAIN
RAIL AND MONKEY RAIL

21'-3 TO   28'-6   49'-0   29'-6 TO
TAFFRAIL   KNIGHTHEADS

RACER #3, 4, 97   207'OA × 42'-6

HOUSE

HOUSE
47' × 18'

CREW IS QUARTERED FORWARD
IN THE TWEEN DECKS.

PARTS OF THIS ARRANGEMENT
BASED ON A PRINT IN REF. 97.

SCALE - FEET   100   150   200   250

405

Figure 26.22. *Weather deck arrangements.*

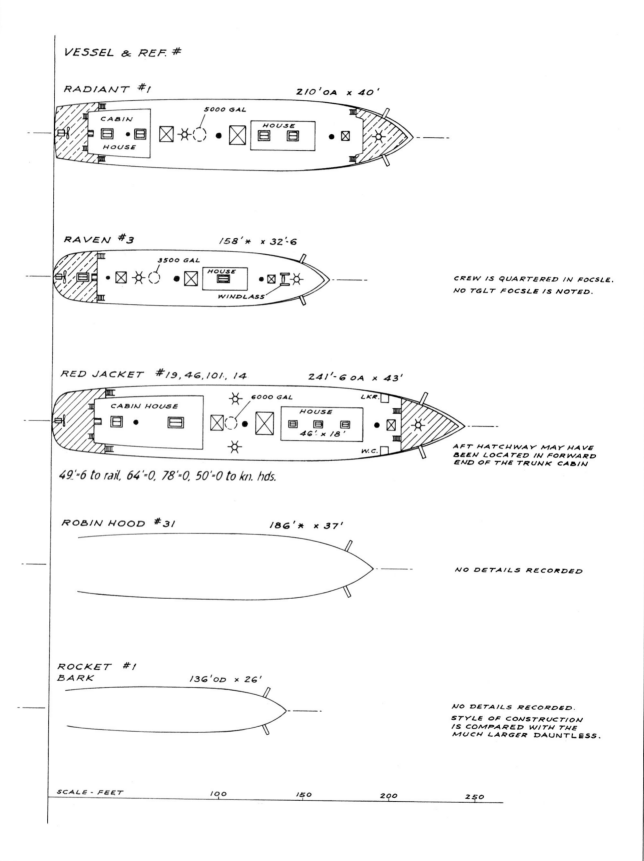

VESSEL & REF. #

RADIANT #1   210' OA × 40'

RAVEN #3   158' * × 32'-6

CREW IS QUARTERED IN FOCSLE.
NO TGLT FOCSLE IS NOTED.

RED JACKET #19, 46, 101, 14   241'-6 OA × 43'

49'-6 to rail, 64'-0, 78'-0, 50'-0 to kn. hds.

AFT HATCHWAY MAY HAVE
BEEN LOCATED IN FORWARD
END OF THE TRUNK CABIN

ROBIN HOOD #31   186' * × 37'

NO DETAILS RECORDED

ROCKET #1
BARK   136' OD × 26'

NO DETAILS RECORDED.
STYLE OF CONSTRUCTION
IS COMPARED WITH THE
MUCH LARGER DAUNTLESS.

SCALE - FEET   100   150   200   250

Figure 26.23. *Weather deck arrangements.*

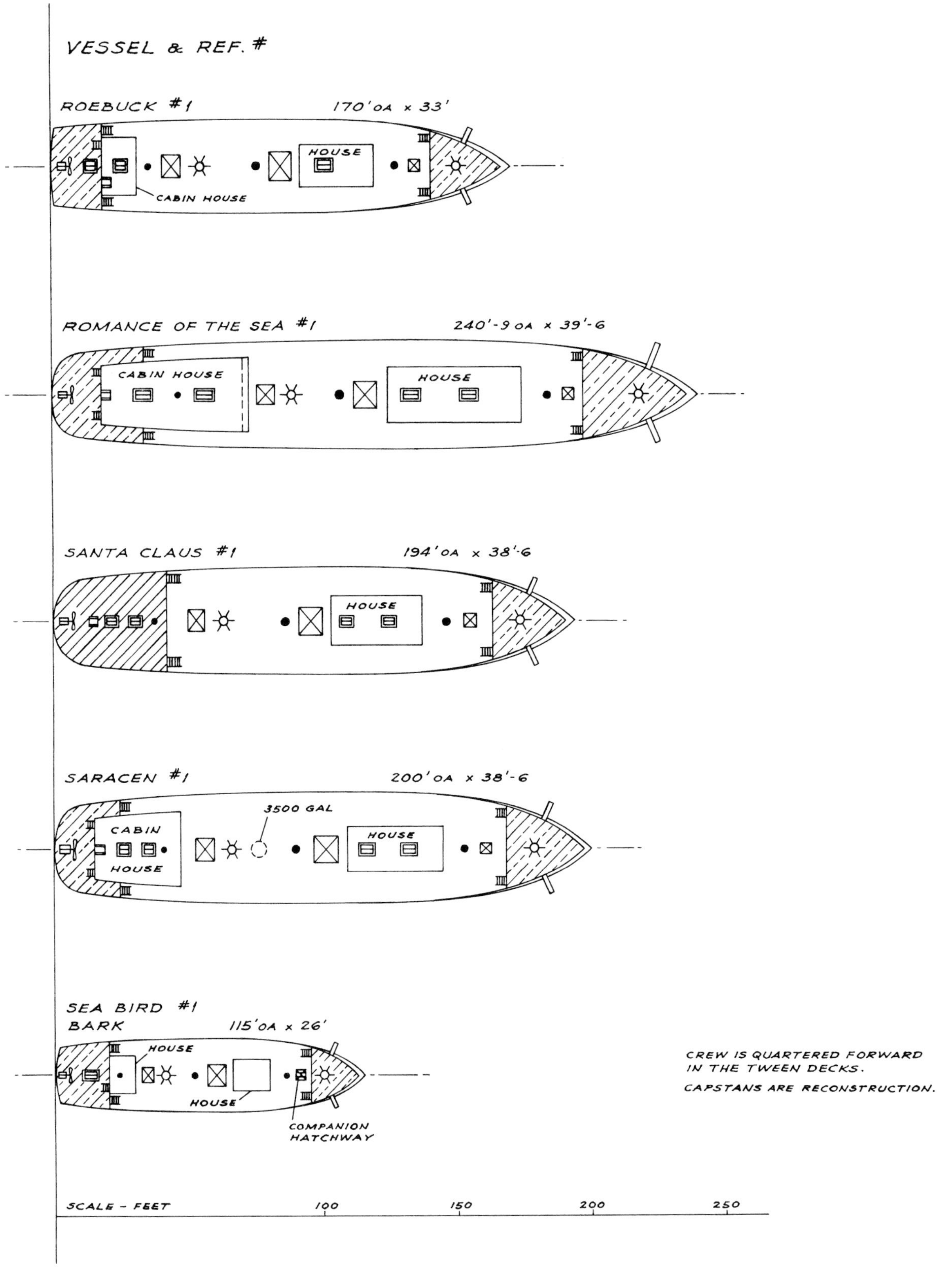

VESSEL & REF. #

ROEBUCK #1   170' OA × 33'

CABIN HOUSE

HOUSE

ROMANCE OF THE SEA #1   240'-9 OA × 39'-6

CABIN HOUSE

HOUSE

SANTA CLAUS #1   194' OA × 38'-6

HOUSE

SARACEN #1   200' OA × 38'-6

3500 GAL

CABIN HOUSE

HOUSE

SEA BIRD #1
BARK   115' OA × 26'

HOUSE

HOUSE

COMPANION HATCHWAY

CREW IS QUARTERED FORWARD
IN THE TWEEN DECKS.

CAPSTANS ARE RECONSTRUCTION.

SCALE – FEET   100   150   200   250

407

Figure 26.24. *Weather deck arrangements.*

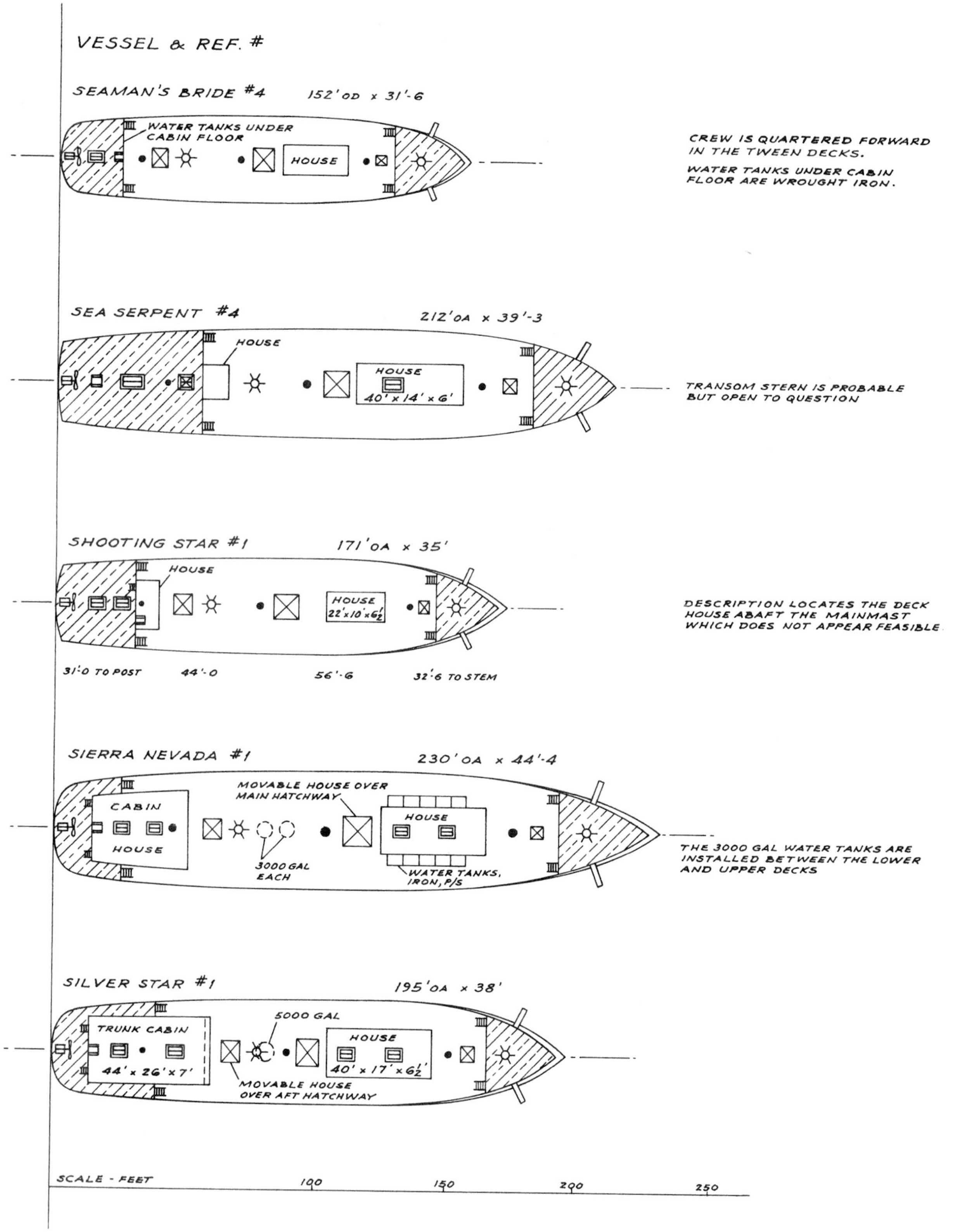

VESSEL & REF. #

SEAMAN'S BRIDE #4   152' OD x 31'-6

CREW IS QUARTERED FORWARD
IN THE TWEEN DECKS.
WATER TANKS UNDER CABIN
FLOOR ARE WROUGHT IRON.

WATER TANKS UNDER
CABIN FLOOR

HOUSE

SEA SERPENT #4   212' OA x 39'-3

TRANSOM STERN IS PROBABLE
BUT OPEN TO QUESTION

HOUSE

HOUSE
40' x 14' x 6'

SHOOTING STAR #1   171' OA x 35'

DESCRIPTION LOCATES THE DECK
HOUSE ABAFT THE MAINMAST
WHICH DOES NOT APPEAR FEASIBLE.

HOUSE

HOUSE
22' x 10' x 6½'

31'-0 TO POST   44'-0   56'-6   32'-6 TO STEM

SIERRA NEVADA #1   230' OA x 44'-4

MOVABLE HOUSE OVER
MAIN HATCHWAY

CABIN
HOUSE

HOUSE

3000 GAL
EACH

WATER TANKS,
IRON, P/S

THE 3000 GAL WATER TANKS ARE
INSTALLED BETWEEN THE LOWER
AND UPPER DECKS

SILVER STAR #1   195' OA x 38'

5000 GAL

TRUNK CABIN
44' x 26' x 7'

HOUSE
40' x 17' x 6½'

MOVABLE HOUSE
OVER AFT HATCHWAY

SCALE - FEET   100   150   200   250

Figure 26.25. *Weather deck arrangements.*

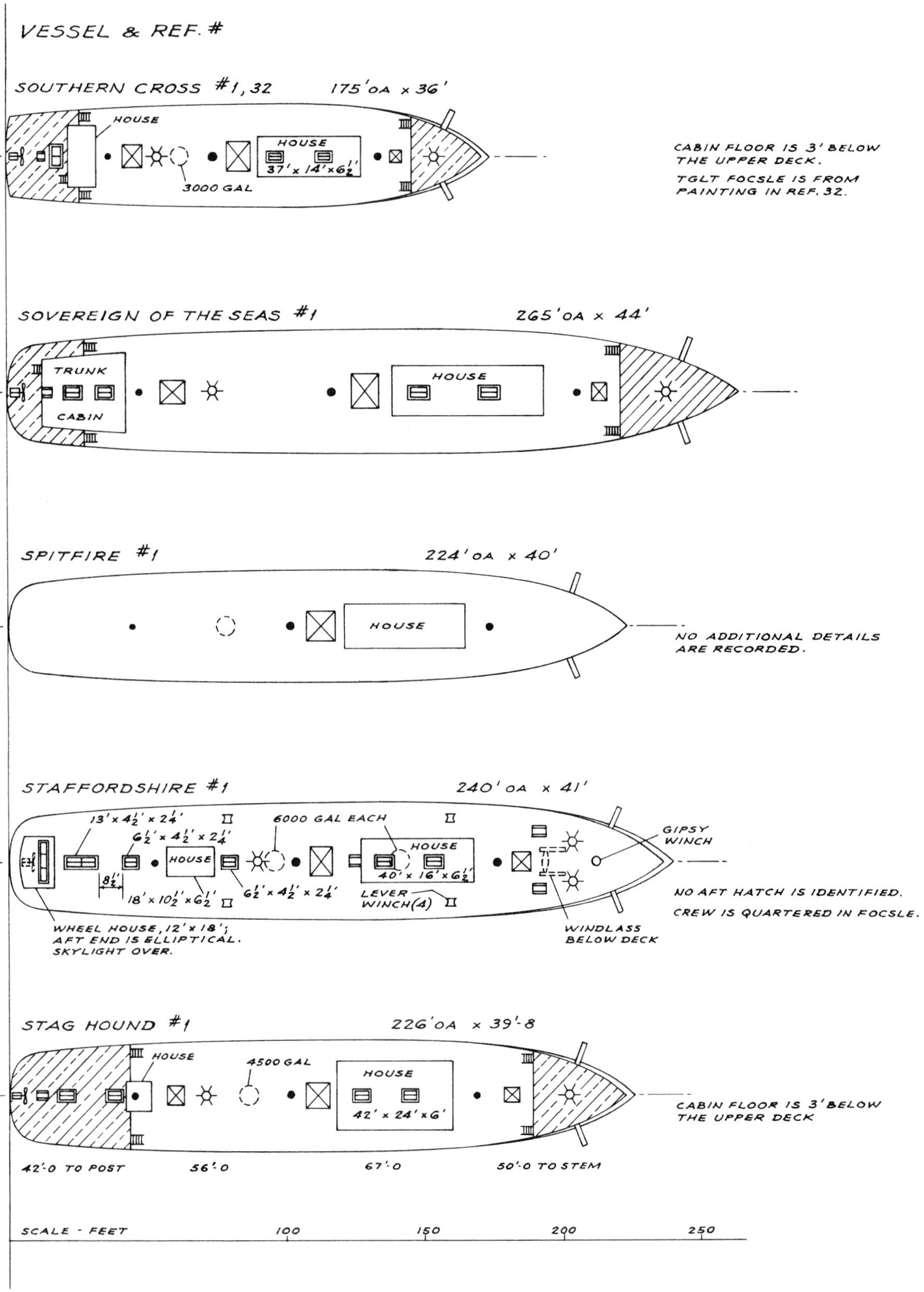

VESSEL & REF. #

SOUTHERN CROSS #1,32   175' OA × 36'

HOUSE

HOUSE
37' × 14' × 6½'

3000 GAL

CABIN FLOOR IS 3' BELOW
THE UPPER DECK.
TGLT FOCSLE IS FROM
PAINTING IN REF. 32.

SOVEREIGN OF THE SEAS #1   265' OA × 44'

TRUNK

CABIN

HOUSE

SPITFIRE #1   224' OA × 40'

HOUSE

NO ADDITIONAL DETAILS
ARE RECORDED.

STAFFORDSHIRE #1   240' OA × 41'

13' × 4½' × 2¼'   6000 GAL EACH   GIPSY
WINCH
6½' × 4½' × 2¼'
HOUSE
8½'   HOUSE
40' × 16' × 6½'
18' × 10½' × 6¼'   6½' × 4½' × 2¼'
LEVER
WINCH(4)

WHEEL HOUSE, 12' × 18';
AFT END IS ELLIPTICAL.
SKYLIGHT OVER.

WINDLASS
BELOW DECK

NO AFT HATCH IS IDENTIFIED.
CREW IS QUARTERED IN FOCSLE.

STAG HOUND #1   226' OA × 39'-8

HOUSE   4500 GAL   HOUSE

HOUSE
42' × 24' × 6'

CABIN FLOOR IS 3' BELOW
THE UPPER DECK

42'-0 TO POST   56'-0   67'-0   50'-0 TO STEM

SCALE - FEET   100   150   200   250

Figure 26.26. *Weather deck arrangements.*

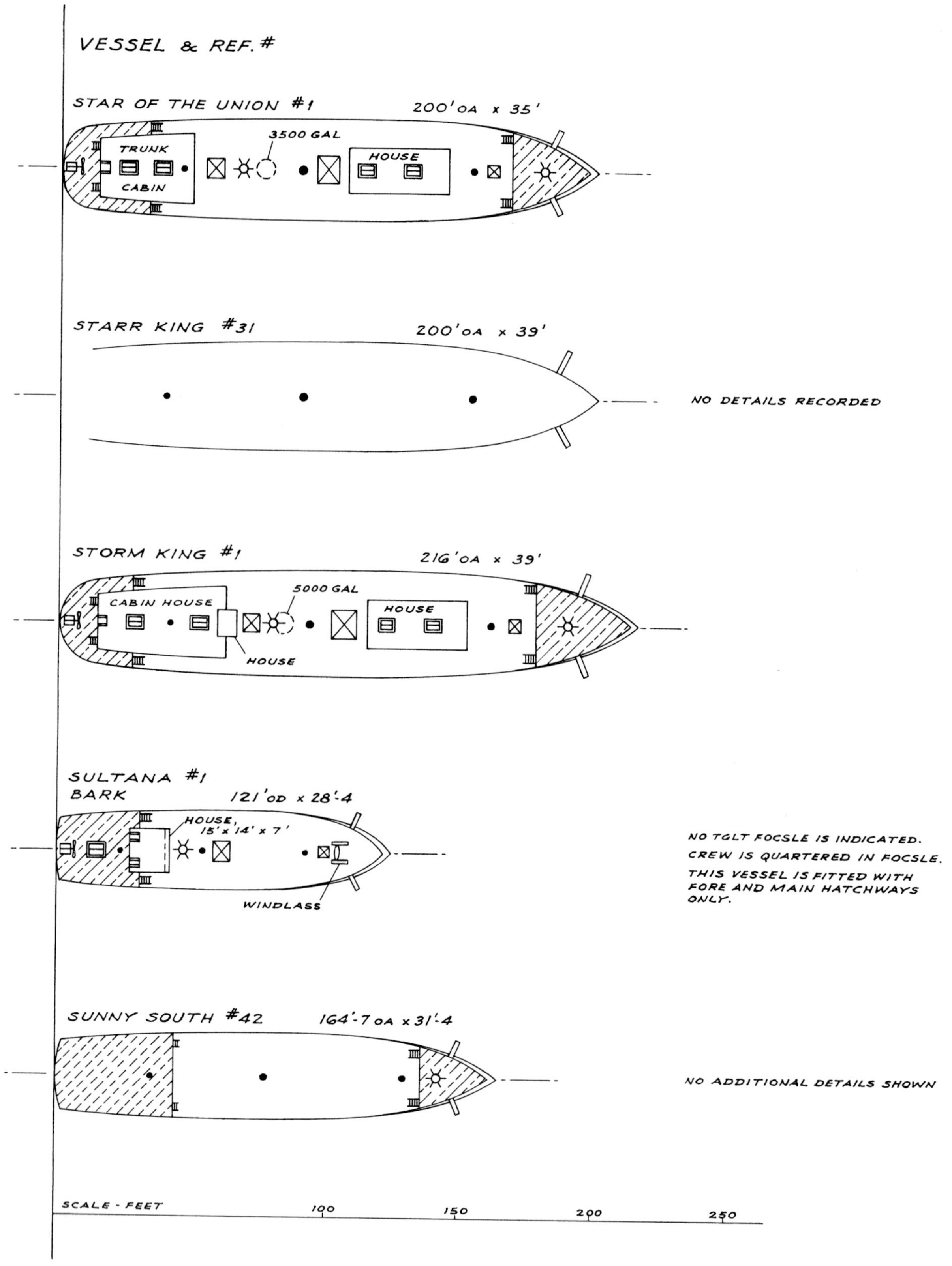

VESSEL & REF. #

STAR OF THE UNION #1   200' OA x 35'

3500 GAL

TRUNK

CABIN

HOUSE

STARR KING #31   200' OA x 39'

NO DETAILS RECORDED

STORM KING #1   216' OA x 39'

CABIN HOUSE

5000 GAL

HOUSE

HOUSE

SULTANA #1
BARK   121' OD x 28'-4

HOUSE,
15' x 14' x 7'

WINDLASS

NO TGLT FOCSLE IS INDICATED.
CREW IS QUARTERED IN FOCSLE.
THIS VESSEL IS FITTED WITH
FORE AND MAIN HATCHWAYS
ONLY.

SUNNY SOUTH #42   164'-7 OA x 31'-4

NO ADDITIONAL DETAILS SHOWN

SCALE - FEET   100   150   200   250

Figure 26.27. *Weather deck arrangements.*

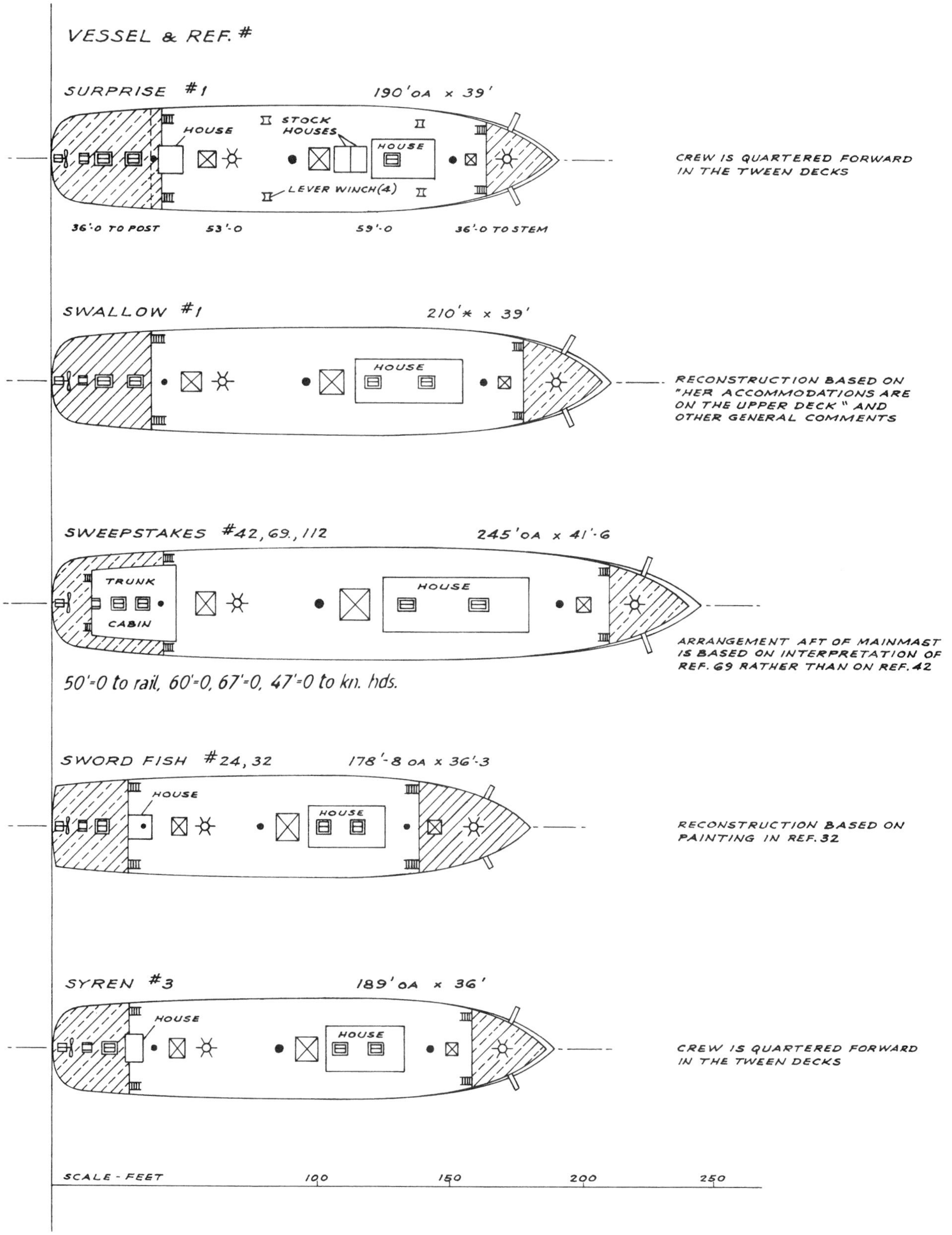

VESSEL & REF. #

SURPRISE #1   190' OA × 39'

HOUSE   II STOCK HOUSES   II

HOUSE

LEVER WINCH (4)   II

CREW IS QUARTERED FORWARD IN THE TWEEN DECKS

36'·0 TO POST   53'·0   59'·0   36'·0 TO STEM

SWALLOW #1   210'* × 39'

HOUSE

RECONSTRUCTION BASED ON "HER ACCOMMODATIONS ARE ON THE UPPER DECK" AND OTHER GENERAL COMMENTS

SWEEPSTAKES #42, 69., 112   245' OA × 41'·6

TRUNK

CABIN

HOUSE

ARRANGEMENT AFT OF MAINMAST IS BASED ON INTERPRETATION OF REF. 69 RATHER THAN ON REF. 42

50'=0 to rail, 60'=0, 67'=0, 47'=0 to kn. hds.

SWORD FISH #24, 32   178'-8 OA × 36'-3

HOUSE

HOUSE

RECONSTRUCTION BASED ON PAINTING IN REF. 32

SYREN #3   189' OA × 36'

HOUSE

HOUSE

CREW IS QUARTERED FORWARD IN THE TWEEN DECKS

SCALE - FEET   100   150   200   250

Figure 26.28. *Weather deck arrangements.*

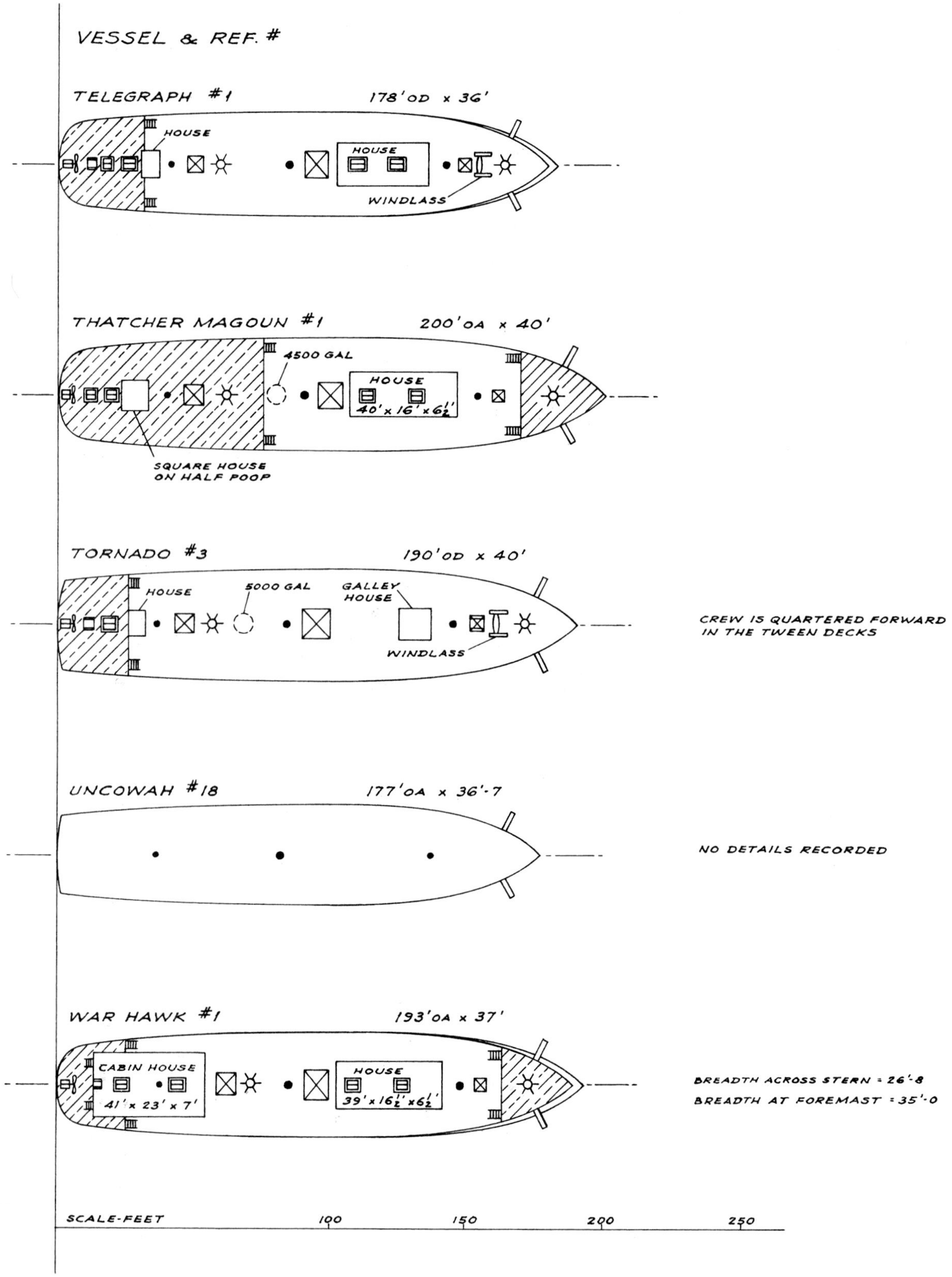

VESSEL & REF. #

TELEGRAPH #1   178'OD x 36'

HOUSE
HOUSE
WINDLASS

THATCHER MAGOUN #1   200'OA x 40'

4500 GAL
HOUSE
40' x 16' x 6½'
SQUARE HOUSE
ON HALF POOP

TORNADO #3   190'OD x 40'

HOUSE
5000 GAL
GALLEY
HOUSE
WINDLASS

CREW IS QUARTERED FORWARD
IN THE TWEEN DECKS

UNCOWAH #18   177'OA x 36'-7

NO DETAILS RECORDED

WAR HAWK #1   193'OA x 37'

CABIN HOUSE
41' x 23' x 7'
HOUSE
39' x 16½' x 6½'

BREADTH ACROSS STERN = 26'-8
BREADTH AT FOREMAST = 35'-0

SCALE-FEET   100   150   200   250

Figure 26.29. *Weather deck arrangements.*

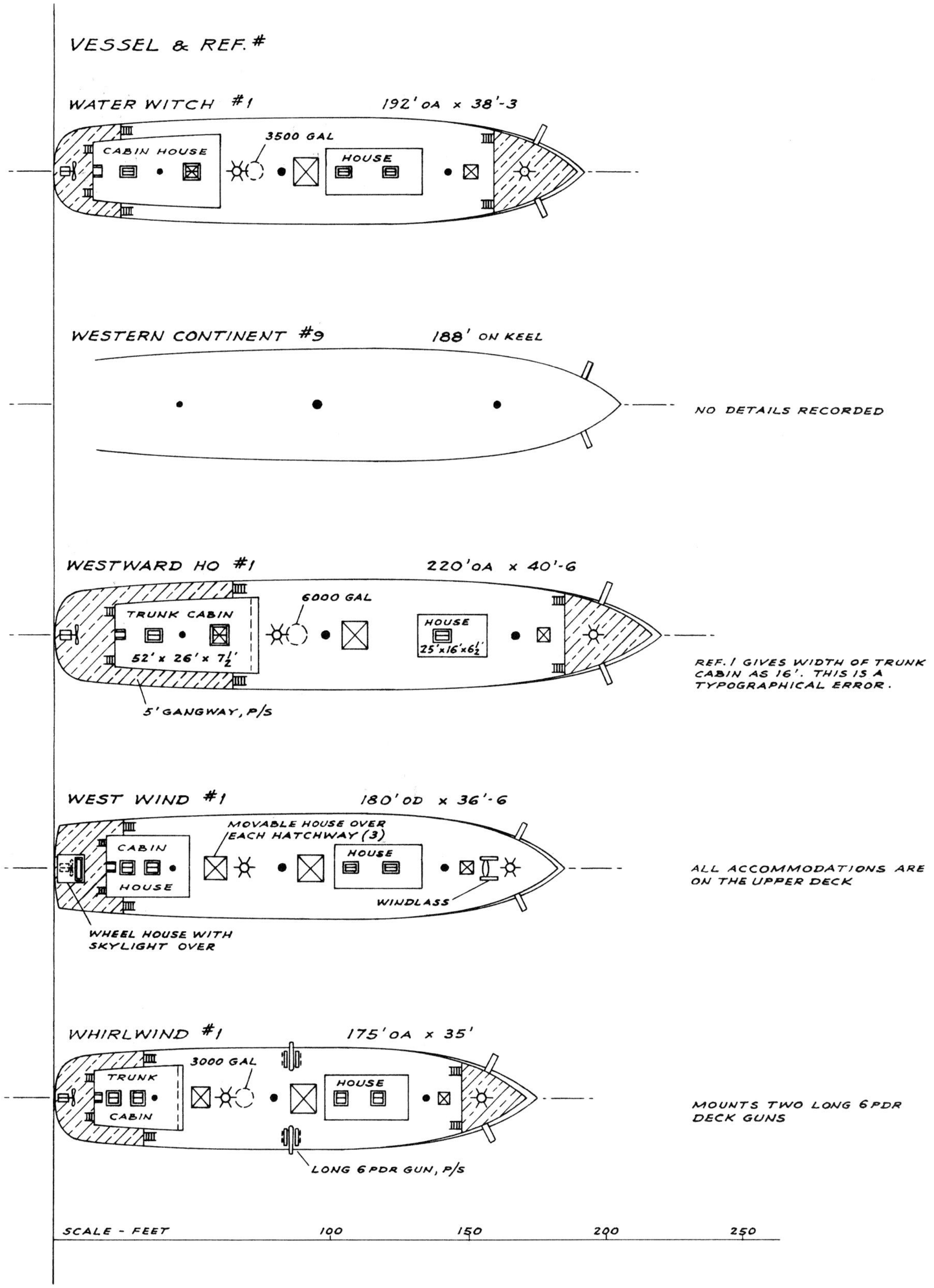

VESSEL & REF. #

WATER WITCH #1   192' OA × 38'-3

CABIN HOUSE   3500 GAL   HOUSE

WESTERN CONTINENT #9   188' ON KEEL

NO DETAILS RECORDED

WESTWARD HO #1   220' OA × 40'-6

TRUNK CABIN   6000 GAL   HOUSE
52' × 26' × 7½'   25'×16'×6½'

5' GANGWAY, P/S

REF. I GIVES WIDTH OF TRUNK
CABIN AS 16'. THIS IS A
TYPOGRAPHICAL ERROR.

WEST WIND #1   180' OD × 36'-6

MOVABLE HOUSE OVER
EACH HATCHWAY (3)
CABIN
HOUSE   HOUSE

WINDLASS

WHEEL HOUSE WITH
SKYLIGHT OVER

ALL ACCOMMODATIONS ARE
ON THE UPPER DECK

WHIRLWIND #1   175' OA × 35'

TRUNK   3000 GAL   HOUSE
CABIN

LONG 6 PDR GUN, P/S

MOUNTS TWO LONG 6 PDR
DECK GUNS

SCALE - FEET   100   150   200   250

413

Figure 26.30. *Weather deck arrangements.*

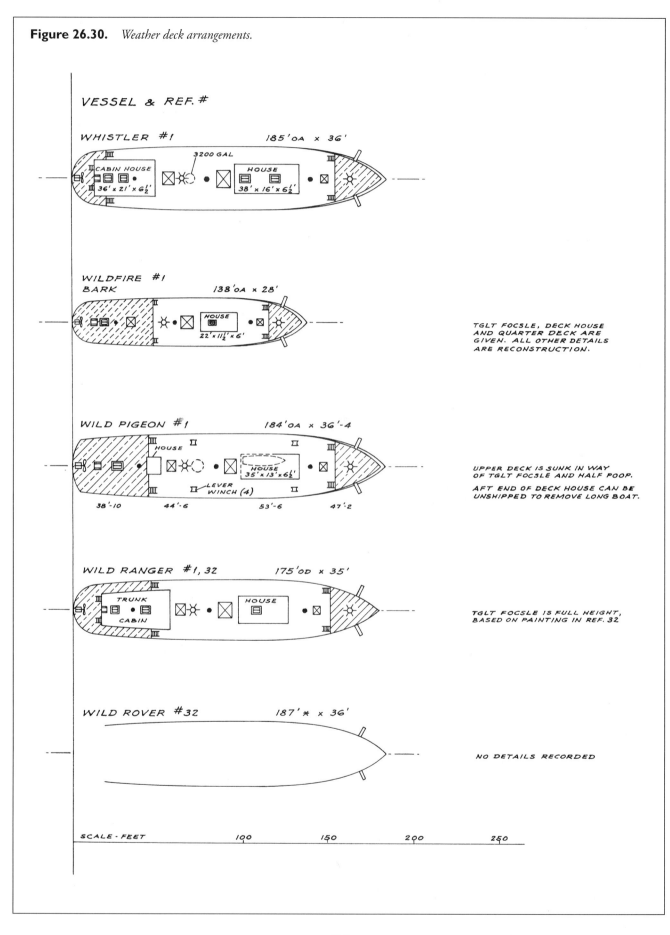

VESSEL & REF. #

WHISTLER #1   185' OA × 36'
CABIN HOUSE   3200 GAL   HOUSE
36' × 21' × 6½'   38' × 16' × 6½'

WILDFIRE #1
BARK   138' OA × 28'
HOUSE
22' × 11½' × 6'

TGLT FOCSLE, DECK HOUSE
AND QUARTER DECK ARE
GIVEN. ALL OTHER DETAILS
ARE RECONSTRUCTION.

WILD PIGEON #1   184' OA × 36'-4
HOUSE
HOUSE
35' × 13' × 6½'
LEVER WINCH (4)
38'-10   44'-6   53'-6   47'-2

UPPER DECK IS SUNK IN WAY
OF TGLT FOCSLE AND HALF POOP.

AFT END OF DECK HOUSE CAN BE
UNSHIPPED TO REMOVE LONG BOAT.

WILD RANGER #1, 32   175' OD × 35'
TRUNK
CABIN   HOUSE

TGLT FOCSLE IS FULL HEIGHT,
BASED ON PAINTING IN REF. 32

WILD ROVER #32   187' * × 36'

NO DETAILS RECORDED

SCALE - FEET   100   150   200   250

Figure 26.31. *Weather deck arrangements.*

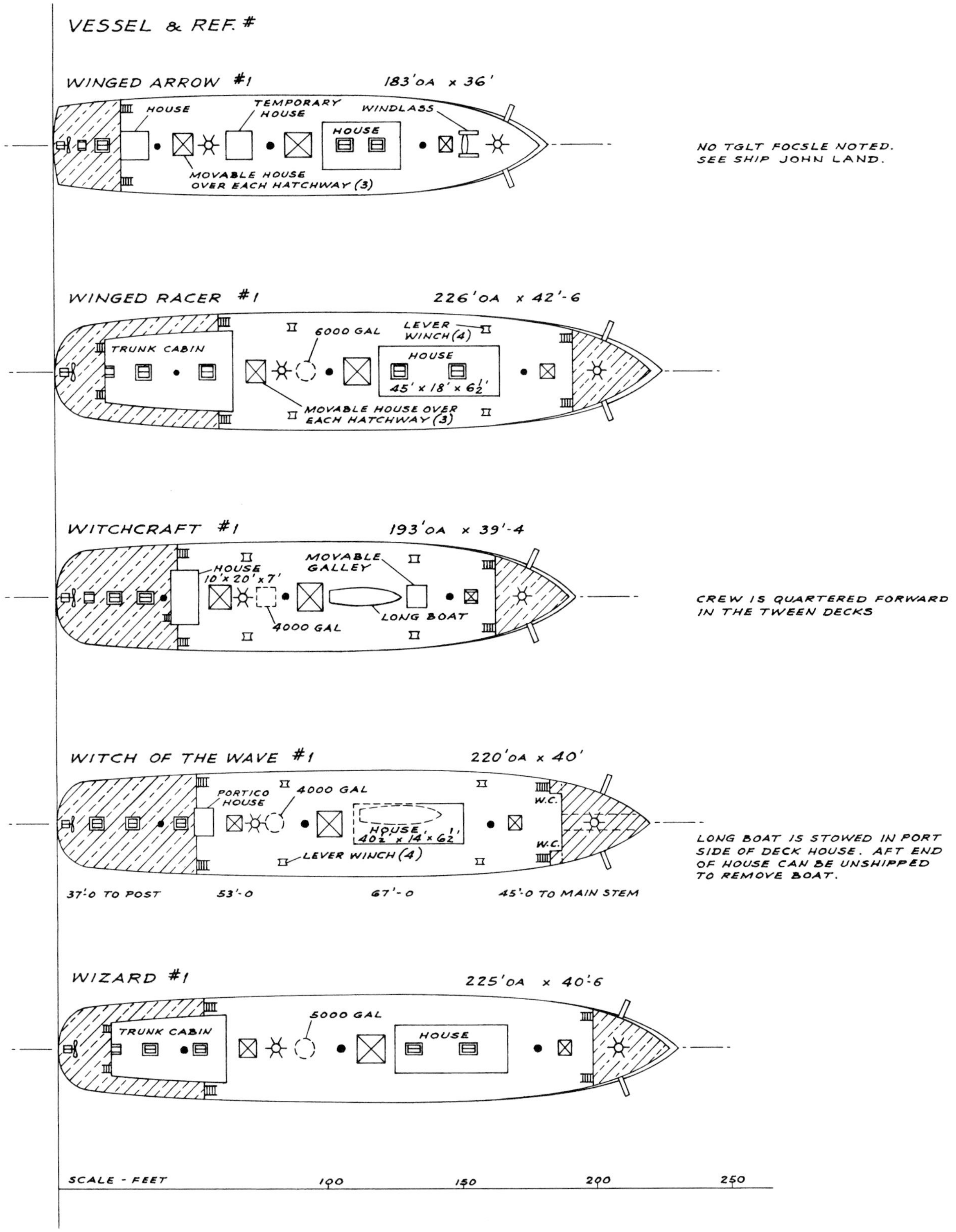

VESSEL & REF. #

WINGED ARROW #1   183'OA x 36'

HOUSE   TEMPORARY   WINDLASS
          HOUSE
HOUSE

MOVABLE HOUSE
OVER EACH HATCHWAY (3)

NO TGLT FOCSLE NOTED.
SEE SHIP JOHN LAND.

WINGED RACER #1   226'OA x 42'-6

6000 GAL   LEVER
            WINCH (4)
TRUNK CABIN
                        HOUSE
                        45' x 18' x 6½'

MOVABLE HOUSE OVER
EACH HATCHWAY (3)

WITCHCRAFT #1   193'OA x 39'-4

                 MOVABLE
HOUSE   GALLEY
10'x 20'x 7'

            4000 GAL   LONG BOAT

CREW IS QUARTERED FORWARD
IN THE TWEEN DECKS

WITCH OF THE WAVE #1   220'OA x 40'

PORTICO   4000 GAL
HOUSE   W.C.
                  HOUSE
                  40½' x 14' x 6½'   W.C.

        LEVER WINCH (4)

37'-0 TO POST   53'-0   67'-0   45'-0 TO MAIN STEM

LONG BOAT IS STOWED IN PORT
SIDE OF DECK HOUSE. AFT END
OF HOUSE CAN BE UNSHIPPED
TO REMOVE BOAT.

WIZARD #1   225'OA x 40'-6

                 5000 GAL
TRUNK CABIN   HOUSE

SCALE - FEET   100   150   200   250

415

Figure 26.32. *Weather deck arrangements.*

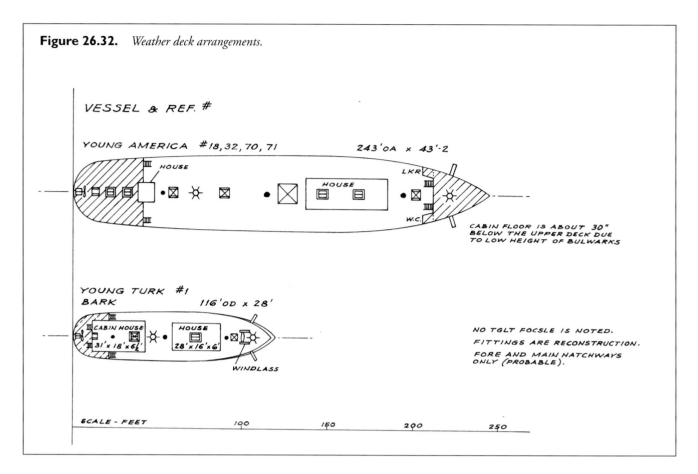

(text continued from page 384)

these poops obviated the need for any form of house to provide access to the interior.

Like all other structures, poop decks were not bound by any rules governing their size and extent; this remained the builder's prerogative. Only for a small percentage of vessels do the descriptions available state the lengths of poop structures and trunk cabins or cabinhouses; however, they often include details of the cabins and staterooms built within the structures, from which the size of the total structure may be ascertained.

In vessels that were not designed as flush-decked ships, the omission of some type of poop deck structure was very rare. However, of the clippers listed herein, *Bald Eagle* and *Champion of the Seas* were described as having their aft accommodations below deck. This left the entire after deck clear, except in *Bald Eagle* there was a small house which covered access to the tween-decks, while in *Champion of the Seas* a combination wheelhouse–smoking room was built over the helm.

A third form of deck construction aft was the *raised quarter deck*, in which the weather deck was raised several feet above its normal level from the area of the mizzenmast to the taffrail. The only recorded instance of this among the vessels herein occurs in the bark *Wildfire*. *Celestial* (Figure 26.4) and *Sunny South* (Figure 26.26) are based on lines drawings shown in *The Search for Speed Under Sail*.[42]

The final form of structural deck design was that of the *flush-decked* vessel, in which no superstructure was built into the ends of the vessel, thus leaving the entire deck available for any houses that might be desired. Two examples of this are included, *Staffordshire* and the original *Great Republic*, both built by Donald McKay.

Hatches

Ships' *hatches* followed some fixed general rules governing their size and location. Provision for hatches was made prior to construction of the decks so that the structure would be spaced and sized to accommodate the required openings. As a matter of arrangement in a vessel, any hatches in a given area were located so as to "plumb" each other through the decks, thus allowing for unimpeded vertical lift when onloading or offloading cargo.

In general, all vessels were fitted with three hatchways—fore, main, and after—and all followed the same general considerations.

The *fore hatch* was the smallest one to pierce the decks due to the restrictions of space in the ship's bows, especially in the lower decks. It was located close abaft the break of the topgallant forecastle, and was of a breadth to fit within the span of the windlass barrel and well clear of its knees and bits. In the fore-and-aft direction this hatch opening was fitted between two deck beams.

After cargo had been onloaded and the fore hatches in the lower decks had been battened down, a companion was fitted over the weather deck hatch and a ladder installed to the deck below. This provided access to and from the crew's spaces when quartered below in the tween-decks, or, if that was not the case, it provided access for the purpose of inspection below deck.

The *main hatch*, as the name implies, was the largest hatch usually found in ships. It was invariably located amidships close before the mainmast, clear of any possible fouling of the pump installation. There was little restraint on the breadth of the clear opening, but in the fore-and-aft direction it was usually kept within the space of three deck beams, the middle one being cut and supported by headers under the longitudinal hatch coamings.

The cover of this hatch was of scantlings well calculated to resist the impact of pounding seas or the introduction of excessive deck loads. However, it is worthy of note that such covers, whether made up of panels or planks, did not contribute to or detract from the structural integrity of the ship; this function was performed by the deck framing in way of the hatch. In many cases the main hatch in the tween-decks was in way of passenger accommodations and, once closed up for a voyage, was covered in a manner consistent with the living quarters in which it was located.

The *after hatch* was generally located close forward of the mizzenmast and sometimes pierced the extended portion of long poop and half poop decks. It was intermediate in size; being located near the ship's run, the space below decks was quickly diminishing, thus precluding the stowage of large individual items of cargo.

The same factors that applied to the main hatch also applied to the after hatch. However, in vessels that had this after hatch located over living spaces, it was not battened down after cargo had been onloaded; instead, the hatch was fitted with a raised skylight that admitted light and much-needed ventilation to the space below.

It was a frequent practice throughout the clipper fleet to fit skylights over hatches that were located in way of living spaces, thus providing light and ventilation, always in short supply. These skylights make an appearance intermittently throughout the illustrations, and are covered below under their own heading.

There were exceptions to the usual practice of installing three hatches. All appear in the illustrations but are worthy of separate mention: *Challenge*, with six hatches, exclusive of the forward companion, which was an individual unit installed over a companionway ladder forward of the fore hatch; *John Stuart*, six hatches, all fitted with skylights; *Great Republic*, the original ship, four hatches and, in addition, a large hatch, port and starboard, on the spar deck outboard of the 25-foot deckhouse, to facilitate spar stowage on the upper deck; *Young America*, four hatches, the fore and two after hatches fitted as companionways; *Lightning*, four hatches, the after hatch fitted as a companionway only. *Staffordshire*, a large vessel, and the barks *Sultana*, *Lamplighter*, and *Young Turk*, all small vessels, had only two hatches each.

Deckhouses

The *deckhouse* was the major individual unit to be found on a vessel's weather deck. In general, the principal house was closely related in size to that of the vessel and was always located immediately abaft the foremast. These houses were long, rectangular structures which usually contained the galley in the forward end and accommodations for the crew in the remaining portion. A long fore-and-aft passage ran amidships dividing the house into port and starboard staterooms or living spaces.

This arrangement, while usual, was by no means exclusive. There were many variations. In some vessels, while the galley was retained, the bulk of the house quartered the ship's boys, and might be fitted out with staterooms, storerooms, carpenter shop, stock pens, etc., in one of many combinations.

Perhaps the most unusual deckhouses were those that, in addition to or in lieu of the above arrangements, were built to house the ship's longboat. In such vessels, one side and the after end of the house in way of the boat was made to allow its being unshipped. The boat, stowed inside on rollers, would be rolled out to be lowered over the side. For reasons not stated, this stowage, except in one vessel, was always located in the after port side of the deckhouse. In this book's listing of clippers the above arrangement was found in *John Bertram*, *Queen of the Seas*, *Wild Pigeon*, and *Witch of the Wave*. The single exception was *Bald Eagle*, whose longboat was stowed on centerline in the forward portion of the deckhouse. Both sides of this house could be unshipped for removal of the boat.

Great Republic, an unusual ship by any standard, carried four large deckhouses on her spar deck when originally built. After her disastrous fire she was rebuilt without a spar deck and was fitted out with two deckhouses on her upper deck, which was now her weather deck.

The dimensions for all deckhouses, large or small, and trunk cabins, which are found in this listing, are given where known.

While the large deckhouse was a customary structure on a ship's weather deck, there were some vessels built with minimal houses, the designer choosing to quarter the facilities below deck. Vessels in this category were *Challenge*, the house being only large enough to accommodate the galley and one stateroom; *Coeur de Lion*, housing the galley and quarters for the ship's boys; *Tornado*, housing only the galley; and the small bark *Sea Bird*, housing the galley, one storeroom, and sleeping quarters for the ship's doctor.

In addition to the above vessels built with small deckhouses, there were some clippers that had no permanent deckhouse but did have small portable or removable houses on deck. Four of these are *Dauntless*, with two movable houses between the foremast and the main hatch; *Witchcraft*, *Flying Childers*, and the bark *Racehorse*, each with only a portable galley.

The clearest deck of all was found in Webb's large *Invincible*, a ship with no deck structures between the forecastle and her small half poop.

An unusual but not uncommon practice in the clipper ships was that of installing movable houses over one or all of the principal hatchways on the weather deck. More than a dozen vessels included herein were built with this feature; all are appropriately noted in the illustrations.

Exterior Doors

The *exterior doors* that were installed in deckhouses and structural bulkheads were all subject to certain general requirements. The first was that each such door be provided with a raised sill height, in order to preclude the penetration of water into the house or structure in the event of wet weather or boarding seas. Such sills were normally about 12 inches high or a similar convenient height over which personnel could easily step.

A second general practice was that of hinging all exterior doors to open out to the weather. In this way, boarding seas tended to force the doors tightly against their jambs, thus enhancing their watertightness.

Exterior doors in transverse bulkheads were hinged along their outboard edge. This minimized the possibility of water being shipped into the interior spaces if a door should be opened against boarding seas.

Finally, the general practice with exterior doors in longitudinal bulkheads or in the sides of deckhouses was to place the hinges along the forward edge of the doors, there being greater chance of seas boarding the ship from forward than from abaft. This arrangement precluded the doors acting as scoops to direct water into the interior.

Quite obviously, these practices did not keep the interiors of ships bone-dry, but in their own way they contributed toward making the vessels more livable.

Skylights

The *skylight* was a desirable and important appurtenance to a ship's on-deck details. As the name implies, skylights allowed for the access of daylight into interiors that otherwise could be dark and unattractive. Equally important, however, was the fact that, when hinged, they could be opened to provide all-important ventilation. They were invariably constructed with frames and trim made of finer woods such as mahogany, finished with varnish, and were sometimes partially glazed with stained glass. The skylights were impressive examples of quality joinerwork.

The most usual locations for skylights were on the tops of deckhouses and trunk cabins, and on half poops, poops, and decks in locations over living spaces. As a general rule, any cabin, saloon, or passage that was bounded on all sides by interior bulkheads was fitted with skylights in the overhead.

In addition to the above usual locations, the ships *Challenge*, *Invincible*, *James Baines*, *John Stuart*, and *Racer* were fitted with skylights over one or more of the weather deck hatches.

Pump Brake Windlass

The *pump brake windlass*, found on the forward deck of all the clippers, was not an item of structure, but, rather, an item of the ship's outfit. However, its size, function, and location mandated that it be considered a major structure when arranging a vessel's deck. In the restricted area of the forecastle deck, the windlass assembly assumed huge proportions and thus required primary consideration for its placement. It was usually located immediately below the break of the topgallant forecastle, the pump brake mechanism extending up through that deck, at which location the pumping motion that operated it was applied.

In the deck arrangements appearing in this chapter, the windlass is not shown in vessels that were built with a topgallant forecastle due to its not being visible. However, categorically, every vessel was fitted with such a windlass.

Capstans

The *capstans*, like the windlass, were part of a vessel's outfit and, due to their function and mode of operation, required definite space considerations. Most ships, except for the very smallest, were fitted with one capstan in the bow close up to the inboard ends of the catheads and one amidships on the weather deck forward of the after hatch, both located on the centerline of the ship.

An area around the center of the capstan was kept relatively clear so that the crew manning the capstan bars would have sufficient room to walk the bars around in a complete circle. The presence of such structure as hatch coamings was regarded as an inconvenience rather than an interference.

Capstans were used for such chores as heavy lifting work, warping a ship into her berth at dockside, and in anchor handling. While most vessels had two capstans, some were fitted with as many as six. Donald McKay's vessels appear to have been the most well-found in this respect. *James Baines* had six capstans, three ranged along the deck on each side of the ship, and on the topgallant forecastle deck a crab winch in lieu of a capstan; *Donald McKay*, six capstans; *Champion of the Seas*, five capstans, one of which was a patent capstan on the topgallant forecastle; *Staffordshire*, three capstans, two of which were on the forecastle deck along with a winch; *Lightning*, three capstans; *Andrew Jackson* and *Red Jacket*, three capstans each (questionable); and the small barks *Mermaid*, *Racehorse*, and *Sultana*, all having one capstan.

In most clippers the capstan located in the waist, even though placed there to perform a practical function, was almost a work of art. The central barrel of these capstans was probably made of oak or a similar hardwood to provide adequate strength, but the surface features were grand. The *whelps*—raised strips that increased the hold of a rope and prevent chafing of the barrel—whelp chocks, and drumhead were fabricated of polished mahogany. The whelps were faced with locust to resist wear, and the drumhead was covered with polished brass; in addition, other brass trim was applied.

Pumps

The ship's *pumps* were a vital item of outfit, absolutely essential to the well-being of the vessel. They were universally located immediately abaft the mainmast, the crank generally being supported at the ends by the main fife rail. Their entire fabrication was conveniently contained within the space occupied by the fife rail, and in this respect they required no space that was exclusively their own.

The principal type of pump in vogue during the early clipper period was the flywheel pump, the flywheels providing centrifugal energy once they were set in motion by the men operating the crank. This feature did much to ease the labor of pumping, which, under extreme conditions, could become a task of long duration.

To the men who operated this type of pump, there was nothing picturesque. However, on a ship's deck they added a small bit of color with their red flywheel rims and their peculiar S-shaped spokes. This type of spoke was not a matter of aesthetics, but of practicality. Most flywheels, consisting of rim, spokes, and hub, were made as a one-piece iron casting. In such a casting, with its large bulk of iron in the rim and its relatively long, slender spokes, it was impossible to achieve a uniform rate of cooling after the molten metal had been poured into the mould; consequently, uneven stresses developed and resulted in cracking, breakage, and deformity of the wheel. The solution was found in the shaping of the spokes. Where the fast-cooling,

straight spoke was a rigid, unyielding column, the S-shaped spoke was free to distort throughout the entire cooling process. The result was a flywheel that could be cast without the threat of initial failure.

In cases where the flywheels were fabricated as an assembly of hubs, spokes, and rims, the S-shaped spoke was a necessity for the assembly process. The hub was cast with short, hollow bosses equally spaced and arranged radially around its periphery. The rim featured similar bosses, also equally spaced, arranged around the inner surface and pointing directly toward the center of the hub. The spokes, instead of being cast, were round wrought iron rods, formed into a similar "S" configuration; but, in this case, each end of the spoke was sharply bent to fit into the round holes in the bosses. The shape of the spokes allowed them to be deflected enough to clear the ends of the bosses and then sprung into their final position.

In this same period, there was a great surge of improvement in all the existing methods of working ship. Inventions were made and patented, and in a short course of time new patent machines such as pumps began to appear and replace the everyday flywheel pump and many other items of outfit, as covered in the next chapter.

Steering

The *steering apparatus* was the final bit of deck furniture which required specific consideration of its location. There were two types of steering mechanisms that were activated by the ship's wheel. The first was the *incumbent mechanism*, which consisted of a short tiller secured to the rudderhead immediately below the steering deck, a gun tackle purchase which was rove below the deck from the tiller and led upward to a barrel built into the wheel shaft, and the steering wheel itself.

This mechanism, which had credibility of long standing, was now finding itself displaced by newer patented mechanisms that were devoid of rope and blocks and consisted of machined iron parts installed on the rudderhead, which now terminated above the steering deck and connected directly with the wheel.

Both systems had their advocates and their detractors as to efficiency and reliability, but each required room on deck to house the steering stand and allow space on either side for the helmsman to function.

Almost all vessels were fitted with one unprotected steering wheel, and the helm was placed as close to the taffrail as the apparatus would permit. There were, however, exceptions to this general rule. Both *Blue Jacket* and the original *Great Republic* were fitted with double wheels, that of *Great Republic* being protected in a wheelhouse. Donald McKay appears to have been an avid proponent of the wheelhouse to protect the helmsman. Other of his clippers to be so built were *Champion of the Seas*, *Donald McKay*, *James Baines*, *Lightning*, and *Staffordshire*. *Ellen Foster*, *Flying Dragon*, and *West Wind* were also provided with houses.

Challenge and *Hoogly* were built with unusual steering arrangements. The wheel of *Challenge* was on the upper deck immediately forward of the break of her half poop, which was about 25 feet long. The wheel was unprotected except for its unusual location. *Hoogly*, built with a full poop deck 60 feet long, had her wheel located under the forward overhang of this deck, thus placing her helm midway between the main and mizzen masts. Both of these wheels were rigged to gun tackle purchases.

Chapter Twenty-Seven

FITTINGS AND OUTFITS

THE PREVIOUS CHAPTER DEALT WITH deck arrangements of the clippers, defining the fittings and items of outfit in generic terms. This chapter refines such terms and lists specific names and types of such furnishings whenever they have been identified in the various references.

Until the late 1840s, the general details of such ship gear as steering arrangements, windlass designs, ships' boats, and (inadequate) provisions for ventilation would have been suitably covered under generic terminology. From year to year little changed, and the improvements that did appear were minor and slow to make their existence known throughout the shipbuilding world.

Late in the 1840s, however, shortly after the appearance of the clipper ships, this lethargic process of change underwent a phenomenal departure from the evolutionary system of adopting improvements. From all quarters and in all details, new mechanical changes and improvements were patented and introduced. These changes occurred in every item of ship's outfit from the hawseholes in the bow to the steering mechanism at the stern.

Where, at one time, only the names of shipbuilders and designers were generally familiar, there now appeared additional new names which would become synonymous with modern, state-of-the-art shipbuilding. Names such as Crane (chain stoppers), Emerson (ventilation), Reed (steering apparatus), Tewksbury and Francis (ships' boats), Litchfield (pumps), Flanders (force pumps), and Perley (capstans) were among the best known and most successful of this new group of inventors. Another name, Harris (lightning conductors), became well known a short time later, although his invention cannot properly be considered an item of outfit in the accepted sense.

Competition among the inventors was as intense as the competition between the ships at sea. New inventions were introduced at a vastly accelerated pace, and existing inventions were constantly being improved. All were immediately protected by patent and widely advertised in the appropriate publications of the day. Thus the names of the men became merged with the names of their inventions.

As with all improvements, whether on land or at sea, there was always a segment of resistance among the potential users of the product. This resistance was found to a great extent among the shipbuilders themselves, some of the best of whom were reluctant to accept changes. An example was William H. Webb, who apparently did not take kindly to the newfangled steering apparatus. However, since improvements must ultimately be embraced in order for any endeavor to survive, the successful inventions were accepted (even though grudgingly) and the impractical ones discarded, and progress proceeded.

No attempt is made here to describe the details of the improvements in the vast array of equipment in use among the clippers, a subject great enough to merit a book in its own right. Unfortunately, to my knowledge, no such work has yet appeared. However, the subject is covered in great depth in a series of articles published in the *Nautical Research Journal* starting in 1987.[100]

Fortunately for posterity, a number of references itemize the specific types and brands of equipment installed in some of the ships that are the subject of this book. The following list contains the equipment in each vessel as it is covered in the appropriate references. Where the coverage is incomplete, or in vessels where no details are recorded, it must be remembered that every oceangoing vessel required such basic fittings and outfit as binnacles in proximity to the steering stand, chain pipes close abaft the windlass, and hawseholes in the eyes of the vessel. These features all required specific space allowances that were not amenable to compromise.

This list is compatible with the deck arrangements illustrated in Chapter 26. Following the name of each vessel is the number of the appropriate reference.

Alarm[1]—Patent windlass; two capstans; copper chambered hold pumps; a force pump; eight trunk ventilators; Emerson's patent ventilators; steering wheel fitted to a gun tackle purchase; "liberally found in boats and ground tackle."

Amphitrite[1]—Windlass; capstans; hold pumps located immediately forward of the aft hatchway; Emerson's patent ventilators; patent steering apparatus; "well found in boats and ground tackle."

Andrew Jackson

Antelope[1]—Patent windlass; one capstan amidship, mahogany, brass mounted; two hold pumps; Emerson's patent ventilators; patent steering apparatus; three boats (two on a gallows frame over the quarterdeck); "liberally found in ground tackle."

Asa Eldridge[1]—Windlass with double gearing; Crane's patent chain stoppers; two capstans; four copper hold pumps, two close abaft the foremast and two (Edson's "Fountain Pumps") near the after hatchway; a patent force pump; five trunk ventilators; patent steering apparatus; four boats; ground tackle in accordance with Lloyd's.

Bald Eagle[1]—Patent windlass; two Perley's patent capstans; Shelton's hold pumps; a force pump; patent steering apparatus; four boats and a metallic lifeboat; "well found in ground tackle"; two long six-pounder deck guns.

Belle of the West[1, 100]—Patent windlass; two patent capstans; Litchfield's hold pumps; Flanders's patent force pump; Emerson's patent ventilators; an improved steering apparatus; "well found in boats and ground tackle."

Beverly[3]—Adams & Hammond's patent windlass; one capstan (known); Emerson's patent ventilators; Robbins's patent steering apparatus; two boats on a gallows frame over the quarterdeck. Ground tackle not noted.

Black Hawk[62, 63, 100]—Two capstans (patent on the topgallant forecastle, wood on the poop); hold pumps; steering apparatus (possibly patent); two boats (stowed on deckhouse); "well found in ground tackle, including two Porter's anchors."

Blue Jacket[32, 101]—Two capstans (probable, one known on the topgallant forecastle); Reed's patent steering apparatus, with double steering wheels; three boats (known).

Bonita[1]—Patent windlass; Crane's self-acting chain stoppers; two patent capstans; hold pumps; a force pump; Emer-son's patent ventilators; patent steering apparatus; "well found in boats and ground tackle."

Bounding Billow, bark[1]—Two capstans; Emerson's patent ventilators; "well found in boats and ground tackle; all other improvements of the day."

Celestial

Challenge[1, 100]—Perley's patent windlass; two capstans with brass-covered drum beads; one double-lever winch; four single-lever winches; copper pumps with 8-inch chambers, operated with engine breaks [sic]; a force pump; five Emerson's patent ventilators; steering wheel at the break of the poop, fitted to a gun tackle purchase. Five boats: launch, 26 feet × 9 feet × 3 feet 6 inches, double planked, sails and twelve oars; two cutters, 27 feet × 7 feet × 2 feet 9 inches, carver [sic] built, sails and 12 oars; third cutter, 25 feet × 5 feet 5 inches × 2 feet 4 inches, five oars; captain's gig, 30 feet × 5 feet × 3 feet 3 inches, clincher [sic] built, six oars. Three anchors, total weight 13,378 pounds; a stream anchor and chain; three cables of 120 fathoms each, one of 1⅞-inch chain, two of 2-inch chain; ground tackle and the details connected therewith "have been made to surpass the strictest requirements of Lloyd's."

Challenger[1, 101]—Patent windlass; Crane's chain stoppers; two capstans; copper pumps; Emerson's corresponding ventilators, forward and aft; Reed's patent steering apparatus; "plenty of good boats and every other improvement now in general use."

Champion of the Seas[1]—Patent windlass; Crane's self-acting chain stoppers; Allyn's patent capstan on the topgallant forecastle; two capstans forward and two aft on the upper deck, one on each side (four total); patent steering apparatus; "ground tackle and boats are of the best quality."

Charger[1]—Windlass; one capstan on the topgallant forecastle, one Allyn's patent capstan on the quarterdeck; two Edson's patent pumps; a force pump; a head pump; trunk ventilators in each corner of the deckhouse; steering apparatus (apparently a patent variety); three boats, two stowed upon the after house and a gallows frame across the quarterdeck; two cables, each 1⅞-inch chain, 90 fathoms long, and anchors to correspond.

Charmer[1]—Patent windlass; Crane's self-acting chain stoppers; two capstans; Emerson's patent ventilators; patent steering apparatus; three boats; heavy ground tackle, each cable 120 fathoms long; "Well supplied with everything that is useful in a first class ship."

Cleopatra[1]—Windlass; Crane's self-acting chain stoppers; two Perley's patent capstans; copper chambered pumps; Emerson's patent ventilators, forward and aft; patent steering apparatus; "plenty of good boats, heavy ground tackle, and all other details of a superior ship."

Climax[1]—Windlass; Crane's self-acting chain stoppers; two Perley's patent capstans; patent hold pumps; steering wheel fitted to a gun tackle purchase; Delano's rudder brace; "very heavy ground tackle."

Coeur de Lion[1]—Patent windlass; two capstans, one being Allyn's patent capstan; copper hold pumps; a force pump; steering wheel fitted to a gun tackle purchase; three boats, the longboat stowed bottom-up forward of the main hatchway, two quarter boats on davits between main and mizzen rigging; "good ground tackle."

Comet[64, 100]—Two capstans; patent steering apparatus; four boats; three Porter's patent anchors, 40 hundredweight, 34 hundredweight and 26 hundredweight; one Porter's patent kedge, 6 hundredweight; three cables, each 90 fathoms long, 1⅞-inch, 1½-inch, and 1-inch chain.

Cyclone[1, 3]—"The ship is amply supplied in her outfits."[1] "Emerson's patent ventilators; patent steering apparatus."[3]

Daring[1]—"In her outfits she is all that a ship ought to be. . . ."

Dauntless[1]—Windlass; one capstan on the topgallant forecastle, one brass-mounted capstan on the quarterdeck; patent copper chambered pumps; Emerson's patent ventilators, forward and aft; patent steering apparatus; "liberally supplied with boats and ground tackle." Longboat stowed lengthwise on the hull centerline, a movable house at each end.

Donald McKay[1]—Patent windlass; Crane's self-acting chain stoppers; six capstans; two copper chambered pumps; patent (probable) steering apparatus; six boats, with Tewksbury's patent seats; "other furniture of a perfect ship."

Don Quixote[1]—Patent windlass; two capstans; Litchfield's patent pumps; Reed's patent steering apparatus; Delano's rudder brace; "plenty of good boats."

Eagle[5]—Windlass; "all the most approved ventilators"; boats stowed on the deckhouse.

Eagle Wing[1, 100]—Allyn's patent capstans; "In ventilation she has all the improvements of the day." "In all her outfits she is most liberally found."

Edwin Forrest[1]—Windlass; Crane's self-acting chain stoppers; Emerson's patent ventilators; patent steering apparatus; "all other improvements of the day."

Electric Spark[1]—Windlass; one capstan on the topgallant forecastle (known); two trunk ventilators under the topgallant forecastle, always open; five ventilators in each side of the house into the tween-decks; six ventilators with circular covers in front of the poop; "her outfits are excellent."

Ellen Foster[1]—Patent windlass; one capstan on the topgallant forecastle; one capstan of locust and mahogany, brass mounted, on the quarterdeck; Litchfield's patent copper pumps; Emerson's patent ventilators; patent steering apparatus; five boats, two stowed on a gallows frame spanning the quarterdeck.

Empress of the Sea[1]—"In all her outfits, such as ground tackle, windlass, capstans, steering apparatus, boats, etc., she is most liberally found, and in these . . . will compare favorably with any ship in the merchant service."

Endeavor[1]—Windlass; two capstans, one on the topgallant forecastle, one on the poop; copper chambered pumps; Reed's patent steering apparatus; four boats. "In all her outfits, such as ground tackle . . . is up to the fullest requirements of Lloyd's best ships."

Eringo, bark[1]—One capstan on the topgallant forecastle; Emerson's patent ventilators; "is well found in boats, ground tackle, etc."

Eureka

Fair Wind[1]—Patent windlass; two capstans; copper chambered pumps; patent steering apparatus; four boats, two of which are Francis's lifeboats. "In all her outfits she has been most liberally found."

Fearless

Fleet Wing[1]—Patent windlass; Crane's self-acting chain stoppers; two capstans; a patent force pump; steering wheel fitted to a gun tackle purchase; three boats stowed on a gallows frame over the quarterdeck, their after ends resting on the house in front of the poop; "she is also liberally found in all her outfits."

Flyaway

Flying Arrow[1]—Crane's self-acting chain stoppers; patent capstans; Litchfield's pumps; Emerson's patent ventilators, forward and aft; patent steering apparatus; boats and ground tackle of the most approved qualities. "In outfits she has all the improvements of the day."

Flying Childers[1, 100]—Patent windlass; Crane's patent chain stoppers; two capstans; patent pumps; Emerson's patent ventilators, forward and aft; patent steering apparatus; five boats, including longboat stowed bottom-up on bitts amidships, clear of the deck; ground tackle in conformity with the requirements of Lloyd's.

Flying Cloud[1, 100]—Allyn's patent capstans; Emerson's patent ventilators.

Flying Dragon[1, 32]—Patent windlass; Crane's self-acting chain stoppers; patent capstans; pumps; Emerson's patent ventilators; patent steering apparatus, in a wheelhouse; "plenty of good boats and the best of ground tackle."

Flying Dutchman

Flying Eagle[1]—Crane's self-acting chain stoppers; Emerson's patent ventilators; patent steering apparatus; "all the other necessary improvements of the day."

Flying Fish[1]—Patent windlass; Crane's patent (self-acting) chain stoppers; one capstan on the topgallant forecastle, one on the quarterdeck, both mahogany, brass mounted; Emerson's corresponding ventilators, forward and aft; Reed's patent steering apparatus; five boats, of most approved models. "Ground tackle in weight and length comes up to the highest requirements of Lloyd's."

Flying Mist[1]—Windlass with double gearing and patent fleeting flange; Crane's self-acting chain stoppers; two Edson's patent hold pumps; a patent force pump, forward; four circular trunk ventilators in each house; patent steering apparatus; four boats stowed on two gallows frames over the forward part of the house; ground tackle of extra weight and strength; "all the other outfits of a well found ship."

Galatea

Game Cock[1]—Patent windlass; two capstans; Emerson's patent ventilators; patent steering apparatus; "she has all the essentials suitable for a ship of her capacity." The longboat was stowed on the deck forward of the main hatchway.

Gazelle[32]—Pumps.

Gem of the Ocean

Golden Eagle[1]—Patent windlass; two capstans; Litchfield's pumps; patent steering apparatus; four boats; superior ground tackle; "everything else pertaining to a clipper."

Golden Fleece (second)[1]—Patent windlass; one capstan on the topgallant forecastle (known); copper chambered pumps; "plenty of good boats; best of ground tackle; in all her outfits she is liberally found."

Golden Light[1, 32, 100]—Patent windlass; Crane's self-acting chain stoppers; two brass-mounted capstans with locust barrels; Emerson's patent ventilators; patent steering apparatus; five boats; "best of ground tackle; every other detail of a perfect ship."

Golden West[1]—Windlass; two Perley's patent capstans; Litchfield's copper pumps; Emerson's patent ventilators; patent steering apparatus; four boats; "best of ground tackle; all other details of a complete clipper."

Grace Darling[1]—Patent windlass; one capstan on the topgallant forecastle, one Allyn's patent capstan on the quarterdeck; copper chambered pumps; patent steering apparatus; "is liberally fitted out in every particular."

Great Republic[4, 10]—No windlass. Anchors handled by a capstan below the weather deck. Double capstan forward, upper barrel on the spar deck for working ship; lower barrel on upper deck for anchor handling. One large Allyn's patent purchase capstan on the quarterdeck; Crane's patent self-acting chain stoppers; six crab winches; four hold pumps. Double steering wheels (protected by a wheelhouse), with an iron tiller fitted to a gun tackle purchase. Four large boats on the spar deck: two 30 feet × 10 feet 6 inches × 5 feet, fitted with sails; one fitted with a propeller operated by a steam engine. Four quarter boats, 26 feet long; captain's gig, 22 feet long. Four anchors: best bower, Porter's patent, 8,500 pounds; working bower, 6,500 pounds; stream anchor, 2,500 pounds; kedge, 1,500 pounds. Bower chains 2½ inches, 120 fathoms; stream chain 1½ inches, 120 fathoms. Harris's lightning conductors on each mast. "Nothing has been omitted in her outfits."

Great Republic (rebuilt)[32, 100, 103]—Crane's self-acting chain stoppers; Allyn's patent capstans (two probable); two double-action pumps located about midway between the mainmast and mizzenmast;[100] four hold pumps;[103] Reed's patent steering apparatus; Harris's lightning conductors; four boats (known); adequate ground tackle, her best bower being Porter's patent anchor of 8,500 pounds.

Henry Hill, bark[1]—Windlass; two capstans; copper chambered pumps; Emerson's patent ventilators, forward and aft;

patent steering apparatus; three boats; "all other outfits of a perfect vessel."

Herald of the Morning[1, 32]—Crane's self-acting chain stoppers; capstans (two probable), one Allyn's patent; pumps; Emerson's patent ventilators; patent steering apparatus; "well found in boats and ground tackle . . . and all other improvements of the day." Two fancy brass cannon were mounted on her poop deck.

Hoogly[1, 100]—Patent windlass; Crane's self-acting chain stoppers; two capstans of mahogany and locust, one on the topgallant forecastle, the other on the quarterdeck. Steering apparatus located under the break of the poop midway between the mainmast and mizzenmast, consisting of a wheel fitted to a gun tackle purchase set up to a yoke on the rudderhead. "She has the best of ground tackle and plenty of good boats."

Hurricane[4]—Emerson's patent ventilators.

Indiaman[1]—Patent windlass; Crane's self-acting chain stoppers; two capstans; hold pumps; Emerson's patent ventilators; patent steering apparatus; three boats fitted with Tewksbury's patent seats (these also acted as life preservers, as described later in this chapter); "the best of ground tackle and all other furniture of a first class ship."

Intrepid[32]—Two nine-pounder cannon.

Invincible[4]—Latest approved windlass; copper pumps with 8-inch chambers, worked with engine brakes; powerful engine (force) pump; six Emerson's patent ventilators along the deck; three Porter's patent anchors of full size for the ship; full-length chain cables of 2-inch and 1⅞-inch wire size.

James Baines[1]—Patent windlass; Crane's self-acting chain stoppers; a crab winch on the topgallant forecastle; six capstans; copper chambered pumps; trunk skylights venting below decks; patent steering apparatus, sheltered in a wheelhouse; two quarter boats on davits; spare boats stowed bottom-up on three gallows frames before the mainmast. Also "a large variety of other modern improvements."

John Bertram[1]—Patent windlass; four patent lever winches, two port and two starboard; two capstans, locust and mahogany, with composition circles and pawls, and brass drum heads; New York patent copper pumps, worked with flywheels and winches; Emerson's patent ventilators;

patent steering apparatus. Longboat stowed in the deckhouse, port side. After end of house could unship when necessary. "She is liberally found."

John Gilpin

John Land[1, 32] (built as a duplicate of *Winged Arrow*)—Windlass; capstans (two probable); pumps; Emerson's corresponding patent ventilators; patent steering apparatus; boats; ground tackle; "she is most substantially found."

John Stuart

John Wade[1]—Two capstans, one on the topgallant forecastle, one on the quarterdeck; "she is liberally found."

Joseph Peabody[1]—Patent windlass; Crane's self-acting chain stoppers; two capstans; copper chambered pumps; a force pump; ventilation trunks in each corner of each house; patent steering apparatus; four boats; extra-sized [sic] ground tackle; "all other outfits of a first-class clipper."

King Fisher[1]—Crane's self-acting chain stoppers; two capstans, one on the topgallant forecastle, one on the quarterdeck; patent hold pumps; a force pump; Emerson's patent ventilators.

Lady Franklin

Lamplighter, bark[1]—A capstan on the topgallant forecastle.

Lightfoot[1, 101]—Emerson's patent ventilators; Reed's patent steering apparatus; "liberally found in every other particular."

Lightning[1]—Windlass; three capstans; copper chambered pumps; patent steering apparatus, protected by a wheelhouse; "amply found in the best of ground tackle."

Mameluke[1]—Patent windlass; two capstans; patent pumps; ventilation trunks in each corner of each house; steering wheel fitted to a gun tackle purchase; four boats; heavy ground tackle; "all other improvements of the day."

Mary Robinson[100]—Allyn's patent capstans (two probable).

Mastiff[1]—Windlass with patent fleeting flange; Crane's patent self-acting chain stoppers; two capstans.

Mermaid, bark[1]—Patent windlass; one capstan (known) of locust and mahogany, inlaid with composition; two copper chambered pumps; patent steering apparatus; three boats, two stowed on a gallows frame over the quarterdeck; "substantial ground tackle."

Morning Light[1, 100]—Crane's self-acting chain stoppers; Allyn's patent capstans, one on the topgallant forecastle (known), one on the quarterdeck (probable); a force pump; five Emerson's patent ventilators, three forward, two aft; patent steering apparatus; "all other improvements of the day."

Mystery[1]—"In all her outfits is as perfect as a ship needs to be. . . ."

Nightingale[3]—Patent windlass; two patent pumps; Emerson's patent ventilators; Andrews's patent steering apparatus; "liberally found in boats and ground tackle."

Noonday[1]—Patent windlass; two capstans; Odion's patent pumps with copper chambers and flywheels; "well found in boats"; two chains 1¾-inch wire size and 90 fathoms long; "as complete as possible in all her other outfits."

Northern Light[100]—Crane's self-acting chain stoppers.

Ocean Express[1]—Crane's self-acting chain stoppers; a force pump; patent steering apparatus; "well found in boats and ground tackle."

Ocean Pearl[1]—Emerson's patent ventilators; "all other improvements of the day."

Ocean Telegraph

Onward[1]—Emerson's patent ventilators, forward and aft; "fitted out in liberal style."

Osborne Howes[32]—Steering wheel fitted to a gun tackle purchase. This based on the fact that, in 1860, off Cape Horn, she reportedly had her tiller broken off.

Panther

Phantom[1, 32]—Patent windlass; Crane's self-acting chain stoppers; a capstan on the topgallant forecastle (known); Litchfield's patent pumps; a force pump; Perley's patent ventilators between every frame; patent steering apparatus; five boats; five anchors, in weight 4,200, 3,700, 3,200, 1,200, and 500 pounds, with four chain cables of 1⅞-, 1¾-, 1⅝-, and 1-inch wire size; "well found in every other requirement of a perfect ship."

Queen of Clippers[1, 101]—Emerson's patent ventilators; Reed's patent steering apparatus; "fitted in superior style."

Queen of the Pacific

Queen of the Seas[1]—Patent windlass; Crane's self-acting chain stoppers; two capstans, one a Perley's patent capstan on the topgallant forecastle, one of mahogany and locust, inlaid with brass, on the poop; Litchfield's patent pumps, which work under the poop; a force pump; Phillips's Fire Annihilators; Emerson's patent ventilators, forward and aft; patent steering apparatus; one longboat stowed in the port side of the deckhouse (after end of the house could be unshipped); four additional longboats; "long, strong ground tackle."

Quickstep, bark[1]—One capstan on the topgallant forecastle.

Racehorse, bark[1, 44]—Patent windlass; a patent winch; pumps; longboat stowed on hull centerline; fittings for guns installed at three gunports on each side of ship.

Racer[3, 97]—Patent windlass; two capstans, one on the topgallant forecastle, one on the quarterdeck; Litchfield's patent pumps; patent steering apparatus; three boats; "usual ground tackle."

Radiant[1]—Crane's self-acting chain stoppers; Perley's patent capstans (two probable); Litchfield's patent pumps; Emerson's patent ventilators; "all other improvements of the day."

Raven[3]—Patent windlass; Emerson's patent ventilators; Robinson's patent steering apparatus; "she has everything which goes to make up a perfect ship in every sense."

Red Jacket[19, 67, 101]—Reed's patent steering apparatus; four boats; chain cables of 2-inch wire size and anchors to suit.

Robin Hood

Rocket, bark

Roebuck[1]—Patent windlass; two capstans, one on the topgallant forecastle, one on the quarterdeck, brass mounted; Emerson's patent ventilators, forward and aft; patent steering apparatus; heavy ground tackle. "Nothing has been omitted in her outfits necessary to make her a perfect ship."

Romance of the Sea[1]—Windlass. "In ground tackle and all her other furniture she is found agreeably to the requirements of Lloyd's."

Santa Claus[1]—Windlass; two capstans, one on the topgallant forecastle, and an Allyn's patent capstan on the quarterdeck; Hubbard's rotary force pump; Reed's patent steering apparatus; four boats, each 26 feet long.

Saracen[1]—Patent windlass; capstans (two probable), one Allyn's patent; four boats, two Francis's metallic lifeboats; "best of ground tackle."

Sea Bird, bark[1]—Windlass. "In boats, ground tackle, and every other detail, she is most liberally found."

Seaman's Bride[4]—Patent pumps; force pumps; Reed's patent ventilators throughout; Reed's patent steering apparatus. (Note: "Reed's" patent ventilators may be an incorrect identity.)

Sea Serpent

Shooting Star[1, 100]—Improved patent windlass; Crane's self-acting chain stoppers; two capstans, one on the topgallant forecastle, one of mahogany and locust, inlaid with brass, on the quarterdeck; pumps; patent steering apparatus. "In boats, ground tackle, and other furniture she is amply found."

Sierra Nevada[1]—Patent windlass; Crane's self-acting chain stoppers; two Allyn's patent capstans, one on the topgallant forecastle, one on the quarterdeck; pumps; a force pump; Emerson's patent ventilators, forward and aft; patent steering apparatus; "best of ground tackle."

Silver Star[1]—Windlass; Crane's self-acting chain stoppers; two capstans, one on the topgallant forecastle, one on the quarterdeck; copper chambered hold pumps, worked with engine brakes; Emerson's patent ventilators, forward and aft; patent steering apparatus; five boats; "all other furniture of a perfect ship."

Southern Cross[1, 3]—Patent windlass; two capstans; Emerson's patent ventilators; Robinson's patent steering apparatus; "good ground tackle and plenty of substantial boats. Her outfits are all that they ought to be to insure safety and success."

Sovereign of the Seas[1]—"Her windlass, pumps, capstans, ground tackle, etc. are all of the first quality, and are made more for wear than show."

Spitfire

Staffordshire[1]—Windlass brakes on the forecastle deck, windlass on the deck below; gypsy winch on the forecastle deck; two capstans on the forecastle deck, another capstan on the quarterdeck; hold pumps of a new patent (probably Litchfield's) abaft the mainmast in the upper tween-decks;

Reed's patent steering apparatus, consisting of a single screw and lever, protected in a wheelhouse; four lever winches, two on each side of ship abaft the fore and main rigging; two nine-pounder cannon forward in the upper tween-decks.

Stag Hound[1, 32, 100]—Perley's patent windlass, with ends that ungeared; Crane's self-acting chain stoppers (apparently installed in late 1851 or early 1852); two capstans of mahogany and locust, inlaid with brass; patent copper chambered pumps; patent steering apparatus; four boats; "ground tackle and other furniture of the first quality."

Star of the Union[1]—Patent windlass; Crane's self-acting chain stoppers; two patent capstans; Litchfield's patent pumps; Emerson's patent ventilators; patent steering apparatus; "all other improvements of the day."

Starr King

Storm King[1]—Windlass, in accordance with Lloyd's requirements; Perley's patent capstans; Litchfield's patent pumps; Emerson's patent ventilators; Sylvester and Cram's steering apparatus; ground tackle in accordance with Lloyd's; "other outfits are of the most approved kind."

Sultana, bark[1]—Patent windlass; one capstan; "well found in boats and ground tackle. Her outfits are all that could be required."

Sunny South[100]—Allyn's patent capstan (one known); Reed's patent steering apparatus.

Surprise[1, 32]—Patent windlass with iron ends that could be ungeared; two patent lever winches on each side, one forward, the other aft; a mahogany capstan inlaid with brass (two capstans probable); patent steering apparatus; five boats (two cutters, two quarter boats, one gig). "In pumps, ground tackle, and every other detail she is amply found."

Swallow[1, 101]—Crane's self-acting chain stoppers; rotary patent pumps; a force pump; Emerson's patent ventilators; Reed's patent steering apparatus; "all the other improvements of the day."

Sweepstakes[69]—Windlass; capstans (two probable); four boats.

Sword Fish

Syren[3]—Windlass; Emerson's patent ventilators; Robinson's patent steering apparatus. "She is well provided with boats, ground tackle and everything which goes to make up a complete craft."

Telegraph

Thatcher Magoun[1, 100]—Patent windlass; two capstans; hold pumps; a force pump; a tier of trunk ventilators along the front of the poop; two square ventilators under the top-gallant forecastle; Reed's patent steering apparatus, with Delano's rudder brace to keep the rudder fair on the pintles; "the best of ground tackle and plenty of boats."

Tornado[3, 100]—Patent windlass; Crane's self-acting chain stoppers.

Uncowah

War Hawk[1, 100]—Patent windlass; Crane's self-acting chain stoppers; two capstans; patent pumps; a force pump; Emerson's patent ventilators; Reed's patent steering apparatus, with Delano's rudder brace to keep the rudder fair on the pintles; four boats; "all other furniture of a first class clipper."

Water Witch[1]—Patent windlass; Crane's self-acting chain stoppers; two patent capstans; patent hold pumps; a force pump; Emerson's patent ventilators. "She has plenty of good boats and the best of ground tackle."

Western Continent—Crane's self-acting chain stoppers.[135]

Westward Ho[1, 100]—Windlass; Crane's self-acting chain stoppers; two Perley's patent capstans; Litchfield's patent pumps; Phillips's Fire Annihilators; a force pump; Emerson's patent ventilators; four boats; "ground tackle, which, in weight and length of chains, exceeds the requirements of Lloyd's."

West Wind[1]—Crane's self-acting chain stoppers; Litchfield's patent pumps; bilge pumps; Flanders' patent force pump; patent steering apparatus, protected in a house; "in all her other outfits she is liberally found."

Whirlwind[1]—Patent windlass; Crane's self-acting chain stoppers; two capstans, brass mounted, one on the topgallant forecastle, one on the quarterdeck; a force pump forward; Emerson's patent ventilators, forward and aft; patent steering apparatus; four boats; two long six-pounder cannon.

Whistler[1]—Patent windlass; Crane's self-acting chain stoppers; Cheney's patent capstans (two probable); improved hold pumps; a force pump; Emerson's patent ventilators; "all other details of a first class clipper."

Wildfire, bark

Wild Pigeon[1]—Perley's patent windlass; lever winches (four total), forward and aft, port and starboard; two capstans; copper chambered pumps, New York patent; Emerson's patent ventilators; patent steering apparatus; longboat, stowed in port side of deckhouse; three patent anchors of 3,052, 2,738, and 2,280 pounds; two kedge anchors, one of 765 pounds, one of 450 pounds; three chains, each 90 fathoms, of 1⅝-, 1½-, and 1-inch wire size.

Wild Ranger[1]—Crane's self-acting chain stoppers; "all other improvements of the day."

Wild Rover

Winged Arrow[1, 3]—Adams & Hammond's patent windlass; Emerson's corresponding patent ventilators, forward and aft; Robinson's patent steering apparatus. "In her outfits, such as ground tackle, capstans, boats, etc., she is most substantially found."

Winged Racer[1, 101]—Patent windlass; Crane's self-acting chain stoppers; two capstans; purchase winches each side (quantity not specified); Emerson's patent ventilators; Reed's patent steering apparatus; four boats; heavy ground tackle.

Witchcraft[1]—Windlass; two capstans; four lever winches, two on each side, one forward and one aft; patent pumps; Emerson's patent ventilators, two forward, one on the quarterdeck made of polished brass, all 10 inches in diameter; patent steering apparatus; "well found in boats and ground tackle." Her longboat stowed on deck amidships.

Witch of the Wave[1, 3]—Patent windlass; two capstans; four lever winches, two on each side, one forward and one aft; pumps with flywheels, New York patent; Emerson's patent ventilators; patent steering apparatus (Lewis H. Priest's patent[1], Joseph E. Andrews's patent[3]); four boats, including longboat stowed in port side of deckhouse; patent anchors.

Wizard[1]—Patent windlass; Crane's self-acting chain stoppers; two patent capstans; two patent hold pumps; a force pump; Emerson's patent ventilators; patent steering apparatus; "stout ground tackle; all other furniture of a perfect ship."

Young America[70, 71, 72]—Windlass; capstans (two probable), one on the topgallant forecastle known; four boats; patent and Admiralty anchors.

Young Turk[1]—"No expense has been spared in her outfit."

Trunk Ventilators

Toward the end of the clipper-building phenomenon, the ship *Mameluke*, launched after mid-year 1855, was built with an improvement in ventilation that was more a method than it was an invention, and as such is briefly mentioned here.

The vessel was built by Briggs Brothers of South Boston, both brothers, as we have seen in Chapter 16, being tremendously progressive and imaginative shipbuilders. In *Mameluke* they introduced *trunk ventilators*, which were structural tubes or boxes built into each corner of her deckhouses. These trunks communicated with the deck below, and their openings to the atmosphere were protected by brass covers that could be opened or closed as desired.

This form of ventilation proved to be eminently successful, it being reported that *Mameluke* delivered one of the best-conditioned cargoes ever landed at San Francisco. From that time the trunk ventilator became a frequent item found in the construction of the clippers.

Ships' Boats

Changes and improvements were being made in ships' boats. George P. Tewksbury patented a boat seat built with flotation properties which allowed them to function as life preservers. By 1854 these seats were routinely found on board most vessels. In this same time frame Francis's metallic lifeboats were introduced and had gained wide acceptance.

Ladders

The ladder is a fitting no ship could function without, yet it receives short shrift in any nautical discussion. The most that is ever stated is that ladders are provided wherever two adjacent but differing levels are encountered. That, in itself, is a most basic truth. However, there is more to a ladder than merely something that prevents you from missing your step and falling to the deck below. Many innocuous details are involved in the fabrication of ladders, and in modern steel ships, particularly naval vessels with their many decks and levels requiring hundreds of such items, the design, fabrication, and installation details of ladders are their own specialty.

In the clippers and other wooden vessels the problem was decidedly less complex and the number of ladders relatively few. Nevertheless, in any ship of quality, the ladders were generally custom built to suit their particular individual location.

The basic consideration controlling the design of a ladder is the height of an average person, which, in the days of the clipper ship, was considerably less than the average today.

The distance between rungs (in vertical ladders) or treads (in inclined ladders) is determined by the normal climbing attitude of an average individual. If the ladders are properly proportioned, the leg action or movement will be approximately the same in all cases. This is why, when a person approaches a ladder or staircase for the first time, it offers no surprises.

Ladders are divided into two categories, vertical and inclined, the former being the simplest and most basic form. *Vertical ladders* are composed of vertical stringers and horizontal rungs, generally square or round in section. The spacing between rungs is greater than that between treads of inclined ladders.

In wooden vessels vertical ladders are usually encountered at the house sides to provide access to the housetop, and between some decks to provide access to the various levels. When installed on a house side, the distance between the roof and the top rung is made to equal the distance between rungs; this eliminates surprise when starting to descend. The bottom rung can be at a variable height above the deck, although uniform spacing throughout the length of the ladder is desirable.

Where vertical ladders are installed against a house side or a bulkhead, a minimum clearance of 4 inches toeroom is required between the ladder rungs and the surface to which the ladder is secured.

Inclined ladders are more complex than their vertical counterparts, and certain factors control their design. The height between the levels to be served is divided into a number of equal parts that are compatible with the normal step taken by the average person. This will give the number of treads, which in turn determines the angle of inclination of the ladder. Steep ladders have narrow treads, but as the angle of inclination from horizontal decreases, the distance between treads also decreases and the width of the treads increases. All of this accommodates the human step.

Inclined ladders whose upper end terminates at a flush surface are fitted with treads of uniform width. However, where a ladder such as an interior companionway ladder, extending from a living area aft up to the poop deck level, terminates at a coaming, certain important details are always considered. In such cases the topmost tread is always placed at the same level as the deck outside; thus, stepping over the coaming, whether ascending or descending, entails the same movement. Also, in these instances, the topmost tread only is made wide enough to accommodate the length of a person's foot, thus providing an actual landing.

In any well-found vessel, the inclined ladders were custom made for the location they were to serve and were very seldom interchangeable. This was due to the camber of the vessel's decks, and was especially a consideration at the outboard ends of the camber curve. This curve necessitated that each stringer be cut to a specific length and angle in order to set the ladder true.

Several details included in the fabrication of inclined ladders were based on preventing possible injury. First, the upper face of the ladder stringers, between the bottom tread and the deck on which the ladder stood, was dubbed off vertically so that it did not protrude beyond the toe of the tread; this eliminated the possibility of tripping over the stringer when hurriedly responding to a command for all hands to work ship. Also, where the top surface of a tread protruded beyond the face of the stringers, the offending corner was chamfered off to line up with the stringer. Relieving these corners helped preclude some nasty injuries when the vessel was sailing in rough seas.

Most ships' ladders of the period were basic functional structures provided to allow convenient access from one level to another. However, in the first-class quarters aft, in the areas of the high-profile living spaces, the joinerwork and artistic treatment of ladders was limited only by the amount of money the client was willing to part with.

Water Tanks

Freshwater tanks are a detail which requires very little discussion but receives even less in discourses about sailing vessels, whether or not they were clippers. As is indicated in many of the deck arrangements shown in Chapter 26, the typical clipper ship was generally fitted with one large water tank whose capacity varied between approximately 2,000 and 8,000 gallons. Such tanks were usually located abaft the mainmast, this location having the least effect on the ship's trim regardless of the level of water in the tank.

In general, water tanks were cylindrical in shape, being made up of rectangular iron plates, rolled to a suitable radius and riveted together. However, in *Challenge* and *Witchcraft* the tanks were fabricated from flat iron plates that were formed with angular square corners and then riveted together to form relatively square tanks. All tanks were provided with an access plate in the side near the top to allow for inspection and cleaning.

It appears logical to assume that internally, these large tanks were fitted with non-tight, vertical partitions, installed in egg-crate fashion, which would restrict the action of water swashing against the tank sides in rough seas. This action is greatest when tanks are but partially filled, and can cause considerable distress to a tank over a period of time. In later shipbuilding these partitions were known as "swash bulkheads" or "swash plates."

A rather small percentage of vessels were fitted with two water tanks. Some of these were *Challenge*, two square tanks; *Hurricane*, *Morning Light*, *Phantom*, *Queen of the Seas*, *Sierra Nevada*, and *Staffordshire*, all having two tanks, apparently cylindrical in form; and *Great Republic*, two tanks that are definitely recorded as being cylindrical.

A valid assumption may be made that, in the above instances, the pairs of tanks were cross-connected so that when water was being drawn or the tanks were being filled, the water level was the same in each tank and thus did not affect the trim of the ship.

In order to achieve their capacity, water tanks were usually stepped directly upon the keelson. Appropriate foundations were fashioned and installed on either side of the keelson assembly in order to support the bottoms of the tanks.

The height of a tank was limited by the height of the weather deck. With the height in feet and the desired capacity of the tank being known, the diameter or square section of a tank can easily be found by using the value of 7.5 gallons to the cubic foot.

There were several deviations from this positioning of water tanks. In *Great Republic* the tanks rose from the keelson to underside of the upper deck rather than to the spar or weather deck. In *Sierra Nevada* her main tanks were stepped on the lower deck rather than on the keelson.

Other unusual installations were to be found, even though the situations were quite rare. In *Seaman's Bride* her principal water tanks were installed under the cabin floor in the after peak. In *Sierra Nevada* square iron tanks were installed on the weather deck along both sides of the deckhouse, while in *Coeur de Lion* secondary water tanks stood on a low platform on the hull centerline between the deckhouse and the main hatchway.

Lightning Conductors

The *lightning conductor* is an item difficult to classify. When installed, such conductors are intimately entwined in the rigging but are not a part thereof; neither are they considered to be fittings. For want of other designation, they are briefly covered in this chapter as part of the ship's outfit.

One day in 1752 Benjamin Franklin proved in his kite-flying experiment that lightning and electricity are identical. He later invented the lightning rod, which is based on the fact that lightning will take either the shortest path or the path of least resistance to reach the ground. Both iron and copper were found to be conductors that provided the path of least resistance through which this electric "fluid" could travel. Man, by providing this path in his structures, was thus able to divert the potentially damaging lightning from the structure into the conductor and thence harmlessly into the ground.

A tall ship standing alone on the flat surface of the sea is an unusually susceptible target for lightning to strike during a storm. Many vessels were destroyed as a result of such strikes, and it was not long after Franklin's discovery that this principle of conductivity was applied to ships.

The initial method was to install long lengths of small chain which extended uninterrupted from a small, fixed rod secured to the vessel's highest masthead or truck, down the mast, thence along a lower shroud to end up overboard in the sea. One feature that made this method attractive was the chain conductor's facility to be easily unshipped and stowed below when masts were struck for repair or replacement, or when worn or damaged rigging prompted its removal.

Sir William Snow Harris, an Englishman, had occupied himself since about 1823 with inventing improved methods of protecting ships from lightning strikes. His principal objections to the use of chain conductors were their lack of positive continuity between links; their liability to being subject to all the injuries incident to ships' rigging; the lack of sufficient contact area between links to carry off the electric fluid; and last, but far from least, the propensity of ships' personnel to contentedly leave the entire chain linkage in the compartment where it had been stowed.

In 1830 Harris invented a new system of rigid, permanent, copper conductors which led continuously down the mast and through the decks to terminate at the mast step at a conductor connected to a fastening which penetrated the hull. Critics were quick to announce their disapproval of this means of introducing the electric fluid into the interior of vessels instead of conducting it overboard into the sea.

In 1853 a well-known American ship captain, Robert Bennett Forbes, submitted to the U.S. Patent Office his own version of a system of solid connectors which followed the course of the old chain system and discharged the electric fluid directly into the sea. It consisted principally of lengths of tubing that were connected to each other by sockets or short lengths of slide-tubes.

Detailed information on this subject and the two inventors may by found in a pamphlet titled "A New Rig for Ships and Other Vessels, combining Economy, Safety and Convenience," by R.B. Forbes,[108] and in Forbes' patent specification No. 11217, dated 4 July 1854, "Improvement in Lightning-rods for Vessels."

From the available information, it appears that categorically, the clipper fleet put to sea without the benefit of protection against lightning. Except for the original *Great Republic*, which was reportedly fitted with Harris's lightning conductors on all her masts, no other clipper among those included in this book is recorded as having had lightning protection provided. Among all the incidental noting of ships' equipment and details by reporter Duncan MacLean, only once does he mention lightning conductors, and in this instance he was critical of their omission. In his report on *Water Witch*, built in 1853, he states " . . . but we regret to add, like all our other fine ships, she has no lightning conductors. For this omission we hold the underwriters alone responsible."[1]

The installation of lightning conductors in American-built clippers can certainly be open to question. What is not open to question, however, is that very little notice was given the subject in contemporary descriptions. The description of one vessel (not a clipper), the packet *Webster*, built in 1853 by George Raynes, at Portsmouth, New Hampshire, includes the following paragraph: "She has chain lightning conductors, upon the old fashioned principle, to lead from the mastheads over the sides, which are better than none; but we think Harris' plan is decidedly the best."[1]

Chapter Twenty-Eight

SHIP INTERIORS

IN ADDITION TO A SOUND hull and tall masts, a sailing vessel required appropriate accommodations for all who would be aboard—sailors, officers, and passengers alike. Basically, this entailed providing living quarters and messing facilities in degrees appropriate to the standing of each category of humans on board.

Space was the controlling factor, and this was doled out in portions that befitted the status of the individual being considered. The meanest of these were the men and boys who served before the mast. It can rightfully be stated that the ordinary seaman was entitled to only the space he occupied at a given moment. If he was occupying his bunk, he could lay claim to this "territory." If he was sitting at a mess table, the space he occupied was his. When performing his shipboard duties, he was entitled to the space he occupied. When he departed the space, however, he also gave up claim to it.

In the effort of the ship's organization to keep body and soul together, the body was accorded as little consideration as could be afforded. The soul was accorded slightly less; in effect, it was on its own. Of course, there were exceptions to these basic philosophies, but the world of the ship was based almost exclusively on practicality, and there was little time for refinements and nonessentials.

In keeping with this philosophy, it was inevitable that, over the centuries, the ordinary sailors' quarters gravitated to the ship's forecastle, the least attractive location on board the average vessel. The clipper ships followed this basic rule to a degree, but far from exclusively. Their fine lines forward, combined with the enormous scantlings of the stem and hook assemblies, severely constricted available space and, in many cases, eliminated it entirely. As a result, most crews were quartered elsewhere. Ultimately, the crews could be found housed in three principal locations: the traditional forecastle (tween decks); the topgallant forecastle, in ships having structures of sufficient height; and in deckhouses built expressly but not exclusively for this purpose.

Forecastle Berthing

Forecastle berthing was the ultimate in simplicity and plainness. Bunks were built of simple structural lumber and were universally about 5 to 6 feet long and 30 inches wide. They were generally two tiers high, but in some ships the available space strongly hinted at bunks in three tiers.

Privacy was a relative condition achieved only to the extent of having the berthing spaces bulkheaded off from the rest of the ship. Individual privacy was unknown. Light and ventilation in the forward tween-decks and the topgallant forecastle were provided by air ports. In deckhouses skylights in the roof augmented side lights. And, regardless of the berthing location, the crew's toilet facilities were generally located in the after wings of the topgallant forecastle. No hint is given of the use of paint in these spaces.

Despite the fact that crews' quarters were severely restricted in terms of space, there was a surprisingly large diversity in the arrangement of bunks in the designated areas. Figure 28.1 illustrates four examples of the use of the topgallant forecastle and the forward tween-decks for housing the crew.

In all berthing, common practice dictated that bunks should be installed in a fore-and-aft direction in order to minimize the possibility of sailors having to sleep with their head lower than their feet. The notable exception occurred in the forecastle bunks which lined the sides of the hull. However, even in this location, the fore-and-aft direction prevailed.

In *Flying Cloud* the berthing in the topgallant forecastle was protected by a transverse structural bulkhead immediately forward of the windlass. In the space available it was possible to install twenty bunks arranged two tiers high as shown. Although this arrangement allows moderate space in which the men can move, the number of men represents but one watch of the crew. The other watch was quartered in the house on the upper deck.[1]

Figure 28.1. *Examples of crew berthing forward.*

CREW BERTHED IN A TGLT FOCSLE
(ONE WATCH ONLY)

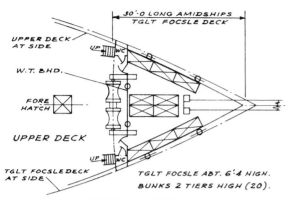

FLYING CLOUD

TGLT FOCSLE HOUSES ONE WATCH OF THE
CREW. OTHER WATCH IS QUARTERED IN
HOUSE ON UPPER DECK.

CREW APPARENTLY ABOUT 40 MEN.

CREW BERTHED IN A TGLT FOCSLE
DIVIDED INTO TWO COMPARTMENTS

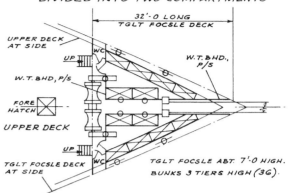

WITCH OF THE WAVE

PORT AND STARBOARD WATCHES ARE
QUARTERED IN SEPARATE COMPARTMENTS.

CREW APPARENTLY ABOUT 35 MEN.

DESCRIPTION STATES THAT THE FOCSLE WAS
"MADE AS COMFORTABLE AS THE SPACE
WOULD ADMIT."

NOTES –

RECONSTRUCTIONS ARE BASED ON DESCRIPTIONS IN REF. 1.

BUNKS ARE ASSUMED TO BE 30" WIDE x 5'·6 LONG.

OPEN TGLT FOCSLE WITH
STATEROOMS FOR SHIP'S BOYS

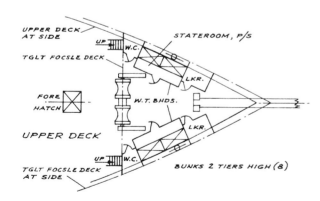

THATCHER MAGOUN

CREW (MEN) QUARTERED IN DECKHOUSE.
EACH WATCH HOUSED IN ITS OWN
APARTMENT.

NO CLOSING BULKHEAD AT BREAK OF
THE TGLT FOCSLE.

CREW BERTHED BETWEEN DECKS
IN THE FOCSLE

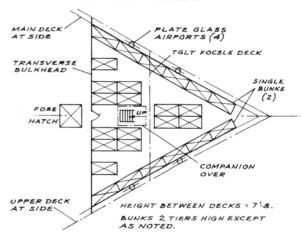

CHALLENGE

ACCOMMODATIONS ARE PROVIDED FOR
HER CREW OF 50 MEN.

433

In *Witch of the Wave* the topgallant forecastle was divided into two separate, tight compartments, one for each watch. The reconstruction shown in Figure 28.1 provides for the maximum number of bunks that each space could accommodate. However, the only way that the two spaces combined were able to house a full crew was to have the bunks installed three tiers high, since this was the only accommodation for the crew.[1] This assumption of three tiers appears to be fortified by the statement that the forecastle was "made as comfortable as the space would admit."[1] In addition, the 7-foot deck height makes such an installation physically possible.

The situation appears to be rather unusual but not unreasonable when one considers that, in a sailor's life on board, he lived a "four hours on, four hours off" existence. If his watch was not on duty, he was expected to rest. There was little time for play. Having bunks in which one could sit upright was not a requisite.

The berthing arrangement in the topgallant forecastle of *Thatcher Magoun* appears to be an unusual departure from common practice. In this instance the open space was fitted with two small staterooms, one on each side of the ship. In these compartments the ship's boys were housed, while the men of the crew were quartered topside in a large deckhouse, each watch having its own separate compartment.

Quartering the ship's boys separately from the men of the crew was strictly a practical matter, as were most all other considerations on board ship. Human nature being what it is, and the confines of a ship being almost stifling in size, brought about a closeness which, if precautions were not taken, fostered corruption and a discontent that was certainly not needed. Crews were not assembled based upon sterling qualities of character. "Separating the men from the boys" was a statement having various connotations, and in this case, the considerations were not elevating.

The final illustration in Figure 28.1 shows the crew berthing of *Challenge*. This example is the arrangement usually thought of in the matter of housing the crew. Here the entire crew was quartered forward in the tween-decks, the compartment being formed by a transverse bulkhead spanning the breadth of the deck in the forecastle. This arrangement was probably the least comfortable of all berthing arrangements. Light and ventilation were meager at best and, in the case of *Challenge*, twenty-five men, or one watch, always occupied the space.

This berthing layout was utterly simple and requires little discussion or description, but if *Challenge* is the example, it was an unsatisfactory condition—too many men in too small a space. Sailors, in general, were a rough, tough, unsavory lot, and the performance of *Challenge* reportedly suffered because of their shortcomings.[32] Whether or not the crew's living quarters contributed to this is moot, but it takes little imagination to conclude that a voyage of one hundred days at sea under these conditions would do little to promote peace and harmony.

For two hundred years, whether serving his king and country or merely serving his ship, the sailor's lot was not a happy one.

A common factor in all forecastle berthing is the lack of space in which to move around. It was virtually impossible to reach some bunks without crawling around others. And all bunks were too intimately close. The examples shown indicate only the overall compartment configurations; none of the many usual structural interferences are detailed.

These conditions might be perceived as instances of a culture that was primitive and inhumane, but such perception should not be too restricted. These same conditions prevailed in the United States steel navy in many classes of smaller vessels in the period of World War II and were accepted as routine characteristics of shipboard life. Crew berthing aboard submarines was assigned to torpedo rooms, and many sailors were obliged to crawl over the torpedoes stowed in these spaces in order to find their 2-by-6-foot bunk. On board small destroyer classes "hot bunks" were the norm, one or the other of the watches always occupying the bunks. None of this was considered primitive or inhuman—merely inconvenient—and was routinely accepted. Such was the romantic life of the sailor.

In the crowded topgallant forecastles, the anchor windlass, hawseholes, and other features of ground tackle had to be considered. Accordingly, all berthing structures that were in the path of incoming or outgoing chain cable and its handling were built of "knock-down" construction so they could be removed and reinstalled as necessary. This procedure was routine not only in the forecastle but elsewhere in the ship. There was never a lack of manpower. There was always a lack of space.

In spite of the many obstacles, there were vessels whose forecastles were fitted out with more than the minimum creature comforts. Among these were *John Bertram*, *Witchcraft*, *Staffordshire*, *Dauntless*, and *Bald Eagle*.

Deckhouses

Large Deckhouse

The *large deckhouse*, 30 to 50 feet long, and as much as 19 feet wide in large clippers, did not originate with and was not an exclusive feature of these ships. Vessels built prior to 1850 were sometimes built with sizable deckhouses, but it remained for the clipper, due to its hull form and projected mission, to use this form of deck superstructure to its greatest advantage. There were two principal assets: The deckhouse freed scarce space below the weather deck for the stowage of cargo, and it virtually transformed the living conditions of crews consigned to the dark, cramped quarters that existed in many forecastles. Here, topsides, light and ventilation were vastly improved. As a result, the large deckhouse became a hallmark of the clipper ship. However, almost a dozen well-known clippers, of those included herein, did not have large deckhouses, and some others still housed their crews in the forward tween-decks.

Figure 28.2 illustrates eight deckhouses with compartmentation based on descriptions found in the reports of Duncan MacLean.[1] Crew berthing is a feature of each example, but taken together the selections illustrate that the diversity of arrangements was probably as varied as the number of deckhouses that were built.

The typical large deckhouse contained the galley, berthing for some of the vessel's junior officers, storerooms, and accommodations for the crew. Generally, in support of the galley, there were the pantry, the cook's stateroom, and, on occasion, an additional galley, as in *Ellen Foster*, or mess spaces, as in *Charger*.

Berthing was generally contained in a single compartment in the deckhouse. There were, however, exceptions, as shown in *Thatcher Magoun*, in which each watch had its own separate space. The ship's boys were also berthed in their own compartment.

The rectangular configuration of the house allowed more space adjacent to the bunks, which contributed to a more inviting ambiance than could be found in the forecastle. This availability of slightly more space, a more refined structure, and the increased availability of light and ventilation through air ports and skylights represented a relatively marked improvement over the basic conditions found in many forecastles.

Deckhouses were constructed with framing calculated to withstand the pounding of boarding seas, hurricane-force wind loads, and superimposed loading such as would be encountered from boat stowage on the housetops. This work was done by ship carpenters. The exterior sheathing and trim were the work of *outside joiners*, their interior counterparts being *inside joiners*, who did the paneling and trim work of the finer interior cabins.

American-built clipper deckhouses received one or the other of two general treatments. They were closed in either with *paneled sides* or with *smooth planked sides* of tongue-and-groove planking. Specific details are not found in abundance, but a few examples serve to indicate the broad general extent of such work.

The details of finishing a deckhouse were apparently the general option of the artisan who was selected to perform the work. Paneled house sides were more intricate and expensive to build than were the smooth-planked sides and, in many minds, presented a richer and more impressive picture than did smooth planking. In general, when paneling was installed it extended the full height of the deckhouse, as in the specific cases of *Whistler* and the bark *Mermaid*. However, in a less common form, the paneling was limited to the upper portion of the house, as was done in *Stag Hound*.

Tongue-and-groove planking was faster and less expensive to install and could be laid up either vertically or horizontally. The latter method allowed for better draining of the joints and also projected a lower profile of a house. *Daring* was smooth-planked, and the observation was made, "It looks better than if it had been paneled."

With both types of siding there were usually generous, overhanging cornices. These employed the standard architectural mouldings such as ovolo, ogee, torus, and combinations of all. *Dentil* (toothed) cornices were not usual but also found their way aboard; two instances are found in *Daring* and *Black Hawk*. The painting of these structures, where known, is covered in Chapter 23.

Movable Houses

The deckhouses that occupied the weather deck of most clippers were generally built as permanent structures, but in many ships some of these were movable. All principal deckhouses were located between the foremast and the mainmast except in the original *Great Republic*, which had three major houses and one minor house strung along her spar deck. Most deckhouses were devoted to providing sleeping quarters for petty officers and crew, but there were exceptions to this general usage, some of which are covered later.

At least five of the clippers included herein devoted a considerable portion of the deckhouse to boat stowage: *Bald Eagle*, *John Bertram*, *Queen of the Seas*, *Wild Pigeon*, and *Witch of the Wave*. In each case the deckhouse was constructed with sides that could be broken down to gain access to the boat, which was stowed on rollers and could be rolled out and lifted over the side with ship's tackle. The same procedure in reverse was used to onload the boat into the house.

With the exception of *Bald Eagle*, all the ships stowed their longboat in the aft port side of the house—apparently the traditional stowage location. *Bald Eagle* stowed a metallic lifeboat on the centerline of the ship, which was also the centerline of the deckhouse. This boat occupied the entire 8-foot breadth of the house and is shown in Figure 28.2.

Certain ships had no large houses on deck but rather confined their structures to small sizes. Typical of such installations were *Game Cock*, with a galley house about 7 feet square; *Tornado*, with a galley house; *Coeur de Lion*, with a house containing her galley and sleeping accommodations for the ship's boys; and *Challenge*, with a house containing the galley and one stateroom fitted with berths. In all of these vessels the crew was quartered in the tween-decks.

Another group of vessels was fitted out with only small

(text continued on page 438)

Figure 28.2. *Some representative deckhouse arrangements.*

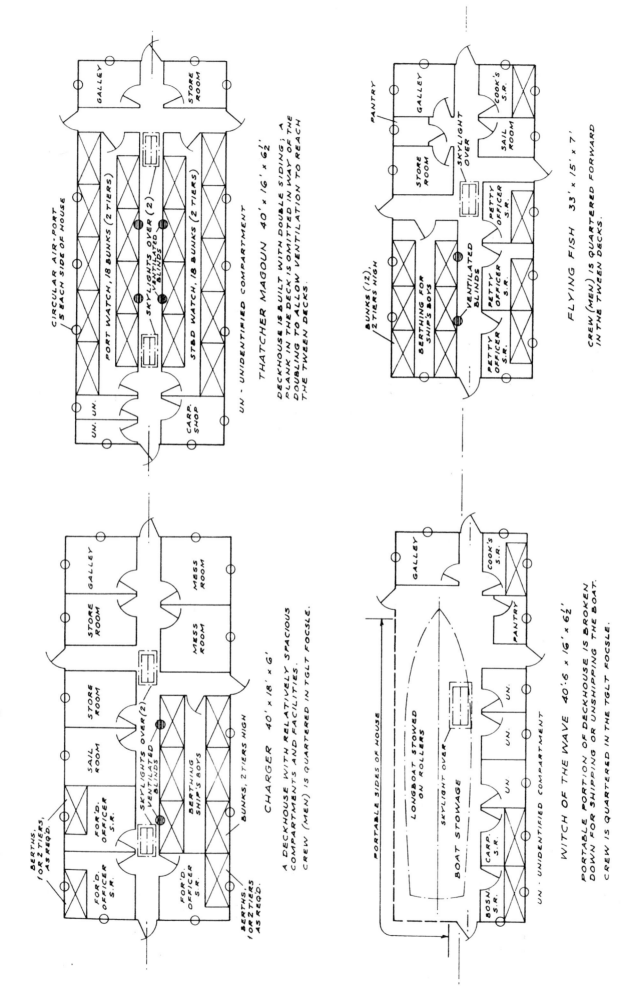

GALLEY

STORE ROOM

CIRCULAR AIR-PORT 5 EACH SIDE OF HOUSE

PORT WATCH, 18 BUNKS (2 TIERS)

SKYLIGHTS OVER (2) VENTILATED BLINDS

ST'B'D WATCH, 18 BUNKS (2 TIERS)

UN. UN.

CARP. SHOP

UN · UNIDENTIFIED COMPARTMENT

THATCHER MAGOUN 40' x 16' x 6½'

DECKHOUSE IS BUILT WITH DOUBLE SIDING; A PLANK IN THE DECK IS OMITTED IN WAY OF THE DOUBLING TO ALLOW VENTILATION TO REACH THE TWEEN DECKS.

PANTRY

STORE ROOM

GALLEY

COOK'S S.R.

SKYLIGHT OVER

SAIL ROOM

BUNKS (12), 2 TIERS HIGH

BERTHING FOR SHIP'S BOYS

VENTILATED BLINDS

PETTY OFFICER S.R.

PETTY OFFICER S.R.

PETTY OFFICER S.R.

FLYING FISH 33' x 15' x 7'

CREW (MEN) IS QUARTERED FORWARD IN THE TWEEN DECKS.

BERTHS, 1 OR 2 TIERS, AS REQ'D.

FOR'D OFFICER S.R.

SAIL ROOM

STORE ROOM

STORE ROOM

GALLEY

FOR'D OFFICER S.R.

SKYLIGHTS OVER (2) VENTILATED BLINDS

BERTHING SHIP'S BOYS

FOR'D OFFICER S.R.

MESS ROOM

MESS ROOM

BERTHS, 1 OR 2 TIERS, AS REQ'D.

BUNKS, 2 TIERS HIGH

CHARGER 40' x 18' x 6'

A DECKHOUSE WITH RELATIVELY SPACIOUS COMPARTMENTS AND FACILITIES. CREW (MEN) IS QUARTERED IN T'GL'T FOCSLE.

PORTABLE SIDES OF HOUSE

LONGBOAT STOWED ON ROLLERS

SKYLIGHT OVER

BOAT STOWAGE

GALLEY

COOK'S S.R.

PANTRY

BOS'N S.R.

CARP. S.R.

UN. UN. UN.

UN · UNIDENTIFIED COMPARTMENT

WITCH OF THE WAVE 40'.6 x 16' x 6½'

PORTABLE PORTION OF DECKHOUSE IS BROKEN DOWN FOR SHIPPING OR UNSHIPPING THE BOAT. CREW IS QUARTERED IN THE T'GL'T FOCSLE.

FORWARD →

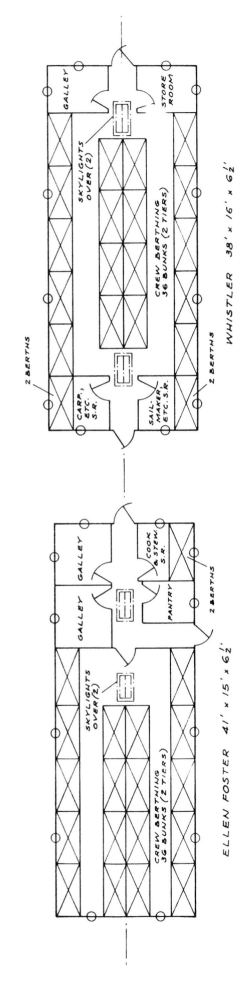

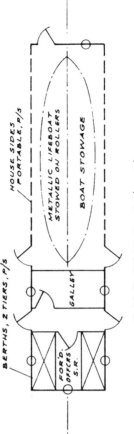

HOUSE SIDES PORTABLE, P/S

METALLIC LIFEBOAT STOWED ON ROLLERS

BOAT STOWAGE

GALLEY

BERTHS, 2 TIERS, P/S

FORD. OFFCRS. S.R.

BALD EAGLE 36' × 8'

EITHER SIDE OF DECKHOUSE CAN BE BROKEN DOWN FOR SHIPPING OR UNSHIPPING THE LIFEBOAT.

CREW IS QUARTERED FORWARD IN THE TWEEN DECKS.

GALLEY

STORE ROOM

SKYLIGHTS OVER (2)

CREW BERTHING 36 BUNKS (2 TIERS)

2 BERTHS

CARP., ETC. S.R.

SAIL-MAKER ETC. S.R.

2 BERTHS

WHISTLER 38' × 16' × 6½'

GALLEY

CREW BERTHING 14 BUNKS (2 TIERS)

BOSN. S.R.

CARP. S.R.

SHOOTING STAR 22' × 10' × 6½'

A SMALL DECKHOUSE.

CREW'S BERTHING APPARENTLY FEATURES "HOT BUNKS". THESE ARE BUNKS WHICH ARE IN CONSTANT USE BY SUCCESSIVE WATCHES. A RARE PRACTICE IN THE CLIPPER FLEET.

GALLEY

GALLEY

COOK & STEW. S.R.

PANTRY

2 BERTHS

SKYLIGHTS OVER (2)

CREW BERTHING 36 BUNKS (2 TIERS)

ELLEN FOSTER 41' × 15' × 6½'

NOTES

RECONSTRUCTIONS ARE BASED ON DESCRIPTIONS IN REF. 1.

COMPARTMENTS ARE FITTED WITH AIRPORTS OR DEADLIGHTS AS REQUIRED.

ALL BUNKS ARE ASSUMED 30" WIDE × 5'-6 LONG. BERTHS ARE SLIGHTLY WIDER.

INTERIOR BULKHEADS IN LARGE COMPARTMENTS ARE SOMETIMES FITTED WITH VENTILATED BLINDS.

(text continued from page 435)

deckhouses, all of which were movable. These were *Dauntless*, with two such houses, one containing the galley, and the second being a storeroom; *Game Cock*, with one unidentified house; and *Winged Arrow*, with a house fitted out as a storeroom and sail room. *John Land*, which was built as a duplicate of *Winged Arrow*, presumably had a similar house.

A third small group of ships was fitted out with movable galley houses. These vessels were *Dauntless*, *Witchcraft*, and the bark *Racehorse*. In addition there was *Flying Childers*, whose movable galley also contained the cook's stateroom.

A final practice which gained considerable acceptance in the clipper fleet involved the installation of small, movable deckhouses over the hatchways. The hatchways themselves were obstacles to the working of a ship; thus, they presented an opportunity for installing houses without additional encroachment on deck space. After a hatch had been battened down, the movable structure was superimposed on the coamings where it would remain until a destination was reached and the hatch must be broken out.

Descriptions of vessels rarely identify the use to which such individual houses were put. Of the vessels covered in this book, only *Flying Mist* is noted as having one house containing berths. It was installed over her aft hatchway.

Of the remaining vessels, *Winged Arrow*, *John Land*, *West Wind*, *Mameluke*, and *Winged Racer* all had a movable house over each of the three hatches. *Daring* had a house over the fore and main hatches only. *Donald McKay*, *Morning Light*, *Onward*, and *Sierra Nevada* each had one house installed over the main hatchway, while *Silver Star* and the bark *Quickstep* each had a house over the aft hatchway. The description of *Golden Eagle* makes no mention of a house over any hatch.[1] However, it is recorded that, during a gale in 1858, her hatch house was stove in.[32] No record is made of which hatch carried the house.

A rare, or possibly unique, vessel was Webb's three-decked *Invincible*, which was built with a clear, unencumbered weather deck. Other than a half poop, which was but 22 feet long, the only structures rising above the deck planking were hatchways with skylights fitted over them and a companionway close abaft the windlass for use of the crew quartered forward in the tween decks. Her forward deck was flush, there being no topgallant forecastle.

Doors and Passages

Doors and passages receive virtually no notice in any discourse about ships of this period. Actually, both were probably considered routine items not subject to designers' whims and fancy. However, it is satisfying to find some rare bit of information from which realistic conclusions can be drawn.

The illustration of the cabin arrangement in *James Baines*, Figure 28.4, also includes the attached cabinhouse in which the dining saloon was located. In the only instance involving the vessels included in this book, an actual dimension is given, from which a rational sizing of doors and passages in the living areas can be made, reasonably based on the location and specific function of each door and passage. (This same rationale was employed in designing ships of the United States navy in the mid-1900s.)

The key dimension is the 30-inch width of the athwartship passage at the forward end of the dining saloon. This width, in a general passage, represents an acceptable space where people in the passage can pass each other with little inconvenience. From this it can be concluded that a 24-inch passage would suffice for a restricted passage such as to an individual cabin, an isolated pantry, or small group of staterooms. Of course, these represent acceptable minimum dimensions.

The passage was fitted with an exterior door in each side of the house. These doors were required to be structural in nature and always opened out. To fit such a door in the 30-inch passage would limit the door size (clear opening) to about 24 inches. Interior doors in such a passage are lightweight and are classed as *joiner doors*. These could conceivably be 26 inches wide if necessary.

Joiner doors were fitted in all interior spaces and could vary in width as traffic dictated. Doors to a bathroom, water closet, pantry, or stateroom could be held to a practical minimum which allowed for access. Doors to galleys, storerooms, and between adjoining cabins required or were assigned a greater width because of necessity or privilege. All interior doors which accessed an individual space were hinged to swing into that space; doors were never deliberately hung to swing into a passage.

Cabins and Saloons

The cabins and saloons represented the most that a clipper could offer in the way of comfort, luxury, and beauty. The interiors, always fitted out in artistic fashion, were to the interior joiner what figureheads were to the woodcarvers—the challenge and the opportunity to indulge and exhibit their consummate skills. Their greatest resource was the plentiful supply of beautiful and exotic woods that were brought home from all corners of the world as cargo or ballast in the holds of returning vessels.

The fervor and interest with which the general public was infected by the introduction of the clipper ship did not end with the designer and the building of a sleek and powerful hull. The associated trades and crafts entered the fray, and in a short time the building and outfitting of clipper ships became a contest. It was a heady, engrossing business, and nowhere did it manifest itself to a greater degree than among the craftsmen who provided the decoration in the cabins and saloons. The greatest competition appeared to be among the joiners. They indulged their craft to an almost shameful degree, each one trying to make his vessel the outstanding example of the craft. The full impact of this indulgence of artistry can be appreciated from the following report.

Duncan MacLean surveyed the great cabin of *Witch of the Wave* in May 1851. In describing the interior treatment and finishing of this cabin, he wrote: "Here is splendor. Gothic panels of bird's eye maple, with frames of satin wood, relieved with zebra, mahogany and rose wood, enameled cornices edged with gold, and dark pilasters, with curiously carved and gilded capitals, and dark imitation marble pedestals. Abaft it is another cabin, finished in the same style, and having three panels of mirrors forward, and another mirror aft in the rudder-casing. The transom is fitted as a semicircular sofa, covered with rich velvet."[1]

Each of these cabins was illuminated by a large skylight in the overhead which allowed all of the cabin treatment to bathe in luxurious natural light—certainly a most impressive sight to behold.

At this particular time, approximately fifty medium and extreme clippers had been produced since the beginning of the previous year (1850), and MacLean had personally inspected about a dozen of them, including *Stag Hound, Challenge, Flying Cloud, Game Cock*, and others which would shortly assume their places in the nautical history of the period. During this same time frame he inspected about a dozen freighters and packets, reporting on them in varying degrees of detail. However, it remained for *Witch of the Wave* to awaken his senses and impress upon him the lavish extremes to which the interior appointments of the luxury spaces were being taken. Descriptions of the various luxury spaces were recorded for ship after ship, from the first one in 1850 to the last one, *Charger*, in 1856, of those covered in this book. Some descriptions are perfunctory, while others go into meticulous detail, but in no other case did reporter MacLean expose his personal impression as he did upon viewing *Witch of the Wave*, quoted above. Here, indeed, was splendor.

From 1850 through 1852 the descriptions of cabin treatments were detailed to a degree which allowed the reader to quite readily visualize the picture seen by the reporter spread out before him. Small details, particular locations, specific woods in specific applications—all were set down in a rather finite form. This was a boon to posterity and to any study of the clipper ships.

However, the beauty and lustre of this form of decoration became routine and commonplace. As ship after ship took to the water, the details appeared to be repetitious. They gave way to generalities such as a recitation of the varieties of wood used in a given ship, and similar statements. After 1853 it was only an occasional vessel that was recorded in the original detailed manner. This is the price that familiarity must pay.

The cabins, saloons, and other superior living accommodations were categorically installed in the after extremities of a ship. Space here was more amenable to providing quarters, the location was far removed from the noisy activity routinely found forward, and the area was drier than the forecastle when a vessel was pounding ahead at a great rate of speed.

There was an infinite array of cabin locations and arrangements in this aftermost area. Figures 28.3 through 28.7 illustrate reconstructed cabin and stateroom configurations that represent almost all available choices ranging from quarters under a full-height poop deck to those fitted out below in the tween-decks.

The overall extent of the cabin enclosures shown in these figures is based on given dimensions or descriptive lengths. This information, combined with detailed descriptions of the types of spaces (such as stateroom, galley, storeroom, and so on), allow for a reasonable reconstruction of an entire area. Certain considerations were necessary and certain rules of arrangement prevailed, so, within the confines of a structure, acceptable accuracy can be achieved.

The general scheme of interior joinerwork and cabinetry in cabins and saloons consisted of wainscoting the bulkheads and embellishing the beams of the deck overhead. As shipboard spaces are not expansive and working space is limited, the practical solution for applying the wainscoting lay in using various woods in relatively small pieces. This also satisfied the limitations imposed by small accesses to ship interiors.

The *wainscoting*, as applied in the various cabins and saloons, was not confined to the lower portion of the bulkheads in the fashion that is commonly found in an ordinary residence. Rather, it consisted of relatively narrow panels of rare and exotic woods, the panels extending for the full deck height. The most common forms of paneling featured the Gothic arch, the semicircular Roman arch, and, on occasion, an elliptical arch as was installed in *Challenge*. Occasionally the panels were of a geometric design, as is noted in *Sultana*, whose panels were octagonal in form. The panels, when installed, presented a tall, slender form which enhanced the illusion of height in the space.

It is a foregone conclusion that, while many cabin areas were fitted out in the same general manner, no two were alike when completed. Without going into endless descriptive detail, much of which would not be absolutely conclusive, the better method appears to rest in describing the typical or most prevalent style of treatment and then noting known exceptions.

Based upon frequency of appearance in MacLean's descriptions,[1] a typical cabin featured mahogany paneling;

(text continued on page 445)

439

Figure 28.3. *Cabin and stateroom arrangements.*

CABINS UNDER A LONG POOP DECK

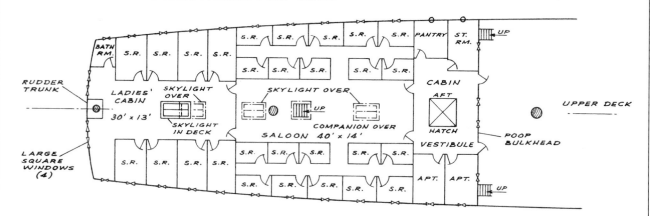

BLUE JACKET RECONSTRUCTION BASED ON DESCRIPTION IN REF. 5.

ALL STATEROOMS ARE FITTED WITH SQUARE WINDOWS AND/OR DECK LIGHTS.

LADIES CABIN IS MAHOGANY, WITH ROSEWOOD PANELS ORNAMENTED WITH FLOWERS SURROUNDED BY GILT WORK; SALOON IS PAINTED WHITE, WITH DECORATED PANELS AND GILT TRIM.

CABINS UNDER A MEDIUM LENGTH POOP DECK

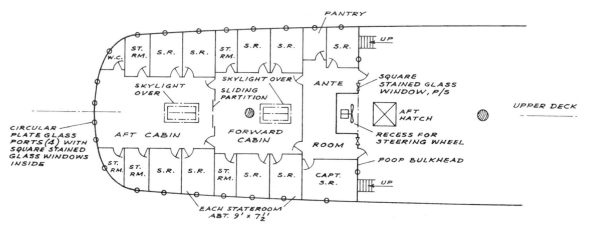

HOOGLY RECONSTRUCTION BASED ON DESCRIPTION IN REF. 1.

ALL STATEROOMS ARE FITTED WITH SIDELIGHTS AND DECKLIGHTS.

CABINS ARE WAINSCOTED WITH SEMI-CIRCULAR ARCHED PANELS IN SATIN WOOD, ZEBRA WOOD, ROSEWOOD AND MAHOGANY, WITH WHITE CEILING; ANTE ROOM IS PAINTED AND GRAINED.

Figure 28.4. *Cabin and stateroom arrangements.*

CABINS UNDER A SHORT POOP DECK, WITH A LARGE HOUSE ADJOINING

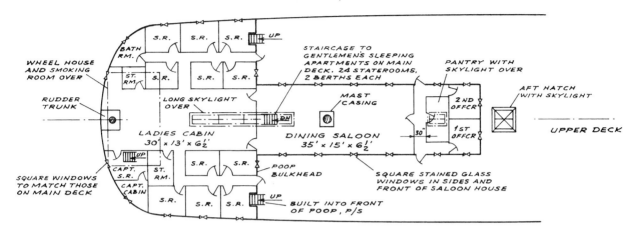

JAMES BAINES — RECONSTRUCTION BASED ON DESCRIPTION IN REF. 1.

INTERIOR STATEROOMS ARE PROBABLY FITTED WITH DECKLIGHTS.

LADIES CABIN IS PAINTED WHITE, WITH PANELS TRIMMED WITH GILDED CARVED WORK; DINING SALOON HAS MAHOGANY WAINSCOTING, WHITE PANELING AND CEILING, WITH FLOWERED AND GILDED ORNAMENTATION.

CABINS UNDER A MEDIUM LENGTH HALF POOP DECK WITH ATTACHED DECKHOUSE

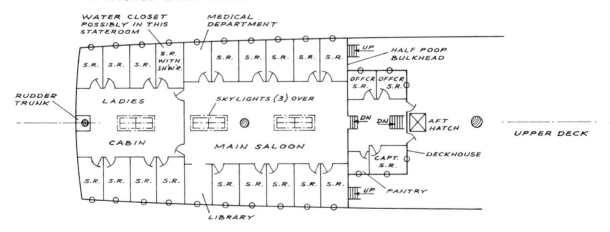

NIGHTINGALE — RECONSTRUCTION BASED ON DESCRIPTION IN REF. 3.

ALL STATEROOMS ARE FITTED WITH OPERATING GLASS AIRPORTS.

SKYLIGHTS OVER THE CABINS HAVE STAINED GLASS SIDES.

MANY STATEROOMS ARE FURNISHED WITH IRON BED-STEADS INSTEAD OF BERTHS.

CABIN AND SALOON ARE FINISHED IN MAHOGANY AND ROSEWOOD, WITH WHITE ENAMELED PANELS AND PILASTERS SET OFF WITH GILT ORNAMENTAL WORK.

Figure 28.5. *Cabin and stateroom arrangements.*

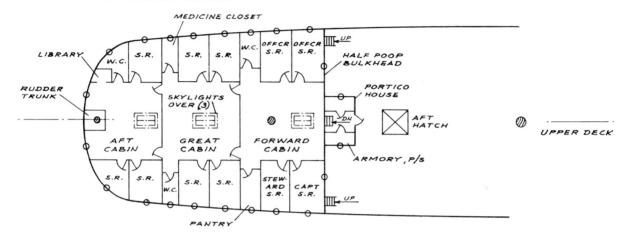

CABINS UNDER A MEDIUM LENGTH HALF POOP DECK WITH A PORTICO HOUSE

WITCH OF THE WAVE RECONSTRUCTION BASED ON DESCRIPTION IN REF. 1.

ALL STATEROOMS ARE FITTED WITH SIDELIGHTS AND DECKLIGHTS.

FORWARD CABIN IS WAINSCOTED AND GRAINED; GREAT CABIN AND AFT CABIN ARE FITTED WITH GOTHIC PANELS OF BIRD'S EYE MAPLE, WITH SATINWOOD FRAMES, TRIMMED WITH ZEBRA WOOD, ROSEWOOD AND MAHOGANY; ENAMELED CORNICES EDGED WITH GOLD; DARK PILASTERS WITH CARVED AND GILDED CAPITALS AND IMITATION MARBLE PEDESTALS.

THE LIBRARY CONTAINS OVER ONE HUNDRED VOLUMES.

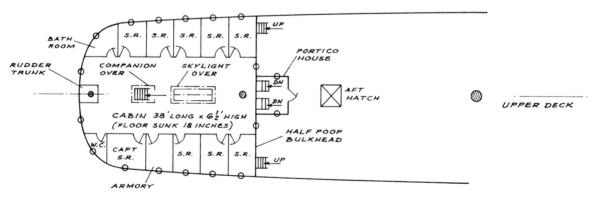

CABIN UNDER A SHORT HALF POOP DECK WITH A PORTICO HOUSE

ENDEAVOR RECONSTRUCTION BASED ON DESCRIPTION IN REF. 1.

ALL STATEROOMS ARE PROBABLY FITTED WITH SIDELIGHTS AND DECKLIGHTS.

NO DECORATIVE DETAILS ARE GIVEN.

Figure 28.6. *Cabin and stateroom arrangements.*

CABIN HOUSE BUILT INTO A HALF POOP

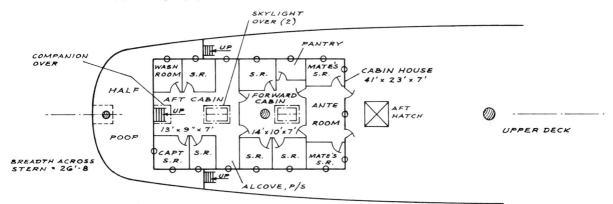

WAR HAWK   RECONSTRUCTION BASED ON DESCRIPTION IN REF. 1.

ALL STATEROOMS WELL LIGHTED AND VENTILATED.
SIDELIGHTS AND DECKLIGHTS PROBABLE.

ALL STATEROOM SEATS AND MATTRESSES ARE TEWKSBURY'S
PATENT LIFE PRESERVERS.

AFTER CABIN IS WAINSCOTED AND ENAMELED WHITE, SET OFF
WITH GILDED MOULDINGS AND FLOWER WORK; FORWARD
CABIN IS WAINSCOTED WITH SATINWOOD, WHITE ASH AND
MAHOGANY, RELIEVED WITH GILDING.

TRUNK CABIN BUILT INTO A HALF POOP

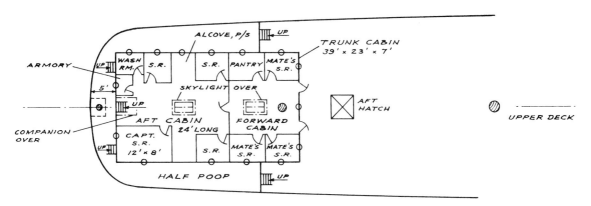

DARING   RECONSTRUCTION BASED ON DESCRIPTION IN REF. 1.

ALL STATEROOMS PROBABLY FITTED WITH SIDELIGHTS
AND DECKLIGHTS.

AFT CABIN IS PANELED AND PAINTED WHITE, EDGED WITH
GILDED FLOWER WORK; FORWARD CABIN IS POLISHED
BLACK WALNUT.

Figure 28.7. *Cabin and stateroom arrangements.*

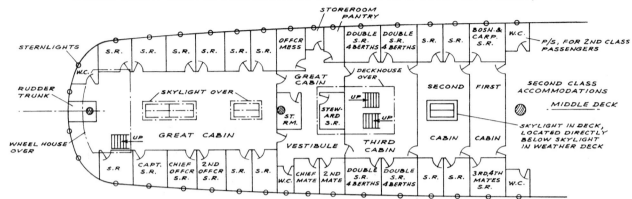

CABINS BELOW DECK IN VESSEL WITH FLUSH DECK AFT (CLIPPER PACKET)

STAFFORDSHIRE   RECONSTRUCTION BASED ON DESCRIPTION IN REF. 1.

ALL STATEROOMS ARE FITTED WITH DECKLIGHTS AND/OR SIDELIGHTS.
ROOMS WITHOUT SKYLIGHTS ARE FITTED WITH DECKLIGHTS.
GREAT CABIN IS MAHOGANY, WITH WHITE GOTHIC PANELS HAVING
GOLD MARGINS AND DECORATED WITH FLOWERED GOLD CENTERS.

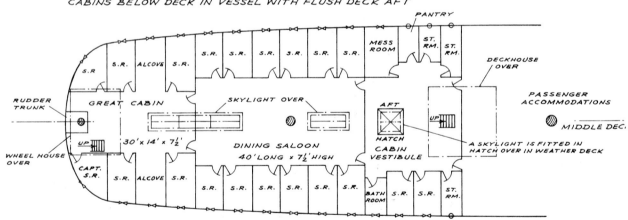

CABINS BELOW DECK IN VESSEL WITH FLUSH DECK AFT

CHAMPION OF THE SEAS   RECONSTRUCTION BASED ON DESCRIPTION IN REF. 1.

ALL STATEROOMS ARE FITTED WITH SQUARE SIDELIGHTS
OR PORTS WHICH CAN BE OPENED, AND WITH DECKLIGHTS.
GREAT CABIN IS MAHOGANY, WITH GOTHIC PANELS RELIEVED
WITH GILDED CARVED-WORK; DINING SALOON IS PAINTED
WHITE RELIEVED WITH GILDING.

444

(text continued from page 439)
satinwood trim around Gothic arches; rosewood pilasters with fancy papier-mâché capitals, gold in color; imitation marble pedestals; gilt cornices; white ceiling and beams, the lower corners of the beams edged in gilt.

Descriptions do not differentiate between gold paint and gold-leafing as applied to interior decor. *China Tea Clippers* [51] contains some mention of the subject, but the information is brief and general.

It would be difficult to find a single vessel which embodied every detail of the above treatment. Artistic license was apparent everywhere. *Hoogly* had panels with semicircular Roman arches. In *Challenge* and *Asa Eldridge* the arches were elliptical. *Southern Cross* had rectangular panels, and *Sultana* had octagonal paneling. In many vessels the trim around the panels was artistic "flower-work," generally painted but possibly carved in some instances, and finished in gilt. Many ceilings and beams were dark in color.

In vessels containing more than one cabin, the forward cabin was very often painted white and trimmed out in gilt. In many minds this was considered to be the most attractive color scheme due to its bright, clean appearance. *Indiaman* had two cabins and an anteroom, all painted white, trimmed out with gilt.

In all cases, the papier-mâché capitals which topped the pilasters were ornate and intricate. Some adhered to classical patterns, and some followed the whim of an individual designer. Flowered motifs were in great favor.

Some vessels strayed rather far from the beaten path. *Seaman's Bride* was finished with polished cherry wood; then the after cabin was painted with white enamel, trimmed out in gilt. *Lightning* used polished ash trim with some of the paneling in the after cabin. *Joseph Peabody* featured chestnut paneling trimmed with black walnut and gilt flowers. *Silver Star*, taking a turn in a different direction, finished her forward cabin in grained imitation oak.

For a better visualization of how the cabins were actually appointed, the following group of descriptions, quoted from the *Boston Daily Atlas*,[1] are representative of the type of cabin decoration found throughout the American-built clipper fleet.

Sultana—"The cabin is wainscotted with mahogany, and the frames are divided into two octagonal panels, edged with rose and zebra woods the whole set off with satin wood pilasters, edged with dark lines and sprigs, and rest upon imitation marble pedestals, and have enameled capitals inlaid with gilding. The cornices are of enamelled white, enclosed between gilded mouldings. The ceiling of the cabin is plain white."

Staffordshire—"Its [the great cabin] frame work is mahogany. The panels are crowned with gothic arches, and are of pure enamelled white, lined along the margins with gold, and flowered with gold in the centers. They are raised, or rather their outlines are indented and form rosewood grooves, outside of which are the pilasters. These last are also lined with gilding, and ornamented with gilded carved work in the middle. Their capitals are richly carved and gilded, and their pedestals are enameled in imitation of dark veined marble."

Hoogly—"The two cabins . . . are separated by a sliding partition, so that they may, when required, be made one. They are beautifully wainscoted with semi-circular arched panels of satin wood, relieved with zebra, rosewood and mahogany, and set off with satin wood cornices between gilded mouldings, and satin wood pilasters with gilded capitals and imitation dark-veined marble pedestals. The ceiling is painted white."

Joseph Peabody—"Both cabins are wainscotted with chestnut panels with double chestnut pillars, black walnut frames, enamelled white cornices, with rosewood ledges, the whole finely relieved with gilded lines and flower-work."

Asa Eldridge—"It contains two handsome cabins. The after one is pure white, with elliptical panels fringed with golden flower-work, and set off with double pillars, having gilded capitals. The panelling of the staircase and of the forward cabin is of chestnut and black walnut."

The merchants who provided furniture for use in cabins and dining saloons vied with the joiners in creating spaces of exquisite richness. Marble-topped walnut tables and sideboards; velvet, damask, and brocaded fabrics; plush carpeting; mirrors—all were used in profusion to complete the spaces.

Large mirrors were installed on rudder and mast casings. Oval, arched, or rectangular in shape, their presence enhanced the illusion of spaciousness whenever they were installed.

In the after cabin, probably the most visible and universal item of furniture was the transom sofa. These were placed aft in way of the rudder casing, and ranged from semicircular in form to slightly curved, depending upon the shape of the deck at the ship's stern. In *Shooting Star* the covering was crimson damask; in *Witch of the Wave*, it was velvet; in *Challenge*, green and gold brocatel; *Dauntless*, damask.

An unusual, perhaps unique, transom sofa installation was found in *Southern Cross*: " . . . she has two transom sofas, one above the other, and on the forward partition, a beautiful mirror, which gives a reflected view of the cabin abaft it."[1]

445

Many vessels had alcoves or recesses built into each side of the aft cabin. Examples are shown in *War Hawk* and *Daring* (Figure 28.6) and *Champion of the Seas* (Figure 28.7). These alcoves were fitted out as lounges and contained a sofa and, generally, a round marble-top table made of walnut. Their popularity grew as time went on. In the years 1850–53 they appeared only in an occasional vessel. Then, in 1854, they seemed to find favor, and their appearance was commonplace through 1856.

Vessels having large dining saloons, similar to that in *James Baines* (Figure 28.4), were fitted with settees along the fore-and-aft partitions. In front of the settees were walnut tables extending fore-and-aft.

A final detail of luxury and beauty was the frequent use of stained glass in skylights and windows. Many of the designs in stained glass were representations of persons, animals, scenes, and inanimate objects such as ships.

Ships' cabins were the beneficiaries of all the art and craftsmanship that mortal man could bestow upon an object which, unfortunately, was soon to be buffeted and abused by nature in her most terrifying moods.

Staterooms

The *staterooms* occupied by cabin-class passengers and the ship's senior officers generally flanked each side of the cabins and saloons and extended outboard to the ship's sides. In some vessels a trunk or a house side formed the outboard limit of these compartments.

Staterooms required a minimum fore-and-aft length of 5 feet 6 inches, this dimension being based upon the stature of a man of the period. Athwartship allowances had to be made for a berth (30 inches) and the swing of the door (about 24 inches) or, if space permitted, a greater dimension to allow for dressing and washing if the stateroom contained a nightstand. These ordinary staterooms were made as sleeping quarters, social activity taking place in the cabins. A stateroom measuring 6 feet by 7 feet was considered "spacious," and the staterooms in *Hoogly*, measuring 9 feet by 7 feet 6 inches, were "very large."

In any vessel the staterooms for officers were made slightly larger than the ordinary stateroom—a nod in deference to their position aboard. These officers' staterooms were not universally installed in given locations but, rather, appear to have been arbitrarily situated.

The captain's stateroom was governed by tradition and his position as the "infallible law" of the ship. The most universal fact about the captain's stateroom was that it was always located on the starboard side of the ship. There appeared to be no exception to this rule.

In most vessels this stateroom was located far aft in proximity to the helm. This facilitated the master's easy access to the wheel if conditions rendered his presence necessary. However, there were vessels in which the helm was located farther forward at the break of the poop. Two were *Hoogly*, shown in Figure 28.3, and *Challenge*. In both ships the wheel was installed on the upper deck, and in both ships the captain's stateroom was moved forward to the starboard side of the poop.

However, as in most cases where definite rules and procedures are in force, there were exceptions. It was not uncommon for the captain's stateroom to be located at the forward end of the poop—still on the starboard side of ship—even though the wheel was positioned over the rudderpost. From this vantage point he had a clear view of the deck before him. Some of the vessels arranged in this manner were *Stag Hound, Shooting Star, Queen of the Seas, John Stuart, Seaman's Bride, Climax, Nightingale* (Figure 28.4), and *Witch of the Wave* (Figure 28.5).

Two perquisites accorded the captain's stateroom were large size and pleasing decor. In cabins where enough information is available to allow reconstruction, the details generally show that the captain's quarters were larger than others. In some vessels the actual dimensions are given. The stateroom in *Charger* was 10 feet by 13 feet, an extremely spacious stateroom, and in *Daring* (Figure 28.6) it is shown as being 12 feet by 8 feet, another spacious compartment. In *James Baines* (Figure 28.4), the captain's quarters were subdivided into a stateroom (sleeping) and a separate cabin (living). This practice was optional and probably not unusual.

Unlike most other staterooms and officers' quarters, the captain's spaces were generally paneled and decorated in a manner similar to the cabins provided in the ship but to a less ostentatious degree. Furniture was most probably custom-provided to suit the individual's own taste and desires.

Light and Ventilation

Light and ventilation were easily provided in the cabin areas. Exterior staterooms, located along the sides of the vessels, were fitted with either square windows or the more approved round air port, and prismatic deck lights which emitted soft, diffused light from the outside. Interior staterooms received their light solely from such deck lights. Ventilation was provided through the air ports, through vent pipes, and a certain amount of ambient air circulation in the general area. Interior staterooms, such as are found in second-class accommodations in the tween-decks, sometimes received air through "ventilated blinds, which admit light as well as air." Such blinds are noted in the description of *James Baines*,[1] but no details are given. These are possibly Venetian-type shutters.

Washrooms and Water Closets

Basic hygienic facilities were provided in all vessels to a degree which appeared appropriate for the personnel on board. The most obvious need was for *water closet* facilities, which were always installed, but in many cases were not specifically noted. In cabin areas, water closets were almost universally located at the extreme stern or aft along the ship's side and were usually their own specific facility. *Staffordshire* (Figure 28.7) shows representative facilities of this type.

Many vessels were noted as having *washrooms* or *bathrooms* included in the cabin areas; examples are shown in Figures 28.3 through 28.7. It appears possible that, in these cases, the water closet facilities may have been included in these spaces.

A final and unusual development was included in *Nightingale* (Figure 28.4). One stateroom in the ladies' cabin was equipped with a shower bath "Which no doubt will prove quite a blessing to those who are in the habit of indulging in this luxury at home." *Nightingale* also had a separate compartment in the main saloon which was designated as the *medical department*. Such features are not noted frequently, but they do serve to point out the prevailing trend of improving general living conditions aboard ship.

Berthing

In keeping with major forms of progress, changes of lesser magnitude were being introduced. An example of such change is apparent in the furnishing of berthing facilities. Various ships appeared to timidly experiment with better ways to provide attractive and adequate berthing. Specific cases were relatively rare but were of sufficient number to suggest a trend.

In *Surprise* the staterooms in the after cabin were outfitted with French bedsteads in lieu of the standard built-in wooden berths. Presumably these were bed frames made up of fancy wrought iron headboards and footboards decorated with flowers and vinery. In *Nightingale* and *Eagle* many of the staterooms in the main cabin were provided with bedsteads.

Improvements of this nature were not confined to only the cabin areas of the ships. In *John Stuart*, a large three-decked vessel, the sleeping accommodations for steerage passengers in the lower tween-decks departed from the usual standing construction of the old-fashioned wooden berths. Instead of these, the berths were iron and were hung from the main deck overhead, "thus securing free access and ventilation beneath and contributing much to the cleanliness and, consequently, the health of the passengers."

The above improvements all took place in 1850–51 at the beginning of the clipper ship period, and it appears logical to assume that such internal progress kept pace with the changes in mechanical gear which were constantly taking place on deck.

Descriptions of the beautiful and lavish interior treatments of the great cabins of the clippers do much toward allowing a reader to visualize the appearance of these spaces in many of the vessels. However, there is no denying that description, no matter how accurate and detailed, can convey only a general idea of the whole picture, which will be different in the mind of each individual.

Unfortunately, there is little else surviving about this artistic work in the clippers, but one artifact still exists which can transport a person back to the past and into the realm of such vessels. While not of a clipper, the artifact is of a period not far removed and, when seen, identifies itself with the descriptions that have been previously noted.

On December 8, 1866, William H. Webb launched his three-masted, bark-rigged side-wheeler *Celestial Empire* into the East River in New York. In June 1867, after having completed a trial trip, she was delivered to the Pacific Mail Steamship Company, bearing her new name, *China*. She performed successfully between California and the Far East until 1879, and a few years later, in 1885, she was sold and burned for her metal at California City, California. Prior to being torched, one of her deck structures was removed in toto and became known as the "*China* Cabin." This structure is presumed to have enclosed the entry from the weather deck to the grand staircase which led to her main saloon. It has been painstakingly restored and can now be seen on exhibit at Belvedere, California. The book *William H. Webb, Shipbuilder*,[26] from which this information has been loosely taken, contains three photographs of this structure. On page 228 is an exterior view which is impressive in its own right; page 229 contains two photographs of the cabin interior. Even in black-and-white, these photographs echo Duncan MacLean's exclamation, "Here is splendor," which he uttered as he gazed into the cabin of *Witch of the Wave* fifteen years earlier.

The intricacy of structure, the delicacy of mouldings and trim, the daintiness of the tracery in the paneling, as seen in the *China* Cabin—all fit the descriptions of the clippers that had been built a scant dozen years before. The entire fabrication belies the sturdy, practical, working exteriors of the ships that contained these artistic jewels.

They, in every way, seem to merit the distinction of being categorized as art rather than craftsmanship.

Chapter Twenty-Nine

MAST AND SPAR ARRANGEMENTS

THE MASTING AND SPARRING OF the clipper ship produced no characteristics or innovations that posterity would come to regard as peculiar to clippers as a class. The construction and details of all spars, particularly the intricate and complex assembly of the various timbers that formed large "made" masts, remained the same as they had been when gathered in a treatise on the subject by John Fincham in 1829[110] and, before him, by David Steel in 1794.[109] Mastmakers could find no reason for changing production of these articles which had functioned so well for so many years.

However, certain evolutionary developments were taking place in shipbuilding, and these found their way into mastmaking. As in all other phases of shipbuilding, change met with grudging resistance and there were always "compelling and logical reasons" why new ideas should not be accepted. Ultimately, though, changes with merit won the day and were slowly absorbed.

From Rope to Metal

The greatest changes in mastmaking did not occur within the timbers but rather came about with the intrusion of iron into shipbuilding. The beginning of the nineteenth century saw the reluctant acceptance of iron fittings, and structural devices become ever more in evidence until, in the end, they superseded rope entirely. For many years the known superiority of the strength of iron over rope, in a ratio approximating eight to one, had made its use seem inevitable. The unbelievers, however, advanced the argument that the inherent flexibility of rope, as compared to the rigidity of iron, allowed for necessary working of parts aloft, which action absorbed shock and sudden stresses.

Practice ultimately laid this argument to rest, and slowly familiar rope parts were replaced by metal. In the body of lower made masts, the old rope "wooldings," with their numerous turns about the diameter of the assembled "side trees" and "fishes," were replaced with iron hoops sized to be heated and shrunk in position. Here was an assembly that was neat and absolutely inflexible; also it was highly efficient.

Higher aloft, the bulky wooden caps were replaced by smaller forged iron assemblies with neatly fitted eyes to accept shackles and bolts. Lower yards were no longer supported by clumsy rope slings, these being superseded by chain of small wire size which was equally capable of supporting the great weights incurred. Rope trusses that confined these yards to the masts disappeared, being replaced by forged iron patent trusses which controlled the position of the yard much more effectively. Rope strops and grommets disappeared from yardarms, and before long ships appeared finer and cleaner aloft.

Mast and Spar Development

The use of iron in the wooden sailing vessel was instrumental in a sudden increase in the length, and thus the size, of ships. In the 1840s the vessel constructed of wood held together with treenails and iron fastenings had reached the practical limits that wood fibers could sustain. In the 1850s the introduction of iron structure into the hulls gave impetus to a new surge of increased size and tonnage. As hulls grew larger, greater driving power was required to complement the increased hull capacity. Masts were thrust higher into the sky. Yards became longer or, as the sailors put it, "squarer." This was the situation into which the clipper ship was introduced.

This chapter will not discuss the construction of masts and spars; such information is available in detail in several excellent references.[109–111] This discussion will be confined to the generalities of clipper masting and details of interest outside of the intricate profession of mastmaking.

Great weights and huge sizes were encountered as ships' masts and spars grew ever larger. The description of *Donald McKay*[1] records weights encountered in her principal spars, and they are repeated here to bring the picture into focus. Her masts and spars were all pitch pine, the lower masts weighing 30, 33, and 18 tons; the topmasts 5, 5½, and 3 tons; and the bowsprit 7 tons. The lower yards weighed 12, 14½, and 6½ tons; the lower topsail yards 8, 8½, and 4 tons; the upper topsail yards 4½, 5, and 3 tons; total weight, 167 tons. The hoops on the fore and main masts were iron, 4 inches wide and ⅝ inch thick. In number there were 30, 31, and 28 hoops, the weights being 3,120, 3,210, and 2,500 pounds—a total of 8,830 pounds. The hoops on the fore and main yards weighed 1,805 and 2,085 pounds—a total of 3,890 pounds. The trusses on the lower yards were 800, 850, and 600 pounds—a total of 2,250 pounds. In addition she spread 16,755 yards of canvas.

As can be seen, this was an imposing aggregation of weights all thrust into the air at considerable height. These were all dry weights; with the addition of rainwater, which would cover all surfaces during wet weather, the weight aloft takes on even more significant numbers.

Another gauge of the size of individual iron fittings can be visualized in the forged iron patent trusses supporting the fore and main yards of *Phantom*. These trusses were of a size that positioned the yards 7 feet clear of the mast at the hounds.

Many additional examples of the magnitude of individual components of ships' masts and spars can be found, but the above dimensions will convey the impression of the massive sizes routinely in evidence.

Sparring Arrangements

Relatively few clippers have left behind detailed records such as offset tables, lines plans, or half models which tell us the exact configuration of their hull. The situation is different with records of these ships' masting. Of the vessels included here, over half have had their masting tables listed in complete detail or with information enough to allow acceptably accurate reconstruction of their principal sparring arrangements. Table 29.1 lists pertinent details pertaining to types of spar plan, type of rig, and associated data, and also identifies the vessels for which mast and spar data is available in very complete form in the noted references. Also included is limited information where complete tables are not recorded for certain vessels.

Any study of the detailed sizes (length and diameter) of clipper masts and spars does not lead the researcher to a definite source of basic information. While the majority of vessels were sparred in a generally similar manner, a close look at details and proportions discloses such disparity as to give no clue suggesting that the builders were adhering to any standard set of rules or governing factors. Individual preference seemed to be more the order of the day. It would

appear, however, that all the basic assumptions were based on rules, written or unwritten, developed over a period of time and modified as conditions demanded.

There was at least one instance in which a set of rules, "ascertained by experience to be pretty correct and easy of application," was recorded in a publication. This information appears in *The U.S. Nautical Magazine and Naval Journal*, October 1856.[113] The information and proportions given are claimed to be the diameters and forms of masts and spars "generally recognized by spar makers in this country and in England."

When this edition of the magazine was published, all but four of the clippers included herein had been launched, and the remaining four would be launched by year's end. The date of the publication indicates that all the clippers covered in this book could have been sparred more or less in accordance with the details of the article. Examination of the various ships' masting tables does little, however, to indicate that this is a fact.

Of great interest in the sparring of the clippers is the wide range of individual spar plans to be found throughout the clipper fleet. Figures 29.1 through 29.4 illustrate twenty-three known examples of sparring arrangements that were installed in clippers. This probably is not the complete representation of what was done because, for many vessels, no details have survived. However, a detailed inspection of the illustrations reveals almost every possible combination of mast assemblies and the crossing of yards. These spar plans are identified by number, and the numbers appear in Table 29.1 beside the name of the individual vessel that wore the rig.

A combination of the timing of clipper ship building and the development of the single topsail resulted in plan No. 6 (Figure 29.1) being the most commonly used spar plan to be found among the clippers, accounting for 30 percent of the total. The next two most frequently used plans were No. 7 and No. 8 (Figure 29.2), accounting for 17 and 20 percent, respectively, of all vessels. Thus, three spar plans, all featuring the single topsail, accounted for the rigging of two-thirds of the vessels listed in this book. (This percentage matches almost precisely the proportion shown in paintings of clippers to be seen today. Even allowing for artistic license, these figures appear to support the contemporary acceptance of artistic accuracy.)

The remaining third were those vessels that carried single topsails and variations in the other sails that they carried, or were rigged with the newly introduced double topsails. Also, as in plans No. 15 (Figure 29.3) and No. 23 (Figure 29.4), one-of-a-kind innovations were advanced.

Many of the spar plans in the figures, if given only a superficial glance, would appear to be duplicates. In actuality, however, no two are exactly alike, and their principal

(text continued on page 455)

Table 29.1. *Masting and rigging data.*

Notes: 1. * = Spar dimensions are given in the reference. Some entries are not complete.
2. Rake of masts is in inches per foot.
3. "Rigging" refers to fore and main lower standing rigging and topmast backstays. All other rigging is always in proportion.
4. "Square", in reference to yard dimensions, refers to their length. It was a sailors' term and appears throughout ref.1.

Fig. 29.1 thru 29.4

Vessel & Ref.#	Spar plan no.	Type of rig	Rake of masts F,Mn,Mz	Rigging See note 3	Remarks
Alarm #1*	13	Howes		Russia hemp,10½"	All chain and iron work in general use.
Amphrite #1*	9	Forbes			Topmasts are fidded before lower mastheads.
Andrew Jackson #32	14	Howes			Rig is taken from painting in ref.32.
Antelope #1		single topsails			Full rigged ship. No additional details.
Asa Eldridge #1*	13	Howes		Russia hemp,10½"; Manila running rigging.	All chain and iron work in general use. Has chain topsail sheets and ties.
Bald Eagle #1*	7	single topsails		Russia hemp, 4-strand, 11"; topmast back-stays, 10½"	Extra long lower mastheads. Topsail halliards, gins and ties are double. Lower rigging has unusual spread.
Belle of the West #1,32	9	Forbes			Ref.1 states that topmasts were fidded before lower mastheads. Ref.32 states that they were fidded abaft.
Beverly #3		single topsails			
Black Hawk #24,62,63	8	single topsails			Original sail plan, ref.24, shows single topsails. The photos are not her original rig.
Blue Jacket #32	17	Howes, mod.			Double topsails on fore and mainmasts only.
Bonita #1	6	single topsails		Russia hemp	Sparred in same style as Golden Light. Skysail yards are rigged aloft.
Bounding Billow Bark #1*	20	single topsails	raked		
Celestial #32,42		single topsails			

Vessel & Ref.#	Spar plan no.	Type of rig	Rake of masts F,Mn,Mz	Rigging See note 3	Remarks
Challenge #1*	6	single topsails	1⅛",1¼",1½"	Russia hemp, 4-strand, without heart, 11"; Manila running rigging.	Wide, solid tops; chain topsail sheets and ties; double ties with gins on yards similar to naval fashion. Shifting topmast and tglt backstays.
Challenger #1*	6	single topsails	"usual rake"	Russia hemp; Manila running rigging.	Spar plan not definite.
Champion of the Seas #1*	8	single topsails	½",⅝",1"	Russia hemp	All chain and iron work in general use. Carries main spencer.
Charger #1	6	single topsails		Russia hemp	Spar plan is based on her 12000 yards spread of canvas.
Charmer #1*,32	6	single topsails		Russia hemp	All chain and iron work in general use. Painting in ref.32 shows skysails at main only and either Forbes or Howes rig. This was apparently a re-rig.
Cleopatra #1,32	6	single topsails			Skysails are noted in ref.32.
Climax #1*,32	13	Howes			The Howes rig is used for the first time. Straight foot of upper topsail laces to jackstay on lower topsail yard, leaving no space between. Skysail yards are rigged aloft. Also see refs.32,44 and chapter text.
Coeur de Lion #1*,32	6	single topsails		Russia hemp; Manila running rigging	Rig is based on painting in ref.32.
Comet #24	6 mod.	single topsails			Tglt masts are separate, headed spars.
Cyclone #1*	7 prob.	single topsails			Mainmast is 80 feet long and main yard is 80 feet square.
Daring #1	13 prob.	Howes			Lower masts 74',79',71' long; Lower yards 68',73',51' square.
Dauntless #1	6 prob.	single topsails			Tglt rigging is fitted over copper cylinders; man-of-war fashion.
Donald McKay #1*	14	Howes	nearly upright	Russia hemp; Manila running rigging	All chain and iron work in general use.
Don Quixote #1	8	single topsails			Mainmast 84' long; main yard 80' square. Spar plan is based on her 9000 yards spread of canvas.

Table 29.1. *Continued.*

Vessel & Ref.#	Spar plan no.	Type of rig	Rake of masts F,Mn,Mz	Rigging See note 3	Remarks
Eagle #5		single topsails			
Eagle Wing #1 *	7	single topsails		Russia hemp	
Edwin Forrest #1 *	6	single topsails			
Electric Spark #1,32	13	Howes			Spar plan is based on text in ref.32.
Ellen Foster #1 *	7	single topsails	1¼",1½",1¾"	Russia hemp	
Empress of the Sea #1 *	7	single topsails	⅞",1",1⅛"	Russia hemp, 4-strand, 11"; fore and main stays, 11". Manila running rigging.	All chain and iron work in general use. Has iron gins for the topsail ties. Carries main spencer.
Endeavor #1 *	7	single topsails		American hemp, 4-strand, 9"; fore and main stays, 8"; mizzen stay, 7"; fore and main topmast stays, 5¼"; mizzen topmast stay, 4½". Manila running rigging.	All chain and iron work in general use.
Eringo Bark #1 *	20	single topsails		Russia hemp	
Eureka		single topsails prob.			
Fair Wind #1	13	Howes		Russia hemp	
Fearless #32	8	single topsails			
Fleet Wing #1	7	single topsails		Russia hemp	Mainmast is 75 feet long; main yard is 68 feet square.
Flyaway #24		single topsails prob.			
Flying Arrow #1 *	6	single topsails			
Flying Childers #1 *	11	Forbes			Fore and main topmasts are fidded abaft the lower masts. Mz topmast fidded before to avoid the trysail mast when sending the mz topmast up or down. Yards on mainmast fit foremast except one stage lower, i.e. the lower main topsail yard fits the fore yard, etc.
Flying Cloud #1 *	6	single topsails	1¼",1¼",1¼"		Carries main spencer.
Flying Dragon #1	8	single topsails			Mainmast is 80 feet long. Yards on fore and mainmasts are alike, 72',56',42' and 31' square.
Flying Dutchman #24	6	single topsails			
Flying Eagle #1 *	8	single topsails		Rope, 9¾"; fore stay, 9"; main stay, 8½". (Not an error.)	All chain and iron work in general use. Royal masts have poles long enough to rig skysails.
Flying Fish #1 *	6	single topsails	1¼",1¼",1¼"	Russia hemp, 4-strand, 10½". Manila running rigging.	All chain and iron work in general use. Has double topsail ties and halliards. Carries fore and main spencers.
Flying Mist #1 *	15	Linnell (Howes' mod.)		Russia hemp, 10"; fore and main stays, 10". Manila running rigging.	Lower topsail yard is fitted with Capt. Linnell's invention. See text for description. Straight foot of upper topsail laces to jackstay on lower topsail yard. Skysail is rigged aloft. Yards on fore and mainmasts are alike.
Galatea #1*,32	8	single topsails			Carries royals only, per painting in ref.32.
Game Cock #1 *	6	single topsails	1",1⅛",1¼"		Built with very long lower masts and short topmasts. This increased reliance on courses which could be kept standing longer.
Gazelle #24	8	single topsails			
Gem of the Ocean #1	8	single topsails			Mainmast is 74 feet long; main yard is 66 feet square.
Golden Eagle #32	6	single topsails			Spars and type of rigging are taken from text in ref.32.
Golden Fleece (2nd) #1 *	14	Howes		Russia hemp, 11"	
Golden Light #1 *	6	single topsails		Russia hemp	Carries skysail yards rigged aloft. Carries main spencer.
Golden West #32	8	single topsails			Spars and type of rigging are taken from painting in ref.32.
Grace Darling #1	7	single topsails		Russia hemp	

Table 29.1. *Continued.*

Vessel & Ref.#	Spar plan no.	Type of rig	Rake of masts F,Mn,Mz	Rigging See note 3	Remarks
Great Republic #4*,10*	1	Forbes		Rope, $12\frac{1}{2}$"; mizzen rigging and topmast backstays, 11"; fore and main topmast rigging, 8".	Spar dimensions in ref.4 (28 Dec 1853) agree with ref.10. Spar dimensions in ref.4 (18 June 1853) are not correct. Double topsails are noted as topsail and tgltsail thus a moonsail appears on fore and mainmasts. Has solid tops.
Great Republic #103 * (rebuilt)	2	Howes		Rope, $12\frac{1}{2}$"	Rig reduced.
Henry Hill Bark #1 *	19	single topsails	$1\frac{1}{8}$", $1\frac{1}{2}$", $1\frac{7}{8}$"		Main skysail yard is rigged aloft.
Herald of the Morning #1*,32	6	single topsails			Skysails on all masts, ref.32.
Hoogly #1 *	8	single topsails	1", $1\frac{1}{4}$", $1\frac{1}{2}$"		Corresponding yards on fore and mainmasts are alike. Yards on mizzen mast are the same except one stage higher, e.g. crojack is same as fore and main topsail yards, etc.
Hurricane #4*,32	4	single topsails			Fitted with Cunningham's rolling topsails, ref.32. Yards on fore and mainmasts are alike. Carried moonsails on fore and mainmasts.
Indiaman #1	6	single topsails			
Intrepid		single topsails prob.			
Invincible #4*,24	8	single topsails	$1\frac{1}{8}$", $1\frac{1}{4}$", $1\frac{1}{2}$"	Russia hemp, 4-strand, $10\frac{3}{4}$".	Rig taken from ref.24.
James Baines #1*,32	7	single topsails			Was able to set moonsails in light winds. Carries main spencer.
John Bertram #1 *	6	single topsails	$1\frac{1}{4}$", $1\frac{1}{2}$", $1\frac{3}{4}$"	Rope, 10"; mizzen rigging and mz topmast backstays, 8".	All chain and iron work in general use.
John Gilpin #1*,32	8	single topsails	"very rakish", ref.32.		Fore and main topmasts and above are alike. All yards on foremast are same as yards on mainmast. Carries main spencer.

Vessel & Ref.#	Spar plan no.	Type of rig	Rake of masts F,Mn,Mz	Rigging See note 3	Remarks
John Land #1,32 (built as a duplicate of Winged Arrow.)	7	single topsails			All chain and iron work in general use. Main skysail yard is rigged aloft.
John Stuart #4 *	8	single topsails			
John Wade #1*,32	7	single topsails			Mainmast is 70 feet long; main yard is 64 feet square. Rig is taken from ref.32.
Joseph Peabody #1 *	13	Howes		Russia hemp, $10\frac{1}{2}$"	
King Fisher #1		single topsails			
Lady Franklin		single topsails			
Lamplighter Bark #1 *	20	single topsails			All yards on foremast same as yards on mainmast.
Lightfoot #1		single topsails			Mainmast is 89 feet long; main yard is 85 feet square.
Lightning #1 *	7	single topsails		Russia hemp, 4-strand, $11\frac{1}{2}$"; lower and topmast stays, $11\frac{1}{2}$"; mz rigging, $8\frac{1}{2}$". Manila running rigging.	All chain and iron work in general use.
Mameluke #1	13	Howes		Russia hemp	
Mary Robinson #32		single topsails			Fore and main yards are 76' square x 20" dia.; fore and main topsail yards are 60' square x 16" dia.
Mastiff #1	7	single topsails		Russia hemp	All chain and iron work in general use. Main skysail yard is rigged aloft.
Mermaid Bark #1 *	22	Forbes			All chain and iron work in general use, and iron futtocks. Lower rigging sets up to iron eyes in a band below masthead in lieu of going over the trestletrees. (This method was favored by R.B. Forbes.) Carries main spencer.
Morning Light #1,78	6	single topsails			Lower masts 86', 90', 80' long; main yard is 85' square. Painting shown in ref.78 is probably a later re-rig.
Mystery #1 *	8	single topsails		Russia hemp	Fore and main topmasts and above are alike. Yards on foremast are same as yards on mainmast. Carries main spencer.
Nightingale #3 *, 32	6	single topsails	$1\frac{1}{4}$", $1\frac{1}{2}$", $1\frac{3}{4}$"		Rake of masts from ref.32.

Table 29.1. *Continued.*

Vessel & Ref.#	Spar plan no.	Type of rig	Rake of masts F,Mn,Mz	Rigging See note 3	Remarks
Noonday #1	7	single topsails		Russia hemp, 10½"	Lower masts 77',80',72' long; lower yards 74',78',64' square.
Northern Light #32	7	single topsails			Based on painting in ref.32.
Ocean Express #1,32	8	single topsails			Rig altered to Howes' after first voyage, ref.32.
Ocean Pearl #1 *	6 or 8	single topsails			Rig not conclusive.
Ocean Telegraph #5				Russia hemp	
Onward #1 *	8	single topsails			Spar plan not conclusive.
Osborne Howes #32	6	single topsails			Crossed skysail yards. Type of rig not conclusive.
Panther #32		single topsails prob.			
Phantom #1 *	6	single topsails		Russia hemp, 10½"	Fore and main yards are slung 7 feet from the trestletrees with stout patent trusses.
Queen of Clippers #1 *	6	single topsails		Russia hemp	All chain and iron work in general use. Carries main spencer.
Queen of the Pacific #32	8	single topsails			Based on painting in ref.32.
Queen of the Seas #1 *	8	single topsails	1",1¼",1½"	4-strand patent rope, 10½"	All chain and iron work in general use. Gins on mastheads and yards, double topsail ties and halliards. Carries main spencer.
Quickstep Bark #1 *	20	single topsails			Rigging sets up with iron eyes on masts and iron bands in the channels. All yards on foremast same as yards on mainmast. Carries main spencer.
Racehorse Bark #1 *	22	Forbes	1½",1½",1½"		Lower rigging sets up to iron eyes in a band below masthead in lieu of going over trestletrees. (This method was approved by R.B. Forbes.) Head yards are same size as after yards except one stage lower, e.g. fore yard is same length as main lower topsail yard, etc. Carries main spencer.
Racer #3 *	8	single topsails	1",1¼",1½"		
Radiant #1 *	8	single topsails		Russia hemp	
Raven #3		single topsails			
Red Jacket #14 *	6	single topsails			
Robin Hood #32		single topsails prob.			
Rocket Bark #1		single topsails			
Roebuck #1 *	8	single topsails			All yards on foremast same as yards on mainmast.
Romance of the Sea #1 *	7	single topsails			Has unusual spread to her lower rigging; 24' at fore and main channels, 18' at mizzen channels. Tops are wide and solid, man-of-war fashion. Carries fore and main spencers.
Santa Claus #1		single topsails			Lower masts 80',84',75' long; lower yards 68',76'56' square.
Saracen #1 *	8	single topsails			
Sea Bird Bark #1 *	21	single topsails	1¼",1½",1¾"		Crosses three yards on fore and mainmasts. Both tglt pole masts are divided into three lengths. Carries main spencer.
Seaman's Bride #4	3	single topsails			Main topmast 40' long; main yard 68' square. One of very few vessels to carry moonsails on all masts.
Sea Serpent #32	6	single topsails	1",1¼",1½"		Lower masts 83',87',78' long.
Shooting Star #1 *	8	single topsails	$1\frac{3}{16}$",$1\frac{3}{8}$",$1\frac{3}{4}$"	Russia hemp, 4-strand; Manila running rigging.	All chain and iron work in general use. Chain topsail sheets, ties and runners. Solid boarded tops, man-of-war fashion. Carries main spencer.
Sierra Nevada #1 *	16	Howes	"graceful rake"	Russia hemp; Manila running rigging.	
Silver Star #1 *	6	single topsails		4-strand rope, 10¼"; fore and main stays, 10"; mizzen rigging, 8"; mizzen topmast backstays, 5"; mizzen stay, 4".	All chain and iron work in general use. Chain topsail sheets and ties. Carries main spencer.
Southern Cross #1 *	6	single topsails		4-strand rope	

Table 29.1. *Continued.*

Vessel & Ref.#	Spar plan no.	Type of rig	Rake of masts F,Mn,Mz	Rigging See note 3	Remarks
Sovereign of the Seas #1 *	7	single topsails	$\frac{3}{4}$", $\frac{7}{8}$", $1\frac{1}{8}$"	12" rope	All chain and iron work in general use. Double gins for topsail ties, gins on the topsail yards and double halliards. Main tglt has a gin at masthead and double ties to the yard. Carries main spencer.
Spitfire #1 *	6	single topsails		Russia hemp	All yards on the foremast are same as yards on the mainmast. Mizzen also, taking the fore topsail yard for the crojack. Skysail yards are rigged aloft.
Staffordshire #1 *	8	single topsails	$1\frac{1}{4}$",$1\frac{1}{4}$",$1\frac{1}{4}$"		Has solid boarded tops, man-of-war fashion. Carries main spencer.
Stag Hound #1*,32	6	single topsails	$1\frac{1}{4}$",$1\frac{1}{4}$",$1\frac{1}{4}$"	4-strand, 10"; mizzen rigging,8"; fore and main stays,$9\frac{1}{2}$"; fore and main topmast backstays,$9\frac{3}{4}$"; topmast rigging,$5\frac{1}{4}$"; mizzen topmast backstays,$7\frac{3}{4}$"; mizzen topmast rigging,$4\frac{3}{4}$"; fore and main tglt backstays and jibboom guys, $6\frac{1}{2}$".	All chain and iron work in general use. Has solid boarded tops, man-of-war fashion. Carries fore and main spencers.
Star of the Union #1 *	8 prob.	single topsails	$1\frac{1}{8}$",$1\frac{3}{8}$",$1\frac{5}{8}$"		Number of yards crossed is not specified.
Starr King #32		single topsails prob.			
Storm King #1 *	8	single topsails	1",$1\frac{1}{4}$",$1\frac{1}{2}$"	4-strand, $10\frac{1}{2}$"	All chain and iron work in general use. Carries main spencer.
Sultana Bark #1 *	19	single topsails	1",$1\frac{1}{4}$",$1\frac{1}{2}$"		Carries main spencer.
Sunny South #32	6 prob.	single topsails			Main yard is $66\frac{1}{2}$' square; main skysail yard is 24' square.
Surprise #1 *	6	single topsails	$\frac{5}{8}$", $\frac{3}{4}$", 1"	Patent rope	Carries fore and main spencers.
Swallow #32		single topsails			
Sweepstakes #32,112*	6 mod.	single topsails			Tglt masts are separate, headed spars.

Vessel & Ref.#	Spar plan no.	Type of rig	Rake of masts F,Mn,Mz	Rigging See note 3	Remarks
Sword Fish #24,32	6	single topsails			Original design shows single topsails. Painting in ref.32 shows double topsails, fore and main only. This was apparently a re-rig, Forbes modified.
Syren #3 *	6	single topsails			
Telegraph #1		single topsails			
Thatcher Magoun #1 *	13	Howes			
Tornado #3		single topsails			Fore and mizzen masts 80' long; mainmast 90' long.
Uncowah #26					
War Hawk #1*,32,47	7	single topsails			She underwent large repairs in Feb. 1869, ref.47, and may have had her rig modified at that time. Painting dated 1880, ref.32, shows her fitted with Howes rig and crossing three skysail yards.
Water Witch #1 *	6	single topsails	1",$1\frac{1}{2}$",$1\frac{3}{4}$"	Russia hemp, 4-strand, $10\frac{1}{2}$".	Carries main spencer.
Western Continent		single topsails prob.			
Westward Ho #1 *	6	single topsails	$\frac{3}{4}$", $\frac{7}{8}$", 1"	Russia hemp,$10\frac{1}{2}$"; Manila running rigging.	Double gins for the topsail ties, gins on the yards and double halliards. Carries main spencer.
West Wind #1 *	7	single topsails			Main skysail yard is rigged aloft.
Whirlwind #1		single topsails			Lower masts 75',80',72' long; main yard 72' square.
Whistler #1 *	6 or 8	single topsails			Spar plan is not conclusive.
Wildfire Bark #1 *	18	single topsails	$1\frac{1}{4}$",$1\frac{1}{2}$",$1\frac{3}{4}$"		Skysail yards are rigged aloft.
Wild Pigeon #1 *	6	single topsails	$1\frac{1}{4}$",$1\frac{3}{8}$",$1\frac{1}{2}$"	Russia hemp	Carries fore and main spencers.
Wild Ranger #32	6	single topsails			
Wild Rover #32		single topsails			
Winged Arrow #1 *	7	single topsails			All chain and iron work in general use. Main skysail yard is rigged aloft.

Table 29.1. *Continued.*

Vessel & Ref.#	Spar plan no.	Type of rig	Rake of masts F,Mn,Mz	Rigging See note 3	Remarks
Winged Racer #1 *	6	single topsails		4-strand rope	All chain and iron work in general use.
Witchcraft #1 *	6	single topsails	1",1¼",1½"	4-strand rope	All chain and iron work in general use. Carries main spencer.
Witch of the Wave #1*,32	6	single topsails	1¼",1½",1¾"	Russia hemp, 4-strand, 10½".	Blocks at topmast head and on topsail yards for double topsail ties. (These are not gins.) Carries fore and main spencers. Painting in ref.32 shows her with double topsails. This is not her original rig.
Wizard #1		single topsails		Russia hemp	Lower masts 86',90',82' long; fore and main yards 80' square; crojack 62' square.
Young America #24	5	single topsails			Spar dimensions appear in a contemporary list, source not identified. Carries moonsail on mainmast. Re-rigged in 1854 with Howes double topsails Rig again modified, possibly in 1870, when she underwent large repairs, ref.47.
Young Turk Bark #1 *	23	Humphrey	1",1¼",1½"		See text for complete description.

Monkey Gaff

(text continued from page 449)
characteristics are briefly noted in the brief subheadings. Where a vessel's name is given, the plan is peculiar to that individual vessel. Naturally, this does not preclude the possibility that some other vessel with details unknown could have been sparred in the same manner.

Monkey Gaff

The *monkey gaff*, not included in any of the spar plans shown, is a small but rather conspicuous spar that was carried by many vessels but is not included in their masting tables. Its sole purpose was to support a halliard for the ship's ensign, in ships that were fitted with reefing spankers and in those that did not carry a spanker gaff. (Ensigns, flags, and signals are covered in Chapter 31.)

There appeared to be no specific dimensions for this spar, but a few drawings indicate a length between 15 and 20 feet. This was sufficient to hoist the ensign clear of all rigging on the mizzenmast. The heel diameter was about 5 inches.

When carried, these gaffs were usually set up to the mizzen topmast crosstrees with a small gooseneck fitting. Their position was fixed, being constrained transversely by *vangs*, port and starboard, which were seized to the aftermost mizzen topmast shroud at about its mid-length, and topped with a lift secured to the topmast cap. It was peaked parallel with the spanker gaff, when one was carried, or with the mizzen topmast stay if no gaff existed.

Single Topsail

The *single topsail*, over the course of the history of the quadrilateral or square sail, came to be the most important sail ever to find its way aloft in both merchant ships and ships-of-war. However, the *square course*, the first squaresail to make its appearance, retained this distinction for many centuries prior to the introduction of a topsail in any form.

No one can surmise just when some ancient boatman discovered that a hide or woven mat, when hoisted on a post in the middle of his raft and spread at the top with a crude branch, could catch the breeze and relieve him of the labor of poling or paddling his craft—at least in one direction. The discovery no doubt took place long before it became a matter of record. Like all discoveries, once brought to light there was no thought of using the innovation without attempting to improve upon it.

Ages later, when records began to be kept in the form of pictures, we come upon valid evidence that this primitive sail had evolved, through many stages, into the sail which we today recognize as a *course*. One of the earliest examples of this sail in the form we know it is shown in a carved relief in the pyramid of Pharaoh Sahure, circa 2400 B.C.[114] It is a basic quadrilateral, spread by a yard slung atop a stubby mast structure forward of amidships, braced from the ends of the yard, and its foot spread with a spar, the clews being brought inboard to the rail. In this general form the squaresail with its single mast powered ships of diverse sizes and shapes through many civilizations including Egyptian, Greek, Roman, and Viking.

The rig in its basic form remained undisturbed until about the mid-1400s, when the slow accumulation of advances in hull design flowed over into the masting of ships.[79] The single mast gave way to a second and then to a third. The institution of three masts proved to be the optimum combination of propulsion compatible with the general form of ships' hulls.

These ships with three masts still carried only the square course on the fore and main masts, and a lateen sail on the mizzen. Invariably the mastheads carried pennants for decorative or recognition purposes. At some time during this period some shipmaster must have noticed that, when underway, his courses filling, these pennants and flags were rippling stiffly in the breeze. If these small rags could do this, was there not a useful breeze blowing above the vessel's sails? Indeed there was, and later in this fifteenth century the first small, insignificant topsail appeared between the lower yard and the masthead.

The increasing efficiency and seaworthiness of hull design, with the additional power apparent in these new "top sails" (so named because they were handled in a ship's tops), altered forever the function of the sailing ship's principal squaresails. Taking advantage of this added power, the designers, by careful degrees, increased the size of topsails.

This growth in size was rather constant until about the middle of the sixteenth century, when it slowed due to the length limitations of pole masts. The combination of topsail and course rigged to a single stick became rather impractical and thus impeded progress for a short time. Then, around the 1570s, the single-stick mast was discarded in favor of a lower mast with separate topmast that was stepped, or *fidded*, on the lower mast. A fid is an iron pin inserted transversely through the foot of a mast. The pin then rests on the trestletree structure, which is contructed at the top of the mast immediately below. This innovation is credited to the Dutch. These smaller sticks were easy to handle, convenient to install, and could be rigged up or sent down as circumstance required.

The result of this innovation was that lower masts remained stationary, while fidded topmasts reached higher into the air and were in turn surmounted by additional fidded lighter masts. It also became routine in this period to fit the third or mizzen mast with a square topsail.

It was at this point in time that the lower squaresail or course, which had seen thousands of years as the backbone of sail, lost its predominance and gave way to the single topsail—the great workhorse of the big, deepwater vessels. As their efficiency kept asserting itself, the topsails grew ever larger, becoming the largest sails to be found on the average square-rigged vessel. It was their great size that would be their undoing as a single, separate fabrication.

Topsails, now elevated to the status of the most important unit of propulsion to be found in a ship, became so large as to require four reef bands, in extreme cases, but more likely three on the average. With so much sail area to expose to every sort of weather condition, it became more important than ever that this sail could be quickly controlled to meet any given change in the weather. The most usual way of accomplishing this was to quickly reef the sail as necessary. To do this, especially in cold, wet, freezing weather, with contrary winds working at the sail, required manpower. In ships-of-war with more than ample manpower at their disposal, this was no problem. Yardmen could be provided in more than sufficient numbers.

Such was not the case with the clippers or any other types of commercial vessels. Crews, for economic reasons, were kept as small as the well-being of a vessel would permit; in many cases the size of the crew could be regarded as marginal at best. In the meantime the sizes of topsails were still growing, and at the zenith of clipper ship construction the topsail yards were measuring as much as 70 feet square. Throughout the nautical community it was a well known but not freely admitted fact that while "big" was an asset, "too big" would be a liability. It was at this stage that a new departure was introduced—an innovation which would ultimately doom the single topsail.

Double Topsails

The Forbes Rig

The *Forbes rig* was first installed in the year 1844 by the American ship captain Robert Bennett Forbes in the topsail schooner *Midas*, with her topmasts fitted abaft, and double topsails. As a topsail schooner she obviously crossed squaresails on her foremast only, and little is reported about this first experiment, one reason being that, shortly after in this same year, he fitted the auxiliary bark *Edith* with his rig. This was the first vessel with squaresails on more than one mast to receive the new invention.

Robert Bennett Forbes, a Bostonian, was an experienced ship captain, born in 1804, who accumulated by the age of thirty-three a modest fortune, which he lost in the Panic of 1837, and subsequently recouped by the early 1840s. In addition to being an accomplished sailor, Forbes was deeply involved in shipbuilding, particularly where the introduction of steam propulsion was concerned.

He operated as an astute businessman with an eye ever cocked toward progress. He also spent considerable time in analyzing existing conditions and shortcomings as he perceived them through his experiences at sea. Among other characteristics, he was an idealist and constantly concerned himself with the dangers, hardships, and safety of the

(text continued on page 461)

Figure 29.1. *Clipper mast and spar arrangements.*

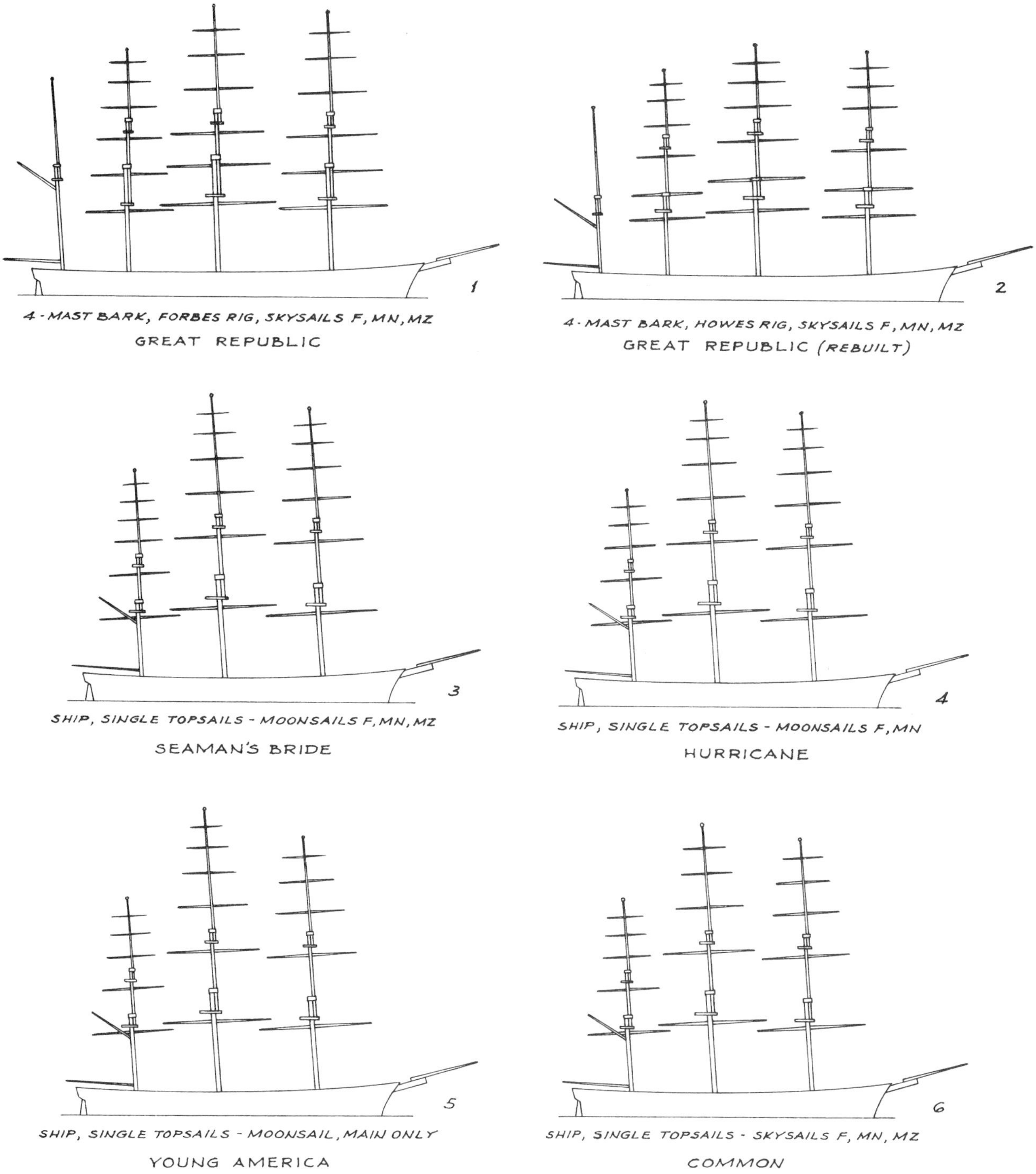

4-MAST BARK, FORBES RIG, SKYSAILS F, MN, MZ
GREAT REPUBLIC

4-MAST BARK, HOWES RIG, SKYSAILS F, MN, MZ
GREAT REPUBLIC (REBUILT)

SHIP, SINGLE TOPSAILS - MOONSAILS F, MN, MZ
SEAMAN'S BRIDE

SHIP, SINGLE TOPSAILS - MOONSAILS F, MN
HURRICANE

SHIP, SINGLE TOPSAILS - MOONSAIL, MAIN ONLY
YOUNG AMERICA

SHIP, SINGLE TOPSAILS - SKYSAILS F, MN, MZ
COMMON

Figure 29.2. *Clipper mast and spar arrangements.*

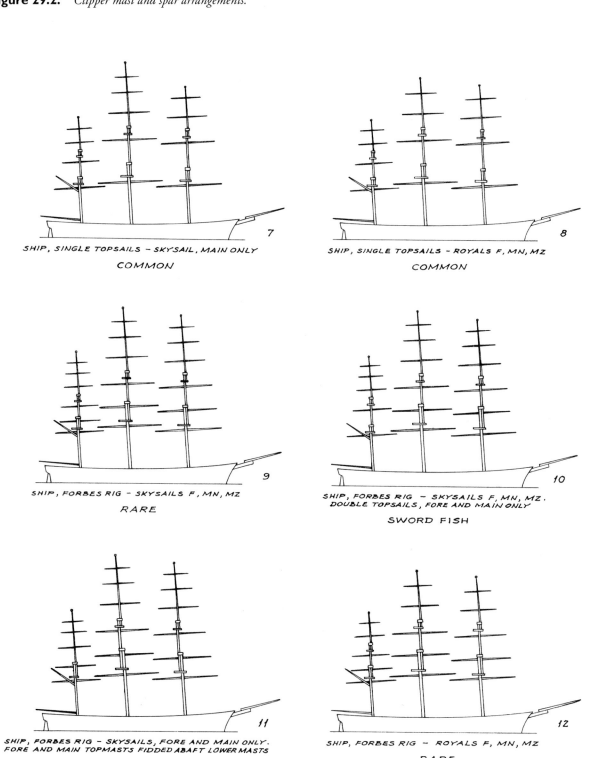

SHIP, SINGLE TOPSAILS – SKYSAIL, MAIN ONLY
COMMON

SHIP, SINGLE TOPSAILS – ROYALS F, MN, MZ
COMMON

SHIP, FORBES RIG – SKYSAILS F, MN, MZ
RARE

SHIP, FORBES RIG – SKYSAILS F, MN, MZ.
DOUBLE TOPSAILS, FORE AND MAIN ONLY
SWORD FISH

SHIP, FORBES RIG – SKYSAILS, FORE AND MAIN ONLY.
FORE AND MAIN TOPMASTS FIDDED ABAFT LOWER MASTS
FLYING CHILDERS

SHIP, FORBES RIG – ROYALS F, MN, MZ
RARE

Figure 29.3. *Clipper mast and spar arrangements.*

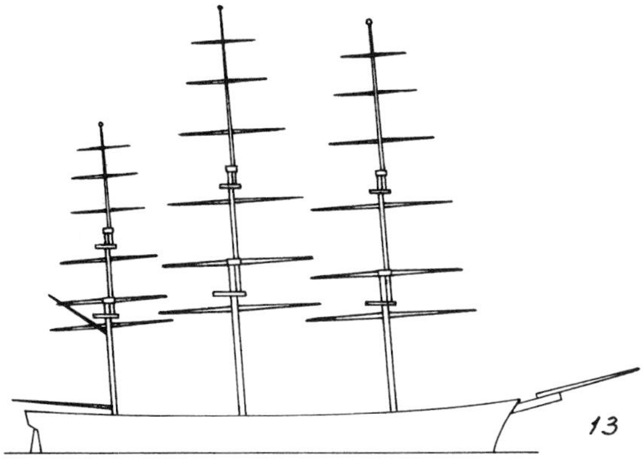

13

SHIP, HOWES RIG – SKYSAILS F, MN, MZ

INFREQUENT

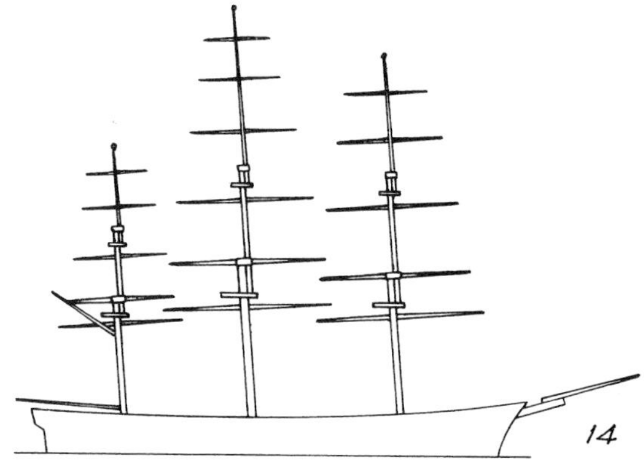

14

SHIP, HOWES RIG – SKYSAIL, MAIN ONLY

RARE

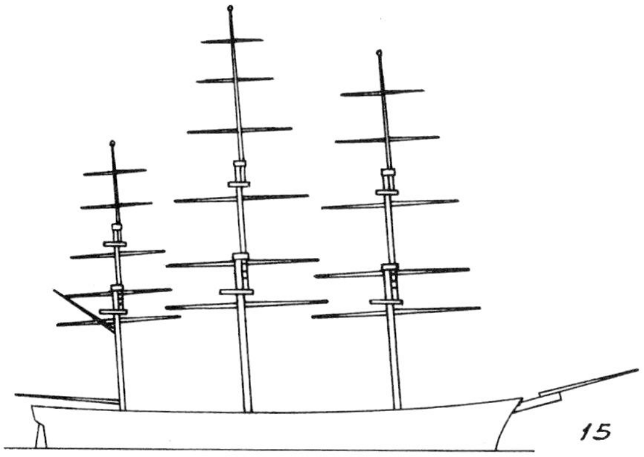

15

SHIP, HOWES RIG – SKYSAIL, MAIN ONLY
RIG MODIFIED BY CAPT. E. H. LINNELL

FLYING MIST

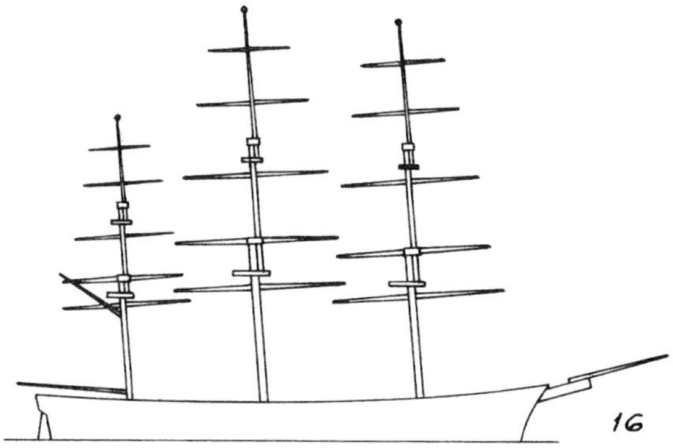

16

SHIP, HOWES RIG – ROYALS F, MN, MZ

RARE

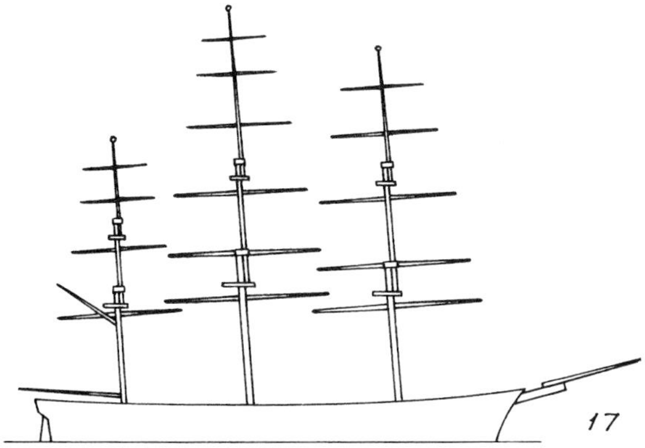

17

SHIP, HOWES RIG – SKYSAIL, MAIN ONLY
DOUBLE TOPSAILS, FORE AND MAIN ONLY

BLUE JACKET

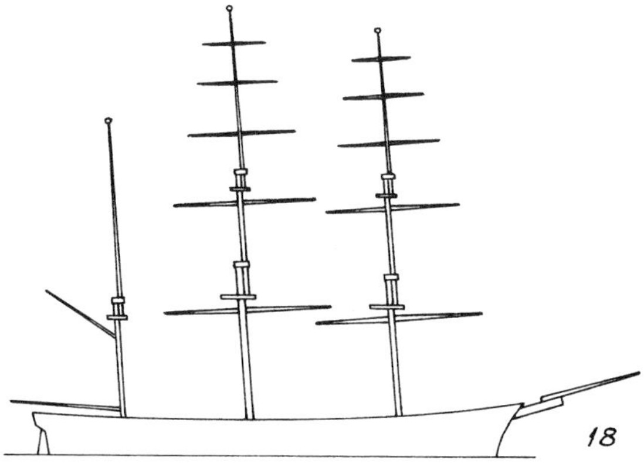

18

BARK, SINGLE TOPSAILS – SKYSAILS F, MN

WILDFIRE

Figure 29.4. *Clipper mast and spar arrangements.*

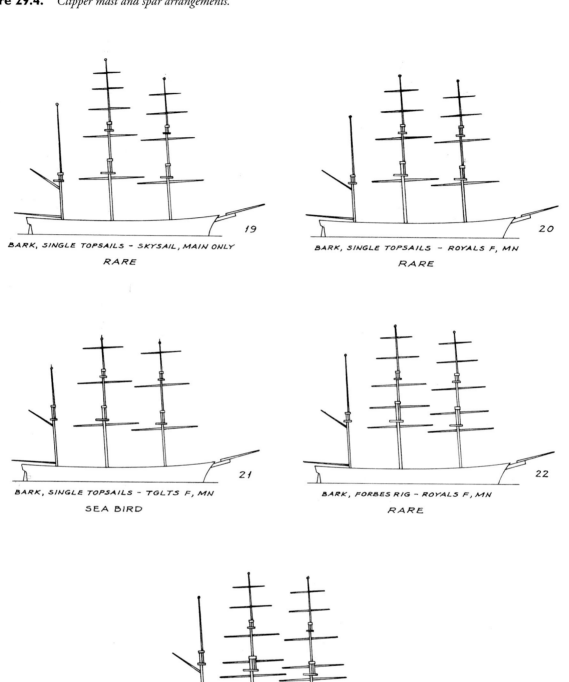

19

BARK, SINGLE TOPSAILS – SKYSAIL, MAIN ONLY

RARE

20

BARK, SINGLE TOPSAILS – ROYALS F, MN

RARE

21

BARK, SINGLE TOPSAILS – TGLTS F, MN

SEA BIRD

22

BARK, FORBES RIG – ROYALS F, MN

RARE

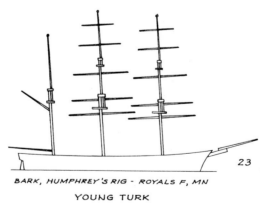

23

BARK, HUMPHREY'S RIG – ROYALS F, MN

YOUNG TURK

(text continued from page 456)

common deckhand. These were conditions he knew very well from firsthand experience.

One of the two deficiencies that bothered him most was the ever-increasing size of topsails and the accompanying hardships in handling them. The second was the lack of protection of ships from lightning strikes by the simple expedient of installing lightning conductors; the system he devised has been described in Chapter 27. Against the former deficiency he devised the double topsail, an invention which, in any form, indelibly etched his name in the annals of the sailing ship. To believe that he alone thought of dividing topsails into two parts in order to facilitate their handling is not realistic, but there is no question that his efforts converted the thought into fact.

Some mysteries and misunderstandings accompany the general perception of details of Forbes's rig, but these are easily dispelled in his own pamphlet,[108] which explains the genesis and development of the rig.

In 1844, after *Midas*, he fitted the auxiliary bark *Edith*, and in 1845, the auxiliary ship *Massachusetts*, with double topsails. All three of these vessels had the topmasts fidded abaft the lower masts. (A model of *Midas* and two paintings of *Edith*[44] do not agree with topmasts being fidded abaft the mizzenmast.) The principal features of the rig were as follows: The large topsails were cut horizontally into an upper and a lower portion, not necessarily equal in depth. The lower mast was increased slightly in length, and its masthead was increased to slightly more than one-third the length of the lower mast from partners to cap; this compared to a masthead length of about 25 percent in conventionally rigged vessels. Originally, in the three vessels already named, the topmasts were fidded abaft the lower masts, the reason being, in Forbes's own words, "the convenience of housing [the topmasts], which as steamships, they might now and then be obliged to do. Whether steamships or not, I consider the fidding abaft as an advantage." The new additional yard was slung as a hoisting yard between the top and the cap of the lower doubling. The original yard was slung above the cap in the customary fashion. Each of these sails was fitted with a reef band. Operation of the two sails, each now only half the original size, remained essentially the same. Obviously, the greatly reduced size and weight of each sail worked directly in favor of the crew.

With all the obvious advantages in place, and the principles of the new rig widely accepted, certain dissatisfactions were immediately voiced, the most prominent one being lack of enthusiasm for the aesthetic picture of topmasts standing abaft lower masts. In deference to this criticism, Forbes rigged a fourth vessel, the ship *Samoset*, in 1847, fidding all the topmasts in conventional fashion, even though, by doing this, he gave up the facility for easily striking or housing the topmasts.

The general misunderstanding of Forbes's rig lies in the fact that the topmasts fitted for the rig are to be found fidded abaft the lower mast in some instances, and before in others. Forbes himself stood firm in his belief that fidding abaft was the better method, but he was not so adamant as to indulge in open warfare with those who did not agree. In the end, the proponents of the old system of fidding topmasts before the lower masts had their way. However, one vessel included in this volume was rigged in Forbes's most approved manner. This was *Flying Childers*, plan No. 11 (Figure 29.2).

Another confusing detail lay in the terminology used in identifying the various yards. In his pamphlet on the subject,[108] Forbes listed the yards on *Samoset* but did not refer to his divided topsail in terms of "upper" and "lower." Consequently, the upper portion of the old topsail appeared as the *topgallant* and the sails above became the *royal* and *skysail*. In later practice this nomenclature did not survive, and the two sails on the topmast were always referred to as the lower and upper topsails.

In addition to the aesthetic criticism of Forbes's original rig, the dissidents voiced other negative aspects. These were, briefly, increased costs incurred by blacksmiths and riggers; increased weight in the form of the extra yard and additional ironwork; and lastly, the relative inefficiency of the smaller expanses of canvas. To each of these arguments Forbes was able to offer fitting rebuttal, and thus they slowly lost their validity.

After *Samoset* the new rig was fitted in Donald McKay's *Reindeer*, in 1849, and in *Lantao*, built by Samuel Hall, also in 1849. The first clipper to be built with Forbes rig was the bark *Racehorse*, designed by Samuel Hartt Pook and built by Samuel Hall in 1850, spar plan No. 22 (Figure 29.4).

The double topsail was on its way to becoming an institution in the sparring and rigging of sailing vessels. However, the vast majority of clippers continued to be built with the old familiar single topsail. Only in later years when undergoing repairs or a refit were those sails replaced by the new invention.

Forbes never received, or even applied for, a patent for his double topsail rig. However, he promoted its use at every turn. Neither did he claim to have "invented" the concept of the double topsail; in fact, he was very quick to point out the opposite.

In one of his writings Forbes discusses having examined a pamphlet containing much evidence in several suits at law (not involving him) by Capt. Frederic Howes. From the pamphlet he notes that in 1823–24 a three-masted vessel, *Pan Matanzas*, was planned by Capt. W. Cammett, and was built at Dover, New Hampshire, by R. Rogers, for himself (Cammett) and W. Savage of Boston. She carried squaresails, but no courses, on two masts. In this vessel her lower topsails hoisted on the heels of the topmasts below the caps, and the sails above were set as usual. Forbes comments that this rig was somewhat similar to his rigging of *Edith* and *Massachusetts*, except that the latter vessels had their topmasts fidded abaft the lower mastheads.[134]

From this same pamphlet, Forbes notes that the ship *Marengo* had double topsails prior to 1840, and *Tremont* in 1841. Further, he points out that one Daniel Tonge, of Liverpool, invented a double topsail rig in 1824, and that, while Howes did not introduce his rig in *Climax* until 1853, he had applied for a patent in 1847.[134]

A final observation on the character of Robert B. Forbes can be observed in his comment, "It seems to me more clear than ever that the double topsail rig came into use long before Howes or I were born; if I have any claim to originality it rests solely on fidding my upper masts abaft the lower masthead, and so arranging the yards as to render them interconvertible. . . ."[134]

While never conceding that his own double topsail rig was not the best, Forbes readily admitted that ". . . the verdict of the public (generally, if not always governed by dollars and cents) has proved the Howes rig to be the most acceptable."[134]

Cunningham's Self-Reefing Topsails

On May 23, 1851, *Cunningham's self-reefing topsails* were patented in England by Henry Duncan Preston Cunningham, paymaster in the British Royal Navy. This patent, British Patent No. 13368, comprised a method of reefing the large single topsails by providing a topsail yard with rigging which literally rolled the yard on the principle of *parbuckling*, the sail spooling around the yard, or unspooling, as the yard was lowered or raised. This invention involved the use of many special parts and, as a mechanical fabrication, was subject to malfunction.[111]

This new rolling topsail first appeared on a new British steamer, *Iberia*.[44] The idea appeared quite feasible and quickly found its way across the Atlantic to the United States. In late October 1851 the extreme clipper *Hurricane* was launched at the yard of Isaac B. Smith, Hoboken, New Jersey. She was fitted with Cunningham's topsails and is the only clipper herein known to have carried them. The spar plan of this vessel, No. 4 (Figure 29.1), is shown because she was one of very few clippers to carry *moonsail* yards—yards that were crossed above the skysail yards. As is evident in the plan, the existence of Cunningham's patent topsails does not affect the arrangement of her spars. This rolling topsail appears to qualify as the progenitor of today's roller furling/reefing rigs.

A short time after the appearance of Cunningham's patent topsail, two other Englishmen, Colling and Pinkney, teamed together and received a patent for a different rolling topsail. With this invention a long roller, mounted on brackets extending forward of the yard at the yardarms, was mounted parallel with the yard. To this roller, which was free to revolve, the sail was bent. In this case the yard itself did not rotate; the sail was furled or unfurled when the roller revolved.[111]

As was the case with the Cunningham patent, this topsail required the installation of special moving or fitted parts

which could be subject to damage. This aspect of both inventions emphasized the negative attributes of both systems. From 1851 through 1852 the two new rigs were promoted and might have achieved considerable success based on their merits. In March 1853, however, Howes's introduction of his version of the double topsail, in *Climax*, dealt them a crucial blow. It was no more than a matter of simplicity versus complexity. The Howes system was here to stay for the duration of sail.

On January 15, 1856, Cunningham was granted Patent No. 14094 by the United States Patent Office for his invention. Later in this same year, two separate advertisements[115] reported that *Donald McKay* was having her topgallant sails fitted with the invention in August and *Champion of the Seas* was having her topsails replaced in like manner shortly thereafter. Both vessels had been built by Donald McKay for James Baines & Co., Liverpool. *Champion of the Seas* was delivered in mid-1854, rigged with single topsails and *Donald McKay* was delivered early in 1855 rigged with Howes double topsails.

Howes Rig

The first *Howes rig* was fitted in the clipper ship *Climax*, built by Hayden & Cudworth, at Medford, Massachusetts, in 1853. Her construction was superintended by Frederic Howes, who was to be her captain. It was he who also dictated the details of her rigging which would contain some innovations that were dear to him personally. This new rig was to ultimately supersede the Forbes rig and become the standard for all future large square-riggers.

It was not unusual for the prospective master of a vessel to suggest or even demand that certain features be incorporated into the masting and rigging of a ship nearing completion. It was a foregone conclusion by owner, builder, and other interested parties that no innovation would be advanced that was not perceived to be in the best interest of the ship and her crew. And, since the life of the master would be as much at risk as that of the least deckhand, he was generally allowed the luxury of details with which he was comfortable.

With one exception, the real or fancied deficiencies in the Forbes rig were quieted and ceased to bear any consideration in its use. The exception, however, was stubborn, and, in the half dozen years after the appearance of the invention, it apparently always lurked in the background when the new double topsail was discussed. Most ship captains could not accept the thought that valuable breeze was escaping between the lower topsail yard and the foot of the upper topsail. Forbes himself had put forward a method of overcoming this apparent deficiency—namely, the simple expedient of making the upper topsail a trifle longer than was customary—but the solution never was incorporated into the making of the affected sails. The condition and its solution must have occupied much of Capt. Howes's thinking and, as a result, he introduced his new idea in the new clipper, *Climax*, spar plan No. 13 (Figure 29.3).

Essentially, Capt. Howes closed the gap between the lower and upper topsails. However, this was accompanied by several other innovations which were so practical and successful that the new rig, bearing Howes's name, immediately became the rig of choice and, in its essential form, remained the standard for the remainder of the age of sail.

Probably more important than closing the gap was the manner in which the lower topsail yard was slung. Basic details of the entire invention are very interesting and are here noted in probable sequence of consideration.

Howes's first diversion from Forbes's ideas was to dispose of the lengthened lower masts and greatly extended mastheads, returning both to the proportions that prevailed in conventional rigs; any inclination to step the topmasts abaft the lower masts was never considered. The second, and most universally accepted change, was incorporated into the installation of his new lower topsail yard. The yard would be a fixed, permanent installation with its iron truss fashioned into the forward portion of the lower cap. The overturning moment generated by the weight of the yard hanging from the cap was countered by an iron crane which extended downward to a band fixed around the heel of the topmast. This yard was stationary and its sail was made without a reef; thus it could be either set or furled as the situation warranted.

The upper topsail yards were slung in the usual manner and could be lowered upon the cap. These sails contained one reef and were cut straight on the foot. The foot was then detailed to be laced to a jackstay on the lower topsail yard. When both sails were set and the lacing completed, the result was, in effect, the setting of a single topsail. The terrible demon—that of the escape of breezes between the two sails—had been exorcised.

Additional advantages were gained in the running rigging. The two yards on the foremast had a *span* rove between them, and from this span a single-brace purchase was applied which worked both yards. The same rig was applied to the mizzenmast. The main topsail yards, however, were braced separately owing to the differences in their angles of leading.

From its very first appearance in *Climax*, in 1853, the Howes rig was viewed with favor and provided the best of all worlds to the overworked sailor. But, in spite of the obvious advantages, most clippers were still being built and rigged with single topsails. Of the vessels covered in this book, *Sierra Nevada*, 1854, is known to have received the Howes rig when built. It was not until 1855–56 that the rig appeared routinely.

In the years that followed, various versions of the Howes rig made their appearance in more and more vessels. Those that had been originally fitted with single topsails were re-rigged with double topsails for one single, universal reason—economy of operation. This rig, perfected by Howes in its very first experiment, became the standard rig of all large square-rigged vessels. However, with some ring of poetic justice, it is the name of Robert Bennett Forbes which is most associated with the double topsail.

Linnell's Rig

In early November 1856, *Linnell's rig* appeared in the clipper *Flying Mist* which was built in Medford, Massachusetts, by James O. Curtis. Capt. Eber H. Linnell, who was to be her master and who superintended her construction, was the inventor of this new rig for which he received a patent, U.S. Patent No. 16650, on February 17, 1857.

One detail of the Howes rig caused great concern among certain shipmasters, one of whom was Capt. Linnell. This concern centered on the overturning moment generated by the lower topsail yard as it hung out forward of the iron cap surmounting the lower masthead. Whether or not this concern was justified can be debated, but its existence cannot. Capt. Linnell was only one of a dozen inventors and shipmasters to attempt eliminating this problem. His solution resulted in a rig fabricated with portions of both the Forbes and the Howes rig incorporated into its construction.

The principal components of the rig were contained in a new method of supporting the lower topsail yard, in which the yard was located below the cap (a feature of the Forbes rig) and worked entirely against the heel of the topmast. It consisted of two supports, one an iron band fitted around the topmast and secured in a fixed, permanent position. Above this was a second iron band fitted loosely around the topmast in the manner of a parrel. Attached to this loose band were two iron rods, one on each side, which terminated in a point under the yard and supported it. The yard itself was parreled to the mast in such a manner as to neatly plumb the lower yard; this permitted it to be braced almost as sharp as the lower yard without touching the topmast rigging, and it also carried the lower topsail clear of the top rim.

The foot of the upper topsail was cut straight and laced to the top of the lower topsail yard (a principal feature of the Howes rig). Other details of her rig were the same as those in general use.

Flying Mist (spar plan No. 15, Figure 29.3) appears to be the only ship to have been fitted with Capt. Linnell's invention. Some credence must be given to the validity of Capt. Linnell's concern inasmuch as he was a master of the first rate and left behind him many noteworthy passages including one run in 1855 from London to China, in *Eagle Wing*, logging a passage which was never to be equalled.

Humphrey's Rig

Late in November 1856, *Humphrey's rig* appeared in the diminutive and little-known bark *Young Turk*. She was built by James O. Curtis at Medford, Massachusetts, for Alpheus Hardy & Co., Boston. One of the masters who skippered vessels for this company was Capt. John Humphrey. His name is not one which has found its way into the realm of sailing records, but he was evidently a thinking man who was caught up in the same concerns that bothered Capt. Linnell. Both men had a connection with James O. Curtis; *Flying Mist* and *Young Turk* were on the stocks together in the same yard at the same time.

Capt. Linnell, as superintendent of construction for *Flying Mist*, was in a favorable position to press his demands in matters of rigging the vessel. This was a prerogative that was routinely recognized. However, in the case of *Young Turk* there is no hint that Capt. Humphrey had any direct connection with the vessel. Whatever the circumstances, Capt. Humphrey was apparently devoting considerable thought to the now-familiar problem of the weight of the lower topsail yard tending to overturn the cap on the lower masthead. It is quite conceivable that he saw Capt. Linnell's invention as it was installed in *Flying Mist*. It might reasonably be conjectured that the two men discussed the problem together, since there appears to be no record of Capt. Humphrey being at sea between late 1855 and late 1857. Together they could have witnessed the construction of both vessels from keel to truck.

Conjecture aside, it is a fact that Capt. Humphrey developed his own version of a cure for the "overturning" disease, and reportedly applied for a patent for his new rig. Unfortunately, no record of the patent appears to exist in the files of the U.S. Patent Office, so details of the rig as laid out cannot be factually reported. However, MacLean's description in *The Boston Daily Atlas* is complete enough to allow a reasonable reconstruction of the invention: "She *[Young Turk]* has a new rig, invented by Capt. John Humphrey. It consists of double topmasts and double topsail yards. The lower topsail has a single reef in it and the lower topmast is just long enough to set this sail. The second topmast has cross trees, doubling and cap, and is fitted for the upper topsail, which also contains a reef. When the upper topsails are furled, the vessel is then under the same surface of canvass represented by double reefs in the old rig, and when the lower topsails are reefed, she is under close reefed topsails."[1] This spar plan is No. 23 (Figure 29.4).

Nothing further was reported as to the success or failure of Humphrey's rig, and, for the period covered by this book, no additional inventions of this nature would appear. In the years that followed, the Howes rig became universally adopted, almost in the form it first appeared. The principal detail that was abandoned was the lacing of the two topsails together. They were soon to become completely separate units, in which form they survived until the end of the days of sail.

It is fitting that the single topsail, which, in the span of four hundred years, had grown from a small, insignificant wisp of cloth into the greatest single spread of canvas to ever

grace a sailing ship's yards, should come into conjunction with the clipper ship, which in about one hundred months etched its name in history as the most universally recognized class of sailing vessel to ever sail the seas.

The two traveled together until the efficiency of the great sail outdid its practicality, and the need for the great clippers succumbed to the economics of the times. They met their demise together. This is not to say that either disappeared overnight. Both were seen at sea for many years after, but these creations were merely living out their days. Age, nature, and progress would take their toll. In due time they were gone with the likelihood of never being seen again. *Sic transit gloria.*

Colors of Masts and Spars

The colors of masts and spars in the clippers covered a minimal spectrum—black, white, and natural wood, generally "hard pine," the then-popular name of longleaf pine. This wood, when left unpainted, was termed "bright" and could be varnished or left untreated. It was of an orange tinge, especially when greased between doublings to facilitate the movement of parrels which loosely confined yards to masts. A fourth color was gilt, which, in masting, was restricted to the coloring of the trucks atop the masts.

The three basic colors were applied to masts, yards, and booms in a variety of combinations, and among the vessels included here, with only one exception, there were two color applications that were universal: All the yards of the vessels listed in Table 29.2 were completely black. Also, the booms, which were always bright, were often tipped with black ends but never tipped with white; the same applied to yards if left bright. The lone exception occurred in *Dauntless*, whose masting and spars were completely white[1]—a rare departure from the general color scheme.

Every general practice has its exception, and the installation of the gilded balls at the mastheads of the vessels was another such category. In the description of the bark *Henry Hill*, her mast trucks are described as being glass balls, the only instance of departure from gilding.

In general, the ball or truck was drilled through with two holes to accommodate reeving flag halyards.

Due to the lack of information for many vessels about the colors of their masting, Table 29.2 has been abridged to include only those vessels about which some definite description of colors has been recorded in the various references.

With the stepping of masts and crossing of yards, the actual construction of the ship reached its conclusion. Rigging was then to be set up and sails bent. The vessel would then be in condition to put to sea.

Table 29.2. *Colors of masts and spars.*

Note: This table is abridged to include only those vessels listed in this volume about which some definite description of colors has been recorded in the various references.

Vessel & Ref.#	Colors	
Asa Eldridge #1	Trucks	– gilded balls
Bald Eagle #1	Masts	– white (extent not specified)
	Yards	– black
	Booms	– bright with black ends
Bounding Billow Bark #1	Masts	– white (extent not specified)
Challenge #1	Lower masts	– black
	Masts, above lower doublings	– bright
	Tops	– bright
	Trucks	– gilded balls
	Yards	– black
Champion of the Seas #1	Lower masts	– white
	Mastheads	– black
	Yards	– black
	Studdingsail booms	– bright with black ends
Charger #1	Lower masts	– white
	Mastheads	– black
	Tops	– black
	Yards	– black
	Studdingsail booms	– bright with black ends
Charmer #1	Lower masts, etc.	– bright and varnished
	Yards	– black
Dauntless #1	Masts	– white
	Yards	– white
Donald McKay #1	Lower masts	– bright and varnished
	Bowsprit	– black
	Yards	– black
Don Quixote #1	Lower masts	– white
	Tops	– black
	Crosstrees	– black
	Caps	– black
	Yards	– black
	Studdingsail booms	– bright with black ends
Edwin Forrest #1	Trucks	– gilded balls
Ellen Foster #1	Lower masts	– white
	Mastheads	– white
	Trucks	– gilded balls
	Yards	– black
	Studdingsail booms	– bright with black ends
Empress of the Sea #1	Lower masts	– white
	Topmast heads	– white
	Yards	– black
	Booms	– bright and varnished
Fleet Wing #1	Trucks	– gilded balls

Vessel & Ref.#	Colors	
Flying Eagle #1	Lower masts	– black
	Topmast heads	– black
	Skysail poles	– black
	Bowsprit	– black
	Studdingsail booms	– bright and varnished with black ends
Flying Fish #1	Lower masts	– white
	Yards	– black
	Trucks	– gilded balls and spires
	Booms	– bright
Flying Mist #1	Lower masts	– white
	Tops	– white
	Masts above	– bright and varnished
	Bowsprit	– black
	Yards	– black
	Studdingsail booms	– bright with black ends
Henry Hill Bark #1	Masts	– bright
	Tops	– bright
	Trucks	– glass balls
	Yards	– black
Invincible #4	Lower masts	– white
	Topmast heads	– white
	Tglt & royal mastheads	– black
	Trucks	– gilded balls
	Yards	– black
James Baines #1	Lower masts, from truss bands down to the fife rails	– bright and varnished with white mast hoops
	Tops, down to truss bands	– white
	Mastheads	– black
	Yards	– black
John Land #1 (built as a duplicate of Winged Arrow.)	Lower masts	– white
	Trucks	– gilded balls
	Bowsprit	– black
	Yards	– black
	Booms	– bright
John Wade #1	Lower masts	– bright
	Tops	– black
	Mastheads	– black
	Yards	– black
Joseph Peabody #1	Lower masts	– white, to the tops
	Tops	– white
	Masts above	– bright and varnished
	Trucks	– gilded balls
	Yards	– black
	Studdingsail booms	– bright
Lightning #1	Lower masts	– white
	Doublings	– white
	Trucks	– gilded balls
	Yards	– black
	Booms	– bright with black ends
Mastiff #1	Masts	– bright
	Bowsprit	– black
	Yards	– black
Nightingale #3	Yards	– black
Noonday #1	Lower masts	– white
	Mastheads	– black
	Bowsprit	– black
	Yards	– black

Table 29.2. *Continued.*

Vessel & Ref.#	Colors		Vessel & Ref.#	Colors	
Ocean Express #1	Lower masts	- white	Storm King #1	Lower masts	- white
	Mastheads	- white		Topmast heads	- white
	Yards	- black		Trucks	- gilded balls
	Studdingsail booms	- bright		Yards	- black
				Booms	- bright and varnished
Queen of Clippers #1	Paintwork on the masts	- white			
	Trucks	- gilded balls	War Hawk #1	Masts	- bright
	Yards	- black		Caps	- black
	Studdingsail booms	- bright and varnished with black ends		Yards	- black
			Westward Ho #1	Masts	- white
				Trucks	- gilded balls
Queen of the Seas #1	Lower masts	- white		Yards	- black
	Topmast heads	- white		Booms	- bright
	Trucks	- gilded balls			
	Yards	- black	Wildfire Bark #1	Lower masts	- white
	Booms	- bright and varnished		Trucks	- gilded balls
				Yards	- black
Radiant #1	Trucks	- gilded balls		Booms	- bright
			Winged Arrow #1	Lower masts	- white
Red Jacket #67	Lower masts	- bright		Bowsprit	- black
	Upper masts	- bright		Trucks	- gilded balls
	Doublings	- black		Yards	- black
	Bowsprit	- black		Booms	- bright
	Trucks	- gilded balls			
	Yards	- black	Winged Racer #1	Lower masts	- white
	Booms	- bright		Trucks	- gilded balls
				Yards	- black
Roebuck #1	Trucks	- gilded balls		Studdingsail booms	- bright with black en
Santa Claus #1	Lower masts	- bright and varnished			
			Witch of the Wave #1	Trucks	- gilded balls and spi
Sea Bird Bark #1	Lower masts	- white			
	Topmast heads	- white			
	Trucks	- gilded balls with spires			
	Yards	- black			
	Booms	- bright with black ends			
Silver Star #1	Trucks	- gilded balls			
Sovereign of the Seas #1	Lower masts	- white			
	Trucks	- gilded balls			
	Yards	- black			
	Booms	- bright			
Staffordshire #1	Lower masts	- white			
	Trucks	- gilded balls and spires			
	Yards	- black			

RIGGING

THE RIGGING OF CLIPPER SHIPS, like the masting, is a wide-ranging subject and, due to the multitude of variations to be found in these vessels, is not a subject that can be suitably covered in a book such as this. However, certain generalities can be discussed and available sources of information can be identified, all with the purpose of completing the picture of the American-built clipper ship.

No neat lists of rope and block sizes in the clippers have been tabulated by contemporary riggers and left for the benefit of posterity. One reason for this probably is the fact that rigging was not newly invented for every ship that entered the water. The rigging of ships developed as the ships were developed, and each individual length of rope was installed in the most practical manner to perform a given task. The craft of rigging was handed down through generations, and riggers were schooled through long periods of apprenticeship and journeyman experience until they reached a stage where they could be called "riggers."

While there was "standard" general practice for setting up and leading a line from its standing end to its position around a belaying pin, there were countless deviations to be found among the many vessels. The only knowledge of specific departures is found in some descriptions that have survived over the years.

The content of this chapter is devoted to identifying authoritative and reliable sources of general rigging information; the descriptions of some detailed departures as described for certain vessels; a tabulation of rope and block sizes which have been taken from United States naval vessels, for reasons that will be explained; and the reconstruction of a representative belaying pin arrangement for a large clipper.

Most descriptions of clipper ship rigging comment on general characteristics of the vessel being discussed. Thus we learn the number and sizes of masts; the number and sizes of yards and spars; the type of vessel—ship-rigged when all masts wear square sails; bark-rigged when the mizzen is rigged with fore-and-aft sails only—and, perhaps, any major peculiarity of her rigging, if such existed. All too rarely is anything specific mentioned about her rope unless, perhaps, a statement is made that she was rigged with Russia or American hemp for her standing rigging, and manila for her running rigging. However, there are occasions when the size of a ship's rigging is given. *Rigging* in this context does not refer to all the lines that are visible aloft; rather, it refers to fore and main lower shrouds and to fore and main topmast backstays. From these particular items the proportions of all other rigging lines are developed, although there does not appear to be any rigid rule governing such sizes.

Standing Rigging

The *standing rigging* comprises those lines that are installed to confine the masts, bowsprit, and jibbooms in their proper positions. The rigging of the mainmast was generally the heaviest, and other rigging was proportioned from this. When definite sizes are quoted, they usually are confined to the items previously referred to as "rigging."

A representative arrangement of standing rigging is shown in Figure 30.1 and contains all the usual lines to be found in the typical clipper. This figure, along with data included in Tables 29.1 and 30.1, portray an accurate general picture of standing rigging as it appeared in the clipper era.

Bowsprit Rigging

The *bowsprit rigging* of the day was very neat and clean. The earlier shrouds and bobstays, made up of rope, had given way to the increasing use of chain, which, due to its superior strength, was furnished in small wire size which did not give an appearance of encumbering the bow. The usual vessel was rigged with one shroud each side of the bowsprit, and two bobstays set up between its outer end and the cutwater at the waterline. There were the usual exceptions;

(text continued on page 476)

Table 30.1. *Rigging details applicable to Figures 30.1, 30.2, and 30.3.*

Notes: Sheaves in blocks - S = single (one sheave); D = double (two sheaves).

Block and rope sizes are in inches.

Rope size refers to circumference.

Chain size refers to the wire diameter in inches.

Belaying pin numbers - Even are port side; Odd are starboard side.

Parts are listed in the order in which they are passed over the various mastheads, reading from the top down.

Part	Rope Quantity	Rope Size	Blocks Sheaves	Blocks Quantity	Blocks Size	Rigging leads
Bowsprit						
Shrouds	2	¾ chn				Shackled to plate in bow, p/s; set up with hearts shackled under the bees.
Lanyards	2	2½				
Bobstays	2	1 chn				Shackled to plates in stem; set up to bowsprit with hearts shackled under the bees.
Lanyards	2	4				
Manropes	2	4				Seized to foot of fore stay and fore topmast stay, p/s.
Jibboom						
Jib stay, inner	1	7½				Goes over the rigging after the fore topmast is rigged. Sets up with collar at fore topmast head, over inner sheave in jibboom, under stbd upper cleat in martingale; sets up on self around bullseye to eyebolt in stbd bow.
Jib stay, outer	1	4½				Goes over the rigging after the fore topmast is rigged. Sets up with collar at fore topmast head, over outer sheave in jibboom, under port upper cleat in martingale; sets up on self around thimble to eyebolt in port bow.
Martingale						
Backropes	2	½ chn				Shackled to yoke band at lower end of martingale; set up with shackle to eyebolt in bow, p/s.
Stay, inner	1	½ chn				Shackled to jibboom inner band and to yoke at lower end of martingale.
Guys	2	5½				Set up to eyes in jibboom inner band, over inner cleat on cathead whisker boom; set up with hearts to eyebolt in bow, p/s.
Lanyards	2	2¾				
Footropes	2	3¾				Spliced to eyebolt in bowsprit cap and to eyebolt in band at outer end of flying jibboom, p/s.
Stirrups		2½				

Part	Rope Quantity	Rope Size	Blocks Sheaves	Blocks Quantity	Blocks Size	Rigging leads
Flying jibboom						
Flying jib stay						See fore topgallant stay.
Martingale stay, outer	1	½ chn				Shackled to band on end of flying jibboom and to yoke at lower end of martingale.
Guys	2	3¾				Set up to eye in band at end of flying jibboom, over outer cleat on cathead whisker boom; set up with hearts to eyebolt in bow, p/s.
Lanyards	2	1¾				
Footropes	2	3¾				See jibboom.
Stirrups		1¾				
Foremast						
Pendants	2	11				Thimble spliced in end. Go over the top first, under the shrouds, p/s. Are set up with a cut-splice over the masthead.
Shrouds, pairs	6	11				Go over the top (over the pendants); set up with 16" deadeyes to chainplates in the channels, p/s.
Lanyards	12	5				
Ratlines		1½				
Stay, double	1	11				Goes over the rigging. Collar over the masthead, goes double between seizings; sets up with separate legs to bullseyes in the knightheads.
Futtock shrouds	6	6½				Eyebolts in mast band; hooks in the crosstrees, p/s.
Ratlines		1¼				
Fore yard						
Sling	1	1½ chn				Shackled to yard sling band and to eyebolt in mast under forward crosstree.
Footropes	2	4½				
Stirrups		3				
Sheet block on yard sling band			2	1	-	This iron block has two iron sheaves on separate pins, in a yoke.
Clew garnets			S	2	13	
Topping lift pendants	2	6				Set up with shackle to eye in band at yardarm, block seized in end, p/s.
Pendant blocks			S	2	10	
Halliards	2	3				Set up to becket in pendant block, p/s, thru block shackled over cap, p/s, thru pendant block, thru cap block, to pins #17, 18.
Cap blocks			D	2	10	
Braces						
Pendants, yard	2	4¼				Set up with shackle to eye in band at yardarm, block shackled to thimble in end, p/s.
Pendant blocks			S	2	15	
Pendants, channel	2	4¼				Set up with shackle to eye in lower main channel, block shackled to thimble in end, p/s.
Pendant blocks			S	2	15	
Falls	2	2				Set up to becket in yard pendant block, p/s, thru channel pendant block, thru yard pendant block, thru fairleader block on main rail, p/s, to pins #81, 82.
Fairleader blocks			S	2	15	

Table 30.1. *Continued.*

Part	Rope Quantity	Rope Size	Blocks Sheaves	Blocks Quantity	Blocks Size	Rigging leads
Fore topmast						
Pendants	2	6½				Thimble spliced in end. Go over the crosstrees first, under the shrouds, p/s. Are set up with a cut-splice over the masthead.
Shrouds, pairs	3	6½				Go over the topmast crosstrees; set up with 9" deadeyes to lower futtock shrouds, p/s.
Lanyards	6	3				
Ratlines		1¼				
Backstays, pairs	2	8¼				Go over the topmast rigging; set up with 12" deadeyes to chainplates in fore channels, p/s.
Lanyards	4	3¼				
Stay, double	1	6½				Goes over all. Collar over masthead, goes double between seizings, separate legs thru the bees, p/s; set up on self around thimble to eyebolt in bow, p/s.
Futtock shrouds	4,iron					
Ratlines		1				
Fore topsail yard						
Footropes	2	4				
Stirrups		2½				
Flemish horses	2	4				
Quarter blocks			D	2	12	
Clewline blocks			S	2	10	
Lifts	2	5				Set up with shackles to eyebolts in band at yardarm and eyebolt in topmast trestletrees, p/s.
Fore topsail yard (cont.)						
Tie	1	3/8 chn	S	1	12" gin	Sets up with shackle to yard sling band, over sheave in topmast below trestletrees, gin shackled in end.
Pendant	1	2 7/8 wire rope				Sets up with hook to eyebolt in upper fore channel, stbd, thimble spliced in upper end.
Runner	1	¼ chn				Shackled to pendant, thru gin, thimble turned in end.
Halliard	1	3½				Sets up to becket in channel block, port, thru fly block shackled to runner, thru channel block, thru fly block, thru fairleader block in waterway, to pin #64.
Fly block			D	1	13	
Channel block			S	1	13	
Waterway block			S	1	12	
Braces						
Pendants	2	4				Set up with shackle to eye in band at yardarm, pendant block shackled to thimble in end, p/s.
Pendant blocks			S	2	16	
Runners	2	3				Hitched around main topmast head, thru pendant block, runner block shackled to thimble in end, p/s.
Runner blocks			S	2	14	
Falls	2	2				Set up with shackle to lower main channel, p/s, thru runner block, thru fairleader block shackled to eyebolt on main rail, p/s, to pins #83, 84.
Fairleader blocks			S	2	11	

Part	Rope Quantity	Rope Size	Blocks Sheaves	Blocks Quantity	Blocks Size	Rigging leads
Fore topgallant mast						
Grommet	1	4				For lift shackles. Goes over stop first.
Stay (flying jib)	1	5				Spliced over tglt stop, thru slot in flying jibboom, under port lower cleat in martingale; sets up on self around thimble to eyebolt in port bow.
Shrouds, pairs	2	5				Go over tglt stop, thimbles turned in ends; set up to thimbles in crosstrees, p/s.
Lanyards	4	2¼				
Ratlines		1				
Backstays	2	6				Go over tglt rigging; set up with 9" deadeyes to chainplates in fore channels, p/s.
Lanyards	2	2¼				
Fore topgallant yard						
Footropes	2	2½				
Stirrups		2				
Quarter blocks			D	2	10	
Clewline blocks			S	2	8	
Lifts	2	4				Set up with shackle and thimble to grommet over tglt stop and to band at yardarm, p/s.
Tie	1	3/8 chn				Sets up with shackle to yard sling band, over sheave in tglt mast below stop, fly block hooked in end.
Halliard	1	2½				Sets up to becket in channel block, stbd, thru fly block hooked to tglt tie, thru channel block, thru fly block, to pin #69.
Fly block			D	1	10	
Channel block			S	1	10	
Braces						
Pendants	2	3				Set up with shackle to eye in band at yardarm, pendant block shackled to thimble in end, p/s.
Pendant blocks			S	2	9	
Falls	2	2¼				Set up with seizing to upper end of main tglt stay, thru pendant block, thru block seized to collar of main topmast stay, p/s, thru lubber hole, to pins #129, 130.
Fairleader blocks			S	2	7	

Table 30.1. *Continued.*

Part	Rope Quantity	Rope Size	Blocks Sheaves	Blocks Quantity	Blocks Size	Rigging leads
Fore royal mast						
Grommet	1	3				For lift shackles. Goes over stop first.
Stay	1	3¼				Spliced over royal stop, thru slot at end of flying jibboom, under stbd lower cleat on martingale; sets up on self around thimble to eyebolt in stbd bow.
Backstays	2	3¾				Go over royal stop; set up with 6" deadeyes to chainplates in fore channels, p/s.
Lanyards	2	1¼				
Fore royal yard						
Footropes	2	2				
Quarter blocks			S	2	8	
Clewline blocks			S	2	6	
Lifts	2	3				Set up with shackle and thimble to grommet over royal stop and to band at yardarm, p/s.
Tie	1	¼ chn				Sets up with shackle to yard sling band, over sheave in royal mast below stop, fly block hooked in end.
Halliard	1	1½				Sets up to becket in channel block, port, thru fly block hooked to royal tie, thru channel block, thru fly block, to pin #72.
Fly block			D	1	8	
Channel block			S	1	8	
Braces	2	2½				Set up with shackle to eye in band at yardarm, p/s, thru blocks seized near collar of main tglt stay, thru lubber hole, to pins #138, 139.
Fairleader blocks			S	2	6	
Fore skysail mast						
Grommet	1	2				For lift shackles.
Stay	1	2¾				Seized to eye in mast band at skysail stop; sets up on self around end of jibboom.
Backstays	2	3				Shackled to eye in band at skysail stop; set up with 4" deadeyes to chainplates in fore channels, p/s.
Lanyards	2	1				
Fore skysail yard						
Footropes	2	1½				
Clewline blocks			S	2	6	
Lifts	2	2				Set up with shackle and thimble to grommet over skysail stop and to band at yardarm, p/s.
Tie	1	2¼				Sets up with shackle to yard sling band, over sheave in skysail mast below stop, fly block hooked in end.
Halliard	1	1				Sets up to becket in fly block, thru block hooked to eyebolt in channel, stbd, thru fly block, to pin #75.
Fly block			S	1	6	
Channel block			S	1	6	
Braces	2	1½				Set up with shackle to eye in band at yardarm, p/s, thru blocks seized near collar of main royal stay, thru lubber hole, to pins #144, 145.
Fairleader blocks			S	2	6	
Flag halliard	1	1½				Reeves thru sheave in fore truck, hitches to sheerpole at skysail backstay.

Part	Rope Quantity	Rope Size	Blocks Sheaves	Blocks Quantity	Blocks Size	Rigging leads
Mainmast						
Pendants	2	11				Same as foremast.
Shrouds, pairs	6	11				Same as foremast.
Lanyards	12	5				Same as foremast.
Ratlines		1½				
Stay, double	1	11				Goes over the rigging. Collar over masthead, goes double between seiz sets up with separate legs, one on side of foremast, to bullseyes in forward of the topsail sheet bitts
Futtock shrouds	6	6½				Same as foremast.
Ratlines		1¼				
Main yard						
Sling	1	1½ chn				Same as fore yard.
Footropes	2	4½				
Stirrups		3				
Sheet block on yard sling band			2	1	-	This iron block has two iron sheaves on separate pins, in a yoke.
Clew garnets			S	2	13	
Topping lift pendants	2	6				Same as fore yard.
Pendant blocks			S	2	10	
Halliards	2	3				Same as fore yard except belay to pins #87, 88.
Cap blocks			D	2	10	
Braces						
Pendants, yard	2	4¼				Same as fore yard.
Pendant blocks			S	2	15	
Pendants, bumpkin	2	4¼				Set up with shackle to outer eyebolt bumpkin, pendant block shackled to thimble in end, p/s.
Pendant blocks			S	2	15	
Main yard (cont.)						
Falls	2	2				Set up to becket in yard pendant bloc thru bumpkin pendant block, thru ya pendant block, thru fairleader bloc on main rail, p/s, to pins #209, 21
Fairleader blocks			S	2	15	
Main topmast						
Pendants	2	6½				Same as fore topmast.
Shrouds, pairs	3	6½				Same as fore topmast.
Lanyards	6	3				Same as fore topmast.
Ratlines		1¼				
Backstays, pairs	2	8¼				Same as fore topmast except set up to main channels, p/s.
Lanyards	4	3¼				
Stay, double	1	6½				Goes over the rigging. Collar over t masthead, goes double between seizi sets up with separate legs, one on each side of foremast, to bullseyes fore fife rail bolster.
Springstay (if carried)	1	7				Goes over all. Single collar at mast head; sets up on self with thimble eyebolt in fore top.
Futtock shrouds	4, iron					
Ratlines		1				
Main topsail yard						
Footropes	2	4				
Stirrups		2½				
Flemish horses	2	4				
Quarter blocks			D	2	12	
Clewline blocks			S	2	10	
Lifts	2	5				Same as fore topsail yard.

Table 30.1. *Continued..*

Part	Quantity	Size	Sheaves	Quantity	Size	Rigging leads
Main topsail yard (cont.)						
Tie	1	3/8 chn	S	1	12" gin	Same as fore topsail yard.
Pendant	1	2 7/8 wire rope				Sets up with hook to eyebolt in upper main channel, port, thimble spliced in upper end.
Runner	1	1/4 chn				Same as fore topsail yard.
Halliard	1	3½				Sets up to becket in channel block, stbd, thru fly block shackled to runner, thru channel block, thru fly block, thru fairleader block in waterway, to pin #137.
Fly block			D	1	13	
Channel block			S	1	13	
Waterway block			S	1	12	
Braces						
Pendants	2	4				Same as fore topsail yard.
Pendant blocks			S	2	16	
Runners	2	3				Hitched around mizzen topmast head, thru pendant block, runner block shackled to thimble in end, p/s.
Runner blocks			S	2	14	
Falls	2	2				Set up with shackle to inner eyebolt in bumpkin, thru runner block, thru fairleader block on main rail, p/s, to pins #211, 212.
Fairleader blocks			S	2	11	
Main topgallant mast						
Grommet	1	4				Same as fore topgallant mast.
Stay	1	5				Spliced over tglt stop, thru fairleader bullseye shackled to fore cap; sets up on self around thimble in fore top.
Shrouds, pairs	2	5				Same as fore topgallant mast.
Lanyards	4	2¼				
Ratlines		1				
Backstays	2	6				Go over tglt rigging; set up with 9" deadeyes to chainplates in main channels, p/s.
Lanyards	2	2¼				
Main topgallant yard						
Footropes	2	2½				
Stirrups		2				
Quarter blocks			D	2	10	
Clewline blocks			S	2	8	
Lifts	2	4				Same as fore topgallant yard.
Tie	1	3/8 chn				Same as fore topgallant yard.
Halliard	1	2½				Sets up to becket in channel block, port, thru fly block hooked to tglt tie, thru channel block, thru fly block, to pin #146.
Fly block			D	1	10	
Channel block			S	1	10	
Braces						
Pendants	2	3				Same as fore topgallant yard.
Pendant blocks			S	2	9	
Falls	2	2¼				Set up with seizing to upper end of mizzen tglt stay, thru pendant block, thru fairleader block seized to collar of mizzen topmast stay, p/s, thru lubber hole, to pins #175, 176.
Fairleader blocks			S	2	7	

Part	Quantity	Size	Sheaves	Quantity	Size	Rigging leads
Main royal mast						
Grommet	1	3				Same as fore royal mast.
Stay	1	3¼				Spliced over royal stop, thru bullseye shackled to fore topmast head; sets up on self to thimble strapped to eye of fore topmast rigging.
Backstays	2	3¾				Go over royal stop; set up with 6" deadeyes to chainplates in main channels, p/s.
Lanyards	2	1¼				
Main royal yard						
Footropes	2	2				
Quarter blocks			S	2	8	
Clewline blocks			S	2	6	
Lifts	2	3				Same as fore royal yard.
Tie	1	1/4 chn				Same as fore royal yard.
Halliard	1	1½				Sets up to becket in channel block, stbd, thru fly block hooked to royal tie, thru channel block, thru fly block, to pin #149.
Fly block			D	1	8	
Channel block			S	1	8	
Braces	2	2½				Set up with shackle to eye in band at yardarm, p/s, thru fairleader block seized near collar of mizzen tglt stay, thru lubber hole, to pins #189, 190.
Fairleader blocks			S	2	6	
Main skysail mast						
Grommet	1	2				Same as fore skysail mast.
Stay	1	2 3/4				Seized to eye in mast band at skysail stop, thru bullseye shackled to fore topmast cap; sets up on self to thimble strapped to eye of fore topmast rigging.
Backstays	2	3				Shackled to eye in band at main skysail stop; set up with 4" deadeyes to chainplates in main channels, p/s.
Lanyards	2	1				
Main skysail yard						
Footropes	2	1½				
Clewline blocks			S	2	6	
Lifts	2	2				Same as fore skysail yard.
Tie	1	2¼				Same as fore skysail yard.
Halliard	1	1				Sets up to becket in fly block, thru block hooked to eyebolt in channel, port, thru fly block, to pin #150.
Fly block			S	1	6	
Channel block			S	1	6	
Braces	2	1½				Set up with shackle to eye in band at yardarm, p/s, thru fairleader block seized near collar of mizzen royal stay, thru lubber hole, to pins #195, 196.
Fairleader blocks			S	2	6	
Flag halliard	1	1½				Reeves thru sheave in main truck, hitches to sheerpole at skysail backstay.

Table 30.1. *Continued.*

Part	Quantity	Rope Size	Sheaves	Blocks Quantity	Blocks Size	Rigging leads
Mizzen mast						
Shrouds, pairs	4	8¼				Go over top; set up with 12" deadeyes to chainplates in channels, p/s.
Lanyards	8	3				
Ratlines		1½				
Stay, single	1	8½				Goes over rigging. Collar over the masthead, thru bullseye shackled to band around mainmast; sets up on self to bullseye shackled to eyebolt in deck on aft side of mainmast. (Mizzen stay parallels main stay.)
Futtock shrouds	6	5½				Same as foremast.
Ratlines		1¼				
Crojack						
Sling	1	1⅛ chn				Same as fore yard.
Footropes	2	4				
Stirrups		2½				
Sheet block on yard sling band				2	1	- This iron block has two iron sheaves on separate pins, in a yoke.
Clew garnets			S	2	9	
Topping lift pendants	2	5				Same as fore yard.
Pendant blocks			S	2	8	
Halliards	2	2½				Set up to becket in block shackled over cap, p/s, thru pendant block, thru cap block, to pins #157, 158.
Cap blocks			S	2	8	
Crojack (cont.)						
Braces	2	3				Set up to becket in block shackled to band at third quarter of crojack, p/s, thru top block shackled to eye in aft end of main trestletrees, p/s, thru yard block, thru fairleader block shackled to hounds of mainmast, p/s, to pins #95, 96.
Yard blocks			S	2	11	
Top blocks			S	2	11	
Fairleader blocks			S	2	9	
Mizzen topmast						
Shrouds, pairs	3	5				Go over topmast crosstrees; set up with 7" deadeyes to lower futtock shrouds, p/s.
Lanyards	6	2¾				
Ratlines		1¼				
Backstays, pairs	2	6				Go over topmast rigging; set up with 9" deadeyes to chainplates in mizzen channels, p/s.
Lanyards	4	2¼				
Stay, single	1	8¼				Goes over all. Single collar at masthead; sets up on self with thimble to eyebolt in main top.
Futtock shrouds	4,iron					
Ratlines		1				

Part	Quantity	Rope Size	Sheaves	Blocks Quantity	Blocks Size	Rigging leads
Mizzen topsail yard						
Footropes	2	3				
Stirrups		2				
Quarter blocks			D	2	10	
Clewline blocks			S	2	8	
Lifts	2	4				Same as fore topsail yard.
Tie	1	⅜ chn	S	1	10" gin	Same as fore topsail yard.
Pendant	1	2½ wire rope				Sets up with hook to eyebolt in upper mizzen channel, stbd, thimble spli in upper end.
Runner	1	¼ chn				Same as fore topsail yard.
Halliard	1	2½				Sets up to becket in channel block, port, thru fly block shackled to runner, thru channel black, thru f block, thru fairleader block in waterway, to pin #198.
Fly block			D	1	10	
Channel block			S	1	10	
Fairleader block			S	1	9	
Braces	2	3				Set up with shackle to eyebolt in main cap, p/s, thru yard block, th block shackled to underside of mai cap, p/s, thru lubber hole, to pin #93, 94.
Yard block			S	2	11	
Cap block			S	2	11	
Mizzen topgallant mast						
Grommet	1	3				Same as fore topgallant mast.
Stay	1	3½				Spliced over tglt stop, thru fairlead bullseye shackled to main cap; sets on self around thimble in main top.
Shrouds, pairs	2	3¼				Same as fore topgallant mast.
Lanyards	4	1¾				Same as fore topgallant mast.
Ratlines		1				
Backstays	2	4¼				Go over tglt rigging; set up with 6" deadeyes to chainplates in mizzen channels, p/s.
Lanyards	2	1¾				
Mizzen topgallant yard						
Footropes	2	2½				
Stirrups		1½				
Quarter blocks			S	2	8	
Clewline blocks			S	2	6	
Lifts	2	3				Same as fore topgallant yard.
Tie	1	¼ chn				Same as fore topgallant yard.
Halliard	1	1½				Sets up to becket in channel block, stbd, thru fly block hooked to tglt tie, thru channel block, thru fly block, to pin #197.
Fly block			D	1	8	
Channel block			S	1	8	
Braces	2	2¼				Set up with shackle to band at yardarm p/s, thru fairleader block shackled eyebolt in aft end of main topmast trestletrees, p/s, thru lubber hole, to pins #97, 98.
Fairleader blocks			S	2	6	

Table 30.1. *Continued.*

Part	Rope Quantity	Rope Size	Blocks Sheaves	Blocks Quantity	Blocks Size	Rigging leads
Mizzen royal mast						
Grommet	1	2				Same as fore royal mast.
Stay	1	2¾				Spliced over royal stop, thru fairleader block shackled to main topmast head, to thimble strapped to eye of main topmast rigging.
Fairleader block			S	1	6	
Backstays	2	2¾				Go over royal stop, set up with 5" deadeyes to chainplates in mizzen channels, p/s.
Lanyards	2	1				
Mizzen royal yard						
Footropes	2	2				
Quarter blocks			S	2	6	
Clewline blocks			S	2	5	
Lifts	2	2				Same as fore royal yard.
Tie	1	2¼				Same as fore royal yard.
Halliard	1	1				Sets up to becket in fly block hooked to royal tie, thru block hooked to channel, port, thru fly block, to pin #206.
Fly block			S	1	6	
Channel block			S	1	6	
Braces	2	1½				Set up with shackle to eye in band at yardarm, p/s, thru block shackled to eyebolt in main topmast cap, p/s, thru lubber hole, to pins #99, 100.
Fairleader blocks			S	2	6	
Mizzen skysail mast						
Grommet	1	1½				Same as fore skysail mast.
Stay	1	2¼				Seized to eye in mast band at skysail stop, thru fairleader block shackled to main topmast cap; sets up on self to thimble strapped to eye of main topmast rigging.
Fairleader block			S	1	5	
Backstays	2	2¼				Shackled to eye in mast band at skysail stop; set up with 3" deadeyes or bullseyes to chainplates in mizzen channels, p/s.
Lanyards	2	1				
Mizzen skysail yard						
Footropes	2	1½				
Clewline blocks			S	2	5	
Lifts	2	1½				Same as fore skysail yard.
Tie	1	2				Same as fore skysail yard.
Halliard	1	1				Sets up to becket in fly block, thru block hooked to eyebolt in channel, stbd, thru fly block, to pin #205.
Fly block			S	1	5	
Channel block			S	1	5	
Braces	2	1¼				Set up with shackle to eye in band at yardarm, p/s, thru fairleader block seized to eye of main tglt rigging, p/s, thru lubber hole , to pins #147, 148.
Fairleader blocks			S	2	5	
Signal halliard	1	1½				Reeves thru sheave in mizzen truck, hitches to sheerpole at skysail backstay.
Spanker boom (sets up to trysail mast)						
Footropes	2	2				Set up to eye in band at end of boom, other end seized to eye in band around boom, inboard of taffrail, p/s.
Boom sheets	2	2¾				Set up, p/s, to eye in band around boom above taffrail, thru block at rail, thru block shackled to boom, thru block at rail, to pins #215, 216.
Boom blocks			S	2	9	
Blocks at rail			D	2	9	
Boom topping lift (sets up on each side of boom)						
Spans	2	3				Set up with thimble in eye of band near end of boom, other end seized to band forward of footrope band; span block reeves between thimbles, p/s.
Span blocks			S	2	9	
Pendants	2	5				Span block turned in end, p/s, thru top block shackled to end of each mizzen trestletree, thimble turned in end, fly block shackled to thimble, p/s.
Top blocks			S	2	12	
Halliards	2	3				Set up to becket in fly block, p/s, thru block shackled to eyebolt in deck at fife rail, p/s, thru fly block, to pins #169,170.
Fly blocks			S	2	9	
Deck blocks			S	2	9	
Spanker gaff (sets up to trysail mast)						
Throat halliard	1	4				Sets up to becket in block shackled to eye in mizzen trestletree, port, thru block shackled to heel of gaff, thru top block, thru gaff block, thru top block, to pin #168.
Top block			D	1	12	
Gaff block			D	1	12	
Vangs						
Pendants	2	5				Spliced over peak stop, pendant block turned in end, p/s.
Pendant blocks			S	2	7	
Halliards	2	2½				Set up to eyebolt in waterway, p/s, thru pendant block, thru fairleader block shackled to eyebolt in waterway, p/s, to pins, #213, 214.
Fairleader blocks			S	2	7	
Peak halliard	1	4				Spliced over peak stop, thru block shackled to eye in mizzen cap, thru block shackled to band at mid-length of gaff, thru cap block, to pin #167.
Cap block			D	1	12	
Gaff block			S	1	11	
Ensign halliard	1	1¼				Reeves thru dasher block in end of gaff, both ends hitch around pins #217 or 218.
Dasher block			S	1	4	

Figure 30.1. *Representative clipper ship standing rigging.*

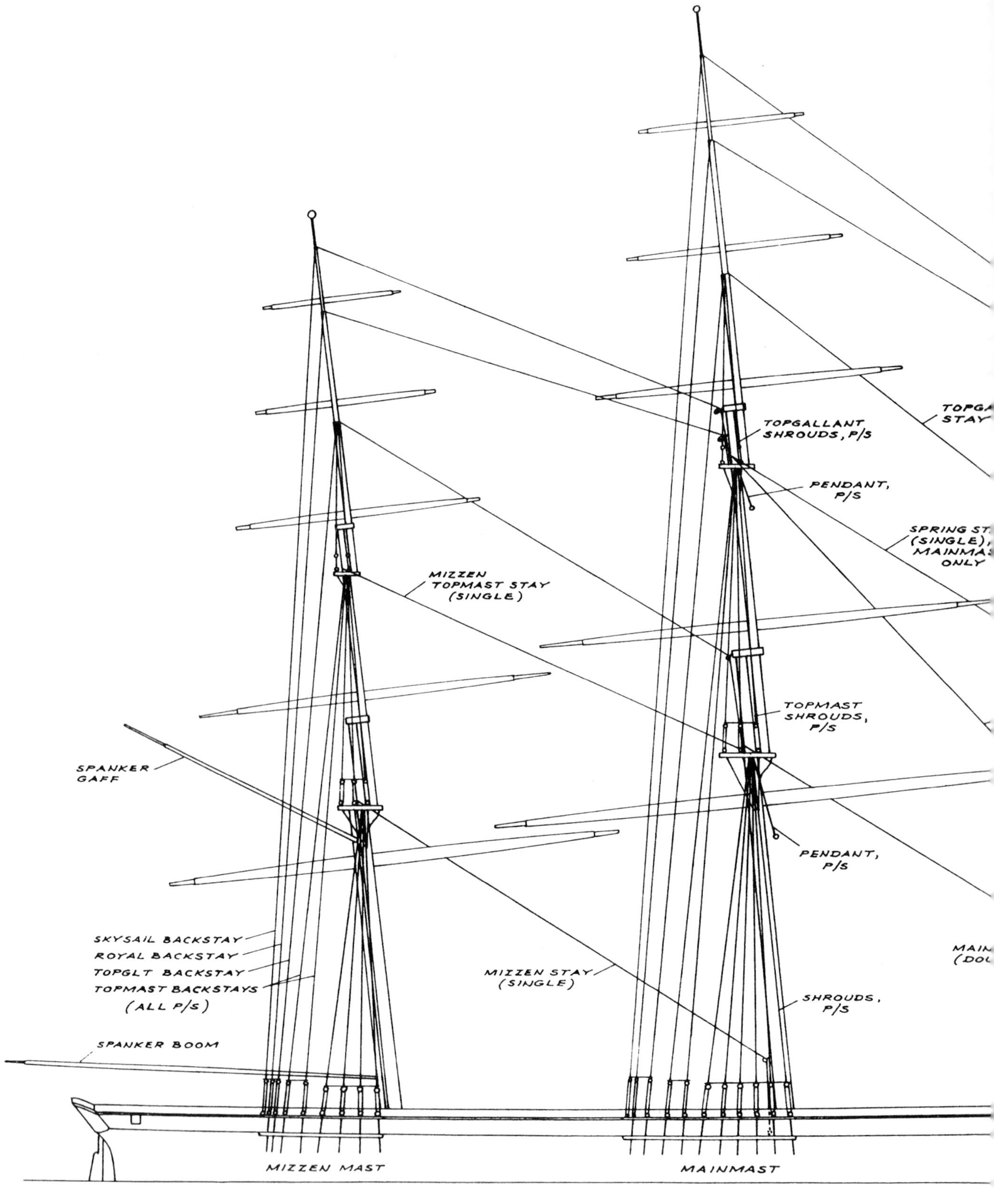

TOPGALLANT
SHROUDS, P/S

PENDANT,
P/S

TOPG
STAY

SPRING ST
(SINGLE),
MAINMAS
ONLY

MIZZEN
TOPMAST STAY
(SINGLE)

TOPMAST
SHROUDS,
P/S

SPANKER
GAFF

PENDANT,
P/S

MAIN
(DOU

SKYSAIL BACKSTAY
ROYAL BACKSTAY
TOPGLT BACKSTAY
TOPMAST BACKSTAYS
(ALL P/S)

MIZZEN STAY
(SINGLE)

SHROUDS,
P/S

SPANKER BOOM

MIZZEN MAST

MAINMAST

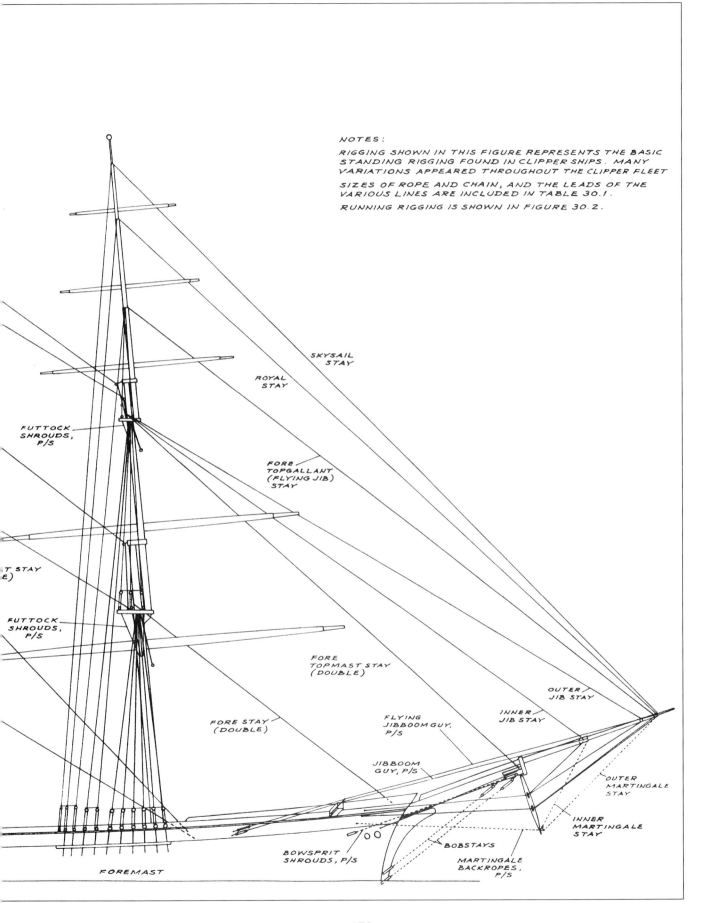

NOTES:
RIGGING SHOWN IN THIS FIGURE REPRESENTS THE BASIC
STANDING RIGGING FOUND IN CLIPPER SHIPS. MANY
VARIATIONS APPEARED THROUGHOUT THE CLIPPER FLEET
SIZES OF ROPE AND CHAIN, AND THE LEADS OF THE
VARIOUS LINES ARE INCLUDED IN TABLE 30.1.
RUNNING RIGGING IS SHOWN IN FIGURE 30.2.

SKYSAIL
STAY

ROYAL
STAY

FUTTOCK
SHROUDS,
P/S

FORE
TOPGALLANT
(FLYING JIB)
STAY

T STAY
E)

FUTTOCK
SHROUDS,
P/S

FORE
TOPMAST STAY
(DOUBLE)

OUTER
JIB STAY

INNER
JIB STAY

FORE STAY
(DOUBLE)

FLYING
JIBBOOM GUY,
P/S

JIBBOOM
GUY, P/S

OUTER
MARTINGALE
STAY

INNER
MARTINGALE
STAY

BOWSPRIT
SHROUDS, P/S

BOBSTAYS

MARTINGALE
BACKROPES,
P/S

FOREMAST

475

(text continued from page 467)

Challenge, with an extremely short bowsprit, and *Queen of the Seas* each had only one bobstay. *Flying Fish* had two bowsprit shrouds each side. These chain bobstays and the shrouds were still set up with hearts and lanyards, as were their predecessors.

Jibboom and Flying Jibboom Rigging

The *jibboom* and *flying jibboom rigging* consisted of a pair of guys, one each side of ship, which were set up to the mid-length of the jibboom and led in to the bows. They resisted any transverse movement of the jibboom.

Upward motion of the jibboom was counteracted by a martingale which was suspended from the bowsprit immediately behind the bowsprit cap. The *martingale*—sometimes called a martingale boom or dolphin striker—was held in position by a chain stay set up to its lower end and to the jibboom inner band, and by two chain backstays leading aft from its end to a point in each bow. These backstays were sometimes brought aft to the inboard ends of the catheads. The triangulation of this arrangement prevented any athwartship movement of the martingale.

In most clippers the martingale was restrained in a position normal (perpendicular) to the steeve of the bowsprit; however, a few vessels were rigged with the martingale suspended vertically, "Navy fashion." In either case, its function of resisting the upward forces of headsails filled with strong breezes was successfully carried out.

The inner jibstay, a collar in its upper end, went over the fore topmast head after the shrouds and backstays were installed. It reeved over a sheave at the mid-length of the jibboom. Even though the foremast was tightly wedged in position, and the bowsprit was solidly implanted in the bow, there was considerable movement between the fore topmast and the jibboom even under normal sailing conditions. This accounted for the sheave in the jibboom which allowed the stay to roll rather than slide where it reeved through the jibboom.

Due to constant wetting, the stay was served from a point about 10 feet above the jibboom for its entire length aft to the bow. This stay was of fixed length and, once installed, remained as it was without provision for adjustment by means of lanyards.

The outer jibstay, with a collar spliced in, was the last part to be passed over the fore topmast head. It, like the inner jibstay, was rove over a sheave to allow it to roll rather than slide due to movement between fore topmast and jibboom.

Jibboom guys restrained the jibboom in the athwartship direction and were set up as noted in Table 30.1.

The elements of the flying jibboom rigging were much smaller in size but were set up essentially the same as were jibboom rigging components. The only major exception was in the fact that, in lieu of a collar, the flying jibstay, which was also the fore topgallant stay, was set up to the fore topgallant masthead with an eye spliced over the stop or shoulder.

The rigging of the masts, shown in Figure 30.1 and detailed in Table 30.1, is representative of an average clipper. The only unusual detail is the inclusion of pendants at the fore and main lower and topmast heads.

Pendants

The *pendants* at the lower mastheads were used as working parts when cargo or material was being onloaded or offloaded. Tackles were hooked into the thimbles, and, after all work was finished, they were removed and the pendants hung idle. They were put over before any other item of rigging; this avoided any possibility of their chafing the eyes of the shrouds when in use.

The pendants that were fitted over the fore topmast head were used mostly to assist in *catting* the anchor.

Both were seldom found in the clipper ship but were standard rigging in men-of-war. They are included as an item of uncommon use but moderate interest.

Shrouds

The *shrouds* of almost all clippers were set up with eyes over the mastheads. In fact, this was the accepted practice in all types and classes of vessel. Of the vessels herein, three departed from this procedure. The barks *Racehorse*, *Mermaid*, and *Quickstep* were fitted with an iron band around the mast at about the height of the futtock band. This band contained iron eyes in its circumference, and the shrouds were set up to these eyes. This mode of setting up shrouds was highly favored by Robert Bennett Forbes.

Shrouds were subject to a variety of treatments to their eyes around the mastheads and to their ends at the channels. In most cases it appears, mainly due to lack of other evidence, that the shrouds were served in way of the deadeyes and the masthead, to an extent that is left unstated. However, in *Stag Hound*, *Shooting Star*, *Southern Cross*, and the bark *Racehorse* the service was carried up the shrouds and the backstays to the height of the bull's-eyes, which were *seized* to them as fairleaders for the running rigging.

Additional protection against the elements is found in *John Bertram*, *Witch of the Wave*, *Westward Ho*, and *Empress of the Sea*, all of which had the eyes of the lower shrouds covered with canvas.

General practice recommended that all *swifters*—the forward shroud in a gang of shrouds—in the lower and topmast rigging be served over their entire length. This was a protection against abrasion by the yards in the course of sailing or working with them.

The shrouds on all lower and topmasts were *middled*—a term applied to dividing their total length into two parts. The middling was served and an eye seized in, thus making a pair, and they were then gotten over the masthead, the starboard pair being shipped first. If the shroud was single, an eye was spliced in its upper end. These lower and topmast shrouds always went over the masthead prior to shipping any stays or backstays over a particular masthead.

Lower shrouds at this period were universally set up with deadeyes and lanyards at the channels. Topmast shrouds, usually three to a side, and topgallant shrouds, usually two to a side, had generally discarded this mode of setting up rigging. The usual practice was to *reeve* the shroud through a thimble at the end of the crosstrees and set it up on itself with several seizings.

Futtock Shrouds

Futtock shrouds of the lower masts, sometimes rope but more often iron rods, were set up to a mast band with shackles and to the deadeyes in the tops with hooks.

In the topmasts they were set up to a band below the topmast crosstrees. The upper end of the futtock shroud passed through the crosstree and had a thimble turned in. These shrouds were inserted downward through a suitable slot in the crosstree when being set up.

Topgallant shrouds were set up in the same general manner as those of the masts below. Customarily they had a thimble seized in their lower end and were then secured by a lanyard to the thimble in the crosstrees. The sequence of setting up the rigging at the topgallant masthead differed from the sequence at the lower and topmast heads. At the topgallant shoulder or stop, the shrouds were put in place *after* the stay had been put over; details are explained under the heading "Stays."

A very rare departure from normal merchant topgallant rigging occurred in *Dauntless*, in which the topgallant rigging was installed over copper cylinders or funnels. This installation was found in men-of-war, its use being to allow the masts to be struck without unshipping any of the attendant rigging.

Topmast Backstays

The topmast backstays were the next parts to go over the mastheads. There were usually two to a side. The middling was served, an eye was seized in similar to that in the shrouds, and they were then pounded down over the shrouds, starboard pair first. After the ends had been served they were turned into the deadeyes and set up to the channels with lanyards.

Larger vessels sometimes were fitted with three topmast backstays. *Empress of the Sea*, *Champion of the Seas*, and *Lightning* are known to have been fitted in this fashion on both the fore and main masts.

In addition to the standing topmast backstays *Challenge* and *Empress of the Sea* carried shifting topmast backstays, which were used when sailing by the wind. No quantity or locations are specified.

Topgallant Backstays

The *topgallant backstays*, and those above, were usually one on each side of a given mast, and all were set up in a like manner. An eye was spliced in the upper end to tightly fit over the masthead. The lower end led to the channels and was there set up similar to the topmast backstays. The topgallant backstays were placed on the masthead immediately over the eyes of the stay and shrouds.

The *royal backstays* went over the masthead immediately on the stay that was installed first. This mast was not fitted with shrouds.

Skysail backstays were seized around eyes in a masthead band of iron which circled the top of the skysail mast and prevented the end of the mast from splitting. Above this was the very slender skysail pole. The lower end of the backstay was fitted as the previous backstays (see Figure 30.1 and Table 30.1).

Most vessels were fitted with *outriggers* on the topmast crosstrees. These outriggers rested on the crosstrees and extended out and aft at an angle which intersected the higher backstays as they passed this level on their way to the channels. *Thumb cleats* were fashioned into the outriggers, and the backstays passed over the cleats. They were served in way of the outriggers and were free to slide, but were restrained; this prevented excessive whipping of the backstays throughout their extended length. Outriggers for the topgallant backstays are specifically mentioned in the descriptions of *Shooting Star*, *Empress of the Sea*, and *Champion of the Seas*.

Some of the larger ships were fitted with two topgallant backstays on each side of the vessel at the fore and main masts. These were made up and shipped over the masthead, same as the topmast shrouds. *Lightning*, *Empress of the Sea*, and *Champion of the Seas* were outfitted in this manner.

A very unusual bit of rigging found in the clippers were topgallant shifting backstays, which were used when sailing by the wind. The only instance noted herein is *Challenge*; no quantity or locations are specified.

Stays

The *stays*, individually, were the largest items of standing rigging to be installed in clipper ships. Lower and topmast stays had collars at their upper ends. These collars were actually large eyes, their length equal to the length of the masthead over which they were passed. A seizing at the lower end of the eye maintained its length. Placing the stays over the tight-fitting shrouds allowed the shrouds to remain intact if a stay was parted or damaged and required replacement; in such a case, the shrouds remained undisturbed.

Fore and main stays and topmast stays went double, generally to a seizing not far removed from the point where they were to be set up. For the forestay, this end was generally at the knightheads; for the mainstay it was in the deck immediately forward of the foot of the foremast, one leg on each side of the mast. In the case of *Young America*, the mainstay went as two separate legs below the seizing of the collar.

The mizzen stay, with a collar seized in the end, went single from the mizzen masthead down to the mainmast, to a point where a bull's-eye strapped to this mast confined the mizzen stay parallel with the mainstay.

The fore and main topmast stays went double in the same manner, the forestay reeving a leg through each *bee* then aft to an eye in each bow where it was set up on itself with a thimble and seizings. The main topmast stay was set up to the fore fife rail bolster in the same fashion.

Some vessels were fitted with main topmast stays which were set up in the manner of the springstay shown in Figure 30.1. In such instances the typical main topmast stay, which was brought to the deck, was omitted. Setting this stay up in the fore top was copied from the naval practice of keeping the deck as clear as possible. Examples of this practice are *Challenge*, *Staffordshire*, and *Flying Fish*.

The mizzen topmast stay, fitted with a collar, went single to an eyebolt in the main crosstree which embraced the masthead on its aft side. There it was set up on itself in the manner of the lower stays.

If a vessel carried a springstay, it was set up between the main topmast head and the fore top in the same manner as the mizzen topmast stay. In direct contradiction to this statement is the description of *Champion of the Seas*, which states that she had "double main topmast stays, which set up in the fore top; and a spring stay, which leads on deck." Either method would appear to be effective since the springstay is actually a preventer in the event that the stay should suffer damage.

All of these stays were served at their collars, ends, in way of fairleads, and in way of masts where the stay passed by the side of the mast. In the case of the fore topmast stay, the lower ends were served for the entire length from a point above the bees to the eyebolts in the bows. This service was protection against the constant wetting due to plunging of the bow.

In addition to the usual protection, the collars of all stays in *Bald Eagle* were covered with leather.

Grommets

Grommets were eyes formed from rope which was then served over its entire surface. The eye fitted tightly over the mast for which it was made and had a thimble seized in each side forming what appeared to be ears. The grommets were pounded down onto the stops of the topgallant and royal masts, with the thimbles resting athwartships; these would later receive the upper shackles of the yard lifts.

The topgallant and royal stays were all put over the masts immediately upon the grommets. In their upper end an eye, small enough to fit tightly on the stop of the appropriate mast, was spliced. The eye was then pounded down solidly on the grommet.

The reason for this sequence of the stays preceding installation of any shrouds and backstays was to allow the stays, which were set up at a relatively flat angle, to act as *preventers* which would prohibit the shrouds and backstays from sliding down the masts if their eyes were to stretch or ease off and tend to slip over the stop.

The fore topgallant stay was rove through the flying jibboom immediately forward of the sheave for the outer jibstay, led inboard under the port lower cleat on the martingale, and was set up on itself to an eyebolt in the port bow.

The fore royal stay was set up and reeved in similar fashion to an eyebolt in the starboard bow.

The main and mizzen topgallant and royal stays each received an eye in the upper end, were put over their respective mastheads and pounded down on the grommets. They then led forward into the lower or topmast doublings, leading through bull's-eyes or thimbles, and were set up in the crosstrees as indicated in Figure 30.1 and Table 30.1.

Skysail stays were set up with shackles to eyes in iron bands around the tops of the skysail masts. Thimbles were spliced in the ends to take the shackles.

The fore skysail stay led to the stop at the end of the flying jibboom, where a tight-fitting eye was spliced in its end and pounded solidly into the stop.

The main and mizzen skysail stays were set up in the same manner to their mast bands and led forward into fore and main topmast caps, respectively, then through fairleads to the crosstrees where they were turned and seized on their own ends.

In most vessels the headstays, those stays that passed over the bowsprit and jibbooms, were set up outboard in the bows, all in proximity to the hawseholes and figurehead. However, in some vessels these stays were brought through the bows and were set up inboard, which rendered the vessel's prow neat and unhampered. Included were *Challenge*, *Queen of the Seas*, *Bald Eagle*, *Storm King*, and *Champion of the Seas*.

Running Rigging

The *running rigging* comprises those lines that are used to control the positions of yards, booms, and gaffs to take advantage of wind conditions when a vessel is underway. Various combinations of pendants, blocks, and purchases are employed to minimize the labor required to work the yards. Also, there is the need to locate the lines in reference to points available for setting up and reeving such lines from their point of origin to their ultimate destination at a belaying point. The requirements result in a maze of ropes stretching between masts in what appears to be a haphazard fashion. A study of Figure 30.2 shows that, while this may be a maze, it is far from being haphazard; it illustrates in general terms the trace of the various individual parts. Table 30.1 contains significant details of these same parts.

Many essential accessories such as yard trusses, parrels, jackstays, and other associated hardware are not covered in this book but are examined in the following references: *The Boston Daily Atlas*;[1] on-site description of *Great Republic*;[10] *The Visual Encyclopedia of Nautical Terms under Sail*;[41] *Kedge Anchor*;[89] *Masting and Rigging*;[111] and *The Shipmodeler*.[116]

Slings

The *slings* supported the weight of the lower yards at the mast. In a previous time, these slings were fabrications of heavy rope that were passed around the yard, reeved up through the tops, and then looped around the after side of the masthead and supported by a thumb cleat.

The use of chain in lieu of rope simplified the installation of slings. Most clippers carried slings that were simple lengths of chain. However, there were vessels that still followed the old system, passing chain over the masthead in lieu of rope; *Challenge* was one vessel rigged in this manner.

Lifts

The *lifts*, which position the yards when they are lowered and no sail is set, supported the yards at the yardarms. They were divided into two categories. Those that supported the lower yards were termed *topping lifts*. They were adjustable, being made up of a pendant and a luff tackle purchase at fore and main and a gun tackle purchase at the mizzen.

The lower yards were suspended in permanent position by the slings, and the topping lifts were used to adjust these yards to a true horizontal position. This flexibility was necessary due to the fact that, in addition to spreading sail, they were working yards used in handling cargo, boats, and other heavy weights, as the situation required. Squaring them after completion of such chores was a matter of pride in any vessel.

The lifts of yards above the lower yards were termed *standing lifts*. They were of a length appropriate to the yard being supported and, when sail was not set, limited the distance the yard could lower on its mast. Under sail, when the yard was raised and hanging in the tie, these lifts draped loosely abaft the sail.

All standing lifts were shackled to an eye in the yardarm band. However, the upper ends at the masts were secured in several ways. The topsail lifts were shackled to eyebolts in the topmast trestletrees. Those of the topgallant and royal yards were shackled to the thimbles of the grommets at their respective stops. The skysail lift was shackled to an eye in the band around the top of the skysail mast.

Halliards

The *halliards* were used to raise the yards to their mastheads in order to set sail. All were arranged in the same general manner, namely a line attached to the middle of the yard, rove up through the mast, and down aft to some point on deck. In detail there were many specific arrangements, all conceived with the purpose of making any yard manageable from the deck. The halliards, as shown in Figure 30.2, represent the simplest form, and were found in any merchant vessel of the same size as the average clipper. The lower yards, having positions fixed by their slings, obviously were devoid of this piece of rigging.

In the arrangement shown, the topmast halliards consisted of a tie attached to the yard and rove over a sheave in the mast below the crosstrees. A *gin* (a sheave made of iron, encased in a flat frame) was shackled to the end. A *runner* passed through the gin. One end of the runner was shackled to a pendant that was secured to an upper channel, and the other end was secured to a tackle that was set up to an eye in an upper channel directly across on the opposite side of the ship.

The accepted practice was to set up the pendant of the fore topsail halliard on the starboard side of ship, and the tackle on the port side. For the mainmast the parts were set up to opposite sides. The mizzen was set up to the same sides as the foremast.

The yards above the topsail yard were of decreasing size, and the halliards were simpler in form and basically alike. These were made up of a tie shackled to the yard and then rove over a sheave in the mast below the stop. To this end the tackle was shackled and brought to an upper channel.

These halliards each used only one side of a vessel. However, their sequence of location is important and follows a pattern which can be seen in Figure 30.2. The fore topgallant halliard was set up to the starboard side of ship. The fore royal halliard (drawn in broken lines in the figure) set up on the port side and the fore skysail halliard on the starboard side. At the mainmast the individual halliards reversed the sides of the ship to which they were set up. At the mizzen they reverted to the same sides as the foremast. The result along the length of the vessel was that no two adjacent halliards were set up side by side. The purpose of this alternate arrangement was to prohibit stresses induced through the halliards from forming a concentration of loads at any given location at the side of the hull and allowed better working space.

The tackles were made up appropriate to the size of the yards they controlled and in a manner which allowed them to be operated by available manpower. In ascending order, and with no consideration of friction over the sheaves, the tackles were made up in the following manner.

(text continued on page 482)

Figure 30.2. *Representative clipper ship running rigging.*

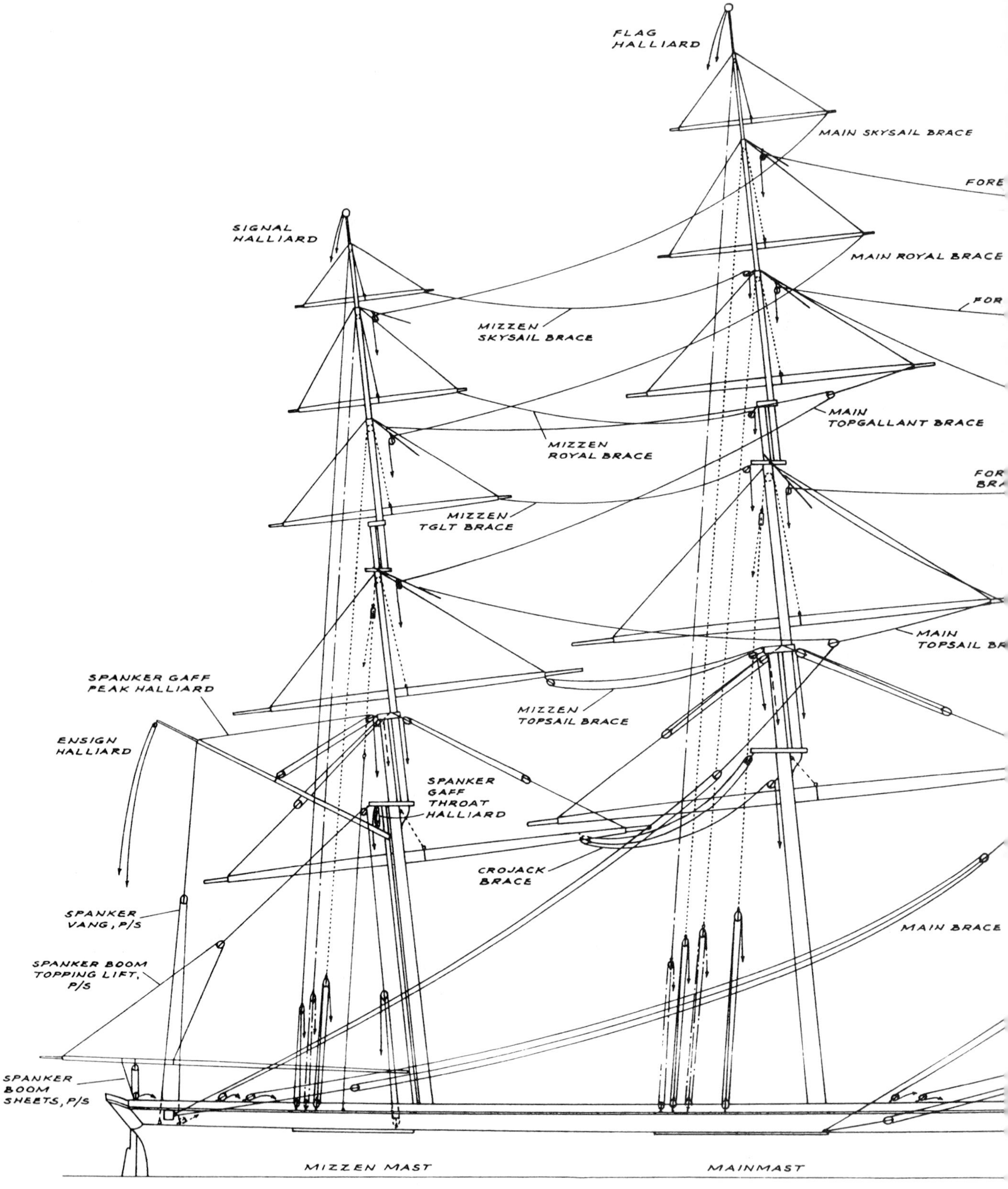

FLAG
HALLIARD

MAIN SKYSAIL BRACE

FORE

MAIN ROYAL BRACE

SIGNAL
HALLIARD

FOR

MIZZEN
SKYSAIL BRACE

MAIN
TOPGALLANT BRACE

MIZZEN
ROYAL BRACE

FOR
BRA

MIZZEN
TGLT BRACE

MAIN
TOPSAIL BR

SPANKER GAFF
PEAK HALLIARD

MAIN
TOPSAIL BR

MIZZEN
TOPSAIL BRACE

ENSIGN
HALLIARD

SPANKER
GAFF
THROAT
HALLIARD

CROJACK
BRACE

SPANKER
VANG, P/S

MAIN BRACE

SPANKER BOOM
TOPPING LIFT,
P/S

SPANKER
BOOM
SHEETS, P/S

MIZZEN MAST

MAINMAST

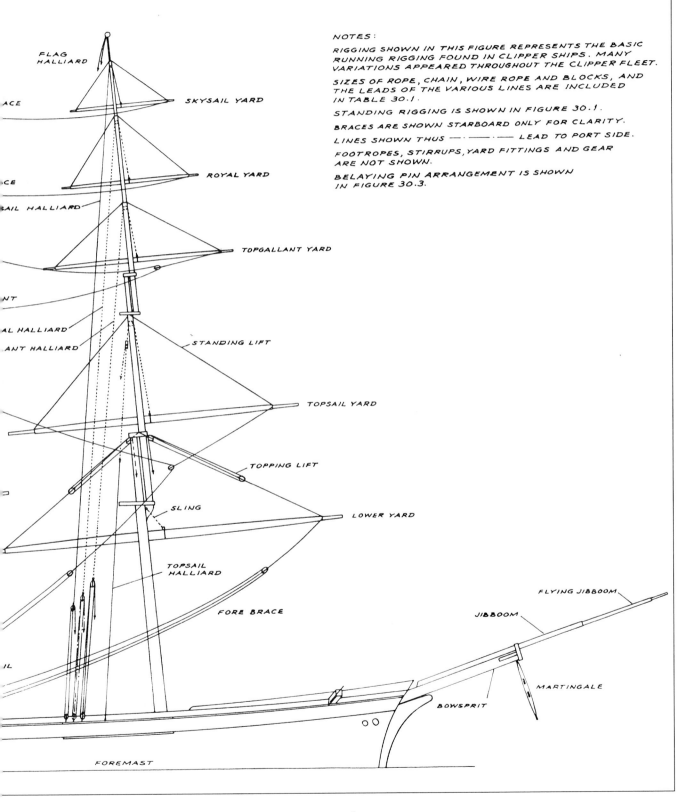

FLAG
HALLIARD

ACE

SKYSAIL YARD

CE

ROYAL YARD

AIL HALLIARD

TOPGALLANT YARD

NT

AL HALLIARD

ANT HALLIARD

STANDING LIFT

TOPSAIL YARD

TOPPING LIFT

SLING

LOWER YARD

TOPSAIL
HALLIARD

FORE BRACE

IL

FLYING JIBBOOM

JIBBOOM

MARTINGALE

BOWSPRIT

FOREMAST

NOTES:

RIGGING SHOWN IN THIS FIGURE REPRESENTS THE BASIC
RUNNING RIGGING FOUND IN CLIPPER SHIPS. MANY
VARIATIONS APPEARED THROUGHOUT THE CLIPPER FLEET.

SIZES OF ROPE, CHAIN, WIRE ROPE AND BLOCKS, AND
THE LEADS OF THE VARIOUS LINES ARE INCLUDED
IN TABLE 30.1.

STANDING RIGGING IS SHOWN IN FIGURE 30.1.

BRACES ARE SHOWN STARBOARD ONLY FOR CLARITY.

LINES SHOWN THUS —·——·—— LEAD TO PORT SIDE.

FOOTROPES, STIRRUPS, YARD FITTINGS AND GEAR
ARE NOT SHOWN.

BELAYING PIN ARRANGEMENT IS SHOWN
IN FIGURE 30.3.

Figure 30.3. *Representative clipper ship belaying arrangement.*

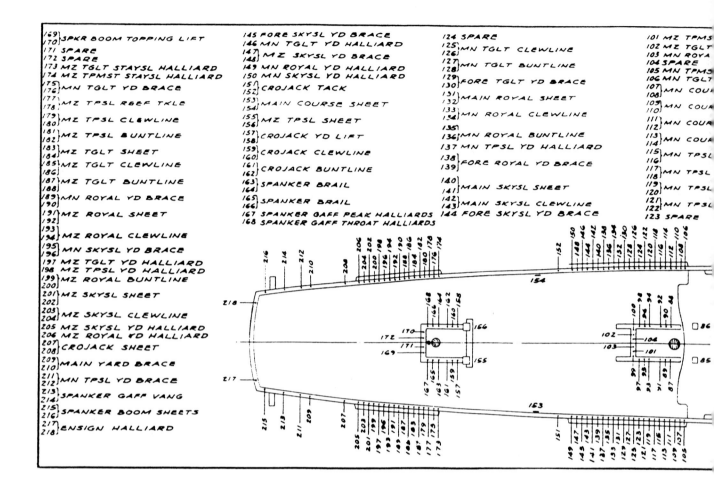

169 170} SPKR BOOM TOPPING LIFT
171 SPARE
172 SPARE
173 MZ TGLT STAYSL HALLIARD
174 MZ TPMST STAYSL HALLIARD
175 176} MN TGLT YD BRACE
177 178} MZ TPSL REEF TKLE
179 180} MZ TPSL CLEWLINE
181 182} MZ TPSL BUNTLINE
183 184} MZ TGLT SHEET
185 186} MZ TGLT CLEWLINE
187 188} MZ TGLT BUNTLINE
189 190} MN ROYAL YD BRACE
191 192} MZ ROYAL SHEET
193 194} MZ ROYAL CLEWLINE
195 196} MN SKYSL YD BRACE
197 MZ TGLT YD HALLIARD
198 MZ TPSL YD HALLIARD
199 200} MZ ROYAL BUNTLINE
201 202} MZ SKYSL SHEET
203 204} MZ SKYSL CLEWLINE
205 MZ SKYSL YD HALLIARD
206 MZ ROYAL YD HALLIARD
207 208} CROJACK SHEET
209 210} MAIN YARD BRACE
211 212} MN TPSL YD BRACE
213 214} SPANKER GAFF VANG
215 216} SPANKER BOOM SHEETS
217 218} ENSIGN HALLIARD

145 FORE SKYSL YD BRACE
146 MN TGLT YD HALLIARD
147 148} MZ SKYSL YD BRACE
149 MN ROYAL YD HALLIARD
150 MN SKYSL YD HALLIARD
151 152} CROJACK TACK
153 154} MAIN COURSE SHEET
155 156} MZ TPSL SHEET
157 158} CROJACK YD LIFT
159 160} CROJACK CLEWLINE
161 162} CROJACK BUNTLINE
163 164} SPANKER BRAIL
165 166} SPANKER BRAIL
167 SPANKER GAFF PEAK HALLIARDS
168 SPANKER GAFF THROAT HALLIARDS

124 SPARE
125 126} MN TGLT CLEWLINE
127 128} MN TGLT BUNTLINE
129 130} FORE TGLT YD BRACE
131 132} MAIN ROYAL SHEET
133 134} MN ROYAL CLEWLINE
135 136} MN ROYAL BUNTLINE
137 MN TPSL YD HALLIARD
138 139} FORE ROYAL YD BRACE
140 141} MAIN SKYSL SHEET
142 143} MAIN SKYSL CLEWLINE
144 FORE SKYSL YD BRACE

101 MZ TPMS
102 MZ TGLT
103 MN ROYA
104 SPARE
105 MN TPMS
106 MN TGLT
107 108} MN COUR
109 110} MN COUR
111 112} MN COUR
113 114} MN COUR
115 116} MN TPSL
117 118} MN TPSL
119 120} MN TPSL
121 122} MN TPSL
123 SPARE

(text continued from page 479)

Topsail halliards—The runner passed over the tie gin; this divided the original load by two. A luff tackle, rove to advantage, was shackled to the runner; this divided the load in the runner by four. The resultant load on the hauling end of the tackle was one-eighth of the original load.

Topgallant halliards—A luff tackle, rove to advantage, was shackled directly to the tie; this divided the load on the hauling end of the tackle by four.

Fore and main royal halliards—Same as topgallant halliards.

Mizzen royal halliard—A gun tackle, rove to advantage, was shackled directly to the tie; this divided the load on the hauling end of the tackle by three.

Skysail halliards—Same as mizzen royal halliard. In all cases the blocks were sized to accommodate the sizes of the falls.

Every yard halliard benefited to some degree from the mechanical advantage which these tackles offered. The higher yards, with smaller initial loads, were fitted with the minimum purchase that would allow expeditious handling of the yards. There was an economic side to this consideration, since the amount of rope required increased directly with the number of sheaves over which the rope passed.

All vessels appear to have followed the previously described rig for the topgallant yard and the yards above. However, some vessels adopted a major departure in rigging their topsail halliards. In these ships double topsail halliards were fitted. Two gins were shackled to the middle of the yard, and two were shackled to the crosstrees under the topmast shrouds, one port and one starboard. The standing ends were set up in the crosstrees; then the ties were rove through a gin on the yard, up through the gin in the crosstrees on the same side of the ship, and down to receive the halliards. This arrangement reduced the initial load of the yard by four at the fly block of the halliards; in addition,

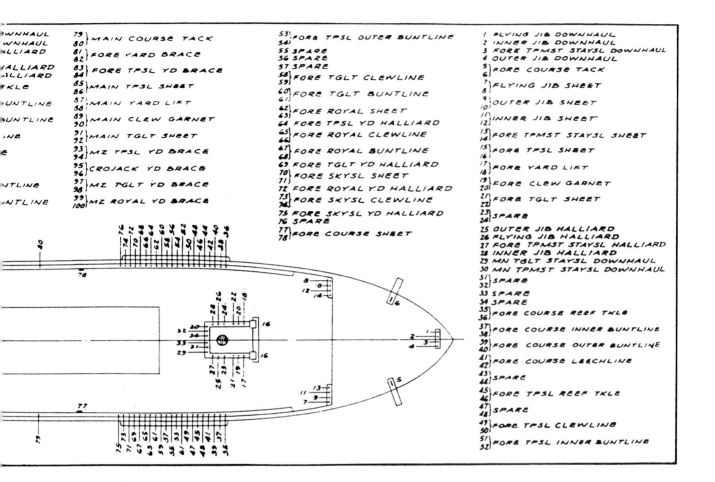

WNHAUL
WNHAUL
ALLIARD
79/80} MAIN COURSE TACK
HALLIARD / ALLIARD
81/82} FORE YARD BRACE
83/84} FORE TPSL YD BRACE
KLE
85/86} MAIN TPSL SHEET
UNTLINE
87/88} MAIN YARD LIFT
UNTLINE
89/90} MAIN CLEW GARNET
INE
91/92} MAIN TGLT SHEET
E
93/94} MZ TPSL YD BRACE
95/96} CROJACK YD BRACE
NTLINE
97/98} MZ TGLT YD BRACE
NTLINE
99/100} MZ ROYAL YD BRACE

53/54} FORE TPSL OUTER BUNTLINE
55 SPARE
56 SPARE
57 SPARE
58/59} FORE TGLT CLEWLINE
60/61} FORE TGLT BUNTLINE
62/63} FORE ROYAL SHEET
64 FORE TPSL YD HALLIARD
65/66} FORE ROYAL CLEWLINE
67/68} FORE ROYAL BUNTLINE
69 FORE TGLT YD HALLIARD
70/71} FORE SKYSL SHEET
72 FORE ROYAL YD HALLIARD
73/74} FORE SKYSL CLEWLINE
75 FORE SKYSL YD HALLIARD
76 SPARE
77/78} FORE COURSE SHEET

1 FLYING JIB DOWNHAUL
2 INNER JIB DOWNHAUL
3 FORE TPMST STAYSL DOWNHAUL
4 OUTER JIB DOWNHAUL
5/6} FORE COURSE TACK
7/8} FLYING JIB SHEET
9/10} OUTER JIB SHEET
11/12} INNER JIB SHEET
13/14} FORE TPMST STAYSL SHEET
15/16} FORE TPSL SHEET
17/18} FORE YARD LIFT
19/20} FORE CLEW GARNET
21/22} FORE TGLT SHEET
23/24} SPARE
25 OUTER JIB HALLIARD
26 FLYING JIB HALLIARD
27 FORE TPMST STAYSL HALLIARD
28 INNER JIB HALLIARD
29 MN TGLT STAYSL DOWNHAUL
30 MN TPMST STAYSL DOWNHAUL
31/32} SPARE
33 SPARE
34 SPARE
35/36} FORE COURSE REEF TKLE
37/38} FORE COURSE INNER BUNTLINE
39/40} FORE COURSE OUTER BUNTLINE
41/42} FORE COURSE LEECHLINE
43/44} SPARE
45/46} FORE TPSL REEF TKLE
47/48} SPARE
49/50} FORE TPSL CLEWLINE
51/52} FORE TPSL INNER BUNTLINE

the mast was not weakened because of the slot that was ordinarily cut through the mast.

Some clippers rigged in this manner were *Challenge, Witch of the Wave, Sovereign of the Seas, Westward Ho, Queen of the Seas,* and *Empress of the Sea*. The main topgallant yard of *Sovereign of the Seas* was also rigged in like manner.

Braces

The *braces*, used to set the yards in reference to the wind, presented a more confusing picture to the viewer, even though no confusion existed. It was merely a case of many lines occupying a relatively small space. The most common arrangement of braces is that shown in Figure 30.2. As with the halliards, various purchases were used to reduce the need for excessive manpower to handle the lines. Table 30.1 contains details of each brace.

Fore and main braces—These were made up of yard pendants, channel pendants on the fore, bumkin pendants on the main, and gun tackle purchases for the falls. The purchases were rove to advantage, thus dividing the load at the hauling end by three. (The addition of fairleads does no more than change the direction of pull on the line.) The pendants were made as long as possible. Long pendants meant short tackles and a great saving of rope.

Crojack brace—Instead of being set up at the yardarm, this brace was shackled to the yard at about the third quarter. By necessity, the mizzen braces led forward to the mainmast. Due to the length of the crojack, the braces, if shackled to the yardarm band, generally fouled the main backstays; to avoid this, they were brought inboard to a point on the yard that eliminated the condition, and there they were set up. The brace consisted wholly of a gun tackle purchase rove to advantage and a fairlead block, there being insufficient space for pendants.

"Crojack" is the corrupted name of "crossjack," the lowest yard on the mizzen mast. It is used to spread the foot of the mizzen topsail and, generally, not fitted with its own sail.

Fore and main topsail braces—These were set up with runners reeved through yard pendants. The falls were shackled to the runners and set up at the main channels and the bumkins, respectively. These purchases combined to reduce the load at the hauling end by four; this was the same as a luff tackle rove to advantage. The arrangement of these braces allowed them to clear other rigging as the yards were braced from one position to another.

Mizzen topsail brace—This brace was set up between the yard and the main cap and, like the crojack brace, was not fitted with pendants. The purchase reduced the load at the hauling end by two.

Fore and main topgallant braces—These braces resembled the topsail braces in arrangement but were made up with pendant and falls only. The purchase used reduced the load on the hauling end by two.

Mizzen topgallant brace—At this height on a mast the yards were becoming shorter and the sail areas were much smaller, and a point was reached where mechanical advantage was no longer a necessity. All that was required was that the leads of the braces be clear of any other lines aloft. Thus the brace was set up at the yardarm and reeved through a fairlead block shackled to an appropriate location on the mainmast. No mechanical advantage was transmitted to the hauling end of the brace, the fairlead only changing the direction of the pull.

Fore and main royal braces—These were set up similar to the mizzen topgallant brace. However, in all cases the fairlead blocks were seized near the eyes of appropriate stays and offered no mechanical advantage.

Mizzen royal brace—Set up similar to the mizzen topgallant brace.

Fore and main skysail braces—Set up similar to the fore and main royal braces.

Mizzen skysail brace—Set up similar to the mizzen topgallant brace.

Many vessels had masts that were built to carry skysails, but these sails were not set up as standing skysails. Instead the yards, sails, and rigging were made up on deck and the skysails sent up only when appropriate weather conditions permitted. These skysails were referred to as being "rigged aloft." *Winged Arrow, John Land, West Wind, Golden Light, Flying Mist, Bonita, Spitfire,* and the barks *Henry Hill* and *Wildfire* were some vessels in this category.

These skysails "rigged aloft" appeared exactly as shown in Figure 30.2 when they had been sent up and set.

Spanker boom—The topping lift, which went double, flat against each side of the sail, was made up of a span, a pendant, and falls. The span was set up with one end approaching the midpoint of the boom, giving support to its considerable slender length; the other end was set up to the after stop of the boom after the span had been rove through a block which had a pendant turned in. The pendant reeved through a block in the mizzen top and thence led down the mast to a halliard that was set up to an eyebolt in the deck at the foot of the mast; this halliard was a gun tackle purchase. Each topping lift was a complete assembly, port and starboard, and together they controlled the height at which the boom hung (see Figure 30.2).

The boom sheets were set up to the boom about as far aft as the taffrail. They consisted of a luff tackle, port and starboard, which secured to an eyebolt in the rail. The sheets controlled the distance that the boom could swing.

The spanker gaff, if it was not a *standing gaff* (one that could not be raised and lowered), was controlled by a *throat halliard* inboard at the jaws and a *peak halliard* at the end. The peak halliard was rigged with a block set up at the midpoint of the gaff, providing support for its length. The vangs restrained its athwartship motion.

Belaying Arrangements

Categorically, all parts of rigging which determined the position of yards required a convenient and logical point of termination on deck from which to control the set of the sails. Depending on the number of yards and sails, and the detailed complexity of rigging, these *belaying points* varied in number and location from ship to ship. However, in general, the belaying points—sometimes as belaying pins, sometimes as cleats—followed a loosely similar pattern. Figure 30.3 represents the belaying arrangement for the rigging shown in Figure 30.2; it also contains belaying locations for all lines that were necessary for the control of sails that could be set in accordance with that figure. The detailed rigging of these sails is a subject in its own right and is not included in this book.

Obviously, there was great scope to the details involved in the construction, masting, and rigging of the American-built clipper ship. All were alike, but, at the same time, all were different. Where detailed information is available, many of the differences have been noted.

With her hull completed and freshly painted, all her masts stepped, her rigging set up, sails bent, and all her outfit on board, the ship was now about to pass from the hands of the builder to the hands of her captain and crew. In a matter of a few weeks she would take on her cargo and put to sea. The rest of her story would be told in the record books.

Chapter Thirty-One

FLAGS AND SIGNALS

NO VESSEL, CLIPPER OR OTHERWISE, would initially leave port without first having received her full complement of flags. Except for the close-range speaking trumpet, these, at sea, were the sole means of identification and communication, and were a vital component of the ship's outfit.

Flags of identification consisted of the appropriate ensign of the country of registry; the house flag of the company that owned (or was temporarily chartering) the vessel, or the flag of the agent who represented the owner; and the flags of a signal code, one portion of which was devoted to numerical or alphabetical combinations designating the identity of individual vessels.

Flags of communication were those designed for a specific signal code and used for "speaking" to other vessels or land-based interests by means of both code and telegraphic signaling.

National Ensigns

American Ensign

The *American ensign* was flown by all vessels built for American owners.[122] Among the vessels listed in this book, there were four exceptions, these being built to order for a British shipping company.

American vessels flew the national ensign—the Stars and Stripes—of the design appropriate at the time of their launching. During the years (1850–1856) covered in this book, the flag contained the usual thirteen stripes, alternating red and white, and the blue union or canton, charged with white stars. In accordance with adopted custom, the number of stars on the ensign was equal to the number of states as of the first July 4th following the date of admission of a state into the union. Thus a flag containing thirty stars would be flown by vessels built in 1850 and the first half of 1851. On September 9, 1850 California became the thirty-first state, and on July 4, 1851 the number of stars was increased to

thirty-one. No additional changes were made after that until 1858, so, theoretically at least, all clippers of our period flew the thirty-one-star ensign.

During the clipper era the universally accepted location of hoist for vessels of this general type was at the mizzenmast. By far the most common location for displaying the ensign was at the peak of the spanker gaff. This was generally a fixed location and applied to vessels that set brailing spankers which could be shortened in to the mast, thus not disturbing the trim of the spanker gaff.

Vessels that set a reefing spanker, with the gaff rigged to be raised and lowered, required a different location for displaying the ensign. This was provided by a monkey gaff (described in Chapter 29), which was set up as a fixed, permanent spar, at the mizzen topmast crosstrees. In either case the ensign, when flown, was in a position of maximum visibility.

British Red Ensign

The British red ensign, the famous "red duster," was the official flag flown by British merchant vessels, and was flown by the few American-built clippers that were constructed to order for British owners.[119] Of the clippers covered here, only four were in this category: *Lightning*, *Champion of the Seas*, *James Baines*, and *Donald McKay*. All four were built for James Baines & Co. of Liverpool and spent most or all of their lives sailing under the British flag.

Two additional vessels, *Red Jacket* and *Blue Jacket*, were built for American owners but are regarded as British vessels. *Red Jacket*, owned by Seccomb & Taylor of Boston, initially sailed from New York to Liverpool in January 1854 under American colors. Upon arrival she was chartered by the British White Star line for a round-trip voyage to Melbourne, Australia. She arrived back in Liverpool in October 1854 and was immediately purchased by Pilkington & Wilson, owners of the White Star line. After only ten months under the American ensign, she sailed for almost twenty-five years under the British flag. In all this time she never again put in to an American port.

Blue Jacket, also owned by Seccomb & Taylor, sailed to Liverpool on her initial passage. Shortly after her arrival she was purchased by John James Frost of London to sail in his Fox line of Australian packets. She, too, sailed the rest of her life— fifteen years—without once putting in to an American port.

It is coincidental that both vessels made their initial passage to Liverpool under command of Capt. Asa Eldridge and both were at some time owned by the White Star line.

House Flags

The *house flag* was the signature of the owner of a vessel or of the agent who operated the vessel for the owner.[121] The official designation of such flags was "private signal." These flags were generally in the form of a rectangle, although there were many of burgee, swallowtail, or pennant configuration. In addition there were a relative few that were of unique shape or combinations of flags.

A house flag was intended to function as a monogram that would be peculiar to a specific owner and therefore identify a vessel as belonging to him. In spite of the great number of owners and agents, this goal was very successfully achieved. Shape, color combinations, and individual initials offered innumerable opportunities to design a very individual flag. In general, most flags were uniquely distinctive, but in a day of distances and slow, inefficient communication, there were instances of duplication.

In addition to the various configurations previously noted, there were colors to be considered. The basic colors of house flags were red, yellow, blue, black, and white, used separately or in combination. Only on rare occasion did green or brown appear.

The most prevalent combination of shape and colors were rectangular red, white, and blue flags. Following these were rectangular flags of red and white, and blue and white. Other shapes and color combinations existed, but not in such prolific numbers as those noted. Most house flags contained some form of geometric design, possibly embellished with an appropriate initial or initials. Very few of these flags were content to display a solitary initial on a solid background.

In cases where a merchant might own only a few vessels, perhaps three or four, each vessel may have flown its own individual flag. When this was done, there would be a consistent principal theme connecting the flags.

Agents who undertook the operation of vessels in the name of an owner had house flags of their own. These were flown in lieu of an owner's flag and in the same manner.

The practical use of these private signals was a matter of everyday business activity. When a vessel was at sea or in port between sailings, the flags were generally stowed in the ship's flag locker or other designated location. The need for the house flag was occasioned by the vessel's imminent arrival at a port. When broken out it was generally hoisted to the main truck, this being the highest, most visible position in a vessel.

Agents, owners' representatives, customs officials, and others constantly scanned the horizon for ships that were arriving at a given port. When their own house flag was sighted through a glass, or its impending presence was passed along, the agent or owner's representative immediately began to prepare for the ritual offloading of cargo. No time was to be lost; every day in port cost money.

It seems rather incongruous that, after perhaps four months at sea, there should be such a rush to get a vessel underway again, but such was the case. In shipping, turnaround time is considered money lost. A day in port was not a day under sail. If commerce could have arranged it, no ship would ever have spent time tied up. That being impossible, the next best thing was to get her in and on her way again.

Rather than flying the house flag of owner or agent, vessels that were sailing under charter flew the flag of the chartering company, for the same reasons as those noted previously.

From what has been noted above, it can be seen that identity was divided into three categories. The broadest form of identity was achieved when a vessel's ensign was broken out and hoisted at the mizzen; this indicated the country under whose protection the vessel was sailing. The private signal, or house flag, narrowed the field of identification. While it generally could not identify a particular vessel by name, it drastically reduced the scope of possibilities. When hoisted it alerted all parties who had a personal or commercial interest in any ship which sailed as the property of a specific individual or organization.

Marryat Signal Code

The third part of the identification process was contained in the *signal code* to which the vessel subscribed. Such codes were tightly organized and dealt with precise details. In the early nineteenth century there was a flurry of activity in the development of flag hoist signal codes. The names of Marryat, Maxwell, Walker, and Watson of Great Britain, Rohde of Denmark, Missiessy of France,[118] Elford of the United States,[123] and others appeared as developers of flag hoist signal systems. With the exception of Marryat, none of these names succeeded in establishing a code that would become competitive.

The *Marryat code* originally appeared in 1817 under the complete title *A Code of Signals for the Merchant Service*.[41, 117] This was the signal code to which the clippers subscribed. Its designer was Capt. Frederick Marryat, Royal Navy. It was a well-developed code, successful from the very start.

The code was divided into several parts which served specific interests. The parts appropriate to general merchant shipping and American-built clippers were the numeral flags, the vocabulary, and vessels' identification numbers. For the purpose of identification, the vocabulary is not relevant.

During its lifetime the code underwent a series of changes. Originally ten numeral flags, 1 through 0; a telegraph flag; the British Union Jack as a pilot signal; a numeral pennant, rendezvous flag, and two distinguishing pennants were provided.

The inclusion of the *pilot jack* (Union Jack) in a merchant signal system was not appreciated by the British naval top brass, and they instantly voiced their displeasure at such usurping of a flag considered to be solely the province of the Royal Navy. The situation was protested vigorously until finally, in 1823, the pilot jack was revised to include a white border.

By 1854 the Marryat code had become so well accepted that available signal numbers were rapidly diminishing. The remedy was simple, and the problem was overcome by the addition of the third distinguishing pennant. There was no change to the existing flags. However, at the same time the title of the code was amended, and it now would be known as the *Universal Code of Signals for the Mercantile Marine of All Nations*.

The final change to the code flags took place in 1869[41] when the fourth distinguishing pennant was added without additional changes. The most remarkable aspect of this modification was that it occurred after the official Commercial Code of Signals, introduced in 1857, had been in existence for twelve years. Due to its immense popularity the Marryat code remained in constant use until at least 1879.

Ships, when built, did not automatically receive an identification number. With the Marryat code, as with all other proposed codes, the ship owner was required to subscribe to the system. Upon doing this a ship was given a number and was entitled to the current codebook. Once assigned, the ship's number was hers for life; the code itself, however, under went numerous revisions.

The identification numbers for all ships subscribing to the code were listed in the codebook, which was consulted whenever two ships met at sea and broke out their appropriate flags. This being a numerical system, all identification and communication was carried out by use of the numerals in various combinations.

Signals of the type under discussion were "made," not "sent," as was the case in later radio transmission. Accordingly, when a vessel hoisted her specific flags, she was "making her number." The term itself first appeared in the British 1799 *Signal Book for the Ships of War* and was soon universally adopted, becoming an ingrained part of nautical terminology. Old habits are difficult to break, so even after the introduction of the alphabetical Commercial Code in 1857, ships were still making their number. It remains that way today. Whenever a ship identifies herself, she "makes her number."

The Marryat system of ships' numbers was a four-digit system, meaning that no number would contain more than four numerals. In addition, no individual number would show a digit more than once in any given hoist. And, since this was a code which did not have repeater or substitute flags, many numbers were automatically omitted from the list. Thus, numbers such as 11, 22, 55, 99, 100, 101, 999, 1,000, 1,001, 1,010, 3,123, etc., could not be made.

The numerical list in the code was made up of numbers 1 through 9,999. Of these, the highest number that could be used for ship identification was 9,876—no digit appearing twice. This characteristic rendered 4,273 numbers unusable due to the repetition of digits, leaving 5,726 numbers available.

Marryat was aware at the outset that if his system were put to full use, this would not provide for all vessels that might wish to use the system. To provide for this eventuality, he included two "distinguishing pennants" in his original code in 1817. This doubled the quantity of available numbers. So, as introduced, all Marryat identification numbers would be made with an assigned distinguishing pennant (first or second) flying immediately over the numerical signal below.

Due to universal acceptance of the code, a third distinguishing pennant was added in 1854 and a fourth in 1869. This latter date obviously did not apply to the clipper period. However, one of the vessels included in this book, the ship *Thatcher Magoun*, 1856, appears in the 1869 edition of the codebook under the fourth distinguishing pennant list.

Marryat numbers for nearly all the clippers included in this book have been found and are listed in Table 31.1. The absence of a number for any given vessel may be due to her not having been listed in the Marryat system, or it might not have been recorded in any of the noted editions of the codebook.[117]

Communication by means of this code was quite similar to the usage of any other code. The same numeral flags could be converted to alphabetical usage by following the procedures set up within the system.

The codebook was made up containing a variety of headings under which various relevant subjects were assigned code numbers employing numerals and a specific identifying flag; for example, in the 1817 code the hoisting of the "rendezvous" flag over the numerals 5–4–0 signified "London." However, due to changes in the code at later date, this was no longer true, even though there was no change in the flags. This same signal in the 1841 code indicated the "Paker Ort Lighthouse."

(text continued on page 490)

Table 31.1. *Vessels' Marryat ID numbers.*

Notes: The signal is generally hoisted to the mizzen truck.

Vessel's number is made with the distinguishing pennant at the top, followed by the numerals reading downward.

1st, 2nd, 3rd and 4th indicate the number of the distinguishing pennant.

Unless otherwise noted all numbers are taken from the 1858 edition of ref.117.

Vessel	Year built	Marryat ID No.	Remarks
Alarm	1856	1st, 1-7-4	
Amphitrite	1853	1st, 3-1-4	
Andrew Jackson	1855	3rd, 8-1-6	
Antelope	1851	1st, 4-8-1	
Asa Eldridge	1856	3rd, 2-5-4-7	
Bald Eagle	1852	3rd, 5-8-6-3	
Belle of the West	1853	3rd, 3-0-7-6	
Beverly	1852	1st, 9-4-3	1856 edition
Black Hawk	1856	1st, 9-5-7-6	
Blue Jacket	1854	3rd, 1-4-2	1856 edition. Sold British upon reaching Liverpool, 1854.
Bonita	1853	1st, 5-9-0-4	
Bounding Billow Bark	1854		
Celestial	1850	1st, 7-6-8-0	
Challenge	1851	2nd, 8-4-2-0	1854 edition
Challenger	1853	1st, 1-7-2-5	
Champion of the Seas	1854	3rd, 9	Built to order for James Baines & Co., Liverpool.
Charger	1856	3rd, 3-6-8-2	
Charmer	1854	3rd, 8-6-0-7	1869 edition
Cleopatra	1853	1st, 2-0-1-8	
Climax	1853		
Coeur de Lion	1854	1st, 2-0-6-8	
Comet	1851	1st, 2-1-3-0	
Cyclone	1853	1st, 8-5-2-0	
Daring	1855	1st, 2-5-6-7	
Dauntless	1851	1st, 2-5-8-1	
Donald McKay	1855	3rd, 5-8-7	Built to order for James Baines & Co., Liverpool.
Don Quixote	1853	1st, 9-2-8-1	
Eagle	1851	1st, 2-9-5-3	1856 edition
Eagle Wing	1853	3rd, 8-9-1	
Edwin Forrest	1853	3rd, 2-1	
Electric Spark	1855	3rd, 4-6-9-5	1869 edition
Ellen Foster	1852	3rd, 5-4-1-2	1869 edition
Empress of the Sea	1853	1st, 9-7-5-3	
Endeavor	1856	1st, 3-5-4-0	
Eringo Bark	1853		
Eureka	1851	1st, 7-3-4-2	1856 edition
Fair Wind	1855	3rd, 8-0-2	
Fearless	1853	3rd, 3-9-7-5	1869 edition
Fleet Wing	1854	1st, 8-7-3-1	
Flyaway	1853	1st, 9-2-7-4	1856 edition
Flying Arrow	1852		
Flying Childers	1852	1st, 8-3-4-0	
Flying Cloud	1851	3rd, 3-4-7-1	
Flying Dragon	1853	1st, 9-1-5-0	
Flying Dutchman	1852	1st, 6-7-1-2	
Flying Eagle	1852		
Flying Fish	1851	1st, 3-9-2-7	
Flying Mist	1856	3rd, 4-0-6-3	
Galatea	1854	1st, 4-1-6-3	
Game Cock	1850	3rd, 3-5-0-1	
Gazelle	1851	1st, 4-2-0-6	1856 edition
Gem of the Ocean	1852	3rd, 9-8-4	
Golden Eagle	1852	1st, 4-6-0-8	
Golden Fleece (2nd)	1855	1st, 4-5-9-1	
Golden Light	1853	3rd, 1-7-9-2	
Golden West	1852	3rd, 6-1-7-4	
Grace Darling	1854	1st, 4-6-5-8	
Great Republic (original)	1853	1st, 9-2-5-3	
Great Republic (rebuilt)	1855	1st, 9-2-5-3	
Henry Hill Bark	1856	3rd, 3-4-6-8	
Herald of the Morning	1853	1st, 9-8-6-7	
Hoogly	1851	1st, 5-2-9-0	
Hurricane	1851	1st, 4-3-7-8	
Indiaman	1854	3rd, 4-0-9-8	
Intrepid	1856	1st, 5-4-9-0	1856 edition
Invincible	1851	1st, 5-6-4-0	
James Baines	1854	3rd, 2-1-8	Built to order for James Baines & Co., Live
John Bertram	1850	1st, 8-5-3-4	
John Gilpin	1852	3rd, 0-3-1-9	1869 edition
John Land	1853		
John Stuart	1851	1st, 7-6-9-5	1856 edition
John Wade	1851	3rd, 2-6-7-8	
Joseph Peabody	1856	3rd, 5-7-6-8	
King Fisher	1853	1st, 6-7-0-9	
Lady Franklin	1852	2nd, 6-8-2-5	
Lamplighter Bark	1854		
Lightfoot	1853	1st, 7-1-4-8	

488

Table 31.1. *Continued.*

Vessel	Year built	Marryat ID No.	Remarks	Vessel	Year built	Marryat ID No.	Remarks
Lightning	1854	1st, 7-1-4-9	Built to order for James Baines & Co., Liverpool.	Storm King	1853	2nd, 1-2-8-9	
Mameluke	1855	3rd, 9-8-3		Sultana Bark	1850	2nd, 1-3-4-5	
Mary Robinson	1854	3rd, 2-7-9-3		Sunny South	1854	3rd, 1-3-9	
Mastiff	1856	3rd, 1-7-8-0		Surprise	1850	2nd, 1-3-6-2	
Mermaid Bark	1851	1st, 8-3-5-9		Swallow	1854	2nd, 1-4-0-3	
Morning Light	1853	1st, 9-1-3-2		Sweepstakes	1853	2nd, 8-6-3-1	
Mystery	1853	1st, 4-0-5-2		Sword Fish	1851	2nd, 4-5-9-7	
Nightingale	1851	1st, 8-9-4-5	1856 edition	Syren	1851	2nd, 1-4-5-8	1856 edition
Noonday	1855	3rd, 1-2-8-7		Telegraph	1851	2nd, 1-5-2-9	
Northern Light	1851	1st, 9-1-6-3		Thatcher Magoun	1856	4th, 1-0-4-7	1869 edition
Ocean Express	1854	3rd, 8-4		Tornado	1850	2nd, 7-6-3-8	1856 edition
Ocean Pearl	1853	3rd, 9-3-4		Uncowah	1856	3rd, 3-9-5-6	1856 edition
Ocean Telegraph	1854	2nd, 9-7-4-5	1856 edition	War Hawk	1855	2nd, 8-7-5-4	
Onward	1852	1st, 6-0-4-2		Water Witch	1853	2nd, 2-5-0-9	
Osborne Howes	1854	3rd, 6-0-9-1	1869 edition	Western Continent	1853		
Panther	1854	1st, 9-3-5-2	1856 edition	Westward Ho	1852	3rd, 4-2-6-5	
Phantom	1852	1st, 9-5-7-4		West Wind	1853		
Queen of Clippers	1853	3rd, 5-0-7		Whirlwind	1852	3rd, 2-6-7	
Queen of the Pacific	1852	3rd, 4-7-9-2		Whistler	1853	2nd, 9-0-4-3	
Queen of the Seas	1852	2nd, 8-2-5-4		Wildfire Bark	1853	2nd, 9-1-5-3	
Quickstep Bark	1855	3rd, 1-7-0		Wild Pigeon	1851	2nd, 7-6-1-5	
Racehorse Bark	1850	2nd, 3-2		Wild Ranger	1853	3rd, 3-8-2-1	
Racer	1851	2nd, 3-4	1856 edition	Wild Rover	1853	3rd, 6-7-5-4	1869 edition
Radiant	1853	2nd, 4-6-1-9		Winged Arrow	1852	3rd, 4-3-8-6	
Raven	1851	2nd, 6-3	1856 edition	Winged Racer	1852	3rd, 7-9-0-4	1869 edition
Red Jacket	1853	2nd, 9-4-5-0	Sold British in 1854 after her first voyage (to Australia).	Witchcraft	1850	2nd, 7-2-4-5	
Robin Hood	1854	2nd, 3-2-7		Witch of the Wave	1851	2nd, 9-1-0-2	
Rocket Bark	1851	2nd, 3-5-1		Wizard	1853	2nd, 2-9-3-4	
Roebuck	1851	3rd, 3-2-4-0		Young America	1853	3rd, 4-2-5-3	
Romance of the Sea	1853	3rd, 1-7-0-3		Young Turk Bark	1856		
Santa Claus	1854	3rd, 2-7-9					
Saracen	1854	2nd, 6-4-9					
Sea Bird Bark	1851	2nd, 7-3-5					
Seaman's Bride	1851						
Sea Serpent	1850	2nd, 7-0-5-1					
Shooting Star	1851	2nd, 7-3-5-9					
Sierra Nevada	1854	3rd, 1-2-7-6					
Silver Star	1856	3rd, 4-0-9-3					
Southern Cross	1851	2nd, 8-2-0-6					
Sovereign of the Seas	1852	2nd, 9-0-2-7	1856 edition				
Spitfire	1853	3rd, 1-4-7-3					
Staffordshire	1851	2nd, 7-3-8-1					
Stag Hound	1850	3rd, 1-4-5-2					
Star of the Union	1852						
Starr King	1854	3rd, 5-4-3-6					

(text continued from page 487)

Letters of the alphabet, words of common usage, and messages germane to ships and the sea, were all assigned combinations of numerals (bound by the same digital restrictions as mentioned before) and entered in the codebook. This was the "code."

Provisions for transmitting numerical quantities were made by the use of the "numeral" pennant. Thus, if one vessel asked another, "How many miles are we from port?", the second vessel could reply "123" by hoisting the numeral pennant over flags 1–2–3. Without the numeral pennant, the flags would probably have had a code meaning.

Provisions for communicating by means of conversation, meaning messages that were outside the provisions of the code, were made by use of the "telegraph" flag. When this was hoisted, it meant that the flags that followed would spell out conversational words. Standard communication within the code consisted of selecting appropriate sentences and then hoisting only the group of numerals that was assigned to the sentence.

There is generally some confusion pertaining to the word "code" in signal systems. To many it seems to imply secrecy and arrangements of letters which must be unscrambled in order to be understood. Such arrangements are really *ciphers*, words or letters which are deliberately given arbitrary meanings that will be known only by those admitted to the cipher as developed. A *code*, in our sense, is merely a collection of words, letters, or numbers arranged in various combinations of convenience. The codebook contains this information, which becomes understandable on sight when the book is available. Its use could be compared to the use of a dictionary.

From the standpoint of the researcher or nautical scholar, it is noteworthy (and very convenient) that in the Marryat code of 1817 no flag or pennant could be confused with another if seen in black-and-white as an illustration on a printed page. All the geometric patterns differ except in the cases of numerals 1 and 8. However, in these two the dark and light colors are reversed, so any problem is eliminated.

In the 1854 revision, the added third distinguishing pennant (red) can be confused with the existing second distinguishing pennant (blue) under the same circumstances.

The addition, in 1869, of the fourth distinguishing pennant appeared to present a similar problem by having the same geometric pattern as the "numeral" pennant and having the darker color at the fly. However, with a ship's number these two would never appear in the same hoist.

Signal halliards were generally reeved through the mizzen truck.

Chapter Thirty-Two

ENTRY INTO VALHALLA: FATE OF THE VESSELS

UPON COMPLETION OF CONSTRUCTION, all clippers would soon put to sea amid high hopes and great expectations. The builders and owners, in many cases, hosted extravagant ceremonies, especially on the occasion of launchings of much-publicized vessels. Huge crowds, more than twenty thousand people in the case of the original *Great Republic,* turned out to watch and cheer as the ships slid into the water. For a few heady hours, everyone was oblivious to the one fact common to all ships, great and small: at some point in time, there would be a report of a disastrous or melancholy end.

Under routine circumstances, any ship was safe while tied up at a dock. However, "safe" was not "successful." The successful ship was the one that was constantly at sea contesting and overcoming the elements. The unavoidable truth that she would "go missing" someday was not a thought to be considered.

The means of "going missing" were as numerous as they were formidable. There was fire spontaneously generated deep in the hold; fire from a strike by lightning; fire from unrelated sources, such as the one that destroyed *Great Republic.* There were collisions with ships or rocks, groundings, bilging, hurricanes, gales, fierce squalls, foundering—all with the potential of destroying the best of vessels.

Paradoxically, of all the above calamities, only lightning strikes could be systematically thwarted, but against these almost nothing was done, as we have seen in Chapter 27. Of all the ships covered in this book, only the original *Great Republic* is reported to have been fitted with lightning conductors. Equally paradoxical is the fact that only one vessel, *Golden Light,* is specifically reported as being destroyed by lightning.

The potentially violent end to the life of a ship was accepted with as little concern as was the knowledge that life at sea was tough, hard, wet, and uncomfortable. There was not even the remote solace that your ship might be the one that would never come face to face with the above realities.

All of these fates were sad to contemplate, not only for the ship but also for the great losses of human life. However, many catastrophes were experienced with little or no loss of life, and the list of heroic rescues and feats of navigation in ships' boats is long and impressive.

Such calamities were considered to be the accepted risks—losses with dignity, in the sense of the vessels having succeeded in the purpose for which they were created. Relatively few losses were followed by sadness, recrimination, and finger pointing. The records show overwhelming support for the shipmasters' judgments.

The saddest fate to befall a ship was to encounter the day that it had outlived its usefulness. Clippers, due to their relatively small cargo space, were particularly subject to this assessment. Having weathered and conquered the sea in all its moods from serene to ugly, they could not overcome the grim statistics of economics. These vessels—ship rigged, with great speed that was no longer an asset, relatively small carrying capacity, and requiring large crews—had been built for a time that had since slipped into the pages of history. However, they were still too valuable to discard or to burn for their metals, so they began a tortuous path through a downgrading process.

Generally, the first step involved modifying the rigging from that of ship to that of a bark. Removing square yards and sails from the mizzenmast also allowed removal of a number of men from the crew. It was the first step in helping her to pay her way. This treatment was given a few ships even in their prime. Bark rig proved to be an excellent compromise between speed and economy.

When trade declined in poor financial times and freights were difficult to find, many vessels were downgraded another step: they were sold into the lumber trade and spent their days ferrying lumber in bulk from any location rich in timber to any port in need of timber. This was a docile, unimpressive existence, and any vessel might find herself in the trade until she came to an ultimate end.

There were, however, still lower types of existence in store for some vessels. Becoming a barge was the next logical step down. Clippers functioned well as barges; their fine ends made for little resistance when under tow. They were shorn of their masts and, for the first time in their existence, were no longer self-propelled. Any movement was now at the end of a tow line.

The ultimate degradation awaited a barge. There was no way up, only down—down to the category of coal hulk. These hulks were nothing more than huge, floating coal bins, and they fulfilled the purpose very well. Even these derelict remnants of a once proud clipper still possessed one redeeming feature. Having strong, solid bottoms, due to the great scantlings of the keelson assemblies that had been built into them, they could handle the great weight of bulk coal which filled their holds. It was a grimy, untidy, unglamorous end for any vessel that had seen the glory days.

There were other variations of this ending of the days of the clippers. Some were taken to Alaska by the salmon fishing industry to serve as floating refrigerators. And one, *James Baines*, was converted to a landing stage.

Finally, all of these proud vessels reached the day of reckoning and disappeared. Some were burned for their metal, some were broken up by the elements. Others grounded and sank, and more than a few rotted into oblivion.

The life span and date of destruction of the ships that were destroyed in their assigned line of work are quite easily found, merely because the event was recorded in a ship's log which survived, or the event was witnessed and reported. Such information about the vessels that lingered on and wasted away is not necessarily in existence due to lack of actual knowledge or lack of interest, or both. When the ship, in some altered form, was able to stubbornly remain afloat, there was often no one left to care when the end did come. In attempting to track such information, the trail slowly fades and, in many instances, the only inkling lies in the fact that the records abruptly cease.

The longevity of individual vessels is always interesting and rather fascinating. Why did some succumb so soon while others sailed the seas for years? Why were some ships favored with good fortune throughout their sailing life while others were constantly dogged by the vagaries of wind and weather? Why did some vessels, which were not lauded to the sky while still on the ways, sail time after time into the record books, as was the case with William H. Webb's wonderful clipper *Comet*, while others like his well-advertised *Challenge* never lived up to expectations? Answers are not really important, because their day has passed and nothing of practical importance can now be gained by knowing.

This book has followed the ships in detail from the day the first timber was laid on the ways until the day the ensign was first broken out. Throughout the pages, as each vessel developed, interest was kindled to a greater or lesser degree and, by the time the ships were launched, it would appear most natural to wonder what became of each vessel about which so much was known in detail. To this end Table 32.1 has been tabulated, and most but not all of the vessels have been accounted for as they made their entry into the Valhalla of ships.

The significant details of loss reveal many unusual circumstances and locations on the face of the globe. The ships probed every coast and port in all the continents except Africa; commercial trade in that region was minimal among the clippers. Also, the coasts of Russia and Japan saw almost nothing of American vessels. The rest of the maritime world was well accustomed to the sight of the American ensign.

In order to present the life spans in some orderly fashion, Table 32.2 has been compiled arranging the ships by longevity, starting with the very short-lived *Golden Light* and concluding with the very aged *Syren*. Among the many clippers not included in this book due to the lack of sufficient data, there might be some with a shorter life span than *Golden Light*. However, it is a fact that, of all the clippers, *Syren* survived the longest in years and was also the last known survivor of this fascinating class of vessels.

The entries in Table 32.2 indicate that specific dates of loss are more numerous for vessels that survived for ten years or less. Then, as the time frame is extended, approximate dates become more prevalent. The most elusive data is that which is required to determine the actual life span of vessels noted as "minimum." In these cases, the ships are accounted for to a certain point, after which they slip into oblivion. There can be no doubt that somewhere, hidden away in unlikely places, some of this data survives. However, it is brought to light more by good fortune than by diligent research.

The known fact, applicable to all the clippers, is that they were created as things of beauty and, after short or long, eventful or mundane lives, they disappeared one by one, each to become a small part of a unique period of wooden shipbuilding history. Now they belong to the ages. *Requiescat in pace.*

Table 32.1. *Life span and fate of the vessels.*

Notes: Sailing life is the length of time spent sailing as a legitimate trader and does not include time spent as a barge, coal hulk or other non-sailing conversion.

Sailing life is indicated as: y - years; m - months; w - weeks.

( ) - Indicates approximate date or life span.
[ ] - Indicates inconclusive life span.
Min. - Indicates minimum life based on data in this table.

Vessels noted as no longer being listed may have been sold and the name changed, rather than actually being lost.

RAFS - Record of American and Foreign Shipping, issued as of 1 January of the year published.

All dates are 1800's except as noted.

Vessel & Ref.#	Date of launch	Date of loss	Sailing life, y,m,w	Circumstances of loss or final end
Alarm #32	3.18.56	11.18.63	7.8.0	Struck on south end of Preparis Reef, enroute to Singapore from Akyab, Burma. Filled and was abandoned 18 November 1863.
Amphitrite #1,32	6. .53	. .	1. 6. min.	Sold British 1855, renamed Result.
Andrew Jackson #32	3. .55	12. 4.68	(13. 9.)	Sold British 1863. Went ashore on reef in Gaspar Straits, between Sumatra and Borneo, enroute to Glasgow from Shanghai. Became a total loss.
Antelope #1,32	11. .51	8. 6.58	(6. 9.)	Struck on Discovery Shoal, Paracels Reef, in China Sea, Lat 17°N, Lon 112°E, enroute to China from Bangkok, Siam, and was abandoned 6 August 1858.
Asa Eldridge #1,32	10. .56	(1. .80)	[23. 2.]	Sold British 1873, renamed Norfolk. Still registered in 1880. Not listed thereafter.
Bald Eagle #32,124	11.25.52	10.15.61	8.10.3	Sailed from Hong Kong 15 October 1861 and went missing. Apparently foundered in a severe typhoon.
Belle of the West #32	3.25.53	6. .68	(15. 3.)	Sold Indian at Calcutta 1864, renamed Fiery Cross. Foundered in May/June 1868, in Bay of Bengal, enroute to Muscat, Arabia, from Calcutta.
Beverly #32	4.19.52	9. .72	[20. 5.]	Sold Batavian (Java) 1864, renamed Alexander. Sold again. Renamed Argonaut 1867, Mauritius registry. Sold September 1872, Nova Scotia registry. Not listed in 1873 Lloyds.
Black Hawk #26,37,126,129	12.29.56	2. .91	(34. 2.)	Sold German 1880. Sold Norwegian 1889, renamed Christiania. Reported damaged by fire and condemned February 1891.
Blue Jacket #32	8.27.54	3.16.69	14. 6.3	Caught fire off Cape Horn 5 March 1869. Abandoned 16 March 1869.
Bonita #32	5.12.53	6.18.57	4. 1.1	Put into Algoa Bay, Port Elizabeth, South Africa, 18 June 1857, leaking badly. There she was abandoned.
Bounding Billow Bark #1,127	9. .54	9. .55	(1. .)	Prior to 8 September 1855, enroute to Smyrna (Izmir), Turkey, from Boston ran ashore at Smyrna.
Celestial #26	6.10.50	. .61	[10. 6.]	Sold Spanish 1858. Owned by Bartolmeo Bianco, New York, in 1861. No further record of her career.
Challenge #32,125	5.24.51	. .79	(27. 7.)	In 1875 was British owned, listed as Golden City. In 1879 lost her rudder off Scilly Islands (Land's End, England), was abandoned, and drifted to Ushant Island off Finisterre, France. Went ashore near Aberfranche and broke up.
Challenger #32	12.19.53	10. .75	(21.10.)	Sold Peruvian 1864, renamed Camille Cavour. Was badly damaged in a gale off the coast of Mexico in October, 1875, enroute to Peru from Port Discovery, N.W. of Seattle, and was abandoned.
Champion of the Seas #32	4.19.54	1. 3.76	21. 8.2	Abandoned off Cape Horn, leaky and in sinking condition 3 January 1876.
Charger #32	10.25.56	12.14.73	17. 1.2	Piled up on reef, 10 miles from Cebu, Philippine Islands, 14 December 1873. Began to break up one week later. The wreck was sold.
Charmer #32	10.28.54	. .77	[22. 2.]	Sold British 1863. Listed in 1877 Lloyds. Not listed in 1878.

Table 32.1. *Continued.*

Vessel & Ref.#	Date of launch	Date of loss	Sailing life, y,m,w	Circumstances of loss or final end
Cleopatra #32	3.28.53	9.25.55	2. 6.0	Struck a submerged wreck 23 September 1855, enroute to New York from Callao, Peru. Wreck was located in Lat 23°31'S, Lon 31°19'W. Vessel foundered 25 September 1855.
Climax #1,32	2. .53	. .65	[11.10.]	Sold Peruvian 1855, renamed Antonio Terry. Sold again at Hong Kong, 1865. Not listed in 1866 Lloyds.
Coeur de Lion #32,78	1. 3.54	8. .1915	(61. 7.)	In May 1872 was Russian, renamed Zaritza. In 1882 was Swedish with the same name but re-rigged as a bark. Wrecked August 1915 in collision off the Skagerak, in the Baltic Sea.
Comet #26,32	7.10.51	(4.22.65)	(13. 9.2)	Sold British 1863, renamed Fiery Star. On 1 April 1865 left Moreton Bay, Queensland, Australia, bound for London. Three weeks later fire broke out in her hold. The captain and 80 persons took to three boats and were never again heard from. Shortly after, the portion of the crew still on board were rescued by the British bark Dauntless when about ready to sink.
Cyclone #32	8.18.53	. .66	[12. 4.]	Sold British 1863, renamed Avon. Registered as owned by M. Nolan, London, 1866.
Daring #32	10. 8.55	(1. .70)	[14. 2.]	Condemned, sold, repaired and went British 1865. Listed 1870. Not listed in 1874 registers.
Dauntless #1,32	12. .51	10.23.53	(1.11.)	Sailed from Boston 23 October 1853, bound for Valparaiso, Chile, and was never again heard from. Lost with all hands.
Donald McKay #32,47	1. .55	(1. .85)	(30. .)	Sold German 1879. Listed in 1885 RAFS. Not listed in 1886 RAFS. Eventually went to Madeira as a coal hulk.
Don Quixote #32	9. .53	. .	20. 3. min.	Sold French 1864, renamed St. Aubin. Classed A-1 by Lloyds in 1874.
Eagle #32	5. 3.51	. .	10. 7. min.	Sold Indian at Calcutta 1862, renamed Turkey.
Eagle Wing #32	10. 4.53	(2.11.65)	(11. 4.1)	Sailed from Boston 11 February 1865, destination Bombay. Was officially posted as missing in October 1865.
Edwin Forrest #32	10. 5.53	(8. 1.60)	(7. .)	Left New York 1 August 1860, destination Hong Kong. Never again heard from.
Electric Spark #32	11.17.55	6.26.69	13. 7.1	Stranded at Blackwater Head, Wexford, Ireland, 26 June 1869. Crew was taken off by a lifeboat. Vessel broke up 28 June 1869.
Ellen Foster #1,32	4. .52	12. .67	(15. 8.)	Condemned and sold at Callao, Peru in July 1867. After repairs went ashore in December 1867 at Neah Bay, close to her destination, enroute to Puget Sound from Callao.
Empress of the Sea #32	1.14.53	12.19.61	8.11.1	Caught fire 19 December 1861 at Queenscliff Bight, Port Phillip, Australia, and became a total loss.
Endeavor #1,32	4. .56	. .75	(18. 8.)	Destroyed by fire in Japan, 1875.
Eringo Bark #1	12. .53	. .	. .	Sold British 1863. Condemned at Calcutta in June 1866.
Eureka #32	2. 9.51	6. .66	(15. 4.)	Sold British 1866. Still sailing 1875.
Fair Wind #32	10.12.55	. .	19. 3. min.	
Fearless #32,44	7.28.53	. .92	38. 5. min.	Sold Norwegian, October 1878, renamed Johanne, re-rigged as a bark. Surveyed at Halifax, Nova Scotia, in June 1885 but no class was assigned. Last reported 1892. End uncertain.
Fleet Wing #1,32	1. .54	3.27.85	(31. 2.)	Inspected at Melbourne, Australia, 27 March 1885. Found in such poor condition that she was condemned.
Flyaway #26	6.23.53	1.20.81	27. 7.0	Sold Spanish, March 1859, renamed Concepcion. In 1875 was British owned, re-rigged as a bark, renamed Bothalwood. On 20 January 1881 she stranded and became a total loss at St. Ouen's Bay, Island of Jersey, enroute to Leith, Scotland from Cartagena, Spain.
Flying Arrow #32	12. .52	3.20.56	(3. 4.)	Sold British 1856, renamed Wings of the Wind. On 20 March 1856 sailed from London, destination Calcutta. Nothing further.

Table 32.1. *Continued.*

Vessel & Ref.#	Date of launch	Date of loss	Sailing life, y,m,w	Circumstances of loss or final end
Flying Childers #32	11.11.52	. .	12. 1. min.	Sold British, January 1863, renamed Golden South. Listed British 1865. Became a coal hulk at Port Jackson and many years later was destroyed by fire due to sparks from another burning ship.
Flying Cloud #32	4.15.51	. .74	(22. 8.)	Sold British 1862. Went ashore on Beacon Island, Newfoundland, bar in 1874. Broke her back, was condemned and sold. Was burned in 1875 for her metals.
Flying Dragon #32	6. .53	1.29.62	(8. 7.)	On 29 January 1862, enroute to San Francisco from Newcastle, New South Wales, struck on Arch Rock in San Francisco harbor and foundered. On the 30th she rolled over on her starboard side and sank from sight.
Flying Dutchman #26	9. 9.52	2.14.58	5. 5.1	On 14 February 1858, enroute to New York from San Francisco, she stranded at Brigantine Beach, New Jersey. On 22 February she was filled and rapidly breaking up.
Flying Eagle #32	12. .52	7.22.79	(26. 7.)	On 22 July 1879 she arrived at Mauritius Island (east of Madagascar) in distress. Was condemned and sold prior to 22 September 1879.
Flying Fish #32	9. .51	. .	7. 2. min.	On 23 November 1858, enroute to New York from Foo Chow, China, she stranded on a sand bank at the mouth of river Min. On the 25th she was got off slightly leaky. A survey reported her badly damaged. Was condemned and sold. Taken to Whampoa she was rebuilt and renamed El Bueno Suceso and, years later, foundered in the China Sea.
Flying Mist #32	9.13.56	8.26.62	5.11.2	Blown ashore 26 August 1862, after being properly anchored, at Bluff Harbor, New Zealand, after arrival from the Clyde (Scotland). Became a total loss. (Of 1760 sheep on board, only 820 were saved.)
Galatea #32	3.16.54	(1. .85)	[30. 9.]	Sold Norwegian, July 1882. Listed in 1885 RAFS. Not listed in 1886 RAFS.
Game Cock #32	12.21.50	2. .80	(29. 2.)	Condemned February 1880 at the Cape of Good Hope.
Gazelle #26,32	1.21.51	(1. .62)	[11. .]	Damaged by typhoon, condemned and sold Peruvian, October 1854, renamed Cora. Later sold British, renamed Harry Puddemsey. Last listed in 1862 registers.
Gem of the Ocean #1,32	8. .52	8. 1.79	(27. .)	In November 1867 struck a sunken rock near Bellingham Bay, Washington. Was refloated, repaired and re-rigged as a bark. Went ashore on Vancouver Island, 1 August 1879, enroute to San Francisco from Seattle, and was a total loss.
Golden Eagle #32	11. 9.52	2.21.63	10. 3.2	On 21 February 1863, in Lat 29°N, Lon 45°W, she was captured and burned by CSS Alabama.
Golden Fleece (2nd) #32	11.20.55	11.19.77	22. 0.0	On 19 November 1877, enroute to San Francisco from New York, grounded on English Bank, at the mouth of Rio de la Plata, Uruguay. Surveyed at Montevideo, she was condemned and ultimately sold.
Golden Light #32	1. 8.53	2.22.53	0. 1.2	On 22 February 1853, enroute to San Francisco from Boston, on her first voyage, she was struck by lightning in Lat 22°23'N, Lon 45°47'W. Four of her five boats, with 27 of her 35 people, were picked up.
Golden West #32	11.16.52	. .	13. 2. min.	Sold British at auction, 1863. In 1866 was in the coolie trade between China and Peru.
Grace Darling #1,32	5. .54	1.18.78	(23. 8.)	Sailed from Nanaimo, British Columbia, 3 January 1878. While hove to in a heavy gale she was sighted by the ship Melancthon on 18 January. Nothing was heard of her thereafter.
Great Republic (1853) #32	10. 4.53	12.27.53	0. 2.3	Burned and sank at her wharf in New York while onloading her first cargo. The fire started in the nearby Novelty Baking Co., 242 Front Street, New York, on 26 December 1853. She was given over to the underwriters on 27 December 1853.

Table 32.1. *Continued.*

Vessel & Ref.#	Date of launch	Date of loss	Sailing life, y,m,w	Circumstances of loss or final end
Great Republic (1855) #28,32	1. .55	3. 5.72	(17. 2.)	Sold Nova Scotian 1866. Sold British 1869, renamed Denmark. On 2 March 1872, enroute to St. John, New Brunswick, from Rio de Janeiro, she started to leak in a strong gale. On 5 March she was abandoned in sinking condition.
Henry Hill Bark #1	6. .56	. . .	. . .	
Herald of the Morning #32	12. .53	1. .91	[38. .]	Sold Norwegian 1879 and was re-rigged as a bark. Sailed British 1890. Not listed 1891.
Hoogly #1,32	12. .51	8.20.52	(0. 9.0)	On 20 August 1852, enroute to Shanghai from San Francisco, she stranded in the Huangp'u Chiang as she arrived at Shanghai, becoming a total loss.
Hurricane #32	10.25.51	(1. .76)	[24. 3.]	Sold British 1860 at Singapore, renamed Shaw-Allum. Listed in 1876 registers.
Indiaman #1,32	11. .54	. .83	(28. .)	Sold British 1862, renamed Indian Merchant. Last reported 1883.
Intrepid #26,128	4.23.56 Ref. 26 gives date of launch as June 1856.	3.31.60	3.11.1	On 31 March 1860, enroute to New York from Macao (southern China), she ran aground on Belvedere Reef, in the Gaspar Straits (the western passage between Sumatra and Borneo.) On 1 April, after battling pirates, the crew fired the ship and took to her boats. They were picked up shortly after. The wreck was reputedly towed to Singapore and sold.
Invincible #32	8. 6.51	9.11.67	16. 1.1	On 11 September 1867, while being onloaded in Brooklyn, fire was discovered on board. She was towed out and beached on Governor's Island becoming a total loss.
James Baines #32	7.25.54	4.22.58	3. 8.3	On 22 April 1858, four days after arriving at Liverpool from Calcutta, fire was discovered in her hold. She was scuttled but the fire burned her to the water's edge. The wreck was sold at auction and was later converted to a landing stage.
John Bertram #32	12. 9.50	3.17.83	32. 3.1	Sold German 1855. Later sold Norwegian. Sailed from New York 22 February 1883, destination Rotterdam. On 17 March her wreck was sighted and her crew picked up.
John Gilpin #1	9. .52	1.30.58	(5. 5.)	On 30 January 1858, enroute to Honolulu from Boston, she was abandoned about 150 miles from the Falkland Islands, having struck the submerged portion of an iceberg. Her hold filled with 15 feet of water and she accidentally caught fire becoming a total loss.
John Land #32	3.26.53	3.25.64	11. 0.0	On 28 February 1864, enroute to New York from Newport, England, she sprang a leak. On 25 March, filling fast, she was abandoned in Lat 39°N, Lon 65°W.
John Stuart #4,32	10. .51	(1. .70)	[18. 2.]	Sold British at Bombay, June 1863. Appears in 1870 register, B.F. Camoa, owner.
John Wade #1,32	8. .51	3.28.59	(7. 7.)	On 28 March 1859, enroute to Hong Kong from Bangkok, Siam, she struck an uncharted rock in the Gulf of Siam and became a total loss.
Joseph Peabody #32	6. 7.56	(1. .74)	[17. 6.]	Sold British 1863, renamed Dagmar. In 1874 register she is listed as a bark. Not listed in 1875 Lloyds.
King Fisher #32	8.18.53	. .90	(36. 5.)	On 20 June 1871, enroute to San Francisco from New York, she sprang a leak and put in to Montevideo, Uruguay, in distress. Was surveyed, condemned and, in November 1871, was sold to the Cibils family of that city. She was repaired, renamed Jaime Cibils and sailed under the Uruguayan flag until 1890 when she was sold at auction and broken up in Montevideo Bay.
Lady Franklin #32	. .52	10. .56	(3.10.)	In October 1856, enroute to Trieste, Austria, from New York, she was abandoned.

Table 32.I. *Continued.*

Vessel & Ref.#	Date of launch	Date of loss	Sailing life, y,m,w	Circumstances of loss or final end
Lamplighter Bark #1	6. .54	3. .77	(22. 9.)	In March 1877, was off Bermuda in distress and was driven out to sea.
Lightfoot #1,32	8. .53	6.29.55	(1.10.)	On 29 June 1855, enroute to Calcutta from London, was totally wrecked near Saugor, mouth of the Hooghly River, Calcutta.
Lightning #32	1. 3.54	10.31.69	15. 9.4	On 31 October 1869, while at her wharf at Geelong, Melbourne, Australia, fire was discovered in her hold. She was towed into the stream and scuttled in 24 feet of water. Was later destroyed as a menace to navigation.
Mameluke #1,32	8.30.55	(1. .74)	[18. 4.]	Sold British 1863, renamed Milton. Listed in 1874 registers.
Mary Robinson #31,32	. .54	6.27.64	(9. 6.)	On 27 June 1864, while loading guano at Howland's Island, in the Pacific, Lat 1°N, Lon 176°W, she was driven on the reef by a squall. Lost her rudder and started to leak. On 28 June slid off the reef and went under in deep water.
Mastiff #1,32	1. .56	9.10.59	(3. 8.)	On 10 September 1859, when five days out, enroute to Hong Kong from San Francisco, caught fire and was lost.
Mermaid Bark #1,14	3.20.51	3. 2.56	4.11.2	On 2 March 1856, enroute to China from Bombay, grounded on Pratas Shoal, about 200 miles east of Hong Kong and was a total loss.
Morning Light #78	8.20.53	. .	15. 4. min.	Sold British 1863, renamed Queen of the South. Sold again 1 February 1867. Sailed under charter 1869.
Mystery #32	1.11.53	. .	17.10. min.	Sold British at London, March 1854. Still sailing 1871.

Vessel & Ref.#	Date of launch	Date of loss	Sailing life, y,m,w	Circumstances of loss or final end
Nightingale #32,47	6.16.51	4.17.93	41.10.0	Sold at auction 6 September 1851 at No. 22, Long Wharf, Boston, and was re-sold shortly after. Sold in 1860 to an American, Capt. Francis Bowen. Sailed to London, fitted out as a "slaver" and, on 24 November 1860, cast off for Africa. At St. Thomas, West Coast Africa, was boarded by the U.S. gun boat Mystic on 14 January 1861. Passed inspection but was under suspicion. On 20 April she was again boarded and 961 slaves were found. Sent as a prize to New York she was purchased by the U.S. Gov't. on 6 July. Was sold out of the navy at auction 11 February 1865. Was sailing Norwegian in the lumber trade in 1882. On 17 April 1893, rigged as a bark, enroute to Halifax, Nova Scotia from Liverpool, was abandoned at sea.
Noonday #32,78	8.25.55	1. 1.63	7. 4.1	On 1 January 1863, approaching San Francisco harbor from Boston, struck a rock at Farallon, glided clear but with her bottom stove in. Started to fill and sank in 40 fathoms. The rock is now known as Noonday Rock.
Northern Light #32	9.25.51	1. 2.62	10. 3.1	On 2 January 1862, enroute to New York from Havre, France, collided with the French brig Nouveau St. Jacques. The brig sank and Northern Light was abandoned a few hours later. All hands of both crews were picked up and landed at Cowes, Isle of Wight, England.
Ocean Express #32	7.10.54	. .90	(16. .)	Sold in Peru, 1871. In December 1872 was under the flag of San Salvador [sic]. Between 1873-1876 sailed under Peruvian and Costa Rican flags. In 1876, in New York, was sold German, renamed Friedrich. In 1890 was under the Norwegian flag and reported abandoned in the North Atlantic.

Table 32.1. *Continued.*

Vessel & Ref.#	Date of launch	Date of loss	Sailing life, y,m,w	Circumstances of loss or final end
Ocean Pearl #32	8.15.53	10.27.64	11. 2.2	On 27 October 1864, enroute to Lisbon from New York, she put in to Tarragona, Spain, and went ashore in a gale, becoming a total loss.
Ocean Telegraph #32	3.29.54	2. .83	(28.10.)	Sold British 1863, renamed Light Brigade. Appeared bark rigged, 1875. In February 1883 arrived at Queenstown (Cobh), Ireland, leaking badly. Was converted to a coal hulk for use at Gibraltar where she served many years.
Onward #32,81	7. 3.52	11.13.84	(32. 4.1)	On 9 September 1861, was sold to the U.S. Gov't. and became a sailing cruiser fourth class; mounted one 30 pdr Parrott rifle and eight 32 pdrs. At close of Civil War became a storeship at Callao, Peru. On 13 November 1884 was sold out of the navy.
Osborne Howes #32	7.27.54	. .70	(15. 5.)	Sold British, June 1864. Her name last appears in 1870 registers.
Panther #32	1 or 2. .54	1.17.84	(20. .)	On 17 January 1874, enroute to San Francisco from Nanaimo, British Columbia, she stranded off Vancouver Island. After the tug cast off she went ashore on a reef. Thirty days later, filled, she was abandoned.
Phantom #32	12. 8.52	7.13.62	9. 7.1	On 13 July 1862, enroute to Hong Kong from San Francisco, she ran on to Pilot Reef, off Pratas Shoal, about 200 miles east of Hong Kong, in thick weather and was abandoned.
Queen of Clippers #32	3.26.53	. .	2. 8. min.	Was under French Gov't. charter during the Crimean War, 1854-1856, as a transport. Sold French at Marsailles, 1856, renamed Reina des Clippers. Apparently met an unknown fate a few years later.
Queen of the Pacific #32	11. .52	9.19.59	(6.10.)	In early 1857 she put in to St. Thomas, Virgin Islands, leaking badly. Was condemned, sold and repaired. On 19 September 1859, enroute to San Francisco from New York she was lost on a reef 180 miles north of Pernambuco, Brazil, breaking in two amidships.
Queen of the Seas #32	9.18.52	9.21.60	8. 0.0	On 21 September 1860, enroute to Shanghai from Liverpool, foundered in the Formosa Channel, in a hurricane.
Quickstep Bark #1	11.17.55	. .	. .	Vanished early 1865.
Racehorse Bark #1,44	6. .50	. .65	(14. 6.)	On 6 May 1856, enroute to New York from Liverpool, struck on Arklow Bank, near Wicklow, east coast of Ireland. Settled on one side and was abandoned.
Racer #3,32	6.18.51	5. 6.56	4.10.2	Sold at Calcutta, 1863. Appears in 1868 register.
Radiant #32	1.24.53	(1. .68)	[14.11.]	Launched fully rigged. In 1863, enroute to San Francisco from New York, put in to Rio de Janeiro, leaking badly and was condemned. At the time was bark rigged. Sold Brazilian 1864, renamed Bessie. In 1871 appears Portugese in American Lloyds, renamed Don Antonia dos Santos. In 1875 is registered Mondego, Portugese.
Raven #32	7. 1.51	. .	23. 5. min.	Sold British, October 1854. In the timber trade in 1882. Was a coal hulk in after 1882.
Red Jacket #32	11. 2.53	. .82	(28. 1.)	On 20 August 1869, at Baker's Island, mid-Pacific Ocean, Lat 1°N, Lon 176°W, she was destroyed by fire, apparently set by some of the crew.
Robin Hood #32	4. .54	8.20.69	(15. 4.)	On 28 January 1859, enroute to Philadelphia from Boston, struck Willie's Rocks, Cohasset, Massachusetts and sank.
Rocket Bark #1	12. .51	. .	. .	On 31 December 1862 departed Hong Kong enroute to New York. Was never again heard from. Officially posted missing April 1863.
Roebuck #1,32	12. .51	1.28.59	(7. 1.)	On 9 August 1863, in Lat 5°N, Lon 45°W, enroute to Hamburg, Germany, from Callao, Peru, she was abandoned in sinking condition off St. Thomas, Virgin Islands.
Romance of the Sea #32	10.23.53	12.31.62	9. 2.1	
Santa Claus #32	9. 5.54	8. 9.63	8.11.1	

Table 32.1. *Continued.*

Vessel & Ref.#	Date of launch	Date of loss	Sailing life, y,m,w	Circumstances of loss or final end
Saracen #1,32	10. .54	. .	11. 2. min.	Sold Italian, December 1865, renamed Teresa.
Sea Bird Bark #1	11. .51			
Seaman's Bride #32	6.25.51		3.10. min.	Sold German about May 1855, renamed Carl Staegoman.
Sea Serpent #78	11.20.50	6.12.91	40. 6.3	Sold Norwegian, May 1874, renamed Progress. On 12 June 1891, enroute to Dublin from Quebec, she was abandoned at sea. She drifted 1120 miles in 93 days. Was sighted 19 times before disappearing.
Shooting Star #32	2. 8.51	. .67	(16. .)	Sold Siamese about 1857. In 1867 was reported wrecked on the coast of Formosa.
Sierra Nevada #32,78	5.30.54	. .77	(22. 6.)	Sold British, March 1863, renamed Royal Dane. In 1877, enroute to Liverpool from Callao, Peru, was wrecked on the coast of Chile.
Silver Star #1,32	4. .56	11.10.60	(4. 6.)	On 10 November 1860, was wrecked at Jarvis Island in the Pacific Ocean, in Lat 0°3′ S, Lon 160°30′W, while loading guano.
Southern Cross #32	3.19.51	6. 6.63	12.11.3	On 6 June 1863 was captured by CSS Florida in the Atlantic Ocean, just south of the equator, and burned.
Sovereign of the Seas #1,32	6. .52	. .59	(6. 6.)	Sold German at Liverpool, 1854. In 1859, enroute to China from Hamburg, she ran on Pyramid Shoal in the Straits of Malacca, between Sumatra and the Malay Peninsula, and became a total loss.
Spitfire #32	9. 3.53	. .	15. 4. min.	Sold British, April 1863. Listed in 1869 registers.
Staffordshire #32	6.17.51	12.24.53	2. 6.1	On 24 December 1853, enroute to Boston from Liverpool, she struck Blonde Rock, about 4 miles from Seal Island, near Cape Sable, Nova Scotia. On the 25th she slid off and sank. Of 214 persons on board, 44 were saved.
Stag Hound #32	12. 7.50	10.12.61	10.10.1	On 12 October 1861, enroute to San Francisco from Sunderland, England, fire was discovered below when she was 45 miles south of Pernambuco, Brazil. Four boats got out with all hands. At 5 P.M. she was burning to the water's edge. All boats made Pernambuco.
Star of the Union #32	12. 9.52	11. .66	(13.11.)	In November 1866 she was reported at Rio de Janeiro, in distress, after collision off Cape Horn with the British bark Simon Habley. Reported condemned and sold. Not in 1869 registers.
Starr King #32	. .54	6. .62	(8. 6.)	In June 1862, enroute to Singapore from Hong Kong, went ashore on Point Romania and became a total loss.
Storm King #1,32	2. .53	(1. .75)	[22.11.]	Sold British in Hong Kong, April 1863. Listed in 1875 registers.
Sultana Bark #1	6. .50	. .	. .	
Sunny South #32	10. 7.54	8.10.60	5.10.0	Sold at Havana 1859, renamed Emanuela, and went into the slave trade. On 10 August 1860 was captured in Mozambique Channel, between Madagascar and Africa, by the British sloop-of-war Brisk. Sold British as a cruiser.
Surprise #32	10. 5.50	2. 4.56	5. 4.0	On 4 February 1856, enroute to Yokohama, Japan from New York, she struck Plymouth Rocks near Yeddo Bay. All hands got off. On 8 February she was found floating bottom up.
Swallow #32	4. 4.54	. .85	(30. 8.)	In 1885, enroute to Sydney, Australia, from Liverpool, began to leak soon after leaving port and was abandoned at sea due to pumps choking.

Table 32.1. Continued.

Vessel & Ref.#	Date of launch	Date of loss	Sailing life, y,m,w	Circumstances of loss or final end
Water Witch #32,78	5. 6.53	6. 1.55	2. 0.4	On 1 June 1855 in the roadstead of Ypala, at San Blas, Mexico, she dragged her anchors, went on the rocks and was bilged. (Ref.78 reports her at Mazatlan, Mexico.)
Western Continent #31	. .53	. .	. .	
Westward Ho #32,124	9.14.52	2.27.64	11. 5.2	On 27 February 1864, caught fire in the harbor at Callao, Peru, and burned until she sank.
West Wind #32	3. .53	. .	10. 1. min.	Sold British in April 1863, renamed Lord Clyde.
Whirlwind #32	9.13.52	11.27.60	8. 2.2	Last reported at Calcutta, 27 November 1860.
Whistler #32	6.15.53	5.23.55	1.11.1	On 23 May 1855, enroute to Singapore from Port Philip, Melbourne, Australia, went ashore on King's Island, Bass Straits, and became a total loss.
Wildfire Bark #1	4. .53	. .	. .	
Wild Pigeon #32	7.31.51	2.17.92	40. 6.2	Sold Spanish about 1865. In 1868 she appears as Bella Juana, later as Voladora. Listed the same in 1882 RAFS. On 17 February 1892, rigged as a bark, she was abandoned in the Atlantic Ocean, in Lat 27°N, Lon 68°W.
Wild Ranger #32	4. 7.53	. .72	(18. 8.)	On 3 January 1862, enroute to Boston from Gravesend, England, collided with British Coleroon. Was libeled, auctioned under writ. Went British 1862 and was renamed Ocean Chief. In 1872, enroute to Rio de Janeiro, is reported to have foundered after collision with a steamer.
Wild Rover #32	. .53	. .71	(18. .)	In 1871 she went ashore at Jones Inlet, Long Island and became a total loss.
Winged Arrow #1	7. .52	. .	18. 5. min.	In 1868 was sold to the Russo-American Fur Co. Listed in 1871 registers.
Winged Racer #32	11. .52	11.10.63	(11. .)	On 10 November 1863, enroute to New York from Manila, was captured in Sunda Straits and burned by CSS Alabama.

Vessel & Ref.#	Date of launch	Date of loss	Sailing life, y,m,w	Circumstances of loss or final end
Sweepstakes #32	6.21.53	5.13.62	8.10.3	On 24 April 1862 arrived at Batavia (Djakarta), Java from Adelaide after spending ten hours on a reef in Sunda Straits between Java and Sumatra. Extensively injured she was sold out of service on 13 May 1862, her career ended.
Sword Fish #26,32	9.20.51	7. 9.62	10. 9.2	On 9 July 1862 left Shanghai for Amoy (Hsiamen), China, in Formosa Strait. Fouled her anchors while still in the Yangtze River and went to pieces on the north shore.
Syren #32	5. 1.51	1. .1920	(68. 7.)	On 25 June 1888 she put in to Rio de Janeiro leaking badly. Was surveyed, condemned, sold, repaired and then re-rigged as the bark Margarida, of Buenos Aires, Argentina. Listed in 1920 Lloyds register. She was the longest lived of all the clippers, whether or not included in this book.
				Note: Dashing Wave, launched 15 July 1853, stranded on the mud flats of Seymour Narrows in March 1920. However, she had been a barge for some years. Life span approx. 66 years, 8 months.
Telegraph #32	5. .51	. .68	(16. 7.)	Sold Peruvian in August, 1865, renamed Compania Maritima del Peru, No.2. Sold Italian 1866, renamed Galileo. In 1868 reported as burned at sea.
Thatcher Magoun #1,14,32	4.25.56	(1. .82)	[25. 8.]	Sold Norwegian about 1874, renamed Hercules. Listed in 1882 RAFS. Reported lost off the coast of Africa in the early 1880's. Not listed 1884.
Tornado #3	12.21.50	. .	. .	
Uncowah #26	10.15.56	9. .70	(13.10.)	Sold Peruvian 1865. In autumn of 1870, enroute to Callao, Peru, from Macao, China, with almost 540 coolies on board, she was fired by the coolies near Neptune (?) Island. She was destroyed along with 425 coolies burned or drowned.
War Hawk #32	1. 3.55	4.12.83	28. 3.1	On 12 April 1883, after arrival at Port Discovery, Puget Sound, Washington, was found to be on fire. She was scuttled and went on her beam ends under water.

Table 32.1. *Continued.*

Vessel and Ref.#	Date of launch	Date of loss	Sailing life, y,m,w	Circumstances of loss or final end
Witchcraft #32	12.21.50	4. 8.61	10. 3.2	On 8 April 1861, enroute to Hampton Roads, Virginia, from Callao, Peru, went ashore on Chickamaconic in sight of Cape Hatteras and Bodie Island lights. Was pounded to pieces.
Witch of the Wave #32,47,78	4. 5.51	(1. .86)	[34. 8.]	Sold Holland 1855, renamed Electra. Listed as bark rigged in 1882 RAFS. Listed in 1886 RAFS. Not listed 1887.
Wizard #1,32	4. .53	. .74	(20. 8.)	Sold British in November 1862, renamed Queen of the Colonies. Reported wrecked enroute to Falmouth, England from Java, in 1874.
Young America #26	4.30.53	(2.17.86)	(32. 9.2)	Sold Austrian in October 1883, renamed Miroslav. Sailed from Delaware Breakwater, 17 February 1886 and was never heard from again.
Young Turk Bark #1	11. 1.56	. .	. .	

Table 32.2. *Progressive longevity of the vessels based on data in Table 32.1.*

Vessel	Sailing life, y,m,w	Vessel	Sailing life, y,m,w	Vessel	Sailing life, y,m,w	Vessel	Sailing life, y,m,w
Golden Light	0. 1.2	Queen of the Pacific	(6.10.)	Saracen	11. 2. min.	Charger	17. 1.2
Great Republic (1853)	0. 2.3	Edwin Forrest	(7. .)	Ocean Pearl	11. 2.2	Great Republic (1855)	(17. 2.)
Hoogly	(0. 9.)	Roebuck	(7. 1.)	Eagle Wing	(11. 4.1)	Joseph Peabody	[17. 6.]
Bounding Billow Bark	(1. .)	Flying Fish	7. 2. min.	Westward Ho	11. 5.2	Mystery	17.10. min.
Amphitrite	1. 6. min.	Noonday	7. 4.1	Climax	[11.10.]	Wild Rover	(18. .)
Lightfoot	(1.10.)	John Wade	(7. 7.)	Flying Childers	12. 1. min.	John Stuart	[18. 2.]
Dauntless	(1.11.)	Alarm	7. 8.0	Cyclone	[12. 4.]	Mameluke	[18. 4.]
Whistler	1.11.1	Queen of the Seas	8. 0.0	Southern Cross	12.11.3	Winged Arrow	18. 5. min.
Water Witch	2. 0.4	Whirlwind	8. 2.2	Golden West	13. 2. min.	Wild Ranger	(18. 8.)
Cleopatra	2. 6.0	Starr King	(8. 6.)	Electric Spark	13. 7.1	Endeavor	(18. 8.)
Staffordshire	2. 6.1	Flying Dragon	(8. 7.)	Andrew Jackson	(13. 9.)	Fair Wind	19. 3. min.
Queen of Clippers	2. 8. min.	Bald Eagle	8.10.3	Comet	(13. 9.2)	Panther	(20. .)
Flying Arrow	(3. 4.)	Sweepstakes	8.10.3	Uncowah	(13.10.)	Don Quixote	20. 3. min.
Mastiff	(3. 8.)	Empress of the Sea	8.11.1	Star of the Union	(13.11.)	Beverly	[20. 5.]
James Baines	3. 8.3	Santa Claus	8.11.1	Daring	[14. 2.]	Wizard	(20. 8.)
Lady Franklin	(3.10.)	Romance of the Sea	9. 2.1	Racehorse Bark	(14. 6.)	Champion of the Seas	21. 8.2
Seaman's Bride	3.10. min.	Mary Robinson	(9. 6.)	Blue Jacket	14. 6.3	Challenger	(21.10.)
Intrepid	3.11.1	Phantom	9. 7.1	Radiant	[14.11.]	Golden Fleece (2nd)	22. 0.0
Bonita	4. 1.1	West Wind	10. 1. min.	Belle of the West	(15. 3.)	Charmer	[22. 2.]
Silver Star	(4. 6.)	Northern Light	10. 3.1	Robin Hood	(15. 4.)	Sierra Nevada	(22. 6.)
Racer	4.10.2	Witchcraft	10. 3.2	Eureka	(15. 4.)	Flying Cloud	(22. 8.)
Mermaid Bark	4.11.2	Golden Eagle	10. 3.2	Spitfire	15. 4. min.	Lamplighter Bark	(22. 9.)
Surprise	5. 4.0	Celestial	[10. 6.]	Morning Light	15. 4. min.	Storm King	[22.11.]
John Gilpin	(5. 5.)	Eagle	10. 7. min.	Osborne Howes	(15. 5.)	Asa Eldridge	[23. 2.]
Flying Dutchman	5. 5.1	Sword Fish	10. 9.2	Ellen Foster	(15. 8.)	Raven	23. 5. min.
Sunny South	5.10.0	Stag Hound	10.10.1	Lightning	15. 9.4	Grace Darling	(23. 8.)
Flying Mist	5.11.2	John Land	11. 0.0	Ocean Express	(16. .)	Hurricane	[24. 3.]
Sovereign of the Seas	(6. 6.)	Winged Racer	(11. .)	Shooting Star	(16. .)	Thatcher Magoun	[25. 8.]
Antelope	(6. 9.)	Gazelle	[11. .]	Invincible	16. 1.1	Flying Eagle	(26. 7.)
				Telegraph	(16. 7.)	Gem of the Ocean	(27. .)

Table 32.2. *Continued.*

Vessel	Sailing life, y,m,w	Vessel	Sailing life, y,m,w
Flyaway	27. 7.0	Eringo Bark	No data for the vessels in this column
Challenge	(27. 7.)	Henry Hill Bark	
Indiaman	(28. .)	Quickstep Bark	
Red Jacket	(28. 1.)	Rocket Bark	
War Hawk	28. 3.1	Sea Bird Bark	
Ocean Telegraph	(28.10.)	Sultana Bark	
Game Cock	(29. 2.)	Tornado	
Donald McKay	(30. .)	Western Continent	
Swallow	(30. 8.)	Wildfire Bark	
Galatea	[30. 9.]	Young Turk Bark	
Fleet Wing	(31. 2.)		
John Bertram	32. 3.1		
Onward	(32. 4.1)		
Young America	(32. 9.2)		
Black Hawk	(34. 2.)		
Witch of the Wave	[34. 8.]		
King Fisher	(36. 5.)		
Herald of the Morning	[38. .]		
Fearless	38. 5. min.		
Wild Pigeon	40. 6.2		
Sea Serpent	40. 6.3		
Nightingale	41.10.0		
Coeur de Lion	(61. 7.)		
Syren	(68. 7.)		

Chapter Thirty-Three

CONCLUSION AND COMMENT

THE CONTENTS OF THIS BOOK, while dealing in particular with the construction of American-built clipper ships, apply to all large sailing vessels of the period. It is an attempt to record in detail all the elements of similarity and difference that can be built into a given class of vessels. Hopefully, it exposes to view a picture of all that is contained within the planking of large wooden merchant sailing ships.

The Clipper Phenonemon

A review of the five hundred years of history of the Western Hemisphere or "New World" from the time of Christopher Columbus gives some validity to the conclusion that the wooden clipper ship could have come into being only in the period of 1845–1860. This period is, of course, not rigidly confined to the dates stated, but these dates accurately define the extent of the clipper phenomenon.

It was a confluence of conditions and events, combined separately and unintentionally, that brought about the concept of a ship with clipper characteristics. The absence of, or shifting of dates, of even one of the contributing factors might have been sufficient to nullify the need or desire for such ships.

The great quantities and sizes of timber required to build any wooden vessel, whether or not it was a clipper, had already drained the once "inexhaustible" supply of suitable trees. Lumbermen were obliged to venture farther west from the Atlantic coast in order to find trees that filled the requirements of the shipbuilders. Timber other than exotic woods was now imported. The long-term outlook for the wooden ship was no longer bright, and this fact was well known by all shipbuilders. However, the construction of the completely wooden ship was still a viable and lucrative practice and would proceed for another ten years or so without noticeable interruption in the United States.

Oceangoing steamships had been built in Great Britain since 1838 and in the United States shortly thereafter. While the hulls were wood, many parts were now being made of iron. This metal, a relatively new commodity, the use of which had once been approached with considerable misgiving, was found to be wonderfully well suited to the requirements of shipwrights. Once its merits had been recognized, it was embraced wholeheartedly and was used in constantly greater quantities. Reliance on wood was now diminishing.

Propulsion by wind alone was being challenged by the use of machinery. Steam-propelled paddlewheels augmented sail power, but paddlewheels were cumbersome and prone to damage in rough seas. As a result, their progress of development was slow and somewhat limited for oceangoing vessels. However, ingenious minds were at work, developing, inventing, and patenting the screw propeller in the mid-1830s. It would doom the sailing ship as the choice of oceangoing commerce, but not for quite a few years.

In the early nineteenth century the use of iron fittings began to replace traditional use of rope. Chain cables were being used for ground tackle; yard slings of rope were superseded by chain slings; patent iron trusses replaced rope trusses; steering mechanisms were fabricated of iron.

Slowly the use of metal in fittings and minor items of ships' outfit gathered momentum, and in the 1840s inventions of every conceivable nautical type were patented. The age of the use of natural materials, such as wood for hulls and rope for many fittings—the philosophy of using natural forms, such as the fish, for determining hull form—was giving way to mathematical, academic design in the form of naval architecture. The forms of ships' hulls were undergoing rapid changes. One of these metamorphoses would be the clipper hull.

On the horizon, but not yet a fact in the United States, loomed the prospect of the iron-hulled ship. In England, due to the severe shortage of suitable timber, this iron construction was developed far ahead of the time when it would be undertaken in the United States, where timber was still available in quantities that made it the most economical form of construction. This situation would last until the Civil War, after which iron would come into its own until, in 1877, it would be superseded by a more sophisticated material—steel.

While these events were transpiring, the use of coal as fuel for oceangoing steamships was being furthered. One of the major stumbling blocks, however, was that of handling coal on board ship in sufficient quantities for long voyages. Over a period of time the efficient use of bunkers was developed. The end of sail was fast approaching.

With progress advancing steadily in the development and building of wooden ships, and the appearance of steam and iron still some years away for commercial shipping, a sudden burst of activity on the Pacific coast, particularly in California, created an unprecedented need for goods and materials to be shipped from the East.

Beginning in the 1830s, many people in the eastern United States had been pulling up their roots and migrating westward in quest of space and individual freedom. This migration eventually reached the Pacific coast in steady, moderate numbers, until the discovery of gold in California in 1848 led to the great Gold Rush of 1849. The overwhelming influx of new people into the far West inevitably led to acute shortages of every type of material. Suddenly there was an immediate need for the fast, voluminous transportation of any conceivable goods the exploding population used in their everyday lives or had left behind in the East. The overland route to the West was much shorter than the sea route by way of Cape Horn. It was, however, an arduous journey and did not lend itself to the transport of materials in great bulk. Thus there was suddenly a need for fast ships.

Since the overland route to the West did not lend itself to the movement of materials in bulk, the answer lay in shipping by sea. It was here that the law of supply and demand took over, along with the economics of the situation. More goods were needed than could be provided in a short period of time. And the fortunate person who could provide these materials first was well on his way to undreamed-of success.

All these developments and events transpired individually, and the timing of each was a crucial part of the total mixture. Progress that had taken place over a long period of time was soon to be superseded; development of new things to come was not quite ready to replace all that had gone before. It was during this window of opportunity that the clipper ship came into being. It was a highly specialized object, created for a highly specialized purpose, at a uniquely special time in history.

The new, fast type of vessel, which would become forever known as "clipper ship," was a super-swift vessel which, due to its potential speed, could overcome its relatively limited carrying capacity. It sailed in the teeth of all normal business

practice, but these were not normal conditions. For a few grand years this new breed of vessel would capture the imagination of all America—East and West.

As the records show, some of these vessels accomplished their objective many times over, while others disappeared almost before they started. Fortunately for the clipper ship as a type, it became more than a success—it became a phenomenon.

In general, merchant vessels were routinely given mundane names. They were named after persons associated with the individual vessel, countries, rivers, historical personages, and other types of rather matter-of-fact identity. However, the clippers brought into being a new trend in names, names associated with speed and freedom—and, perhaps, over-active imaginations. *Bounding Billow, Empress of the Sea, Flying Arrow, Eagle Wing, Gazelle, Lightning, Racehorse, War Hawk, Winged Racer*—these were names considered appropriate for the speedy clippers. The long list of these vessels reveals a relatively small percentage being named after some obscure individual. It was all a part of this wonderful fever.

The new trend in names denoted speed above all else, but speed was not the only attribute of the clippers. As a class these ships performed the greatest feats of nonstop movement that man had ever experienced. The average passage between our east and west coasts took more than one hundred days—days during which the vessels were in constant motion, rarely in sight of, and never touching land. Such accomplishments were routine and neatly fitted into the time slot occupied by the clippers. However, the required elements would soon disappear, since time and development do not stand still. The records of these sailings, though, are etched in history forever.

Transport of Slaves and Coolies

The lustre of the clipper ship is tarnished by involvement in two trades that were despised by most people. One was the slave trade between Africa and United States. The other was the coolie trade between China and Peru for the mining of the guano deposits on the Chincha Islands, which lie close to the coastline, about seventy-five miles north of Lima. Of course, being involved in such activities is the fault of people, not of ships.

Fortunately, from our point of view today, the clipper involvement in the slave trade was minimal and was not entered into by recognized American shipping firms. Certain individuals bought ships and operated in clandestine fashion, as was the case with Capt. Francis Bowen and *Nightingale*, and *Sunny South*, which operated in the trade after being sold at Havana. Both of these events took place in 1860.

Because slavery is an integral part of the history of the

United States, the general details of the institution are quite well known to most Americans. Not so the coolie trade, which never became a part of our early historical legacy. A brief accounting of details is of interest. The term "coolie" belonged to a predatory tribe living near the Gulf of Cutch, north of Bombay, India.

Unlike the transport of slaves, which was an involuntary matter from start to finish, the transport of coolies was voluntary and legal. Also, unlike the slave trade which was carried on as a straightforward, albeit repugnant, business venture, the coolie trade, even though voluntary, was dishonest and deceitful from start to finish.

At any of the principal Chinese seaports, the lowest class of unskilled laborers was offered a "contract" which included free transportation to the destination, an indentured service for a period of about five years, a stipulated annual wage, and freedom at the end of the indenture period. Coolies by the thousands accepted this welcome and promising offer.

The poor unfortunates who signed on had no inkling that they were departing for certain death as surely as if they had made a date with the gallows. The incoming ships at Chincha were loaded to the gunwales with coolie laborers; the outgoing vessels were loaded to the gunwales with guano, the product of their labors; the laborers died from sheer exhaustion; they were replaced by new laborers. That was the never-ending cycle. There is no record of a Chinese coolie ever returning to China where he might warn all who would listen against accepting the promises offered to them.

In spite of slavery being an involuntary condition, all first-hand accounts of the servitude of Chinese coolies in the guano deposits agree that this was by far the lowest level of human existence that could be devised by man. A grim report about the coolies is included in the description of *Joseph Peabody*.[32]

Sources and Endnotes

In the development and final format of this book the constant, and perhaps repetitious, inclusion of numbers keyed to endnotes throughout the text and tables is the result of years of frustration and dissatisfaction generated by inadequate referral to sources of specific information in many authoritative books dealing with ships. The thoroughgoing use of endnotes herein is admittedly a drastic departure from usual practice.

Most of such books contain generous quantities of both original data and necessary reconstruction required to fill in the blanks. However well-intentioned and accurate such reconstruction may be, it is always subject to the personal approach and interpretation of the individual writer. My intent herein is to extend an invitation to the reader: "Refer to the original source. Enjoy the satisfaction of seeing it yourself."

Reliance on a work can only be promoted through its authenticity. Authenticity is only achieved through close relationship with original data. Original data is best made known through convenient and ready reference to it in any given text.

Many readers appreciate an opportunity to examine the available original information and perhaps form their own opinions agreeing or dissenting. Also, original sources often contain much more detailed information than an author includes in his work.

Such is the case with certain references in this book, especially Duncan MacLean's reports in *The Boston Daily Atlas*.[1] Almost certainly there is no other source of detailed information that can rival these descriptions of American-built clipper ships, either in quality or quantity. The information taken from this source and included in this book represents only a portion of the data available in some of MacLean's descriptions. This also applies to other references which are as informative if not as voluminous.

There is a downside to exhaustive research and the resultant findings. On a subject such as clipper ships the possibility of discovering conflicting data, such as measurements, dates, and details, increases with the amount of research attempted. These are instances where the user is entitled to enough background and source data to draw his own conclusions. Ship measurements are particularly prone to discrepancies, many of which are based upon the points where measurements are taken and are not necessarily in error. In any case, the result is puzzling and can foment considerable cause for argument and question.

One of the more gratifying aspects of attempting completion of this book was the discovery of dates involving the fate of the vessels. After following the ships through all the stages of construction, it was satisfying to learn when, where, and how they met their inevitable end. It was a fitting manner in which to bring the book to its conclusion.

The vessels have long since disappeared, and much of their detail along with them. Still, great amounts of information might exist. The problem is that this information is scattered and hidden in countless museums, libraries, and personal collections of such data. It is hoped that this effort to bring much of the data together between the covers of one book will preclude the necessity for others to engage in a long quest for the same information. Perhaps they will start where this book ends and produce additional details that will further enhance the total picture.

REFERENCES

Notes: ** Original and/or contemporary source.

* Secondary source.

References are identified by number throughout the text and tables to provide direct access to the basic sources.

**1   Clipper ship descriptions, 1850–1856. (Scantlings, size, arrangements, masting, fittings, colors, etc.) *The Boston Daily Atlas*, 1844–1857, by Duncan MacLean. (Microfilm available in the Library of Congress, 26 reels, Shelf NP4736, Reel #3277.) Note: Between April 1850 and March 1857 Duncan MacLean, marine reporter for the *Boston Daily Atlas*, described in varying depth of detail the principal features of 161 vessels, of which 110 were clipper ships, and 51 were packets and freighters. Especially complete are descriptions of *Stag Hound, Challenge, Flying Fish, Queen of the Seas, Lightning*, and *Empress of the Sea*. The number may exceed this total due to the absence of some issues of the paper from this collection of microfilm.

*2   *Models and Measurements* (scantlings of 20 vessels designed by Donald McKay). Notebook by Henry Hall, 1883. (In possession of Penobscot Marine Museum, Searsport, Maine.) Note: This ledger-type notebook spells out the scantlings of 20 vessels designed and built by Donald McKay between 1846 and 1855. Of these vessels 12 were clippers and 8 were packets. The information in this notebook is based on original papers of Donald McKay, which were passed on to Mr. Hall by Mrs. McKay. Also included are some brief statistics in reference to the ships built by William H. Webb.

**3   Clipper ship descriptions, 1850–1853. *The Boston Daily Evening Traveller*, 23 December 1850 to 21 September 1853.

**4   Clipper ship descriptions, 1850–1853. *The New York Herald*, 11 December 1850 to 28 December 1853.

**5   Clipper ship descriptions, 1851–1854. *The New York Commercial Advertiser*, 22 May 1851 to 30 September 1854.

*6   *The Practical Shipbuilder*, 1839. Lauchlan McKay, 1839. (Published privately by Richard C. McKay, New York, 1940.)

*7   *Rudiments of Naval Architecture: Practical Principles of Science*. James Peake. London: John Weale, 1851.

*8   *Naval Architecture—A Treatise on Laying Off and Building Wood, Iron and Composite Ships*. Samuel J.P. Thearle. London and Glasgow: Wm. Collins, Sons & Co., Ltd., 1874.

*9   *The Merchant's and Mechanic's Assistant*. I.R. Butts. Boston: I.R. Butts & Co., 1856.

**10   *Description of the Largest Ship in the World, the New Clipper* Great Republic, *of Boston. Designed, built and owned by Donald McKay*. Written by a Sailor. Boston: Eastburn's Press, 1853. This is an on-site description of *Great Republic* noting pertinent details and containing five line drawings.

**11   "Clipper Ship *Lightning*—Lines." *U.S. Nautical Magazine and Naval Journal*, Vol. III, 1855. New York: Griffiths, Bates and Co.

**12   "Clipper Ship *Herald of the Morning*—Body Plan, Lines and Scantlings." *U.S. Nautical Magazine and Naval Journal*, Vol. III, No. 6, March 1856. New York: Griffiths, Bates and Co.

*13   "Clipper Ship *Comet*—Critical evaluation." *U.S. Nautical Magazine and Naval Journal*, Vol. IV, 1856. New York: Griffiths, Bates and Co.

**14   "Clipper Ship *Red Jacket*—Lines and spar dimensions." *U.S. Nautical Magazine and Naval Journal*, Vol. IV, No. 3, June 1856. New York: Griffiths, Bates and Co.

**15   "*Ocean Monarch*, 1856—General trader." *U.S. Nautical Magazine and Naval Journal*, Vol. IV, 1857. New York: Griffiths, Bates and Co. (Article reproduced in *Nautical Research Journal*, Vol. 31, No. 4, December 1985.)

*16   Clipper Ship *Lightning*—Lines. Waterman Collection, Peabody Museum, Salem, MA, and Clark Collection, M.I.T. Museum, Cambridge, MA.

*17   Tables of Moulded Offsets, Lines—*Sea Witch*, 1846. Museum of History and Technology, Smithsonian Institution, Washington, DC. (See article in *Nautical Research Journal*, Vol. 26, No. 2, June 1980.)

**18   Tables of Moulded Offsets—William H. Webb's clippers. Webb Institute of Naval Architecture, Livingston Library, Glen Cove, NY.

**19   *Red Jacket*, 1853—Details of ship and description of launching. *Limerock Gazette*, November 5, 1853. (As reprinted in the *Rockland Gazette*, Rockland, ME, circa 1920s.) Courtesy of the Farnsworth Museum, Rockland, ME, and Stephen Hopkins.

*20   Partial description of *Celestial*, 1850, *Sword Fish*, 1851, and *Andrew Jackson*, 1855. *The American Neptune*, Vol. I, 1941. Salem, MA: The American Neptune, Inc.

*21   *New York Marine Register: A Standard of Classification of American Vessels, And of Such Other Vessels as Visit American Ports—1858*. New York: Board of Underwriters. (Phillips Library, Peabody Museum, Salem, MA.)

*22   "Laying Out in the Mould Loft" (as excerpted from "A Method of Comparing the Lines and Draughting Vessels, Propelled by Sail and Steam"). Samuel M. Pook. New York: D. Van Nostrand, 1866. (See article in *Nautical Research Journal*, Vol. 35, No. 3, September 1990.)

*23   *Report on the Ship building Industry of the United States*. Henry Hall. Washington, DC: U.S. Government Printing Office, 1884.

**24   Plans of Wooden Vessels—from a fishing smack to the Largest Clipper Ships, etc. from 1840 to 1869. William H. Webb, New York, 1895.

25 *Architectura Navalis Mercatoria.* Fredrik Henry of Chapman, 1768. (Reprint published by Praeger Publishers, New York, 1971.)

*26 *William H. Webb: Shipbuilder.* E. Dunbaugh and Wm. DuB. Thomas. Glen Cove, NY: Webb Institute of Naval Architecture, 1989.

**27 *Red Jacket*, passenger accommodations. Diagram of passenger accommodations after being modified as a packet by Pilkington & Wilson, Liverpool, in 1855. (Courtesy of Stephen Hopkins, New Rochelle, NY.)

*28 *The Clipper Ship Era, 1843–1869.* Arthur H. Clark, revised edition. Riverside, CT: 7C's Press, 1970. (Original published in 1910.)

*29 Clipper ship *Fearless*—Lines and Body Plan. Historic American Merchant Marine Survey, Plan 2-59, Smithsonian Institution, Washington, DC.

*30 Clipper ships *Donald McKay* and *Flying Fish*—Lines and Body Plan. Bergen Sjøfartsmuseum, Bergen, Norway. (Reproduction of *Flying Fish* drawn by H. S. Scott, Nautical Research Guild, 1952.)

*31 *Greyhounds of the Sea, The Story of the American Clipper Ship.* Carl C. Cutler. New York: Halcyon House, 1930.

*32 *American Clipper Ships, 1833–1858.* Howe and Matthews. New York: Argosy Antiquarian, Ltd., 1967. (Original published in 1926.)

33 *The Shipwright's Trade.* Sir Wescott Abel. London: Conway Maritime Press, 1981.

*34 *Know Your Woods.* Albert Constantine, Jr. New York: Charles Scribner's Sons, 1987.

*35 *The Audobon Society Field Guide to North American Trees–Eastern Region.* Elbert L. Little. New York: Alfred A. Knopf, 1988.

36 *The Building of a Wooden Ship.* Charles G. Davis. Philadelphia: United States Shipping Board Emergency Fleet Corp., 1918.

37 *How Wooden Ships Are Built.* H. Cole Estep. New York: W. W. Norton and Co. (Original by Penton Publishing Co., Cleveland, OH, 1918.)

38 *Wooden Ship-building.* Charles Desmond. Vestal, NY: The Vestal Press, Ltd., 1984. (Original published by The Rudder Publishing Co., 1919.)

39 *The Building of a Wooden Ship.* Dana A. Story. Barre, MA: Barre Publishers, 1971.

40 *The Oxford Companion to Ships and the Sea.* Peter W. Kemp, editor. London: Oxford University Press, 1976.

41 *The Visual Encyclopedia of Nautical Terms under Sail.* Basil W. Bathe. New York: Crown Publishers, Inc., 1978. A volume replete with excellent data on fittings, ropework, tackle, nautical terms, and general information.

42 *The Search for Speed under Sail.* Howard I. Chapelle. New York: W. W. Norton and Co., Inc., 1967.

43 *The Built-up Ship Model.* Charles G. Davis. Portland, ME: The Southworth Press, 1933.

44 *American Ships.* Alexander Laing. New York: American Heritage Press, 1971.

45 *Clipper Ships and Their Makers.* Alexander Laing. New York: Bonanza Books, 1966.

**46 Clipper ship *Red Jacket*—Details and Launching. The Rockland *Courier-Gazette*, 27 February 1971, quoting the *Rockland Gazette* of 2 November 1853. Courtesy of the Farnsworth Museum, Rockland, ME.

*47 *Record of American and Foreign Shipping.* New York: American Shipmasters' Association, established 1867.

*48 *Textbook of Dendrology, Covering the important Forest Trees of the United States and Canada.* William Morehouse Harlow. New York: McGraw-Hill Book Co., Inc., 1958. (Free Library of Philadelphia, Call No. 582 H22lt.)

49 *Picture History of the U.S. Navy.* Roscoe and Freeman. New York: Bonanza Books, 1956.

50 *Machinery's Handbook, Strength of Materials,* 13th edition. New York: The Industrial Press, 1946.

51 *China Tea Clippers.* George F. Campbell. New York: David McKay, Inc., 1974.

52 *Tropical Timbers of the World.* Martin Chudnoff. Washington, DC: U.S. Department of Agriculture, Forest Service, 1984.

53 *Wood Handbook.* Washington, DC: U.S. Department of Agriculture, Forest Service.

*54 McKay packets *Star of Empire* and *Chariot of Fame.* Midship section and longitudinal section on center line of ship. Color illustration in possession of The Peabody Museum, Salem, MA. Negative No. 19625.

*55 *The Shipwright's Handbook and Draughtsman's Guide, etc.* L. H. Boole. Milwaukee, WI: Ben Franklin Printing House of Burdick & Treyser, 1958. (See article in *Nautical Research Journal,* Vol. 37, No. 2, June 1992.)

56 *The Ship of the Line, Vol. II: Design, Construction and Fittings.* Brian Lavery. Annapolis, MD: Naval Institute Press, 1984.

**57 Daguerreotype of *Seaman's Bride.* Reproduced in Ref. 90, courtesy of the Maryland Historical Society.

58 *History of the American-built clipper* Red Jacket. Compiled by Robert R. O'Loughlin, Bronxville, New York.

**59 Clipper ship *Andrew Jackson*—Lines and Body Plan. Ships Plans Division, Mystic Seaport Museum, Mystic, CT.

60 "Report of the Secretary of the Navy to the United States Senate on 15 January 1861 pertaining to the Naval Establishment." Report issued by the Navy Department in compliance with a Senate Resolution of 23 June 1860.

**61 Daguerreotype of *Champion of the Seas* by Southworth and Hawes, Boston. *The American Neptune,* Vol. XIX, No. 2, April 1959. Salem, MA: The American Neptune, Inc. (See Ref. 97.)

**62 Photograph of *Black Hawk*, port side. (No. Al. 1234n.) Fireman's Fund, National Maritime Museum, San Francisco, CA.

**63 Photograph of *Black Hawk*, stbd. bow. (Negative No. P1840.) National Maritime Museum, London.

64 Clipper ship *Comet* of New York in a Hurricane off Bermuda, October 1852. Print by N. Currier, New York. Copy in the Shelburne Museum, Shelburne, VT. (See Ref. 97.)

65 Clipper ship *Hurricane* of New York. Print by N. Currier, New York. Copy in the Shelburne Museum, Shelburne, VT. (See Ref. 97.)

66 Clipper ship *Ocean Express*, outward bound "Discharging the pilot." Print by Currier & Ives, New York. Copy in the Shelburne Museum, Shelburne, VT. (See Ref. 97.)

67 Clipper ship *Red Jacket* in the Ice off Cape Horn, 1855. Print by N. Currier, New York. Copy in the Penobscot Marine Museum, Searsport, ME. (This print is widely distributed.)

68 Clipper ship *Red Jacket*. Painting by Percy Sanborn, 1849–1929, in Penobscot Marine Museum Collection, Searsport, ME.

69 Clipper ship *Sweepstakes*. Print by N. Currier, New York. Copy in the Shelburne Museum, Shelburne, VT. (See Ref. 97.)

**70 *Young America*, contemporary builder's half model. Smithsonian Institution, Washington, DC. Photograph, Negative No. 45608-D, Catalog No. 160.135.

**71 *Young America*, port side and starboard side. Photographs from the Fireman's Fund, Vols. I and II, San Francisco Maritime Museum.

**72 *Young America*, port side off the bow; starboard side off the quarter. Photographs in the Peabody Museum, Salem, MA. Negatives Nos. 5232 and 11895.

*73 Mr. Lang, Master Shipwright, Woolwich Royal Dockyard, England, 1826–1832. Correspondence with the National Maritime Museum, Greenwich, 3 July 1991.

74 Clipper ship *Nightingale* getting under weigh off the Battery, New York. Print by N. Currier, New York. Copy in the Shelburne Museum, Shelburne, VT. (See Ref. 97.)

**75 Clipper ship *Great Republic* as rebuilt in 1855. Photograph taken in 1860, in possession of the Peabody Museum, Salem, MA.

76 *The New Columbia Encyclopedia*. New York: Columbia University Press, 1975.

77 *The Coppering of 19th Century American Merchant Sailing Ships*. Erik A. R. Ronnberg, Jr. A compilation of data, published in the *Nautical Research Journal*, Vol. 26, No. 3, September 1980.

*78 *Clippers of the Port of Portsmouth and the Men who Built Them*. Ray Brighton. Portsmouth, NH: The Portsmouth Marine Society, 1985.

79 *The Lore of Ships*. Tre Trykare. New York: Holt, Rinehart and Winston, 1963.

80 *A History of Seafaring based on Underwater Archeology*. George F. Bass. New York: Walker & Co., 1972.

81 *Dictionary of American Naval Fighting Ships*. Washington, DC: U.S. Government Printing Office.

82 *"Mystic Built" Ships and Shipyards of the Mystic River, Connecticut, 1784–1919*. Mystic, CT: William N. Peterson. Mystic Seaport Museum, 1989.

83 *American Sail: A Pictorial History*. Alexander Laing. New York: Bonanza Books, 1961.

*84 Clipper ships etchings, photographs, and paintings; also a half model of *Don Quixote*. *The American Neptune*, Vol. XIX, 1959. Salem, MA: The American Neptune, Inc. (See Ref. 97.)

**85 Half model of *Stag Hound*. Old State House Museum of the Marine Society, Boston, MA. (Noted in Ref. 42.)

86 *The Colonial Clippers*. Basil Lubbock. Glasgow: James Brown and Son, Ltd., 1921.

87 *The Clipper Ships*. A.B.C. Whipple. Alexandria, VA: Time-Life Books, 1980.

88 *Paint and Colors for American Merchant Vessels, 1800–1920: Their study and interpretation for model making*. Erik A. R. Ronnberg, Jr. Compilation of data, published in *Nautical Research Journal*, Vol. 36, No. 4, December 1991.

**89 *The Kedge Anchor or Young Sailor's Assistant*. William N. Brady, Sailing-master, U.S.N. New York: D. Appleton and Co., 1847. A book devoted to rigging details of United States naval vessels. Its value lies in the tables of rigging and block sizes, which are useful in determining the proper proportions for rope sizes in their various functions and locations. It is very easily adaptable to clipper ships, which were regarded as being in the general category of first- and second-class frigates.

*90 *Shipcarvers of North America*. Marion V. Brewington. New York: Dover Publications, Inc., 1972.

*91 *Figureheads and Ship Carvings at Mystic Seaport*. Edouard A. Stackpole. Mystic, CT: The Marine Historical Association, Inc., 1964.

**92 Contemporary builder's half model of the clipper *Comet*. Housed in the Smithsonian Institution, Washington, DC.

93 Clipper ship *Great Republic*. Lithograph by N. Currier, New York, 1853, inscribed "To Donald McKay, Esq., builder of the *Leviathan*."

94 Clipper ship *Great Republic*. Wood engraving in *Gleason's Pictorial*, 1853.

95 Painting of *John Wade*, 1851, attributed to Clement Drew. *The American Neptune*, Pictorial Supplement I. Salem, MA: The American Neptune, Inc., 1959. (See Ref. 97.)

96 Clipper ship *Racer* of New York. Print by N. Currier, New York. Copy in the Shelburne Museum, Shelburne, VT. (See Ref. 97.)

97 Prints, photographs and paintings of American sailing vessels. *The American Neptune*, Pictorial Supplement I. Salem, MA: The American Neptune, Inc., 1959.

98 *The Ways of the Sea*. Charles G. Davis. New York: The Rudder Publishing Co., 1930.

**99 Clipper ship *Challenge*—Lines and Body Plan. Admiralty take-off while the ship was in dry dock at London, November 1852. (This take-off is noted in Ref. 32.)

*100 "Deck Furniture and Machinery of large mid-19th century Sailing Ships." Robert C. and Grisel M. Leavitt. Articles in *Nautical Research Journal*, beginning Vol. 32, No. 2, June 1987.

**101 "Reed's Patent Steering Apparatus, Some ships using." Advertisement in the *Boston Shipping List*, February 13, 1858. Courtesy of Robert C. and Grisel M. Leavitt, Miami, FL.

*102 *A Museum of Early American Tools*. Eric Sloane. New York: Henry Holt & Co., 1990. (Originally published by Funk and Wagnalls, 1964.)

**103 The clipper *Great Republic*, 1855, as rebuilt. *U.S. Nautical Magazine and Naval Journal*, April 1855. New York: Griffiths, Bates & Co., New York. (Article reproduced in *Nautical Research Journal*, Vol. 21, No. 1, January 1975.)

**104 *American Lloyd's Registry of American and Foreign Shipping, 1859*. American Lloyd's. New York: E. & G.W. Blunt, 1859.

105 *The Passage Makers*. Michael K. Stammers. Brighton, Sussex, England: Teredo Books, Ltd., 1978.

*106 *The History of the United States Flag*. Quafe, Weig and Appleman. New York: Harper & Row, 1961. (U.S. arms, as of 1841, pp. 119, 120, 138.)

107 *Architectural Graphic Standards*, 5th edition. Ramsey and Sleeper. New York: John Wiley & Sons, Inc, 1956.

**108 "A New Rig for Ships and Other Vessels, combining economy safety and convenience." R. B. Forbes. Printed by Wier and White, 11 Cornhill, Boston, 1849.

**109 *Steel's Elements of Mastmaking, Sailmaking and Rigging, from the 1794 edition*. Arranged by Claude S. Gill. New York: Edward W. Sweetman, 1932.

**110 *A Treatise on Masting ships and Mast Making*. John Fincham, Esq. London: Conway Maritime Press, Ltd., 1982. (First published in 1829.)

111 *Masting and Rigging the Clipper Ship and Ocean Carrier*. Harold A. Underhill. Glasgow: Brown, Son and Ferguson, Ltd., 1946. A complete book on the masting and rigging of the later British clippers but, in details, applicable to the earlier American-built clippers. It is very detailed and contains many drawings and tables. It is probably one of the best single sources of general information on this particular subject.

112 *The Ship Model Builder's Assistant*. Charles G. Davis. Salem, MA: Marine Research Society, 1926.

**113 "On Mast and Spar-making." *U.S. Nautical Magazine and Naval Journal*, Vol. V, No. 1, October 1856. New York: Griffiths, Bates and Co.

114 *Ships and the Sea—A Chronological Review*. Duncan Hawes. New York: Thomas Y. Crowell Company, Inc., 1975.

*115 "Cunningham's Self-reefing Topsails, etc." Advertisements in the *Liverpool Telegraph and Shipping Gazette*, editions of 17 September 1856 and 22 November 1856.

*116 *The Shipmodeler—Official Journal of the Ship Model Maker's Club*. Capt. E. Armitage McCann. Published monthly by A.C. & H.W. Dickens, New York, from February 1929 through November 1933; 45 issues. (Clipper ship rigging detailed from February 1930 through June 1932, issues Nos. 11 through 35.) A magazine devoted to nautical subjects that featured a series of articles on clipper ship rigging. The author, a man who had sailed in the later square riggers, covers the subject well and includes many line drawings. These drawings are not refined but are simple and easily understood. The articles must be classed as worthy of the subject.

**117 *The Universal Code of Signals for the Mercantile Marine of all Nations, by the late Capt. Frederick Marryat, R.N.* G. B. Richardson. London: Richardson Brothers. (Editions used are 1854, 1856, 1858, 1869.)

118 *The Evolution of Visual Signals on Land and Sea* (1976). David Lyndon Woods. Published on demand by University Microfilms International, 300 N. Zeeb Road, Ann Arbor, MI, 48106.

119 *Flags at Sea*. Timothy Wilson. Greenwich: National Maritime Museum, 1986.

*120 *So Proudly We Hail*. Furlong and McCandless. Washington, DC: Smithsonian Institution Press, 1981. (Thirty-one-star flag pattern, Fig. 163, page 199.)

*121 Private Signals (House flags) of American Merchant Sail. Collections of handbills, broadsides, sailing cards, paintings and miscellaneous sources, all housed in museums such as Mystic Seaport, Peabody, Shelburne, Penobscot Marine, Independence Seaport (Philadelphia), and private collections.

122 *The Stars and the Stripes*. Boleslaw and Mastai. New York: Alfred A. Knopf, 1973.

**123 *Marine Telegraph; or Universal Signal Book*. James M. Elford, publisher. Printed by Archibald E. Miller, No. 4 Broad Street, Charleston, SC, 1823.

*124 *Merchant Sail*. William Armstrong Fairburn. Center Lovell, ME: Fairburn Marine Educational Foundation, Inc., 1945. (Information from Volume 2.)

*125 Fate of *Challenge*, built by William H. Webb, 1851. Letter from City of Liverpool Museums, William Brown Street, Liverpool L3 8EN, England, 13 November 1973. (States circumstances of loss in 1879.)

**126 Launching date of clipper *Black Hawk*, 29 December 1856. Certificate book of William H. Webb. Webb Institute of Naval Architecture, Glen Cove, Long Island, NY.

**127 Bark *Bounding Billow*, 1854; loss reported. *U.S. Nautical Magazine and Naval Journal*, Vol. III, No. 5, December 1855. New York: Griffiths, Bates and Co.

**128 Launching date of clipper *Intrepid* reported. *U.S. Nautical Magazine and Naval Journal*, Vol. IV, No. 2, May 1856.

**129 Launching date of clipper *Black Hawk* reported. *U.S. Nautical Magazine and Naval Journal*, Vol. V, No. 5, February 1857. New York: Griffiths, Bates and Co.

**130 Abstract log of *Flying Cloud*, New York to San Francisco, 22 January 1854–20 April 1854; record passage. National Archives Microfilm Publications, Washington, DC 20408. (Record Group (RG)27, Weather Bureau/Maury Logs, Microcopy Number M1160, Roll #21, Vol. 70.)

**131 Abstract log of *Comet*, San Francisco to New York, 27 December 1853–14 March 1854; record passage. National Archives Microfilm Publications, Washington, DC, 20408. (Record Group (RG)27, Weather Bureau/Maury Logs, Microcopy Number M1160, Roll #4, Vol. 6.)

132 Goode's Interrupted Homolosine Projection. *Goode's World Atlas*, 12th edition. Edited by Edward B. Espinshade, Jr. Chicago: Rand, McNally & Company, 1964.

133 *The Elements of Wood Ship Construction*. W.H. Curtis. New York: McGraw-Hill Book Company, 1919.

**134 *Notes on Ships of the Past*. R.B. Forbes. Boston: J.F. Cotter & Co., printers, 1888. Copy in possession of Clemson University Library, Clemson, SC.

**135 Clipper ship description. *The Boston Daily Atlas*, Friday, March 3, 1854.

*136 *The National Watercraft Collection (Smithsonian)*. Howard I. Chapelle. Washington, D.C.: U.S. Government Printing Office, 1960.

INDEX

The "data" entry after each vessel's name, where applicable, includes the vessel's dimensions, date of launch, building location, and the names of its designer, builder, and owner.

Boldface type indicates an illustration.

A

Adams, W., and A. Hammond, inventors
  windlass, 422, 428
Air circulation, 273
Air strakes
  description, 273
  function, 273
  locations, 87 (**Fig. 6.2**), **266** (**Fig. 17.1**) 267-271 (Table 17.1), 273
Alarm, 1856, xii, **386** (**Fig. 26.2**)
  data, xix
  Briggs mast truss, 261, **262** (**Fig. 16.2**)
  ceiling fastenings, 214
  deckhouse colors, 347
  transoms, 191, 193 (Table 11.1)
Alarm, HMS, 1761
  copper sheathing, 328
Allowing the seam, 294, 304, **306-307** (**Fig. 20.1**)
Allyn, Edwin
  patent assignee of a capstan invented by Joseph E. Andrews. *See* Fittings and Outfits; and Andrews, Joseph E.
Allyn's capstan, 422-427
America, schooner-yacht, 1850, 38
American ensign, 1850-58, 485
American Lloyds Register of American and Foreign Shipping, published by Hartshorne and King, New York, xxv
American Lloyds Universal
  See New York Marine Register:
American Lloyds Universal Register of Shipping, published by Thomas D. Taylor, New York, xxv
American Shipmasters Association

See Record of American and Foreign Shipping
American Shipmasters Association: Rules for Construction of Wooden Vessels, 1867
  floor timbers, 152
Amphitrite, 1853, xii, **386** (**Fig. 26.2**)
  data, xvii
Anchors
  designations, 183
  Porter's, 422-425
  quantity, 183
  sizes, 181
  space requirements, 48
  up-and-down, 181
Andrew Jackson, 1859, xii, **386** (**Fig. 26.2**)
  data, xix
  capstans, 419
  wales, 309-314 (Table 20.1), 315, 316
Andrews, Joseph E., inventor
  capstan, later assigned to Edwin Allyn
  steering apparatus, 426, 428
  See Fittings and Outfits; and Allyn, Edwin
Angle of floor, 9
Antelope, 1851, xii, **386** (**Fig. 26.2**)
  data, xvi
  color of bulwarks, 345
  deadwood, 169
  transoms, 193 (Table 11.1)
Apron
  description, **130** (**Fig. 8.1**), 134, 135
  fabrication, 134, 135
  fastenings, 131-133 (Table 8.1), 135
  function, 134
  material, 131-133 (Table 8.1), 134
  moulding, 134
  scarphs, 135
  siding, 131-133 (Table 8.1), 134
  in *Charger*, 171
  in *Great Republic*, 22
Arey, James, and Co., Frankfort, ME
  shipbuilders, xviii
Asa Eldridge, 1856, xii, **386** (**Fig. 26.2**)
  data xix

Briggs mast braces, **263** (**Fig. 16.3**), 264
Briggs mast truss, 261, **262** (**Fig. 16.2**)
  cabin decoration, 445
  cargo ports, 321
  hawse holes, 183
  transoms, 193 (Table 11.1), 194
  waterways "let over," **266** (**Fig. 17.1**), 267-271 (Table 17.1), 272
Austin and Hall, Damariscotta, ME
  shipbuilders, xviii

B

Bacon, Daniel C., Boston
  ship owner, xv
  et al, ship owners, xv
  and Sons, ship owners, xvi
Badger, Samuel, Portsmouth, NH
  builder, packet *Cathedral*, 348
Baines, James, and Co., Liverpool
  ship owners, xviii, xix, 98, 462
  clippers built for, 53, 485
  cross bracing in *Lightning*, **210-211** (**Fig. 12.4**), 273
Baker and Morrill, Boston
  ship owners, xv-xvii, xix
  et al, ship owners, xviii
Baker, Matthew, 1530-1613
  first Master of the Shipwrights' Company of England, 1572,
Bald Eagle, 1852, xii, **387** (**Fig. 26.3**)
  data, xvi
  advantages of solid bulwarks, 288
  beaded bulwarks, **318-319** (**Fig. 20.2**)
  boat stowage in deckhouse, 417, 435, **436-437** (**Fig. 28.2**)
  ceiling fastenings, quantity, 273
  collars of stays leathered, 478
  crew berthing, 434
  diagonal wooden braces, 257
  fastenings in tween decks, 75
  flare of bow, negative effect, 48
  gunports, 278-284 (Table 18.1), 289
  headstays set up inboard, 478
  weather deck flush aft, 416

Bangs, Benjamin, Boston
  ship owner, xvii
Barclay and Livingston, New York
  ship owners, xvi
Barnacles (Lepas), 328, 329
  See also Metal sheathing
Barstow, Capt.
  sheathing vessels with copper, 336
Beaded edges, **318-319** (**Fig. 20.2**), 320
Beakhead bulkhead, 317
  deck, 317
Beal, J., Boston
  ship owner, xvii
  See also Nickerson, F., et. al.
Beam mould, 56, **57** (**Fig. 3.5**)
  See also Camber curve
Beams
  carlings, **242** (**Fig. 14.2**), 244, 246, 247
  description, 228, 229, 244, **245** (**Fig. 14.3**), 246, 247
  fabrication, 229, 244, 246
  fastenings, 229, 230-238 (Table 14.1), 246
  function, 228, 244, 246
  half beam **242** (**Fig. 14.2**), 244
  headers, **242** (**Fig. 14.2**), 244
  installation, 229, **242** (**Fig. 14.2**), 244, 246, 247
  ledges, **242** (**Fig. 14.2**), 244, 246
  locations, 228, 229, 244, 246, 247
  material, 228, 230-238 (Table 14.1), 246
  salting, preparation for, 229
  scarphs, 229, 230-238 (Table 14.1)
  sizes, 229, 230-238 (Table 14.1)
Bearding
  false stem, 135, 136
  rudder, 323, **324** (**Fig. 21.1**), 325
  sternpost, 139, 140, 325
Bearding line, deadwood, 169
Beaufoy, Henry, c. 1830, 31
Beaufoy, Mark, c. 1775
  nautical experimenter, 31
Belaying pin arrangement, **482-483** (**Fig. 30.3**), 484